Mexico

a Lonely Planet travel survival kit

John Noble
Wayne Bernhardson
Tom Brosnahan
Susan Forsyth
Nancy Keller
James Lyon

Mexico

5th edition

Published by
Lonely Planet Publications
Head Office: PO Box 617, Hawthorn, Vic 3122, Australia
Branches: 155 Filbert St, Suite 251, Oakland, CA 94607, USA ì
  10 Barley Mow Passage, Chiswick, London W4 4PH, UK
  71 bis rue du Cardinal Lemoine, 75005 Paris, France

Printed by
SNP Printing Pte Ltd, Singapore

Photographs by
Ross Barnett (RB)   Peter Ptschelinzew (PP)
Greg Elms (GE)   Jason Rubinsteen (JR)
Susan Forsyth (SF)   David Trembath (DT)
Nancy Keller (NK)   Scott Wayne (SW)
James Lyon (JL)   Paul Wentford (PW)
John Noble (JN)   Tony Wheeler (TW)

Front cover: Convent Bells – Yucatán, by Tom Owen Edmunds (The Image Bar

First Published
1982

This Edition
July 1995

**Although the authors and publisher have tried to make the information as
accurate as possible, they accept no responsibility for any loss, injury or
inconvenience sustained by any person using this book.**

National Library of Australia Cataloguing in Publication Data

Mexico – a travel survival kit.

5th ed.
Includes index.
ISBN 0 86442 291 1.

1. Mexico – Guidebooks. I. Noble, John, 1951 Oct 11 - .
(Series : Lonely Planet travel survival kit).

917.204835

text & maps © Lonely Planet 1995
photos © photographers as indicated 1995
climate charts compiled from information supplied by Patrick J Tyson © Patrick J Tyson, 1995

John Noble

John was born and grew up in the cool, green and lovely valley of the River Ribble, England. He escaped intermittently from a career in English newspaper journalism by taking lengthy trips around Europe, North and Central America and South-East Asia, before Lonely Planet answered his call and sent him to Sri Lanka, where he met his wife and co-author Susan Forsyth. Since then John has co-authored three editions of *Mexico* for Lonely Planet, and also worked on LP's *Australia, Indonesia, USSR, Baltic States, Central Asia* and *Russia, Ukraine & Belarus* guides. John and Susan and their children Isabella and Jack (also experienced Mexico travellers) now live in southern Spain, where they are trying to improve their Spanish.

Wayne Bernhardson

Wayne was born in North Dakota, grew up in Tacoma, Washington, and spent most of the 1980s shuttling between North and South America en route to a PhD in geography from the University of California, Berkeley. He is co-author, with María Massolo, of LP's *Argentina, Uruguay & Paraguay*, author of *Chile & Easter Island* and *Baja California*, and a contributor to *South America*. Wayne lives in Oakland, California with María, their daughter Clío and their Alaskan malamute Gardel.

Tom Brosnahan

Tom was born and raised in Pennsylvania, went to college in Boston, then set out on the road. After travelling in Europe he joined the Peace Corps, and saw Mexico for the first time as part of the Peace Corps training programme. A short term of teaching English in a Mexico City school whetted his appetite for more exploration. After graduate school he travelled throughout Mexico, Guatemala and Belize writing travel articles and guidebooks for various publishers, and in the past two decades his 20 books covering numerous destinations have sold over two million copies in 12 languages. For Lonely Planet, Tom has worked on *Turkey, Guatemala, Belize & Yucatán – La Ruta Maya, Central America, Mediterranean Europe* and *New England*.

Susan Forsyth

Susan grew up in semitropical Melbourne. She narrowly survived several years' teaching in the Victorian state education system before activating long-postponed travel plans and heading off for a year as a volunteer lecturer in Sri Lanka, where she met her future husband John Noble. Susan has since helped update LP's *Australia, Indonesia* and *Sri Lanka* guides, travelled lengthily in the ex-USSR and Mexico, and found time to give birth to and nurture two little Vikings in England's cold, wet Ribble Valley. The whole family temporarily relocated to Mexico while Susan and John were researching this edition. Having weathered five years based in England, Susan now happily soaks up the almost-Australian climate of southern Spain.

Nancy Keller

Nancy was born and raised in Northern California, and worked in the alternative press for several years, doing every aspect of newspaper work from editorial and reporting to delivering the papers. She returned to university to earn a master's degree in journalism, finally graduating in 1986 after many breaks for extended stays on the west coast of Mexico. Since then she's been travelling and writing in Mexico, Israel, Egypt, Europe, various South Pacific islands, New Zealand and Central America. She has worked on several LP books, including *Central America, Rarotonga & the Cook Islands, New Zealand* and *California & Nevada*.

James Lyon

James is an Australian by birth, a sceptic by nature and a social scientist by training. He was unsuccessful as a government bureaucrat because of an unfortunate tendency to put his itchy foot in his mouth. James eventually became an editor at Lonely Planet's Melbourne office, where his warped sense of humour was generally tolerated and the time he had spent travelling was not regarded as a black spot on his CV. After a couple of years, James jumped at the chance to update LP's *Bali & Lombok* guide. Trying to reconcile guidebook-writing with family life, he then travelled to Mexico with his wife, Pauline, and their two young sons, where they lived for five months while working on this book.

From the Authors

John Noble & Susan Forsyth For invaluable help of many kinds in the preparation of this edition, John and Susan would especially like to thank Oscar Dinero of Mud City Loop, Vermont; Mike Saxby and Silvia Soria de Saxby of Oxford; la familia Soria of Mexico City; Colin 'Cuttings' Richardson of London; Carey Egger-Díaz, Checo Díaz and Suzanne López of Puerto Ángel; Chris Schroeder of Portland, Oregon; Donald Chamberlain of Seattle; Chris & Anna Barry of Melbourne; the staff of the Guanajuato tourist office; Mauricio Rivas of the Mexican Government Tourism Office in London; and Rosario Graham Zapata of the Secretaría de Turismo in Mexico City.

John would also like to thank James, Nancy, Susan, Tom and Wayne for getting everything in on time and in good order. John and Susan both thank Katie Purvis and the team in Melbourne for seeing the book through with a minimum of headaches, and not least for managing to stay in touch with moving targets!

Wayne Bernhardson Special mention to James J Parsons of the Department of Geography at the University of California, Berkeley, for his knowledge and enthusiasm over the years. Further thanks to Rey and Marta Ayala of Calexico, California; Serge Dedina and Emily Young of the Department of Geography at the University of Texas, Austin; Justin Hyland of the Department of Anthropology at the University of California, Berkeley; Dan Arreola of the Department of Geography at Arizona State University, Tempe; Lucero Gutiérrez of INAH, San Ignacio; and Almudena Ortiz and Jorge Lizárraga of Berkeley. Other significant contributors include Francisco Javier Sotelo Leyva of Tijuana, Angel Carlos Covarrubias R of Ensenada, Rigoberto González Peralta of La Paz, Dr Aldo Piñeda of La Paz, John Spencer of La Rivera, Baja California Sur and Union City, California, and John Laragy of Cabo San Lucas.

James Lyon To all the Mexicans who helped me to enjoy their rich culture and beautiful country – muchas gracias. In San Miguel de Allende, thanks to the staff at the library, and to Richard Gütter who saved my computer from a dreaded virus. I am also indebted to the Opies in San Diego, who sustained me in my traumatic search for a cheap used car; to Rob and Shirl, who paid the bills in my absence; and as ever to Pauline, my research assistant, administrator, wife and nurse.

Nancy Keller Muchas gracias a la familia Ozuna Morales en Mazatlán, que es mi familia adoptada – a mis amigas Rosa María, Mirla, Quina y todos; a Doña Petra y su familia en Mexcaltitán, y a Margarita en Creel. Thanks also to Molly Muir and John in Puerto Vallarta, Philomena ('Phil') and Trini in San Patricio-Melaque, and Suzanne and Gordon in Alamos.

From the Publisher

This edition of LP's Mexico guide was edited and coordinated by Katie Purvis. For editing/proofing help, thanks to everyone who pitched in, especially Janet Austin, Adrienne Costanzo, Rowan McKinnon, Mary Neighbour, Sarah Parkes, Paul Smitz, Stephen Townshend and Ian Ward. The maps were drawn by Chris Klep, Chris Love and Andrew Smith, with help from Kay Dancey, Jane Hart and Maliza Kruh. Design, illustration and layout were by Ann Jeffree, and the cover was the work of Tamsin Wilson. Additional illustrations were provided by Trudi Canavan and Jacqui Saunders. Thanks to Janet Austin and Ann Jeffree for indexing, and to Adrienne Costanzo, Jane Hart and Tamsin Wilson for general assistance. Katie would like to thank Lou Byrnes, Helen Castle and the Wondrous Rumbleweed for keeping her sane during this project, and Ann would like to thank Katie. Nice book – shame about the peso!

This Book

This is the fifth edition of Lonely Planet's Mexico guide. Past authors have included Doug Richmond, Dan Spitzer, Scott Wayne, Mark Balla, John Noble, Tom Brosnahan and Nancy Keller.

John was the coordinating author for this edition, which has undergone substantial reorganisation. He and Susan Forsyth wrote the Mexico City, Western Central Highlands, Northern Central Highlands and Oaxaca chapters, while James Lyon contributed the Around Mexico City, Central North Mexico, North-East Mexico and Central Gulf Coast chapters. Nancy Keller covered North-West Mexico and the Central Pacific Coast, and Tom Brosnahan was responsible for Tabasco & Chiapas and Yucatán. Wayne Bernhardson took care of Baja California.

Thanks to the many travellers who wrote in; a list of your names is on pages 969-70.

Warning & Request

Things change – prices go up, schedules change, good places go bad and bad places go bankrupt – nothing stays the same. So if you find things better or worse, recently opened or long since closed, please write and tell us and help make the next edition better.

Your letters will be used to help update future editions and, where possible, important changes will also be included in a Stop Press section in reprints.

We greatly appreciate all information that is sent to us by travellers. Back at Lonely Planet we employ a hard-working readers' letters team to sort through the many letters we receive. The best ones will be rewarded with a free copy of the next edition or another Lonely Planet guide if you prefer. We give away lots of books, but, unfortunately, not every letter/postcard receives one.

Contents

INTRODUCTION 11

FACTS ABOUT THE COUNTRY 12

History 12
Geography 35
Climate 36
Flora & Fauna 39

Government 41
Economy 41
Population 44
People 44

Arts & Culture 46
Religion 53
Language 54

FACTS FOR THE VISITOR 60

Visas & Embassies 60
Documents 63
Customs 64
Money 65
When to Go 68
What to Bring 68
Tourist Offices 69
Business Hours 69
Festivals & Public Holidays 69
Post 71

Telecommunications 72
Time 74
Electricity 74
Weights & Measures 74
Books 74
Maps 77
Media 77
Radio & TV 77
Film & Photography 78
Health 78

Women Travellers 85
Dangers & Annoyances 85
Work 86
Activities 87
Accommodation 88
Food 89
Drinks 94
Entertainment 96
Things to Buy 96

ARTESANÍAS 97

Buying Handicrafts 100
Textiles 102
Pottery 110
Masks & Headdresses 116
Lacquerware & Woodwork 118

Bark Paintings 121
Leather 122
Jewellery & Metalwork 122
Retablos 125
Baskets, Hats & Hammocks ... 125

Festival Crafts 127
Books on Mexican
Handicrafts 128

GETTING THERE & AWAY 129

Air 129
Land 133

River 137
Tours 137

GETTING AROUND 139

Air 139
Bus 139
Train 141

Car & Motorbike 142
Bicycle 144
Hitching 145

Boat 145
Local Transport 145

MEXICO CITY 146

History 146
Orientation 149
Information 150
Around the Zócalo 162
Around the Alameda 166
La Ciudadela 170
Around Plaza de la
República 170
Paseo de la Reforma &
Bosque de Chapultepec 172
Polanco 177

Lomas de Chapultepec 178
Tlatelolco & Guadalupe 178
Tlatelolco – Plaza de las
Tres Culturas 178
Tenayuca & Santa Cecilia
Acatitlán 180
Insurgentes Sur 180
San Ángel 181
Ciudad Universitaria 184
Cuicuilco 185
Coyoacán 186

Xochimilco 190
Parque Nacional Desierto
de Los Leones 191
Language Courses 191
Festivals 191
Places to Stay 192
Places to Eat 198
Entertainment 206
Things to Buy 210
Getting There & Away 211
Getting Around 219

AROUND MEXICO CITY 224

North of Mexico City 225
Tepotzotlán 225
Tula 228
Acolman 231
Teotihuacán 232
Pachuca 236
Around Pachuca 238
North of Pachuca – Hwy 105   239
East of Pachuca – Hwy 130 ... 239
East of Mexico City 239
Popocatépetl & Iztaccíhuatl ... 240
Tlaxcala 244
Cacaxtla 247
La Malinche 248

Huamantla 248
Puebla 248
Cholula 260
Around Cholula 263
Sierra Norte de Puebla 263
Pico de Orizaba 264
Southern Puebla 264
South of Mexico City 265
Tepoztlán 265
Oaxtepec 268
Cuautla 269
Cuernavaca 271
Around Cuernavaca 282
Taxco 283

Around Taxco 292
Iguala 293
West of Mexico City 293
Toluca 294
Around Toluca 297
Nevado de Toluca 297
Valle de Bravo 297
Tenango del Valle
& Teotenango 298
Tenancingo 298
Malinalco 298
Chalma 299
Ixtapan de La Sal 299

BAJA CALIFORNIA 300

**La Frontera & the
Desierto del Colorado** 300
Tijuana 302
Around Tijuana 308
Ensenada 308
Around Ensenada 313
Parque Nacional Constitución
de 1857 313
Parque Nacional Sierra San
Pedro Mártir 313
Mexicali 314
San Felipe 320

**The Desierto Central &
the Llano de Magdalena.** 320
Guerrero Negro 320
Around Guerrero Negro 321
Isla Cedros 321
Around Isla Cedros 323
San Ignacio 323
Around San Ignacio 324
Santa Rosalía 324
Mulegé 325
Loreto 326
Around Loreto 328

Ciudad Constitución 329
Around Ciudad Constitución . 329
**La Paz & the
Cape Region** 330
La Paz 330
Around La Paz 336
Los Barriles 336
Sierra de La Laguna 336
Todos Santos 337
San José del Cabo 338
The Los Cabos Corridor 341
Cabo San Lucas 341

NORTH-WEST MEXICO 347

Nogales 347
Other Border Crossings 351
Around Northern Sonora 351
Hermosillo 351
Bahía Kino (Kino Nuevo &
Kino Viejo) 356
Guaymas 357

Around Guaymas 360
Ciudad Obregón & Navojoa.. 361
Alamos 361
Around Alamos 367
Los Mochis 367
Topolobampo 370
El Fuerte 370

Culiacán 371
Barranca Del Cobre
(Copper Canyon) 371
Creel 376
Batopilas 380

CENTRAL NORTH MEXICO 381

Ciudad Juárez & El Paso
(Texas) 381
Other Border Crossings 388
Casas Grandes &
Nuevo Casas Grandes 389

Around Nuevo Casas
Grandes 390
Madera 390
Chihuahua 391
Around Chihuahua 396
Hidalgo del Parral 396

Around Hidalgo del Parral 397
Torreón, Gómez Palacio
& Ciudad Lerdo 397
Around Torreón 398
Durango 399
Around Durango 402

NORTH-EAST MEXICO 403

Tamaulipas 405
Nuevo Laredo 405
Reynosa 409
Matamoros 412
South of Matamoros 417
Ciudad Victoria 418

South of Ciudad Victoria 420
Nuevo León 420
Monterrey 420
Around Monterrey 434
North of Monterrey 435
South of Monterrey 435

Coahuila 436
Border Crossings 436
Monclova 436
Saltillo 436
Parras 442

CENTRAL PACIFIC COAST 443

Mazatlán 443	Puerto Vallarta 465	Playa Azul 495
Around Mazatlán 454	Chamela 480	Zihuatanejo & Ixtapa 497
Santiago Ixcuintla 455	San Patricio-Melaque 480	Around Zihuatanejo & Ixtapa 507
Mexcaltitán 455	Barra de Navidad 483	Acapulco 508
San Blas 457	Manzanillo 486	Around Acapulco 520
Tepic 461	Cuyutlán & Paraíso 492	Chilpancingo 522
Around Tepic 464	Lázaro Cárdenas 494	

WESTERN CENTRAL HIGHLANDS 523

Guadalajara & Around 525	Santuario de Mariposas	Zamora 579
Guadalajara 525	El Rosario 558	**Inland Colima 579**
Lago de Chapala 546	Pátzcuaro 560	Colima 580
Tequila 548	Around Pátzcuaro 568	Around Colima 586
Inland Michoacán 548	Uruapan 571	
Morelia 549	Around Uruapan 576	

NORTHERN CENTRAL HIGHLANDS 589

Zacatecas 590	San Luis Potosí 609	Dolores Hidalgo 634
Zacatecas 591	Santa María del Río 617	San Miguel de Allende 637
Around Zacatecas 599	Gogorrón 617	Around San Miguel 649
Fresnillo 600	Matehuala 618	**Querétaro 651**
Jerez 601	Real de Catorce 619	Querétaro 651
La Quemada 601	**Guanajuato 622**	San Juan del Río 658
Aguascalientes 602	Guanajuato 622	Tequisquiapan 659
Aguascalientes 602	Around Guanajuato 632	
San Luis Potosí 608	León 633	

CENTRAL GULF COAST 661

History 661	Around Tuxpan 673	Orizaba 702
Geography & Climate 663	Poza Rica 673	Around Orizaba 704
People 663	Poza Rica to Pachuca 674	**Southern Veracruz 704**
Tampico & the Huasteca 663	Papantla 674	Alvarado 704
Tampico-Ciudad Madero 664	El Tajín 676	Tlacotalpan 705
Ciudad Valles 668	South of Papantla 680	Santiago Tuxtla 705
Tamuín 669	**Central Veracruz 681**	Tres Zapotes 706
Tancanhuitz 669	Zempoala 681	San Andrés Tuxtla 707
Aquismón 669	Around Zempoala 682	Catemaco 709
Xilitla 670	Xalapa (Jalapa) 682	The Coast near Catemaco 711
Tamazunchale 670	Around Xalapa 688	Acayucan 712
Huejutla 670	La Antigua 688	San Lorenzo 712
South of Huejutla 670	Veracruz 688	Minatitlán & Coatzacoalcos .. 713
Northern Veracruz 670	Córdoba 699	
Tuxpan 671	Fortín de las Flores 701	

OAXACA STATE 714

History 714	Tlacolula 742	Ejutla 747
Geography & Climate 715	Santa Ana del Valle 742	**Mixteca Alta & Mixteca**
People 717	Yagul 742	**Baja 747**
Oaxaca City 717	Mitla 744	**Northern Oaxaca 749**
Central Valleys 736	Mixe Region 745	Tuxtepec & Guelatao 749
Monte Albán 737	Cuilapan 745	Huautla de Jiménez 749
El Tule 741	Zaachila 746	**Oaxaca Coast 750**
Dainzú 741	San Bartolo Coyotepec 746	Puerto Escondido 750
Teotitlán del Valle 741	Santo Tomás Jalieza 747	West of Puerto Escondido 758
Lambityeco 742	Ocotlán 747	Pochutla 759

Puerto Ángel 760
Zipolite 763
Beyond Zipolite 764
Bahías de Huatulco 765
Isthmus of Tehuantepec 770
Tehuantepec 770
Salina Cruz 772
Juchitán 773

TABASCO & CHIAPAS 775

Tabasco 775
History 775
Geography & Climate 777
Villahermosa 777
Comalcalco Ruins 786
Río Usumacinta 787
Chiapas 787
History 787
Geography & Climate 790
Economy 791
People 791

Tuxtla Gutiérrez 791
Tuxtla Gutiérrez to
Villahermosa 798
Chiapa de Corzo 798
Cañón del Sumidero 800
San Cristóbal de Las Casas ... 800
Around San Cristóbal
de Las Casas 815
San Cristóbal to Palenque 817
Palenque 821

Bonampak & Yaxchilán
Ruins 833
Comitán 836
Lagos de Montebello 839
Motozintla 841
Ciudad Cuauhtémoc 841
The Soconusco 842
Tapachula 844
Zapa 847
Talismán & Ciudad Hidalgo 848

THE YUCATÁN PENINSULA 849

History 849
Geography 852
Campeche State 852
Escárcega 852
Xpujil & Surrounds 853
Campeche 854
Campeche to Mérida –
Short Route (Hwy 180) 860
Campeche to Mérida –
Long Route (Hwy 261) 860
Yucatán 861
Mérida 861
Dzibilchaltún 875
Progreso 875
Celestún 877
Uxmal 878
The Puuc Route 883

Ticul 886
Ticul to Mérida 888
Ruinas de Mayapán 888
Ruinas de Mayapán
to Mérida 889
Izamal 889
Chichén Itzá 890
Valladolid 897
Tizimin 901
Río Lagartos 901
San Felipe 902
Quintana Roo 903
Cancún 903
Isla Mujeres 914
Around Isla Mujeres 920
Isla Holbox 921
Puerto Morelos 921

Playa del Carmen 922
Cozumel 925
Around Cozumel 932
Beaches – Cancún to Tulum   933
Tulum 935
Tulum to Boca Paila
& Punta Allen 939
Cobá 940
Felipe Carrillo Puerto 943
Laguna Bacalar 944
Chetumal 945
Around Chetumal 949
Kohunlich Ruins 949
South to Belize
& Guatemala 950

GLOSSARY 951

INDEX 957

Map Index 957
Text 958

Map Legend

BOUNDARIES

.... International Boundary

.... State Boundary

ROUTES

.... Freeway

.... Highway

.... Major Road

.... Unsealed Road or Track

.... City Road

.... City Street

.... Railway

.... Underground Railway

.... Metro

.... Walking Track

.... Walking Tour

.... Ferry Route

.... Cable Car or Chairlift

AREA FEATURES

.... Park, Gardens

.... National Park

.... Built-Up Area

.... Pedestrian Mall

.... Market

.... Cemetery

.... Reef

.... Beach or Desert

.... Rocks

HYDROGRAPHIC FEATURES

.... Coastline

.... River, Creek

.... Intermittent River or Creek

.... Lake, Intermittent Lake

.... Canal

.... Swamp

SYMBOLS

⊙ CAPITAL	.... National Capital	
◉ Capital	.... Regional Capital	
CITY	.... Major City	
● City	.... City	
● TOWN	.... Town	
● Village	.... Village	
■	.... Place to Stay	
▼	.... Place to Eat	
⛉	.... Pub, Bar	
✉ ☎	.... Post Office, Telephone	
❶ ❸	.... Tourist Information, Bank	
⊖ 🄿	.... Transport, Parking	
⛉ ⌂	.... Museum, Youth Hostel	
⚑ ⚐	Caravan Park, Camping Ground	
† ➡ †	.... Church, Cathedral	
⚊ ⚌	Buddhist Temple, Hindu Temple	
✚ ★	.... Hospital, Police Station	

✈ ✝	.... Airport, Airfield	
▱ ✿	.... Swimming Pool, Gardens	
❖ 🐘	.... Shopping Centre, Zoo	
⚘ ⛺	...Winery or Vineyard, Picnic Site	
← A25	One Way Street, Route Number	
⚶	...... Archaeological Site or Ruins	
🏛 ⚑	.... Stately Home, Monument	
⚔ ▣	.... Castle, Tomb	
⌒ ⌂	.... Cave, Hut or Chalet	
▲ ※	.... Mountain or Hill, Lookout	
⛯ ⚓	.... Lighthouse, Shipwreck	
)(⚷	.... Pass, Spring	
	.... Ancient or City Wall	
	.... Rapids, Waterfalls	
	.... Railway Station	
	.... Underground Station	
	...... Cliff or Escarpment, Tunnel	

Note: not all symbols displayed above appear in this book

Map Legend

BOUNDARIES

International Boundary

State Boundary

ROUTES

Freeway

Highway

Major Road

Unsealed Road or Track

City Road

City Street

Railway

Underground Railway

Metro

Walking Track

Walking Tour

Ferry Route

Cable Car or Chairlift

AREA FEATURES

Park, Gardens

National Park

Built-Up Area

Pedestrian Mall

Market

Cemetery

Trail

Beach or Desert

Rocks

HYDROGRAPHIC FEATURES

Coastline

River, Creek

Intermittent River or Creek

Lake, Intermittent Lake

Canal

Swamp

SYMBOLS

⊙ CAPITAL	National Capital		✈	Airport, Airfield
⊛ Capital	Regional Capital		⌕	Swimming Pool, Gardens
● CITY	Major City		◇	Shopping Centre, Zoo
⊙ City	City		⌖	Winery or Vineyard, Picnic Site
● TOWN	Town		—	One-Way Street, Route Number
• Village	Village		⋏	Archaeological Site or Ruins
●	Place to Stay		⚓	Battle, Home, Monument
▼	Place to Eat		⊞	Castle, Tomb
♥	Pub, Bar		⚑	Cave, Hut or Chalet
⊠	Post Office, Telephone		▲	Mountain or Hill, Lookout
⊕	Tourist Information, Bank		⚓	Lighthouse, Shipwreck
Ⓟ	Transport, Parking		)(	Pass, Spring
⌂	Museum, Youth Hostel			Ancient or City Wall
⚑	Caravan Park, Camping Ground		≋	Rapids, Waterfalls
✝	Church, Cathedral			Railway Station
☩	Buddhist Temple, Hindu Temple		⊖	Underground Station
✛	Hospital, Police Station			Cliff or Escarpment, Tunnel

Note: not all symbols displayed here appear on the maps in this book.

Introduction

Mexico is a land of extraordinary diversity. Great cultures and empires flourished here centuries ago, and their descendants – over 50 distinct Indian peoples, each with its own language – maintain vestiges of traditional lifestyles even in the midst of rampant modernisation. Traditional sources of wealth such as mining, fishing and agriculture coexist with modern manufacturing industries and services. Tourism is very important.

The country's diversity stems partly from topography: mountains and more mountains allowed indigenous peoples to pursue their destiny in some degree of isolation. Only in this century have modern roads, aeroplanes, radio and television knitted the various regions together into a national consciousness. Even so, being Mexican still means very different things to people in the nation's many distinct regions.

For the traveller, Mexico holds inexhaustible fascination in its cultures, cuisines, handicrafts, art and history. To explore Mexico is to travel through vast deserts, past snow-capped volcanoes, along tropical jungle-clad beaches, amidst ancient ruins, in teeming modern cities, timeless villages and posh resorts. The adventure is endless. Mexico has it all. What you make of it is up to you.

> **Stop Press**
> As this book went to press, the Mexican peso was in a state of crisis and subject to an international bail-out package. The research for the book was carried out before the collapse of the peso, so many of the prices quoted could be out of date. See the Money section on pages 65 to 68 for more details.

Facts about the Country

HISTORY

There is nothing new about the 'New World', as a look at Mexico's history reveals. The first people to inhabit this land may have arrived as many as 20,000 years before Columbus. Their descendants built a succession of brilliant, highly developed civilisations which flourished from 1200 BC to 1500 AD. Among these, the Maya and Aztec cultures are the best known. But in your travels through Mexico you'll have the opportunity to explore the achievements of the mysterious Olmecs of the Gulf Coast, the Zapotecs of Oaxaca, the great imperial city of Teotihuacán near Mexico City, the warlike Toltecs from Tula, the artistically accomplished Totonacs from Veracruz, and the Tarascans of Michoacán.

Historians divide Mexico's history before the Spanish conquest (the pre-Hispanic era) into four periods – Archaic, up to 1500 BC; Preclassic or Formative, 1500 BC to 250 AD; Classic, 250 to 900 AD; and Postclassic, 900 to the conquest of the Aztec Empire in 1521. However you divide it, Mexico's history is a fascinating procession of peoples and cultures.

Beginnings

The first inhabitants of the Americas came from Siberia during the last ice age in migrations that probably began about 50,000 BC and lasted until about 8000 BC. They came across a land bridge now submerged beneath the Bering Strait. The earliest human traces so far found in Mexico date from about 20,000 BC. These first Mexicans hunted the big herds of mammals that grazed the cool wet grasslands of the highland valleys. With the rise in temperatures at the end of the ice age, the valleys became much drier, ceasing to support such animal life and forcing the people to derive more food from plants.

Archaeologists have traced the slow beginnings of agriculture in the Tehuacán valley in Puebla state, where soon after 6500 BC people were planting seeds of chile pepper and a kind of squash. Between 5000 and 3500 BC they started to plant mutant forms of a tiny wild maize and to grind it into meal. After 3500 BC a much better variety of maize, and also beans, enabled the Tehuacán valley people to live semi-permanently in villages and spend less time in seasonal hunting camps. Pottery appeared by 2300 BC.

Mexico's earliest year-round villages were probably coastal, living by a combination of agriculture and seafood. There is evidence of such settlements on the Pacific coast of Chiapas from about 1500 BC, and there were probably similar places on the Gulf coast.

The Olmecs

Mexico's first civilisation arose near the Gulf coast, in the humid lowlands of southern Veracruz and neighbouring Tabasco. These were the Olmecs, or People from the Region of Rubber, a name coined in the 1920s. Olmec civilisation is famed for the awesome 'Olmec heads', stone sculptures of human heads up to three metres high with grim, pug-nosed features and wearing curious helmets. If the snarls and pitiless gazes on these heads are any guide, Olmec society was held together by fear – of terrifying gods, priests and rulers. The heads, typical of Olmec art, combine the features of human babies and jaguars – a mixture referred to as the 'were-jaguar'.

The first known great Olmec centre, San Lorenzo near Acayucan in Veracruz, flourished from about 1200 to 900 BC. The centre may well have been the creation of a ruling elite that emerged out of conflicts for the flood-fertilised lands of the area. San Lorenzo is a plateau about 1.25 km long and 50 metres high, at least partly human-made, that served chiefly as a politico-religious centre. Eight Olmec heads and many other carved stone monuments have been identified as originating here. Their basalt material was probably dragged, rolled or rafted from 60 to 80 km away. Finds there of objects from far away, such as artefacts of obsidian, a glasslike volcanic stone, from Guatemala and the Mexican highlands, suggest that San Lorenzo may have controlled trade over a very large area.

The second great Olmec centre was La Venta in Tabasco, which flourished from about 800 to 400 BC. Several tombs have been found here. In one of them, jade, a favourite pre-Hispanic ornamental material, makes its appearance. La Venta produced many more fine stone carvings, including at least five Olmec heads. Like San Lorenzo, it was violently destroyed long ago.

Olmec sites found far from the Gulf coast heartland may well have been trading posts-cum-garrisons placed to ensure the supply of jade, iron ore for mirrors, and other luxuries for the Olmec elite. The most impressive is Chalcatzingo, Morelos.

The Olmecs were Mexico's ancestral civilisation. Their art, religious beliefs and quite possibly their social organisation strongly influenced the civilisations that followed. Apart from the were-jaguar, which seems to have been linked with rain, Olmec gods included fire and maize deities and the feathered serpent, all of which persisted throughout the pre-Hispanic era.

Early Monte Albán
By 300 BC settled village life, based on agriculture but supported by hunting, had developed throughout the southern half of Mexico. At this time Monte Albán, the

hilltop centre of the Zapotec people of Oaxaca, was growing into a town of perhaps 10,000. Some of the stone carvings known as Danzantes (Dancers) from this era at Monte Albán show figures with Olmec-like downturned mouths and are considered 'Olmecoid' in style. Many of them have hieroglyphs or dates in a dot-and-bar system, which quite possibly means that the elite of Monte Albán were the inventors of writing and the written calendar in Mexico and Central America. The Zapotecs seem never to have tried extending their control beyond the mountainous Oaxaca region.

Izapa & the Early Maya
The large temple centre of Izapa near the Pacific coast of Chiapas, almost on the border of Guatemala, flourished from about 200 BC to 200 AD. Among its pyramids stood many tall stone slabs, called stelae, fronted by round altars and carved with mythological scenes showing Olmec-derived gods. Izapan culture was distributed from the former Olmec heartland to the Guatemalan highlands and is considered the link between the Olmec and the next great civilisation in southern Mexico, the Maya. Izapa and the early Maya shared several characteristics like the stele-altar pairing and 'Long Count' dates (see Mayan Writing & the Calendar later in this chapter).

Izapan civilisation may have been carried to the Maya by way of Kaminaljuyú, an ancient centre on the outskirts of modern Guatemala City. By the close of the Preclassic period in 250 AD, people in the

---

The Ball Game
Probably all pre-Hispanic Mexican cultures played the ball game, which may have varied from place to place and era to era but had certain lasting features. Special I-shaped ball courts appear at archaeological sites all over the country. The game seems to have been played between two teams and its essence was apparently to keep a rubber ball off the ground by flicking it with hips, thighs and possibly knees or elbows. The vertical or sloping walls around the courts were probably part of the playing area, not stands for spectators. The game had – at least sometimes – deep religious significance. It perhaps served as an oracle, with the result indicating which of two courses of action should be taken. Games could be followed by the sacrifice of one or more of the players – whether winners or losers, no one is sure! ∎

lowland Mayan areas – the Yucatán Peninsula and the Petén forest of northern Guatemala – were already building stepped temple pyramids and a characteristically Mayan type of roof, the corbel vault.

Teotihuacán

The first great civilisation of central Mexico emerged in a side-valley off the Valley of Mexico, about 50 km north-east of the centre of modern Mexico City. Teotihuacán grew into Mexico's biggest pre-Hispanic city, with an estimated 200,000 people at its height in the 6th century AD, controlling probably the biggest pre-Hispanic empire.

The building of a magnificent planned city began about the time of Christ. The greatest of its buildings, the 70-metre-high, 220-metre-square Pyramid of the Sun, the second biggest pyramid in Mexico and third biggest in the world, was constructed within the first 150 years AD. Most of the rest of the city, including the almost-as-big Pyramid of the Moon, was built between about 250 and 600 AD.

Culture & Economy Teotihuacán was a true city in that many classes of people lived and worked in it. It had writing and books, the bar-and-dot number system and the 260-day sacred year (see Mayan Writing & the Calendar). Literacy probably spread throughout its empire, except perhaps in the west. But the nature of its economic base, in a not especially fertile valley, has long been debated. Some suggest irrigation, others *chinampa* agriculture – the cultivating of the swampy margins of the lakes which then filled the Valley of Mexico. Exports of locally mined obsidian may also have been crucial.

Empire Teotihuacán probably became an imperialistic state after 400 AD. At its peak it may have controlled, one way or another, the southern two-thirds of Mexico, all of Guatemala and Belize, and bits of Honduras and El Salvador. But it was an empire probably geared to tribute-gathering, to feed the mouths and tastes of Teotihuacán's big population, rather than to full-scale occupation.

Cholula, near Puebla, with a pyramid

bigger even than the Pyramid of the Sun, was part of Teotihuacán's cultural sphere. Teotihuacán may also have had hegemony over the Zapotecs of Oaxaca during the zenith of their capital Monte Albán, which grew into a city of perhaps 25,000 people between about 300 and 600 AD. In about 400 AD Teotihuacán invaders built almost a miniature replica of their home city in Kaminaljuyú, Guatemala. From there they probably extended their sway over some of the Maya in the Petén.

Fall of Teotihuacán In the 7th century the heart of Teotihuacán was put to the torch and the city was plundered and largely abandoned. It is likely that the state had already been economically weakened – perhaps by the rise of rival powers in central Mexico, by a drying-up of the climate, or by desiccation caused by the denuding of the surrounding hillsides for wood.

Teotihuacán's influence on Mexico's later cultures was huge. Many of its gods, such as the feathered serpent Quetzalcóatl, an all-important symbol of fertility and life itself, and Tláloc, the rain god, were still being worshipped by the Aztecs a millennium later.

The Classic Maya

The Mayan region falls into three areas. The northern area is the Yucatán Peninsula; the central area is the Petén forest of northern Guatemala and adjacent lowlands in Mexico (to the west) and Belize (east); the southern area is the highlands and Pacific coast of Guatemala. It was the northern and central areas – the lowlands – that produced pre-Hispanic America's most brilliant civilisation, the Classic Maya, between about 250 and 900 AD.

Most of the major Classic Mayan sites are outside Mexico, in the Petén, with Tikál supreme among them. Since the early Classic Maya were probably partly controlled by Teotihuacán, it is not surprising that the era of Teotihuacán's decline was also one of disturbances among the Maya. But in the 7th century Mayan life seems to have resumed much as before.

Mayan Cities Mayan 'cities' were probably ceremonial, political and market centres for groups of farming hamlets. The rulers and artisans are thought to have lived close to these centres. The impossibility of intensive agriculture amid forests made large settlements unlikely, but the ceremonial centres and their associated settlements constituted city states.

A typical ceremonial centre focused on plazas surrounded by tall temple pyramids (usually the tombs of probably deified rulers), and lower buildings, so-called 'palaces', with warrens of small rooms. Stelae and altars were carved with dates and elaborate human and divine figures. Stone causeways called *sacbeob*, probably for ceremonial use, led out from the plazas.

Classic Mayan centres in Mexico fall into four zones: Chiapas in the central Mayan area, and Río Bec, Chenes and Puuc, all on the Yucatán Peninsula.

Chiapas The chief Chiapas sites are Yaxchilán, its tributary Bonampak (where vivid battle murals were found in 1948), and Palenque, which to many people is the most beautiful of all Mayan sites. Palenque rose to prominence under the 7th-century ruler Pakal, whose treasure-loaded tomb deep inside the fine Temple of the Inscriptions was discovered in 1952. Perhaps the most exquisite buildings at Palenque are the three delicate Temples of the Cross, built around a single plaza by Pakal's son Chan-Balum.

Río Bec & Chenes In Campeche state are the wild, little-investigated Río Bec and Chenes zones, noted for their lavishly carved buildings. Río Bec pyramids and palaces tend to be fronted by unclimbable false stairways leading to dummy rooms, and flanked by false towers.

Puuc The Puuc zone in Yucatán state was the focus of northern Classic Mayan culture. The most important of the many Puuc ceremonial centres was Uxmal, an architectural treasure trove south of Mérida. Puuc ornamentation, which reached its peak on the Governor's Palace at Uxmal, featured intricate stone mosaics on building façades, part-geometric but also incorporating faces of the hook-nosed, sky-serpent-cum-rain-god Chac. The façade of the amazing Palace of Masks at Kabah, 18.5 km south of Uxmal, is covered with over 300 Chac faces. The splendid Chichén Itzá, about 200 km east of Mérida, is another Puuc site, though it also owes much to a later era (see the Toltecs section following).

Mayan Art The art of the Maya was typically elegant but cluttered, and narrative in content. Fine carved stelae showing historical and mythological events have survived, with those in the central area generally superior. Mayan potters achieved marvellous multicoloured effects on grave vessels to accompany the dead to the next world. Jade, the most precious substance, was turned into beads or thin carved plaques.

Mayan Writing & the Calendar Classic Mayan intellectual achievements were among their greatest of all. They had a very complex writing system with 300 to 500 symbols, which only a minority then, and no one today, could fully understand.

The Maya also refined a calendar possessed by other pre-Hispanic peoples into a tool for exact recording of earthly and heavenly events. They could predict eclipses of the sun and the movements of the moon and Venus. Time was counted in three ways:

- in sacred or almanac years *(tzolkins)* composed of 13 periods of 20 days;
- in 'vague' solar years *(haabs)* of 18 20-day 'months' followed by a special five-day 'portentous' period called the Uayeb; the last day of each 'month' was known as the 'seating' of the next month, in line with the Mayan belief that the future influences the present;
- in units of one, 20, 360, 7200 and 144,000 days.

All Mexico's pre-Hispanic civilisations used the first two counts, whose interlocking enabled a date to be located precisely within a period of 52 years called a Calendar Round. But the Maya were the pre-eminent users of the third count, known as the Long Count, and was infinitely extendable. Their inscriptions

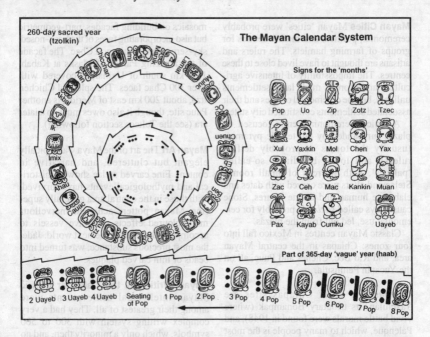

The Mayan Calendar System

260-day sacred year (tzolkin)

Part of 365-day 'vague' year (haab)

2 Uayeb 3 Uayeb 4 Uayeb Seating of Pop 1 Pop 2 Pop 3 Pop 4 Pop 5 Pop 6 Pop 7 Pop 8 Pop

Signs for the 'months'

Pop Uo Zip Zotz Tzec

Xul Yaxkin Mol Chen Yax

Zac Ceh Mac Kankin Muan

Pax Kayab Cumku Uayeb

enumerate the Long Count units elapsed from a starting (Creation) point of 13 August 3114 BC. Numbers were written in a system of dots (counted as one) and bars (counted as five).

Mayan Religion Religion permeated every facet of Mayan life. The Maya believed in predestination, and had a complex astrology. But they also carried out elaborate rituals, involving incense offerings, the alcoholic drink *balche*, bloodletting from ears, tongues or penises, and dances, feasts and sacrifices, to win the gods' favours. The Classic Maya seem to have practised human sacrifice on a small scale, the Postclassic on a bigger scale. Beheading was probably the most common method. At Chichén Itzá, victims were thrown into a deep *cenote* (well) to bring rain.

The Maya inhabited a universe with a centre and four directions (each associated with a colour – east, red; north, white; west, black; south, yellow; the centre, green), plus 13 layers of heavens and nine layers of

underworld to which the dead descended. The earth was thought of as the back of a giant reptile floating on a pond. (It's not *too* hard to imagine yourself as a flea on this creature's back as you look across a Mayan landscape!)

The Maya believed themselves descended from people made from maize gruel. The current world was just one of a succession of worlds destined to end in cataclysm and be succeeded by another. This cyclical nature of things enabled the future to be predicted by looking at the past.

Important Mayan gods included Itzamná (who was the fire deity and either the supreme creator or the son of the supreme creator), Chac the rain god, Yum Kaax the maize and vegetation god, and Ah Puch the death god. The feathered serpent, known to the Maya as Kukulcán, was introduced from central Mexico in the Postclassic period. Also worshipped were dead ancestors, particularly rulers, who were thought to be descended from the gods.

Flora & Fauna
Top: Desert scenery (JL); Reclamation (DT)
Bottom: Lizard, Cancún (TW); Parrot (SW)

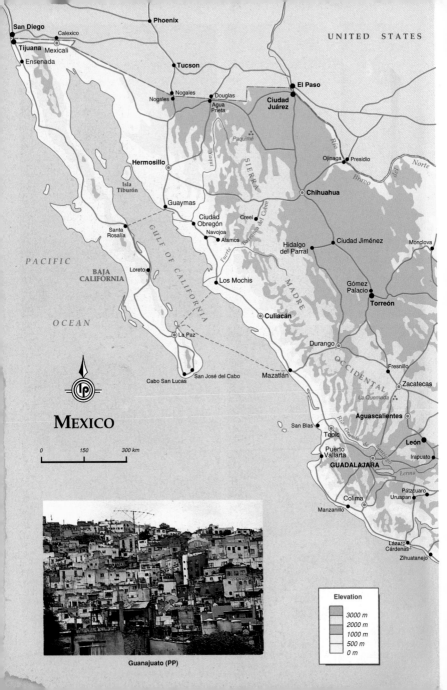

MEXICO

United States

San Diego
Phoenix
Tijuana
Mexicali
Calexico
Ensenada

Tucson

El Paso
Nogales
Nogales
Douglas
Ciudad
Agua
Juárez
Prieta

Paquimé

SIERRA

Hermosillo

Ojinaga   Presidio

Isla
Tiburón

Chihuahua

Guaymas

Creel
Ciudad
Obregón
Navojoa
Álamos

Hidalgo
del Parral
Ciudad Jiménez
Monclova

PACIFIC

Santa
Rosalía

BAJA
CALIFORNIA

Loreto

Los Mochis

Gómez
Palacio
Torreón

OCEAN

La Paz

Culiacán

Durango

Fresnillo

Zacatecas
La Quemada

Cabo San Lucas   San José del Cabo
Mazatlán

OCCIDENTAL

Aguascalientes

San Blas

Tepic
León
Irapuato

Puerto
Vallarta
GUADALAJARA

Lerma

Pátzcuaro
Uruapan

Colima

Manzanillo

Lázaro
Cárdenas
Zihuatanejo

0   150   300 km

Elevation

3000 m
2000 m
1000 m
500 m
0 m

Guanajuato (PP)

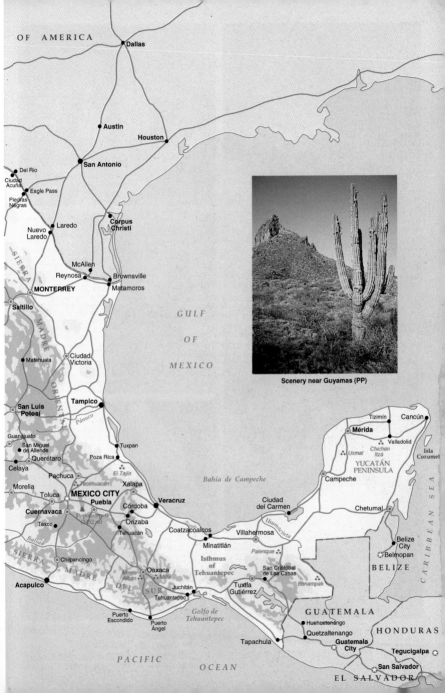

Scenery near Guyamas (PP)

People

A Tziscao children (JN)
B Washing radishes, Mérida (GE)

C Cleaning fish, Zacatecas (PP)
D Carnaval, San Andrés Larrainzar (JN)
E Woman from Pátzcuaro (PP)

The Mayan Collapse In the second half of the 8th century, trade between Mayan states started to shrink and conflict began to grow. By the early 10th century the central Mayan area was virtually abandoned, most of its people probably migrating to the northern area or the highlands of Chiapas. Population pressure and ecological damage are considered likely causes of the collapse.

Classic Veracruz Civilisation
Along the Gulf coast, in what are now central and northern Veracruz, the Classic period saw the rise of a number of independent power centres with a shared culture – together known as the Classic Veracruz civilisation. Their hallmark is a style of abstract carving featuring pairs of curved and interwoven parallel lines. Classic Veracruz appears to have been particularly obsessed with the ball game; its most important centre, El Tajín near Papantla, which was at its height from about 600 to 900 AD, contains at least 11 ball courts.

The Toltecs
In central Mexico, one chief power centre after the decline of Teotihuacán was Xochicalco, a hilltop site in Morelos with both Mayan influence and impressive evidence of a feathered-serpent cult. Another may have been Cholula. A third was Tula, 65 km north of Mexico City. Tula is widely thought to have been the capital of a great empire referred to by later Aztec 'histories' as that of the Toltecs (Artificers).

It is particularly hard to disentangle myth and history in the Tula/Toltec story because the annals which form part of the evidence may be more legend than fact. A widely accepted version is that the Toltecs were one of a number of semicivilised tribes from dry northern Mexico who moved into the Valley of Mexico area after the fall of Teotihuacán. Tula became their capital, probably in the 10th century, growing into a city of 30,000 or 40,000. The Tula ceremonial centre is dedicated primarily to the feathered serpent god Quetzalcóatl, but the annals relate that Quetzalcóatl was displaced by Tezcatlipoca

(Smoking Mirror), a newcomer god of warriors and sorcery, who demanded a regular diet of the hearts of sacrificed warriors. A Quetzalcóatl king fled to the Gulf coast and set sail eastward on a raft of snakes, promising one day to return.

Tula seems to have become the capital of a militaristic kingdom that dominated central Mexico. Warriors were organised in orders dedicated to different animal-gods – the coyote, jaguar and eagle knights. Mass human sacrifice may have started at Tula.

The influence of Tula was enormous. It is seen at Paquimé in Chihuahua, at Gulf coast sites like Castillo de Teayo, and in western Mexico. Pottery from as far south as Costa Rica has been found at Tula, and there's even probable Tula influence in temple mounds and artefacts found in Tennessee and Illinois.

Tula was abandoned about the start of the 13th century, seemingly destroyed by Chichimecs, as the periodic hordes of barbarian raiders from the north came to be known. Its people apparently dispersed to the southern part of the Valley of Mexico and further afield. Many later Mexican peoples revered the Toltec era as a golden age. Some rulers, including Mayan leaders and Aztec emperors, claimed to be descended from the Toltecs.

Chichén Itzá Mayan scripts relate that towards the end of the 10th century much of the northern Yucatán Peninsula was conquered by one Kukulcán (Feathered Serpent). The Puuc Mayan site of Chichén Itzá in northern Yucatán contains many Tula-like features, from flat beam-and-masonry roofs (contrasting with the Mayan corbel roof) to gruesome chac-mools – reclining human figures holding dishes which were probably receptacles for human hearts torn out in sacrifices. There's a resemblance that can hardly be coincidental between Tula's Pyramid B and Chichén Itzá's Temple of the Warriors. Many writers therefore believe Toltec exiles invaded Yucatán and created a new, even grander version of Tula at Chichén Itzá.

To confuse matters, however, there's a respectable body of opinion that believes the

Tula-style features at Chichén Itzá *predated* Tula, implying that Chichén Itzá, not Tula, was the epicentre of whatever culture this was. Some even argue that the great Toltecs referred to in the Aztec annals may not have been the people of Tula, but those of another great earlier city, Teotihuacán.

The Aztecs

Rise of the Aztecs The Aztecs' own legends relate that they were the chosen people of their tribal god Huizilopochtli. Originally nomads from the north or west of Mexico who were led to the Valley of Mexico by their priests, they settled on islands in the series of lakes that then filled much of the valley, because they saw there an eagle standing on a cactus, eating a snake – the sign, their prophecies had told them, to show where to stop their wandering.

The Aztec capital Tenochtitlán was founded on one of these islands in the first half of the 14th century. For half a century or more the Aztecs served the rulers of Azcapotzalco on the lake shore, which was gaining control over some of the dozens of rival statelets in the valley. Then, around 1426, the Aztecs rebelled against Azcapotzalco and themselves became the most powerful people in the valley.

The Aztec Empire In the mid-1400s, with their sense of being a chosen people growing, the Aztecs formed the Triple Alliance with two other valley states, Texcoco and Tlacopan, to wage war against Tlaxcala and Huejotzingo, outside the valley to the east. The prisoners they took would form the diet of sacrificed warriors that their god Huizilopochtli demanded, to keep the sun rising every day. For the dedication of Tenochtitlán's Great Temple in 1487, the Aztec emperor Ahuízotl had 20,000 captives sacrificed.

In the second half of the 15th century the Triple Alliance, led by the Aztec emperors Moctezuma I Ilhuicamina, Axayácatl and Ahuízotl, brought most of central Mexico from the Gulf coast to the Pacific (though not Tlaxcala) under its control. The total popu-lation of the empire's 38 provinces may have been about five million. The empire's purpose was to exact tribute of resources absent from the heartland – such as jade, turquoise, cotton, paper, tobacco, rubber, lowland fruits and vegetables, cacao, and precious feathers – which were needed for the glorification of its elite and to support the many nonproductive servants of its war-oriented state.

Ahuízotl's successor was Moctezuma II Xocoyotzin, a reflective character who believed – perhaps fatally – that the Spaniard Hernán Cortés, who arrived on the Gulf Coast in 1519, might be the feathered serpent god Quetzalcóatl, returned from the east to reclaim his throne.

Economy & Society By 1519 Tenochtitlán and the adjoining Aztec city of Tlatelolco probably had over 200,000 inhabitants and the Valley of Mexico as a whole probably over a million. These were supported by a variety of intensive farming methods using only stone and wooden tools, but including irrigation, terracing and lake and swamp rec-lamation.

The basic unit of Aztec society was the *calpulli*, consisting of a few dozen to a few hundred extended families, owning land communally. The Aztec king held absolute power but delegated important roles like priest or tax collector to members of the *pilli* (nobles). Military leaders were usually *tec-uhtli*, elite professional soldiers. Another special group was the *pochteca*, militarised merchants who helped extend the empire, brought goods to the capital and organised large, important markets, held daily in big towns. At the bottom of society were pawns (paupers who could sell themselves for a specified period), serfs and slaves.

Culture & Religion Tenochtitlán-Tlatelolco had hundreds of temple complexes, the greatest of which was located on and around modern Mexico City's Zócalo. Its main temple pyramid, dedicated to Huizilopochtli and the rain god Tláloc, was 40 metres high and 100 metres long on each side.

Much Aztec culture was drawn from earlier Mexican civilisations. They had writing, bark-paper books, and the Calendar Round. They observed the heavenly bodies in great detail for astrological purposes. A routine of great ceremonies, many of them public, was performed by celibate priests. Typically these would include offerings, sacrifices, and masked dances or processions enacting myths.

Like the Maya, the Aztecs believed they lived in a world whose predecessors had been destroyed – in this case the fifth world. The previous four had each been ended by the death of the sun, wiping out humanity each time. Aztec human sacrifices were designed to keep the sun alive. Like the Maya, the Aztecs saw the world as having four directions, 13 heavens and nine hells. Those who died by drowning, leprosy, lightning, gout, dropsy or lung disease went to the paradisiac gardens of Tláloc, the god who had killed them; warriors who were sacrificed or died in battle, merchants killed travelling far away, and women who died giving birth to their first child all went to heaven as companions of the sun; everyone else travelled for four years under the northern deserts, in the subterranean abode of the death god Mictlantecuhtli, before reaching the ninth hell where they vanished altogether.

Other Postclassic Civilisations

On the eve of the Spanish conquest many Mexican societies, including the Aztecs, held deep similarities. Each was politically centralised and divided into classes, with many people occupied in specialist tasks, including professional priests. Agriculture was productive despite the lack of draft animals, metal tools and the wheel. Maize tortillas and *pozol* (maize gruel) were staple foods. Beans provided important protein, and a great variety of other crops were grown in different regions, from squashes, tomatoes and chiles to avocados, peanuts, papayas and pineapples. Luxury foods for the elite included turkey, domesticated hairless dog, game, and chocolate drinks. Exchange of foods between different regions was an important reason for trade. All peoples worshipped a variety of powerful gods (often shared with other cultures), some of which demanded human sacrifices. War was widespread, often in connection with the need to take prisoners for sacrifice.

Maya The 'Toltec' phase at Chichén Itzá lasted until about 1200. Chichén's subsequent rulers are thought to have been a Mayan people called the Itzá, who went on to found the town of Mayapán, south of modern Mérida. Mayapán, under the Cocom line of the Itzá, came to dominate most of the Yucatán Peninsula city states until the 15th century, when the Cocom were overthrown in a rebellion and Mayapán was destroyed. The peninsula became a quarrelling-ground of numerous city states with a culture much decayed from Classic Mayan glories.

Oaxaca Zapotec civilisation had declined since the 8th century. From about 1200 the remaining Zapotec settlements, such as

Knife used in Aztec human sacrifice

Mitla and Yagul, were increasingly dominated by the Mixtecs, famed metalsmiths and potters from the uplands around the Oaxaca-Puebla border. Mixtec and Zapotec cultures became entangled before much of their territory fell to the Aztecs in the 15th and 16th centuries.

Gulf Coast The Totonacs, a people who may have occupied El Tajín in its later years, established themselves in much of what is now Veracruz state. To their north, the Huastec civilisation, another web of probably independent statelets, flourished from 800 to 1200. In the 15th century the Aztecs subdued most of the Totonac and Huastec areas.

The West One civilised people who avoided conquest by the Aztecs were the Tarascans, who ruled the area of modern Michoacán from their capital Tzintzuntzan, about 200 km west of Mexico City. Like the Mixtecs they were skilled artisans and jewellers; fire and the moon were among their chief deities.

The Spanish Conquest

Ancient Mexican civilisation, nearly 3000 years old, was shattered in two short years from 1519 to 1521. A tiny group of invaders destroyed the Aztec empire, brought a new religion and reduced the native people to second-class citizens and slaves. So alien to each other were the newcomers and the Indians that each doubted whether the other was human (the Pope gave the Indians the benefit of the doubt in 1537).

From this traumatic encounter arose modern Mexico. Most Mexicans, being *mestizo* (of mixed Indian and European blood), are descendants of both cultures. But while Cuauhtémoc, the last Aztec emperor, is now an official hero, Cortés, the leader of the Spanish conquerors, is a villain, and Indians who helped him are seen as traitors.

Early Expeditions The Spaniards had been in the Caribbean since Christopher Columbus arrived in 1492, with their main bases on the islands of Hispaniola and Cuba. Realis-

ing that they had not reached the East Indies, they began looking for a passage through the land mass to their west but were distracted by tales of gold, silver and a rich empire there. Trading, slaving and exploring expeditions from Cuba, led by Francisco Hernández de Córdoba in 1517 and Juan de Grijalva in 1518, were driven back from Mexico's Gulf coast by hostile natives.

In 1518 the governor of Cuba, Diego Velázquez, asked Hernán Cortés, a Spanish colonist on the island, to lead a new expedition westward. As Cortés gathered ships and men, Velázquez became uneasy about the costs and Cortés's loyalty, and cancelled the expedition. Cortés ignored him and set sail on 15 February 1519 with 11 ships, 550 men and 16 horses.

Cortés's cunning and Machiavellian tactics are legendary, but the Aztecs played military politics too. The story of their confrontation is one of the most bizarre in history.

Cortés & the Aztecs Landing first at Cozumel off the Yucatán Peninsula, the Spaniards were joined by Jerónimo de Aguilar, a Spaniard who had been shipwrecked there several years earlier, and who now spoke the Indians' language. Moving west along the coast to Tabasco, they defeated some hostile Indians and Cortés delivered the first of many lectures to Indians on the importance of Christianity and the greatness of King Carlos I of Spain. The Indians gave him 20 maidens, among them Doña Marina (La Malinche) who became his interpreter, aide and lover.

The expedition next put in near the present city of Veracruz, where the local Totonac Indians were friendly. Meanwhile, in the Aztec capital Tenochtitlán, tales of 'towers floating on water' bearing fair-skinned beings had been carried to Moctezuma II, the Aztec god-king. Lightning struck a temple, a comet sailed through the night skies, a bird 'with a mirror in its head' was brought to Moctezuma, who saw warriors in it. According to the Aztec calendar, 1519 would see the legendary god-king Quetzalcóatl's return from the east. Moctezuma tried to discourage Cortés from travelling to Tenochtitlán by sending messages about the difficult terrain and hostile tribes that lay between them.

The Spaniards were well received at the Totonac towns of Zempoala and Quiahuiztlán, which resented Aztec domination. Cortés thus gained his first Indian allies. Cortés set up a settlement called Villa Rica de la Vera Cruz, and then apparently scuttled his ships to remove any ideas of retreat from his men's minds. Leaving about 150 men at Villa Rica, Cortés set off inland for Tenochtitlán. On the way he convinced the Tlaxcalan Indians that he was their friend, and they became his most valuable allies.

Moctezuma finally invited Cortés to meet him, denying responsibility for an ambush at Cholula which had resulted in the Spanish massacring many of that town's inhabitants. The Spaniards and 6000 Indian allies thus approached the Aztecs' island capital – a city bigger than any in Spain. Entering Tenochtitlán on 8 November 1519 along one of the causeways which joined it to the lake shore, Cortés was met by Moctezuma, who was carried by nobles in a litter with a canopy of feathers and gold. The Spaniards were lodged – as befitted gods – in the former palace of Axayácatl, Moctezuma's father.

Hernán Cortés

Though attended to with considerable luxury, the Spaniards were trapped. Some of the Aztec leaders advised Moctezuma to attack them, even though they might be gods. Moctezuma hesitated and the Spaniards took him hostage instead. Moctezuma, believing Cortés a god, kept his people from rebelling by telling them that he went willingly. But hostility rose in the city, aggravated by the Spaniards' destruction of Aztec idols.

The Fall of Tenochtitlán After the Spaniards had been in Tenochtitlán about six months, Moctezuma informed Cortés that another fleet had arrived on the Veracruz coast. This was led by Pánfilo de Narváez, sent by Diego Velázquez to arrest Cortés. Cortés left 140 Spaniards under Pedro de Alvarado in Tenochtitlán and sped to the coast with his remaining forces. They routed Narváez' much bigger force one night in May 1520 and most of the defeated men joined Cortés.

But in their absence the long-feared confrontation took place in Tenochtitlán. Apparently fearing an attack, the Spaniards had struck first and killed about 200 Aztec nobles trapped in a square during a festival. Cortés and his enlarged force returned to the Aztec capital and were allowed to rejoin their comrades – only then to come under fierce attack. Trapped in Axayácatl's palace, Cortés persuaded Moctezuma to try to pacify his people. According to one version, the king went on to the roof to address the crowds but was unable to calm them and, wounded by missiles, died soon afterwards; other versions have it that the Spaniards killed him.

The Spaniards fled on the night of 30 June 1520, but several hundred of them, and thousands of their Indian allies, were killed on this Noche Triste (Sad Night). The survivors were however welcomed at Tlaxcala, where they prepared for another campaign by building boats in sections which could be carried across the mountains for a waterborne assault on Tenochtitlán. When the 900 Spaniards re-entered the Valley of Mexico, they were accompanied by 100,000 native allies. For the first time, the odds were in their favour.

Moctezuma had been replaced by his nephew, Cuitláhuac, who then died of smallpox, brought to Mexico by one of Narváez' soldiers. He was succeeded by another nephew, the 18-year-old Cuauhtémoc. The attack started in May 1521 and the Spaniards' boats soon bested the Aztecs' canoes. But the besieged Aztecs refused to surrender, and Cortés resorted to razing Tenochtitlán to the ground, building by building. By 13 August 1521 the resistance ended. The captured Cuauhtémoc asked Cortés to kill him, but was denied his request.

The Colonial Era
The Encomienda System Establishing their headquarters at Coyoacán on the southern shore of the lake, the Spaniards organised the rebuilding of Tenochtitlán as the capital of Nueva España (New Spain), as the new colony was called. In an unsuccessful bid to discover the whereabouts of the fabled treasure hoards, they reputedly tortured Cuauhtémoc and other Aztec nobles by burning the soles of their feet.

By 1524 virtually all the Aztec empire, plus some outlying regions such as Colima, the Huasteca and the Tehuantepec area, had been brought under at least loose Spanish control.

To reward his soldiers, Cortés granted them *encomiendas* – rights to the labour or tribute of groups of Indians. Under this system the settlers were also supposed to convert and 'civilise' their Indians, but in reality the system often produced little more than slavery. In 1528 Cortés was himself granted 22 towns as encomiendas and given the title Marqués del Valle de Oaxaca, but was denied the role of governor. He returned to Spain in 1540 and died near Seville in 1547. The rest of the 16th century saw a long, eventually successful struggle by the Spanish crown to control the conquistadors, who often resisted its attempts to restrict their power in the land they had conquered in its name. By the 17th century the number of encomiendas had fallen drastically (partly because of an

appalling decline in the Indian population) and the system was abolished in the 18th century.

New Spain In 1527 the Spanish king set up New Spain's first *audiencia*, a high court with government functions. Its leader, Nuño de Guzmán, was among the worst of Mexican history's long list of corrupt, violent leaders. Guzmán made an enemy of Mexico City's first bishop, Juan de Zumárraga, who was shocked by the maltreatment of the Indians. Guzmán then set off on a bloody expedition to conquer western Mexico, from Michoacán up to Sonora. Eventually he was recalled to Spain.

The second audiencia (1530-35) brought some order to the colony. The king then appointed Antonio de Mendoza as New Spain's first viceroy – his personal representative to govern the colony. Mendoza, who ruled for 15 years, gave New Spain the stability it badly needed, limited the worst exploitation of the Indians, encouraged the spread of Christianity and ensured steady revenue to the Spanish crown.

The Yucatán Peninsula was subdued in the 1540s by two men both called Francisco de Montejo. This meant that all the southern half of Mexico was in Spanish hands, as well as Central America, which had been conquered in the 1520s by Spanish forces from Mexico and Panama. That left the huge 'Chichimec frontier' – roughly, the area north of a line between modern Tampico and Guadalajara – inhabited by the fierce seminomads known as Chichimecs (Barbarians). The discovery of big silver deposits in Zacatecas in the mid-1540s, followed by major finds at Guanajuato, San Luis Potosí and Pachuca, spurred Spanish attempts to subdue the Chichimec area. These were only successful in the 1590s, after the Spanish offered the Chichimecs food and clothing in return for peace.

New Spain, the area governed by the viceroy in Mexico City, stretched from these northern frontiers to the border of Panama in the south, and by 1700 it would also officially include Spain's Caribbean islands and the Philippines. In practice, however, Central America, the Caribbean and the Philippines were governed separately.

The northern borders were slowly extended by missionaries and a scattering of settlers. By the early 19th century, New Spain included most of the modern US states of Texas, New Mexico, Arizona, California, Utah and Colorado, though its control over much of this area was tenuous.

Indians & Missionaries Despite the efforts of Bishop Zumárraga and Viceroy Mendoza, the position of the conquered peoples deteriorated disastrously, not only because of harsh treatment at the hands of the colonists but also because of a series of plagues, many of them new diseases brought by the Spaniards. The Indian population of New Spain fell from an estimated 25 million at the time of conquest to a little over one million by 1605.

The Indians' only real allies were some of the monks who started arriving in New Spain in 1523 to convert them. Many of the monks were compassionate and brave men; the Franciscans and Dominicans distinguished themselves by protecting the Indians from the colonists' worst excesses. One Dominican monk, Bartolomé de Las Casas, persuaded the king to enact new laws in the 1540s to protect the Indians. But when this nearly caused a rebellion among the encomienda holders the laws were not put into practice.

The monks' missionary work helped extend Spanish control over Mexico. By 1560 they had built over 100 monasteries, some fortified, and had carried out millions of conversions. Under the second viceroy, Luis de Velasco, Indian slavery was abolished in the 1550s, to be partly replaced by black slavery. Forced labour on encomiendas was also stopped, but since the population of workers was plummeting, a new system of about 45 days' forced labour a year (the *cuatequil*) for all Indians was introduced. This too was widely abused by the Spaniards until abolished about half a century later.

The Criollos From the 16th to 19th centuries, a sort of apartheid system was in effect in Mexico. A person's place in society was determined by skin colour, parentage and birthplace. Spanish-born colonists – known as *peninsulares* or, derisively, *gachupines*, were a minuscule part of the population but were at the top of the socioeconomic ladder and were considered nobility in New Spain, however humble their status in Spain.

Next on the ladder were *criollos*, people born of Spanish parents in New Spain. By the 18th century some criollos had managed to acquire fortunes in mining, commerce, ranching and agriculture *(haciendas*, large landed estates, had begun to grow up as early as the 16th century); not surprisingly criollos sought political power commensurate with their wealth.

Below the criollos were the *mestizos*, people of mixed Spanish and Indian or African slave ancestry, and at the bottom of the pile were the remaining Indians and the Africans. Though the poor were now paid for their labour, they were paid very little, and many were *peones*, bonded labourers tied by debt to their employers. Indians still had to pay tribute to the crown.

King Carlos III (1759-88), aware of the threat to New Spain from British and French expansion in North America, sought to bring the colony under firmer, more centralised control and improve the flow of funds to the crown, which desperately needed the additional revenue. Several effective changes were made, such as replacing a whole tier of the colonial administration – the 200 notoriously corrupt and oppressive *alcaldes mayores* and *corregidores* who supposedly acted as New Spain's district administrators – with 12 *intendants*. These officials would oversee much larger areas and were charged with improving justice, public facilities and defence; collecting taxes; controlling royal monopolies; and stopping smuggling. Equally importantly, Charles expelled the Jesuits, whom he suspected of disloyalty and intrigues, from the entire Spanish empire. The Jesuits in New Spain had played major roles in missionary work, education and

A Different Sort of Liberator

The Spanish invaders of the New World acquired, and in many cases earned, a reputation for brutality towards the peoples of the Americas and often amongst themselves. Such cruelty contributed to the notorious 'Black Legend' of the invaders' 'deliberate sadism', in the words of respected historian Charles Gibson.

While the Black Legend allowed northern European powers like the British to claim a moral high ground to which, in historical context, they probably had no right, there is no lack of evidence for the legend. For instance, the Spaniards imported vicious mastiffs for combat, intimidation, punishment, torture, blood sports, guard duty and tracking Indian fugitives. In the invaders' footsteps followed representatives of the Catholic Church, enforcing 'Christian principles' among peoples they regarded as pagans. Since those early days, the official Church has often been identified with brutal authority, but a strong counter-current of thought began in early colonial times and has survived to the present.

Of several figures, the outstanding one was Father Bartolomé de Las Casas – though he was at first glance an unlikely figure to protest maltreatment of the Indians. Born in Seville in 1474, he first reached the Americas in 1502 as part of an expedition against the Indians of Higuey, on the island of Hispaniola; he soon held encomiendas there and in Cuba. However, he experienced a conversion which convinced him of the evils of the system, and devoted the rest of his life to the cause of justice for the indigenous peoples of Spanish America.

Renouncing his encomiendas, Las Casas returned to Spain to argue for reform of the abuses he had observed in the Indies. His impassioned advocacy of indigenous causes led to a failed attempt at peaceful evangelisation on the Venezuelan coast – Las Casas detested the idea of forced conversion – but his polemical *Very Brief Account of the Destruction of the Indies* persuaded King Carlos V to enact the New Laws of 1542, which included a major reform of the encomienda system. Though the New Laws proved difficult to enforce, Las Casas continued to speak out against corrupt officials and encomenderos from his position as bishop of Chiapas (Mexico) and then as Protector of the Indians at the Spanish court in Madrid until his death in 1566.

Before the court, the audacious Dominican reported one cacique's statement that, if Spaniards went to heaven, the Indians would prefer hell, and went so far as to defend the practice of cannibalism, to advocate restitution for all the wealth that Spain had plundered from the Americas, and even to imply the return of the lands themselves to the Indians in the interests of good government:

When we entered there...would we have found such great unions of peoples in their towns and cities if they had lacked the order of a good way of life, peace, concord and justice?

While Las Casas never achieved such utopian goals, his advocacy undoubtedly mitigated some of the worst abuses against the Indians. In this sense, he was a role model for the Latin American activist clergy of recent decades which, inspired by 'Liberation Theology', has worked to alleviate poverty and human rights abuses despite great personal risk. Las Casas was the original liberation theologist.

In addition to his sense of commitment, Las Casas left valuable and accurate observations of Indian customs and history. His estimates of the dense population of Hispaniola, which he counted about four million, have been confirmed and even augmented by modern researchers. His is a broad and complex legacy with great modern relevance.

Wayne Bernhardson

administration, and two-thirds of them were criollos.

Continuing its attack on the increasingly powerful Catholic church in New Spain, which had amassed a big enough fortune from bequests to allow it to lend money to local entrepreneurs, the crown in 1804 decreed the immediate transfer of all church charitable fund assets to the royal coffers. As a result the church had to call in many debts, which hit many criollos hard and created widespread discontent against the crown. The catalyst for rebellion came in 1808 when Napoleon Bonaparte occupied most of Spain and forced King Carlos IV to abdicate, putting his own brother on the throne. Direct

Spanish control over New Spain suddenly ceased. Rivalry between peninsulares and criollos in the colony intensified, with criollos setting up a junta which was then dissolved by peninsulares loyal to the crown.

Independence

War of Independence In 1810 a coterie based in Querétaro, 200 km north-west of Mexico City, began actively planning a rebellion. News of the plans leaked to the government, so the group acted immediately. On 16 September one of its members, Miguel Hidalgo y Costilla, the criollo parish priest of the town of Dolores, summoned his parishioners to the church and issued his now-famous call to rebellion, the Grito de Dolores, whose exact words have been lost to history but whose gist was:

My children, a new dispensation comes to us this day. Are you ready to receive it? Will you be free? Will you make the effort to recover from the hated Spaniards the lands stolen from your forefathers 300 years ago? We must act at once... Long live Our Lady of Guadalupe! Death to bad government!

An angry mob formed and marched quickly on San Miguel, Celaya and Guanajuato, massacring the peninsulares in Guanajuato. Over the next month and a half the rebels captured Zacatecas, San Luis Potosí and Valladolid (Morelia). On 30 October the rebel army, now numbering about 80,000, defeated loyalist forces at Las Cruces outside Mexico City, but Hidalgo hesitated to attack the capital. The rebels occupied Guadalajara instead but thereafter they were pushed northward by their opponents, their numbers shrank, and eventually the leaders, including Hidalgo, were captured and executed in 1811.

José María Morelos y Pavón, an former student of Hidalgo and also a parish priest, assumed leadership of the rebel forces, leading them back to Mexico City, which they blockaded for several months. Meanwhile he convened a congress at Chilpancingo (in modern Guerrero state). The congress adopted guiding principles for the independence movement, including the abolition of slavery, elimination of royal monopolies, universal male suffrage and, most importantly, popular sovereignty. Morelos, however, was captured and executed in 1815 and his forces dispersed into several bands of guerrillas, the most successful of which was led by Vicente Guerrero in the southern state of Oaxaca.

Emperor Agustín I Sporadic fighting continued until 1821 when the royalist general Agustín de Iturbide defected during an offensive against Guerrero, and conspired with the rebels to declare independence from Spain. Iturbide and Guerrero worked out a deal called the Plan de Iguala, which established 'three guarantees' – religious dominance by the Catholic church, a constitutional monarchy, and equality of rights for criollos and peninsulares. The plan won the support of all influential sections of society and the incoming Spanish viceroy in 1821 agreed to Mexican independence. Iturbide, who under the terms of the Plan de Iguala had command of the army, soon arranged his own nomination to the throne, which he ascended as Emperor Agustín I in 1822.

The Mexican Republic

Iturbide was deposed in 1823 by a rebel army led by another opportunist soldier, Antonio López de Santa Anna. A new constitution was drawn up in 1824, establishing a federal Mexican republic of 19 states and four territories. Guadalupe Victoria, a former independence fighter, became its first president. Mexico's southern boundary was the same as today, Central America having set up a separate federation in 1823. In the north, Mexico stretched as far as New Spain had, to include most of modern Texas, New Mexico, Arizona, California, Utah and Colorado.

Vicente Guerrero, the independence war hero, stood as a liberal candidate in the 1828 presidential elections and was defeated, but was eventually awarded the presidency after another Santa Anna-led revolt. Guerrero abolished slavery but was deposed, and later executed, by his conservative vice-president Anastasio Bustamante. The struggle between liberals, who favoured social reform, and conservatives, who opposed it, would be a constant theme in the twists and turns of Mexican 19th-century politics.

Santa Anna Intervention in politics by ambitious military men was also becoming a habit. Santa Anna, now a national hero after defeating a small Spanish invasion force at Tampico in 1829, overthrew Bustamante and was himself elected president in 1833. Now began 22 years of chronic instability in which the presidency changed hands 36 times; 11 of these terms went to Santa Anna. Economic decline and corruption became endemic and Santa Anna quickly turned into a conservative. His main contributions to Mexico were manifestations of his megalomaniac personality. Most memorably, he had his amputated, mummified leg (which he lost in an 1838 battle with the French) disinterred in 1842 and paraded through Mexico City with a full military guard in attendance.

Santa Anna is also remembered for helping to lose large chunks of Mexican territory to the USA. North American settlers in Texas, initially welcomed by the Mexican authorities, grew restless under Mexican rule and declared Texas independent in 1836. Santa Anna led an army north, besieged and wiped out the defenders of an old mission called the Alamo in San Antonio, but was routed on the San Jacinto River a few weeks later. Texan independence was recognised by the USA but not by Mexico.

In 1845 the US congress voted to annex Texas and US President Polk demanded further Mexican territory stretching as far west as California. This led to the Mexican-American War, in which US troops captured Mexico City. At the end of the war, by the Treaty of Guadalupe Hidalgo (1848), Mexico ceded modern Texas, California, Utah, Colorado, and most of New Mexico and Arizona to the USA. Santa Anna's government sold the remaining bits of New Mexico and Arizona to the USA in 1853 for US$10 million, in what's known as the Gadsden Purchase. This loss precipitated the liberal-led Revolution of Ayutla, which ousted Santa Anna once and for all in 1855.

Mexico almost lost the Yucatán Peninsula, too, in the so-called War of the Castes in the late 1840s, when the Mayan Indians rose up against their criollo overlords and narrowly failed to drive them off the peninsula.

Juárez & the French Intervention The new liberal government ushered in the era known as the Reform, in which it set about dismantling the conservative state that had developed in Mexico. The key figure of the movement was Benito Juárez, a Zapotec Indian from Oaxaca who had become a leading lawyer and politician. A new constitution, and laws requiring the church to sell much of its property, were among the moves that precipitated the internal War of the Reform (1858-61) between the liberals, with their 'capital' at Veracruz, and conservatives based in Mexico City. The liberals eventually won and Juárez became president in 1861. But the country was in a shambles – roads, bridges, public buildings and fields of crops were all in ruins – and heavily in debt to Britain, France and Spain. These three countries sent a joint force to Mexico to collect their debts, but France under the hawkish Napoleon III decided to go even further and colonise Mexico, leading to yet another war.

Though the French army was defeated at Puebla by General Ignacio Zaragoza on 5 May 1862, the French took Puebla a year later, and went on to capture Mexico City. In 1864 Napoleon invited the Austrian archduke, Maximilian of Hapsburg, to become emperor of Mexico. Juárez and his government were forced by the French army to withdraw to the provinces.

Emperor Maximilian and Empress Carlota entered Mexico City on 12 June 1864 and moved into Chapultepec Castle. But their reign was brief. In 1866, under pressure from the USA, Napoleon III began to withdraw many of the troops who enforced Maximilian's rule. Maximilian – in some ways a noble, tragic figure who refused to abandon his task though Napoleon had abandoned him – was defeated at Querétaro by forces loyal to Juárez in May 1867, and executed there by firing squad on 19 June.

Juárez immediately set an agenda emphasising economic and educational reform. The education system was completely revamped and, for the first time, schooling was made mandatory. A railway was built between Mexico City and Veracruz. A rural police force, the *rurales*, was organised to secure the transport of cargo through Mexico.

The Porfiriato Juárez died in 1872. When his successor, Sebastián Lerdo de Tejada, stood for re-election in 1876, Porfirio Díaz, an ambitious liberal from Oaxaca, launched a rebellion under the banner of the Plan de Tuxtepec, which took the view that presidents should not serve more than one term of office. The following year Díaz, the sole candidate, won presidential elections, and for the next 33 years he ran Mexico. Though he stepped down from the presidency in 1881 in accordance with his own no re-election rule, he remained the power behind the scenes. Old principles now brushed aside, Díaz returned to the presidency in 1884 for the first of six successive terms known as the Porfiriato. With the slogan 'order and progress', Díaz brought Mexico into the industrial age. Building and public-works projects were launched throughout the country, particularly in Mexico City. Telephone and telegraph lines were strung and underwater cables laid. In 1876, Mexico had 640 km of railway track; by the 1890s, 3200 km, and by 1911, more than 20,000 km. The country's stability and prosperity attracted foreign investors.

Díaz kept Mexico free of the civil wars which had plagued it for over 60 years, but La Paz Porfiriana (the Porfirian Peace) came at a cost. Political opposition, free elections and a free press were banned. Many of Mexico's resources went into foreign ownership, peasants were cheated out of their land by new laws weighted against them, agricultural and industrial workers suffered some appalling conditions, and the country was kept under control by a ruthless army and the now feared rurales. Land and wealth became concentrated in the hands of a small minority. Some hacienda owners amassed truly vast landholdings – Don Luis Terrazas in the northern state of Chihuahua, for instance, owned at least 14,000 sq km – and along with them, commensurate political power. Many rural workers were tied by debt to their bosses just like their colonial forebears.

In the early 1900s a liberal opposition formed, but was forced into exile in the USA. In 1906 the most important group of exiles, which included Juan Sarábia and the Flores Magón brothers, issued a new liberal plan for Mexico from St Louis, Missouri. Their actions precipitated strikes throughout Mexico – some violently suppressed – which led, in late 1910, to the Mexican Revolution.

The Mexican Revolution
The revolution was no clear-cut struggle between oppression and liberty, but a 10-year period of shifting allegiances between a spectrum of leaders, in which successive attempts to create stable governments and peace were wrecked by new outbreaks of devastating fighting.

Madero & Zapata In 1910, Francisco Madero, a wealthy liberal from the northern state of Coahuila, campaigned for the presidency and probably would have won if Díaz hadn't jailed him during the election period. On his release, Madero immediately began organising an anti-Díaz opposition and drafted the Plan of San Luis Potosí, which called for the nation to rise up in revolution on 20 November. The call was heard, and the revolution spread quickly across the country. When revolutionaries under the leadership of Francisco 'Pancho' Villa (born Doroteo Arango) took Ciudad Juárez, a city on the US border, in May 1911, Díaz resigned. Madero was elected president in November 1911.

But Madero was unable to create a stable government or contain the various factions fighting for power throughout the country.

The basic divide that was to dog the whole of the revolution was between liberal reformers like Madero and more radical leaders such as Emiliano Zapata from the state of Morelos, who was fighting for the transfer of hacienda land to the peasants, with the cry *'Tierra y Libertad'* ('Land and Liberty'). Zapata withdrew his support from Madero because of Madero's reluctance to do this. Madero sent federal troops to Morelos to disband Zapata's rebel forces, and the Zapatista movement was born.

In November 1911, Zapata promulgated the Plan of Ayala, calling for the restoration of all land to the peasants. Zapatista forces won several battles against government troops in central Mexico. Other forces of various political complexions took up local causes in other parts of the country. Soon all of Mexico was plunged into military chaos.

Huerta In February 1913, two conservative leaders – Félix Díaz, nephew of Porfirio, and Bernardo Reyes – were sprung from prison in Mexico City and commenced a counter-revolution which brought 10 days of fierce fighting, known as the 'Decena Trágica', to the capital. Thousands of civilians and soldiers were killed or wounded and many buildings destroyed. The fighting ended only after the US ambassador to Mexico, Henry Lane Wilson, negotiated for Madero's general, Victoriano Huerta, to switch to the rebel side and help depose Madero's government. Huerta himself became president and Madero and his vice president, José María Pino Suárez, were executed.

Huerta did nothing for Mexico except foment greater strife. In March 1913, three revolutionary leaders in the north united against him under the Plan of Guadalupe: Venustiano Carranza, a Madero supporter, in Coahuila, Pancho Villa in Chihuahua, and Alvaro Obregón in Sonora. Zapata and his forces were also fighting against the government. Terror reigned in the countryside as Huerta's troops fought, pillaged and plundered. Finally Huerta was defeated and forced to resign in July 1914.

Constitutionalists vs Radicals Carranza called all the revolutionary factions to a conference in Aguascalientes to try bring some unity to the movement, but the plan failed and another civil war broke out. This time, in broad terms, supporters of Obregón and the far-from-radical Carranza – the 'Constitutionalists', with their capital at Veracruz – were pitted against followers of the populist Villa and the radical Zapata. Villa and Zapata, however, despite a famous meeting in Mexico City, never formed a serious alliance and the war became increasingly anarchic. Villa never recovered from defeat by Obregón in the big battle of Celaya (1915), and Carranza eventually emerged the victor, to form a government that was recognised by the USA. A new reformist constitution, still largely in force today, was enacted in 1917. Carranza was sworn in as president the same year.

But the revolution continued, especially in Morelos where the Zapatistas continued to demand more social reforms. Carranza was able to eliminate the Zapata threat by having Zapata assassinated in Chinameca, Morelos, on 10 April 1919. The following year, however, Obregón turned against Carranza and, together with fellow Sonorans Adolfo de la Huerta and Plutarco Elías Calles, raised an army, chased Carranza out of office and had him assassinated.

The 10 years of violent civil war had cost an estimated 1.5 to two million lives – roughly one in eight Mexicans – and totally disrupted the economy.

From Revolution to WW II
Obregón & Calles The 1920s brought relative stability. President Alvaro Obregón (1920-24) turned to national reconstruction. Over 1000 rural schools were built and some land was redistributed from big landowners to the peasants. Obregón's education minister, José Vasconcelos, regarded the arts as an important part of national revival and commissioned Mexico's top artists, such as Diego Rivera, David Alfaro Siqueiros and José Clemente Orozco, to decorate import-

ant public buildings with large, vivid murals on social and historical themes.

Plutarco Elías Calles, who succeeded Obregón in 1924, presided over economic growth. Calles expanded rural education by 2000 schools and distributed over 30,000 sq km of land to small farmers. He also took measures against the Catholic church, including the closure of monasteries, convents and church schools, deportation of foreign priests and nuns, and prohibition of religious processions. These drastic measures precipitated the bloody Cristero Rebellion by Catholics, which lasted until 1929.

At the end of his term in 1928, Calles called for the return of Obregón to office, for the newly expanded presidential term of six years. Obregón won re-election, but was assassinated by a Cristero soon after. On Calles' recommendation, Emilio Portes Gil was then chosen for a two-year interim term while Calles reorganised his supporters to found the National Revolutionary Party (El Partido Nacional Revolucionario, or PNR), Mexico's first well-organised political party and initiator of a long tradition of official acronyms.

Cárdenas & Camacho In 1934 Lázaro Cárdenas, formerly governor of Michoacán, won the presidency with the support of the PNR and actively continued the reform programme. During his six-year term, Cárdenas carried out extensive land reform by redistributing almost 20,000 sq km – nearly double the amount distributed by all his predecessors since 1920 – mostly through the establishment of *ejidos* (peasant landholding cooperatives). This meant that most of Mexico's arable land had been redistributed and nearly one-third of the population had received land. Cárdenas strengthened the labour movement by forming the one-million-member Confederation of Mexican Workers (Confederación de Trabajadores Mexicanos, or CTM).

He also boldly expropriated foreign oil company operations in Mexico (1938), formed the Mexican Petroleum Company (Petróleos Mexicanos, or Pemex), and

reorganised the PNR into the Party of the Mexican Revolution (Partido de la Revolución Mexicana or PRM), a coalition of representatives from four sectors of Mexican society – agrarian, military, labour and the people at large.

After the oil expropriation, foreign investors avoided Mexico. Combined with the tremendous cost of implementing various social programmes, this slowed the Mexican economy, but only temporarily. In 1940, his last year in office, Cárdenas established the tradition of the *dedazo* (laying-on of the finger), by which the outgoing president recommends a successor who receives the ruling party's candidacy and is then elected president. Cárdenas recommended a conservative candidate, Manuel Avila Camacho, who easily won. The transition from Cárdenas to Camacho is now seen as the moment the scales tipped towards more conservative government after the reforming presidencies of the two post-revolutionary decades.

WW II was the key event during Camacho's presidency (1940-46). As a supporter of the Allied war effort, he sent Mexican troops to help the Allies in the Pacific, and supplied raw materials and labour to the USA. At home, the war proved a valuable boost to Mexico's economy: because many manufactured goods could no longer be imported from the industrialised countries, they had to be produced in Mexico. This fostered local industry as well as increasing exports.

After WW II

As the Mexican economy expanded, new economic and political groups demanded influence in the ruling PRM. To recognise their inclusion, the party was renamed the Institutional Revolutionary Party (El Partido Revolucionario Institucional, or PRI). In the postwar boom, President Miguel Alemán Valdés (1946-52) continued industrialisation and development by building hydroelectric stations, irrigation projects and the National Autonomous University of Mexico (Universidad Nacional Autónoma de México or

UNAM), and by expanding Mexico's road system fourfold. Pemex drilling operations and refineries grew dramatically and, with the rapid rise of other industries, spawned some of Mexico's worst corruption.

Alemán's successor, Adolfo Ruiz Cortines (1952-58), tried to eliminate much of the graft and corruption, and also began to confront a new problem – explosive population growth. In the previous two decades Mexico's population had doubled and many people began migrating to urban areas to search for work.

The poor were a priority for Cortínes' successor, Adolfo López Mateos (1958-64), one of Mexico's most popular post-WW II presidents, who redistributed 120,000 more sq km of land to small farmers, nationalised foreign utility concessions, implemented social welfare programmes for the poor, and launched campaigns to combat tuberculosis, malaria and polio. Almost every village was given assistance in the construction of schools and provided with teachers and textbooks. These programmes were helped by strong economic growth, particularly in tourism and exports.

Unrest, Boom & Bust

President Gustavo Díaz Ordaz (1964-70) was a conservative who came to power with a platform that emphasised business more than social programmes. He sacked the president of the PRI, Carlos Madrazo, whose attempts to democratise the party had upset its hierarchy. Groups of university students in Mexico City were the first to express their outrage with the Díaz Ordaz administration.

Protests began at the National University in spring 1966, and discontent came to a head in 1968 in the run-up to the Mexico City Olympic Games, the first ever held in a Third World country. Single-party rule, restricted freedom of speech, and spending on the Olympics were among the objects of protest. More than half a million people rallied in Mexico City's Zócalo on 27 August; in mid-September troops seized the National University campus to break up a student occupation. On 2 October, with the Olym-

pics only a few days away, a rally was organised in Tlatelolco, Mexico City. The government, fearing the rally would disrupt the games, sent in heavily armed troops and police. In the ensuing massacre, several hundred people died.

Though Díaz Ordaz fostered education and tourism, and the Mexican economy grew by 6% a year during his term, he is much better remembered for the repressive attitude to civil liberties and political change, symbolised by Tlatelolco.

President Luis Echeverría (1970-76) sought to deliver Mexico from its political mess by distributing wealth more equitably. He instituted government credit projects in the troubled agriculture sector, to bring in badly needed technical assistance and forestall a financial collapse. He also expanded rural health clinics, the social security system and family planning. But civil unrest increased, including political kidnappings, bank robberies, and a guerrilla insurrection in Guerrero – all of which were partly fuelled by the corruption that was now rife among government officials.

Echeverría's successor, José López Portillo (1976-82), presided during the jump in world oil prices following the Arab boycott. For Mexico this meant rapidly rising oil revenues, which could be applied to both industrial and agricultural investments. International banks and lending institutions suddenly began lending Mexico billions of dollars until, just as suddenly, a glut of oil on the world market sent oil prices plunging. Mexico's worst recession for decades began.

López Portillo's administration was considered the most corrupt in living memory. Mexico City's chief of police, Arturo Durazo, earning officially US$65 a week, bought race horses, built palatial residences in Mexico City, Zihuatanejo and various foreign cities, and funnelled more than US$600 million into Swiss bank accounts.

Miguel de la Madrid (1982-88) was largely unsuccessful in coping with the problems he inherited. The population continued to grow at Malthusian rates; the economy made only weak progress, crushed by the huge debt burden from the oil boom years; and the social pot continued to simmer.

De la Madrid's economic policies were not helped by the earthquake of 19 September 1985, which registered eight on the Richter scale, and caused more than US$4 billion in damage. Hundreds of buildings in Mexico City were destroyed, thousands of people were dislocated, and at least 8000 were killed.

Not surprisingly, in this climate of economic helplessness, there was an increase in organised political dissent on both the left and the right, and even within the PRI. There were sometimes violent protests at the electoral fraud and strong-arm tactics of which the PRI was now routinely accused.

The Salinas Presidency

Discontent mounted to the point where it made a historic impact on the 1988 presidential election. Cuauhtémoc Cárdenas, son of the charismatic 1930s president Lázaro Cárdenas, walked out of the PRI to stand for a new centre-left National Democratic Front (Frente Democrático Nacional, or FDN). It was and is widely believed that more voters chose Cárdenas than the PRI candidate, Carlos Salinas de Gortari, and as counting proceeded after the voting, Cárdenas looked to be heading for victory – until a mysterious computer failure halted the tallying of results. In the end Cárdenas was awarded only 31% of the vote, while Salinas received 50.7% – still the lowest up to that point of any PRI presidential candidate in history.

But once he had weathered the storm of electoral protest, Salinas, young, softspoken and hard-working, developed into one of Mexico's most popular modern presidents during his term of office. He made early moves against corruption in local elections, the police, financial circles and the powerful oil workers' union, and brought an end to the century-old conflict between the Mexican state and the Catholic church, which since 1917 had been officially banned from owning property or running schools or newspapers. Mexico and the Vatican established full diplomatic relations in 1992.

A Historical Who's Who

Ahuízotl (d. 1502)
Aztec emperor from 1486 to 1502, who expanded the empire.

Ignacio Allende (1779-1811)
One of the instigators of the independence struggle in 1810.

Pedro de Alvarado (1486-1541)
One of the leading conquistadors who accompanied Cortés; later he conquered Guatemala and El Salvador.

Axayácatl
Aztec emperor from 1469 to 1481, father of Moctezuma II Xocoyotzin.

Plutarco Elías Calles (1877-1945)
Mexican Revolution leader, and president from 1924 to 1928. As president he started to unite regional political elites into a national party, precursor to the modern PRI, thereby creating a modicum of political stability.

Lázaro Cárdenas (1895-1970)
A general and a statesman, he was considered a true president of the people, serving from 1934 to 1940. Cárdenas carried out major land reforms, expanding the system of ejidos, expropriated foreign oil company operations, and reorganised the governing party into the PRM (Party of the Mexican Revolution), consolidating one-party domination.

Empress Carlota Marie Charlotte Amélie (1840-1927)
Daughter of King Leopold I of Belgium, she married Archduke Maximilian of Hapsburg (1857), and accompanied him to Mexico in 1864 to become empress. After her husband's execution in 1867, she lived on for 60 years, mentally unstable, a ward of the Vatican.

Venustiano Carranza (1859-1920)
Leader of the Constitutionalist side, opposed to Pancho Villa and Emiliano Zapata, in the revolution. President from 1917 to 1920, Carranza had Zapata assassinated in 1919. The next year he himself was overthrown by an alliance led by Alvaro Obregón and assassinated while fleeing the country, which effectively ended the revolution.

Hernán Cortés (1485-1547)
Spanish conquistador, sometimes known as Hernando or Fernando, who invaded Mexico and conquered the Aztecs. Much maligned today in Mexico, Cortés was the person chiefly responsible for introducing Hispanic civilisation into Mexico.

Cuauhtémoc (c. 1495-1525)
Last Aztec emperor, successor to Moctezuma II Xocoyotzin and Cuitláhuac. Cuauhtémoc was defeated and later executed by Cortés.

Cuitláhuac (d. 1520)
Aztec emperor who succeeded Moctezuma II Xocoyotzin in 1520, but died in the same year.

Porfirio Díaz (1830-1915)
Elected president in 1877 and re-elected on numerous occasions on a slogan of 'order and progress', he became a dictator who pursued public-works projects and encouraged foreign investment, at the expense of the poor and civil liberties. His policies precipitated the Mexican Revolution in 1910 and forced his resignation in 1911.

Bernal Díaz del Castillo (1492-1581)
Captain in the army of Cortés. He was the author of the *History of the Conquest of New Spain*, an eyewitness account of the Spanish conquest of Mexico and Guatemala.

Luis Echeverría (1922-)
President of Mexico from 1970 to 1976, he increased government technical assistance for agriculture and expanded rural social services. His administration, however, was blighted by violent civil unrest and the beginnings of severe corruption.

Vicente Guerrero (1782-1831)
A leader in the later stages of the struggle for independence from Spain. Subsequently a liberal president but deposed by the conservative Anastasio Bustamante in 1829 and executed in 1831.

Miguel Hidalgo y Costilla (1753-1811)
Parish priest of Dolores who sparked the independence struggle in 1810 with his famous Grito or call for independence. He led an unsuccessful attempt to take Mexico City.

Victoriano Huerta (1854-1916)
Leader of Madero's forces against a 1913 counter-revolution, he switched sides to become president himself. One of Mexico's most disliked and ineffective leaders, he was forced to resign in 1914.

Agustín de Iturbide (1783-1824)
An officer in the royalist army sent to lead forces against the independence fighters led by Guerrero, he instead negotiated with the rebels to achieve independence from Spain (1821). Iturbide established a conservative state with himself as Emperor Agustín I of Mexico, but his reign lasted less than a year (1822-23).

Benito Juárez (1806-72)
A Zapotec Indian lawyer from Oaxaca, Juárez was prominent in the group of liberals who deposed Santa Anna, then passed laws against the church that precipitated the three-year War of the Reform. Elected president in 1861, he was forced to flee because of the French takeover by Napoleon III and Emperor Maximilian. After Napoleon recalled his soldiers from Mexico, Juárez resumed the presidency until his death.

Bartolomé de Las Casas (1474-1566)
Spanish missionary and a leading campaigner for Indian rights; Bishop of Chiapas in the 1540s.

José López Portillo (1920-)
President from 1976 to 1982, López Portillo's administration borrowed enormous sums from foreign banks on the strength of Mexico's oil wealth. When the price of oil crashed, Mexico's debt all but crushed the economy. His administration is thought by many to have marked a high point in government corruption.

Francisco Madero (1873-1913)

A liberal politician, Madero began the Mexican Revolution, leading the first major opposition to Porfirio Díaz and forcing him to resign. But he proved unable to quell factional fighting throughout Mexico and his presidential term (1911-13) ended in front of a firing squad.

La Malinche (Doña Marina) (c. 1501-50)

Cortés' Indian mistress and interpreter, she is considered to have had a major influence on Cortés's strategy in subduing the Aztecs.

Ferdinand Maximilian (1832-67)

Hapsburg archduke sent by Napoleon III of France to rule as emperor of Mexico. His rule was short-lived (1864-67) and he was forced to surrender to Benito Juárez' forces, who executed him by firing squad in 1867.

Moctezuma I Ilhuicamina

Aztec emperor from 1440 to 1469.

Moctezuma II Xocoyotzin (1466-1520)

Aztec emperor from 1502 to 1520. An indecisive leader, he failed to fend off the Spanish invasion led by Cortés.

José María Morelos y Pavón (1765-1815)

A liberal priest like Hidalgo, he proved to be a brilliant leader and military strategist. Assumed leadership of the independence movement after Hidalgo's execution, but was himself captured and executed in 1815. He was succeeded in his struggle by Vicente Guerrero and Guadalupe Victoria.

Alvaro Obregón (1880-1928)

An enlightened farmer and revolutionary leader, he led a force from Sonora in support of Madero, and later supported Carranza against Huerta and Villa. After serving as Carranza's minister of war, he rebelled when Carranza tried to keep power illegally. Obregón's term as president (1920-24) saw the implementation of revolutionary reforms, especially in education. He was assassinated in 1928.

Carlos Salinas de Gortari

President from 1988 to 1994, Salinas revived the economy with important free-market reforms and led Mexico into the North American Free Trade Agreement (NAFTA). His final year in power was clouded by a peasant uprising in Chiapas and the assassination of his chosen successor, Luis Donaldo Colosio.

Antonio López de Santa Anna (1794-1876)

Santa Anna unseated Iturbide in 1823, and himself headed 11 of the 50 governments that held office during Mexico's first 35 years of independence, a period of endemic economic decline and corruption. Santa Anna was a leading player in conflicts with the USA, in which Mexico lost huge tracts of territory – and famous in the USA for his massacre of the US defenders of the Alamo mission in what is today San Antonio, Texas.

Guadalupe Victoria (1786-1843)

Born Manuel Félix Fernández, he fought alongside Hidalgo and Morelos, and contested (along with Santa Anna) Iturbide's accession as emperor of Mexico. After Iturbide's removal in 1823, he was a member of the provisional government, then (1824-28) the first president of the Mexican republic.

Francisco 'Pancho' Villa (1877-1923)

Born Doroteo Arango, he rebelled from his *peon* (peasant) roots and became a Robin Hood-style bandit in Chihuahua and Durango. A charismatic fighting leader in the Revolution, his support was an important element in the victories of Madero over Díaz. He also supported Carranza against Huerta, but Carranza fell out with him when Huerta was out of the way. After a string of military defeats, Villa's forces raided the USA, and General Pershing invaded Mexico in pursuit of him – but never caught him. Villa was assassinated in 1923.

Emiliano Zapata (1879-1919)

A peasant leader from the state of Morelos, Zapata was the most politically radical of the revolution leaders, fighting principally for the return of land to the peasants. He was at odds not only with the conservative supporters of the old regime but also with their liberal opponents. After winning numerous battles during the revolution (some in association with Pancho Villa), he was ambushed and killed in 1919 on Carranza's orders. ■

The Harvard-educated Salinas set about replacing Mexico's state-dominated, protectionist economy with private enterprise and free trade. State monopolies were privatised and in a bid to make agriculture more productive, the ejido system of communal ownership for most agricultural land was reformed. Salinas succeeded in renegotiating Mexico's crippling national debt and bringing down inflation.

The apex of his programme was NAFTA, the North American Free Trade Agreement, known to Mexicans as the TLC, or Tratado de Libre Comercio. The product of several years of negotiations, NAFTA came into effect on 1 January 1994 (see Economy later in this chapter).

Mexican opinion was divided on the benefits of NAFTA, and fears of its effects on the poor were among the causes of the event which set the tone for the troubled final year of Salinas' presidency – the uprising in the southern state of Chiapas by the EZLN (Ejército Zapatista de Liberación Nacional, or Zapatista National Liberation Army). The day NAFTA took effect, this group of 2000 or so Indian-peasant rebels shocked Mexico by taking over San Cristóbal de Las Casas and other towns. As their name, harking back to the land-reform goals of the revolutionary Emiliano Zapata, indicated, they were fighting to end decades of evictions from land, discrimination and disappearances in their impoverished state, where a wealthy minority had maintained a near-feudal grip on land, resources and political power since before the Mexican Revolution. Though the EZLN was driven out of the towns within a few days (around 150 people were killed in the uprising), it struck a chord nationally among all who felt that the Mexican system prevented real social or political change and believed that Salinas, in his rush to economic reform, had only widened the gap between rich and poor.

The government exercised some restraint in its handling of the uprising, and the rebels were able to retreat under a truce to a secure base in the Chiapas jungle. The uprising precipitated a social upheaval in Chiapas, with peasants forcibly taking over hundreds of estates, farms and ranches. The rebels' leader, a balaclava-clad figure known only as Subcomandante Marcos, became something of a national folk hero.

Things took a further turn for the worse when Luis Donaldo Colosio, Salinas' chosen successor as PRI presidential candidate, was assassinated in Tijuana in March 1994. The finger of blame was pointed by many at the conservative old-guard faction of the PRI, opposed to the economic and political changes that Salinas and Colosio stood for.

After the EZLN uprising, Salinas sensibly pushed through electoral reforms to prevent ballot-stuffing and double voting in the August presidential election, which was regarded as the cleanest ever – though that's a very qualified accolade, as on polling day at least one million voters with valid credentials mysteriously found they were not on the electoral roll. In addition, a reported 200 opposition activists had been killed during the Salinas presidency, and the PRI had no doubt, as usual, won many votes through subsidies, bribes, threats and its control of trade unions and peasant organisations.

Colosio's replacement as PRI candidate, 43-year-old Ernesto Zedillo, won the election but with only 49% of the vote.

Crisis under Zedillo

Within weeks of Zedillo taking office in late 1994, a series of political and economic shocks rocked Mexico and gave him little chance to show whether the PRI could respond to growing calls for more democracy and civil rights. The peso suddenly collapsed, leaving Mexico almost bankrupt and dependent on an emergency US$50 billion credit package from US and international financial bodies. Mexico had to put up its oil earnings – a key symbol of national self-reliance – as collateral for this aid. The financial crisis looked sure to bring a recession, and most of the blame was laid on Salinas for having held the peso at an artificially high level during his presidency. In the wake of this, the PRI suffered a very rare electoral defeat, by the right-wing Partido

Ernesto Zedillo

the Yucatán Peninsula. The southern part of the Gulf is called the Bahía de Campeche (Bay of Campeche). The east coast of the Yucatán Peninsula faces the Caribbean Sea.

Mexico is big: it's nearly 3500 km as the crow flies from Tijuana in the north-west to Cancún in the south-east, or about 4600 km by road. To travel from the US border at Ciudad Juárez to Mexico City, one must ride 1800 km (about 24 hours). From Mexico City to the Guatemalan border at Ciudad Cuauhtémoc is 1200 km by road.

Mexico has a 3326-km northern border with the USA, the eastern half of which is formed by the Río Bravo del Norte (or Rio Grande as Americans call it). In the south and south-east, there is an 871-km border with Guatemala and a 251-km border with Belize.

Acción Nacional (PAN), for the state governorship of Jalisco.

In Chiapas, Zedillo negotiated with the EZLN but then suddenly sent in the army to 'arrest' Subcomandante Marcos and its other leaders. Marcos and most of his followers escaped, accompanied by thousands of peasants fleeing the army. The credibility of the PRI took a further blow when Salinas' brother Raoul, linked with the party's old guard, was arrested in March 1995 in connection with the murder of a leading PRI 'progressive', Francisco Ruiz Massieu.

All this left the PRI facing its most serious struggle yet to maintain its unity and grip on power – and national stability.

GEOGRAPHY
Size & Borders

Covering almost two million sq km, Mexico curves from north-west to south-east, narrowing to the Isthmus of Tehuantepec in the south then continuing north-east to the Yucatán Peninsula. On the west and south it's bordered by the Pacific Ocean, with the Gulf of California, also called the Sea of Cortés, lying between the Baja California peninsula and the mainland. Mexico's east coast is bordered by the Gulf of Mexico all the way from the US border to the north-east tip of

Topography

Northern and central Mexico – as far south as Mexico City – have coastal plains on the east and west, and two north-south mountain ranges framing a group of broad central plateaux known as the Altiplano Central.

On the west coast, a relatively dry coastal plain stretches south from Mexicali on the US border almost to Tepic. Several rivers flow across the plain and empty into the Gulf of California or the Pacific Ocean. They begin in the rugged Sierra Madre Occidental mountain range, which is crossed by only two main surface transport routes – the Copper Canyon railway from Los Mochis to Chihuahua and the dramatic highway from Mazatlán to Durango.

The plateaux are divided into northern and central parts, themselves divided by minor ranges, and vary in altitude from about 1000 metres in the north to 1500 metres around Guadalajara, 2000 metres near San Luis Potosí, and 2300 metres around Mexico City. The northern plateau extends northward into the southern fringes of Arizona and California. The central plateau is mostly a series of rolling hills and broad valleys, and includes some of the best farming and ranching land and the two largest cities (Mexico City and Guadalajara) in the country. Not surprisingly, more than half the population lives on this plateau.

Both plateaux are bound on the east by the Sierra Madre Oriental mountain range, which runs as far south as the state of Puebla and includes peaks as high as 3700 metres.

On the east side of the Sierra Madre Oriental is the Gulf coast plain, an extension of a similar coastal plain in Texas. In northeastern Mexico the plain is a wide area, semi-marshy near the coast, but it gradually narrows as it nears the major port of Veracruz. Like the Pacific coastal plain it is crossed by many rivers.

The central plateau, the Sierra Madre Oriental and the Gulf coast plain reach as far as the Cordillera Neovolcánica mountain range, just south of Mexico City. This range runs east-west and includes Mexico's highest peaks – Pico de Orizaba (5610 metres), Popocatépetl (5452 metres) and Iztaccíhuatl (5286 metres) – as well as Mexico's most active volcano, the Volcán de Fuego de Colima (3960 metres), and its youngest volcano, Paricutín (2800 metres), which only appeared in 1943.

The Pacific coastal lowlands south of Cabo Corrientes (west of Guadalajara) narrow to a thin strip. The main mountain range in the south of the country is the Sierra Madre del Sur which stretches across the states of Guerrero and Oaxaca to the Isthmus of Tehuantepec, the narrowest part of Mexico, just 220 km wide. The Sierra Madre de Oaxaca runs south from the Cordillera Neovolcánica to meet the Sierra Madre del Sur in the region of Oaxaca city. The north side of the isthmus is part of a wide, well watered, often marshy plain stretching from Veracruz to the Yucatán Peninsula.

From the Isthmus of Tehuantepec a narrow stretch of lowlands runs along the Pacific coast south to Guatemala. The lowlands are backed by the Sierra Madre de Chiapas, beyond which is the Río Grijalva basin and then the Chiapas highlands. Northeast of the highlands is a tropical rainforest area stretching over into northern Guatemala. The jungle melts into a region of tropical savanna on the flat, low Yucatán Peninsula and, at the tip of the peninsula, an arid desert-like region.

The other major geographical feature of Mexico is Baja California, the world's longest peninsula – 1300 km of mountains, deserts, plains and beaches.

CLIMATE

The Tropic of Cancer cuts across Mexico north of Mazatlán and Tampico. It's hot and humid along the coastal plains on both sides of the country south of the tropic. Inland, at higher elevations, such as in Guadalajara or Mexico City, the climate is much more dry and temperate, with mountain peaks that are often capped with snow. Inland and coastal temperatures both get higher as you travel south.

The hot, wet season is May to October, with the hottest and wettest months of all falling between June and September over most of the country. Low-lying coastal areas get more rain and higher temperatures than elevated inland ones – though there's considerable local variation: among coastal resorts, Acapulco receives twice as much rain in a year as Mazatlán (nearly all of it, over 1700 mm, from May to October); Cozumel and Cancún receive only about 20% less rain than Acapulco but it's not as intensely concentrated in the six wettest months. Acapulco and Cancún share similar temperatures, but Mazatlán and Cozumel are a few degrees cooler.

Mexico City's rainfall and temperatures are both on the low side for an inland city: Taxco and Pátzcuaro both have about twice as much rain as the capital and are generally a few degrees warmer; Oaxaca is also a few degrees warmer but similarly dry. Northwestern Mexico, Baja California and inland areas in the northern half of the country are drier than the rest of Mexico. In the east, rainfall is particularly high on the eastern slopes of the Sierra Madre Oriental and on the northern side of the Isthmus of Tehuantepec. December to February are generally the coolest months and north winds can make inland northern Mexico decidedly chilly, with temperatures (in °C) often in single figures, sometimes approaching freezing.

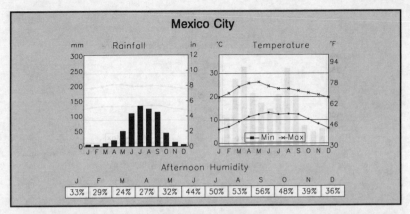

Mexico City

Rainfall / Temperature / Afternoon Humidity

J	F	M	A	M	J	J	A	S	O	N	D
33%	29%	24%	27%	32%	44%	50%	53%	56%	48%	39%	36%

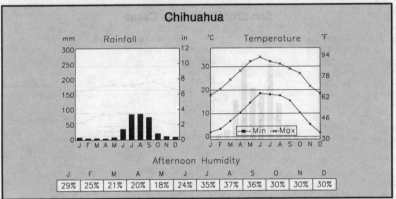

Chihuahua

Rainfall / Temperature / Afternoon Humidity

J	F	M	A	M	J	J	A	S	O	N	D
29%	25%	21%	20%	18%	24%	35%	37%	36%	30%	30%	30%

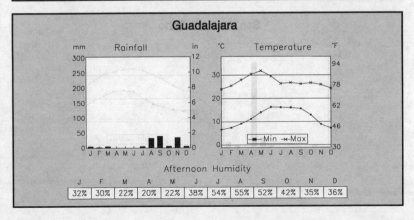

Guadalajara

Rainfall / Temperature / Afternoon Humidity

J	F	M	A	M	J	J	A	S	O	N	D
32%	30%	22%	20%	22%	38%	54%	55%	52%	42%	35%	36%

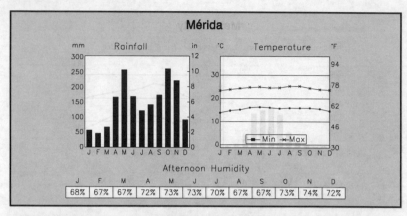

Mérida

	J	F	M	A	M	J	J	A	S	O	N	D
	68%	67%	67%	72%	73%	73%	70%	67%	67%	73%	74%	72%

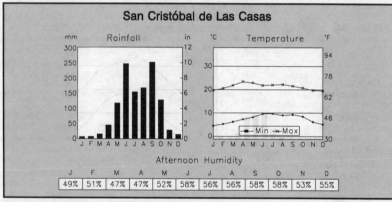

San Cristóbal de Las Casas

	J	F	M	A	M	J	J	A	S	O	N	D
	49%	51%	47%	47%	52%	58%	56%	56%	58%	58%	53%	55%

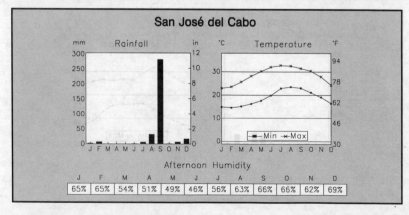

San José del Cabo

	J	F	M	A	M	J	J	A	S	O	N	D
	65%	65%	54%	51%	49%	46%	56%	63%	66%	66%	62%	69%

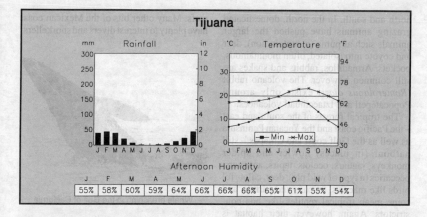

Tijuana

Rainfall / Temperature / Afternoon Humidity

J	F	M	A	M	J	J	A	S	O	N	D
55%	58%	60%	59%	64%	66%	66%	66%	65%	61%	55%	54%

FLORA & FAUNA

Bridging temperate and tropical regions, and lying in the latitudes which contain most of the world's deserts, Mexico has an enormous range of natural environments and vegetation zones. Its rugged mountainous topography adds to the variety by creating countless microclimates. The human impact has been enormous. Before the Spanish conquest about two-thirds of the country was forested. Now only one-fifth is, mainly in the south and east.

Vegetation Zones

North-west and central north Mexico are dominated by two deserts – the Desierto Sonorense (Sonoran Desert) west of the Sierra Madre Occidental, and the Desierto Chihuahuaense (Chihuahuan Desert) occupying much of the Altiplano Central, the series of upland plateaux lying between the Sierra Madre Occidental and the Sierra Madre Oriental. The deserts are sparsely vegetated with cacti, agaves, yucca, scrub and short grasses. Both deserts stretch north into the USA; the Sonoran desert also extends down into Baja California (although Baja has a surprising range of other habitats too, and, thanks to its isolation, a rather specialised flora and fauna). Most of the world's estimated 800 to 1500 species of cacti are found in Mexico: an interesting

place to scrutinise many of them is the still-being-developed botanical garden at San Miguel de Allende, Guanajuato.

The Sierra Madre Occidental and Oriental, along with the Cordillera Neovolcánica, running east-west across the middle of the country, and the Sierra Madre del Sur, still have some big stretches of pine and oak forest, though human occupation has stripped away much of the forest cover around the valleys.

The natural vegetation of the damper east side of the country is tropical rainforest. Dominated by broadleaf evergreen trees, these dense forests are highly diversified and contain ferns, epiphytes and palms as well as tropical hardwoods. Again, however, human impact has destroyed much: the largest remaining tropical forest area is the Selva Lacandona (Lacandón Forest) in eastern Chiapas, and it too is shrinking as new land is cleared for agriculture. The Yucatán Peninsula changes from rainforest in the south to dry thorny forest in the north.

The drier Pacific side of Mexico has deciduous or semi-deciduous tropical forest, less varied than the eastern evergreen tropical forests. There are big stretches of thorn forest and savannah along the coastal plain.

Fauna

Land Fauna show a similar contrast between

north and south. In the north, domesticated grazing animals have pushed the larger animals such as puma (mountain lion), deer and coyote into isolated, often mountainous, pockets. Armadillos, rabbits and snakes are still common however. The volcano rabbit *(Romerolagus diazi)* exists only around Popocatépetl and Iztaccíhuatl volcanoes.

The tropical forests of the south and east – the Pacific coast and the Yucatán Peninsula as well as the Gulf coast and Chiapas – still harbour (in places) howler and spider monkeys, jaguars, ocelots, tapirs, anteaters, peccaries (a type of wild pig), deer, colourful birds like macaws, toucans and parrots, and some mean tropical reptiles like boa constrictors. Again, however, their habitat is being eroded.

In all warm parts of Mexico you'll come across two harmless though sometimes alarming reptiles: the iguana, a lizard which can grow a metre or so long and comes in many different colours; and the gecko, a tiny, usually green, lizard that may shoot out from behind a curtain or cupboard in your room when disturbed. Geckos might make you jump, but they're good news – they eat mosquitoes. Less welcome are scorpions, also common in warmer parts of the country.

Sea & Coast Mexico's coasts are one of the world's chief breeding grounds for sea turtles: six of the world's seven species come to Mexican beaches – from Baja California to Oaxaca and from the north-east to the Yucatán Peninsula – to lay eggs. Laying takes place between July and March. At Mazunte, Oaxaca, a national turtle centre is being created.

Dolphins can be seen in the seas off much of the Pacific coast, while some wetlands, mainly in the south of the country, harbour crocodiles, alligators or caymans.

Baja California is famous for whale-watching in the early months of the year but it's also a breeding ground for other big sea creatures like sea lions and elephant seals.

Underwater life is richest off parts of the Yucatán Peninsula, where there are coral reefs. Many other bits of the Mexican coast have plenty to interest divers and snorkellers.

Whale breaching in the Gulf of California

Birds Coastal Mexico is also a major bird habitat, especially on the estuaries, lagoons, islands, mangroves and wetlands in the north-east, the Yucatán Peninsula and the Pacific Coast. Inland, northern Mexico abounds with eagles, hawks and buzzards, while innumerable ducks and geese winter in the northern Sierra Madre Occidental. Altogether Mexico has over 1000 bird species. If you'd like to do some bird-spotting in Mexico, take along the excellent paperback *A Field Guide to Mexican Birds* by Roger Tory Peterson and Edward L Chalif (Houghton Mifflin, Boston, 1973).

Seeing Wildlife
You're not likely to bump into a great variety of Mexico's land-bound wildlife unless you visit remote coastal, mountain or forest areas. Mexican national parks are a mixed bag, ranging from expanses of wilderness with no visitor infrastructure to small, heavily-visited areas with roads and car parks for weekend picnickers. There are also a few *Reservas Biósferas* (biosphere reserves) dedicated mainly to conservation and research, with visits usually allowed only by permit. Probably the most concentrated selection of purely Mexican wildlife is to be found at the zoo in Tuxtla Gutiérrez, Chiapas, devoted solely to the very varied fauna of that state. Awareness of visitors'

interest in Mexican nature is increasing, however, and there's a growing range of possibilities for visiting interesting natural areas.

Here's a selection of good places to see some Mexican fauna in the wild (see the relevant sections in the regional chapters for more information):

Birds – Parque Nacional Constitución de 1857 and Laguna San Ignacio, Baja California; Alamos area, Sonora; Creel area, Chihuahua; coastal lagoons and wetlands, Tamaulipas and northern Veracruz; Mexcaltitán and San Blas, Nayarit; Pie de la Cuesta, Acapulco, Guerrero; Laguna Manialtepec and Lagunas de Chacahua, Oaxaca; Isla Contoy off Isla Mujeres, Quintana Roo (see also Flamingos)

Elephant Seals – Isla Cedros and Islas San Benito, Baja California

Flamingos – Celestún and Río Lagartos, Yucatán

Monarch Butterflies – Santuario de Mariposas El Rosario, Michoacán

Sea Lions – Isla Cedros, Baja California

Tropical Forest Fauna (howler monkeys, pumas, crocodiles, ocelots, jaguars) – Sian Ka'an Biosphere Reserve, Quintana Roo

Whales – Ensenada, Laguna Ojo de Liebre, Laguna San Ignacio, Puerto López Mateos and Puerto San Carlos (all Baja California); Bahía de las Banderas, Jalisco

GOVERNMENT

Mexico is a federal republic of 31 states and one federal district, further divided into 2394 municipalities *(municipios)*. The system has some similarities to both the American and European styles of democracy. A two-chamber legislature, with a Senate of 128 members and a Chamber of Deputies of 500 members, makes the laws, a directly-elected president carries them out, and an independent judiciary decides disputes according to Napoleonic law. Women gained the vote in 1955, and achieved passage of an Equal Rights Amendment to the constitution in 1974. The governors and legislatures of Mexico's states, which need not be of the same party as that which dominates the federal government, are elected by their citizens.

So much for theory. In practice, Mexican political life has been dominated for more than half a century by the Institutional Rev-olutionary Party (PRI) and its predecessors, and the president of Mexico has ruled in the tradition of strong, centralised leadership going back to Moctezuma. Though the Chamber of Deputies and the Senate may debate the president's proposals, his will is rarely denied. The fiscal and political power of the states is very much subordinate to the federal government. Elections at all levels routinely raise accusations of fraud, bribery, intimidation and violence against the all-conquering PRI.

Each president serves one six-year term of office *(sexenio)* and is not eligible for re-election. At the end of his term, the president selects a candidate to succeed him from within PRI ranks, and since 1929 that candidate has invariably won.

Carlos Salinas de Gortari, president from 1988 to 1994, signalled the tentative beginnings of a democratisation of the Mexican system. Some measures to reduce corruption were enforced for the election to choose his successor in 1994, and during Salinas' term non-PRI governors were elected in three Mexican states (Baja California, Chihuahua and Guanajuato) – the first time ever that the PRI or its predecessors had conceded any state governorship. Salinas also pushed through some democratic reforms within the PRI itself. However all this was no more than a beginning, and the frustration of the majority of Mexicans about their effective exclusion from the political process – expressed most dramatically in the 1994 EZLN uprising in Chiapas – is something that President Ernesto Zedillo, Salinas' successor, is having to take very seriously.

ECONOMY
Resources & Products

Mexico, an almost entirely agricultural country before the 1910 revolution, is now one of Latin America's most industrialised nations. Manufacturing, largely concentrated in and near Mexico City, employs about 18% of the workforce and produces about a quarter of national output. Motor vehicles, processed food, steel, chemicals, paper, glass and textiles have joined more

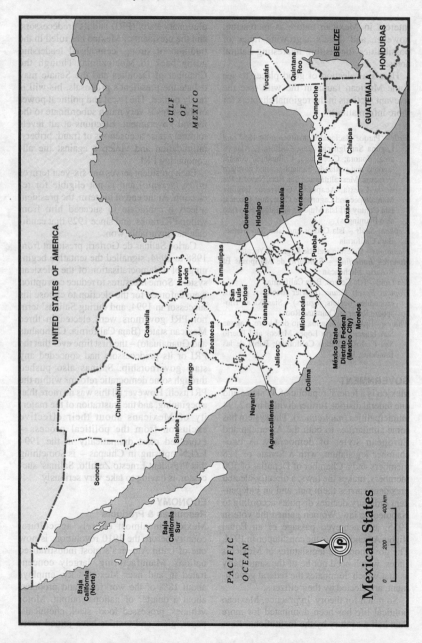

Mexican States

UNITED STATES OF AMERICA

GULF OF MEXICO

PACIFIC OCEAN

BELIZE

GUATEMALA

HONDURAS

0   200   400 km

Baja California (Norte)

Baja California Sur

Sonora

Chihuahua

Sinaloa

Durango

Coahuila

Nuevo León

Tamaulipas

Zacatecas

San Luis Potosí

Nayarit

Aguascalientes

Jalisco

Guanajuato

Querétaro

Hidalgo

Tlaxcala

Veracruz

Colima

Michoacán

México State

Distrito Federal (Mexico City)

Morelos

Puebla

Guerrero

Oaxaca

Tabasco

Chiapas

Campeche

Yucatán

Quintana Roo

traditional sources of income such as sugar, coffee, silver, lead, copper and zinc. Mexico's biggest national assets are its oil reserves, the fifth largest in the world, and gas reserves. These contribute 28% of the country's export earnings. Oil and gas production are concentrated mainly along the Gulf coast. About 30% of the workforce is occupied in service industries.

Mining, the source of most of Mexico's income in the colonial era, remains fairly important in the northern half of the country, and accounts for about 3% of the national product. Mexico is still the world's largest silver producer.

Agriculture occupies about 25% of the workforce but only produces about 8% of the national product. Around 10% to 12% of Mexico is planted to crops, chiefly maize, wheat, rice and beans, but Mexico is still a net grain importer. Small farming plots became prevalent after the redistribution of hacienda land to ejidos following the revolution. These are often farmed at subsistence level, lacking technology and investment to render the land more productive. Moves to change this, permitting the sale of ejido land and joint ventures with the private sector, were made by President Salinas in the early 1990s. Larger-scale commercial farming goes on primarily along the Gulf coastal plain (coffee and sugar cane), in the north and north-west (livestock ranching and, in irrigated areas, wheat and cotton), and in the Bajío area north of Mexico City (wheat and vegetables).

Policy

After WW II, Mexico entered an era of statism, with the federal government taking control of many aspects of the economy. By the 1970s, the government ran the telephone company, the oil monopoly, railways, airlines, and some banks, hotels and other enterprises. Many of these enterprises were inefficient, with jobs given out as political favours and subsidies granted to make up for losses. Nevertheless Mexican business and commerce grew substantially in the postwar decades.

The oil boom of the 1970s encouraged Mexico to undertake ambitious public spending projects, piling up a big burden of national debt, which could not be paid when revenues slumped in the oil bust of the early 1980s. In response to this, particularly under President Salinas from 1988 to 1994, debt was rescheduled, austerity measures were introduced, and government enterprises were privatised. Inflation was cut from well over 100% to under 10% during Salinas' presidency, with help from a prices-and-incomes pact. By the early 1990s the Mexican economy was showing healthy growth again and the peso, which had slumped disastrously through the 1980s, had been stabilised.

The Harvard-trained Salinas aimed to transform Mexico from a closed, state-dominated economy into a country of private enterprise and free trade. He encouraged private investment, relaxing restrictions on private business and on foreign control of Mexican companies. The key plank in his programme was the North American Free Trade Agreement (NAFTA), agreed between Mexico, the USA and Canada in 1992, ratified by their legislatures in 1993, and effective from 1994. By eliminating restrictions on trade and investment between the three countries, step by step over a 15-year period, it was hoped that NAFTA will bring labour-cheap Mexico increased employment and growing exports, as well as cheaper imports. Some Mexicans however were fearful of becoming an economic colony of the USA, of being exploited as cheap labour, and of deadly competition from the north for less efficient sectors of their economy such as grain and livestock farming and small-scale industry and agriculture.

By the end of 1993 Salinas' economic policies were widely seen as a success, particularly among the rich and middle class who definitely benefited from them. But the EZLN peasant rebellion in Chiapas, which began on 1 January 1994, the day NAFTA came into effect, drew the spotlight back to the big, seemingly widening gap between rich and poor. Wealth remains concentrated in relatively few hands, and by government figures 13.5 million Mexicans live in extreme poverty, with another 23.6 million in poverty. Living standards are close to subsistence level for the majority of the rural population (especially in the centre and south of the country) and many of the urban poor, whose squatter settlements can be seen on the fringes of most of the larger cities. Mexico's fast-growing population contributes over a million extra job seekers every year.

Salinas' policies took a crushing blow shortly after he handed over the presidency to Ernesto Zedillo at the end of 1994. In an attempt to curb Mexico's ballooning current account deficit, caused partly by a flood of imports since NAFTA took effect, Zedillo devalued the peso by 15%, to a level of 4 pesos to US$1. This unleashed a rush of capital out of Mexico and the government, unable to hold the peso even at its new low value, floated the currency to find its own level. The peso slumped to nearly six to the dollar, creating a major flurry in world financial markets. Most of the blame for the economic crisis was laid on Salinas, for having held the peso at too high a level in order to control inflation and maintain international confidence.

Though the peso was expected eventually to regain some of the lost ground, partly in response to lines of credit and other support from the USA, Canada and other countries, the consequences of its fall for the Mexican economy were grim. Prices, especially of imported goods, had immediately started rising; the Bank of Mexico had spent most of its dollar reserves trying to defend the peso; the government had to cut public spending in order to curb its deficit and limit the inevitable jump in inflation; foreign investor confidence had been badly hit; and hopes of high economic growth and lots of new jobs in the near future were wrecked.

Although the cheaper peso was likely to stimulate exports, the medium-term economic prospects for most Mexicans were bad, with wages highly unlikely to keep pace with prices, and economic growth severely curtailed.

POPULATION

Mexico's population according to the 1990 census was 81 million, but there are claims that this figure was several million too low. The official increase since 1980 was much lower than that between 1970 and 1980. One United Nations estimate for 1991 gave the figure of 87,836,000. Mexico's population in 1940 was counted at 20 million, in 1960 at 35 million, in 1970 at 49 million and in 1980 at 67 million.

About two-thirds of the people live in towns or cities, and around 40% are aged under 15. The biggest cities are Mexico City (with officially 15 million in its metropolitan area but perhaps 20 million if you include fringe settlements), Guadalajara (officially 2.8 million, estimated 4 million), Monterrey (estimated 2.6 million), Tijuana, Acapulco and Puebla (all estimated 1.5 million) and Ciudad Juárez (estimated 1.1 million).

PEOPLE
Ethnic Groups

The major ethnic division is between *mestizos* and *indígenas* (Indians). Mestizos are people of mixed ancestry – usually Spanish and Indian, although African slaves and other Europeans were also significant elements. Indians are descendants of Mexico's pre-Hispanic inhabitants who have retained their distinct identity. Mestizos are the overwhelming majority, and together with the few people considered to be of pure Spanish descent, hold most positions of power in Mexican society.

Researchers have listed at least 139 vanished Indian languages. The 50 or so Indian cultures that have survived, some now with only a few hundred people, have done so largely because of rural isolation. Indians in general remain second-class citizens, often restricted to the worst land or forced to migrate to city slums in search of work. Their main wealth is traditional and spiritual, their way of life imbued with communal customs and rituals bound up with nature. Indian traditions, religions, arts, crafts and their colourful costumes are fascinating subjects of study. There is more information on them in the various regional chapters, in this chapter under Arts & Culture and Religion, and in the colour Artesanías section.

Official figures count as Indians only those who list themselves in censuses as speakers of Indian languages. The real number may be around 10 million. The biggest Indian people is the Nahua, 1.5 million or more of whom are spread over at least 12 states, with the greatest numbers in Puebla, Veracruz, Hidalgo, Guerrero and San Luis Potosí. The ancient Aztecs were Nahua. The 900,000 Maya of the Yucatán Peninsula, the 500,000 Zapotecs of Oaxaca, the 500,000 Mixtecs of Oaxaca, Guerrero and Puebla, the 260,000 Totonacs of Veracruz and Puebla, and the 120,000 Tarascos or Purépecha in Michoacán are all descendants of well-known pre-Hispanic peoples.

Descendants of lesser-known pre-Hispanic peoples include the 360,000 Otomí (mainly in Hidalgo and México states), the 170,000 Mazahua in México state, and the 150,000 Huastecs in San Luis Potosí and northern Veracruz. The 300,000 Tzotzils and 330,000 Tzeltals of the Chiapas highlands are probably descendants of lowland Maya who migrated into the hills at the time of the Classic Maya downfall. Among smaller Indian peoples, the Huichol of Jalisco and Nayarit are renowned for the importance of *peyote* (hallucinogenic cactus) in their religious life, and the Mazatecs of northern Oaxaca for their use of hallucinogenic mushrooms.

Meeting Mexicans

Despite strong currents of machismo and nationalism in their make-up, Mexicans are in general friendly, humorous, and helpful to visitors – the more so if you address them in Spanish, however rudimentary.

Machismo is an exaggerated masculinity, aimed perhaps at impressing other males rather than women. Its manifestations range from aggressive driving and the carrying of weapons to heavy drinking. Women, in turn, exaggerate their femininity and don't question male authority. Such extreme sexual stereotyping, however, is far from universal, and seems to be under pressure from more modern influences.

The macho image may have its roots in Mexico's violent past, and seems to hinge on a curious network of family relationships: as several writers have pointed out, it's not uncommon for Mexican husbands to have mistresses. In response, wives lavish affection on their sons, who end up idolising their mothers and, unable to find similar perfection in a wife, take a mistress... The strong mother-son bond also means that it's crucial for a Mexican wife to get along with her mother-in-law. And while the virtue of daughters and sisters has to be protected at all costs, other women – including foreign tourists without male companions – may be seen as 'fair game' by Mexican men.

Despite tensions, family loyalty is very strong. One gringo who lived in Mexico for

---

Questions of Geography

Non-American travellers who make their nationality known may receive some amusing responses, especially in rural areas. Reactions to the revelation that I was *Inglés* have included 'How many days in the bus to England?' (from a trainee teacher in Chiapas); 'England...that is Germany? Or France?' (a Oaxaca restaurant-owner); 'What part of England is Britain in?' (a Mexico City telephone operator); and, from a fisherman on the Chiapas coast, 'Is England that way' (pointing out to sea) 'or that way?' (inland), to which I pointed inland (the more accurate of the two choices) and he replied, 'Ah, in the sierra'. A New Zealander with whom I travelled for a few days usually evoked blank incomprehension with the words *'Nueva Zelandia'*, nor did the addition of *'cerca de Australia'* help much.

But then, how much would the average European or Australasian person-in-the-street be able to tell you about Mexico?

John Noble

several years commented that Mexicans never really reveal their true selves outside the family: 'However well you think you know someone, you eventually realise that everything they say or do is an act of one kind or another – but that doesn't stop them being friendly, loyal or charming'. An invitation to a Mexican home is quite an honour for an outsider; as a guest you will be treated royally and will enter a part of real Mexico to which few outsiders are admitted.

Nationalism stems from Mexico's 11-year war for independence from Spain in the early 19th century and subsequent struggles against US and French invaders on Mexican soil. Foreign economic domination – by the British and Americans around the turn of this century and more recently by the US again – has also been impossible to forget. The classic Mexican attitude to the USA is a combination of the envy and resentment that a poor neighbour feels for a rich one. The word 'gringo' isn't exactly a compliment but it's not really an insult either.

Tourists and travellers in Mexico are usually assumed to be citizens of the USA. Away from the main tourist cities, your presence may bring any reaction from curiosity or wonder to fear or, very occasionally, brusqueness. But any negative response will usually evaporate as soon as you show that you're friendly.

Language difficulties may be the biggest barrier to friendly contact: some people are shy or will ignore you because they don't imagine a conversation is possible – just a few words of Spanish will often bring smiles and warmth, not to mention lots of questions. Then someone who speaks a few words of English will pluck up the courage to try them out.

Some Indian peoples adopt a cool attitude to visitors: they have learned to mistrust outsiders after five centuries of exploitation by whites and mestizos. They don't like being gaped at by crowds of tourists and are sensitive about cameras, particularly in churches and at religious festivals.

As for the fabled Mexican attitude toward time – 'mañana, mañana...' – it's actually no more casual than in any other developing country and has probably become legendary simply from comparison with the USA. In fact, Mexicans seem to be getting gradually more businesslike in their attitude to time and arrangements. However it's still true, especially outside the big cities, that the urgency Europeans and North Americans are used to is lacking. Most Mexicans value *simpatía* (congeniality) over promptness. If something is really worth doing, it gets done. If not, it can wait. Life should not be a succession of pressures and deadlines. In the 'business-like' cultures, life (according to many Mexicans) has been de-sympathised. You may come away from Mexico convinced that the Mexicans are right!

ARTS & CULTURE

Art

Mexicans have had a talent for art – and an excitement about bright colours – since pre-Hispanic times. Today Mexico is spattered with murals and littered with galleries of contemporary and historic art which are a highlight of the country for many visitors. On another level, Mexican creativity is expressed in its myriad folk arts which are still very much a living tradition – see the Artesanías colour section for more on them.

Pre-Hispanic Art The Olmec of the Gulf coast (about 1200 to 400 BC) produced some of the most remarkable pre-Hispanic stone sculpture, depicting deities, animals, and wonderfully lifelike human forms. Most awesome are the huge Olmec heads which combine the features of human babies and jaguars. The earliest outstanding Mexican murals are found at the city of Teotihuacán outside modern Mexico City (about 100 BC to 600 AD), where the *Paradise of Tláloc* depicts in a detailed, colourful way the delights awaiting those whose deaths were believed to have been caused by the water god Tláloc. The Teotihuacán mural style spread to other parts of Mexico such as Monte Albán in Oaxaca. The Maya of south-eastern Mexico, at their cultural height from about 250 to 900 AD, were perhaps ancient

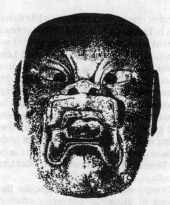

Olmec jaguar mask

as well as original works. Outstanding pre-Hispanic museums elsewhere include the Museo de Antropología in Xalapa, Veracruz, and Parque-Museo La Venta in Villahermosa, Tabasco. The exhibits in the Anahuacalli in Mexico City, the Museo Amparo in Puebla, and the Museo Rufino Tamayo in Oaxaca are selected for their specifically artistic, rather than archaeological or historical, value. More information on pre-Hispanic art can be found in the History section in this chapter and in the regional chapters of this book.

Mexico's most artistic people and have left countless beautiful stone carvings, of complicated design and meaning but with an easily appreciable delicacy of touch – a talent also expressed in their unique architecture. Subjects are typically rulers, deities and ceremonies. The Maya also created some marvellous multicoloured murals and pottery, most famously the murals of Bonampak in Chiapas. The art of the Aztecs (about 1350 to 1521) is a little less accessible and more reflective of their harsh worldview, with many carvings of skulls and complicated, symbolic representations of gods. But there are also some fine, simpler carvings of gods and people, and frescos too.

Other pre-Hispanic peoples with major artistic legacies include the Toltecs of central Mexico (10th to 13th centuries AD) with a harsh, militaristic style of carving; the Mixtecs from Oaxaca and Puebla (13th to 16th centuries) who were excellent goldsmiths and jewellers; the Classic Veracruz civilisation (about 400 to 900 AD) with a great wealth of pottery and stone carving; and the people of Cacaxtla near Puebla (650 to 900 AD) who left some vivid murals.

Pre-Hispanic art can be found at archaeological sites and museums throughout Mexico: the Museo Nacional de Antropología in Mexico City provides an excellent overview, with some very fine reproductions

Colonial Period Mexican art during Spanish rule was prolific, heavily Spanish-influenced in style, and chiefly religious in subject – though portraits grew in popularity under wealthy patrons later in the period. The influence of Indian artisans is seen in the highly elaborate altarpieces and sculpted walls and ceilings, overflowing with tiny detail, in churches and monasteries, as well as in some fine frescos such as those at Actopan monastery in Hidalgo state. Miguel Cabrera (1695-1768), a Zapotec Indian from Oaxaca, was probably the leading painter of the era – his scenes and figures have a simple sureness of touch lacking in the more laboured efforts of many others. His works can be seen in churches and museums scattered all over Mexico.

Independent Mexico Juan Cordero (1824-84) began the modern Mexican mural tradition, starting on church domes but progressing to murals expressing historical and philosophical ideas on public buildings such as the Escuela Nacional Preparatoria (now Museo de San Ildefonso) in Mexico City.

José María Velasco (1840-1912) was among the finest of all Mexican landscape painters. His canvases capture the magical qualities of the country around Mexico City and areas further afield such as Oaxaca.

The years before the 1910 revolution saw the beginnings of socially-conscious art in Mexico, and of a real break from the European traditions fostered by the national art academy, San Carlos, in Mexico City. Slums, brothels and Indian poverty began to appear on canvases. The cartoons and engravings of José Guadalupe Posada (1852-1913), with his characteristic *calavera* (skull) motif, carried a strong message of political satire against the injustices of the Porfiriato period and were aimed at a wider audience than most previous Mexican art. Gerardo Murillo (1875-1964), who took the name Dr Atl (from a Nahuatl word meaning 'water'), displayed some scandalously orgiastic paintings at a show marking the 1910 centenary of the independence movement. Dr Atl went on to become director of the San Carlos academy during the revolution.

The Muralists Immediately after the revolution, in the 1920s, the education minister José Vasconcelos commissioned leading young artists to paint a series of murals on public buildings designed to spread awareness of Mexican history and culture. This launched the first Mexican art movement of world importance. The trio of great muralists were Diego Rivera (1885-1957), José Clemente Orozco (1883-1949) and David Alfaro Siqueiros (1896-1974).

Rivera's work carried a clear left-wing message, emphasising the oppression suffered by Indians and peasants at the hands of the conquistadors, the colonial rulers and 19th-century reactionaries such as Porfirio Díaz. Rivera had an intense interest in Indian Mexico, past and present, and tried hard to pull together the country's Indian and Spanish roots into one national identity. Typically, his murals are colourful, crowded tableaux depicting historical people and events or symbolic scenes of Mexican life, with a simple, very clear-cut moral message. They're realistic, if not always lifelike. To appreciate them you need a bit of knowledge of Mexican history and, preferably, an explanation of the details. Some of Rivera's greatest works can be seen in Mexico City at the Palacio Nacional, the Secretaría de Educación Pública, the Palacio de Bellas Artes and the Museo Mural Diego Rivera, and in Cuernavaca at the Palacio de Cortés.

Siqueiros, who fought on the Constitu-tionalist side in the revolution (while Rivera was in Europe), remained a serious political activist afterwards, spending time in jail as a result, and leading an attempt to kill Leon Trotsky in Mexico City in 1940. Siqueiros' murals lack Rivera's detailed realism but convey a more clearly Marxist message through dramatic, symbolic depictions of concepts like the oppressed and the people, and grotesque caricatures of the oppressors. Some of his best works can be seen at the Palacio de Bellas Artes, Chapultepec Castle, the Siqueiros Poliforum and the Ciudad Universitaria, all in Mexico City.

Orozco was less of a propagandist than Rivera or Siqueiros, conveying emotion, character and atmosphere, and focusing more on the universal human condition than specific historical or political contexts. More of a pessimist than Rivera or Siqueiros, by the 1930s Orozco grew disillusioned with the revolution. Some of his most powerful works, such as those in the Palacio de Bellas Artes and the Suprema Corte de Justicia in Mexico City, depict oppressive scenes of degradation, violence or injustice but do not offer any simplistic political solution. His work is reckoned to have reached its peak in Guadalajara from 1936 to 1939, particularly the 53 frescos on the theme of Mexican history and the four elements in the Instituto Cultural Cabañas.

Rivera, Siqueiros and Orozco were also great artists on a smaller scale, and some of their portraits, drawings and other works are among Mexico's finest. Some can be seen in the Museo de Arte Moderno and Museo de Arte Carrillo Gil in Mexico City, and in personal museums devoted to Siqueiros and Rivera in Mexico City and Guanajuato.

The mural movement continued well after WW II. Other leading figures included Rufino Tamayo (1899-1991), a Zapotec Indian from Oaxaca, and Juan O'Gorman (1905-81), a Mexican of Irish ancestry. Tamayo, also represented in the Palacio de Bellas Artes, was relatively unconcerned with politics and history but absorbed by abstract and mythological scenes and effects of colour. O'Gorman's approach was even more realistic and detailed than Rivera's. His mosaic covering the Biblioteca Central at Mexico City's Ciudad Universitaria is probably his best known work, but atypical.

Other 20th-Century Artists Frida Kahlo (1907-54), physically crippled by a road accident in her teens and mentally tormented in her marriage to an unfaithful Diego Rivera, painted anguished, penetrating self-portraits and grotesque, surreal images that expressed her left-wing views and externalised her inner tumult. After several decades of being seen as an interesting oddball, Kahlo suddenly seemed to strike an international chord in the late 1980s and early 1990s, almost overnight becoming hugely popular and almost as well known as Rivera.

After WW II, young Mexican artists reacted against the muralist movement, which they saw as too didactic and too obsessed with *Mexicanidad* (Mexicanness). They opened Mexico up to world trends like abstract expressionism, op art and so on. The Museo José Luis Cuevas, a major modern-art museum in Mexico City, is named after and partly devoted to one of the leaders of this movement. Other interesting artists to look for in galleries of modern art include Zacatecans Francisco Goitia and Pedro Coronel and Francisco Toledo from Oaxaca.

Architecture

Pre-Hispanic Architecture The ancient civilisations of Mexico produced some of the most spectacular and eye-pleasing architecture ever built. At sites like Teotihuacán near Mexico City, Monte Albán in Oaxaca, and Chichén Itzá and Uxmal in Yucatán, you can still see largely intact pre-Hispanic cities. Most spectacular are the ancient cities' ceremonial centres. These complexes, used by the pre-Hispanic religious and political elites, were designed to impress with their great stone pyramids, palaces and ball courts. Pyramids usually functioned as the bases for small shrines on their summits. Mexico's three biggest pyramids are the Pyramid of the Sun (70 metres high on a base

over 200 metres square) and the Pyramid of the Moon at Teotihuacán, and the Great Pyramid of Cholula near Puebla.

There are many differences in style between the architectures of the pre-Hispanic civilisations: while Teotihuacán, Monte Albán and Aztec buildings were relatively simple, designed to awe by their grand scale, Mayan architecture paid more attention to aesthetics with intricately patterned façades, delicate 'combs' on temple roofs, and sinuous carvings. The buildings at Mayan sites like Uxmal, Chichén Itzá, and Palenque in Chiapas are undoubtedly some of the most beautiful human creations in Mexico.

Colonial Architecture One of the Spaniards' first preoccupations on their arrival in Mexico was to replace pagan temples with Christian churches. A classic case is the Great Pyramid of Cholula, which is now topped by a small colonial church. Many of the fine mansions, churches, monasteries and plazas which today contribute so much to the country's beauty were created during the 300 years of Spanish rule. Most of them were in basically Spanish styles, but often with unique local variations.

Gothic & Renaissance These styles dominated in Mexico in the 16th and early 17th centuries. The Gothic style, which originated in medieval Europe, is typified by soaring buttresses, pointed arches, clusters of round columns and ribbed vaults (ceilings). The Renaissance style saw a return to disciplined ancient Greek and Roman ideals of harmony and proportion: columns, and classical shapes like the square and the circle, predominated. The usual Renaissance style in Mexico was plateresque – from *platero* (silversmith), because it resembled the elaborate ornamentation that went into silverwork. Plateresque was commonly a style of decoration for the façades of buildings, particularly church doorways, which had round arches bordered by classical columns and stone sculpture. A later, more austere Renaissance style was called Herreresque after the Spanish architect Juan de Herrera.

Two of Mexico's outstanding Renaissance buildings are in Yucatán: Mérida's cathedral and Casa de Montejo. Mexico City and Puebla cathedrals mingle Renaissance and the later baroque styles.

Gothic and Renaissance influences were combined in many of the fortified monasteries that were built as Spanish monks carried their missionary work to all corners of the country. Monasteries usually had a large church, a cloister where the monks lived and worked, a big atrium (churchyard), and often a *capilla abierta* (open chapel) from which priests could address large crowds of Indians gathered in the atrium. Capillas abiertas are rare outside Mexico. Notable monasteries include Actopan, Acolman and Huejotzingo (all in central Mexico), and Yanhuitlán, Coixtlahuaca and Teposcolula in Oaxaca.

The influence of the Arabs, who had ruled much of Spain until the 13th century, was also carried to Mexico. Examples of the Spanish Arabic style, known as *Mudéjar*, can be seen in some beautifully carved wooden ceilings and in the *alfíz*, a rectangle framing a round arch. The 49 domes of the Capilla Real in Cholula almost resemble a mosque.

Baroque Baroque style, which reached Mexico in the early 17th century, was a reaction against the strictness of Renaissance styles, combining classical influences with other elements and aiming at dramatic effect rather than pure proportion. Curves, colour, contrasts of light and dark, and increasingly elaborate decoration were among its hallmarks. Painting and sculpture were integrated with architecture for further elaborate effect – most notably in ornate, often enormous altarpieces. Classical columns were used, but often with the heavier or simpler columns placed above the lighter or more elaborate ones.

Examples of early, more restrained baroque buildings include the churches of Santiago Tlatelolco in Mexico City, San Felipe Neri in Oaxaca and San Francisco in San Luis Potosí. Later baroque structures are the churches of San Cristóbal in Puebla and La Soledad in Oaxaca, and the Zacatecas cathedral façade.

Mexican baroque reached its final form, known as Churrigueresque, between 1730 and 1780. Named after a Barcelona carver and architect, José Benito de Churriguera, this style was characterised by riotous surface ornamentation of which the hallmark is the *estípite* – a pilaster (vertical pillar projecting only partly from the wall) in the form of a very narrow upside-down pyramid. The estípite helped give Churrigueresque its typical 'top-heavy' effect.

Outstanding Churrigueresque churches include the Sagrario Metropolitano in Mexico City; San Martín in Tepotzotlán; San Francisco, La Compañía and La Valenciana in Guanajuato; Santa Prisca and San Sebastián in Taxco; and the Ocotlán sanctuary at Tlaxcala.

Mexican Indian artisanry added a profusion of detailed sculpture in stone and coloured stucco to many baroque buildings. Among its most exuberant examples are the Capilla del Rosario in Santo Domingo church, Puebla, and the village church of Tonantzintla, near Puebla. Arabic influence continued with the popularity of coloured tiles *(azulejos)* on the outside of buildings, particularly in and around the city of Puebla.

Neoclassic Neoclassical style was another return to Greek and Roman ideals. In Mexico it lasted from about 1780 to 1830. Outstanding examples are the Colegio de Minería in Mexico City, the Alhóndiga de Granaditas in Guanajuato and the second tier of the Mexico City cathedral towers.

19th & 20th Centuries Independent Mexico saw revivals of earlier Gothic and colonial styles. Towards the end of the 19th century many buildings copied contemporary French or Italian styles. The Palacio de Bellas Artes in Mexico City is one of the finest buildings from this era.

After the revolution of 1910 to 1921, art deco appeared in buildings like the Lotería Nacional and Frontón México in Mexico City, but more important was an attempt to return to pre-Hispanic roots in the search for a national identity. This trend was known as

Toltecism and many public buildings exhibit the heaviness of Aztec or Toltec monuments. This movement culminated in the Mexico City university campus, built in the early 1950s, where many buildings are covered with colourful murals.

Music

In Mexico live music may start up at any time on streets, plazas or even buses. The musicians are playing for a living and range from marimba teams and mariachi bands (trumpeters, violinists, guitarists and a singer, all dressed in 'cowboy' costume) to ragged lone buskers with out-of-tune guitars and hoarse voices. Mariachi music – perhaps the most 'typical' Mexican music of all – originated in Guadalajara but is played nationwide. Marimbas are particularly popular in the south-east and on the Gulf coast.

On a more organised level, Mexico has a thriving popular music business. Its outpourings can be heard live at clubs, fiestas, nightspots and concerts, or bought in recorded form from music shops or cheap bootleg cassette vendors. (Always ask bootleg vendors to try out the particular cassette you're buying as there are many defective or even blank copies.)

Popular music ranges from the simple melodies accompanying Indian traditional dances through Mexican regional styles to foreign imports such as Latin *música tropical* and Western rock and pop. Indian dance music is typically played by flute, drum and perhaps guitar or violin, and tends to be solemn, even stately. Regional popular music is basically dance music rooted in a strong rhythm from several guitars, with voice, accordion, violin or brass taking the lead – the brass-led Mariachi is one regional style that has gained national popularity. *Música ranchera* is Mexico's version of country music – it's vocalist-and-combo music, sometimes with a sentimental touch, fairly bland and repetitive to some ears.

Latin and Caribbean music under generic headings like *música Afro-Antillana, salsa* or *música tropical* didn't originate in Mexico but has become highly popular. Again it's dance music, with percussion and often electric guitars providing infectious rhythms. Mambo, merengue, rumba and bossanova are specific dances within these categories. Andean-style pan-pipe music, another import from the south, can be heard particularly at *peñas*, Latin American folk song evenings.

Western-style pop and rock are popular in Mexico and concerts by home-grown and international stars draw big crowds. Top groups include El Tri (raucous rock), Maná (with a sound not unlike the Police), and the more original Fobia and Café Tacuba. El General is Mexico's leading rap artist.

Jazz and classical music are far from neglected, with frequent concerts and festivals taking place in Mexico City and elsewhere.

Dance

Indian Dance Colourful traditional Indian dances are an important part of many of the fiestas on the Mexican calendar. Though often performed as part of Christian festivals, many bear traces of pre-Hispanic ritual. There are hundreds of traditional dances, some popular in many parts of the country, others danced only in a single town or village. Nearly all of them require special costumes, often including masks. Among the most superb of all dance costumes are those of the Zapotec feather dance in Oaxaca and the Nahua quetzal dance in Puebla, which feature enormous feathered headdresses or shields.

One of the most spectacular dances is the *voladores*, performed by Totonac Indians from the states of Veracruz and Puebla. Four men 'fly' (with ropes attached to one leg) from the top of a 20-metre-high pole in re-enactment of an old fertility rite. Other dances tell stories that are clearly Spanish or colonial in origin. The Zapotec feather dance represents the Spanish conquest of Mexico. *Moros y Cristianos* is a fairly widespread dance which re-enacts the victory of Christians over Moors in medieval Spain. The costumes of Los Viejitos (The Old Men), which can be seen in Pátzcuaro, Michoacán, originated in mockery of the Spanish, whom the local Tarasco Indians thought aged very fast! Some dances are these days performed outside their religious context as simple spectacles. The voladores, for instance, can regularly be seen at the Museo Nacional de Antropología in Mexico City and at the El Tajín and Zempoala archaeological sites – and in Acapulco. The Ballet Folklórico in Mexico City brings together traditional dances from all over the country. Other folkloric dance performances can be seen in several cities, and annual festivals like the Guelaguetza in Oaxaca and the Atlixcáyotl in Atlixco, Puebla, gather performers from wide areas.

Sport

The Bullfight To gringo eyes, the *corrida de toros* (bullfight) hardly seems to be sport or, for that matter, entertainment. Mexicans, however, see it as both and more. It's a traditional spectacle, more a ritualistic dance than a fight, that originated in Spain and readily lends itself to a variety of symbolic interpretations, mostly related to machismo. It's said that Mexicans arrive on time for only two events – funerals and bullfights.

The bullfight begins with the presentation of the matador and his assistants. Everyone leaves the ring except for the matador and his 'cape men', then the first of the day's six or seven bulls is released from its pen. The cape men try to tire the bull by working him around the ring.

After a few minutes, a trumpet sounds to mark the beginning of the first of three parts (*tercios*) of each 'fight'. Two men called *picadores* enter the ring on thickly padded horses with long lances and get close enough to the bull to stick their lances into its shoulder muscles. They weaken the bull just enough to make it manageable.

After the picadores leave the ring, the second tercio begins. Men with *banderillas*, one-metre-long darts, enter the ring on foot. Their objective is to jam three pairs of banderillas into the bull's shoulders without being gored.

With that done, the third tercio – the part everyone has been waiting for – begins. The matador has exactly 16 minutes to kill the bull. First he tires it with fancy cape work. When he feels the time is right, he trades his large cape for a smaller one (the *muleta*) and takes up a sword. He baits the bull towards him and gives it what he hopes will be the death blow, the final *estocada*, or sword-lunge, between the shoulders. If the matador succeeds, and he usually does, the bull collapses and an assistant dashes into the ring to slice its jugular. If the applause from the crowd warrants, he will also cut off an ear or two and sometimes the tail for the matador.

A 'good' bullfight depends not only on the skill and courage of the matador but also the spirit of the bulls. Animals that lack heart for the fight bring shame on the ranch that bred them. Very occasionally, a bull that has fought outstandingly is spared (*indultado*) – an occasion for great celebration – and will then retire to stud. *The News* carries an informative weekly bullfighting column, usually on Tuesdays.

Football (Soccer) *Fútbol* is just about as popular as bullfighting. There is a thriving 20-team national *primera división*, and several impressive stadiums. Mexico hosted the World Cup finals in 1970 and 1986.

The two most popular teams in the country – and usually two of the best – are América of Mexico City (nicknamed Las Águilas), and Guadalajara (Las Chivas). They attract large followings wherever they play. The two major cities also provide several other teams in the primera división: UNAM (Las Pumas), Cruz Azul (Los Cementeros), Atlante (Los Potros) and Necaxa (Los Rayos) all come from the capital, while Guadalajara is home to Universidad de Guadalajara (Los Leones Negros), Universidad Autónoma de Guadalajara (Los Tecos), and Atlas (Los Zorros). Leading provincial clubs include Toluca (Los Diablos Rojos), Puebla (Los Camoteros), Santos of Torreón, Monterrey (Los Rayados), and Universidad de Nuevo León (Los Tigres) also of Monterrey.

The biggest games of the year are those between América and Guadalajara, known as 'Los Clásicos'. These teams attract crowds of 100,000 when they meet at the Estadio Azteca in Mexico City. Crowds at other games range from a few thousand to around 70,000 depending on the attractions of the fixture. Games are normally spaced over the weekend from Friday to Sunday: details are printed in *The News* and the Spanish-language press. The season runs from August to May, culminating in championship play-offs between the leaders of four groups into which the 20 primera división teams are divided.

Attending a game is fun: rivalry between opposing fans is generally good-humoured. Tickets can be bought at the gate and normally cost from 5 to 50 pesos, depending on the quality of your seat.

Other Sports *Beisbol* (baseball) is popular, and there is a national professional league. Mexican stars often move to the United States, and ageing Americans sometimes stretch out their careers south of the border.

Charreada is the rodeo, held particularly in the northern half of the country, both during fiestas and at regular venues often called *lienzos charros*.

Horse racing is held at several *hipódromos* (racecourses) around the country. It's popular in towns on the US border and at the Hipódromo de las Américas in Mexico City.

Jai Alai ('HIGH-lie') is the Basque game *pelota*, brought to Mexico by the Spanish. It is a bit like squash with a hard ball on a very long court, played with curved baskets attached to the arm – and it can be fast and exciting. You can see it played by semi-professionals in Mexico City and Tijuana, among other places.

Lucha libre is a type of free-style wrestling that's as much showbiz as sport. Participants wear lurid masks and sport attractive names like Bestia Salvaje, Shocker, Los Karate Boy, Heavy Metal, El Hijo del Diablo and Los Camikasis.

RELIGION
Christianity
Almost 90% of the population professes Roman Catholicism and about 4% Protestantism. The dominance of Catholicism is remarkable considering the rocky history

that the Catholic church has had in Mexico, particularly in the last two centuries.

The church was present in Mexico from the very first days of the Spanish conquest. Until independence it remained the second most important institution after the crown's representatives (the viceroy etc), and was really the only unifying force in Mexican society. Almost everyone – Indians, mestizos and whites – belonged to the church because, spirituality aside, it was the principal provider of social services and education.

The Jesuits were among the foremost providers and administrators, establishing several missions and settlements throughout Mexico by the second half of the 18th century. Their expulsion then from the Spanish empire by the Bourbon king Carlos III, who suspected them of disloyalty, marked the beginning of stormy church-state relations in Mexico.

In the 19th and 20th centuries (up to 1940), Mexico passed numerous measures restricting the church's power and influence. The bottom line was money and property, both of which the church was amassing faster than the generals and political bosses. The 1917 Mexican constitution prevented the church from owning property or running schools or newspapers, and banned clergy from wearing clerical garb or speaking out on government policies and decisions. In practice most of these provisions ceased to be enforced in the second half of the 20th century, and in the 1990s President Salinas formally recognised the church's role in Mexican society by having such measures removed from the constitution and establishing diplomatic relations with the Vatican.

The church remains the unifying force that it was when Mexico was a Spanish colony. Its most binding symbol is the dark-skinned Virgin of Guadalupe *(Nuestra Señora de Guadalupe)*, a manifestation of the Virgin Mary who appeared to a Mexican Indian in 1531 on a hill near Mexico City where Aztec gods had long been worshipped. The Virgin of Guadalupe became a crucial link between Catholic and Indian spirituality and, as Mexico grew into a predominantly mestizo society, she became the most potent symbol of Mexican

Catholicism. Today she is the country's patron, her blue-cloaked image is ubiquitous, and her name is invoked in religious ceremonies, political speeches and literature.

Mexico's patron saint, the Virgin of Guadalupe

Indian Religion

The Spanish missionaries of the 16th and 17th centuries won the indigenous people over to Catholicism as much by grafting it on to pre-Hispanic religions as by full-scale conversion. Often old gods were simply identified with Christian saints and old festivals continued to be celebrated, little changed, on the nearest saint's day. Acceptance of the new religion was greatly helped by the appearance of the Virgin of Guadalupe in 1531.

Today, despite some decline in traditional practices as the modern world makes inroads into Indian life, Indian Christianity is still fused with more ancient beliefs. In some remote regions, Christianity is only a veneer at most. Triqui Indian witch doctors in Oaxaca, for instance, reputedly carry out magical cures in churches after services, and for the Day of the Dead, Triquis pour a broth made from sacrificed oxen over the church

floor to feed the dead. The Huichol Indians of Jalisco have two Christs but neither is a major deity. Much more important is Nakawé, the fertility goddess. The hallucinogenic plant peyote is a crucial source of wisdom in the Huichol world. Elsewhere, especially among the Tarahumara in the Copper Canyon, drunkenness is an almost sacred element at festival times.

Even among the more orthodox Indians it is not uncommon for saints' festivals in spring, or the pre-Lent carnival, to be accompanied by remnants of fertility rites. The famous Totonac voladores dance of Veracruz is one such ritual, though it is losing sacredness today through being performed as a tourist spectacle. The Guelaguetza dance festival, which draws thousands of visitors to Oaxaca every summer, has its roots in pre-Hispanic maize-god rituals.

In the traditional Indian world almost everything has a spiritual (some would say superstitious) dimension – trees, rivers, plants, wind, rain, sun, animals and hills have their own gods or spirits. Even Coca-Cola bottles can be seen among offerings in the Tzotzil Indian church at Chamula, Chiapas. Whole hierarchies of 'pagan' gods sometimes coexist side by side with the Christian Trinity and saints.

Witchcraft and magic survive. Illness may be seen as a 'loss of soul' caused by the sufferer's wrongdoing or by the influence of someone with magical powers. A soul can be 'regained' if the appropriate ritual is performed by a witch doctor *(brujo)*. Another belief is in the *tono* or *tona* – a person's animal 'double' in the spirit world whose welfare closely parallels that of the person's.

Judaism

Jews make up 0.1% of Mexico's population. Most of them live in the state of México and in Mexico City, where there are several synagogues.

LANGUAGE

Spanish is the predominant language of Mexico. Mexican Spanish is unlike Castilian Spanish, the literary and official language of

Spain, in two respects: in Mexico, the Castilian lisp has more or less disappeared, and numerous Indian words have been adopted.

Travellers in the cities, towns and larger villages can almost always find someone who speaks at least some English. All the same, it is still advantageous and courteous to know at least a few words and phrases of Spanish. Mexicans will generally respond much more positively if you attempt to speak to them in their own language.

About 50 Indian languages are spoken by five million or more people in Mexico, of whom perhaps 15% don't speak Spanish.

Pronunciation

Vowels & Consonants Spanish has five vowels: **a**, **e**, **i**, **o** and **u**. They are pronounced something like the highlighted letters of the following English words: f**a**ther, **e**nd, mar**i**ne, **o**r and p**u**ll.

Most of the consonants in Spanish are pronounced in much the same way as their English counterparts, but there are a few exceptions:

c is pronounced like 's' in 'sit' when before e or i; elsewhere it is like 'k'

g is pronounced like English 'h' (with more friction) before e or i; before a or o it is like the 'g' in 'go'

gu is pronounced like the 'g' in 'go', but the u is not pronounced

h is not pronounced at all

j is pronounced like English 'h', only with a lot more friction

ll is similar to English 'y'

ñ is like the 'ny' in 'canyon'

qu is the same as English 'k' (the u is not pronounced)

r is a very short rolled r

rr is a longer rolled 'r'

x is like the English 'h' when it comes after e or i, otherwise it is like English 'x' as in 'taxi'; in many Indian words (particularly Mayan ones), 'x' is pronounced like English 'sh'

z is the same as the English 's'; under no circumstances should s or z be pronounced like English 'z' – this sound does not exist in Spanish

There are a few other minor pronunciation problems, but the longer you spend in Mexico, the easier they will become. The letter **ñ** is considered a separate letter of the Spanish alphabet and follows n in alphabetical lists like indexes, dictionaries or phone books. Until 1994, **ch** and **ll** were also considered separate letters, coming after c and l in the alphabet, but a congress of scholars from the Spanish-speaking world changed things to aid translation and computer work.

Accents & Stress Knowing which part of a word to stress in Spanish is a big aid to being understood. The rule is: if the word has an accent, put the stress on the syllable containing the accent; if not, stress the last syllable unless the word ends in a vowel or n or s, in which cases stress the second-last syllable. Examples:

kilómetro	ki-LOH-meh-tro
México	MEH-hee-ko
Cortés	cor-TESS
favor	fa-VOR
catedral	cat-eh-DRAL
comer	coh-MEHR
estoy	es-TOY
Acapulco	ah-cah-POOL-co
naranja	na-RAN-ha
casa	CA-sa
joven	HO-ven
Estados Unidos	es-TA-dos oo-NEE-dos

Gender

Nouns in Spanish are either masculine or feminine. Nouns ending in 'o', 'e', or 'ma' are usually masculine. Nouns ending in 'a', 'ión' or 'dad' are usually feminine. Some nouns take either a masculine or feminine form, depending on the ending, eg *viajero* is a male traveller; *viajera* is a female traveller. An adjective usually comes after the noun it describes, and must take the same gender form.

Greetings & Civilities

Hello/Hi.
  Hola.

Good morning/Good day.
Buenos días.
Good afternoon.
Buenas tardes.
Good evening/Good night.
Buenas noches.
See you.
Hasta luego.
Goodbye.
Adiós.
Pleased to meet you.
Mucho gusto.
How are you? (to one person)
¿Como está?
How are you? (to more than one person)
¿Como están?
I am fine.
Estoy bien.
Please.
Por favor.
Thank you.
Gracias.
You're welcome.
De nada.
Excuse me.
Perdóneme.

People

I	*yo*
you (familiar)	*tu*
you (formal)	*usted*
you (pl, formal)	*ustedes*
he/it	*el*
she/it	*ella*
we	*nosotros*
they (m)	*ellos*
they (f)	*ellas*
my wife	*mi esposa*
my husband	*mi esposo*
my sister	*mi hermana*
my brother	*mi hermano*
sir/Mr	*señor*
madam/Mrs	*señora*
miss	*señorita*

Useful Words & Phrases

For words pertaining to food and restaurants, see the Food and Drinks sections of the Facts for the Visitor chapter.

Yes.	*Sí.*
No.	*No.*
What did you say?	*¿Mande?* (colloq)
good/OK	*bueno*
bad	*malo*
better	*mejor*
best	*lo mejor*
more	*más*
less	*menos*
very little	*poco* or *poquito*

I am... *Estoy...*
(location or
temporary condition)

here	*aquí*
tired	*cansado*
sick/ill	*enfermo*

I am... *Soy...*
(permanent state)

a worker	*trabajador*
married	*casado*

Buying

How much?
¿Cuanto?
How much does it cost?
¿Cuanto cuesta? or *¿Cuanto se cobra?*
How much is it worth?
¿Cuanto vale?
I want...
Quiero...
I do not want...
No quiero...
I would like...
Quisiera...
Give me ...
Deme...
What do you want?
¿Que quiere?
Do you have ...?
¿Tiene...?
Is/are there ...?
¿Hay ...?

Nationalities

American (m/f)	*(norte-) americano/a*
Australian (m/f)	*australiano/a*
British (m/f)	*británico/a*
Canadian (m & f)	*canadiense*

English (m & f)	*inglés*
French (m/f)	*francés/francesa*
German (m/f)	*alemán/alemana*

Languages

I speak...	*Yo hablo...*
I do not speak...	*No hablo...*
Do you speak...?	*¿Usted habla...?*
Spanish	*español*
English	*inglés*
German	*alemán*
French	*francés*

I understand.
   Entiendo.
I do not understand.
   No entiendo.
Do you understand?
   ¿Entiende usted?
Please speak slowly.
   Por favor hable despacio.

Crossing the Border

border (frontier)	*la frontera*
car-owner's title	*título de propiedad*
car registration	*registración*
customs	*aduana*
driver's licence	*licencia de manejar*
identification	*identificación*
immigration	*inmigración*
passport	*pasaporte*
tourist card	*tarjeta de turista*
visa	*visado*
birth certificate	*certificado de nacimiento*

Getting Around

street	*calle*
boulevard	*bulevar*
avenue	*avenida*
road	*camino*
highway	*carretera*
corner (of)	*esquina (de)*
corner/bend	*vuelta*
block	*cuadra*
to the left	*a la izquierda*
to the right	*a la derecha*
on the left side	*al lado izquierdo*
on the right side	*al lado derecho*

straight ahead	*adelante*
straight on	*todo recto* or *derecho*
this way	*por aquí*
that way	*por allí*
north	*norte*
south	*sur*
east	*este*
east (in an address)	*oriente* (abbrev. *ote*)
west	*oeste*
west (in an address)	*poniente* (abbrev. *pte*)

Where is ...?	*¿Donde está...?*
the bus station	*el terminal de auto-buses/central camionera*
the train station	*la estación del ferrocarril*
the airport	*el aeropuerto*
the post office	*el correo*
a long-distance telephone	*un teléfono de larga distancia*

bus	*camión* or *autobús*
minibus	*colectivo, combi* or
(in Mexico City)	*pesero*
train	*tren*
taxi	*taxi*
ticket sales counter	*taquilla*
waiting room	*sala de espera*
baggage check-in	*(Recibo de) Equipaje*
toilet	*sanitario*
departure	*salida*
arrival	*llegada*
platform	*andén*
left luggage room/ checkroom	*guardería* (or *guarda*) *de equipaje*

How far is ...?
   ¿Á que distancia está ...?
How long? (how much time?)
   ¿Cuanto tiempo?
short route (usually a toll highway)
   vía corta

Driving in Mexico

gasoline/petrol	*gasolina*
fuel station	*gasolinera*
unleaded	*sin plomo, Magna Sin*

regular/leaded	regular/con plomo, Nova
fill the tank	llene el tanque; llenarlo
full	lleno; 'ful'
oil	aceite
tyre	llanta
spare tyre	llanta de repuesto
puncture	agujero
flat tyre	llanta desinflada

How much is a litre of gasoline (petrol)?
    ¿Cuanto cuesta el litro de gasolina?
My car has broken down.
    Se me ha descompuesto el carro.
I need a tow truck.
    Necesito un remolque.
Is there a garage near here?
    ¿Hay un garaje cerca de aqui?

Highway Signs

Though Mexico mostly uses the familiar international road signs, you should be prepared to encounter these other signs as well.

road repairs	camino en reparación
keep to the right	conserva su derecha
do not overtake	no rebase
dangerous curve	curva peligrosa
landslides or subsidence	derrumbes
slow	despacio
detour	desviación
slow down	disminuya su velocidad
school (zone)	escuela, zona escolar
men working	hombres trabajando
road closed	no hay paso
danger	peligro
have toll ready	prepare su cuota
continuous white line	raya continua
speed bumps	topes or vibradores
road under repair	tramo en reparación
narrow bridge	puente angosto
toll highway	vía cuota
short route (often a toll road)	vía corta

| free, older road beside a toll highway | libramiento |
| one-lane road 100 metres ahead | un solo carril a 100 m |

Accommodation

hotel	hotel
guesthouse	casa de huéspedes
inn	posada
room	cuarto, habitación
room with one bed	cuarto sencillo
room with two beds	cuarto doble
room for one person	cuarto para una persona
room for two people	cuarto para dos personas
double bed	cama matrimonial
twin beds	camas gemelas
with bath	con baño
shower	ducha or regadera
hot water	agua caliente
air-conditioning	aire acondicionado
blanket	manta
towel	toalla
soap	jabón
toilet paper	papel higiénico
the bill	la cuenta

What is the price?
    ¿Cual es el precio?
Does that include taxes?
    ¿Están incluidos los impuestos?
Does that include service?
    ¿Está incluido el servicio?

Money

money	dinero
travellers' cheques	cheques de viajero
bank	banco
exchange bureau	casa de cambio
credit card	tarjeta de crédito
exchange rate	tipo de cambio

I want to change some money.
    Quiero cambiar dinero.
What is the exchange rate?
    ¿Cual es el tipo de cambio?
Is there a commission?
    ¿Hay comisión?

Telephones

telephone	*teléfono*
telephone call	*llamada*
telephone number	*numero telefónico*
area or city code	*clave*
local call	*llamada local*
long-distance call	*llamada de larga distancia*
long-distance telephone	*teléfono de larga distancia, Ladatel*
coin-operated telephone	*teléfono de monedas*
credit card phone	*teléfono de tarjetas de crédito*
telephone card phone	*teléfono de tarjetas telefónicas* or *teléfono de tarjetas de débito*
long-distance telephone office	*caseta de larga distancia*
tone	*tono*
operator	*operador(a)*
person to person (collect call)	*persona a persona por cobrar*
insert credit card	*inserta tarjeta de crédito*
remove credit card	*remueva tarjeta de crédito*
dial the number	*marque el numero*
please wait	*favor de esperar*
busy	*ocupado*
toll/cost (of call)	*cuota/costo*
time & charges	*tiempo y costo*

Times & Dates

Monday	*lunes*
Tuesday	*martes*
Wednesday	*miércoles*
Thursday	*jueves*
Friday	*viernes*
Saturday	*sábado*
Sunday	*domingo*
yesterday	*ayer*
today	*hoy*
right now (i.e. in a few minutes)	*horita, ahorita*
already	*ya*

tomorrow (also some time, maybe)	*mañana*
morning	*mañana*
tomorrow morning	*mañana por la mañana*
afternoon	*tarde*
night	*noche*
What time is it?	*¿Que hora es?*

Numbers

0	*cero*
1	*un, uno* (m), *una* (f)
2	*dos*
3	*tres*
4	*cuatro*
5	*cinco*
6	*seis*
7	*siete*
8	*ocho*
9	*nueve*
10	*diez*
11	*once*
12	*doce*
13	*trece*
14	*catorce*
15	*quince*
16	*dieciséis*
17	*diecisiete*
18	*dieciocho*
19	*diecinueve*
20	*veinte*
21	*veintiuno*
22	*veintidós*
30	*treinta*
31	*treinta y uno*
32	*treinta y dos*
40	*cuarenta*
50	*cincuenta*
60	*sesenta*
70	*setenta*
80	*ochenta*
90	*noventa*
100	*cien*
101	*ciento uno*
143	*ciento cuarenta y tres*
200	*doscientos*
500	*quinientos*
1000	*mil*
2000	*dos mil*

Facts for the Visitor

VISAS & EMBASSIES

Visitors to Mexico should have a valid passport. Some nationalities have to obtain visas, but most Western nationalities only require the easily obtained Mexican government tourist card. Since the regulations sometimes change, it would be wise to confirm them at a Mexican government tourist office or Mexican embassy or consulate before you go.

Passports

Though it is not recommended, US tourists can enter Mexico without a passport if they have some other proof of their citizenship, such as a birth certificate certified by the government agency that issued it, or a voter's registration, or armed forces ID, or a notarised affidavit of citizenship, or a certificate of naturalisation or citizenship. Canadian tourists may enter Mexico without a passport if they carry a birth certificate issued within Canada.

However, it is much better to have a passport, because officials are used to passports and may delay those with other documents. This applies to officials you have to deal with on re-entry to North America as well as to Mexican officials: the only proof of citizenship recognised by the US customs is a passport or (for non-naturalised citizens) a birth certificate. In Mexico, you will often need your passport when you change money.

Citizens of other countries need to show a current passport.

Visas & Tourist Cards

Citizens of many countries – including the USA, Canada, Australia, New Zealand, and all Western European countries except France and Andorra – do not require visas to enter Mexico as tourists. Nationalities who do not need visas must obtain a Mexican government tourist card *(tarjeta de turista)*.

Travellers under 18 who are not accompanied by *both* parents must have special documentation – see Minors in the Documents section following.

Visas Countries whose nationals *do* have to obtain visas include South Africa, France, Andorra and Hong Kong.

Visa application procedures vary with your nationality and the country in which you are applying – check with your local Mexican embassy or consulate. You may have to show an outward ticket from Mexico, a passport valid for at least six months, and two or three photos. Some nationalities have to pay a fee.

Remember that everyone is normally governed by the regulations applying to their country of *citizenship*, not their country of residence. In particular, non-US citizens with permanent resident status in the USA should not assume that a US residence visa in their passport will always suffice for entry to Mexico. Mexican consulates in the USA may not know the appropriate rules (even if they think they do). Check with the embassy or consulate of your country of citizenship.

Non-US citizens passing through the USA on the way to or from Mexico, or making a visit to Mexico from the USA, should check the US visa requirements before leaving for Mexico.

Tourist Cards The tourist card – officially the Forma Migratoria de Turista (FMT) – is a brief paper document which you have to fill in and get validated (stamped). The card is available free of charge at Mexican immigration points at official border crossings, international airports and ports, which will also validate it. At the US-Mexico border you won't usually be given one automatically – you have to ask for it at the Mexican immigration office. You can also get tourist cards from Mexican embassies, consulates and tourist offices in other countries; from most airlines flying to Mexico; from some travel agencies outside Mexico;

and from several automobile clubs in the USA and Canada: some of these places may also be able to validate your card, but if not, you must get it validated at immigration when you enter Mexico. At many US-Mexico border crossings, you don't *have* to get the card validated at the border itself, as there are other immigration offices a little further into Mexico where it's possible to do it – but it's highly advisable to do it at the border, since there may be difficulties elsewhere.

If you don't fill in the part of the card detailing the length of your stay in Mexico, Mexican immigration officials will often put '30 days', on the assumption you're there for a short vacation. If you want more than this, fill in the number of days you want yourself, or make sure to tell the officer before he or she does so. In any case it's often advisable to put down more days than you think you'll need, in case you change your plans. The normal maximum is 180 days but the decision rests with the immigration official who validates your card.

If no one looks at your tourist card when you leave or re-enter Mexico, as often happens on the US border, there would be nothing to stop you using the same card more than once provided it was still valid.

Look after your tourist card, as Mexican law requires you to hand it in when you leave Mexico and to carry it with you at all times. (In large cities, it may be a good idea to put your tourist card in the hotel safe and carry a photocopy instead, in case of theft.)

If you overstay the time limit on your card you may be subject to a fine (normally 150 pesos for up to one month). The chances are slim that you will be asked to show your card if you walk or take a bus across the Mexico-US border, but you may be asked for your card if you fly into a border city airport from elsewhere in Mexico.

US citizens do not need a tourist card for visits of less than 72 hours to Mexican towns on the US border. From Tijuana, such visitors can go as far as Maneadero (south of Ensenada), and from Mexicali as far as San Felipe.

Extensions & Lost Cards If your tourist card is for less than 180 days, its validity may be extended one or more times, at no cost, to a maximum of 180 days. But not everyone, especially people applying for a second or subsequent extension, is automatically allowed the maximum. To get a card extended you have to apply to a Delegación de Servicios Migratorios (Immigration Office). These exist in many towns and cities. The procedure should be straightforward but it's advisable to enquire at least two weeks before your card is due to expire. If the wording on your extension *(ampliación)* states that you must leave *(abandonar)* Mexico at the end of the period, no further extension will be allowed.

A convenient immigration office in Mexico City is in the Secretaría de Gobernación (Interior Ministry) building at Avenida Chapultepec 284, outside Insurgentes metro station, open from 9 am to 2 pm Monday to Friday. Take your passport and tourist card to the Departamento de No Inmigrantes (Non-Immigrant Department) on the 2nd floor. The procedure normally takes about one hour.

If you lose your card or need further information, you can call the SECTUR tourist office in Mexico City (☎ (5) 250-01-23 or (5) 250-01-51) at any time, seven days a week. If you are outside Mexico City, you can call these numbers collect or use the free number 800-9-03-92 preceded by the 91 long-distance access code. Your embassy or consulate may also be able to help with lost or expired cards. In any case prepare to spend some time with your local Delegación de Servicios Migratorios, which will have to issue a duplicate.

Mexican Embassies & Consulates

Unless otherwise noted, details are for embassies or their consular sections.

Australia
14 Perth Ave, Yarralumla, Canberra, ACT 2600 (☎ (06) 273-3963)
Consulate: 135-153 New South Head Rd, Edgecliff, Sydney, NSW 2027 (☎ (02) 326-1311)

Austria
    Renngasse 4, 1010 Wien (Vienna) (☎ (0222) 535-1776 to 79)
Belgium
    1st floor, 164 Chaussée de la Hulpe, 1170 Brussels (☎ (02) 676-0711)
Belize
    20 North Park St, Fort George Area, Belize City (☎ (02) 30-193/194)
Canada
    130 Albert St, Suite 1800, Ottawa, Ontario K1P 5G4 (☎ (613) 722-1563/3876)
    Consulate: 2000 Rue Mansfield, Suite 1015, Montreal, Quebec H3A 2Z7 (☎ (514) 288-2502)
    Consulate: 60 Bloor St West, Suite 203, Toronto, Ontario M4W 3B8 (☎ (416) 922-2718/3196)
    Consulate: 810-1130 West Pender St, Vancouver, BC V6E 4A4 (☎ (604) 684-3547/1859)
Costa Rica
    7a Avenida No 1371, San José (☎ 57-06-33)
Denmark
    Gammel Vartov Vej 18, Hellerup, 2900 Copenhagen (☎ 3120-8081)
El Salvador
    Paseo General Escalon No 3832, Escalon, San Salvador (☎ 98-10-84, 98-11-76)
France
    9 rue de Longchamps, 75116 Paris (☎ (1) 45.53.99.34, 45.53.76.43)
    Consulate: 4 rue Notre-Dame des Victoires, 75002 Paris (☎ (1) 42.61.51.80)
Germany
    Adenauerallee 100, 5300 Bonn 1 (☎ (0228) 914-8603)
    Consulate: Kurfurstendamm 72, D-W-1000, Berlin 31 (☎ (030) 324-9047/48)
    Consulate: Neue Mainzer Str 57, 6000 Frankfurt-am-Main (☎ (069) 23-05-14/15)
Guatemala
    16 Calle 1-45, Zona 10, Guatemala City (☎ (02) 68-32-89, 68-28-67)
    Consulate: 13a Calle No 7-30, Zona 9, Guatemala City (☎ (02) 31-95-73, 32-52-49)
    Consulate: 9a Avenida No 6-19, Zona 1, Quetzaltenango (☎ (9) 61-25-47)
Honduras
    República del Brasil Suroeste 2028, Colonia Palmira, Tegucigalpa (☎ 32-40-39, 32-64-71)
Ireland
    43 Ailesbury Rd, Dublin 4 (☎ (01) 2-600-627/699)
Israel
    Bograshov 3, 63808 Tel Aviv (☎ (03) 523-0367 to 69)
Italy
    Via Lazzaro Spallanzani 16, 00161 Rome (☎ (06) 440-2319/2323)
    Consulate:Via Cappuccini 4, Milan (☎ (02) 7602-0541)

Japan
    2-15-1 Nagata-cho, Chiyoda-ku, Tokyo 100 (☎ (3) 3584-4065)
Netherlands
    Nassauplein 17, 2585 EB The Hague (☎ (070) 60-2900/6857)
New Zealand
    PO Box 11-510, Manners St, Wellington (☎ (04) 472-5555/56)
Nicaragua
    Del Km 4.5 Carretera a Masaya, 25 Varas Arriba, Altamira, Managua (☎ (2) 75-380, 75-275 to 79)
Norway
    Drammensveien 108-B, 0244 Oslo 2 (☎ (22) 43-1165/1477)
Panama
    Edificio Plaza Bancomer 5o Piso, Calle 50 y Calle San José, Panama City (☎ 63-5021)
Spain
    Avenida Paseo de la Castellana No 93, 7o Piso, Madrid 28046 (☎ (91) 556-1263/1496)
    Consulate: Avenida Diagonal Sur 626, 4o Piso, Barcelona 08021 (☎ (93) 201-1822)
    Consulate: Calle San Roque No 6, Seville 41001 (☎ (95) 456-3944)
Sweden
    Grevgatan 3, 11453 Stockholm (☎ (08) 661-2213, 663-5170)
Switzerland
    Bernestrasse 57, 3005 Bern (☎ (031) 43-18-75)
UK
    8 Halkin St, London SW1X 7DW (☎ (0171) 235-6393/9165)
USA
    1911 Pennsylvania Ave, Washington DC 20006 (☎ (202) 728-1630/1600)

Mexican Consulates in the USA Besides the Mexican embassy in Washington DC, there are consulates in many other US cities, particularly in the border states:

Arizona
    Nogales: 480 Grand Ave, Terminal St, 85621 (☎ (602) 287-2521)
    Phoenix: 1990 W Camelback Rd, Suite 110, 95015 (☎ (602) 242-7398)
    Tucson: 553 S Stone Ave, 85701 (☎ (602) 882-5595/96)
California
    Calexico: 331 West 2nd St, 92231 (☎ (619) 357-3863/3880)
    Fresno: 905 N Fulton St, 93728 (☎ (209) 233-3065/9770)
    Los Angeles: 2401 West 6th St, 90057 (☎ (213) 351-6800/07)
    Sacramento: 9812 Old Winery Place, Suite 10, 95827 (☎ (916) 363-3885/0403)

San Bernardino: 588 West 6th St, 92401 (☎ (714) 889-3155/9836)

San Diego: 1549 India St, 92101 (☎ (619) 231-8414)

San Francisco: 870 Market St, Suite 528, 94102 (☎ (415) 392-5554)

San Jose: 380 North First St, Suite 102, 95112 (☎ (408) 294-3414/5)

Colorado

Denver: 707 Washington St, Suite A, 80203 (☎ (303) 830-6702/0601)

Florida

Miami: 780 NW 42nd Ave, Suite 525, 33126 (☎ (305) 441-8781 to 83)

Georgia

Atlanta: 3220 Peachtree Rd NE, 30305 (☎ (404) 266-2233/1204)

Illinois

Chicago: 300 North Michigan Ave, 2nd floor, 60601 (☎ (312) 855-1367/80)

Louisiana

New Orleans: World Trade Center Building, 2 Canal St, Suite 840, 70130 (☎ (504) 522-3596/7)

Massachusetts

Boston: 20 Park Plaza, 5th floor, Suite 506, 02116 (☎ (617) 426-4942/8782)

Michigan

Detroit: 600 Renaissance Center, Suite 1510, 48243 (☎ (313) 567-7709/7713)

Missouri

St Louis: 1015 Locust St, Suite 922, 63101 (☎ (314) 436-3233/3065)

New Mexico

Albuquerque: Western Bank Building, 1st floor, 401 Fifth St NW, 87102 (☎ (505) 247-2139/2147)

New York

New York: 8 East 41st St, 10017 (☎ (212) 689-0456/58/60)

Pennsylvania

Philadelphia: 575 Bourse Building, 21 S 5th St, 19106 (☎ (215) 922-4262/3834)

Texas

Austin: 200 East 6th St, Suite 200, 78701 (☎ (512) 478-2300/2866)

Brownsville: 724 E Elizabeth, 78520 (☎ (512) 542-4431/2051)

Corpus Christi: 800 North Shoreline Boulevard, Suite 410 North Tower, 78401 (☎ (512) 882-3375/5964)

Dallas: 1349 Empire Central, Suite 100, 75247 (☎ (214) 630-7341/43)

Del Rio: 300 East Losoya, 78840 (☎ (512) 775-2352/5031)

Eagle Pass: 140 Adams St, 78852 (☎ (512) 773-9255/6)

El Paso: 910 East San Antonio St, 79901 (☎ (915) 533-3644/5)

Houston: 3015 Richmond, Suite 100, 77098 (☎ (713) 524-2300)

Laredo: 1612 Farragut St, 78040 (☎ (512) 723-6360/69)

McAllen: 1418 Beech St, Suite 102, 104, 106, 78501 (☎ (512) 686-0243/44)

Midland: 511 W Ohio, Suite 121, 79701 (☎ (915) 687-2334/35)

San Antonio: 127 Navarro St, 78205 (☎ (512) 227-9145/46)

Utah

Salt Lake City: 182 South 600 East, Suite 202, 84102 (☎ (801) 521-8502/03)

Washington State

Seattle: 2132 3rd Ave, 98121 (☎ (206) 448-3526/6819)

DOCUMENTS

See the Visas & Embassies section for information on passport, visa and Mexican tourist card requirements. See the Getting There & Away chapter for the paperwork needed to take a vehicle into Mexico.

Minors

Every year numerous North American parents run away to Mexico with their children in order to escape the legal machinations of the children's other parent. In order to prevent this escape from the law, the Mexican authorities may – and often do – require a notarised letter of consent *signed by both parents* permitting a minor (a person under 18) to enter Mexico if alone or with just one parent. Don't risk hassles. Write out an affidavit (statement) of permission to travel, have it notarised, or authenticated at a Mexican consulate, and take it with you to Mexico. If both parents are going, no affidavit is needed. This rule is aimed primarily at North Americans but apparently applies to all nationalities – if in doubt, call a Mexican consulate.

Student Cards

Though notices at museums, archaeological sites and so on generally state that reduced prices for students are only for those with Mexican education system credentials, in practice the ISIC card will sometimes get you a reduction in any case. Take it along.

La Mordida

A border official trying to extract a small 'tip' or unofficial 'fee' from a traveller usually puts the *mordida*, the 'bite', on you in an official tone of voice: the officer will scribble something on your tourist card, or in a ledger, or stamp your passport, or do some other little action, then say 'Too dallah'. There are several things you can do to avoid paying.

The first is to look very important by dressing in a suit and tie or other such intimidating clothing. If you are male, wearing dark sunglasses (a favourite expression of machismo) can help.

The second is to scowl quietly and act worldly-wise – but whatever you do, keep everything formal. Appear quietly superior and unruffled at all times.

The third thing is to ask for a receipt: '*un recibo*'. Some fees, such as charging for the disinfection of your car, are official and legitimate. If so, you'll be given an official-looking receipt; often the official will show you the receipt booklet when he makes the request, to prove to you that the fee is legitimate. If you don't get a receipt, you've succumbed to the mordida.

The fourth thing is to offer some weird currency such as Thai baht or Australian dollars. Border officials are usually used to seeing only US dollars (and some Canadian ones), Mexican pesos, or perhaps Belizean dollars or Guatemalan quetzals. At the sight of strange money the officer will probably drop the request. If he doesn't, or if the fee turns out to be legitimate, 'search' for several minutes in your belongings and come up with the dollars you need. ∎

Hunting & Fishing Permits

Regulations on hunting licences and taking firearms into Mexico are quite stringent – contact a Mexican consulate well in advance of your planned trip. To take any of your catch out of Mexico you may have to meet further Mexican requirements as well as import requirements for the country and/or state you are taking it to.

Anglers need fishing permits, which can be obtained from the Mexico Secretariat of Fisheries (☎ (619) 233-6956), 2550 5th Avenue, Suite 101, San Diego, California 92103, or from authorities at principal ports and resorts. To take a boat into Mexico, contact the Mexico Secretariat of Fisheries in San Diego or a Mexican consulate for a permit and information on the regulations.

Spear fishing also requires a permit – if your nearest Mexican consulate can't help you, contact the Dirección General de Administración de Pesquerías (☎ (5) 211-00-63), 1st floor, Alvaro Obregón 269, Colonia Roma, Mexico City.

CUSTOMS

Motor vehicles entering Mexico (except within the limits of the US border towns) must have vehicle permits and should have Mexican insurance (see the Getting There & Away chapter).

Officially, adult visitors are allowed to bring in duty-free three litres of liquor or wine, 50 cigars or 20 packets of cigarettes (two cartons) or 250 grams of tobacco, one still camera with 12 rolls of film, and one other still, movie or video camera (with 12 cassettes), but these limits are rarely applied strictly.

If you're unsure about what you'll be able to bring back into your home country from Mexico, contact your local customs department before you go. The US Customs Service, PO Box 7407, Washington, DC 20044, can provide a brochure, *Know Before You Go*. Canadian residents can contact the Customs & Excise Department in Ottawa (☎ (613) 993-0534). British residents should contact HM Customs & Excise Office in London (☎ (0171) 928-3344). Australians can ask at an office of the Australian Customs Service for the booklet *Customs Information for All Travellers*, and New Zealanders should get the booklet *New Zealand Customs Guide for Travellers*.

Luggage Inspection

Normally Mexican customs officers will not look seriously in your luggage, and they may not look at all. Mexico made an effort to reduce corruption by replacing all its customs personnel on the US border in 1991. But there may still exist here and there the type of official who likes a tip to ease your passage through customs. If you have an expensive camera, electronic gizmo, or jewellery, there is a risk that it may be seen as leverage, or deemed liable for duty at customs' discretion. Be prepared, and be firm but flexible. Whatever you do, keep it all formal and polite. Anger, surliness or rudeness can get you thrown out of the country, or into jail, or worse.

One of our authors, who found himself a significant sum poorer after one passage through US customs, comments: 'I personally think the corruption factor is greater *north* of the border'.

MONEY

It's useful to carry your money in US dollars or major-brand US dollar travellers' cheques. Though you should be able to change other sorts of currency (especially Canadian dollars) in main cities, it can require some time-consuming hassles, and in smaller cities and towns it may be impossible.

If crossing from Mexico into Guatemala or Belize, or vice versa, try to spend all your local currency beforehand, because exchange rates across the border – for instance if you want to change pesos into quetzals in Guatemala – are often terrible.

For some useful Spanish words dealing with money, see the Language section in the Facts about the Country chapter.

Exchanging Cash & Travellers' Cheques

You can change money in banks or in *casas de cambio* ('exchange houses', often single-window kiosks). Banks go through a more time-consuming procedure than casas de cambio and have shorter exchange hours (typically 9 or 10 am to noon or 1 pm, Monday to Friday). Casas de cambio can easily be found in just about every large or medium-sized town and many smaller ones. They're quick, and often open afternoons, evenings or weekends, but often won't accept travellers' cheques, something that happens rarely in banks.

Exchange rates vary a little from from one bank or casa de cambio to another. Different rates are also often posted for cash (*efectivo*) and travellers' cheques (*documento*). On the whole, though not invariably, banks give better rates for travellers' cheques than for cash, and casas de cambio do the opposite.

If you have trouble finding somewhere to change money, particularly at a weekend, you can always try some of the bigger hotels – though the exchange rate is likely to be poor.

American Express in Mexico City maintains a 24-hour hotline – ☎ (5) 326-36-25 – for lost travellers' cheques: you can call collect from anywhere in Mexico.

Currency

Mexico has two currencies in circulation together, and this will continue until at least 1996. These are the new peso (*nuevo peso*) and the old peso (*viejo peso*). Both are often referred to simply as pesos, but once you have been in the country a couple of days it quickly becomes obvious which type of peso is being talked about.

This situation came about because of Mexico's 1993 currency reform, which simply divided every old-peso price figure by 1000 to give the new-peso figure, and put new-peso coins and banknotes into circulation alongside the old-peso ones.

The new peso is divided into 100 centavos. Coins come in denominations of five, 10, 20 and 50 centavos, and one, two, five and 10 pesos; and there are notes of two, five, 10, 20, 50 and 100 pesos.

Old pesos come in coins of 50, 100, 200, 500 and 1000 pesos and notes of 2000, 5000, 10,000, 20,000, 50,000 and 100,000 pesos.

Most prices are now quoted in new pesos, but you'll still find some – especially small ones like bus fares – quoted in old pesos. Confusing though this may sound, in practice it all quickly becomes obvious once you're in Mexico. As long as the old currency remains legal tender, you can use either new or old to pay for anything.

Prices in this book are in new pesos.

The $ sign is used to refer to pesos in Mexico (so don't panic if you find everything is costing many more $ than you expected!). The designations 'N$', 'NP' and 'Nuevos Pesos' all refer to new pesos. Prices quoted in US dollars will normally be written 'US$5', '$5 Dlls' or '5 USD' to avoid misunderstanding.

In heavily touristed areas like Acapulco, Cancún, Cozumel and Baja California you can often spend US currency as easily as pesos at hotels, restaurants and shops. Often you'll get a worse exchange rate than if you had changed your dollars for pesos, and at times it can be downright outrageous. In some establishments, however, dollars are accepted at an exchange rate as good as or better than that available at the banks, to get you to spend your money there.

Exchange Rates

As this book went to press the value of the peso was still in flux following a currency crisis, having fallen at one point to nearly six to the US dollar. Here are the approximate exchange rates at which economists reckoned the peso would settle once the crisis was over:

A$1	=	3.90 pesos
C$1	=	3.50 pesos
DM1	=	3.30 pesos
FFr1	=	0.95 pesos
NZ$1	=	3.25 pesos
100 pta	=	3.80 pesos
UK£1	=	7.75 pesos
US$1	=	5.00 pesos

Credit Cards & Bank Cards

Major credit cards such as Visa and MasterCard (Eurocard, Access) are accepted by virtually all airline, car rental companies and travel agents in Mexico, and by many hotels, restaurants and shops; American Express cards are widely accepted too. Many smaller establishments will readily accept your card for charges as little as US$5 or US$10; the big cities and resorts live on credit cards. Just a few establishments slap on a surcharge if you pay by credit card.

Major credit cards have other uses too. They can be used to operate a growing number of public telephones (see the Telecommunications section). And along with some bank cash cards, they enable you to withdraw cash pesos from cash-dispensing machines (automated teller machines or ATMs), which are open 24 hours, seven days a week. ATMs are common at bank branches in big cities and increasingly found in smaller places. Though a significant percentage of them don't work, and though a handling charge is normally added to your bill, they can be an easy source of cash if your other funds have run out, or other sources are closed or queue-bound.

Mexican banks call their ATMs by a variety of names – usually something like *caja permanente* or *cajero automático*. Each ATM displays the cards it will accept. Two major banks with hundreds of ATMs around the country are Banamex (accepting Visa, MasterCard, Cirrus and Plus System cards),

---

The Peso Crisis

As this book went to press, the value of the Mexican peso was in a state of flux following a currency crisis precipitated by Mexico's balance of payments problems. After several years of stability in the region of 3 pesos to US$1, the peso suddenly plunged to almost 6 pesos to the dollar. Economists reckoned that when the dust had settled, the currency would probably stabilise again at around 5 pesos to the dollar.

This means that Mexico will, for a while at least, be a cheaper place to visit. Visitors will get more pesos for their dollar and, though prices in Mexico started rising as soon as the peso fell, it will take time for them to return to their previous US$ equivalents. Exceptions will be places such as many top-end hotels which set their room rates in US$ terms.

Price information in this book was collected before the fall of the peso, so you must expect everything to cost more in peso terms, if not in dollar terms. At the time of going to press, peso prices were on average somewhere around 40% higher than given in this book. ∎

and Bancomer (Visa and MasterCard). In big cities, it's probably wise to take precautions against robbery when using ATMs.

Costs

The dramatic fall in the peso's value in late 1994 and early 1995 made Mexico, for a while at least, a cheaper place to visit. Price details in this book were gathered before the peso's plunge, so expect prices in Mexico to be higher in peso terms. The lower value of the peso against foreign currencies, however, should more than make up for this for some time.

Mexico has low prices in the smaller towns but still-high prices in resorts such as Acapulco, Cancún and Cozumel. A single budget traveller staying in bottom-end accommodation and eating two meals a day in restaurants will pay anywhere between US$10 to US$30 a day for those basics. Add in other costs (snacks, purified water and soft drinks, entry to archaeological sites, about US$3 per hour on long-distance buses, etc), and you'll spend more like US$15 to US$40 a day. If there are two or more of you sharing accommodation, costs per person come down considerably. Double rooms are often only a few pesos more than singles, and triples or quadruples only a little more expensive than doubles.

Camping is the cheapest way to go. You can camp for nothing on almost any beach in Mexico (all beaches are public property). Most organised campgrounds are designed for mobile homes and trailers. Electrical hook-ups, running water and sewerage are normally provided, and clean bathrooms with hot showers are sometimes available. Prices for two people and a vehicle average around US$10 a night. To pitch a tent is less expensive; the price may be subject to negotiation.

In the middle range, you can live quite well for US$35 to US$50 per person per day, even in the large cities and expensive resorts. In most places two people can easily find a clean, modern room with private bath and TV for US$25 to US$40, and have the other US$50 or so to pay for food, admission fees, transport and incidentals.

At the top of the scale, there are hotels and resorts that charge upwards of US$200 for a room, and restaurants where you can pay US$50 per person, but you can also stay at very comfortable smaller hotels for US$40 to US$75 a double, and eat extremely well for US$20 to US$40 per person per day.

These figures do not include extra expenses like internal air fares or car hire, which you're more likely to need if you're on a quick trip, or any souvenirs or clothes you buy in Mexico.

Tipping

In general, staff in the smaller, cheaper places don't expect much in the way of tips, while those in the expensive resort establishments expect you to be lavish in your largesse. Tipping in the resorts frequented by foreigners (Acapulco, Cancún, Cozumel, Ixtapa, Huatulco, etc) is up to American levels of 15% to 20%; elsewhere, 10% is usually sufficient. In small, cheap eateries you needn't tip – though you may be more inclined to do so!

Bargaining

Though you can attempt to haggle down the price of a hotel room, especially in cheaper places, the rates are normally set and fairly firm, especially during the busy winter season. In markets, bargaining is the rule, and you may pay several times the going price if you pay the first price quoted. You should also bargain with drivers of un-metered taxis.

Consumer Taxes

IVA Mexico's *Impuesto de Valor Agregado* (Value-Added Tax), abbreviated *IVA* ('EE-bah'), is levied at 15%. By law the tax must be included in virtually any price quoted to you; it should not be added afterwards. Prices in this book all, to the best of our knowledge, include IVA. Signs in shops and notices on restaurant menus often state *'incluye el IVA'* or *'IVA incluido'*. Occasionally they state instead that IVA must be added to the quoted prices. Sometimes – especially it seems in top-end hotels – a price is given as, say, '100 pesos *más IVA*' ('plus IVA'), so you must add 15% to the figure. When in doubt, ask '*¿Está incluido el IVA?*' ('Is IVA included?').

Airport Taxes Mexico levies airport taxes on all passengers: domestic (25 pesos) and international (35 pesos). These taxes are normally included in quoted fares and paid when you buy the ticket, but if you have bought your ticket abroad, they may not be levied till you check in for the flight in Mexico – you can check with your airline.

WHEN TO GO

The coastal regions of Mexico, particularly in the southern half of the country, are pretty hot from May to September, and can get extremely and unpleasantly humid, especially from July to September. If you can avoid these areas at these times, you'll have a more comfortable trip, the more so because July and August are peak holiday months and the coastal resorts attract big tourist crowds.

Mexico's other peak holiday seasons are between mid-December and early January (for both foreigners and Mexicans), and a week either side of Easter (for Mexicans). At these times accommodation and public transport of all kinds are heavily booked and advance reservations are often advisable. Despite this, you'll nearly always be able to get to where you want and find somewhere to stay – even if it's not exactly when you want to go or exactly where you would have chosen to stay.

The interior of the country has a more moderate climate than the coasts, although it's sometimes decidedly chilly in the north in winter.

WHAT TO BRING

The clothing you bring should depend upon how, when and where you want to travel, and how you would like to be perceived by Mexicans. You might want to conform to Mexican norms.

Mexicans tend to dress informally but conservatively. In the hot regions, men of all classes, from taxi drivers to business executives, wear long trousers and sports shirts or *guayaberas*, the fancy shirts decorated with tucks and worn outside the belt, which substitute for jacket and tie. Many women still dress traditionally in Indian costume, or stylishly in dresses, or blouses and skirts. In the largest cities, stylish, fashionable clothing is the rule for those who can afford it.

The local people do not expect you to dress as they do. They allow for foreign ways, but know that, except in beach resorts, shorts and T-shirts are the marks of the tourist.

In lowland areas such as the Pacific and Gulf coasts, Yucatán and Tabasco, everyone should have a hat and sunblock cream. If your complexion is particularly fair or if you burn easily, consider wearing light cotton shirts with long sleeves and light cotton slacks. Jeans are often uncomfortably heavy in these warm, humid areas – but bring a light sweater or jacket for evening boat rides.

Otherwise, men can wear light cotton trousers or shorts, tennis shoes or sandals and T-shirts, although more conservative wear is in order when visiting churches.

Women can dress similarly, except off the beaten track in villages unaccustomed to tourists. In general, it is better for women to dress somewhat more conservatively when in town – no shorts, sleeveless tops, etc. Seaside resorts are the exception; in resorts such as Acapulco, Cancún, Cozumel, Huatulco and Zihuatanejo, wear whatever you like.

In the mountainous interior you will need warmer clothing – a pair of trousers or jeans for sure – plus a sweater or jacket, perhaps both. A light rain-jacket, preferably a loose-fitting poncho, is good to have from October to May, and is a necessity from May to October.

Toiletries such as shampoo, shaving cream, razors, soap and toothpaste are readily available throughout Mexico in all but the smallest villages. You should bring your own contact lens solution, tampons, contraceptives and insect repellent – these items are available in Mexico, but not always readily so.

Other recommended items are sunglasses, torch (flashlight), pocket knife, two to three metres of cord, small sewing kit, money belt or pouch, and a small Spanish-English dictionary.

TOURIST OFFICES
Local Tourist Offices
There are national, state and city/town tourist offices. Just about every place of touristic interest has one. They're often helpful and English-speaking, with maps and brochures to hand out. Details are given in city/town sections of this book.

Representatives Abroad
Mexican government tourist offices are a fair source of information; they also distribute tourist cards. In the USA and Canada you should address enquiries to the Mexican Government Tourism Office at these locations:

Chicago
70 East Lake St, Suite 1413, 60601 (☎ (312) 565-2786)
Houston
2707 North Loop West, Suite 450, 77008 (☎ (713) 880-5153)
Los Angeles
10100 Santa Monica Boulevard, Suite 224, 90067 (☎ (310) 203-8191)
Miami
128 Aragon Avenue, Coral Gables, 33134 (☎ (305) 443-9160)
Montreal
1 Place Ville Marie, Suite 2409, H3B 3M9 (☎ (514) 871-1052)
New York
405 Park Ave, Suite 1401, 10022 (☎ (212) 755-7261)
San Antonio
Centre Plaza, Building 45 NE, Loop 410, Suite 125, 78216 (☎ (512) 366-3242)
Toronto
2 Bloor St West, Suite 1801, M4W 3E2 (☎ (416) 925-0704)
Vancouver
999 W Hastings St, Suite 1610, V6C 1M3 (☎ (604) 669-2845)
Washington DC
1911 Pennsylvania Ave NW, 20006 (☎ (202) 728-1750)

In Europe there are offices in these countries:
France
4 rue Notre Dame des Victoires, Paris 75002 (☎ 40-20-07-34)
Germany
Wiesenhuettenplatz 26, D600 Frankfurt-am-Main 1 (☎ (069) 25-34-13)
Italy
Via Barberini 3, 00187 Rome (☎ (06) 474-2986)
Spain
Calle Velázquez No 126, Madrid (☎ (91) 261-3120)
UK
60-61 Trafalgar Square, 3rd floor, London WC2N 5DS (☎ (0171) 734-1058)

BUSINESS HOURS
Businesses generally open from 9 am to 2 pm, close for siesta, then reopen from 4 to 7 pm, Monday to Friday. Outside Mexico City, some shops and offices in hot regions close roughly from 1 to 4 pm, then stay open until 7 or 8 pm.

Most Mexican churches are in frequent use, so be careful not to disturb services when you visit them. Some – particularly those that contain valuable works of art – are locked when not in use.

Archaeological sites are usually open from 8, 9 or 10 am to 5 pm seven days a week. This is unfortunate, because in many hot regions the hours before 8 am and after 5 pm, especially in summer, are cooler and much more pleasant for touring, and there's plenty of golden light. Most museums have one closing day a week, often Monday. On Sundays nearly all archaeological sites and museums are free, and the major ones can get very crowded.

FESTIVALS & PUBLIC HOLIDAYS
The abundance of fiestas in the Mexican calendar has been explained by some writers, notably Octavio Paz, as a way of escape from the problems of day-to-day existence. Another explanation is that many of them are modern successors to pre-Hispanic seasonal rituals. Whatever the reason, Mexico's frequent fiestas are full-blooded, highly colourful affairs which often go on for several days and add a great deal of spice to

life. There's a major national holiday or celebration almost every month, to which each town adds almost as many local saints' days, fairs, arts festivals and so on.

Christmas-New Year and Semana Santa, the week leading up to Easter, are the chief Mexican holiday periods. If you're travelling at these times, try to book transport and accommodation in advance.

National Holidays

Banks, post offices, government offices and many shops throughout Mexico are closed on these days:

1 January
Año Nuevo – New Year's Day

5 February
Día de la Constitución – Constitution Day

24 February
Día de la Bandera – Flag Day

21 March
Día de Nacimiento de Benito Juárez – Anniversary of Benito Juárez' Birth

1 May
Día del Trabajo – Labour Day

5 May
Cinco de Mayo – anniversary of Mexico's victory over the French Army at Puebla in 1862, celebrated grandly in Puebla

10 May
Día de la Madre – Mother's Day

16 September
Día de la Independencia – Independence Day (commemoration of the beginning of Mexico's war for independence from Spain); the biggest celebrations take place in Mexico City

12 October
Día de la Raza – commemorating Columbus' discovery of the New World, and the founding of the Mexican (mestizo) people

1 November
Informe Presidencial – the president's state of the nation address to the legislature, coinciding with the Catholic *Día de Todos Santos* (All Saints' Day)

20 November
Día de la Revolución – Revolution Day (anniversary of the Mexican Revolution of 1910)

25 December
Día de Navidad – Christmas Day; the Christmas feast traditionally takes place in the early hours of 25 December, after midnight mass

Other National Celebrations

Though not official holidays, some of these are among the most important festivals in the Mexican calendar. Many offices and businesses close.

6 January
Día de los Reyes Magos – Three Kings' Day (Epiphany); children traditionally receive gifts this day, rather than at Christmas (nowadays some get two lots of presents!)

2 February
Día de la Candelaría – Candlemas: processions, bullfights, dancing in many towns

Late February or early March
Carnaval – Carnival; held the week or so before Ash Wednesday, this is the big bash before the 40-day penance of Lent; it's celebrated most festively in Veracruz and Mazatlán, with huge parades and masses of music, food, drink, dancing, fireworks and fun

March or April
Semana Santa – Holy Week, the week leading up to Easter; this is one of Mexico's biggest holiday periods, starting on Palm Sunday (Domingo de Ramos); closures are usually from Good Friday to Easter Sunday; particularly colourful celebrations are held in San Miguel de Allende, Taxco and Pátzcuaro, among other places; most of Mexico seems to be on the move at this time

2 November
Día de los Muertos – Day of the Dead; perhaps Mexico's most characteristic fiesta; the souls of the dead are believed to return to earth this day. Families build altars in their homes, and visit graveyards to commune with their dead on the preceding night and the day itself, taking garlands and gifts of the dead one's favourite foods, etc. A happy atmosphere prevails. The souls of dead children, called Angelitos because they are believed to have automatically become angels, are celebrated the previous day, All Souls' Day. The events probably have roots in pre-Hispanic ancestor worship. Those around Pátzcuaro are most famous, but every cemetery in the country comes alive this day. Sweets resembling human skeletons and skulls are sold in almost every market.

12 December

> *Día de Nuestra Señora de Guadalupe* – Day of Our Lady of Guadalupe, Mexico's national patroness, the manifestation of the Virgin Mary who appeared to a Mexican Indian, Juan Diego, in 1531; a week or more of celebrations leads up to the big day, with children taken to church dressed as little Juan Diegos or Indian girls; festivities are nationwide but the biggest of all are at the Basílica de Guadalupe in Mexico City

16-24 December

> *Posadas* – Candlelit parades of children and adults, re-enacting the journey of Mary and Joseph to Bethlehem, held nightly for nine nights (the tradition is more alive in small towns than cities); at the end of each procession the participants break *piñatas* – clay or papier-mâché animals, fruits or stars, stuffed with sweets; the ninth procession, on Christmas Eve, goes to the church. Also around Christmas, Pastorelas – dramas enacting the journey of the shepherds to see the infant Jesus – are staged.

Local Fiestas

Every city, town, *barrio* (neighbourhood) and village has its own fiestas, often in honour of its patron saint(s). Many are religious at heart but also serve as an excuse for general merrymaking. Parades of holy images through the streets, special costumes, fireworks, dancing, lots of music, plenty of drinking, even bull-running through the streets in some places, are all part of the scene. There are festivals of arts, dance, music and handicrafts, and celebrations for harvests of products like avocados, grapes, even radishes. Even trade and business fairs often serve as a focus for wider festivities.

Highlight local events are listed in city and town sections of this book. Colourful Indian dances are performed at many of them (see Arts & Culture in Facts About the Country).

POST

Almost every town in Mexico has an *oficina de correos* (post office) where you can buy stamps and send or receive mail. They're usually open Saturday mornings as well as long hours Monday to Friday.

Sending Mail

The table shows air-mail rates in pesos at the time of writing.

Destination	Postcard	Letter up to 20 grams	Letter 20 to 50 grams
Mexico	0.90	1.30	1.70*
USA, Canada	1.50	2.00	3.70
Europe	1.80	2.50	4.40
Australasia, Asia	2.10	2.80	5.20

* up to 40 grams

Postal service is unpredictable: delivery times are elastic and packages, in particular, sometimes go missing. If you are sending something by air mail, be sure to clearly mark it 'Correo Aéreo' or 'Por Avión'. An air-mail letter from Mexico to the USA or Canada may take between four to 14 days, but don't be surprised if it takes longer. Mail to Europe may take between one and three weeks; to Australasia a month or more. The Mexpost EMS express mail service, available at some post offices, is quicker: charges for up to 50 grams are 51 pesos to North America or 65 pesos to Europe.

If you need assured and speedy delivery, use one of the expensive international courier services such as United Parcel Service, Federal Express, or DHL, all of which have agents or offices in Mexico. Minimum rates to North America, Europe or Australia are around 130 to 140 pesos.

Receiving Mail

You can receive letters and packages care of a post office if they're addressed as follows:

Jane SMITH (last name in capitals)
Lista de Correos
Acapulco
Guerrero 00000 (postcode)
MEXICO

When the letter reaches the post office, the name of the addressee is placed on an alphabetical list which is updated daily. If you can, check the list yourself – it's often pinned up on the wall – because the letter may be listed under your first name instead of your last. To claim your mail, present your passport or other identification; there's no charge. The snag is that many post offices only hold 'Lista' mail for 10 days before returning it to the sender. If you think you're going to pick mail up more than 10 days after it has arrived, have it sent to (eg):

Jane SMITH (last name in capitals)
Poste Restante
Correo Central
Acapulco
Guerrero 00000 (postcode)
MEXICO

Poste Restante may hold mail for up to a month but no list of what has been received is posted. Again, there's no charge for collection.

If you can arrange a private address to send mail to, do so. There's less chance of your mail getting put aside, or returned to the sender if you're late in picking it up.

Delivery times for mail to Mexico from other countries are similar to those for mail from Mexico (see above). International packages coming into Mexico may go missing just like outbound ones.

American Express If you have an American Express card or American Express travellers' cheques, you can have mail sent to you c/o any of the 50-plus American Express offices in Mexico (the Mexico City office holds it for one month before returning it to sender). Take along your card or a travellers' cheque to show when you collect the mail.

TELECOMMUNICATIONS
Telephone
Local calls are cheap; international calls can be very expensive – but needn't be if you call from the right place at the right time. Beware of making any call from a hotel: hotels can – and do – charge what they like for this service. Always ask the cost *before* calling from a hotel: you'll find it's nearly always far cheaper to go elsewhere.

For some useful words when making telephone calls, see Language in the Facts About the Country chapter.

Local Calls Calls within the town you're in are easy to place from any public payphone or from a *caseta de teléfono* (a call station in a shop – look for 'Teléfono' signs). The most a caseta is likely to charge is 1 peso – and that's expensive compared to a payphone, where your only difficulty (after finding one that works) is making sure you have the minuscule-denomination coins you need. Payphones are gradually being converted to accept new pesos instead of old. You just dial the number you need – seven digits in Mexico City, Guadalajara or Monterrey, six digits in other major cities, and five elsewhere – without any area code.

Long-Distance Calls The Mexican term for 'long-distance' is *larga distancia*, often shortened to *Lada*, and this refers both to calls within Mexico, beyond the city code you're in, and to international calls.

You can make long-distance calls from special direct-dial long-distance payphones, marked 'Ladatel' or 'Larga Distancia', which are conveniently located around the centres of most big and a few smaller towns, at airports, and so on. You can also call long-distance – more expensively – from *casetas de larga distancia* (Lada casetas), which are public call stations, often in shops or restaurants, identified by the words 'Lada' or 'Larga Distancia'. In Baja California Lada casetas are known as *cabinas*. Locations of some Ladatel phones and Lada casetas are given in city and town sections of this book.

Most Ladatel phones work on coins (*monedas*), but some work on credit cards (*tarjetas de crédito*) and others on special telephone cards (called *tarjetas telefónicas* or *tarjetas de débito*) sold by some shops (you have to ask around to find out which) and Telmex (Teléfonos de México) offices.

Lada casetas may charge two or three times what Ladatel phones cost – ask the rate before you order a call. You tell the person at the desk the number you want and wait till they connect you and call you to a booth. The wait is usually short unless there are a lot of other people waiting.

Costs The cost of a long-distance call depends on not just where you call to, but also where you call from, and when you call.

The cheapest phones to call from are private phones or Ladatel phones, with basic rates per minute of around 0.70 to 2.50 pesos within Mexico (depending how far you call), 4.50 pesos to North America, 10 pesos to Europe and 13 pesos to Australasia. But long-distance calls within Mexico are discounted 50% from 8 pm to 7.59 am Monday to Saturday, and Sunday all day. Station-to-station calls to the USA and Canada are discounted 33% from 7 pm to 6.59 am Monday to Friday, all day Saturday, and on Sunday till 4.59 pm (except calls to Alaska and Hawaii). Calls to Europe or Australasia are discounted 33% all day Saturday and Sunday, and (to Europe) from 6 pm to 5.59 am Monday to Friday, (to Australasia) from 5 am to 4.59 pm Monday to Friday.

Lada casetas generally charge two or three times as much, and don't give off-peak discounts. Calls from hotels are even dearer.

Placing a Call Calling from a Ladatel phone, insert your coins or card and begin with the access code for the service you want:

Mexico long-distance station-to-station:	91
Mexico long-distance person-to-person, collect (reverse-charge):	92
USA & Canada station-to-station:	95
USA & Canada person-to-person, collect:	96
Other countries, station-to-station:	98

Follow the access code with the country code (not needed for calls within Mexico or to the USA or Canada), then the city code, then the local number. Mexican city codes may be one, two or three digits, but the code plus the local number always totals eight digits.

Collect Calls You can make a collect (reverse charge) call *(llamada por cobrar)* within Mexico or to North America by using the 92 or 96 access codes given above.

You can call collect anywhere in the world from any Mexican payphone (it doesn't have to be a Ladatel phone), by dialling 02 for the domestic operator or 09 for the international operator, then asking for a llamada por cobrar. But since you have to go through an operator, this can be very time-consuming. In provincial towns it can take hours to get the international operator.

Another disadvantage of collect calls is that they normally cost the receiving party much more than if *they* called *you* (around three times as much to Britain, for instance, and up to eight or nine times as much for Mexican domestic calls!).

You can avoid these problems by finding a phone where you can receive an incoming call, then making a very quick direct-dial call to ask the other party to call you back.

Some Lada casetas and hotels will get collect calls for you, but they usually charge for the service.

Home Country Direct These services, by which you make an international collect call via an operator in the country you want to call, are available to several countries. The Mexican term for Home Country Direct is País Directo. It's wise to get information on these services, and their costs, from your international operator before you leave for Mexico. In Mexico, a few Ladatel phones in tourist areas have País Directo instructions; otherwise you can get information from Telmex, the national telephone company. AT&T and MCI both operate services to the USA for around US$5.75, plus a little under US$2 per minute.

Fax
Public fax service is offered in many Mexican towns by the *telégrafos* (telegraph) office – which may go under the name Telecomm. Also look for *'Fax Público'* signs on shops, businesses and telephone Lada casetas, and in bus stations and airports. The charge for a one or two-page fax sent within Mexico from a telégrafos office is 4.30 pesos plus the cost of the phone call. A fax to Europe or Australia is around 15 pesos a minute.

Telegrams & Giros
Domestic and international telegrams can be sent from telégrafos offices. The usual cost within Mexico is 3.25 pesos for up to 10 words, and around double that for *urgente*

service. Telegrams to North America cost around three times, and to Europe seven or eight times as much.

Another service offered by telégrafos offices is *giros* ('HEE-ros'), telegraphic money transfers, which can be useful if, for instance, you have a pay a deposit on a hotel booking in a distant city. You fill in a form and pay the cash over at your local telégrafos and the recipients collect it at theirs.

TIME

Most of Mexico is on Greenwich Mean Time minus six hours, the same time as Chicago, Dallas and Winnipeg in wintertime. The states of Baja California Sur, Sinaloa, Sonora and Nayarit are on Greenwich Mean Time minus seven hours, the same as Calgary, Salt Lake City and Tucson in winter. Baja California Norte always keeps the same time as the US state of California: Greenwich Mean Time minus eight hours in winter, and minus seven hours in summer when Daylight Saving Time is observed. (Baja California Norte is the only Mexican state to observe Daylight Saving.)

ELECTRICITY

Electrical current in Mexico is the same as in the USA and Canada: 110 volts, 60 cycles. Mexico has three different types of electrical socket; older ones with two equally-sized flat slots, newer ones with two flat slots of different sizes, and a few with a round hole for an earth pin. If the plug on your foreign appliance doesn't fit your Mexican socket, you must either change the plug, or cut/file/bend its pins, or get an adaptor. Fortunately Mexican electrical goods shops have a variety of adaptors and extensions which should solve the problem.

WEIGHTS & MEASURES

Mexico uses the metric system. For conversion between metric and US or Imperial measures, see the back of this book.

BOOKS

Although you can find books in English in most major centres, only Mexico City has an extensive choice. The Mexican-published titles mentioned here – such as the guides to pre-Hispanic sites – are widely available in Mexico, but with other books it is wise to find what you want before arriving in the country.

History & Society

General *Sons of the Shaking Earth* by Eric Wolf (University of Chicago Press, 1959) is a wonderfully readable introduction to Mexican history. Other good general introductions include *A Short History of Mexico* by J Patrick McHenry (Doubleday) and *The Course of Mexican History* by Michael C Meyer & William L Sherman (Oxford University Press).

Ancient Mexico Two books by Michael D Coe, both available as Thames & Hudson paperbacks, give a learned but well-illustrated and not over-long picture of the great cultures of ancient Mexico. *The Maya* (fourth edition, 1987) traces the history, art and culture of the Maya while *Mexico* (third edition, 1988) concentrates on Mexico's other pre-Hispanic civilisations.

Nigel Davies' *The Ancient Kingdoms of Mexico* (Pelican) is a succinct but scholarly study of the Olmec, Teotihuacán, Toltec and Aztec civilisations. Diagrams, illustrations, plans and maps complement the text.

The Daily Life of the Aztecs by Jacques Soustelle (New York, 1962) is something of a classic on its subject. *Of Gods & Men* by Anna Benson Gyles & Chlo Sayer (BBC, London, 1980) traces the paths of several Indian peoples from pre-Hispanic to modern times.

Spanish Conquest & Colonial Period

William Henry Prescott's mammoth *History of the Conquest of Mexico* remains a classic, even though published in 1843 by an author who never went to Mexico. Only with Hugh Thomas' 812-page *The Conquest of Mexico* (Hutchinson, 1993; Simon & Schuster, 1994) has the 20th century produced an equivalent tome. *History of the Conquest of New Spain* by Bernal Díaz del Castillo

(Penguin paperback, abridged version) is an eye-witness account of the Spanish arrival by one of Cortés's lieutenants.

Charles Gibson's *The Aztecs Under Spanish Rule* (Stanford, 1964) and *Spain in America* (Harper Colophon, New York, 1966) are authoritative, worthwhile books on the colonial period.

19th & 20th Centuries *The Caste War of Yucatán* by Nelson Reed (Stanford, 1964) tells how the Mayan Indians nearly threw their overlords off the peninsula in the 1840s. *Barbarous Mexico* by John Kenneth Turner (University of Texas Press, 1969) was written by a US journalist to tell North Americans the truth about the barbarity of the Porfirio Díaz regime – a job in which it succeeds admirably.

Distant Neighbors: A Portrait of the Mexicans by Alan Riding (Viking), first published in 1984, remains an excellent guide to understanding modern Mexico and its love-hate relationship with the United States. The author was based in Mexico as a *New York Times* correspondent.

Octavio Paz, a master of Mexican letters and winner of the 1990 Nobel Prize, has written perhaps the most probing examination of Mexico's myths and the Mexican character in *The Labyrinth of Solitude* (Penguin). *The Children of Sánchez* by Oscar Lewis (Penguin) is essential reading if you want to understand the family dynamics that are crucial to Mexican society.

Culture, Art & Architecture
Books on Mexico's great 20th-century artists include Diego Rivera's autobiography *My Art, My Life* (Citadel Press, New York), *The Fabulous Life of Diego Rivera* by B D Wolfe (Stein & Day, New York), and *The Mexican Muralists* by Alma M Reed (Crown, New York).

Mexico City bookshops are full of beautifully illustrated coffee-table books in English on Mexican art, archaeology and anthropology. Many are written by experts, and though they're often very expensive, you might want to take one home with you

or note its details so you can order it back home.

Art & Time in Mexico by Elizabeth Wilder Weismann & Judith Hancock Sandoval (Harper & Row) is a good, fairly handy, recent book on colonial architecture, with many photos. *A Guide to Mexican Art* by Justino Fernández (University of Chicago Press, 1969) covers architecture as well as art fairly thoroughly.

Chloe Sayer has written two fascinating, authoritative books on Mexican folk art, both tracing its evolution from pre-Hispanic times to the present. *Arts & Crafts of Mexico* (Thames & Hudson, 1990) is a wide-ranging overview, while *Mexican Costume* (British Museum Publications, 1985) is a comprehensive treatment of this absorbing topic, with a wealth of intriguing detail about Mexican life. Both books have dozens of beautiful photos.

Travel Guides
Lonely Planet has two guides covering specific regions of Mexico in detail. *Guatemala, Belize & Yucatán: La Ruta Maya* by Tom Brosnahan covers south-eastern Mexico and its neighbours, with emphasis on the Maya and their culture. *Baja California* details the many attractions of the Baja peninsula. A handy companion for this book and the two mentioned above is Lonely Planet's *Latin American Spanish Phrasebook*, which contains practical, up-to-date words and expressions in Latin-American Spanish.

The People's Guide to Mexico and *The People's Guide to RV Camping in Mexico* by Carl Franz (John Muir Publications, Santa Fe) have long been invaluable, amusing resources for anyone planning an extended trip. They do not attempt to give hotel-restaurant-transport-sightseeing specifics but provide an all-round general introduction to Mexico.

A number of guides cater to travellers who want to get out into back-country Mexico. *Bicycling Mexico* by Ericka Weisbroth and Eric Ellman (Hunter Publishing, Edison, New Jersey, 1990) covers numerous routes in the south, west and north-west in an amusing, anecdotal style, while Jim Conrad's *No Frills Guide to Hiking in Mexico* (Bradt Publications, Chalfont St Peter, UK, 1992) details 33 walks, over half of them in Baja California and the northwest. *Mexico's Volcanoes* by R J Secor (The Mountaineers, Seattle, 1981) is a thorough guide to routes up the seven main peaks of Mexico's central volcanic belt. *Backpacking in Mexico & Central America* by Hilary Bradt and Rob Rachowiecki (Bradt) covers just a few hikes in Mexico, and also some in the Central American countries.

Those with a big interest in pre-Hispanic sites should find *A Guide to Ancient Mexican Ruins* and *A Guide to Ancient Maya Ruins*, both by C Bruce Hunter (University of Oklahoma Press). The two books provide maps and details of over 40 sites between them.

Several useful series of straightforward guides to single sites or regions are fairly widely available in Mexico. One is the INAH-SALVAT *Official Guide* booklets, published in Mexico, on important museums and archaeological sites. Most cost 20 to 30 pesos. Also useful is the *Easy Guide* series by Richard Bloomgarden, with about 20 titles on main sites at about 15 to 20 pesos.

Travel & Description

Incidents of Travel in Central America, Chiapas & Yucatán and *Incidents of Travel in Yucatán* by John L Stephens are fascinating accounts of adventure, discovery and archaeology by the enthusiastic 19th-century amateur archaeologist. Both are available in Dover paperback.

Graham Greene's *The Lawless Roads* (Penguin) traces his wanderings down the eastern side of Mexico to Chiapas in the 1930s, a troubled time of conflict between Catholics and the atheistic state. Greene wasn't impressed with Mexican food, which he characterised as 'pieces of anonymous meat, a plate of beans, fish from which the taste of the sea has long been squeezed away...a little heap of bones and skin they call a chicken...all a hideous red and yellow, green and brown'! Aldous Huxley travelled through Mexico too: *Beyond the Mexique*

Bay, first published in 1934, has interesting observations on the Maya. It's also worth reading if you're going to be staying long in Oaxaca.

So Far from God by Patrick Marnham (Penguin) is an insightful, amusing account of a 1980s journey from Texas through Mexico into Central America. Paul Theroux rides the rails through Mexico on *The Old Patagonian Express*.

Other interesting books by foreigners who have lived in or travelled in Mexico include *Life in Mexico* by Frances Calderón de La Barca, the Scottish wife of Spain's ambassador to Mexico in the turbulent 1840s (reissued by Dent, London in 1970); *Viva Mexico!* by Charles Macomb Flandrau (Eland paperback) which tells of life on a coffee plantation at the turn of this century; and *Thomas Gage's Travels in the New World* (University of Oklahoma Press, 1969), by a 17th-century English Puritan.

Fiction

Mexico's most internationally-known novelist is probably Carlos Fuentes. His most highly regarded novel is *Where the Air is Clear* (Farrar Straus & Giroux, New York, 1971), written in the 1950s. Like *The Death of Artemio Cruz* (Panther), it's an attack on the failure of the Mexican Revolution. *Aura* is a magical book with one of the most stunning endings of any novel. In Mexico, Juan Rulfo is generally regarded as the country's supreme novelist. His *Pedro Páramo* (Serpent's Tail Publishers) has been described as '*Wuthering Heights* set in Mexico and written by Kafka'. Set before and during the Mexican Revolution, it's a short, simple but highly symbolic tale of a brutal landowner obsessed with a woman he has loved since his orphan childhood.

Many foreign novelists too have been inspired by Mexico. Graham Greene's *The Power and the Glory* dramatises the violent state-church conflict that followed the Mexican Revolution. D H Lawrence's *The Plumed Serpent* asks the big questions about life, death and relationships in a Mexican setting – heavy going even for Lawrence fans. Lawrence's *Mornings in Mexico* is a collection of short stories set in both New Mexico and Mexico. *Under the Volcano* by the British dipsomaniac Malcolm Lowry follows a British diplomat who drinks himself to death on the Day of the Dead in a fictionalised Cuernavaca. Sounds simple, but it delves deeply into the Mexican psyche, as well as Lowry's own, at a time (1938) of deep conflict.

Carlos Castaneda's *Don Juan* series of novels (Penguin), which reached serious cult status in the 1970s, tells of a North American's experiences with a peyote guru somewhere in northern Mexico.

Books Published in Mexico
Mexican publisher Minutiae Mexicana produces a range of interesting booklets on various aspects of Mexico including *A Bird Watcher's Guide to Mexico, A Guide to Mexican Mammals & Reptiles, The Maya World, The Aztecs Then and Now, A Guide to Mexican Archaeology, A Guide to Mexican Ceramics* and even *A Guide to Tequila, Mezcal & Pulque*. They're widely available in Mexico at about 15 pesos each.

A similar Mexican-produced paperback series with many titles in English is Panorama. These include *History of Mexico, The Conquest of Mexico, The Mexican Revolution, Truth & Legend on Pancho Villa, Pre-Hispanic Gods of Mexico, Mural Painting of Mexico* and *Indian Costumes of Mexico*.

MAPS
International Travel Map Productions publishes a good 1 cm:33 km *México* map, which has considerable detail but is easy to read, as well as the 1 cm:11 km regional maps *Baja California, Mexico South* and *Yucatán Peninsula*, and a *Mexico City* map. If you can't get these maps from your local map shop, contact ITM c/o World Wide Books & Maps (☎ (604) 687-3320, fax 687-5925), 736A Granville St, Vancouver, BC, V6Z 1G3, Canada. *Mexico* in the Bartholomew World Travel Map series is

another good overall map, strong on geographical features like altitudes and rivers.

A useful *Mapa Turístico* of Mexico is given away by tourist offices in Mexico City and some other places. *Mapa de la República Mexicana 9600*, available at some Sanborns stores, shows 9600 towns and villages, all indexed. For information on road maps, see the Car section of the Getting Around chapter.

MEDIA
Newspapers & Magazines
English-Language *The News*, a daily newspaper published in Mexico City, is distributed throughout Mexico. It covers the main items of Mexican and foreign news, and will keep you in touch with North American and European sports results! Almost every city or region that attracts long-stay English-speakers – San Miguel de Allende, Guadalajara and Puerto Vallarta, for example – has a small English-language newspaper or newsletter.

Spanish-Language Mexico has a thriving local press as well as national newspapers such as *Excelsior* and *El Tiempo*. Even small cities often have two or three newspapers of their own. *La Jornada* is a good national daily with a non-establishment viewpoint; it covers a lot of stories other papers don't.

México Desconocido (Unknown Mexico) is a colourful monthly magazine with intelligent coverage of many interesting places. Buy it at newsstands for 6 pesos. You can often find back copies or special supplements with features about local areas.

Radio & TV
Broadcasting is run by private enterprise. Mexican radio announcers are much given to the use of the dramatic echo chamber. Apart from that, they offer a variety of music, often that of the region where you're listening. In tourist areas such as Mexico City, Acapulco and Cancún, some stations give news reports several times a day in English. In the evening you may be able to pick up US stations on the AM (medium wave) band.

Many, if not most, hotel rooms above the low end have television sets. The news reports can help you to improve your Spanish. Many top-end hotels have satellite dishes and receive some US stations. Most popular are ESPN (the sports channel) and UNO, the Spanish-language US network. Local Spanish-language programming includes hours and hours of talk shows and soap operas *(telenovelas)*, some sports, and reruns of old American movies dubbed in Spanish.

FILM & PHOTOGRAPHY

According to Mexican customs laws you are allowed to bring in no more than one still camera and one other still, movie or video camera, with 12 rolls of film and 12 cassettes, but these limits are rarely applied strictly. Camera and film processing shops, pharmacies and hotels all sell film. Most types of film are available in the larger cities and resorts. Prices in Mexico are usually about US$1 or US$2 higher than in North America. Be suspicious of film that is being sold at prices lower than what you might pay in North America – it is often outdated. If the date on the box is obscured by a sticker bearing the price, look under the sticker.

Mexico is a photographer's paradise. A wide-angle lens is useful and it helps to have a polarising filter to cut down glare from reflections of sunlight on the ocean. Be sensitive about taking pictures of people: if in doubt, ask first. Indian peoples in particular can be reluctant to be photographed.

If your camera breaks down, you'll be able to find a repair shop in most sizeable towns – and prices will be agreeably low.

HEALTH
Predeparture Preparations

Specific immunisations are not normally required for travel in Mexico. All the same, it's a good idea to be up to date on tetanus, typhoid and polio, and to check your immunity to measles (catching measles is not a pleasant prospect for an adult: those who had it as children are definitely immune). You may also want to take antimalarial medicine and have vaccinations against hepatitis A,

cholera, diphtheria, tuberculosis (for children) or even rabies. Consult a doctor: much depends on which parts of Mexico you're going to and what you'll be doing. Some diseases are more prevalent in isolated country areas than elsewhere; malaria is much less of a risk in the highlands than in cities than on the coast and in isolated villages. See the later sections on some individual diseases for more information.

You only need a yellow fever certificate to enter the country if, within the last six months, you have been to a country where yellow fever is present.

Insurance Mexican medical treatment is generally inexpensive for common diseases and minor surgery, but if you suffer some serious disease or injury you may want to attend a private hospital in Mexico or return home for treatment. Travel insurance can cover the costs of this. If you're a frequent traveller it's possible to get year-round travel insurance at reasonable rates (one such policy is offered by American Express).

Medical Kit It is always a good idea to travel with a small first-aid kit. Some of the items that should be included are: adhesive bandages, a sterilised gauze bandage, elastic bandage, cotton wool, thermometer, tweezers, scissors, antiseptic (Dettol or Betadine), burn cream (Caladryl is good for sunburn, minor burns and itchy bites), and insect repellent (see Protection against Mosquitoes). Multivitamins can be useful too.

Don't forget a full supply of any medication you're already taking; the prescription may be difficult to match abroad.

Basic Rules
Mexico is partly in the tropics where food spoils easily, mosquitoes roam freely, and sanitation is not always the best, so be careful about what you eat and drink, and stay away from mosquitoes (or make them stay away from you). These measures are particularly important for travellers who enjoy getting off the beaten track and mingling with the locals.

Food & Water Food can be contaminated when it is harvested, shipped, handled, washed or prepared. Cooking, peeling and/or washing food in pure water is the way to get rid of the germs. To avoid gastrointestinal diseases, steer clear of salads, uncooked vegetables, and unpasteurised milk or milk products (including cheese). Make sure the food you eat has been freshly cooked and is still hot. Squeezing lime on salads may help, as may eating lots of raw garlic, but these habits are far from foolproof. Do not eat raw or rare meat, fish or shellfish. Peel fruit yourself with clean hands and a clean knife.

As for beverages, don't trust any water unless it has been boiled for 20 minutes or treated with purifiers, or it comes in an unopened bottle labelled *agua purificada*. Most hotels have large bottles of purified water from which you can fill your carafe or canteen. Local people may drink the water from the tap or from the well and their systems may be used to it – or they may have chronic gastric diseases! Purified water is available from supermarkets, grocery shops and liquor stores.

Use only pure water for drinking, washing food, brushing your teeth, and ice. Tea, coffee, and other hot beverages should be made with properly boiled water. If the waiter swears that the ice in your drink is made from agua purificada, you may feel you can take a chance with it.

Canned or bottled carbonated beverages, including carbonated water, are usually safe, as are beer, wine and liquor.

If you plan to travel off the beaten track, you may have to purify water yourself. Your method might be one of these:

- Water purification drops or tablets containing tetraglycine hydroperiodide or hydroclonazone, sold under brand names such as Globaline, Potable-Agua or Coughlan's in pharmacies and sporting goods stores in the USA. In Mexico, ask for *gotas* (drops) or *pastillas* (tablets) *para purificar agua*, in pharmacies and supermarkets.
- Boiled water; you must boil it for at least 20 minutes to kill parasites.
- A portable water filter that eliminates bacteria. Compact units are available from major camping supply stores in the USA such as Recreational

Equipment Inc (REI) of Seattle (☎ 800-426-4840) or Mountain Equipment Inc (MEI) of Fresno, California (☎ 800-344-7422), or through outfitters such as Eddie Bauer and L L Bean.

Protection against Mosquitoes Many serious tropical diseases are spread by infected mosquitoes. In general, mosquitoes are most bothersome in the evening and early morning, and on overcast days, and most prevalent in lowland and coastal regions and during the rainy season (May to October).

Mosquitoes seem to be attracted more to dark colours than to light, so in mosquito-infested areas wear light-coloured long trousers, socks, a long-sleeved shirt and a hat. Clothes should be loose-fitting. Mosquitoes also seem to be attracted by scents such as those in perfume, lotions, hair spray, etc. Sleep in screened rooms or beneath mosquito netting after you have disposed of the little suckers who have somehow got in there with you. Check that all openings to the outside are either screened or blocked.

Use insect repellent which has at least a 20% concentration of diethylmetatoluamide (DEET) on any exposed skin. It's best to buy this before leaving home. To avoid reactions apply it sparingly, and don't get it in your eyes or mouth or on broken or irritated skin. It's probably best not to use a repellent with an especially high concentration of DEET (concentrations reach 95%!).

Another mosquito deterrent is mosquito coils, which you can buy under brand names like Raidolitos or Baygon from groceries or supermarkets in Mexico. A packet of 16 costs about 5 pesos. Once you've figured out how to get a coil smoking without breaking it, it'll keep mosquitoes away for six to eight hours.

Heat You can avoid heat problems by drinking lots of fluids (see the Heatstroke section) and generally not overdoing things. Remember that the sun is much fiercer in the middle of the day than in the morning or afternoon. Take it easy climbing pyramids and trekking through the jungle. Wear a hat, and light cotton clothing. Take frequent rest breaks in the shade. Use sunblock to prevent bad sunburn. Near water, the glare from sand and water can double your exposure to the sun. You may want to wear a T-shirt and hat while swimming or boating.

Medical Problems & Treatment

Mexico is partly in the tropics, and has tropical diseases, but before presenting the following somewhat alarming catalogue of potential illnesses, let us say from our own experience that it is possible to take dozens of journeys in every region of Mexico, climbing volcanoes, trekking to pyramids in remote jungle, camping out, staying in cheap hotels and eating in all sorts of markets and restaurants, without getting anything more serious than occasional traveller's diarrhoea. But we *have* experienced hepatitis and dysentery, and we have known people with dengue fever and typhoid fever, so we know that these things can happen.

If you come down with a serious illness, be careful to find a competent doctor, and don't be afraid to get second opinions. You may want to telephone your doctor at home for consultation as well. In some cases it may be best to fly home for treatment, difficult as this may be. Medical treatment in Mexico is not always what it should be.

Traveller's Diarrhoea The food and water in Mexico will have different bacteria from those your digestive system is used to – germs that your immune system may not be prepared to combat. Travellers to many less developed countries suffer from what is known medically as traveller's diarrhoea (TD) and informally in Mexico as Moctezuma's revenge or *turista*. The condition is defined as having twice as many (or more) unformed bowel movements as normal. Other possible symptoms include abdominal cramps, nausea, fever and urgency of bowel movements. TD hits people most often within the first week of travel, but may hit at any time. A bout typically lasts three or four days. It seems to affect younger travellers more than older ones. Note that heatstroke (see below) can resemble the symptoms of TD.

Doctors recommend that you do *not* take medicines in the hope they will prevent TD. These can actually kill off the benign digestive bacteria that help to protect you from 'foreign' bacteria. Instead, observe the rules of safe eating and drinking, and for the first week of your trip, be conservative in your eating habits, don't get overtired, and don't drink lots of alcohol or coffee.

If you come down with TD, take it easy; stay in bed if you can. Make sure you replace fluids and electrolytes (potassium, sodium, etc) by drinking caffeine-free soft drinks or glasses of fruit juice, with honey and a pinch of salt added, plus a glass of pure water with a quarter teaspoon of sodium bicarbonate (baking soda) added; weak tea, preferably unsweetened and without milk, is all right. Avoid dairy products. Eat only salted crackers or dry toast for a day or so. After that, eat easily digested foods that are not fatty or overly acidic. Yoghurt with live cultures is good as it helps to repopulate the bowel with benign digestive organisms. When you feel better, be particularly careful about what you eat and drink from then on.

Traveller's diarrhoea is self-limiting, and you're usually better off if you can get through it without medication. If you feel that you need medicine, go to a doctor. Make sure that you have TD and not some other gastrointestinal ailment.

Doctors may recommend one of the treatments described in the US Public Health Service's book *Health Information for International Travel*, such as bismuth subsalicylate (Pepto-Bismol), diphenoxylate (Lomotil), loperamide (Imodium), doxycycline, trimethoprim or TMP/SMX. Treatments and dosages should be determined by a competent doctor who can tell you about side effects and contraindications. Bismuth subsalicylate is not recommended if symptoms last more than 48 hours, or if you have high fever, blood in the stool, kidney problems or are allergic to salicylates. Children under the age of two should not be given it. Diphenoxylate and loperamide temporarily slow down the diarrhoea but do not cure it, and they increase the risk of getting TD again. They should not be used if you have a high fever, or blood in the stool, or are driving a motor vehicle or operating machinery (your alertness is impaired). Don't use them for longer than two full days. Doxycycline, trimethoprim and TMP/SMX – this last is sold in Mexico as Bactrim F (Roche) – are antibiotics that may be indicated if there are three or more loose stools in an eight-hour period, especially with nausea, vomiting, abdominal cramps and fever.

Medicines Not to Take Pharmacies in Mexico may sell medicines – often without a prescription – which might be banned for good reason in your home country. Incompetent doctors or pharmacists might recommend such medicines for gastrointestinal ailments, but they may cause other sorts of harm such as neurological damage.

Medicines called halogenated hydroxyquinoline derivatives are among these, and may bear the chemical names clioquinol or iodoquinol, or brand names Entero-Vioform, Mexaform or Intestopan, or something similar.

Cholera In recent years this serious disease has spread into Mexico from South and Central America. About 700 cases were reported in Mexico in the first half of 1994. Vaccination against cholera is not all that effective, but the disease does respond to treatment if caught early. Food and drink hygiene minimises the chance of contracting it.

Cholera is a disease of insanitation, and spreads quickly where sewerage and water supplies are rudimentary. It can also be spread in foods that are partly cooked or uncooked, such as the popular *ceviche*, made from marinated raw fish, as well as salads and raw vegetables.

Cholera is characterised by a sudden onset of acute diarrhoea with 'rice water' stools, vomiting, muscular cramps and extreme weakness. With the onset of these symptoms you should seek medical help – but first treat for dehydration, which can be extreme. If

there is an appreciable delay in getting to the hospital, begin taking tetracycline (adults, one 250 mg capsule four times a day; children under eight, one-third of this dose; other children, half this dose).

Dysentery Like cholera, dysentery is a disease of insanitation. There are two types of dysentery, both characterised by diarrhoea containing blood and/or mucus. You require a stool test to determine which type you have.

Bacillary dysentery, the more common variety, is sharp and nasty but short. It lays you out suddenly with fever, nausea, cramps and diarrhoea, but it is self-limiting. Treatment is the same as for traveller's diarrhoea; the disease responds well to antibiotics if needed.

Amoebic dysentery is caused by amoebic parasites and is more dangerous. It builds up slowly, cannot be starved out and if untreated will get worse and can permanently damage your intestines. Do not have anyone other than a doctor diagnose your symptoms and administer treatment.

Giardia (Giardiasis) This is caused by a parasite named *Giardia lamblia*, contracted from faecally contaminated food or beverages or by contact with a contaminated surface. Symptoms usually last for more than five days (perhaps months!), may be mild or serious, and may include diarrhoea, abdominal cramps, weight loss, anorexia and nausea. If you have gastrointestinal gripes for a length of time, talk to a doctor and have a stool sample analysed for giardia. Medicine is available to cure you easily and safely.

Hepatitis This is a viral disease of the liver for which there are no medicines, and it can be very serious – even fatal – if not treated with bed rest. Symptoms appear 15 to 50 days after infection (generally around 25 days) and consist of fever, loss of appetite and energy, nausea, depression, and pains around the base of the rib cage. Skin turns yellow, the whites of the eyes yellow to orange, and urine deep orange or brown. Do *not* take antibiotics. The only cure is complete rest and careful diet. The worst is over in about 10 days, but rest is still important.

The hepatitis A virus can be spread by contaminated food, beverages, cutlery or crockery, or by intimate contact with an infected person. You can protect yourself against it short-term by getting a gamma-globulin injection before you travel, and by being careful of what you eat and how you have sex. If you're a frequent traveller, it's probably a good idea to have the Havrix vaccination which gives long-term immunity against hepatitis A.

Hepatitis B is spread by direct contact with blood, secretions, or intimate sexual contact with an infected person. Risk is very low if you avoid these situations.

The mysterious hepatitis virus known as Non-A, Non-B is spread in the same way as Hepatitis A, by contaminated food and beverages. Yet another variant, Hepatitis C, is similar to the B virus, but is fairly rare.

Hepatitis may also be spread by use of contaminated, unsterilised needles for tattooing, acupuncture, drug use or medicinal injections. It can be avoided by making sure that needles are sterile.

If you get hepatitis, see a doctor immediately. The treatment is simple: go to bed and stay there for several weeks, eat only easily digestible low-fat foods and drink no alcohol for at least six months. The only medicine which helps cure hepatitis is B vitamins. Many medicines such as antibiotics, which must be detoxified by the already-weakened liver, can cause fatal liver failure.

Typhoid Fever This serious disease, spread by contaminated food and beverages, has symptoms similar to traveller's diarrhoea. If you get it, you should be under close supervision by a competent doctor for a while, and perhaps spend a short time in hospital. Inoculation can give you some protection, but is not 100% effective. If diagnosed and treated early, typhoid can be treated effectively.

Heatstroke Only slightly less common than traveller's diarrhoea are illnesses caused by

excessive heat and dehydration. These are more dangerous because they display fewer symptoms.

If you exercise excessively in hot regions, or if you fail to replace lost fluids and electrolytes (salt, potassium, etc), you can suffer dizziness, weakness, headaches, nausea, and greater susceptibility to other illnesses. This is heat exhaustion, heat prostration or, in severe cases, heatstroke. In this last case, exposure to intense heat can cause convulsions and coma.

Protect yourself by drinking lots of fluids. In hot regions, make it a habit to drink frequently, whether you're thirsty or not. If you urinate infrequently and in small amounts, or if you feel tired and have a headache, you're not drinking enough. Drink pure water, fruit juices and soft drinks. Alcohol, coffee and tea are not good for dehydration: they make you urinate and lose fluids. Salty food is good as the salt helps your body to retain fluids.

Altitude Sickness Acute Mountain Sickness is the result of the lower levels of oxygen and barometric pressure at altitudes of 1500 metres or higher. Many interesting places in Mexico are above these altitudes: Mexico City is over 2000 metres. Your body will adjust to higher altitude in time, but it may take a week or more. When you arrive at an altitude over 1500 metres, refrain from strenuous activity for a few days – no jogging, fast walking or climbing. Drink extra fluids, but avoid alcohol. If you have respiratory or heart disease, talk to your doctor about pollution in Mexico City, and about what to do at altitudes above 2500 metres.

Symptoms of Acute Mountain Sickness are shortness of breath, fatigue, headache, and sometimes nausea. (Some further information on severe altitude sickness, which can be fatal, is given in the Popocatépetl section of the Around Mexico City chapter.)

Dengue Fever Dengue is spread by mosquitoes. See the earlier section on Protection against Mosquitoes. Symptoms include fast onset of high fever, severe frontal headache, and pain in muscles and joints; there may be nausea and vomiting, and a skin rash may develop three to five days after the first symptoms, spreading from the torso to arms, legs and face.

There are four different dengue viruses, but no medicines to combat them. The disease is usually self-limiting. If you are generally healthy and have a healthy immune system, dengue may be unpleasant but it is rarely serious. It is, however, possible to contract dengue haemorrhagic fever (DHF), a very serious and potentially fatal disease.

Malaria Symptoms of this serious disease may include jaundice (a yellow cast to the skin and/or eyes), headaches, fever, chills and abdominal pains. These may appear as early as eight days after infection, or as late as several months. Seek examination immediately if there is any suggestion of malaria.

Malaria is spread by mosquitoes. See the section on Protection against Mosquitoes. You can also take medicines to protect against malaria, though these do not guarantee that you won't get it. Most visitors to Mexico do not take antimalarial medicine, and do not get malaria, but adventurous travellers – especially those who visit some remote rural areas – are more at risk than package tourists in Cancún or Acapulco.

There is a variety of antimalarial medicines – chloroquine (under various brand names) is commonly used for Mexico. Chiapas is the only state where chloroquine-resistant strains of malaria are suspected. Talk to your doctor or an appropriate information service. In the USA, call the Centers for Disease Control on (404) 332-4555. In the UK, the Malaria Reference Laboratory has a 24-hour helpline on (0891) 600 350. In Australia, call the Australian Government Health Service (part of the Commonwealth Department of Human Services & Health), or consult a clinic like the Travellers Medical & Vaccination Centre (☎ (03) 670 3969), at Level 2, 393 Little Bourke St, Melbourne.

You need a prescription to buy antimalarials: be careful to follow the correct dosage and frequency. You will usually be told to start taking the medicine one or two weeks *before* you arrive in a malarial area, continue taking it while you're there, and also for a month after you leave the area.

Rabies Rabies is caused by a bite or scratch by an infected animal. Dogs are noted carriers, as are monkeys and cats. Any bite, scratch or even lick from a warm-blooded, furry animal should be immediately and thoroughly scrubbed with soap and running water, then cleaned with an alcohol solution. If there is any possibility that the animal is infected, medical help should be sought immediately. Rabies is potentially fatal, but can be cured by prompt and proper treatment. Even if the animal is not rabid, all bites should be treated seriously as they can become infected or can result in tetanus. A rabies vaccination is now available and should be considered if you are in a high-risk category – eg, if you intend to explore caves (bat bites could be dangerous) or work with animals.

Schistosomiasis A parasitic worm makes its way into certain tiny freshwater snails and then into humans touching the infected water. Two or three weeks later you may experience fever, weakness, headache, nausea, coughing, loss of appetite or weight, and pain in the gut, joints or muscles. Six to eight weeks after infection, evidence of the worm can be found in the stools, schistosomiasis can be diagnosed, and you can get rid of it quickly with an inexpensive medicine. To guard against it, don't swim in fresh water that may be infected by sewage or other pollution. If you accidentally expose your skin to schistosomiasis-infected water, rub the skin vigorously with a towel and/or alcohol.

Typhus If you go to a mountain town and get head lice, they can give you typhus; otherwise, the risk is extremely low. Typhus is treated by antibiotics.

Sexually Transmitted Diseases Sexual contact with an infected partner spreads these diseases. Abstinence is the only 100% preventative, but condoms are also effective. Gonorrhoea and syphilis are the most common of these diseases; sores, blisters or rashes around the genitals, discharges or pain when urinating are common symptoms. Symptoms may be less marked or not observed at all in women. Syphilis symptoms eventually disappear but the disease continues and can cause severe problems in later years. Gonorrhoea and syphilis are treated with antibiotics.

There is no cure for herpes or, currently, for AIDS. Condoms are usually effective but, as one doctor put it, if your partner is infected with HIV (the AIDS virus) and the condom breaks, you may die.

AIDS can also be spread through infected blood transfusions or dirty needles: vaccinations, acupuncture and tattooing are potentially as dangerous as intravenous drug use if the equipment is not clean. If you need an injection it may be a good idea to buy a new syringe from a pharmacy and ask the doctor to use it.

Over 18,000 AIDS cases had been reported in Mexico by 1994. One in 10 Tijuana prostitutes is HIV-positive. Foreigners applying for permanent residence in Mexico need an HIV-negative certificate.

Cuts & Stings Skin punctures can easily become infected in hot climates. Treat them with antiseptic and Mercurochrome. Scorpion stings are painful and can even be fatal. Scorpions may shelter in shoes or clothing, so in rural areas shake these out before you put them on. An effective folk remedy for jellyfish stings is immediate application of fresh urine. Ammonia is also used, but you may need to seek further help too.

Hospitals & Clinics

Almost every Mexican town and city now has either a hospital or clinic, and Cruz Roja (Red Cross) emergency facilities, all of which are indicated by road signs showing a red cross. Hospitals are generally inexpensive for common ailments (diarrhoea, dysentery) and minor surgery (stitches, sprains). Clinics are often too overburdened with local problems to be of much help, but they are linked by a radio network to emergency services.

If you must use these services, try to ascertain the competence of the staff treating you. If you have questions, call your embassy for recommendation of a doctor, or call your own doctor back home.

Women's Health

Gynaecological problems, poor diet, use of antibiotics for stomach upsets, and even contraceptive pills, can lead to vaginal infections in hot climates. Keeping the genital area clean, and wearing skirts or loose-fitting trousers and cotton underwear will help to prevent them.

Yeast infections, characterised by a rash, itch and discharge, can be treated with a vinegar or lemon-juice douche or plain yoghurt. Nystatin suppositories are the usual medical prescription. Trichomonas is a more serious infection; symptoms are a discharge and a burning sensation when urinating. If a vinegar-water douche is not effective medical attention should be sought. Flagyl is the prescribed drug. Male sexual partners must also be treated. Those prone to cystitis should drink plenty of fluids, and as soon as the first twinges are felt must drink as much water as possible and take a teaspoon of bicarbonate of soda in water every couple of hours. If this doesn't work, an antibiotic should be prescribed.

Pregnancy Most miscarriages occur during the first three months of pregnancy, so this is the most risky time to travel. The last three months should also be spent within reasonable distance of good medical care. Pregnant women should avoid all unnecessary medication, but vaccinations and malarial prophylactics should still be taken where possible. Extra care should be taken to prevent illness and particular attention should be paid to diet and nutrition.

WOMEN TRAVELLERS

In this land of machismo, women must make some concessions to local customs. In general, Mexicans are great believers in the *difference* (rather than the equality) between the sexes. Lone women have to expect some catcalls and attempts to chat them up. Normally these men only want to talk to you, but it can get tiresome; the best way to discourage unwanted attention is to avoid eye contact and, if possible, ignore it altogether. Otherwise use a cool but polite initial response and a consistent, firm 'No'. It is possible to turn uninvited attention into a worthwhile conversation by making clear that you *are* willing to talk, but no more.

Travelling alone presents unlimited opportunities for meeting people, but don't put yourself in peril by doing things Mexican women would not do, such as challenging a man's masculinity, drinking in a cantina, hitchhiking without a male companion, or going alone to isolated places.

Wearing a bra will spare you a lot of unwanted attention. A wedding ring may help too. Except in beach resorts, it's advisable to wear shorts only at a swimming pool. You might even consider swimming in shorts and a T-shirt, as many Mexican women do.

DANGERS & ANNOYANCES

Mexico has some reputation as a violent country, thanks mainly to Pancho Villa, foreign movies and machismo. However, there's really little to fear for your physical safety unless you get deeply involved in a quarrel. More at risk are your possessions, particularly those you carry around with you.

Theft & Robbery

Theft, particularly pocket-picking and purse-snatching, is common in all large Mexican cities, and epidemic in Mexico City. Tourists are particularly singled out for theft as they are presumed to be wealthy (by Mexican standards) and to be carrying valuables. Buses, the metro in Mexico City, markets, pedestrian underpasses, thronged streets and plazas, and remote beach spots are all prime locations for theft.

Robberies and muggings are much less common than pocket-picking and purse-snatching, but they are on the increase. One of this book's authors was robbed at gun and knife-point in Mexico City on a quiet Sunday afternoon – he was not harmed, and lost little, as his valuables were in the hotel safe. Robbery is easier to avoid than theft, but more serious when it happens as the robbers may force you to remove your moneybelt or neckstrap pouch, watch, rings etc. Usually robbers will not harm you. What they want is your money, fast.

To avoid being robbed in cities, do not go where there are few other people. This includes empty streets at night, empty metro carriages at night, little-used pedestrian underpasses, and similar lonely places.

On beaches and in the countryside, do not camp overnight in lonely places unless you can be sure it's safe.

You must protect yourself, or you can expect to lose a considerable amount. In Mexican cities, follow the precautions listed below *without fail*.

- Unless you have immediate need of them, leave most of your cash, travellers' cheques, passport, jewellery, air tickets, credit cards, watch etc (and perhaps your camera) in a sealed, signed envelope in your hotel's safe. Virtually all hotels except the very cheapest provide safe-keeping for guests' valuables. You may have to provide the envelope (buy some at a *papelería*, or stationery shop). Your signature on the envelope and a receipt for it help to ensure that hotel staff won't pilfer your things.
- Leaving valuable items in a locked suitcase in your hotel room is often safer than carrying them on the streets of a Mexican city.
- Have a moneybelt or a pouch on a string around your neck, place your remaining valuables in it, and preferably wear it *underneath your clothing*. You can carry a small amount of ready money in a pocket or bag.
- Be aware that any purse or bag in plain sight may be slashed or grabbed. At ticket counters in airports and bus stations, keep your bag between your feet, particularly when you're busy with a ticket agent.
- On trains and lower-grade long-distance buses, keep your baggage with you if you can. If you let it disappear into the baggage hold of a 2nd or 3rd-class bus, the chances of not seeing it again increase.
- Do not leave any valuables visible in your vehicle when you park it in a city.

Pickpockets Crowded buses, bus stops and the Mexico City metro are among pickpockets' favourite haunts. They often work in teams: one or two of them may grab your bag or camera (or your arm and leg), and while you're trying to get it free another will pick your pocket. Or one may 'drop' a coin or other object in a crowded bus and as he 'looks for it', a pocket will be picked or a bag slashed in the jostling. Pickpockets often carry razor blades with which they slit pockets, bags or straps. The operative principle is to outnumber you, confuse you, and to get you off balance. If your valuables are *underneath* your clothing, the chances of losing them are greatly reduced.

Highway Robbery Occasionally bandits stop buses and take luggage or valuables from passengers. Robberies are also a risk on trains east of the Isthmus of Tehuantepec. The only sure way to avoid highway robbery is not to travel at night except by deluxe buses on toll highways, especially in Oaxaca, Chiapas, Tabasco and Campeche states. If the situation in Chiapas remains tense, seek local advice before venturing off major roads at all.

Reporting a Theft or Robbery There's little point in going to the police unless your loss is insured, in which case you'll need a police statement to present to your insurance company. You'll probably have to communicate with the police in Spanish, so if your Spanish is poor take a more fluent speaker. Also take your passport and tourist card, if you still have them. Say you want to *'poner una acta de un robo'* (make a record of a robbery). This should make it clear that you merely want a piece of paper and aren't going to ask the police to do anything inconvenient like look for the thieves or recover your goods. You should get the required piece of paper without too much trouble.

SECTUR in Mexico City maintains a telephone hotline, open 24 hours daily, to help tourists with problems and emergencies. The numbers are ☎ (5) 250-01-23 and ☎ (5) 250-01-51. If you are outside Mexico City, you can call them collect or use the free number ☎ 800-9-03-92, preceded by the 91 long-distance access code.

Legal Assistance

If you should encounter legal troubles with public officials or local businesspeople anywhere in Mexico, you can contact the Procuraduría de Protección al Turista (Attorney-General for the Protection of the Tourist). There's an office in every state capital and in some other cities as well, with English-speaking staff members. Use the SECTUR hotline (above) to make contact. For consumer problems, you can file a complaint with one of the 54 offices of the Procuradoría Federal del Consumador (Attorney-General for Consumers). Written evidence of the purchase or service is required.

WORK

Work is not particularly easy to find in Mexico as Mexicans themselves need jobs. English-speakers may find teaching work in language schools, high schools *(preparatorias)* or universities, or can offer personal tutoring. Mexico City is the best place to pick up English-teaching work; Guadalajara is also good. It should also be possible in Monterrey, Puebla and other sizeable cities. The pay is low, but you can live on it.

Positions in high schools or universities are more likely to become available with the beginning of the new term. *The News* and the telephone yellow pages in large towns are good sources of job opportunities. Contact the institutions that offer bilingual programmes or classes in English. For universities, arrange an appointment with the director of the language department.

Language schools tend to offer short courses, so that opportunities come up more often, and any commitment is for a shorter time, but they pay less than high schools and universities.

By law, a foreigner working in Mexico must have a permit, but a school will often pay a foreign teacher in the form of a scholarship or *beca*, and thus circumvent the law, or the school's administration will procure the appropriate papers.

It's helpful to know at least a little Spanish, even though some institutes insist that only English be spoken in class.

The Council on International Educational Exchange, 205 East 42nd St, New York, NY 10017 (☎ (212) 661-1414), has information on volunteer programmes in various countries including Mexico.

ACTIVITIES

Outdoor Sports

Interest in the wilderness experience is only beginning to develop in Mexico. For many middle-class Mexicans, the countryside is either a place where *campesinos* work or, if it's picturesque, somewhere to go in your car, have a family picnic, and look at the view. There are a few popular day trails; the one up Popocatépetl volcano outside Mexico City can get pretty busy. Fishing and hunting are bigger news. There is also a small mountaineering fraternity (see the section below).

This general lack of interest doesn't stop growing numbers of intrepid gringos trekking off into what Mexicans may consider absurdly rough country. Trails around the Copper Canyon (see the North-West Mexico chapter) and Baja California are among the most popular. Long-distance cycling is similarly rare among Mexicans, but that doesn't stop gringos enjoying cycling trips in Mexico. (See Books, earlier in this chapter, for some useful books on these activities.) In a few places there are bicycles for rent or horses for hire to visit specific sites.

Sport fishing is especially popular off the Pacific coast and in the Gulf of California. Check the *Angler's Guide to Baja California* by Tom Miller (Baja Trail Publications).

Water sports are popular in the coastal resorts, snorkelling and diving particularly so on the Yucatán Peninsula, in Baja California and in some Pacific coast resorts. Most Mexican coastal resorts and surrounding towns have shops that will rent equipment such as snorkels, masks and fins, and arrange boat excursions. Inland, there are many *balnearios*, bathing places with swimming pools, often centred on hot springs in picturesque surroundings.

Surfing is popular on the Pacific coast. Some of the best surf spots are Punta Mesquite and Santa Rosalillita in Baja California, Bahía de Matanchén near San Blas (which claims the world's longest wave), Ixtapa and Puerto Escondido (with the 'Mexican Pipeline').

Sport fishing is popular off the Pacific coast

Mountain Guides & Climbs A number of Mexico City-based organisations conduct hiking and climbing trips on Mexico's volcanoes, including Popocatépetl, Iztaccíhuatl, Pico de Orizaba, Nevado de Toluca and La Malinche. You should make a booking at least a week ahead, and you will probably need at least two people. Transport is usually included in the cost, but food and equipment may cost extra.

Coordinadores de Guías de Montaña (☎ (5) 584-46-95), at Tlaxcala 47 in Colonia Roma, Mexico City, is a professional organisation which provides qualified guides for most Mexican mountain peaks. A 28-hour trip from Mexico City to the top of Popo and back is around 900 pesos per person including accommodation and two meals.

Club Alpino Mexicano (☎ (5) 564-71-64), at Baja California 75, Mexico City, organises climbing trips for nonmembers. They quote, for instance, 600 pesos per person for a climb on Popo, but you may have to arrange your own food and acommodation.

Socorro Alpino de Mexico, the volunteer mountain rescue association, with an office at Orozco Iberra 26 No 5, Colonia Guerrero,

Mexico City, conducts some private climbing and trekking trips. The prices are reasonable and some of the proceeds go to support their rescue work.

Study Programmes

There are Spanish-language schools in many cities – some private, some attached to universities. Course lengths range from a week to a year. Often you can enrol in a course on the spot, though some places prefer you to make the arrangements before you come to Mexico.

You may be offered accommodation with a local family as part of the deal – and living with Spanish speakers will help your Spanish-language skills as much as any formal tuition. Mexico City, Guadalajara, Guanajuato, Cuernavaca, San Miguel de Allende, Morelia, Taxco, Oaxaca and Puerto Vallarta are all among the cities with college courses or private language schools – see those city sections for more information. In some places courses in art, crafts or in-depth study of Mexico and Latin America are also available. The Universidad de las Américas at Cholula near Puebla is another college with Mexican or Latin American studies courses.

Many Mexican towns have Casas de la Cultura, which are adult education centres offering part-time, usually cheap courses in a wide variety of arts and crafts. Foreigners are often welcome to join these.

Information about Spanish-language programmes in Mexico is available from the National Registration Center for Study Abroad, 823 North Second St, Milwaukee, WI 53203 (☎ (414) 278-0631). The Council on International Educational Exchange (see Work) also has information on study in Mexico.

ACCOMMODATION

Accommodation in Mexico ranges from campsites, guesthouses (casas de huéspedes) and hostels, through budget hotels and motels, to world-class luxury high-rise hotels and lavish holiday resorts.

Reservations

It's often advisable to reserve your room in advance at particularly popular hotels, or if you plan to visit busy areas during the Christmas-New Year holidays, Semana Santa, or the summer holiday period during July and August. You should request a reservation by telephone or fax, asking whether a deposit is required and how to send it, and requesting confirmation. Within Mexico, giro is a useful method of sending a deposit – see the Telecommunications section in this chapter.

Camping

All beaches in Mexico are public property. You can camp for nothing on most of them, but you must be very conscious of safety.

Most equipped campgrounds are actually trailer parks, set up for trailers, RVs (camper vans) and caravans, but accept tent campers at lower rates. Some are very basic, others are quite luxurious. You may pay five to 20 pesos a person to pitch your tent, or up to 70 pesos for two people to use the full facilities of a good campground.

You'll find tent camping a more practicable proposition on the Yucatán Peninsula, in Baja California and along the Pacific Coast than in most other areas, where campgrounds are rarer. If you plan to camp much, we highly recommend *The People's Guide to RV Camping in Mexico* by Carl Franz (see the Books section in this chapter).

Cabañas & Hammocks

These are two of the cheapest forms of accommodation, usually found in low-key beach spots. Cabañas are palm-thatched huts – some have dirt floors and nothing inside but a bed; others may have electric light, mosquito nets, fans and even fridges. Prices per person range from around 10 to 60 pesos.

You can rent a hammock and a place to hang it for a few pesos in some beach places – usually under a palm roof outside a small casa de huéspedes or a fishing family's shack. If you bring your own hammock the cost may be even less. It's easy enough to buy hammocks in Mexico; Mérida in

Yucatán and Mitla in Oaxaca are two places specialising in them.

Hostels

Villas juveniles or *albergues de juventud* (youth hostels) exist in about 20 university and resort towns. Many of them are attached to sports centres. Sometimes they are of use to travellers; other times cheap hotels are preferable. Hostels have basic but usually clean single-sex dormitories and a variety of other facilities. No membership is needed and a bed usually costs 10 to 15 pesos. You may get a small discount with an IYHA card. Lists of hostels can be obtained from the Coordinación Nacional de Turismo Juvenil (☎ (5) 533-12-91) at Local C-11, Glorieta Metro Insurgentes (outside Insurgentes metro station), Mexico City.

In one or two places such as Oaxaca and San Miguel de Allende there are privately run hostels aimed at international backpackers, but these are as yet a rarity.

Casas de Huéspedes

The cheapest and most congenial lodging is often a casa de huéspedes, a home converted into simple guest lodgings. Good casas de huéspedes have a relaxed, friendly atmosphere. Rooms may or may not have a private bathroom. A double can cost anywhere from 20 to 75 pesos.

Cheap Hotels

These exist in virtually every Mexican city and town. There are many clean, friendly ones; there are also dark, dirty ones. You can get a decent double room with private shower and hot water in the centre of Mexico City for 50 to 60 pesos. In Cancún you may have to pay 130 pesos for a comparable room. In many smaller, less touristed towns you can get one for 40 pesos. Many hotels have rooms for three, four or five people which cost little more than a double. Bargaining may bring prices down a bit in places that don't get a big flow of foreign tourists.

Note that *cuarto sencillo*, which translates literally as 'single room', usually means a room with one bed, which is often a *cama*

matrimonial (double bed). One person can usually occupy such a room for a lower price than two people. A *cuarto doble* is usually a room with two beds, often both doubles.

Middle & Top-End Hotels

Mexico specialises in good middle-range hotels where two people can usually get a room with private bathroom, TV, perhaps air-con and a lift, and maybe a restaurant and bar, for between 75 and 150 pesos. These places are generally pleasant, comfortable without being luxurious, respectable and safe.

Among the most charming middle-range hotels are many old mansions and inns turned into hotels. Some date from colonial times, others from the 19th century. Most are wonderfully atmospheric. Some are 'authentic' and a bit spartan (but lower in price), others have been 'updated' with modern facilities, and can be quite posh. These are often the lodgings you will remember most fondly after your trip.

Mexico has a full selection of large, modern hotels, particularly in the largest cities and resorts. These offer expected levels of luxury at expectedly lofty prices. If you like to stay in luxury but also enjoy saving some money, choose a Mexican hotel, not one that's part of an international chain. If you're on a short holiday from the USA and want as much as possible for your money, sign up for one of the many package deals offered in Sunday newspaper travel sections. Most travel agents should also be able to help you. The packages often include 25% to 45% discounts on room rates, a rented car and airport transfers.

FOOD

Mexican food is enormously varied, full of regional differences and subtle surprises. You'll eat well in Mexico and the range of restaurants is wide in all sizeable cities. In addition to the Mexican fare that we describe here, there's all sorts of international food available too, even some very good vegetarian restaurants. If you need the reassurance of familiar flavours and familiar ambience, there are many North American-style eateries including reliable chain restaurants like VIPS, Denny's and Sanborns.

Staples

Mexicans eat three meals a day: breakfast *(desayuno)*, lunch *(comida)*, and supper *(cena)*. Each includes one or more of three national staples: *tortillas, frijoles* and *chiles*.

Tortillas are thin round patties of pressed corn *(maíz)* or wheat flour *(harina)* dough cooked on griddles. Both can be wrapped around or served under any type of food. Frijoles are beans, eaten boiled, fried or refried, in soups, on tortillas, or with just about anything.

Chiles are spicy-hot peppers which come in dozens of varieties and are consumed in hundreds of ways. Some types such as the *habanero* and *serrano* are always very hot, while others such as the *poblano* vary in spiciness according to when they were picked. If you are unsure about your tolerance for hot chiles, ask if the chile is *dulce* (sweet), *picante* (spicy-hot), or *muy picante* (very spicy-hot).

Breakfast

The simplest breakfast is coffee or tea and *pan dulce* (sweet rolls), a basket of which is set on the table; you pay for the number consumed. Many restaurants offer combination breakfasts for about eight to 18 pesos, typically composed of fruit juice *(jugo de fruta)*, coffee *(café)*, bread roll *(bolillo)* or toast *(pan tostado)* with butter *(mantequilla)* and jam *(mermelada)*, and eggs *(huevos)*, which are served in a variety of ways:

huevos pasados por agua – lightly boiled eggs (too lightly for many visitors' taste)
huevos cocidos – harder-boiled eggs (specify the number of minutes if you're in doubt)
huevos estrellados – fried eggs
huevos fritos (con jamón/tocino) – fried eggs (with ham/bacon)
huevos mexicanos – eggs scrambled with tomatoes, chiles, onions and garlic (representing the red, green and white of the Mexican flag)

huevos motuleños – tortilla topped with slices of ham, then fried eggs, topped with cheese, peas and tomato sauce
huevos rancheros – fried eggs on tortillas, covered in *salsa*
huevos poches – poached eggs

Mexicans may eat hunks of meat for breakfast but this isn't to many visitors' taste.

Lunch

La comida, the biggest meal of the day, is usually served between 1 and 3 or 4 pm. Most restaurants offer special fixed-price menus called *comida corrida, cubierto, menú del día, platillo del día*, or even *lonch comercial*. These constitute the best food bargains, because you get several courses (often with some choice) for much less than such a meal would cost à la carte. Prices range from a mere 7 or 8 pesos for a very simple three-course meal of soup, a meat dish, rice and coffee, to 40 pesos or more for elaborate repasts beginning with oyster stew and finishing with profiteroles – but typically you'll get four or five courses for 10 to 20 pesos. Drinks are usually extra.

Dinner/Supper

La cena, the evening meal, is usually lighter than the comida. Fixed-price multi-course value-for-money meals are rarely offered, so plan to eat your main meal at lunchtime.

Snacks

Antojitos, or 'little whims', are Mexican traditional snacks or light dishes – some are actually small meals in themselves. Here are some of the standard ones:

burrito – any combination of beans, cheese, meat, chicken or seafood seasoned with salsa or chile and wrapped in a wheat-flour tortilla
chilaquiles – fried tortilla chips with scrambled eggs or sauce, often with grated cheese on top
chiles rellenos – chiles stuffed with cheese, meat or other foods, deep fried and baked in sauce

empanada – small pastry with savoury or sweet filling

enchilada – ingredients similar to those used in tacos and burritos rolled up in a tortilla, dipped in sauce and then baked or semi-fried. Enchiladas Suizas (Swiss enchiladas) come smothered in a blanket of thick cream

enfrijolada – soft tortilla in a frijole sauce with cheese and onion on top

entomatada – soft tortilla in a tomato sauce with cheese and onion on top

gordita – fried maize dough filled with refried beans, topped with cream, cheese and lettuce

guacamole – mashed avocados mixed with onion, chile, lemon, tomato and other ingredients

machaca – cured, dried and shredded beef or pork mixed with eggs, onions, cilantro (coriander leaves) and chiles

quesadilla – flour tortilla topped or filled with cheese and occasionally other ingredients and then heated

queso fundido – melted cheese served with tortillas

sincronizada – a lightly grilled or fried tortilla 'sandwich', usually with a ham and cheese filling

taco – soft corn tortilla wrapped or folded around the same fillings as a burrito

tamale – corn dough stuffed with meat, beans, chiles or nothing at all, wrapped in corn husks or banana leaves and then steamed

torta – Mexican-style sandwich in a roll

tostada – crisp-fried tortilla topped with meat or cheese, tomatoes, beans and lettuce

Soup

There are many soups (*sopas*) made from meats, vegetables and seafoods, including:

caldo – broth

gazpacho – chilled vegetable soup spiced with hot chiles

menudo – tripe soup made with the spiced entrails of various four-legged beasts

pozole – rich, spicy stew of hominy (large maize kernels) with meat and vegetables.

Note that *sopa de arroz* is not soup at all but rice pilaf.

Seafood

Seafood is good along the coasts, and in the major cities where customers abound. Be suspicious of seafood in out-of-the-way mountain towns, and take care with uncooked seafood.

Fish is often eaten as a *filete* (fillet), *frito* (fried whole fish), or *al mojo de ajo* (fried in butter and garlic). *Ceviche*, the popular Mexican cocktail, is raw seafood (fish, shrimp, etc) marinated in lime and mixed with onions, chiles, garlic and tomatoes. There are other seafood *cocteles* (cocktails) as well. *Tortuga* (turtle) is sometimes served in restaurants. In the interests of wildlife conservation, give it a miss.

Fish

atún – tuna

corvina – bass

filete de pescado – fish fillet

huachinango – red snapper

mojarra – perch

pescado – fish after it has been caught

pez espada – swordfish

pez – fish which is alive in the water

robalo – sea bass

salmón (ahumada) – (smoked) salmon

tiburón – shark

trucha – trout

Other Seafood

abulón – abalone

almejas – clams

calamar – squid

camarones – shrimp
camarones gigantes – prawns
cangrejo – large crab
caracol – snail
jaiba – small crab
langosta – lobster
mariscos – shellfish
ostiones – oysters

Meat & Poultry

Meat and poultry are often listed separately as *Carnes* and *Aves* on Mexican menus.

Meat

bistec, bistec de res – beefsteak
borrego – sheep
cabra – goat
cabrito – kid (small goat)
carne – meat, usually beef if not otherwise specified
carne asada – tough but tasty grilled beef
carnero – mutton
carnitas – deep-fried pork
cerdo – pork
chicharrón – deep-fried pork rind; pigskin cracklings
chorizo – spicy pork sausage
conejo – rabbit
cordero – lamb
hígado – liver
jamón – ham
puerco – pork
res – beef
salchicha – spicy pork sausage
ternera – veal
tocino – bacon
venado – deer (venison)

Poultry

faisán – pheasant; turkey
ganso – goose

guajolote – turkey
pato – duck
pavo – turkey
pechuga – chicken breast
pollo – chicken

Cuts & Preparation

In Mexico, you will come across meat, poultry and seafood prepared and served in many ways, including the following.

adobado – marinated, seasoned and dried
ahumado – smoked
a la parrilla – grilled, perhaps over charcoal
a la plancha – 'planked', split and roasted
a la tampiqueña – sautéed thin slice of meat, officially also marinated in garlic, oil and oregano
a la veracruzana – topped with tomato, olive and onion sauce
al carbón – charcoal-grilled
al horno – baked
al mojo de ajo – in garlic sauce
alambre – shish kebab, 'en brochette'
barbacoa – literally 'barbecued', but meat is covered and placed under hot coals
bien cocido – well done
birria – a mutton or goat stew
cabeza – head
chuleta – chop (eg lamb chop)
cocido – boiled
coctel – appetiser (seafood, fruit, etc) in sauce
costillas – ribs
empanizado – breaded
filete – fillet of fish or meat
frito – fried
hamburguesa – hamburger
lengua – tongue
lomo – loin
milanesa – breaded (Italian-style)
mole – sauce made from chiles and other ingredients, often served over chicken or turkey
mole poblano – Puebla-style mole, especially delicious, with many ingredients including hot chiles and bitter chocolate
patas – trotters (feet)
pechuga – chicken breast
pibil – roasted (Yucatán)

pierna – leg
poco cocido – rare

Vegetables & Fruit

Legumbres and *verduras* (vegetables) are rarely served as separate dishes, but are often mixed into salads, soups and sauces, or used as garnishes. Vegetarians needn't worry: there are usually plenty of options for them, and many Mexican towns have good vegetarian restaurants.

Vegetables

aguacate – avocado
betabel – beetroot
calabaza – squash or pumpkin
cebolla – onion
champiñones – mushrooms
chícharos – peas
col – cabbage
coliflor – cauliflower
ejotes – green beans
elote – corn on the cob; commonly served from steaming bins on street carts
ensalada verde – green salad
espárragos – asparagus
espinaca – spinach
frijoles – beans, usually black
hongos – mushrooms
lechuga – lettuce
lentejas – lentils
nopales – green prickly-pear cactus ears
papas – potatoes
papas fritas – fried potatoes, chips
pepino – cucumber
rábano – radish
tomate – tomato
zanahoria – carrot

Fruit

chabacano – apricot
coco – coconut
durazno – peach
ensalada de frutas – plain mixed seasonal fruits
fresas – strawberries, but also used to refer to any berries
fruta – fruit
granada – pomegranate
guanabana – green pear-like fruit
guayaba – guava
higo – fig
limón – lime or lemon
mamey – sweet orange tropical fruit
mango – mango
manzana – apple
melón – melon
naranja – orange
papaya – papaya
pera – pear
piña – pineapple
plátano – banana
toronja – grapefruit
tuna – nopal (prickly-pear) cactus fruit
uva – grape
zapote – sweet fruit of chicle tree

Desserts

Most desserts *(postres)* are small afterthoughts to a meal.

arroz con leche – rice pudding
crepa – crepe, thin pancake
flan – custard; crème caramel
galletas – cookies/biscuits
gelatina – jelly, jello
helado – ice cream
nieve – powdered, flavoured ice
pastel – pastry or cake
pay – fruit pie

Other Foods

Some other food words you may find useful are:

aceite – oil
aceitunas – olives
arroz – rice
azúcar – sugar
catsup – ketchup; US-style spiced tomato sauce
cilantro – fresh coriander leaf
crema – cream
entremeses – hors d'oeuvres
leche – milk
mantequilla – butter
margarina – margarine
paleta – flavoured ice on a stick
pan (integral) – (whole-grain) bread
pimienta – pepper

queso – cheese
salsa – red or green sauce made with chiles, onions, tomato, lemon or lime juice and spices
sel – salt

At the Table

Note that *el menú* can mean either the menu, or the special set-price meal of the day. If you want the menu, ask for *la lista* or *la carta* or you may inadvertently order the set-price meal.

copa – wineglass
cuchara – spoon
cuchillo – knife
cuenta – bill
plato – plate
propina – the tip; 10% to 15% of the bill
servilleta – napkin
taza – cup
tenedor – fork
vaso – glass

DRINKS

A big variety of drinks *(bebidas)*, both alcoholic and non-alcoholic, is available – as befits a country with such a warm climate.

Tea & Coffee

Mexican *café*, grown mostly near Córdoba and Orizaba and in Chiapas, can be somewhat coarse like the African varieties, but is always flavourful. Mexican tea, invariably from bags, is usually a profound disappointment to any real tea drinker.

café americano – black coffee
café con leche – coffee with hot milk, half and half
café con crema – coffee with cream, served separately
café instantaneo – instant coffee
café negro – black coffee
espresso – espresso, brewed by steam pressure
Nescafé – instant coffee
té de manzanilla – camomile tea
té negro – black tea

Fruit & Vegetable Drinks

Pure fresh juices *(jugos)* are popular in Mexico, and readily available from streetside stalls, where the fruit is normally squeezed before your eyes. Every fruit and a few of the squeezable vegetables are used. Ever tried pure beetroot juice?

Licuados are blends of fruit or juice with water and sugar. *Licuados con leche* use milk instead of water. Possible additions include raw egg, ice, and flavourings such as vanilla or nutmeg. The delicious combinations are practically limitless. You may want to check that *agua purificada* is being used.

Aguas frescas or *aguas de fruta* are made by mixing fruit juice or a syrup made from mashed grains or seeds with sugar and water. You will usually see them in big glass jars on the counters of juice stands. *Agua fresca de arroz* (literally 'rice water') has a sweet nutty taste.

Refrescos

Refrescos are bottled soft drinks, and there are some interesting and tasty local varieties. Sidral and Manzanita are two reasonable apple-flavoured carbonated drinks. There's also a non-alcoholic variety of sangría (see Wine & Brandy following). *Toronja* (grapefruit) flavoured drinks are tart and refreshing. Flavours such as *fresa* (strawberry), *limón* (lime) and *cereza* (cherry) tend to be too sweet for most travellers' taste.

There are many good brands of mineral water *(agua mineral)* from Mexican springs – Tehuacán and Garci Crespo are two of the best and can sometimes be obtained with refreshing flavours as well as plain.

Alcohol

Mexico produces a fascinating variety of intoxicating drinks from grapes, grains and cacti. Many foreign liquors are widely available too.

Drinking Places Everyone knows about Mexican cantinas, those pits of wild drinking and even wilder displays of machismo. One of this book's authors has been in a cantina in Mexico City where it was hardly noticed when a man drew his pistol and fired several rounds into the ceiling. Cantinas are generally loud, but not that loud.

Cantinas are not usually marked as such, but can be identified by signs prohibiting minors from entering, wild-west type swinging half-doors, and the generally raucous atmosphere.

Cantinas are usually for men only – no women or children are allowed. Those who enter must be prepared to drink hard. They might be challenged by a local to go one-for-one at a bottle of tequila, mezcal or brandy. If you're not up to this, excuse yourself and beat a retreat.

Some of the nicer cantinas don't get upset about the presence of a woman if accompanied by a regular patron. Leave judgement of the situation up to a local, though, and tread lightly or there could be trouble.

Besides cantinas, Mexico has lots of bars, lounges, 'pubs' and cafés to which all are welcome and where the excesses of machismo are toned down. However, there are no signs that differentiate a cantina from a bar or lounge.

Mezcal, Tequila & Pulque Mezcal can be made from the sap of several species of the *maguey* plant, a spray of long, thick spikes sticking out of the ground. Tequila is made only from the maguey *agave tequilana* that grows in and around the town of Tequila. The spikes of the maguey are stripped away to expose the plant's core or *piña*. The piña is chopped, roasted, shredded and then pressed to remove the juice. Sugar is added to the juice and, after the resulting mixture has fermented for four days, it is put through two distillation processes. After distillation the mezcal and tequila are aged in wooden casks for periods ranging from four months to seven years. The final product is a clear liquid (sometimes artificially tinted to gold) which is at its most potent as tequila. The longer the ageing, the smoother the drink and the higher the price. A repugnant worm (*gusano*) is added to each bottle of mezcal.

The traditional steps in drinking mezcal or tequila are:

1) lick the back of your hand and sprinkle salt on it
2) lick the salt
3) suck on a lime
4) down a shot of mezcal or tequila in one gulp
5) lick more salt

When the bottle is empty, you are supposed to eat the worm.

For foreigners not used to the potency of straight tequila, Mexican bartenders invented the margarita, a concoction of tequila, lime juice and liqueur served in a salt-rimmed glass. *Pulque* is a mildly alcoholic drink derived directly from the sap of the maguey. The foamy, milky drink spoils quickly and thus cannot easily be bottled and shipped. Most pulque is produced in the region around Mexico City and served in *pulquerías*. There are several excellent pulquerías in Mexico City around the Plaza Garibaldi.

Beer Breweries were established in Mexico by German immigrants in the late 19th century. Mexico's several large brewing companies now produce more than 25 brands of beer (*cerveza*), many of which are excellent. Each major company has a premium beer such as Bohemia and Corona de Barril (usually served in bottles), several standard beers such as Carta Blanca, Superior and Dos Equis, and 'popular' brands such as Corona, Tecate and Modelo. All are blond lagers meant to be served chilled. Some places serve beer barely cooled, so it's a good idea to ask for *una cerveza fría* (a cold beer).

Each of the large companies also produces a dark beer such as Modelo Negro and Tres Equis, but these are sometimes difficult to find in the smaller towns.

There are some regional beers as well, brewed to similar tastes.

Wine & Brandy Wine is not as popular in Mexico as beer and tequila, but the country's three large wine growers produce some quite drinkable vintages.

Pedro Domecq is best known for its Los Reyes table wines and various brandies. Formex-Ybarra has more than 324 hectares of vineyards in the Valle de Guadalupe and is known for its Terrasola table wine. Bodegas de Santo Tomás hopes eventually to produce wines which can compete with California's. It is run by the Tchelistcheffs, a California-based wine-growing family. They have planted several varieties of grapes from California and have begun producing Pinot Noir, Chardonnay and Cabernet wines which are worth a try.

Wine mixed with fruit juice makes the tasty *sangría*.

ENTERTAINMENT

Nothing beats a Mexican fiesta for entertainment, but if none is being celebrated, you have alternatives. People-watching from a café on a plaza is high on the list. In the larger cities, the range of entertainments is extensive, with opera, classical concerts, theatre (in Spanish), music clubs (jazz, salsa, mariachi, rock, etc), spectator sports, coffee houses, discos, bars and lounges abounding. Cinemas screen both local and foreign films, with the foreign ones normally dubbed into Spanish.

Performances of folk dance range from the simple, local and authentic, at a village fiesta, to the dazzlingly elaborate, such as Mexico City's Ballet Folklórico (see Arts & Culture in Facts about the Country).

Sporting events such as soccer matches, lucha libre sessions, bullfights and charreadas can be fascinating: even if the sport on view doesn't especially grab you, the crowd probably will. (See the Sport section in Facts About the Country for more information.)

In smaller towns, the best you can expect is a primitive cinema and a bar, perhaps with entertainment, in the best local hotel.

THINGS TO BUY

See the Artesanías colour section for information on Mexican *artesanías* (handicrafts) and where to buy them.

Artesanías

exico is so richly endowed with appealing *artesanías* (handicrafts) that even the most hardened non-souvenir-hunter finds it hard to get home without at least one pair of earrings or a little model animal. There's such a huge and colourful range of arts and crafts, many of them sold at reasonable prices, that virtually every visitor is irresistibly attracted to something, somewhere along the way.

The tourist and collectors' market in folk art has been a growing money-earner for Mexican artisans since before WW II. In the face of so many souvenir-type handicrafts, it's easy to forget that bringing in foreign tourist dollars is only one of the roles played by handicrafts in Mexican life. For one thing, Mexicans themselves are eager buyers and collectors as well as creators of such handicrafts. More fundamentally, Mexicans have been producing artesanías, both for everyday use and for more special purposes, for millennia. The origins of many modern Mexican crafts are easily traceable to pre-Hispanic origins, and some techniques, designs and materials have remained unchanged since long before the coming of Europeans. The colourful, highly decorative artesanías that catch the eye in shops and markets today are in a way the counterpart of the splendid costumes, beautiful ceramics and elaborate jewellery used by Aztec, Mayan and other pre-Hispanic nobility. On a more mundane level, Mexican artisans continue to turn out countless handmade objects of everyday use – pots, hats, baskets, toys, clothes, sandals, to name but a few – just as they did centuries before the Spanish came. Despite its rapid modernisation, Mexico is still a country where handmade artefacts are in constant, widespread production and use.

The Spanish brought their own methods, styles and products,

Ceramic sculpture with a pre-Hispanic motif, showing the three stages of life – young man, old man, dead man (JL)

and while these mingled to some extent with older traditions, indigenous crafts were generally regarded as inferior during the colonial period. But with the new search for a national identity after the Mexican Revolution in the early 20th century, a new interest – inspired partly by artists like Frida Kahlo and Diego Rivera – arose in older, specifically Mexican, craft traditions. A lot of craftwork today shows a clear fusion of pre-Hispanic and Spanish inspirations, sometimes with eclectic modern influences too. Many of Mexico's Indian peoples, whose ancestors were the originators of so many crafts, still maintain age-old skills and traditions. It's no surprise that the areas producing the most exciting artesanías today are often those with prominent Indian populations, in states like Chiapas, Guerrero, México, Michoacán, Nayarit, Oaxaca, Puebla and Sonora. ■

European motifs are given a distinctively Mexican treatment in this mask from Guerrero state (NK)

BUYING HANDICRAFTS

The villages where many crafts are produced are often not the best places to buy them. Items intended for sale to tourists or collectors make their way to shops and markets in the bigger urban centres, and here you'll find a big range of wares, usually of the best quality, from many smaller places. This saves the time and effort of seeking out the sometimes remote spots where particular items are made. Some bigger towns and cities also have workshops where you can see artisans at work (though this should not put you off making your way to a village whose products or techniques you're particularly interested in).

Nor are prices necessarily higher in the bigger centres – on occasions they may even be higher in the villages, where an artisan may see the chance of bargaining more advantageously with a single tourist than with a local wholesaler. In Oaxaca city,

Detail of Huichol Indian yarn painting (JL)

for instance, which is the major clearing-house for handicrafts from all over the state of Oaxaca, the number of stores and markets selling crafts helps keep prices competitive. On the other hand, goods from Oaxaca become more expensive when they're transported to Mexico City or elsewhere.

City shops devoted to artesanías will give you a good overview of what's available. Some towns and cities – notably those with large numbers of long-stay foreigners or craft-aware tourists, such as Mexico City, Guadalajara, San Miguel de Allende, Puerto Vallarta and Oaxaca – have shops offering handicrafts from all over the country. In shops in other cities you'll find wares from all around the local region. Even if you don't buy in these shops, they'll show you good-quality crafts, and give you a basis for price comparisons.

Museums can also be good for information and examples of handicrafts: many towns have artesanías museums showing local craft products and techniques, sometimes also with items for sale. The upper floor of the Museo Nacional de Antropología in Mexico City, for one, is devoted to the modern lifestyles of many of Mexico's Indian peoples, including displays on their handicrafts. It's interesting to compare these with the products of their pre-Hispanic ancestors in the ground-floor archaeological sections of the museum.

Markets, of course, are another major source of handicrafts. A few cities have special markets devoted exclusively to crafts, while ordinary daily or weekly markets everywhere always have some handicrafts on sale – often regional specialities which attract buyers from further afield, as well as the everyday pots, baskets etc used by local people. The quality of market goods may not be as high as in shops, but you'll normally pay less – bargaining is expected in markets, while shops generally have fixed prices.

Specific shops, markets, villages and museums with interesting handicrafts are listed in this book's regional sections. ■

Detail of natural-dyed rug from Oaxaca, with a motif in the style of Mitla mosaics (JL)

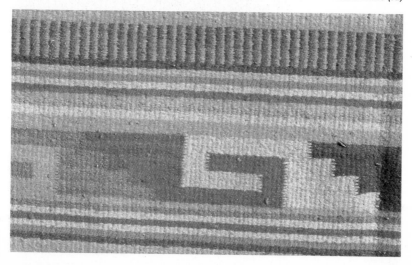

TEXTILES
Traditional Costume

Though traditional Indian clothing is rarely worn in towns nowadays, if you get out into some of Mexico's Indian villages you can't fail to be intrigued by the variety of colourful everyday costumes, differing from area to area and often from village to village. In general, the remoter the area and the less open to outside influences, the more intact its costume traditions tend to be. One town where you will come across Indians in traditional dress is San Cristóbal de Las Casas in Chiapas, which is visited every day by numerous Indians from nearby villages.

Traditional costume – more widely worn by women than men – serves as a mark of the community to which a person belongs, and may also have more specific meanings related to a person's status in a community, or to religious or magical beliefs. A great deal of laborious, highly skilled work goes into creating it. Many of the types of garment and the methods by which they are made, and even some of the designs worked into them, are little changed since before the Spanish reached Mexico, and Indian clothing is a remarkable reminder of the continued identity of these peoples.

Eye-catching huipiles, such as this one from Puebla state have been worn by Indian women for centuries (JL)

The following four important types of female Indian garment have all been in use since long before the Spanish conquest:

Huipil – a sleeveless tunic, often reaching as low as the thighs or ankles, though some are shorter and may be tucked into a skirt. The huipil is now mainly found in the southern half of the country.

Quechquémitl – a shoulder cape with an opening for the head, now mainly worn in the centre and north of the country

Enredo – a wrap-around skirt, almost invisible if worn beneath a long huipil

Faja – a waist sash which holds the enredo in place

Blouses, introduced by Spanish missionaries who thought the quechquémitl immodest when worn without a huipil, are now often embroidered with just as much care and detail as the more traditional garments. They have caused quechquémitls to shrink in size and have replaced huipiles in some places.

The *rebozo*, which also probably appeared in the Spanish era, is a long shawl which may cover the shoulders or head, or be used for carrying.

Indian men's garments are less traditional than women's: in Spanish times modesty was encouraged by the church, so loose shirts and *calzones* (long baggy shorts, often held up by a woollen sash) were introduced. Indian men may carry shoulder bags because their clothes lack pockets. In more modern times, many Indian men have adopted ordinary Mexican clothing.

The male equivalent of the rebozo, also dating from the Spanish era, is the *sarape*, a blanket with an opening for the head.

What's most eye-catching about Indian costumes – especially women's – is the colourful, intricate designs woven into or embroidered on them. Some garments are covered in a multicoloured web of stylised animal, human, plant and mythical shapes which can take many months to complete.

Modern-style sarapes coloured with synthetic dyes (JL)

The basic materials of Indian weaving are cotton and wool, which were once always home-produced and home-spun. Labour-saving factory yarn, including synthetic fibres, is increasingly common today, however.

Colours too are often synthetic – Mexicans use bright modern shades in some highly original combinations – but some natural dyes are still in use, among them deep blues from the indigo plant; reds and browns from various woods; reds, pinks and purples from the cochineal insect (chiefly used in Oaxaca state); and purples and mauves from a secretion of the *caracol púrpura* or purple sea snail, found on rocks along the south-western coast of Oaxaca and used by some Mixtec weavers in that region. Cloth with natural dyes is highly valued but it's very difficult for the non-expert to tell the difference between natural and artificial colours. Thread dyed from the caracol púrpura, however, is said always to retain the smell of the sea!

Mexicans' love of vibrant colours spills over from traditional Indian textiles to contemporary fashion clothing like this embroidered waistcoat found in Oaxaca (JN)

The basic Indian weaver's tool – invented before the Spanish conquest and, now as then, used only by women – is the backstrap loom *(telar de cintura)*. In simple terms, the warp (long) threads are stretched between two horizontal bars, one of which is fixed to a post or tree, while the other is attached to a strap which goes around the weaver's lower back; the weft (cross) threads are then woven in. The length of a cloth woven on a backstrap loom is almost unlimited but the width is restricted to the weaver's armspan.

A variety of highly skilled weaving techniques, including tapestry and brocading, is used to create amazingly sophisticated patterns in the cloth. Embroidery of already-woven cloth – either home-made or bought – is another widespread decorative technique. The intricacy of some final products has to be seen to be believed. Huipiles, skirts, blouses, sashes, quechquémitls and other cloths used for various purposes are all decorated in these ways.

Among Mexico's most intricate and eye-catching clothing are the huipiles worn by Indian women in some villages and towns in the south and south-east of the country. There's immense variety of colour and pattern between the costumes of different Indian peoples. In the state of Oaxaca the Mazatecs, Chinantecs, Triquis, the coastal Mixtecs and some Zapotecs, in villages like Yalalag, create some of the finest, most colourful designs. The Amuzgos, who straddle the southern part of the Oaxaca/Guerrero state border, are also superb textile artisans. In Chiapas state the most skilled weavers are the highland Tzotzils. The Maya of the Yucatán peninsula also wear some attractive huipiles. There may also be big differences between the styles of even neighbouring villages. This is especially noticeable around San Cristóbal de Las Casas in Chiapas, where each of the dozen or so Indian villages within

Indian weaver at an open-air market in Oaxaca (JN)

about 30 km of the town has an entirely distinct costume design. There are also differences between everyday huipiles and special ceremonial huipiles. In addition each individual huipil is likely to have its own unique features.

Some especially beautiful embroidered blouses and quechquémitls are created by Nahua women in Puebla state, the Mazahua in the west of México state, and by the Huichol people who live in a remote region on the borders of Nayarit, Jalisco and Durango states.

An exception to the generally less elaborate design of Indian men's clothing is the garb of the Tacuate Indian people in the south-west of Oaxaca state, which is embroidered with hundreds of tiny, colourful birds, animals and insects – an idea now widely copied on commercially produced clothing elsewhere.

The care that goes into embellishing Indian clothing is not just for simple joy in decoration. Costume and its patterning may have a magical or religious role too, usually of pre-Hispanic origins. In some cases the exact significance has been forgotten, but among the Huichol, for instance, waist sashes are identified with snakes, which are themselves rain and fertility symbols, so the wearing of a waist sash is a symbolic prayer for rain. To some Indian weavers of Chiapas, scorpion motifs serve a similar function, as scorpions are believed to attract lightning. Diamond shapes on some huipils from San Andrés Larrainzar in Chiapas represent the universe of the ancient Maya, ancestors of these villagers, who believed that the earth was a cube and the sky had four corners. Wearing a garment with a saint's figure on it is also a form of prayer, and the sacredness of traditional costume in general is shown by the widespread practice of dressing saints' images in old, revered garments at festival times.

Indian costume is not something you're often likely to buy for practical use, but many items are purchased by collectors as works of art, which the finest examples certainly are. Outstanding work doesn't come cheap: many hundreds of pesos are asked for the very best huipiles in shops in Oaxaca and San Cristóbal de Las Casas. A less expensive reminder of Mexican costume comes in the form of the cloth dolls found in several parts of the country. Some of these are quite detailed in their representation of Indian dress. ■

Intricate embroidery in different styles adorns clothing from many regions. Dresses like this one are seen in many parts of Mexico (NK)

Other Textiles

One textile art that's practised by men is weaving on the treadle loom, introduced to Mexico by the Spanish and operated by foot pedals. This machine can weave wider cloth than the backstrap loom and tends to be used for blankets, rugs and wall hangings as well as rebozos, sarapes and skirt material. Like the backstrap loom, it's capable of great intricacy in design. Mexico's most famous blanket and rug-weaving village is Teotitlán del Valle near Oaxaca city, which produces, among other things, fine textile copies of pre-Hispanic and modern art, including versions of works by Picasso, Escher and Miró, as well as more sober pre-Hispanic-influenced geometric patterns.

Rugs from Teotitlán del Valle: (above) based on an ancient Mixtec design; (below) a modern butterfly composition (JN)

Wall hanging from Jocotepec depicting village girls going to church (JN)

Textile art can be hung on walls as well as worn or spread on beds or floors. Many Teotitlán products can serve this purpose, and smaller examples of the weaver's art, specifically designed as wall hangings, can be found around the country. Some appealing wall hangings, depicting simple village and other scenes, are woven in Jocotepec, near Lago de Chapala, Jalisco, and sold in local towns.

The Huichol Indians make colourful and interesting 'yarn paintings' by pressing strands of wool or acrylic yarn on to a wax-covered board. The resulting scenes resemble visions experienced under the influence of the hallucinatory cactus *peyote*, which is central to Huichol culture and believed to put people in contact with the gods. Huichol artefacts are mainly to be found in the states of Nayarit and Jalisco, on whose remote borders the Huichol live. There's a museum where you can buy Huichol crafts in Zapopan, Guadalajara, and Huichol artisans can be found at work most of the year at the Centro Huichol in Santiago Ixcuintla, Nayarit. Some galleries in Puerto Vallarta sell Huichol work too.

Top: Detail of Huichol Indian yarn painting (JL)

Bottom: Huichol Indian yarn painting, Galería Pyrámide, Puerto Vallarta (NK)

Detail of embroidered cloth from San Pablito area: note the eagle and snake, amongst other motifs (JL)

Also suitable as wall hangings are the cloths embroidered with multitudes of highly colourful birds, animals and insects by the Otomí Indian villagers of San Pablito in northern Puebla state. A remote, traditional village, San Pablito is a source of many other varied crafts. The embroidered cloths are found fairly widely in shops and markets around central Mexico.

Not to be forgotten beside the more authentic textile products is the wide range of commercially produced clothing, based to varying extents on traditional designs and widely available in shops and markets throughout Mexico. Some of these clothes are very attractive and of obvious practical use.

Also useful and decorative are the many tablecloths and shoulder bags found around the country. Commercially woven tablecloths can be a good buy as they're often reasonably priced and can serve a variety of purposes. Attractive ones are found in Oaxaca and Michoacán, among other places. Bags come in all shapes and sizes, many incorporating pre-Hispanic or Indian-style designs. Those produced and used by the Huichol are among the most authentic and original. ■

POTTERY

Mexicans have been making pottery of both simple and sophisticated designs for several millennia. Owing to its preservability, pottery tells us a great deal of what we know about Mexico's ancient cultures, among many of which this was a highly developed art. Wonderful human, animal and mythical pottery figures are to be seen in almost any archaeological museum.

Today the country still has many small-scale, often one-person, potters' workshops, turning out anything from the plain, everyday cooking or storage pots that you'll see in markets to elaborate decorative pieces that are really works of art.

Some village potters work without a wheel. Moulds are employed by some; others use a board resting on a stone, or two upturned dishes one on top of the other, as devices to turn their pots on. Two villages producing attractive, inexpensive but unique styles of unglazed pottery by such unsophisticated methods are Amatenango del Valle, near San Cristóbal de Las Casas in Chiapas, and San Bartolo Coyotepec near Oaxaca city. Amatenango women make jars and plates turned on boards, but the village is best known for its *animalitos* (tiny animal figures), many of which are made by children. (Infant potters will surround you with baskets of their creations if you set foot in the village.) Amatenango pottery is painted with colours made by mixing local earths with water, then fired not in a kiln but by the pre-Hispanic method of burning a mound of wood around a pile of pots.

Cow figurine from Oaxaca (JN)

San Bartolo is the source of all the shiny, black, surprisingly light pottery you'll see in Oaxaca and, increasingly nowadays, further afield. It comes in hundreds of shapes and forms – candlesticks, jugs and vases, decorative animal and bird figures, you name it. Turning here is by the two-dish method. The distinctive black colour is achieved by firing in pit-kilns in the ground, which minimise oxygen intake and turn the iron oxide in the local clay black. Burnishing and polishing give the shine.

Ceramic suns, bowls and fish (NK)

Animalitos from Amatenango del Valle (JN)

A more sophisticated and highly attractive type of Mexican pottery is Talavera, named after a town in Spain whose pottery it resembles. Talavera has been made in the city of Puebla since colonial times. Dolores Hidalgo is a lesser Talavera production centre. Talavera comes in two main forms – tableware and tiles. Bright colours, with blue and yellow often prominent, and floral designs are typical – but tiles in particular may bear any kind of design. In Puebla, Talavera tiles adorn the exteriors of many colonial-era buildings to very pretty effect, some even painted with people or animals. The basic Talavera method involves two firings, with a tin and lead glaze and the painted design applied between the two.

Talavera plates from Puebla (JL)

Dolores Hidalgo tiling (JL)

Earthenware pottery from Dolores Hidalgo (JL)

Talavera tilework in Puebla (JL)
Moulded ceramics (NK)

Another of Mexico's most distinctive pottery forms is the 'tree of life' *(árbol de la vida)*. These highly elaborate candelabra-like objects, often a metre or more high, are moulded by hand and decorated with numerous tiny figures of people, animals, plants and so on. Packing one to take home would be a big challenge! Trees of life may be brightly or more soberly coloured. The commonest themes are Christian, with the Garden of Eden a frequent subject, but trees of life may be devoted to any theme the potter wishes. The works of Herón Martínez, a renowned potter from Acatlán in Puebla state, are among the best, but others are produced in Izucar de Matamoros, also in Puebla, and in Metepec in the state of México. It's not necessary to go to these out-of-the-way places to find the work, however, as artesanías shops in several major centres sell them. The same goes for the striking clay suns, sometimes painted with very bright colours, from Metepec.

The Guadalajara suburbs of Tonalá and Tlaquepaque are two other renowned Mexican pottery centres. Tonalá is actually the source of most of the better work, and its products are sold in both places (as well as further afield). A wide variety of ceramics is produced, and the outstanding work is

Ceramic sun from Metepec (NK)

Tree of life (JL)

the heavy 'stoneware' of Jorge Wilmot, mostly tableware in delicate blue colours, fired at very high temperatures.

One very eye-catching method of decorating pottery, used by the Huichol Indians, practitioners of so many unusual craft techniques, is to cover it in dramatic, bright patterns of glass beads pressed into a wax coating. The Huichol also use this technique on some masks and gourds, and even to make pictures.

A walk around almost any Mexican market or craft shop will reveal interesting pottery. All kinds of decorative animal and human figurines, often with strong pre-Hispanic influence, are sold around the country. Some of them make pleasing souvenirs – but before you go overboard on buying pottery, remember that it all needs very careful packing if you want to get it home in one piece! Copies of pre-Hispanic pottery can be attractive too, a notable example being figures of the podgy, playful, hairless *Izcuintli* dogs which formed part of the diet of ancient western Mexicans. Many pottery Izcuintlis have been unearthed around the city of Colima and skilful reproductions of these are sold in several places in the city. ■

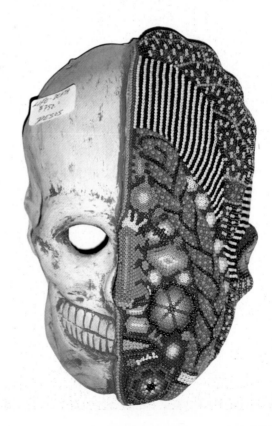

Huichol Indian beadwork mask, Galería Pyrámide, Puerto Vallarta (NK)

Opposite page: Huichol Indian beadwork iguana, Galería Pyrámide, Puerto Vallarta (NK)

*Mask from
Guerrero state (NK)*

*Left: European-faced
mask (JL)
Right: Miniature wooden
jaguar mask (JN)*

MASKS & HEADDRESSES

Like so many other Mexican crafts, mask-making and mask-wearing goes back to pre-Hispanic times. In authentic use, masks were and are worn for magical and religious purposes in dances, ceremonies and shamanistic rites. The wearer temporarily becomes the creature, person or deity depicted by the mask. Many Indian festivals still involve masked dances, whose exact meanings may have been forgotten but which often enact a mythical story intended to bring fertility or scare away enemies or evil forces. These dances often have a curious mixture of pre-Hispanic and Christian or Spanish themes. In some cities traditional dances, some with masks, are regularly performed in *folklórico* shows for tourists.

A huge range of masks is employed, differing from region to region and dance to dance. Though masks obviously have much more life when in use, you can still admire their variety and artisanry at museums in cities like San Luis Potosí, Zacatecas, Morelia and Colima, and at artesanías shops and markets around the country. The southern state of Guerrero has produced probably the most varied range of fine masks.

Wood is the usual basic material of masks but papier-mâché, clay, wax, leather and other things are also used. A mask will often be painted and/or embellished with real feathers, hair, teeth or other adornments. 'Tigers' – often looking more like leopards or jaguars – are fairly common masks, as are other animals and birds, actual and mythical. Christs and Devils are also quite numerous, as well as masks depicting Europeans, whose pale, wide-eyed, usually moustachioed features may look as bizarre and comical to

visitors today as the original Europeans in Mexico looked to the native Mexicans.

Today masks are also made for simple decoration, to hang on walls. While these may not have the mystique that surrounds genuine ceremonial masks, some of which are of considerable age, they're often brighter and in better condition. Even miniature masks can be attractive. Distinguishing genuine dance masks from imitations can be near-impossible for the uninitiated. Some new masks are even treated so that they will look old.

There's also a steady, quite separate business in papier-mâché masks of cartoon and movie characters, animals and so on, which can be fun for children.

Unless you know something about masks or have expert guidance, the best policy when buying masks is simply to go for what you like – if the price seems right!

Another spectacular element of some dance costumes is brilliant feather headdresses, recalling the famous ones which adorned the Aztec emperor Moctezuma and other ancient Mexican nobles. Unless you're lucky enough to be present at a festival in Puebla state where the *Danza de los Quetzales* (Quetzal Dance) is being performed, or in Oaxaca state for the Zapotec Indians' stately *Danza de las Plumas* (Feather Dance), the best chance you'll have of seeing these magnificent creations is at some folklórico dance shows. The *conchero* dance, frequently staged as a form of busking by groups in the Mexico City Zócalo to the accompaniment of loud, upbeat drumming, features some not-quite-so-superb but still eye-catching feather headdresses. Huichol Indians also adorn some of their hats with impressive feather arrays. ■

Mask from Guerrero state (NK)

Totonac headdress (JL)

LACQUERWARE & WOODWORK

Gourds, the hard shells of certain squash-type fruits, have been used since time immemorial in Mexico as bowls, cups and small storage vessels. Today they're also turned to many other uses, including children's rattles, maracas or even hats. Since pre-Hispanic times, too, gourds have been decorated. The most eye-catching technique is the lacquer process, in which the outside of the gourd is coated with layers of paste or paint, each of which is left to harden before the next is applied. The final layer is painted with the artisan's chosen design, then coated with oil, or, sometimes today, varnish, to seal the lacquer. All this makes the gourd non-porous, and to some extent heat-resistant. The painted designs often show birds, plants or animals, but there are infinite possibilities.

Left: Gourd drinking vessels (NK)

Right: The ironwood carvings of the Seri Indians of Sonora state depict dramatic human and animal forms (NK)

Bottom: Mazatlán wood-carver (NK)

Wood too can be lacquered, and today the majority of lacquerware you'll see in Mexico – sold all over the centre and south of the country – is pine or a sweetly scented local wood from the remote village of Olinalá in the north-east of Guerrero state. Characteristic of Olinalá are boxes, trays, chests and furniture lacquered by the *rayado* method, in which designs are created by scraping off part of the top coat of paint to expose a different-coloured layer below. Other lacquering centres are the towns of Chiapa de Corzo in Chiapas, and Uruapan and Pátzcuaro in Michoacán state. Some lacquer artists in Uruapan practise the *embutido* method, in which they scrape a design in the top layer of lacquer and fill in the resulting depressions in different colours, sometimes with beautiful results.

Among the finest wooden artefacts made in Mexico are the polished *palo fierro* (ironwood) carvings done by the Seri Indians of the north-western state of Sonora. This hard wood is worked into a variety of dramatic human, animal and sea-creature shapes. Seris sell their work in Hermosillo, Kino Viejo and Kino Nuevo.

Another attractive woodcraft is the brightly painted copal animals, dragons and imaginary beasts produced by villagers in San Martín Tilcajete, Arrazola and La Unión Tejalapan near Oaxaca city. Multitudes of these creatures are arrayed in shops and markets in Oaxaca. This craft only emerged in the late 1980s from toys that local people had been carving for their children for generations. It has brought relative wealth to many families in the villages concerned.

Some less sophisticated but still pleasing wood carving is produced by the Tarahumara Indians of the Barranca del Cobre (Copper Canyon) area in north-west Mexico. Dolls, toys and animals are among their products.

Quiroga, near Pátzcuaro in Michoacán, is known for its very brightly painted wooden furniture. San Miguel de Allende and Cuernavaca are other centres for wooden furniture. ■

Tarahumara Indian dolls from Divisadero (JL)

Detail of lacquered wooden tray from Olinalá (JN)

Musical Instruments

Many musical instruments are made of wood. Mexico's finest guitars are undoubtedly produced in Paracho, near Uruapan in Michoacán, which also turns out violins, cellos and other instruments. There are many shops and workshops in the town, which also holds a guitar festival every August. The Tarahumara Indians also make violins.

Elsewhere, you'll come across maracas, tambourines, whistles, scrapeboards and a variety of drums in markets and shops. Interesting to look out for, though not particularly common, are tongue drums – hollowed-out pieces of wood, often cylindrical in shape and interestingly carved or decorated, with two central tongues of wood each giving a different note when struck. ■

Maraca, tambourine, miniature tongue drum and guiro fashioned from a hollowed-out gourd (JN)

BARK PAINTINGS

Colourful paintings on *amate*, paper made from tree bark, are sold in countless souvenir shops. While many are cheap, humdrum productions for an undiscriminating tourist market, others are art, showing village life in revealing and skilful detail.

Bark paper has been made in Mexico since pre-Hispanic times, when some codices – pictorial manuscripts – were painted on it. It has always been held sacred. The skill of making it survives only in one small remote area of central Mexico, where the states of Hidalgo, Puebla and Veracruz converge. One chief source of the paper is the traditional Otomí Indian village of San Pablito, where Christianity has only a toehold and non-Christian nature deities are still believed to control life. The paper is made by women, who boil the bark, then lay out the fibres and beat them till they merge together. The resulting paper is dried in the sun. Most of it is then bought by Nahua Indian villagers from the southern state of Guerrero, who have been doing bark paintings since the 1960s. More recently San Pablito villagers have taken up bark painting too, some producing unorthodox designs representing San Pablito's traditional deities.

Bark paper cutouts portraying the same deities are still used in fertility and medicinal rites in San Pablito as a means by which shamans bring the gods to life, and some of these highly unusual works are also sold. ■

Detail of bark painting (NK)

LEATHER

Leather belts, bags, sandals *(huaraches)*, shoes, boots and clothes are often of good quality in Mexico, and usually much cheaper than at home. They're widely available in shops and markets all over the country, but towns and cities in the northern and central ranching regions, such as Zacatecas, Jerez, Hermosillo, Monterrey, Saltillo, León and Guadalajara, have some especially well crafted gear. These are also the places to look if you want to make a present of a Mexican cowboy saddle or pair of spurs to your steed back home.

León is renowned as Mexico's shoe capital, and does indeed have dozens of shoe shops, but in fact every other sizeable city has plenty of good ones too. Check quality and fit carefully before you buy. Mexicans use metric footwear sizes. ■

Left: Huaraches (NK)

Right: Mexican saddlery (NK)

JEWELLERY & METALWORK

Some ancient Mexicans were expert metalsmiths and jewellers, as museum exhibits show. The Spanish fever for Mexico's reserves of gold and silver led to Indians being banned from working these metals for a time during the colonial period, during which European styles of jewellery predominated. Indigenous artisanry was revived in the 20th century, however – most famously in the central Mexican town of Taxco by the American William Spratling, who initiated a silver craft industry that now boasts over 300 shops in Taxco. Silver is much more widely available than gold in Mexico today, in all manner of styles and designs and with artisanry ranging from the dully imitative to the superb. Earrings are particularly popular among Mexicans. It's quite possible to buy good pieces at sensible prices – see the Taxco section in this book's Around Mexico City chapter for hints on judging and buying silver jewellery. For gold, including some delicate filigree work, Oaxaca and Guanajuato cities are two of the best places to look.

Necklaces of a wide variety of materials, including glass or stone beads, wood, seeds and coral, are worn by many Mexican women and are quite easy to come by. Many original jewellery creations, mostly from inexpensive materials, are also sold at the weekend bohemian market in the Mexico City suburb of Coyoacán and by vendors in travellers' haunts like Oaxaca city and San Cristóbal de Las Casas.

Precious stones are much less common than precious metals. True jade, beloved of ancient Mexicans, is a rarity and most 'jade' jewellery is actually jadeite, serpentine or calcite. One abundant stone, however, is the opal, mined in Querétaro state, where the town of San Juan del Río has become quite a gem and jewellery centre.

Though silver and goldsmithing are probably Mexico's two most prominent metal crafts, other skills stand out in a few specific areas. The town of Santa Clara del Cobre, near Pátzcuaro in Michoacán, is a centre for copperwork, turning out shining plates, pots, candlesticks, lamps and more from dozens of workshops.

Silver earrings (NK)

Beaten copper basins from the Bajío area (JL)

Oaxaca city is the scene of a thriving craft in tinplate, stamped into low relief and painted into hundreds of attractive, colourful, small shapes – birds, people, mermaids, fruits, animals, churches, suns, moons, fishes, butterflies. They hang quite beautifully on Christmas trees. ■

Oaxacan stamped tinplate may come as small Christmas decorations (above) or in more elaborate sculptural forms (below) (JN & NK)

RETABLOS

An engaging Mexican custom is the practice of adorning the sanctuaries of specially revered saints or holy images with *retablos*, small paintings giving thanks to the saint in question for answered prayers. Typically done on small sheets of tin, but sometimes on glass, wood, cardboard or another material, retablos depict these miracles in touchingly literal images painted by their beneficiaries. They may show a cyclist's hair's-breadth escape from a hurtling bus, a sailor's survival of a shipwreck, or an invalid rising from a sickbed, beside a representation of the saint and a brief message along the lines of 'Thanks to San Milagro for curing my rheumatism – María Suárez González, 6 June 1990'. The Basilica of Guadalupe in Mexico City, the Plateros Sanctuary near Fresnillo, and the church at Real de Catorce in San Luis Potosí state all have fascinating collections of retablos. Diego Rivera was among the first people to treat these tiny works as real folk art, and the house he shared with Frida Kahlo in Coyoacán, Mexico City, displays some of his collection of old retablos. ■

BASKETS, HATS & HAMMOCKS

Handmade baskets of multifarious shapes and sizes are common in Mexican markets. If you take a liking to one or two, at least you can use them to carry other souvenirs home. Materials used to make baskets include cane, bamboo, and rush or palm-leaf strips. The latter may be wound around a filling of grasses. The more pliable materials enable a coiled construction, but weaving is more common. Many baskets are attractively patterned or coloured.

Woven basket from Amecameca (JN)

Woven palm baskets and boxes (JL)

The classic wide-brimmed, high-crowned Mexican *sombrero* is now largely a thing of the past except on a few mariachi musicians and in a few souvenir shops. Contemporary everyday men's hats are smaller but still often woven from palm strips, either in factories or by hand. The best are considered to be the *jipijapa* hats made in caves at Becal, Campeche, where the humidity prevents the fibres becoming too brittle during the production process. Mérida in the adjacent state of Yucatán is a good place to buy a Becal hat.

Another Mexican product of practical use to many travellers is the hammock. Hammocks can be the most comfortable and economical places to sleep in many hot, southern areas. Generally made of cotton or nylon, they come in a variety of widths and an infinite number of colour patterns. Notable places where they're made and/or sold include Mérida (Yucatán state), Palenque (Chiapas), and Mitla and Juchitán (Oaxaca). You can watch them being made in the village of Tixcocob near Mérida. Some useful information for anyone thinking of buying a hammock can be found in the Mérida section of this book's Yucatán Peninsula chapter. ∎

Tarahumara girl selling baskets (JL)

Tarahumara woman selling handicrafts at the train station in Divisadero, Copper Canyon (NK)

FESTIVAL CRAFTS

Some Mexican crafts are produced for specific events in the annual calendar. The national obsession with skull and skeleton motifs, by which Mexicans continually remind themselves of their own mortality, reaches a crescendo in the run-up to *el Día de los Muertos* (the Day of the Dead), 2 November, when the souls of the dead are believed to revisit the earth and people gather in grave-yards with gifts for them. As the Day of the Dead approaches, families build altars in their homes, and shops and markets fill with countless toy coffins and paper, cardboard and clay skeletons, many of these engaged in eminently lively activities like riding bicycles, playing music or getting married. Most amazing are the rows of chocolate and sugar-candy skulls, skeletons and coffins which appear on market stalls at this time – proof of the almost joyful nature of this festival which reunites the living with their dead.

Left: Miniature coffin made of icing sugar (JN)

Right: Chocolate and candy skulls, Guanajuato (JN)

Bottom: Day of the Dead altar at the Templo Mayor, Mexico City (JN)

Most Mexican children's birthdays would be incomplete without a *piñata*, a large, brightly decorated papier-mâché star, animal, fruit or other figure, constructed around a clay pot or papier-mâché mould. At party time the piñata is stuffed with small toys, sweets and fruit and suspended on a rope. Blindfolded children take turns at bashing it with a stick until it breaks open and, with luck, showers everyone with the gifts inside. Piñatas are also broken after the traditional pre-Christmas processions called posadas which are still held in some towns.

Another Christmas craft is the creation of *nacimientos*, nativity scenes, in homes or town plazas. Clay or wood figures of the personages in these scenes may be reused year after year. Some larger-scale nacimientos even feature live sheep and goats! ■

The piñata, stuffed with sweets and small gifts, is a feature of many Mexican celebrations (NK)

Nacimiento at Guadalajara: angels and animals surround a glittering 'stable' (SF)

BOOKS ON MEXICAN HANDICRAFTS

There are countless books on the subject but two fairly recent works by Chloe Sayer are excellent sources if you want to delve into the field. *Arts and Crafts of Mexico* (Thames & Hudson, 1990) is a general introduction covering almost every craft you could think of, and a good starting point for further research. *Costumes of Mexico* (1985, published in Britain as *Mexican Costume*) concentrates on the textile arts, and will answer most questions you could ask about the bewildering array of techniques, materials, styles and designs employed in Mexican Indian clothing, as well as digging back into their history. ■

Getting There & Away

Most visitors to Mexico arrive by air. You can also approach by road from the USA, Guatemala and Belize, and reach both sides of the US-Mexican border (but not actually cross it) by rail. There's also a back-country jungle route by bus and river-boat between Flores in Guatemala's El Petén and Palenque in Chiapas.

AIR

Round-the-World Tickets

Round-the-World (RTW) tickets are often real bargains, and from Australasia can work out no more expensive or even cheaper than an ordinary return ticket to Mexico. Prices start at about UK£850 or A$1800 though they tend to be more expensive if you want to include Mexico.

Official airline RTW tickets are usually put together by a combination of two airlines, and permit you to fly anywhere you want on their route systems so long as you do not backtrack. An alternative type of RTW ticket is one put together by a travel agent using a combination of discounted tickets.

To/From the USA & Canada

The airlines with most services to Mexico include Alaska Airlines, American, Canadian Airlines International, Continental, Delta and United, and the Mexican lines Aeroméxico and Mexicana. You can fly without changing planes to Mexico from at least these North American cities: Atlanta, Chicago, Dallas/Fort Worth, Denver, Houston, Los Angeles, McAllen (Texas), Miami, New Orleans, New York, Orlando, Phoenix, San Antonio, San Diego, San Francisco, San Jose, Seattle, Tampa/St Petersburg, Toronto, Tucson and Washington, DC. There are one-stop connecting flights from many others.

About 30 Mexican cities receive direct flights from North America. Mexico City receives most, followed by Guadalajara, Cancún, Monterrey and Acapulco. There are connections to many other places in Mexico, the majority through Mexico City. See the relevant city sections of this book for more information.

If you want to travel overland through northern Mexico, you can still fly to a US city on the Mexican border. Continental, for instance, serves El Paso, Brownsville, Laredo, McAllen (Texas) and San Diego.

Fares There are dozens of airfares for any given route. Travel agents are the first people to consult about fares and routes. Once you've discovered the basics of the airlines flying, the routes taken and the various discounted tickets available, you can consult your favourite discount ticket agent, consolidator or charter airline to see if their fares are better. Consolidators buy bulk seats from airlines at considerable discounts and resell them to the public, usually through travel agents. Though there are some shady dealers, most consolidators are quite legitimate. Ask your travel agent about buying a consolidator ticket, or look for the consolidator advertisements in the travel section of the newspaper (they're the ones with tables of destinations and fares and toll-free '800' numbers to call). Fares depend among other things on what time of year you fly (expect to pay more around Christmas-New Year and in the summer holiday season), how far ahead you book, and how long you're going for (usually the longer the dearer). Here are some typical examples of full fares and cheapest discounted or excursion tickets, return trip to Mexico City.

City	Full fare	Lowest rate
Chicago	US$660	US$370
Dallas/		
Fort Worth	US$500	US$250
Los Angeles	US$640	US$280
Miami	US$550	US$300
New York	US$1050	US$450
Toronto	US$750	US$350

Air Travel Glossary

Apex Apex, or 'advance purchase excursion' is a discounted ticket which must be paid for in advance. There are penalties if you wish to change it.

Baggage Allowance This will be written on your ticket: usually one 20 kg item to go in the hold, plus one item of hand luggage.

Bucket Shop An unbonded travel agency specialising in discounted airline tickets.

Bumped Just because you have a confirmed seat doesn't mean you're going to get on the plane – see Overbooking.

Cancellation Penalties If you have to cancel or change an Apex ticket there are often heavy penalties involved; insurance can sometimes be taken out against these penalties. Some airlines impose penalties on regular tickets as well, particularly against 'no show' passengers.

Check-In Airlines ask you to check in a certain time ahead of the flight departure (usually 1½ hours on international flights). If you fail to check in on time and the flight is overbooked the airline can cancel your booking and give your seat to somebody else.

Confirmation Having a ticket written out with the flight and date you want doesn't mean you have a seat until the agent has checked with the airline that your status is 'OK' or confirmed. Meanwhile you could just be 'on request'.

Discounted Tickets There are two types of discounted fares – officially discounted (see Promotional Fares) and unofficially discounted. The lowest prices often impose drawbacks like flying with unpopular airlines, inconvenient schedules, or unpleasant routes and connections. A discounted ticket can save you other things than money – you may be able to pay Apex prices without the associated Apex advance booking and other requirements. Discounted tickets only exist where there is fierce competition.

Full Fares Airlines traditionally offer first class (coded F), business class (coded J) and economy class (coded Y) tickets. These days there are so many promotional and discounted fares available from the regular economy class that few passengers pay full economy fare.

Lost Tickets If you lose your airline ticket an airline will usually treat it like a travellers' cheque and, after inquiries, issue you with another one. Legally, however, an airline is entitled to treat it like cash and if you lose it then it's gone forever. Take good care of your tickets.

No-Shows No shows are passengers who fail to show up for their flight, sometimes due to unexpected delays or disasters, sometimes due to simply forgetting, sometimes because they made more than one booking and didn't bother to cancel the one they didn't want. Full-fare passengers who fail to turn up are sometimes entitled to travel on a later flight. The rest of us are penalised (see Cancellation Penalties).

On Request An unconfirmed booking for a flight; see Confirmation.

Open Jaws A return ticket where you fly out to one place but return from another. If available, this can save you backtracking to your arrival point.

To/From Europe

Only a few airlines fly nonstop from Europe to Mexico, among them Aeroméxico, British Airways, Iberia and KLM. On some of these you can fly straight into Cancún instead of Mexico City if you wish. Other airlines take you to one of the US hub cities (Atlanta, Dallas/Fort Worth, New York, Miami), where you will at least touch down and may change planes, even to another airline. Fares are not necessarily cheaper on the indirect routes.

If you want to stop over in the USA on the way to Mexico, several airlines, including Aeroméxico, American, Continental, Delta

and United, serve Europe, the USA and Mexico. Or you can simply get a ticket to the USA and buy another ticket to Mexico or the border from there. You may have to show 'sufficient funds' to enter the USA if you haven't already got an onward ticket. Also check US visa requirements.

The most common type of ticket from Europe to Mexico is a fixed-date return, but one-ways, open returns, circle trips and 'open-jaws' are also possible. Most of them are available at discount rates from cheap ticket agencies in Europe's bargain flight centres like London, Amsterdam, Paris and Frankfurt.

Overbooking Airlines hate to fly empty seats and since every flight has some passengers who fail to show up (see No Shows) airlines often book more passengers than they have seats. Usually the excess passengers balance those who fail to show up, but occasionally somebody gets bumped. If this happens guess who it is most likely to be? The passengers who check in late.

Promotional Fares Officially discounted fares like Apex fares which are available from travel agents or direct from the airline.

Reconfirmation At least 72 hours prior to departure time of an onward or return flight you must contact the airline and 'reconfirm' that you intend to be on the flight. If you don't do this the airline can delete your name from the passenger list and you could lose your seat. You don't have to reconfirm the first flight on your itinerary or if your stopover is less than 72 hours. It doesn't hurt to reconfirm more than once.

Restrictions Discounted tickets often have various restrictions on them – advance purchase is the most usual one (see Apex). Others are restrictions on the minimum and maximum period you must be away, such as a minimum of 14 days or a maximum of one year. See Cancellation Penalties.

Standby A discounted ticket where you only fly if there is a seat free at the last moment. Standby fares are usually only available on domestic routes.

Tickets Out An entry requirement for many countries is that you have an onward or return ticket, in other words, a ticket out of the country. If you're not sure what you intend to do next, the easiest solution is to buy the cheapest onward ticket to a neighbouring country or a ticket from a reliable airline which can later be refunded if you do not use it.

Transferred Tickets Airline tickets cannot be transferred from one person to another. Travellers sometimes try to sell the return half of their ticket, but officials can ask you to prove that you are the person named on the ticket. This is unlikely to happen on domestic flights; on an international flight tickets may be compared with passports.

Travel Agencies Travel agencies vary widely and you should ensure you use one that suits your needs. Some simply handle tours while full-service agencies handle everything from tours and tickets to car rental and hotel bookings. A good one will do all these things and can save you a lot of money but if all you want is a ticket at the lowest possible price, then you really need an agency specialising in discounted tickets. A discounted ticket agency, however, may not be useful for other things, like hotel bookings.

Travel Periods Some officially discounted fares, Apex fares in particular, vary with the time of year. There is often a low (off-peak) season and a high (peak) season. Sometimes there's an intermediate or shoulder season as well. At peak times, when everyone wants to fly, not only will the officially discounted fares be higher but so will unofficially discounted fares or there may simply be no discounted tickets available. Usually the fare depends on your outward flight – if you depart in the high season and return in the low season, you pay the high-season fare. ∎

A typical fixed-date return from Europe to Mexico for up to three months is likely to cost US$450 or US$500 – not much more than from North America. The sooner you buy, the cheaper the ticket may be. Fares can also vary between high and low seasons. Open returns, and fixed-date returns for longer than three months, are a bit more expensive than three-month fixed-date returns.

Circle trips and open-jaws are useful if you want to hop from one part of Mexico to another, or between Mexico and elsewhere in the Americas, without backtracking. You usually depart from, and return to, the same city in Europe: circle trips give you flights between your different destinations en route, while with open-jaw tickets you make your own way between your arrival and departure points.

Ticket Agents in the UK For cheap tickets, pick up a good weekend newspaper travel section such as the Saturday *Independent*, or *Time Out* or any of the other London magazines that advertise discount or bucket shop flights, and check out a few of the advertisers. Most bucket shops are trustworthy and reliable but the occasional sharp operator appears. If a travel agent is registered with the ABTA (Association of British Travel Agents), as most are, ABTA will guarantee a refund or an alternative if the agent goes out of business after you have paid for your flight. Reputable agents offering good-value fares to Mexico include Journey Latin America (☎ (0181) 747-3108) at 16 Devonshire Rd, Chiswick, London W4 2HD; Campus Travel (☎ (0171) 730-3402) at 52 Grosvenor Gardens, London SW1; STA (☎ (0171) 937-9962) at 86 Old Brompton Rd, London SW7, or 117 Euston Rd, London NW1; and Trailfinders (☎ (0171) 938-3939) at 194 Kensington High St, London W8, or (☎ (0171) 938-3366) at 42-50 Earls Court Rd, London W8. The last three have branches in other cities too.

Ticket Agents Elsewhere in Europe

Agencies which specialise in cheap tickets and youth/student travel include:

France – Council Travel (☎ (1) 42.66.20.87), 31 rue Saint Augustine, Paris 2ème, a branch of the USA's biggest student and budget travel agency; another office (☎ (1) 44.55.55.44) is at 22 Rue des Pyramides, Paris 1er

Germany – Cheap flights are advertised in the Berlin magazine *Zitty*. Agents include Alternativ Tours (☎ (030) 881-2089), Wilmersdorfer Strasse 94, Berlin; SRID Reisen (☎ (069) 43-01-91), Berger Strasse 1178, Frankfurt; and SRS Studenten Reise Service (☎ (030) 281-5033), Marienstrasse 23, Berlin.

Ireland – USIT Travel Office (☎ (01) 679-8833), 19 Aston Quay, Dublin

Italy – CTS (☎ (06) 46 791), Via Genova 16, off Via Nazionale, Rome; other branches all over Italy

Netherlands – NBBS (☎ (020) 624-0989), Rokin 38, Amsterdam; Malibu Travel (☎ (020) 623-6814) Damrak 30, Amsterdam

Scandinavia – Kilroy Travels, with branches in Copenhagen, Stockholm, Oslo, Helsinki and several other towns, a well-established cheap flight agent, often especially good if you're under 26 or a student under 35

Spain – TIVE (☎ (91) 401-1300), Calle José Ortega y Gasset, Madrid

Switzerland – SSR (☎ (01) 261-2956), Leonhardstrasse 5 & 10, Zurich; branches in several other Swiss cities

To/From Australasia

There are no direct flights from Australia or New Zealand to Mexico. The cheapest way to get there is via the USA, often through Los Angeles. From Sydney/Melbourne to Mexico City via Los Angeles the cheapest low-season single fare is A$950, return A$1600; the cheapest high-season return is A$1850. You might be able to do it cheaper by buying a ticket to Los Angeles then getting your Los Angeles-Mexico ticket there. You may have to show 'sufficient funds' to enter the USA if you haven't already got an onward ticket. Also check US visa requirements.

STA Travel, and Flight Centres International, with numberous offices in main towns and cities, are major dealers in cheap air fares in both Australia and New Zealand. Check the travel agents' ads in the yellow pages and ring around.

To combine Mexico with other destinations in one trip, Round-the-World tickets are one option (see the earlier section). Another is a Circle Pacific ticket, which uses a combination of airlines to circle the Pacific – combining Australia, New Zealand, North America and Asia. You may be able to get a Circle Pacific ticket which includes Mexico City for around A$2800.

To/From Guatemala & Belize

Aviateca (Guatemala's national airline), Mexicana and TACA (of El Salvador) fly daily between Guatemala City and Mexico City. These flights are easily bookable through travel agents. Smaller airlines provide quicker, cheaper connections between smaller cities: you may have to contact them directly for schedules and fares.

Aerocaribe (Mexicana Inter), Aviateca (in Guatemala City ☎ (02) 31-82-22/27, fax 34-74-01), and the small Guatemalan airline Aeroquetzal (in Guatemala City ☎ (02) 37-34-67/68/69, fax 34-76-89) fly daily between Guatemala City and Cancún; some routes are via Belize City. Aviateca also flies between Guatemala City and Mérida. Fares are US$120 to US$185 one way. The small Guatemalan airline Aerovías (in Guatemala City ☎ (02) 34-79-35, 31-96-63; fax 32-56-86) flies between Guatemala City and Chetumal, sometimes with stops in Belize

City. There are also flights between Tikal and Mérida, and Flores and Cancún.

Aviacsa flies three times a week between Guatemala City and Tuxtla Gutiérrez, its hub, where there are connections for other south and south-eastern Mexico cities.

For more information see this book's city sections.

To/From Latin America & the Caribbean

Mexicana flies between Mexico City and Bogotá, Havana, San José (Costa Rica) and San Juan (Puerto Rico). Mexicana flies to Havana from Mexico City, Mérida and Cancún. Cubana also flies between Mexico City and Havana. The airlines of most Central and South American countries fly to/from Mexico City (see Mexico City's Getting There & Away section for contact details).

Leaving Mexico by Air

A departure tax equivalent to about US$12 is levied for international flights from Mexico. If you buy your ticket in Mexico, the tax will be included in your ticket cost. If you bought it outside Mexico, the tax may not be included (you can check with the airline). If it isn't, you will have to pay the tax in cash at the airport check-in.

Buying international air tickets in Mexico is an expensive business as no substantial discounts are available. You're looking at at least US$800 one way or return to Europe, for example. Icelandair has some of the lowest fares to Europe. To North America, some of the smaller Mexican airlines flying there, such as TAESA, may have lower fares than the big airlines. In Mexico City, the travel agency Consejeros de Viajes México (☎ (5) 525-75-20), Génova 30, Zona Rosa, offers some of the best international fares.

LAND

You can enter Mexico by road from the USA or Belize, and by road or boat from Guatemala. You can also reach a few US towns on the Mexican border by train, and/or travel on from some Mexican border towns by train.

To/From the USA

There are over 20 official road crossing points on the USA-Mexico border:

Arizona: Douglas/Agua Prieta, Nogales/Nogales and San Luis/San Luis Río Colorado (all open 24 hours); Naco/Naco, Sasabe/El Sásabe and Lukeville/Sonoita
California: Calexico/Mexicali and San Ysidro/Tijuana (both open 24 hours); Andrade/Algodones (open from 6 am to 8 pm); Tecate/Tecate (open from 7 am to midnight); and Otay Mesa/Mesa de Otay (near Tijuana's international airport; open from 6 am to 10 pm)
New Mexico: Columbus/Palomas (open 24 hours)
Texas: Brownsville/Matamoros, Laredo/Nuevo Laredo, Eagle Pass/Piedras Negras, Del Rio/Ciudad Acuña and El Paso/Ciudad Juárez (all open 24 hours); Progreso/Nuevo Progreso, McAllen/Reynosa, Rio Grande City/Camargo, Los Saenz/Ciudad Alemán, Falcon/Nueva Ciudad Guerrero, Presidio/Ojinaga, Fort Hancock/Praxedis Guerrero, and Fabens/Guadalupe de Bravo

More information on many of these crossings can be found in the regional chapters.

Bus There are no long-distance buses linking cities in the US interior with cities in the Mexican interior. You have to take one bus to the border, then another onward. A few buses from US cities cross to cities on the Mexican side of the border: routes include Los Angeles to Tijuana, Mexicali and Ciudad Juárez; Albuquerque and Denver to Ciudad Juárez; and San Antonio, Dallas and Houston to Nuevo Laredo and Reynosa. But more often you must get a bus to a city on the US side of the border, then walk, or take a local bus or taxi, across the border. Greyhound buses serve Brownsville, El Paso, McAllen, Laredo, Del Rio, Calexico and San Diego. To reach other border cities, transfer from Greyhound to a smaller line.

A few buses start for Mexican destinations from cities on the US side of the border, but you'll find a much better selection of companies and routes (and usually significantly better fares) by crossing to the Mexican bus terminal.

See the sections on the Mexican border towns for more information.

Train You can reach some US border cities by train, and you can travel on from some Mexican border cities by train, but you can't cross the border by train.

Taking a train to the Mexican border can be quite enjoyable, but it may not be much cheaper than flying when you add meals and other expenses. Trains tend to be a little slower, a little cheaper, and less frequent than buses. Amtrak (☎ (800-872-7245) serves three US cities from which access to Mexico is easy. From El Paso (Texas) you cross to Ciudad Juárez; from San Antonio (Texas) you can take a bus to the border at Eagle Pass/Piedas Negras, Del Rio/Ciudad Acuña, or Laredo/Nuevo Laredo; from San Diego (California) you can cross to Tijuana.

The main services from Mexican border cities, all daily, are from Nuevo Laredo to Mexico City via Monterrey, Saltillo, San Luis Potosí and San Miguel de Allende; from Ciudad Juárez to Mexico City via Chihuahua, Zacatecas and Querétaro; and from Nogales and Mexicali to Guadalajara via Hermosillo, El Sufragio and Mazatlán. The relatively comfortable *primera especial* seats are only available from Nuevo Laredo, Nogales and Mexicali. There are also daily trains from Matamoros and Reynosa to Monterrey, and Piedas Negras to Saltillo, connecting (more or less) with the Mexico City trains. See the Mexico City and Guadalajara Getting There & Away sections for schedules, and the Getting Around chapter for information on bookings and Mexican train classes.

Car & Motorbike Driving into Mexico is not for everyone – you should have some Spanish, basic mechanical aptitude, large reserves of patience, and access to some extra cash for emergencies. Cars are most useful for travellers who:

- have plenty of time
- plan to go to remote places
- will be camping out a lot
- have surfboards/climbing gear/diving equipment or other cumbersome luggage
- will be travelling with a group/family of four or more
- want to buy lots of bulky handicrafts.

Don't take a car if you:

- are on a tight schedule
- have a low budget
- plan to spend most time in urban areas
- will be travelling alone
- want a relaxing trip with minimum risks.

Cars are expensive to buy or rent in Mexico, so the best option is to take one in from North America. If this means buying it first, you may need several weeks to find a good vehicle at a reasonable price. It may also take some time at the end of your trip to sell the thing. It's not worth it for just a short trip. The rules for taking a vehicle into Mexico, described in what follows, have in the past changed from time to time. You can check them with a Mexican consulate, Mexican government tourist office (the one in San Antonio, Texas (☎ (512) 366-3242) reportedly specialises in temporary import of vehicles), or the toll-free information number 1-800-446-8277 in the USA.

Buying a Car in the USA The border states, particularly California and Texas, are good places to buy – there are many car lots, and every town has magazines and newspapers with ads from private sellers. Cars are more likely to have air-con – desirable in Mexico. Most local libraries have copies of the 'Blue Book' which lists wholesale and retail prices of second-hand cars. About US$1200 to US$2200 should buy a car that will take you round Mexico and still be worth something at the end.

It's a good idea to get a car made by Volkswagen, Nissan/Datsun, Chrysler, General Motors or Ford, which have manufacturing or assembly plants in Mexico, and dealers in most big Mexican towns. Other makes may be difficult to obtain spare parts for. Big cars are unwieldy on narrow roads and streets, and use a lot more petrol. A sedan with a boot (trunk) provides safer, more discreet storage than a station wagon or a hatchback. Volkswagen camper vans are economical, and parts and service are easy to find. Tyres (including spare), shock absorbers and suspension should be in good condition.

To avoid delay in getting your certificate of title or ownership for the vehicle – which you must take with you to Mexico – you can ask the state department of motor vehicles for rush service on the transfer of ownership (this may cost a few bucks but it's worth it). Alternatively, ask for an official letter stating that you have bought the vehicle and applied for a transfer. If a lienholder's name is shown on the certificate of title (eg a bank which has lent money on the vehicle) then you'll need a notarised affidavit giving their permission for the vehicle to be taken into Mexico.

Motor Insurance It is very foolish to drive in Mexico without Mexican liability insurance. If you are involved in an accident, you can be jailed or forbidden to leave the immediate area until all claims are settled, which could take weeks or months. A valid insurance policy is regarded as a guarantee that restitution will be paid, and will expedite release of the driver. Mexican law only recognises Mexican car insurance *(seguro)*, so a US or Canadian policy won't help.

Mexican insurance is sold in US towns near the Mexican border. Approaching the border from the USA you will see billboards advertising offices selling Mexican policies. At the busiest border-crossing points (Tijuana, Mexicali, Nogales, Agua Prieta, Ciudad Juárez, Nuevo Laredo, Reynosa and Matamoros), there are insurance offices open 24 hours a day. Some deals are better than others. Check the yellow pages in US border towns. Three organisations worth checking are the American Automobile Association (AAA), International Gateway Insurance Brokers, and Sanborns (the latter offers lots of useful free travel information). Short-term cover is about US$6 a day for full coverage of a US$5000 car, but a policy for a whole year can be obtained for as little as US$200.

Driver's Licence To drive a motor vehicle – car, RV (camper van), motorbike or truck – in Mexico, you need a valid driver's licence from your home country. Mexican police are familiar with US and Canadian licences; licences from other countries or an International Driving Permit may be scrutinised more closely, but they are still legal.

Vehicle Permit You will need a *permiso de importación temporal de vehículos* (a temporary import permit for vehicles) if you want to take a vehicle beyond Baja California or the border zone which extends about 20 km into Mexico. Customs officials at posts a few km south of each border town, and at the mainland ports for ferries from Baja (and sometimes at the Baja ports too), will want to see the permit for your vehicle. You must get one at the *aduana* (customs) office at a border crossing or, in Baja, at the Registro Federal de Vehículos in either Tijuana or La Paz. The purpose of the permit is to prevent people selling vehicles in Mexico illegally, ie without paying import duties.

In addition to a passport or proof of US or Canadian citizenship, the person importing the vehicle will need originals of the following documents, which must all be in his/her own name: a tourist card (go to *migración* before you go to aduana); a certificate of title or ownership for the vehicle (in California this means the 'pink slip'); a current registration card or notice; a driver's licence (see above); and either a valid international credit card (Visa, MasterCard, Amex or Diners) issued by a non-Mexican bank or cash to pay a very large bond (see below). You need one photocopy of each of these documents as well as the original, but people at the office will make all the copies for a dollar or so.

If it's a company car and you do not have a certificate of title in your own name, bring a notarised affidavit that certifies you work for the company and are allowed to take the car into Mexico. If the vehicle is leased or rented, bring the original contract (plus a copy), which must be in the name of the person importing the car, and a notarised affidavit from the rental company authorising the driver to take it into Mexico.

One person cannot bring in two vehicles. If, for example, you have a motorcycle attached to your car, you'll need another adult travelling with you to obtain a permit for the motorcycle, and they will need to have all the right papers for it. If the motorcycle is in your name, you'll need a notarised affidavit authorising the other person to take it into Mexico.

At the border there'll be a parking area for vehicles awaiting issue of a permit. Go inside and find the right counter to present your papers. After some signing and stamping of papers, you sign a promise to take the car out of the country, the Banco del Ejército (also called Banjército; it's the army bank) charges US$10 to your credit card, and you are sent out to wait with your vehicle. Make sure you get back the originals of all the documents. Eventually someone will come out, check the details of your vehicle, put a hologram sticker on the top corner of the windshield, and give you a permit (with another hologram sticker) and your tourist card stamped *'con automóvil'*.

If you don't have an international credit card, you will have to deposit a cash bond (not a cheque) with the Banco del Ejército or an authorised Mexican bonding company (*afianzadora*). The required amounts for medium or small cars in 1994 were US$6000 for a vehicle up to two years old, US$3000 (three to five years old), US$1000 (six to eight years old), US$750 (nine to 14 years old), and US$500 (15 years or older). Bigger vehicles require higher bonds. The bond should be refunded, plus any interest, when the vehicle finally leaves Mexico and the temporary import permit is cancelled. If you plan to leave Mexico at a different border crossing, make sure that the bonding company will give you a refund there. There are Banco del Ejército modules and authorised Mexican bonding company offices at all the major border crossings. Mostly they're open 24 hours every day but the Tijuana office closes at night.

The permit entitles you to take the vehicle in and out of Mexico for the next 180 days; multiple entries are permitted. If the car is still in Mexico after that time, aduana will start charging fines to your credit card. Cars in Mexico without a current permit can be confiscated. The vehicle may be driven by the owner's spouse or adult children, and by other people if the owner is in the vehicle.

When you leave Mexico for the last time you must have the permit cancelled by the Mexican authorities, no later than the day before it expires. An official may cancel the permit as you enter the border zone, about 20 km before the border itself. If not, you will have to find the right official from aduana and/or Banco del Ejército at the border crossing. If you leave Mexico without having the permit cancelled, once the permit expires the authorities will assume that you've left the vehicle in the country illegally and start charging fines to your credit card.

Only the owner can take the vehicle out of Mexico – and as a rule, the owner cannot leave Mexico without it. If it's wrecked completely, you must obtain permission to leave it in the country from either the Registro Federal de Vehículos (Federal Registry of Vehicles) in Mexico City, or a Hacienda (Treasury Department) office in another city or town; your insurance company can help with this. If it breaks down, you can get permission to leave Mexico while it's being fixed (you'll need a statement signed by the mechanic). If you have to leave the country in an emergency, the vehicle can be left in bonded storage with Hacienda, usually at an airport. In the last two cases, you must return personally and collect the vehicle within 45 days, or before the original permit expires.

To/From Guatemala & Belize

For detailed information on travel in and through Central America, see *Guatemala, Belize & Yucatán: La Ruta Maya* or *Central America*, both published by Lonely Planet.

There are three official highway border crossings between Guatemala and Mexico: La Mesilla/Ciudad Cuauhtémoc on the Pan-American Highway in the highlands (on the way to San Cristóbal de Las Casas), and Ciudad Tecún Umán/Ciudad Hidalgo and El Carmen/Talismán, both on the Pacific slope near Tapachula.

There is one official crossing point between Belize and Mexico, at Santa

Elena/Subteniente López (near Corozal and Chetumal respectively).

Bus Direct buses connect Guatemala City with all three Guatemalan border crossings. On the Pacific slope, Tecún Umán is preferred to El Carmen as there are fewer hassles. There's more information on these border points in the Tabasco & Chiapas chapter.

From Guatemala City to La Mesilla is 342 km (seven hours). Transportes El Condor (☎ (02) 2-85-04), 19 Calle 2-01, Zona 1, goes to La Mesilla at 4, 8 and 10 am, and 1 and 5 pm daily, for US$4.

From Guatemala City to Ciudad Tecún Umán is 253 km (five hours). Fortaleza (☎ (02) 51-79-94), 19 Calle 8-70, Zona 1, has buses at 5.30 and 9.30 am for US$4.50, stopping at Escuintla, Mazatenango, Retalhuleu and Coatepeque.

From Flores, near Tikal in Guatemala's Petén province, there is a direct 1st-class bus each morning to Chetumal in Mexico; it's 350 km and takes nine hours, bypassing Belize City. The fare is US$35. To go 2nd class you must take the Transportes Pinita and Novelo buses to Belize City (US$5.75), then a Batty bus (US$5) to Chetumal. This is slower, less convenient and less comfortable than the 1st-class bus, but only a third of the price.

From Belize City there are frequent services north, via Orange Walk and Corozal, to Chetumal, a journey of 160 km (four hours; express 3¼ hours, US$). Venus has buses departing from Belize City every hour on the hour from noon to 7 pm. Batty's has buses every two hours on the hour.

RIVER

There are currently three routes through the jungle from Flores (Petén, Guatemala) to Palenque (Chiapas, Mexico).

The El Naranjo route takes you by bus to El Naranjo, then by boat down the Río San Pedro to La Palma, then by bus via Tenosique to Palenque.

Another route is by bus to Bethel, then down the Río Usumacinta to Frontera Corozal (also called Frontera Echeverría) and Yaxchilán, and eventually to Palenque.

The third route takes you to Sayaxché by bus, then down the Río de la Pasión via Pipiles to Benemerito, where you can catch a bus to Palenque or detour to Bonampak and Yaxchilán archaeological sites.

For details of these routes, see the Tabasco & Chiapas chapter. It may only be a matter of time before robbers wake up to the prospect of easy pickings from gringo tourists on these remote routes.

TOURS

Package holidays to Mexico are available from many countries. Many of them are of the 'nine nights in Acapulco, two in Taxco' variety. Mexican government tourist offices and travel agents around the world can give you armfuls of brochures about these trips, and travel agents can book them for you. Costs depend on where you go, your accommodation, how many meals are included, the time of year (peak time is usually December to February), and where you're coming from. To take one example, a typical seven-night off-season trip from Southern California costs around US$310 to US$380 to Puerto Vallarta or US$400 to US$600 to Cancún, including flights.

Quite a few companies offer 'adventure tours' or 'eco-tours', featuring activities like kayaking, diving, horse riding and wildlife viewing. They often advertise in magazines devoted to these activities. You'd probably pay US$120 to US$220 a day on such tours

if the accommodation is of reasonable standard, plus airfares. Escorted tours to the Mexican cultural heartland, away from the seaside resorts, are a bit rarer. Some of the more unusual possibilities include:

Expeditions Inc (☎ (817) 861-9298), PO Box 13594, Arlington, Texas 76094-0594, USA, can take you to about 16 archaeological or colonial destinations in two weeks.

Explore Worldwide runs small-group trips. It has offices in several countries, including Aldershot, England (☎ (01252) 344-161) and Oakland, California (☎ (415) 654-1879).

Journey Latin America (☎ (0181) 747-8315), 14-16 Devonshire Rd, Chiswick, London W4 2HD, UK, runs a few small-group tours using local transport.

Mayan Adventures (☎ (206) 523-5309), PO Box 15204, Wedgwood Station, Seattle, Washington 98115-15204, USA, offers small-group tours of obscure Mayan sites that are not easily accessible.

Mexican Trails (☎ (914) 365-6698, 1-800-487-4783) of Orangeburg, NY, USA, offers tours to colonial cities, mainly in Central Mexico.

Pacific Adventures (☎ (714) 684-1227), PO Box 5041, Riverside, California 92517, USA, offers trips oriented to horse riding, kayaking, scuba diving and sailing.

Getting Around

The peak travel periods of Semana Santa (the week before Easter) and Christmas/New Year are hectic and heavily booked throughout Mexico: try to book transport in advance for these periods.

For some useful words and phrases when travelling, see the Language section in Facts about the Country.

AIR

All sizeable cities in Mexico, and many smaller ones, have passenger airports. Aeroméxico and Mexicana are the country's two largest airlines. In recent years numerous smaller airlines have also emerged, often flying useful routes between provincial cities that the big two don't bother with. These include Aero California (serving the west and north-west of Mexico, including Baja California), Aerocaribe (the south-east and Gulf coast), Aerolitoral (central highlands and Gulf coast), Aeromar (central highlands), Aviacsa (south-east), Saro (about a dozen cities around the country) and TAESA (about 20 cities around the country). Most of these will be included in travel agents' computerised reservation systems both in Mexico and abroad, but you may find it difficult or impossible to get information on the smallest airlines until you get to a city served by them.

Aerolitoral and Aeromar are feeder airlines for Aeroméxico and normally share its ticket offices. A similar arrangement applies between Aerocaribe and its owner Mexicana.

Information on flights is given in the city sections of this book. It's well worth shopping around between airlines as fares can vary a lot. Some real bargain-basement fares may be offered by the smaller airlines – often with similar comfort, service and safety standards to Mexicana and Aeroméxico. Though a few excursion (fixed-date return) fares are available, generally return fares are simply twice the price of one-ways. If you're going to fly a lot in south-east Mexico, you might consider Aerocaribe's Mayapass deal (see the Cancún section).

Depending on what fare you get, flying can still represent good value for money, especially considering the long, hot bus trip that may be the alternative. Here are some sample Aeroméxico/Mexicana one-way fares from Mexico City (including domestic airport tax of 25 pesos and the 10% IVA consumer tax, which are usually included in quoted fares):

Acapulco	350 pesos
Cancún	900 pesos
Ciudad Juárez	1040 pesos
Guadalajara	390 pesos
Monterrey	530 pesos
Oaxaca	310 pesos
Tijuana	990 pesos
Villahermosa	520 pesos

Smaller airlines may offer much lower fares.

BUS

Intercity buses are frequent and go almost everywhere, typically for 7 to 10 pesos per hour (50 to 80 km) of travel on deluxe or 1st-class buses. For trips of up to three or four hours on busy routes, you can usually just go to the bus terminal, buy a ticket and head out without too much delay. For longer trips, or trips on routes with infrequent service, book a ticket at least a day in advance and preferably two or three.

Immediate cash refunds of 80% to 100% are often available if you cancel your ticket more than three hours before the listed departure time. This allows you to book ahead, but to change your mind as well. To check whether it applies, ask '¿Hay cancelaciones?'.

On long journeys it helps to work out which side of the bus the sun will be on, and sit on the other side. If the bus is not air-con, it's a good idea to get a seat where you can control the opening and shutting of the window – Mexicans often have different ideas from yours about what's too warm or too cool! If the bus is air-con, carry a sweater or jacket with you.

Conventional wisdom on luggage is of two minds. One says you should keep your luggage with you in the passenger compartment, where, under your watchful eye, it will be safer. The other says you should have it safely locked in the luggage compartment underneath. We suggest that you carry your valuables on your person in a money belt or pouch, and store most of your stuff in the luggage compartment on deluxe and 1st-class buses. Don't allow it to be hoisted on to the open luggage rack atop a 2nd-class bus unless you feel you can keep an eye on it (which is nearly impossible).

Food and drink in bus stations is overpriced: you'd do well to stock up before reaching the bus station. Drinks and snacks are provided on some deluxe services. The better buses have toilets but it's worth carrying some toilet paper.

Terminals & Schedules

Most cities and towns have a single, modern, main bus station where all long-distance buses arrive and depart. This is called the Central Camionera, Central de Autobuses, Terminal de Autobuses, Central de Camiones or simply El Central, and is usually on the outskirts, a long way from the centre of town, to reduce heavy city-centre traffic. Frequent city buses link bus stations with town centres. Note the crucial difference between the *Central* (bus station) and the *Centro* (town centre). Sometimes there are separate Centrales for deluxe/1st-class and 2nd-class buses.

If there is no single main terminal, the different bus companies will have their own terminals scattered around town.

Most bus lines have schedules posted at their ticket desks in the bus station, but these aren't always comprehensive, so ask. If your destination isn't listed, it may be en route to one that is. From big towns, many different bus companies may be competing on the same routes, so compare fares and classes of service before you buy a ticket.

Classes

Long-distance buses range enormously in quality from comfortable, nonstop, air-con deluxe services to decaying, suspensionless ex-city buses grinding out their dying years on dirt tracks to remote settlements. The differences between classes are no longer clear-cut and the terms *de lujo* and *primera clase* can cover quite a wide range of levels of comfort. All of them offer a combination of features like extra legroom, reclining seats, drinks, snacks or videos. (You'll get heartily sick of *Rambo*-type movies if you spend much time on Mexican intercity buses!) But broadly, buses fall into three categories:

Deluxe – *De lujo* services run mainly on the busier routes. They bear names like Plus, GL or Ejecutivo. The buses are swift, new, comfortable and air-con. The cost may be just 10% or 20% higher than 1st-class, or may be double for the most luxurious lines like ETN and UNO, which offer reclining seats, plenty of legroom, few or no stops, and snacks, hot and cold drinks, videos and toilets on board. Cheaper deluxe buses have fewer of these amenities. Except on the busiest routes you should book your ticket in advance.

1st-class – *Primera (1a) clase* buses have a comfortable numbered (*numerado*) seat for each passenger, and often videos. They may have air-con, and usually a toilet. They make infrequent stops and serve all sizeable towns. As with deluxe buses you must buy your ticket in the bus station before boarding. From smaller towns these may be the best buses available – their standards of comfort are usually perfectly adequate.

2nd-class – *Segunda (2a) clase* buses serve small towns and villages, and also offer cheaper, slower travel on some intercity routes. A few are almost as quick and comfortable as 1st-class buses and may even have videos; others are old, tatty, uncomfortable, more prone to break down, and considerably slower because they'll stop anywhere for someone to get on or off. Except on some major runs, there's usually no apparent limit on capacity, which means that if you board mid-route you might not be seated (*sentado*) but standing (*parado*). (Don't confuse parado with parada, bus stop.) If you board mid-route you pay your fare to the conductor. Fares are about 10% or 20% less than 1st class.

Types of Service

It is also important to know the type of service offered.

Sin escalas – nonstop
Directo – very few stops
Semi-directo – a few more stops than directo
Ordinario – stops wherever passengers want to get on or off; deluxe and 1st-class buses are never ordinario
Express – nonstop on short to medium trips, very few stops on longer trips
Local – bus that starts its journey at the bus station you're in: you usually get a numbered seat in advance on *locales*, and they usually leave on time
De paso – a bus which started its journey somewhere else, but which is stopping to let down and take on passengers. Often late, a de paso bus may or may not have empty seats, and you may have to wait until it arrives before any tickets are sold.
Viaje redondo – return (round trip); return tickets are only available on some journeys, most starting in Mexico City.

TRAIN

The Ferrocarriles Nacionales de México (Mexican National Railways) have a chequered reputation, perhaps because they offer chequered service. Some trains are fairly comfortable and, though slower than buses, are sometimes cheaper and more atmospheric. One Mexican rail trip, the spectacular Copper Canyon railway between Chihuahua and Los Mochis, is deservedly a major visitor attraction in its own right. Unhappily, the better trains are decreasing in number as the railways decline in the face of fierce

competition from buses. Other trains are mediocre to unpleasant; yet others are ridiculous and downright unsafe.

As a rule, major trains north and west of the Isthmus of Tehuantepec (Mexico's narrow 'waist') are worth considering. East of the isthmus, service is very poor and the trains are renowned for theft and robbery. Take a bus or the plane, or prepare for unpleasantness.

Classes

Most travellers will probably prefer to take 1st-class seats or sleepers; 2nd class is strictly for the more adventurous. Many trains have only one or two classes, and the better the classes, the less slow the train is likely to be, with fewer stops. *Rápido* or *express* trains may lack segunda clase carriages; slow *local* trains may be segunda-clase only, or even *mixto* (mixed 2nd-class and freight).

Primera (1a) especial – 'special 1st-class' carriages are air-con, with reclining seats better than those in primera regular. It's advisable to buy tickets in advance. Fares are around the same as 1st-class buses, and may include boxed meals of a decent standard (though you should take extra drinks and supplementary food). Some top trains are all primera especial. Middle-class Mexicans consider primera especial the 'basic' class of train service.

Primera (1a) regular – 'regular 1st-class' carriages are better than 2nd-class, but not air-con. Fares are little more than half those in primera especial. You must beware of pickpockets and luggage thieves. Seats can be booked in advance.

Segunda (2a) clase – 2nd-class carriages are usually dirty, hot, overcrowded and uncomfortable, and sometimes rife with pickpockets and livestock. The poorest Mexicans walk; the next poorest ride segunda. Fares are little over half those of primera regular. If you're an adventurous sort with plenty of time at your disposal who wants to see the 'real Mexico' at the lowest possible cost, you might consider segunda. Most of the best trains don't have 2nd-class carriages.

Coche dormitorio – Sleeping car, only available on a handful of trains. The fare includes good presentable meals in a dining car. There are two types of accommodation, both of acceptable but not exceptional cleanliness:

Camarín – private 'roomette' with washbasin and toilet (under the seat/bed, which must be moved for use). At night, a berth folds out to fill the entire compartment. Camarines can take one or two people, each paying around double the cost of a primera especial seat.

Alcoba – private 'bedroom' with separate upper and lower berths which convert to seats during the day. The berths are comfortable for one adult each and minimum occupancy is two adults, but up to four adults and one child are permitted. Washbasin and toilet are always accessible. The fare per person is a little more than in a camarín.

Schedules & Ticketing

Information about rail services to/from particular cities, where they exist, is given in this book's city sections. Since nearly all the better trains terminate in Mexico City or Guadalajara, the fullest schedule and fare information is given in those cities' Getting There & Away sections. Details of schedules change quite often but the basics are fairly constant.

Mexico's top trains are listed in the *Thomas Cook Overseas Timetable*, perhaps the most convenient way to check current schedules outside Mexico. The timetable, published 12 times a year, is available in the UK from bookshops or from Thomas Cook Timetable Publishing Office (☎ (01733) 63961), PO Box 36, Peterborough PE3 6SB. In the USA it is on sale in good travel bookshops or by mail from Forsyth Travel Library (☎ (913) 384-3440), PO Box 2975, Shawnee Mission, KS 66201.

In Mexico you can get train schedule and ticketing information in English by calling ☎ 800-9-03-92, a toll-free number operated by the tourism ministry SECTUR. Start with the 91 long-distance access code if calling from outside Mexico City. At Mexico City's Buenavista Station you can pick up the free monthly *Rutas Ferroviarias* timetable from the Departamento Tráfico de Pasajeros.

Coche dormitorio, primera especial and primera regular tickets can be bought up to one month ahead; for some trains they will still be available on the day of travel but it's advisable to buy them in advance if you can. You can buy tickets for trains from Mexico City at stations in other main Mexican cities

– allow two or three days for the procedures to go through. Segunda clase tickets are sold only on the day of departure.

In the USA you can book Mexican train tickets (coche dormitorio or primera clase only), at some extra cost, through Mexico by Rail (☎ 1-800-321-1699), PO Box 2782, Laredo, TX 78044. You must pay 10 days before you travel.

CAR & MOTORBIKE

Driving in Mexico is not as easy as it is in North America, but it is often easier and more convenient than the bus and sometimes the only way to get to some of the most beautiful places or isolated towns and villages. See the Getting There & Away chapter for information about the requirements for bringing a vehicle into Mexico, and the Language section in Facts about the Country for some useful Spanish words and phrases for drivers.

Traffic laws, speed limits etc rarely seem to be enforced on the highways. In the cities, you'll want to obey the laws strictly so as not to give the police an excuse to hit you with a 'fine' payable on the spot.

Fuel & Service

All petrol *(gasolina)* and diesel in Mexico is sold by the government's monopoly, Pemex (Petróleos Mexicanos), for cash (no credit cards). Motor oil and other automotive fluids are sold by Pemex and by foreign companies. Most towns, even small ones, have a Pemex station and they are pretty common on most major roads; new Pemex stations are going up everywhere. Nevertheless, in remote areas it's better to fill up when you can.

Unleaded petrol is now available at just about every Pemex station. It's called Magna Sin and is sold from green pumps. It's 87 octane by US standards (92 octane by Mexican standards). If you have an old car that needs leaded fuel, get Nova, from the blue pump, which is 80 octane by US standards (82 by Mexican standards). A higher-octane Nova Plus is available in some places. Diesel fuel, in red or purple pumps, is also widely available.

At 1994 rates Magna Sin cost 1.33 pesos per litre; about 5 pesos (US$1.50) per US gallon. This is more than the typical US price for unleaded, and the fuel is of a lower octane rating as well. Standard Nova leaded cost 1.27 pesos per litre. Unleaded Diesel Sin cost 1.02 pesos per litre. Mexican fuel is cheap compared with European, Asian or Australian prices.

All stations have pump attendants, but they are not always trustworthy. When buying fuel, it's better to ask for a peso amount than to say *lleno* (full) – lleno usually finishes with fuel gushing down the side of your car. Check that the pump registers zero pesos to start, and be quick to check afterwards that you have been given the amount you requested – the attendants often reset the pump immediately and start to serve another customer. Don't have the attendants do your petrol, oil and water all at once or you may not get what you paid for. Pressure gauges on air hoses are often absent, so carry and use your own.

Road Conditions

Mexican highways, even the new toll highways, are not up to the standards of European or North American ones. Still, the main roads are serviceable and fairly fast when traffic is not heavy. A common problem is very steep shoulders, so if your wheels go off the road surface the car tilts alarmingly. Sometimes there's a deep gutter, and if you go into it you may roll the car. Driving at night is especially dangerous – unlit vehicles, rocks and livestock on the roads are common. Hijacks and robberies do occur.

Road tolls (*cuotas*) have become more common and more expensive. There are usually alternative free roads, but if the toll road is overpriced the free road becomes overloaded – it's not uncommon for a brand new four-lane highway (*autopista*) to be deserted while a parallel road is breaking up under the burden of every truck, bus and car on the route. State and federal toll roads can be relatively cheap, but they may also be second-rate, undivided roads with potholes. Some of the privatised highways are excellent, but the tolls can be exorbitant, like the 400-km Mexico City to Acapulco stretch which costs a total of 255 pesos.

In towns and cities you must be especially wary of stop (*alto*) signs, speed bumps (*topes*) and potholes. These are often not where you'd expect, and missing one can cost you in traffic fines or car damage. One-way streets are the rule in towns: usually alternating streets run in opposite directions – if you cross one that's west-bound only, the next one will probably go east.

Maps

Town and country roads are often poorly or idiosyncratically signposted. It pays to get the best road maps you can. Michelin are excellent but hard to find in Mexico. The American Automobile Association (AAA) map is quite good but not detailed enough. The 'Travelogs' which Sanborns insurance supplies free to its customers are very detailed and can be very useful. Many Mexican road maps of Mexico are available, especially in Mexico City. Guía Roja maps are just adequate, but hard to read. The *Mapa de la República Mexicana 9600* is pretty clear and fairly up-to-date.

Parking

It's difficult to park in many cities. If a vehicle is parked illegally the inspectors remove its licence plates (*placadas*) and the owner has to go to the municipal office, *transito* headquarters or police station and pay a fine to get them back. It's inadvisable to park in the street overnight, and most cheap city hotels don't provide parking. Sometimes you can leave a car out front and the night porter will keep an eye on it. Usually you have to use a commercial *estacionamiento*, which might cost 30 pesos overnight and 3 pesos per hour during the day. Hotels with parking tend to be more expensive.

Breakdown Assistance

Ángeles Verdes (Green Angels) are bilingual mechanics in bright green trucks. They patrol each major stretch of highway in

Mexico at least twice daily searching for motorists in trouble. They make minor repairs, replace small parts, provide fuel and oil, and arrange towing and other assistance by radio if necessary. Service is free; parts, petrol and oil are provided at cost. If you are near a telephone when your car has problems, you can contact them through the national 24-hour tourist information number in Mexico City (☎ (5) 250-01-23/51).

Most serious mechanical problems can be fixed efficiently and inexpensively by mechanics in towns and cities as long as the parts are available. Volkswagen, Ford, Nissan/Datsun, Chrysler and General Motors parts are the easiest to obtain; others may have to be ordered from the USA. For parts suppliers, consult the Yellow Pages telephone directory under *Refacciones y Acesorios para Automóviles y Camiones*. For authorised dealer service, look under *Automóviles – Agencias*.

Accidents

Under Mexico's legal system, persons involved in an incident are assumed to be guilty until proven innocent. They can be detained until the matter is resolved, perhaps weeks or months later. For minor accidents, drivers will probably be released if they have insurance to cover any property damage they may have caused. If it's a serious accident, involving injury or death, the drivers may be held until the authorities determine who is responsible. The guilty party will not be released until he/she guarantees restitution to the victims and payment of any fines. Your embassy can help only by recommending a lawyer, and contacting friends or family at home. Adequate insurance cover is the only real protection.

Rental

Car rental is expensive, but can be worthwhile if you want to visit several places in a short time and have three or four people to share the cost. It can also be useful for going off the beaten track where public transport is slow or scarce.

Cars can be hired in most of Mexico's

cities, at airports and sometimes at bus and train stations. Most big hotels can arrange a car. Sometimes it is necessary to book a week or more ahead.

Renters must have valid driver's licences and passports, and are usually required to be at least 21 years of age (sometimes 25). A major credit card is needed, or a huge cash deposit. You should ensure that the price you're quoted includes all taxes, insurance costs, drop-off charges etc. You should also get a signed rental agreement and read its small print.

In addition to the basic daily or weekly rental rate, you must pay for insurance, tax, a per-km charge, and fuel. Some agencies offer rates for unlimited distance, which are often preferable if you intend to do some hard driving (if you don't, why are you renting a car?). Prices vary a lot from city to city, and tend to be lower in the biggest cities and major tourist resorts. Within each city, rates are often fairly similar, but it's still worth shopping around. For one day in a Volkswagen Beetle – often the cheapest car available – you could pay a total of anywhere between 170 and 380 pesos.

Major international companies like Hertz, National, Budget and Avis all operate in Mexico. There are also local firms. With the large firms, reserving from outside Mexico may sometimes get you lower rates. In the USA call Hertz (☎ 800-654-3131), National (☎ 800-328-4567), Budget (☎ 800-527-0700) or Avis (☎ 800-331-2112).

Where car hire is particularly useful, and where good deals exist, we've put details in city sections.

BICYCLE

Cycling can be a great way to travel Mexico if you're prepared for some rough roads and climatic challenges like altitude and tropical heat, are experienced in long-distance cycling, and, preferably, have a companion. You can get off the beaten track and take routes along minor roads that other travellers miss – but be careful with safety in isolated rural areas. Mexico is reasonably well supplied with bike shops, but of course you should take as many spares as you can. Mirrors on your handlebars are useful for warning of the approach of inconsiderate drivers who come too close. *Bicycling Mexico* by Ericka Weisbroth & Eric Ellman (Hunter Publishing, Edison, NJ, 1990) is a useful guide.

HITCHING

Travellers who decide to hitch should understand that they are taking a small but potentially serious risk. A woman alone certainly should not hitch in Mexico, and two women alone are not advised to. However, many people do choose to hitch, and it's not an uncommon way of getting to or from off-the-beaten-track archaeological sites and other places that are poorly served by bus. It's less common along the highways and main roads, but possible if you have a sign and don't look scruffy. Be alert to possible dangers wherever you are. If in doubt, ask local advice about safety.

If the driver is another tourist or a private motorist, you may get the ride for free. If it is a work or commercial vehicle, you should expect (and offer) to pay.

BOAT

Vehicle and passenger ferries connect Baja California with the Mexican mainland at Santa Rosalía/Guaymas, La Paz/Mazatlán and La Paz/Topolobampo. Ferries also run to the islands Isla Mujeres, Cozumel and Isla Holbox off the Yucatán Peninsula. For details, see the relevant town or island sections.

LOCAL TRANSPORT
Bus

Generally known as *camiones*, local buses are the cheapest way of getting around cities and to nearby villages. They run everywhere, frequently, and are dirt cheap (fares in cities are rarely more than 1 peso). Older buses are often noisy, dirty and crowded but in some cities there are fleets of small, modern microbuses which are more pleasant. In cities buses halt only at specific points (*paradas*), which may or may not be marked.

Mexico City buses are notorious haunts for thieves and pickpockets, so be careful.

Colectivo, Combi & Pesero

Colectivos are minibuses, minivans or big cars functioning as a halfway house between taxis and buses. (A *combi* is a VW minibus and a *pesero* is Mexico City's word for colectivo.) They're cheaper than taxis, quicker and less crowded than buses. They run along set routes – sometimes displayed on the windscreen – and will pick you up or drop you on any corner along that route.

If you're not at the start of a colectivo route, go to the kerb and wave your hand when you see one. As the driver approaches, he may indicate how many places are free by holding up the appropriate number of fingers. Tell the driver where you want to go; you normally pay at the end of the trip. The fare usually depends on how far you go.

Taxi

Taxis are common in towns and cities. They're often surprisingly economical, and useful if you have a lot of baggage, or need to get from A to B quickly, or are worried about theft on public transport. In many cities most taxis are Volkswagen Beetles. Some taxis, especially in Mexico City, have meters. If a taxi has a meter, ask the driver if it's working (*'¿Funciona el taxímetro?'*). If it's not, or if the taxi doesn't have a meter, establish the price of the ride *before* getting in (this usually involves a bit of haggling).

Some airports and big bus stations have taxi *taquillas* (kiosks) where you buy a fixed-price ticket to your destination then hand it to the driver instead of paying cash. This can save haggling and major rip-offs but fares are usually higher than you could get outside on the street.

Finding Your Way in Cities

Mexican street naming and numbering can be quite confusing. When asking directions, it's better to ask for a specific place, such as the Hotel Central or the Museo Regional, than for the street it's on. To achieve any degree of certainty, ask at least three people.

Mexico City

• *pop: 20 million* • *alt: 2240 metres*

Mexico City is a place to love and loathe. Spread across more than 2000 sq km of a single highland valley, it encapsulates the best and worst of Mexico the country. The result is a seething, cosmopolitan megalopolis that is in turn exhilarating and overpowering. One moment Mexico City is music, colour and life; the next it's drabness, overcrowding and bad smells. This is a city of colonial palaces, world-renowned cultural treasures – and sprawling slums; of ear-splitting traffic and quiet, peaceful plazas; of surprising wealth and miserable poverty; of green parks and brown air.

Mexico City is known to Mexicans simply as México – pronounced, like the country, 'MEH-hee-ko'. If they want to distinguish it from Mexico the country, they call it either *la ciudad de México* or *el DF* ('el de EFF-e') – the Distrito Federal (Federal District) in which half the city, including all its central areas, lies. (The outlying parts of Mexico City are in the state of México, which rings the Distrito Federal on three sides.)

HISTORY

As early as 10,000 BC, humans and animals were attracted to the shores of a lake, Lago de Texcoco, that covered much of the floor of the Valley of Mexico. Some time after 7500 BC the lake began to shrink and hunting became more difficult, so the inhabitants turned to agriculture, developing techniques such as chinampas, or 'floating gardens', versions of which are still seen in Xochimilco on the southern outskirts of Mexico City.

A loose federation of farming villages had evolved around Lago de Texcoco by approximately 200 BC, but the big influence in the region was Teotihuacán, a rapidly developing city 25 km north-east of the lake. After centuries as the capital of an empire stretching to Guatemala and beyond, Teotihuacán fell in the 7th century AD. The power vacuum was eventually filled by an empire based at Tula, 65 km north of modern Mexico City, whose people, known as the Toltecs, had probably arrived as a nomadic Chichimec tribe from the north.

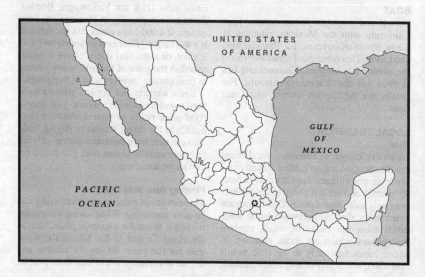

The Aztecs

By the 13th century the Tula empire had also collapsed, leaving a number of small city-states around the lake to compete for control of the Valley of Mexico. But it was the Mexica ('meh-SHEE-kah') or Aztecs, another Chichimec tribe from the north, who eventually came out on top.

The Aztecs had settled on the western shore of the Lago de Texcoco, but other valley inhabitants objected to Aztec interference in their relations, and to practices like wife-stealing, and human sacrifice to appease their guardian god, Huizilopochtli. By the early 14th century Coxcox, the leader of Culhuacán on the southern shore of the lake, had the Aztecs working as serfs, but when they won a battle against nearby Xochimilco for him (sending him 8000 human ears as proof of their victory), he granted them land and even agreed that they could make his daughter an Aztec goddess. He didn't know what this would entail, however. As described in *The Course of Mexican History* by Michael Meyer & William Sherman:

...the princess was sacrificed and flayed. When her father attended the banquet in his honour, he was horrified to find that the entertainment included a dancer dressed in the skin of his daughter...Coxcox raised an army which scattered the barbarians...

Some time between 1325 and 1345 the Aztecs, wandering around the swampy fringes of the lake, finally founded their own city, Tenochtitlán, on an island near the lake's western shore. The site was chosen, according to legend, because there they saw an eagle standing on a cactus eating a snake – a sign, they believed, that they should stop their wanderings and build a city.

About 1370 the Aztecs began to serve as successful mercenaries for the expanding kingdom of Azcapotzalco on the western shore of the lake. When the Aztecs' own growing strength finally led them to rebel against Azcapotzalco about 1427, they became the greatest power in the valley.

Tenochtitlán rapidly grew into a sophisti-cated city-state whose empire would, by the early 16th century, extend across most of central Mexico from the Pacific to the Gulf and down into far southern Mexico. At the same time the Aztecs' sense of their own importance as the chosen people of the voracious Huizilopochtli was growing too. In the mid-15th century they formed a Triple Alliance with the lakeshore states Texcoco and Tlacopan, to conduct the so-called 'Flowery Wars' against Tlaxcala and Huejotzingo, which lay east of the valley. The purpose was to gain a steady supply of the prisoners needed to satisfy Huizilopochtli's vast hunger for sacrificial victims, so that the sun would continue to rise each day and floods and famines could be avoided. On one occasion in 1487, no less than 20,000 prisoners were sacrificed in four days to dedicate Tenochtitlán's newly rebuilt main temple.

The peace and prosperity at the heart of the Aztec empire allowed them to build an immense city of canals, streets, gardens and pyramid-temples. At its heart, roughly where the Mexico City Zócalo is today, stood the main temple with its double pyramid dedicated to Huizilopochtli and the water god Tláloc; three causeways linked the city to the lake shore. This was the city that amazed the Spanish when they arrived in 1519, by which time its population was an estimated 200,000. (See Facts about the Country for the story of the Spanish conquest.)

Capital of New Spain

Wrecked during and after the Spanish conquest, Tenochtitlán was rebuilt as a Spanish city. By 1550 it was the beautiful, thriving capital of New Spain. Broad, straight streets were laid out and buildings constructed to Spanish designs in local materials such as *tezontle*, a light-red, porous volcanic rock that the Aztecs had used for their temples. Hospitals, schools, churches, palaces, cathedrals, parks, a university and even an insane asylum were built.

During the 16th and 17th centuries the city flourished as the prosperous and elegant, if somewhat insanitary, hub of a politically centralised New Spain. But it was not without problems. In 1779-80 nearly 20% of its population died of smallpox, and right up to the late 19th century the city suffered floods caused by the partial destruction in the 1520s of the Aztecs' canals. Lago de Texcoco often overflowed into the city, damaging streets and buildings, causing disease and forcing the relocation of thousands of people.

Independence

On 30 October 1810, 80,000 pro-independence rebels, led by the priest Miguel Hidalgo, had Mexico City at their mercy after defeating Spanish forces at Las Cruces outside the capital. But Hidalgo decided against advancing on the city – a mistake which cost Mexico 11 more years of fighting before independence was achieved. Eventually the former royalist general Agustín de Iturbide entered Mexico City with a victorious pro-independence army in 1821. The city at this time had a population of 160,000, which made it the biggest in the Americas.

Mexico City entered the modern age under the despotic Porfirio Díaz, who held power for most of the period from 1876 to 1911 and attracted a great deal of foreign investment. Díaz ushered in an unprecedented building boom in the city and had railways constructed to link it to the provinces and the USA. Some 150 km of electric tramways provided urban transport. Industry expanded and by 1910 the city had 471,000 inhabitants. A drainage canal with two tunnels finally succeeded in drying up a large part of the Lago de Texcoco, allowing the city to expand further, but this brought a host of new problems by causing ground levels to sink – which they continue to do today, with damage to many notable buildings. Díaz's most famous project was one of his last: *El Ángel,* the monument to Mexico's independence on Paseo de la Reforma.

The 20th Century

After Díaz fell in 1911, the chaos of the Mexican revolution stopped most new building projects, and brought warfare and hunger to the city's streets.

The 1920s ushered in peace and a modicum of prosperity as political stability was regained and the economy was rebuilt. The post-revolution Minister of Education, José Vasconcelos, commissioned Mexico's top artists – among them Diego Rivera, David Alfaro Siqueiros and José Clemente Orozco – to decorate numerous public buildings with dramatic, large-scale murals conveying a clear sense of Mexico's past and present. This was the start of a major trend in Mexican art, with a lasting impact on the face of the capital.

The growth and reconstruction of Mexico City were halted by the Depression, but afterwards a drive to industrialise attracted more and more money and people to the city; the population was 1,726,858 by 1940. Mexico City was growing into the urban monster of both great beauty and extreme ugliness that we know today. In the 1940s and 1950s factories and skyscrapers rose almost as quickly as the population, which was growing at an average 7% a year. But the supply of housing, jobs and social services could not keep pace with the influx of people; shanty towns started to appear around the city's fringes, and Mexico City's modern problems began to take shape.

Recent Times

Despite continued economic growth into the 1960s, political and social reform lagged far behind. Student-led discontent with the government came to a head as Mexico City prepared for the 1968 Olympic Games, the first ever held in a Third World country. Half a million people rallied against the government in the Zócalo on 27 August. On 2 October, 10 days before the games started, about 5000 to 10,000 people gathering at the Plaza de las Tres Culturas in Tlatelolco, north of the city centre, were encircled by troops and police. To this day, no one is certain how many people died in the ensuing massacre, but estimates have been put at 300 to 400.

Mexico City continued to grow at a frightening rate in the 1970s, spreading beyond the Distrito Federal into the state of México and developing some of the world's worst traffic and pollution problems, only partly alleviated by the metro system opened in 1969. In the mid-1970s rises in world oil prices spawned an economic boom in the city, but when the price dropped again in the early 1980s the ensuing recession brought people migrating in droves – 2000 to 3000 a day – from the countryside hoping to find work in the capital.

People have continued to pour into Mexico City despite the earthquake on 19 September 1985, which registered more than eight on the Richter scale, killed at least 8000 people (possibly 20,000), displaced thousands more, and caused more than US$4 billion in damage to hundreds of buildings.

By 1990 the population of Mexico City and adjacent areas was estimated at 20 million, about a quarter of the national total, making it one of the world's most populous and most crowded metropolitan areas. Overcrowding and extremes of wealth have brought high crime rates. Predictions have been made of over 30 million people by the year 2000.

Mexico City is the centre of Mexico's industry, retail trade, finance, communication and culture. It has more than 450 industrial plants – about half the country's industries – and as many as 70% of Mexico's banking transactions occur here. Tourism is also a big industry: more than a million tourists visit annually. The city has 20 daily newspapers (whose circulation accounts for more than half of the country's total), 30 radio stations and several TV stations.

Efforts to move industry and government jobs away from the capital have so far been minimal, and there's little reason to believe that Mexico City's difficulties won't get worse. But it remains a magnet to Mexicans and visitors alike because, as one Mexican put it, *'Lo que ocurre en México, ocurre en el DF'* (What happens in Mexico, happens in Mexico City).

ORIENTATION

Mexico City's 350 *colonias*, or neighbourhoods, sprawl across the ancient bed of Lago de Texcoco and beyond. Though this vast urban expanse is daunting at first, the main areas of interest to visitors are fairly well defined and easily traversable.

El Zócalo

The historic heart of the city is the wide plaza known as El Zócalo (metro: Zócalo), surrounded by the Palacio Nacional, the Catedral Metropolitana and the excavated site of the Templo Mayor, the main temple of Aztec Tenochtitlán. The neighbourhoods north, west and south of the Zócalo have many good, economical hotels and restaurants.

Alameda Central & Bellas Artes

Avenida Madero (for eastbound traffic) and Avenida Cinco de Mayo (or 5 de Mayo, for westbound traffic) link the Zócalo with the verdant park named the Alameda Central, seven blocks to the west (metro: Hidalgo or Bellas Artes). On the east side of the Alameda stands the magnificent Palacio de Bellas Artes. The major north-south thoroughfare running along the east side of the Bellas Artes is Avenida Lázaro Cárdenas. The landmark Torre Latinoamericana (Latin American Tower) pierces the sky a block south of the Bellas Artes on Lázaro Cárdenas.

Plaza de la República

Some 750 metres west of the Alameda across Paseo de la Reforma is the Plaza de la República (metro: Revolución), marked by the sombre, domed art deco-style Monumento a la Revolución. This is a fairly quiet, mostly residential area with many decent, moderately priced hotels.

Paseo de la Reforma

Mexico City's grandest boulevard runs for many km across the city's heart, connecting the Alameda to the Zona Rosa and Bosque de Chapultepec. Major hotels, embassies and banks rise on either side. Landmark *glorietas* (traffic circles) along its route are marked with statues, including those commemorating Cristóbal Colón (Christopher Columbus);

Cuauhtémoc, the last Aztec emperor (at the intersection with Avenida Insurgentes); and Mexican independence (the Monumento a la Independencia, or *El Ángel*).

Zona Rosa

The Zona Rosa (Pink Zone; metro: Insurgentes) is the high-life and nightlife district anchored on the Monumento a la Independencia and bounded by Paseo de la Reforma on the north, Avenida Insurgentes on the east, and Avenida Varsovia on the west. Many top hotels, restaurants, clubs and boutiques cluster here. It's a fascinating place for a stroll, and if you know where to look, it can yield some good budget surprises as well.

Bosque de Chapultepec

The Wood of Chapultepec, generally known to gringos as Chapultepec Park, is to the west of the aforementioned districts (metro: Chapultepec or Auditorio). It's Mexico City's 'lungs', a large expanse of trees, gardens and artificial lakes, and holds most of the city's major museums, including the renowned Museo Nacional de Antropología, and Chapultepec Castle, now officially the Museo Nacional de Historia. Polanco and Lomas de Chapultepec, two wealthy residential areas, lie north and west of the park respectively.

North of the Centre

Estación Buenavista, the city's train station, is 1.2 km north of the Plaza de la República. The Plaza de las Tres Culturas at Tlatelolco (metro: Tlatelolco), with Indian, colonial and modern buildings, is two km north of the Alameda. Five km north of the Alameda is the Terminal Norte, the largest of the city's four major bus terminals (metro: Autobuses del Norte). Six km north of the Zócalo is the Basílica de Guadalupe (metro: La Villa), Mexico's most revered shrine.

South of the Centre

Avenida Insurgentes, the city's major north-south axis, connects the centre to most points of interest in the south. Ten to 15 km south of the Alameda are the charming former villages of San Ángel (metro: M A de Quevedo) and Coyoacán (metro: Viveros, Coyoacán or General Anaya), and the vast campus of the Universidad Nacional Autónoma de México (National Autonomous University of Mexico; metro: Copilco). Also down here is the Terminal Sur (metro: Tasqueña), the southern intercity bus station. Further south, about 20 km from the Alameda, are the floating gardens of Xochimilco.

Finding an Address

Some major streets, such as Avenida Insurgentes, keep the same name for many km, but the names – and numbering systems – of many lesser streets change every few blocks. In some neighbourhoods, street names concentrate on a particular subject, such as famous writers, rivers, or Mexican states. Many of the streets near the Zócalo are named after Latin American countries while streets in the Zona Rosa are named after European cities.

Street addresses normally include the name of the colonia. Except for well-known city centre districts, you may need help in finding a particular colonia. Often the easiest way to find an address is by asking where it is in relation to the nearest metro station.

INFORMATION
Tourist Offices

Mexico City has three tourist information offices in central areas. There are others at the airport and the Terminal Oriente (TAPO) bus station (see the Getting There & Away section).

SECTUR (☎ (5) 250-01-23 or (5) 250-01-51) at Avenida Presidente Masaryk 172, on the corner of Hegel, in the Polanco district about 600 metres north of the Museo Nacional de Antropología, stocks lots of information for tourists on the city and country of Mexico, including a good free map of both. The office, open Monday to Friday from 8 am to 8 pm, is helpful and has multilingual staff – but is less conveniently located than the Mexico City tourism office in the Zona Rosa. You can take the metro to

Polanco and walk one block south on Avenida Arquímedes, then four blocks east on Avenida Masaryk.

SECTUR's ☎ 250-01-23 and ☎ 250-01-51 phone lines are open 24 hours, seven days a week to provide tourist information and help with tourist problems and emergencies. If you are not in Mexico City, you can call these numbers collect (reverse charge).

Mexico City's own tourism office, the Dirección General de Turismo de la Ciudad de México (☎ (5) 525-93-80 to -83), is at Amberes 54, corner of Londres, in the Zona Rosa (metro: Insurgentes). The English-speaking staff are helpful and can provide a good free map of the city and country. Hours are from 9 am to 9 pm daily. During these hours, telephone queries can also be answered in English.

The Mexico City National Chamber of Commerce (Cámara Nacional de Comercio de la Ciudad de México; ☎ (5) 592-26-77), at Paseo de la Reforma 42 between Avenidas Juárez and Morelos, also has a helpful tourist office – though its map is not free. Hours are Monday to Friday from 9 am to 2 pm and 3 to 6 pm.

Money

Exchange rates can vary a few per cent between Mexico City's numerous money-changing outlets, so if you have time, it's worth checking two or three before you part with your money. Most banks and casas de cambio (exchange houses) will change both cash and travellers' cheques; some give a better rate for cash, others for travellers' cheques. Some places will only change US or Canadian dollars.

Banks Mexico City is full of banks, most open Monday to Friday from 9 am to 1.30 pm. Some branches will only do currency exchange at certain hours. But many banks have ATMs open 24 hours, seven days a week, and if you have a major international bank credit card or an ATM cash card you can usually withdraw money quickly and easily from these. The greatest concentration of banks, and of ATMs, in Mexico City is on

Paseo de la Reforma between the Monumento a Cristóbal Colón and the Monumento a la Independencia, but there are many others all over the city, including at the airport. See Money in the Facts for the Visitor chapter for more on using ATMs.

Casas de Cambio Casas de cambio have longer hours and quicker procedures than banks. For this you may get a worse exchange rate. There are dozens of casas de cambio in Mexico City: they're particularly numerous in the Zona Rosa and on Paseo de la Reforma between the Cristóbal Colón and Independencia monuments. Here are some we've found useful:

Near the Zócalo
   Casa de Cambio Bancomer, corner of 16 de Septiembre and Bolívar, open Monday to Friday from 9 am to 1.30 pm and 3 to 5 pm; reasonable rates for cash and travellers' cheques
Near the Alameda
   Casa de Cambio Plus, on the south side of Avenida Juárez facing the Alameda, open Monday to Friday from 9 am to 4 pm, Saturday 9.30 am to 2 pm; good rates for cash and travellers' cheques
Near Plaza de la República
   Casa de Cambio Catorce, Reforma 51 at Antonio Caso, open Monday to Friday from 9 am to 4 pm; good rates for cash and travellers' cheques
Zona Rosa & Nearby
   Asesorería Cambiaria, on Florencia at Reforma, open Monday to Friday from 9 am to 5.30 pm, Saturday 9 am to 1 pm; good rate for travellers' cheques, reasonable rate for cash
   Casa de Cambio Mexicana de Devisas, on Florencia at Reforma, open Monday to Friday from 9 am to 5 pm; good rates for cash and travellers' cheques
   Casa de Cambio Tiber, Río Tiber 112, 200 metres north of the Monumento a la Independencia, open Monday to Friday from 8.30 am to 5 pm, Saturday 8.30 am to 2 pm, Sunday 11.30 am to 6 pm; reasonable rates for cash and travellers' cheques
   Dollar Express, Liverpool 161 between Amberes and Florencia, open Monday to Friday from 8.30 am to 6 pm, Saturday 10.30 am to 5 pm; reasonable rates for cash and travellers' cheques
Airport
   There are several casas de cambio in the airport terminal. Some, including Tamize in Sala E, are open 24 hours.

MEXICO CITY

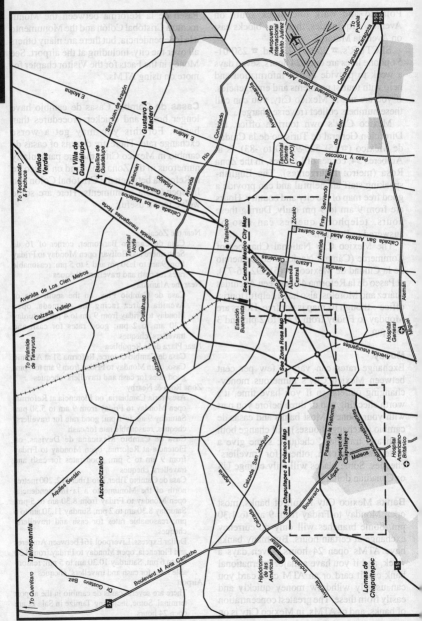

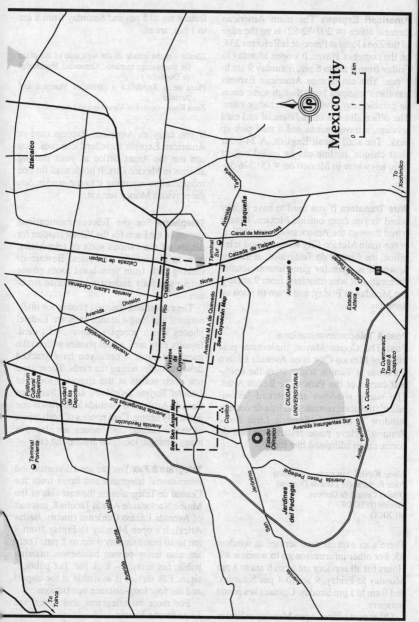

American Express The main American Express office (☎ 207-72-82) is on the edge of the Zona Rosa at Paseo de la Reforma 234, on the corner of Havre. It's open Monday to Friday from 9 am to 6 pm, Saturday 9 am to 1 pm. You can change American Express travellers' cheques here, though some casas de cambio may give better exchange rates. The office also has other financial and card services, a travel bureau and a mail pick-up desk. The staff speak English. A 24-hour 'lost cheque' hotline can be called collect from anywhere in Mexico on ☎ (5) 326-36-25.

Wire Transfers If you need to have money wired to you from outside Mexico, have it wired through the American Express office, or the main Mexico City telegram and telex office, the Central de Telégrafos, at Tacuba 8, which is open for giros internacionales (international wire transfers) from 9 am to 7 pm Monday to Friday, and 9 am to noon on Saturday.

Post & Telecommunications

Post The Correo Mayor, the central post office of Mexico City, is on Avenida Lázaro Cárdenas at Tacuba across from the north-east corner of the Palacio de Bellas Artes. The stamp windows are marked '*estampillas*'; the poste restante and lista de correos window is marked '*Entrega Lista Poste Restante*'. Have poste restante or lista de correos mail addressed like this:

Albert JONES (last name in capitals)
Poste Restante (or Lista de Correos)
Oficina Central de Correos
México 06002 DF
MEXICO

There's an express mail service at window 33. For other information go to window 49. Hours for all services are from 8 am to 8 pm Monday to Friday, 9 am to 4 pm Saturday, and 9 am to 1 pm Sunday. Upstairs is a postal museum.

Other post offices, open Monday to Friday from 8 am to 5 pm and Saturday from 8 am to 1 pm, are at:

Zócalo – in the arcade on the west side of the plaza (in the passage marked 'Almacenes Nacionales de Depósito')
Plaza de la República – corner of Mariscal and Arriaga
Zona Rosa – corner of Varsovia and Londres.

If you carry an American Express card or American Express travellers' cheques, you can use the Amex office as your mailing address in Mexico City. It holds mail for one month before returning it to the sender. See the previous Money section.

Telephone See the Telecommunications section of the Facts for the Visitor chapter for details on the various sorts of telephones, how to place calls, and rates. Beware of making calls from your hotel room phone before you fully understand the price structure!

The easiest and cheapest phones for international and long-distance calls are Ladatel phones which accept a major credit card. Equally easy are Ladatel phones which take telephone cards – once you have tracked down an outlet selling the cards. There are a few such outlets at the airport – look for *Ladatel Tarjeta Telefónica* signs; Sanborns Casa de Azulejos at Avenida Madero 4 is one in the city centre. Card phones of both types, as well as Ladatel coin phones, are placed in many strategic locations around the city.

Telegram & Fax You can send domestic and international telegrams and faxes from the Central de Telégrafos on the east side of the Museo Nacional de Arte at Tacuba 8, just east of Avenida Lázaro Cárdenas (metro: Bellas Artes). It's open Monday to Friday from 8 am to 10 pm, Saturday 9 am to 1 pm. There are also many private businesses offering public fax service – look for 'fax público' signs. Fax service is available at the airport and the four long-distance bus stations.

For more on telegrams and faxes, see Facts for the Visitor.

Foreign Embassies & Consulates

Embassies and consulates often keep limited business hours, and close on both Mexican and their own national holidays. It's best to telephone ahead to check hours and confirm that the address you're heading for is the right one for the service you want. The numbers at the end of the following addresses are postcodes, which can help you locate an embassy's street in an atlas such as the *Guía Roji Ciudad de México* (see Maps in this section), or on another map which gives postcodes.

Australia
Jaime Balmes 11, Plaza Polanco Torre B, 10th floor, Los Morales, 11510 (☎ (5) 395-99-88); open Monday to Friday from 10 am to 2 pm; metro: Polanco

Austria
Campos Elíseos 305, Polanco, 11560 (☎ (5) 280-69-19); metro: Auditorio

Belgium (Bélgica)
Musset 41, Polanco, 11550 (☎ (5) 545-00-08); metro: Polanco

Belize (Belice)
Thiers 152B, Anzures, 11590 (☎ (5) 203-56-42, 203-59-60); metro: Sevilla

Canada
Schiller 529, Polanco, 11560, 400 metres north of the Museo Nacional de Antropología (☎ (5) 254-32-88; emergencies 724-79-00); open Monday to Friday from 9 am to 1 pm and 2 to 5 pm; metro: Polanco

Colombia
Paseo de la Reforma 195, Cuauhtémoc, 06600, 500 metres east of the Monumento a la Independencia (☎ (5) 535-27-35)

Costa Rica
Río Po 113, Cuauhtémoc, 06500, near the Monumento a la Independencia (☎ (5) 525-77-64)

Cuba
Avenida Presidente Masaryk 554, Polanco, 11560 (☎ (5) 280-80-39); metro: Polanco

Denmark (Dinamarca)
Tres Picos 43, Polanco, 11580 (☎ (5) 255-34-05, 255-41-45); open Monday to Friday from 9 am to 1 pm; metro: Polanco

El Salvador
Paseo de las Palmas 1930, Lomas de Chapultepec, 11000 (☎ (5) 596-33-90, 596-73-66)

France (Francia)
Consulate: Alejandro Dumas 16, Polanco, 11560 (☎ (5) 281-44-64); open Monday to Friday from 9 am to 1 pm (for emergencies at other times, if no telephone reply at the consulate, call the embassy); metro: Auditorio

Embassy: Havre 15 between Reforma and Hamburgo, Zona Rosa, 06600 (☎ (5) 533-13-60 to 64)

Germany (Alemania)
Lord Byron 737, Polanco, 11560 (☎ (5) 280-54-09); open Monday to Friday from 9 am to noon; metro: Auditorio

Guatemala
Explanada 1025, Lomas de Chapultepec, 11000 (☎ (5) 540-75-20; consulate 520-92-49); consulate open Monday to Friday from 9 am to 1.30 pm

Honduras
Alfonso Reyes 220, Hipódromo Condesa, 06140 (☎ (5) 211-52-50, 515-66-89); metro: Juanacatlán

Israel
Sierra Madre 215, Lomas de Chapultepec, 11000 (☎ (5) 540-63-40)

Italy (Italia)
Paseo de las Palmas 1994, Lomas de Chapultepec, 11000 (☎ (5) 596-36-55)

Japan (Japón)
Paseo de la Reforma 395, 2nd floor, Cuauhtémoc, 06500, near the Monumento a la Independencia (☎ (5) 211-00-28, consulate 514-45-07)

Netherlands (Reino de los Paises Bajos)
Montes Urales Sur 635, 2nd floor, Lomas de Chapultepec, 11000 (☎ (5) 202-84-53, 202-83-46)

New Zealand (Nueva Zelandia)
Homero 229, 8th floor, Chapultepec Morales, 11570 (☎ (5) 250-59-99); open Monday to Friday from 9 am to 1.30 pm; metro: Polanco

Nicaragua
Avenida Nuevo León 144, Hipódromo, 06170 (☎ (5) 553-97-91); metro: Chilpancingo

Norway (Noruega)
Boulevard Virreyes 1460, Lomas de Chapultepec, 11000 (☎ (5) 540-34-86)

Panama
Campos Elíseos 111-1, Polanco, 11560 (☎ (5) 250-42-29; consulate ☎ 250-40-45); metro: Auditorio

Spain (España)
Consulate: Edgar A Poe 91, Polanco, 11560 (☎ (5) 280-45-08)

Embassy: Parque Vía Reforma 2105, Lomas de Chapultepec, 11000 (☎ (5) 596-18-33)

Sweden (Suecia)
Boulevard M Ávila Camacho 1, 6th floor, Lomas de Chapultepec, 11000 (☎ (5) 540-63-93)

Switzerland (Suiza)
Hamburgo 66, 4th floor, Zona Rosa, 06600 (☎ (5) 533-0735); metro: Insurgentes

UK (Gran Bretaña, Reino Unido)
Río Lerma 71 at Río Sena, Cuauhtémoc, 06500, not far from the Monumento a la Independencia (☎ (5) 207-24-49, 207-25-69; emergencies 207-20-89); open Monday to Friday from 8.30 am to 3.30 pm

USA (Estados Unidos de Norteamérica)
Paseo de la Reforma 305, Cuauhtémoc, 06500, not far from the Monumento a la Independencia (☎ (5) 211-00-42, always attended); open from 8.30 am to 5.30 pm Monday to Friday, closed on Mexican and American holidays; visa office at rear, on corner of Río Danubio and Río Lerma, open Monday to Friday from 8.30 to 11 am

Laundry & Dry Cleaning

Lavandería Automática at Edison 91, between Iglesias and Arriaga near the Plaza de la República (metro: Revolución), charges 9 pesos for five lb (2.25 kg) of washing and the same for drying. They will do it for you for a further 9 pesos. Hours are Monday to Friday from 10 am to 7 pm, Saturday 10 am to 6 pm.

Slightly further from the Plaza de la República, Lavandería Cocó at Antonio Caso 31A between Ignacio Vallarta and Montes (metro: Revolución), charges 9.60 pesos for three kg of washing, and a further 9.60 pesos for drying. They will do it all for you for 9.60 pesos. Hours are Monday to Saturday from 9 am to 8 pm, Sunday 9 am to 3 pm.

A reliable dry cleaner is Jiffy ('HEE-fee') on the corner of Río Tiber and Río Lerma, two blocks north of the Monumento a la Independencia on Reforma.

Bookshops

Mexico City has many bookshops with a good range of English-language titles. Top-end hotels and major museums often have bookstalls selling English-language books and other print media.

City Centre All these bookshops except the Templo Mayor are near Bellas Artes metro station:

American Bookstore, Avenida Madero 25, has many English-language books, and magazines and newspapers that are two or three days old. Hours are from 9.30 am to 6 pm daily except Sunday.
Gandhi, Avenida Juárez 4, a few steps west of Avenida Lázaro Cárdenas, is a good source of English-language books about Mexico and Mexico City.

Librería Británica, Madero 30A in the Hotel Ritz building, specialises in English-language books and magazines.
The Palacio de Bellas Artes has an excellent bookshop focusing mainly on the arts, with a fair range of English titles.
Templo Mayor, Calle Seminario just east of the Catedral Metropolitana, has a good little bookshop covering archaeological and anthropological topics (metro: Zócalo).

Near the Plaza de la República Sanborns on Reforma on the corner of Lafragua (metro: Revolución) has a good range of maps and English-language books and magazines.

Zona Rosa Useful bookshops in and around the Zona Rosa include the following:

Librairie Française, Génova 2 in the Zona Rosa (metro: Insurgentes), has a wide range of French books and French newspapers.
Librería Británica (☎ 705-05-85), Serapio Rendón 125, two blocks north-west of the intersection of Insurgentes and Reforma (metro: San Cosme), carries Lonely Planet and other English-language travel guides, plus books on Mexico, and many novels, in English.
Sanborns has at least three branches in the Zona Rosa area with good English-language book and magazine sections. Insurgentes is the nearest metro station. They're on the corner of Niza and Hamburgo (this branch has a good range of maps of Mexico); on Londres between Génova and Amberes; and on the north side of the Monumento a la Independencia traffic circle on Reforma.

San Ángel & Coyoacán There are several good bookshops in these two southern suburbs:

American Bookstore (☎ 550-01-62), Avenida Revolución 1570, San Ángel.
Gandhi, Avenida M A de Quevedo 128 to 132, one block west of Avenida Universidad, San Ángel, is a Mexico City institution with a big range of books on most subjects, mostly in Spanish, and a popular upstairs café. It's open daily (metro: M A de Quevedo).
Librería Británica, Avenidas Universidad and México, Coyoacán, has a good general collection (metro: Coyoacán).

Maps

The various tourist offices, bookshops and hotel bookstalls can all provide useful street plans of the city. Most of those from tourist offices are free. A thorough, attractive street atlas is the *Guía Roji Ciudad de México*, which costs 40 pesos at the American Bookstore, Avenida Madero 25, and some other bookshops.

Libraries

There are several useful foreign-run libraries in Mexico City:

Biblioteca Benjamín Franklin (Benjamin Franklin Library, ☎ 591-02-44), Londres 16 west of Berlin, two blocks south-east of the Reforma/Insurgentes intersection (metro: Cuauhtémoc), is run by the US embassy. A wide range of books about the USA, Mexico and other parts of Latin America is available, as well as current English-language periodicals. Opening hours are Monday and Friday from 3 to 7.30 pm, Tuesday to Thursday 10 am to 3 pm.

Canadian Embassy Library (☎ 254-32-88), Schiller 529, Polanco, 400 metres north of the Museo Nacional de Antropología (metro: Polanco), has a wide selection of Canadian books and periodicals in English and French. Hours are Monday to Friday from 9 am to 12.30 pm.

Consejo Británico (British Council, ☎ 566-61-44), Antonio Caso 127, corner of Altamirano, one block north and one west of the Jardín del Arte (metro: San Cosme), has a library with lots of books and magazines in English, plus British newspapers a couple of weeks old. Hours are Monday to Friday from 9 am to 7 pm or later, Saturday 10 am to 1 pm.

Institut Français d'Amérique Latine (☎ 566-07-77) at Río Nazas 43 (metro: San Cosme or Insurgentes) has a library with French newspapers, magazines and many books. Hours are Monday to Friday from 9 am to 7 pm, Saturday 10 am to 1 pm.

Instituto Goethe (☎ 207-04-87), Tonalá 43, Colonia Roma (metro: Insurgentes), has a German library.

Media

The News, Mexico's most popular and oldest English-language newspaper, is the best source of information in English about concerts, exhibitions, plays, movies and English-language teaching positions in Mexico City. Price is 2.50 pesos. Some city centre newsstands carry it, as do several of the bookshops mentioned earlier in this section.

The *Mexico City Daily Bulletin* is a 20-page tabloid distributed free every day except Monday in some shops and many hotels (usually the ones which advertise in it). There are snippets of news as well as bits of tourist-oriented information, some of it useful, not all of it accurate.

The essential Spanish-language what's-on directory for entertainment in Mexico City is the weekly magazine *Tiempo Libre* – see the Entertainment section for details.

Some North American and European newspapers and magazines are sold at major hotel newsstands and at the bookstores listed earlier. La Casa de la Prensa at Avenida Florencia 59 in the Zona Rosa stocks major British and American newspapers and magazines, plus a few French and German ones; it's closed Sunday. La Torre del Papel at Filomeno Mata 6A north of Cinco de Mayo, five blocks west of the Zócalo, carries some American regional newspapers.

Medical Services

For the recommendation of a doctor, dentist or hospital, call your embassy or the 24-hour telephone help-lines (☎ 250-01-23/51) operated by SECTUR.

One of the best hospitals in Mexico City is undoubtedly the Hospital Americano-Británico (American-British Hospital, ☎ 272-85-00, emergencies 515-83-59) at Calle Sur 138 just south off Avenida Observatorio in Colonia Las Américas. There's an outpatients section and many of the staff speak English – but fees can be steep so adequate medical insurance is a big help. Observatorio metro station is 500 metres south of the hospital.

Emergency

Tourist Hotline SECTUR, the Secretaría de Turismo, maintains a telephone hotline, open 24 hours daily, to help tourists with problems and emergencies. The numbers are ☎ (5) 250-01-23 and (5) 250-01-51. From outside Mexico City, you can call these numbers collect.

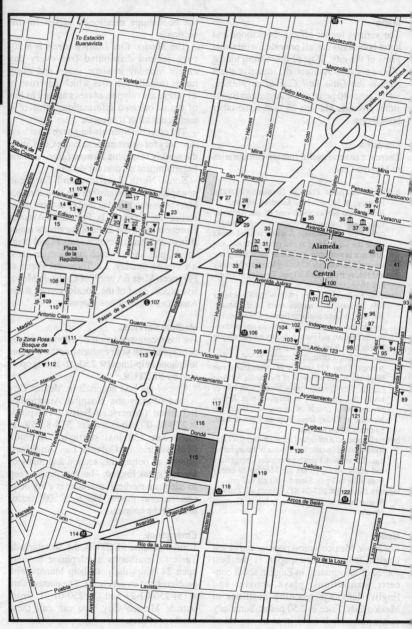

Central Mexico City

0   150   300 m

MEXICO CITY

PLACES TO STAY

4   Hotel Antillas
11 Gran Hotel Texas
12 Hotel Pensylvania
14 La Casa de los
      Amigos
15 Hotel Edison
19 Hotel Oxford
20 Hotel Carlton
22 Hotel New York
23 Hotel Jena
25 Hotel Frimont
35 Hotel de Cortés
39 Hotel Hidalgo
52 Hotel Ritz
54 Hotel Gillow
55 Hotel Juárez
56 Hotel Zamora &
      Café El Popular
57 Hotel Washington
58 Hotels Canada & Rioja
60 Hotel San Antonio
63 Hotel Catedral
74 Hotel Roble
77 Hotel Majestic
80 Gran Hotel Ciudad
      de México
82 Hotel Isabel
83 Hotel La Fayette
86 Hotel Principal
91 Hotel Capitol
95 Hotel Toledo
97 Hotel Marlowe
101 Hotel Bamer
102 Hotel Metropol
105 Hotel Fleming
108 Palace Hotel
109 Hotel Corinto
119 Hotel Fornos
120 Hotel San Diego

PLACES TO EAT

5   Hostería de Santo
      Domingo
10 Potzollcalli
13 Restaurante María
      Candelaria
21 Restaurante Regis
24 Restaurante Samy
27 'No Name' Restaurant
28 La Hostería del
      Bohemio
31 Café Trevi
42 Frutería Frutivida &
      El Taquería y Pollería
      Correo

47 La Ópera Bar
48 Sanborns Casa
      de Azulejos
49 Café de Tacuba
51 Restaurante Jampel
53 Café La Blanca
59 Restaurante El
      Vegetariano I
78 Cafetería Los Metates
79 Restaurant El Gallo Z
81 Pastelería Madrid
84 La Casa del Pavo
87 Hong King (Bolívar)
88 Rincón Mexicano &
      Antojitos Tere
89 Restaurant Danubio
90 Restaurant Centro
      Castellano
92 Pastelería Ideal
94 Taquería Tlaquepaque
96 Centro Naturista
      de México
98 Hong King (Chinatown)
103 Los Faroles
104 Restaurant Lincoln
110 Tacos El Caminero
112 Shirley's (Reforma)
113 Café La Habana

OTHER

2   Mercado La Lagunilla
3   Plaza Garibaldi
6   Iglesia de Santo
      Domingo
7   Plaza Santo Domingo
8   Secretaría de
      Educación Pública
      (murals)
16 Frontón México
17 Museo de San Carlos
18 Plaza Buenavista
26 Lotería Nacional
30 Pinacoteca Virreinal de
      San Diego
32 Museo Mural Diego
      Rivera
33 Exposición Nacional
      de Arte Popular
34 Jardín de la Solidaridad
36 Museo Franz Mayer &
      Cafetería del Claustro
37 Plaza de Santa
      Veracruz
38 Museo de la Estampa
41 Palacio de Bellas Artes
43 Central de Telégrafos
44 Museo Nacional de Arte

45 Main Post Office
46 Colegio de Minería
48 Casa de Azulejos
      (Sanborns)
61 Nacional Monte de
      Piedad (Pawn Shop)
62 Museo de la Caricatura
64 Catedral Metropolitana
      & El Sagrario
66 Museo de San
      Ildefonso (murals)
67 Templo Mayor & Museo
68 Museo José Luis
      Cuevas
69 Templo de La
      Santísima
70 Museo Nacional de las
      Culturas
71 Palacio Nacional
72 Suprema Corte de
      Justicia (murals)
73 Museo de la Ciudad
      de México
75 Departamento del
      Distrito Federal
76 Branch Post Office
85 Palacio de Iturbide
93 Torre Latinoamericana
99 Museo Nacional de
      Artes e Industrias
      Populares
100 Juárez Hemiciclo
107 Cámara Nacional
      de Comercio
      (Information Office)
111 Monumento a Cristóbal
      Colón
115 La Ciudadela
116 Plaza Ciudadela
117 Centro Artesanal
      La Ciudadela
121 Mercado de Artesanías
      San Juan

METRO STATIONS

1   Guerrero
9   Revolución
29 Hidalgo
40 Bellas Artes
50 Allende
65 Zócalo
106 Juárez
114 Cuauhtémoc
118 Balderas
122 Salto del Agua
123 Isabel la Católica
124 Pino Suárez

Tourist Police The Procuraduría General de Justicia del Distrito Federal (Solicitor-General of Justice of the Federal District) maintains two offices to aid tourists with legal questions and problems, including theft and robbery. Offices are at Florencia 20 in the Zona Rosa (☎ 625-86-64 or 625-86-66, 24 hours daily), and on Argentina on the corner of San Ildefonso (☎ 789-08-33), three blocks north of the Zócalo.

Lost & Found If you've lost something on the metro, you can call the Oficina de Objetos Extraviados (☎ 627-46-63). If it's something that 10 million people wouldn't want, you may find it there.

Dangers & Annoyances

Crime Mexico City is among the more likely places to be robbed in Mexico. But there's no need to walk in fear whenever you step outside your hotel: a few basic precautions will greatly reduce the risks. Please read the section under the same heading in the Facts for the Visitor chapter.

Mexico City's buses and metro are notorious for pickpockets and thieves, particularly when they're crowded. Happily, the increasing use of smaller *peseros* (minibuses) instead of large buses reduces the risk of theft. The riskiest places are those where lots of foreigners go: central metro stations, the Bosque de Chapultepec, buses along Paseo de la Reforma, around the Museo Nacional de Antropología. If you're worried, you can walk or take taxis instead of buses.

If you take taxis, make sure they are licensed and properly authorised (look for the windscreen stickers, rooftop light, driver's permit, meter, etc). When in doubt, ask your hotel to help you find a taxi.

Do not use guides who are not properly licensed or officially authorised.

Do not walk into a pedestrian underpass which is empty or nearly so; robbers may post spotters at each end, and intercept you after you enter. One of our authors was robbed in the pedestrian underpass beneath Reforma near the Cine Diana and Bosque de Chapultepec. Robbers work these underpasses regularly.

If you participate in any Mexican festivities (rallies or celebrations in the Zócalo, etc) be aware that half the pickpockets in the city will be there too. At the airport and bus stations, keep your bag or pack between your feet, particularly when you are checking in. On the metro, the first and last carriages are usually less crowded, but during rush hour (6.30 to 9 am and 4 to 7 pm) all trains and buses in the central area are sardine cans, which suits pickpockets. You may want to walk or take a taxi instead.

If you are the victim of a crime, you can report it through the offices of the Procuraduría General de Justicia (see Emergency in this section).

Pollution Mexico City's severe traffic and industrial pollution is made worse by the mountains which ring the Valley of Mexico and prevent air from dispersing, by the altitude and consequent lack of oxygen, and by a phenomenon called thermal inversion, which occurs particularly in the cooler months. Thermal inversion happens when warmer air passing over the Valley of Mexico traps the pollution in the valley near ground level and puts at risk people suffering from severe asthma, bronchitis or other respiratory problems. At any time, the pollution and altitude may make any visitor feel a little breathless or cause a sore throat, headache or runny nose.

The News publishes daily pollution reports and forecasts. Air contamination is measured by the Índice Metropolitana de Calidad de Aire (Imeca, Metropolitan Air Quality Index). When readings top 250 Imeca points – which happens several times a year – an atmospheric contingency plan is triggered. This requires over 200 big industrial plants to reduce activity by 30%, traffic to be deterred with roadblocks at some major intersections and a 50% cut in the use of official vehicles, and city building projects to be suspended. People are also advised to stop driving, to refrain from intense physical activity between 11 am and 4 pm, and to stay indoors from 1 to 3 pm.

AROUND THE ZÓCALO

Start your explorations of the city where it began. The historic centre of Mexico City is the Plaza de la Constitución, more commonly known as the Zócalo (metro: Zócalo).

The Aztec word *zócalo*, which means plinth or stone base, was adopted in 1843 when a tall monument to independence commissioned by President Santa Anna was constructed only as far as the base. The plinth is long gone, but the name remains, and has been adopted informally by many (but by no means all) other Mexican cities and towns for their main plazas.

The plaza was first paved in the 1520s by Cortés with stones from the ruins of the grandest and most important set of temples and palaces of the Aztec empire. Until the early 20th century, the plaza was often more a maze of market stalls and narrow passageways than an open plaza. With each side measuring 240 metres, it is one of the world's largest city plazas. To get a true sense of its size, visit the open-air terrace restaurant on the 7th floor of the Hotel Majestic, on the plaza's west side.

The Zócalo is the home of the powers-that-be in Mexico City. On its east side is the Palacio Nacional, on the north the Catedral Metropolitana. The buildings on the south side house the Departamento del Distrito Federal (Federal District Government). Just off the south-west corner of the plaza at Avenida 16 de Septiembre 82 is the Gran Hotel Ciudad de México, with ornate birdcage elevators rising towards a spectacular stained-glass canopy floating above its lobby.

The large Mexican flag flying in the middle of the Zócalo is ceremonially lowered by the Mexican army at 6 pm daily, and carried into the Palacio Nacional.

The whole area stretching for several blocks in each direction from the Zócalo – to the west, as far as Avenida Lázaro Cárdenas – is known as the Centro Histórico, or the Historic Centre of Mexico City. In a bid to make the Centro Histórico cleaner and less crowded, many streets are being pedestrianised, and in 1993 thousands of street vendors operating from small stalls were compulsorily moved to sites away from the centre.

Palacio Nacional

Home to the offices of the president of Mexico, the Federal Treasury, the National Archives, and dramatic murals by Rivera, the National Palace fills the entire east side of the Zócalo. The first palace on this spot was built of tezontle by the Aztec emperor Moctezuma II in the early 16th century before Cortés and his conquistadors arrived. Cortés destroyed the palace in 1521 and rebuilt it with a large courtyard so that he could entertain visitors with New Spain's first recorded bullfights. The palace remained in Cortés's family until the king of Spain bought it in 1562 to house the viceroys of New Spain. It was destroyed during riots in 1692, reconstructed again in tezontle and continued to be used as the viceregal residence until Mexican independence in the 1820s.

As you face the palace you see three portals. On the right (south) is the guarded entrance for the president of Mexico and other officials. Above the centre door hangs the **Campana de Dolores** (Bell of Dolores), rung in the town of Dolores by Padre Miguel Hidalgo in 1810 to signal the start of the Mexican War of Independence, and later moved to this place of honour in Mexico City. The bell is rung by the president of Mexico during the independence anniversary celebrations on 15 September every year.

Enter the palace through the centre door. The colourful **Diego Rivera murals** around the courtyard are the prime attraction of the palace. They present Rivera's view of the history of Mexican civilisation from the arrival of Quetzalcóatl – the plumed serpent god whom some believed to be personified in Hernán Cortés – to the 1910 revolution. The murals are open for public viewing from 9 am to 5 pm daily. Admission is free. Detailed guides to the murals are sold for 12 pesos at the foot of the stairs just inside the entrance gate.

The third (north) door of the palace leads to a courtyard where the seldom-visited **Recinto de Homenaje a Benito Juárez** (Place of Homage to Benito Juárez) is normally located. Owing to building work, the Recinto display had temporarily been moved to Avenida Hidalgo 79, near the Alameda Central, at the time of writing. But it was due to return to the Palacio Nacional some time in 1995. It's worth a visit if you have time. Juárez led Mexico's reform movement in the 1850s and the fight against the French invaders in the 1860s. He served as president until his death in this wing of the Palacio Nacional in 1872. His library, the room in which he died, and various personal effects have been preserved. Opening hours before the recinto was temporarily moved were from 10 am to 6 pm Tuesday to Friday, 10 am to 3 pm Saturday and Sunday. Admission is free.

Catedral Metropolitana

The Metropolitan Cathedral facing the north side of the Zócalo was built between 1573 and 1813. Though disfigured in recent years by scaffolding, as builders struggle to arrest its uneven descent into the soft ground on which it's built, the cathedral is still impressive. Extraction of water from the subsoil – the source of 70% of Mexico City's water – is reckoned to be the main reason for the subsidence. The existing building replaced an earlier cathedral, built between 1524 and 1532 on the southern part of the present site, where the main *tzompantli*, or rack for skulls of sacrifice victims, of the Aztecs' *teocalli* (sacred precinct) had stood. Cortés reportedly found over 136,000 skulls of sacrificial victims here and nearby.

Exterior With a three-naved basilica design of vaults on semicircular arches, the cathedral was built to resemble cathedrals in the Spanish cities of Toledo and Granada. Parts were added or replaced over the years and as a result the cathedral, together with its adjoining sacristy, El Sagrario, is a compendium of the architectural styles of colonial Mexico. The grand portals facing the Zócalo were built in the 17th century in baroque style. They have three levels of columns and marble panels with bas-reliefs. The central panel shows the Assumption of the Virgin Mary, to whom the cathedral is dedicated. The tall north portals facing Calle Guatemala are older, dating from 1615, and are in pure Renaissance style.

The upper levels of the towers, with their unique bell-shaped tops, were not added till the end of the 18th century, and the exterior was finally completed in 1813 when architect Manuel Tolsá added the clock tower topped by statues of Faith, Hope and Charity, and a great central dome, all in neoclassical style, to create a sense of unity and balance.

Interior The cathedral has a central nave, two processional or side naves and two chapel naves with 14 heavily decorated chapels. Much of the interior is a forest of scaffolding. Its chief artistic treasure is the gilded 18th-century Altar de los Reyes (Altar of the Kings), behind the main altar, a masterly exercise in controlled elaboration and a high point of the Churrigueresque style in Mexico. The Capilla de los Santos Ángeles y Archángeles (Chapel of the Holy Angels & Archangels) at the cathedral's south-west corner is an exquisite example of baroque sculpture and painting, with a huge main altarpiece and two smaller altarpieces decorated by the 18th-century painter Juan Correa. Four oval paintings by another leading 18th-century Mexican artist, Miguel Cabrera, grace the cathedral's side entrances.

A lot of other artwork in the cathedral was, unfortunately, damaged or destroyed in a 1967 fire. The intricately carved late 17th-century wooden choir stalls by Juan de Rojas, and the huge gilded Altar de Perdón (Altar of Pardon), all in the central nave, have been restored, and work continues.

El Sagrario Adjoining the east side of the cathedral is the 18th-century parish church, the Sagrario Metropolitano. Originally built as the cathedral's sacristy, to house the archives and vestments of the archbishop, it is a prime example of the ultradecorative Churrigueresque style.

Templo Mayor

The teocalli of Aztec Tenochtitlán, demolished by the Spaniards in the 1520s, stood on the site of the cathedral and the blocks to its north and east. Archaeologists established the location of the teocalli's Templo Mayor (Great Temple) in the first half of the 20th century, but the decision to excavate it, with the demolition of colonial buildings that this entailed, wasn't made until 1978 after electricity workers digging north-east of the cathedral happened upon an eight-tonne stone-disc carving of the Aztec goddess Coyolxauhqui. The temple is thought to be on the exact spot where the Aztecs saw their symbolic eagle with a snake in its beak perching on a cactus – still the symbol of Mexico today. In Aztec belief it was, literally, the centre of the universe.

The entrance to the temple site is just east of the cathedral, on the pedestrianised Calle Seminario. On your way from the Zócalo to the site, stop at the Fountain of Tenochtitlán, on the east side of the cathedral. A brass model of the ancient island city is displayed in the pool, with causeways linking it to the lake shore.

The temple site is open Tuesday to Sunday from 9 am to 5 pm. Admission is 13 pesos and includes entrance to the excellent adjoining Museo del Templo Mayor; on Sunday, both are free. There's a good little bookshop next to the ticket office. *The Great Temple and the Aztec Gods* in the Minutiae Mexicana series is a good short guide to the Templo Mayor and its background.

A walkway round the site reveals the temple's multiple layers of construction. There's plenty of explanatory material but it's all in Spanish. Like many other sacred buildings in Tenochtitlán, the temple, first begun in 1375, was enlarged several times, to express growing Aztec political dominance. Each rebuilding was accompanied by the sacrifice of captured warriors. In 1487 these rituals were performed at a frenzied pace to rededicate the temple after one major reconstruction. Michael Meyer & William Sherman write in *The Course of Mexican History*:

In a ceremony lasting four days sacrificial victims taken during campaigns were formed in four columns, each stretching three miles. At least twenty thousand human hearts were torn out to please the god...In the frenzy of this ghastly pageant, the priests were finally overcome by exhaustion.

What we see today are sections of several of the temple's different phases, though hardly anything is left of the seventh and final version, built about 1502 and seen by the Spanish conquistadors. A replica of the Coyolxauhqui stone is laid near the west side of the site. At the centre of the site is an early platform dating from about 1400. On the southern half of the platform, a sacrificial stone stands in front of a shrine to Huizilopochtli, the Aztec tribal god to whom human sacrifices were made to ensure that the sun would continue to rise. On the northern half is a chac-mool figure in front of a shrine to the water god Tláloc. A century later, a 40-metre-high pyramid would tower above this spot, with steep twin stairways leading up to shrines to the same two gods.

Other highlights of the site are a late 15th-century stone replica of a tzompantli, carved with 240 stone skulls, and the mid-15th century Recinto de los Guerreros Águila (Sanctuary of the Eagle Warriors, an elite band of Aztec fighters), decorated with coloured bas-reliefs of military processions.

Museo del Templo Mayor

The beautiful, modern museum on the north-east part of the Templo Mayor site houses artefacts from the site and gives an excellent overview (in Spanish) of Aztec civilisation. Pride of place is given to the great wheel-like stone of Coyolxauhqui, *She of Bells on her Cheek*, who is shown decapitated – the result of her murder by Huizilopochtli, her brother, who also killed her 400 brothers en route to becoming top god. Other outstanding exhibits include full-size terracotta eagle warriors, and a model of the Templo Mayor.

Here is an outline of the exhibit rooms:

Sala 1, Antecedentes – the early days of Tenochtitlán
Sala 2, Guerra y Sacrificio – Aztec beliefs and practices of war and human sacrifice

Sala 3, Tributo y Comercio – Aztec government and trade
Sala 4, Huizilopochtli – lord of the Templo Mayor and demander of sacrifices
Sala 5, Tláloc – the water and fertility god
Sala 6, Fauna – animals of the Aztecs and their empire
Sala 7, Agricultura – the chinampa system and its products
Sala 8, Arqueología Histórica – archaeological finds from the post-conquest era

Calle Moneda

As you walk back towards the Zócalo from the Templo Mayor, the first street on the left is Calle Moneda. Many of the buildings along Moneda are made of tezontle.

The **Museo Nacional de las Culturas** (National Museum of Cultures) at Moneda 13, in a building constructed in 1567 as the colonial mint, has a collection of exhibits showing the art, dress and handicrafts of several world cultures. Hours are Tuesday to Saturday from 9.30 am to 6 pm, and Sunday 9.30 am to 4 pm. Admission is free.

A block east of the Museo Nacional de las Culturas, then a few steps north at Calle Academía 13, is a former convent housing the fine **Museo José Luis Cuevas**, founded by the leading modern Mexican artist, José Luis Cuevas. There are works by Picasso and other modern artists as well as by Cuevas himself. The museum attracted controversy with the opening of a new Sala de Erótica (Erotica Room) in 1993. Hours are Tuesday to Friday from 10 am to 6.30 pm, Saturday and Sunday 10 am to 5.30 pm. Admission is 3 pesos.

The fine Churrigueresque-style **Templo de la Santísima** (Church of the Holy Sacrament) is three blocks east of the Museo Nacional de las Culturas on the corner of Moneda and Calle de la Santísima. Among the profusion of ornamental sculpture on the façade are ghostly busts of the 12 apostles and a depiction of Christ with his head in God's lap. Most of the carving was done by Lorenzo Rodríguez between 1755 and 1783.

Nacional Monte de Piedad

Facing the west side of the cathedral on the corner of Cinco de Mayo is Mexico's national pawnshop, founded in 1775. As one of the world's largest second-hand shops, it's worth a visit. It is housed in a large, dark building, open daily except Sunday. The site was once occupied by the Palace of Axayácatl, where Cortés and his intrepid companions were first lodged by Moctezuma II in 1519.

Museo de la Caricatura

One and a half blocks north of the Nacional Monte de Piedad, then a few steps to the right at Donceles 99, is a small museum dedicated to the cartoon, which has a long history in Mexico as a form of political comment as well as a source of humour. It's worth a visit if you're not in a hurry. Entry costs 1 peso.

Plaza & Iglesia de Santo Domingo

Plaza Santo Domingo, two blocks north of the cathedral on the corner of Calles Brasil and Cuba, is a scruffier affair than the Zócalo. Modern-day scribes, with typewriters and antique printing machines, work beneath the Portal de Evangelistas along its west side.

At the north end of the plaza is the Iglesia de Santo Domingo, dating from 1736, a beautiful example of baroque architecture, decorated on its east side with carved stone figures of Santo Domingo (St Dominic) and San Francisco (St Francis). Below the figures, the arms of both saints are symbolically entwined as if to convey a unity of purpose in their lives. The front or southern façade is equally beautiful with 12 columns around the main entrance. Between the columns are statues of San Francisco and San Agustín (St Augustine), and in the centre at the top is a bas-relief of the Assumption of the Virgin Mary.

Murals

In addition to the Palacio Nacional, several other buildings near the Zócalo hold important works by Rivera or other great Mexican muralists like Orozco and Siqueiros.

The first is the **Secretaría de Educación Pública**, on Calle Argentina north of Calle San Ildefonso, 3½ blocks north of the Zócalo. As the building houses government offices, it's only open Monday to Friday from 9 am to 3 pm. At these times you can walk into the two courtyards to see some of the 235 mural panels done by Rivera in 1921-22, when the building was constructed. Themes include agriculture, handicrafts, industry and festivals. There are also panels by Jean Charlot, Juan O'Gorman, Carlos Mérida and others.

From the Secretaría de Educación Pública, walk 1½ blocks back towards the Zócalo along Argentina, then turn east into Calle Justo Sierra. The **Museo de San Ildefonso**, half a block along at Justo Sierra 16, is open daily except Monday from 11 am to 6 pm (Wednesday to 9 pm). Originally the Jesuit college of San Ildefonso, it became the Escuela Nacional Preparatoria, a teacher training college, under President Benito Juárez. Juan Cordero, the first modern Mexican muralist, completed a painting depicting Mexican progress through science and industry on the main staircase in 1874. From 1923 to 1933, Rivera, Orozco, Siqueiros and others were brought in to add many more murals. Most of the work in the main court and on the grand staircase is by Orozco, inspired by the Mexican revolution (recently ended at the time). In a small patio are Siqueiros's works. The amphitheatre holds a gigantic Creation mural by Rivera.

Walk three blocks south (through the Zócalo) to reach the **Suprema Corte de Justicia**, Mexico's Supreme Court, on the corner of Pino Suárez and Corregidora. Four big murals were painted here by Orozco during WW II. Enter and go to the top of the stairs straight in front. Orozco chose this judicial setting to express ideas about justice – or rather, injustice. In the mural on the east wall, facing you at the top of the stairs, a great jaguar bestrides scenes of rottenness and decay. The mural opposite, on the west wall, shows images of destruction, violence and mayhem. The other two murals show Justice sleeping while its scales are upset and robbery and looting go unchecked.

Opposite the Supreme Court, on the west side of Pino Suárez, is a sculptural group showing the Aztecs' legendary discovery of an eagle standing on a cactus eating a snake.

The sculpture's positioning in such a prominent location demonstrates the importance of pre-Hispanic, particularly Aztec, roots in Mexico's modern national consciousness.

The strip of garden along the middle of Corregidora, between the Supreme Court and the Palacio Nacional, was once a section of one of Mexico City's main canals, the Acequia Real, used for bringing food into the centre of the city in Aztec and colonial times.

Museo de la Ciudad de México

The Museum of Mexico City, Pino Suárez 30 at Calle República del Salvador (metro: Pino Suárez), three blocks south of the Zócalo, was closed for renovation at the time of research, but will be worth a visit when it reopens as it provides an interesting overview of the city's history, starting as far back as the volcanic eruptions that created the Valley of Mexico. The museum is housed in a mansion originally built in 1528 as a residence for one of Cortés's cousins. A stone sculpture of a feathered serpent embedded in its cornerstone at Pino Suárez and República del Salvador shows that the mansion was partly constructed from Aztec ruins.

AROUND THE ALAMEDA

A little less than one km west of the Zócalo, west of Avenida Lázaro Cárdenas and north of Avenida Juárez, is the pretty Alameda Central, Mexico City's only sizeable central park. In the blocks around the Alameda are about a dozen interesting sights, from colonial mansions to skyscrapers.

If you walk from the Zócalo to the Alameda along Avenida Madero, you'll pass streets filled with hotels, restaurants, shops and old buildings. Stop and have a look at the Palacio de Iturbide and the Casa de Azulejos (see the following sections).

Bellas Artes and Hidalgo metro stations are at the north-east and north-west corners of the Alameda Central respectively. You can also reach the Alameda from the Zócalo area on any 'Km 15.5' or 'Auditorio' bus along Avenida Cinco de Mayo, or an 'Alameda', 'Bellas Artes' or 'M(etro) Revolución' pesero or bus west on Belisario Domínguez.

Alameda Central

What is now a pleasant, verdant park was once an Aztec marketplace. In early colonial times, it became the site of the church's *autos-da-fé*, where heretics were burned or hanged. Then in 1593 Viceroy Luis de Velasco decided the growing city needed a pleasant area of pathways, fountains and trees. By the late 19th century the park was dotted with European-style statuary, a bandstand was the venue for free concerts, and gas lamps illuminated it at night. Today, the park is a popular, easily accessible refuge from the crowds and traffic of the city. It's busiest on Sunday.

On the south side of the Alameda, facing Avenida Juárez, is the Juárez Hemiciclo, a gleaming white semicircle of marble columns about a regally seated statue of Benito Juárez (1806-72). Born a poor Zapotec Indian in the state of Oaxaca, Juárez rose to become president of Mexico and victor over the armies of Maximilian of Hapsburg.

West of the Alameda across Calle Dr Mora is the Jardín de la Solidaridad (Solidarity Garden). Created in 1986 on the site of the old Hotel Regis, it commemorates the struggle of Mexico City's residents to rebuild their city after the disastrous earthquake of 1985. The Alameda is surrounded by museums. Here they are, starting on the east side, moving to the north, then west and south.

Palacio de Bellas Artes

This splendid white marble concert hall and arts centre, commissioned by President Porfirio Díaz, dominates the east end of the Alameda . Construction of the Palace of Fine Arts began in 1904 under Italian architect Adamo Boari, who favoured neoclassical and art nouveau styles. It was supposed to be completed by 1910 for the grandiose centennial celebration of Mexican independence. But the heavy marble shell of the building began to sink into the spongy subsoil, and work was halted. Then came the Mexican revolution, which delayed completion until 1934. Architect Federico Mariscal finished the interior with new designs reflecting the art deco style of the 1920s and 1930s.

The palace houses some of Mexico's finest murals, which dominate immense wall spaces on the second and third levels. If you can understand Spanish, the written interpretations alongside add greatly to their interest.

On the second level are two large, striking, early 1950s works by Tamayo: *México de Hoy* (Mexico Today), and *Nacimiento de la Nacionalidad* (Birth of Nationality), a symbolic depiction of the creation of the Mexican mestizo identity.

At the west end of the third level is Rivera's famous *El Hombre, Contralor del Universo* (Man, Controller of the Universe), which was first commissioned for the Rockefeller Center in New York. The Rockefeller family had the original destroyed because of its anticapitalist themes, but Rivera re-created it even more dramatically here in 1934. Capitalism, with accompanying death and war, is shown on the left; socialism, with health and peace, is on the right. Lenses in the centre project images of the cosmos and the microscopic world, suggesting the power which science has given humanity to determine its own destiny.

On the north side of the third level are Siqueiros's three-part *La Nueva Democracía* (New Democracy), painted in 1944-45, and Rivera's four-part *Carnaval de la Vida Mexicana* (Carnival of Mexican Life), from 1936. At the east end of this level is Orozco's eye-catching *La Katharsis* (Catharsis), from 1934-35. Contradictory 'natural' and 'social' poles of human nature are symbolised by naked and clothed figures fighting each other. Violence and degradation result from this conflict, but a giant bonfire threatens to consume all and provide a spiritual rebirth.

Another highlight of the palace is the beautiful stained-glass stage curtain in the theatre, depicting the highlands of Mexico, based on a design by Mexican painter Gerardo Murillo ('Dr Atl'). Tiffany Studios of New York assembled the curtain from almost a million pieces of coloured glass. On Sunday mornings and just before performances, it is lit up for public viewing.

You can view the murals and look around the palacio Tuesday to Sunday from 10 am to 6 pm (free). A good bookshop and an arty little café are on the premises too. The palacio is also home to the Ballet Folklórico, a dazzling spectacle of Mexican music and dance that should not be missed. See the Entertainment section for more on this and other events in the palacio.

Palacio de Iturbide

East of the Bellas Artes at Avenida Madero 17, between Bolívar and Gante, rises the beautiful baroque façade of the Iturbide Palace. Built between 1779 and 1785 for a family of colonial nobility, it was claimed in 1821 by General Agustín Iturbide, a hero of the Mexican struggle for independence from Spain. The general responded favourably to a crowd which gathered in front of the palace in 1822 beseeching him to be their emperor (Iturbide is thought to have instigated the gathering). Iturbide proclaimed himself Emperor Agustín I but reigned over Mexico for less than a year, abdicating in 1823 after General Santa Anna announced the birth of the Mexican republic.

The palace was restored in 1972 and now houses the Fomento Cultural Banamex, the bank's cultural promotion section. Some excellent art exhibitions are hung in the fine courtyard and several of the rooms; there's a bookshop as well.

Casa de Azulejos

A block west of the Iturbide Palace at Avenida Madero 4, on the north side of the street on the corner of Condesa, stands one of the city's gems. The Casa de Azulejos (House of Tiles) dates from 1596, when it was built for the counts of the valley of Orizaba. Although the tiles which have adorned its outside walls since the 18th century are Spanish and Moorish in style, most of them were actually produced in China and shipped to Mexico on the Manila *naos* (Spanish galleons used up to the early 19th century).

The building now houses a Sanborns store and is a good place to buy a newspaper or

have refreshments. The main restaurant (see Places to Eat) is set in a lovely courtyard with a Moorish fountain. The staircase on the north side of the restaurant has a 1925 mural by Orozco.

Torre Latinoamericana

The Latin American Tower, the landmark 1950s skyscraper on the corner of Avenidas Madero and Lázaro Cárdenas, has an observation deck on its 42nd floor, open every day between 10 am and 11 pm. The view at night is just as spectacular, in its way, as the daytime vista. Admission is 10 pesos. Tickets are sold at the entrance, on the Lázaro Cárdenas side of the building. If you want to use the pay telescopes, buy tokens for them at the same time.

Museo Nacional de Arte

The National Museum of Art at Tacuba 8, just east of Avenida Lázaro Cárdenas and the Bellas Artes, contains exclusively Mexican work. You'll recognise the building by the distinctive bronze equestrian statue in front of the Spanish king Carlos IV (1788-1808) by the Mexican sculptor and architect Manuel Tolsá. Called *El Caballito* (The Little Horse), this originally stood in the Zócalo. It was moved here in 1852. Note that Mexicans refer to the horse, not to the rider, who reigned shortly before Mexico gained its independence. A sign points out that the statue is preserved as a work of art (and not, presumably, out of political loyalty).

The museum – which originally housed the Communications Ministry – was built at the turn of this century in the style of an Italian Renaissance palace. A grand marble staircase greets you as you enter. The collections represent every style and school of Mexican art. The works on the 1st floor by José María Velasco, depicting Mexico City and the countryside in the late 19th and early 20th centuries, are among the highlights. One shows the city still surrounded by lakes even in the late 19th century.

Second-floor collections include 17th-century religious paintings by Antonio Rodríguez, Juan Correa and José de Ibarra;

18th and 19th-century sculptures; portraits by Antonio Poblano; prints of skeletal figures sweeping streets; and anonymous paintings with social and political themes. Hours are from 10 am to 5.30 pm Tuesday to Sunday. Admission is 10 pesos.

Colegio de Minería

Opposite the museum, at Tacuba 5, is the College of Mining, a beautiful neoclassical building designed by Manuel Tolsá and built between 1797 and 1813. Four meteorites found in Mexico are on display in the entrance, echoing the time when this first engineering school in the Americas was the centre of Mexican mining activity. The building is now used by the UNAM engineering faculty and related organisations. It can be visited for free, Monday to Friday from 8.30 am to 9 pm.

Museo Franz Mayer

The Franz Mayer Museum, a sumptuous, once-private collection of mainly Mexican art and craft, is housed in the lovely 16th-century Hospital de San Juan de Dios at Avenida Hidalgo 45, on the little Plaza de Santa Veracruz opposite the north side of the Alameda. It's an oasis of calm and beauty in the city.

Franz Mayer, born in Mannheim, Germany, in 1882, moved to Mexico, became a citizen, earned the name 'Don Pancho', and began to collect Mexican silver, textile and furniture masterpieces.

The museum is open Tuesday to Sunday from 10 am to 5 pm. Admission is 8 pesos (free on Sunday). As you enter, rooms to the right hold changing exhibits and displays of antique furnishings. To the left is a gorgeous colonial garden courtyard. The suite of rooms on the courtyard's south side is done in antique furnishings, and is very fine, especially the lovely chapel. On the north side is the delightful Cafetería del Claustro (see Places to Eat). The best gold and silver items are in one room on the upper floor of the courtyard (follow signs to 'Obras maestras de la colección de plata del Museo Franz Mayer').

Museo de la Estampa

Also on the Plaza de Santa Veracruz is the Museum of Engraving, Avenida Hidalgo 39. It has a permanent collection of engravings, lithographs, etc by top Mexican artists, as well as the tools of these techniques and changing exhibits of the graphic arts. Hours are Tuesday to Sunday from 10 am to 6 pm. Admission is 10 pesos. The Iglesia de la Santa Veracruz next door leans noticeably, a result of land subsidence.

Recinto de Homenaje a Benito Juárez

At the time of writing the exhibit of the Place of Homage to Benito Juárez (see the earlier Palacio Nacional section) was temporarily housed at Avenida Hidalgo 79, a block west of the Museo Franz Mayer. It was due to return to the Palacio Nacional during 1995. Opening hours at the temporary site were Tuesday to Sunday from 10 am to 6 pm. Entry is free.

Museo Mural Diego Rivera

Among Rivera's most famous murals is *Sueño de una Tarde Dominical en la Alameda* (Dream of a Sunday Afternoon in the Alameda), a large work, 15 metres long by four metres high, painted in 1947. The artist imagines many of the figures who walked in the city from colonial times onward, from Cortés through Juárez, Santa Anna, Emperor Maximilian and Empress Carlota, to Porfirio Díaz, and Francisco Madero and his nemesis, General Victoriano Huerta. All are grouped around a central skeleton dressed in pre-revolutionary ladies' garb. Rivera himself, and his artist wife Frida Kahlo, appear next to the skeleton.

The mural was painted in the Hotel del Prado which stood across the street, on the south side of Avenida Juárez, until it was badly damaged in the earthquake of 1985. The museum was built in 1986 to house just this mural. It's just west of the Alameda, fronting the Jardín de la Solidaridad. Hours are Tuesday to Sunday from 10 am to 2 pm and 3 to 6 pm. There's a sound-and-light show at 11 am and 4 pm Tuesday to Friday, and at 11 am and 1, 4 and 5 pm Saturday and Sunday. Admission costs 7 pesos.

Pinacoteca Virreinal de San Diego
At Calle Dr Mora 7, facing the west side of the Alameda, is the Viceregal Picture Gallery, a former church and monastery that is now home to a collection of 17th and 18th-century baroque and religious paintings. A contemporary mural by Federico Cantú is also displayed. Hours are from 9 am to 5 pm Tuesday to Sunday. Admission is 7 pesos, free on Sunday.

LA CIUDADELA
About 700 metres south of the Alameda, near Balderas metro station, is the Citadel, an extensive colonial building now housing the **Biblioteca de México** (Library of Mexico). It was from their base here in February 1913, during the Mexican Revolution, that supporters of the ousted dictatorial president Porfirio Díaz waged bloody street battles that resulted in the deposition and execution of President Francisco Madero. Nearby is an excellent handicrafts market – see Things to Buy for more information.

AROUND PLAZA DE LA REPÚBLICA
There are a few sights of interest around the plaza, starting with the huge, domed Monumento a la Revolución in its centre. The metro station for most of the sights in this district is Revolución. 'M(etro) Revolución' buses and peseros run west along Belisario Domínguez, four blocks north of the Zócalo, then south on Allende and west on Tacuba and Avenida Hidalgo.

Monumento a la Revolución
Begun in the early 1900s under Porfirio Díaz, the Revolution Monument was originally supposed to be a meeting-chamber for senators and deputies, but construction (not to mention Díaz's term as president) was interrupted by the revolution. The structure was modified and given its new role in the 1930s. The tombs of the revolutionary and post-revolutionary heroes Pancho Villa,

Francisco Madero, Venustiano Carranza, Plutarco Elías Calles and Lázaro Cárdenas are inside its wide pillars (not open to the public).

Beneath the monument lies the interesting little **Museo Nacional de la Revolución**, with exhibits on the revolution and the decades leading up to it. It's entered from the small garden on the south-east side of the monument. Hours are Tuesday to Saturday from 9 am to 5 pm, Sunday 9 am to 3 pm. Admission is free.

Frontón México
On the north side of the Plaza de la República is the recently restored Frontón México, Mexico City's art deco jai alai arena. Games are open to spectators most evenings. See the Entertainment section for more details.

Museo de San Carlos
The Museum of San Carlos at Puente de Alvarado 50, on the corner of Ramos Arizpe 1½ blocks east of Revolución metro station, has a fine collection of European art. It's housed in the former mansion of the Conde (Count) de Buenavista, designed by Manuel Tolsá in the early 1800s. For a long time it housed the country's leading art academy; Rivera, Siqueiros and Orozco all studied here. Ground-floor rooms hold temporary exhibits. The museum's permanent collection of European paintings from the 14th to 19th century, upstairs, includes works by Bruegel, Goya, Rembrandt and Titian. There's also a collection of Mexican and international contemporary art. Hours are Wednesday to Monday from 10 am to 6 pm. Admission is 7 pesos, free on Sunday. After you visit, stroll into the pretty little park on the museum's south side.

Lotería Nacional
Mexico's national lottery is a national passion. The tall art deco tower on the west side of Paseo de la Reforma opposite Avenida Juárez (metro: Hidalgo) is the game's headquarters. Walk into the building and up the stairs almost any Sunday, Tuesday

The Lottery

Lottery tickets are sold all over Mexico by street vendors and at kiosks, and normally cost 3 or 4 pesos. Anyone can buy them. Each ticket is for a particular draw *(sorteo)* on a specific date. Prizes range from a few hundred to over one million pesos. The winning numbers are published in newspapers the next day, and posted at ticket sales points. Buying a ticket at least enables you to fantasise for a day or two about what you would do with a million pesos. Retire to Mexico? Travel the world for ever? Give it to charity? Buy a lifetime supply of Bohemia lager? Since the ticket numbering system is a bit complicated, get a ticket seller or someone else who understands it to check your ticket against the list of winners. Each draw usually has several series of tickets, each of which gets a share of the many prizes. If the winning ticket hasn't been sold, other numbers close to the winner may also qualify for prizes.

Mexicans resort to all sorts of calculations, hunches and superstitions to decide which numbers may be lucky. Added spice is provided by regular *zodiaco* draws, where each ticket bears a sign of the zodiac as well as a number. At Christmas and other special times, there may be draws with ultra-big prizes: other draws will be suspended for a couple of weeks beforehand to ensure good sales for the big one, whose tickets may cost up to 40 pesos.

Profits from the lottery go to government charity projects. ■

or Friday after 7.30 pm, take a seat in the cosy auditorium, and at exactly 8 pm the *sorteo*, the ceremony of picking the winning numbers, begins. Cylindrical cages spew out numbered wooden balls which are plucked out by uniformed pages who announce the winning numbers and the amounts they have won. Admission is free.

PASEO DE LA REFORMA & ZONA ROSA

Paseo de la Reforma, Mexico City's main boulevard and status address, runs south-west from the Alameda Central down through the Bosque de Chapultepec. It's said that Emperor Maximilian of Hapsburg laid out the boulevard to connect his palace on Chapultepec Hill with the older section of the city. He could look eastward straight along it from his bedroom, and ride along it to work in the Palacio Nacional on the Zócalo.

Today the traffic along Reforma means that it's not a very pleasant place for a prolonged stroll, but most visitors are likely to pass along it on the way to somewhere else, or to call at one of its banks, shops, hotels, restaurants or embassies. The Zona Rosa (Pink Zone), Mexico City's high-life and nightlife district, lies on the south side of Reforma west of the Avenida Insurgentes intersection, roughly two km from the Alameda Central.

Westbound 'Km 15.5' and 'Auditorio' buses and peseros, which you can catch on Avenida Cinco de Mayo west of the Zócalo, or on Avenida Hidalgo on the north side of the Alameda, go along Reforma. A westbound 'M(etro) Chapultepec' bus or pesero on Reforma itself will go as far as Chapultepec metro station, beyond the end of the Zona Rosa. In the opposite direction, 'Villa' buses and peseros go up Reforma to La Villa, several km beyond the Alameda; there are also vehicles to 'M(etro) Hidalgo', 'Alameda', 'Bellas Artes' and 'Zócalo'.

Many modern skyscrapers have now joined the older buildings on Reforma. The paseo is also – surprisingly – dotted with noteworthy pieces of art. A few blocks due south of the Plaza de la República on Reforma is the **Glorieta Cristóbal Colón**, with a statue to Christopher Columbus created by French sculptor Charles Cordier in 1877. About 600 metres further south-west, in the main hall of the Prime Internacional bank building at Reforma 156, is a large fresco painted in 1965 by Juan O'Gorman.

Reforma's busy intersection with Avenida Insurgentes is marked by the **Monumento a Cuauhtémoc**, the last Aztec emperor. Two blocks north-west of this intersection is the **Jardín del Arte**, a sliver of shady park which becomes an interesting open-air artists' bazaar on Sunday. Come for a stroll and a browse, if not to buy.

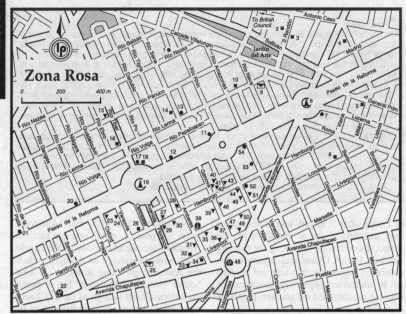

Zona Rosa

0   200   400 m

The most striking of the modern buildings on Reforma is the **Centro Bursatil**, Mexico City's stock exchange, an arrow of reflecting glass at Reforma 255, six blocks south-west of Insurgentes. You can visit the gallery overlooking the exchange's trading floor between 11 am and 1 pm Monday to Friday. Entry is free but you need to show ID such as your passport.

The **Zona Rosa** (metro: Insurgentes) is not a tourist ghetto, as its glossy appearance might lead you to believe. It's an integral piece of the Mexico City jigsaw, interesting to visit whether or not you plan to use its hotels, restaurants, shops and nightclubs. People-watching from one of its sidewalk cafés reveals a fascinating variety among the passing parade of pedestrians. For details of how to spend money here, see Places to Stay, Places to Eat, Things to Buy and Entertainment.

On the north-west flank of the Zona Rosa, at Reforma's intersection with Avenida Río Tiber and Avenida Florencia, stands the symbol of Mexico City, the **Monumento a**

la Independencia, a gilded statue of Liberty on a pedestal, called by locals simply El Ángel. The statue was created by sculptor Antonio Rivas Mercado and erected in 1910, just as the Mexican revolution got under way. South-west from the Angel the boulevard is lined mostly with large, impersonal modern office buildings until you reach the intersection with Calzada General Escobedo and Calzada Melchor Ocampo. On the south-west side of this intersection, marking the entrance to the Bosque de Chapultepec, stand the six slender columns of the **Monumento a los Niños Héroes** (see the section following).

At this point the monumental part of Reforma ends, though the road continues through the park, veering almost due west, to become the start of the main road to Toluca.

BOSQUE DE CHAPULTEPEC

According to legend, Chapultepec first gained prominence when one of the last kings of the

PLACES TO STAY

2	Hotel Mallorca
3	Hotel Sevilla
4	Hotel Regente
5	Mi Casa
6	Hotel Vasco de Quiroga
10	Hotel María Cristina
14	Casa González
16	San Marino Hotel-Suites
18	María Isabel-Sheraton Hotel
21	Hotel Marquis Reforma
26	Hotel Westin Galería Plaza
28	Hotel Marco Polo
32	Hotel Krystal Rosa
34	Hotel Century
37	Hotel Calinda Geneve & Sanborns Bookshop

PLACES TO EAT

15	Restaurante Vegetariano Las Fuentes
23	Anderson's de Reforma
24	Restaurante Vegetariano Yug
27	Auseba
29	Salon de Te Duca d'Este
30	Parri
31	Harry's Bar
33	Fonda El Refugio
35	El Faisán
36	Sanborns
39	Konditori
40	Piccadilly Pub
41	Pizza Real
42	El Perro d'Enfrente
43	Mesón del Perro Andaluz
44	Carrousel Internacional
45	Chalet Suizo
46	Restaurante Jacarandas
47	Salón Luz
49	Restaurante El Gallito
50	Shirley's Pink Zone
51	Luaú

OTHER

1	Institut Français d'Amérique Latine
7	Prime Internacional Bank
8	Monumento a Cuauhtémoc
9	Post Office
11	Centro Bursatil
12	US Embassy
13	UK Embassy
17	Sanborns
19	Monumento a la Independencia (El Ángel)
20	Japanese Embassy
25	Post Office
38	City Tourist Office
52	Sanborns
53	French Embassy
54	American Express

METRO STATIONS

22	Sevilla
48	Insurgentes

Toltecs took refuge in its woods after fleeing from Tula. Later, the hill in the park (Chapultepec means Hill of Grasshoppers in the Nahua language) served as a refuge for the wandering Mexica (Aztec) tribe and then as a fortress for Moctezuma I before becoming a summer residence for Aztec nobles. Nezahualcóyotl, the ruler of nearby Texcoco, gave his sanction for the area to be made a forest reserve. At that time Chapultepec was still separated from Tenochtitlán, the site of modern central Mexico City, by the waters of the Lago de Texcoco.

The Bosque de Chapultepec has remained Mexico City's largest park for almost 500 years. Today it covers more than four sq km and has lakes, a zoo and several world-class museums. It attracts thousands of visitors daily, and is particularly popular on Sunday when vendors line its main paths and throngs of families come to relax and crowd into the museums. The park is divided into two sections by two big roads – Calzada Molino del Rey and Boulevard López Mateos – which run north-south across the middle. The major attractions are in the eastern or first section (1a sección) which lies nearer the city centre. Most of the museums in the park offer free admission on Sunday.

Monumento a los Niños Héroes
The six columns of the Monument to the Boy Heroes, near Chapultepec metro, mark the main entrance to the park. They commemorate six brave cadets at the national military academy, which was once housed in Chapultepec Castle. On 13 September 1847, when invading American troops reached Mexico City, the six cadets, having defended their school as long as they could, wrapped themselves in Mexican flags and leapt to their deaths rather than surrender. An annual ceremony on the date remembers their heroism.

Castillo de Chapultepec
Part of the castle on Chapultepec Hill was built in 1785 as a residence for the viceroys of New Spain. Briefly abandoned after independence, the building was converted into a military academy in 1843. When Emperor

Maximilian and Empress Carlota arrived in 1864, they refurbished the castle as their main residence. After their fall from power the castle remained a residence for Mexico's presidents until 1940, when President Lázaro Cárdenas converted it into the National Museum of History.

Today the **Museo Nacional de Historia** has two floors of exhibits chronicling the rise and fall of New Spain, the establishment of independent Mexico, the dictatorship of Porfirio Díaz and the Mexican revolution. Several of the ground-floor rooms are decorated with impressive murals on historical themes by leading Mexican artists. These include Juan O'Gorman's *Retablo de la Independencia* (Thanksgiving Panel for Independence) in room 5, Orozco's *La Reforma y la Caída del Imperio* (The Reform and Fall of the Empire) in room 7, and Siqueiros's *Del Porfirismo a la Revolución* (From Porfirism to the Revolution) in room 13. Don't miss the rooms entered from a garden walkway around the east end of the castle. This is the portion where Maximilian and Carlota lived and is furnished in period style, including Carlota's marble bath.

The museum is open Tuesday to Sunday from 9 am to 5 pm. Admission is 13 pesos, free on Sunday. To reach the castle, walk up the road that curves up the right-hand side of the hill behind the Monumento a los Niños Héroes.

Museo del Caracol

From Chapultepec Castle, the Museo del Caracol is just a short distance back down the approach road. Shaped somewhat like a snail shell *(caracol)*, this is officially the Museo Galería de la Lucha del Pueblo Mexicano por su Libertad (Museum Gallery of the Mexican People's Struggle for its Liberty). Displays cover social and political life from Spanish colonial days, the divisions of New Spain in the 18th century, Miguel Hidalgo's leadership in the struggle for independence, and Francisco Madero's leadership in the revolution.

The self-guided tour ends in a circular hall that contains only one item – the 1917 Constitution of Mexico. The museum's hours are

Tuesday to Saturday from 9 am to 5 pm, Sunday 10 am to 4 pm. Admission is free.

Museo de Arte Moderno

The two rounded buildings of the Museum of Modern Art stand in their own sculpture garden just north-west of the Monumento a los Niños Héroes. The entrance is from the north side of the museum, facing Paseo de la Reforma. The museum's permanent collection is of work by Mexico's most famous 20th-century artists, including Dr Atl, Rivera, Siqueiros, Orozco, Kahlo, Tamayo and O'Gorman. In contrast to the large murals for which many of these are best known, some of their more intimate work such as portraits is shown here. In addition there are always several temporary exhibitions by prominent artists from Mexico and abroad. The museum's hours are Tuesday to Sunday from 10 am to 5.30 pm. Admission is 10 pesos.

Museo Nacional de Antropología

The National Museum of Anthropology is one of the finest museums of its kind in the world, and ranks with the Zócalo and the Alameda among Mexico City's not-to-be-missed attractions. It stands in the Bosque de Chapultepec on the north side of Paseo de la Reforma. Opening hours are Tuesday to Saturday from 9 am to 7 pm, Sunday and holidays 10 am to 6 pm. Admission is 16 pesos, free on Sunday.

The museum is fascinating and very large, with more than most people can absorb (without brain strain) in a single visit. Unless you have time to come more than once, a good plan is to concentrate on the regions of Mexico that you plan to visit or have visited, with a quick look at some of the most eye-catching exhibits in other rooms. All labelling is in Spanish, but some of the spectacular exhibits justify a visit even if you can't decipher a word of the explanations.

In a clearing in the park about 100 metres in front of the museum's entrance, Totonac Indians perform their spectacular voladores dance – 'flying' from a 20-metre-high pole – several times a day, collecting money from onlookers afterwards. More information on the voladores rite is given under El Tajín in the Central Gulf Coast chapter.

The spacious modern museum building is the work of Mexican architect Pedro Ramírez Vásquez and was constructed in the early 1960s at a cost of more than US$20 million. Through the high glass windows of the entrance hall you can see a long, rectangular courtyard flanked on three sides by the museum's two-storey display halls, with over one km of hallways. An immense umbrella-like stone fountain rises from the centre of the courtyard.

The museum's ground-floor halls are dedicated to Mexican societies and civilisations before the Spanish conquest. Rooms on the upper level cover the way Mexico's Indian peoples, the direct descendants of those pre-Hispanic civilisations, live today. With a few exceptions, each ethnological section upstairs covers the same territory as the archaeological exhibit below it, so you can see the great Mayan city of Palenque as it was in the 700s, then go upstairs and see how the Mayan people live today. Here's a brief guide to the regions and archaeological sites covered on the ground floor, in anticlockwise order around the courtyard:

Introducción a la Antropología – The exhibits introduce the studies of anthropology and ethnology, and pre-Hispanic culture in general.

Sala Origenes – The Origins Room shows evidence of the first men and women in this hemisphere, explaining their arrival from Asia, and displays findings from the Valley of Mexico.

Sala Preclásica – The preclassic period lasted from about 1500 BC to 250 AD. The exhibits highlight the transition from a nomadic hunting life to a more settled farming life in Mexico around 1000 BC.

Sala Teotihuacana – The Teotihuacán Room has models of the awesome city of Teotihuacán near Mexico City, the Western Hemisphere's first great and powerful state. A highlight is the full-sized model of part of the Temple of Quetzalcóatl.

Sala Tolteca – The predominant people in Mexico from about 900 to 1200 AD, known as the Toltecs, had a capital at Tula, near Mexico City, and carved huge stone statues of the god Quetzal-

cóatl. This room has one such statue from Tula's Temple of Tlahuizcalpantecuhtli.

Sala Mexica – At the west end of the courtyard is the hall devoted to the Mexica or Aztecs. Come here to see the famous sun (or 'calendar') stone, with the face of the sun god Tonatiuh at the centre of a web of symbols representing the five worlds, the four directions, the 20 days and more; the statue of Coatlicue ('She of the Skirt of Snakes'), the mother of the Aztec gods, found – like the sun stone – beneath the Zócalo in 1790; a replica of a carved stone tzompantli; an 'aerial view' painting of Tenochtitlán, the Aztecs' island capital; and other graphic reminders of the Aztec age.

Sala Oaxaca – In the southern state of Oaxaca great artistic heights were reached by the Zapotecs (about 300 BC to 700 AD) and the Mixtecs (about 1200 to 1500 AD). Two tombs from the great hilltop site of Monte Albán are reproduced full-size here – one inside the room, one on the outside patio.

Sala Golfo de México – Important civilisations along the coast of the Gulf of Mexico included the Olmec, Classic Veracruz, Totonac and Huastec. There are very fine stone carvings here, including one of the awesome Olmec heads.

Sala Maya – The Maya Room includes wonderful exhibits not only from south-eastern Mexico (including Palenque, Yaxchilán, and Bonampak), but from Guatemala, Belize and Honduras too. The full-scale model of the tomb of King Pakal, discovered deep in the Temple of the Inscriptions at Palenque, is breathtaking. On the outside patio are replicas of the famous wall paintings of Bonampak (looking much better than the damaged originals) and of Edificio II at Hochob in Campeche, constructed as a giant mask of the rain god Chac.

Cafetería – Just past the Maya Room is a flight of stairs down to the museum's cafeteria (see Places to Eat).

Sala Norte – The Northern Mexico room covers the Casas Grandes (Paquimé) site in Chihuahua and other cultures from the dry north. Similarities can be seen with the Indian cultures of the American south-west.

Sala Occidente – The Western Mexico room deals with the cultures of Nayarit, Jalisco, Michoacán, Colima and Guerrero states, chief among them the Tarascans of Michoacán, who were one of the few peoples able to repel the invading Aztecs.

Museo Rufino Tamayo

The Tamayo Museum, a multilevel concrete and glass structure about 250 metres east of the Museo Nacional de Antropología, houses the fine collection of international modern art donated by Rufino Tamayo and his wife,

MEXICO CITY

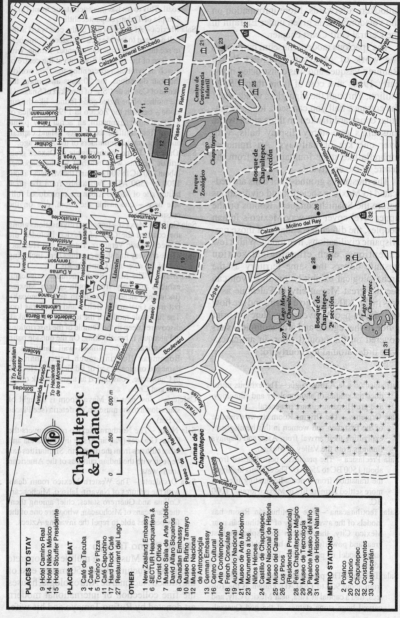

Chapultepec & Polanco

PLACES TO STAY
9 Hotel Camino Real
14 Hotel Nikko México
15 Hotel Stouffer Presidente

PLACES TO EAT
3 Café de Tacuba
4 Cafés
5 Tonino's Pizza
11 Café Capuchino
17 Hard Rock Café
27 Restaurant del Lago

OTHER
1 New Zealand Embassy
6 SECTUR Headquarters &
    Tourist Office
7 Museo Sala de Arte Público
    David Alfaro Siqueiros
8 Canadian Embassy
10 Museo Rufino Tamayo
12 Museo Nacional
    de Antropología
13 German Embassy
16 Centro Cultural
    Arte Contemporáneo
18 French Consulate
19 Auditorio Nacional
21 Museo de Arte Moderno
23 Monumento a los
    Niños Héroes
24 Castillo de Chapultepec,
    Museo Nacional de Historia
25 Museo del Caracol
26 Los Pinos
    (Residencia Presidencial)
28 Feria Chapultepec Mágico
29 Museo de Tecnología
30 Papalote Museo del Niño
31 Museo de Historia Natural

METRO STATIONS
2 Polanco
20 Auditorio
22 Chapultepec
32 Constituyentes
33 Juanacatlán

Olga, to the people of Mexico. Over 150 artists including Picasso, Warhol and Tamayo himself are represented in the permanent collection. Among the more unusual offerings is a model of a Rolls-Royce made from twigs and branches. The museum also hosts world-class travelling shows with works by top contemporary artists. It's open Tuesday to Sunday from 10 am to 6 pm. Admission is 10 pesos, free on Sunday.

Parque Zoológico de Chapultepec

The first zoo in Chapultepec – and the Americas – is said to have been established by King Nezahualcóyotl well before the Spanish arrived. Cortés added a bird sanctuary. In 1975 a gift from China brought pandas. In 1993 the zoo closed for rebuilding, but it may have reopened by the time you visit. It's fun, particularly for children, and admission – before reconstruction at least – was free. Hours before reconstruction were Wednesday to Sunday from 9 am to 5 pm. The zoo is on the south side of Paseo de la Reforma a short distance west of the lake (Lago de Chapultepec).

Segunda (2a) Sección

The second section of the Bosque de Chapultepec lies west of Boulevard López Mateos. It's most easily reached from Constituyentes metro station near its southern perimeter.

Two highlights of the second section are the **Feria Chapultepec Mágico**, a funfair with some hair-raising rides, which was closed at the time of research but may have now reopened after a bout of reconstruction (hours before the closure were Wednesday and Thursday from 10.30 am to 6 pm, Saturday and Sunday 10.30 am to 8 pm); and **Papalote Museo del Niño**, a hands-on children's museum opened in 1993, with themes ranging from the arts through computers to the human body. Children must be accompanied by adults and vice versa. Hours are Monday to Friday from 9 am to 6 pm, Saturday and Sunday 9 am to 1 pm and 2 to 6 pm. Entry costs 15 pesos for adults, 10 pesos for children (two to 12 years).

You'll also find two lakes, some large fountains, the **Museo de Tecnología**, which includes a planetarium and sections on oil and railways, and the **Museo de Historia Natural**, which focuses on the evolution of the planet and its species. Both these museums are open Tuesday to Sunday from 9 or 10 am to 5 pm.

Getting There & Away

Chapultepec metro station is at the east end of the Bosque de Chapultepec, near the Monumento a los Niños Héroes and the Castillo de Chapultepec. Auditorio metro station is on the north side of the park, 500 metres west of the Museo Nacional de Antropología.

'Km 15.5', 'Auditorio' and 'M(etro) Chapultepec' buses and peseros heading west on Avenida Cinco de Mayo, between the Zócalo and the Alameda Central, all go to Bosque de Chapultepec. The first two cross the park on Paseo de la Reforma – you can get off right outside the Museo Nacional de Antropología (but watch out for pickpockets). 'M(etro) Chapultepec' vehicles stop at the east end of the park. You can catch the same vehicles on Avenida Hidalgo (the north side of the Alameda Central) or on Reforma near the Alameda or the Plaza de la República.

Returning to the city centre, 'M(etro) Hidalgo', 'Alameda', 'Bellas Artes', 'Zócalo' and 'Villa' buses and peseros heading east on Reforma all pass within a short walk of the Zona Rosa, the Plaza de la República and the Alameda Central. Those marked 'Zócalo' continue along Avenida Madero to the Zócalo; 'Villa' vehicles continue up Reforma to La Villa, several km north of the Zócalo.

POLANCO

The smart residential quarter north of Bosque de Chapultepec, known as Polanco, contains a couple of interesting museums, numerous restaurants, several embassies, some expensive hotels and shops, and the SECTUR tourist office (see the earlier Information section). You could visit this relatively peaceful part of the city before or after the Museo Nacional de Antropología, which is close by. There's a market area along Virgilio, off Julio Verne north of Parque Lincoln.

Centro Cultural Arte Contemporáneo

The Contemporary Art Cultural Centre on Campos Elíseos on the corner of Jorge Eliot (metro: Auditorio) focuses on avant-garde art, a generation or two after the artists displayed in the Modern Art or Tamayo museums. Some of the exhibits are beautiful or arresting, others may make you wonder why the artists bothered! The ground and 1st floors display varied visiting exhibitions; the 2nd floor holds permanent collections of Mexican and international art and photographs; the 3rd floor is devoted to 'electronic art' – strange (or just boring?) arrangements of light and screens.

Hours are Tuesday from 10 am to 6 pm, Wednesday 10 am to 8 pm, Thursday to Sunday 10 am to 6 pm. Entry costs 5 pesos but is free on Wednesday and Sunday.

Museo Sala de Arte Público David Alfaro Siqueiros

Shortly before his death in 1974, Siqueiros donated his house and studio at Tres Picos 29, on the corner of Hegel (metro: Auditorio or Polanco), to the government for use as a museum. His private papers and photographs, along with a lot of his art, are on display. Hours are Monday to Friday from 10 am to 5 pm, Saturday 10 am to 2 pm. Entry costs 6 pesos. The house is 300 metres north-west of the Museo Nacional de Antropología.

LOMAS DE CHAPULTEPEC

West of Polanco and Bosque de Chapultepec is Lomas de Chapultepec, one of Mexico City's wealthiest residential areas, full of large houses protected by high walls. You can take a quick tour of the area by boarding bus 'Km 15.5 por Palmas' westbound on Paseo de la Reforma in the Bosque de Chapultepec. The bus goes along Avenida de las Palmas, the main boulevard of Lomas de

Chapultepec, before re-emerging on Paseo de la Reforma four or five km west of Bosque de Chapultepec. Here you can either take a 'M(etro) Auditorio', 'M(etro) Chapultepec' or 'Zócalo' bus or pesero back towards the city centre, or stay on the bus as it climbs towards the city's fringes past exclusive housing precincts where ID is needed to enter.

TLATELOLCO & GUADALUPE

Tlatelolco – Plaza de las Tres Culturas

About two km north of the Alameda Central up Avenida Lázaro Cárdenas is the Plaza de las Tres Culturas, so called because it symbolises the fusion of pre-Hispanic and Spanish roots into the modern Mexican mestizo identity. The Aztec pyramids of Tlatelolco, the 17th-century Spanish colonial church of Santiago, and the modern Foreign Affairs building on the plaza's south side represent the three cultures.

Founded by Aztecs in the 14th century as a separate dynasty from Tenochtitlán, on what was then a separate island, Tlatelolco was annexed by Tenochtitlán in 1473. In pre-Hispanic times it was the scene of the largest market in the Valley of Mexico. Spaniards under Cortés defeated Tlatelolco's Aztec defenders, led by Cuauhtémoc, here in 1521. An inscription about that battle in the plaza today translates: 'This was neither victory nor defeat. It was the sad birth of the mestizo people which is Mexico today'.

Today Tlatelolco is also a symbol of more modern conflict. On 2 October 1968, an estimated 300 to 400 people among a crowd of political protesters were massacred by government troops on the eve of the Mexico City Olympic Games. The plaza, situated in the middle of a high-rise housing estate, is a calm oasis among the hurly-burly of the city, but is haunted by echoes of its sombre history.

You can view the ruins of Tlatelolco's main pyramid-temple and other Aztec buildings from a walkway erected around them. The Spanish, recognising the religious significance of the place, built a monastery and then, in 1609, the Church of Santiago that stands today. Just inside the main (west)

doors of the church is the baptismal font of Juan Diego (see the following Basílica de Guadalupe section for background on Juan Diego). Outside the north wall of the church stands a monument to the victims of the 1968 massacre, erected in 1993. The full truth about the massacre has never come out: the traces were hastily cleaned away, and not until 1993 were Mexican schoolbooks permitted to refer to it.

'Eje Central, Central Camionera, Tenayuca' peseros or buses, running north on Avenida Lázaro Cárdenas by the Palacio de Bellas Artes, pass right by the Plaza de las Tres Culturas. Alternatively, take the metro to Tlatelolco station, exit on to the busy Calle Manuel González, and turn right. Walk to the first major intersection (Avenida Lázaro Cárdenas), turn right again and you will soon see the plaza on the far (east) side of the road – 900 metres from the metro station in all. Returning to the city centre, you can get a 'M(etro) Hidalgo' pesero southbound on Calle Lerdo, one block west of Avenida Lázaro Cárdenas.

Basílica de Guadalupe

On 9 December 1531 a Mexican Indian Christian convert named Juan Diego, standing on the Cerro del Tepeyac hill, site of an old Aztec shrine about six km north of the Zócalo, saw a vision of a beautiful lady in a blue mantle trimmed with gold. He told the local priest that he had seen the Virgin Mary, but the priest didn't believe him. Juan returned to the hill, saw the vision again, and an image of the lady was miraculously emblazoned on his cloak. Eventually the church authorities believed his story, and a cult grew up around the place.

Over the following centuries Nuestra Señora de Guadalupe (Our Lady of Guadalupe), as this manifestation of the Virgin became known, came to receive the credit for all manner of miracles, hugely aiding the acceptance of Catholicism by Mexican Indians. In 1737, after she had extinguished an outbreak of typhoid in Mexico City, she was officially declared the Principal Patroness of New Spain. Today her image is to be seen throughout the country, and her shrines around the Cerro del Tepeyac are the most revered in Mexico, attracting thousands of pilgrims daily from all over the country – and hundreds of thousands on the days leading up to her feast day, 12 December. See the Festivals section in this chapter for more on these festivities.

The pilgrims' main goal is the Basílica de Nuestra Señora de Guadalupe, at the foot of the Cerro del Tepeyac. Some pilgrims travel the last few hundred metres to this church on their knees. By the 1970s the first basilica here, built around 1700, was being swamped by the numbers of worshippers and was also leaning alarmingly as it slowly sank into the soft earth beneath. So a **new basilica** was built next door, on the west side of the large plaza. Designed by Pedro Ramírez Vásquez, already famous for his Museo Nacional de Antropología, the new basilica is a vast, rounded, open-plan structure able to hold many thousands of worshippers at once. The sound of so many singing together is quite thrilling. The Virgin's miraculous image hangs above the main altar, with moving walkways beneath it to bring visitors as close as possible. The rear of the old basilica is now the **Museo de la Basílica de Guadalupe**, with a fine collection of *retablos* (small tin panels painted by pilgrims in thanks for miracles), plus plenty of colonial religious art. It's open Tuesday to Sunday from 10 am to 6 pm; admission is 1 peso.

Steps behind the old basilica climb about 100 metres up to the hilltop **Capilla del Cerrito** (Hill Chapel) on the spot where Juan Diego saw his vision. The church dates from the 17th or 18th century. From here, steps lead down the east side of the hill to the **Jardín del Tepeyac** (Tepeyac Garden), where the modern monument *La Ofrenda* (The Offering) shows the Virgin of Guadalupe receiving gifts from Mexican Indians and a Spanish priest. From the Jardín de Tepeyac a path leads back to the main plaza, re-entering it beside the 17th-century **Capilla de Indios** (Chapel of Indians), next to the place where, according to tradition, Juan Diego lived from 1531 to his death in 1548.

An easy way to reach the Basílica de Guadalupe is to take the metro to La Villa station then walk two blocks north along Calzada de Guadalupe (follow the crowds). You can also reach La Villa metro station by taking any 'M(etro) La Villa' pesero or bus running north-east on Paseo de la Reforma. A 'M(etro) Hidalgo' or 'M(etro) Chapultepec' pesero heading south down Calzada de los Misterios, a block west of Calzada de Guadalupe, will return you to the city centre.

TENAYUCA & SANTA CECILIA ACATITLÁN

Ruins enthusiasts might find it's worth making a day trip to two Aztec sites just beyond the Distrito Federal's northern border, now surrounded by Mexico City's urban sprawl.

Tenayuca was settled at least as far back as the 11th century but its last ruler was a son of Moctezuma and the pyramid he left is a dead ringer for what the Templo Mayor in the Mexico City Zócalo looked like, though smaller. Striking serpent sculptures surround three sides of its base – imagine what they looked like when they were painted bright red, yellow and green. There's a small museum on the site, with some artefacts, diagrams showing the various stages of the pyramid's construction, and a model of the pyramid with the two temples which originally surmounted it.

The site is open from 10 am to 5 pm daily except Monday (10 pesos; free Sunday). The pyramid is next to Tenayuca zócalo – take a 'Pirámide' pesero from La Raza metro station, or an 'Eje Central, Central Camionera, Tenayuca' pesero north on Lázaro Cárdenas from Bellas Artes.

Santa Cecilia Acatitlán, two km north of Tenayuca, is a small but fine pyramid topped with a temple dedicated to the war god Huizilopochtli. It's one of the few surviving pyramids which still has a complete Aztec temple on top. It's surrounded by a pleasant garden which is accessed through the Plazuela & Museo Hurtado. The museum was being renovated in 1994, and was not open, though it was possible to visit the pyramid. Opening hours were irregular but they weren't charging admission. The entrance to the plazuela is in a lane behind the 16th-century Parroquia Santa Cecilia church. If the site is closed, you may be able to look at the pyramid through iron railings in the fence.

You can reach Santa Cecilia Acatitlán by taking a pesero or bus that's going north up Avenida Santa Cecilia, west of the Tenayuca pyramid. Get off at Calle Pirámide de Tula and walk a few blocks east to the church. You'll probably need to ask for directions – the people at Tenayuca will get you started. A taxi would be much easier. There are also peseros between Basílica metro and Santa Cecilia.

INSURGENTES SUR

Avenida Insurgentes, the longest street in Mexico City, runs from La Villa de Guadalupe in the north to Cuicuilco in the south. Its southern section, Avenida Insurgentes Sur, passes one or two places of interest between Paseo de la Reforma and the attractive suburb of San Ángel. 'San Ángel' and 'Tlalpan' peseros and buses south on Insurgentes, from anywhere at least as far north as Estación Buenavista, will take you to these places. Returning north, 'M(etro) Indios Verdes' buses and peseros travel the whole length of Insurgentes to the north of the city; 'M(etro) Insurgentes' vehicles go to Insurgentes metro station, one km south of Paseo de la Reforma.

Poliforum Cultural Siqueiros

The bizarre Siqueiros Poliforum, on Insurgentes Sur on the corner of Filadelfia, 4.5 km south of Reforma, was designed by muralist Siqueiros and opened in 1971. It's an arts centre, and is open daily from 10 am to 7.30 pm.

The 12-sided exterior of the building is covered with murals: the atom as the triumph of peace over destruction, and dramas of love during the Spanish conquest, among other subjects. The wall backing Insurgentes shows five leaders of the Mexican artistic resurgence of the late 19th and 20th centuries: Rivera, Orozco, the cartoonist and print-maker José Guadalupe Posada, the engraver Leopoldo Méndez, and Dr Atl. Inside, the ground floor houses contemporary art exhibitions, while the auditorium, upstairs, is covered with Siqueiros's last, enormous mural, *The March of Humanity on Earth and Towards the Cosmos*. Grand in scale and concept – it took six years and a team of 50 to finish it – the mural is meant to be seen from a rotating, tilting central platform in a sound-and-light show, but this only happens when a group books it. The 50-storey Hotel de México towering behind the poliforum was for a long time a white elephant, that stood unfinished for years after its funding ran out. But it has now been converted into a World Trade Centre.

Ciudad de los Deportes & Parque Hundido

'Sports City', 1.5 km south of the poliforum, consists of Mexico City's major bullring, the Monumental Plaza México (reputedly the largest in the world, holding 64,000 spectators) and a 65,000-capacity sports stadium called the Estadio Ciudad de los Deportes. Calle Maximino A Camacho leads a few blocks west from Insurgentes Sur to both places. See the Entertainment section for information on events here.

An alternative way to reach the Ciudad de los Deportes is to ride the metro to San Antonio station on línea 7, take the exit to Avenida San Antonio and Calle Balderas and walk east along Balderas (one km).

Parque Luis Urbina, also known as the Parque Hundido (Sunken Garden), half a km south along Insurgentes Sur from Sports City, is a leafy park containing 51 copies of famous pre-Hispanic Mexican artworks.

SAN ÁNGEL

Sixty years ago San Ángel ('san ANN-hell'), 8.5 km south of Paseo de la Reforma, was a village separated from Mexico City by open fields. Today it's one of the city's most charming suburbs, with many quiet cobbled streets lined by both old colonial houses and expensive modern homes. San Ángel is best known for its weekly arts and craft market, the Bazar

Sábado (Saturday Bazaar), but there's plenty of things to do on other days too (don't come on Monday though, as the museums will be closed). Coyoacán, another fascinating southern suburb, lies only three km east of San Ángel and it's quite feasible to visit both in one day although a full day in either won't be wasted. Also within easy reach is the Ciudad Universitaria, 1.5 km south of San Ángel.

The two main roads through San Ángel are Avenida Insurgentes Sur, which runs north-south through the eastern side of the suburb, and Avenida Revolución, parallel to Insurgentes around 200 metres west.

Plaza San Jacinto & Bazar Sábado

Every Saturday the Bazar Sábado market (see Things to Buy later in this chapter) brings a festive atmosphere, masses of colour and crowds of people to San Ángel's pretty little Plaza San Jacinto. To reach it walk uphill, south-west from Avenida Revolución, on Calle Madero.

The 16th-century **Iglesia de San Jacinto**, off the west side of the plaza, has a peaceful garden where you can take refuge from the crowded market areas. It's entered from Calle Juárez. The 18th-century **Casa del Risco**, on the north side of Plaza San Jacinto at No 15, contains two courtyards with beautiful tiled fountains and two museums. One, the Museo Colonial Casa del Risco, is dedicated to European and colonial art, furniture and domestic objects. The other, the Centro Cultural y Biblioteca Isidro Fábela, has a library and a display of colonial art. Both are open from 10 am to 5 pm daily except Monday and entry is free.

Museo Estudio Diego Rivera & San Ángel Inn

One km (a 10-minute walk) north-west of Plaza San Jacinto, at Calle Diego Rivera 2 on the corner of Altavista, is the Diego Rivera Studio Museum. Rivera lived here for several years with Frida Kahlo. The ground floor is a gallery for temporary exhibitions. The studio itself, upstairs, contains 6000 items, including Aztec statuettes, dozens of fanciful skeleton shapes in various media, self-portraits, portraits of women, and much other Riveriana. The museum is open daily from 10 am to 6 pm except Monday; admission is 7 pesos.

To walk from Plaza de San Jacinto, head north from the north-west corner of the plaza to reach Calle General Rivera. Turn left, then take the third street on the right (Reina), then the first left off Reina. This is Lazcano. The museum is a short distance to the right from the end of Lazcano.

Just to the left (south-west) of the Museo Estudio Diego Rivera, on the corner of Santa Catarina, Palmas and Altavista, the 18th-century ex-Hacienda de Goicoechea has a beautiful verdant courtyard, a fountain, a chapel and colonial gardens. Once the home of the marquises of Selva Nevada and the counts of Pinillos, it is now the San Ángel Inn, a luxurious restaurant.

You can reach the Museo Estudio Diego Rivera and the San Ángel Inn by pesero along Comunal and Altavista from the corner of Avenida Revolución.

Diego Rivera

Museo de Arte Carrillo Gil

The Carrillo Gil Art Museum at Avenida Revolución 1608 is one of Mexico City's best art galleries. It has a permanent collection of Mexican and foreign artists of the first rank, with many works by Rivera, Siqueiros, Orozco (including some of his grotesque, satirical early drawings and watercolours), Picasso and others. Temporary exhibits are also excellent. Hours are Tuesday to Sunday from 10 am to 6 pm; admission is 7 pesos. There's also a pleasant bookshop-café in the basement.

To reach the museum from Plaza San Jacinto, walk down to Avenida Revolución, then go two blocks north past a picturesque streetside flower market to the corner of Revolución and Camino Desierto de los Leones. From the San Ángel Inn, you can take any bus or pesero heading east down Altavista, and get out at Avenida Revolución.

Museo del Carmen

The tile-domed church and museum of El Carmen are at Avenida Revolución 4, on the corner of Calle Monasterio opposite the end of Calle Madero. The cool, peaceful church was built between 1615 and 1617 to the designs of Andrés de San Miguel, a Carmelite monk. The museum occupies the former monastic quarters to one side of the church and is mainly devoted to colonial religious art – but its big tourist attraction is the mummified bodies in the crypt, which are thought to be 18th-century monks, nuns and gentry. You can also walk out into the pretty garden, once much bigger, which was a source for cuttings and seeds sent all over colonial Mexico, including to California. The museum is open Tuesday to Sunday from 10 am to 5 pm. Admission costs 7 pesos.

Parque de la Bombilla

This pleasant park lies just east of Avenida Insurgentes, along the south side of Avenida La Paz. Near the Insurgentes end is a monument to Álvaro Obregón, the Mexican revolutionary and president who was assassinated on this spot during a banquet in 1928, soon after he had won a new presidential

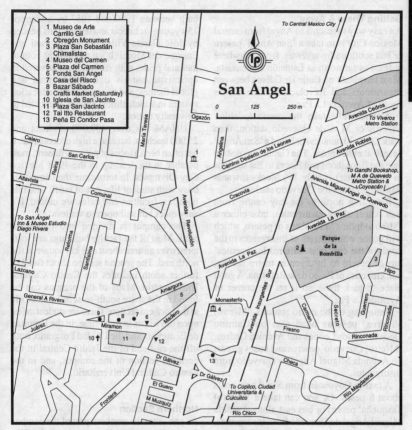

1 Museo de Arte
  Carrillo Gil
2 Obregón Monument
3 Plaza San Sebastián
  Chimalistac
4 Museo del Carmen
5 Plaza del Carmen
6 Fonda San Ángel
7 Casa del Risco
8 Bazar Sábado
9 Crafts Market (Saturday)
10 Iglesia de San Jacinto
11 Plaza San Jacinto
12 Tai Itto Restaurant
13 Peña El Condor Pasa

San Ángel

term. The killer was a young Christian fanatic, José de León Toral, who was involved in the Cristero rebellion against the government's anti-Church policies. Just beyond the far (east) end of the park is the Plaza San Sebastián Chimalistac, surrounded by old colonial houses and a little church with a 16th-century open chapel.

Copilco

One km south of Avenida La Paz along Insurgentes, then 500 metres east along Avenida Copilco and Calle Victoria, is the site of one of the earliest villages in the Valley of Mexico. Copilco probably already existed in 1200 BC, and remained inhabited until 400 BC. It is thought to have been a trade and religious centre for a large agricultural area and may have been ruled by priests.

The village was buried by an eruption of the volcano Xitle between about 100 BC and 100 AD. Archaeologists have found several tombs containing skeletons, stone implements and clay figurines beneath three metres of lava. Some of these are displayed in a museum which is open from 10 am to 5 pm daily except Monday. The nearest metro station is M A de Quevedo, one km northeast of the site.

Getting There & Away

An easy way to reach San Ángel from central Mexico City is to take a 'San Ángel' pesero or bus south on Insurgentes, from anywhere at least as far north as Estación Buenavista. Most terminate on Calle Dr Gálvez between Insurgentes and Revolución, three blocks south of Avenida La Paz.

Alternatively, take the metro to either Viveros or M A de Quevedo station, then walk (20 to 30 minutes) or board a 'San Ángel' pesero at either place. The Gandhi bookshop (see the Bookshops and Places to Eat sections in this chapter) is only 1½ blocks towards San Ángel from the Quevedo station.

Returning north to the city centre from San Ángel along Insurgentes, take either a 'M(etro) Indios Verdes' bus or pesero, which will go the whole length of Insurgentes to the north of the city, or a 'M(etro) Insurgentes' bus or pesero to Insurgentes metro station, one km south of Paseo de la Reforma. A good place to pick these up is on the corner of Avenida La Paz.

Returning to the metro stations, 'M(etro) Viveros' peseros head east on Camino Desierto de los Leones and Avenida Cedros. 'M(etro) Quevedo' peseros and buses go east on Avenida Miguel Ángel de Quevedo from Insurgentes.

A taxi to Coyoacán from San Ángel costs about 8 pesos. Or you can take a 'M(etro) Tasqueña' pesero or bus east along Avenida Miguel Ángel de Quevedo from Insurgentes. Get off on the corner of Calle Carrillo Puerto, after 2.5 km, and walk five blocks north to Coyoacán's Plaza Central.

CIUDAD UNIVERSITARIA

The University City, on the east side of Avenida Insurgentes two km south of San Ángel, is the main campus of Latin America's biggest university, the Universidad Nacional Autónoma de México (UNAM), and one of the nation's modern architectural showpieces. It stands on part of a vast dried-up lava field called El Pedregal.

The university was originally founded in the 1550s but was suppressed from 1833 to 1910. Most of the Ciudad Universitaria was built between 1950 and 1953 by a team of 150 young architects and technicians headed by José García Villagrán, Mario Pani and Enrique del Moral. It's a monument both to national pride, with its buildings covered in optimistic murals linking Mexican and global themes, and to an idealistic education system in which almost anyone is entitled to university tuition.

UNAM has over 400,000 students and 25,000 teachers, but also a high dropout rate. It has often been a focus of political dissent, most notably in the lead-up to the 1968 Mexico City Olympics. In term-time the campus is busy with student life; out of term, when its libraries, faculties and cafés are closed, it's very quiet but still open to visitors.

The campus is divided into two main parts. Most of the faculty buildings are scattered over an area about one km square at the north end. The second section about two km further south includes the Centro Cultural Universitario. Maps of the campus can be found in the space south-west of La Rectoría in the northern section. There are student cafés, open to visitors in term-time, in the Facultad de Economía and the Unidad Posgrado, both off the east end of the Jardín Central in the northern section of the campus, and in the Centro Cultural Universitario.

Northern Section

As you enter the northern part of the campus from Insurgentes, it's easy to spot the **Biblioteca Central** (Central Library), one of Mexico's most eye-catching modern buildings – 10 floors high, almost windowless, and covered on every side with mosaics by Juan O'Gorman. The south wall, with two prominent circles towards the top, covers colonial times. The theme of the north wall is Aztec culture. The east wall shows the creation of modern Mexico. The mosaic on the west wall is harder to interpret but may be dedicated to Latin American culture as a whole.

La Rectoría, the Rectorate administration building south-west of the library, at the top (west) end of the wide, grassy Jardín Central, has a spectacular 3-D mosaic by Siqueiros on its south wall, showing students urged on by the people.

The building to the south of La Rectoría contains a post office, the campus's Librería Central (Central Bookshop), and the university's own modern art museum, the **Museo Universitario Contemporáneo de Arte**, with some worthwhile visiting shows.

The **Auditorio Alfonso Caso**, at the bottom (east) end of the Jardín Central, has on its north end a mural by José Chávez Morado showing the conquest of energy. Humanity progresses from the shadow of a primitive jaguar god to the use of fire and then the atom, before emerging into an ethereal, apparently female, future. A little further east, on the west wall of the **Facultad de Medicina**, a mosaic in Italian stone by Francisco Eppens interprets the theme of life and death in Mexican terms. The central mask has a Spanish profile on the left, an Indian one on the right, together making up a mestizo face in the middle. A maize cob and symbols of Aztec and Mayan gods represent the forces of life and death.

Estadio Olímpico

The Olympic Stadium, on the west side of Insurgentes opposite the northern part of the campus, is designed to resemble a somewhat elliptical volcano cone and holds 80,000 people. There's a Rivera mosaic over its main entrance. The stadium is home to the UNAM soccer team, known as the Pumas. You can peep inside when it's closed by going to Gate 38 at the south end.

Southern Section

The **Centro Cultural Universitario** is the focus of the southern part of the campus. To reach it take a bus or pesero south on Insurgentes to the second footbridge south of the Estadio Olímpico, then walk the short distance into the campus. Find the Estacionamiento No 2 parking area and take the steps down behind Rufino Tamayo's tall black sculpture, *La Universidad Germen de Humanismo y Sabiduría* (The University, Seed of Humanism and Wisdom). You'll find the Sala Nezahualcóyotl, one of Mexico

City's main concert halls, down here on the left, and a collection of theatres, cinemas and smaller concert halls to the right. About 200 metres north of the Centro Cultural is the large **Unidad Bibliográfica** (Bibliographic Unit), which houses part of Mexico's National Library.

About 300 metres north of the Unidad Bibliográfica is the **Espacio Escultórico** (Sculptural Space), focused on a work by Mathias Goeritz which no one can explain but most people agree is striking. It consists of concrete shapes about a round platform, set on a bare lava bed.

Getting There & Away

Any pesero or bus marked 'Imán', 'Tlalpan', 'Villa Olímpica' or 'Perisur' travelling south on Avenida Insurgentes from the city centre or San Ángel will take you to the Ciudad Universitaria. If none of these shows up, take one marked 'San Ángel' and change at San Ángel.

For the northern part of the campus, get off at the first yellow footbridge crossing Insurgentes a little over one km from San Ángel, just before the Estadio Olímpico. For the southern part of the campus, get off at the third yellow footbridge from San Ángel (the second after the Estadio Olímpico).

Returning north, 'San Ángel', 'M(etro) Insurgentes' or 'M(etro) Indios Verdes' buses or peseros will take you along Insurgentes as far as their respective destinations.

The university's handiest metro station is Copilco, near the north-east edge of the campus, one km east of the Biblioteca Central. Universidad station, further south, is less convenient.

CUICUILCO

The early archaeological site of Cuicuilco is set in the Parque Ecológico Cuicuilco, on the east side of Insurgentes 1.5 km south of the south end of the Ciudad Universitaria. The 1968 Olympic Village, now turned into housing, is on the west side of Insurgentes opposite the park. To get there, take a 'Tlalpan', 'Villa Olímpica' or 'Perisur' pesero or bus south on Insurgentes from San

Ángel or the Ciudad Universitaria, and get off immediately after going under the Periférico Sur ring road.

Cuicuilco was probably the biggest settlement in the Valley of Mexico from approximately 600 to 200 BC. At this time the valley was something of a backwater, far from the centres of Mexican civilisation on the Gulf Coast, but Cuicuilco is estimated to have had a population of 20,000 on a 4.5-sq-km area, and traces of a street layout have been found. It was still occupied when it was buried by the eruption of Xitle volcano, to the south, some time between 100 BC and 100 AD.

The site, which has a museum, is open from 9 am to 4.30 pm daily. Entry is free. The main structure is a round pyramid, 118 metres wide. A 10-metre layer of lava has been removed from its lower levels. The pyramid shows that Cuicuilco must have been a ceremonial centre of an organised, priest-dominated society. Earlier temples in the Valley of Mexico were thatch-roofed affairs on low earth mounds.

COYOACÁN

About 10 km south of central Mexico City, Coyoacán ('Place of Coyotes' in Nahuatl) was Cortés's base after the fall of Tenochtitlán. It remained a small town outside Mexico City until the urban sprawl surrounded it 50 years ago. Close to the university and once home to Leon Trotsky, Diego Rivera and Frida Kahlo (whose old houses are among several excellent museums in the area), it still has its own identity, with narrow colonial-era streets, plazas, cafés and a Bohemian atmosphere. Coyoacán's special day is Sunday, when musicians, mime artists and craft markets (see Things to Buy later in this chapter) draw relaxed weekend crowds from all over the city to its central plazas.

Plaza Hidalgo & Jardín del Centenario

The focuses of Coyoacán life, and scene of most of the weekend festivities, are its twin central plazas – the eastern Plaza Hidalgo, with its statue of Miguel Hidalgo, and the western Jardín del Centenario, with its coyote fountain. Calle Aguayo/Carrillo Puerto divides the two parts. Several cafés and restaurants are located on or near the twin plazas (see Places to Eat).

The former town hall (Ayuntamiento) of Coyoacán, on the north side of Plaza Hidalgo, is also called the **Casa de Cortés**. It's said that on this spot the Spanish tortured the defeated Aztec emperor Cuauhtémoc to try to make him reveal the whereabouts of treasure. The existing 18th-century building was the headquarters of the Marquesado del Valle de Oaxaca, the Cortés family's lands in Mexico, which included Coyoacán. Above the entrance is the coat of arms bestowed on Coyoacán by King Carlos IV of Spain.

The **Parroquia de San Juan Bautista**, Coyoacán's parish church, and the adjacent ex-monastery, on the south side of Plaza Hidalgo, were built for Dominican monks in the 16th century. Half a block east of Plaza Hidalgo, at Avenida Hidalgo 289, is the **Museo Nacional de Culturas Populares**, which has good temporary exhibitions on popular cultural forms like lucha libre (freestyle wrestling), *nacimientos* (nativity models) and circuses. It's free, and open Tuesday to Sunday from 10 am to 5 or 6 pm.

Plaza de la Conchita

Formally called Plaza de la Concepción, this peaceful little square is two blocks east of Plaza Hidalgo, along Calle Higuera. The red house (not open to the public) on the corner of Higuera is the 'Casa Colorada'. Cortés is said to have built it for La Malinche, his Mexican interpreter and mistress, and to have had his Spanish wife, Catalina Juárez de Marcaida, murdered here. On the east side of the plaza stands the pretty little 18th-century baroque church of La Concepción. Beyond (east of) the Plaza de la Conchita is the Jardín Frida Kahlo, a park with a statue of the artist atop a pyramidal base in pre-Hispanic style.

Viveros & Jardín de Santa Catarina

One of the most pleasant ways of approaching Coyoacán is from Viveros metro station via the Viveros de Coyoacán. The Viveros (plant nurseries) are a swath of greenery,

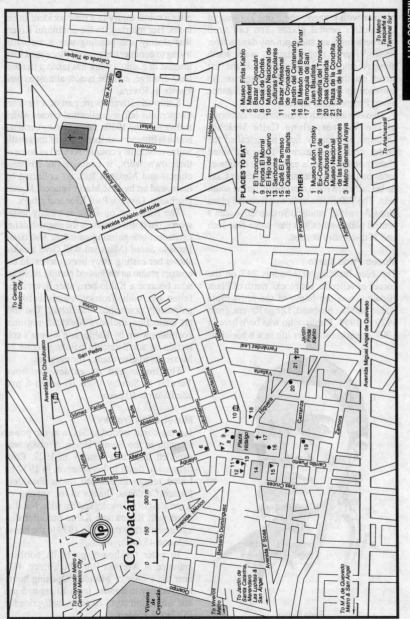

Coyoacán

0   150   300 m

PLACES TO EAT

7   El Tizoncito
9   Fonda El Morral
12 El Hijo del Cuervo
15 Sanborns
16 Café El Parnaso
18 Quesadilla Stands

OTHER

1   Museo León Trotsky
2   Ex-Convento de
    Churubusco &
    Museo Nacional
    de las Intervenciones
3   Metro General Anaya
4   Museo Frida Kahlo
5   Market
6   Bazar Coyoacán
8   Casa de Cortés
10 Museo Nacional de
    Culturas Populares
11 Bazar Artesanal
    de Coyoacán
14 Jardín del Centenario
16 El Mesón del Buen Tunar
17 Parroquia de San
    Juan Bautista
19 Hostería del Trovador
20 Casa Colorada
21 Plaza de la Conchita
22 Iglesia de la Concepción

To Central Mexico City

To Viveros Metro

To Coyoacán Metro & Central Mexico City

To Metro Tasqueña & Terminal Sur

To Anahuacalli

To Jardín de Santa Catarina, Merendero Las Lupitas & San Ángel

To M A de Quevedo Metro & San Ángel

popular with joggers, about one km west of Coyoacán's central plazas. You can stroll here between 6 am and 6 pm any day for free. From Viveros metro station, walk south along Avenida Universidad then take the first street on the left, Avenida Progreso. An entrance to the Viveros is a short distance along Progreso, on the left.

Two blocks south of the south-east corner of the Viveros, along Calle Melchor Ocampo, is a pretty little plaza called the Jardín de Santa Catarina. There's a small church on the plaza's east side, a couple of cafés on the west side, and Coyoacan's Casa de la Cultura, a local arts centre, on the south side. The 700-metre walk east from the plaza along Avenida Francisco Sosa to Coyoacán's central plazas takes you past some fine 16th and 17th-century houses.

Museo Frida Kahlo

The blue building at Londres 247 on the corner of Allende, six blocks north of Plaza Hidalgo, was the home of the artist Frida Kahlo and her husband, Diego Rivera, from 1929 to 1954. Kahlo, who was born here in 1907, spent most of her life in a wheelchair

Frida Kahlo

after a spinal injury in a road accident in her teens. Her marriage to the unfaithful Rivera was stormy and painting was a means of trying to conquer her misery. Since the 1980s interest in Kahlo's work has taken a tremendous upsurge, and she is now almost as well known as Rivera.

Kahlo and Rivera were part of a far from harmonious leftist intellectual circle (which included, in the 1930s, Leon Trotsky), and the house is littered with mementos of the artistic and revolutionary couple. As well as some of their own work, it contains pre-Hispanic objects and Mexican folk art collected by them, and art by José María Velasco, Marcel Duchamp, Orozco, Paul Klee and others.

The Kahlo art on show is mostly lesser works, but it still expresses the anguish of her existence: one painting called *El Marxismo Dará la Salud* (Marxism Will Give Health) shows her casting away her crutches. In the upstairs studio an unfinished portrait of Stalin, who became a Kahlo hero after Rivera had fallen out with Trotsky, stands before a poignantly positioned wheelchair. The folk art collection includes Mexican regional costumes worn by Kahlo, and Rivera's collection of small retablo paintings done by Mexicans to give thanks for miracles.

The house and its garden are open Tuesday to Sunday from 10 am to 6 pm; admission is 10 pesos.

Museo Léon Trotsky

Having come second to Stalin in the power struggle in the Soviet Union, Trotsky was expelled from that country in 1929. Condemned to death in his absence, in 1937 he found refuge in Mexico under President Lázaro Cárdenas, thanks to the support of Rivera. At first Trotsky and his wife, Natalia, lived with Rivera and Kahlo but after disagreements they moved in 1939 to the house at Viena 45 in Coyoacán.

To enter the house, go to its northern entrance at Avenida Río Churubusco 410, near the corner of Morelos. Opening hours are Tuesday to Sunday from 10 am to 5 pm and admission costs 10 pesos, half-price for ISIC card-holders.

The house has been left pretty much as it was on the day in 1940 when a Stalin agent finally caught up with Trotsky and killed him here. High walls and watchtowers – once manned by armed bodyguards – surround the house and small garden. These defences were built after a first attempt on Trotsky's life on 24 May 1940, when attackers led by the Mexican artist Siqueiros pumped bullets into the house. Trotsky and Natalia survived by hiding under their bedroom furniture. The bullet holes remain.

The final fatal attack took place in Trotsky's study. The assassin had several identities but is usually referred to as Ramón Mercader, a Spaniard. He had managed to become the lover of Trotsky's secretary and gain the confidence of the household. On 20 August 1940 he went to Trotsky at his desk, and asked him to look at a document. Mercader then pulled an ice-axe from under his coat and smashed it into the back of Trotsky's skull. Trotsky died next day; Mercader was arrested and spent 20 years in prison. Trotsky's desk has been left much as it was at the time of his death: the books and magazines lying on it give an intriguing glimpse of his preoccupations.

A display in an outbuilding shows photos of Trotsky's time in Mexico, plus biographical notes (in Spanish). The garden contains a tomb holding the Trotskys' ashes.

Ex-Convento de Churubusco

Less than 1.5 km east of the Trotsky Museum stands the 17th-century former Monastery of Churubusco, scene of one of Mexico's heroic military defeats. It's on Calle 20 de Agosto at General Anaya, two blocks east of Avenida División del Norte along Catita.

On 20 August 1847, an invading American army was advancing on Mexico City from Veracruz. Mexicans who had fortified the old monastery fought until they ran out of ammunition and were only finally beaten in hand-to-hand fighting. General Pedro Anaya, asked by US general Twiggs to surrender his ammunition, is said to have answered: 'If there was any, you wouldn't be

here'. Cannons and memorials outside the monastery recall these events.

The monastery's church, on its west side, still functions, but most of the monastery is occupied by the interesting **Museo Nacional de las Intervenciones** (National Interventions Museum), open from 9 am to 6 pm Tuesday to Sunday (admission 10 pesos). Displays include an American map showing operations in 1847 (note how far outside the city Churubusco was then), and material on the French occupation in the 1860s and the plot by US ambassador Henry Lane Wilson to bring down the Madero government in 1913. Parts of the peaceful old monastery gardens are also open to visitors.

You can reach Churubusco on a 'M(etro) Gral Anaya' pesero or bus going east on Xicoténcatl at Allende, a few blocks north of Coyoacán's Plaza Hidalgo. Alternatively it's a 500-metre walk west along Calle 20 de Agosto from General Anaya metro station.

Anahuacalli

This dramatic museum was designed by Diego Rivera to house his own excellent collection of pre-Hispanic art. It also contains one of his studios and some of his own work. It's at Calle del Museo 150, 3.5 km south of central Coyoacán.

The fortress-like building is made of dark volcanic stone and incorporates stylistic features from many pre-Hispanic cultures. Its name means House of Anáhuac (Anáhuac was the Aztec name for the Valley of Mexico). An inscription over the door reads: 'To return to the people the artistic inheritance I was able to redeem from their ancestors'. If the air is clear, there's a great view over the city from the roof.

The archaeological exhibits are mostly pottery and stone figures, selected primarily for their artistic qualities. Among Rivera's own art, the most interesting are studies for major murals like *El Hombre en el Cruce de los Caminos* (Man at the Crossroads) whose final version, *El Hombre, Contralor del Universo*, can be seen at the Palacio de Bellas Artes. The Anahuacalli is open daily, except Monday, from 10 am to 2 pm and 3 to 6 pm.

Entry is free. To get there from Coyoacán, catch a 'Huipulco' or 'Espartaco' bus or pesero south down Avenida División del Norte, which is just over one km east of Coyoacán's Plaza Hidalgo. Get off after three km at Calle del Museo (there are traffic lights and a church at the intersection), and walk six blocks west along Calle del Museo, curving to the left at first, then going slightly uphill. Returning northwards, take a 'M(etro) División del Norte' pesero or bus along Avenida División del Norte.

From central Mexico City, take the metro to Tasqueña, then the Tren Ligero (tram) from Tasqueña metro station to Xotepingo. The Tren Ligero costs 0.40 pesos, paid in coins at the Tasqueña platform entrance. Follow 'Salida a Museo' signs at Xotepingo station and go three short blocks along Calle Xotepingo to the traffic lights at Avenida División del Norte. Then continue ahead along Calle del Museo for six blocks as described in the previous paragraph.

Getting There & Away

The nearest metro stations to Coyoacán are Viveros, Coyoacán and General Anaya, all 1.5 to two km away. From Viveros station you can walk via the pleasant Viveros (plant nurseries) and Jardín de Santa Catarina to the centre of Coyoacán. If you don't fancy a walk, from Viveros station, walk south to Avenida Progreso and catch an eastbound 'M(etro) Gral Anaya' pesero to Calle Allende; from Coyoacán station take the 'Coyoacán' exit, walk a few metres south along Avenida Universidad, and catch a 'Coyoacán' pesero going south-east (half left) on Avenida México; from General Anaya station, take a 'Río Guadalupe' bus to Avenida Hidalgo.

To get back to these metro stations from central Coyoacán, there are 'M(etro) Viveros' peseros going west on Malitzin at Allende, 'M(etro) Coyoacán' peseros north on Calle Aguayo, and 'Gral Anaya' peseros and buses east on Xicoténcatl at Allende.

To reach San Ángel from Coyoacán, take a taxi (about 8 pesos), or an 'Insurgentes' or 'Revolución' pesero west on Malitzin at

Allende, or a 'San Ángel' pesero west on Avenida Miguel Ángel de Quevedo, five blocks south of Plaza Hidalgo. To reach the Ciudad Universitaria from Coyoacán, take a 'M(etro) Copilco' pesero west on Malitzin at Allende.

XOCHIMILCO

Xochimilco is a suburb of 'floating gardens' 20 km south of the Zócalo. Its name is Nahuatl for 'place where flowers grow'. Pre-Hispanic inhabitants here built rafts of matted mud and vegetation, named chinampas, on the shallow waters of the Lago de Xochimilco, a southern offshoot of the Lago de Texcoco, to grow food. The chinampas were very fertile, giving three or four harvests a year, and became one of the bases of the economic success of the Aztec empire. As they proliferated, many became rooted to the bottom, and much of the lake was transformed into a series of canals, about 100 km of which are navigable today.

More than 3000 boats, mostly colourful *trajineras* (gondolas) propelled by one man with a pole, now cruise the canals with parties of Mexican merrymakers, mariachi bands, photographers, floating flower stalls, taco bars and big pots of steaming corn. At weekends, especially Sunday, the town and waterways of Xochimilco are jammed with people trying to arrange a boat, cruising the canals or fast-talking you into buying something. Foreign tourists of course attract special attention. The hawkers can be bothersome because they hound you even when you're on the canals. Many of them disappear during the week, so that's a much quieter time to visit, but then you have to pretend that you don't see the mounds of weekend rubbish floating on the water.

You won't have trouble finding a boat: the boatmen will find you as you approach the boat landing. The going rate for an hour's ride is about 30 pesos, but you must negotiate, and the price may have something to do with the condition of the boat. Inspect your craft before you embark. When you've had enough, tell the boatman to return. Remember, he's getting paid by the hour.

To reach Xochimilco, take the metro to Tasqueña station, then take the Tren Ligero, which starts at the station, to its last stop, Xochimilco. It costs 0.40 pesos, paid in coins at the platform entrance. Alternatively you can get on a 'Xochimilco' bus or pesero outside Tasqueña metro station. It's about 45 minutes from Tasqueña to Xochimilco either way. When you reach Xochimilco, look for 'Embarcaderos' signs directing you to the boat landing. The last Tren Ligero back to Tasqueña leaves Xochimilco at about 11 pm.

PARQUE NACIONAL DESIERTO DE LOS LEONES

The name of this 2000-hectare national park, 25 km west of Mexico City, means Desert of the Lions but it is actually a cool pine forest, 800 metres higher than the capital. The name comes from Desierto de Santa Fe, the 17th-century Carmelite monastery in the park – the Carmelites called all their monasteries 'deserts' to commemorate Elijah, who lived as a recluse in the desert near Mt Carmel. The Leones were a family of lawyers who represented the Carmelites and eventually were believed to own the area, hence Desierto de los Leones. The ex-monastery has pleasant gardens and is sometimes the setting for exhibitions and Sunday concerts. The surrounding park has pleasant walking trails and is popular with picnickers on weekends. Robberies have been reported in the park, so take care of your things and don't wander away from the main paths. A bus goes to the park from Observatorio metro station. With a car, you take highway 15 (the road to Toluca) or Camino del Desierto from the suburb of San Ángel (this road is closed from 6 pm to 7 am).

LANGUAGE COURSES

The Centro de Enseñanza para Extranjeros (Foreigners' Teaching Centre, ☎ 550-51-72, fax 548-99-39) at UNAM offers six-week intensive Spanish language courses five times a year. Though classes can be quite large, the courses have received good reports from students we have met. For a fee of about 750 pesos, you get three hours in the class-room, on the main Ciudad Universitaria campus, five days a week. For more information write to: CEPE, Apartado Postal 70-391, Ciudad Universitaria, Delegación Coyoacán, 04510 México DF, Mexico.

FESTIVALS

Every major festival described in Facts for the Visitor is celebrated in Mexico City. Among those with a special flavour in the capital are the following.

Cinco de Mayo

On Cerro del Peñon hill near the airport (metro: Oceanía), a mock battle between 'French' and Mexican 'soldiers' is conducted in the afternoon of 5 May to commemorate the Battle of Puebla (1862), one of Mexico's rare military victories.

Día de la Independencia

On the evening of 15 September thousands of people gather in the Zócalo to hear the president of Mexico recite a version of the *Grito de Dolores* (Cry of Dolores), Miguel Hidalgo's famous rallying call to rebellion against the Spanish in 1810, from the central balcony of the National Palace. The president then rings the ceremonial Bell of Dolores, and there's lots of cheering, fireworks and throwing of confetti, usually in the faces of other merrymakers. If you go, leave your valuables in the hotel safe.

Día de Nuestra Señora de Guadalupe

At the Basílica de Guadalupe in the north of the city, 12 December, the Day of Our Lady of Guadalupe, caps 10 days of festivities venerating and celebrating Mexico's religious patron, the Virgin of Guadalupe. From 3 December onwards, ever-growing crowds flood towards the basilica and its huge plaza. Vendors sell a special Virgin-shaped corn cake called *la gordita de la Virgen*, eaten only at this time. On 11 and 12 December groups of brightly costumed Indian dancers and musicians from all over Mexico perform in an uninterrupted sequence on the plaza for two days. The numbers of pilgrims reach the hundreds of thousands by 12 December, when religious services go on in the basilica almost round the clock.

Christmas & Día de los Reyes Magos

For the couple of weeks before Christmas the Alameda Central is ringed with brightly lit fairy-tale castles and polar grottoes, where children pose for photos with Mexican Santa Clauses and their reindeer. Between Christmas and 6 January – the Day of the Three Kings (los Reyes Magos) – Santa Claus is replaced by the Three Kings, who are equally popular and look, if anything, even more ill-at-ease. Families flock in and hosts of stalls selling anything from tacos to music tapes pop up too.

PLACES TO STAY

Mexico City has a full range of hotels, from basic but centrally located places (for 30 to 75 pesos a double) through comfortable middle-range hostelries (75 to 210 pesos a double) to luxurious high-rises (210 pesos up to the sky). In general, the best cheap and moderately priced rooms are in the areas west of the Zócalo, near the Alameda, and near the Plaza de la República; luxury hotels are in the Zona Rosa, along Paseo de la Reforma, and in the Polanco district.

Hotels are described here in order of preference. If two prices are given for double rooms, the lower is for two people in one bed, the higher for twin beds. Many hotels have rooms for three or four people, costing not very much more than a double. The numbers in brackets, '(06000)', are postcodes, which are useful if you want to write for reservations.

Places to Stay – bottom end

Rooms in the hotels recommended here have private baths unless otherwise mentioned. Many also have TV and carafes or bottles of purified water.

West of the Zócalo There are many suitable hotels on Avenida Cinco de Mayo and the streets to its north and south, between the Zócalo and Avenida Lázaro Cárdenas. Hot water supplies are erratic in some places. All

are in the 06000 postcode zone unless otherwise stated.

Hotel Juárez (☎ (5) 512-69-29), at 1a Cerrada de Cinco de Mayo 17, has 39 rooms on a quiet side street only 1½ blocks west of the Zócalo (metro: Zócalo or Allende). Recently refurbished, it's simple but very clean and presentable, with an excellent location, 24-hour hot water, and low prices of 50 pesos a single, 55 or 60 pesos a double. It's a popular place but if you're there by 2 pm you should get a room. The side street *(cerrada)* is off Cinco de Mayo between La Palma and Isabel la Católica.

Hotel San Antonio (☎ (5) 512-99-06), at 2a Cerrada de Cinco de Mayo 29, is just south of the Hotel Juárez across Cinco de Mayo, on the corresponding side street (metro: Zócalo or Allende). They're not quite as used to gringos here, but many of the 40 small, clean rooms have TV, and it's quiet and convenient. Rooms on the street side are brighter. Singles/doubles are 45/50 pesos.

Hotel Isabel (☎ (5) 518-12-13), Isabel la Católica 63 at República del Salvador (metro: Isabel la Católica), is popular with backpackers because of its convenient location, agreeable management, comfy if old-fashioned rooms, and inexpensive little restaurant. Some of the rooms are very large: those overlooking the street are noisy but brighter. There are views from some upper-floor rooms. Singles/doubles cost 40/45 pesos with shared bath, 60/75 pesos with private bath.

Hotel Antillas (☎ (5) 526-56-74), Belisario Domínguez 34 at Allende (06010; metro: Allende), seven blocks north-west of the Zócalo, has 100 clean, good-sized rooms with carpeting and bright bedspreads for 65 pesos a single, 70/80 pesos a double. The staff are agreeable and there's an attractive restaurant off the lobby. Parking is available.

Hotel La Fayette (☎ (5) 521-96-40), Motolinía 40 near the corner of 16 de Septiembre (metro: Zócalo), looks like a plastic sofa showroom as you enter, but in fact is a hotel popular with Mexican families. Rooms are quite big, slightly worn but clean enough, and the staff are friendly. The cost is 50 pesos a single, 55/60 pesos a double.

Mexico City
Top Left: Christmas Day clean-up in the Zócalo (GE)
Top Right: Museo Frida Kahlo, Coyoacán (PW)
Bottom: Dancers in Bosque de Chapultepec (PW)

Mexico City
Top: The Zócalo at dusk (PP)
Bottom Left: Centro Bursatil (JN)
Bottom Right: Infant Jesus dolls in a market (PW)

Hotel Washington (☎ (5) 512-35-02), Cinco de Mayo 54 at La Palma, near the aforementioned Hotel Juárez (metro: Allende or Zócalo), has noisy front rooms, offhand staff and slightly higher prices, but is well located. Singles are 55 pesos, doubles 60/65 pesos; all rooms have baths.

Hotel Rioja (☎ (5) 521-83-83), Cinco de Mayo 45 at Isabel la Católica (metro: Allende), is worn and fairly noisy, with small rooms, but popular with travellers on slim budgets. With shared shower facilities, singles are 26/30 pesos, doubles are 30 to 35 pesos; with private bath, singles are 35 pesos, doubles 40/50 pesos.

Hotel Zamora at Cinco de Mayo 50 a couple of doors west of the Hotel Washington (metro: Allende or Zócalo), has a grotty entrance and bare, well-used rooms, but is friendly, with low prices. Doubles are 35 pesos using shared showers and sagging beds, or 50 pesos with private bath.

Hotel Principal (☎ (5) 521-13-33) at Bolívar 29, between Madero and 16 de Septiembre (metro: Allende or Zócalo), is a friendly place with most rooms opening on to a plant-draped central hall. Doubles are 50/60 pesos, with private bath. The twin rooms are quite large.

South of the Alameda Many hotels in this convenient area upgraded as they rebuilt after the 1985 earthquake, leaving only a few in the bottom range.

Hotel Toledo (☎ (5) 521-32-49) at López 22 (06050), one block south of the south-east corner of the Alameda (metro: Bellas Artes), is conveniently located and good value at 45 pesos a single, 50/60 pesos a double. Rooms are clean and medium-sized, with windows on a fairly quiet street. There are some bright, inexpensive eateries nearby.

Hotel Fornos (☎ (5) 512-60-01) at Revillagigedo 92 (06070), 700 metres south of the west end of the Alameda (metro: Balderas), was being modernised when we visited but work should be completed by the time you go. Rooms are smallish but pleasant, with tiled bathrooms and carpets – and the price of 60 pesos for a single or double compen-

sates for its rather distant location. The hotel is popular with Mexicans and has a car park and restaurant.

North of Plaza de la República This area, about one km west of the Alameda, is drab and slightly less convenient, but prices are good and the neighbourhood is quiet and residential, with an amiable feel. The postcode is 06030 and the metro station is Revolución; walk east from the station along Puente de Alvarado, then turn right (south) on Arriaga or Ramos Arizpe.

The excellent *La Casa de los Amigos* (☎ (5) 705-05-21) at Mariscal 132, half a block west of Arriaga, is run by the Quakers, but anyone can stay there and there's no religious pressure on guests. Many people working on social justice projects in Mexico and Central America stay here, so it's a great place for meeting people with an informed interest in the region. Facilities include a guest kitchen and living room, information files, and a library which was once the studio of artist Orozco. A big 8-peso breakfast is served Monday to Friday. There's room for 40 people in single-sex dormitories and private rooms. Dorm beds cost 24 pesos; rooms with shared bath are 28 or 35 pesos a single, 50 pesos a double; singles/doubles with private bath are 40/55 pesos. Reservations are advisable, especially in August and September and December to February. Minimum stay is two nights. Alcohol and smoking are banned inside the building.

Hotel Carlton (☎ (5) 566-29-11), Mariscal 32B at Ramos Arizpe on the quiet little Plaza Buenavista, is a favourite among budget travellers. Get here early if you want a room. The management is helpful and the rooms are clean, carpeted and equipped with TV, for 50/60 pesos a single/double. The hotel restaurant serves a comida corrida for just 7 pesos.

Hotel Oxford (☎ (5) 566-05-00), Mariscal 67 at Alcázar, also on Plaza Buenavista, always seems redolent of flyspray, but it has large, clean, carpeted singles or doubles with TV for 50 to 70 pesos. Rooms higher up overlook the park.

Hotel Pensylvania (☎ (5) 703-13-84), Mariscal 101 at Arriaga, is a recently modernised place whose 82 decent rooms all have TV and tiled bathrooms. Standard singles/doubles cost 40/50 pesos but there's also a *'zona de kingsize'* with bigger beds in mostly bigger rooms, at 60/70 pesos.

Hotel Frimont (☎ (5) 705-41-69) at Terán 35, 250 metres east of the Plaza de la República, is a bit more expensive but fair value for what you get. The 100 clean, decent-sized rooms, all with TV, cost 66 pesos a single, 71.50/82.50 pesos a double. The hotel has its own restaurant, with a four-course comida corrida at 15 pesos.

Near Estación Buenavista There are only a few cheap lodgings in the Buenavista train station area (postcode 06300). To reach the following places, walk out of the front of the station and turn left (east) along Mosqueta. The nearest metro station is Guerrero, 500 metres east of the hotels.

Hotel Yale (☎ (5) 591-14-88) at Mosqueta 200, 2½ blocks east of the station, has clean, recently decorated rooms with TV and tiled bathrooms for 50 pesos a single or double, or 80 pesos a double in larger twin rooms.

One block nearer the station, *Hotel Central* (☎ (5) 535-57-24), Mosqueta 248, is all right for one night if you're exhausted, but get a room at the back or the noise will prevent you from sleeping. Singles/doubles with private bath are 35/40 pesos.

Near the Zona Rosa The pricey Zona Rosa is no place to stay on a low budget. But just on the far (north) side of Reforma is a low-priced gem.

Casa González (☎ (5) 514-33-02) at Río Sena 69 between Río Lerma and Río Pánuco (06500), is a 500-metre walk from the heart of the Zona Rosa. Two beautiful houses set in small plots of lawn have been converted to a charming guesthouse. It's a friendly place, perfect for those staying more than one or two nights, and cheap at 60 to 78 pesos for a single or double. Good home-cooked meals are available in the pretty dining room. They may have parking. Reserve in advance

if you can. No sign marks the houses, and the gate is locked. Ring the bell for admittance.

Places to Stay – middle

Hotels in this range provide comfortable and attractive, if often small, rooms, in well-located modern or colonial buildings. All rooms have private bath (usually with shower, sometimes with tub) and colour TV (sometimes with satellite hook-ups).

North of the Zócalo This convenient neighbourhood, though hardly posh, has lots of small shops and interesting streetlife.

Hotel Catedral (☎ (5) 518-52-32; fax 512-43-44), Donceles 95 (06020; metro: Zócalo), just around the corner from the Templo Mayor and a block north of the cathedral, is shiny, bright and efficient, with a good restaurant off the bright lobby. The 140 rooms are well kept, pleasant and comfortable at 100/125 pesos a single/double. Some have views of the cathedral. There's parking nearby.

West & South of the Zócalo The area between the Zócalo and Avenida Lázaro Cárdenas (postcode 06000) has some excellent moderately priced choices.

Hotel Canada (☎ (5) 518-21-06, fax 521-12-33), Cinco de Mayo 47 east of Isabel la Católica (metro: Allende), is one of our favourites. It's bright, modern and tidy, the staff are welcoming, and the location is excellent. The 100 rooms cost 90 pesos a single, 100/110 pesos a double. Parking is available.

Hotel Gillow (☎ (5) 518-14-40), Isabel la Católica 17 at Cinco de Mayo (metro: Allende), has a pleasant leafy lobby and clean, cheerful, up-to-date rooms. Singles/doubles are 100/120 pesos. There's a popular, moderately priced restaurant, too.

Hotel Roble (☎ (5) 522-78-30), Uruguay 109 at Pino Suárez (metro: Zócalo or Pino Suárez), is two blocks south of the Zócalo on a noisy corner. Used mostly by Mexicans with dealings in the nearby markets, it's at the cheaper end of the middle range, with doubles at 75/85 pesos. The rooms are of a reasonable size and clean – better than the exterior suggests. A bright, busy, moderately priced restaurant adjoins the hotel.

Hotel Capitol (☎ (5) 512-04-60, fax 521-11-49) is a recently upgraded hotel at Uruguay 12, less than half a block east of Avenida Lázaro Cárdenas (metro: Isabel La Católica). Rooms, mostly around a central hall with a fountain, are modern and pleasant, and cost 90 pesos a single, 100/120 pesos a double.

Hotel Ritz (☎ (5) 518-13-40, fax 518-34-66), Avenida Madero 30 east of Bolívar (metro: Allende), caters to business travellers and North American tour groups, offering 140 quite comfortable singles and doubles with mini-bars and an upscale atmosphere at 200 pesos. There's live music in the lobby daily, a restaurant, a good little bar, and parking. For reservations in the USA call Best Western on ☎ 800-528-1234.

North of the Alameda The neighbourhood just north of the Alameda Central is quiet yet convenient.

Hotel Hidalgo (☎ (5) 521-87-71), Santa Veracruz 37 at Dos (2) de Abril, one block from the Alameda (06030; metro: Bellas Artes), is grey and monolithic, but modern. The 100 rooms are carpeted and quite clean. There's a restaurant and a garage. Rates are good at 80/95 pesos a single/double.

South of the Alameda Except for one hotel right on Avenida Juárez, these hotels are in a slightly drab area not quite fully recovered from the ravages of the 1985 earthquake.

Hotel Bamer (☎ (5) 521-90-60; fax 510-17-93) faces the Alameda at Avenida Juárez 52 (06050; metro: Hidalgo or Bellas Artes). Many of the 111 large, comfortable rooms have fantastic views of the Alameda. Singles/doubles cost 170/180 pesos. There are some smaller twin rooms at the sides of the hotel, without Alameda views, for 110 pesos. The ground-floor cafeteria serves four-course lunches for 20 to 38.50 pesos.

Hotel Fleming (☎ (5) 510-45-30), Revillagigedo 35 south of Artículo 123 (06050; metro: Juárez), 2½ blocks south of the Alameda, has 100 comfortably modernised rooms with large tiled bathrooms; some on the higher floors have great views. Rates are 130/140 pesos. There's a café.

Hotel San Diego (☎ (5) 521-60-10), Luis Moya 98 south of Pugibet (06070; metro: Salto del Agua), 5½ blocks south of the Alameda, is a bit far from the action, but offers good value. The 87 spacious modern rooms boast satellite TV, tiled bathrooms, and prices of 70/100 pesos. There's a good restaurant, a bar and a garage.

Hotel Marlowe (☎ (5) 521-95-40, fax 518-68-62), Independencia 17 between Dolores and López (06050; metro: Bellas Artes) is just one short block south of the Alameda, near many cheap restaurants. It's being modernised and the rooms already completed are pleasant, tasteful and quite big. Corner rooms – especially those higher up – tend to be the brightest. Rates are 90/100 pesos.

The *Hotel Metropol* (☎ (5) 510-86-60, fax 512-12-73), Luis Moya 39 south of Independencia (06050; metro: Juárez or Hidalgo), was totally modernised in 1991 and now rates four stars. Rooms, though not enormous, are pleasant and comfortable. They're on the expensive side at 165/187 pesos, but the hotel's location, just over a block from the Alameda, is good.

Near Plaza de la República Within a few blocks of the Plaza de la República are several comfortable hotels offering very good value. The location, one km west of the Alameda, is only a bit inconvenient. The postcode is 06030 and the nearest metro station, unless otherwise specified, is Revolución.

Hotel Edison (☎ (5) 566-09-33) at Edison 106 east of Iglesias, has 45 pleasant, clean rooms around a small, plant-filled courtyard. It's good value, with rates at the low end of the middle range – 70/80 pesos for singles/doubles. There's a bakery just across the street, and several small restaurants nearby.

Gran Hotel Texas (☎ (5) 705-57-82), Mariscal 129 near Arriaga, charges the same prices as the Edison. It was undergoing a bout of reconstruction when we researched this edition, which should make the rooms cosier but may raise prices. Rooms are clean and the staff friendly. There's a car park.

Hotel Corinto (☎ (5) 566-65-55), 1½ blocks south of the Plaza de la República at Ignacio Vallarta 24, is sleek, modern and polished, with a good restaurant, a bar, and even a small swimming pool on the 9th-floor roof. The 155 rooms, though small, are comfortable and quiet. Singles cost 110 pesos, doubles 121/143 pesos.

Palace Hotel (☎ (5) 566-24-00, fax 535-75-20) at Ramírez 7, half a block south of Plaza de la República, always has lots of bustle in its lobby as guests (mostly foreigners) arrive and depart. The 200 rooms are modernised and comfortable, and cost 110/132 pesos for singles/doubles. There's a restaurant, bar and garage.

Hotel New York (☎ (5) 566-97-00), Edison 45 at Baranda, three short blocks north-east of the Plaza de la República, is a friendly little place with 45 reasonably sized though well-used rooms at 75/100 pesos. It has a good, busy little restaurant, and a garage.

Hotel Jena (☎ (5) 566-02-77, fax 566-04-55), Terán 12 at Mariscal (metro: Hidalgo), is a modern, gleaming building with a posh feel. Its 120-plus rooms are ultra-clean and among the most luxurious in the middle range. Singles are 143 pesos, doubles 165/176 pesos. There's a piano bar, open from noon to 2 am, and a slightly pricey restaurant.

Near Estación Buenavista *Hotel Pontevedra* (☎ (5) 541-31-60 to -64), Insurgentes Norte 226 (06400), stands opposite the west side of Buenavista train station. Modern, clean and decently priced, it has good singles for 70 pesos and doubles for 80 to 110 pesos. Use buses and peseros on Insurgentes for transport.

Near Terminal Norte *Hotel Brasilia* (☎ (5) 587-85-77), Avenida de los Cien Metros 4823 (07370; metro: Autobuses del Norte), is a five to eight-minute walk (2½ blocks)

south of the northern bus terminal; turn left out of the terminal's front door. It has 200 comfortable, TV-equipped rooms at 90 pesos a single, 90 to 130 pesos a double. There's a restaurant and bar.

Near Jardín del Arte There are several hotels near the Jardín del Arte, one km north of the Zona Rosa and close to the Reforma/Insurgentes intersection (see the Zona Rosa map). There is no very convenient metro station but buses and peseros pass nearby on Insurgentes and Reforma.

Hotel Sevilla (☎ /fax (5) 566-18-66), at Serapio Rendón 126 (06470) north of Sullivan, is popular with Mexican couples and families. It has 150 quiet rooms just half a block from the park. There are purified water taps in all bathrooms, a shop, travel agency, restaurant-bar, and garage. Prices are good at 79 pesos a single, 88 to 96 pesos a double. Many rooms have views of the park (unless they build something next door).

Hotel Mallorca (☎ (5) 566-48-33), Serapio Rendón 119, across from the Sevilla and under the same management, has similar services and slightly lower prices.

Hotel Regente (☎ (5) 566-89-33; fax 592-57-94), at Paris 9 north of Madrid (06030), is three blocks north-east of the park, on the far side of Insurgentes. The 130 clean, small, comfortable rooms are favoured by European (often Dutch) tour groups. Singles/doubles are 110/132 pesos, and service is quiet and polished. The hotel's Restaurant Korinto serves a decent 20-peso comida corrida. Parking is available.

Near the Zona Rosa Accommodation right in the posh Zona Rosa is expensive, but there are one or two good middle-range places on the fringes.

Hotel María Cristina (☎ (5) 703-17-87; fax 566-91-94), Río Lerma 31 (06500), between Río Amazonas and Río Neva, north of Reforma 600 metres from the centre of the Zona Rosa, is a colonial-style gem. It has 150 comfy rooms, manicured lawns, baronial public rooms, and a patio with a fountain. There's a fine restaurant (comida: 27 pesos), a bar and parking. Rooms are 165 pesos a single, 187 pesos a double. Suites cost 209 pesos and up. The hotel is popular with Mexican business executives, families, and foreign tourists, and is often fully booked. Reserve in advance if you can. There is no convenient metro station but buses and peseros on Reforma are only 1½ blocks away.

Hotel Vasco de Quiroga (☎ (5) 546-26-14 to -16), Londres 15 north-east of Dinamarca (06600; metro: Cuauhtémoc), has 50 elegant, well-furnished rooms, though some are small. The public rooms are large and formal, and the place has a quality feel. Singles/doubles are 170/183 pesos.

Mi Casa (☎ (5) 566-67-11, fax 566-60-10), at General Prim 106 (08600; metro: Cuauhtémoc), is nearly a km east of the centre of the Zona Rosa, but only 1½ short blocks from Paseo de la Reforma. Accommodation here is in 27 comfortable self-catering suites. Each has twin beds, a sitting room, bathroom, TV and fully equipped kitchen, at a reasonably priced 150/180 pesos for singles/doubles.

Places to Stay – top end

Zócalo Two long-established hotels beside the Zócalo are hard to beat for location, but not quite up to the standards of luxury offered by some of the newer hotels elsewhere.

Hotel Majestic (☎ (5) 521-86-00, fax 512-66-62), Avenida Madero 73 (06000) on the west side of the Zócalo, has lots of colourful tiles in the lobby, and a few rooms (the more expensive ones) overlooking the vast plaza. Avoid the rooms facing Avenida Madero (too noisy) and around the inner glass-floored courtyard (unless you don't mind people looking in through your windows). Rates are 286 pesos a room or 330 pesos a suite, single or double. The 7th-floor café-restaurant has a great view of the Zócalo and occasionally, if the smog clears, the peaks of Popocatépetl and Iztaccíhuatl. The hotel is part of the Best Western group: for reservations in the USA you can call ☎ 800-528-1234.

Gran Hotel Ciudad de México (☎ (5) 510-40-40 to -49; fax 512-20-85), Avenida 16 de Septiembre 82 just off the Zócalo (06000), is a feast of Mexican rococo-Victoriana operated, oddly enough, by the Howard Johnson chain. Sit on one of the plush settees in the spacious lobby, listen to the songbirds in the large cages, and watch the open ironwork elevator glide towards the brilliant canopy of stained glass high above you. Rates for the 125 large, comfortable singles and doubles are 297 pesos. Suites with a view of the Zócalo are 375 pesos. There's a branch of the Delmonico's restaurant chain, plus a 4th-floor cafeteria overlooking the Zócalo. For reservations in the USA call ☎ 800-654-2000.

Alameda The *Hotel de Cortés* (☎ (5) 518-21-84, fax 512-18-63) at Avenida Hidalgo 85, facing the north side of the Alameda Central (06030; metro: Hidalgo), has a somewhat forbidding façade of dark stone, but inside is a charming colonial courtyard hotel. Built in 1780 as a hospice for Augustinian friars, its 29 rooms and suites are now modern and comfortable with TV, mini-bars, and small windows that look out on the courtyard. Noise can be a problem, though. Singles/doubles are 258/270 pesos. The four-course lunch is 42 pesos. The hotel is part of the Best Western group: for reservations in the USA call ☎ 800-528-1234.

Zona Rosa Hotels in the Zona Rosa are mostly at the low end of the luxury market in terms of price, and offer excellent locations. The metro station is Insurgentes; postcode is 06600.

Hotel Calinda Geneve (☎ (5) 211-00-71), Londres 130 at Génova, is the dowager of Zona Rosa hotels, being older but well kept, with a formal colonial lobby from which you can walk through to a grand, glass-canopied Sanborns restaurant. Rooms have two double beds, mini-bars, and other luxuries, and cost 395 pesos a single or double.

Hotel Century (☎ (5) 726-99-11, fax 525-74-75), Liverpool 152 at Amberes, is a dramatic high-rise with 143 small rooms furnished in outspoken modern style, including sunken bathtubs and curved balconies. The hotel has all the services – bars, restaurants, rooftop pool, garage – yet charges less than many others: 480 pesos a single or double.

Hotel Westin Galería Plaza (☎ (5) 211-00-14, fax 207-58-67), Hamburgo 195 between Lancaster and Varsovia, is classy, comfortable and well located, with smooth service and a reputation for good, varied cuisine. The 434 air-con rooms cost 545 pesos a single or double.

Hotel Marco Polo (☎ (5) 207-18-93, fax 533-37-27), at Amberes 27 between Reforma and Hamburgo, is Mexico City's most trendy lodging. Arts and entertainment types gravitate to its 60 very comfortable, soundproofed, stylishly modern rooms priced at 525 pesos a single or double. For reservations in the USA or Canada call ☎ 800-888-1199.

Hotel Krystal Rosa (☎ (5) 511-87-79, fax 511-34-90), Liverpool 155 between Amberes and Florencia, is best described as glitzy: it has a mirrored lobby ceiling and walls above a white marble floor, plush rooms with good city views, a heated swimming pool, a rooftop Japanese restaurant and so on. Rates are 537 pesos and up.

Along Paseo de la Reforma These places (postcode 06500) are within an easy walk of the Zona Rosa.

Hotel Marquis Reforma (☎ (5) 211-36-00, fax 211-55-61), Paseo de la Reforma 465 at Río de la Plata, is among the city's newest hotels, with 125 deluxe rooms and 85 lavish executive suites. Design and decor draw from the city's rich art deco heritage, and update it for the 21st century. It has lots of coloured marble, well-trained multilingual staff, and facilities such as an outdoor spa with whirlpool baths. The hotel is within walking distance of Bosque de Chapultepec. Rates are 644/743 pesos for rooms, 1000 to 1733 pesos for suites, single or double. For reservations in the USA, call ☎ 800-223-6510.

María Isabel-Sheraton Hotel (☎ (5) 207-39-33, fax 207-06-84), Paseo de la Reforma 325 at the Monumento a la Independencia

(El Ángel), is Mexico City's standard for solid comfort. Though older (built in 1962), it is as plush and attractive as ever with spacious public rooms, excellent food and drink, and all the services of a top-class hotel, including pool, health club, two lighted tennis courts, and nightly mariachi entertainment. The 752 deluxe rooms and suites offer all the comforts. Standard singles/doubles are 760/810 pesos. For reservations in the USA call ☎ 800-325-3535.

San Marino Hotel-Suites (☎ (5) 525-48-86), Río Tiber 107 at Río Lerma, two blocks north of the Monumento a la Independencia, is well-located, well-kept, and offers suites with fully equipped kitchenettes for 350 to 950 pesos, single or double, including breakfast. The cheaper ones cost much less than a room in many other luxury hotels. They have a restaurant and a car park.

Polanco The Polanco area just north of Bosque de Chapultepec has another cluster of top hotels. Probably the best is the *Hotel Nikko México* (☎ (5) 280-11-11, fax 280-91-91) at Campos Elíseos 204 (11560; metro: Auditorio). It successfully blends modern luxury with Asian traditions of service in a dramatically designed building within walking distance of the Museo Nacional de Antropología. The hotel features a formal French restaurant, a Japanese steakhouse and a Mexican café, as well as a heated pool, three tennis courts and a health club. Singles/doubles are 660/693 pesos.

PLACES TO EAT

This cosmopolitan capital has eateries for all tastes and budgets. Price categories in what follows are not strictly defined, so you might want to look through a few sections before making a choice, whatever your budget. Some of the best places are the cheapest, and some of the more expensive places are well worth the extra money. Of the city's many top-end restaurants, we include only a few which offer exceptional Mexican experiences. At these it's usually best to reserve a table, and to dress semi-formally (a dress for women, a jacket for men).

Chain Restaurants

Mexico City is liberally provided with modern chain restaurants whose predictable food is a sound fallback if you fancy somewhere easy and reliable to eat. Prices are slightly higher than you'd like but many of these places are very popular with locals. Numerous branches of *VIPS*, *Denny's* and the *Sanborns* store chain, all with mixtures of Mexican and international food and main dishes at around 18 to 28 pesos, can be found in affluent and touristed parts of the city like the Zona Rosa, the Alameda area and Paseo de la Reforma.

Around the Zócalo

Inexpensive *Café El Popular*, Cinco de Mayo 52, between La Palma and Isabel la Católica, just west of the Hotel Washington, is a good neighbourhood place open 24 hours a day. They serve good breakfasts (fruit, eggs, ham, rolls, beans and coffee for 10 pesos), a four-course comida corrida for 10 pesos, and light meals.

Almost across the street from El Popular, on the corner of Cinco de Mayo and the side street 2a Cerrada de Cinco de Mayo, *Jugos Canada* is a great place to pop into for a refreshing pure fruit juice, a licuado, or a fruit salad. A big orange or carrot juice, squeezed before your eyes, is yours for 4 pesos.

Cafetería Los Metates, Avenida Madero 71 east of La Palma, just west of the Hotel Majestic, is a modern lonchería serving tacos, sandwiches, enchiladas, sincronizadas (ham and cheese in tortillas) and pozole for 6 to 10 pesos, or chicken or meat dishes up to 14 pesos. A dozen set-price breakfasts go for 7 to 12 pesos. Hours are from 8 am to 9 pm, closed Sunday.

Café La Blanca, Avenida Cinco de Mayo 40 west of Isabel la Católica, is big, always busy, and good for people-watching over a café con leche. Prices are not the lowest, but you can have their three-course lunch for 21 pesos. It's open every day.

Restaurante El Gallo Z, La Palma 28 on the corner of Madero, is marked by a sign which reads 'Restaurante Zenón'. Since 1939 this restaurant has been satisfying singles, couples and families with platters of meat, potatoes, beans and guacamole for under 18 pesos. Breakfasts are a bit expensive at 7 to 16 pesos. It's open every day till 8.30 pm.

At *La Casa del Pavo*, three blocks west of the Zócalo at Motolinía 40A north of 16 de Septiembre, chefs in white aprons slice roast turkeys all day long and serve them up at low prices. The four-course comida corrida offers excellent value at 10 pesos. Also on Motolinía – mostly on the northern half of the street, near Allende metro station – are several big, bare eateries selling tacos, enchiladas and other Mexican snacks at low prices (four tacos for 3 to 6 pesos).

Rincón Mexicano, Uruguay 27 west of Bolívar, and *Antojitos Tere*, Uruguay 29, are tiny hole-in-the-wall eateries with home cooking and very low prices. Set meals at both places cost 9 pesos. They're open daily, but close at 5 pm.

Hong King, on Bolívar between Uruguay and Carranza, is a branch of a Chinatown eatery (see Around the Alameda) which has much cheaper set-price meals than the original place. A four-course lunch here will cost just 8 or 8.50 pesos.

Vegetarian Restaurants *Restaurante El Vegetariano I*, Avenida Madero 56 west of La Palma, is up a flight of stairs between two jewellers' shops. Don't be put off by the unimpressive entrance: upstairs are three busy, high-ceilinged rooms where a pianist plunks out old favourites as you dine. The food is tasty, filling, and excellent value; the five-course daily set-price meal goes for 15 pesos. Opening hours are from 9 am to 6.30 pm daily except Sunday.

Bakeries & Pastry Shops There are always good snacks or light breakfasts to be bought at *pastelerías* (pastry shops). You enter the pastelería, take a tray and tongs, fill the tray with what you like, then an attendant will price and bag it.

Pastelería Madrid, Cinco (5) de Febrero 25 at República del Salvador, 2½ blocks south of the Zócalo, is huge, with fresh breads and pastries issuing from the ovens all the time.

Pastelería Ideal, 16 de Septiembre 14 west of Gante, looks fancy but prices are still low. All the breads and rolls are at the back. Upstairs, Mexico's ultimate array of wedding cakes is on offer: this is the place to come if you need a 1500-peso, multistorey gâteau for your nuptials.

Mid-Range *Café de Tacuba* (☎ 512-84-82), Tacuba 28 east of Bolívar, just west of Allende metro station, is a gem of old-time Mexico City, opened in 1912. Coloured tiles, brass lamps and oil paintings set the mood. The cuisine is traditional Mexican and delicious. There's a four-course set-price lunch for 42 pesos. Hours are from 8 am to 11.30 pm every day.

Hostería de Santo Domingo (☎ 510-14-34), Belisario Domínguez 72 east of Chile, six blocks north-west of the Zócalo, is small but intense. Handicrafts crowd the walls and ceiling, good and unusual regional cooking fills the menu and the customers. Full three-course à la carte meals cost about 45 pesos per person, though you can easily eat for 30 pesos. If you want somewhere atmospheric, this is it. Come any day between 9 am and 11 pm. Lunch (with live music) is best; in the evening the restaurant is fairly empty.

Restaurante Jampel (☎ 521-75-71), Bolívar 8 north of Cinco de Mayo, is three establishments in one. On the left is the fancy Restaurant-Bar Ejecutivo, open from 2 to 11 pm, with live music and a moderately priced international menu. On the right is a big cafeteria section (open from 7.30 am to 11 pm Monday to Saturday, 1 to 6 pm Sunday), with quick, smooth service and a variety of three-course comidas priced from 16 to 28 pesos, plus an à la carte menu. And in the Salón Fuente (Fountain Room), at the back of the cafeteria, there's a self-service buffet for 16.75 pesos from 1 to 4.30 pm daily except Saturday.

Several hotels have good-value restaurants. Two bright, very popular ones are at the *Hotel Catedral*, Donceles 95 a block north of the cathedral, where set-price lunches go for 20 to 28 pesos; and the *Restaurante-Bar Maple* at the Hotel Roble, Uruguay 109 two blocks south of the Zócalo, where four-course lunches cost 15.50 to 26 pesos. The *Hotel Gillow*, Isabel la Católica 17 at Cinco de Mayo, does a popular lunch for 20 pesos.

For a meal with a view, head up to the 7th-floor restaurant of the *Hotel Majestic* at Avenida Madero 73, which overlooks the Zócalo. Four-course set lunches cost from 26 to 44 pesos but you can have something lighter or à la carte if you wish.

Around the Alameda

Inexpensive One of the prettiest and most peaceful restaurants in the area is the *Cafetería del Claustro* (Cloister Café) in the Museo Franz Mayer, opposite the north side of the Alameda at Avenida Hidalgo 45. The museum and café are open Tuesday to Sunday from 10 am to 5 pm: if you only want to visit the café there's a 2-peso fee for entry to the cloister. Marble-top tables are set in the lovely courtyard: the good, self-service food includes sandwiches, salads and quiche for 3 to 9 pesos; there are also coffee, juices, yoghurt, and excellent cakes at 4 pesos.

On the west side of the Alameda *Café Trevi*, on the corner of Dr Mora and Colón, is a good, popular Italian and Mexican restaurant. It serves breakfasts from 8 am to noon for 8 to 12 pesos, and its five-course set-price daily meal costs just 14 pesos. Pasta dishes and one-person pizzas range from 13 to 20 pesos.

One block south of the south-east corner of the Alameda, there's a cluster of bright, inexpensive eateries around the corner from Independencia and López. Pick of the bunch is the clean, bustling *Taquería Tlaquepaque* at Independencia 4, east of López (don't confuse it with the Ostionería Tlaquepaque a couple of doors away). Bow-tied waiters serve up several dozen types of taco, priced at 4.50 to 17 pesos for three. The chuletas, nopales y queso variety (chopped pork, cactus tips and cheese), at the top of the range, is delicious.

Also south of the Alameda, at Luis Moya

41, south of Independencia, is *Los Faroles*. Beneath the brick arches white-aproned señoras ladle steaming caldo (stew) from huge earthenware *cazuelas* (cooking pots), and prepare authentic and tasty tacos and enchiladas. The dining room can be dark and hot, but prices are low. There's a five-course comida corrida for just 11 pesos. Hours are from 8 am to 7 pm every day.

The café inside the *Palacio de Bellas Artes* serves salads for 16 pesos, and other light meals and snacks from 10 to 20 pesos. For cheaper eats close to the Palacio de Bellas Artes, head one block north to the intersection of Avenida Lázaro Cárdenas and Donceles, where *Taquería y Pollería El Correo* serves a big variety of tacos – from 0.80 to 1.50 pesos each for the cheapest fillings up to 12 pesos for three superior tacos. Next door is *Frutería Frutivida*, with lots of fresh fruit juices, licuados, fruit salads, tortas – and more tacos. There are several other inexpensive *taquerías* (taco places) nearby on Donceles, most open till 3 am.

Vegetarian Restaurants The *Centro Naturista de México*, Dolores 10B, half a block south of Avenida Juárez, has a vegetarian restaurant serving full meals for 9 to 11 pesos. Hours are from 12.30 to 5.30 pm every day. The shop at the front sells natural foods including pan integral (wholegrain bread).

Mid-Range *Sanborns Casa de Azulejos* (☎ 512-98-20), Avenida Madero 4 east of Avenida Lázaro Cárdenas, is worth a visit just to see its superb 16th-century tile-bedecked building (see Around the Alameda for details). The restaurant is in the covered courtyard around a Moorish fountain, with odd murals of mythical landscapes covering its walls. The food is Mexican and good, if not exceptional, at 15 to 30 pesos per main dish, or 17 to 25 pesos for a three-course comida. The lunch counter section in the north-west corner of the building has similar prices but less atmosphere. Both eating areas are open from 7.30 am to 10 pm.

Restaurant Danubio (☎ 512-09-12), Uruguay 3 at Avenida Lázaro Cárdenas, is a city tradition. It's been here, specialising in seafood, for half a century, and still does it well. It serves an excellent six-course set-price menú for 30 pesos. À la carte fish main courses are mostly 30 to 45 pesos. Lobster (langosta) and crayfish (langostinos) are the specialities, but prices for them are stratospheric. Hours are from 1 to 10 pm every day.

Restaurant Centro Castellano (☎ 510-14-61), close to the Danubio at Uruguay 16, is huge, occupying three floors of its building. The decor is colonial, the menu is long and heavy on seafood such as red snapper (huachinango) and octopus in its own ink. There's also veal, roast kid – just about everything. The five-course comida corrida costs 35 pesos; most à la carte dishes are 30 to 40 pesos. Hours are from 1 to 10 pm (till 7 pm on Sunday).

Mexico City has a small Chinatown district centred on Calle Dolores south of Independencia. One of the best restaurants on the street is the *Hong King* (☎ 512-67-03), Dolores 25, which is small and attractive, with set meals from 21 to 42 pesos per person (minimum two people) and menus in Chinese, Spanish and English. Hours are from 11.30 am to 11 pm every day.

Restaurant Lincoln (☎ 510-14-68) at Revillagigedo 24, 1½ blocks south of the Alameda, is formal and dignified, with dark wood, white tablecloths and black-coated waiters. The food is delicious and prices are moderate, with most meat and fish dishes costing 25 to 45 pesos. They offer no set-price lunch. Hours are from 8 am to 10 pm Monday to Saturday, 1 to 6 pm Sunday.

Near Plaza de la República
There are several small, cheap, neighbourhood restaurants as well as a few slightly smarter places.

Inexpensive *Restaurante Samy*, Mariscal 42, just south-west of the Hotel Jena, doesn't look much from outside but is clean and pleasant, offering fixed-price breakfasts for 6 to 14 pesos, and a four-course comida corrida for 13 pesos.

Restaurante Regis is the real name of the

place with the 'Restaurant Bisquets' sign on the corner of Edison and Alcázar. It's clean, unpretentious and cheap, with five choices of a four-course comida corrida priced from 9.90 to 23 pesos.

The restaurant of the *Hotel New York*, Edison 45 between Emparán and Alcázar, is popular for its good food and moderate prices. You'd do well to come early (1 pm) or late (3.30 pm) for the 15-peso comida corrida. For a really cheap, quick (if not enormous) comida you can't beat the restaurant of the *Hotel Carlton*, nearby at Mariscal 32B, where four courses will set you back just 7 pesos.

A great place for a quick lunch is the seafood cocktail stand on Emparán just north of Edison. It has stood here daily (except Sunday) for at least a decade and includes many office workers in suits among its regular customers. A *mediano* (medium-size) prawn or crab cocktail at 10 pesos is filling. The neighbouring stand offers a range of good tortas.

About 100 metres south of Plaza de la República on Ramírez, next door to a branch of VIPS, *Tacos El Caminero* is a busy, slightly upscale taco joint doling out serves of three good tacos for 9 pesos, or six for 16 pesos. There's draft beer (cerveza de barril) too, at 4 pesos a mug. El Caminero's hours are from 10 am to 1 am Monday to Friday, 1 pm to 1 am Saturday, and 1 pm to 11 pm Sunday.

The large *Café La Habana*, on the corner of Bucareli and Morelos, is a half-km southeast of the Plaza de la República, on the south side of Reforma, but worth the walk for its good, strong coffee and good four-course 'lunch comercial' at 17 pesos. It's open from 8 am to midnight every day. Journalists and staff from nearby newspaper offices are among the clientele.

Among the very cheapest restaurants in the district is one with no apparent name at Plaza San Fernando 1, north of Puente de Alvarado and just east of Guerrero. Between the Café Paris (more expensive) on the corner, and the Restaurante El Pedregal (a noisy cantina) to the north, is the drab high-ceilinged room where señoras cook up a four-course comida corrida every day for 7.50 pesos. Local workers come to fill the tables and themselves at lunchtime. Breakfast and supper are offered too.

Mid-Range *Potzollcalli*, on Arriaga just south of Puente de Alvarado, is a clean and brightly lit branch of a Mexican chain restaurant, with good specialities like taquiza mixta (five types of taco with rice, 18.50 pesos), meat dishes from 21 to 32 pesos, and pozole at 17 to 24 pesos. There's a popular four-course comida for 14 pesos. It opens at 8 am daily, closing at 12.30 am Monday to Thursday, 1 am Friday and Saturday, and 10 pm Sunday.

Restaurante María Candelaría, on Arriaga north of Edison, does a good four-course comida, from 1 pm, for 20 pesos – including a drink of agua de fruta.

Shirley's, south of the Plaza de la República at Reforma 108, is a big, American-style place serving gringo and Mexican food in clean, modern surroundings with efficient service. Though all meals are served (they're open from 7.30 am to 11.30 pm every day), it's the eat-all-you-want lunch buffet from 1 to 4.30 pm which packs 'em in. This costs 27 pesos Monday to Friday, 32 pesos on weekends and holidays.

Near Estación Buenavista

There's a cheap station cafeteria near the segunda-clase ticket windows, but it's better to go out the front of the station and cross Mosqueta to a good chain restaurant called *El Portón*, which serves Mexican food at moderate prices (breakfast 9 to 11 pesos, light dishes 6 to 15 pesos, main dishes 16 to 25 pesos). Across Insurgentes is *Shakey's Pizza*.

Around the Zona Rosa

The Zona Rosa is packed with restaurants. Many streets are closed to traffic, making the sidewalk cafés very pleasant.

Inexpensive Believe it or not, there are a few good budget eateries in the Zona Rosa.

El Faisán, Londres 136A between

Génova and Amberes, serves excellent Yucatecan food at good prices. The menu (in English and Spanish) offers lime soup, papadzules (tacos of boiled egg with a pumpkin-seed sauce), barbecued spicy pork, turkey with onions and beans, and other Mayan favourites. Soup and a main course can be had for about 18 pesos. Hours are from 8 am to 10 pm daily except Sunday.

Restaurante Jacarandas at Génova 44, in an alley off the east side of Génova just south of Hamburgo, is busy at lunchtimes, Monday to Saturday, serving up its good three-course lunch for just 11 or 12 pesos. The menu changes daily but 'pollo al orange' is a good choice when available.

Restaurante El Gallito, on Liverpool between Insurgentes and Génova, is a bright, quick place with good, basic fare like tacos and quesadillas (4 pesos each), pozole (16 pesos) and enchiladas (17 pesos). It's open from 10 am to midnight every day.

Parri, Hamburgo 154 between Florencia and Amberes, is a busy, barn-like grill house serving grilled chicken, beef or pork in various ways, from tacos to whole beasts. Chefs tend the grill and waiters scurry about. You can eat for 12 pesos, but you're more likely to spend 20 or 25 pesos. Breakfasts are around 10 pesos.

Mid-Range *Konditori* (☎ 511-15-89), Génova 61 between Londres and Hamburgo, serves a mixture of Italian, Scandinavian and Mexican fare in its elegant small dining rooms and spacious sidewalk café, which is a great place to observe the passing parade on one of the Zona Rosa's busiest pedestrian streets. Pasta or good crepa (pancake) dishes cost 19 to 22 pesos, meat or fish 26 to 36 pesos. There are good pastries too. Coffee is expensive at 12 pesos and up. It's open from 7 am to midnight daily.

Salón Luz, Génova 70A between Liverpool and Londres, is another sidewalk café, which is quick, popular and good for people-watching on Génova. A snack and a drink will set you back about 15 pesos. Some evenings there's live music inside.

Shirley's Pink Zone (☎ 514-77-60), Lon-

dres 102 between Niza and Génova, is efficient and friendly. The big lunch buffet costs just 20 pesos on weekdays, 30 pesos on Saturday and Sunday. Hours for this tried-and-true place are from 7.30 am to 11.30 pm.

Chalet Suizo (☎ 511-75-29), Niza 37 between Hamburgo and Londres, has dependably good food well served in pseudo-Swiss rusticity. They have fondues (29 to 68 pesos for two), pasta plates at 20 pesos, and a range of meat dishes between 22 and 40 pesos, including pig's knuckles with sauerkraut, and duck in orange or blackberry sauce. Full meals usually cost 30 to 60 pesos. It's open from 12.30 to 11.45 pm every day. The menu is in English.

Luaú (☎ 525-74-74), Niza 38 between Hamburgo and Londres, is an elaborate Chinese-Polynesian fantasy with fountains and miniature gardens. The best bargains are the set-price Cantonese meals priced at 28.50 to 53.50 pesos per person. It's open daily from noon to 10.45 pm.

Pizza Real (☎ 511-88-34), Génova 28 at Estrasburgo, serves pizza in dozens of different ways (12 to 60 pesos), as well as moderately priced pasta and other Italian specialities; there are indoor and outdoor tables. Hours are from 8 am to 11.30 pm daily.

Carrousel Internacional (☎ 533-64-17), Niza 33 at Hamburgo, is a lively bar/restaurant with mariachis singing energetically most of the time. Come for a sandwich, spaghetti or tuna steak (16 to 40 pesos), or a drink, and enjoy the music. It's open from 11.30 am to midnight every day.

Harry's Bar, Liverpool 155 (the entrance is round the corner on Amberes), is a bright, loud place popular with groups – often many gringos among them – out for a bit of fun. Steaks, chicken and seafood are the standard fare and a meal will cost 45 to 75 pesos. It's open daily except Sunday. Video screens show sport most of the time.

Vegetarian Restaurants *Restaurante Vegetariano Las Fuentes* (☎ 207-64-14), at Río Pánuco 127 on the corner of Río Tiber, two blocks north of the Monumento a la Independencia, is among our favourites. Big, modern and attractive, it serves delicious food in huge portions for moderate prices. Full meals cost 24 to 30 pesos; big breakfasts (8 am to 1 pm) are 15 pesos. Wine and beer are served too. It's open from 8 am to 6 pm daily.

Restaurante Vegetariano Yug (☎ 533-32-96), Varsovia 3 just south of Reforma, also does decent vegetarian food, at lower prices. There's a lunch buffet for 20 pesos from 1 to 5 pm daily except Saturday (upstairs), or daily four-course comidas corridas, with good wholewheat bread, for 13 or 18.50 pesos (downstairs). The clientele are mostly office workers from the neighbourhood. Hours are Monday to Friday from 7 am to 9 pm, Saturday 8.30 am to 7 pm, Sunday 1 to 9 pm.

Tearooms The Zona Rosa has two wonderful tearooms serving good drinks, pastries, breakfasts and light meals.

Auseba, at Hamburgo 159B north-east of Avenida Florencia, has glass cases filled with enticing sweet offerings, and large windows for watching the Hamburgo pedestrian parade. Cakes and pastries are around 9 pesos each, but you can get by with a pan dulce (sweet biscuit) for 2.50 pesos.

Salon de Te Duca d'Este at Hamburgo 164B, on the corner of Florencia almost facing the Auseba, has formal French decor and polite service. A tea or coffee and a pastry costs 7.50 pesos and up. A breakfast is only around 12 pesos. Hours are from 6 am to 10.30 pm every day.

Expensive The Zona Rosa's swankiest restaurant street is Copenhague, which is lined with busy upscale eateries. Two of the best and most popular are the *Mesón del Perro Andaluz*, serving meat and seafood, on the east side of the street, and *El Perro d'Enfrente*, opposite, with good Italian food. Main dishes in both are mostly in the 30 to 50-peso range and a full meal is likely to cost 60 to 75 pesos.

Prices are similar at *Piccadilly Pub* (☎ 514-15-15), Copenhague 23 on the west side of the street. This is a Mexican conception of an Olde English pub; that is, far from the real thing. It's a posh restaurant, heavy on fantasy English decor, with quiet live music and both indoor and outdoor seating. Most dishes are Mexican and international, but they do serve steak and oyster pie, Cambridge sausages, and lots of beefsteak. Hours are from noon to 1 am (to 6 pm on Sunday).

Fonda El Refugio (☎ 528-58-23), Liverpool 166 between Florencia and Amberes, is a charming old house decorated with antiques and crafts. The chef prepares many of the less well known Mexican regional dishes with great care. In season, they even have tacos de cuitlacoche, made with that curious corn mould beloved of the Aztecs. You'll pay 60 to 75 pesos for a full meal. Make reservations for dinner; it's closed on Sunday.

Anderson's de Reforma, Reforma 382 at Oxford, is a branch of a bright, reliable Mexican grill/steakhouse chain. Like most of the others, this one is very popular. The many varieties of steak and seafood go for 45 pesos and up. There's a cover charge of 6 pesos.

Chapultepec & Polanco
Inexpensive & Mid-Range The *Museo Nacional de Antropología* has a reasonable cafeteria for its visitors with a lunch buffet at 35 pesos, and individual Mexican and international dishes mostly between 15 and 24 pesos. The nearest cheap food is at *Café Capuchino*, beside Calzada Mahatma Gandhi 100 metres north of the museum entrance – a basic, open-air eatery with tortas or sincronizadas at 4.50 pesos, and chicken, salad and fries at 10.50 pesos.

Café de Tacuba in Polanco, at Newton 88 north-east of Arquímedes, about 700 metres north of the Museo Nacional de Antropología, is a pleasant little place with coloured windows, a beamed ceiling and a bit of character. Polanco metro station is 2½ blocks away. Good breakfasts, served till 11.30 am, cost from 12 to 18 pesos and include Mexican offerings like tacos and enchiladas as well as the standard egg combinations. Main dishes later in the day range from 28 to 42 pesos.

For other moderately priced fare in Polanco, head for Avenida Presidente Masaryk, between Alejandro Dumas and

Oscar Wilde, where a string of sidewalk cafés lines the south side of the street. Among them are two branches of *Klein's*, serving antojitos at around 12 to 20 pesos, meat or chicken dishes in the 25-peso bracket, or breakfasts for about 13 pesos. Between the two is *Taconova* which concentrates on enchiladas (three for 10 pesos) and other antojitos. A block south is the busy little *Tonino's Pizza* at Julio Verne 104D, doling out pizzas for 19 to 36 pesos, or spaghetti for 17 pesos.

Expensive The *Hard Rock Café* at Campos Elíseos 290 on the corner of Paseo de la Reforma is directly inspired by the London original of the same name, with background rock music and rock-paraphernalia decor. It's favoured by groups of Mexicans, plus a few foreigners, who come to enjoy the scene and the good burgers (around 30 pesos). Grills go up to 54 pesos; a beer is 9 pesos. Hours are from 1 pm to 2 am daily and it's always busy, but you should be able to walk in before about 6 pm.

Hacienda de los Morales (☎ 540-32-25), Calle Vázquez de Mella 525, is about 1.5 km north-west of the middle of Polanco, south of Avenida Ejército Nacional. It's easiest to go by taxi. Once a grand colonial country house, it is now surrounded by the city, which makes the spacious rooms and pretty gardens all the more appealing. Popular Mexican, American and European dishes are served in numerous dining rooms by experienced waiters. A full dinner costs about 75 to 90 pesos. It's open daily from 1.30 to 11.30 pm (till 10.30 on Sunday).

Restaurant del Lago (☎ 515-95-86), Lago Mayor, Segunda Sección del Bosque de Chapultepec, stands at the lakeside west of Boulevard López Mateos. The lofty, dramatic modern building has a fine view of the lake and the park, an excellent international menu (in English) with an emphasis on French cuisine, one of Mexico's best wine lists, smooth service, and a dance band for postprandial exercise. A jacket and tie are required for men. Expect to spend 75 to 100 pesos per person. It's open daily.

San Ángel

Inexpensive & Mid-Range The *Fonda San Ángel*, a few doors from the Bazar Sábado at Plaza San Jacinto 9, has an excellent location which makes it a popular place on Saturday, but the food is nothing very special. Most main dishes are 35 pesos or more. Better value is found in several of the smaller places along Calle Madero. The nameless little place on the east side of the plaza, next to the Tai Itto Japanese restaurant, offers a good comida corrida for only 12 pesos, and at weekends great caldo de camarón (prawn soup) for 7.50 pesos.

The *Museo de Arte Carrillo Gil* at Avenida Revolución 1608 on the corner of Camino Desierto de los Leones, has a pleasant basement café and bookshop, with good, reasonably priced snacks and drinks and quiet background classical music. It's open from 10 am to 9 pm daily except Monday, and you can get into the café and bookshop without paying to enter the museum.

San Ángel's most renowned bookshop café is upstairs in *Gandhi* at Avenida M A de Quevedo 128 to 132, 400 metres east of Parque de la Bombilla. Customers linger over coffee, snacks, books, newspapers and chess in this haunt of Mexico City intelligentsia. It's open daily. M A de Quevedo metro station is 1½ blocks away.

Expensive For very fancy meals, head for the *San Ángel Inn* (☎ 548-68-40), at Diego Rivera 50, on the corner of Altavista, one km (a 15-minute walk) north-west of Plaza San Jacinto. This is an ex-hacienda with a lovely courtyard, fountain and gardens, now transformed into a luxurious restaurant serving delicious traditional Mexican and European cuisine. If you order carefully you can lunch for 35 pesos per person; choose whatever you like and a three-course meal costs about 60 to 75 pesos. See the earlier San Ángel section for how to get there.

Other upscale restaurants including several steakhouses are to be found on Avenida La Paz and Camino Desierto de los Leones between Avenida Revolución and

Avenida Insurgentes Sur, and on Insurgentes Sur north of Camino Desierto de los Leones.

Coyoacán

There are many places on or near Coyoacán's central plazas. To find some of the cheapest food, leave Plaza Hidalgo along Higuera. The municipal building on the left is filled with stands charging 2.50 pesos apiece for quesadillas with various tasty fillings.

Café El Parnaso, at Carrillo Puerto 2 on the south side of the Jardín del Centenario, is a fashionable sidewalk café with a good bookshop in the back. Good burritas and croissants cost 8 pesos. Hours are from 9 am to 9.30 pm daily. There are three other cafés on this south side of the Jardín del Centenario. On the north side are *El Hijo del Cuervo*, a fashionable café-cum-bar (open in the evenings) with a young clientele, and a branch of *Sanborns*.

Half a block north of Plaza Hidalgo at Aguayo 3, *El Tizoncito* is a cheerful, bustling taco hall, serving up several varieties at 3 pesos each. One excellent choice is nopal y queso (cactus tips and cheese).

Fonda El Morral, Allende at Moctezuma, a half-block north of the east side of Plaza Hidalgo, is a big, busy restaurant with two sections, between them open from 9 am to 9 pm Monday to Saturday and 9 am to 7 pm on Sunday and holidays. Both are decorated in colourful tiles, and serve bountiful breakfasts for 11 to 20 pesos, and a four-course comida corrida for 32 pesos. Orders of enchiladas, tacos and pozole cost 8 to 21 pesos.

Coyoacán's main *market*, two blocks further north on Allende at Malitzin, has a couple of popular seafood comedores serving fish platters at around 20 or 25 pesos, or seafood cocktails at 10 to 20 pesos.

Merendero Las Lupitas, one of Coyoacán's most enjoyable restaurants, is 700 metres west of the Jardín del Centenario, on the little Plaza Santa Catarina, conveniently close to the Viveros (plant nurseries) if you're approaching or leaving Coyoacán by that route. This is a colourful, friendly little place serving a variety of typical Mexican dishes. All three meals are served: snacks and antojitos go for about 8 to 18 pesos, main courses for 20 to 45 pesos.

ENTERTAINMENT

There's a vast choice of entertainment in Mexico City, as a glance through *Tiempo Libre* (Free Time), the city's comprehensive what's-on magazine, will show. *Tiempo Libre* is published every Thursday and can be bought at newsstands for 3 pesos. Even with limited Spanish, it's not too hard to work out what's on where and when. *The News* also carries some what's-on information.

Tickets for many major concerts (popular and classical), dance and opera performances can be bought through Ticketmaster (☎ 325-90-00), which has outlets in the Palacio de Bellas Artes, the Teatro de la Ciudad, and elsewhere.

Dance, Classical Music & Opera

The Palacio de Bellas Artes, home of the national symphony orchestra, is a main venue for classical concerts and opera, but its most famous show is the Ballet Folklórico de México, a two-hour festive blur of coloured lights and regional costumes, music and dance from all over Mexico. The world-famous company has been doing shows like this for decades, so it's a sure hit – although tickets are now expensive at 90, 115 and 125 pesos. Performances are normally at 9 pm on Wednesday and 9.30 am on Sunday. Tickets are usually available on the day or the day before the show at the ticket windows *(taquillas)* in the Bellas Artes lobby, open Monday to Saturday from 11 am to 3 pm and 5 pm to 9 pm, Sunday 10.30 am to 1 pm and 4 to 7 pm. Travel agencies and hotels also have tickets but mark up prices. For information call ☎ 529-93-18 to -22.

A second Mexican folk dance spectacular, cheaper than that of the Bellas Artes but said to be just as good, is staged by the Ballet Folklórico Nacional Aztlán at the Teatro de la Ciudad (☎ 510-21-97) at Donceles 36, between Bolívar and Chile (metro: Allende). Shows are normally at 8.30 pm on Tuesday and 9.30 am on Sunday, and tickets are 30, 60 or 80 pesos. The Teatro de la Ciudad has a ticket office in its lobby.

Cinema

Most non-Mexican movies are dubbed into Spanish, though some have subtitles. The best places to catch serious films, either in Spanish or in foreign languages with subtitles, are both in the south of the city: the Cineteca Nacional (☎ 688-32-72) at Avenida México-Coyoacán 389 (metro: Coyoacán) and the Centro Cultural Universitario (☎ 665-25-80) in the Ciudad Universitaria. Both have full programmes; *The News* and *Tiempo Libre* carry listings.

Mariachis

Plaza Garibaldi, six blocks north of the Palacio de Bellas Artes along Avenida Lázaro Cárdenas (metro: Bellas Artes or Guerrero), is where the city's mariachi bands gather in the evenings. Fitted out in their fancy costumes, they tune their guitars and stand around with a drink until someone who is ready to pay for a song (about 30 to 50 pesos) approaches them. You can wander and listen to the mariachis in the plaza for free, and perhaps have a drink in one of the bars or clubs around the plaza, some of which have live salsa or tropical music as a change from the mariachis. Don't bring any valuables, and look out for pickpockets;

they'll certainly be looking out for you. Come earlier (8 to 10 pm) rather than later, and be careful if you wander in the neighbouring streets.

Nightlife

High cover charges in some places mean you must choose carefully. Check drink prices – which can be astronomical – before you go in, too. There are dozens of live music venues all over the city – look through *Tiempo Libre's* 'Espectáculos' and 'Espectáculos Populares' sections for details. Many good bars and nightspots are closed on Sunday.

Zona Rosa Mexico City's biggest concentration of discos, along with a smattering of live music spots, is in the Zona Rosa (metro: Insurgentes). This is where the city's non-poor converge for a good time. Friday and Saturday are the busiest nights and the clubs are fullest from about 11 pm to 2 or 3 am.

Most Zona Rosa discos have a free bar *(barra libre)*, along with a cover charge of 80 to 120 pesos for men (free for women), on Friday, Saturday and sometimes Thursday. Earlier in the week the cover charge is lower (40 to 60 pesos) but drinks have to be paid for. The trendiest discos – *Mekano* at Génova 44 just south of Hamburgo, *Rockstock* on the south-west side of the Reforma/Niza intersection, and *Caligula* at Londres 77 east of Niza – attract a young, fashionably drab crowd. Rockstock has some live music in its programme. One place that's busy and bright, with live as well as recorded music, and lower-than-average cover charges – free on Wednesday, 65 pesos for men (women free) Thursday to Saturday – is *Papa's* on Amberes just south of Londres. There's no cover charge at all at *Yarda's Bar*, Niza 40 south of Hamburgo, or *Xcess*, across the street, two cafés with video screens and small dance floors. They can be fun on Friday and Saturday. There are more discos, and even a karaoke bar, on Avenida Florencia.

Live heavy rock can be experienced nightly, except Monday, from 9 pm at *Bar*

Osiris, Niza 22 north of Hamburgo, or nightly from 6 pm at *La Casa del Canto*, Glorieta Insurgentes CC-04 (near the exit of Insurgentes metro station). Both are small places which allow the decibels full effect. The cover charge is 10 or 15 pesos in each place; there may be a minimum 10-peso charge for drinks. At the other end of the volume scale, *El Chato* at Londres 117 east of Amberes has a calm piano bar (no cover charge). The *Carrousel Internacional* restaurant/bar, Niza 33 at Hamburgo, has mariachis singing energetically most of the time.

El Taller, Florencia 37 south of Hamburgo, is Mexico City's best known club for gay men. It's open Wednesday to Saturday from 9 pm, cover charge 20 pesos. It has no sign: the entrance is next to the Multy Sexy Boutique.

Near the Zócalo & Alameda *La Ópera Bar* (☎ 512-89-59) at Avenida Cinco de Mayo 14, a block east of the Palacio de Bellas Artes, is an ornate turn-of-the-century watering hole which, after decades as a bastion of masculinity, opened its doors to women in the 1970s. Gilded ceilings, dark wood booths and a massive bar are all original. Drinks cost 7.50 pesos and up, lots of food is served at moderate prices, and mariachis serenade the tables. It's a fun place to spend a couple of hours – open Monday to Saturday from noon to midnight.

A small, lively place for live salsa, merengue, rumba and other Afro-Antillano music is the *Restaurante-Bar León* (☎ 510-30-93) at Brasil 5, half a block north of the Catedral Metropolitana (metro: Allende or Zócalo). The rhythms drive customers to the tightly packed dance floor from 9 pm to 3 am Tuesday to Saturday – cover charge is 25 pesos, drinks are 25 pesos and up.

La Hostería del Bohemio at Avenida Hidalgo 107, a few steps west of Reforma near the Alameda Central, is an apt setting for nightly performances of *música romántica* by singers and guitarists. Tables are set around a leafy, candlelit, open-air courtyard and snacks and soft drinks are served – open daily from 5 to 11 pm, no cover charge, minimum consumption 12 pesos.

Southern Suburbs For free entertainment, you can't beat the musicians, comedians and mime artists who turn the Plaza Central in Coyoacán into a big open-air party every Saturday evening and Sunday. There are good cafés around the plaza where you can take in the atmosphere. Coyoacán also has a few indoor music venues, including *El Mesón del Buen Tunar*, off the south side of Plaza Hidalgo, a small café where customers pass the guitar around on Wednesday to Sunday afternoons and evenings; and the *Hostería del Trovador* (☎ 554-72-47) at Presidente Carranza 82, on the corner of 5 de Febrero, where *peñas* – evenings of Latin-American folk songs, often with a political protest theme – are held most Fridays and Saturdays (no cover or minimum drink charge).

The neighbouring suburb of San Ángel has perhaps Mexico City's best peña – *El Condor Pasa* (☎ 548-20-50) at Calle Rafael Checa 1, between Avenida Revolución and Avenida Insurgentes two blocks south of Avenida La Paz. It's open Tuesday to Saturday from 8 pm to 2 am – the cover charge is 10 pesos.

See the earlier Coyoacán and San Ángel sections for information on how to get to these places.

Elsewhere *Antillano's* (☎ 592-04-39) at Francisco Pimentel 78 in Colonia San Rafael, 1.5 km north of the Zona Rosa (metro: San Cosme), is the top place in the city for salsa and other Afro-Antillano music. It's a large dance hall with room for 1000 or more people, and busy every night except Sunday and Monday, when it's closed. Top bands from Mexico, Cuba, Puerto Rico and Colombia grind out their infectious rhythms from 9.30 pm to 3.30 am. Cover charge is 40 pesos: tequila, rum and whisky are the only drinks, served by the bottle at 175 pesos.

Two upscale places for live rock are *Bulldog's Cafe* (☎ 566-81-77) at Avenida

Insurgentes Centro 149 on the corner of Sullivan, two blocks north of Reforma – open Thursday to Saturday from 10 pm (cover charge 120 pesos) – and the *Hard Rock Café* on the corner of Campos Elíseos and Paseo de la Reforma in Polanco, with music Thursday to Saturday from 9 pm (cover charge 70 pesos).

Top Mexican bands and a growing number of major foreign rock stars – after the government started allowing them into Mexico in 1993 – tour at various big venues around the city. Watch the press – including *Tiempo Libre's* 'Espectáculos Populares' section – for upcoming events.

Spectator Sports

Football (Soccer) Mexico City stages two or three matches in the national Primera División every weekend from August to April. Watch the press, including *Tiempo Libre's* 'Deportes' section, for details. The Mexico City club América, known to its fans as las Águilas (the Eagles), is easily the most popular in the country, and usually one of the best. The Pumas of UNAM (the Universidad Autónoma de México) come second in popularity in the capital. Mexico City's other teams include Cruz Azul (known as los Cementeros), Atlante (los Potros) and Necaxa (los Rayos).

The biggest game of the year in the capital is 'El Clásico', between América and their traditional rivals Guadalajara (las Chivas), which fills the awesome Estadio Azteca (Aztec Stadium) with 100,000 flag-waving fans – an occasion well worth attending if you happen to be around, and surprising for the friendliness of the rivalry between the two bands of supporters. Particularly big crowds also attend América-Pumas and Pumas-Guadalajara games.

Most main games are played at the Azteca. The metro to Tasqueña, then the Tren Ligero to Estadio Azteca is the easiest way of reaching the Azteca from central Mexico City. The Pumas' home is the Estadio Olímpico at the Ciudad Universitaria. A few matches are also played at the Estadio Ciudad de los Deportes – see the Insurgentes Sur section earlier in this chapter. Even for the biggest games, there are usually tickets available at the gate right up to kick-off – prices range between 5 and 50 pesos.

Bullfights Mexico City's main bullring, the Monumental Plaza México, is the largest in the world, holding 64,000 spectators. It's on Calle Maximino A Camacho, a few blocks west of Avenida Insurgentes Sur, 5.5 km south of Paseo de la Reforma. From November or December to April or May, professional fights are held here every Sunday at 4 pm. (Junior matadors fight young bulls the rest of the year.) The cheapest seats, in the Sol (Sun) section, cost 7 pesos and are OK if there's a cool breeze. Seats in the Sombra (Shade) section cost 10 pesos or more, and may need to be reserved in advance. Tickets for these can be bought at most major hotels and travel agencies in central Mexico City. Six or seven bulls will be fought in the afternoon. See the earlier Insurgentes Sur section for how to reach the Plaza México.

Horse Racing Horse races are held from Wednesday to Sunday all year (except for a few weeks in September and October) at the Hipódromo de las Américas in the west of the city. The track opens at 2.30 pm and admission is just 1 peso. Bets cost 2 pesos and up. The course is on Avenida Industria Militar, off the Anillo Periférico, Colonia Lomas de Sotelo, eight km west of the Alameda Central. To get there, take a 'Hipódromo' pesero going west on Paseo de la Reforma.

Jai Alai This old Basque game, introduced to Mexico by the Spanish, is fast and elegant when played by experts, and some of the best can be seen at the Frontón México on the Plaza de la República (metro: Revolución). The attraction for spectators is not just the game but the chance to bet on it, which you can do at the Frontón. Admission is 20 pesos. Games are played nightly except Monday almost all year, starting at 8 pm. It's something of an upper-class sport but formal dress is not required. However, a notice at the door translates: 'No entry with guns, cellular phones, radios or cameras'. For more information on jai alai, see the Arts & Culture (Sport) section of the Facts about the Country chapter.

THINGS TO BUY

For boutiques, art and antiques, stroll the streets of the Zona Rosa. For specialist shops in more everyday things, from shoes or screws to fireworks or cakes, wander the streets south or west of the Zócalo.

Mexican Sweets

For delicate Mexican sweets such as candied fruits, sugared almonds, crystallised strawberries, as well as honey and fruit jams, go directly to the Dulcería de Celaya, Cinco de Mayo 39 west of Isabel la Católica. These treats are not cheap, costing 2.50 pesos or more apiece, but anyone can afford at least one or two. The dulcería is open every day from 10.30 am to 7 pm.

Dulcería La Gardenia, Cinco de Mayo 46C (it has no name sign), east of Isabel la Católica, is not nearly so fancy, and prices are lower, but the sweets are still delicious.

Crafts

There are two permanent exhibitions selling quality Indian handicrafts from all over Mexico on Avenida Juárez a few steps from the Alameda Central (metro: Hidalgo). The **Exposición Nacional de Arte Popular** (National Exhibition of Popular Art) at Juárez 89, open Monday to Saturday from 10 am to 7 pm, is just west of the Jardín de la Solidaridad. You'll find colourful glassware, lacquerware and ceramics, hand-woven blankets, wooden animals, baskets and many other items from all over the country. Prices are fixed. The exhibition is run by Fonart, the National Handicrafts Promotion Fund.

The **Museo Nacional de Artes e Industrias Populares INI** (Museum of Popular Arts and Industries of the National Indigenous Peoples' Institute) at Juárez 44, faces the south side of the Alameda. Its shop is open from 9 am to 6 pm every day. A small museum section, entered through the door marked 'Edificio F' at the rear of the building, is open Monday to Friday from 9 am to 3 pm. Entry is free but sadly the exhibits are unlabelled.

Markets

There are several interesting markets dotted around the city where you can buy all sorts of Mexican handicrafts, souvenirs and everyday goods.

San Ángel The Bazar Sábado, held in Plaza San Jacinto 11, one of the houses on the north side of the square, is a market for some of Mexico's best folk art and crafts like jewellery, pottery and textiles. Prices aren't low but quality is high. It's open Saturday only, from 10 am to 7 pm. Also on Saturday, other artists and artisans display their work in the plaza itself and streets leading off it. See the earlier San Ángel section for information on how to reach San Ángel. To reach the Plaza San Jacinto, walk uphill south-west from Avenida Revolución, on Calle Madero.

Coyoacán The busy main market is three blocks north of Plaza Hidalgo on the east side of Calle Allende. It's worth a look on the way to the houses of Frida Kahlo and Leon Trotsky. On Saturday and Sunday a colourful Bohemian jewellery and craft market spreads over much of Coyoacán's central Jardín del Centenario. Hippie jewellery, Rasta hats and reggae tapes are among the stock-in-trade. Also on Saturday and Sunday, two more traditional craft markets are held. These are the Bazar Artesanal de Coyoacán on the west side of Plaza Hidalgo, and the Bazar Coyoacán 1½ blocks further north on the corner of Aguayo and Cuauhtémoc. See the earlier Coyoacán section for information on getting to Coyoacán.

La Ciudadela & San Juan About 600 metres south of the Alameda, on Balderas on the corner of Aten30 (metro: Balderas), the Centro Artesanal La Ciudadela, open daily, has stalls selling handicrafts from all over Mexico at prices that are fair even before you begin bargaining. You'll find brightly dyed sarapes, multicoloured ceramic parrots, pretty lacquerware boxes and trays, masks, silver jewellery, guitars, maracas – and baskets of every shape and size, some large enough to hide in.

The Mercado de Artesanías San Juan, four blocks east of the Centro Artesanal La Ciudadela, on the corner of Dolores and Ayuntamiento (metro: Salto del Agua), has a similar range of goods and prices. It's open Monday to Saturday from 9 am to 7 pm, Sunday 9 am to 4 pm.

Centro Artesanal Buenavista Just east of the Buenavista train station at Aldama 187, this vast handicrafts 'market' is actually a huge fixed-price store. Much advertised and often visited by foreign tour groups, it has a huge assortment of stuff ('110,000 Mexican typical articles'). Some of it is rubbish, some is quality – but bargains can be scarce. Hours are Monday to Saturday from 9 am to 6 pm, Sunday 9 am to 2 pm.

La Lagunilla From Monday to Saturday this is an unspectacular market in household and practical goods, but on Sunday it becomes a sprawling flea-market of over 1500 stalls selling antiques, old books, stamps, pottery, watches, guitars, leather, clothes, blankets, hats and much more. It spreads out from the corner of Rayón and Allende, just east of the intersection of Reforma and Avenida Lázaro Cárdenas, one km north-east of the Alameda. Guerrero is the nearest metro station; 'Lagunilla' peseros run from there, or you can pick them up heading north on Isabel la Católica from Cinco de Mayo near the Zócalo.

La Merced & Sonora Mercado La Merced, about one km south-east of the Zócalo, is a vast area – four whole blocks – dedicated to the buying and selling of Mexicans' daily needs, which makes for an interesting wander. It's also worth straying down to the Mercado Sonora, two blocks south of La Merced, on the south side of Avenida Fray Servando Teresa de Mier, which has four diverse specialities: toys, cage birds, herbs

and folk medicine. Merced metro station is in the middle of La Merced market.

Tianguis del Chopo From around 10 am to 4 pm on Saturday, Calle Aldama just north of the Centro Artesanal Buenavista becomes the gathering place of Mexico City's punks, with black-clad youths squeezing between stalls selling tapes, CDs, T-shirts, leather gear and so on. It's a glimpse of a little-expected side of the city's life.

GETTING THERE & AWAY
Air

For international flight information, see the Getting There & Away chapter. For general information on air travel within Mexico, see the Getting Around chapter. For transport to/from the airport, see the following Getting Around section. For information on airport taxes, see Costs in the Facts for the Visitor chapter.

Airport Aeropuerto Internacional Benito Juárez, Mexico City's only major airport, is six km east of the Zócalo (metro: Terminal Aérea).

The single terminal is divided into six *salas* or halls, lettered A to F: Sala A – domestic arrivals; Sala B – domestic departures, ticket sales for Aeroméxico and a few other domestic airlines, Aeroméxico check-in; Sala C – Mexicana ticket sales and check-in; Sala D – check-in and departure for most international airlines; Sala E – international arrivals; Sala F – United Airlines and American Airlines check-in and departures (other international airlines may move to this new sala, which opened in 1993).

The terminal has hosts of shops and facilities, though eating options are poor: best value are the fast-food places upstairs in Sala F. There are many casas de cambio and bank branches where you can change money: Tamize in Sala E is one that stays open 24 hours. You can also obtain pesos from ATMs at several bank branches in Salas A, D and F. There are Ladatel credit-card, telephone-card and coin phones all over the place, plus several shops selling telephone cards (look for 'Ladatel Tarjeta Telefónica' signs). In Sala A you'll find guarded left-luggage lockers (12 pesos for 24 hours), a tourist information office, open from 8 am to 10 pm daily, and post and telegraph offices (the latter has a fax service). Most car rental agencies are in Sala E.

Airlines If you already have an onward air ticket from Mexico City, you're all set. If not, a visit to one or two of the city's many travel agencies *(agencias de viajes)* is a good way of finding a suitable ticket. Ask at your hotel for the nearest full-service agency. Consejeros de Viajes México (☎ 525-75-20) at Génova 30 in the Zona Rosa is one conveniently located agency that offers some good fares on domestic and international flights. Here's where to find the offices of the major domestic and international airlines:

Aero California
    Paseo de la Reforma 332, 4th floor (☎ 207-13-92, 207-53-31)
Aerolíneas Argentinas
    Estocolmo 8, Zona Rosa (☎ 208-10-50)
Aeromar
    Sevilla 4, Zona Rosa (☎ 207-66-66)
Aeroméxico
    Paseo de la Reforma 76 (☎ 546-60-62); Paseo de la Reforma 445 (☎ 228-99-10, 207-63-11); and eight other offices around the city
Aeroperú
    Paseo de la Reforma 195 (☎ 566-18-55)
Air France
    Paseo de la Reforma 404, 15th floor (☎ 627-60-60, 546-91-40)
Air New Zealand
    Río Nilo 80, Colonia Cuauhtémoc (☎ 525-12-90)
Alitalia
    Paseo de la Reforma 390, 10th floor (☎ 533-12-40 to 43)
Alaska Airlines
    Hamburgo 213-1004, Zona Rosa (☎ 533-17-46)
American Airlines
    Paseo de la Reforma 300 (☎ 203-94-44, 399-92-22, 208-63-96)
Avensa (Venezuela)
    María Isabel-Sheraton Hotel, Paseo de la Reforma 325 (☎ 208-49-98)
Aviacsa
    Campos Elíseos 169, 3rd floor, Polanco (☎ 281-19-25, 280-81-01)

Avianca (Colombia)
    Paseo de la Reforma 195 (☎ 566-85-50)
Aviateca (Guatemala)
    Paseo de la Reforma 56 (☎ 592-52-89, 566-59-66)
British Airways
    Paseo de la Reforma 10, 14th floor (☎ 628-05-00)
Canadian Airlines International
    María Isabel-Sheraton Hotel, Paseo de la Reforma 325 (☎ 208-18-83)
Continental Airlines
    Andrés Bello 45, Polanco (☎ 280-34-34, 571-40-41)
COPA (Panama)
    Paseo de la Reforma 87, 1st floor (☎ 592-35-35)
Cubana
    Temístocles 246, Polanco (☎ 250-63-55)
Delta Airlines
    Paseo de la Reforma 381 (☎ 202-16-08, 207-34-11)
Ecuatoriana (Ecuador)
    Hamburgo 213, Zona Rosa (☎ 533-31-20)
Iberia
    Paseo de la Reforma 24 (☎ 705-07-16, 703-07-09)
Icelandair
    Durango 193, 3rd floor, Colonia Roma (☎ 511-84-61)
Japan Air Lines
    Paseo de la Reforma 295 (☎ 533-55-15)
KLM
    Paseo de las Palmas 735, 7th floor, Lomas de Chapultepec (☎ 202-39-36)
LACSA (Costa Rica)
    Río Nilo 88, Colonia Cuauhtémoc (☎ 208-46-54, 525-00-25)
Ladeco (Chile)
    Hamburgo 175, 3rd floor, Zona Rosa (☎ 208-01-46, 208-65-55)
LanChile
    Paseo de la Reforma 87 (☎ 566-52-11)
Lloyd Aéreo Boliviano
    Campos Elíseos 169, 3rd floor, Polanco (☎ 280-52-28)
Lufthansa
    Paseo de las Palmas 239, Lomas de Chapultepec (☎ 202-88-66)
Mexicana
    Paseo de la Reforma 312 on the corner of Amberes, Zona Rosa (☎ 511-04-24) and more than a dozen other offices throughout the city (reservations ☎ 325-09-90)
Qantas
    Avenida Insurgentes Sur 520 (☎ 687-77-13)
Saro
    Paseo de la Reforma 34 (☎ 273-17-66, 592-07-87)

SAS
  Hamburgo 61 at Havre, Zona Rosa (☎ 202-85-33)
Singapore Airlines
  Dante 14, 8th floor, Colonia Nueva Anzures (☎ 574-92-11)
Swissair
  Hamburgo 66, 3rd floor, Zona Rosa (☎ 207-24-55)
TACA International (El Salvador)
  Paseo de la Reforma 87 (☎ 566-18-50, 546-88-09)
TAESA
  Paseo de la Reforma 30 (☎ 705-08-80)
United Airlines
  Hamburgo 213, Zona Rosa (☎ 627-02-22)
Varig (Brazil)
  Hotel Holiday Inn Crowne Plaza, Paseo de la Reforma 80 (☎ 591-17-44)

Bus

Mexico City has four main long-distance bus terminals serving the four points of the compass: Terminal Norte (north), Terminal Oriente (TAPO; east), Terminal Sur (south), and Terminal Poniente (west). Information on how to get to/from them is given in the Getting Around section. All terminals have left-luggage rooms or lockers, toilets, newsstands, Ladatel phones or Lada casetas where you can make long-distance calls, post, telegraph and fax offices, cafeterias and snack stands.

Here are some long-distance bus travel tips:

- For shorter trips (one to five hours), just go to the bus station, buy your ticket and go.
- For longer trips (six hours or more), many buses leave in the evening or at night, and service (except to Monterrey and Guadalajara) may be limited, so buy your ticket in advance. If you speak some Spanish, you can telephone bus companies to ask about schedules – they're listed in the yellow-pages phone book under 'Camiones y Automóviles Foráneos para Pasajeros'.
- Large companies have ticket counters in several bus stations, so you may be able to buy a ticket at the Terminal Norte for a bus departing later from the Terminal Sur, etc.
- Ticket prices vary from company to company, and for different classes of service within each company. You pay more for better facilities (more leg room, toilets, drink service, air-con, video) and for faster services such as directo or express.
- Many companies require you to check in luggage at their counter at least 30 minutes before departure.

Terminal Norte The Terminal Central Autobuses del Norte (☎ (5) 587-59-73), Avenida de los Cien Metros 4907, is half a km north off Avenida Insurgentes Norte and five km north of the Zócalo (metro: Autobuses del Norte). The largest of the four terminals, its name has many variations, including Autobuses del Norte, Central del Norte, Central Camionera del Norte, Camiones Norte, or just CN. It serves places north of Mexico City, including Guadalajara and Puerto Vallarta, which are more to the west than the north; Pachuca, Papantla and Tuxpan which are to the north-east; and even the state of Colima, to the west.

There's a guardería, open from 6 am to 10 pm, at the far south end of the terminal, charging 12 pesos per item per 24 hours; there are also lockers in the waiting areas for which you have to buy a token (ficha), costing 8 pesos per 24 hours for a small locker or 16 pesos for a big one, from a desk in the central passage of the terminal. Don't leave valuables in your bags.

The casa de cambio at the centre of the main hall, near the entrance, is open Monday to Friday from 8 am to 8 pm, Saturday 9 am to 4 pm.

Over 30 different bus companies run services from the terminal. In the main, though not exclusively, deluxe and 1st-class ticket counters are in the southern half of the building (to the right as you enter from the metro or the street), and 2nd-class counters are in the northern half.

Terminal Oriente (TAPO) The Terminal de Autobuses de Pasajeros de Oriente (☎ (5) 762-59-77), usually known by its acronym TAPO, is at Calzada Ignacio Zaragoza 200, between Avenida Eduardo Molina and Avenida Oceanía, about two km east of the Zócalo (metro: San Lázaro). This is the terminal for buses serving places east and south-east of Mexico City, including Puebla, central and southern Veracruz, Yucatán, Oaxaca and Chiapas.

A tourist information office and a Banamex ATM, where you can get cash if you have a Visa, Cirrus, MasterCard or Plus

System card, are located in the passage between the metro and the terminal's circular main hall. Left-luggage lockers are underneath the ticket hall of the Sur bus company.

Terminal Sur The Terminal Central de Autobuses del Sur (☎ (5) 689-97-45) at Avenida Tasqueña 1320, 10 km south of the Zócalo (metro: Tasqueña), is busy with services to Tepoztlán, Cuernavaca, Taxco, Acapulco, Zihuatanejo and a few other destinations.

There are no money-changing facilities in this bus station. A left-luggage room, and lockers operated by fichas, are in the waiting hall. A hotel kiosk at the terminal entrance is open from 10 am to 5 pm Monday to Friday for making reservations in Acapulco. When you get to an Acapulco hotel you have booked this way, ask the price *before* you tell them that you have a reservation. Sometimes 'reserved' prices are higher than walk-in prices.

Terminal Poniente The Terminal Poniente de Autobuses (☎ (5) 271-00-38), at Avenida Sur 122 on the corner of Avenida Río Tacubaya, is eight km south-west of the Zócalo (metro: Observatorio). This is the place to come for very frequent shuttle services to nearby Toluca, and for most buses to the state of Michoacán. There are no money-changing facilities.

Destinations Here are the main daily services to a selection of major destinations from Mexico City, with distances, travel times, bus companies, classes and fares. The name of the terminal from which each destination is served is in brackets. More information can be found in other town and city sections of this book. It is all subject to change, of course.

Acapulco – 400 km, five to six hours (Sur); four deluxe buses each by Estrella de Oro and Turistar (130 pesos) and 16 by Futura (85 pesos); 19 1st-class buses by Estrella de Oro and 21 by Turistar (65 or 77 pesos)

Aguascalientes – 468 km, seven hours (Norte); six deluxe buses by ETN (100 pesos) and 10 each by Primera Plus and Expreso Futura (77 pesos); 12 1st-class buses by Omnibus de México (65 pesos)

Campeche – 1360 km, 21 hours (Oriente); one deluxe bus (180 pesos) and five 1st-class (143 or 158 pesos) by ADO

Cancún – 1772 km, 27 hours (Oriente); one deluxe bus (216 pesos) and four 1st-class (190 or 209 pesos) by ADO

Chetumal – 1450 km, 24 hours (Oriente); four 1st-class buses by ADO (154 or 169 pesos)

Chihuahua – 1412 km, 20 hours (Norte); four deluxe buses by Expreso Futura (217 pesos); 11 1st-class by Transportes Chihuahuaenses (184 pesos)

Ciudad Juárez – 1830 km, 24 to 26 hours (Norte); three deluxe buses by Expreso Futura (272 pesos); 11 1st-class by Transportes Chihuahuaenses (230 pesos) and eight by Omnibus de México (227 pesos)

Colima – 740 km, 11 hours (Norte); one deluxe bus by ETN (155 pesos) and two each by Primera Plus (112 pesos) and Tres Estrellas de Oro (102 pesos); two 1st-class buses by Tres Estrellas de Oro (86 pesos) and three by Omnibus de México (83 pesos)

Cuernavaca – 85 km, 1½ hours (Sur); buses half-hourly, 6.30 am to 8.30 pm, by Flecha Roja (15 pesos deluxe, 11 or 12 pesos 1st-class); frequent buses until 11 pm by Autos Pullman de Morelos (18 pesos deluxe, 12 or 13 pesos 1st-class)

Guadalajara – 535 km, seven to eight hours (Norte); 19 deluxe buses by ETN (120 pesos) and 65 by Primera Plus, Tres Estrellas de Oro or Expreso Futura (95 pesos); 23 1st-class buses by Omnibus de México, Servicios Coordinados or Tres Estrellas de Oro (79 or 81 pesos); 35 2nd-class by Flecha Amarilla (65 pesos)

Guanajuato – 355 km, 4½ hours (Norte); two deluxe buses by ETN (70 pesos), four by Expreso Futura and three by Primera Plus (both 56 pesos); two 1st-class by Servicios Coordinados (48 pesos)

Jalapa – see Xalapa

Los Mochis – 1583 km, 24 hours (Norte); one deluxe bus (231 pesos) and three 1st-class (197 pesos) by Tres Estrellas de Oro; four 1st-class by Autobuses Blancos (197 pesos); seven 2nd-class by Transportes Norte de Sonora (165 pesos)

Matamoros – 960 km, 15½ hours (Norte); one deluxe bus by Turistar Ejecutivo (197 pesos) and three by Expreso Futura (153 pesos); five 1st-class by Transportes del Norte (129 pesos)

Mazatlán – 1085 km, 18½ hours (Norte); four deluxe (189 pesos) and six 1st-class buses (155 pesos) by Tres Estrellas de Oro; seven 2nd-class by Transportes Norte de Sonora (139 pesos)

Mérida – 1550 km, 24 hours (Oriente); one deluxe bus (200 pesos) and five 1st-class (162 or 178.50 pesos) by ADO

Mexicali – 2650 km, 40 hours (Norte); four to six deluxe or 1st-class buses each by Autobuses Blancos, Expreso Futura and Tres Estrellas de Oro (all 282 pesos)

Monterrey – 960 km, 11 hours (Norte); five deluxe buses by Turistar Ejecutivo (177 pesos), 11 by Autobuses Blancos and eight by Expreso Futura (both 137 pesos); 17 1st-class buses by Transportes del Norte (117 pesos)

Morelia – 310 km, four hours (Poniente, Norte); from Terminal Poniente, 22 deluxe buses by ETN (70 pesos), 27 1st-class by Herradura de Plata (40 or 47 pesos), and about 50 2nd-class by Autobuses de Occidente (34 pesos); from Terminal Norte, more than 50 departures of all classes

Nogales – 2325 km, 32 hours (Norte); one deluxe bus each by Expreso Futura and Autobuses Blancos (295 pesos); two 1st-class by Transportes del Pacifico (270 pesos)

Nuevo Laredo – 1191 km, 15 hours (Norte); three deluxe buses by Turistar Ejecutivo (229 pesos) and five by Expreso Futura (177 pesos); 12 1st-class by Transportes del Norte (151 pesos); nine 2nd-class by Transportes Frontera (131 pesos)

Oaxaca – 500 km, nine hours (Oriente); six deluxe buses by ADO (72 pesos) and three each by UNO (119 pesos) and Cristóbal Colón (66 pesos); 25 1st-class buses by ADO and six by Cristóbal Colón (58 to 64 pesos); 12 2nd-class buses by AU (50 pesos)

Palenque – 1020 km, 14 to 16 hours (Oriente); two 1st-class buses by ADO (113 pesos)

Papantla – 290 km, 5½ hours, (Norte); four 1st-class buses by ADO (36 pesos)

Pátzcuaro – 370 km, 6½ hours (Poniente); 13 buses by Herradura de Plata (54 pesos 1st-class, 48 pesos 2nd-class)

Playa del Carmen – 1840 km, 28 hours (Oriente); three 1st-class buses by ADO (183 or 202 pesos)

Puebla – 130 km, two hours (Oriente); 35 deluxe buses by Pullman Plus (23 pesos); 84 1st-class buses by ADO (21 pesos); 64 1st-class 'Pullman' buses by Estrella Roja (17 pesos); one-stop 'directo inmediato' service every five minutes, 6 am to 9.30 pm, by Estrella Roja (15 pesos); nonstop 2nd-class 'Premier' service by AU every five or 10 minutes, 5 am to 11 pm (15 pesos)

Puerto Escondido – 790 km, 15 hours (Sur); two deluxe buses (125 pesos) and one 1st-class (118 pesos) by Turistar

Puerto Vallarta – 932 km, 14 to 15 hours (Norte); seven deluxe buses by Elite (140 to 202 pesos) and one by ETN (195 pesos); one 1st-class bus by Transportes del Pacifico (140 pesos)

Querétaro – 220 km, 2½ to three hours (Norte); buses by at least 14 different companies including 31 deluxe by ETN (43 pesos) and 15 or more each by Expresso Futura, Autobuses Blancos and Primera Plus (33 pesos); 1st-class buses every 30 minutes by Omnibus de México (28 pesos); over 70 2nd-class buses by Flecha Amarilla, 34 by Estrella Blanca, and frequent service by Herradura de Plata (all 24 or 25 pesos)

San Cristóbal de Las Casas – 1085 km, 21 hours (Oriente); one deluxe bus (163 pesos) and four 1st-class (123.50 pesos), by Cristóbal Colón

San Luis Potosí – 400 km, five to six hours (Norte); 18 deluxe buses each by ETN (80 pesos) and Expreso Futura (62 pesos); 13 to 19 1st-class buses each by Transportes Chihuahuaenses and Estrella Blanca (53 pesos); about 12 2nd-class buses each by Transportes Frontera (46 pesos) and Flecha Amarilla (45 pesos)

San Miguel de Allende – 280 km, 3¼ to four hours (Norte); four deluxe buses by Primera Plus (41 pesos); three 1st-class nonstop by Herradura de Plata (41.70 pesos); 2nd-class buses every 30 minutes, 5.30 am to 7 pm, by Herradura de Plata (31.50 pesos) and Flecha Amarilla (31 pesos)

Taxco – 140 km, three hours (Sur); 11 deluxe buses by Cuauhtémoc and three by Estrella de Oro (26 or 32 pesos); two 1st-class buses by Cuauhtémoc and three by Estrella de Oro (22 pesos)

Teotihuacán – 50 km, one hour (Norte); 2nd-class buses every 20 or 30 minutes, 7 am to 3 pm, by Autobuses San Juan Teotihuacán (6 pesos). For the archaeological zone, make sure your bus is going to 'Los Pirámides' – some go to the town of San Juan Teotihuacán instead

Tijuana – 2841 km, 42 hours (Norte); four to 10 deluxe or 1st-class buses each by Transportes del Pacifico, Tres Estrellas de Oro, Expreso Futura and Autobuses Blancos (300 to 305 pesos); four 2nd-class buses by Transportes Norte de Sonora (262 pesos)

Toluca – 66 km, one hour (Poniente); 18 deluxe buses by ETN (15 pesos); 1st-class 'Caminante' service every five minutes, 6 am to 10.30 pm, by TMT (10 pesos)

Tula – 65 km, one hour (Norte); 1st-class buses every 30 minutes, 6.30 am to 8 pm, by Ovni (15 pesos); 2nd-class buses every 15 or 30 minutes, 5 am to 10 pm, by Autotransportes Valle de Mezquital (13 pesos)

Tuxtla Gutiérrez – 1000 km, 19 hours (Oriente); three deluxe buses (145 or 154 pesos) and six 1st-class (115.50 or 126.50 pesos), by Cristóbal Colón

Uruapan – 430 km, six hours (Poniente); six deluxe buses by ETN (85 pesos); six 1st-class buses by Vía 2000 Plus (67 pesos); seven 2nd-class buses by Autobuses de Occidente and five by Vía 2000 (60 pesos)

Veracruz – 430 km, six hours (Oriente); eight deluxe buses by UNO (108 pesos), 17 by ADO (62 pesos) and one by Cristóbal Colón (57 pesos); 25 1st-class buses by ADO (50 to 60 pesos); 22 2nd-class buses by AU

Villahermosa – 820 km, 14 hours (Oriente); four deluxe buses by UNO (198 pesos), six by ADO (130 pesos) and two by Cristóbal Colón (118 pesos); 21 1st-class buses by ADO (98.50 or 108.50 pesos)

Xalapa – 315 km, five hours (Oriente); seven deluxe buses by UNO (85 pesos) and six by ADO (52 pesos); 29 1st-class buses by ADO (35 to 40 pesos); 31 2nd-class buses by AU (31 pesos)

Zacatecas – 615 km, eight to nine hours (Norte); one deluxe bus by Turistar Ejecutivo (120 pesos) and nine by Expreso Futura (93 pesos); six 1st-class buses by Transportes Chihuahuaenses (79 pesos) and seven by Omnibus de México (72 pesos)

Zihuatanejo – 640 km, nine hours (Sur); three deluxe buses by Estrella de Oro (110 or 160 pesos) and two each by Futura (125 pesos) and Turistar (105 pesos); three 1st-class buses by Estrella de Oro (87 pesos), others by Flecha Roja (90 pesos)

Train

Estación Buenavista The city's central station is the Terminal de Ferrocarriles Nacionales de México (FNM), better known as Estación Buenavista (Buenavista Station). It's a cavernous building at the intersection of Insurgentes Norte and Mosqueta (Eje 1 Norte), 1.2 km (a 20-minute walk) north of the Plaza de la República. For local transport to/from the station, see Getting Around.

The main hall has taquillas for primera clase and coche dormitorio accommodation, open from 6 am to 9 pm daily, plus an information desk (open from 6.30 am to 9 pm daily, English not spoken) and a Banamex ATM where you can withdraw cash pesos with a Visa, MasterCard, Cirrus or Plus System card. Downstairs from the main hall are the segunda-clase ticket windows, and a left-luggage office *(Guarda Equipaje)* open from 6.30 am to 9.30 pm daily, charging 4 pesos per item per day. You can make long-distance phone calls from the Lada coin phones upstairs or the Lada caseta in the main hall (which also has a fax service).

Telephone information in English on train services, ticketing and so on, can be obtained by calling ☎ 800-9-03-92, a free number operated by SECTUR. Use the 91 long-distance access code if you're calling from outside Mexico City. Information in Spanish is available on ☎ 547-10-84, ☎ 547-10-97 or ☎ 547-65-93. If you need help in English at the station, go to the Departamento Tráfico de Pasajeros (Passenger Traffic Department) next to the Lada caseta in the main hall, or

the Gerencia de Tráfico de Pasajeros (Passenger Traffic Management) upstairs.

You can also buy tickets for trains from Mexico City at stations in other main Mexican cities – allow two or three days for the procedures to go through. For more on ticketing and an explanation of the accommodation class system, see the Train section of the Getting Around chapter.

For hotels and eateries within walking distance of the station, see Places to Stay and Places to Eat.

Top Trains Here are the daily schedules of the most important trains. The named trains (El División del Norte, El Regiomontano, etc) are generally less slow, more comfortable and more expensive, but worth it. The schedules and fares will probably change at least slightly by the time you travel, so please confirm these and other details in advance of travel.

To/From Ciudad Juárez El División del Norte, train Nos 7 and 8, has primera regular and segunda clase seats only. Fares in primera regular are 38.70 pesos to Aguascalientes, 46.30 pesos to Zacatecas, 106.45 pesos to Chihuahua, and 130.25 pesos to Ciudad Juárez.

departs	Train 7
Mexico City	8.00 pm
Querétaro	11.30 pm
León	3.35 am
Aguascalientes	6.50 am
Zacatecas	9.50 am
Torreón	5.20 pm
Chihuahua	1.30 am
arrives	
Ciudad Juárez	6.45 am

departs	Train 8
Ciudad Juárez	10.00 pm
Chihuahua	3.25 am
Torreón	12.10 pm
Zacatecas	8.15 am
Aguascalientes	10.40 pm
León	2.02 am
Querétaro	5.45 am
arrives	
Mexico City	9.30 am

To/From Monterrey & Nuevo Laredo El Regiomontano, train Nos 71 and 72, running between Mexico City and Monterrey, carries primera especial and coche dormitorio accommodation only. Fares (primera especial/one-person camarín) are 53.55/111.10 pesos to San Luis Potosí, 101/209.60 pesos to Saltillo, and 114.35/237.35 pesos to Monterrey.

Train Nos 1 and 2, the Águila Azteca, between Mexico City and Nuevo Laredo, has primera especial, primera regular and segunda clase seats. Fares in primera regular/primera especial are 21.50/33.05 pesos to San Miguel de Allende, 29.10/44.75 pesos to San Luis Potosí, 62.15/95.60 pesos to Monterrey, and 83.95/129.15 pesos to Nuevo Laredo.

El Regiomontano connects at Saltillo with El Coahuilense, train Nos 181 and 182, hauling primera regular and primera especial coaches between Saltillo and Piedras Negras (9½ hours); and at Monterrey with El Tamaulipeco, train Nos 141 and 142, which hauls primera especial coaches between Monterrey, Reynosa and Matamoros, taking a scheduled 4½ hours from Monterrey to Reynosa and 2½ hours from Reynosa to Matamoros.

departs	Train 71	Train 1
Mexico City	6.00 pm	9.00 am
Querétaro	–	1.00 pm
San Miguel de Allende	–	2.35 pm
San Luis Potosí	12.11 am	5.15 pm
Saltillo	5.45 am	11.55 pm
Monterrey		2.20 am
arrives		
Monterrey	8.10 am	–
Nuevo Laredo	–	7.20 am

departs	Train 72	Train 2
Nuevo Laredo	–	6.55 pm
Monterrey	7.50 pm	11.30 pm
Saltillo	10.15 pm	2.35 am
San Luis Potosí	3.55 am	10.05 am
San Miguel de Allende	–	1.09 pm
Querétaro	–	2.40 pm
arrives		
Mexico City	10.00 am	7.00 pm

To/From Guadalajara El Tapatío, train Nos 5 and 6, hauls primera regular, primera especial and coche dormitorio accommodation. Primera regular/primera especial/one-person camarín fares between Mexico City and Guadalajara are 40.30/80.65/161.35 pesos.

Barring delays, El Tapatío connects at Guadalajara with Estrella del Pacífico running along the Pacific Coast to/from Mexicali. See the Guadalajara section in the Western Central Highlands chapter for information on this and other connections.

departs	Train 5
Mexico City	8.30 pm
arrives	
Guadalajara	8.15 am

departs	Train 6
Guadalajara	9.00 pm
arrives	
Mexico City	8.25 am

To/From Guanajuato El Constitucionalista, train Nos 9 and 10, hauls primera especial coaches only. The fare from Mexico City is 30.40 pesos to Querétaro, 50.35 pesos to Guanajuato.

departs	Train 9
Mexico City	7.00 am
Tula	8.03 am
Querétaro	10.20 am
arrives	
Guanajuato	1.25 pm

departs	Train 10
Guanajuato	2.25 pm
Querétaro	5.35 pm
Tula	7.45 pm
arrives	
Mexico City	9.15 pm

To/From Veracruz El Jarocho hauls primera regular, primera especial and coche dormitorio accommodation. Fares from Mexico City (primera regular/primera especial/one-person camarín) are 21.50/39.95/85.95 pesos to Fortín de las Flores, and 28.75/53.55/115.05 pesos to Veracruz.

departs	El Jarocho
Mexico City	9.15 pm
Fortín de las Flores	4.33 am
Córdoba	4.45 am
arrives	
Veracruz	7.10 am

departs	El Jarocho
Veracruz	9.30 pm
Córdoba	11.35 pm
Fortín de las Flores	12.08 am
arrives	
Mexico City	7.40 am

To/From Lázaro Cárdenas El Purépecha, train Nos 31 and 32, hauls primera especial, primera regular and segunda clase coaches. Fares (primera regular/primera especial) are 24.45/46 pesos to Morelia, 28.75/54.10 pesos to Pátzcuaro, 33.70/63.35 pesos to Uruapan, and 52.90/99.45 pesos to Lázaro Cárdenas.

departs	Train 31
Mexico City	9.00 pm
Morelia	5.30 am
Pátzcuaro	6.45 am
Uruapan	9.00 am
arrives	
Lázaro Cárdenas	4.00 pm

departs	Train 32
Lázaro Cárdenas	noon
Uruapan	6.10 pm
Pátzcuaro	9.00 pm
Morelia	10.55 pm
arrives	
Mexico City	7.30 am

To/From Oaxaca El Oaxaqueño, train Nos 111-112 and 112-111, is supposed to haul primera regular and primera especial coaches, but at the time of writing it had only primera regular and segunda clase. Fares (primera regular/primera especial) are 14.20/28.70 pesos to Puebla, 38.35/77.50 pesos to Oaxaca.

departs	Train 111-112
Mexico City	7.00 pm
Puebla	11.50 pm
Tehuacán	2.35 am
arrives	
Oaxaca	9.25 am

departs	Train 112-111
Oaxaca	7.00 pm
Tehuacán	1.35 am
Puebla	4.05 am
arrives	
Mexico City	9.20 am

Car

Touring Mexico City by car is strongly discouraged, unless you are familiar with the streets and have a healthy reserve of stamina and patience. You may, however, want to rent a car here for a trip outside the city. If you're travelling through Mexico by car, pick a hotel that has off-street parking (many do, including some in the bottom-end price range).

Any hotel above the lowest class can put you in touch with a car rental agency, often the hotel owner's brother-in-law. Most of the international car rental companies have offices in or near the Zona Rosa; ask at any of the large hotels there. Prices vary little between agencies. The seemingly better deals offered by some small agencies should be compared carefully with a larger international chain before you take the plunge. For more information on car rentals, see the Getting Around chapter.

As part of its efforts to combat pollution, Mexico City operates an 'Hoy No Circula' ('Don't Drive Today') programme banning every vehicle, no matter where it is registered, from being driven in the city from 5 am to 10 pm on one day each week. The last digit of the vehicle's registration number determines the day. Any car may operate on Saturday and Sunday. The system works as follows:

Last Digit	Prohibited Day
1, 2	Thursday
3, 4	Wednesday
5, 6	Monday
7, 8	Tuesday
9, 0	Friday

The programme's days may be numbered because it is unpopular and widely seen as a failure, partly because many wealthier people have bought a second car – often a polluting old rustbucket – to get round the regulations.

GETTING AROUND

Mexico City has a good, cheap, easy-to-use metro (underground railway) system. Peseros (minibuses) and buses ply all main routes and are also cheap and useful. Taxis are plentiful.

Obvious though it may sound, always make sure you look both ways when you walk across a street. Some one-way streets have bus lanes running counter to the flow of the rest of the traffic, and traffic on some divided streets runs in the same direction on both sides.

Besides their street names, many major north-south and east-west routes in Mexico City are termed *Eje* (axis). The Eje system superimposes a comprehensible grid of priority roads on this sprawling city's maze of smaller streets, making transport easier and quicker. Eje Central is Avenida Lázaro Cárdenas. Major avenues to the west of it are termed Eje 1 Poniente, Eje 2 Poniente, etc; to the east of it, Eje 1 Oriente, Eje 2 Oriente and so on. The same goes for major avenues to the north and south of the Alameda Central and Zócalo: Avenida Rayón is Eje 1 Norte, and Avenida Fray Servando Teresa de Mier is Eje 1 Sur.

To/From the Airport

Unless you are renting a car (not recommended for travel in this city), use the metro or a taxi to travel to/from the airport. No bus or pesero runs directly between the airport and the city centre.

Metro Officially, you're not supposed to travel on the metro with anything larger than a shoulder bag – and at busy times the crowds make it inadvisable in any case. However, this rule is often not enforced at quieter times, especially before 7 am and after 9 pm, and on Sunday.

The airport metro station is Terminal Aérea on línea 5 *(not* Aeropuerto on línea 1). It's 200 metres from the terminal: leave the terminal by the exit at the end of Sala A – the domestic flight arrivals area – and continue walking in the same direction until you see the metro logo, a stylised 'M', and the steps down to the station. A ticket costs 0.40 pesos.

To get to the hotel areas in the city centre, follow signs for 'Dirección Pantitlán'; at Pantitlán, you have to change trains: follow signs for 'Dirección Tacubaya' (línea 9). Change trains again at Chabacano, where you follow signs for 'Dirección Cuatro Caminos' (línea 2), which takes you to the Zócalo, Allende, Bellas Artes, Hidalgo and Revolución stations.

Taxi The comfortable 'Transporte Terrestre' taxis from the airport terminal give good service and are controlled by a fixed-price ticket system. Street taxis picked up outside the airport are cheaper, however.

Two kiosks at the terminal sell Transporte Terrestre tickets: one is outside the exit of Sala E (one of the international flight arrivals areas); the other is in Sala A (domestic arrivals). Maps on display at the kiosks show the *zonas* (fare zones) the city is divided into. The Zócalo and the Alameda Central are in zona 3 (27 pesos); the Plaza de la República and the Zona Rosa are in zona 4 (32 pesos). One ticket is valid for up to four people and a reasonable amount of luggage. If you simply mention a landmark such as 'Zócalo' or 'Plaza de la República' to the ticket agent, you should receive a ticket for the correct zone – but it's advisable to check the map, and count your change, as rip-offs are not unknown. Walk to the taxi rank, put your luggage in the car's trunk (boot), and hand the ticket to the driver only after getting into the car. (Various 'assistants' will want to take your ticket and your luggage the few steps to the taxi, and will then importune you for a tip.) At the end of a trip the driver is not supposed to expect a tip.

For a normal street taxi, don't go with the drivers of nonregulated taxis who hang out in the terminal calling 'Taxi? Taxi?', but walk to the metro station (see the previous section). Just beyond it is the busy Boulevard Puerto Aéreo, with lots of small Volkswagen, Nissan and other normal taxis. They're not as comfortable as the Transporte Terrestre cars, but they do the job for half the price.

Going to the airport from the city centre, use a normal taxi or the metro.

To/From the Bus Terminals

The metro is the fastest and cheapest way to get to any bus terminal, but the prohibition against luggage bigger than a shoulder bag may keep you from using it. Each terminal is reachable by bus, pesero and/or trolleybus. Ticket-taxis from the terminals are much cheaper than from the airport, with fares similar to normal street taxis.

Terminal Norte The metro station (on línea 5) just outside the front door is named Autobuses del Norte, but on some maps it's marked 'TAN' for Terminal de Autobuses del Norte. If you're travelling from the Terminal Norte into the centre, enter the metro station and follow signs for 'Dirección Pantitlán', then change at La Raza or at Consulado and Candelaria. If you change at La Raza, you must walk for seven or eight minutes and negotiate a long flight of steps in La Raza station.

You can also get to the centre by trolleybus, bus or pesero. Trolleybuses marked 'Eje Central' waiting in front of the terminal head south along Avenida Lázaro Cárdenas, going within one block of the Alameda Central and six blocks from the Zócalo. Those marked 'Tasqueña' or 'Terminal Sur' take the same route and continue to the southern bus station at Tasqueña some 15 km south. 'M(etro) Insurgentes' buses travel down Avenida Insurgentes as far as Insurgentes metro station, one km south of Paseo de la Reforma: these take you close to the Plaza de la República and the Zona Rosa.

For peseros or other buses going downtown, cross under the road through the underpass. Vehicles heading for central areas include those marked 'M(etro) Revolución', 'M(etro) Hidalgo', 'M(etro) Bellas Artes' or 'M(etro) Salto del Agua'.

To reach the Terminal Norte from central areas, there are trolleybuses and peseros north on Avenida Lázaro Cárdenas at the Palacio de Bellas Artes, and buses and peseros north on Avenida Insurgentes, anywhere north of Chapultepec metro station. Vehicles going to the Terminal Norte are marked with some variation of the terminal's name – often 'Central Camionera Norte' or just 'Central Norte' or 'Central Camionera'.

The terminal's taxi ticket kiosk is in the central passageway: a ticket to the Plaza de la República, Alameda, Zócalo or Terminal Oriente (TAPO), all in zona 3, costs 15 pesos; to Bosque de Chapultepec or the airport (zona 4) it's 17 pesos; and to the Terminal Sur at Tasqueña (zona 6) it's 24 pesos.

Terminal Oriente (TAPO) TAPO is next door to San Lázaro metro station. For peseros or city buses from TAPO, follow the signs to Calle Eduardo Molina and when you hit the street the bus stop is 50 metres to the right. Ruta 22 peseros marked 'Zócalo, M(etro) Allende, M(etro) Bellas Artes, Alameda', or some combination of these, run to the city centre, passing along Calle Venezuela, four blocks north of the Zócalo, and terminating on Calle Trujano opposite the north side of the Alameda Central.

The taxi ticket fare to the Zócalo (zona 1) is 11 pesos; to the Alameda, Plaza de la República or airport (zona 2), 13 pesos; to the Zona Rosa or Terminal Norte (zona 3), 16 pesos; to Bosque de Chapultepec or Coyoacán (zona 4), 22 pesos.

To get to TAPO from the centre, you can take a 'Santa Martha' bus from the west side of Calle Trujano. Some Ruta 22 peseros from the same place also go to TAPO. If you're starting from the Plaza de la República area, there are 'M(etro) San Lázaro' peseros leaving from the corner of Arriaga and Mariscal.

Terminal Sur Tasqueña metro station is just across the street from the Terminal Sur. 'Eje Central' and 'Central Camionera Norte' trolleybuses run from the Terminal Sur to Avenida Lázaro Cárdenas in the city centre, then all the way to the Terminal Norte. If you walk to the left outside the Terminal Sur's main exit, you'll find the trolleybuses waiting on the far side of the main road.

Running south to the Terminal Sur, these trolleybuses are marked with some combination of 'Eje Central', 'Tasqueña/Taxqueña', 'Autobuses Sur' and 'Terminal Sur'. You can pick them up on Avenida Lázaro Cárdenas by the Palacio de Bellas Artes. You can reach the Terminal Sur from San Ángel or Coyoacán on a 'M(etro) Tasqueña' pesero or bus east along Avenida Miguel Ángel de Quevedo from either place.

A taxi ticket from the Terminal Sur to Plaza Hidalgo in Coyoacán (zona 1) is 10 pesos; to the Zona Rosa, Alameda or Zócalo (zona 4), 17 pesos; to the Plaza de la República or the airport (zona 5), 19 pesos; and to the Terminal Norte (zona 6), 24 pesos.

Terminal Poniente The metro station is Observatorio. A taxi ticket to the Zócalo costs 19 pesos.

To/From the Train Station

Many peseros and buses run along Avenida Insurgentes right past Estación Buenavista. To catch them, turn to the right when you emerge from the station and cross to the far side of Insurgentes. Ones marked 'M(etro) Insurgentes' run as far as the intersection with Avenida Chapultepec, one km south of Paseo de la Reforma; ones marked 'San Ángel' continue to the southern suburb of that name. The frequent 'M(etro) Insurgentes' express bus makes only a few stops, including Ribera de San Cosme (close to the Plaza de la República) and Sullivan (just north of Insurgentes's intersection with Reforma).

If you want a cab you must go outside the station and get one on the forecourt or the street. The fare to any of the major hotel areas should be 10 pesos or less.

The nearest metro station to Estación Buenavista is Guerrero, 900 metres east of the station along Mosqueta, the road in front of the station. 'M(etro) Guerrero', 'M(etro) Morelos' or 'M(etro) Oceanía' peseros along Mosqueta will take you there.

To reach Estación Buenavista from central areas of the city, there are many buses and peseros going north on Avenida Insurgentes. Any saying 'Buenavista', 'Central Camionera', 'M(etro) La Raza' or 'M(etro) Indios Verdes' will do. To identify your stop as you head north on Insurgentes, look for street signs saying 'Eje 1 Norte' and 'Aeropuerto':

these point east along Mosqueta. The station building is topped with the words 'Ferrocarriles Nacionales de México', and has a small antique locomotive out the front.

Metro

Mexico City's metro system offers the quickest and most crowded way to get around Mexico City. The fare is 0.40 pesos a ride, including transfers.

About five million people ride the metro on an average day, making it the third-busiest underground railway in the world, after Moscow's and Tokyo's. It has 135 stations and 158 km of track on nine lines *(líneas)*. Another line (línea 8) was due to open before mid-1995.

The stations are generally clean and well organised, but always crowded, sometimes fearfully so. The carriages at the ends of trains are usually the least crowded. The platforms can become dangerously packed with passengers during the morning and evening rush hours (roughly from 6.30 to 9 am and 4 to 7 pm). At these times carriages are reserved for women and children on some trains. Boarding for these is done through special *'Solo Mujeres y Niños'* lanes. The best times to ride the metro are midday, in the evening and Sunday. From Monday to Friday, trains run from 5 am to 12.30 am on líneas 1, 2, 3 and A, and from 6 am to 12.30 am on the other lines. On Saturday they run from 6 am to 1.30 am on all lines, and on Sunday and holidays from 7 am to 12.30 am on all lines.

With such crowded conditions, it's not surprising that pickpocketing is rife and that luggage bigger than a shoulder bag is not allowed. Be careful with your belongings (see Crime, in the introduction to this chapter, and Dangers & Annoyances in the Facts for the Visitor chapter).

The metro is easy to use. Signs in stations reading 'Dirección Pantitlán', 'Dirección Universidad' and so on name the stations at the end of the metro lines. Check a map for the dirección you want. Buy a ticket *(boleto)* – or several at once to save queueing next time – at the booth, feed it into the turnstile, and you're on your way.

Mexico City Metro

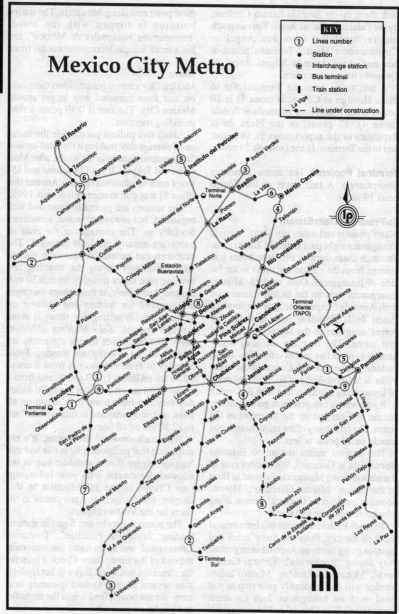

When changing trains, look for *'Correspondencia'* (transfer) signs. Information desks give out maps of the system at La Raza, Hidalgo, Insurgentes, Pino Suárez and other stations.

Bus & Pesero

Over 15 million people use Mexico City's thousands of buses and peseros daily; they run from 5 am to midnight. They are most crowded during the rush hours – roughly from 6.30 to 9 am and 4 to 7 pm. During other hours, routes of interest to the traveller are not too crowded. Pickpockets and thieves are worst on the routes frequented by tourists, especially along Paseo de la Reforma – though the replacement of many larger buses by peseros has reduced the danger here. See Crime at the beginning of this chapter, and Theft & Robbery under Dangers & Annoyances in Facts for the Visitor, for ways to protect yourself.

Full-sized buses are operated by the city government. Peseros (usually green minibuses, but occasionally Volkswagen combi-type vehicles) are privately run but their routes and fares are determined by the city government. Peseros will stop at virtually any street corner; buses have more limited stops. There are a few express buses which stop only every km or so. Bus and pesero routes often begin and/or end at metro stations. Route information is displayed on the front of vehicles, often painted in random order on the windscreen. Peseros also have route *(ruta)* numbers on their sides, but these are of limited use because a vehicle may not travel the whole ruta, and because some rutas have several branches.

Information on bus and pesero services to specific places around the city is given in the relevant sections of this chapter.

Fares on buses (and the few trolleybus services) are 0.40 pesos. Peseros are 0.50 pesos for trips of up to five km, 0.80 pesos for five to 12 km, 0.90 pesos for 12 to 17 km, and 1.10 pesos for more than 17 km.

Taxi

Mexico City has several classes of taxi. The cheapest are the normal street cabs – Volkswagen Beetles, small Nissans and other Japanese models. Slightly more expensive are the larger *sitio* (taxi rank) cars. Both these types are painted green if they run on unleaded fuel. Most expensive are the large, comfortable Transporte Terrestre vehicles from the airport, and the full-size American sedans with black bags over the meters and no taxi markings. These last operate more like hired limousines than taxis, charging set prices rather than metered fares.

In the street taxis, fares are computed by digital meters. The meter should show 2 pesos when you start, then rise by 0.25 pesos every 40 seconds. In average city centre traffic this works out to about 2 pesos per km. Some drivers will try to get you to agree to a fare before you start, or claim that their meter is not working. This will be to your disadvantage, so insist on paying what the meter shows (*'lo que marce el taxímetro'*), and if the driver still refuses, leave him and stop another cab. At night, however, many drivers just cannot be persuaded to use the meter, so you have to negotiate a fare, which is likely to be higher than the daytime rate.

You need not tip taxi drivers unless they have provided some special service.

Around Mexico City

Some of the best things to see and do in Mexico are within a day's travel of the capital. Many of them, such as the ancient city of Teotihuacán or the quaint town of Tepoztlán, can easily be visited as day trips. Other destinations, such as the colonial cities of Puebla and Taxco, are a bit further away and have so many attractions that you should plan to spend at least one night.

Alternatively, you can stop at most of the places covered in this chapter on your way between the capital and other parts of Mexico. The chapter is divided into four sections – north, east, south and west of Mexico City – and each covers at least one major route to/from the capital. Another option is a circular tour around the capital, which would make a fascinating trip. The roads going around the Distrito Federal are not as good as those going to and from it (especially between the north and the west), but it is still quite feasible to take this option, either in your own vehicle or on the local buses.

Geographically, the whole area is elevated. South of Mexico City the Cordillera Neovolcánica, with Mexico's highest volcanoes, runs from Pico de Orizaba in the east to Nevado de Toluca in the west (and continues as far west as Colima). North of this range is the central plateau, or Altiplano Central. The altitude makes for a very pleasant climate, cooler and less humid than the lowlands, with rain falling in brief summer downpours. It also makes for a variety of landscapes, from dramatic gorges to fertile plains, fragrant pine forests and snow-capped peaks. Geologically, it has been an active area, with some still-smoking volcanoes and natural hot springs which have been developed as spa resorts.

Historically the area was home to a succession of important indigenous civilisations (notably Teotihuacán, Toltec and Aztec), and a crossroads of trade and cultural exchange. By the late 15th century, all but one of the small states of central Mexico were under the domination of the Aztec empire. Remnants

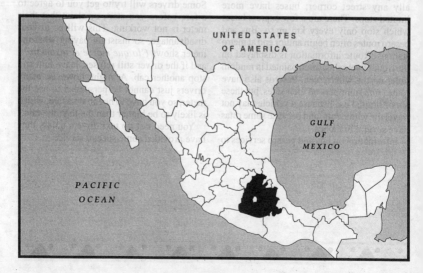

Mexico City
Top: Sculpture garden, Biblioteca Central, Ciudad Universitaria (JN)
Bottom Left: Choosing a sweet (PW)
Bottom Right: Palacio de Bellas Artes (GE)

Around Mexico City
Top: Cosmo Vitral Jardín Botanico, Toluca (JL)
Bottom Left: Templo de Santa Maria, Tonantzintla (PW)
Bottom Right: Market day in Toluca (JL)

of pre-Hispanic history can be seen at the many archaeological sites, and in museums rich with artefacts – the Museo Amparo in Puebla gives an excellent overview of the area's history and culture.

After the conquest, the Spanish transformed central Mexico, establishing ceramic industries at Puebla, mines at Taxco and Pachuca, and haciendas producing wheat, sugar and cattle. Nearly all towns and cities still have a central plaza surrounded by dignified Spanish colonial buildings. The Catholic church used the area as a base for its missionary activity in Mexico, and left a series of fortified monasteries and imposing churches.

Despite the rich historical heritage, this is a modern part of Mexico, with some very large industrial developments and up-to-date transport and urban infrastructure. A common feature of many places near Mexico City is a weekend influx of visitors from the capital. Generally this means that there are ample facilities available during the week, and if a place is crowded it probably won't be with foreigners.

North of Mexico City

Two main routes go to the north of Mexico City. Highway 57 goes past the colonial town of Tepotzotlán, swings north-west past Tula with its Toltec archaeological site, and continues to Querétaro (see the Northern Central Highlands chapter). Highway 85 goes northeast from the capital to Pachuca, a mining town since colonial times. Highway 132D branches east, past the old monastery at Acolman and the vast archaeological zone of Teotihuacán. From Pachuca, a number of routes go north to the Huasteca or east to the Gulf Coast (see the Central Gulf Coast chapter). Most of this area is flat or undulating, and not particularly scenic, but beyond Pachuca, where the fringes of the Sierra Madre descend to the coastal plain, it can be quite spectacular.

TEPOTZOTLÁN

About 35 km north of central Mexico City, but only just past the edge of its urban sprawl, the little town of Tepotzotlán has a pleasant central plaza and park, a riotous example of Churrigueresque church architecture and the Museo Nacional del Virreinato (National Museum of the Viceregal (Colonial) Period).

The Jesuit **church of San Francisco Javier**, beside the zócalo, was originally built from 1670 to 1682, but it was the elaborations carried out in the 18th century that made it one of Mexico's most lavish churches. The façade, with its single tower, is a phantasmagoric array of carved saints, angels, people, plants and more, while the interior walls, and the Camarín del Virgen adjacent to the altar, are covered with a circus of gilded and multicoloured ornamentation. One sparkling altarpiece gives way artfully to another, each adorned with mirrors accentuating the dazzle.

In the 1960s the church and adjacent monastery – including its peaceful gardens – were restored and transformed into the **Museo Nacional del Virreinato**. Among the fine art and folk art gathered here are silver chalices, pictures created from inlaid wood, porcelain, furniture and some of the finest religious paintings and statues from the epoch. Don't miss the Capilla Doméstica (Domestic Chapel) whose Churrigueresque main altarpiece is thick with mirrors.

Opening hours are from 10 am to 5 pm on weekdays and 10 am to 6 pm on weekends (closed Monday), and admission is 13 pesos (free on Sunday and holidays). Classical concerts are sometimes given on the premises.

Places to Stay & Eat

Tepotzotlán is geared to day-trippers – accommodation options are limited but there are plenty of restaurants serving expensive lunches. On the west side of the zócalo, the *Posada San José* (☎ (5) 876-05-20) has small rooms in traditional style for around 60/70 pesos a single/double. Four blocks to the east, the *Posada El Cid* is much more

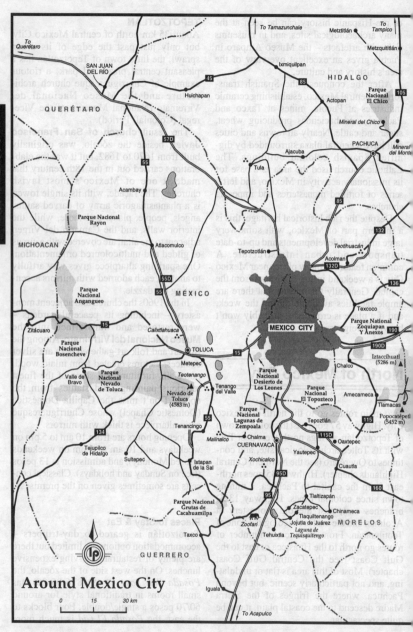

Around Mexico City

To Querétaro

To Tamazunchale

To Tampico

SAN JUAN
DEL RÍO

Metztitlán

Metzquititlán

Ixmiquilpan

HIDALGO

45

85

105

Huichapan

Actopan

Parque
Nacional
El Chico

QUERÉTARO

Mineral del Chico

57D

Ajacuba

PACHUCA

Mineral
del Monte

55

Tula

85

Acambay

MÉXICO

Atlacomulco

Tepotzotlán

Teotihuacán

132

Acolman

132D

136

Parque Nacional
Rayón

55D

Texcoco

MICHOACÁN

55

Calixtlahuaca

MEXICO CITY

Parque National
Zoquiapan
Y Anexos

190

Parque
Nacional
Angangueo

TOLUCA

190D

Zitácuaro

Metepec

15

Iztaccíhuatl
(5286 m)

Parque
Nacional
Bosencheve

Teotenango

190D

Parque
Nacional
Nevado
de Toluca

Chalco

Valle de
Bravo

Nevado de
Toluca (4583 m)

Tenango
del Valle

Parque Nacional
Desierto de
Los Leones

Parque
Nacional
El Topozteco

Amecameca

Tlamacas

Popocatépetl
(5452 m)

134

Tenancingo

55

Parque
Nacional
Lagunas de
Zempoala

Tepoztlán

115

Tejupilco
de Hidalgo

Malinalco

Chalma

Oaxtepec

115D

Sultepec

Ixtapan
de la Sal

CUERNAVACA

Yautepec

Cuautla

160

Xochicalco

95D

Tlaltizapán

Zacatepec

Chinameca

MORELOS

Parque Nacional
Grutas de
Cacahuamilpa

Zoofari

Tlaquiltenango
Jojutla de Juárez

Laguna de
Tequisquitengo

Tehuixtla

GUERRERO

Taxco

Iguala

To Acapulco

N

0   15   30 km

To Querétaro

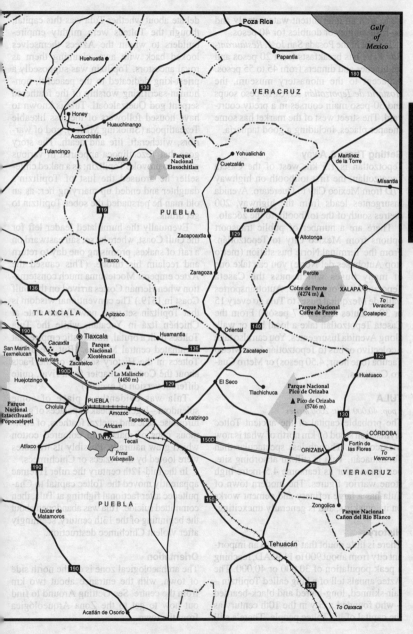

basic with an intermittent water supply and no-frills singles or doubles for 40 pesos.

In front of the Posada San José, *Restaurant-Bar Pepe* has breakfasts from 20 pesos and set lunches and dinners from 45 to 55 pesos. Adjacent to the monastery museum, the *Hostería de Tepotzotlán* serves 16-peso soups and 30-peso main courses in a pretty courtyard. The street west of the market has some cheaper places, including a good taquería.

Getting There & Away

Tepotzotlán is 1.5 km west of the Caseta Tepotzotlán, the first tollbooth on highway 57D from Mexico City to Querétaro. Avenida Insurgentes leads from the highway, 200 metres south of the tollbooth, to the zócalo.

There are a number of public transport options from Mexico City to Tepotzotlán. From the Terminal Norte bus station (metro stop Autobuses del Norte) you can take one of many buses which pass the Caseta Tepotzotlán. (For example, Autotransportes Valle de Mezquital buses to Tula go every 15 or 30 minutes and cost 7 pesos.) From the Caseta Tepotzotlán take a local bus or walk along Avenida Insurgentes. You can also take a colectivo or bus to Tepotzotlán from Metro Tacuba (one hour; 4.50 pesos) or Metro Cuatro Caminos.

TULA

• *pop: 40,000* • *alt: 2060 metres*

The probable capital of the ancient Toltec civilisation stood 65 km north of what is now Mexico City. Though less spectacular than Teotihuacán, Tula is still an absorbing site, best known for its fearsome 4.5-metre-high stone warrior figures. The modern town of Tula has a large refinery and cement works on its outskirts, and is generally unexciting.

History

There is little doubt that Tula was an important city from about 900 to 1150 AD, reaching a peak population of 30,000 or 40,000. The Aztec annals tell of a king called Topiltzin – fair-skinned, long-haired and black-bearded – who founded a city in the 10th century as the capital of his Toltec people. There's still

debate about whether Tula was this capital, though the Toltecs were mighty empire-builders to whom the Aztecs themselves looked back with awe, claiming them as royal ancestors. Topiltzin was supposedly a priest-king dedicated to the peaceful, non-human-sacrificing worship of the feathered serpent god Quetzalcóatl. Tula is known to have housed followers of the less likeable Tezcatlipoca (Smoking Mirror), god of warriors, witchcraft, life and death. The story goes that Tezcatlipoca appeared in various guises to provoke Topiltzin: as a naked chile-seller he aroused the lust of Topiltzin's daughter and ended up marrying her; as an old man he persuaded the sober Topiltzin to get drunk.

Eventually the humiliated leader left for the Gulf Coast, where he set sail eastward on a raft of snakes, promising one day to return and reclaim his throne. (This caused the Aztec emperor Moctezuma much consternation when Hernán Cortés arrived on the Gulf Coast in 1519.) The conventional wisdom is that Topiltzin set up a new Toltec state at Chichén Itzá in Yucatán, while the Tula Toltecs built a brutal, militaristic empire that dominated central Mexico. (But see under Toltecs in the History section of the Facts about the Country chapter for a rival, quite different version of events.)

Tula was evidently a place of some splendour – legends speak of palaces of gold, turquoise, jade and quetzal feathers, of enormous cobs of maize and coloured cotton which grew naturally. Possibly its treasures were looted by the Aztecs or Chichimecs.

In the mid-12th century the ruler Huémac apparently moved the Toltec capital to Chapultepec after factional fighting at Tula, then committed suicide. Tula was abandoned about the beginning of the 13th century, seemingly after violent Chichimec destruction.

Orientation

The archaeological zone is on the north side of town, with the entrance about two km from the centre. See Getting Around to find out how to get to the Zona Arqueológica from the town.

AROUND MEXICO CITY

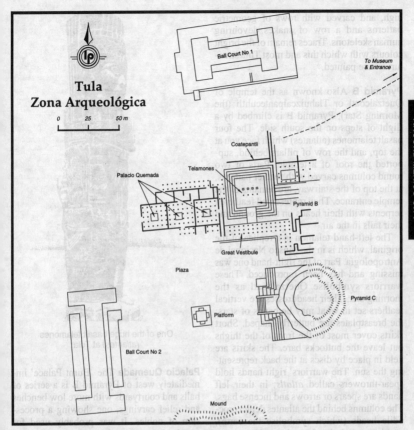

Tula
Zona Arqueológica

0   25   50 m

To Museum
& Entrance

Ball Court No 1

Coatepantli

Telamones

Palacio Quemada

Pyramid B

Great Vestibule

Plaza

Pyramid C

Platform

Ball Court No 2

Mound

Town Centre

The fortress-like church on Zaragoza was part of the 16th-century fortified monastery of San José. Inside, its vault ribs are picked out in gold. On the library wall in the zócalo is a mural of Tula's history.

Zona Arqueológica

The site itself is on a hilltop, with a rural feel and good views over rolling countryside. The old settlement of Tula covered nearly 13 sq km and stretched to the far side of the modern town, but the present focus is the ruins of the main ceremonial centre. The visitors' centre and museum (☎ (773) 9-17-73) were closed for renovations at the time of writing. Tula's ruins are open daily from 9.30 am to 4.30 pm; admission is 13 pesos (free on Sunday and holidays).

Ball Court No 1 This is the first structure you reach from the museum. It's I-shaped, 37 metres long, and a copy of an earlier one at Xochicalco.

Coatepantli A few metres from the north side of Pyramid B stands the Coatepantli (Serpent Wall), 40 metres long, 2.25 metres high, and carved with rows of geometric patterns and a row of snakes devouring human skeletons. Traces remain of the bright colours with which this and most Tula structures were painted.

Pyramid B Also known as the temple of Quetzalcóatl or Tlahuizcalpantecuhtli (the Morning Star), Pyramid B is climbed by a flight of steps on the south side. The four basalt telamones (atlantes) which face you at the top, and the row of pillars behind, supported the roof of a temple. Parts of two round columns carved with feather patterns, at the top of the stairway, are remains of the temple entrance. They represented feathered serpents with their heads on the ground and their tails in the air.

The left-hand telamon is a replica of the original, which is in the Museo Nacional de Antropología. Part of the right-hand one was missing and has been reproduced. These warriors symbolise Quetzalcóatl as the morning star. Their headdresses are vertical feathers set in what may be bands of stars; the breastplates are butterfly-shaped. Short skirts cover most of the front of the thighs but leave the buttocks bare. The skirts are held in place by discs at the back representing the sun. The warriors' right hands hold spear-throwers called *atlatls*; in their left hands are spears or arrows and incense bags. The columns behind the atlantes depict crocodile heads (which symbolise the earth), warriors, symbols of warrior orders, weapons and the head of Quetzalcóatl.

On the north wall of the pyramid, protected by scaffolding, are some of the carvings which once surrounded all four sides. These show the symbols of the warrior orders: jaguars, coyotes, eagles eating hearts, and what may be a human head in the mouth of Quetzalcóatl.

Great Vestibule A now roofless colonnaded hall, this extends along the front of the pyramid, facing the open plaza. The stone bench carved with warriors originally ran the length of the hall, possibly for priests and nobles observing ceremonies in the plaza.

One of the huge basalt telamones *(atlantes)* at Tula

Palacio Quemada The 'Burnt Palace' immediately west of Pyramid B is a series of halls and courtyards with more low benches and relief carvings, one showing a procession of nobles. It was probably used for meetings or ceremonies, and the walls were painted with frescos.

Plaza The plaza in front of Pyramid B would have been the scene of religious and military displays. At its centre is a small altar or ceremonial platform. **Pyramid C**, on the east side of the plaza, is Tula's biggest structure but is largely unexcavated. To the west is **Ball Court No 2**, the largest in central Mexico at over 100 metres long, with alarming chac-mools at each end.

Places to Stay

Casa de Huéspedes Agua Caliente Regadera, at Zaragoza 20, has basic but tolerably clean singles/doubles for 38/45 pesos, with communal bathrooms which may actually have hot-water showers. It's at the far end of Zaragoza from the plaza, on the right.

Auto Hotel Cuéllar (☎ (773) 2-04-42) at 5 de Mayo 23 (turn left at the end of Zaragoza) has bare, smallish rooms with private baths for 50/60 pesos, or 10 pesos extra with TV. *Motel Lisbeth* (☎ (773) 2-00-45) at Ocampo 42 is an ordinary, clean motel charging 99/110 pesos for comfortable rooms with private bath and colour TV. The best place is probably the new, multistorey *Hotel Sharon* (☎ (773) 2-09-76), at the turnoff to the archaeological site, with singles/doubles at 120/135 pesos and suites up to 295 pesos.

Places to Eat

The large, clean *Restaurant Casa Blanca*, on the corner of Zaragoza and Hidalgo, does antojitos for around 13 pesos and meat courses for 18 to 24 pesos. *Cafetería El Cisne*, 100 metres from the zócalo at the end of the pedestrian street Juárez, has bright orange decor and does Western-type snacks and light meals. Hamburguesas are 6 pesos, and fried chicken and salad 12 pesos.

Getting There & Away

Autotransportes Valle de Mezquital runs 2nd-class buses to Tula from Mexico City's Terminal Norte every 15 to 30 minutes from 5 am to 10 pm (13 pesos). The ticket office is at the northern end of the terminal – to the left as you enter. There are a few 'Directo' buses, more frequent 'Directo vía Refinería' services (half-hourly or hourly; 1¼ hours) and 'Ordinario vía Refinería' buses which are even more frequent but slower; 'Vía Cruz Azul' services take a more round-about route.

In Tula, Autotransportes Valle de Mezquital has its own amazingly gleaming terminal on Xicoténcatl. The last 'Directo vía Refinería' bus to Mexico City leaves at 8 pm, though there are ordinarios up to 11 pm. Buses to Pachuca (12 pesos) leave every 15 minutes or so. From the same terminal, Flecha Amarilla has nine daily services to

Querétaro, one at 10 am to Guanajuato, and also buses to León and Morelia.

Getting Around

If you arrive in Tula at the Autotransportes Valle de Mezquital bus terminal, the easiest way to the site is to catch a taxi from outside the terminal (6 pesos). If you prefer to walk, turn right from the bus station, go 1½ blocks to Ocampo, turn right, go a few more blocks and cross the river bridge. You'll see the multistorey Hotel Sharon on a corner on the left, with a replica warrior statue in the middle of the side road in front of it. Turn left at the statue and follow the road 1.75 km to the archaeological zone entrance on the left. The car park and museum are 500 metres from the entrance, and it's another 700 metres, past souvenir stalls, to the centre of the archaeological site.

Motorists can reach the site by following 'Parque Nacional Tula' and 'Zona Arqueo-lógica' signs.

ACOLMAN

About 40 km north of Mexico City, just beside highway 132D (the toll road to Teotihuacán), you'll see what look like battlements surrounding the **Ex-Convento de San Agustín Acolman**. The adjacent church of San Agustín, built between 1539 and 1560, has a spacious Gothic interior and one of the earliest examples of a plateresque façade. The old monastery now houses a museum with artefacts and paintings from the early Christian missionary period (open from 10 am to 5 pm Tuesday to Sunday; entry 10 pesos). The historic building, with its massive thick walls, colonnaded court-yards and carved stonework, is in the process of restoration – plaster and paint are being stripped away to reveal the original frescos. If you have the time, this is a very pleasant stop on the way to or from Teotihuacán. Buses go to Acolman from Metro Indios Verdes. It's not far to Teotihuacán, so if there's no convenient bus you can get a taxi for a few pesos.

AROUND MEXICO CITY

TEOTIHUACÁN

If there is any 'must see' attraction in the vicinity of Mexico City, it is Teotihuacán ('teh-oh-tih-wah-KAN'), some 50 km north-east of the city centre in a mountain-ringed offshoot of the Valley of Mexico. Site of the huge pyramids of the Sun and Moon, Teotihuacán was Mexico's biggest ancient city, with perhaps 200,000 people at its peak, and the capital of probably Mexico's biggest pre-Hispanic empire. If you don't let the hawkers get you down, a day here can be an awesome experience. Using some of the less-trodden paths off the Avenue of the Dead helps you appreciate the place. It's most beautiful after the rains, when wildflowers colour much of this surprisingly rural site.

See History in the Facts about the Country chapter for an outline of Teotihuacán's importance. A grid plan for the city was used from the early years AD and the Pyramid of the Sun was built – over an earlier cave shrine – by 150 AD. Most of the rest of the city was built between about 250 and 600 AD. At its peak in the 6th century it was the sixth-largest city in the world. It declined, was plundered and then was virtually abandoned in the 7th century.

The city was divided into quarters by two great avenues which met near the so-called Ciudadela (Citadel). One, running roughly north-south, is the famous Avenida de los Muertes (Avenue of the Dead) – so called because the later Aztecs believed the great buildings lining it were vast tombs, built by giants for Teotihuacán's first rulers. The major buildings are typified by a *talud-tablero* style, in which the rising portions of stepped, pyramid-like buildings consist of both sloping (talud) and upright (tablero) sections. They were often covered in lime and colourfully painted. Most of the city consisted of residential compounds within walls, about 50 or 60 metres square. Some of these, thought to be residences of nobility or priests, contain elegant and refined frescos.

Centuries after its fall, Teotihuacán was still a pilgrimage site for Aztec royalty, who believed that all the gods had sacrificed themselves here to start the sun moving at the beginning of the 'fifth world', which the Aztecs inhabited.

Orientation

Ancient Teotihuacán covered over 20 sq km. Most of what there is to see now lies along nearly two km of the Avenue of the Dead, running north from La Ciudadela. Buses arrive at a traffic circle by the south-west entrance to the site, near the museum. One of the site's five car parks can be entered from the same traffic circle; the others are reached from the road which circles the site, and you can buy a ticket and enter the site from any of them.

Information

Most of the year you should bring a hat and water. You may walk several km and the midday sun can be brutal. Soft-drink vendors on the site charge muchos pesos. From June to September, afternoon showers are common and an umbrella may be equally valuable. Because of the heat and the 2300-metre altitude, take your time exploring the expansive ruins and climbing the steep pyramids.

The ruins are open daily from 8 am to 5 pm, but you can stay till around sunset, or even later if there's a *son et lumière* (October to June; call the site office ☎ (595) 6-01-88) for details). Admission is 16 pesos, plus 25 pesos for a video camera (free on Sunday and holidays). Crowds are at their thickest from about 10 am to 2 pm, and it can be busy on Sunday, holidays and in the peak tourist seasons, but outside these times there is plenty of room for everyone.

Museo

The museum has recently been renovated and has excellent displays of artefacts, models of the site and explanatory maps and diagrams. It's worth spending an hour here before starting to trek around the site itself – the site entry fee includes admission to the museum. If you come into the site at the south-west entrance, cross the car park, go through the row of souvenir shops and walk right around the box-like three-storey building – the museum entrance is on the east side.

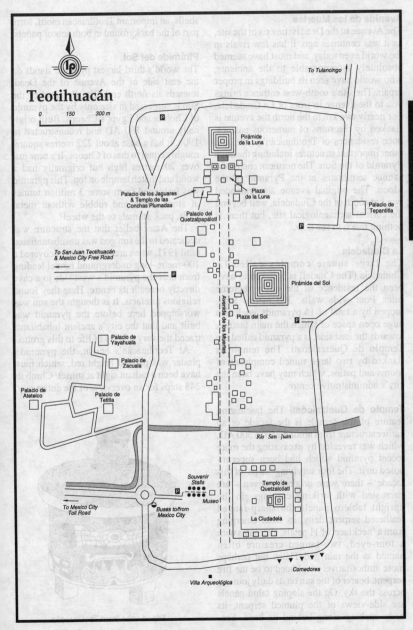

Teotihuacán

0   150   300 m

To Tulancingo

P Pirámide de la Luna

Plaza de la Luna

Palacio de los Jaguares & Templo de las Conchas Plumadas

Palacio del Quetzalpapálotl

Palacio de Tepantitla

P

To San Juan Teotihuacán & Mexico City Free Road

P

Pirámide del Sol

Plaza del Sol

Avenida de los Muertos

Palacio de Yayahuala

Palacio de Zacuala

Palacio de Atetelco

Palacio de Tetitla

Río San Juan

To Mexico City Toll Road

Souvenir Stalls

P Museo

Buses to/from Mexico City

Templo de Quetzalcóatl

La Ciudadela

Comedores

Villa Arqueológica

Avenida de los Muertes

The Avenue of the Dead is the axis of the site, as it was centuries ago. It has few rivals in the world even today, and must have seemed absolutely incomparable to the ancients, who would have seen its buildings in proper repair. The site's south-west entrance brings you to the avenue in front of La Ciudadela. For nearly two km to the north the avenue is flanked by the ruins of numerous palaces, once residences of Teotihuacán's elite, and other important structures including the huge Pyramid of the Sun. The northern end of the avenue terminates at the Pyramid of the Moon. The original avenue also extended two km south of the Ciudadela, well beyond the current archaeological site, but there is nothing much to see now.

La Ciudadela

The large square complex called La Ciudadela (The Citadel) is believed to have been the residence of the city's supreme ruler. Four wide walls, 390 metres long, topped by a total of 15 pyramids, enclose a huge open space of which the main feature, towards the east side, is a pyramid called the Templo de Quetzalcóatl. The temple is flanked by two large ruined complexes of rooms and patios, which may have been the city's administrative centre.

Templo de Quetzalcóatl The fascinating feature of this temple is the façade of an earlier structure from around 250 to 300 AD, which was revealed by excavating the more recent pyramid which had been superimposed on it. The four surviving 'steps' of this façade – there were originally seven – are encrusted with striking carvings. In the upright tablero panels the sharp-fanged feathered serpent deity, its head emerging from a 'necklace' of 11 petals, alternates with a four-eyed, two-fanged creature often named as the rain god Tláloc but perhaps more authoritatively reckoned to be the fire serpent, bearer of the sun on its daily journey across the sky. On the sloping talud panels are side-views of the plumed serpent, its body snaking along behind its head. Sea-

shells, an important Teotihuacán motif, form part of the background in both sets of panels.

Pirámide del Sol

The world's third-largest pyramid stands on the east side of the Avenue of the Dead, towards its north end. The Pyramid of the Sun is surpassed in size only by the pyramid of Cholula and Egypt's Cheops. Built originally around 100 AD and reconstructed in 1908, it has a base about 222 metres square, roughly equal to that of Cheops. It's now just over 70 metres high but originally had a wood and thatch temple on top. This pyramid was fashioned from some 3 million tonnes of stone, brick and rubble without metal tools, pack animals or the wheel!

The Aztec belief that the structure was dedicated to the sun god was unsubstantiated until 1971, when archaeologists uncovered a 100-metre-long underground tunnel leading from near the pyramid's west side to a cave directly beneath its centre. Here they found religious artefacts. It is thought the sun was worshipped here before the pyramid was built and that the city's ancient inhabitants traced the very origins of life to this grotto.

At Teotihuacán's height, the pyramid's plaster was painted bright red, which must have been a radiant sight at sunset. Climb its 248 steps for an overview of the entire city.

Tripod vase from Teotihuacán

Pirámide de la Luna

The Pyramid of the Moon, at the north end of the Avenue of the Dead, is not as expansive or tall as the Pyramid of the Sun, but seems more gracefully proportioned. Its summit is virtually at the same height, because it is built on higher ground. It was finished about 300 AD.

The Plaza de la Luna, in front of the pyramid, is a handsome arrangement of 12 temple platforms. Some archaeologists attribute astronomical symbolism to the total 13 (made by the 12 platforms plus the pyramid). The altar in the plaza's centre is thought to have been the site of religious dancing.

Palacio del Quetzalpapálotl

Off the south-west corner of the Plaza of the Moon is the Palace of the Quetzalpapálotl, or Quetzal Butterfly, where it is thought a high priest or ruler lived. A flight of steps leads up to a roofed portico with an abstract mural, off which is a well-restored patio with thick columns carved with designs representing the quetzal bird or a hybrid quetzal-butterfly.

Palacio de los Jaguares & Templo de las Conchas Plumadas

These structures lie behind and below the Palace of the Quetzal Butterfly. On the lower walls of several of the chambers off the patio of the Jaguar Palace are parts of murals showing the jaguar god in feathered head-dresses, blowing conch shells and apparently praying to the rain god Tláloc.

The Temple of the Plumed Conch Shells, entered from the Jaguar Palace patio, is a now-subterranean structure of the 2nd or 3rd century AD. Carvings on what was its façade show large shells – possibly used as musical instruments – decorated with feathers, and four-petalled flowers. The base on which the façade stands has a green, blue, red and yellow mural of birds with water streaming from their beaks.

Palacio de Tepantitla

Teotihuacán's most famous fresco, the *Paradise of Tláloc*, is in the Tepantitla Palace, a priest's residence about 500 metres north-east of the Pyramid of the Sun. The full-size copy of the mural in the Museo Nacional de Antropología is easier to make out than the original, so don't hike out to Tepantitla unless you are keen. The mural flanks a doorway in a covered patio in the north-east corner of the building. The rain god Tláloc, attended by priests, is shown on both sides. Below, on the right of the door, appears his paradise, a garden-like place with tiny people, animals and fish swimming in a river flowing from a mountain. Left of the door, tiny human figures are engaged in a unique ball game. Frescos in other rooms show priests with feather headdresses.

Palacio de Tetitla & Palacio de Atetelco

Another group of palaces lies west of the main part of the site, several hundred metres from the south-west entrance. Their many murals, discovered in the 1940s, are often well preserved or restored and perfectly intelligible. The Tetitla Palace is a large complex, perhaps of several adjoining houses. No less than 120 walls have murals, with Tláloc, jaguars, serpents and eagles among the easiest to make out. Some 400 metres west is the Atetelco Palace, whose vivid jaguar or coyote murals – a mixture of originals and restoration – are in the so-called Patio Blanco in the north-west corner. Processions of these creatures in shades of red perhaps symbolise warrior orders. There are also crisscross designs of priests with Tláloc and coyote costumes.

Places to Stay & Eat

The Club Med-run *Villa Arqueológica* (☎ (595) 9-15-95) at the south end of the site ring road has very comfortable air-con singles/doubles/triples for 184/215/245 pesos. There is a pool, library, tennis court and French-Mexican restaurant.

On the 3rd floor of the museum building there's a pretty expensive restaurant with a great panorama of the site, set meals from around 40 pesos and main courses from 40 to 50 pesos. The floor below has a bar with almost as good a view and pricey drinks.

Cheaper restaurants and *comedores típicos* (food stalls) are lined up on the ring road on the south side of the site.

Getting There & Away

The 2nd-class buses of Autobuses San Juan Teotihuacán run from Mexico City's Terminal Norte to the ruins every 20 or 30 minutes during the day, costing 6 pesos for the journey of about an hour. The ticket office is at the north end of the terminal. Make sure your bus is going to 'Los Piramides', because some only go to the village of San Juan Teotihuacán, two km west of the ruins.

Buses arrive and depart from the traffic circle outside the site's south-west entrance. Return buses are more frequent after about 1 pm: if you get sick of waiting at the site, get a taxi to San Juan Teotihuacán, from where buses leave every 20 minutes. The last bus back to the capital from the traffic circle leaves about 6 pm. Some terminate at Indios Verdes metro station on Insurgentes Norte in the north of Mexico City, but most continue to Terminal Norte. If you don't fancy taking the metro from Indios Verdes, you can get a pesero or taxi down Insurgentes to the city centre.

Numerous tours from Mexico City go to Teotihuacán.

PACHUCA

• *pop: 320,000* • *alt: 2426 metres*

Pachuca, capital of the state of Hidalgo, lies 90 km north-east of Mexico City. It has grown rapidly in the last few years and brightly painted houses climb the dry hillsides around the town. There are a few interesting things to see, and Pachuca is a good departure point for trips north and east to the dramatic fringes of the Sierra Madre.

Silver was found in the area by the Spanish as early as 1534, and the mines of Pachuca and Real del Monte, nine km northeast, still produce substantial amounts of the metal. Pachuca was also the gateway by which fútbol (soccer) entered Mexico, brought by miners from Cornwall, England, in the 19th century.

Orientation

Pachuca's centre is the rectangular Plaza de la Independencia, with its central clock tower. The main market is on Plaza Constitución, a couple of blocks north-east of the Plaza de la Independencia.

Important streets include Matamoros, along the east side of Plaza de la Independencia, and Allende, running south from the plaza's south-west corner. Guerrero runs roughly parallel to the plaza, about 100 metres west. To the south, both Guerrero and Matamoros reach the modern Plaza Juárez after about 700 metres.

Information

There's a tourist information office (☎ (771) 5-14-11) in the base of the central clock tower, supposedly but not reliably open from 9 am to 6 pm Monday to Friday. The Hidalgo state tourist office (☎ (771) 4-00-06) at Allende 406, near the corner of Matamoros, may also be helpful, and has similar opening hours.

There are banks (with ATMs) on the Plaza de la Independencia. The post office is on the corner of Juárez and Iglesias.

City Centre

A couple of streets east of the Plaza de la Independencia have been pedestrianised and several small modern plazas have been added to the older ones. The Plaza de la Independencia clock tower, the **Reloj Monumental**, was built in 1904 in the French style then popular. Four marble sculptures, one on each side, represent Independence, Liberty, the Constitution and Reform.

The old **Cajas Reales** (Royal Treasuries) are behind the north side of the Plaza Constitución.

Centro Cultural Hidalgo

The former monastery of San Francisco has become the Centro Cultural Hidalgo, which incorporates two museums, a theatre, a library and an exhibition gallery. Admission is free (except for performances) and the centre is open from 10 am to 6 pm, Tuesday to Sunday.

From the Plaza de la Independencia go three blocks south down Matamoros to a crossroads with a fountain. A fine **mural**, depicting animals and plants, inspired by Hidalgo's Otomí Indian heritage, covers a wall just south of this fountain. From the fountain go two blocks east along Arista to the monastery, which is behind the San Francisco church beside the Jardín Colón.

The **Museo Nacional de la Fotografía** has exhibits of early photographic technology (such as a re-created daguerreotype studio) with selections from the 1.5 million photos in the archive of INAH, the national anthropology and history institute. Some of the images are from early European and North American photographers who worked in Mexico, while many more are from the Archivo Casasola. Agustín Victor Casasola was one of Mexico's first press photographers, and he established Mexico's first photojournalism agency; its archive has now been acquired by INAH. The photos provide fascinating glimpses of Mexico's past (since 1873) and present.

The **Museo Regional de Hidalgo** has exhibits on Indian life, clothing and crafts as well as the state's archaeology and history. There is a fine stone jaguar from Tula. The 17th-century **La Asunción church** next door contains the mummified body of Santa Columba (who died in Europe in 273 AD) on one of the side altars.

Places to Stay

The *Hotel Grenfell* (☎ (771) 2-02-77) occupies an imposing building on the west side of Plaza de la Independencia but is much less impressive inside. Sizeable but bare rooms cost 39/44/50 pesos for singles/doubles/triples with private bath, or 22/28/33 with shared bathroom. There's a large courtyard for parking.

The *Hotel Noriega* (☎ (771) 2-50-00) at Matamoros 305, two blocks south of Plaza de la Independencia, is an excellent-value colonial-style place with a good restaurant. There's a covered courtyard, a fine staircase, wide rambling corridors and lots of plants. Pleasant rooms with TV and private bath cost 54/64/75 pesos. *Hotel Plaza Eldorado* (☎ (771) 2-52-85) at Guerrero 721 has 92 pleasant and sizeable rooms at 56 pesos. Take the short street off the middle of the west side of the Plaza de la Independencia and turn left along Guerrero at the first corner.

The modern *Hotel Emily* (☎ (771) 2-65-17), on the south side of Plaza de la Independencia, is about the best place in town, with comfortable rooms from 100 pesos.

Places to Eat

The Cornish miners who brought soccer to Pachuca also brought Cornish pasties – meat, potato, carrot and onion in a pastry shell – and you can still find *pastes* in Pachuca shops, though the filling nowadays is likely to contain its share of chile or mole. There are quite a few places to eat on or near the plaza.

The large *Restaurant La Blanca* (☎ 2-18-96), on the plaza on the corner of Matamoros and Valle a few metres from the clock tower, serves fairly ordinary Mexican snacks from 10 pesos, a good set breakfast for 17 pesos, main courses from 17 to 30 pesos, and a substantial comida corrida. Get some tasty pastes to take away for 1.50 pesos a piece.

The *Restaurant Noriega* in the Hotel Noriega has a touch of elegance (including prints of old London on the walls), and prices are reasonable, particularly the set lunch. *Chip's Restaurant*, in the Hotel Emily, is more of an upscale snack and coffee bar, but it does breakfasts (12 to 16 pesos) and a comida corrida (30 pesos).

Restaurant Ciro's is a few steps down from street level on the north side of the plaza. The usual aves and carnes are in the 15 to 30-peso range. *Cafe Reforma*, on the east side, does a good breakfast for 10 pesos.

Things to Buy

The Casa de las Artesanías (☎ 3-04-12), by the Glorieta Independencia traffic circle on Avenida Juárez (the Mexico City road), two km south-west of Plaza de la Independencia, displays and sells Hidalgo crafts.

Getting There & Away

First-class ADO buses leave Mexico City's Terminal Norte for Pachuca every 10 or 15 minutes (1½ hours; 10 pesos). There are several daily ADO buses from Pachuca to Poza Rica (four hours; 23 pesos), Ciudad Valles (eight hours; 33 pesos), Tampico (nine hours; 54 pesos) and Puebla (32 pesos). Buses serving destinations closer to Pachuca are nearly all 2nd class – frequent buses go to/from Tula (1½ hours; 12 pesos), Tulancingo (one hour; 6 pesos) and Tamazunchale (six hours); several daily to/from Huejutla (six hours) and Querétaro (five hours via the surfaced but rough highway 45 between Ixmiquilpan and San Juan del Río; 22 pesos).

Getting Around

The bus station is some way south-west of the centre, not far off the road to Mexico City. Green and white colectivos marked 'El Centro' take you to Plaza Constitución (1 peso), a short walk from Plaza de la Independencia. Regular taxis cost 3 pesos.

AROUND PACHUCA

Highway 85, the Pan-American, goes via Actopan and Ixmiquilpan, across the forested, sometimes foggy Sierra Madre to Tamazunchale and Ciudad Valles in the Huasteca (see the Central Gulf Coast chapter). Two other scenic roads descend from the Sierra Madre: highway 105 goes north to Huejutla and Tampico, and highway 130 goes east to Tulancingo and Poza Rica.

Actopan

Actopan (population 26,000), 37 km northwest of Pachuca on highway 85, has one of the finest of Hidalgo's many 16th-century fortress-monasteries. Founded in 1548, the **monastery** is in an excellent state of preservation. Its church has a lovely plateresque façade and a single tower showing Mudéjar (Moorish) influence. The nave has Gothic vaulting. Mexico's best 16th-century frescos are in the cloister: hermits are depicted in the Sala De Profundis, while on the stairs are shown saints, leading Augustinian monks and a meeting between Fray Martín de Acevedo, an important early monk at Actopan, and two Indian nobles, Juan Inica Actopa and Pedro Ixcuincuitlapilco. To the left of the church a large, vaulted capilla abierta is also decorated with frescos.

Wednesday is **market day** in Actopan, and has been for at least 400 years. Local handicrafts are sold, along with regional dishes like barbecued meat.

Getting There & Away There are frequent 2nd-class buses from Pachuca (45 minutes) and from Mexico City's Terminal Norte.

Ixmiquilpan

Ixmiquilpan (population 35,000), 75 km from Pachuca on highway 85 (1½ hours by frequent buses), is a former capital of the Otomí Indians, very anciently established inhabitants of Hidalgo. The arid Mezquital valley in which the town stands remains an Otomí enclave. About 125,000 of Mexico's 300,000 Otomí live in Hidalgo, more than in any other state. Traditional Otomí women's dress is a quechquémitl worn over an embroidered cloth blouse. The Mezquital valley Otomí make Mexico's finest *ayates*, cloths woven from *ixtle*, the fibre of the maguey cactus. The Otomí also use maguey to make food, drink, soap and needles.

The **Casa de Artesanías**, on Felipe Ángeles, displays and sells Otomí crafts, but the busy Monday **market** is the best place to find products like miniature musical instruments made of juniper wood with pearl or shell inlay, colourful drawstring bags or embroidered textiles.

The **church** of Ixmiquilpan's monastery has a huge Gothic vault. In the cloister are old frescos by Indian artists showing combats between Indians and mythical pre-Hispanic figures, as well as religious scenes.

Places to Stay You can stay at the *Hotel Saisa* (☎ (772) 3-01-12) at Insurgentes 99, the *Hotel Jardín* (☎ (772) 3-03-08) and *Hotel Palacio* (☎ (772) 3-01-08), both on Plaza Juárez, and the more expensive *Hotel Club Alcantara* (☎ (772) 3-04-90), which has a swimming pool, at Peña Juárez 8.

North of Pachuca – Highway 105

About nine km north of Pachuca, a road branches north-west left off highway 105 and winds 10 km or so to the picturesque old mining town of **Mineral del Chico**, located in the small but attractive **Parque Nacional El Chico**. The park has spectacular rock formations popular with climbers, pine forests with lovely walks, and rivers and dams for fishing. There are places to eat and several camping areas, but otherwise accommodation is limited.

A few km past the national park turnoff, about 10 km from Pachuca, **Mineral del Monte** (also called Real del Monte and Mineral del Real del Monte) was the scene of a miners' strike in 1776 – commemorated as the first strike in the Americas. Most of the town was settled in the 19th century, after a British company took over the mines. Cornish-style cottages line many of the steep cobbled streets, and there is an English cemetery nearby. There are regular buses from Pachuca.

Eleven km north of Mineral del Monte is a turnoff east to **Huasca** (or Huasca de Ocampo), with a 17th-century church, balnearios and a variety of local crafts. Some old haciendas have been converted to comfortable hotels. Nearby is a canyon with some imposing natural basalt columns and a waterfall.

At **Atotonilco el Grande**, 34 km from Pachuca, there's a 16th-century fortress-monastery, and a balneario at some nearby hot springs. Market day is Thursday. The highway then descends steeply to Metzquititlán, in the fertile Río Tulancingo valley – see Tampico & the Huasteca in the Central Gulf Coast chapter for information about other places on this route.

East of Pachuca – Highway 130

Just 46 km east of Pachuca is **Tulancingo** (population 70,000, altitude 2222 metres), the second-biggest town in Hidalgo. Before Tula, it was the Toltec capital for a short time. There's a Toltec pyramid at the foot of a cliff at **Huapalcalco**, three km north. Market day is Thursday.

The remote Otomí village of **Tenango de Doria** is 40 rugged km north of Tulancingo by sometimes impassable dirt roads. Indians here make cotton cloths colourfully embroidered with animals and plants. In **Huehuetla**, 50 km north of Tulancingo, one of the few communities of the tiny Tepehua Indian group embroiders colourful floral and geometric patterns on its quechquémitls and enredos.

Beyond Tulancingo, highway 130 descends towards Huauchinango in the state of Puebla – see the section on Northern Veracruz in the Central Gulf Coast chapter.

East of Mexico City

Highway 190D, the toll autopista, goes east to Puebla across a high, dry region studded with volcanic peaks, including Popocatépetl, Iztaccíhuatl and La Malinche. In the mountains, you can try anything from pleasant alpine strolls to demanding technical climbs. Just north of the highway, the tiny state of Tlaxcala (population 800,000) features a charming little capital, and relics from a rich pre-Hispanic and colonial history. Puebla itself is one of Mexico's best preserved colonial cities, a pivot of its history, and a lively modern metropolis with a lot to see. Nevertheless, the state of Puebla is predominantly rural, with about half a million Indians. The Indian presence helps give Puebla a rich handicraft output, including pottery, carved onyx and fine handwoven and embroidered textiles.

You can continue east from Puebla on highway 150D, past Pico de Orizaba (Mexico's highest mountain), and descend from the highlands to the coast of Veracruz state (see the Central Gulf Coast chapter). An alternative is to swing north on highway 140 towards the remote Sierra Norte de Puebla, or descend to the Gulf Coast via Xalapa. South and east of Puebla there are two main routes, both scenic, through the mountains to the state and city of Oaxaca.

POPOCATÉPETL & IZTACCÍHUATL

The snow-capped peaks of Mexico's two most famous mountains ('po-po-ka-TEH-pettle' and 'iss-ta-SEE-wattle') form the eastern rim of the Valley of Mexico, 60 km south-east of Mexico City and 45 km west of Puebla. They are usually visible from the Mexico City-Puebla road – from where Iztaccíhuatl (5286 metres) is the nearer, and Popocatépetl (5452 metres) is the more cone-shaped peak. From Mexico City and Cuernavaca they are almost always obscured by cloud – or smog. From the east side they often make a stunning morning backdrop for Puebla. The peaks are Mexico's second and third highest and they are classified as dormant volcanoes, but while Iztaccíhuatl is now craterless, Popocatépetl sometimes belches steam. As recently as 1921, a small new cone formed on the floor of its crater.

The mountains are easily reached by road from Mexico City, and this is a popular weekend jaunt for people from the capital. When the weather's clear the mountains are magnificent – but be ready for winds which can produce a distinct chill even in sunshine. There is a lodge at Tlamacas, between the two mountains at 3950 metres, on the edge of a pine forest; from there you can make plenty of strolls, walks and climbs. It is possible to walk from Tlamacas to the top of Popo and back in a strenuous day if you have the right equipment (see below). For information about the more challenging options, check the books by Bradt & Rachowiecki and Secor listed under Travel Guides in the Facts for the Visitor chapter. To arrange a climb in advance, see the organisations listed in the Activities section of the Facts for the Visitor chapter.

In Nahuatl, Popocatépetl means Smoking Mountain, and Iztaccíhuatl means White Woman. The legend is that Popo was a warrior, in love with Izta, the emperor's daughter. She died of grief while he was away at war. On his return, he built the two mountains, laid her body on one and stood holding her funeral torch on the other. Steam still sometimes rises from Popo's crater and, with a touch of imagination, Izta – popularly

known as La Mujer Dormida (The Sleeping Woman) – does look a bit like a woman lying on her back. From the Mexico City side you can, if the weather's clear, make out four peaks from left to right known as La Cabeza (head), El Pecho (breast), Las Rodillas (knees) and Los Pies (feet). Between head and breast is El Cuello (neck).

History

High on the Ventorrillo, Popocatépetl's rugged lower peak, is a small enclosure dating from 900 AD, reckoned to be the work of Toltecs. In the Aztec era, Moctezuma sent runners up the mountain every day to collect ice for his drinks. Cortés reached Cholula in October 1519, and sent a party of 10 Spaniards and some Indians up Popo, which was erupting at the time. They didn't quite reach the top because of snow, flying ashes, wind and cold, but the conquistadors crossed the pass between the two volcanoes on their way to Tenochtitlán. It doesn't seem like the easiest choice of route, but it was from this pass, the Paso de Cortés, that the conquistadors saw for the first time the lake cities at the heart of the great empire they were to conquer.

After the fall of Tenochtitlán in 1521, five conquistadors were sent back to collect sulphur from Popo's crater for making gunpowder. Again it was erupting. The expedition managed to dodge the flying hot rocks and four reached the top, one having retired exhausted. Two men were lowered by rope towards the molten lava in the crater, 13 times between them, each time coming up with a bag of sulphur. They were received as heroes by Indians waiting at the foot of the mountain. Their exploits were equalled on a daily basis nearly four centuries later by workers of a sulphur-mining company.

Information

Some information is available from the desk at the Tlamacas lodge, with Popo routes marked on aerial photos, but there are no maps for sale. The people at the Brigada de Rescate del Socorro Alpino (mountain rescue service) station may be able to help with specific enquiries. They are in the small building across the paved area from the main lodge. In any case you should register there, at the Caseta de Registro, before venturing up the mountains, and notify them when you return.

Conditions & Seasons It can be windy and well below freezing on the upper slopes of either mountain any time of year and it is nearly always below freezing near the summits at night. Ice and snow are permanent; the average snow line is 4200 metres. The best months for ascents are from October to February, when there is a reasonable amount of hard snow for cramponing. February and March are sometimes prone to storms and poor visibility. The rainy season, April to September, is least suitable because there can be clouds, whiteouts, thunderstorms and even avalanches. The snow line may be much higher in summer, but the snow can be soft and difficult to walk on. A climb can still be rewarding though – it's usually clearest early in the day, around sunrise, when the snow is firmer. Crevasses (*grietas*) exist on parts of Popo at any time of year.

Altitude Anyone can be affected by altitude problems, including altitude sickness which can be fatal. Even the Paso de Cortés, at 3650 metres, is at a level where you should be aware of the symptoms – see the Health section in the Facts for the Visitor chapter. If you are planning to climb higher, spending a day at Tlamacas to acclimatise is a good idea. It is wise to sleep at a lower altitude than the highest you have reached during the day. Take it easy at first, increase your liquid intake and eat well. Even with acclimatisation you may still have trouble adjusting. Breathlessness, a dry, irritative cough – which may progress to the production of pink, frothy sputum – severe headache, loss of appetite, nausea and sometimes vomiting are all danger signs. Increasing tiredness, confusion and lack of coordination and balance are even more serious. Any of these symptoms, even a persistent headache, can be a warning. If the symptoms persist or become worse, the only treatment is to descend.

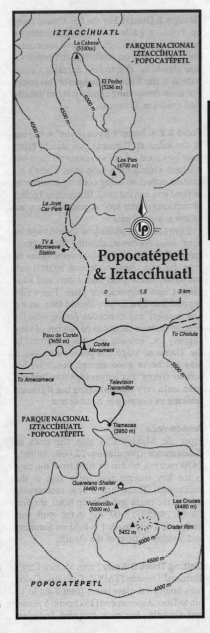

AROUND MEXICO CITY

Groups & Guides For the Las Cruces route on Popo, a guide is not really necessary because the trail is well worn and sometimes busy, especially on weekends and holidays. You should be able to find a trekking companion at the Tlamacas lodge for this route. For more demanding climbs you can usually find guides at Tlamacas.

Food & Equipment Even if you're staying in the lodge at Tlamacas you should bring your own food – there's a restaurant there but it's been closed for a long time. There's no kitchen either, so bring cooking equipment or food you can eat cold. Bring some bottles of drinking water too. A padlock for your locker is a good idea.

Even for short walks you should have, at least: solid footwear; clothing for temperatures below freezing and, at some times of year, for rain; head protection against sun and cold; snack food and water; and sunglasses and sunblock for glare. For walks beyond Las Cruces you should take an ice axe *(peolet)* and crampons *(crampones)* – even in summer there can be patches of very slippery ice. You can rent this equipment at the Tlamacas lodge (20 pesos each), but it may not be in good enough condition for serious climbs. For longer trips take first-aid gear, and a very warm sleeping bag if you are thinking of sleeping in a hut or tent.

Amecameca

From the Mexico City side, the town of Amecameca (population 22,000; altitude 2470 metres), 60 km by road from the city, is the key staging post for a visit to the volcanoes. There are a few restaurants around the plaza and a cheap hotel, the *San Carlos* (☎ (597) 8-07-46), in the south-east corner. A lively market is held on Saturday and Sunday in front of the church.

Getting There & Away From Mexico City's Terminal Oriente (TAPO), Cristóbal Colón runs hourly 1st-class buses from 6 am to 10 pm to/from Amecameca (1¼ hours; 5 pesos) and Cuautla. Sur runs frequent 2nd-class buses on the same route. From the bus station, turn right and walk two blocks to the plaza. On weekends and holidays, colectivos go up the mountains to Tlamacas from the north-west corner of the plaza (7 am to noon; 7 pesos). At other times you can take a taxi (45 to 50 pesos for up to five passengers). Alternatively, walk a couple of km south to the turnoff and hitch up the road which branches east to the pass, though traffic may be light on weekdays.

Paso de Cortés & Tlamacas

The road to Paso de Cortés, 25 km from Amecameca, winds its way up through pine woods. On the pass is a junction and a traffic circle with a monument to Hernán Cortés – one of only two in the country. Cortés isn't too popular among Mexicans! The dirt road to the left goes eight km to La Joya car park on the south-west side of Iztaccíhuatl, passing a TV transmitter on the way. The road straight ahead goes east down to Cholula, 45 km away; it's pretty rough, especially in the wet season, but it's passable in a robust vehicle. The paved road to the right goes another four km to the Tlamacas lodge (3950 metres), at the base of the black, towering cone of Popo.

The lodge, *Albergue Vicente Guerrero*, is a large, modern 98-bed establishment which charges 10 pesos per person for a dormitory bed and locker. It's an imposing, well-built structure but it's poorly maintained and managed. There may be hot water at certain hours, if there's running water at all. The bar and restaurant have been closed for years, and there's no kitchen or eating area. At holiday times it's advisable to make a reservation through the lodge's Mexico City office (☎ (5) 553-58-96, from 9 am to 2 pm) at Río Elba 20, Noveno Piso (9th floor), Colonia Cuauhtémoc.

There's a camping area on the left of the road just before the lodge, with no fees but no facilities either (except for the toilet block to the right of the steps up to the lodge). This is also the parking area, and it has a security attendant; elsewhere it would be unwise to leave valuables in a tent or vehicle.

Easy Walks The saddle between the mountains has lovely meadows and pine forests. Look for the *genciana*, a small shrub with upright stems of purple flowers, and the *cardo*, a thistle-like cactus with a large, pale mauve flower, which only grows at high altitudes. For an easy walk, or to help you acclimatise, take a ramble through the woods around Tlamacas or a stroll in the general direction of Popo. For a longer trek, walk the four km between Paso de Cortés and Tlamacas, which are 300 metres apart in altitude; there are several short cuts between the bends in the road. Longer but flatter is the eight km from Paso de Cortés to La Joya car park on the flank of Izta – take drinks (at least) with you. From La Joya there are trails across the west flank of Izta to the Chalchoapan hut beneath El Cuello, and back down to Amecameca (six hours).

Walk to Las Cruces

Las Cruces is a small group of memorial crosses on the eastern shoulder of Popo, at about 4480 metres. It's well above the tree line, and the only ground cover is rock and loose volcanic sand. The views across to Izta and east to Malinche and Orizaba are superb. On the way up you may get whiffs of sulphur from the crater, and you might be able to see the valley of Mexico City as Cortés did, but a view of cloud and smog is more likely. Las Cruces is a two or three-hour walk from Tlamacas – take the clear trail going east across the base of the volcano, and keep going. It's only about four km, but there is a 530-metre gain in height, and at this altitude it can be quite a strenuous outing. The walk down will take only around 45 minutes.

Climbing Popocatépetl

Las Cruces Route The summit of Popocatépetl is 1500 metres above Tlamacas. The route via Las Cruces requires no technical climbing, but you should take an ice axe and crampons for safety on the icy sections. It is physically demanding, and takes an average of eight hours to reach the summit, a bit less just to the crater rim, and two to three hours to come down, so a 3 am start is normal.

Start by walking to Las Cruces, then continue almost straight up the long, steep section known as La Naranja to the lower edge of the crater at 5100 metres – this is by far the hardest part. From the rim you can look down the sheer sides into the 380-metre-deep crater, with its small lake and a few minor cones. If you turn right on reaching the rim and follow it round, you reach the shelter on the 5452-metre summit after an hour or so.

Ventorrillo Route The trip to the Queretano shelter on the Ventorrillo – the craggy formation visible between Tlamacas and the crater – is a possibility for adventurous hikers. You fork right off the Las Cruces trail at 4100 metres, following the path to the north-east ridge of the Ventorrillo, from where it reaches the Queretano shelter hut at 4460 metres, overlooking the canyon between the Ventorrillo and Popocatépetl's glaciers. Continuing from here to the summit requires technical climbing, and the steep valley on Popo's north-east side can present avalanche dangers.

Shelters on Popo The Queretano and summit shelters *(refugios)* have no equipment or facilities. They hold eight people each and at weekends and holidays can be full.

Climbing Iztaccíhuatl

Izta's highest peak is El Pecho at 5286 metres, and though it is not quite as high as Popo, in many ways it is a more beautiful mountain, more exposed and with better views. All the routes to the peaks involve some technical climbing and a night on the mountain. The usual routes are from La Joya car park, where there is a box with a registration book for the mountain rescue people. Between there and Las Rodillas there are two shelter huts (between 4500 and 4900 metres) which could be used during an ascent of El Pecho. On average, it takes five hours from La Joya to the huts, another four hours from the huts to El Pecho, and four hours to descend. There are a few other huts and many other routes on Izta. Before tackling any of them, make sure you are well prepared physically and have up-to-date information.

TLAXCALA
* *pop: 50,000* * *alt: 2252 metres*

About 120 km east of Mexico City and 30 km north of Puebla, this quiet colonial town is the capital of Mexico's smallest state. It makes a pleasant, off-the-beaten-track trip from either city.

History
In the last centuries before the Spanish conquest, a number of small warrior kingdoms (*señoríos*) arose in the Tlaxcala area. Some of them formed a loose federation which managed to stay independent of the Aztec empire as it spread from the Valley of Mexico in the 15th century. The most important kingdom seems to have been Tizatlán, now on the outskirts of Tlaxcala town.

When the Spanish arrived in 1519 the Tlaxcalans fought them fiercely at first, but then became Cortés's staunchest allies against the Aztecs (with the exception of one chief, Xicoténcatl the Younger, who tried at least twice to rouse his people against the Spanish and is now a Mexican hero). The Spanish rewarded the Tlaxcalans with privileges and used them to help pacify and settle Chichimec areas to the north. In 1527 Tlaxcala became the seat of the first bishopric in New Spain, but a plague in the 1540s decimated the population and the town never played an important role again.

Orientation
Two central plazas meet on the corner of Independencia and Diego Muñoz. The northern one, surrounded by colonial buildings, is the zócalo, called Plaza de la Constitución. The other one, Plaza Xicohténcatl, has a craft market on Saturday. Tlaxcala's bus station (Central Camionera) is a km south-west of the town centre.

Information
The Tlaxcala state tourist office (☎ (246) 2-00-27) is on the corner of Juárez and

Lardizabal, just off the zócalo. It's open from 9 am to 7 pm Monday to Friday, 10 am to 6 pm on weekends. It has leaflets and a computerised information system, and the helpful staff speak some English. The post office is on the west side of the zócalo, with Bancomer and Banamex branches (with ATMs) nearby.

Zócalo
The spacious, shady zócalo is one of the best-looking in Mexico. Most of its north side is taken up by the 16th-century Palacio Municipal, a former grain storehouse, and **Palacio de Gobierno**; inside the latter are vivid murals of Tlaxcala's history by local artist Desiderio Hernández Xochitiotzin. Just off the zócalo's north-west corner is the pretty brick, tile and stucco **parish church of San José**.

Ex-Convento San Francisco
This former monastery is up a short, steep path from the south-east corner of Plaza Xicohténcatl. This was one of Mexico's earliest monasteries, built between 1537 and 1540, and its church has a beautiful Moorish-style wooden ceiling. Next to the church is the Museo Regional de Tlaxcala, which was being renovated at the time of writing but should re-open soon.

Museo de Artes y Tradiciones Populares
This museum, on Boulevard Mariano Sánchez at the end of Lardizabal, has displays on Tlaxcalan village life, mask carving, weaving, pulque making etc, sometimes with actual demonstrations. It's open from 10 am to 5.30 pm daily except Monday; admission is 6 pesos. Next door, the Casa de Artesanías has modern handicrafts like pottery and textiles – quality and prices vary, but it's worth a look.

Santuario de la Virgen de Ocotlán
This is one of Mexico's most spectacular churches, and an important pilgrimage goal because the Virgin is believed to have appeared here in 1541. The 18th-century

façade is a classic example of the Churrigue-resque style, with white stucco 'wedding-cake' decoration contrasting with plain red tiles. Inside, the 18th-century Indian Francisco Miguel spent 25 years decorating the *camarín* (chapel beside the main altar) and altarpieces with a riot of colour and gilding – look up. An image of the Virgin stands on the main altar in memory of the 1541 apparition, and on the third Monday in May it is carried round other churches in a procession that attracts large crowds of pilgrims and onlookers.

The church is on a hill one km north-east of the zócalo – walk north on Juárez for three blocks, then turn right up Zitlalpopocatl, or take an Ocotlán bus or colectivo from the bus station.

Santa Ana Chiautempan

This adjoining village, just east of Tlaxcala, is known for its weaving and embroidery. There's a market on Sunday, but you should be able to see examples in shops any time. Take a local bus, or keep walking east of Ocotlán.

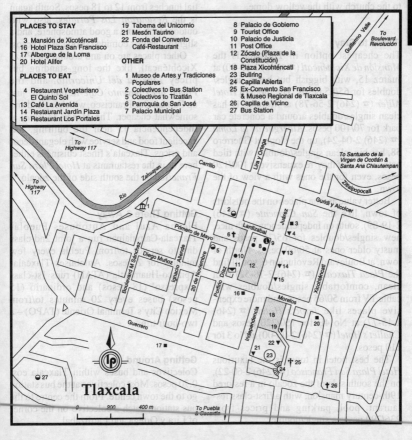

PLACES TO STAY

3   Mansión de Xicoténcatl
16 Hotel Plaza San Francisco
17 Albergue de la Loma
20 Hotel Alifer

PLACES TO EAT

4   Restaurant Vegetariano El Quinto Sol
13 Café La Avenida
14 Restaurant Jardín Plaza
15 Restaurant Los Portales

19 Taberna del Unicornio
21 Mesón Taurino
22 Fonda del Convento Café-Restaurant

OTHER

1   Museo de Artes y Tradiciones Populares
2   Colectivos to Bus Station
5   Colectivos to Tizatlán
6   Parroquia de San José
7   Palacio Municipal

8   Palacio de Gobierno
9   Tourist Office
10 Palacio de Justicia
11 Post Office
12 Zócalo (Plaza de la Constitución)
18 Plaza Xicohténcatl
23 Bullring
24 Capilla Abierta
25 Ex-Convento San Francisco & Museo Regional de Tlaxcala
26 Capilla de Vicino
27 Bus Station

To Highway 117

To Highway 117

To Santuario de la Virgen de Ocotlán & Santa Ana Chiautempan

To Boulevard Revolución

Río Zahuapan

Carrillo

Guillermo Valle

Zitlalpopocatl

Guridi y Alcocer

Primero de Mayo

Lardizabal

Lira y Ortega

Juárez

Diego Muñoz

Ignacio Allende

20 de Noviembre

Porfirio Díaz

Xicohténcatl

Boulevard M Sánchez

Guerrero

Morelos

Independencia

Tlaxcala

0   200   400 m

To Puebla & Cacaxtla

Tizatlán

These ruins are the scant remains of Xicoténcatl's palace. Under a shelter are two altars with some faded frescos showing gods like Tezcatlipoca (Smoking Mirror), Tlahuizcalpantecuhtli (Morning Star) and Mictlantecuhtli (Underworld). Templo San Estéban, next to the ruins, has a 16th-century Franciscan capilla abierta and frescos showing angels playing medieval instruments. The site is on a small hill four km north of the town centre – take a 'Tizatlán' colectivo from the corner of Primero de Mayo and 20 de Noviembre. From the highway, a lane goes north-west up the hill to the church with the yellow dome.

Places to Stay

The cheapest option in Tlaxcala is the *Mansión de Xicoténcatl* (☎ (246) 2-19-00) at Juárez 15, with biggish but basic singles/doubles for 65/85 pesos. The modern *Hotel Alifer* (☎ (246) 2-56-78) at Morelos 11 has clean singles/doubles around a concrete car park for 70/100 pesos. *Albergue de la Loma* (☎ (246) 2-04-24), up the slope at Guerrero 58, has big, clean singles/doubles with tiled bathrooms, but they're expensive at 100/120 pesos, even for the ones with a view of the town.

Better value are the places on the outskirts of town, like the *San Clemente* (☎ (246) 2-19-89), south on Independencia, with nice, new singles/doubles for 65/75 pesos and musty older ones at 50/60 pesos. North of town, at Boulevard Revolución 6, you'll find the *Plaza Tlaxcala* (☎ (246) 2-78-52) with clean, comfortable singles/doubles with cable TV from 50/65 pesos, and more expensive places like *Jeroc's Hotel* (☎ (246) 2-15-77) at No 4B for 150/220 pesos and *Challet's Hotel* (☎ (246) 2-03-00) at No 3 for 110 pesos.

The best hotel in town is the luxurious *Hotel Plaza San Francisco* (☎ (246) 2-60-22), on the south side of the zócalo in a restored 19th-century mansion, with a first-class restaurant, pool, parking and prices from 236/299 pesos a single/double.

Places to Eat

For breakfast and healthy snacks and meals, try the *Restaurant Vegetariano El Quinto Sol* on Juárez, next to the Mansión Xicohténcatl hotel. Fixed-price meals at 12, 15 and 18 pesos are good value, with fresh salads and fish available, as well as yoghurt, fruit, granola and juices.

There's a row of places under the *portales* (arcades) on the east side of the zócalo. The furthest north, and perhaps the classiest, is *Café La Avenida*, with well-dressed patrons enjoying good coffee. Going south you find the *Restaurant Jardín Plaza*, with a very pleasant indoor-outdoor setting and substantial lunches from 12 to 18 pesos. South again is the *Restaurant Los Portales*, also with outdoor tables and a good atmosphere, and a slightly cheaper comida corrida at 10 pesos.

Other places are on and around the Plaza Xicohténcatl, like the long-standing but pricey *Taberna del Unicornio*, and the *Fonda del Convento Café-Restaurant*, just up Calzada San Francisco, which is good and somewhat cheaper. The *Mesón Taurino*, at Independencia 15 near the bullring, has excellent food and service with elegant decor and prices. Tlaxcala's finest cuisine is either here or in the restaurants at *Hotel Plaza San Francisco* on the south side of the zócalo.

Getting There & Away

Flecha Azul and Autobuses Puebla-Tlaxcala-Calpulalpan run a joint 2nd-class directo service to/from Puebla every few minutes for 2 pesos. Autobuses Tlaxcala-Apizaco-Huamantla (ATAH) runs 1st-class 'expresso' (18 pesos) and ordinario (15 pesos) buses every 20 minutes to/from Mexico City's Terminal Oriente (TAPO) – a two-hour trip.

Getting Around

Colectivos and buses within Tlaxcala cost 0.70 pesos. Most colectivos at the bus station go to the town centre. From the centre to the bus station, catch a colectivo on the corner of Lira y Ortega and Lardizabal.

CACAXTLA

The hilltop ruins at Cacaxtla feature vividly coloured and well-preserved frescos showing nearly life-sized jaguar and eagle warriors in ancient battles. The ruins, 35 km north-west of Puebla and 20 km south-west of Tlaxcala, were discovered in 1974 when looters dug up bits of the mural.

History

Cacaxtla was the capital of a group of Olmeca-Xicallanca or Putún Maya, who first came to central Mexico as early as 400 AD. After the decline of Cholula about 600 AD (which they may have helped bring about), they became the chief power in southern Tlaxcala and the Puebla valley. Cacaxtla peaked from 650 to 900 AD before being abandoned around 1000 or 1100 in the face of possibly Chichimec newcomers.

Orientation & Information

From the car park it's about a 200-metre walk to the ticket office, small museum, shop and cafeteria. Then it's 500 metres to the main part of the site, a natural platform 200 metres long and 25 metres high called the Gran Basamento (Great Base), which is now protected by a huge roof – an impressive structure in its own right, but hardly beautiful. A number of smaller pyramids surround the site, with a larger one on a knoll to the west – this structure is being restored and should offer a great view when it's open to visitors.

The site is open daily from 10 am to 4.30 pm (museum closed Monday). Entry is 13 pesos; free on Sunday and holidays. The shop sells a 'mini-guide' (3 pesos) with a plan of the site and some historical details (in Spanish), but you don't really need it as the site is easy to get around, and has good explanatory signs in English as well as Spanish.

Gran Basamento

On this platform stood Cacaxtla's main religious and civil buildings and the residences of its ruling priestly classes. In front at the top of the entry stairs is an open space called the Plaza Norte. From here you follow a clockwise path around the ruins till you reach the murals.

Murals Facing the north side of the Plaza Norte is the long, low Battle Mural, dating from just before 750 AD. It shows people dressed as jaguars and birds engaged in a battle, possibly a real one, with the Olmeca-Xicallanca (the jaguar-warriors, with round shields) repelling invading Huastecs (the bird-warriors, with green stone ornaments and deformed skulls).

At the end of the Battle Mural, turn left and climb some steps to see the second main group of murals, to your right behind a fence. The two main murals, also from about 750 AD, show a figure in bird costume with black-painted body (who may be the Aquiyach Amapane, the Olmeca-Xicallanca priest-governor) and a figure in jaguar costume.

Getting There & Away

The Cacaxtla site is 1.5 km uphill from the 'main' road 1.5 km west of the village of Nativitas – a sign points to Cacaxtla and the nearby village San Miguel del Milagro. Some local buses go right to the site, but if not, the hike isn't *too* steep and offers views of Popocatépetl and Iztaccíhuatl. Nativitas is on a back road between San Martín Texmelucan (near highway 190D) and highway 119, which is the secondary road between Puebla and Tlaxcala. By car, turn west off highway 119 at the 'Cacaxtla' sign just north of Zacatelco. From there it's about 7.5 km to the Cacaxtla turnoff.

By public transport from Tlaxcala, take a 'Texoloc-Tlaxcala-Nativitas' colectivo from the corner of Porfirio Díaz and Guerrero, or an Autobuses Tepetitla 'Nativitas' bus from the bus station. From Puebla bus station, take a 'Zacatelco-San Martín' bus. These leave about every 10 minutes; tickets are sold at the Flecha Azul desk. Alternatively, get a bus (from either town) to Zacatelco, then a micro to San Miguel del Milagro, which will drop you a few hundred metres from the site. Some ATAH buses from Mexico City to Tlaxcala go via Nativitas (11 pesos).

LA MALINCHE

This dormant 4450-metre volcano, named after Cortés's Indian interpreter and lover, is 30 km south-east of Tlaxcala and 30 km north-east of Puebla. Its long, sweeping slopes dominate the skyline north of Puebla.

The main approach to the summit is from the Apizaco-Huamantla road, highway 136. Turn south on the road (mostly paved) to *Centro Vacacional Malintzi* (☎ (246) 2-38-22), a government-run resort about 15 km from the highway. It's mainly for groups, with six and nine-bed cabins for 260/390 pesos (high season), or campsites at 20 pesos per adult. There's a shop, restaurant and recreational facilities. The road gets rougher past the resort, and becomes impassable at 3000 metres. Then it's 1000 metres by footpath, through trees at first, on to the ridge leading to the summit. La Malinche has snow only for a few months of the year.

HUAMANTLA

This town dates from 1534 and is a national historic monument. Two of the most notable buildings are the 16th-century **Ex-Convento San Francisco** and the 18th-century baroque **Iglesia de San Luis**. The state of Tlaxcala breeds many of Mexico's fighting bulls, and Huamantla boasts a **Museo Taurino** which will interest aficionados. The annual **fiesta**, during the first two weeks of August, sees the town's streets covered with beautiful patterns made of flowers. A 'running of the bulls' similar to that in Pamplona, Spain, is held on the Sunday following the feast of the Assumption. A quieter attraction is the **Museo Nacional del Títere**, with exhibits on puppets and puppetry.

There are two hotels in town, the *Vallejo* (☎ (247) 2-02-13) at Parque Juárez 9 and *El Centenario* (☎ (247) 2-05-87) at Juárez Norte 209.

PUEBLA

• *pop: 1.5 million* • *alt: 2162 metres*

Few Mexican cities preserve the Spanish imprint as faithfully as Puebla. There are over 70 churches and 1000 other colonial buildings in the central area alone – many adorned with the hand-painted tiles for which the city is famous. Strategically located on the Veracruz-Mexico City road, and set in a broad valley with Popocatépetl and Iztaccíhuatl rising to the west, Puebla has always played a major role in national affairs.

Strongly Catholic, criollo and conservative, its people (Poblanos) maintained Spanish affinities longer than most in Mexico. In the 19th century their patriotism was regarded as suspect and today Puebla's wealthy, Spanish-descended families have a reputation among other Mexicans for snobbishness. Nevertheless it's a lively city with much to see and do. The historic centre, where a great deal of conservation and restoration has taken place, has a prosperous modern dimension too, with its share of slick dressers, boutiques and burger bars. The Hill of Guadalupe is a peaceful retreat from city noises and smells, as well as the site of a celebrated Mexican military victory in 1862 and a clutch of museums. On the negative side, accommodation in Puebla is expensive and some areas of the city are as noisy, squalid and polluted as any in Mexico.

History

Founded by Spanish settlers in 1531 as Ciudad de los Ángeles, with the aim of overshadowing the nearby pre-Hispanic religious centre of Cholula, the city became Puebla de los Ángeles eight years later and quickly grew into an important Catholic religious centre. Fine pottery had always been made from the local clay, and after the colonists introduced new materials and techniques, Puebla pottery became an art and an industry. By the late 18th century the city was also an important textile and glass producer. With 50,000 people by 1811, it remained Mexico's second-biggest city until Guadalajara overtook it in the late 19th century.

The French invaders of 1862 expected a welcome in Puebla, but General Ignacio de Zaragoza fortified the hill of Guadalupe and on 5 May his 2000 men defeated a frontal attack by 6000 French, many of whom were

The Nahua

Puebla has about 400,000 of Mexico's most numerous Indian people, the Nahua – more than any other state. Another 200,000 Nahua live in western parts of Veracruz state adjoining Puebla. The Nahua language (Nahuatl) was spoken by the Aztecs and, like the Aztecs, the Nahua were probably of Chichimec origin. Traditional Nahua women's dress consists of a black wool enredo (waist sash) and embroidered blouse and quechquémitl (shoulder cape). The Nahua are Christian but often also believe in a pantheon of supernatural beings including *tonos*, people's animal 'doubles', and witches who can become blood-sucking birds and cause illness. ■

handicapped by diarrhoea. About 1000 French were killed. This rare Mexican military success is the excuse for annual national celebrations and hundreds of streets named in honour of Cinco de Mayo (5 May). No one seems to remember that the following year the reinforced French took Puebla after a two-month siege and several days' bombardment, occupying it until 1867.

In recent decades Puebla has seen huge industrial growth, the most obvious sign of which is a vast Volkswagen plant built in 1970 on the approach from Mexico City.

Arts

Architecture In the 17th century local tiles – some in Arabic designs – began to be used to fine effect on church domes and, with red brick, on buildings' façades. In the 18th century *alfeñique* – elaborate white stucco ornamentation named after a candy made from egg whites and sugar – became popular. Throughout the colonial period the local grey stone was carved into a variety of forms to embellish many buildings. Also notable is the local Indian influence, best seen in the prolific stucco decoration of buildings like the Capilla del Rosario in Santo Domingo church and Tonantzintla village church (see Around Cholula later in this chapter).

Pottery Puebla's colourful hand-painted ceramics, known as Talavera after a town in Spain, take many forms – plates, cups, vases, fountains, azulejos (tiles) – and designs show Asian, Spanish-Arabic and Mexican-Indian influences. Before the conquest, Cholula was the most important town in the area, and it had artistic influence from the Mixtecs to

the south. The colourful glazed Mixteca-Cholula-Puebla pottery was the finest in the land when the Spanish arrived: Moctezuma, it was said, would eat off no other. In colonial times Puebla pottery was not used by the rich, who preferred silver or Chinese porcelain. The finest Puebla pottery of all is the white ware called *majolica*.

Orientation

The centre of the city is the spacious, shady zócalo, with the cathedral on its south side. The majority of places to stay, eat and visit are within a few of blocks of here. Further away, particularly to the north or west, you soon enter dirtier, poorer streets. The area of smart, modern restaurants and shops along Avenida Juárez, one to two km west of the zócalo, is known as the Zona Esmeralda.

Buses arrive at a big modern bus station, the Central de Autobuses de Puebla, or CAPU, on the northern corner of the city. (See Getting Around for transport to/from the centre.)

The crucial intersection for the complicated naming system of Puebla's grid-plan of streets is the north-west corner of the zócalo. From here, Avenida 5 de Mayo goes north, Avenida 16 de Septiembre goes south, Avenida Reforma goes west and Avenida Maximino Avila Camacho goes east. Other north-south streets are called Calles and east-west streets are called Avenidas. These are designated with rising sequences of either odd or even numbers as you move away from the centre. Calles are suffixed Norte (Nte) or Sur, Avenidas Poniente (Pte) or Oriente (Ote).

Don't confuse the downtown Avenida 5 de

Mayo with Boulevard Héroes del 5 de Mayo, an inner ring road a few blocks east of the zócalo.

Information

Tourist Office The helpful tourist office (☎ (22) 46-12-85) is at Avenida 5 Oriente 3, facing the cathedral yard. Some English is spoken and there's an interactive computerised information unit which is actually useful. It's open from 10 am to 8 pm daily.

Money Several city-centre banks change money and travellers' cheques, including Banamex, Bancomer and Banco Internacional, all on Avenida Reforma within a block west of the zócalo, and all with ATMs.

Post & Telecommunications The main post office is on Avenida 16 de Septiembre, a couple of doors south of the cathedral. The Centro de Servicios Integrados de Telecomunicaciones, offering public telegram, fax and telex services, is next door.

Museum Hours Nearly all of Puebla's many museums are open from 10 am to 5 pm daily except Monday, but you usually can't enter after 4.30 pm. Admission prices vary but most are free on Sunday. The main exception to these rules is the Museo Amparo.

Things to See – Zócalo & South

Puebla's central plaza was a marketplace where hangings, bullfights and theatre took place before it acquired its current garden-like appearance in 1854. The portales date from the 16th century.

Catedral The massive cathedral occupying the block south of the zócalo is considered one of Mexico's best proportioned. It blends severe Herreresque Renaissance style and early baroque. Building began in 1550 but most of it took place under the dynamic bishop Juan de Palafox in the 1640s. The towers are the highest in the country at 69 metres; some of the cathedral guides may let

you climb the southern tower between 11 am and noon. The cathedral's bells are celebrated in the traditional rhyme *'Para mujeres y campanas, las Poblanas'* – 'For women and bells, Puebla's (are best)'.

Casa de la Cultura Occupying the whole block facing the south side of the cathedral, this former bishop's palace is a classic brick-and-tile Puebla building which now houses government offices, including the tourist office and the Casa de la Cultura, devoted to local cultural activities. Upstairs is the Biblioteca Palafoxiana (Palafox Library), with thousands of valuable books, including the 1493 Nuremberg Chronicle with more than 2000 engravings. Look for the wooden Ferris wheel, which held half a dozen heavy tomes open and revolved so you could consult them quickly – a not very compact disk ROM. Entry is 5 pesos during normal museum hours.

Museo Amparo This excellent modern museum, opened in 1991 at 2 Sur on the corner of Avenida 9 Oriente, is an absolute must. It is attractively housed in two linked colonial buildings. The first has eight rooms with superb pre-Hispanic artefacts, well displayed with explanations, in English and Spanish, of their production techniques, regional and historical context and anthropological significance. An audiovisual system offers more information in Spanish, English, French, German and Japanese. Crossing to the second building, one enters a series of rooms rich with the finest art and furnishings from the colonial period. The contrast between the pre-Hispanic and European styles is so radical it could induce culture shock – it's a lesson in the enormity of the clash of civilisations which commenced with the Conquest.

The museum is open from 10 am to 6 pm daily except Tuesday, and entry is 10 pesos (free on Monday). Rental of the headphones for the audiovisual system costs another 7 pesos, plus a deposit. The museum also has a library, cafeteria and very good bookshop.

Museo Bello This house at Avenida 3 Poniente 302 is filled with the very diverse art and craft collection of 19th-century industrialist José Luis Bello and his son Mariano. There is beautiful French, English, Japanese and Chinese porcelain, and a large collection of Pueblan Talavera. Other items include nuns' spiked flagellation chains and a door of glass columns, each with a different musical pitch. Admission is 4 pesos (free on Saturday). Tours are given in Spanish and English and guides ask for a tip.

Things to See – East & North-East

Casa de los Muñecos The big tiles on the House of the Puppets on 2 Norte, just off the north-east corner of the zócalo, caricature the city fathers who took the house's owner, Agustín de Ovando y Villavicencio, to court because his building was taller than theirs. Inside is the Museo Universitario (5 pesos), telling the story of education in Puebla.

Templo de La Compañía This Jesuit church with a 1767 Churrigueresque façade, on the corner of Avenida Camacho and 4 Sur, is also called Espíritu Santo. Beneath the altar is a tomb said to be that of a 17th-century Asian princess who was sold into slavery in Mexico and later freed. She is supposed to have originated the colourful China Poblana costume of shawl, frilled blouse, embroidered skirt and gold and silver adornments – a kind of peasant chic fashionable in the 19th century. But *china* also meant maidservant and the style may have developed from Spanish peasant costumes. Next door, the 16th-century Edificio Carolino, formerly a Jesuit college, is now the main building of Puebla University.

Casa del Alfeñique This house, on the corner of 6 Norte and Avenida 4 Oriente, is an outstanding example of the 18th-century decorative style alfeñique. Inside is the Museo del Estado (entry 4 pesos) with 18th and 19th-century Puebla paraphernalia such as China Poblana gear, carriages and furniture.

Teatro Principal & Barrio del Artista The theatre on 6 Norte between Avenidas 6 and 8 Oriente dates from 1756, which makes it one of the oldest in the Americas – sort of. It went up in flames in 1902 but was rebuilt in the 1930s. You can look inside between 10 am and 5 pm when it's not in use. Nearby, the pedestrian-only Calle 8 Norte, between Avenidas 4 and 6 Oriente, is the Barrio del Artista, with open studios where you can see artists and buy their work.

Templo de San Francisco The north doorway of San Francisco, just east of Boulevard Héroes del 5 de Mayo on Avenida 14 Oriente, is a good example of 16th-century plateresque; the tower and fine brick-and-tile façade were added in the 18th century. In a glass case in the church's north chapel is the body of San Sebastián de Aparicio, a Spaniard who came to Mexico in 1533 and planned many of the country's roads before becoming a monk. His body is in a remarkable state of preservation and attracts a stream of worshippers. The chapel contains many paintings of his life, and his statue stands outside the church.

Things to See – North

Museo de la Revolución This house at Avenida 6 Oriente 206 was the scene of the first battle of the 1910 revolution. Betrayed only two days before a planned uprising against Porfirio Díaz's dictatorship, the Serdán family (Aquiles, Máximo, Carmen and Natalia) and 17 others fought 500 soldiers and police until only Aquiles, their leader, and Carmen were left alive. Aquiles, hidden under the floorboards, might have survived if the damp hadn't provoked a cough which gave him away. The house retains its bullet holes and other memorabilia, including a room dedicated to women of the revolution, including Carmen Serdán and 'Mariá Pistolas'. Entry is 4 pesos.

Templo de Santo Domingo Santo Domingo, 2½ blocks north of the zócalo on Avenida 5 de Mayo, is a fine church, but its Capilla del Rosario (Rosary Chapel), south

AROUND MEXICO CITY

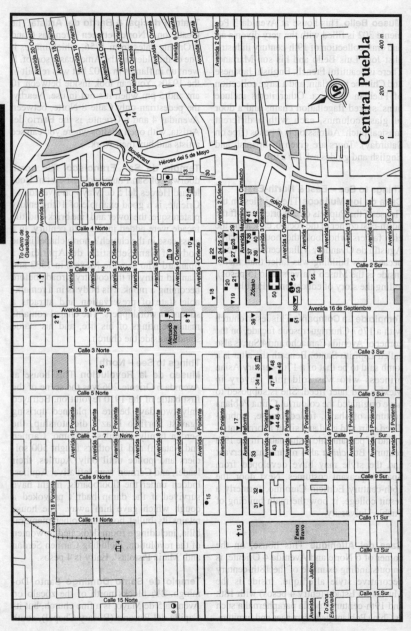

Central Puebla

PLACES TO STAY		
7	Hotel Embajadoras	
10	Hotel Imperial	
20	Hotel Palace	
21	Hotel & Restaurant/Bar Royalty	
22	Hotel Posada San Pedro	
25	Hotel Palacio San Leonardo	
32	Hotel Virrey de Mendoza	
34	Hotel Victoria	
37	Hotel Del Portal	
40	Hotel Colonial	
43	Hotel San Miguel	
45	Hotel San Agustín	
47	Hotel Teresita	
49	Hotel Avenida	
51	Hotel Santander	

PLACES TO EAT		
17	Teorema Bookshop/Café	
18	Sanborns	
19	Café Foto Aguirre	
23	VIPS	
24	Restaurant Concordia	

26	Restaurant Nevados Hermilo
29	Tacos Tito
31	Fonda Santa Clara, 3 Pte 920 Branch
36	Restaurant-Café El Vasco
38	Café El Carolo
39	Vittorio's
44	Mesón de los Frailes
46	El Vegetariano
48	Fonda Santa Clara, 3 Pte 307 Branch
55	Los Arbanos

OTHER	
1	Templo San José
2	Ex-Convento de Santa Monica
3	Mercado Cinco de Mayo
4	Museo del Ferrocarril
5	Ex-Convento de Santa Rosa & Museo de Artesanías

6	Colectivos to Cholula
8	Templo de Santo Domingo
9	Museo de la Revolución
11	Teatro Principal
12	Casa del Alfeñique
13	Barrio del Artista
14	Templo de San Francisco
15	Talavera Uriarte
16	Templo de Guadalupe
27	Casa de los Muñecos
28	Cervecería Vaquero
30	El Parián Craft Market
33	Palacio de Gobierno
35	Museo Bello
41	Templo de La Compañía
42	University
50	Catedral
52	Post Office & Centro de Servicios Integrados de Telecomunicaciones
53	Tourist Office
54	Casa de la Cultura
56	Museo Amparo

of the main altar, is a gem. Built between 1680 and 1720, it has a sumptuous baroque proliferation of gilded plaster and carved stone with angels and cherubim popping out from behind every leaf. See if you can spot the heavenly orchestra.

Ex-Convento de Santa Rosa & Museo de Artesanías
This 17th-century former nunnery houses an extensive collection of Puebla state handicrafts. You must do a tour with a guide, who may hustle you too quickly through the fine displays of Indian costumes, pottery, onyx, glass and metal work. Finally you reach the old convent kitchen where *mole poblano* (see Puebla Specialities in the Places to Eat section) is said to have been invented. Enter from Avenida 14 Poniente between Calles 3 and 5 Norte (4 pesos).

Ex-Convento de Santa Monica
Another nunnery-museum, Santa Monica has an exquisite tiled courtyard, a collection of religious art, and old nuns' cells where you can see instruments of self-flagellation if you're interested. It's at Avenida 18 Poniente 101 near the corner of Avenida 5 de Mayo (7 pesos).

Museo del Ferrocarril
A dozen vintage locomotives ranging from the majestic to the quaint repose with fresh coats of paint outside the city's old station, facing the junction of 11 Norte and Avenida 12 Poniente. You can reminisce about the age of steam and wonder whether trains were ever a really serious transport option in Mexico. Entry is free.

Cerro de Guadalupe
The hilltop park stretching a km east of 2 Norte, two km north-east of the zócalo, contains the historic forts of Loreto and Guadalupe and the Centro Civico 5 de Mayo, a group of museums and exhibitions. Good views, relatively fresh air and eucalyptus woods add to the appeal. Take a 'Loreto' bus

(1 peso) from the corner of Avenidas 5 de Mayo and 10 Poniente to get there.

The **Fuerte de Loreto** at the west end of the hilltop was one of the Mexican defence points on 5 May 1862, during the famous victory over the invading French. Today it houses the Museo de la Intervención, with displays of uniforms and documents relating to the French invasion and occupation of Mexico (7 pesos).

A short walk east of the fort, beyond the domed auditorium, are the **Museo Regional de Antropología** (10 pesos), tracing human history in the state, the **Museo de Historia Natural** (4 pesos) and the pyramid-shaped **Planetario de Puebla**. At the east end of the hilltop is the **Fuerte de Guadalupe** (10 pesos), which also played a part in the battle of 5 May 1862.

Africam Safari Park

One of the best places in Mexico to see African wildlife is 16 km south-east of Puebla, on the road to Presa Valsequillo. The animals are in 'natural' settings. Estrella Roja runs direct buses from CAPU, or ring the park for details (☎ 35-87-00).

Places to Stay

Basic bottom-end places cost around 40/50 pesos for singles/doubles, and that can be pretty rudimentary in Puebla. Always ask if, and when, hot water is available. For colonial ambience you need to move into the middle range and pay at least 120/140 pesos. The better-value places are often full. Most hotels have a large, red 'H' sign outside.

Places to Stay – bottom end

Some of Puebla's cheapest budget hotels bear a strong resemblance to prisons. A good example is the *Hotel Santander*, on Avenida 5 Poniente just west of the cathedral, where the cheapest cells cost 30 pesos and have clanging steel doors, no windows and shared bathrooms with uncertain hot water. The more expensive rooms are better, and the location's good.

Another lower bottom-end place is the *Hotel Avenida* (☎ (22) 32-21-04) at Avenida

5 Poniente 141, two blocks west of the centre. It's an old building with rooms facing a courtyard or the (noisy) street, some with shared bathroom for 20 pesos, others with private facilities for 30 pesos. With one double bed the price is the same for one or two people. Staff are friendly and it's about as clean as a hotel can be with flaking plaster and missing tiles.

The little *Hotel Teresita* (☎ (22) 32-70-72) at Avenida 3 Poniente 309, 1½ blocks west of the zócalo, has small, windowless rooms with little escape from other guests' noise, but it's clean, friendly and often full. Singles/doubles with one bed are 40/50 pesos with private bath, but hot water is limited. The *Hotel Victoria* (☎ (22) 32-89-92), across the street at 3 Poniente 306, is gloomy and faded, but friendly enough and just about clean. Singles/doubles with private bath are 45/50 pesos, or 60 pesos with two beds. A block west at Avenida 3 Poniente 531, the *Hotel San Agustín* has an imposing lobby but more modest singles/doubles, small and a bit dark, from 50/70 pesos, or 80/100 pesos with TV. They all have bathrooms and there's a car park nearby.

North of the centre, rooms at the *Hotel Embajadoras* (☎ (22) 32-26-37), on 5 de Mayo between 6 and 8 Oriente, are 20/35 pesos for a single/double with shared bath, 40/50 pesos with private shower. They're on three floors around a big, covered courtyard, and are quite big and reasonably clean, but dark, bare and very worn.

Places to Stay – middle

The cheaper mid-range hotels are acceptable, but nothing special – these three all cost 80/100 pesos for singles/doubles with one bed, or 120 pesos for a room with two beds. The *Hotel Imperial* (☎ (22) 42-49-80) at Avenida 4 Oriente 212 is the most central and the staff are friendly. Rooms are clean, with TV and phone – upstairs rooms are bigger and airier than those below, with tiles to brighten the bare walls. West of the zócalo, *Hotel Virrey de Mendoza* (☎ (22) 42-39-03) at Avenida 3 Poniente 912 has large, clean, wood-beamed rooms along two wide balconies above a courtyard car park (not too disturbing). It's a bit run down, but not bad for this price range. The *Hotel San Miguel* (☎ (22) 42-48-60), nearby at Avenida 3 Poniente 721, has clean, respectably sized rooms with private bath but not much character.

Some of the more expensive mid-range places have a lot of charm, and may be better value if you can afford it. *Hotel Colonial* (☎ (22) 46-47-09) at 4 Sur 105 on the corner of 3 Oriente, a block east of the zócalo, has singles/doubles from 110/145 pesos. Once part of an old Jesuit monastery, it maintains a colonial atmosphere despite being comfortably modernised. Most of the 70 rooms are spacious and tiled, with TVs. Upstairs exterior rooms are among the brightest and best. The hotel has an old glass-domed dining room with a carved stone fountain and several attractive sitting areas. Call between 9 am and 1 pm for a room reservation – it's often full.

The 54-room *Hotel Royalty* (☎ (22) 42-47-40) is another friendly, well-kept colonial-style place, located right on the zócalo at Portal Hidalgo 8. Rooms are comfortable, with carpet and TV, though mostly only moderately sized. Older singles/doubles are 121/160 pesos; newer ones are 150/180 pesos. Prices include breakfast but parking costs extra. The *Hotel Palace* (☎ (22) 32-24-30), at Avenida 2 Oriente 13, is another comfortable, centrally located mid-range place charging 120/150 pesos for singles/doubles, or 170 pesos for rooms with two beds.

The outwardly colonial *Hotel Del Portal* (☎ (22) 46-02-11), at Avenida Camacho 205 on the north-east corner of the zócalo, has been modernised inside. The rooms are comfortable, if small, and cost 193 pesos for singles or doubles including breakfast and parking.

Places to Stay – top end

The *Hotel Posada San Pedro* (☎ (22) 46-50-77), in a colonial building at Avenida 2 Oriente 202, has a small pool and two restaurants but the rooms, while pleasant, are none too big and some could be noisy. They cost 176/220

pesos a single/double. The central *Hotel Palacio San Leonardo* (☎ (22) 46-05-55), at Avenida 2 Oriente 211, has an elegant lobby with a coloured glass ceiling, and spacious modern singles/doubles for 205/235 pesos.

The 52-room *Hotel Lastra* (☎ (22) 35-97-55) at Calzada de los Fuertes 2633, two km north-east of the zócalo on the Cerro de Guadalupe, is worth considering for its peaceful location, good views, easy parking and pleasant garden. Rooms (193/242/290 pesos for singles/doubles/triples) are comfortable, sizeable and come in assorted shapes. It's a longish but pleasant walk to the city centre.

There are three top hotels outside the city centre charging around 360 pesos for a room. They're all suitably luxurious, but you miss out on the charm of central Puebla. The best is generally reckoned to be the 190-room *Hotel El Mesón del Ángel* (☎ (22) 24-30-00, toll-free 800-22333) at Avenida Hermanos Serdán 807, six km north-west of the centre, just off the Mexico City autopista. There are two pools, tennis courts, several restaurants, bars etc. The others are the 400-room *Gran Hotel de Alba* (☎ (22) 48-60-55), three km nearer the centre at Avenida Hermanos Serdán 141, and the *Hotel Misión Park Plaza* (☎ (22) 48-96-00) at Avenida 5 Poniente 2522, between 25 and 27 Sur in the Zona Esmeralda.

Places to Eat

Specialities An excellent place to sample Poblano food is the *Fonda Santa Clara* which has two branches on Avenida 3 Poniente. Both have the same menu. The one at No 307 (☎ 42-26-59), which closes on Monday, is nearer to the city centre and usually busier, but the cooking at No 920 (☎ 46-19-19), which closes on Tuesday, is equally good. The Santa Clara's delicious mole poblano comes with chicken for 24 pesos or on enchiladas for 22 pesos. Also enjoyable are mixiotes – seasoned lamb steamed in cactus leaves, with guacamole – at 28 pesos for two.

The little *Mesón de los Frailes*, in the Hotel San Agustín at Avenida 3 Poniente

531, serves up cheaper but still tasty Poblano fare. The *Restaurant Nevados Hermilo* (☎ 32-55-46), on the corner of Avenida 2 Oriente and 4 Norte, is another favourite for its tortas (5 pesos), enchiladas in mole poblano (18 pesos) and the tasty little cocktails called nevados. Breakfast is good too – huevos a la Mexicana for 7 pesos and good fruit cocktails for 5 pesos.

Cheap Eats & Snacks A pan árabe taco (see box) costs around 3 pesos – try one at *Tacos Tito*, which has a few branches in the blocks around the zócalo, or *Los Arbanos* on Avenida 7 Oriente.

Vegetarian *El Vegetariano* at Avenida 3 Poniente 525, open from 7.30 am to 10 pm, has a long menu of meatless dishes like chiles rellenos, nopales rellenos (stuffed cactus ears), crepas or enchiladas Suizas, all of which come with salad, soup and a drink for around 14 pesos, or on their own for about 10 pesos.

Zócalo & Nearby The zócalo culinary highlight is *Vittorio's* (☎ 32-79-00), on the east side at Portal Morelos 106. This Italian-run restaurant bills itself 'La Casa de la Pizza Increíble' in memory of a 20-sq-metre monster pizza it baked as a stunt back in 1981. The pizzas are still good, but not cheap

at 20 to 32 pesos for a chico (one-person) size, up to 44 to 80 pesos for a grande (three or four-person). You can eat in or take away. Spaghetti bolognese is 16 pesos and fresh salads around 10 pesos.

Other places around the zócalo have lots of atmosphere, but they tend to be expensive. The *Restaurant-Café El Vasco* is in Portal Juárez on the west side. It's the kind of place where couples and old friends meet for a chat, with a varied menu of good food. Delicious smells may entice you in. On the north side, the smart *Restaurant-Bar Royalty* (☎ 42-47-40) has outdoor tables where you can watch the world go by, but the view doesn't come cheap – even a café con leche will cost you 6 pesos.

Places off the zócalo are more reasonably priced, like the *Café Foto Aguirre* on Avenida 5 de Mayo. It's a busy but clean and orderly place, popular with locals. Set breakfasts, with juice, coffee and eggs, cost around 12 pesos, and the comidas corridas run from 12 to 18 pesos. There's a *Sanborns* at Avenida 2 Oriente No 6 and a *VIPs* café and bookshop in a beautifully restored 19th-century cast-iron building on the corner of Avenida 2 Oriente and 2 Norte. Just east of VIPS on Avenida 2 Oriente are some good, cheap local places like the popular *Restaurant Concordia*, with a range of four-course comidas corridas for around 15 pesos. *Café El Carolo*, on Avenida Camacho half a block

---

Puebla Specialities

Mole poblano, found on almost every menu in Puebla and imitated Mexico-wide, is a spicy chocolate sauce usually served over turkey (pavo or guajolote) or chicken – a real taste sensation . if well prepared. Supposedly invented by Sor (Sister) Andrea de la Asunción of Santa Rosa Convent for a visit by the viceroy, it traditionally contains fresh chile, chipotle (smoked chile), pepper, peanuts, almonds, cinnamon, aniseed, tomato, onion, garlic and, of course, chocolate.

A seasonal Puebla dish, available in July, August and September, is *chiles en nogada*, said to have been created in 1821 to honour Agustín de Iturbide, the first ruler of independent Mexico. Its colours are those of the national flag: large green chiles stuffed with meat and fruit are covered with a creamy white walnut sauce and sprinkled with red pomegranate seeds.

In April and May you can try *gusanos de maguey* and in March *escamoles* – respectively maguey worms and their eggs, prepared with avocados or hen eggs.

A *pan árabe* taco is Puebla's improvement on the taco – it's bigger, because it's made using pita bread. Another substantial Poblano snack is the *cemita*, a lightly toasted bread roll with cheese, chile, chicken, ham, onion, lettuce...sort of a super torta. *Camotes* are a local sticky sweet – sticks of fruit-flavoured jelly. ■

east of the zócalo, serves up fruit salad, yoghurt and other healthy stuff, and a budget comida corrida for only 8 pesos.

Zona Esmeralda The upscale stretch of Avenida Juárez has lots of swish international-style restaurants – including German, Italian and Chinese. For a splash-out meal in semi-Westernised surroundings (enjoyed by many Mexicans), go to *Charlie's China Poblana* (☎ 46-31-59) at Juárez 1918. Now part of the Carlos Anderson chain, this venerable establishment serves meals from 1 pm to midnight, and the bar keeps going much later. Salads cost 15 pesos and main courses around 30 pesos – a full meal with wine could easily run to 100 pesos.

Entertainment

Teorema, on the corner of Avenida Reforma and 7 Norte, is a bookshop-cum-café which fills up in the evenings with an arty/studenty crowd attracted by live music from about 8.30 pm to 1 am nightly. There's a good atmosphere, excellent coffee (5 pesos), cakes (8 pesos), beer (6 pesos) and stronger drinks by the glass or bottle.

The serious nightlife is at Cholula, a few km west (see separate section), and as a consequence the Puebla-Cholula road is an accident blackspot! The bar at *Charlie's China Poblana* restaurant at Juárez 1918 in the Zona Esmeralda has a reputation as a pick-up spot. At night mariachis lurk around the Callejón del Sapo, a pedestrian street between Avenidas 5 and 7 Oriente, just east of 4 Sur.

For cultural events check the noticeboards in the tourist office and Casa de la Cultura on Avenida 5 Oriente and the university building on 4 Sur.

Things to Buy

Quite a few shops along Avenida 18 Poniente, west of the Ex-Convento de Santa Monica, display and sell the pretty Puebla ceramics. The big pieces are very expensive and difficult for a traveller to carry, but you could buy a small hand-painted Talavera tile for 12 to 18 pesos, or a 15-cm plate for

around 45 pesos. Few of these places manufacture pottery on site, but one that still does is Talavera Uriarte (☎ 32-15-98), with a factory and showroom at Avenida 4 Poniente 911. The showroom is open every day, but you can only see the factory at work on weekdays till 3 pm. It's well worth a visit.

The city is also a good place to look for crafts from elsewhere in the state, like Indian textiles, Tecali onyx and pottery from Acatlán de Osorio, Amozoc or Izúcar de Matamoros. There's a government shop selling good examples of the state's crafts next to the tourist office at Avenida 5 Oriente 3. It's open weekdays till 8 pm and, theoretically, on weekends as well.

El Parián craft market, between 6 and 8 Norte and Avenidas 2 and 4 Oriente, has, besides the sorts of leather, jewellery and textiles that you find in other cities, local Talavera, onyx and trees of life. Much of the work is crappy souvenirs, but there is some good stuff and prices are generally reasonable. There are lots of antique shops on and near Callejón del Sapo, between Avenidas 5 and 7 Oriente just east of 4 Sur, with a wonderful variety of old books, furniture, bric-a-brac and junk. It's great for browsing – most of them close for a long lunch break.

The three smart shopping areas are the streets just north of the zócalo, the Zona Esmeralda, and the Plaza Dorada beside Boulevard Héroes del 5 de Mayo.

Getting There & Away

Air The only scheduled flights into Aeropuerto Hermanos Serdán, 22 km west of Puebla on the Cholula-Huejotzingo road, are to/from Guadalajara and Tijuana by Aero-California (☎ 30-48-55). Mexicana (☎ 48-56-00) has an office at 23 Sur 506 on the corner of Avenida Juárez; Aeroméxico (☎ 32-00-13/14) is at Avenida Juárez 1514A.

Bus Puebla's big modern bus station, the Central de Autobuses de Puebla (CAPO), is four km north of the zócalo and 1.5 km off the autopista, by the corner of Boulevards Norte and Carmen Serdán. It has a left-luggage facility, phone office, Banca Serfin branch (with ATM), restaurant and various shops.

Buses to/from Puebla use Mexico City's Terminal Oriente (TAPO). The 130-km trip takes around two hours. Three bus lines have very frequent services: ADO (☎ 49-71-44) has some deluxe services (25 pesos) and a 1st-class directo service (21 pesos) goes every 10 or 20 minutes from 6 am to 10 pm; AU's 2nd-class directo service goes every five to 15 minutes from 6 am to 10 pm; and Estrella Roja has continuous 2nd-class ordinario buses (16.50 pesos) 24 hours a day. After 7 pm, there can be long queues for the Estrella Roja continuous service. Estrella Roja also runs direct buses to Mexico City airport every one or two hours from 4 am to 8 pm, for 33 pesos.

There are bus services from Puebla to just about everywhere in the south and east of Mexico, including:

Acapulco – 510 km, seven hours; one deluxe bus (100 pesos) and six 1st-class buses (88 pesos) daily by Autobuses Oro

Córdoba – 170 km, three hours; 10 1st-class buses (28 pesos) daily by ADO, 30 2nd-class buses (23 pesos) by AU

Cuernavaca – 180 km, three hours; two deluxe buses (25 pesos) and 28 1st-class buses (20 pesos) daily by Autobuses Oro; regular 2nd-class buses by Estrella Blanca

Mérida – 1390 km, 22 hours; one 1st-class bus (186 pesos) daily by ADO

Oaxaca – 450 km, eight hours; one deluxe bus (58 pesos) and five 1st-class locales (48 pesos) daily by ADO; two 1st-class buses by Cristóbal Colón; 2nd-class directos (43 pesos) by AU

Tampico – 730 km, 14 hours; three 1st-class buses (68 pesos) daily by ADO

Tuxtla Gutiérrez – 1070 km, 17 hours; one 1st-class bus daily (129 pesos) each by ADO and Cristóbal Colón

Veracruz – 300 km, five hours; eight 1st-class buses (41 pesos) daily by ADO; 15 2nd-class buses by AU (36 pesos)

Villahermosa – 690 km, 12 hours; one deluxe evening bus (110 pesos) by UNO; three 1st-class buses (99 pesos) daily by ADO

Xalapa – 185 km, 3½ hours; two deluxe morning buses (28 pesos) by UNO; eight 1st-class buses (28 pesos) daily by ADO; 13 2nd-class buses (20 pesos) daily by AU

Train Trains to/from Mexico City are ridiculously slow (between five and 12 hours) but the train ride to Oaxaca is scenic and popular. The best train is the daily El Oaxaqueño from Mexico City to Oaxaca, which is scheduled to leave Puebla at 11.50 pm and reach Oaxaca at 9.25 am, but is usually an hour or so late out of Puebla and two or three hours late reaching Oaxaca. It therefore passes through the dramatic Sierra Madre de Oaxaca in daylight. Puebla-Oaxaca fares are 55 pesos for primera especial, 27 pesos for primera regular. Primera especial tickets are sold at the station from noon to 2 pm Monday to Friday and 11 am to noon on Saturday, though some trains apparently run with no primera especial seats. Primera regular tickets are sold during the hour before the scheduled departure. Camarines and alcobas are not available. The Oaxaqueño's reverse trip from Oaxaca to Puebla is nearly all in darkness.

Other trains to Oaxaca are a segunda clase only (16 pesos) at 7.20 am daily, and a mixed primera regular and segunda clase at noon daily. Seats are sold only in the hour before scheduled departure.

Puebla station is in the north of the city, about 200 metres north of the corner of 9 Norte and Avenida 80 Poniente. Ruta 1 'Estación Nueva' colectivos take 20 minutes from 9 Sur on the corner of Avenida 5 Poniente in the city centre. They run until about 9 pm. In the reverse direction, board the colectivo about 200 metres straight ahead from the station entrance and get off at Paseo Bravo. A taxi between the station and zócalo will cost about 11 pesos.

Car Puebla is 130 km from Mexico City by a fast autopista, highway 190D (tolls total about 30 pesos). East of Puebla, the toll highway continues as 150D to just east of Córdoba (about 175 km), negotiating a cloudy, winding 22-km descent from the 2385-metre Cumbres de Maltrata en route.

Getting Around

Most hotels and places of interest are within walking distance of the zócalo. From the bus

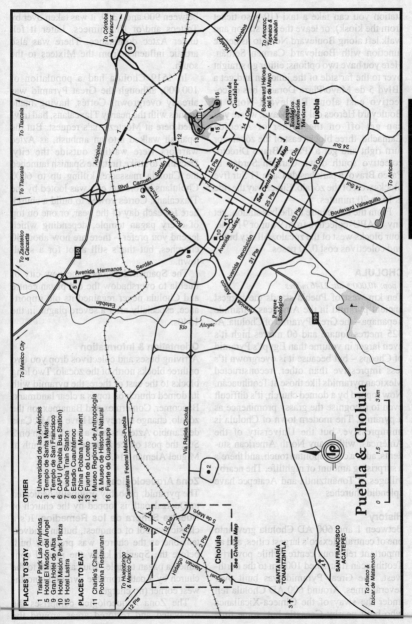

Puebla & Cholula

0   1.5   3 km

PLACES TO STAY

1 Trailer Park Las Américas
5 Hotel El Mesón del Angel
9 Gran Hotel de Alba
10 Hotel Misión Park Plaza
15 Hotel Lastra

PLACES TO EAT

11 Charlie's China
Poblana Restaurant

OTHER

2 Universidad de las Américas
3 Templo de Santa María
6 Templo de San Francisco
7 CPU (Puebla Bus Station)
8 Puebla Train Station
12 China Poblana Monument
13 Fuerte de Loreto
14 Museo Regional de Antropología
   & Museo de Historia Natural
16 Fuerte de Guadalupe

station you can take a taxi (10-peso ticket from the kiosk), or leave the bus station and walk left along Boulevard Norte to its hectic junction with Boulevard Carmen Serdán. Here you have two options: either go straight over to the far side of the junction and get a 'Blvd 5 de Mayo/Plaza Dorada' bus or colectivo east along Boulevard Norte to Boulevard Héroes del 5 de Mayo, where you can get off on the corner of Avenida Camacho, three blocks east of the zócalo; or turn right and get a 'Paseo Bravo Directo' colectivo south down Carmen Serdán to Paseo Bravo, a park beside Calle 11 Sur five blocks west of the zócalo. Either way the ride is 15 to 20 minutes.

From the city centre to the bus station, get any 'CAPU' colectivo from 9 Sur or 9 Norte, four blocks west of the zócalo. All city buses and colectivos cost 0.70 pesos.

CHOLULA
• *pop: 40,000* • *alt: 2146 metres*
Ten km west of Puebla stands the biggest ancient pyramid in the Americas, Pirámide Tepanapa – the Great Pyramid of Cholula. At 425 metres square and 60 metres high it's even larger in volume than Egypt's Pyramid of Cheops – but because it is overgrown it's less impressive than other, reconstructed Mexican pyramids like those at Teotihuacán. Now topped by a domed church, it's difficult even to recognise the grassy prominence as a pyramid. The modern town of Cholula is unimpressive, but the University of the Americas, with many North American students, adds a cosmopolitan touch, and there's a surprising amount of nightlife. The nearby villages of Tonantzintla and Acatepec have splendid churches.

History
Between 1 and 600 AD Cholula grew into one of central Mexico's largest cities, and an important religious centre, while powerful Teotihuacán flourished 100 km to the northwest. The Great Pyramid was built over several times. Around 600 AD Cholula fell under the sway of the Olmeca-Xicallanca who built nearby Cacaxtla but, some time

between 900 and 1300, it was taken over by Toltecs and/or Chichimecs. Later it fell under Aztec dominance. There was also artistic influence from the Mixtecs to the south.

In 1519 Cholula had a population of 100,000, although the Great Pyramid was already overgrown. Cortés, having made friends with the nearby Tlaxcalans, had travelled here at Moctezuma's request. But the Spanish walked into an ambush, as Aztec warriors were waiting outside the city. Deciding to strike first, the Spanish launched the Cholula massacre, killing up to 6000 Cholulans before the city was looted by the Tlaxcalans. Cortés vowed to build a church here for each day of the year, or one on top of every pagan temple, depending which legend you prefer – there are now about 40 churches, but that's still a lot for a small town.

The Spanish developed the new city of Puebla to overshadow the old pagan centre and Cholula never regained its old importance, especially after a severe plague in the 1540s.

Orientation & Information
Arriving buses and colectivos drop you two or three blocks north of the zócalo. Two long blocks to the east of there, the pyramid with its domed church on top is a clear landmark. Bancomer, Comermex and Banamex, on the zócalo, change money and have ATMs. Casa de Cambio Azteca is half a block south on 2 Sur; the post office is three blocks south at Miguel Alemán 314.

Zona Arqueológica
The pyramid, probably originally dedicated to Quetzalcóatl, is topped by the church of **Nuestra Señora de los Remedios**. It's a classic symbol of conquest, but an inadvertent one as the church was probably built before the Spanish knew the mound contained a pagan temple. You can climb to the church by a path from the pyramid's northwest corner (no charge).

The Zona Arqueológica comprises the excavated and restored areas around the

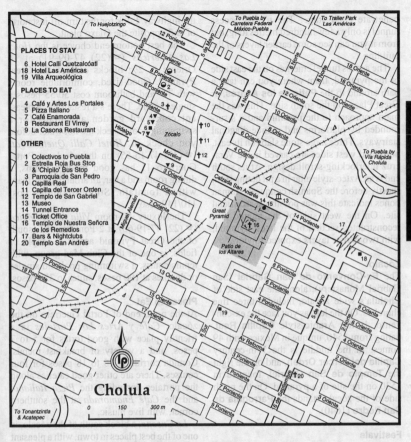

PLACES TO STAY

6 Hotel Calli Quetzalcóatl
18 Hotel Las Américas
19 Villa Arqueológica

PLACES TO EAT

4 Café y Artes Los Portales
5 Pizza Italiano
7 Café Enamorada
8 Restaurant El Virrey
9 La Casona Restaurant

OTHER

1 Colectivos to Puebla
2 Estrella Roja Bus Stop
   & 'Chipilo' Bus Stop
3 Parroquia de San Pedro
10 Capilla Real
11 Capilla del Tercer Orden
12 Templo de San Gabriel
13 Museo
14 Tunnel Entrance
15 Ticket Office
16 Templo de Nuestra Señora
   de los Remedios
17 Bars & Nightclubs
20 Templo San Andrés

Cholula

0   150   300 m

To Tonantzintla
& Acatepec

Great Pyramid, and the tunnels underneath it. The entry to the zona is via the tunnel on the north side, open from 10 am to 5 pm daily. Pay your 14 pesos at the ticket office (free on Sunday and holidays), plus 25 pesos if you have a video camera.

Guides at the tunnel entrance will suggest you take a guided tour (25/30 pesos in Spanish/English for a one-hour tour; longer tours for 60/70 pesos and 70/80 pesos). You won't need a guide to follow the tunnel through to the structures on the south and west sides of the pyramid, but they can be useful in pointing out and explaining various features in and around the site – nothing is labelled.

The small **museum**, across the road from the ticket office and down some steps, has the best introduction to the site – a large cutaway model of the pyramid mound showing the various superimposed structures. Museum admission is included with your site ticket. The nearby bookshop may have a useful small guide booklet.

Several pyramids were built over the top of each other in various reconstructions. Over eight km of **tunnels** have been dug beneath the pyramid by archaeologists, to penetrate each stage. The tourist access tunnel is only a few hundred metres long, but from it you can see some earlier layers of the building.

The access tunnel emerges on the east side of the pyramid, from where you can take a path around to the **Patio de los Altares**, or Great Plaza, on the south side. This was the main approach to the pyramid and it's surrounded by platforms and unique diagonal stairways. Three large stone slabs on its east, north and west sides are carved in the Veracruz interlocking-scroll design. At its south end is an Aztec-style altar in a pit dating from shortly before the Spanish conquest. Human bones indicate this was possibly a sacrificial site. On the west side of the mound is a reconstructed section of the latest pyramid, with two earlier layers exposed to view.

Zócalo

The **Ex-Convento de San Gabriel** (San Gabriel Monastery), along the east side of Cholula's wide zócalo, includes three fine churches. On the left, as you face the ex-convento, is the Arabic-style **Capilla Real**, dating from 1540, unique in Mexico with 49 domes. In the middle is the 17th-century **Capilla del Tercer Orden**, and on the right the **Templo de San Gabriel**, founded in 1530 on the site of a pyramid. On the north side of the zócalo stands the **Parroquia de San Pedro** (1640).

Festivals

Cholula's firework-makers are renowned for their spectacular shows. Of the many festivals, one of the most important is the Festival de la Virgen de los Remedios and regional feria in the first week of September, with daily traditional dances on the Great Pyramid.

Places to Stay

Cholula is a very easy day trip from Puebla but there are options if you fancy staying. The well-kept *Trailer Park Las Américas* (☎ (22) 47-01-34) charges 20 pesos for a tent site and has hook-ups for trailers. It's 200 metres north of Cholula on the east side of

the highway. Look for the turn-off just north of and opposite the Glaxo plant.

The best bottom-end choice is the *Hotel Las Américas* (☎ (22) 47-09-91) at 14 Oriente 6, 2½ blocks east of the Great Pyramid. Good-sized, comfortable rooms with TV and bathroom cost 50/55 pesos a single/double. There's a restaurant, a pleasant courtyard garden and plans for a swimming pool. Check the hot water before you check in. *Hotel Calli Quetzalcóatl* (☎ (22) 47-15-55) on the zócalo at Portal Guerrero 11 has good modern rooms, a dining room and a bar, all around a courtyard with a fountain. Singles/doubles cost 110/140 pesos.

The luxury, 50-room *Villa Arqueológica* (☎ (22) 47-19-66) at 2 Poniente 601, south of the Great Pyramid across a couple of fields, is one of the Club Med group, with tennis courts, a swimming pool and singles or doubles at 190 pesos, suites to 350 pesos.

Places to Eat

At the north end of Portal Guerrero on the zócalo, *Café y Artes Los Portales* is a friendly place with good tortas for 5 to 7 pesos, and a variety of breakfast menus. Comida corrida is 15 to 18 pesos for four courses. There are other good eateries along the portales, including the *Pizza Italiano*, and the *Café Enamorada* at the southern corner, with live music.

La Casona, a block south of the zócalo, is one of the best places in town, with a pleasant courtyard and a variety of local specialities. Main courses are around 30 pesos, soups and starters from 7 to 15 pesos.

Entertainment

The nightclubs are in the dusty streets around the corner of 14 Poniente and 5 de Mayo. They look like nothing during the day, but after about 10 pm from Thursday to Saturday, there are bright lights and loud music at *Faces, Blue Jeans, Paradise* and *San Marcos* among others. The cover price in the better establishments is about 20 pesos. Women may feel uncomfortable walking around this area alone at night.

Getting There & Away

Frequent local buses to Cholula leave from the corner of Avenida 6 Poniente and 15 Norte in Puebla. They cost 1.50 pesos and take about 20 minutes.

Estrella Roja has frequent buses between Mexico City's Terminal Oriente (TAPO) and Puebla which stop in Cholula on the corner of 3 Norte and 6 Poniente (15 pesos).

AROUND CHOLULA
Tonantzintla & Acatepec

The interior of the small **Templo de Santa María** in Tonantzintla is among the most exuberant in Mexico. Under the dome, every available surface is covered with colourful stucco saints, devils, flowers, fruit, birds and more – a great example of Indian artisanship applied to Christian themes. Tonantzintla holds a procession and traditional dances for the Festival of the Assumption on 15 August.

The **Templo de San Francisco** in Acatepec, 1.5 km south-east of Tonantzintla, dates from about 1730. The brilliant exterior is beautifully decorated with blue, green and yellow Puebla tiles set in red brick on an ornate Churrigueresque façade.

Both of these small churches are open to visitors from 10 am to 1 pm and 3 to 5 pm daily.

Getting There & Away

Autobuses Puebla-Cholula runs 'Chipilo' buses from Puebla bus station to Tonantzintla and Acatepec. In Cholula you can pick them up on the corner of 6 Poniente and 3 Norte. Between the two villages you can wait for the next bus or walk.

Huejotzingo

Huejotzingo ('weh-hot-ZIN-goh'), 14 km north-west of Cholula on highway 150, is a town of 25,000 known for its cider and sarapes. The fine 16th-century platoresque-style monastery has been restored as a museum, with exhibits on the Spanish missions and monastic life (open from 10 am to 5 pm Tuesday to Sunday; 7 pesos, free Sunday). The fortified church is stark but imposing, with Gothic ribbing on its ceiling. There are some old frescos and excellent carved stonework. On Shrove Tuesday, a masked Carnaval dance in Huejotzingo re-enacts a battle between French and Mexicans. Estrella Roja buses serve Huejotzingo to/from Puebla, Cholula and Mexico City.

SIERRA NORTE DE PUEBLA

The Sierra Norte de Puebla covers much of the remote northern arm of Puebla state. The mountains rise to over 2500 metres before falling away to the gulf coastal plain. Even though some of the land is deforested, it's fertile and beautiful with pine forests at higher altitudes and luxuriant semitropical vegetation lower down. The main town is Teziutlán, but Cuetzalán is the most attractive initial destination. Sierra Norte handicrafts – among them rebozos, quechquémitls, wood-carving and baskets – are sold in markets at Cuetzalán, Zacapoaxtla, Teziutlán, Tlatlauquitepec and elsewhere, as well as in Puebla and Mexico City.

The area has a high Indian population, mostly Nahua and Totonac. The ancestors of these Nahua are thought to have reached the Sierra Norte in the 14th century, probably from the Valley of Mexico and southern and central Puebla. For more on the Nahua see the box at the beginning of the East of Mexico City section; for the Totonacs see the Central Gulf Coast chapter, which also covers some places in the low-lying far north of Puebla state.

Cuetzalán

The colonial town of Cuetzalán, 1200 metres high in a lush coffee-growing area and dominated by its large church, is famed for its Sunday market. Indian handicrafts include embroidered blouses and quechquémitls.

Festivals For several days around 4 October Cuetzalán holds lively celebrations of the festival of San Francisco de Assisi, combined with the Feria del Café y del Huipil. A traditional dance festival in mid-July attracts groups from all over the area.

Places to Stay There are a few places to stay, all pretty basic. Try the *Posada Las Garzas* or the *Posada Jackelin*, both on the zócalo, or the *Posada Cuetzalán* (☎ (233) 1-01-54) at Zaragoza 8. On weekends, find a room early or book ahead.

Getting There & Away Cuetzalán is where the paved roads end, some 50 km north of highway 129. From Puebla, there's a 1st-class ADO bus at 4 pm (four hours; 25 pesos) and several 2nd-class buses. Autotransportes México-Texcoco has five buses daily from Mexico City's Terminal Oriente (TAPO).

Yohualichán

Eight km from Cuetzalán by a poor dirt road, this pre-Hispanic site has niche pyramids similar to those at El Tajín, though smaller. The site is adjacent to the Yohualichán town plaza, and is open from Wednesday to Sunday.

PICO DE ORIZABA

Mexico's highest mountain, the 5746-metre Pico de Orizaba (also called Volcán Citlaltépetl), is 25 km north-west of the town of Orizaba. From that town at least one company does tours to the mountain (see the Central Gulf Coast chapter). For climbers the main approach is from the village of Tlachichuca (2700 metres), 30 km east of the Puebla-Xalapa road, where there's some basic accommodation. The dormant volcano has a small crater, a permanent snow-cap and a seasonal pattern similar to Popocatépetl. The only higher peaks in North America are Mt McKinley in Alaska and Mt Logan in Canada.

The most common route to the top is a crevasse-ridden glacier, and crampons are required. From Tlachichuca a rough dirt road, requiring 4WD, leads 23 km east to two huts at Piedra Grande (4230 metres) on the north flank of the mountain, from where the ascent is six to nine hours. In Tlachichuca, Señor José Amador Reyes (☎ (245) 1-50-09/19) can arrange lodging and transport to Piedra Grande. His representative in Mexico City is Señor Francisco Reyes Rodríguez (☎ (5) 595-12-03). The organisations listed in the Activities section of the Facts for the Visitor chapter may be able to help arrange a climb.

SOUTHERN PUEBLA

Two main routes go through the south-east of the state of Puebla towards Oaxaca.

Highway 150

Heading east from Puebla, this road starts parallel to the Orizaba autopista, but it's a lot slower and more congested. Second-class buses stop at the towns en route. **Amozoc**, 16 km from Puebla, produces pottery and many of the fancy metal and silver decorations worn by charros. **Tepeaca** (population 16,000), 40 km from Puebla, has a big Friday market, mainly for everyday goods rather than handicrafts, and a 16th-century Franciscan monastery. The village of **Tecali**, 11 km south-west of Tepeaca, is a centre for the carving of onyx from the nearby quarries.

Tehuacán

Modern Tehuacán (population 139,500), 115 km south-east of Puebla, is a pretty town with a fine zócalo. It's famed for its mineral water, sold in bottles all over Mexico – nearby spas include Peñafiel and San Lorenzo. The high, dry Tehuacán valley was the site of some of the earliest agriculture in Mexico. By 7000 to 5000 BC people were planting avocados, chiles, cotton and squashes, and around 5000 BC they were cultivating the first tiny forms of maize. Pottery, the sign of a truly settled existence, appeared about 2000 BC. The **Museo del Valle de Tehuacán**, three blocks north-west of the zócalo, explains some of the archaeological discoveries and exhibits tiny preserved cobs of maize which were among the first to be cultivated.

Places to Stay Cheap lodgings include the *Hotel Madrid* (☎ (238) 2-02-72) at 3 Sur 105, with singles/doubles around 35/45 pesos, and the *Hotel Posada de Tehuacán* (☎ (238) 2-04-91) at Reforma Norte 213. The *Hotel Iberia* (☎ (238) 2-11-22), just east of the zócalo, is old but cared-for, and slightly more expensive. The nicest place is the *Hotel México* (☎ (238) 2-00-19), at Independencia Poniente 101 a block west of the zócalo; it's a restored colonial building with comfortable singles/doubles for around 220/260 pesos.

Getting There & Away ADO, at Independencia 119, has frequent 1st-class buses to/from Puebla (16 pesos), and several per day to/from Mexico City and Veracruz. AU runs frequent 2nd-class services. Buses to/from Oaxaca go via Huajuapan de León (longer but smoother) or Teotitlán del Camino (slightly quicker but rougher). Frequent buses to Orizaba (25 pesos) cross the dramatic Cumbres de Acultzingo, where the road zigzags 800 metres down an often cloudy mountainside in just four km.

Highway 190
This road swings west from Puebla then goes south-west to reach **Atlixco** (population 50,000), 31 km away. It is known for its therapeutic mineral springs, avocados and near-perfect climate. The Atlixcáyotl festival, held during the last weekend in September, has traditional costumes, dances and music. Another 36 km brings you to **Izúcar de Matamoros**, which also has therapeutic balnearios but is best known for ceramic handicrafts. **Acatlán de Osorio** is also a centre for imaginative handmade pottery.

South of Mexico City

Coming south from Mexico City, highway 95 and highway 95D (the toll road) climb to more than 3000 metres from the Valley of Mexico into refreshing pine forests, then descend to Cuernavaca, capital of Morelos state and long-time popular retreat from Mexico City. On the way, highway 115D branches south-east to Tepoztlán, nestled beneath high cliffs, and to balnearios at Oaxtepec and Cuautla. South of Cuernavaca, in the state of Guerrero, highway 95 detours to the unforgettable silver town of Taxco.

Morelos is one of Mexico's smallest and most densely populated states. Valleys at different elevations have a variety of microclimates, and many fruits, vegetables and grains have been cultivated since pre-Hispanic times. Archaeological sites at Cuernavaca, Tepoztlán and Xochicalco show signs of both the agricultural Tlahuica civilisation, and the Aztecs who subjugated them. In the colonial era, most of the state was controlled by a few wealthy families, including descendants of Cortés. Their palaces and haciendas can still be seen, along with churches and monasteries from as early as the 16th century. Unsurprisingly, the campesinos of Morelos became fervent supporters of the Mexican Revolution, and Emiliano Zapata is the state's revolutionary hero.

A branch of highway 95D goes to Iguala, the capital of mountainous Guerrero state, and continues as highway 95 (no autopista pretensions) to Chilpancingo and Acapulco (see the Central Pacific Coast chapter). The real highway 95D, the newly completed toll road, bypasses Iguala completely and takes a more direct route to Chilpancingo. On this exorbitantly expensive privatised road you can reportedly drive the 400 km between Mexico City and Acapulco in 3½ hours – the tolls total 255 pesos. The alternative sections of free road are consequently heavily used, slow and dangerous. Driving at night in Guerrero is inadvisable because cars are sometimes stopped and robbed. The route from Iguala to Ixtapa via highways 51 and 134 is said to be particularly risky.

TEPOZTLÁN
• *pop: 12,300* • *alt: 1701 metres*
Just off highway 95D, about 80 km from Mexico City, Tepoztlán (Place of Copper) is situated in a beautiful valley surrounded by high, jagged cliffs. It's a magical place, the legendary birthplace, more than 1200 years ago, of Quetzalcóatl, the omnipotent serpent god of the Aztecs. The town retains Indian traditions, with many older people still speaking Nahuatl, and younger people now learning it in the local secondary school. Now something of a hippy/New Age venue, Tepoztlán attracts writers, artists, palm readers and astrologists, as well as many more conventional weekend visitors from Mexico City.

Orientation & Information

The town is small, and everything is easily accessible by walking, except the Pyramid of Tepozteco on the cliff-top to the north which is more of a climb than a walk. Street names change in the centre of town, eg Avenida 5 de Mayo becomes Avenida Tepozteco north of the plaza, and the east-west streets change names as they cross this axis.

Post and telegraph offices are on the north side of the main plaza. Long-distance and local telephone calls can be made from the Farmacia Villamar, on Avenida 5 de Mayo on the west side of the main plaza. It's open every day from 9 am to 9 pm.

Ex-Convento Dominico de la Natividad

This large monastery and the attached church were built by Dominican priests between 1560 and 1588 and are the dominant feature of the town. The church is still in use, and school children play in the grounds, part of which were a capilla abierta. The plateresque church façade has Dominican seals interspersed with indigenous symbols, floral designs and various figures including the sun, moon and stars, animals, angels and the Virgin Mary. The church is open every day from around 7 am to 8 pm.

The monastery section to one side of the church is no longer in everyday use, but is being restored as a museum. It is quiet and impressive, with remnants of murals from centuries past on the walls. The rear terrace on the upper floor offers a magnificent view of the valley of Tepoztlán. The monastery is open Wednesday to Sunday from 9.30 am to 4.30 pm; admission is 5 pesos.

Museo Arqueológico Carlos Pellicer

The museum at Calle Pablo González 2 (behind the Dominican church) has a small but interesting collection of pieces from many parts of Mexico, donated to the people of Tepoztlán by the Tabascan poet Carlos Pellicer Cámara. Pellicer had a great love for Mexico's pre-Hispanic art; the objects on display here are lively and vibrant, with an emphasis on human figures but also including some animals. Unfortunately it's not well

lit, and the labels give only general information, in Spanish. The museum is open Tuesday to Sunday from 10 am to 6 pm, for a donation of 3 pesos.

Pyramid of Tepozteco

The 10-metre-high Pyramid of Tepozteco was built on a cliff 400 metres above Tepoztlán. It honours Tepoztécatl, the Aztec god of the harvest, fertility and pulque. The pyramid is just visible at the top of the cliffs to the north. It's accessible by a steep, narrow path beginning at the end of Avenida Tepozteco; the three-km walk/climb takes about one to 1½ hours, depending how athletic you are. At the top you're rewarded with a spectacular view of Tepoztlán and the valley, and an expensive refresco from one of the vendors. Admission is 10 pesos. The pyramid site is officially open every day from 9 am to 4.30 pm; the opening time seems to be elastic, but you can start climbing earlier as it takes some time to reach the entrance. It's best to climb early, when the air is clear and before it's too hot.

Festivals

Tepoztlán is a festive place, with many Christian festivals superimposed on 'pagan' celebrations. Each of the seven neighbourhood churches has two festivals a year, in addition to the following larger festivals:

Feria de Santa Catarina Celebrated in the nearby village of Santa Catarina, with various regional dances; 16 January

Carnaval On the five days preceding Ash Wednesday, Carnaval features the colourful dances of the Huehuenches and Chinelos with feather headdresses and beautifully embroidered costumes; late February or early March

Fiesta del Brinco del Chinelo The three-day 'Festival of the Hop' during Semana Santa, has dancers in bright costumes of feathers and silk jumping around like gymnasts to amuse the spectators; week before Easter

El Reto del Tepozteco This festival is celebrated on Tepozteco hill near the pyramid, with copious consumption of pulque (locally known as *ponche*) in honour of the god Tepoztécatl; 7 September

Fiesta del Templo A Catholic celebration which features theatre performances in the Nahuatl language.

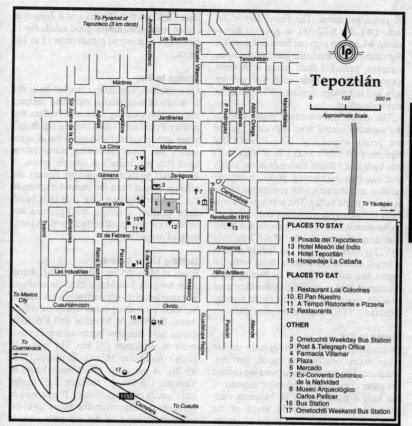

Tepoztlán

0   150   300 m
Approximate Scale

To Pyramid of
Tepozteco (3 km climb)

To Yautepec

To Mexico
City

To Cuernavaca

To Cuautla

PLACES TO STAY

9 Posada del Tepozteco
13 Hotel Mesón del Indio
14 Hotel Tepoztlán
15 Hospedaje La Cabaña

PLACES TO EAT

1 Restaurant Los Colorines
10 El Pan Nuestro
11 A Tempo Ristorante e Pizzeria
12 Restaurants

OTHER

2 Ometochtli Weekday Bus Station
3 Post & Telegraph Office
4 Farmacia Villamar
5 Plaza
6 Mercado
7 Ex-Convento Dominico
  de la Natividad
8 Museo Arqueológico
  Carlos Pellicer
16 Bus Station
17 Ometochtli Weekend Bus Station

It was originally intended to coincide with, and perhaps supplant, the pagan Tepoztécatl festival, but the pulque drinkers get a jump on it by starting the night before; 8 September

Festival Cultural de Tepoztlán A more recent innovation, this event presents music, dance, theatre, art and artesanías, with local artists and big-name visitors; 1 to 10 November

Places to Stay

Hotel prices are high in Tepoztlán, particularly for the bottom-end establishments. They tend to be full on weekends, so check in early or call ahead; on other days, try haggling for a discount. Cuernavaca and

Cuautla, both less than an hour's distance away, have cheaper accommodation.

For camping, try *Campamento Meztitla* (☎ (739) 5-00-68), about two km from Tepoztlán, on the road to Yautepec. Another camping ground is a further three km down the same road.

About the cheapest place in town is the *Hospedaje La Cabaña*, on the left as you come in at Avenida 5 de Mayo 54, almost opposite the Autos Pullman bus stop. It has 10 very basic rooms sharing two toilets and two showers (sporadic hot water). It's clean, with a good-sized garden, but expensive at

60 pesos per room. The *Hotel Mesón del Indio* (☎ (739) 5-02-38), at Avenida Revolución 44, has no sign out front but there's a big number '44' beside the gate. It's a simple, pleasant, peaceful little place with eight rooms beside a garden, each with private bath and hot water, costing 65/75 pesos for singles/doubles.

The middle and top-range places cater to the weekend crowd from Mexico City, and are pretty expensive. The *Posada del Tepozteco* (☎ (739) 5-00-10), at Paraíso 3, was built as a hillside hacienda in the 1920s and has two swimming pools, a restaurant/bar and terraces with panoramic views of the town and valley. The seven rooms cost from 135 pesos on weekdays and 180 pesos on weekends; suites with private spa baths cost from 235 pesos. The *Hotel Tepoztlán* (☎ (739) 5-05-22/23), at Las Industrias 6, is a larger health-resort-style hotel with 36 rooms, two suites, a heated swimming pool, restaurant and bar. Singles/doubles cost 194/268 pesos on Saturday (with Sunday breakfast), 157/200 pesos on other days.

Places to Eat

On market days, the food stalls in the market serve exceptionally tasty tacos, gorditas, tortas etc. The restaurants around the market are more comfortable and more expensive, but have a good variety of Mexican standards. Avenida Revolución, south of the market, has a more varied string of restaurants, including the *Restaurante Vegetariano* at No 12, which may only be open on weekends, and *Naty's* at No 7, between the market and the street. Fancier and more expensive places like *Coquis* at No 10 and *La Luna Mextli* at No 16 are combination restaurants, bars and art galleries.

For good traditional Mexican food, try the *Restaurant Los Colorines* at Avenida Tepozteco 13, 1½ blocks north of the main plaza. A popular restaurant with attractive decor, it offers a variety of dishes from 6-peso snacks to 25-peso main courses. South of the plaza on the same street, *El Pan Nuestro* is a pleasant cafeteria and cake shop with good desserts and coffee (open daily

from 10.30 am to 8.30 pm), and *A Tempo*, an Italian restaurant, makes good salads for 15 pesos and a variety of pizzas from 12 to 140 pesos.

Things to Buy

On weekends, Tepoztlán's market stalls sell a variety of handicrafts, including sarapes, embroidery, weaving, carvings, baskets and pottery. Prices aren't rock bottom, but there's some quite good stuff. Shops in the adjacent streets also have interesting wares (some from Bali and India!) at upscale prices. A local craft product is miniature houses and villages carved from the cork-like spines of the local *pochote* tree – the cute little buildings against a rough background are reminiscent of Tepoztlán itself, with its backdrop of rugged cliffs.

Getting There & Away

Buses to Mexico City (Terminal Sur) depart from Avenida 5 de Mayo 35 at the southern entrance to town – it's not really a bus station, but there's a waiting room and ticket office. Autos Pullman de Morelos and Cristóbal Colón have frequent buses during the day, more on weekends (70 km, 1¼ hours; 11 pesos). Autobuses México-Zacatepec (☎ 5-05-20), at the same office, runs buses to Yautepec (18 km, 30 minutes; 2.50 pesos) and Cuautla eight times daily. If you need to get to or from Tepoztlán after hours, go to the tollbooth (caseta) on the autopista outside town, where lots of buses pass all day and night going to or from the capital.

Ometochtli buses to Cuernavaca go every 15 minutes from 5 am to 9 pm (23 km, one hour; 2.50 pesos). On weekdays they go from their terminal one block north of the plaza, but on weekends, when traffic in the centre is restricted, they go from the depot on the road south of town.

OAXTEPEC

The attraction here is the 20-hectare Centro Vacacional Oaxtepec ('wahs-teh-PEC'), a balneario and holiday centre sponsored by the Mexican Social Security Institute (IMSS), with 25 pools for swimming, diving and the therapeutic benefits of soaking in sulphur springs. The giant park can accommodate 42,000 bathers at once, and often does on weekends and holidays. There are restaurants, picnic areas, a supermarket, sports areas, a theatre, movies and a cable car (funicular) taking you to the top of a hill for a bird's-eye view of the centre. The balneario is open every day from 8 am to 6 pm, and a day ticket is 18 pesos for adults, and half-price for children aged four to 11 and seniors over 60.

Places to Stay

If you want to stay longer than a day, there are campgrounds (12 pesos per adult), four-person rooms in the *Hotel Económico* (130 to 200 pesos), six-person rooms in the *Hotel Familiar* (250 pesos) and four-person cabins with private pools (300 pesos). Information and reservation offices are in Mexico City (☎ (5) 639-42-00) or the centre itself (☎ (735) 6-01-01/02).

Getting There & Away

Oaxtepec is just north of highway 115D, about 100 km south of Mexico City. Frequent buses go from Terminal Sur by Cristóbal Colón, Autos Pullman de Morelos and Estrella Roja (1½ hours; 14 pesos). The bus station is beside the entrance to the springs complex. There are also buses to/from Tepoztlán, Cuernavaca and Cuautla.

CUAUTLA

• *pop: 110,250* • *alt: 1291 metres*

The mineral springs (balnearios) at Cuautla ('KWOUT-la') and its pleasant year-round climate have been attractions as far back as the time of Moctezuma, who reputedly enjoyed soaking in the sun and sulphur springs. These days, however, the city is uninspiring, flat and spread out, though the centre is pleasant enough.

José María Morelos y Pavón, one of Mexico's first leaders in the independence struggle, used Cuautla as a base, but the royalist army besieged the city from 19 February to 2 May 1812 (both dates are now street names in Cuautla). Morelos and his army were forced to evacuate when their food gave out and many people were dying of starvation. A century later, Cuautla was a centre of support for the revolutionary army of Emiliano Zapata. In 1919 Zapata was assassinated by treacherous federalists at Chinameca, 31 km south of Cuautla. Now, on 10 April every year, the Agrarian Reform Minister lays a wreath at Zapata's statue in Cuautla, and makes a speech quoting Zapata's principles of land reform.

Orientation

Cuautla spreads north to south approximately parallel to the Río Cuautla. The main avenue into town, Avenida Insurgentes, changes its name to Batalla 19 de Febrero, then becomes Galeana, then Los Bravos, then Guerrero (in the pedestrian area past the main plaza) and then Zemano. Street names change a lot in Cuautla.

The zócalo has portales with restaurants, a church on the east side, the Palacio Municipal on the west and the Hotel Colón on the south. Bus companies have separate terminals, on the blocks east of the plaza.

Information

The tourist office (☎ (735) 2-52-21) is three blocks north of the plaza, in the 16th-century Ex-Convento de San Diego. This building was the terminal of the Ferrocarril Escénica (Scenic Train), which unfortunately is no longer running. The tourist office is behind the first door on the platform (open weekdays from 10 am to 6 pm; weekends from 10 am to 3 pm). The staff are helpful and have a useful city map.

Things to See

The **Museo José María Morelos**, in the same building as the tourist office, is open Monday to Friday from 9 am to 3 pm. The museum displays a few of the hero's personal items – there's not much to see but it's free. Morelos's old house, on the plaza, now houses the **Museo Histórico del Oriente de Morelos**, with some ethnographic exhibits (masks and costumes) and early photos of Cuautla and Zapata.

Balnearios

The best known balneario in Cuautla itself is Agua Hedionda (☎ (735) 2-00-44), on the east side of the river. Its warm (27°C) mineral waters smell faintly of sulphur, and fill two giant swimming pools. The complex is open every day from 7 am to 6 pm; admission is 10 pesos, more for a private pool. Get there on an 'Agua Hedionda' combi (1 peso).

Other balnearios in town include El Almeal (four blocks east from the tourist office and then two blocks north on Centinela Gabriel Tepepa), Agua Linda (just across the Niños Héroes bridge) and Las Tazas (in the colonia of the same name).

There are other balnearios in the area around Cuautla – the largest and best known is the huge complex at Oaxtepec, 10 km to the north-west (see previous section). Minibuses (combis) make the trip every few minutes from Cuautla.

Places to Stay

One of the best reasons to stop in Cuautla is the comfortable, budget-priced youth hostel, the *Villa Deportiva Juvenil* (☎ (735) 2-02-18), commonly known as the albergue. It's around behind the swimming pool and bleachers of the Balneario Agua Linda, in the Unidad Deportiva sports centre on the east side of the bridge where Niños Héroes crosses the river. A bed in one of the segregated dorms costs 10 pesos with bedding included. The clean, communal washrooms usually have hot water. It's open all day and evening, there's no age limit and a hostel card is not required.

Cheap hotels include the *Hotel Colón* (☎ (735) 2-29-90), on the main plaza, where rooms with private bath cost from 35 pesos. The *Hotel España* (☎ (735) 2-21-86), half a block east at Calle 2 de Mayo 22, has 27 clean, comfortable rooms with private bath and hot water, and limited car parking. Single/double rates are 35/45 pesos on weeknights, 60 pesos on weekends. *Hotel Jardines de Cuautla* (☎ (735) 2-00-88), opposite the Cristóbal Colón bus terminal at Calle 2 de Mayo 94, has cool, stark rooms with private bath, car parking, a garden and two tiny swimming pools. Singles/doubles are 40/70 pesos.

Hotel Sevilla (☎ (735) 2-52-00), at Con-

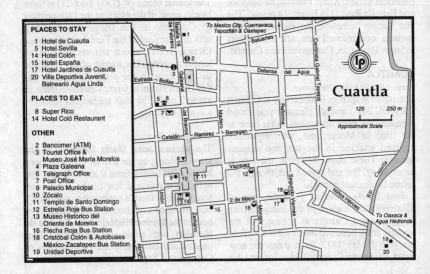

PLACES TO STAY

1 Hotel de Cuautla
5 Hotel Sevilla
14 Hotel Colón
15 Hotel España
17 Hotel Jardines de Cuautla
20 Villa Deportiva Juvenil,
   Balneario Agua Linda

PLACES TO EAT

8 Super Rico
14 Hotel Coló Restaurant

OTHER

2 Bancomer (ATM)
3 Tourist Office &
   Museo José María Morelos
4 Plaza Galeana
6 Telegraph Office
7 Post Office
9 Palacio Municipal
10 Zócalo
11 Templo de Santo Domingo
12 Estrella Roja Bus Station
13 Museo Historico del
   Oriente de Morelos
16 Flecha Roja Bus Station
18 Cristóbal Colón & Autobuses
   México-Zacatepec Bus Station
19 Unidad Deportiva

To Mexico City, Cuernavaca,
Tepoztlán & Oaxtepec

Cuautla

0   125   250 m

Approximate Scale

To Oaxaca &
Agua Hedionda

spiradores 9, is a good-value, mid-range motel-style place, with clean, comfortable rooms with phone, TV and secure parking for 72/88 pesos, or 110 pesos with two beds. The modern *Hotel de Cuautla* (☎ (735) 2-72-33) has the works, but was closed for renovations at the time of writing – it will reopen at around 180 pesos.

Places to Eat

The places around the plaza are the most fun, especially the tables under the arches. Most of them have fixed-price breakfasts and lunches for around 10 to 15 pesos. The corner restaurant at the *Hotel Colón* is popular, from 8 am to midnight.

On the north side, *Super Rico* has snacks like hot dogs and hamburgers. Next door, the *Restaurant/Bar El Portal* is open from 7 am to midnight every day. The specialities are the charcoal-grilled meats (10 to 17 pesos for big burgers) and the pizzas (from 17 pesos for a small cheese pizza up to 44 pesos for a large deluxe with the lot).

North of the main plaza, Galeana has many little restaurants, cafés, fruit-juice stalls and ice-cream shops.

Getting There & Away

Cristóbal Colón, Pullman de Morelos and Autobuses México-Zacatepec share a bus station at Calle 2 de Mayo 97. The Flecha Roja bus station (☎ (735) 2-20-65) is a block away, at Calle 2 de Mayo 74, on the corner of Mongoy. A block north of this, on the corner of Vazquez and Mongoy, is the Estrella Roja bus station (☎ (735) 2-09-59). The most useful 1st-class services include:

Cuernavaca – 42 km, one hour; every 20 minutes, 5 am to 8 pm, by Estrella Roja (7 pesos)
Mexico City (TAPO) – 70 km, 2½ hours via Amecameca; every hour, by Cristóbal Colón (16 pesos)
Mexico City (Terminal Sur) – two hours via Tepoztlán; every 15 or 20 minutes, 5 am to 7.30 pm, by Estrella Roja or Cristóbal Colón (14 pesos)
Oaxaca – 410 km, seven hours; three buses daily, by Cristóbal Colón (42 pesos)
Puebla – 125 km, 2½ hours; hourly, 5.45 am to 6.45 pm, by Estrella Roja (15 pesos)

CUERNAVACA

• *pop: 450,000* • *alt: 1542 metres*

With a mild climate, once described as 'eternal spring', Cuernavaca ('kwehr-nah-VAH-cah') has been a retreat from Mexico City since colonial times. It has attracted the wealthy and fashionable from Mexico and abroad, many of whom stayed on to become temporary or semipermanent residents. A number of their residences have become attractions in themselves, now housing museums, galleries, expensive restaurants and hotels. As the local population grows and more and more visitors come, especially on weekends, Cuernavaca is unfortunately losing some of its charm and acquiring the problems which people from the capital try to escape – crowds, traffic, smog and crime.

Much of the city's elegance is hidden behind high walls and in colonial courtyards, and is largely inaccessible to the casual visitor on a tight budget. A stroll through the lively zócalo costs nothing, but try to allow a few extra pesos to enjoy the food and ambience at some of the better restaurants. Cuernavaca is also worth visiting to see the famed Palacio de Cortés, and the nearby pre-Hispanic sites and balnearios. A lot of visitors stay longer to enrol in one of the many Spanish-language courses, and they find it is a pleasant city with an enjoyable social life.

History

Indians settling in the valleys of modern Morelos around 1220 developed a highly productive agricultural society based at Cuauhnáhuac (Place at the Edge of the Forest). The Mexica, who dominated the Valley of Mexico, called them 'Tlahuica', which means 'people who work the land'. In 1379, a Mexica warlord conquered Cuauhnáhuac, subdued the Tlahuica and required them to pay an annual tribute which included 8000 sets of clothing, 16,000 pieces of amate bark paper and 20,000 bushels of maize. The tributes payable by the subject states were set out in a register called the *Códice Mendocino* in which Cuauhnáhuac was represented by a three-branched tree; this symbol now appears on the city's coat of arms.

The successor to the Mexica *señor* (lord) married the daughter of the Cuauhnáhuac leader, and from this marriage was born Moctezuma I, the great Aztec king. The Tlahuica prospered under the Aztec empire, themselves dominating small states to the south and trading extensively with other regions. Their city was also a centre for religious ceremonies and learning, and archaeological remains show that they had a considerable knowledge of astronomy.

When the Spanish arrived, the Tlahuica were fiercely loyal to the Aztec empire, savagely resisting the advance of the conquistadors. In April 1521 they were finally overcome, and Cortés torched the city. Destroying the city pyramid, Cortés used the stones to build a fortress-palace on the pyramid's base. He also had constructed from the rubble the Catedral de la Asunción, another fortress-like structure in a walled compound – in the 1520s there was not much reason to trust in the benign favour of the new Catholic 'converts'. Soon the city became known as Cuernavaca, a more pronounceable (to the Spanish) version of its original name.

In 1529 Cortés received his somewhat belated reward from the Spanish crown when he was named Marqués del Valle de Oaxaca, with an estate which covered 22 towns, including Cuernavaca, and an encomienda of 23,000 Indians. He introduced sugar cane and other cash crops, and new agricultural methods, which resulted in Cuernavaca becoming a centre of agriculture for the Spanish empire, as it had been for the Aztecs. Cortés made Cuernavaca his home for the rest of his stay in Mexico, and his descendants dominated the area for nearly 300 years.

With its pleasant climate, rural surroundings and colonial elite, Cuernavaca became a refuge and a retreat for the rich and powerful. One of these was José de la Borda, the Taxco silver magnate said to have been the richest man in Mexico at one time in the 18th century. His lavish home and garden were later a retreat for Emperor Maximilian and Empress Carlota. Cuernavaca also attracted

artists and writers, and achieved literary fame as the setting for Malcolm Lowry's 1965 novel *Under the Volcano*. The very rich of Mexico City are now just as likely to go to Pachuca or Acapulco or Dallas for the weekend, but many still have magnificent properties in the suburbs of Cuernavaca.

Orientation

The zócalo, also called the Plaza de Armas or Plaza de la Constitución, is the heart of the city and the best place to begin a tour of Cuernavaca. Most of the budget accommodation and essential places to see are nearby. The various bus companies use different terminals, most of which are within walking distance of the zócalo.

Highway 95D, the toll road, skirts the east side of Cuernavaca; coming from the north, take the Cuernavaca exit and cross to highway 95 – the intersection has a large statue of Zapata on horseback. Highway 95 becomes Boulevard Zapata as you go south into town, and then becomes Avenida Morelos; south of Avenida Matamoros, Morelos is one-way, northbound only. To reach the centre, veer left and go down Matamoros.

Information

Tourist Office The Dirección General de Turismo (☎ (73) 14-37-90, 14-09-94), at Avenida Morelos Sur 802, is a few blocks south of the cathedral and one block north of the Estrella de Oro bus station. It's open from 9 am to 3 pm and 6 to 8 pm, Monday to Friday; weekends from 9 am to 6 pm with fewer staff. The staff are friendly and helpful and can provide information (in Spanish only) on hotels, language schools, archaeological sites, balnearios and cultural activities in Morelos.

The same office operates a small information kiosk in the Plaza de Armas, opposite the Palacio de Cortés; it's open every day from 9 am to 6 pm.

Post & Telecommunications The post office is on the south side of the Plaza de Armas. It's open Monday to Friday from 8 am to 7 pm, Saturday from 9 am to 1 pm. It offers a public fax service. There are several public telephones in front of the post office which take credit cards, and a Lada caseta at the Farmacia Central, on Galeana facing Jardín Juárez (open every day from 7 am to 10 pm).

Plaza de Armas & Jardín Juárez

The Plaza de Armas is Cuernavaca's main plaza. It is flanked on the east by the Palacio de Cortés, on the west by the Palacio del Gobierno (the seat of the state government) and on the north-east and south by a number of restaurants.

The smaller Jardín Juárez adjoins the north-west corner of the zócalo, and has a central gazebo designed by Gustave Eiffel, the tower and ironwork specialist. The booths on the gazebo's ground floor sell fruit and a wide selection of juices. Various stalls sell ice cream, hot dogs and other snacks, and you can enjoy them on a wrought-iron seat under the trees (but beware of sitting under a bird's nest).

Numerous sidewalk restaurants around the jardín and the zócalo will serve you anything from desayuno to an after-dinner drink while you watch the world go by. It's quite a scene. It's also the only main plaza in Mexico *without* a church, chapel, convent or cathedral overlooking it.

Palacio de Cortés & Museo de Cuauhnáhuac

Cortés's imposing medieval-style fortress stands at the south-eastern end of the Plaza de Armas. Construction of this two-storey stone palace was accomplished between 1522 and 1532, on the base of the large pyramid which Cortés destroyed. Cortés resided here until he departed for Spain in 1540. The palace remained with Cortés's family for most of the next century, but by the 18th century it was being used as a prison, and during the days of Porfirio Díaz in the late 19th century it was used by various government offices.

Today the palace houses the Museo de Cuauhnáhuac, with two floors of exhibits highlighting the history and cultures of Mexico. On the ground floor, exhibits focus on pre-Hispanic cultures, including the local

Tlahuica and their relationship with the Aztec empire. The base of the original pyramid can still be seen at various places around the museum's ground floor.

Upstairs, exhibits cover events from the Spanish conquest to today. On the balcony is a fascinating mural by Diego Rivera, said to be one of his best. It was commissioned in the mid-1920s as a gift to the people of Cuernavaca by Dwight Morrow, the US ambassador to Mexico. Reading from right to left, the giant mural shows scenes from the conquest to the 1910 revolution, emphasising the cruelty, oppression and violence which have characterised Mexican history.

The museum is open Tuesday to Sunday from 10 am to 5 pm. Admission is 13 pesos (free on Sunday).

Jardín Borda

The Jardín Borda (Borda Garden) was constructed in 1783 for Manuel de la Borda, as an addition to the stately residence built by his father, José de la Borda, the Taxco silver magnate. From 1866, the house was the summer residence of Emperor Maximilian and Empress Carlota, who entertained their courtiers in the gardens. Now restored, the Jardín Borda, with its various buildings, is one of Cuernavaca's main tourist attractions.

From the entrance on Avenida Morelos, opposite the cathedral compound, you can tour the house and gardens to get an idea of how Mexico's aristocracy lived. In typical colonial style, there are a number of buildings arranged around courtyards. In one wing, the **Museo de Sitio**, has exhibits on daily life in the empire period, and original documents with signatures of Morelos, Juárez and Maximilian. Several large, romantic paintings show scenes of the garden in Maximilian's time, with ladies and gentlemen rowing on the pond; one of the most famous paintings depicts Maximilian in the garden and La India Bonita, 'the pretty Indian' who was to become his lover. Another part of the house has a gallery for temporary exhibitions.

The gardens are formally laid out on a series of terraces, with paths, steps and foun-

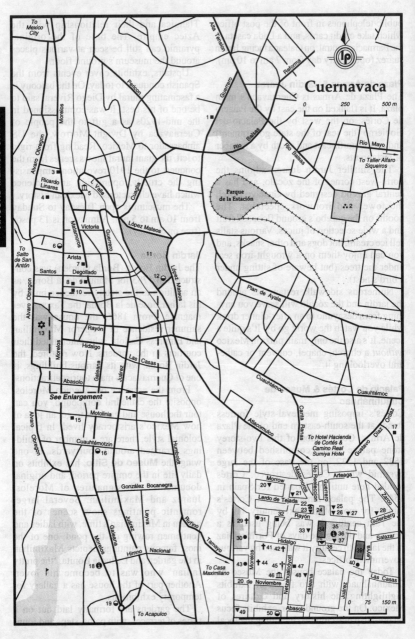

Cuernavaca

AROUND MEXICO CITY

PLACES TO STAY		33	El Portal, La Cueva	29	Parroquia de
			& Pollo y Más		Guadalupe
1	Hotel de la Selva	37	Restaurant Los Arcos	30	Jardín Borda Entrance
3	Motel Los Canarios	48	Restaurants Taxco	31	Cinema Morelos
4	Hotel & Restaurant		& Vegetariana	34	Palacio de Gobierno
	Las Mañanitas	49	Casa de Campo	35	Plaza de Armas
7	Hotel Roma				(Zócalo)
8	Hotels América	**OTHER**		36	Tourist Information
	& Marilú				Kiosk
9	Motel Royal	2	Pirámide de	38	Post Office &
10	Hotel Colonial		Teopanzolco		Telecomm
14	Posada María Cristina	5	Museo Fotográfico	39	Palacio de
15	Hotel Papagayo	6	Flecha Roja		Cortés/Museo de
17	Hostería Las Quintas		Bus Station		Cuauhnáhuac
32	Hotel Iberia	11	Mercado	40	Handicraft & Souvenir
47	Hotel Juárez	12	Local Buses		Stalls
		13	Jardín Borda	41	Templo de la Tercera
PLACES TO EAT		16	Estrella Roja		Orden de San
			Bus Station		Francisco
20	La India Bonita	18	Dirección General	42	Capilla del Carmen
21	Restaurant Vienés		de Turismo	43	Palacio Municipal
	& Los Pasteles		(Tourist Office)	44	Capilla Abierta de
	del Vienés	19	Estrella de Oro		San José
23	Restaurant Diana		Bus Station	45	Templo de la Asunción
25	La Parroquia	22	Farmacia Central		de María (Cathedral)
26	La Universal		(Long-Distance	46	Museo Robert Brady
27	McDonald's &		Telephones)	50	Autos Pullman de
	Other Restaurants	24	Jardín Juárez		Morelos Bus Station
28	Harry's Grill				

tains, and they originally featured a botanical collection with hundreds of varieties of fruit trees and ornamental plants. The vegetation is still exuberant, with large trees and semi-tropical shrubs, though there is no longer a huge range of species, and the pretty pond you see in the painting now looks more like a dirty concrete swimming pool. You can hire a little boat and go rowing for 9 pesos an hour, but it's a lot less classy than it was in Maximilian's day. The house and garden are open Tuesday to Sunday from 10 am to 5.30 pm; admission is 2 pesos.

Beside the house is the Parroquia de Guadalupe church, also built by José de la Borda, and dedicated on 12 December 1784. The schedule of masses is posted behind the iron gate; the church may not be open at other times.

Cathedral Compound

Cuernavaca's cathedral stands in a large high-walled compound on the corner of Morelos and Hidalgo – the entrance gate is on Hidalgo. Like the Palacio de Cortés, the cathedral was built on a grand scale and in a fortress-like style, as a defence against the natives and to impress and intimidate them. Franciscans started work under Cortés in 1526, using Indian labour and stones from the rubble of Cuauhnáhuac; it was one of the earliest Christian missions in Mexico. The first part to be constructed was the **Capilla Abierta de San José**, the open chapel on the west side of the cathedral.

The cathedral itself, the **Templo de la Asunción de María**, is plain and solid, with an unembellished façade. The side door, which faces north to the compound's entrance, shows a mixture of indigenous and European features – the skull and crossbones above it is a symbol of the Franciscan order. Inside are frescos which were accidentally discovered early this century. They are said to show the persecution of Christian missionaries in Japan, though it takes imagination (or faith) to make them out. Cuernavaca was in fact a centre for Franciscan missionary activities in Asia, and the frescos were supposedly painted in the 17th century by a Japanese convert to Christianity.

The cathedral compound also holds two smaller churches, one on either side of the Calle Hidalgo entrance. On the right as you enter is the **Templo de la Tercera Orden de San Francisco**, commenced in 1723, with its exterior carved in 18th-century baroque style by Indian artisans, and its interior with ornate, gilded decorations. On the left of the entrance is the late 19th-century **Capilla del Carmen**, where believers seek cures for illness.

Museo Robert Brady

Robert Brady (1928-86), an American artist and collector, lived in Cuernavaca for 24 years. His home, the Casa de la Torre, was originally part of the monastery within the Cathedral compound, and he had it extensively renovated and decorated. Brady was from a wealthy family and he travelled widely, acquiring paintings, carvings, textiles, antiques and decorative and folk arts from around the world. There are several paintings by well-known Mexican artists, including Tamayo, Kahlo and Covarrubias, but the main attraction is the sheer size and diversity of the collection, and the way it is arranged with fascinating combinations and contrasts of many styles, periods and places. One wall displays masks from Mexico, Bali and Central Africa. New Guinea carvings stand next to a Mexican table on a Persian carpet. Cushions are covered in embroidered fabrics from Asia, America and the Middle East.

The museum (☎ 18-85-54, 14-35-29) is open Thursday to Saturday from 10 am to 6 pm. All visitors must be accompanied by one of the guides – they're very informative, they don't rush you, and some speak English. It's a good idea to call first to check the hours (they can be flexible) and to ensure there's an English-speaking guide available, if you'd prefer. The museum is a short walk from the zócalo, at Netzahualcóyotl 4, just south of Hidalgo.

Palacio Municipal

The 1883 Palacio Municipal is on Avenida Morelos, just south of the Jardín Borda. A collection of large and colourful paintings is displayed around the courtyard, upstairs and down. They depict the history of the region, particularly pre-Hispanic history, in a somewhat romantic light and definitely not in chronological order. The building is open Monday to Friday from around 8 am until 6 pm, and you can come in for nothing to see the paintings. Temporary exhibitions by visiting artists are often held in the courtyard, so it's always worth a look.

Salto de San Antón

For a pleasant walk less than a km from the city centre, follow the small streets west of the Jardín Borda to the *salto*, a 40-metre waterfall. A walkway is built into the cliff face so you can walk right behind the falls. It's a picturesque place, with many trees, and the village of San Antón, above the falls, is a traditional centre for pottery.

Casa Maximiliano & Jardín Etnobotánico

Now in the suburbs of Cuernavaca, about 1.5 km south-east of the centre, this 1866 house was once a rural retreat for the Emperor Maximilian, where he would meet his Indian lover La India Bonita. It was sometimes called La Casa del Olvido (The House of Forgetfulness), reputedly because Maximilian 'forgot' to include a room for his wife there. He did remember to include a small house in the back for La India Bonita, and this is now the **Museo de la Herbolaria**, a museum of traditional herbal medicine. Around the museum, the Jardín Etnobotánico has an extensive collection of herbs and medicinal plants from Mexico and around the world, all clearly labelled with their botanical names.

The main house has INAH offices, and a library which is open to researchers

(Monday to Friday, 9 to 11.30 am and 1.30 to 4.30 pm). The site is open daily from 9 am to 5 pm; the museum closes at 4.30 pm. Admission is free. The address is Calle Matamoros 200 in Colonia Acapantzingo; it's about 200 metres south of Avenida Rufino Tamayo. It's a bit difficult to reach, so ask at the tourist office or your hotel for directions. Local buses on Ruta 6 go along Rufino Tamayo.

Pirámide de Teopanzolco

This small archaeological site is on Calle Río Balsas in the colonia Vista Hermosa. The pyramid is actually two pyramids, one inside the other – this was a typical Tlahuica Indian method of expanding pyramids by using an original pyramid as a base and building a second one all around it.

The older (inside) pyramid was built over 800 years ago; the outside one was under construction when Cortés arrived and was never completed. The name Teopanzolco translates as 'Place of the Ancient Temple' (*teopantli* = temple, *zol-tic* = ancient or old, *co* = place), and may relate to an ancient construction to the west of the current pyramid, where artefacts dating from around 7000 BC have been found, as well as others with an Olmec influence.

Several other smaller platform structures surround the pyramid. The rectangular platform west of the double pyramid is notable because human remains, mixed with ceramic pieces, were found there. They are believed to be products of human sacrifice in which decapitation and dismemberment were practised.

The site is open Tuesday to Sunday from 10 am to 5 pm (10 pesos; free on Sunday). It's over a km from the centre, and quite a walk as you have to go around the north side of the old train station. Try a local bus on Ruta 9.

Other Sights

If you're going to be in Cuernavaca for a while, there are quite a few other sights. Those out in the suburbs can be difficult to reach – see the Getting Around section.

The great Mexican muralist Alfaro Siqueiros had his workshop *(taller)* in Cuer-

navaca from 1964 until his death in 1974. The **Taller Alfaro Siqueiros**, at Calle Venus 7 in Fraccionamiento Jardines de Cuernavaca, is open Tuesday to Sunday from 10 am to 2 pm and 4 to 6 pm (free admission). On display are four murals left unfinished at the artist's death, a photographic display of his principal works, various writings and other mementos of his life.

The **Hacienda de San Antonio Atlacomulco** was built in the 17th century by Martín Cortés, who succeeded Hernán Cortés as Marqués del Valle de Oaxaca. The hacienda was nationalised in 1833 and, after various changes, it became an aguardiente factory in 1852. During the revolution, Emiliano Zapata took it over and used it as a base for his troops. After the revolution the estate deteriorated, but in 1980 it was renovated to become the Hotel Hacienda de Cortés. It's about four km south-east of the centre, in Atlacomulco.

Another notable residence converted to a hotel is **Sumiya**, former house of Baroness Barbara Hutton, heiress to the Woolworth's fortune. Constructed in Japanese style, at great expense, it uses fittings, tiles and even boulders imported from Japan, and has a kabuki theatre, meditation garden and wooden bridges between the rooms. The whole estate is now incorporated in the Camino Real Sumiya Hotel (see Places to Stay). A splurge meal at the Sumiya Restaurant is the best excuse to look at the place.

The **Museo Fotográfico de Cuernavaca** has a few early photos and maps of the city. It's in a very cute little 1897 building called the Castellito, at Güemes 1, a km north of the zócalo. It's free, and open daily from 9 am to 3 pm and 4 to 6 pm.

The **Balneario Ex-Hacienda de Temixco** is just to the south of the city and accessible by a local city bus route. It was founded in the 16th century as a sugar hacienda, but now boasts 15 swimming pools, wading pools and a water slide. There are quite a few other balnearios within an hour's drive of Cuernavaca – the tourist office has information about them. Several provide camping areas.

Language Courses

Many foreigners come to Cuernavaca to study Spanish. The best schools offer small-group (four or five students) or private instruction, at all levels from beginners to advanced, with four to five hours per day of intensive instruction plus a couple of hours' conversation practice. They usually also have optional activities such as weekend tours to archaeological and cultural sites and extracurricular classes in Mexican and Latin American history, culture, politics, music etc. Classes begin each Monday, and most schools recommend a minimum enrolment of four weeks, though you can study for as many weeks as you want. You can take time out to travel, then come back and resume your studies, but this should be arranged in advance.

Tuition fees (always quoted in US$) vary from US$400 to US$600 for four weeks, usually more for shorter periods and usually payable in advance. You may get a discount outside the peak months of January, February, July and August. Most schools also charge a nonrefundable enrolment fee of US$60 to US$100.

The schools can generally arrange for students to live with a Mexican family and experience 'total immersion' in the culture and language. The host families are screened for suitability by the schools, and the cost is around US$16 (50 pesos) per day with shared room and bath, or around US$22 (72 pesos) per day with private room and bath, including three daily meals. The schools can usually help you find rented accommodation too.

The tourist office has a list of 11 language institutes in the city, and any of them will send you a free brochure explaining their programmes and fees. Try contacting the following schools – their postal addresses (all in Morelos, Mexico) are given:

Cemanahuac Educational Community
  Apdo Postal 5-21, Cuernavaca; also offers a range of field studies in villages (☎ (73) 12-64-19, fax 12-54-18)
Center for Bilingual Multicultural Studies
  Apdo Postal 1520, Cuernavaca 62170; instruc-

tors and students are *sworn* to speak only Spanish (☎ (73) 17-10-87, fax 17-05-33)
Cuauhnáhuac – Instituto Colectivo de Lengua y Cultura
  Apdo Postal 5-26, Cuernavaca 62051; a well-established school, but possibly more expensive (☎ (73) 12-36-73, fax 18-26-93)
Cuernavaca Language School
  Apdo Postal 4-254, Cuernavaca 62430; one of the cheapest, but still very professional (☎ (73) 15-46-43)
Experiencia – Centro de Intercambio Bilingüe y Cultural
  Apdo Postal C-96, Cuernavaca; another popular, reputable school, not too expensive (☎ /fax (73) 18-52-09)
IDEAL – Instituto de Estudios de América Latina
  Apdo Postal 22-B, Cuernavaca 62191; best acronym, and a well-established school (☎ (73) 17-04-55, fax 17-57-10)
IDEL – Instituto de Idiomas y Culturas Latinoamericanas
  Apdo Postal 12771-1, Cuernavaca 62001; one of the longest established, they can arrange programmes for children from the age of eight (☎ /fax (73) 13-01-57)

Festivals

These are among the festivals and special events you can see in Cuernavaca:

Carnaval In the five days before Ash Wednesday, this colourful week-long celebration of Mardi Gras includes street performances by the Chinelo dancers of Tepoztlán, among others, and parades, art exhibits, music and more; late February or early March
Feria de la Primavera Cuernavaca's Spring Fair includes cultural and artistic events, concerts and a beautiful exhibit of the city's spring flowers; 21 March to 10 April
San Isidro Labrador On the day of Saint Isidro the Farmer, local farmers adorn their mules and oxen with flowers and bring them to town for an annual blessing; 15 May
Día de la Virgen de Guadalupe The day of the Virgen de Guadalupe is celebrated in Cuernavaca, as it is everywhere in Mexico, on 12 December.

Places to Stay

Accommodation in Cuernavaca doesn't offer great value for money. The cheap places tend to be depressingly basic, the mid-range ones are lacking in charm and the top-end hotels are wonderful but very expensive. On weekends and holidays the town fills up with visitors from the capital, so phone ahead or try to secure your room early in the day.

Places to Stay – bottom end

The cheapest places are on Aragón y León between Morelos and Matamoros. Some of them are disreputable dives but others, like the *América* and the *Marilú*, look OK – check the rooms and the vibes before you check in. The *Hotel Colonial* (☎ (73) 18-64-14), at No 104, is definitely respectable, clean and quiet with 14 rooms arranged around a small courtyard. They charge around 50/70 pesos for singles/doubles, around 85 pesos for two-bed rooms; some rooms are better and brighter than others.

Round the corner, at Matamoros 405, the *Hotel Roma* (☎ (73) 18-87-78) is pretty cheap at 40/50 pesos for small rooms, but they're tolerably clean and have bathrooms with hot water in the morning and evening. The *Motel Royal* (☎ (73) 18-64-80), at Matamoros 19, has clean but characterless rooms around a central car park at 60/65/75 pesos for singles/doubles/triples, or 25 pesos more with TV.

The *Hotel Juárez* (☎ (73) 14-02-19), at Netzahualcóyotl 117 about a block southwest of the zócalo, is a good place to stay, centrally located but quiet, with a large garden and swimming pool behind the hotel. The 13 rooms are simple but light and airy, some with windows to the street and others to the garden; singles/doubles are 55/75 pesos. Get there early if you want the parking space (there's only one!).

Places to Stay – middle

The *Hotel Iberia* (☎ (73) 12-60-40) at Rayón 9, just west of the Jardín Juárez, has long been patronised by travellers and foreign students. Its small rooms are set around a courtyard with lots of tiles, plants and a couple of parking spaces for cars. It's OK and quite clean, but no bargain at 62/81 pesos.

A few blocks north of the zócalo, the *Motel Los Canarios* (☎ (73) 13-00-00, 13-44-44) at Avenida Morelos 713 has two swimming pools and a children's play-

ground. The rooms are a bit worn, with functional metal furniture, but light and spacious enough. At 55/110 pesos for singles/doubles, it's extra-good value for solo travellers, and they give a 20% discount for longer stays. The restaurant is being renovated – it used to serve good meals all day.

The *Hotel Papagayo* (☎ (73) 14-17-11, 14-19-24) at Motolinia 13, between Avenida Morelos and Calle Netzahualcóyotl, is one of the most pleasant places, with 77 modern rooms around a large garden with two swimming pools, children's play equipment and plenty of parking spaces. During the week, it costs 70/110 pesos for a single/double including breakfast. On Friday and Saturday it's 110/180 pesos with breakfast and either lunch or dinner.

Places to Stay – top end

If price is no object, stay in one of the finest colonial-era hotels anywhere in Mexico, *Las Mañanitas* (☎ (73) 14-14-66, fax 18-36-72), at Ricardo Linares 107. Prices run from 260/325 pesos for standard rooms up to 700/775 pesos for incredibly beautiful garden suites. The establishment is very impressive, with every luxury including a large private garden where peacocks stroll around while you enjoy the elegant pool. This hotel has been included in several listings of the world's best hotels and its restaurant is also justly famous.

Now occupying the former home of Baroness Barbara Hutton, the *Camino Real Sumiya* (☎ (73) 20-91-99, fax 20-91-55) is a beautiful place in Fraccionamiento Sumiya on the southern outskirts of town. The surrounding gardens have established trees, fountains and ponds, and the elegant Japanese style of the place is unique in Mexico. Prices start at around 350 pesos a double, but ask about their special rates and packages.

Hostería Las Quintas (☎ (73) 18-39-49) at Avenida Las Quintas 107 is a couple of km from the centre. It has a pool, restaurant and bar, and offers a range of health and beauty treatments. Rooms are set around a lush garden and start at 190 pesos a double; terrace suites are 395 pesos and jacuzzi suites

470 pesos. The more centrally located *Posada María Cristina* (☎ (73) 18-69-84) at Leyva 200, on the corner of Abasolo, is not as luxurious but it's one of Cuernavaca's long-time favourites, in a nicely restored colonial building, at 250 pesos for singles or doubles.

Places to Eat

Cuernavaca has a good range of eating places for all budgets.

Inexpensive For a simple healthy snack or breakfast of yoghurt with fruit, escamochas (a kind of fruit salad), corn on the cob, ice cream, or fresh fruit/vegetable juice, you could patronise one of the booths on the ground floor of the *Jardín Juárez gazebo*, then eat it on one of the park benches. There are a number of places to eat along the east side of the zócalo, including a *McDonald's* and some other fast-food joints.

Food gets cheaper as you move away from the fashionable areas of the central plazas. The west side of Jardín Juárez seems to be less classy, and the *Restaurant Diana* does a good five-course set meal, for lunch or dinner, for around 16 pesos. A block to the south down Galeana, *El Portal* has budget-priced burgers, chicken and fries, and *La Cueva* has a slightly more expensive menu with seafood and Mexican standards. In the afternoon they have a comida corrida at around 18 pesos for a three or four-course meal. Another block down Galeana is the popular *Restaurant Taxco*, with a choice of comidas corridas from 17 to 25 pesos. Next door is the small, simple *Restaurant Vegetariana*, with a delicious four-course comida corrida of salad, vegetable soup, a hot main dish with brown rice, tea and dessert for 10 pesos.

Going away from the plazas on Rayón, you pass a number of cheap eateries going up the hill. A few places have hamburgers, others serve tacos, ice cream or fruit juices – there's even a Chinese restaurant.

Mid-Range On the east side of Jardín Juárez, *La Parroquia*, open every day from 7.30 am to 11.30 pm, is one of Cuernavaca's favourite restaurants. It serves all meals, is open long hours and has a good view of the plaza, but you pay for the position – main meat dishes, for example, cost around 35 pesos. Its extensive menu of meals, coffees and desserts includes some Middle Eastern specialities. Nearby, *La Universal* occupies a strategic position on the corner of the two plazas, with tables under an awning facing the Plaza de Armas. It's open from 9 am to midnight and is a popular place to be seen, but it's quite expensive.

On the south side of the Plaza de Armas, the umbrella-covered tables of the *Restaurant Los Arcos* are a pleasant place for a meal or just to hang out, sip coffee or a soda and watch the action on the plaza. Their varied bilingual menu has something for everyone and is not too expensive. It's open every day from 8 am to 11 pm.

La India Bonita, north-west of Jardín Juárez at Calle Morrow 6, is a lovely courtyard restaurant with good traditional Mexican food. The house specialities are chicken mole, with that great mole sauce which is a combination of chocolate, chiles and about 20 other ingredients (38 pesos); charcoal-grilled filet mignon (45 pesos); or a special Mexican plate with seven different selections (28 pesos). Breakfast costs from 10 to 28 pesos, and is the cheapest way to enjoy this nice little place. It's open Tuesday to Saturday from 8.30 am to 7.30 pm, Sunday from 8.30 am to 6.30 pm.

Restaurant Vienés, at Tejada 201 a block from Jardín Juárez, offers a delicious variety of traditional European dishes, like the 'farmer's plate' (smoked pork ribs, roast veal, frankfurter, potatoes and sauerkraut), knackwurst with sauerkraut and German fried potatoes, or stuffed roast meatloaf served with potatoes, vegetables and salad. Main courses are around 40 pesos. It's open every day except Tuesday, from 1 to 10 pm. The same owners run *Los Pasteles del Vienés*, next door, which serves the best cakes, cookies, cream puffs and chocolate/rum truffles you've seen since the last time you were in Vienna. Their coffee, probably the best in the city, comes with free refills. Hours are from 8 am to 10 pm every day, so it's good for a splurge breakfast (eggs are 12 to 20 pesos).

Harry's Grill, at Juan Gutenberg 3 just off the Plaza de Armas, is one of the Carlos Anderson chain of bar/restaurants where rock'n'roll music shakes the photos and posters lining every inch of wall space. All the Anderson restaurants provide a good time for the gringos, and this one is no exception. Main courses cost around 25 to 30 pesos. The grill is open from 1 pm to midnight, but the bar stays open later.

Expensive As a haven for the rich, Cuernavaca boasts a number of sumptuous restaurants. There are Lebanese, Japanese, Chinese, Italian, Spanish and seafood places, but if you can afford an indulgence, try the *Restaurant Las Mañanitas* (☎ 14-14-66, 12-46-46), at the hotel of the same name at Ricardo Linares 107. One of Mexico's best and most famous restaurants, it has tables inside the mansion or on the garden terrace where you can see peacocks and flamingos strolling through an emerald-green garden and swans gliding around on the pond. The menu features meals from around the world, and you should bring at least 80 pesos in cash per person (no credit cards). It's open every day from 1 to 5 pm and from 7 to 10.30 pm; reservations are recommended.

Other top-end hotels have top-end restaurants offering elegant surroundings as well as fine food – try the colonial dining room at *Hostería Las Quintas* (☎ 18-39-49) or the Japanese-style *Camino Real Sumiya* (☎ 20-91-99). The *Casa de Campo*, on Abasolo 101, is strictly a restaurant but definitely top-end, serving excellent food in a classic colonial courtyard with lots of greenery and tinkling fountains. Of course all these places are a little pricey – expect to pay 25 pesos for salads, 20 pesos for soup, 50 pesos for pasta and 60 pesos for main courses.

Entertainment

Hanging around the central plazas is always a popular activity in Cuernavaca, especially on Sunday and Thursday at around 6 pm,

when open-air concerts are held. The good discos in Cuernavaca are usually open only on Friday and Saturday nights; *Barba Azul*, at Prado 10, Colonia San Jeronimo, and *Kaova*, near the corner of Motolini and Morelos, are two of the best. For live salsa dance music, try *Sammaná*, at Domingo Diez 1522, open Thursday, Friday and Saturday nights.

Some of Cuernavaca's better hotels have live music in their bars every night; you could try the bars at the *Villa Bejar*, Domingo Diez 2350, or the *Villa del Conquistador*, Paseo del Conquistador 134. These places are mostly way out in the posh suburbs – get a taxi. (If you can't afford a taxi, you can't afford to go there anyway.)

The bar at *Harry's Grill* is a fun place to meet people. For quieter drinks in elegant surroundings, the garden bar at the *Hotel Las Mañanitas* is hard to beat; it's open every day from noon to midnight.

The *Cinema Morelos* (☎ 18-82-50), on the corner of Morelos and Rayón, is the state theatre of Morelos, hosting a variety of cultural offerings including quality film series, plays, dance performances etc.

Things to Buy

Cuernavaca has no distinctive handicrafts, but if you want an onyx ashtray, a leather belt or some second-rate silver, try the souvenir stalls south of the Palacio de Cortés.

Getting There & Away

Bus Quite a few bus companies serve Cuernavaca. There are four separate terminals, operated by the main companies:

Autos Pullman de Morelos – corner of Abasolo & Netzahualcóyotl (☎ 14-36-50)
Estrella de Oro – Avenida Morelos Sur 900 (☎ 12-30-55, 12-82-96)
Estrella Roja – corner of Galeana & Cuauhtémotzin (☎ 18-59-34, 12-06-34)
Flecha Roja – Avenida Morelos 503, between Arista & Victoria (☎ 12-81-90)

You might want to get a local bus to/from the Estrella de Oro terminal, which is 1.5 km south, but the others are within walking distance of the zócalo. Many local buses and those to nearby towns go from the southern corner of the mercado (market). First-class buses from Cuernavaca include:

Acapulco – 315 km, three to five hours; 11 buses daily by Estrella de Oro; seven buses daily by Flecha Roja (same prices: ordinario 44 pesos, directo 64 pesos, deluxe 70 pesos)

Chilpancingo – 180 km, three hours; same buses as to Acapulco (ordinario 24 pesos, directo 45 pesos)

Cuautla – 42 km, one hour; every 20 minutes, 5 am to 10 pm, by Estrella Roja (6 pesos)

Grutas de Cacahuamilpa – 80 km, 2½ hours; hourly, 6 am to 6 pm, by Flecha Roja (8 pesos)

Iguala – 90 km, 1½ hours; same buses as to Acapulco (15 pesos)

Izúcar de Matamoros – 100 km, two hours; hourly, 5 am to 8 pm, by Estrella Roja (12 pesos)

Mexico City (Terminal Sur) – 85 km, 1½ hours; every 15 minutes, 5 am to 9.30 pm, by Pullman de Morelos (ordinario 12 pesos, deluxe 18 pesos); every 30 minutes, 6.30 am to 10 pm, by Flecha Roja (14 pesos); six daily by Estrella de Oro (12 pesos)

Mexico City Airport – 100 km, two hours; five per day by Pullman de Morelos (30 pesos)

Puebla – 175 km, 3½ hours; hourly, 5 am to 8 pm, by Estrella Roja (20 pesos)

Taxco – 80 km, 1½ hours; 10 per day, 9 am to 8 pm, by Flecha Roja (14 pesos); three daily by Estrella de Oro (9 pesos)

Tepoztlán – 23 km, one hour; every 15 minutes, 5.30 am to 10 pm, from the local bus terminal at the mercado (2.50 pesos)

Zihuatanejo – 550 km, nine hours; two daily by Flecha Roja (75 pesos)

Car Cuernavaca is 85 km south of Mexico City, a 1½-hour drive on highway 95, but quicker on the toll road (highway 95D). Both these roads continue south to Acapulco. Highway 95 goes via Taxco, which is a must; highway 95D is more direct and much faster, but the tolls will total around 200 pesos.

Getting Around

You can walk around most of the places of interest in central Cuernavaca, but it's difficult to get to places in the suburbs. The local buses cost only a peso, but the system is hard to figure out. They usually have the colonia (neighbourhood) they're going to marked on their windscreen, and many of them do a

circuit which includes going up Avenida Morelos – the tourist office can help you catch one to a particular destination. Taxis will go to most places in town for 6 to 8 pesos.

AROUND CUERNAVACA

Quite a few places can be visited on day trips from Cuernavaca, or perhaps on the way north to Mexico City or south to Taxco (thus avoiding some stretches of the expensive toll road).

Parque Nacional Lagunas de Zempoala

Only 25 km north-west of Cuernavaca, by winding roads, is a group of seven lakes high in the hills. Some of them are stocked with fish for anglers, and the surrounding forest offers some pleasant walks and camping.

Xochicalco

Atop a desolate plateau 15 km south-west of Cuernavaca as the crow flies, but about 38 km by road, is the ancient ceremonial centre of Xochicalco ('so-chee-CAL-co'), one of the most important archaeological sites in central Mexico. In Nahuatl, the language of the Aztecs, Xochicalco means 'Place of the House of Flowers', which it probably was for Toltecs in the 7th century.

Today it is a collection of white stone ruins covering approximately 10 sq km, some of them yet to be excavated. They represent the various cultures – Toltec, Olmec, Zapotec, Mixtec and Aztec – for which Xochicalco was a commercial, cultural and religious centre. When Teotihuacán began to weaken around 650 to 700 AD, Xochicalco began to rise in importance, achieving its maximum splendour between 650 and 850 AD with far-reaching commercial and cultural relations. Around the year 650 a congress of spiritual leaders met in Xochicalco, representing the Zapotec, Mayan and Gulf Coast peoples, to correlate their respective calendars.

The most famous monument here is the Pyramid of the Plumed Serpent; from its well-preserved bas-reliefs archaeologists have surmised that astronomer-priests met here at the beginning and end of each 52-year cycle of the Aztec calendar. Xochicalco remained an important centre until around 1200, when its excessive growth caused a fall similar to that of Teotihuacán.

Getting There & Away Unless you have your own transport, getting to Xochicalco can be difficult. Flecha Roja supposedly runs one bus per hour directly to Xochicalco (5 pesos). Autos Pullman de Morelos buses to Miacatlán will drop you off at the crossroads, about four km from the site, from where you can walk (uphill) or catch a taxi (6 pesos). Or get one of the regular buses to Alpuyeca, and a taxi from there. The site is open Tuesday to Sunday from 10 am to 5 pm (admission 13 pesos; free on Sunday).

Laguna de Tequisquitengo

This lake, 37 km south of Cuernavaca, is a popular location for water sports, particularly water-skiing. There are hotels, restaurants and other facilities around the lake shore. There are several balnearios nearby, including **Tehuixtla** and **Las Estacas**, and old Franciscan monasteries at **Tlaquiltenango** and **Tlaltizapán**.

Zoofari

Over 150 animal species inhabit this drive-through zoo, many wandering freely in large fenced areas, but quite a few in miserable cages as well. It's a good chance to see the difference between an emu and an ostrich, and children will enjoy seeing the giraffes and zebras. Zoofari (☎ (73) 20-97-94) is open every day from 9 am to 5 pm; the *Restaurant Timbuktu* is open only on weekends. It's 55 km from Cuernavaca on highway 95 (the non-toll road) to Taxco; Flecha Roja buses between the two cities will drop you at the gate. A zoofari minibus will take you around for 3 pesos; it costs 20 pesos for a private car.

TAXCO
• *pop: 60,000* • *alt: 1755 metres*

The old silver-mining town of Taxco ('TASS-co'), 180 km south-east of Mexico City, is a gorgeous colonial antique, and one of the most picturesque and pleasant places in Mexico. Clinging to a steep hillside, its narrow, cobblestoned streets twist and turn between well-worn buildings, open unexpectedly onto pretty plazas and reveal delightful vistas at every corner – no colonial grid plan here. Unlike many Mexican towns from the colonial era, it has not surrounded itself with industrial suburbs, and even the traffic in Taxco has a certain charm. Rather than the daily tides of commuting cars and commercial vehicles, a fleet of Volkswagen taxis and combis beetle through the labyrinth like ants in an anthill, seldom going fast enough to be a serious threat to life. And very few streetscapes are defaced with rows of parked cars, because there's simply no room for them.

The federal government has declared the entire city a national historical monument, and local laws preserve Taxco's colonial-style architecture and heritage. Old buildings are preserved and restored wherever possible, and any new buildings must conform to the old in scale, style and materials – have a look at the colonial Pemex station.

Though Taxco's silver mines are almost exhausted, handmade silver jewellery is one of the town's main industries. There are hundreds of silver shops, and browsing from one to another is a perfect pretext for wandering through the streets and alleys. The other main industry is tourism, which has suffered a setback with the completion of the Mexico City to Acapulco toll road that bypasses the town. Though Taxco still attracts lots of visitors, their numbers have fallen and they don't overwhelm the place. The hotels and restaurants are reasonably priced, and generally so appealing that they are good value for money.

History

Taxco was called Tlachco (literally, 'place where ball is played') by the Aztecs, who dominated the region from 1440 until the Spanish arrived. In 1529 the colonial city was founded by Captain Rodrigo de Castañeda, acting under a mandate from Hernán Cortés. The town's first residents were three Spanish miners – Juan de Cabra, Juan Salcedo and Diego de Nava – and the carpenter Pedro Muriel. In 1531 they established the first Spanish mine on the North American continent.

The Spaniards came searching for tin, which they found in small quantities, but by 1534 they had also discovered tremendous lodes of silver. That year the Hacienda del Chorrillo was built, complete with water wheel, smelter and aqueduct. The old arches (Los Arcos) standing over the highway to Mexico City at the northern end of Taxco are all that remains of the aqueduct. The water wheel and smelter have long since vanished, but the hacienda has gone through several metamorphoses and is now part of an art school.

The prospectors quickly emptied the first veins of silver from the hacienda and left Taxco. Further significant quantities of silver were not discovered until two centuries later, in 1743. Don José de la Borda, who had arrived in 1716 from France at the age of 16 to work with his miner brother, accidentally uncovered one of the area's richest veins. According to a frequently related Taxco legend, Borda was riding near where the church of Santa Prisca now stands when his horse stumbled, dislodged a stone and exposed the silver.

Borda went on to make three fortunes, and lose two. He introduced new techniques of draining and repairing mines, and he reportedly treated his Indian workers much better than those working in other colonial mines. A devout man, his two children both joined the clergy, and the church of Santa Prisca was his gift to Taxco. He is remembered for the saying *'Dios da a Borda, Borda da a Dios'* ('God gives to Borda, Borda gives to God').

His success attracted many more prospectors and miners, and new veins of silver were found, and emptied. With most of the silver gone, Taxco became a quiet town with a dwindling population and economy. In 1932 an American professor named William (Guillermo) Spratling arrived and, at the suggestion of then US Ambassador Dwight Morrow, set up a small silver workshop as a

way to rejuvenate the town. (Another version has it that Spratling was writing a book in Taxco and resorted to the silver business because his publisher went broke.) The workshop became a factory and Spratling's apprentices began establishing their own shops. Today there are more than 300 silver shops in Taxco selling some of the finest silverwork in the world.

Orientation

Taxco's twisting streets may make you feel like a mouse in a maze, and even maps of the town look confusing at first, but you'll quickly learn your way around, and in any case it's a nice place to get lost. Plaza Borda, sometimes called the zócalo, is the heart of the town, and its spectacular church, Santa Prisca, is a good landmark.

Highway 95 is called Avenida John F Kennedy as it winds its way around the eastern side of central Taxco. Both bus stations are on Kennedy. Calle La Garita branches west from Kennedy opposite the Pemex station, and it becomes the main thoroughfare through the middle of town. It follows a convoluted route, more or less south-west (one way only), to the Plaza Borda, changing its name to Calle Juárez on the way. Past the plaza, this main artery becomes Cuauhtémoc, and goes down to the Plazuela de San Juan. Most of the essentials are along this La Garita-Juárez-Cuauhtémoc route, or pretty close to it. It's actually quite easy to follow and a standard route for the combis. Several side roads go east back to Kennedy, which is two way and therefore the only way a vehicle can get back to the north end of town. The basic combi route is an anticlockwise loop going north on Kennedy and south through the centre of town, but there are several variants on this.

Information

Tourist Office The Secretaría de Fomento Turístico (☎ (762) 2-22-74) has an office in the Centro de Convenciones de Taxco, on Avenida Kennedy at the north end of town, where the old aqueduct crosses the highway. It's open Monday to Friday from 9 am to

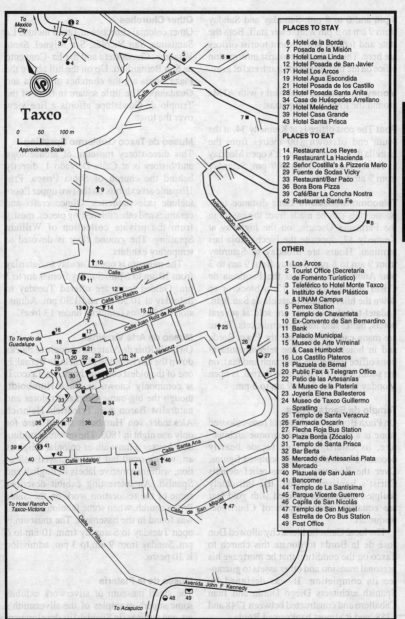

Taxco

To Mexico City

0   50   100 m
Approximate Scale

To Templo de Guadalupe

To Hotel Rancho Taxco-Victoria

To Acapulco

PLACES TO STAY

6   Hotel de la Borda
7   Posada de la Misión
8   Hotel Loma Linda
17 Hotel Posada de San Javier
17 Hotel Los Arcos
19 Hotel Agua Escondida
21 Hotel Posada de los Castillo
28 Hotel Posada Santa Anita
34 Casa de Huéspedes Arrellano
37 Hotel Meléndez
39 Hotel Casa Grande
43 Hotel Santa Prisca

PLACES TO EAT

14 Restaurant Los Reyes
19 Restaurant La Hacienda
22 Señor Costilla's & Pizzería Mario
29 Fuente de Sodas Vicky
33 Restaurant/Bar Paco
36 Bora Bora Pizza
39 Café/Bar La Concha Nostra
42 Restaurant Santa Fe

OTHER

1   Los Arcos
2   Tourist Office (Secretaría de Fomento Turístico)
3   Teleférico to Hotel Monte Taxco
4   Instituto de Artes Plásticos & UNAM Campus
5   Pemex Station
9   Templo de Chavarrieta
10 Ex-Convento de San Bernardino
11 Bank
13 Palacio Municipal
15 Museo de Arte Virreinal & Casa Humboldt
16 Los Castillo Plateros
18 Plazuela de Bernal
20 Public Fax & Telegram Office
22 Patio de las Artesanías & Museo de la Platería
23 Joyería Elena Ballesteros
24 Museo de Taxco Guillermo Spratling
25 Templo de Santa Veracruz
26 Farmacia Oscarín
27 Flecha Roja Bus Station
30 Plaza Borda (Zócalo)
31 Templo de Santa Prisca
32 Bar Berta
35 Mercado de Artesanías Plata
38 Mercado
40 Plazuela de San Juan
41 Bancomer
44 Templo de La Santísima
45 Parque Vicente Guerrero
46 Capilla de San Nicolás
47 Templo de San Miguel
48 Estrella de Oro Bus Station
49 Post Office

3 pm and 6 to 8 pm, Saturday and Sunday from 9 am to 3 pm with fewer staff. Both the state and federal government tourist offices are here. There's another tourist information office on the highway at the south end of town.

Money There are several banks with ATMs around the town's main plazas.

Post The post office is at Kennedy 34, at the south end of town 100 metres from the Estrella de Oro bus station. It's open Monday to Friday from 8.30 am to 7 pm, Saturday from 9 am to 1 pm.

Telecommunications Long-distance telephone calls can be made from the caseta in the Farmacia Oscarín, on the highway at Kennedy 47, opposite the Flecha Roja bus terminal. Hours are Monday to Saturday from 9 am to 8 pm, Sunday from 9 am to 3 pm. Another caseta is at the Farmacia de Cristo at Calle Hidalgo 12, a block or so down the hill from the Plazuela de San Juan. Ladatel telephone cards are sold at several hotels, banks and mini-supermarkets. There are many card phones near the Plaza Borda and in hotel lobbies. The telecommunications office (telegram, telegraph and fax), on the south side of Plazuela de Bernal, is open Monday to Friday from 9 am to 3 pm.

Templo de Santa Prisca
On Plaza Borda, this church of rose-coloured stone is a masterpiece of baroque architecture, its Churrigueresque façade heavily decorated with elaborately sculpted figures. Over the doorway, the bas-relief depicts Christ's baptism. Inside, the intricately sculpted altarpieces covered with gold leaf are equally fine examples of Churrigueresque art.

The local Catholic hierarchy allowed Don José de la Borda to donate this church to Taxco on the condition that he mortgage his personal mansion and other assets to guarantee its completion. It was designed by Spanish architects Diego Durán and Juan Caballero and constructed between 1748 and 1758, and it almost bankrupted Borda.

Other Churches
Other colonial churches in Taxco include La Santísima, San Nicolás, San Miguel, Santa Veracruz, Chavarrieta and the Ex-Convento de San Bernardino. Up on the hill above the Plaza Borda are the churches of Ojeda and Guadalupe. The little square in front of the Templo de Guadalupe affords a fine view over the town.

Museo de Taxco Guillermo Spratling
This three-storey museum of archaeology and history is at Calle Delgado 1, directly behind the church of Santa Prisca. Pre-Hispanic art exhibits on the two upper floors include jade statuettes, Olmec crafts and ceramics and other interesting pieces, mostly from the private collection of William Spratling. The ground floor is devoted to temporary exhibits.

The museum is open Tuesday to Saturday from 10 am to 5 pm, Sunday from 9 am to 3 pm. Guided tours are offered Tuesday to Saturday at 10.30 am and 1.30 pm. Admission is 10 pesos (children under 13 free).

Museo de Arte Virreinal
On Calle Ruíz de Alarcón, a couple of blocks down the hill from the Plazuela de Bernal, is one of the oldest colonial homes in Taxco. It is commonly known as **Casa Humboldt**, though the big-name German explorer and naturalist Baron von Friedrich Heinrich Alexander von Humboldt stayed here for only one night in 1803. The restored building now houses a museum of colonial religious art, with a small but well-displayed collection, with informative labels in English and Spanish. An interesting exhibit describes some of the restoration work on the Santa Prisca church, when some fabulous material was found in the basement. The museum is open Tuesday to Saturday from 10 am to 6 pm, Sunday from 9 am to 3 pm; admission is 10 pesos.

Museo de la Platería
The small museum of silverwork exhibits some superb examples of the silversmith's art, and outlines (in Spanish) its development

in Taxco. Included are some classic designs by William Spratling, and prize-winning pieces from national and international competitions. Notice the very colourful, sculptural combinations of silver with semi-precious minerals such as jade, lapis lazuli, turquoise, malachite, agate and obsidian – a feature of much of the silverwork for sale in the town, and a link with pre-Hispanic stone-carving traditions.

The museum is at Plaza Borda 1, downstairs from the Patio de las Artesanías (enter from the sidewalk as if you were going to Señor Costilla's restaurant, turn left instead of right on the patio and go down the stairs). The museum is open every day from 10 am to 5 pm; admission is 3 pesos.

Silver Shops

Shopping for silver is the main activity of many tourists in Taxco, and among the hundreds of silver shops some are particularly noteworthy. Even if you can't afford to buy the best, it's definitely worth looking in some of the top places to see the finest work and the most creative designs. Several are in the Patio de las Artesanías building on the corner of Plaza Borda, on your left as you face Santa Prisca. Pineda's, on the corner of Calle Muñoz and the plaza, is a famous shop; a couple of doors down Muñoz, at No 4, the Joyería Elena Ballesteros is another.

Los Castillo Plateros, on Plazuela de Bernal, is worth visiting. They display not only jewellery, but also statues, vases, tableware and other unusual items, and you can visit the workshop to see things being made. The shop is open daily from 9 am to 1 pm and 3 to 7 pm, Sunday from 9 am to 3 pm. For quantity rather than quality, see the numerous stalls in the Mercado de Artesanías Plata, with vast quantities of smaller items – rings, chains, pendants etc. The work is not as well displayed here, but you can often spot something special.

Teleférico & Monte Taxco

From the northern end of Taxco, near Los Arcos, a Swiss-made cable car ascends 173 metres to the luxurious Monte Taxco resort hotel. The view of Taxco and the surrounding mountains from the cable car and resort is fantastic. The cable car runs daily from 7.30 am to 7 pm, and costs 6 pesos one way or 10 pesos return (children half-price). Walk uphill from Los Arcos, and turn right into the gate of the Instituto de Artes Plásticos; you can see the cable-car terminal from the gate.

You can use the resort facilities for a price: it's 20 pesos for an hour of tennis or horse riding or for all-day use of the swimming pool, 100 pesos for nine holes of golf. The bar overlooking the pool has a superb view of Taxco, and there's also a restaurant and a discotheque.

Courses

Just up the hill from Los Arcos, the Universidad Nacional Autónomo de México (UNAM) has a campus which offers intensive six-week courses in Spanish language. Tuition and registration cost US$250. Accommodation and meals are extra, but the

---

El Día del Jumil

Jumiles are small beetles, about one cm long, which migrate annually to the Cerro de Huixteco (the hill behind Taxco) to reproduce. They begin to arrive around September; the last ones are gone by about January or February. During this time, the jumiles are a great delicacy for the people of Taxco, who eat them alone or mixed in salsa with tomatoes, garlic, onion, chiles etc, or even alive, rolled into tortillas. (You can buy live jumiles in the mercado during this time; the Restaurant Santa Fe serves salsa de jumil prepared in the traditional way.)

Traditionally, the entire population of the town climbs the Cerro de Huixteco on this day, collecting jumiles, bringing picnics and sharing food and fellowship. Many families come early and camp on the hill over the preceding weekend. The celebration is said to represent the jumiles giving energy and life to the people of Taxco for another year. ∎

school can help find a suitable place. For details of admission requirements, enrolment and course dates, contact CEPE (Centro de Enseñanza Para Extranjeros; ☎ /fax (762) 2-01-24), Apto 70, Taxco 40200, Guerrero. On the same site, the Instituto de Artes Plásticos offers courses in painting, sculpture, printmaking etc.

Festivals

Try to time your visit to Taxco during one of its several annual festivals, but be sure to reserve your hotel room in advance. During Semana Santa, in particular, visitors from around the world pour into the city to see the processions and events.

Santa Prisca & San Sebastián The festivals of Taxco's two patron saints are celebrated on 18 January (Santa Prisca) and 20 January (San Sebastián). Mass is celebrated in the Templo de Santa Prisca while people parade by the entrance with their pets and farm animals in tow for an annual blessing. Game booths are set up outside the church's gates and groups of dancers entertain the many pilgrims who come for the mass.

Palm Sunday Christ's triumphant entry into Jerusalem on a donkey is re-enacted in the streets of Taxco on the Sunday before Easter.

Maundy Thursday On the Thursday before Easter, the institution of the Eucharist is commemorated with beautiful presentations and street processions of hooded penitents. Some of the penitents, bearing crosses, flagellate themselves with thorns as the procession winds through the streets.

Día de San Miguel Regional dance groups perform in the front court of the beautiful 18th-century chapel of Archangel San Miguel on 29 September.

Día del Jumíl El Día del Jumíl is celebrated on the first Monday after the Day of the Dead (which is on 2 November). See box for details of this unusual festival.

Feria de la Plata The week-long national silver fair is held during the last week in November or the first week in December (check with the tourist office for exact dates). National silverwork competitions are held in various categories (statuary, jewellery etc) and some of Mexico's best silverwork is on display. Other festivities include organ recitals in Santa Prisca, rodeos, burro races, concerts and dances.

Las Posadas From 16 to 24 December, nightly candlelit processions pass through the streets of Taxco singing from door to door, going from one church to another each night, and finally arriving at Santa Prisca on Christmas Eve. Children are dressed up to resemble various Biblical characters, and at the end of the processions they attack piñatas.

Places to Stay – bottom end

The *Casa de Huéspedes Arrellano* (☎ (762) 2-02-15), at Calle los Pajaritos 23, offers 10 simple but clean rooms in a central location, tucked away in a back street across from the Mercado de Artesanías Plata. It's a family-run place with terraces for sitting and a place on the roof for washing clothes. Single rooms cost 30 pesos with shared bath (hot water) or 35 pesos with private bath; doubles are 40 pesos. To find it, walk down the alley on the right (south) side of Santa Prisca until you reach a staircase going down to your right. Follow it down past the stalls and shops until you see a flight of stairs down to your left; walk down these and the Casa de Huéspedes is 30 steps down, on your left as you enter the tiny plaza with the Mercado de Artesanías.

Much easier to find is the *Hotel Casa Grande* (☎ (762) 2-11-08), on the Plazuela de San Juan, through the archway and upstairs. It has 12 clean, basic rooms arranged around an inner courtyard; the rooftop rooms are the most pleasant, with plenty of windows and cross-ventilation, opening onto a large rooftop terrace. On one side is a *lavadero* (laundry) where you can wash clothes. Singles/doubles are 45/60 pesos, bigger rooms 80 and 90 pesos; all have private bath and hot water.

The *Hotel Posada Santa Anita* (☎ (762) 2-07-52), at Avenida Kennedy 106, is a basic place with small, dark but OK rooms at 50 pesos a double with shared bathroom, 40/70 pesos for singles/doubles with private bath. It's nearly a km to the centre of town, but it's close to the 2nd-class bus station and has plenty of parking.

Places to Stay – middle

One of the most attractive places to stay in Taxco at any price is the *Hotel Posada San*

Around Mexico City
Top Left: Puebla window (JL)
Top Right: Children (JL)
Bottom: View from Las Cruces, Popocatépetl (JL)

Around Mexico City
Top: Valley south of Toluca (JL); Puebla policia (JL)
Bottom: Templo de Santa Prisca, Taxco (JL); Catedral, Puebla (PW)

Javier (☎ (762) 2-31-77, 2-02-31), at Calle Ex-Rastro 4, half a block down the hill from the Palacio Municipal. Though it's centrally located, it's quiet and peaceful, with a private parking area and a lovely, large enclosed garden with a big swimming pool. The high-ceilinged rooms are clean, spacious, comfortable and pleasant, and many have private terraces. There's a variety of accommodation and prices, from 66/88/110 pesos for singles/doubles/triples, to 88/110 pesos for a 'junior suite', and several apartments which rent by the month.

The *Hotel Los Arcos* (☎ (762) 2-18-36), Juan Ruíz de Alarcón 2, is near the Plaza Borda and has 26 clean and spacious rooms at 65/90/120 pesos for singles/doubles/triples, all with private bath. In 1620 the building was a monastery, and it retains a pleasant courtyard, sitting areas, a rooftop terrace and a lot of character. Across the road, the *Hotel Posada de los Castillo* (☎ (762) 2-13-96, fax 2-29-35), at Juan Ruíz de Alarcón 3, is another place with colonial charm and similar prices – 65/90/110 pesos.

The *Hotel Meléndez* (☎ (762) 2-00-06), at Cuauhtémoc 6, is an older place, but has many pleasant terrace sitting areas, a nice off-street restaurant and a good location between the Plazuela de San Juan and the Plaza Borda. Singles/doubles are 65/90 pesos.

Right on the zócalo, the *Hotel Agua Escondida* (☎ (762) 2-07-26/36), Calle Spratling 4, has several attractive terraces, a large swimming pool and a basement car park. The comfortable, airy rooms cost 90/135/165 pesos.

On the south side of the Plazuela de San Juan, the colonial-style *Hotel Santa Prisca* (☎ (762) 2-00-80, 2-09-80), Cena Obscuras 1, is an elegant place with a quiet interior patio, a bright, comfortable sitting room with a library of books in English, and a pleasant restaurant where breakfast is served from 7.30 to 9.30 am. Rooms, most with private terraces, are 81/115 pesos, or 93/138 pesos with breakfast.

On the highway near town, the motel-style *Hotel Loma Linda* (☎ (762) 2-02-06, 2-07-53) at Avenida Kennedy 52 is perched on the ledge of a vast and beautiful chasm; each of the rooms has a private terrace with a sweeping vista, and they're far enough back from the highway to be quiet and peaceful. There's a swimming pool with a slide for the kids, and a restaurant. Singles/doubles are 99/127 pesos. It's worth considering whether you've come by car or not; combis pass by on the highway every few minutes to take you up the hill to town.

The four-star *Hotel de la Borda* (☎ (762) 2-00-25), at Cerro del Pedregal 2 opposite the junction of Avenida Kennedy and Calle La Garita, is a 120-room, modern, mission-style hotel with a pool and large, clean standard rooms from 140/150 pesos, suites from 180 pesos. Some rooms offer panoramic views of the city. On the other side of town at Nibbi 5, *Hotel Rancho Taxco-Victoria* (☎ (762) 2-02-10, fax 2-00-10) has a pool, dining room and 64 rooms overlooking the town, from 120 pesos for one or two people.

Places to Stay – top end
The *Posada de la Misión* (☎ (762) 2-00-63, 2-05-33, fax 2-21-98), on the highway at Avenida Kennedy 32, is a luxurious place whose 120 large rooms have private terraces with views of Taxco. Overlooking the large swimming pool is a mosaic mural designed by Juan O'Gorman. A standard single or double is 240 pesos; a junior suite is 300 pesos.

Way up on top of the mountain overlooking Taxco, the five-star *Hotel Monte Taxco* (☎ (762) 2-13-00/1/2, fax 2-14-28) is probably the most luxurious place to stay in Taxco. It can be reached by car, taxi or cable car; the rates of 335 pesos for standard rooms, or 400 pesos for suites, include use of the hotel's tennis courts, gym, steam baths, swimming pool and marvellous view. Horseback riding and golf cost extra. There are also restaurants, bars and a disco.

Places to Eat
The *Restaurant Santa Fe* at Hidalgo 2, a few doors downhill from the Plazuela de San Juan, is the one that locals most often recommend for good food at a good price, and it does

indeed serve delicious food. Main courses are 15 to 20 pesos, good set breakfasts cost 10 to 14 pesos and the comida corrida includes four courses for around 18 pesos.

Overlooking the Plaza Borda, the open-air *Restaurant/Bar Paco* is great for people-watching, and is open every day from noon to 11 pm. One of the house specialities is ensalada Popeye (a spinach salad with mushrooms, bacon and nuts) for 22 pesos; other salads are from 11 pesos, and there's a good selection of soups, meat dishes (25 to 45 pesos) and chicken (23 to 30 pesos). The food and the atmosphere are both very enjoyable.

Señor Costilla's, upstairs in the Patio de las Artesanías overlooking the Plaza Borda, is one of the Carlos Anderson chain and resembles the gringo-style Carlos 'n Charlie's restaurants that have sprouted up all over Mexico, with loud rock'n'roll music and prodigious decorations. A lot of gringos and Mexicans come here to party and the prices, though a bit high by Mexican standards, are not unreasonable. It's open for meals every day from 1 pm to midnight; the bar sometimes stays open later.

In the same building, up the stairs on the left from Señor Costilla's, is the *Pizzería Mario*, a small open-air restaurant with a few tiny tables on a terrace and one of the best views in Taxco. It's worth eating here just to see it, and the pizza, spaghetti and garlic bread are pretty good too.

Bora Bora Pizza has a good address – Delicias 4. It's just off Calle Cuauhtémoc not far from the Plaza Borda, and locals swear it serves the best pizza in Taxco. Prices range from 13 to 25 pesos for a small, up to 27 to 54 pesos for a maxi; they also serve spaghetti, cheese fondue and good desserts, dishing it up every day from 1 pm to midnight.

Restaurant La Hacienda, just off the Plaza Borda, can be reached through the lobby of the Hotel Agua Escondida or through the separate entrance around the corner. Their speciality, *cecina hacienda*, is a large, delicious special Mexican meal of tender beefsteak served with sausage, rice, beans, guacamole, cheese, *chicharrones* (crisp pork rinds) and a *chalupita* (a tiny tostada). They

serve breakfast (10/15/20 pesos), a substantial comida corrida (22 pesos) and dinner until 10 pm.

Opposite the Palacio Municipal, the *Restaurant Los Reyes* at Juárez 9 is a quieter place for a meal, away from the Plaza Borda. It's another upstairs restaurant, with colourful woven tablecloths and some tables out on the terrace; it's open every day from 8 am to 10 pm.

For good coffee, ice cream and atmosphere, try the *Fuente de Sodas Vicky*, upstairs overlooking the north-west corner of the plaza. Also pleasant is the *Café/Bar La Concha Nostra*, with coffee and pizza, and a few tables on tiny terraces overlooking the Plazuela de San Juan. It's open every day until 10 pm or later.

If you want to spend more at one of Taxco's fancier restaurants, try *La Taberna* at Juárez 8, beside the Palacio Municipal. The restaurant at *Hotel Monte Taxco*, on the mountaintop overlooking the city, has correspondingly high prices, but very good food. You might settle for a drink at the bar overlooking the swimming pool and that great view; a refresco is 6 pesos.

Entertainment
For drinks and people-watching over the Plaza Borda, try the terraces of the *Restaurant/Bar Paco*, *Señor Costilla's* or the *Bar Berta* beside Santa Prisca. The Berta, opened by a woman of the same name in the early 1930s, is known for its house drink, also called Berta; another claim to fame is that William Spratling supposedly invented the margarita here.

Taxco has several discotheques, including *Güiri Güiri* on Calle Cuauhtémoc, *Tequilas Dominos* a block uphill from the plaza, and *Windows* at the Hotel Monte Taxco.

Things to Buy
Silver With more than 300 shops selling silverwork, the selection is mind-boggling. Look at some of the best places first, to see what's available, then try to focus on the things you're really interested in, and shop around for those. If you are careful and

willing to bargain a bit, you can buy wonderful pieces at very reasonable prices. Most shops advertise themselves as *menudeo* and *mayoreo* (retail and wholesale) – to get the wholesale price you will have to buy maybe 10 examples of a piece. The shops in and around the Plaza Borda tend to have higher prices than shops further from the centre, but they also tend to have more interesting work. The shops on Avenida Kennedy are often branches of downtown businesses, set up for the tourist buses which can't make it through the narrow streets.

The price of a piece is principally determined by its weight – the creative work serves mainly to make it saleable, though items with exceptional artisanship do command a premium. In mid-1994, the retail price of silverwork in Taxco was around 2.5 pesos per gram, and if a piece cost more than that it was either overpriced or of quite exceptional quality. The wholesale price was 2.1 or 2.2 pesos per gram – around 15% less. (For comparison, the world price for silver bullion was US$15 per troy ounce, or 1.6 pesos per gram.) If you're serious about buying silver, find out the current pesos-per-gram rate when you're in Taxco and weigh any piece before you agree on a price. All the silver shops have scales – mostly electronic devices which should be honest and accurate.

An example of the jewellery to be found in Taxco

If a piece costs less than the going price per gram, it's probably not real silver. Don't buy anything that doesn't have the Mexican government '.925' stamp and spread-eagle hallmark (sometimes only one symbol appears), which certify that the piece is 92.5% pure sterling silver. Anything else might be silver-plated tin or copper or alpaca, a cheap silver-like metal. If a piece is too small or delicate to stamp, a reputable shop will supply a certificate as to its purity. Anyone who is discovered selling forged .925 pieces is sent to prison.

Other Crafts It's easy to overlook them amongst the silver, but there are other things to buy in Taxco. Finely painted wood and papier-mâché trays, platters and boxes are sold on the street, along with bark paintings and wood carvings. Quite a few shops sell semiprecious stones, fossils and mineral crystals, and some have a good selection of masks, puppets and semi-antique carvings.

Getting There & Away

Taxco has two long-distance bus terminals, both on Avenida Kennedy (highway 95). The Flecha Roja terminal (☎ (762) 2-01-31), at Kennedy 104, also serves as the terminal for Cuauhtémoc and some other 2nd-class bus lines. The Estrella de Oro terminal (☎ (762) 2-06-48) is at Kennedy 126, at the south end of town. Combis pass these terminals every few minutes and will take you up the hill to the Plaza Borda for 0.50 pesos (get one marked 'Zócalo'). Book early for buses out of Taxco as it can be hard to get a seat. Long-distance services (1st class unless otherwise stated) include:

Acapulco – 260 km, 4½ to five hours; three daily (40 pesos) by Cuauhtémoc; four daily (1st class 40 pesos, deluxe 47 pesos) by Estrella de Oro
Chilpancingo – 151 km, three hours; four daily (1st class 18 pesos, deluxe 25 pesos) by Estrella de Oro; three daily (22 pesos) by Cuauhtémoc
Cuernavaca – 80 km, 1½ to 2½ hours; hourly directo buses from 6.30 am to 6.30 pm (11 pesos) and more frequent ordinarios (9 pesos) by Flecha Roja; two daily (9 pesos) by Estrella de Oro

Grutas de Cacahuamilpa – 30 km, 45 minutes; take a Toluca bus and get off at the 'Grutas' crossroads, or an hourly combi from in front of the Flecha Roja terminal (5 pesos)

Iguala – 35 km, one hour; every 15 minutes from 5 am to 9 pm (5.50 pesos) by Cuauhtémoc

Ixtapan de la Sal – 68 km, two hours; every half-hour from 6.20 to 5.30 pm (14.50 pesos) by Flecha Roja

Mexico City (Terminal Sur) – 140 km, three hours; 15 per day (22 to 32 pesos) by Flecha Roja; five daily (1st class 22 pesos, deluxe 26 pesos) by Estrella de Oro

Toluca – 145 km, three hours; five daily (27 pesos) by Cuauhtémoc

Getting Around

Apart from walking, combis and taxis are the most popular ways of getting around the steep, winding streets of Taxco.

Combi Combis (white Volkswagen buses) are frequent and cheap (0.50 pesos) and operate from 7 am to 8 pm.

The 'Zócalo' combi departs from Plaza Borda, goes down Cuauhtémoc to the Plazuela de San Juan, then heads down the hill on Hidalgo, turns right at San Miguel, left at the highway (Avenida Kennedy) and follows it northwards until La Garita, where it turns left and goes back to the zócalo. The 'Arcos/Zócalo' combi follows basically the same route except that it continues past La Garita to Los Arcos, where it does a U-turn and heads back to La Garita. Combis marked 'Pedro Martín' (PM) go to the south end of town, past the Estrella de Oro bus station.

For great views, take a 'Guadalupe' combi from Plaza Borda up to the Templo de Guadalupe, or a 'Panorámica' combi from the Plazuela de San Miguel to the top of the mountain overlooking town.

Taxi Taxis are plentiful in Taxco and cost from 4 to 6 pesos for trips around town. You can phone for a taxi (☎ 2-03-01).

AROUND TAXCO
Las Grutas de Cacahuamilpa

The caverns of Cacahuamilpa are a beautiful natural wonder of stalactites, stalagmites and twisted rock formations, with huge chambers up to 82 metres high. The caves, 30 km north-east of Taxco, are protected as a national park and well worth visiting.

You must tour the caves with one of the guides, who lead groups two km along an illuminated walkway. Many of the formations are named for some fanciful resemblance – 'the elephant', 'the champagne bottle', 'Dante's head', 'the tortillas' and so on – and the lighting is used to enhance these resemblances. Much of the guide's commentary focuses on these and can be quite amusing, but the geological information is minimal. When you reach the end of the guided part, you return to the entrance at your own pace, but you can't enjoy it much as most of the cave lights are turned off. The entire tour takes about two hours.

As you leave the caves, a path goes down the steep valley to Río dos Bocas, where two rivers emerge from the caves. The walk down and back takes 30 minutes if you do it slowly, and it's very pretty.

Cave tours depart from the visitors' centre at the entrance every hour on the hour from 10 am to 4 pm; the cost is 15 pesos (12 pesos for children aged five to 12). They *might* be able to arrange an English-speaking tour guide if there is a big group of foreigners. There are restaurants, snacks and souvenir shops etc at the visitors' centre.

Places to Stay If you want to stay near the caves, the *Hotel Las Bugambilias* is about a 10-minute drive away, at Km 2 on the highway from Michapa to Puente de Ixtla. A map at the visitors' centre shows you how to get there.

Getting There & Away From Taxco, hourly combis depart from in front of the Flecha Roja bus terminal and go right to the visitors' centre at the caves (30 km, 45 minutes; 5 pesos). Alternatively, you can take any bus heading for Toluca or Ixtapan de la Sal, get off at the 'Grutas' crossroads and walk one km down the road to the entrance, on your right. From Cuernavaca, Flecha Roja buses make the trip hourly from 6 am to 6 pm (80 km, 2½ hours; 8 pesos). Autos Pullman de

Morelos buses go to the Grutas from Mexico City's Terminal Sur. The last combis leave the site at 5 pm on weekdays, 6 pm on weekends; after this you might be able to catch a bus to Taxco at the crossroads, but don't count on it.

Tehuilotepec

In the village of Tehuilotepec (or simply 'Tehui'), five km north of Taxco on the road to Cuernavaca, is a mining museum, the **Museo de la Minería**, in a historic house built by José de la Borda. The museum is right on the town plaza, where there is also an old colonial church. Take a 'Tehui' combi from in front of the Flecha Roja terminal in Taxco (4 pesos).

Ixcateopan

The village of Ixcateopan, south-west of Taxco, was the birthplace of Cuauhtémoc, the final Aztec emperor, who was defeated and later executed by Cortés. After the emperor's death his remains were returned to his native village; they are entombed in the church on the town plaza. A historical museum, the **Museo de la Mexicanidad**, is also on the plaza. Marble is quarried nearby and, being the most common stone in the area, was often used in construction; Ixcateopan is one of the few towns in the world with marble streets.

Getting There & Away A combi marked 'Ixcateopan' departs Taxco from in front of the Seguro Social where Calle de San Miguel meets the highway, approximately every hour from around 7 am to 5 pm (26 km, one or two hours; 6 pesos).

IGUALA

• pop: 83,400

Iguala is an industrial city on highway 95 about 35 km south of Taxco and 170 km south of Mexico City. The city is of interest for its past rather than its present.

On 24 February 1821, at the height of Mexico's struggle for independence from Spain, Agustín Iturbide, an officer in the Spanish royal army, and Vicente Guerrero,

leader of the rebels, met here and issued the historic Plan de Iguala, an unusual declaration of independence. The declaration was the result of Iturbide's defection from the Spanish crown and offer to make peace with Guerrero.

Iturbide and Guerrero recognised the need for conservative support in Mexico for a new government to succeed. They also wanted to appease liberal factions clamouring for an independent republic. Consequently, rather than berate Spain in the declaration, they stated that Spain was the most magnanimous of nations but, after 300 years as a colony, it was time for Mexico to become a nation in its own right. After some badgering, Spain agreed to the plan, Mexico's first flag was sewn and raised in Iguala and a provisional junta was installed in Mexico City as a prelude to an independent congress.

Iguala's only interesting sight is the block-like **Monumento a la Bandera** (Monument to the Flag) on the main plaza. Built in 1942, it features the sculpted figures of Mexico's independence heroes: Morelos, Guerrero and Hidalgo. Tamarind trees planted around the plaza in 1832 in honour of the Plan de Iguala established tamarind as the city's fruit. Try an *agua de tamarindo* at any of the juice stands near the plaza.

Every year, from 17 to 28 February, Iguala hosts the Feria de la Bandera, a colourful celebration with rodeos, horse racing, a parade and exhibits from local farms and businesses.

West of Mexico City

The main road west of the capital, highway 15, goes to Toluca, which has a pleasant centre, an interesting museum and several art galleries. There are archaeological sites nearby, and some of the surrounding villages are known for various types of handicrafts. The countryside to the east, south and west of Toluca is particularly scenic, with pine forests, rivers and a huge volcano. Valle de Bravo, a lakeside resort 70 km west of Toluca, is a fashionable weekend getaway. The road south towards Taxco (highway 55) passes a number of interesting places, including the spa at Ixtapan de la Sal, 80 km south of Toluca.

TOLUCA
• *pop: 490,000* • *alt: 2680 metres*

Toluca, 67 km west of Mexico City, is 400 metres higher than the capital and the extra altitude is noticeable. The eastern outskirts are a developing industrial area, but the colonial-era city centre has been renovated and has attractive plazas and lively portales. Its cultural attractions include a surprising number of museums and art galleries.

Toluca was an Indian settlement from at least the 13th century; the Spanish founded the city in the 16th century after defeating the Aztecs and Matlazincas who lived in the valley. It became part of the Marquesado del Valle de Oaxaca, Hernán Cortés's personal estates in Mexico. Since 1830 it has been capital of the State of México, which surrounds the Distrito Federal on three sides like an upturned U.

Orientation

Highway 15, the main road from Mexico City, becomes Paseo Tollocan, a dual carriageway, as it approaches Toluca. On reaching the east side of the city proper, Paseo Tollocan bears south-west and becomes a ring road around the south side of the city centre. The bus station and the large Mercado Juárez are two km south-east of the city centre, just off Paseo Tollocan.

The vast, open Plaza de los Mártires, with the Palacio de Gobierno and the cathedral, is the centre of town, but most of the life is in the block to the south which is surrounded by arched colonnades on its east, south and west sides. These portales are lined with shops and restaurants and thronged with people most of the day and the evening. The block itself, and the street to the east, is a pedestrian precinct. The pleasant Parque Alameda is three blocks to the west along Hidalgo.

Information

Tourist Office The Dirección General de Turismo of the State of México (☎ (17) 14-

03-04) is in office E307, upstairs in the Edificio Oriente (East Building) of the Plaza Toluca, on Lerdo de Tejada facing Plaza Garibay. It's in the same building as two cinemas. They can answer some questions and have an excellent map of Toluca and the State of México.

Money You can change money or travellers' cheques at Banamex at Hidalgo Poniente 223 on the corner of Galeana, opposite Portal Madero, and Bancomer at Hidalgo Poniente 100, under Portal Madero. Both have ATMs.

Post & Telecommunications The main post office is on the corner of Hidalgo and de la Cruz, 500 metres east of Portal Madero. There's a phone office at the north end of the underground car park, west of the cathedral. It's open from 7.30 am to 8.45 pm daily for long-distance phone calls and faxes. There are Ladatel phones all around the portales.

City Centre

The 19th-century Portal Madero (Madero Arcade), running 250 metres along Avenida Hidalgo, is lively and bustling, as is the arcade on the pedestrian street to the east. A block north, the big, open expanse of the Plaza de los Mártires may induce agoraphobia, but it's surrounded by fine old government buildings; the 19th-century Catedral and the 18th-century Templo Santa Veracruz are on its south side.

Immediately north-east of the Plaza de los Mártires is the fountained Plaza Garibay, at the east end of which stands the unique Cosmo Vitral Jardín Botanico (Cosmic Glass Botanic Garden). Built in 1909 as a market, and until 1975 the site of the weekly *tianguis* (Indian market), this now houses 3500 sq metres of tranquil and lovely botanic garden, lit since 1980 through 48 colourful stained-glass panels by the Tolucan artist Leopoldo Flores. It's open from 9 am to 5 pm, Tuesday to Sunday, for 5 pesos. On the north side of Plaza Garibay is the 18th-century Templo del Carmen.

AROUND MEXICO CITY

Mercado Juárez & Casart

The Juárez Market, on Isidro Fabela behind the bus station, is open daily. On Friday it becomes a tianguis, and villagers from all around swarm in to buy and sell fruit, flowers, pots, plastic goods and every type of clothing from socks to sombreros. The market is huge, pungent, colourful and chaotic, but it's not a great place to buy local handicrafts. There are baskets, blankets and big earthenware bowls, but mostly they are everyday domestic requirements rather than the finely made decorative objects produced in the surrounding villages.

You can see good-quality local arts and crafts in more peaceful surroundings at Casart (Casa de Artesanía; ☎ 17-51-08), the excellent State of México crafts store on Paseo Tollocan. There's a big range and the quality is often better than you will find in the villages where the crafts are made. Prices are fixed, and considerably higher than you can get with some haggling in the markets,

but you can gauge prices and quality here first. It seems that much of the best work is now being sold to bigger retail outlets rather than in village workshops and markets.

Centro Cultural Mexiquense

The impressive State of México Cultural Centre, eight km west of the city centre, comprises three very good museums and a library. The **Museo de Culturas Populares** has superb examples of the traditional arts and crafts of México state, with some astounding trees of life, very whimsical Day of the Dead figures, textiles and a fine display of charro equipment – saddles, sombreros, swords, pistols, ropes and spurs. The **Museo de Antropología e Historia** has fine displays from prehistoric times to the 20th century, with a good collection of pre-Hispanic artefacts. The **Museo de Arte Moderno** traces the development of Mexican art from the late 19th-century Academia de San

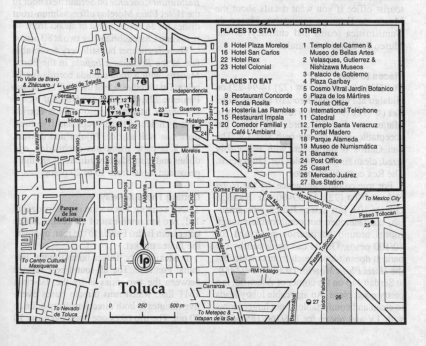

PLACES TO STAY
8 Hotel Plaza Morelos
16 Hotel San Carlos
22 Hotel Rex
23 Hotel Colonial

PLACES TO EAT
9 Restaurant Concorde
13 Fonda Rosita
14 Hostería Las Ramblas
15 Restaurant Impala
20 Comedor Familiar y Café L'Ambiant

OTHER
1 Templo del Carmen & Museo de Bellas Artes
2 Velasques, Gutierrez & Nishizawa Museos
3 Palacio de Gobierno
4 Plaza Garibay
5 Cosmo Vitral Jardín Botanico
6 Plaza de los Mártires
7 Tourist Office
10 International Telephone
11 Catedral
12 Templo Santa Veracruz
17 Portal Madero
18 Parque Alameda
19 Museo de Numismática
21 Banamex
24 Post Office
25 Casart
26 Mercado Juárez
27 Bus Station

Toluca

Carlos to the Nueva Plastica, and includes paintings by Tamayo, Orozco and many more.

The museums are open daily, except Monday, from 10 am to 6 pm. It costs 5 pesos to see one museum or 10 pesos for a ticket to all three, but they're free on Wednesday. Buses marked 'Hipico' or 'Centro Cultural' go there about every 20 minutes from the corner of Independencia and Juárez.

Other Museums

The ex-convent buildings adjacent to the Plaza Garibay house Toluca's **Museo de Bellas Artes**, with paintings from the colonial period to the early 20th century. On Bravo, opposite the Palacio de Gobierno, are three museums devoted to the work of specific artists, from south to north **José María Velasques**, **Felipe Gutierrez** and **Luis Nishizawa**. The latter is an artist of Mexican-Japanese parentage whose work shows influences from both cultures. Ask at the tourist office if you want details about the Museo de Estampa (philately), Museo de Numismática (coins and currency) or the Museo de Ciencias Naturales.

Places to Stay

The *Hotel San Carlos* (☎ (72) 14-94-22) on Hidalgo at Portal Madero 210 and the *Hotel Rex* (☎ (72) 15-93-00), a few metres away at Matamoros Sur 101, are both basic but acceptable, with private bath and TV. The San Carlos is the better, with reasonably sized, clean singles/doubles for 33/60 pesos. The Rex costs 50/60 pesos.

For true colonial ambience, try the *Hotel Colonial* (☎ (72) 15-97-00) at Hidalgo Oriente 103, just east of Juárez, with smallish, old-fashioned but comfortable enough rooms around an interior courtyard for 80/100 pesos. Guests can use a nearby car park. It doesn't look much from outside, but the *Hotel Plaza Morelos* (☎ (72) 15-92-00), at Serdán 115 on the corner of Ascensio, is a pretty good place. An agreeable lobby leads to clean and comfortable, if not huge, rooms with TV and phone for 125/160/185 pesos.

There's car parking, a pleasant stairwell-lounge and a reasonable restaurant too.

Top-end places include the *Del Rey Inn Motel* (☎ (72) 12-21-22) and the *Holiday Inn* (☎ (72) 16-46-66), on the highway to Mexico City, respectively three km and 10 km east of town.

Places to Eat

Orange liqueur *(moscos)*, preserved fruits and chorizo (sausage) are local specialities. In the city centre, one of the best and most atmospheric places is the *Hostería Las Ramblas* at Portal 20 de Noviembre 105 (the pedestrian mall). Antojitos, served only from 6 pm, are around 7 to 9 pesos. Meat courses are mainly 15 to 18 pesos.

The *Fonda Rosita*, in the passage between Portal Madero and the cathedral, has a slightly more cosmopolitan menu – eg avocado salad for 8 pesos, main courses around 23 pesos and a weekend buffet lunch for 35 pesos. The upscale Franco-Mexican *Restaurant Concorde* on Serdán next door to the Hotel Plaza Morelos offers salmon-trout dishes for 38 pesos, a host of steaks from 40 pesos and Chateaubriand for two at 80 pesos.

There is cheaper but still very acceptable fare at the *Restaurant Impala* in the Portal Madero, with a good comida corrida for 16 pesos. On the other side of the road, at Hidalgo Poniente 229, the *Comedor Familial y Café L'Ambiant* has an 11-peso comida corrida with a choice of three soups and five meat dishes as well as rice, frijoles and dessert. The à la carte menu has enchiladas, egg dishes and ensalada de verduras all around 8 pesos and meats from 15 to 20 pesos.

Getting There & Away

Toluca's chaotic bus station is at Berriozábal 101, two km south-east of the centre. Buses enter from Isidro Fabela to the rear, opposite the Juárez market.

In Mexico City, Toluca buses use the Terminal Poniente. The all-round best service between the two cities is by the 1st-class TMT line, which runs directo buses every five minutes in both directions from 6 am to 10 pm. The trip takes one hour and costs 10 pesos. The deluxe buses of ETN make the trip hourly for 15 pesos. Other departures from Toluca include Taxco (44 pesos), Querétaro (27 pesos), Pátzcuaro and:

Cuernavaca – 110 km, three hours; 2nd-class buses (9 pesos) by Lineas Unidas del Sur half-hourly, 5.30 am to 7 pm; buy tickets at the platform

Guadalajara – 500 km, nine hours; one deluxe bus (110 pesos) daily by ETN; two 1st-class buses (79 pesos) daily

Morelia – 250 km, four hours; a few 1st-class buses (26 pesos) daily

Uruapan – 360 km, five hours; a few 1st-class buses (44 pesos) daily

Getting Around

Taxis from the bus station or market to the city centre cost between 10 and 15 pesos. The city bus system is difficult to decipher – ask at your hotel for the bus route to your destination. 'Centro' buses go from outside the bus station to the town centre; 'Terminal' buses go from Juárez (just south of Lerdo de Tejada) in the centre to the bus station. Hertz and Autos San Carlos provide rental cars, which are expensive but may be worthwhile for exploring the surrounding area.

AROUND TOLUCA

Calixtlahuaca

This Aztec site is two km west of highway 55, eight km north of Toluca. It's partly excavated and restored, with some unusual features such as a circular pyramid, which supported a temple to Quetzalcóatl, and the Calmecac, believed to have been a school for the children of priests and nobles. Entry is 13 pesos (free on Sunday); the site is closed on Monday. A bus goes to within 10 minutes' walk of the site.

Metepec

Virtually a suburb of Toluca, seven km to the south on highway 55, Metepec is the centre for producing elaborate and symbolic *arboles de vida* (trees of life) and 'Metepec suns' (earthenware discs brightly painted with sun and moon faces). Unfortunately it is not a centre for selling these wonderful creations. The potters' workshops (*alfare-*

rías) are spread out all over town, and many seem to specialise in large pieces and Disney characters rather than traditional styles. There is only a limited selection of small, well-detailed pieces that a traveller might feasibly carry – prices start around 30 pesos. The triangular building beside the bus stop has a map which may be some help locating the workshops. Frequent 2nd-class buses go from Toluca bus station.

NEVADO DE TOLUCA

The extinct volcano Nevado de Toluca (or Xinantécatl), 4583 metres high, lies across the horizon south of Toluca. A road runs 48 km up to its spectacular crater, with the two lakes, El Sol and La Luna. The earlier you reach the summit, the better the chance of clear views – expect to see clouds after noon. The summit area is *nevado* (snowy) from about November to March, and sometimes OK for cross-country skiing. Buses on highway 134, the Toluca-Tejupilco road, will stop at the turnoff, and on weekends it should be possible to hitch a lift for the 27 km up to the crater. Buses on highway 10 to Sultepec will get you eight km closer to the top. There's an attendant, a boom gate and a café (lunch on weekends) six km by rough road from the crater, or 1.5 km by a very scenic walking track.

Places to Stay & Eat

You can stay at the *Posada Familiar* near the entrance gate (20 pesos) or the *Albergue Ejidal* (15 pesos) 10 km further up. Food is available at both, but only on weekends, and you should bring a sleeping bag.

VALLE DE BRAVO

About 70 km west of Toluca, this was a quiet colonial-era village in the hills until the 1940s when it became a base for construction of a dam and hydroelectric station. The new lake gave the town a waterside location and it was soon a popular weekend and holiday spot for the wealthy. Sailing on the lake is the main activity, while water-skiing, horse riding and hang-gliding are also popular. You can walk and camp in the forested hills around town, which attract monarch butterflies between December and March. The tourist office is due to re-open, probably somewhere near the Casa de Cultura by the lakeside. Until then, you can find a map of the town, and useful information, in one of the free local newspapers.

Places to Stay & Eat
Hotel Mary and *Hotel Blanquita* (☎ (726) 2-00-60) are both on the plaza and cost 60/80 pesos and 40/60 pesos respectively for singles/doubles. The *Hotel ISSEMYM* (☎ (726) 2-00-04) at Independencia 404 is a holiday centre for state government employees, but it accepts other guests and is good value at 63/90 pesos, or 110/220 pesos with three meals. It has parking, a big pool and other recreation facilities. There are a number of nice mid-range hospedajes at around 80 pesos for a room, and luxury places like the tasteful *Hotel Los Arcos* (☎ (726) 2-00-42), at Bocanegra 310, for around 330 pesos per room with breakfast and lunch or dinner. There are lots of restaurants, cafés and food stalls.

Getting There & Away
There are 14 buses a day to Toluca (10 pesos) and Mexico City (19 pesos) from the Valle de Bravo terminal (☎ 2-02-13). Buses from Toluca are de paso, and it might be hard to get a seat. If you're driving between Toluca and Valle de Bravo, the southern route via highway 134 is both quicker and more scenic.

TENANGO DEL VALLE & TEOTENANGO
Tenango, 25 km south of Toluca on highway 55, is overlooked from the west by the large, well-restored hilltop ruins of Teotenango, a Matlazinca ceremonial centre dating from the 9th century. The site, with several pyramids, plazas and a ball court, is quite extensive, with great views. It's open daily except Monday (13 pesos). The road to the site is on the north side of the hill – from Toluca, pass the toll road and turn right into town. Turn right again to find the road. There

is a museum at the final turning up to the hilltop. Buses run from Toluca bus station to Tenango every 10 minutes, and you'll have a 20 to 30-minute walk up to the site.

TENANCINGO
This pleasant colonial town of 50,000, 50 km from Toluca on highway 55, is famous for its brightly coloured rebozos and fruit liqueurs. There's a market on Sunday. You can stay in the budget-priced *Hotel Jardín* on the plaza, and explore the attractions in the surrounding area, including the nearby **El Salto** waterfall, the ex-convent of **Santo Desierto del Carmen**, 12 km south-east in the national park of the same name, and the Malinalco ruins (see below).

MALINALCO
One of the few reasonably well-preserved Aztec temples stands on a hillside above Malinalco, 20 km east of Tenancingo. The site is about one km uphill west of the town centre by a good dirt road.

The Aztecs conquered this area in 1476 and were still building a ritual centre here when they were themselves conquered by the Spanish. The Temple of Eagle & Jaguar Warriors, where sons of Aztec nobles were initiated into the Jaguar and Eagle orders of warriors, survived because it is hewn from the mountainside itself. It is recognisable by its reconstructed thatched roof. Its entrance is carved in the form of a fanged serpent or earth god – you walk over its tongue to enter the temple. The site is open daily except Monday from 10 am to 4.30 pm; admission is 13 pesos.

Getting There & Away
You can reach Malinalco by bus or colectivo pick-up from Tenancingo, by 2nd-class Lineas Unidas del Sur bus from Toluca bus station (every 1½ or two hours) or from Mexico City's Terminal Poniente. By car from Toluca you can turn off highway 55, 12 km south of Tenango, and reach Malinalco via Joquicingo.

CHALMA

One of Mexico's most important shrines is at the small village of Chalma, 12 km east of Malinalco. In 1533 an image of Christ, El Señor de Chalma, 'miraculously' appeared in a cave to replace one of the local gods, Oxtéotl, and proceeded to stamp out dangerous beasts locally and do other wondrous things. The Señor now resides in Chalma's 17th-century church. The biggest of many annual pilgrimages here is for Pentecost (3 May) when thousands of people from Mexico City and elsewhere camp, hold a market and perform traditional dances.

Getting There & Away

Lineas Unidas del Sur has 2nd-class buses from Toluca. There are also four buses a day (morning and early afternoon) from Cuernavaca's Flecha Roja bus station, and a number of companies run 2nd-class buses from Mexico City's Terminal Poniente.

IXTAPAN DE LA SAL

• *pop: 13,260* • *alt: 1925 metres*

The spa town of Balneario Nuevo Ixtapan features a kind of giant curative water fun park, combining thermal water pools with waterfalls, lakes, waterslides, a wave pool and a miniature railway. It's unashamedly a tourist town, where people stroll around in their bathing gear, but it's worth a stop if you want to take the waters or give your kids a fun day. The spa is open from 10 am to 6 pm and costs 25 pesos for adults, 15 pesos for kids. The **Parque Acuatico** (with the waterslides and stuff) operates for slightly shorter hours and costs a few pesos extra on weekends and holidays.

Orientation

Highway 55 is called Boulevard San Román as it makes an arc around the west side of town. Avenida Juárez cuts across the arc from north to south, from balneario to bus station.

Places to Stay & Eat

The cheapest places to stay are the casas de huéspedes on the side streets, with very ordinary rooms at 50/60 pesos. Hotels in the mid-range, like the *Hotel Avenida* (☎ (724) 3-10-39) and the *Hotel Casablanca* (☎ (724) 3-00-36), are down Juárez; these hotels run to about 100/120 pesos for singles/doubles. Most of the top hotels are on San Román near the balneario. The *Hotel Spa Ixtapan* (☎ (724) 3-00-21) is probably the most luxurious, with rooms for 354 pesos a day including meals, or 406 pesos on weekends. Restaurants at the north end of Juárez offer set meals for 20 pesos, but the food gets cheaper as you go south.

Getting There & Away

From the Tres Estrellas de Oro bus station on Juárez there are regular buses to Toluca (10 pesos), Taxco (10 to 14 pesos), Cuernavaca (11 pesos) and Mexico City (15 pesos). For Tenancingo, take a Lineas Unidas del Sur bus from their terminal further up the street. Going north, a toll highway (9 pesos) parallels part of highway 55, by-passing Tenango and Tenancingo. Going south to Taxco, you could give the Grutas (caves) de la Estrella a miss, but the Grutas de Cacahuamilpa are a must (see Around Taxco, in the South of Mexico City section).

Baja California

Baja California's native peoples left memorable murals in caves and on canyon walls, but permanent European settlement failed to reach the world's longest peninsula until the Jesuit missions of the 17th and 18th centuries, which collapsed as Indians fell prey to European diseases.

Mainland ranchers, miners and fishermen settled in the 19th century, when foreigners built port facilities and acquired huge land grants. During US Prohibition, Baja became a popular destination for gamblers, drinkers and other 'sinners' south of the border; it still attracts over 50 million visitors annually for duty-free shopping, sumptuous seafood, and activities like horse riding, diving or snorkelling, windsurfing, clam-digging, whale-watching, fishing, sailing, kayaking, cycling, surfing and hiking.

Though prices in this chapter, as throughout the book, are given in pesos, many places in Baja California quote prices in dollars and expect to be paid in US currency.

La Frontera & the Desierto del Colorado

La Frontera, the northernmost part of the State of Baja California, corresponds roughly to the colonial Dominican mission frontier. Many view its cities and beaches as hedonistic enclaves, but Tijuana and Mexicali are major manufacturing centres, and Mexicali's Río Colorado hinterland is a key agricultural zone. The region attracts many undocumented border crossers, consisting of

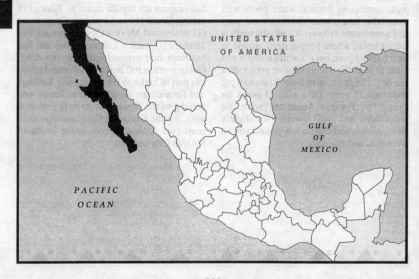

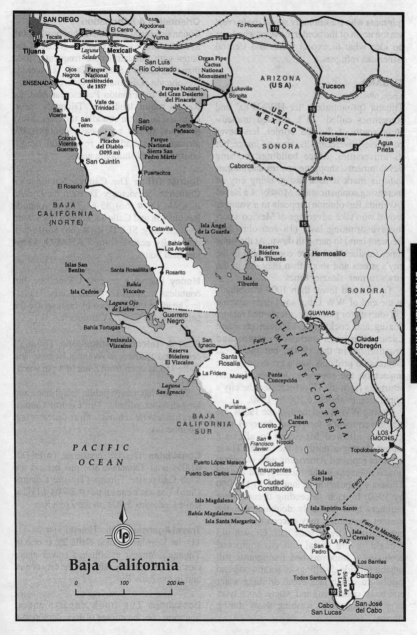

BAJA CALIFORNIA

Baja California

0   100   200 km

migrants who traditionally spend the harvest season north of the border, novices who have no idea what to expect there, and Central American refugees.

TIJUANA

• *pop: 698,752*

Tijuana (pronounced 'tee-HWAH-na' and sometimes called 'TJ'), situated immediately south of the US border, has never completely overcome its 'sin city' image, but its universities, office buildings, housing developments, shopping centres and *maquiladoras* mark it as a fast-growing city of increasing sophistication. Most of 'La Revo' (Avenida Revolución) appeals to a younger crowd who take advantage of Mexico's permissive drinking laws (18-year-olds may frequent bars) to party till dawn. At the same time, families feel more comfortable in the city's streets and shops than they did in the city's former, sleazier times.

Tijuana had fewer than 1000 inhabitants at the end of WW I, but soon drew upscale US tourists for gambling, greyhound racing, boxing and cockfights. Mexican president Lázaro Cárdenas outlawed casinos and prostitution in the 1930s, but the Great Depression probably had a greater negative impact on the economy. Jobless Mexican returnees from the USA increased the city's population to about 16,500 by 1940.

During WW II and through the 1950s, the US government's temporary *bracero* programme allowed Mexicans to alleviate labour shortages north of the border. These workers replaced Americans who were stationed overseas in the military, and caused Tijuana's population to increase to 180,000 by 1960. In each succeeding decade these numbers have probably doubled, and the present population may exceed the official census figure by at least half. Growth has brought severe social and environmental problems – impoverished immigrants still inhabit hillside dwellings of scrapwood and cardboard which lack clean drinking water and trash collection, and where worn tyres keep the soil from washing away during storms.

Orientation & Information

Tijuana's central grid consists of north-south avenidas and east-west calles (most of the latter with numbers more frequently used than their names). South of Calle 1a, Avenida Revolución is the main commercial centre.

East of the Frontón Palacio Jai Alai, La Revo's major landmark, Tijuana's 'new' commercial centre straddles the river; Mesa de Otay, to the north-east, contains the airport, maquiladoras, residential neighbourhoods and shopping areas.

Tourist Office The Cámara Nacional de Comercio, Servicios y Turismo de Tijuana (CANACO; ☎ (66) 85-84-72), at Avenida Revolución and Calle 1a, is open from 9 am to 7 pm daily. SECTUR (☎ (66) 88-05-55), diagonally across from CANACO, keeps identical hours.

Money Everyone accepts US dollars, but countless cambios keep long hours. Travellers heading south or east by bus can use the cambio at the Central Camionera.

Post & Telecommunications Tijuana's central post office, at Avenida Negrete and Calle 11a, is open from 8 am to 4 pm weekdays.

Tijuana has many public telephones and long-distance offices. The Central Camionera has several cabinas with an operator and a public fax.

Consulates The US consulate (☎ 86-00-01/05) is at Tapachula 96, just behind the Club Campestre Tijuana (Tijuana Country Club). Canada's consulate (☎ 84-04-61) is at Calle Gedovius 5-202, in the Zona Río.

Travel Agencies Viajes Honold's (☎ 88-11-11), on Revolución near Calle 2a, is one of Tijuana's longest established travel agencies. There are many others in the city centre and in the Zona Río.

Bookshops The book department at Sanborns, on the corner of Revolución and

Calle 8a, has a large selection of US and Mexican newspapers and magazines.

Librería El Día (☎ 84-09-08), Boulevard Sánchez Taboada 61-A in the Zona Río, specialises in Mexican history and culture, with a small selection in English. In the Plaza Fiesta mall, at Paseo de Los Héroes and Independencia, La Capilla de Frida (☎ 34-14-19) carries new books on Baja (in Spanish) and second-hand items.

Medical Services The Cruz Roja (☎ 132) is at Calle 10a and Avenida Pío Pico. The Hospital General (☎ 84-09-22) is north of the river on Avenida Padre Kino, west of Rodríguez, but many clinics cater to US visitors. Low-priced dentists do fillings, crowns, bridges and dentures, while cut-rate pharmaceutical suppliers and physicians undercut the USA's drug companies, doctors and insurers.

Dangers & Annoyances Coyotes and polleros – human smugglers – and their clients congregate along the river, west of the San Ysidro crossing. After dark, avoid this area and Colonia Libertad, east of the crossing.

La Revo
South of Calle 1a, Avenida Revolución ('La Revo') is Tijuana's tourist heart. Every visitor braves at least a brief stroll up this raucous avenue of futuristic discos, fine restaurants, seedy bars with bellowing hawkers, brash taxi drivers, tacky souvenir shops, and street photographers with zebra-striped burros.

Frontón Palacio Jai Alai
Fast-moving jai alai matches at the Frontón (☎ 85-25-24), on Revolución between Calles 7a and 8a, resemble a hybrid between tennis and handball. Frontón staff explain details to neophyte betters, and the bilingual narration is also helpful. General admission is 6 pesos; it's open most evenings and some afternoons, but closed Wednesday.

Vinícola L A Cetto
The L A Cetto winery (☎ 85-30-31) offers tours and tasting from 10 am to 5.30 pm Tuesday to Sunday, for a modest charge. It's at Cañón Johnson 2108, diagonally southwest of Avenida Constitución.

Centro Cultural Tijuana (CECUT)
Mexico's federal government built this modern cultural centre (☎ 84-11-11), at Paseo de Los Héroes and Avenida Independencia, to reinforce the Mexican identity of its border populations. CECUT houses the **Museo de Las Identidades Mexicanas** (Museum of Mexican Identities), an art gallery, a theatre, and the globular **Cine Planetario** (colloquially known as La Bola – 'The Ball').

Museum admission is 3 pesos; the gallery is free of charge. Hours are 11 am to 8 pm weekdays, to 9 pm weekends.

Tijuana's Cine Planetario ('The Ball')

Places to Stay – bottom end
Hotel del Mar (☎ (66) 85-73-02), on Calle 1a near Revolución, borders a sleazy part of town, but the shared baths are clean, a double costs only 50 pesos, and the English-speaking manager is obliging. The basic *Hotel Tecate* (☎ (66) 85-92-75), at Calle 6a and Constitución, has similar rates.

BAJA CALIFORNIA

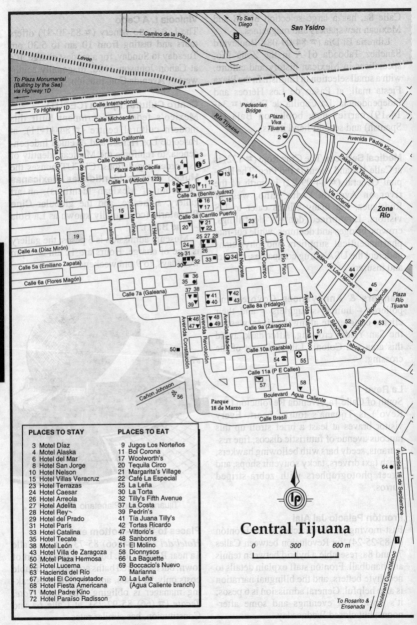

Central Tijuana

0   300   600 m

PLACES TO STAY

3   Motel Díaz
4   Motel Alaska
6   Hotel del Mar
8   Hotel San Jorge
10 Hotel Nelson
15 Hotel Villas Veracruz
23 Hotel Terrazas
24 Hotel Caesar
26 Hotel Arreola
27 Hotel Adelita
28 Hotel Rey
29 Hotel del Prado
31 Hotel París
33 Hotel Catalina
35 Hotel Tecate
38 Motel León
43 Hotel Villa de Zaragoza
50 Hotel Plaza Hermosa
62 Hotel Lucerna
67 Hacienda del Río
67 Hotel El Conquistador
68 Hotel Fiesta Americana
71 Motel Padre Kino
72 Hotel Paraíso Radisson

PLACES TO EAT

9   Jugos Los Norteños
11 Bol Corona
17 Woolworth's
20 Tequila Circo
21 Margarita's Village
22 Café La Especial
25 La Leña
30 La Torta
32 Tilly's Fifth Avenue
37 La Costa
39 Pedrín's
41 Tía Juana Tilly's
42 Tortas Ricardo
47 Vittorio's
48 Sanborns
51 El Molino
58 Dionnysos
66 La Baguette
69 Boccacio's Nuevo Marianna
70 La Leña
     (Agua Caliente branch)

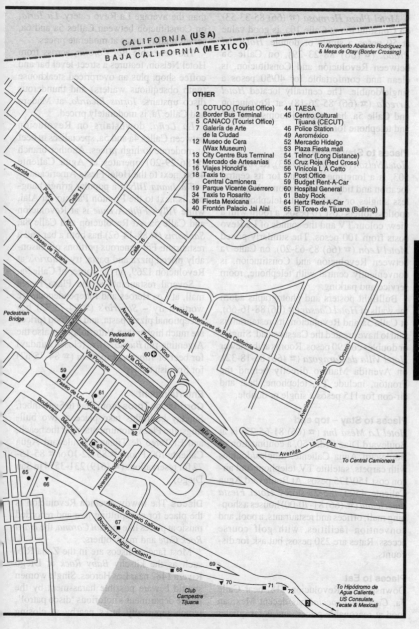

CALIFORNIA (USA)

BAJA CALIFORNIA (MEXICO)

To Aeropuerto Abelardo Rodríguez
& Mesa de Otay (Border Crossing)

OTHER

1	COTUCO (Tourist Office)
2	Border Bus Terminal
5	CANACO (Tourist Office)
7	Galería de Arte de la Ciudad
12	Museo de Cera (Wax Museum)
13	City Centre Bus Terminal
14	Mercado de Artesanías
16	Viajes Honold's
18	Taxis to Central Camionera
19	Parque Vicente Guerrero
34	Taxis to Rosarito
36	Fiesta Mexicana
40	Frontón Palacio Jai Alai
44	TAESA
45	Centro Cultural Tijuana (CECUT)
46	Police Station
49	Aeroméxico
52	Mercado Hidalgo
53	Plaza Fiesta mall
54	Telnor (Long Distance)
55	Cruz Roja (Red Cross)
57	Post Office
56	Vinícola L A Cetto
59	Hospital General
60	Budget Rent-A-Car
61	Baby Rock
64	Hertz Rent-A-Car
65	El Toreo de Tijuana (Bullring)

Avenida Padre Kino

Calle 11

Calle 16

Pedestrian Bridge

Avenida Constitución

Pedestrian Bridge

Avenida Defensores de Baja California

Avenida Padre Kino

Via Poniente

Via Oriente

Avenida Soledad Orozco

Paseo de Los Héroes

Boulevard Sánchez Taboada

Paseo de Tijuana

Río Tijuana

Avenida La Paz

To Central Camionera

Boulevard Agua Caliente

Avenida Gustavo Salinas

Avenida Rodríguez

Club Campestre Tijuana

To Hipódromo de Agua Caliente, US Consulate, Tecate & Mexicali

BAJA CALIFORNIA

Motel Plaza Hermosa (☎ (66) 85-33-53) on Constitución at Calle 10a, is good value at 50 pesos a single or double. *Hotel del Prado* (☎ (66) 88-23-29), on Calle 5a between Revolución and Constitución, is clean and comfortable for 40/50 pesos a single/double. The centrally located *Hotel Arreola* (☎ (66) 85-26-18), at Revolución and Calle 5a, has carpeted rooms with TV and telephone for 60 pesos.

Places to Stay – middle
Hotel Nelson (☎ (66) 85-43-03), Revolución 503, is a longtime favourite for its central location and tidy, carpeted rooms. Windowless singles or doubles with telephone and spotless toilets cost 70 pesos; a room with a view, colour TV and the sounds of La Revo costs from 100 pesos. The similarly priced *Motel León* (☎ (66) 85-63-20), on Calle 7a between Revolución and Constitución, is conveniently central with telephone, room service and parking.

Bullfight posters and photographs adorn the walls of *Hotel Caesar* (☎ (66) 88-16-66), at Calle 5a and Revolución; its restaurant is said to have created the Caesar salad. Singles or doubles cost 90 pesos. Rooms at the newer *Hotel Villa de Zaragoza* (☎ (66) 85-18-32), on Avenida Madero directly behind the Frontón, include TV, telephone, heat and air-con for 115 pesos a single or double.

Places to Stay – top end
Hotel La Mesa Inn (☎ (66) 81-65-22) is at Boulevard Díaz Ordaz 50, a continuation of Boulevard Agua Caliente. Singles/doubles with carpets, satellite TV, telephone and air-con cost 150/175 pesos. At Boulevard Agua Caliente 4500, the 23-storey *Hotel Fiesta Americana* (☎ (66) 81-70-00) houses a shopping mall, offices and restaurants, a pool, and convention facilities, with golf course access. Rates are 230 pesos, but ask for discounts.

Places to Eat
Downstairs at Revolución 718, near Calle 3a, *Café La Especial* has decent Mexican food at reasonable prices, and is far quieter

than the average La Revo eatery. *La Torta*, on Constitución between Calles 5a and 6a, serves quality tortas at moderate prices.

The venerable *Bol Corona*, across from Hotel Nelson, features a street-level bar and coffee shop, plus an overpriced steakhouse (with obsequious waiters) and thunderous disco upstairs. *Tortas Ricardo*, at Madero and Calle 7a, is moderately priced.

La Leña, downstairs on Revolución between Calles 4a and 5a, specialises in beef at moderate to high prices. Another branch (☎ 86-29-20) operates at Agua Caliente 4560, next to the Hotel Fiesta Americana.

Tía Juana Tilly's, a popular gringo hangout, is next to the Frontón Palacio Jai Alai, while *Tilly's Fifth Avenue* is at Revolución and Calle 5a. At Revolución and Calle 8a, *Sanborns* (☎ 88-14-62) has both a bar and a restaurant. For generous portions of reasonably priced pizza and pasta, try *Vittorio's* at Revolución 1269, on the corner of Calle 9a.

Several restaurants at the Plaza Fiesta mall, at Los Héroes and Independencia, are worth a try – *Saverio's* (☎ 84-73-72) has exceptional pizza, pasta, and seafood (prices are much higher than Vittorio's). Try also the Argentine-run *Buenos Aires* (closed Sunday) for beef or *Taberna Española* (☎ 84-75-62) for Spanish tapas.

Entertainment
Corridas de Toros From May to September, Sunday bullfights take place at two bullrings: the Plaza Monumental near the beach, and El Toreo de Tijuana, Boulevard Agua Caliente 100. Phone ☎ 85-22-10 or ☎ 85-15-72 for reservations (☎ (619) 231-3554 in San Diego).

Discos The rowdy Avenida Revolución is the place for ear-splitting live and recorded music at places like the *Bol Corona*, the *Hard Rock Café* and many others.

Most fancier discos are in the Zona Río, such as the kitschy *Baby Rock* at Diego Rivera 1482 near Los Heroes. Single women should beware possible harassment by the police department's notorious 'disco patrol', which reportedly lurks nearby at closing time; for the unsavoury details, see Luis Alberto Urrea's *Across the Wire* (New York, Anchor Books, 1993).

Jazz *Jazz Alley* (☎ 81-87-30) is at Agua Caliente 3401, Colonia Chapultepec. Doors open at 8 pm on Wednesday, Friday and Saturday; there is no cover charge.

Things to Buy
Jewellery, wrought-iron furniture, baskets, silver, blown glass, pottery and leather goods are available on Revolución and Constitución, at the municipal market on Niños Héroes between Calles 1a and 2a, and at the sprawling Mercado de Artesanías at Calle 1a and Ocampo. Auto body and upholstery shops along Ocampo offer real bargains.

Getting There & Away
Air Aeroméxico (☎ 85-15-30; ☎ 83-27-00 at the airport), on Revolución between Calles 8a and 9a, flies to Mexico City, Cancún and intermediate points, as well as Los Angeles. Mexicana (☎ 82-41-83 at the airport) has similar routes within Mexico. TAESA (☎ 84-84-83, 83-55-93 at the airport), at Los Héroes 9288, serves mostly Mexican destinations, but has five Chicago flights weekly.

Aero California (☎ 84-21-00), in the Plaza Río Tijuana at Los Héroes and Independencia, flies to Mexico City and intermediate destinations. AirLA (☎ 800-010-0413 in Mexico; ☎ 800-933-5952 in the USA, both toll-free) provides frequent service to Los Angeles; its office is at the airport.

Bus Only ABC (local buses, ☎ 86-90-10) and the US-based Greyhound use the handy but dilapidated downtown terminal, at Avenida Madero and Calle 1a. From the Plaza Viva Tijuana, near the border, ABC and Autotransportes Aragón go to Ensenada.

Both ABC (☎ 86-90-10) and Greyhound also use the Central Camionera (☎ 26-17-01), about five km south-east of downtown. From Calle 2a, east of Constitución, take any 'Buena Vista', 'Centro' or 'Central Camionera' bus, or a quicker and more convenient

gold-and-white cab (Mesa de Otay) from Avenida Madero between Calles 2a and 3a for 1.50 pesos.

To/From the USA Buses from San Diego (US$4) and San Ysidro depart almost hourly between about 5.30 am and 12.30 am; there are two or three Chula Vista departures daily. Greyhound starts from the Central Camionera and also has connections to Los Angeles (US$18). Mexicoach (☎ (619) 232-5049 in San Diego; ☎ 85-69-13 in Tijuana) has seven daily buses between San Diego's Amtrak station and the Frontón Palacio Jai Alai.

To/From Elsewhere in Mexico Tres Estrellas de Oro's Servicio Elite offers 1st-class buses with air-con and toilets to mainland Mexico. Autotransportes del Pacífico, Norte de Sonora and ABC operate mostly 2nd-class buses to mainland Mexico's Pacific coast and around Baja California. ABC's Servicio Plus resembles Tres Estrellas' Servicio Elite.

Frequent buses leave downtown for Ensenada (15 pesos), Rosarito (3 pesos; try also route taxis from Madero between Calles 5a and 6a), and Tecate (5 pesos).

From the Central Camionera (☎ 21-29-82), there are services to Ensenada, Tecate, Mexicali (four hours, 23 pesos), San Felipe (six hours, 50 pesos), Bahía de Los Angeles (8½ hours, 80 pesos, Saturday only), and La Paz (24 hours, 170 pesos). Tres Estrellas' express buses to Guadalajara/Mexico City (235/305 pesos) take 36 and 46 hours respectively. Transportes del Pacífico and Norte de Sonora are cheaper but less comfortable. All lines stop at major mainland destinations.

From Plaza Viva Tijuana, near the border, Autotransportes Aragón and ABC (☎ 83-56-81) offer inexpensive Ensenada buses. Aragón leaves hourly between 8 am and 9 pm for 15/22 pesos one way/return.

Trolley San Diego's popular light-rail trolley (☎ (619) 233-3004) runs from downtown to San Ysidro every 15 minutes from about 5 am to midnight, for about US$1.50. From

San Diego's Lindbergh Field airport, city bus No 2 goes directly to the Plaza America trolley stop, across from the Amtrak depot.

Car San Diego is cheaper, but try Central Rent de Mexicali (☎ 84-22-57), Los Héroes 104, Zona Río.

Border Crossings The San Ysidro crossing, a 10-minute walk from downtown, is open 24 hours, but Mesa de Otay (open from 6 am to 10 pm) is much less congested.

Getting Around

To/From the Airport Sharing can reduce the cost of a taxi (about 30 pesos if hailed on the street) to the busy Aeropuerto Internacional Abelardo L Rodríguez (☎ 83-20-21) on Mesa de Otay, east of downtown. Alternatively, take any 'Aeropuerto' bus from the street just past the border taxi stand, for about 1.30 pesos; from downtown, catch it on Calle 5a between Constitución and Los Héroes.

Bus & Taxi For about 1.30 pesos, local buses go everywhere, but slightly dearer route taxis are much quicker. From Avenida Madero and Calle 3a, gold-and-white station wagons (Mesa de Otay) go frequently to the Central Camionera. Tijuana taxis lack meters, but most rides cost about 6 to 15 pesos. However, beware of the occasional unscrupulous taxi driver - one traveller told us he'd been quoted $US22 to get from the Central Camionera to the city centre.

AROUND TIJUANA

Rosarito

• *pop: 40,000*

South of Tijuana, the valley of Rosarito marks the original boundary between Alta and Baja California. The town (21 km from Tijuana) dates from 1885, but the Hotel Rosarito (now the landmark Rosarito Beach Hotel) and its long, sandy beach pioneered local tourism in the late 1920s. Its main street, the noisy commercial strip of Boulevard Benito Juárez (a segment of the Transpeninsular highway 1), has many good restaurants.

The amphitheatre at the beachfront **Parque Municipal Abelardo L Rodríguez** contains Juan Zuñiga Padilla's impressive 1987 mural 'Tierra y Libertad' (Land and Liberty).

Tecate

• *pop: 40,000*

About 55 km east of Tijuana by highway 2, the east-west route linking Tijuana and Mexicali, Tecate resembles a mainland Mexican village more than a border town, but hosts several popular tourist events, like biathlons and bicycle races. Its landmark brewery, open for tours by reservation only, produces two of Mexico's best known beers, Tecate and Carta Blanca, but maquiladoras drive the local economy. The border crossing is less crowded than either Tijuana or Mesa de Otay.

ENSENADA

• *pop: 170,000*

Ensenada is a major fishing and commercial port, 110 km south of Tijuana. Ensenada de Todos los Santos occasionally sheltered Acapulco-bound galleons returning from Manila, but the first permanent settlement was established in 1804. The discovery of gold in 1870 at Real del Castillo, 35 km inland, brought a short-lived boom. Ensenada was capital of Baja territory from 1882 to 1915, but the capital shifted to Mexicali during the revolution. After the revolution the city catered to 'sin' industries until the federal government outlawed gambling in the 1930s.

Ageing Americans stroll the streets with shopping lists of pharmaceuticals, but the state's third-largest city is also its biggest party town. Outdoor activities like fishing and surfing are popular, and it's the centre of Baja's wine industry. US visitors sometimes make Ensenada a reluctant host for spontaneous Fourth of July celebrations, when guests from the north should avoid offensive behavior.

Orientation

Hotels and restaurants line the waterfront Boulevard Costero, also known as Boulevard Lázaro Cárdenas. Avenida López Mateos (Calle 1a) parallels Boulevard Costero for a short distance, one block inland (north), beyond which is the 'party district' – Avenidas Gastelum and Ruiz.

North of town, highway 3 heads northeast to Tecate; at the south end of town, it leads east towards Ojos Negros and Laguna Hanson, before continuing south to the Valle de Trinidad and San Felipe.

Information

Tourist Office Ensenada's Comité de Turismo y Convenciones (COTUCO, ☎ (617) 8-24-11), at Costero and Gastelum, carries maps, brochures and current hotel information. Hours are from 9 am to 7 pm Monday to Saturday, 9 am to 2 pm Sunday.

SECTUR (☎ (617) 2-30-22) has moved to Boulevard Costero 1477, near Calle Las Rocas. Hours are from 9 am to 7 pm weekdays, 10 am to 3 pm Saturday and 10 am to 2 pm Sunday.

Money Most banks and cambios are on Avenidas Ruiz and Juárez; only banks provide cash advances. Servicio La Comercial, on Uribe just north of Gastelum, charges 1.5% for cashing travellers' cheques.

Post & Telecommunications The main post office, at López Mateos and Riviera, is open on weekdays from 8 am to 7 pm, weekends 9 am to 1 pm.

Public telephones are widespread, but the bus terminal's Computel Ensenada office allows calls to be paid for by credit card.

Immigration At Azueta 100, near Boulevard Costero, Servicios Migratorios (☎ 4-10-64) are open daily from 8 am to 8 pm.

Wineries

Bodegas de Santo Tomás (☎ 8-33-33), Miramar 666, holds tours and tastings at 11 am, and 1 and 3 pm daily for 6 pesos. Cavas Valmar (☎ 8-64-05), at the north end of Avenida Miramar, offers free tours and tastings by appointment.

Centro Social, Cívico y Cultural de Ensenada (Riviera del Pacífico)

Opened in the early 1930s as Hotel Playa Ensenada, this extravagant Spanish-style former casino on Boulevard Costero features an impressive three-dimensional mural of the Californias, emphasising mission sites. Now a cultural centre, it offers retrospective film cycles, art exhibitions, a museum (recently under renovation), and the atmospheric Bar Andaluz.

Museo (ex-Aduana Marítima de Ensenada)

Built by the US-owned International Company of Mexico, Ensenada's oldest public building (1886) and new historical-cultural museum passed to the British-owned Mexican Land & Colonization Company before Mexican customs acquired it in 1922. At Avenida Ryerson 1, it's open Tuesday to Sunday from 10 am to 5 pm. Admission is free.

Whale-Watching

From December to March, the Museo de Ciencias de Ensenada (☎ 8-71-92), Obregón 1463, arranges offshore whale-watching cruises.

Language Courses

The Colegio de Idiomas de Ensenada (☎ 6-01-09, 6-65-87), Boulevard J A Rodríguez 377, offers intensive Spanish instruction, as does the Center of Languages & Latin American Studies (☎ 7-18-40), Riveroll 1287.

Festivals

The festivals listed below are a tiny sample of the 70-plus sporting, tourist and cultural events that take place each year. Dates change, so contact tourist offices for details.

Carnaval Mardi Gras; mid-February
Fiesta de la Vendimia Wine harvest; mid-August
Fiestas Patrias Mexican independence days; mid-September
Desfile Navideño Club Amigos de Ensenada Christmas parade; mid-December

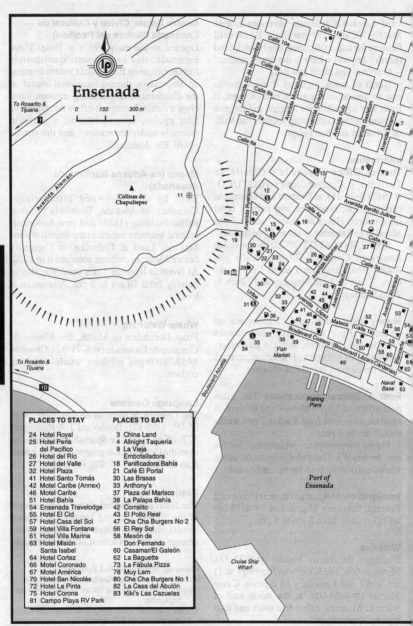

Ensenada

0   150   300 m

To Rosarito & Tijuana

Colinas de Chapultepec

Fishing Piers

Fish Market

Port of Ensenada

Cruise Ship Wharf

Naval Base

To Rosarito & Tijuana

PLACES TO STAY

24 Hotel Royal
25 Hotel Perla del Pacífico
26 Hotel del Río
27 Hotel del Valle
32 Hotel Plaza
41 Hotel Santo Tomás
42 Motel Caribe (Annex)
46 Motel Caribe
51 Hotel Bahía
54 Ensenada Travelodge
55 Hotel El Cid
57 Hotel Casa del Sol
59 Hotel Villa Fontana
61 Hotel Villa Marina
63 Hotel Misión Santa Isabel
64 Hotel Cortez
66 Motel Coronado
67 Motel América
70 Hotel San Nicolás
72 Hotel La Pinta
75 Hotel Corona
81 Campo Playa RV Park

PLACES TO EAT

3   China Land
4   Allnight Taquería
9   La Vieja Embotelladora
18 Panificadora Bahía
21 Café El Portal
30 Las Brasas
33 Anthony's
37 Plaza del Marisco
38 La Palapa Bahía
42 Corralito
43 El Pollo Real
47 Cha Cha Burgers No 2
56 El Rey Sol
58 Mesón de Don Fernando
60 Casamar/El Galeón
62 La Baguette
73 La Fábula Pizza
78 Muy Lam
80 Cha Cha Burgers No 1
82 La Casa del Abulón
83 Kiki's Las Cazuelas

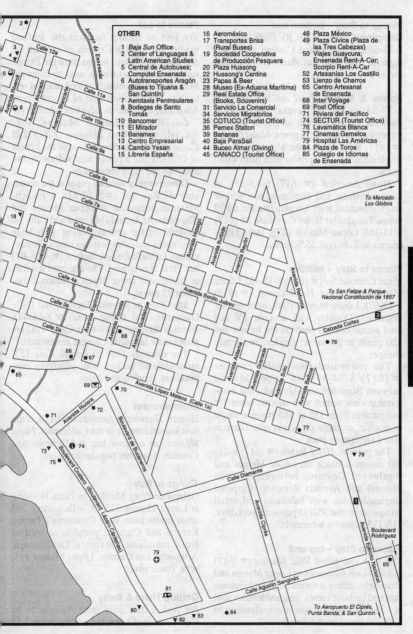

OTHER

1 *Baja Sun* Office
2 Center of Languages & Latin American Studies
5 Central de Autobuses; Computel Ensenada
6 Autotransportes Aragón (Buses to Tijuana & San Quintín)
7 Aerotaxis Peninsulares
8 Bodegas de Santo Tomás
10 Bancomer
11 El Mirador
12 Banamex
13 Centro Empresarial
14 Cambio Yesan
15 Librería España
16 Aeroméxico
17 Transportes Brisa (Rural Buses)
19 Sociedad Cooperativa de Producción Pesquera
20 Plaza Hussong
22 Hussong's Cantina
23 Papas & Beer
28 Museo (Ex-Aduana Marítima)
29 Real Estate Office (Books, Souvenirs)
31 Servicio La Comercial
34 Servicios Migratorios
35 COTUCO (Tourist Office)
36 Pemex Station
39 Bananas
40 Baja ParaSail
44 Buceo Almar (Diving)
45 CANACO (Tourist Office)
48 Plaza México
49 Plaza Cívica (Plaza de las Tres Cabezas)
50 Viajes Guaycura; Ensenada Rent-A-Car; Scorpio Rent-A-Car
52 Artesanías Los Castillo
53 Lienzo de Charros
65 Centro Artesanal de Ensenada
68 Inter Voyage
69 Post Office
71 Riviera del Pacífico
74 SECTUR (Tourist Office)
76 Lavamática Blanca
77 Cinemas Gemelos
79 Hospital Las Américas
84 Plaza de Toros
85 Colegio de Idiomas de Ensenada

To Mercado Los Globos

To San Felipe & Parque Nacional Constitución de 1857

To Aeropuerto El Ciprés, Punta Banda, & San Quintín

BAJA CALIFORNIA

Places to Stay – bottom end

Camping *Campo Playa RV Park* (☎ (617) 8-37-68), at Boulevard Costero and Calle Agustín Sanginés, has shady RV/tent sites for 30 pesos.

Hotels & Motels *Hotel del Río* (☎ (617) 8-37-33) is one of several cheapies on Avenida Miramar north of López Mateos; rooms cost as little as 25 pesos. *Motel Caribe* (☎ (617) 8-34-81), López Mateos 628, has singles/doubles with private bath from 45/60 pesos.

Motel América (☎ (617) 6-13-33), at López Mateos and Espinosa, has simple singles/doubles with kitchenettes for 60/90 pesos. The similar *Motel Coronado* (☎ (617) 6-14-16), López Mateos 1275, lacks kitchenettes and charges 55/60 pesos.

Places to Stay – middle

Hotel Casa del Sol (☎ (617) 8-15-70), López Mateos 1001, and *Hotel Cortez* (☎ (617) 8-23-07), López Mateos 1089, offer similar amenities. Doubles with air-con, TV and pool access cost 95 pesos at the former and 120 pesos at the latter; singles are slightly cheaper.

The renovated *Hotel Villa Fontana* (☎ (617) 8-34-34), on López Mateos between Blancarte and Alvarado, has comfortable view rooms with air-con, cable TV and jacuzzi from 135 to 165 pesos a single or double, or more on weekends. There is also a swimming pool.

The popular *Hotel Bahía* (☎ (617) 8-21-03) covers a block on López Mateos and Boulevard Costero, between Avenida Riveroll and Avenida Alvarado. Carpeted singles/doubles with balconies and small refrigerators cost 95/135 pesos on weekdays, 115/135 pesos on weekends.

Places to Stay – top end

The high-rise *Hotel Villa Marina* (☎ (617) 8-33-21), on the corner of López Mateos and Blancarte, offers a swimming pool, restaurant and harbour views. Singles/doubles start at 135/165 pesos on weekdays, climbing to 230/265 pesos on weekends.

Places to Eat

Try fish or shrimp tacos at the seafood market just south of Costero, or at *Plaza del Marisco*, on Costero across from the Pemex station. *La Palapa Bahía*, next to Plaza del Marisco, is a moderately priced seafood restaurant. On the north side of Costero, near Alvarado, *Casamar* is a costlier alternative.

Las Brasas, López Mateos 486, specialises in roast chicken. *Kiki's Las Cazuelas*, at Calle Sanginés near the corner of Costero, has a pricey seafood menu, but antojitos are more reasonable.

Dinners run around 60 pesos at the venerable *El Rey Sol* (☎ 8-17-33), a French-Mexican institution at López Mateos and Blancarte. At Avenida Miramar and Calle 7a, modernised for upscale dining with huge wine casks and other features intact, the cavernous *La Vieja Embotelladora* (☎ 4-08-07) has great atmosphere. The cheapest lunches or dinners cost about 30 pesos, lobster dishes about 75 pesos.

Muy Lam, at Avenida Ejército and Calle Diamante, and *China Land* (☎ 8-66-44), Avenida Riveroll 1149 near Calle 11a, are Ensenada's favourite Chinese restaurants.

The sidewalk *Café El Portal*, Ruiz 153, lures caffeine junkies with satisfying cappuccinos, mochas and lattes.

Entertainment

Historic *Hussong's*, Avenida Ruiz 113, is the best known cantina in the Californias. *Plaza México*, an outdoor bar at Macheros and Costero, is another popular hang-out.

Things to Buy

Galería de Pérez Meillon, in Plaza Hussong at López Mateos 335-13, sells pottery and other crafts from Baja California's Paipai, Kumiai and Cucapah peoples, as well as from mainland Mexico's Tarahumara. Artesanías Los Castillo, López Mateos 815, sells Taxco silver.

Getting There & Away

Air AirLA flies daily from Aeropuerto El Ciprés, south of town, to Los Angeles at 5.45

pm (US$85 one way); purchase tickets from downtown travel agencies.

Book at least a week in advance at El Ciprés (☎ (617) 6-60-76) for flights run by the Sociedad de Producción Pesquera to Isla Cedros, near the border of Baja California Sur. Flights (285 pesos one way) leave Wednesday and Saturday at 9 am; cheaper, more frequent flights leave from Guerrero Negro (see the Desierto Central section later in this chapter).

Bus Ensenada's Central de Autobuses (☎ 8-65-50) is at Avenida Riveroll 1075. Tres Estrellas de Oro (☎ 8-67-70) and Norte de Sonora (☎ 8-66-77) serve mainland Mexican destinations as far as Guadalajara (245 pesos) and Mexico City (315 pesos). Norte de Sonora's 2nd-class fares are about 15% cheaper.

ABC (☎ 8-66-80) serves La Paz (23 hours, 150 pesos), Mexicali (3½ hours, 30 pesos), San Felipe (five hours, 30 pesos), Tecate (1½ hours, 12 pesos) and Tijuana (1½ hours, 15 pesos). Autotransportes Aragón (☎ 4-04-86), Riveroll 861, goes hourly to Tijuana (22 pesos round trip).

AROUND ENSENADA
Guadalupe
North of Ensenada on highway 3, some Dominican mission ruins remain at the village of Guadalupe. Turn-of-the-century Russian immigrants settled here; their history is now documented by the **Museo Comunitario de Guadalupe**. The **Fiesta de la Vendimia** (wine-harvest festival) takes place in August; the Domecq and Cetto wineries are open for tours.

PARQUE NACIONAL CONSTITUCIÓN DE 1857
From Ojos Negros, east of Ensenada at Km 39 on highway 3, a 43-km dirt road climbs to the Sierra de Juárez and Parque Nacional Constitución de 1857, whose highlight is the marshy, pine-sheltered **Laguna Hanson**. At 1200 metres, the lake abounds with migratory birds in autumn, as well as catfish, bluegill and large-mouth bass.

Camping is pleasant, but livestock have contaminated the water. Firewood is scarce along the lake, but abundant in the hills. Only pit toilets are available. Nearby granite outcrops offer stupendous views but tiring ascents through dense brush and massive rockfalls – beware of ticks and rattlesnakes. Technical climbers will find short but challenging routes.

The park is also accessible by a steeper road east of Km 55, 16 km south-east of Ojos Negros junction. There's no public transport, but many ranchers have pick-up trucks.

PARQUE NACIONAL SIERRA SAN PEDRO MÁRTIR
In the Sierra San Pedro Mártir, east of San Telmo and west of San Felipe, Baja's most notable national park comprises 630 sq km of coniferous forests and granite peaks exceeding 3000 metres, plus deep canyons cutting into its steep eastern scarp; the elusive desert bighorn sheep inhabits some remote areas. Snow falls in winter, but the area also gets summer thunderstorms.

Camping areas and hiking trails are numerous, but maintenance is limited; carry a compass and a topographic map along with cold and wet-weather supplies, canteens and water purification tablets. Below about 1800 metres, beware of rattlesnakes.

The **Observatorio Astronómico Nacional**, Mexico's national observatory, is two km from the parking area at the end of the San Telmo road. It's open on Saturday only, from 11 am to 1 pm.

Picacho del Diablo
Few climbers who attempt Picacho del Diablo, the highest point on the peninsula, reach the 3095-metre summit because finding routes is so difficult. The 2nd edition of Walt Peterson's *The Baja Adventure Book* (Wilderness Press, 1992) includes a good map and describes possible routes. Even better is *Parque Nacional San Pedro Mártir*, a detailed topographic map from Centra Publications, 4705 Laurel St, San Diego, CA 92105, USA.

BAJA CALIFORNIA

Places to Stay

The *San José Meling Ranch*, 44 km south-east of San Telmo, is a Baja institution offering accommodation, meals, horse riding and back-country trips. For the latest information, write or phone Meling Hunting Service (☎ (617) 6-98-85) at Apartado Postal 1326, Ensenada, or c/o Dal Potter, PO Box 189003, No 73, Coronado, CA 92178, USA.

Getting There & Away

From San Telmo de Abajo, south of Km 140 on the Transpeninsular (highway 1), a graded dirt road climbs through San Telmo past Rancho Meling (Rancho San José) to the park entrance, about 80 km east. The road is passable to most passenger vehicles, but snowmelt can raise the river to hazardous levels.

MEXICALI
• *pop: 800,000*

European settlement came late to the Río Colorado lowlands, but the Mexicali area grew rapidly in the 20th century as irrigation made it possible for farmers to take advantage of a long and productive growing season. Many visitors pass through the state capital en route to San Felipe or mainland Mexico. The city does not pander to tourists, but a new Centro Cívico-Comercial (Civic & Commercial Centre) features local, state and federal government offices, a medical school, a bullring, cinemas, a bus station, hospitals and restaurants. Mexicali is also the north-western terminus of Mexico's passenger rail system.

Orientation

Mexicali is on the east bank of the Río Nuevo, opposite Calexico, California. Most of the city's main streets parallel the border. Avenida Francisco Madero passes through the central business district of modest restaurants and shops, bars and bottom-end hotels, while the broad diagonal Calzada López Mateos heads south-east through newer industrial and commercial areas before dividing into highway 5 (to San Felipe) and highway 2 (to Sonora).

Information

Tourist Offices The Comité de Turismo y Convenciones (COTUCO; ☎ (65) 57-23-76) is at Calzada López Mateos and Calle Camelias, about three km south-east of the border. Hours are from 8 am to 7 pm weekdays.

In the Plaza Baja California mall on Avenida Calafia, opposite the Plaza de Toros, SECTUR (☎ (65) 56-10-72) is open on weekdays from 8 am to 7 pm, Saturday 9 am to 3 pm, Sunday 9 am to 1 pm.

Money Cambios are abundant, while banks offer exchange services on weekday mornings only. Several banks in Mexicali and Calexico have 24-hour ATMs.

Post & Telecommunications The post office is on Avenida Madero near Calle Morelos. Telephone cabinas are common in pharmacies and similar businesses, but most public telephones work.

Bookshops Librería Universitaria, across from the Universidad Autónoma on Calzada Benito Juárez, has a good selection on Mexican history, archaeology, anthropology and literature. It also carries the Guías Urbanas series of Mexican city maps.

Medical Services The Hospital Civil (☎ 57-37-00) is at Calle del Hospital and Avenida de la Libertad, near the Centro Cívico. Near the border are many clinics, laboratories and hospitals. Locally trained dentists offer quality work at bargain prices.

La Chinesca

Mexicali's Chinatown, the country's largest, is concentrated along an axis formed by Avenida Juárez and Calle Altamirano, south of Calzada López Mateos.

Historic Buildings

The **Catedral de la Virgen de Guadalupe**, at Avenida Reforma and Calle Morelos, is Mexicali's major religious landmark.

Now the rectory of the Universidad Autónoma, the former **Palacio de Gobierno** (Government Palace, built between 1919 and 1922) interrupts Avenida Obregón just east of Calle E. To the north, at Avenida Reforma and Calle F, the ex-headquarters of the **Colorado River Land Company** dates from 1924.

At Avenida Zaragoza and Calle E, two blocks south-west of the rectory, the former brewery, **Cervecería Mexicali** (opened in 1923) now sits vacant.

Museo Regional de la Universidad Autónoma de Baja California

This modest eight-room museum (☎ 52-57-15), at Avenida Reforma and Calle L, features exhibits on geology, paleontology, human evolution, colonial history and photography. It's open from 9 am to 6 pm Tuesday to Friday, 10 am to 4 pm Saturday.

Teatro del Estado

On the east side of López Mateos, just north of Avenida Tapiceros, the ultramodern state theatre (☎ 52-92-29) seats 1100 spectators. The Instituto de Cultura de Baja California (☎ 54-64-18) presents film cycles at the Teatro's Café Literario.

Festivals & Events

From mid-October to early November, the Fiesta del Sol (Festival of the Sun) commemorates the city's founding in 1903. Events include concerts, art exhibits, a crafts exposition, theatrical performances and parades. It also features local industrial and agricultural products.

In 1993, the legendary Baja 1000 off-road race relocated from Ensenada to a course south of Mexicali. It is held annually in November.

Places to Stay – bottom end

Central Mexicali's best bargain is the family-oriented *Hotel México* (☎ (65) 54-06-09), Lerdo de Tejada 476 between Altamirano and Morelos, with singles from 30 pesos. Amenities like air-con, TV, private bath and parking are dearer. The respectable *Hotel*

Plaza (☎ (65) 52-97-57), Madero 366, charges a reasonable 50/60 pesos a single/double. Near the train station, *Motel Las Fuentes* (☎ (65) 57-15-25), López Mateos 1655, has singles/doubles with TV for 60/80 pesos on weekdays, 70/95 pesos on weekends.

Places to Stay – middle

The greatly improved *Hotel Casa Grande* (☎ (65) 53-66-51), Cristóbal Colón 612, now has air-con and TV for 100/120 pesos a single/double. It also has a swimming pool. Convenient to the border at Calle Melgar 205, the landmark *Hotel del Norte* (☎ (65) 52-81-01) has 52 rooms, some with colour TV and air-con, for 120/135 pesos with breakfast.

Across the border in Calexico, the noteworthy *De Anza Hotel* (☎ (619) 357-1112), 233 East Fourth St, opened during Prohibition in 1931. It's good value at the discount rate of US$29.50 a single or double (with AAA membership card).

Places to Stay – top end

The highly regarded *Hotel Colonial* (☎ (65) 56-53-12), López Mateos 1048, charges 180 pesos for a double. The popular *Hotel Lucerna* (☎ (65) 66-10-00), about five km from downtown at Benito Juárez 2151, has singles/doubles for 200/210 pesos.

Places to Eat

One good, inexpensive breakfast place is *Petunia 2*, on Reforma between Altamirano and Madero. Part of Hotel del Norte, *Restaurant del Norte* is a coffee shop offering cheap but mediocre specials. *El Sarape* (☎ 54-22-87), Calle Bravo 140 between Madero and Reforma, is a raucous spot with live music.

The moderately priced *La Placita* (☎ 68-10-51), in a pleasant atmosphere at Calzada Justo Sierra 377 at Honduras, is tremendous value for Mexican and international dishes. The pricier *La Villa del Seri* (☎ 53-55-03), at Reforma and Calle D, specialises in Sonoran beef, but also has excellent seafood and antojitos. *Cenaduría Selecta* (☎ 52-40-47), an institution at Arista 1510 and Calle G,

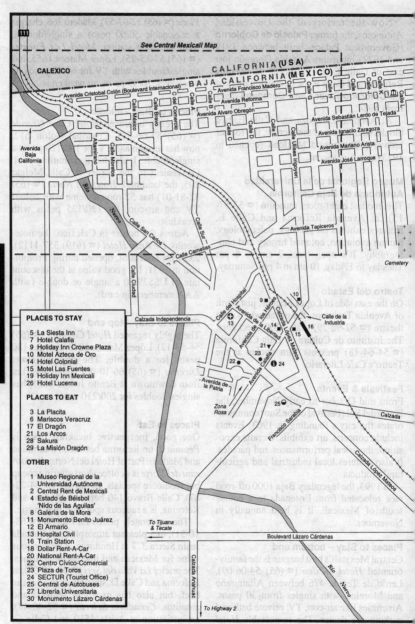

See Central Mexicali Map

CALEXICO

CALIFORNIA (USA)

CALIFORNIA (MEXICO)

BAJA CALIFORNIA (MEXICO)

Avenida Cristobal Colón (Boulevard Internacional)

Avenida Francisco Madero

Avenida Reforma

Avenida Alvaro Obregón

Avenida Sebastián Lerdo de Tejada

Avenida Ignacio Zaragoza

Avenida Mariano Arista

Avenida José Larroque

Avenida Baja California

Calle México
Altamirano
Calle Morelos
Calle Bravo
del Comercio
Calle A
Calle B
Calle C
Calle D
Calle E
Calle F
Calle G
Calle H
Calle I
Calle J
Calle K

Calle Ulises Irrigoyen

Río Nuevo

Calle San Carlos

Calle Sur

Calle Ciudad

Calle Camelias

Cemetery

Avenida Tapiceros

Calzada Independencia

Calle del Hospital
Avenida de los Héroes
Avenida de la Libertad
Calzada López Mateos

Calle de la Industria

9
10
13
16
14
15
21
23
22
24
25

Avenida Calafia
Avenida de la Patria
Zona Rosa

Francisco Sarabia

Calzada

Calzada López Mateos

To Tijuana & Tecate

Boulevard Lázaro Cárdenas

Calzada Anáhuac
Río Nuevo

To Highway 2

PLACES TO STAY

5   La Siesta Inn
7   Hotel Calafia
9   Holiday Inn Crowne Plaza
10 Motel Azteca de Oro
14 Hotel Colonial
15 Motel Las Fuentes
19 Holiday Inn Mexicali
26 Hotel Lucerna

PLACES TO EAT

3   La Placita
6   Mariscos Veracruz
17 El Dragón
21 Los Arcos
28 Sakura
29 La Misión Dragón

OTHER

1   Museo Regional de la
    Universidad Autónoma
2   Central Rent de Mexicali
4   Estado de Béisbol
    'Nido de las Aguilas'
8   Galería de la Mora
11 Monumento Benito Juárez
12 El Armario
13 Hospital Civil
16 Train Station
18 Dollar Rent-A-Car
20 National Rent-A-Car
22 Centro Cívico-Comercial
24 SECTUR (Tourist Office)
27 Central de Autobuses
27 Librería Universitaria
30 Monumento Lázaro Cárdenas

BAJA CALIFORNIA

Avenida Cristobal Colón
(Boulevard Internacional)
Avenida Francisco Madero
Avenida Reforma
Avenida Alvaro Obregón

Calzada de las Américas

To Airport
& Algodones

● 2

▼ 3

Calzada Cuauhtémoc

To Airport
& Algodones

Calzada Justo Sierra

● 4

■ 5

6 ▼

■ 7

● 8

Mexicali

0   250   500 m

11 ▲

● 12

Calzada Benito Juárez

17 ▼   ● 18

● 20

19 ■

■ 26

Independencia

27 ●

Universidad
Autónoma de
Baja California

▼ 28   29 ▼

▲ 30

To Aeropuerto
Internacional &
San Luís Río
Colorado

To San
Luís

To San Felipe

specialises in antojitos, but recent improvements have raised prices.

Opened in 1928, at Juárez 8 near Azueta, the inexpensive *Alley 19* is Mexicali's oldest continuously operating Chinese restaurant. The highly regarded *El Dragón* (☎ 66-20-20), occupying a huge pagoda at Calzada Benito Juárez 1830, is dearer.

Mandolino (☎ 52-95-44), Reforma 1070, has excellent Italian food. *La Fábula*, a pizza chain, has a large branch at Reforma 1150.

Mexicali's most popular seafood restaurant is *Los Arcos* (☎ 56-09-03), at Calafia 454 near the Plaza de Toros in the Centro Cívico-Comercial.

Entertainment
Baseball Starting in October, Mexicali's Las Águilas hosts other professional teams from the Liga Mexicana del Pacífico at El Nido de Las Águilas (Eagles' Nest), on Calzada Cuauhtémoc about five km east of the border. Weeknight games begin at 7 pm, Sunday games at 1 pm. Ticket prices range from 3 to 20 pesos, and a taxi to the ballpark costs around 20 pesos.

Nightclubs *Guaycura,* open from 8 pm to 2 am at the Holiday Inn on Benito Juárez, has a dance floor, live music and floor shows. *La Capilla* at Hotel Lucerna, Benito Juárez 2151, is a dance club popular with university students.

Los Cristales, at López Mateos 570, features performances by nationally known musicians.

Things to Buy
Shops selling cheap leather goods and kitsch souvenirs fill Calle Melgar and Avenida Reforma, near the border. For a more sophisticated selection, try El Armario, Justo Sierra 1700, Suite 1A, in the Plaza Azteca shopping centre.

Getting There & Away
Air Mexicana (☎ 53-54-01, 52-93-91 at the airport), Avenida Madero 832, flies daily to Acapulco. Aero California (☎ 56-04-56,

BAJA CALIFORNIA

BAJA CALIFORNIA

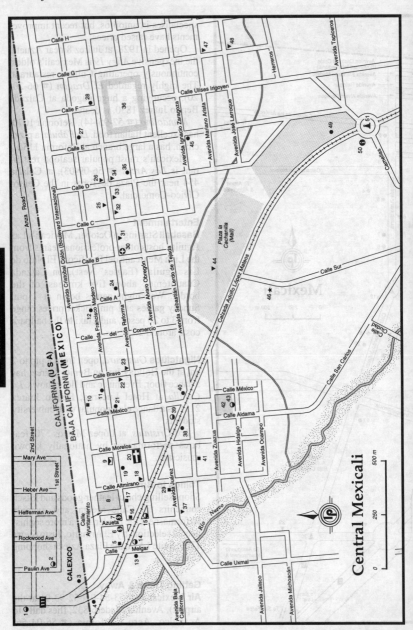

Central Mexicali

PLACES TO STAY		OTHER		30	Hospital
5	Hotel & Restaurant del Norte	1	Golden State Lines	35	México-Americano
10	Hotel Casa Grande	2	Greyhound		Galería de la Ciudad
16	Hotel Imperial	3	US Customs	36	Ex-Palacio de
17	Hotel Plaza	4	Mexican Customs		Gobierno (Rectory of
29	Hotel Nuevo Pacífico	6	Bancomer		the Universidad
41	Hotel México	7	Banca Serfin		Autónoma)
		8	Parque Niños Héroes	38	Los Cristales
PLACES TO EAT			de Chapultepec	39	Tebacsa (Buses to
		9	Post Office		San Felipe, San Luis
18	Petunia 2	11	Aerolímpico Tours		Río Colorado)
22	El Sarape	12	Mexicana	40	Central Rent de
23	China Town	13	LF Caliente Foreign		Mexicali
25	Del Mar		Book		(Car Rental)
26	La Villa del Seri	14	Transportes Golden	42	Plaza del Mariachi
31	Mandolino		State		(Parque
32	Rinconcito Gaucho	15	City Bus Terminal		Constitución)
33	La Fábula Pizza	19	Librería Madero	43	Buses to Algodones
34	La Parroquia/LF	20	Catedral de la Virgen	45	Ex-Cervecería
	Caliente Sports Book		de Guadalupe		Mexicali
37	Alley 19	21	Berlin 77	46	Police
44	Los Buffalos &	24	Támez Tours	49	Teatro del Estado
	Mar y Mar	27	Ana Sol Tours	50	COTUCO (Tourist
47	Cenaduría Selecta	28	Ex-Colorado River		Office)
48	El Rincón del Sabor		Land Company	51	Monumento Vicente
					Guerrero

53-49-00 at the airport), Calafia 672, flies daily to Mexico City and intermediates.

AirLA (☎ 800-010-0413 in Mexico, ☎ 800-933-5952 in the USA, both toll-free) flies to Los Angeles on weekdays at 9.15 am and 5.45 pm, Sunday at 1.20 pm. Return fares are US$138.

Bus Long-distance bus companies leave from the Central de Autobuses on Independencia near López Mateos. Autotransportes del Pacífico (☎ 57-24-61) and Norte de Sonora (☎ 57-24-22) serve mainland Mexican destinations like Mazatlán (170 pesos), Guadalajara (225 pesos) and Mexico City (280 pesos).

Tres Estrellas (☎ 57-24-10) and ABC (☎ 57-24-20) fares within Baja California include Tijuana (22 pesos), Ensenada (35 pesos), Guerrero Negro (105 pesos), Loreto (150 pesos) and La Paz (195 pesos). ABC buses to San Felipe (22 pesos) depart at 8 am, noon, and 4 and 8 pm.

From a stop on the south side of Calzada

López Mateos near Calle Melgar, Transportes Golden State (☎ 53-61-59) serves Palm Springs (US$22), Los Angeles (US$27) and intermediates at 8 am, and 2.30 and 8 pm. Its Calexico stop is Church's Fried Chicken, 344 Imperial Avenue.

In Calexico, Greyhound (☎ (619) 357-1895) is at 121 East First St, directly across from the border. There are five departures daily from the Los Angeles terminal (☎ (213) 629-8400) to Calexico (US$18/35 one way/return) and back.

Train The train station (Ferrocarril Sonora-Baja California; ☎ (65) 57-23-86 or 57-21-01, ext 213, 222 or 223) is at Calle Ulíses Irigoyen (Calle F) near López Mateos. The Estrella del Pacífico 'express' to Hermosillo, El Sufragio, Mazatlán and Guadalajara (train No 2, also referred to as Servicio Estrella) departs daily at 9 am. It has primera especial seating only, and dining facilities. Tickets for this train are on sale from 8 am to 2 pm daily and you can also reserve them in advance by telephone. The trip to Guadalajara takes a scheduled 33½ hours (see the Guadalajara Train section in the Western Central Highlands chapter for further schedule and fare information). A segunda clase train (No 4) to Guadalajara departs at 8.50 pm, taking a scheduled 44 hours for 97 pesos; tickets are sold only from 5 to 10 pm on the day of travel.

Border Crossing The border is open 24 hours. US and Mexican authorities intend to open a second border complex east of downtown to ease congestion.

Getting Around

To/From the Airport Cabs to Aeropuerto Internacional General Rodolfo Sánchez Taboada (☎ 53-67-42), 12 km east of town, cost 60 pesos but may be shared.

Bus Most city buses start from Avenida Reforma, just west of López Mateos; check the placard for the destination. Local fares are about 1.30 pesos.

Taxi A taxi to the train station or Centro Cívico averages about 20 pesos; agree on the fare first.

SAN FELIPE
• *pop: 20,000*

This once tranquil fishing community on the Gulf of California, 200 km south of Mexicali, suffers blistering summer temperatures, roaring motorcycles, firecrackers, property speculators and aggressive restaurateurs who almost yank patrons off the sidewalk. Sport fishing and warm winters have attracted many retirees to sprawling trailer parks, while younger people flock here to party. Farther south, **Puertecitos** is the starting point for a rugged southbound alternative to the Transpeninsular.

Buses to Mexicali (22 pesos, two hours) leave at 7.30 am, noon and 4 and 8 pm; Ensenada-bound buses (30 pesos, four hours) leave at 8 am and 6 pm daily.

The Desierto Central & the Llano de Magdalena

Cochimí Indians once foraged the vast Desierto Central (Central Desert), which extends from El Rosario to Loreto, and its coastline along the Gulf of California (Sea of Cortés). Baja's colonial and later historical heritage is more palpable here than it is further north – well-preserved or restored mission churches and modest plazas reveal close links to mainland Mexico.

The sinuous 125-km stretch of highway between El Rosario and the desert pit stop of Cataviña traverses a surrealistic desert landscape of granite boulders among *cardón* cactus and the twisted *cirio* or 'boojum'. Beyond Guerrero Negro and the harsh, desolate Desierto de Vizcaíno, the oasis of San Ignacio augurs the semitropical gulf coast between Mulegé and Cabo San Lucas. Paralleling the gulf, the Sierra de la Giganta divides the region into an eastern subtropical zone and a western section of elevated plateaus and dry lowlands. South of Loreto, the Transpeninsular turns west to the Llano de Magdalena (Magdalena Plain), a rich farming zone that also offers fishing, whale-watching, surfing and windsurfing.

South of the 28th parallel, the border between the states of Baja California and Baja California Sur, the hour changes; 'Pacific' time (to the north) is an hour behind 'Mountain' time (to the south).

GUERRERO NEGRO
• *pop: 7886*

The town of Guerrero Negro is renowned for the Laguna Ojo de Liebre (Scammon's Lagoon), which annually becomes the mating and breeding ground of California grey whales. Each year, the whales migrate 6000 miles from the Bering Sea to the lagoon, where they stay from early January to early March. The lagoon is south of the town's evaporative salt works (the largest of their kind in the world), about 24 km from the junction of highway 1.

Baja California
Top: Rock formations at Land's End, Los Cabos (RB)
Bottom: Sea of Cortés (JR)

Baja California
Top: Agua Caliente Tower, Tijuana (SW); Across the breakwater, Cabo San Lucas (RB)
Bottom: Bahía de Magdalena (JR); Church, La Paz (SW)

The town comprises two distinct sectors: a disorderly strip along Boulevard Emiliano Zapata, west of the Transpeninsular, and an orderly company town run by Exportadora de Sal (ESSA). Nearly all accommodation, restaurants and other services are along Boulevard Zapata.

Places to Stay

The whale-watching season can strain local accommodation; reservations are advisable from January to March.

The barren *Malarrimo Trailer Park* (☎ (115) 7-02-50), at the eastern entrance to town, charges from 15 pesos and permits tents. Hot water is plentiful and toilets are clean, but check electrical outlets. The new, clean and tidy *Motel Las Ballenas* has hot water and colour TV in every room, for 50 pesos a single or double. It's just north of the recently upgraded *Hotel El Morro* (☎ (115) 7-04-14), on the north side of Boulevard Zapata, which has clean, pleasant singles/doubles for 75/85 pesos. *Cabañas Don Miguelito*, part of the Malarrimo complex, has detached singles/doubles for 65/75 pesos.

Places to Eat

Guerrero Negro's many taco stands keep erratic hours. *El Taco Feliz*, on the south side of Boulevard Zapata, has superb fish and shrimp tacos; others specialise in carne asada, birria (goat) and other fillings.

Cocina Económica Letty, a good breakfast choice on the south side of Boulevard Zapata, has moderately priced antojitos and seafood. Specialising in seafood, both as antojitos and sophisticated international dishes, *Malarrimo* is no longer cheap, but portions are abundant.

Getting There & Away

Air Daily except Sunday, Aerolíneas California Pacifico flies rickety DC-3s to Isla Cedros (75 pesos one way). Reserve at least a day in advance and arrive by 8 am for a 10 am departure. Offices are on the west side of the airfield, in a yellow shed with blue trim.

Bus The bus station is on the south side of Boulevard Zapata. Northbound fares include Ensenada (65 pesos) and Tijuana (80 pesos); southbound fares include Mulegé (32 pesos), Loreto (50 pesos) and La Paz (85 pesos).

AROUND GUERRERO NEGRO
Reserva Biósfera El Vizcaíno

The 25,000-sq-km reserve sprawls from Laguna San Ignacio, Guerrero Negro and Isla Cedros, across to the Gulf of California. Local *pangueros* (boatmen) take visitors for whale-watching excursions in the shallow waters of Laguna Ojo de Liebre; Guerrero Negro travel agencies arrange trips for about 90 pesos.

Eight km south of Guerrero Negro, a graded road leads 25 km west to Ojo de Liebre; inexpensive camping is available after 1 January, the official start of the whale-watching season. Day-trippers pay 10 pesos for parking.

ISLA CEDROS

Isla Cedros is not a touristy destination – it has no bank, no phones, and you can't even get a margarita – but this mountainous northward extension of Península Vizcaíno supports unusual flora, marine mammals like elephant seals and sea lions, and the endangered Cedros mule deer. Most of its 2696 inhabitants live in the port of Cedros on the eastern shore, but many live at Punta Morro Redondo, the transshipment point for salt barged over from Guerrero Negro.

Places to Stay & Eat

The basic *Casa de Huéspedes Elsa García*, uphill from the port's dusty triangular plaza, has clean singles or doubles for 35 pesos. *Restaurant El Marino* has good, reasonably priced antojitos, fish and shrimp. A friendly taco stand up the main drag from El Marino serves only carne asada.

Getting There & Away

Taxis charge about 20 pesos per person to Cedros's airfield at Punta Morro Redondo, eight km south of town, but even the police stop to offer lifts!

Tracking the Turtle

The great whales get all the press. Few travellers know as much about the sea turtles that, historically, have been as important to the peoples of the tropics as whales have to the peoples of the Arctic. Called 'the world's most valuable reptile' by geographer James Parsons, the green turtle *Chelonia mydas* is endangered throughout the world, and its conservation should be a major priority in Baja California and Mexico.

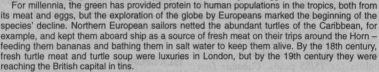
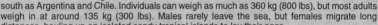

The green turtle *(caguama negra* or *tortuga prieta* in Baja California) is a grazing reptile that feeds on the marine grasses of tropical and subtropical seas, though wandering individuals have been found as far north as England and as far south as Argentina and Chile. Individuals can weigh as much as 360 kg (800 lbs), but most adults weigh in at around 135 kg (300 lbs). Males rarely leave the sea, but females migrate long distances, hauling up on isolated sandy tropical islands to lay their eggs.

For millennia, the green has provided protein to human populations in the tropics, both from its meat and eggs, but the exploration of the globe by Europeans marked the beginning of the species' decline. Northern European sailors netted the abundant turtles of the Caribbean, for example, and kept them aboard ship as a source of fresh meat on their trips around the Horn – feeding them bananas and bathing them in salt water to keep them alive. By the 18th century, fresh turtle meat and turtle soup were luxuries in London, but by the 19th century they were reaching the British capital in tins.

Outside the tropics, where meat was otherwise scarce, turtle always remained a delicacy, but commercial pressures resulted in overhunting in such important areas as the Caribbean coasts of Nicaragua and Costa Rica (where nesting beaches at Tortuguero were frequently raided of eggs as well). The result was a transfer of meat protein from the poor countries of the tropics to the rich countries of the mid-latitudes.

Baja California's turtles shared this unfortunate history. At Bahía Tortugas, on Península Vizcaíno, one 19th-century ship netted almost 200 turtles in a single pass offshore. Many were canned or shipped north to San Francisco or San Diego for sale or further processing. As recently as the 1960s, the Ruffo family's Empacadora Baja California was canning as much as 100 tonnes of turtle soup in a season in Ensenada (Ernesto Ruffo Appel, a member of the family, is the present governor of Baja California).

In the 1970s, increasing concern over the green's declining numbers resulted in its placement (and that of all other sea turtles) on Appendix I of the Convention on International Trade in Endangered Species (CITES). Still, it is not unusual to find surreptitious trade in turtle products. A casual inquiry at a taco stand once led to my being told where to find caguama for sale. Perhaps, some time in the future, the species will recover enough to permit it to resume the role it once played in the human ecology of the tropics, but environmental opponents of NAFTA argue, with some credibility, that the Mexican government has done a poor job of enforcing international agreements on turtle conservation.

Baja visitors are unlikely to come across nesting sites, which are usually at remote spots like Isla Socorro in the Revillagigedo group, some 450 km (280 miles) south of Cabo San Lucas, but greens and other turtle species are not unusual in Baja waters. In Baja California (Norte), sightings of the green have been recorded at Gulf island sites like Ángel de la Guarda, Rasa, Salsipuedes, San Luis and San Lorenzo, as well as Bahía de los Angeles, Bahía San Luis Gonzaga, Puertecitos, San Felipe and even the mouth of the Río Colorado. On the Pacific side, sightings include Isla Cedros, Bahía San Quintín, and Ensenada.

The warmer waters of Baja California Sur are a better turtle habitat, in many of the same areas frequented by calving grey whales: Laguna Ojo de Liebre (Scammon's Lagoon), Laguna San Ignacio and Bahía Magdalena.

Wayne Bernhardson

Aerolíneas California Pacífico flights to Guerrero Negro (75 pesos) ostensibly leave at 1 pm (Pacific time), but to be on the safe side you should arrive at the airport at least an hour early. Purchase tickets at Licores La Panga, up the hill from Cedros's plaza. Tickets for Ensenada (275 pesos one way) are available at the Sociedad Cooperativa de Producción Pesquera.

AROUND ISLA CEDROS
Islas San Benito

This tiny archipelago consists of three small islands, 30 nautical miles west of Cedros. The largest supports a winter camp of abalone divers, their families, and a colony of northern elephant seals *(Mirounga angustirostis)*. The seals start to arrive in December, but are most numerous in January and February.

Budget travellers can catch a free lift from Cedros with the daily supply ship *Tito I*. If you want to do this, visit the Sociedad de Producción Pesquera in Cedros village before 1 pm; with the chief's approval, the secretary issues a letter to present to the captain that evening for the next morning's voyage. If you are prone to seasickness, avoid eating; the four-hour voyage out is generally rougher than the one back.

Bring camping equipment, food and water if you hope to spend more than an hour on shore. Avoid getting too close to the elephants – frightened bulls may accidentally crush or injure newborn pups.

SAN IGNACIO

Jesuits located Misión San Ignacio de Kadakaamán in this soothing oasis in 1728, planting dense groves of date palms and citrus trees, but it was Dominicans who supervised the striking church (finished 1786) that still dominates the cool, laurel-shaded plaza. With lava-block walls nearly 1.2 metres thick, this is one of Baja's most beautiful churches.

The lush village of San Ignacio proper is about 1.6 km south of the Transpeninsular, and is a welcome sight after the scrub brush and dense cacti of the Vizcaíno Desert. Most services are around the plaza, including public telephones and Bancomer, which changes money on weekday mornings.

Places to Stay & Eat

Just south of Hotel La Pinta, on the west side of the road into town, the palm-shaded *El Padrino RV Park* (☎ (115) 4-00-89) has only a single toilet/shower for 25-plus sites, some with full hook-ups. Fees are 15 pesos for camping, slightly higher for large RVs.

At Calle Venustiano Carranza 22, southeast of the plaza, *Motel La Posada* (☎ (115) 4-03-13) has spartan doubles with hot shower for about 60 pesos. The pseudocolonial *Hotel La Pinta* (☎ /fax (115) 4-03-00), on the main road just before entering San Ignacio, appeals to more affluent travellers with singles/doubles at 165/180 pesos.

Specialising in local beef, Hotel La Pinta's restaurant serves typical antojitos at upscale prices. *Tota*, up the block from the plaza, serves good, reasonably priced antojitos and seafood dishes. *Flojo's*, at El Padrino RV Park, prepares good, fresh seafood; its lobster is cheaper than Tota's.

Getting There & Away

At least five buses daily in each direction pick up passengers on the south side of the plaza. Drivers may not stop at the old San Lino terminal on the Transpeninsular.

San Ignacio Mission

AROUND SAN IGNACIO
San Francisco de la Sierra

At Km 118, 43 km north-west of San Ignacio, a graded but poorly consolidated road climbs east to San Francisco de la Sierra, gateway to the Desierto Central's most spectacular pre-Columbian rock art. About 2.5 km before San Francisco, **Cueva del Ratón** is the most accessible site, but independent visitors need a local guide to open the locked gate. Oscar Fischer, at Motel La Posada, charges about 60 pesos per person to visit Cueva del Ratón, with representations of *monos* (human figures), *borregos* (bighorn sheep) and deer.

In the dramatic Cañón San Pablo, **Cueva Pintada**, **Cueva de Las Flechas** and other sites are better preserved; Cueva Pintada's rock overhang is the most impressive. The awesome muleback descent of Cañón San Pablo requires at least two days, preferably three; visitors must refrain from touching the paintings, smoking at sites and employing flash photography (400 ASA film suffices even in dim light).

Entrance to Cueva del Ratón requires a modest tip to the guide, but visitors to Cañón San Pablo must hire a guide with mule through INAH for US$20 a day, plus a mule for each person for US$9 a day, and additional pack animals for supplies (also US$9 a day each). You must also feed the guide. The best season is early spring, when the days are fairly long but temperatures not yet unpleasantly hot. Backpacking is permitted, but you must still hire a guide and mule.

Laguna San Ignacio

Along with Laguna Ojo de Liebre and Bahía Magdalena, Laguna San Ignacio is one of the Pacific coast's major winter whale-watching sites, with three-hour excursions costing around 75 pesos per person. At other seasons the area offers outstanding bird-watching in the stunted mangroves and at **Isla Pelícanos**, where ospreys and cormorants nest (landing on the island is prohibited).

The newly improved road from the village of San Ignacio to the lagoon is a dubious blessing – most vehicles can make the 61 km

to La Fridera in about 1½ hours, but it may also assist ESSA in developing an even larger salt works than Guerrero Negro. There is no public transport to the site.

SANTA ROSALÍA
• *pop: 10,637*

Imported timber frames the clapboard houses lining the main streets of Santa Rosalía, a copper town built by the French-owned Compañía del Boleo in the 1880s. The French also assembled a prefabricated church, designed by Alexandre Gustave Eiffel (the same!) for Paris's 1889 World's Fair, and bequeathed a bakery that sells Baja's best baguettes.

Orientation & Information

Central Santa Rosalía nestles in the canyon of its namesake arroyo, west of the Transpeninsular, but French administrators built their houses on the northern Mesa Francia, now home to municipal authorities and the historic Hotel Francés. Santa Rosalía's narrow avenidas run east-west, while its short calles run north-south; one-way traffic is the rule. Plaza Benito Juárez, four blocks west of the highway, is the town centre.

Money Travellers bound for Mulegé, which has no banks, should change US cash or travellers' cheques at Bancomer or Banamex, both on Avenida Obregón.

Post & Telecommunications The post office is at Avenida Constitución and Calle 2. The Telmex office at the west end of Obregón has a phone outside for collect calls. Hotel del Real, on the exit road from town, also has long-distance cabinas.

Iglesia Santa Bárbara

Designed and erected in Paris, disassembled and stored in Brussels, intended for West Africa and finally shipped here when a Compañía del Boleo director chanced upon it 1895, Gustave Eiffel's prefab church was reassembled by 1897. It has attractive stained-glass windows.

Places to Stay & Eat

Just south of town, *Las Palmas RV Park* (☎ (115) 2-01-09) has grassy camp sites, with hot showers and clean toilets, from about 15 pesos.

Travellers have recommended the 'very quaint' *Hotel Blanco y Negro* (☎ (115) 2-00-80), up a spiral staircase on the 2nd floor of a small building at Avenida Sarabia 1, with clean, basic singles/doubles with hot water for about 30/35 pesos. The family-run *Motel San Victor* (☎ (115) 2-01-16), Avenida Progreso 36, has a dozen tidy rooms with ceiling fans, air-con and tiled baths for 60 pesos a single or double. *Hotel Francés* (☎ (115) 2-08-29), on Mesa Francia, offers an atmospheric bar, views of the rusting copperworks and air-con singles/doubles for 75/90 pesos.

Taco stands are numerous along Avenida Obregón, where the popular *Tokyo Café* serves cheap antojitos and beer; only the calligraphy is Japanese. *Cenaduría Gaby* on Calle 4 just north of Obregón serves reasonably priced antojitos. South of downtown, the waterfront *Restaurant Selene* serves sumptuous seafood at upscale prices.

Panadería El Boleo, on Obregón between Calles 3 and 4, is an obligatory stop for Mexican and French-style baked goods. Baguettes usually sell out by 10 am.

Getting There & Away

Bus At least six buses daily in each direction stop at the terminal, which is south of town on the west side of the Transpeninsular. Sample northbound fares include San Ignacio (10 pesos), Guerrero Negro (30 pesos), Ensenada (90 pesos) and Tijuana (105 pesos); southbound fares include Mulegé (10 pesos), Loreto (22 pesos), Ciudad Constitución (35 pesos) and La Paz (65 pesos).

Ferry Sematur passenger/auto ferries sail to Guaymas on Sunday and Wednesday at 8 am, arriving at 3 pm; the return ferry to Santa Rosalía sails at 8 am Tuesday and Friday, arriving at 3 pm. Strong winter winds may cause delays.

Ticket windows at the terminal (☎ (115) 2-00-13), right along the highway, are open Tuesday and Friday from 8 am to 1 pm and 3 to 6 pm; Sunday and Wednesday from 6 to 7.30 am; and Thursday and Saturday from 8 am to 3 pm. See the accompanying chart for fares and schedules. Make reservations at least three days in advance and, even if you have reservations, arrive early at the ticket office. Passenger fares are 40 pesos in *salón* (numbered seats) and 80 pesos in *turista* (two-to four-bunk cabins with shared bath). Vehicle rates, in pesos, vary with vehicle length:

Vehicle	Length	Rate (pesos)
Car	Up to five metres	307
	5.01 to 6.5 metres	399
	With trailer up to nine metres	553
	9.01 to 17 metres	1043
Bus		524
Motorcycle		45

Details of the documents you need to ship a vehicle to the mainland are given in the introductory Getting There & Away chapter. You should be able to obtain vehicle permits in Santa Rosalía, but it's better to get them in advance from the Registro Federal de Vehículos in Tijuana or La Paz.

MULEGÉ
• *pop: 3341*
Beyond Santa Rosalía, the Transpeninsular hugs the eastern scarp of the Sierra de La Giganta before winding through the Sierra Azteca and dropping into the subtropical oasis of Mulegé, a popular destination for divers. Straddling the Arroyo de Santa Rosalía (Río Mulegé), Mulegé is three km inland from the Gulf. It is a small tropical town with thatched huts, lots of palm trees, and an 18th-century mission.

Information
Most services, including the post office, are on or near Jardín Corona, the town plaza. Mulegé has no bank, but merchants change cash dollars or accept them in payment. For long-distance phones and fax visit the grocery on Calle Zaragoza at Avenida Martínez, or dial an international operator (☎ 09) from payphones on the plaza.

Things to See

Across the highway near the south bank of the arroyo, the hilltop **Misión Santa Rosalía de Mulegé** was founded in 1705, completed in 1766, and abandoned in 1828. A short path climbs to a scenic overlook of the palm-lined arroyo.

Currently undergoing a major restoration, the former territorial prison is now the **Museo Mulegé**, overlooking the town. Its eclectic artefacts include cotton gins, antique diving equipment and firearms.

Activities

Diving Owners Miguel and Claudia Quintana of Mulegé Divers (☎ 3-00-59), on Avenida General Francisco Martínez, specialise in diving instruction and excursions (Claudia is American). The shop also sells fins and masks, fishing equipment and other supplies, T-shirts, and Baja books and maps. Open from 9 am to 1 pm and 3 to 6 pm daily except Sunday, it's also a friendly source of information.

Places to Stay

The friendly *Huerta Saucedo RV Park* (☎ (115) 3-03-00), south of town on the gulf side of the highway, rents RV spaces for about 30 pesos (half that without hook-ups).

The *Canett Casa de Huéspedes* on Calle Madero isn't bad for 25 pesos a single, but the church bells next door start ringing at 6 am. *Casa de Huéspedes Manuelita* (☎ (115) 3-01-75), across from Lavamática Claudia on Calle Moctezuma, and *Casa de Huéspedes Nachita*, half a block north-west, are comparable.

The family-oriented *Hotel Suites Rosita* (☎ (115) 3-02-70), on Madero east of the plaza, has air-con rooms with kitchenettes for 60 pesos a double. The poet Alán Gorosave once inhabited the shady *Hotel Las Casitas* (☎ (115) 3-00-19), on Madero near General Martínez, where the rooms all have hot showers and air-con for 60/85 pesos. The remodelled *Hotel Hacienda* (☎ (115) 3-00-21), Madero 3, has twin-bedded rooms with fridge, air-con and hot shower for 75 pesos a double.

Places to Eat

Dany's is the closest the humble taco will ever get to *haute cuisine*, with various fillings and a cornucopia of tasty condiments at reasonable prices. It's at the intersection of Romero Rubio and Madero. Try the upscale *Las Casitas* for antojitos and a few seafood dishes, or *Los Equipales*, on General Martínez just west of Zaragoza, for outstanding meals which are good value for money. *El Candil*, near the plaza, has filling meat and seafood dishes at moderate prices; its bar is a popular meeting place.

Getting There & Away

Half a dozen buses pass daily in each direction at the Y-junction ('La Y Griega') on the Transpeninsular, at the western edge of town.

LORETO
• *pop: 7845*

In 1697 Jesuit Juan María Salvatierra established the first permanent European settlement in the Californias at this modest port of cobbled streets, which lies some 135 km south of Mulegé, between the Transpeninsular and the Gulf. Aggressive tourist development in nearby Nopoló threatens to dehydrate Loreto by siphoning off its water, or to turn it into Cabo San Lucas Norte. Fishing, diving, snorkelling and kayaking are popular around the reefs and islands of the Gulf.

Orientation & Information

Loreto has an irregular street plan. Most hotels and services are near the landmark mission church on Calle Salvatierra, while the attractive *malecón* by the waterfront is ideal for sunset strolls.The Plaza Cívica is just north of Salvatierra, between Calles Madero and Davis.

Tourist Office The former tourist office on the Plaza Cívica has closed and, at the time of writing, a new office on the Transpeninsular bypass stood empty and apparently abandoned. A good source of information on the town and its surrounding area is the monthly (more or less) newsletter *Loreto Avanza*, which is available at various places around town.

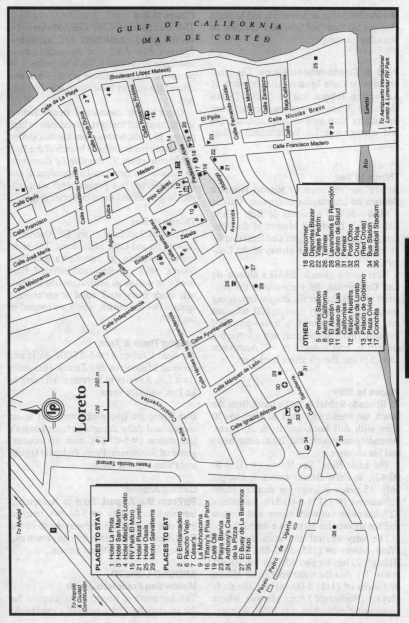

BAJA CALIFORNIA

GULF OF CALIFORNIA
(MAR DE CORTÉS)

(Boulevard López Mateos)

Calle de La Playa

Calle Agua Dulce

Calle Anastacio Carrillo

Calle Davis

Calle Francisco

Calle José María

Calle Misioneros

Calle Rosendo Robles

Zaragoza

Madero

Pino Suárez

Calle Agua

Calle Emiliano

Calle Benito Juárez

Zapata

Dulce

Calle Independencia

Calle Márquez de León

Calle Ignacio Allende

Calle Ayuntamiento

Calle Héroes de la Independencia

El Pipila

Calle Morelos

Calle Zaragoza

Calle Fernando Jordán

Calle Nicolás Bravo

Calle Baja California

Calle Francisco Madero

Hidalgo

Avenida

Pedestrian Area

Río

To Aeropuerto Internacional
Loreto & Loremar RV Park

Loreto

Calle Salvatierra

Constituyentes

Paseo Nicolás Tamaral

Paseo Pedro de Ugarte

Loreto

0   125   250 m

To Mulegé

To Napoló
& Ciudad
Constitución

PLACES TO STAY
1   Hotel La Pinta
3   Hotel San Martín
4   Hotel Misión de Loreto
15   RV Park El Moro
21   Hotel Plaza Loreto
25   Hotel Oasis
29   Motel Salvatierra

PLACES TO EAT
2   El Embarcadero
6   Rancho Viejo
9   César's
10   La Michoacana
16   Tiffany's Pisa Parlor
19   Café Olé
23   Playa Blanca
24   Anthony's Casa
27   El Buey de La Barranca
35   El Nido

OTHER
5   Pemex Station
8   Aero California
11   Museo de Las
     Californias
12   Misión Nuestra
     Señora de Loreto
13   Palacio de Gobierno
14   Plaza Cívica
17   Conchita
18   Bancomer
20   Deportes Blazer
22   Viajes Pedrín
26   Telmex
28   Lavandería El Remojón
30   Centro de Salud
31   Pemex
32   Post Office
33   Cruz Roja
     (Red Cross)
34   Bus Station
36   Baseball Stadium

Money Bancomer, at Salvatierra and Madero, changes US cash and travellers' cheques on weekday mornings.

Post & Telecommunications The post office is on Calle Ignacio Allende, north of Salvatierra. Telmex is at Salvatierra 75, but closes by 7 pm. Several businesses along Salvatierra have long-distance cabinas, but add a surcharge for international collect calls.

Things to See

Above the entrance to **Misión Nuestra Señora de Loreto**, the inscription 'Cabeza y Madre de Las Misiones de Baja y Alta California' (Head and Mother of the Missions of Lower and Upper California) aptly describes its role in the history of the Californias.

Next to the church, INAH's **Museo de Las Californias** dully chronicles the conquest of Baja California, despite interesting artefacts like an early mission bell, religious art, antique weapons, a horse-powered *trapiche* (mill), horse gear, and a kettle big enough to boil a Jesuit in oil. Admission costs 5 pesos; there's also a bookshop.

Places to Stay

At Rosendo Robles 8, half a block from the beach, the friendly *RV Park El Moro* has 20 sites with full hook-ups from 20 pesos, depending on vehicle size. It has clean baths and hot showers.

The basic *Hotel San Martín* (☎ (113) 5-00-42), at Calle Benito Juárez 4, charges only 35 pesos a single or double. *Motel Salvatierra* (☎ (113) 5-00-21), Salvatierra 123, has clean but worn rooms with air-con and hot shower for 80 pesos a double.

The very central and attractive *Hotel Plaza Loreto* (☎ (113) 5-02-80), Avenida Hidalgo 2, has singles/doubles for 90/105 pesos. Try also the waterfront *Hotel Misión de Loreto* (☎ (113) 5-00-48) at Calle de la Playa 1 (Boulevard López Mateos), whose air-con singles/doubles cost 105/120 pesos.

Places to Eat

The inexpensive *Café Olé*, Madero 14, serves good breakfasts and antojitos. *Tiffany's Pisa Parlor*, at Avenida Hidalgo and Calle Pino Suárez, has high prices – 30 pesos for a small cheese pizza – but also offers high-quality food. Smoking is prohibited.

César's, near Zapata and Benito Juárez, serves meat and seafood at moderate to high prices. *El Nido*, across from the bus station on Salvatierra, is the local branch of the Baja steakhouse chain. *El Buey de La Barranca*, on Salvatierra between Independencia and Ayuntamiento, is a popular grill with outstanding tacos and more elaborate dishes.

Things to Buy

For varied handicrafts, try El Alacrán at Salvatierra and Calle Misioneros. The high-priced Conchita, at Salvatierra and Pino Suárez, sells jewellery and selected Baja books, as well as an unpleasant line in products made from black coral or endangered species like sea turtles, which are banned in the USA.

Getting There & Away

Air Aero California (☎ 5-05-00), on Juárez between Misioneros and Zapata, flies daily from Los Angeles to Loreto, continuing to La Paz, and vice versa.

Bus There are five northbound and seven southbound daily departures from Loreto's bus station (☎ 5-07-67), near the convergence of Salvatierra, Paseo Pedro de Ugarte and Paseo Nicolás Tamaral.

Getting Around

To/From the Airport Taxis to Aeropuerto Internacional Loreto (☎ 5-04-54), reached by a side road off the highway south of the Río Loreto, cost 22 pesos for one person and 7 pesos for each additional person.

AROUND LORETO
Misión San Francisco Javier

Two km south of Loreto is the junction for the spectacular 35-km mountain road to the beautifully preserved San Francisco Javier de Viggé-Biaundó (founded in 1699). Every 3 December, pilgrims celebrate the saint's fiesta here. *Restaurant Palapa San Javier* serves simple meals and cold sodas (no beer).

CIUDAD CONSTITUCIÓN
• *pop: 37,480*
Set conveniently close to whale-watching sites, Ciudad Constitución, 215 km northwest of La Paz, has grown dramatically with commercial agriculture. Most services are within a block or two of the north-south Transpeninsular, commonly known as Boulevard Olachea. The post office is on Calle Galeana, west of Olachea; for phone service, try the cabinas on the east side of Olachea between Matamoros and Francisco J Mina.

Places to Stay
Follow the signs to *Campestre La Pila* (☎ (113) 2-05-62), south of town and west of the Transpeninsular, where rates for a single or double are 25 pesos with cold showers, electricity and toilets. There is also a swimming pool.

Hotel Casino (☎ (113) 2-04-55), on Guadalupe Victoria east of Hotel Maribel, has spartan rooms for 60 pesos a single or double. *Hotel Conchita* (☎ (113) 2-02-66), Olachea 180, has similar rates. *Hotel Maribel* (☎ (113) 2-01-55), Calle Guadalupe Victoria 156 near Boulevard Olachea, is comfortable enough at 120/135 pesos a single/double.

Places to Eat
Constitución's many taco stands and the *Mercado Central*, on Avenida Juárez between Calles Hidalgo and Bravo, have the cheapest eats. *Super Pollo*, at the north end of Olachea, specialises in grilled chicken. Next door, *Estrella del Mar* and *Rincón Jarocho*, on the east side of Olachea, are seafood restaurants. Other seafood choices include *Mariscos El Delfín* at Olachea and Zapata, and the upscale *Marlín Sonriente*, on Avenida Juárez between Hidalgo and Bravo.

Getting There & Away
Long-distance buses stop at the terminal at Avenida Juárez and Calle Pino Suárez, one block east of Olachea, but there are also buses to Puerto San Carlos, Puerto López Mateos, La Purísima and San Isidro.

AROUND CIUDAD CONSTITUCIÓN
Puerto López Mateos
Protected by the offshore barrier of Isla Magdalena, Puerto Adolfo López Mateos is one of Baja's best whale-watching sites. Whales are visible from the shore near Playa El Faro, where camping is possible (lock your car). Three-hour *panga* (skiff) excursions cost 90 pesos per hour for up to eight persons.

Places to Stay & Eat *María del Rosario González* offers basic accommodation for 30 pesos per person. *Restaurant El Faro* is open all year, *Restaurant Ballena Gris* only during the whale-watching season, and there are a couple of taco stands.

Getting There & Away Puerto López Mateos is 32 km west of Ciudad Insurgentes, which is 26 km north of Ciudad Constitución. Autotransportes Águila buses leave Ciudad Constitución for López Mateos at 11.30 am and 7 pm; return buses leave López Mateos at 7 am and 12.30 pm.

Puerto San Carlos
On Bahía Magdalena, 58 km west of Constitución, Puerto San Carlos is a deepwater port shipping produce from the Llano de Magdalena. From January to March pangueros take up to five or six passengers for whale-watching excursions for 60 pesos per hour.

Places to Stay & Eat Free camping is possible north of town on the shabby public beach, but the whale-watching season strains regular accommodation. *Motel Las Brisas* (☎ (113) 6-01-52), on Calle Madero, has basic but clean rooms from 35 pesos. *Hotel Palmar* (☎ (113) 6-00-35) charges 50/60 pesos a single/double, while *Hotel Alcatraz* (☎ (113) 6-00-17) has singles/doubles with

TV for 60/70 pesos; its *Restaurant Bar El Patio* is the town's best eatery.

An inexpensive stand at Calle Puerto La Paz and Calle Puerto Madero, around the corner from Las Brisas, has tremendous shrimp tacos.

Getting There & Away Autotransportes Águilar has buses to Constitución (10 pesos) and La Paz (30 pesos) at 7.30 am and 1.45 pm daily.

La Paz & the Cape Region

LA PAZ
* *pop: 149,360*

Hernán Cortés established Baja's first European outpost near La Paz, but permanent settlement waited until 1811. It was occupied by US troops during the Mexican-American War (1846-48). The quixotic William Walker proclaimed a 'Republic of Lower California' in 1853, but left under Mexican pressure.

After the Walker fiasco, La Paz settled

down, but its pearl industry nearly disappeared during the revolution of 1910. Today the capital of Baja California Sur is a peaceful place with beautiful beaches, a palm-lined malecón, old colonial buildings and spectacular sunsets over the bay. It is also a popular winter resort, whose port of Pichilingue receives ferries from the mainland ports of Topolobampo and Mazatlán.

Orientation
Approaching La Paz, the Transpeninsular becomes Calzada (Calle) Abasolo as it runs parallel to the bay. Four blocks east of 5 de Febrero, Abasolo becomes Paseo Alvaro Obregón, leading along the palm-lined malecón towards Península Pichilingue.

La Paz's grid makes basic orientation easy, but the centre's crooked streets and alleys change names almost every block. Four blocks south of the tourist pier, Jardín Velasco (Plaza Constitución) is the city's heart.

Information
Tourist Office Helpful, English-speaking staff are available from 8 am to 8 pm on

---

William Walker & the Cape
William Walker, the infamously quixotic American adventurer who spent (and lost) his life trying to build an Anglo empire in Mexico and Central America, was the first to try to bring the sleepy Cape Region into the modern world. In 1853, planning to establish a self-styled 'Republic of Sonora and Lower California', he sailed south from San Francisco, touching at Cabo San Lucas before anchoring at the territorial capital of La Paz.

Misrepresenting themselves as commercial voyagers to gain permission to land, Walker's forces arrested the governor, took possession of public buildings, and raised the flag of the new republic under the legal code of Louisiana – which permitted slavery. Walker, a native of Tennessee, later made slavery a cornerstone of his proposed Central American empire in an apparent attempt to gain political support from the slave states.

Improvised Mexican resistance failed to dislodge Walker from La Paz, but the threat of a more organised force from Todos Santos and the failure of his own reinforcements to arrive drove him back to Cabo San Lucas. Concerned that a Mexican warship was trailing him, he gave up plans to establish a new capital at Bahía Magdalena, returning to Ensenada, where he led a foolish attempt to cross to Sonora. Eventually, he straggled across the US border to hatch the Central American schemes that led to his death in Honduras.

Despite Walker's failures in Baja California, some have argued that his adventures brought territorial gains to the USA – the Gadsden Purchase of southern Arizona and New Mexico finally brought to the USA part of what Walker had tried to obtain by force. Today, given the overwhelming Americanisation of Cabo San Lucas, concerned Mexicans might well wonder if, in the long run, Walker triumphed in spite of his self-imposed disasters. ∎

weekdays, 9 am to 1 pm weekends, at the Oficina de Información Turística (☎ (112) 2-59-39), Paseo Alvaro Obregón and Calle 16 de Septiembre.

Money Most banks and cambios are on or around Calle 16 de Septiembre.

Post & Telecommunications The post office is at Constitución and Revolución. Most public telephones are out of order; private cabinas along Obregón and elsewhere impose surcharges for collect calls. Verify rates, which vary up to 50% between offices, before calling.

Immigration Servicios Migratorios (☎ 5-34-93), on the 2nd floor at Paseo Obregón 2140, between Calles Juárez and Allende, is open from from 8 am to 8 pm on weekdays. On weekends, officials staff the ferry terminal and the airport (☎ 2-18-29).

Travel Agencies Turismo La Paz (☎ 2-83-00), Calle Esquerro 1679, is the American Express representative.

Bookshops The Museo Regional de Antropología e Historia (see below) has a good selection of Spanish-language books on Baja California and mainland Mexico. Next door, Librería Ágora de La Paz (☎ 2-62-04) is better and cheaper.

Things to See
At Cinco de Mayo and Ignacio Altamirano, the **Museo Regional de Antropología e Historia** chronicles the peninsula from prehistory to the revolution of 1910. Open weekdays from 8 am to 6 pm, Saturday 9 am to 1 pm, it also has an attractive cactus garden.

The **Teatro de la Ciudad** (☎ 5-19-17), a sprawling edifice at Gómez Farías and Legaspí, is part of a major cultural centre whose **Rotunda de los Hombres Ilustres** (Rotunda of Distinguished Men) is a sculptural tribute to those who resisted Walker's invasion.

Activities
Diving & Snorkelling Arrange equipment rentals and day trips with Baja Buceo y Servicio (☎ 2-18-26), Avenida Independencia 107-B.

Fishing The Dorado Vélez Fleet (☎ 2-00-38) has a desk in the lobby of Hotel Los Arcos, but other major hotels and travel agencies can also arrange trips.

Festivals
La Paz's pre-Lenten Carnaval is among the country's best. In early May, Paceños celebrate Hernán Cortés's 1535 landing for two weeks in the Fundación de La Ciudad. June 1 is Día de La Marina (Navy Day). Late November witnesses the Festival de Artes (Arts Festival).

Places to Stay – bottom end
Camping At Km 4 on the Transpeninsular, west of downtown, the well-organised *El Cardón Trailer Park* (☎ (112) 2-00-78) offers full hook-ups, electricity and small *palapas* (thatched-roof shelters). Tent spaces cost 20 pesos, vehicle spaces 25 pesos. West of El Cardón, the shady, secure and well-maintained *RV Park Casa Blanca* (☎ (112) 2-00-09) has a pool, a restaurant, and full hook-ups from 30 pesos.

Hostel Bunks in single-sex dormitories cost 20 pesos at the hostel (*CONADE* or *Casa Juvenil*; ☎ (112) 2-46-15), open from 6 am to 11 pm. It's 20 blocks south-west of downtown, near the convergence of Calle 5 de Febrero, Camino A Las Garzas and the southbound Transpeninsular; catch any 'Universidad' bus from Mercado Francisco Madero at Degollado and Revolución.

Pensiones, Hosterías & Casas de Huéspedes Shaded by tropical plants, its walls lined with quirky art, *Pensión California* (☎ (112) 2-28-96), Degollado 209, is a budget favourite at 25/40 pesos a single/double with ceiling fan and shower. Rates are identical at the clean and basic but dark and dilapidated *Hostería del Convento* (☎ (112)

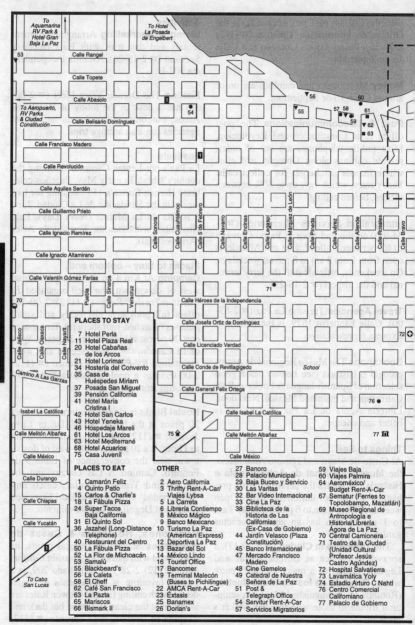

PLACES TO STAY

7 Hotel Perla
11 Hotel Plaza Real
20 Hotel Cabañas
    de los Arcos
21 Hotel Lorimar
34 Hostería del Convento
35 Casa de
    Huéspedes Miriam
37 Posada San Miguel
39 Pensión California
41 Hotel María
    Cristina I
42 Hotel San Carlos
43 Hotel Yeneka
46 Hospedaje Mareli
61 Hotel Los Arcos
63 Hotel Mediterrané
68 Hotel Acuarios
75 Casa Juvenil

PLACES TO EAT

1 Camarón Feliz
4 Quinto Patio
15 Carlos & Charlie's
18 La Fábula Pizza
24 Super Tacos
31 El Quinto Sol
36 Jazahel (Long-Distance
    Telephone)
40 Restaurant del Centro
50 La Fábula Pizza
52 La Flor de Michoacán
53 Samalú
55 Blackbeard's
58 La Caleta
58 El Cheff
62 Café San Francisco
63 La Pazta
65 Mariscos
66 Bismark II

OTHER

2 Aero California
3 Thrifty Rent-A-Car/
  Viajes Lybsa
5 La Carreta
6 Librería Contiempo
8 México Mágico
9 Banco Mexicano
10 Turismo La Paz
   (American Express)
12 Deportiva La Paz
13 Bazar del Sol
14 México Lindo
16 Tourist Office
17 Bancomer
19 Terminal Malecón
   (Buses to Pichilingue)
22 AMCA Rent-A-Car
23 Éxtasis
25 Banamex
26 Dorian's
27 Banoro
28 Palacio Municipal
29 Baja Buceo y Servicio
30 Las Varitas
32 Bar Video Internacional
33 Cine La Paz
38 Biblioteca de la
   Historia de Las
   Californias
   (Ex-Casa de Gobierno)
44 Jardín Velasco (Plaza
   Constitución)
45 Banco Internacional
47 Mercado Francisco
   Madero
48 Cine Gemelos
49 Catedral de Nuestra
   Señora de La Paz
51 Post &
   Telegraph Office
54 Servitur Rent-A-Car
57 Servicios Migratorios
59 Viajes Baja
60 Viajes Palmira
64 Aeroméxico/
   Budget Rent-A-Car
67 Sematur (Ferries to
   Topolobampo, Mazatlán)
69 Museo Regional de
   Antropología e
   Historia/Librería
   Agora de La Paz
70 Central Camionera
71 Teatro de la Ciudad
   (Unidad Cultural
   Profesor Jesús
   Castro Agúndez)
72 Hospital Salvatierra
73 Lavamática Yoly
74 Estadio Arturo C Nahtl
76 Centro Comercial
   Californiano
77 Palacio de Gobierno

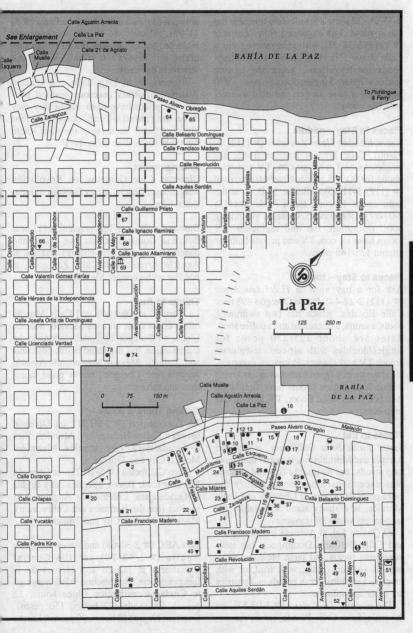

BAJA CALIFORNIA

2-35-08), Madero 85; toilets are tolerable but not spotless. The expanded *Hotel Lorimar* (☎ (112) 5-38-22), with an attractive patio at Calle Bravo 110, is becoming 'a real crossroads for travellers', according to one reader's letter. Singles/doubles cost 55/70 pesos; most have air-con and tiled showers with hot water.

Places to Stay – middle
Recommended *Hotel Acuarios* (☎ (112) 2-92-66), Calle Ignacio Ramírez 1665, has singles/doubles with air-con, TV and telephone for 90/105 pesos. *Hotel Mediterrané* (☎ (112) 5-11-95), Allende 36-B, is in the same range. Historic *Hotel Perla* (☎ (112) 2-07-77), Obregón 1570, has a swimming pool, restaurant, bar and nightclub. All rooms have air-con, TV and private bath for around 125/145 pesos.

Places to Stay – top end
Ask for a bay view at *Hotel Los Arcos* (☎ (112) 2-27-44), Paseo Obregón 498 near Calle Rosales, which has two swimming pools, a sauna, a restaurant and a coffee shop. Rates are about 225/230 pesos for singles/doubles with air-con, telephone, colour TV and shower. Prices are comparable at the nearby *Hotel Cabañas de los Arcos*, whose lush garden rooms have fireplaces, thatched roofs, tiled floors, TV, air-con and mini-bars.

Places to Eat
Super Tacos Baja California, at Agustín Arreola and Mutualismo, is dearer than most taco stands, but its quality fish and shrimp, plus exceptional condiments, justify the extra peso. *Mariscos*, at Obregón and Calle Morelos, is a shady stand with tables for taco-lovers weary of standing.

El Quinto Sol, at Avenida Independencia and Calle Belisario Domínguez, has tasty vegetarian meals and large breakfast servings of yoghurt (plain, with fruit, or with muesli). Licuados, fresh breads and pastries are other specialities.

The popular *La Caleta* (☎ 3-02-87), on the malecón at Calle Pineda, serves reasonably priced meals and drinks. *La Pazta* (☎ 5-11-95), Allende 36-B just south of the malecón, has moderately priced Italian specials, but drinks are small, weak and relatively expensive.

Bismark II, at Degollado and Ignacio Altamirano, offers generous seafood platters, but prices have risen and quality may have stagnated – one correspondent observed that it 'seems to be the place where the yacht snobs dine these days'.

Entertainment
Cinemas Cine Gemelos, on Revolución near Independencia, offers first-run international films.

Discos *Las Varitas,* Independencia 111 near Belisario Domínguez, has live music and dancing (10-peso cover charge). *Éxtasis,* at Agustín Arreola and Calle Zaragoza, is popular with younger Mexicans.

Things to Buy
La Carreta, at Obregón and Calle Muelle, offers crafts from all over Mexico. México Lindo, on Obregón diagonally opposite the tourist office, has mainland items, postcards and T-shirts. México Mágico, on Agustín Arreola near Obregón, boasts good tapestries and sarapes.

Getting There & Away
Air Aeroméxico (☎ 2-00-91), on Obregón between Calles Hidalgo and Morelos, flies to Guadalajara, Los Angeles, Mazatlán, Mexico City and Tijuana.

Aero California (☎ 5-10-23), at Obregón 550 near Calle Bravo, operates daily flights to Guadalajara, Loreto, Los Angeles, Los Mochis (for the Barranca del Cobre train), Mazatlán, Mexico City and Tijuana.

Bus ABC (☎ 2-30-63) and Autotransportes Águila (☎ 2-42-70) use the Central Camionera at Jalisco and Héroes de la Independencia. Northbound ABC buses go to Ciudad Constitución (three hours, 22 pesos), Ensenada (22 hours, 150 pesos), Guerrero Negro (12 hours, 90 pesos), Loreto

(5½ hours, 40 pesos), Mulegé (eight hours, 60 pesos), San Ignacio (10 hours, 70 pesos) and Tijuana (24 hours, 180 pesos).

Frequent southbound ABC buses serve San José del Cabo (25 pesos) and intermediates via the Transpeninsular. Autotransportes Águila takes highway 19 to Todos Santos (12 pesos) and Cabo San Lucas (25 pesos) at least five times daily.

Autotransportes de La Paz (☎ 2-21-57) buses leave the Mercado Francisco Madero at Revolución and Degollado for Todos Santos, Cabo San Lucas and San José del Cabo five times daily.

Car Daily rates at local agencies like AMCA (☎ 3-03-35), Madero 1715, and Servitur (☎ 2-14-48), Abasolo 57, start around 180 pesos with insurance and unlimited km. Budget (☎ 2-10-97) is on Obregón between Morelos and Hidalgo.

Motorbike Camarón Feliz Restaurant (☎ 2-09-11), at Obregón and Calle Bravo, rents mopeds and small cycles.

Ferry Ferries to Mazatlán and Topolobampo leave from Pichilingue, 23 km north of La Paz, but Sematur (☎ 5-38-33) offices are at Calle Guillermo Prieto and Calle 5 de Mayo in La Paz. Before shipping any vehicle to the mainland, officials require a vehicle permit (see the Car section of the introductory Getting There & Away chapter for the documents needed to obtain this). Vehicle permits are supposedly obtainable at Pichilingue on weekdays from 8 am to 3 pm, weekends 9 am to 1 pm, but it's probably safer to get them from the Registro Federal de Vehículos in Tijuana. Confirm tickets by 2 pm the day before departure; at 3 pm, unconfirmed cabins are sold on a first-come, first-served basis.

Weather permitting (high winds often delay winter sailings), the ferry to Mazatlán departs at 3 pm daily except Saturday (Saturday sailings take place in vacation periods only), arriving at 9 am the following day; the return schedule is identical. Approximate passenger fares are 60 pesos in salón, 120 pesos in turista, 179 pesos in *cabina* (two

Ferries to the mainland leave from Pichilingue

bunks with private bath), and 239 pesos in *especial* (suite).

The ferry to Topolobampo sails at 8 pm daily except Tuesday, arriving at 6 am; the return schedule is at 9 am daily except Monday, arriving in La Paz at 6 pm. The fare (salón class only) is 40 pesos.

Vehicle rates (given here in pesos) vary with vehicle length:

Vehicle	Length	Fare to Mazatlán	Fare to Topolobampo
Car	Up to five metres	437	267
	5.01 to 6.5 metres	569	346
	With trailer up to nine metres	788	480
	9.01 to 17 metres	1489	906
Motorcycle		57	33

Yacht Between November and March, the La Paz marina can be a good place to hitch a lift on a yacht to mainland Mexico.

Getting Around

To/From the Airport Taxis charge 60 pesos to Aeropuerto General Manuel Márquez de León, 10 minutes from downtown (bargaining may be necessary). Shared cabs *from* the airport are cheaper.

Bus Most local buses leave from the Mercado Francisco Madero, at Calle Degollado and Calle Revolución.

Bicycle You can hire bicycles at Viajes Palmira (☎ 2-40-30), on Obregón across from Hotel Los Arcos.

BAJA CALIFORNIA

To/From the Ferry Terminal From the Terminal Malecón, at Paseo Obregón and Avenida Independencia, Autotransportes Águila goes to Pichilingue nine or 10 times daily (3 pesos).

AROUND LA PAZ
Beaches
On Península Pichilingue, the nearest beaches are Playa Palmira (with the Hotel Palmira and a marina), and Playa Coromuel and Playa Caimancito (both with restaurant-bars, toilets and palapas). Playa Tesoro, the next beach north, also has a restaurant.

Camping is possible at Playa Pichilingue, 100 metres north of the ferry terminal, which has a restaurant and bar, toilets and shade. The road is paved to Playa Balandra and Playa Tecolote (windsurf rentals). Balandra is problematical for camping because of insects in the mangroves, and Tecolote lacks potable water. Playa Coyote, on the Gulf, is more isolated. Particularly stealthy thieves break into campers' vehicles in these areas.

LOS BARRILES
South of La Paz, the Transpeninsular brushes the Gulf at Los Barriles, Baja's windsurfing capital. Brisk winds averaging 20 to 25 knots descend the 1800-metre cordillera.

Several fairly good dirt roads follow the coast south. Beyond Cabo Pulmo and Bahía Los Frailes, these are rough but passable for vehicles with good clearance and a short wheelbase. South of the junction with the road to the village of Palo Escopeta and San José del Cabo's international airport, however, the rains of November 1993 made the road impassable for everyone except pedestrians, mountain bikers, burros and mules.

Places to Stay & Eat
The crowded *Martín Verdugo's Trailer Park* charges 25 pesos for a small vehicle or 30 pesos for a larger one, with hot showers, full hook-ups, laundry and a sizeable paperback book exchange. Camping costs 15 pesos.

The well-organised, Chilean-run *Juanito's Garden* charges 18 pesos with full hook-ups.

Other than camping, Los Barriles lacks inexpensive accommodation. *Casa de Rafa* (☎ (112) 5-36-36), at Km 109, is a B&B catering mostly to windsurfers. Rates are 105/135 pesos a single/double. *Hotel Playa del Sol* offers clean, comfortable singles/doubles for 165/240 pesos, including meals. Rates are comparable at *Hotel Palmas de Cortez*.

Popular with gringos, *Tío Pablo* has a good pizza menu plus massive portions of Mexican specialities like chicken fajitas, but the margaritas are weak. Despite the raucous decor and satellite TV, it's fairly sedate.

SIERRA DE LA LAGUNA
Even travellers who deplore the Cape Region's ugly coastal development will enjoy the Sierra de La Laguna, an ecological treasure that deserves national park status. Several foothill villages provide access to these unique interior mountains.

Tranquil **Santiago**, 10 km south of La Rivera junction and 2.5 km west of the Transpeninsular, once witnessed a bloody Pericú revolt against the Jesuits.

The modest *Hotel Palomar* has singles/doubles amid pleasant grounds, for about 60/75 pesos, but the place is more notable for moderately priced seafood than for accommodation. The English-speaking owner is a good source of information.

Cañón San Dionisio, about 25 km west of Santiago, is the northernmost of three major east-west walking routes across the Sierra; the others are **Cañón San Bernardo**, west of Miraflores, and **Cañón San Pedro**, west of Caduaño. San Dionisio offers scenic hiking in an ecologically unique area where cacti, palms, oaks, aspens and pines grow side by side. The trail requires scrambling over large granite boulders. If rainfall has been sufficient, there are pools suitable for swimming.

The best guide for hiking these routes is Walt Peterson's *The Baja Adventure Book* (Wilderness Press, 1992).

TODOS SANTOS

Created in 1734 but nearly destroyed by the Pericú rebellion, Misión Santa Rosa de Todos Los Santos limped along until its abandonment in 1840. In the late 19th century, it became a prosperous sugar town with several brick *trapiches* (mills), but depleted aquifers have nearly eliminated this thirsty industry. In recent years, Todos Santos has seen a North American invasion, including artists from Santa Fe and Taos.

Orientation & Information

Todos Santos has a regular grid, but residents rely more on landmarks than street names for directions. The de facto tourist office is El Tecolote (☎ (114) 5-03-72), an American-owned bookstore that distributes a detailed town map and a sketch map of nearby beaches. In a cluster of shops at Benito Juárez and Hidalgo, it maintains a good selection of English-language books and magazines, specialising in Baja California.

Money You can change money on weekday mornings at Bancomer, on the corner of Benito Juárez and Obregón.

Post & Telecommunications The post office is on Heróico Colegio Militar, between Hidalgo and Márquez de León. Pilar's Tacos, at Heróico Colegio Militar and Zaragoza, is the de facto phone office, but a new phone/fax/message centre is due to open in the same complex as El Tecolote (see Orientation & Information above).

Things to See

Scattered around town are several former trapiches, including **Molino El Progreso** at El Molino restaurant, and **Molino de los Santana**, on Juárez opposite the hospital. The restored **Teatro Cine General Manuel Márquez** de León is on the north side of the plaza.

Murals at the **Centro Cultural Todosanteño**, a former schoolhouse on Juárez across from Bancomer, date from 1933. They contain nationalist and revolutionary motifs like missionaries and Indians,

Spanish conquistadores, Emiliano Zapata, rural labour and industry, athletics and 'emancipation of the rural spirit'.

Festivals & Events

Todos Santos's late January Festival de Artes (Arts Festival) lasts two days. At other times, it's possible to visit local artists in their homes/studios. A tour of historic homes takes place in late February.

Places to Stay

El Molino Trailer Park, behind the Pemex station, has a laundry, spotless toilets, spacious showers, and a book exchange. It charges from 20 pesos with hook-ups.

Hotel Miramar, on a quiet side street in Barrio San Vicente south of Calle Degollado, is a bargain at 45/55 pesos a single/double. The remodelled *Motel Guluarte*, at Benito Juárez and Morelos, now has a swimming pool; doubles are about 60 pesos.

The Canadian-run *Hostería Las Casitas*, a B&B on Calle Rangel between Obregón and Hidalgo, charges 75/135 pesos a single/double. It also offers inexpensive tent sites, and the restaurant is open to the public. The distinctive *Hotel California*, on Juárez between Márquez de León and Morelos, has a pool and clean singles/doubles, each with private bath and ceiling fan, for about 105/135 pesos.

Places to Eat

Taco stands along Calle Heróico Colegio Militar between Márquez de León and Degollado offer fish, chicken, shrimp or beef at bargain prices. The family-run *Casa de Margarita*, in Barrio San Vicente, has attracted a devoted following for antojitos and seafood, but has no liquor licence. It's on a street whose name is disputed and which lies in between Calles Villarino and Progreso.

The coffee-conscious can consume their cappuccinos among savoury pastries and enticing fruit salads at *Caffé Todos Santos*, at Centenario and Topete. Expats also praise *El Molino*, situated on the grounds of its namesake trailer park, for its salad bar and Sunday brunches. The moderately priced *Las*

Fuentes, in a bougainvillea-shaded patio with three refreshing fountains on Calle Degollado at Heróico Colegio Militar, has antojitos (try the chicken with mole sauce) and seafood specialities.

Prices are high at *Café Santa Fe*, which attracts patrons from La Paz and Cabo San Lucas to its plaza location for Italian dining, but it's worth a holiday splurge.

Things to Buy

For local artwork try Casa Franco, on Benito Juárez between Márquez de León and Hidalgo; Santa Fe Gallery alongside Café Santa Fe; or Stewart Gallery on Obregón between Legaspí and Centenario.

Getting There & Away

At least six buses go daily to La Paz (15 pesos) and to Cabo San Lucas (12 pesos) from the bus station at Calle Heróico Colegio Militar and Calle Zaragoza.

SAN JOSÉ DEL CABO

• *pop: 19,029*

Developers have not yet totally transformed San José del Cabo, 180 km south of La Paz, but this once quaint town of small streets, Spanish-style buildings and a tree-shaded plaza is fast becoming a major tourist resort. Thankfully, plans for a grandiose marina near the ecologically sensitive Arroyo San José recently fizzled because of local opposition, and while this scheme is not completely dead, for now central San José retains its village ambience.

Orientation

San José del Cabo consists of San José proper, about 1.5 km inland, and a series of tacky beachfront hotels, condominiums and time-shares. Boulevard José Antonio Mijares links the two areas. Just south of the shady Plaza Mijares, it's a gringoland of restaurants and souvenir shops (but tasteful and tranquil compared to Cabo San Lucas).

Information

Tourist Office From 8 am to 3 pm, staff at the Dirección General de Turismo Municipal

(☎ (114) 2-04-46), on Plaza Mijares, will stop chatting on the phone just long enough to say they can't answer your questions. Try instead the talkative, English-speaking owner of Hotel Señor Mañana (see Places to Stay).

Money The cambio at Aeropuerto Internacional Los Cabos pays poor rates; avoid changing money until you get to town.

Bancomer is at Calle Zaragoza and Calle Morelos; Banca Serfin is at Zaragoza and Degollado. The cambio on Zaragoza between Guerrero and Morelos gives poor rates (though better than the airport), but keeps longer hours.

Post & Telecommunications The post office is at Boulevard Mijares and Valerio González. Direct and collect calls to the USA are easy from the public telephone office on Calle Doblado, but several other offices exist.

Jardín del Arte

On Sunday, from 10 am to 2 pm, artists and artisans sell paintings, photographs, sculptures, jewellery and other crafts in Plaza Mijares.

Beaches

Playa del Nuevo Sol and its eastward extension, Playa de California, are at the south end of Boulevard Mijares. **Pueblo La Playa** is a small fishing community about 2.5 km east of the junction of Calle Benito Juárez and Boulevard Mijares.

Activities

Fishing In San José proper, Deportiva Piscis (☎ 2-03-02), on Calle Mauricio Castro, arranges fishing excursions and also sells and rents tackle. Fishermen at Pueblo La Playa arrange similar trips; look for them in the late afternoon as they cut up the day's catch on the beach.

Surfing The best source of surfing information is Killer Hook Surf Shop (☎ 2-24-30), on Calle Hidalgo between Zaragoza and

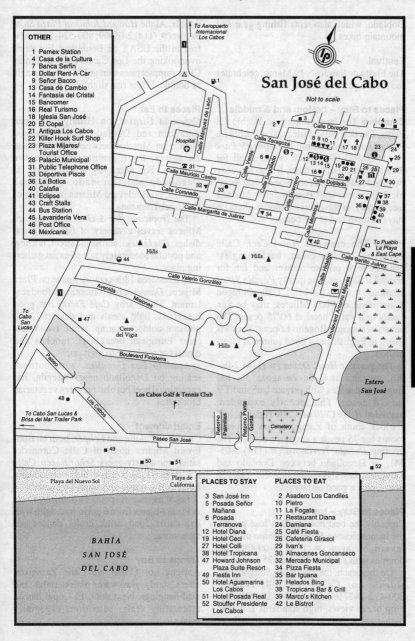

BAJA CALIFORNIA

Doblado, which also rents fishing gear and mountain bikes.

Festival

The Fiesta de San José, 19 March, celebrates the town's patron saint.

Places to Stay – bottom end & middle

Camping Try free camping at Pueblo La Playa. The best paying site, also at Pueblo La Playa, is the Swedish-run *El Delfín RV Park* (☎ (114) 2-11-99), which is too small for RVs but excellent for tents. It also has cosy twin-bedded cabañas for 75 pesos and reciprocal discounts with Posada Señor Mañana (see below) for travellers wishing to alternate stays in town and at the beach.

Hotels The crowded *Hotel Ceci*, Calle Zaragoza 22, has clean, basic singles/doubles with private shower and fan for about 45/50 pesos. The quirky *Posada Señor Mañana* (☎ (114) 2-04-62), Calle Obregón 1 just north of Plaza Mijares, may be San José's best value hotel at 60/75 pesos. The talkative manager Rogelio López ('Yuca') is fluent in English and a good source of information.

The popular *Hotel Diana* (☎ (114) 2-04-90), upstairs at Calle Zaragoza 30, has singles or doubles with private bath and TV for 70 pesos. The recently expanded, upgraded *Hotel Colli* on Calle Hidalgo, half a block south of Zaragoza, has carpeted rooms for 75 pesos a single or double. The inviting *Posada Terranova* (☎ (114) 2-05-34), on Degollado between Doblado and Zaragoza, has singles/doubles for 135/150 pesos, plus a good restaurant.

Places to Stay – top end

Probably the best hotel in San José proper, the inconspicuous *Hotel Tropicana* on Boulevard Mijares (☎ (114) 2-09-09) has doubles with satellite TV for 195 pesos.

On the beach, the 250-room *Stouffer Presidente Los Cabos* (☎ (114) 2-00-38; 800-472-2427 toll-free in the USA) has stunning ocean views, high standards and even higher rates: 250 to 375 pesos a single or double. At the *Howard Johnson Plaza Suite Resort* (☎ (114) 2-09-09; 800-524-5104 toll-free in the USA), on Boulevard Finisterra overlooking the Los Cabos Golf & Tennis Club, summer rates start at 275 pesos a single or double. Prices rise slightly in winter.

Places to Eat

Cafetería Girasol, on Hidalgo between Zaragoza and Doblado, and *Restaurant Diana*, on Morelos between Obregón and Zaragoza, have simple, inexpensive antojitos. For pizza, try *Pizza Fiesta*, at Degollado and Coronado, or *Marco's Kitchen*, on Boulevard Mijares just south of the Hotel Tropicana.

The *Tropicana Bar & Grill* on Boulevard Mijares serves a variety of fish and meat dishes. *Bar Iguana*, across the street, is a new and popular moderately priced expat gathering place.

In a restored 18th-century house on Plaza Mijares, *Damiana* is a romantic seafood restaurant. The nearby *Café Fiesta* has good breakfasts, light meals and desserts, with pleasant outdoor seating, while *Ivan's* features European breakfasts, lunches and dinners at moderate to high prices.

Asadero Los Candiles, with outdoor seating on Degollado near Obregón, has exceptional beef but also prepares vegetarian brochettes.

Entertainment

Clubs like *Calafia* and *Eclipse*, both on Boulevard Mijares north of Calle Coronado, satisfy most party-goers. *Señor Bacco*, Calle Zaragoza 71, is a disco that occasionally features live music and stand-up comedy.

Local merchants sponsor a Saturday fiesta in Plaza Mijares from 6 am to midnight, with live music, food, drink, crafts, dances and other attractions.

Things to Buy

Antigua Los Cabos, on Calle Zaragoza, offers sturdy glassware, plates, mugs and wall-hangings. Next door, El Copal has an interesting crafts selection, especially masks.

Fantasía del Cristal, on Calle Zaragoza alongside Bancomer, sells stained-glass artwork. A series of stalls on Boulevard Mijares, south of Coronado, sells quality souvenirs from all over Mexico.

Getting There & Away

Air Mexicana, with offices at the Plaza Los Cabos, on the beachfront Paseo San José, has daily flights to the USA and Mexico City. At the airport, Alaska Airlines (☎ 2-10-15/16) flies to San Diego, Los Angeles, San Francisco, Seattle and Anchorage. Aero California (☎ 2-09-42) flies to Los Angeles, Phoenix and Denver.

Bus Frequent buses leave for Cabo San Lucas (30 minutes, 7 pesos) and La Paz (two hours, 28 pesos) from the new station (☎ 2-11-00) on Valerio González east of the Transpeninsular.

Car The reasonably priced AMCA (☎ 2-13-14), at Km 33.5 on the Transpeninsular, will arrange airport pick-ups.

Getting Around

To/From the Airport Aeroterrestre runs bright-yellow taxis and minibuses to Aeropuerto Internacional Los Cabos (☎ 2-03-99), 10 km north of San José, for about 35 pesos. Local buses from the station to the airport junction cost only 3 pesos, but this means a half-hour walk to the terminal.

THE LOS CABOS CORRIDOR

West of San José, a string of tacky luxury resorts blights the once scenic coastline. Since the 1993 floods, the divided highway to Cabo San Lucas may not be completely restored for years, but temporary arroyo crossings permit motor traffic. Around Km 27, near the pricey *Hotel Palmilla*, are choice surfing beaches at **Punta Mirador** and at **Km 28** of the Transpeninsular. Experienced surfers claim that, during summer, reef and point breaks at Km 28 (popularly known as Zipper's) match Hawaii's best.

CABO SAN LUCAS

Cabo San Lucas, 220 km south of La Paz, is a resort of international stature, but its quintessential experience might be to stagger out of a bar at 3 am, pass out on the beach, and be crushed or smothered at daybreak by a rampaging bulldozer. Survivors can call the handy therapist at the Hacienda Beach Resort 'to help you strengthen, empower and revitalize your life'.

Cabo's most sinister ocean-floor scavengers are not bloodthirsty sharks, but developers and time-share sellers who have metamorphosed a placid fishing village into a depressing jumble of exorbitant hotels, pretentious restaurants, rowdy bars and tacky souvenir stands – an achievement comparable to turning Cinderella into her stepsisters. Its status as a North American tourist enclave and retirement retreat has engendered resentment among local Mexicans.

Orientation

Central Cabo lies north of Calle Lázaro Cárdenas, and has a fairly regular grid. Lázaro Cárdenas leads out of town to the highway junction. South of Lázaro Cárdenas, Boulevard Marina curves along the western harbour towards Land's End. Few places have street addresses; refer to the map to locate them.

Information

Cabo lacks a tourist office, but time-share sellers on Boulevard Marina distribute town maps and happily provide information (along with their sales pitch). Tourist publications are available free in restaurants and hotel lobbies.

Money Banks are open on weekday mornings. Baja Money Exchange, on Plaza Naútica on Boulevard Marina, changes US cash or travellers' cheques at poor rates, or gives cash advances on credit cards (with 10% commission!); hours are from 9 am to 7 pm weekdays, 9 am to 5.30 pm Saturday. A branch in the Baja Business Center, at Madero and Guerrero, is open from 8 am to 7 pm weekdays, 8.30 am to 5.30 pm Saturday.

Post & Telecommunications The post office is on the south side of Lázaro Cárdenas, near Calle 16 de Noviembre, east of downtown.

Long-distance cabinas have sprung up in many shops and pharmacies.

Consulate The US Consulate (☎ 3-35-36) is on the west side of Boulevard Marina, just south of Plaza Las Glorias.

Immigration Servicios Migratorios is at Lázaro Cárdenas and Gómez Farías.

Beaches

For sunbathing and calm waters try Playa Médano, in front of the Hacienda Beach Resort. Playa Solmar, on the Pacific side, has dangerously unpredictable breakers. Playa del Amor (Lover's Beach), near Land's End, is accessible by boat or a class 3 scramble over the rocks (at high tide) from Hotel Solmar.

Activities

Diving Locals report that poor underwater visibility near Land's End, due to raw sewage from tourist hotels, has improved somewhat, but ask dive shops about current conditions.

Amigos del Mar (☎ 3-05-05; 800-447-8999 toll-free in the USA) is across from the sportfishing dock at the south end of Boulevard Marina. Cabo Diving Services (☎ 3-16-58), located in El Coral restaurant at Boulevard Marina and Calle Hidalgo, is open daily from 9 am to 7 pm. Cabo Acuadeportes (☎ 3-01-17), in front of the Hacienda Beach Resort, is open daily from 9 am to 5 pm. The newest is Baja Diving Explorers (☎ 3-36-01), on Calle Hidalgo at Madero.

Fishing Packages are the best value. Hotel Solmar offers three nights' accommodation and one day of fishing for US$190 per person, but non-guests pay at least US$235 per day, including tackle and a two-person crew, for three passengers. Minerva's Baja Tackle, at Madero and Boulevard Marina, rents fishing gear.

Boat Trips Trips to El Arco (the natural arch at Land's End), the sea-lion colony, and Playa del Amor on the yacht *Trinidad* (☎ 3-14-17) cost about 45 to 90 pesos per hour. Dos Mares (☎ 3-32-66) sails glass-bottomed boats every 20 minutes from 9 am to 4 pm, and will drop off and pick up passengers on Playa del Amor.

From the Plaza Las Glorias dock, *Pez Gato I* and *Pez Gato II* (☎ 3-24-58) offer two-hour sunset sailings on catamarans which, reflecting Cabo's schizophrenic ethos, segregate their clientele into 'booze cruises' and 'romantic cruises'; prices are 90 pesos for adults, 45 pesos for children. The semisubmersible *Nautilus VII* offers similarly priced one-hour tours to view whales, dolphins and sea turtles. Make reservations (☎ 3-30-33) at Boulevard Marina 39-F or at Baja Tourist & Travel Services (☎ 3-19-34).

Land's End

Festivals & Events

Cabo San Lucas is a popular staging ground for fishing tournaments in October and November. One legitimately local celebration is Día de San Lucas, the festival of the town's patron saint, held on 18 October.

Places to Stay

Except for camping and RV parks, even mid-range accommodation is scarce. Some visitors may prefer the cheaper San José del Cabo, which is close enough for day trips.

Places to Stay – bottom end

Camping Tenters and RVs are welcome at *Surf Camp Club Cabo* (☎ (114) 3-33-48), about 1.6 km east of trendy Club Cascadas de Baja by a narrow dirt road. Rates are 15 pesos per person; a cabaña and two kitchenette apartments are available for 90/120 pesos a single/double.

About three km east of Cabo on the Transpeninsular, the spacious but shadeless *Cabo Cielo* (☎ (114) 3-07-21) has full hook-ups, spotless baths and excellent hot showers for 30 pesos.

Hotels

For 65/80 pesos a single/double, *Hotel Casablanca* (☎ (114) 3-02-60), on Calle Revolución near Morelos, has clean but dark rooms with hot showers and ceiling fans. *Hotel Marina*, Boulevard Marina at Calle Madero, has modest poolside rooms with air-con for 75/120 pesos. The comparable *Hotel Dos Mares* (☎ (114) 3-03-30), on Calle Zapata between Hidalgo and Guerrero, charges 80/90 pesos.

Places to Stay – middle

The pseudo-colonial *Hotel Mar de Cortez* (☎ (114) 3-14-32), at Lázaro Cárdenas and Guerrero, has a pool and an outdoor bar/restaurant. Newer air-con singles/doubles cost 115/130 pesos in the high season, but older rooms are good value for 85/100 pesos. Low-season rates (June to October) are about 25% less.

Siesta Suites Hotel (☎/fax (114) 3-27-73), on Calle Zapata between Hidalgo and Guerrero, has new kitchenette apartments for 105 to 135 pesos for two people, plus 15 pesos for each additional person.

Places to Stay – top end

The *Hacienda Beach Resort* (☎ (114) 3-01-22) has fountains, tropical gardens, tennis and paddle-tennis courts, a swimming pool and a putting green. Garden patio rooms start around 350 pesos, but beach cabañas cost 450 to 500 pesos.

All rooms face the Pacific at *Hotel Solmar* (☎ (114) 3-00-22), a secluded beachfront resort near Land's End which has tennis courts, a pool and horse riding. Singles and doubles start at 350 pesos in the low season (June to October), plus 10% tax and 10% service.

Places to Eat

Broken Surfboard, on Calle Hidalgo between Madero and Zapata, has inexpensive burritos, burgers, fish with rice, salads, tortillas and beans and similar items. *Cabo Gourmet*, on Lázaro Cárdenas between Matamoros and Ocampo, offers takeaway sandwiches, cold cuts and cheeses.

El Coral, at Boulevard Marina and Calle Hidalgo, proclaims 'authentic Mexican food', but their cheap double margaritas are better value than their mediocre meals. *Cabo Wabo Cantina*, on Calle Guerrero between Niños Héroes and Lázaro Cárdenas, is better known for its sound system than its cuisine, but the food is palatable and, by some accounts, rapidly improving.

The highly regarded *Salsitas*, in the Plaza Bonita mall on Boulevard Marina just south of Lázaro Cárdenas, serves Mexican specialities. For a variety of salsas, try *Chile Willie's* at Hidalgo and Zapata. *Manuel's*, at Boulevard Marina and Calle Cabo San Lucas, earns raves for its carnitas.

Just south of Lázaro Cárdenas, across from the Pemex station near the eastern entrance to town, the popular *La Golondrina* is expensive, but offers large portions. *El Rey Sol*, two blocks south of the Golondrina, serves appealing Mexican food and seafood; prices are moderate by Cabo standards. *Alfonso's*, at Playa El Médano, serves nouvelle cuisine, usually a 90-peso, five-course set menu.

Faro Viejo Trailer Park Restaurant, at Matamoros and Rosario Morales, lures the wealthy from their beachfront hotels for barbecued ribs, steaks and seafood. *Mi Casa*, on Calle Cabo San Lucas across from Parque Amelia Wilkes, has a pleasant homey environment and excellent seafood. *Romeo y Julieta*, west of the point where Boulevard Marina turns east towards Land's End, is a local institution for pizza and pasta.

Mobeso's sells pastries and a variety of

BAJA CALIFORNIA

PLACES TO STAY

- 3 Hotel Casablanca
- 18 Hotel Mar de Cortez
- 21 Giggling Marlin Inn
- 35 Hotel Dos Mares
- 36 Siesta Suites Hotel
- 37 Hotel Marina
- 43 El Faro Viejo
  Trailer Park
- 44 Medusa Suites
- 53 Hotel Meliá
  San Lucas
- 58 Hacienda Beach
  Resort
- 64 Hotel Finisterra
- 68 Hotel Solmar

PLACES TO EAT

- 1 Mercado Castro
- 2 Super Tacos de
  Baja California
- 4 Jugos Tuti Fruti
- 7 Panadería
  San Angel
- 9 El Squid Roe
  Cabo Grill
- 13 Cabo Wabo Cantina
- 16 Mercado Aramburo
- 19 Cabo Gourmet
- 22 Giggling Marlin
  Restaurant & Bar
- 24 Salsitas
- 26 Mi Casa
- 31 Broken Surfboard
- 34 Chile Willie's
- 38 Shrimp Factory
- 40 El Coral
- 49 Señor Sushi's
- 43 El Faro Viejo Trailer
  Park Restaurant
- 46 La Golondrina
- 49 Peacock's
- 50 El Rey Sol
- 51 Alfonso's
- 54 El Delfín
- 55 The Office
- 56 Mama's

- 59 Manuel's
- 61 Mobeso's Bakery
- 63 Romeo y Julieta
- 65 El Galeón

OTHER

- 5 Main Bus Station
- 6 Los Delfines
  (Travel Agency)
- 8 Bus Station
  (Autotransportes
  de La Paz)
- 10 Banca Serfín
- 11 Budget Rent-A-Car
- 12 Farmacia Aramburo
- 14 Long-Distance
  Telephone/Fax
- 15 Faces of Mexico
- 17 Bancomer
- 20 Giggling Marlin Co
  Store
- 23 Books Books/
  Libros Libros
- 25 Marina Cabo San Lucas
- 26 Casas Mexicanas
- 27 Parque Amelia
  Wilkes/Aero
  California
- 28 Banco Unión
- 29 Baja Business Center
- 30 Minerva's Baja Tackle
- 32 Baja Diving Explorers
- 33 Mercado Mexicano
- 39 Pancho's
- 40 Cabo Diving Services
- 42 Baja Money Exchange
- 45 Servicios Migratorios
- 47 Lukas
- 48 Post Office
- 52 Club Cascadas de Baja
- 57 Cabo Acuadeportes
- 60 AMCA Rent-A-Car
- 62 US Consulate
- 66 Government Crafts
  Centre/Cruise
  Ship Landing
- 67 Amigos del Mar

To Todos Santos
& La Paz

Calle Rosario Morales
Calle Alikán
Calle 12 de Octubre
Calle Alvaro Obregón
Calle Carranza
Calle Revolución
Calle Niños Héroes
Calle Lázaro Cárdenas
Calle Madero

Calle Cabo San Lucas
Calle Hidalgo
Calle Matamoros
Calle Abasolo
Calle Ocampo
Calle Zaragoza
Calle Morelos
Calle Leona Vicario
Calle Narciso Mendoza
Calle Mendoza

See Enlargement

Plaza las Glorias

Calle Ortiz de
Domínguez

Marina

Boulevard Marina

Avenida Solmar

Playa Médano

Playa Solmar

PACIFIC OCEAN

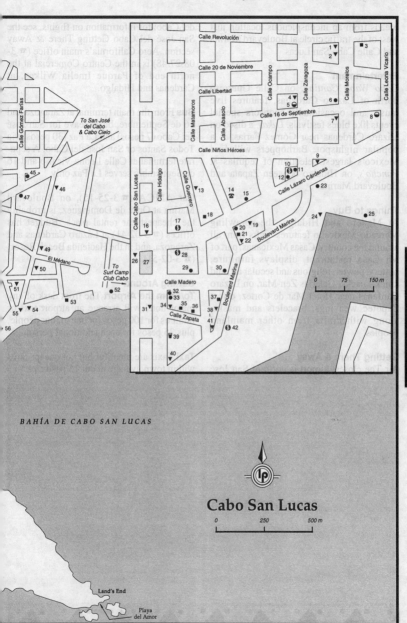

Calle Revolución

Calle 20 de Noviembre

Calle Libertad

Calle Matamoros

Calle Abasolo

Calle Ocampo

Calle Zaragoza

Calle Morelos

Calle Leona Vicario

Calle 16 de Septiembre

Calle Niños Héroes

Calle Hidalgo

Calle Cabo San Lucas

Calle Guerrero

Calle Lázaro Cárdenas

Boulevard Marina

Boulevard Marina

Calle Madero

Calle Zapata

To San José
del Cabo
& Cabo Cielo

Calle Gómez Farías

To Surf Camp
Club Cabo

El Médano

BAHÍA DE CABO SAN LUCAS

Land's End

Playa
del Amor

Cabo San Lucas

0   250   500 m

0   75   150 m

breads from an inconspicuous location just west of the traffic circle at Boulevard Marina and Calle Cabo San Lucas.

Entertainment

Cabo Wabo Cantina, on Calle Guerrero north of Lázaro Cárdenas, features live music and occasionally sponsors special events like blues festivals. *Lukas,* a disco on Lázaro Cárdenas near Gómez Farías, is a popular nightspot. Barhoppers will find Mexico's largest selection of tequilas at *Pancho's,* on Hidalgo between Zapata and Boulevard Marina.

Things to Buy

At Madero and Hidalgo, the sprawling Mercado Mexicano features crafts from all around the country. Casas Mexicanas, part of Mi Casa restaurant, displays furniture, pottery, pewter, religious and secular art, and knick-knacks. Galerías Zen-Mar, on Lázaro Cárdenas near Hotel Mar de Cortez, offers Zapotec weavings, bracelets and masks, along with crafts from other mainland peoples.

Getting There & Away

Air The closest airport is north of San José del Cabo; for information on flights, see the San José del Cabo Getting There & Away section. Aero California's main office (☎ 3-08-27/48) is in the Centro Comercial at the north end of Parque Imelia Wilkes, at Cárdenas and Hidalgo.

Bus From the main terminal at Zaragoza and 16 de Septiembre, buses leave for San José del Cabo (7 pesos) and La Paz (30 pesos) via Todos Santos or San José del Cabo. A separate terminal at Calle Leona Vicario and 16 de Septiembre serves La Paz only.

Car AMCA (☎ 3-25-15), on Boulevard Marina at Ortiz de Domínguez, is probably the cheapest car rental place. Budget has offices (☎ 3-02-41) at Lázaro Cárdenas and Zaragoza, and in the Hacienda Beach Resort (☎ 3-02-51).

Getting Around

To/From the Airport The front desk of any major hotel will arrange an airport taxi or minibus for 100 pesos for one to four people, plus 25 pesos for each additional person.

Taxi Taxis are plentiful but not cheap; fares within town average about 15 pesos.

North-West Mexico

This chapter covers the north-western state of Sonora, Los Mochis and Culiacán in the north of Sinaloa state, and the spectacular Copper Canyon railway from Los Mochis to Chihuahua.

Many travellers pass through Sonora, a large state known for its beef, agriculture (principally wheat and cotton) and the great Sonora Desert which covers much of the state. Highway 15, Mexico's principal Pacific coast highway, begins at the border town of Nogales, Sonora, opposite Nogales, Arizona, about 1½ hours' drive south of Tucson. This is one of the most convenient border crossings between western Mexico and the western USA. From Nogales, highway 15 heads south through the Sonora Desert for about four hours' drive to Hermosillo and then cuts over to the coast at Guaymas, about 1½ hours south of Hermosillo. From Guaymas the highway hugs the beautiful Pacific coast for about 1000 km, finally turning inland at Tepic and heading on to Guadalajara and Mexico City.

The Copper Canyon railway (the Chihuahua al Pacífico) is a highlight of travel in Mexico, traversing a canyon justifiably called the 'Grand Canyon of Mexico'. Its coastal terminus, Los Mochis, is near Topolobampo, where the ferry from La Paz in Baja California connects to the mainland.

NOGALES
• *pop: 108,000* • *alt: 1170 metres*

Like its border-city cousins Tijuana, Ciudad Juárez, Nuevo Laredo and Matamoros, Nogales is a major transit point for goods and people travelling between the USA and Mexico. On the northern side of the border in Arizona is its US counterpart, also named Nogales (walnuts) because of the many walnut trees that once flourished here.

On the Mexico side of Nogales, the bus and train stations, opposite one another on the south side of the city, have convenient connections to other parts of Mexico. On the Arizona side, the Greyhound bus station one block from the border crossing has frequent

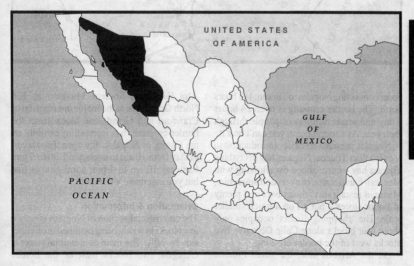

347

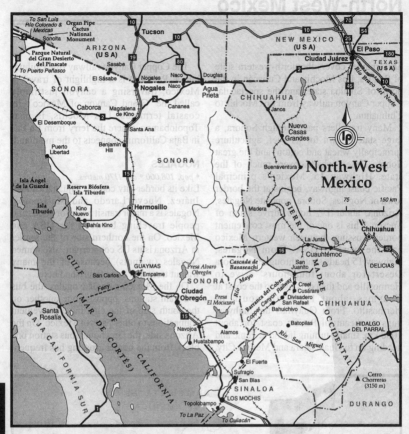

North-West Mexico

buses connecting Nogales to Tucson, 1½ hours north. The border crossing is open 24 hours a day and sends millions of people through each year. As a transit point, you can't beat it.

Nogales presents an easier introduction to Mexico than Tijuana. Nogales has everything Tijuana has – curio shops overflowing with Mexican handicrafts, trinkets and souvenirs, Mexican restaurants, cheap bars and plenty of liquor stores – but all on a much smaller scale. The 'shopping district' occupies only about four blocks along Calle Obregón, two blocks west of the border crossing.

On the Arizona side, the small Pimería

Alta Historical Society Museum at 136 North Grand Ave at the major intersection of Crawford and Grand, one block from the border crossing, has interesting exhibits on the history of Nogales. It's open Tuesday to Friday from 10 am to noon and 1.30 to 5 pm, Saturday 10 am to 4 pm; admission is free but you can make a donation.

Orientation & Information

The commercial section of Nogales is only a few blocks in width, being hemmed in on either side by hills. The main commercial street is Obregón, two blocks west of the border crossing, which eventually runs south into Mexico's highway 15. Almost everything is within walking distance of the border crossing; it's virtually impossible to get lost here.

Tourist Office The Secretaría de Fomento al Turismo (☎ (631) 2-06-66), in the large, modern, white building on the west end of the big white arches over the border crossing, is open every day from 8 am to 4 pm. It hands out a small map of the Mexican side of Nogales, but if you need a good map of the entire city (both sides) you might stop at the Pimería Alta Historical Society Museum on the Arizona side and ask to look at theirs.

Money Plenty of casas de cambio, where you can change US dollars to pesos or vice versa, are on both sides of the border crossing. On the Mexican side of Nogales, dollars and pesos are used interchangeably.

Post & Telecommunications The post office on the Mexican side, on the corner of Juárez and Campillo, is open Monday to Friday from 8 am to 7 pm, Saturday 8 am to noon. Next door, the Telecomm office is open the same hours, with telegram, telex and fax. Lada casetas for long-distance phone calls are everywhere in the small Nogales shopping district.

Places to Stay & Eat
The *Hotel San Carlos* (☎ (631) 2-13-46, fax 2-15-57) at Juárez 22 is very clean; singles/doubles are 72/77 pesos with one double bed, 94 pesos with two beds. In the same block, the *Hotel Regis* (☎ (631) 2-51-81) at Juárez 34 has singles/doubles at 85/100 pesos. Across the street, the very basic *Hotel Orizaba* (☎ (631) 2-58-55) at Juárez 29 has rooms at 55 pesos, some with private bath, some without. The *Hotel Olivia* (☎ (631) 2-22-00/67, fax 2-46-95) at Obregón 125 is a good hotel with parking, a restaurant and 51 clean air-con rooms at 94/105 pesos, a restaurant and enclosed parking. If you just want to clean up before crossing the border, the *Hotel Martinez* at Juárez 33 will rent you a shower for 15 pesos.

Café Olga at Juárez 37 is a basic café open every day from 7 am to 2 am. The similar *Copacabana* at Obregón 38 is open every day from 7 am to 10 pm. For something fancier, try the *Restaurant/Bar El Cid* upstairs at Obregón 124; the entrance is up some stairs at the rear of a shopping arcade. It's open every day from 11 am to midnight, later (till 2 am) on Friday and Saturday.

Getting There & Away
Bus The bus station is on highway 15, about eight km south of the city centre, opposite the train station. It has a cafeteria, a Lada caseta and a customs and immigration desk open every day from 6 am to 10 pm; you can also get your tourist card here.

Tres Estrellas de Oro, Elite, Transportes Norte de Sonora (TNS) and Transportes del Pacífico all have 1st-class air-con buses operating on basically the same routes. Each company offers around two to four buses daily to each destination, except to Herm osillo and Guaymas which have much more frequent service. Buses include:

Chihuahua – 962 km, 12 hours (95 pesos)
Guadalajara – 1737 km, 26 hours (186 to 220 pesos)
Guaymas – 393 km, five hours; every half hour from 4 am to 11 pm by Transportes Norte de Sonora (45 to 52 pesos)
Hermosillo – 282 km, three to four hours; every half hour from 4 am to 11 pm by Transportes Norte de Sonora; 14 daily by Tres Estrellas de Oro (30 to 35 pesos)
Los Mochis – 742 km, 10 hours (80 to 98 pesos)
Mazatlán – 1169 km, 16 hours (131 to 151 pesos)
Mexico City (Terminal Norte) – 2325 km, 32 hours (256 to 295 pesos)
Tepic – 1458 km, 24 hours (161 to 185 pesos)

Train The train station (☎ (631) 3-10-91) is opposite the bus station, about eight km south of the city centre on highway 15. Schedules for the primera especial Estrella del Pacífico and the segunda clase Burro trains are given in the Guadalajara section of the Western Central Highlands chapter. The ticket office sells Estrella del Pacífico tickets every day from 8 am to noon and from 2 to 3.30 pm. Tickets for the Burro go on sale a couple of hours before the train departs.

To/From the USA Nogales is one of the busiest border crossings for people travelling to/from the USA.

By Car Coming south from Tucson, the left lanes go to central Nogales; the right lanes, which go to a vehicular border crossing outside the city, are the quickest way to enter Mexico, but the crossing is only open from 6 am to 10 pm. Outside these hours you'll have to come through the city, where the border crossing is open 24 hours a day. As you approach Nogales you'll see plenty of signs for Mexican auto insurance, which you'll need if you're bringing a vehicle into Mexico. See the Getting There & Away chapter for more information on bringing a vehicle into Mexico.

By Bus The CAS bus coming from the Greyhound bus station in Tucson arrives in Nogales, Arizona at the Greyhound bus station on Terrace Ave, a block from the border crossing. There are luggage lockers here if you want to stash your belongings while you wander around the town. Buses to Tucson depart from this station daily at 7, 9, 10 and 11 am, noon, 1, 2.30, 4, 6 and 8 pm, with additional buses at 5 pm on Friday, Saturday and Sunday. The cost is US$6.50 for the 1½-hour ride.

You can't take a bus or taxi through the border crossing – you must either walk or drive. If you have a lot to carry, men and boys with handcarts will help to carry your luggage across for a small tip.

If you'll be heading further south into Mexico, stop and pick up a Mexican tourist card at the Migración office (see the Tourist Office section; it's in the same building). If you're staying within 21 km of the border you don't need a tourist card; you can easily walk across the border without one, but 21 km south of the border there's a checkpoint and if you don't have the proper paperwork, you'll be turned back. See the Facts for the Visitor chapter for more information on crossing the border between Mexico and the USA.

Getting Around
Everything you'll need in Nogales is within easy walking distance of the border crossing, except the bus and train stations on the Mexican side, which are opposite one another on highway 15, about eight km south of the border crossing. City buses marked 'Central' or 'Central Camionera' shuttle frequently between the stations and the border crossing, departing from a corner on Avenida López Mateos two blocks south of the crossing; the cost is 0.25 pesos. A taxi costs around 20 pesos.

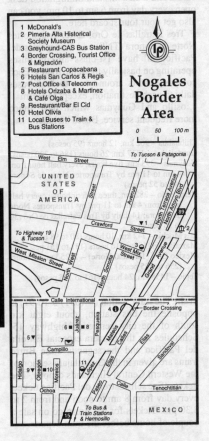

1 McDonald's
2 Pimería Alta Historical Society Museum
3 Greyhound-CAS Bus Station
4 Border Crossing, Tourist Office & Migración
5 Restaurant Copacabana
6 Hotels San Carlos & Regis
7 Post Office & Telecomm
8 Hotels Orizaba & Martinez & Café Olga
9 Restaurant/Bar El Cid
10 Hotel Olivia
11 Local Buses to Train & Bus Stations

Nogales Border Area

0   50   100 m

OTHER BORDER CROSSINGS

The Nogales border crossing is the quickest and easiest route when crossing the border in this region. There are other border crossings between Sonora and Arizona, however. West of Nogales, **San Luis Río Colorado** on the banks of the Río Colorado (Colorado River), 42 km south-west of Yuma, Arizona, has a 24-hour border crossing. **Sonoita**, opposite Lukeville, Arizona and immediately south of the picturesque Organ Pipe Cactus National Monument on the Arizona side of the border, has a crossing open daily from 8 am to midnight. About 130 km east of Nogales, **Agua Prieta** opposite Douglas, Arizona also has a 24-hour crossing. All are on Mexican highway 2, with frequent bus connections on the Mexican side (though possibly not on the USA side between San Luis Río Colorado and Yuma).

El Sásabe, opposite Sasabe, Arizona, about 60 km west of Nogales, is out in the middle of nowhere, with no bus connections on either side of the border and nowhere to get your Mexican car insurance if you're driving down from the north. The border crossing is open daily from 8 am to 10 pm but you're probably better off crossing somewhere else. About 90 km east of Nogales, **Naco**, opposite Naco, Arizona, is another small place in the middle of nowhere.

AROUND NORTHERN SONORA

On the north-east coast of the Gulf of California, **Puerto Peñasco** is a popular place for residents of Arizona and southern California to bring trailers (caravans) and RVs; the small town has 14 hotels and 10 trailer parks, making tourism an even more profitable industry than the shrimping and fishing the town is also known for. About 1½ hours' drive south of the Sonoita border crossing, this is the nearest beach if you live in Arizona.

Between Puerto Peñasco and the border, the **Parque Natural del Gran Desierto del Pinacate** is a large nature reserve with several extinct volcanic craters, a large lava flow, cinder cones, a cinder mine and vast sand dunes. Visitors must register at the park entrance, reached by going down a 10-km gravel road heading south from a turnoff about 10 km east of Los Vidrios, on highway 2 due north of Puerto Peñasco.

The small town of **Cananea**, on highway 2 about halfway between Santa Ana and Agua Prieta, is a mining town which is not of much note today, but it is significant in Mexican history because the miners' revolt that broke out here on 1 June 1906, near the end of the rule of Porfirio Díaz, helped to precipitate the Mexican Revolution. Displays in the small town museum tell the story of the strike.

HERMOSILLO

• *pop: 500,000* • *alt: 238 metres*

Founded in 1700 by Juan Bautista Escalante for the resettlement of Pima Indians, Hermosillo ('ehrr-mo-SEE-yo') is the large, bustling capital of the state of Sonora, on highway 15 about 280 km south of Nogales. Like many cities in Mexico, Hermosillo is quickly industrialising; in little more than a decade the city has gone from being primarily an agricultural and administrative centre of 45,000 to a multi-industry city of more than 500,000. Many travellers pass through Hermosillo heading north or south. Smack in the middle of the great Sonora Desert, Hermosillo gets very hot in summer; the rest of the year it's quite pleasant.

Orientation & Information

Highway 15 enters Hermosillo from the north-east and becomes Boulevard Francisco Eusebio Kino, a wide street lined with orange and laurel trees. Boulevard Kino continues west through the city, curves south-west and becomes Boulevard Rodríguez, then Boulevard Rosales where it passes through the city centre, then Boulevard Agustín de Vildosola before becoming highway 15 again south of the city. The major business and administrative sections of town lie on either side of Boulevard Rosales and along Boulevard Encinas which transects the centre from north-west to south-east. The Periférico, once a belt around

Hermosillo, has become practically an inner loop due to the city's rapid expansion.

Tourist Office The Secretaría de Fomento al Turismo (☎ (62) 17-29-64, fax 17-00-60) is on the 3rd floor of the east wing of the giant Centro de Gobierno building, which straddles Calle Comonfort just south of Paseo Canal, on the south side of the city centre. It's open Monday to Friday from 8 am to 3 pm and 5 to 9 pm, Saturday 10 am to 1 pm.

The tourist office hands out a free city map; a better city map is sold for 15 pesos at the bookshop of the Hotel San Alberto, on Boulevard Rosales opposite the post office.

Money Banks and casas de cambio are scattered along Boulevards Rosales and Encinas. The banks are open Monday to Friday from 9 am to 1 pm; the casas de cambio are open longer hours. The American Express agent, Hermex Travel (☎ 13-44-15, 17-17-18) on the corner of Boulevard Rosales and Monterrey, is open Monday to Friday from 8.30 am to 1 pm and 3 to 6 pm, Saturday 9 am to noon.

Post & Telecommunications The main post office is on the corner of Boulevard Rosales and Avenida Serdán. It's open Monday to Friday from 8 am to 7 pm, Saturday and Sunday 8 am to noon. The Telecomm office, with telegram, telex and fax, is in the same building; it's open Monday to Friday from 8 am to 7 pm, Saturday 8 am to noon. Lada casetas and Ladatel phones are everywhere in central Hermosillo.

Laundry Lavandería Automática de Hermosillo, on the corner of Yañez and Sonora, is open Monday to Saturday from 8 am to 8 pm, Sunday 8 am to 2 pm. Lavandería Automática Dania at Yañez 114, between Niños Héroes and Oaxaca, is open every day from 8.30 am to 1.30 pm and 3.30 to 8 pm. Lavandería La Burbuja on the corner of Niños Héroes and Guerrero is open Monday to Saturday from 9 am to 1 pm and 3 to 7 pm.

Things to See & Do
Hermosillo has two principal plazas: Plaza Zaragoza and Jardín Juárez. Plaza Zaragoza is especially pleasant at sundown when thousands of yellow-headed blackbirds flock in to roost in the trees for the night. On the west side is the lovely **Catedral de la Ascensión**, also called the Catedral Metropolitana. On the east side of the plaza, the grey-and-white **Palacio de Gobierno** has a courtyard full of colourful, dramatic murals depicting episodes in the history of Sonora. The cathedral and palace are open every day. The **Capilla del Carmen** on Avenida Jesús García facing Calle No Reelección is not as impressive as the cathedral but it's a fine little 19th-century chapel, built from 1837 to 1842.

The **Cerro de la Campana** (Hill of the Bell) is the most prominent landmark in the area and an easy point of reference night or day. The panoramic view from the top is beautiful and well worth the climb or drive to get up there. Hugging the east side of the hill, the **Museo de Sonora** has fine exhibits on the history and anthropology of Sonora, other parts of Mexico and Central America. The building itself is also interesting; it served as the Sonora state penitentiary from 1907 to 1979, reopening as a museum in 1985. It's open Wednesday to Saturday from 10 am to 5 pm, Sunday 9 am to 4 pm; admission is 10 pesos (children free), free on Sunday. To get there, walk south from the centre on Calle Jesús García, turn left on Avenida California at the base of the hill and go half a block to the museum. Local bus No 8 will drop you at the entrance.

The University of Sonora has a fine arts complex across from the campus on the corner of Rosales and Encinas; inside, the **Museo Regional de la Universidad de Sonora** has a history section on the ground floor and an archaeology section upstairs. Both are open Monday to Saturday from 9 am to 1 pm; the history section is also open weekday afternoons from 4 to 6 pm; admission is free. Also upstairs, the **university art gallery** is open Monday to Friday from 9 am to noon and 3 to 7 pm, Saturday and Sunday 10 am to 5 pm; admission is free. Events and exhibits are presented at the university throughout the year; check with the university or the tourist office for details.

The **Centro Ecológico de Sonora** is a zoo and botanical garden with plants and animals of the Sonora Desert and other ecosystems of north-west Mexico. There's more variety of desert life than you'd probably expect. The zoo also contains animals from around the world. It's open Wednesday to Sunday from 8 am to 5.30 pm (5 pm December to March); admission is 4 pesos. Also here is an observatory, with telescope viewing sessions on Friday and Saturday from 7 to 9 pm and 9 to 11 pm; admission is 4 pesos. The centre is about five km south of central Hermosillo, past the Periférico Sur and just off highway 15. The Luis Orcí local bus, departing from the west side of Jardín Juárez and heading south on Boulevard Rosales, stops at a gate about 500 metres from the entrance.

Hermosillo has some impressively large government buildings, including the huge, brown **Centro de Gobierno** complex, just south of Paseo Canal on the south side of the city centre, and the **Palacio Administrativo del Estado de Sonora** on Avenida Tehuántepec between Comonfort and Allende.

Some examples of Mexican flora

Festivals

The city's major annual event, the Exposición Ganadera (the Sonora state fair) is held in the Unión Ganadero each year from 28 April to 8 May. La Vendimia, or the Fiesta de la Uva (Festival of the Grape), is held on a weekend in June.

Places to Stay

If you spend a night here in summer, you must have a room with air-con that works. Some hotels advertise air-con, but the cool air may blow with barely more force than a whisper. Check the room before you accept it.

Places to Stay – bottom end

The *Hotel Monte Carlo* (☎ (62) 12-33-54, fax 12-08-53), on the corner of Juárez and Sonora on the north-east corner of Jardín Juárez, is a reasonably priced older hotel with clean air-con rooms; singles/doubles are 68/74 pesos. The *Hotel Washington* (☎ (62) 13-11-83, fax 13-65-02) at Dr Noriega 68, between Guerrero and Matamoros, has clean air-con rooms for 60/65 pesos. The *Hotel América Colonial* (☎ (62) 12-24-48) at Juárez 171 Sur, between Avenida Serdán and Chihuahua, is a basic hotel with rooms that are a bit dark but they do have TV and air-con; prices are 60/80/90 pesos for a room with one/two/three double beds.

The cheapest places to stay are the few dingy casas de huéspedes on Sonora between Garmendia and Matamoros, but even there it's hard to find a single for under 30 pesos. Most of the rooms seem to be rented out long term to students or short term to prostitutes. At night the prostitutes tend to be noisy.

Places to Stay – middle

The *Hotel Kino* (☎ (62) 13-31-31, fax 13-38-52) at Pino Suárez 151 Sur, conveniently situated near Boulevard Rosales, has a small indoor swimming pool, sauna, parking, a pleasant restaurant, and cool air-con throughout; singles/doubles are 100/120 pesos. Right on Boulevard Rosales, the *Hotel San Alberto* (☎ (62) 13-18-40, fax 12-58-98) on the corner of Avenida Serdán has a swimming pool, parking, cafeteria, bar,

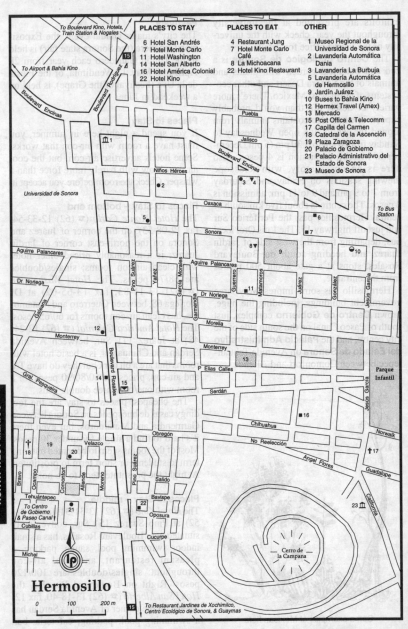

PLACES TO STAY
6 Hotel San Andrés
7 Hotel Monte Carlo
11 Hotel Washington
14 Hotel San Alberto
16 Hotel América Colonial
22 Hotel Kino

PLACES TO EAT
4 Restaurant Jung
7 Hotel Monte Carlo
   Café
8 La Michoacana
22 Hotel Kino Restaurant

OTHER
1 Museo Regional de la
   Universidad de Sonora
2 Lavandería Automática
   Dania
3 Lavandería La Burbuja
5 Lavandería Automática
   de Hermosillo
9 Jardín Juárez
10 Buses to Bahía Kino
12 Hermex Travel (Amex)
13 Mercado
15 Post Office & Telecomm
17 Capilla del Carmen
18 Catedral de la Ascensión
19 Plaza Zaragoza
20 Palacio de Gobierno
21 Palacio Administrativo del
    Estado de Sonora
23 Museo de Sonora

To Boulevard Kino, Hotels,
Train Station & Nogales

To Airport & Bahía Kino

Boulevard Encinas

Boulevard Rodríguez

Universidad de Sonora

Puebla

Jalisco

Boulevard Encinas

Niños Héroes

Oaxaca

Sonora

Aguirre Palancares

Dr Noriega

Aguirre Palancares

Dr Noriega

Morelia

Monterrey

Pino Suárez

Yáñez

García Morales

Garmendia

Guerrero

Matamoros

Juárez

González

Jesús García

To Bus
Station

Monterrey

P Elías Calles

Serdán

Chihuahua

No Reelección

Ángel Flores

Gral. Pesqueira

Boulevard Rosales

Obregón

Velazco

Comonfort

Allende

Moreno

Salido

Bavispe

Oposura

Cucurpe

Pino Suárez

Parque
Infantil

Jesús García

Norwalk

Guadalupe

California

Bravo

Ocampo

Tehuántepec

To Centro
de Gobierno
& Paseo Canal

Cubillas

Michel

Cerro de
la Campana

Hermosillo

0   100   200 m

To Restaurant Jardines de Xochimilco,
Centro Ecológico de Sonora, & Guaymas

travel agency, bookshop and 174 air-con rooms at 150/170 pesos, breakfast included. The *Hotel San Andrés* (☎ (62) 17-30-99) at Oaxaca 14 near Juárez, a block from Jardín Juárez, has parking and 80 refurbished rooms with air-con at 120 pesos with one bed, 150 to 170 pesos with two beds.

Places to Stay – top end

Many of Hermosillo's better hotels and motels are strung out along Boulevard Francisco Eusebio Kino in the north-east corner of the city. Top hotels include the *Fiesta Americana* (☎ (62) 50-60-00, 59-60-11; fax 59-60-62) at Boulevard Eusebio Kino 369 and the *Araiza Inn* (☎ (62) 15-82-37) at Boulevard Eusebio Kino 353. Boulevard Eusebio Kino also has upscale hotels including the *Señorial, Valle Grande Bugambilia, Valle Grande Pitic, Hotel Ganadera* and others.

Places to Eat

Cheap Eats Some of the cheapest food in Hermosillo can be bought from the hot-dog carts on every street corner. The hot dogs, for 4 or 5 pesos, are surprisingly good, especially when piled high with guacamole, refried beans, chiles, relish and/or mustard; the ones at the university are said to be especially tasty. Another street-cart treat is the pico de gallo – chunks of orange, apple, pineapple, cucumber, jícama, watermelon and coconut – refreshing on a hot day.

For a cool fruit salad, yoghurt with fruit, ice cream, fruit or vegetable juice or other cold drinks, check out the many branches of *La Michoacana* and *La Flor de Michoacán*. The one on the west side of Jardín Juárez, open till 10 pm, is a good place to get a snack to take out on the plaza.

There are cheap food stalls in the *Mercado Municipal*, on Calle Matamoros between Avenidas Calles and Monterrey.

Restaurants *Restaurant Jung* is a clean, cheerful air-con vegetarian restaurant and health food store on Niños Héroes between Matamoros and Guerrero, near Boulevard Encinas, open Monday to Saturday from 8 am to 8 pm, with a big comida corrida from

1 to 4 pm. The simple air-con restaurant at the *Hotel Kino* has good inexpensive meals, including a comida corrida; it's open Monday to Saturday from 7 am to 10 pm, Sunday 8 am to 4 pm. The *Hotel Monte Carlo* has a café open Monday to Saturday from 7 am to 10 pm.

Probably the best known restaurant in the city is the *Jardines de Xochimilco*, a pleasant restaurant where mariachis play and you can eat the beef for which Sonora is famous. The dinner special for two, for 80 pesos, is a memorable feast. It's in Villa de Seris, an old part of town just south of the centre. Come in a taxi at night, as the neighbourhood is not the best; anyone can direct you to it in the daytime. It's open every day from 1 pm to midnight; reservations are advised in the evening (☎ 50-40-89). Another branch is on highway 15. The *Restaurant La Huerta* at San Luis Potosí 109 is noted for its seafood.

Things to Buy

If you always wanted to buy a pair of cowboy boots and a 10-gallon hat, you'll probably find what you want in Hermosillo – the city has one of the best selections of cowboy gear in Mexico. Seri Indian ironwood carvings, another distinctive product of the region, are sold in front of the post office and at other places around town.

Getting There & Away

Air The airport (☎ 61-05-45/72) is about 10 km from central Hermosillo, on the road to Bahía Kino. Aero California has direct flights to Guadalajara and Mexicali; Aeroméxico has direct flights to Ciudad Obregón, Chihuahua, Guadalajara, Los Mochis, Mexico City, Tijuana and Tucson; Mexicana has direct flights to Mexicali and Mexico City; and TAESA has direct flights to Ciudad Obregón and Mexico City, all with connections to other centres. Hermex Travel (☎ 13-44-15, 17-17-18), on the corner of Rosales and Monterrey, and Turismo Palo Verde (☎ 13-47-01, 13-18-45), at the Hotel San Alberto on Boulevard Rosales at Avenida Serdán, are helpful travel agencies with details on all flights.

NORTH-WEST MEXICO

The Seris

The Seris are the smallest Indian tribe in Sonora, but one of the most recognised due to their distinctive handicrafts. Traditionally a nomadic tribe living by hunting, gathering and fishing – not agriculture, as was prevalent among many other tribes of Mexico – the tribe's area ranges along the Gulf of California from roughly the areas of El Desemboque in the north to Bahía Kino in the south, and inland to the area around Hermosillo.

The Seris are one of the few indigenous tribes that do not work for others, preferring to live by fishing, hunting and handicrafts. Their most famous handicrafts are their ironwood carvings of animals, humans and other figures; other important traditional handicrafts, including pottery and basketry, are no longer as important. The old-time Seris were one of very few tribes in the world that were nomadic and also made pottery. Though the Seris are no longer strictly nomadic, they still often move from place to place in groups; sometimes you can see them camped at Bahía Kino, on their way travelling up and down the coast or to and from Desemboque.

A visit to the Museo de los Seris in Kino Nuevo is a rewarding experience – it has illuminating exhibits on many aspects of Seri culture, including their distinctive clothing, traditional houses with frames of *ocotillo* cactus, musical instruments and traditional handicrafts, nomadic social structure, nature-based religion and more.

You will see Seris in Bahía Kino and in Hermosillo – a few sell ironwood carvings outside the Hermosillo post office. Many, though, live far from modern civilisation – the large Isla Tiburón belongs to them, and they live in many other inconspicuous places up and down the Sonora coast, still maintaining many of their old traditions and living between the desert and the sea. ■

Bus The Central de Autobuses is on Boulevard Encinas, about two km south-east of the city centre. First-class buses include:

Guadalajara – 1455 km, 24 hours; hourly buses, 24 hours, by Tres Estrellas de Oro and Transportes del Pacífico; 21 daily by Elite; 10 daily by Transportes Norte de Sonora (129 to 157 pesos), all via coastal highway 15 (passing Guaymas, Los Mochis, Mazatlán, Tepic etc)

Guaymas – 111 km, 1¾ hours; buses every half hour, 24 hours, by Transportes Norte de Sonora; hourly buses, 24 hours, by Tres Estrellas de Oro and Transportes del Pacífico (12 to 17 pesos)

Mexico City (Terminal Norte) – 2043 km, 32 hours; same as to Guadalajara (215 to 287 pesos)

Nogales – 282 km, four hours; buses every half hour by Transportes Norte de Sonora (25 to 35 pesos)

Tijuana – 995 km, 13 hours; 24 buses daily by Transportes Norte de Sonora; 16 daily by Elite; 14 daily by Transportes del Pacífico; 12 daily by Tres Estrellas de Oro (80 to 106 pesos)

Buses to Bahía Kino depart not from the main bus station, but from another one in the centre; see the Bahía Kino section following.

Train The train station (☎ 17-17-11) is just off Boulevard Eusebio Kino about four km north-east of the centre. The primera especial Estrella del Pacífico and the segunda clase

Burro trains stop here; see their schedules in the Guadalajara section of the Western Central Highlands chapter.

Getting Around

Bus Local buses operate every day from 5.30 am to 10 pm; the cost is 1 peso. To get to the Central de Autobuses, take any bus marked 'Central' from Calle Juárez on the east side of Jardín Juárez. Buses heading south on Boulevard Rosales depart from Calle Matamoros on the west side of Jardín Juárez.

BAHÍA KINO (KINO NUEVO & KINO VIEJO)

Named for Father Eusebio Kino, a Jesuit missionary who established a small mission here for Seri Indians in the late 17th century, the bayfront town of Kino, 110 km west of Hermosillo, is divided into old and new parts that are as different as night and day.

Kino Viejo, the old quarter on your left as you drive into Kino, is a dusty, run-down fishing village. Kino Nuevo, on your right, is basically a single beachfront road stretching for about eight km north along the beach, lined with the holiday homes and retreats of wealthy gringos and Mexicans. It's a fine beach with soft sand and safe swimming.

From around November to March the 'snowbirds' drift down in their trailers from colder climes. The rest of the time it's not crowded – but it's always a popular day outing for families from Hermosillo escaping the city, especially in summer. The beach has many palapas providing welcome shade.

The **Museo de los Seris** about halfway along the beachfront road in Kino Nuevo has fascinating exhibits about the Seri Indians, the traditionally nomadic indigenous tribe of this area. It's open Wednesday to Sunday from 8 am to 5.30 pm; admission is free. Seri ironwood carvings are sold in both Kinos.

Places to Stay & Eat

Kino Nuevo Most people come to Kino for the day from Hermosillo, but there are several places to stay. Prices tend to be considerably higher than in Hermosillo. There are plenty of palapas all along the beach – you could easily string up a hammock and camp out under these for free.

At the far (north) end of Kino Nuevo, at the end of the bus line, the clean, attractive and well-equipped *Kino Bay RV Park* (☎ (624) 2-02-16, 2-00-83; fax 2-00-37) has trailer or tent spaces at 42 pesos per day (cheaper by the week or month) and motel rooms at 180 pesos per day. The *Parador Bellavista* (☎ (624) 2-01-39), right on the beach, has camping spaces at 20 pesos for tents, 42 pesos for trailers, and two rooms with fridge and private bath at 150/120 pesos with/without air-con. The *Posada Santa Gemma* (☎ (624) 2-00-02, fax Hermosillo (62) 14-55-79), also on the beach, has camping spaces at 60 pesos for one night, 45 pesos nightly for more than one night, and expensive rooms. The beachfront *Restaurant & Hotel Saro* (☎ (624) 2-00-07) has 16 rooms with fridge for 150 pesos (singles 120 pesos on weekdays). The 50-room *Hotel Posada del Mar* (☎ (624) 2-01-55, fax Hermosillo (62) 18-12-37) is the luxury place to stay in Kino, with singles/doubles at 155/180 pesos.

Various places to eat – all specialising in fresh seafood, of course – are found along the beachfront road and in some of the hotels. The *Restaurant Palapa* has a good reputation.

Kino Viejo The *Islandia Marina* (☎ (624) 2-00-81), right on the beach in Kino Viejo, is a trailer park with spaces at 15 pesos for tents and 30 pesos for trailers, plus eight free-standing self-contained bungalows at 100 pesos for up to four people; you must provide your own bed linen and dishes. A block away, the air-con *Restaurant Marlin* is a popular place open from 1 to 10 pm every day except Monday. Other small eateries – open-air places serving fresh barbecued fish – are dotted around Kino Viejo.

Getting There & Away

Bus Buses to Bahía Kino depart from the AMH & TCH bus terminal (☎ 12-25-56) in central Hermosillo, on Sonora between González and Jesús García, 1½ blocks east of Jardín Juárez. Second-class buses depart at 5.40, 6.30, 7.30, 8.30, 9.30 and 11.30 am, and 12.30, 1.30, 3.30 and 5.30 pm; the cost is 11 pesos for the two-hour trip.

The return buses from Kino to Hermosillo run on a similar schedule, with the last bus departing from Kino at 5.30 pm. If you come at a busy time – on a Sunday, for example, when lots of families are there – and you want to get the last bus of the day – catch it at the first stop, on the north end of Kino Nuevo, while it still has space. Fortunately it's an easy hitch back to Hermosillo, if the bus is too crowded.

Car If you're driving, you can make the trip from Hermosillo to Bahía Kino in about an hour. From central Hermosillo, head north-west out of town on Boulevard Encinas and just keep going.

GUAYMAS

• *pop: 130,000*

Founded in 1769 by the Spaniards at the site of Yaqui and Guaymas Indian villages on the shores of a sparkling blue bay, Guaymas is Sonora's main port, with significant fishing and commerce as its main economic activities; the tourist resort town of San Carlos, on

Bahía San Carlos, is 20 km north-west. A ferry connects Guaymas with Santa Rosalía, Baja California.

Orientation & Information

Highway 15 becomes Boulevard García López as it passes along the northern edge of Guaymas. Central Guaymas and the port area are along Avenida Serdán, the town's main drag; everything you'll need is on or near this avenue.

Tourist Office The Delegación de Turismo (☎ (622) 1-14-36, 1-16-45) is several km west of the centre on Avenida Serdán, just before the bridge at the turnoff to Miramar Beach. It's open Monday to Friday from 9 am to 1.30 pm and 4.30 to 6.30 pm.

Money There are several banks and casas de cambio along Avenida Serdán. Most of the banks exchange money Monday to Friday from 8.30 to 11.30 am.

Post & Telecommunications The post office on Avenida 10 between Calles 19 and 20 is open Monday to Friday from 8 am to 7 pm, Saturday 8 am to noon. The Telecomm office, next door to the post office, has telegram, telex and fax; it's open Monday to Friday from 8 am to 7.30 pm, Saturday 8 to 11 am. Lada casetas are found in two pharmacies on Avenida Serdán: Farmacia Bell, between Calles 21 and 22, with phone and fax, open every day from 8 am to 10 pm; and Farmacia León, on the corner of Calle 19.

Places to Stay

For budget accommodation you can't beat the *Casa de Huéspedes Lupita* (☎ (622) 2-84-09) at Calle 15 No 125, between Avenidas 10 and 12, 1½ blocks from the bus stations and directly in front of the jail. Clean rooms opening onto a pleasant courtyard cost 25/35 pesos with shared/private bath. The *Casa de Huéspedes Martha* on Calle 13 (also called Calle Dr Pradeau) between Avenidas 8 and 9 has a similar friendly atmosphere and twelve rooms at 35 pesos, all with private bath, opening onto a courtyard with parking.

The *Hotel Rubí* (☎ (622) 4-01-69, 2-04-95), Avenida Serdán between Calles 29 and 30, is clean and pleasant, with 20 air-con rooms opening onto a pleasant courtyard; singles/doubles are 50/60 pesos. *Hotel Ana* (☎ 2-30-48, fax 2-68-66) at Calle 25 No 135 has 35 air-con rooms around a courtyard at 60/70 pesos for singles/doubles.

On Avenida Serdán at the west end of town there are a couple of US-style motels with not much personality but they're clean, with air-con and parking. The *Hotel Santa Rita* (☎ (622) 4-14-64, fax 2-81-00) on the corner of Avenida Serdán and Calle 9 (also called Calle Mesa) has singles/doubles at 70/85 pesos; in the next block, the *Motel Santa Rita* (☎ (622) 4-19-19, fax 4-16-17) on the corner of Avenida Serdán and Calle 10 charges 85/105 pesos.

Places to Eat

As in most Mexican towns, the mercado has stalls where you can sit down to eat; it's a block south of Avenida Serdán, on Avenida Rodríguez between Calles 19 and 20. Along Avenida Serdán there are many other places to eat. The small air-con *Todos Comen* between Calles 15 and 16 has economical meals, with a 12-peso comida corrida daily from 11.30 am to 4 pm; it's open every day from 7 am to midnight. *Jax Snax* on the corner of Calle 14 is a small air-con restaurant with pizza, snacks and meals, open from 8 am to 11 pm every day except Monday. *Las 1000 Tortas* between Calles 17 and 18 is a snack shop open every day from 7 am to 11 pm. *El Pollo Feliz* between Calles 12 and 13, with char-grilled chicken and beef, is open every day from 11 am to 11 pm; you can phone for free delivery (☎ 2-11-61, 4-17-81). *La Michoacana* on the corner of Calle 17 is a large open-air place with many cool snacks, open every day from 8 am to 10 pm. The *Restaurant/Bar del Mar* on the corner of Calle 17 is a higher-class seafood restaurant, pleasant, dark and cool, open every day from noon to 11 pm.

Getting There & Away

Air The small Guaymas airport (☎ 1-11-22,

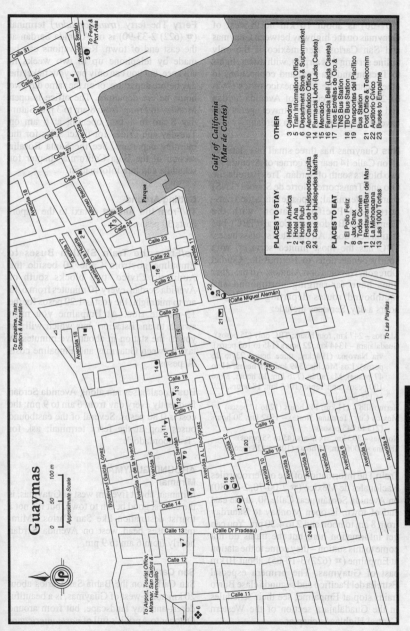

Guaymas

Approximate Scale

0   50   100 m

Gulf of California
(Mar de Cortés)

To Ferry &
Port Area

Avenida Serdán

To Empalme, Train
Station & Mazatlán

To Airport, Tourist Office,
Miramar, San Carlos &
Hermosillo

To Las Playitas

Calle 31
Calle 30
Calle 29
Calle 28
Calle 27
Calle 26
Calle 25
Calle 24
Calle 23
Calle 22
Calle 21
Calle 20
Calle 19
Calle 18
Calle 17
Calle 16
Calle 15
Calle 14
Calle 13
Calle 12
Calle 11

Avenida 18
Avenida 17
Avenida 16
Avenida 15
Avenida de la Huerta
Avenida A de la Huerta
Avenida 11

Boulevard García López
Avenida Serdán
Avenida A L Rodríguez
Avenida 12
Avenida 10
Avenida 9
Avenida 8
Avenida 7
Avenida 6
Avenida 5
Avenida 4

Alfonso Iberri
Calle Yáñez
Parque

(Calle Miguel Alemán)
(Calle Dr Pradeau)

PLACES TO STAY

1   Hotel América
2   Hotel Ana
4   Hotel Rubí
20 Casa de Huéspedes Lupita
24 Casa de Huéspedes Martha

PLACES TO EAT

7   El Pollo Feliz
8   Jax Snax
9   Todos Comen
11 Restaurant/Bar del Mar
12 La Michoacana
13 Las 1000 Tortas

OTHER

3   Catedral
5   Train Information Office
6   Department Store & Supermarket
10 Aeroméxico Office
14 Farmacia León (Lada Caseta)
15 Mercado
16 Farmacia Bell (Lada Caseta)
17 Tres Estrellas de Oro &
    Tres Bus Station
18 TBC Bus Station
19 Transportes del Pacifico
    Bus Station
21 Post Office & Telecomm
22 Auditorio Cívico
23 Buses to Empalme

NORTH-WEST MEXICO

1-07-66) is about 10 km north-west of Guaymas on the highway between Guaymas and San Carlos. Aeroméxico is the only airline serving this airport, with direct flights to Tucson and La Paz, and connections to other centres. The Aeroméxico office (☎ 2-01-23) is on the corner of Avenida Serdán and Calle 16; a couple of travel agents also have offices along Avenida Serdán.

Bus Guaymas has three small bus stations, all on Calle 14 near the corner of Avenida 12, two blocks south of Serdán. Tres Estrellas de Oro and Transportes Norte de Sonora (TNS) share one terminal; opposite this is the Transportes del Pacífico station, with the Transportes Baldomero Corral (TBC) bus station next door. All operate 1st-class buses. TBC has the most limited services, with hourly connections to Hermosillo, Ciudad Obregón, Navojoa and Alamos. All the other lines have far-ranging northbound and southbound routes departing hourly, 24 hours a day. Services include:

Alamos – 247 km, four hours; TBC only (25 pesos)
Guadalajara – 1344 km, 22 hours (145 to 165 pesos),
  via Navojoa (194 km, three hours, 23 to 26 pesos), Los Mochis (349 km, six hours, 41 to 47 pesos), Mazatlán (776 km, 12 hours, 89 to 100 pesos) and Tepic (1065 km, 18 hours, 120 to 138 pesos)
Hermosillo – 111 km, 1¾ hours (12 to 17 pesos)
Mexico City (Terminal Norte) – 1932 km, 30 hours (215 to 245 pesos)
Nogales – 393 km, six hours (45 to 55 pesos)
Tijuana – 1006 km, 15 hours (105 to 125 pesos)

Train The information office of Ferrocarriles Nacionales de México (☎ 2-00-70, 2-49-80) on Avenida Serdán near Calle 30, at the east end of town, is open Monday to Saturday from 8 am to noon and 2 to 4.30 pm. You can get information here but the trains do not come to this station – they come to the station at Empalme (☎ (622) 3-10-65), about 10 km east of Guaymas. The primera especial Estrella del Pacífico and segunda clase Burro trains stop at Empalme; see their schedules in the Guadalajara section of the Western Central Highlands chapter.

Ferry The ferry *(transbordador)* terminal (☎ (622) 2-33-90) is on Avenida Serdán at the east end of town. Reservations can be made by telephone up to two weeks in advance, but you can only buy your ticket the day before departure, or on the same day two hours before departure. The office is open Monday to Friday from 8 am to 3 pm, Saturday 8 am to 1 pm, opening at 6 am on Tuesday and Friday for ticket sales for the morning departure. See the Santa Rosalía section of the Baja California chapter for schedule and fare information.

Getting Around
To/From the Airport A taxi to the airport costs 30 pesos.

To/From the Train Station Buses to Empalme go from Calle 20 beside the Auditorio Cívico, two blocks south of Avenida Serdán, every 10 minutes from 6.15 am to midnight; the cost is 1.20 pesos for the 15-minute ride. At Empalme you must switch to an 'Estación' bus which will get you to the station in about five minutes. A taxi between Guaymas and Empalme costs 30 pesos.

Bus Local buses run along Avenida Serdán frequently every day from 6 am to 9 pm; the cost is 0.80 pesos. Several of the eastbound buses stop at the ferry terminal; ask for 'Transbordador'.

AROUND GUAYMAS
Miramar
Miramar, about five km west of Guaymas, is the closest good beach to town, but it's not a tourist destination like San Carlos. 'Miramar' buses head west on Avenida Serdán hourly from 6 am to 9 pm.

San Carlos
San Carlos, on the Bahía San Carlos about 20 km north-west of Guaymas, is a beautiful desert-and-bay landscape, but from around October to April it's full of *norteamericanos*

and trailer parks, and the accommodation is overpriced; the rest of the year it's pretty quiet. Part of *Catch-22* was filmed on the beach near the Club Méditerranée; only a few rusty pieces of the set remain.

The *Teta Kawi Trailer Park* (☎ (622) 6-02-20, fax 6-02-48), 9.5 km west of the highway 15 San Carlos exit, has tent/trailer spaces at 24/42 pesos and a hotel with rooms costing from 168 to 229 pesos. Near the marina the *Shangri-la Terrazas Trailer Park* (☎ (622) 6-00-75) also has sites with full hook-ups.

The most economical hotel in San Carlos is *Apartamentos Ferrer* (☎ /fax (622) 6-04-67), overlooking the marina, with seven basic air-con studio apartments with kitchen. Four small apartments for up to three people cost 82 pesos for one day, 67 pesos per day for two days or more, or 427/1650 pesos by the week/month. Three larger apartments cost 100 pesos for one day, 85 pesos per day for two days or more, or 555/2190 pesos per week/month. The *Motel Creston* (☎ (622) 6-00-20) at Km 15 on the main road into San Carlos has a swimming pool and 24 air-con rooms at 110 pesos.

Beside the Motel Creston, the San Carlos Diving Center (☎ (622) 6-00-49, fax 6-00-24), also called simply 'Gary's', rents scuba and snorkelling gear and conducts boat trips for sightseeing, fishing, scuba diving, snorkelling, whale-watching (November to March) and a Margarita sunset cruise.

Buses to San Carlos from Guaymas run west along Avenida Serdán every half-hour from 6 am to 8 pm; the cost is 2.20 pesos.

CIUDAD OBREGÓN & NAVOJOA

Heading south-east from Guaymas, highway 15 passes through Ciudad Obregón (125 km from Guaymas), a modern agricultural centre with nothing of touristic interest, and Navojoa (194 km from Guaymas), a similarly mundane place. From Navojoa a side road leaves highway 15 and heads east 53 km into the foothills of the Sierra Madre Occidental to the picturesque town of Alamos.

Navojoa has five bus stations, all within six blocks of each other. Second-class buses to Alamos depart from the station on the corner of V Guerrero and Rincón hourly every day from 6.30 am to 7 pm; the 45-minute trip costs 5 pesos. In the evening, buses to Alamos depart from the TBC station on the corner of V Guerrero and No Reelección at 5, 8 and 10 pm and at midnight. Navojoa is a stop on the Pacific coast train route; see the schedule for the primera especial Estrella del Pacífico and segunda clase Burro trains in the Guadalajara section of the Western Central Highlands chapter.

ALAMOS
• *pop: 8000* • *alt: 432 metres*
This small, quiet town in the foothills of the Sierra Madre Occidental, 53 km east of Navojoa, has been declared a national historical monument. Its beautifully restored Spanish colonial architecture has a Moorish influence, brought by architects from 17th-century Andalusia in southern Spain. The façades of colonial mansions line narrow cobblestoned streets, concealing courtyards

Navojoa Bus Stations

0   75   150 m
Approximate Scale

1 Local buses to Alamos & Huatabampo
2 TBC Bus Station
3 Transportes del Pacífico Bus Station
4 ADG Bus Station
5 Transportes Norte de Sonora Bus Station
6 Tres Estrellas de Oro & Elite Bus Station

lush with bougainvilleas; several of the old mansions have been converted to hotels and restaurants.

Alamos is also becoming known for its natural surroundings. On the border of two large ecosystem areas – the great Sonora Desert to the north and the lush tropical jungles of Sinaloa to the south – Alamos attracts nature-lovers to its 450 species of birds and animals, including some 50 endangered species, a number of species found only in the local area, and over 1000 species of plants. Horse riding, hunting, fishing, hiking, swimming and dining in opulent colonial mansions are also popular activities.

From mid-October to mid-April, when the air is cool and fresh, norteamericanos arrive to live in their winter homes and the town hums with foreign visitors. Mexican tourists come in the scorching hot summer months of July and August, when school is out. At other times you may find scarcely another visitor.

History

In 1540, this was the campsite of Francisco Vázquez de Coronado, future governor of Nueva Galicia in western Mexico, during his wars against the Mayo and Yaqui Indians (the Yaqui resisted all invaders until 1928). If he had known about the vast amounts of gold and silver that prospectors would later find, he would have stayed permanently.

In 1683 silver was discovered at Promontorios, near Alamos, and the Europa mine was opened. Other mines soon followed and Alamos became a boom town of more than 30,000 and one of Mexico's principal 18th-century mining centres. Mansions, haciendas, a cathedral, tanneries, metal works, blacksmiths' shops and later a mint were built. El Camino Real (the 'king's highway'), a well-trodden Spanish mule trail through the foothills, connected Alamos with Culiacán and El Fuerte to the south.

After independence, Alamos became the capital of the newly formed state of Occidente, a vast area which included all of the present states of Sonora and Sinaloa. Don José María Almada, owner of the richest silver mine in Alamos, was appointed as governor.

During the turmoil of the 19th century and up to the Mexican Revolution, Alamos was attacked repeatedly, both by rebels seeking its vast silver wealth and by the fiercely independent Yaqui Indians. The years of the revolution took a great toll on the town. By the 1920s, most of the population had left and many of the once-beautiful haciendas had fallen into disrepair. Alamos became practically a ghost town.

In 1948 Alamos was awakened by the arrival of William Levant Alcorn, a dairy farmer from Pennsylvania who moved to Alamos, bought the 15-room Almada mansion on Plaza de Armas and restored it as the Hotel Los Portales. Alcorn brought publicity to the town and made a fortune selling Alamos's real estate. A number of norteamericanos crossed the border, bought the crumbling old mansions for good prices – many were literally in ruins – and set about the task of lovingly restoring them to their former glory. Many of these people still live in Alamos today. Alcorn is also alive and well; you may find him sitting on the verandah of his hotel recounting intriguing stories of Alamos.

Orientation & Information

The paved road from Navojoa enters Alamos from the west and leads to the green, shady Plaza Alameda, with outdoor cafés at either end where you can get a drink and sit and watch the world go by. The mercado is on the east end of Plaza Alameda; the other main square, Plaza de Armas, is two blocks south of the mercado.

The Arroyo La Aduana (Customs House Stream, which is usually dry) runs along the town's northern edge; the Arroyo Agua Escondida (Hidden Waters Stream, also usually dry) runs along the southern edge. Both converge at the east end of town with the Arroyo La Barranca (Ravine Stream) which runs from the north-west.

Tourist Office The Delegación Regional de Turismo (☎ (642) 8-04-50) at Calle Juárez 6, under the Hotel Los Portales on the west side of the Plaza de Armas, is open Monday to

Friday from 9 am to 2 pm and 4 to 7 pm, Saturday 9 am to 2 pm.

Money The Bancomer bank on the south-east corner of the Plaza de Armas, facing the cathedral, is open Monday to Friday from 8.30 am to 1 pm; you can change money there until 12.30 pm.

Post & Telecommunications The post office on Calle Madero, at the entrance to town, is open Monday to Friday from 8 am to 3 pm. Polo's Restaurant on the corner of Calles Zaragoza and Allende, one block off the Plaza de Armas, has a Lada caseta; it's open every day from 7 am to 9.30 pm.

Books Several interesting books have been written about Alamos. *A Brief History of Alamos*, available at the gift shop of the Hotel Casa de los Tesoros, is an excellent short history of the town. *Las Casas Grandes de Alamos* by Leila Gillette tells stories of many of the town's old homes. Several books about Alamos by Ida Luisa Franklin are sold at her former home, Las Delicias, and at other places around town.

Laundry The town laundry is at the Dolisa Motel & Trailer Park, on Calle Madero at the entrance to town.

Things to See & Do

The **cathedral** is the tallest building in Alamos and also one of its oldest, constructed from 1786 to 1804 on the site of a 1630 adobe Jesuit mission. Legend relates that every family in Alamos contributed to the construction of the church – every high-ranking Spanish lady of the town contributed a plate from her finest set of china, to be placed at the base of the pilasters in the church tower. There is also a three-tiered belfry. Inside, the altar rail, lamps, censers and candelabra were fashioned from silver, but were all ordered to be melted down in 1866 by General Ángel Martínez after he booted French imperialist troops out of Alamos. Subterranean passageways between the church and several of the mansions –

probably built as escape routes for the safety of the rich families in time of attack – were blocked off in the 1950s.

The **Museo Costumbrista de Sonora**, on the east side of the Plaza de Armas, is a fine little museum open Wednesday to Saturday from 9 am to 1 pm and 3 to 6 pm, Sunday 9 am to 6 pm; admission is 2 pesos. About a km east of the town centre, opposite the cemetery, **Las Delicias** was the home of Ida Luisa Franklin. It's a charming restored mansion full of antiques and interesting stories; the 2-peso admission includes a guided tour. It's open every day from 7 to 11 am, 1 to 4 pm and 5.30 to 7 pm.

There are a couple of good vantage points for a view over the town. One is the **Mirador**, on top of a small hill on the south side of town; it's worth the climb or drive up. The other is the **jail**, on a small hill just west of the cathedral. The jail is closer to the centre, but the view is better from the Mirador.

A **tianguis** is held every Sunday from around 6 am to 2 pm beside the Arroyo La Aduana, near Calle Matamoros.

Organised Tours

A Home & Garden Tour sponsored by Friends of the Library leaves on Saturday at 10 am from in front of the bank on the Plaza de Armas, culminating in refreshments back at the library; the cost is 20 pesos. The tour is given from around mid-October to mid-May; at other times, Alamos's tourist guides can take you to some of the homes. Alamos has four professional tourist guides who can take you around to the sights and tell you the stories of the town. Ask at the tourist office; the cost is around 15 to 20 pesos for a two-hour tour.

Festivals

The biggest yearly fiesta is that of the Virgen de Concepción, the town's patron saint, on 8 December. On the night of 1 November everyone goes to the cemetery for the Día de los Muertos; the cemetery is cleaned up, and people bring candles, flowers and food and walk around visiting the graves in an almost festive atmosphere.

Places to Stay

Camping The *Dolisa Motel & Trailer Park*
(☎ /fax (642) 8-01-31) at the entrance to
town has 42 spaces with full hook-ups.
About two km west of town is the *Real de
los Alamos* trailer park (☎ (642) 8-05-57),
with a swimming pool. The *Acosta Trailer
Rancho* (☎ (642) 8-02-46) on a fruit farm
about a km east of the town centre has 30
sites with full hook-ups, barbecue areas,
plenty of shady trees and two swimming
pools; follow the signs across town. All of
these charge around 38 pesos for trailers, half
price for tents.

The 65-space *El Caracol Trailer Resort*
(cellular ☎ (9064) 84-07-01), on a 1120-
hectare cattle ranch 13 km west of Alamos
on the road to Navojoa, has good bird-watching, a swimming pool, a children's pool and
a fine restaurant/bar; it's the least expensive
trailer park in Alamos, with tent/trailer
spaces at 24/28 pesos. The Navojoa-Alamos
bus stops at the gate.

Hotels The *Hotel Enríquez*, on the west side
of Plaza de Armas, is in a 250-year-old building with rooms around a central courtyard at
30 pesos per person. At the entrance to town,
Motel Somar (☎ (642) 8-01-95) at Madero
110 has 30 basic rooms with singles/doubles
from 60/65 pesos to 80/85 pesos. The *Dolisa
Motel & Trailer Park* (see Camping above)
has clean, basic rooms with air-con, some
with fireplace, at 80/90 pesos for singles/
doubles and a suite with kitchen for 120
pesos.

Alamos has several beautifully restored
Spanish colonial mansions that have been
turned into hotels. The *Hotel Los Portales*
(☎ (642) 8-02-01) on the west side of the Plaza
de Armas is in the restored mansion of the
Almada family, with a courtyard surrounded by
stone arches and cool, comfortable rooms with
fireplaces; singles/doubles are 100/120 pesos.

Three other places are even more lux-
uriously restored. The *Hotel Mansión de la
Condesa Magdalena* (☎ /fax (642) 8-02-21)
at Calle Obregón 2, a block behind the cathedral, was built in 1685 for one of the region's
first major mining families, the Salidos. The

12 rooms have fireplaces, stone floors and
fans; some also have air-con. Its restaurant is
open from October to April. Prices start at
120/150 pesos for singles/doubles from
April to October; from November to March
they're 150/185 pesos. Opposite this is the
similarly luxurious *Posada Casa Encantada*
(☎ /fax (642) 8-04-82) at Calle Juárez 20, a
nine-room B&B with a beautiful courtyard,
a swimming pool and singles/doubles at
150/185 pesos from June to September,
220/270 pesos from November to March.

The *Hotel Casa de los Tesoros* (☎ (642)
8-00-10, fax 8-04-00) at Obregón 10 is a
14-room hotel in an 18th-century convent.
Like the other restored hotels, it's a fine
example of Spanish colonial architecture.
There's a swimming pool, a cosy bar and a
courtyard restaurant with entertainment; the
rooms all have air-con and fireplaces.
Singles/doubles are 165/198 pesos from
May to October; the rest of the year they're
208 pesos for singles, 240 to 272 pesos for
doubles, with breakfast included.

About a km south of town, across the dry
stream bed, the *Hotel La Posada* (☎ (642)
8-00-45) at Calle 2 de Abril, Prolongación
Sur, in the Barrio El Perico, has a restaurant,
bar, and some rooms with private kitchens
and sleeping lofts; all have air-con and fireplaces and cost 105 to 135 pesos.

Places to Eat

Some of the cheapest food can be had at the
food stalls in the mercado. On the outside of
the mercado building, the simple *Taquería
La Blanquita* is open every day from around
6 am to 10.30 pm. The *María Bonita* restaurant is opposite the south-east corner of the
mercado.

Good 'home cooking' is served by Doña
Celsa at *Las Palmeras Restaurant*, on the
north side of the Plaza de Armas, every day
from around 6 am to 10 pm. The food is tasty
and the prices are good too – this is a favourite among expatriate residents. *Polo's* on the
corner of Zaragoza and Allende, just off the
Plaza de Armas, is another simple restaurant
with a good reputation, open every day from
7 am to 9.30 pm.

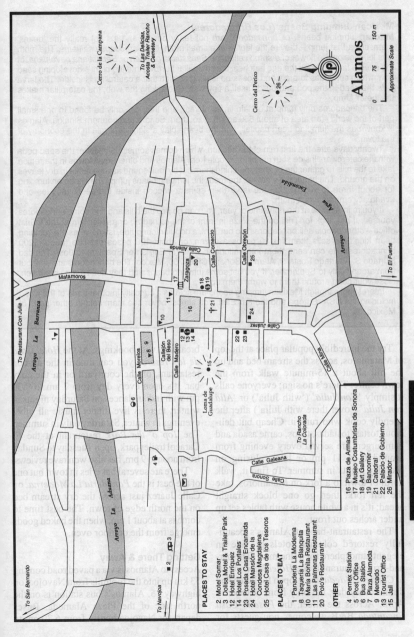

Alamos

Approximate Scale

0   75   150 m

NORTH-WEST MEXICO

PLACES TO STAY

2 Motel Somar
3 Dolisa Motel & Trailer Park
12 Hotel Enriquez
14 Hotel Los Portales
23 Posada Casa Encantada
24 Hotel Mansión de la
   Condesa Magdalena
25 Hotel Casa de los Tesoros

PLACES TO EAT

1 Panadería La Moderna
8 Taquería La Banquita
10 María Bonita Restaurant
11 Las Palmeras Restaurant
20 Polo's Restaurant

OTHER

4 Pemex Station
5 Post Office
6 Bus Station
9 Mercado
13 Tourist Office
15 Jail
16 Plaza de Armas
17 Museo Costumbrista de Sonora
18 Art Gallery
19 Bancomer
21 Catedral
22 Palacio de Gobierno
26 Mirador

Mexican Jumping Beans (Los Brincadores)

Mexican jumping beans, or *brincadores*, are not really beans, and it's not really the 'beans' themselves that jump – they're the larvae of a small moth, the *Carpocapsa saltitans*. The moth lays its eggs on the flower of a shrub called the *Sebastiana palmieri* or *Sebastiana pavoniana*, of the spurge family. When the egg hatches, the caterpillar burrows into the plant's developing seed pod, which continues to grow and closes up leaving no sign that a caterpillar is inside. The larva eats the seed in the pod and builds itself a tiny web. By yanking the web, the caterpillar makes the 'bean' jump.

The brincadores only jump at certain times of year, and they can only be found in one small part of the world – an area of about 650 sq km in southern Sonora and northern Sinaloa. Alamos is known as the 'jumping bean capital', and the beans play a significant role in the economy of the town.

Twenty days after the first rain of the season, which comes sometime in June, the seed pods with the caterpillars inside start jumping. People from Alamos and other small towns in the region take to the hills to gather the beans, searching them out by their sound as they rustle in dry leaves on the ground. The hotter the weather, the more the jumping beans jump. They keep on jumping for about three to six months; the larva then spins a cocoon inside the seed, mutates and eventually emerges as a moth.

If you're in Alamos at the right time of year, you can go into the hills and find some brincadores yourself. If not, look for Trini on the plaza in front of the cathedral, or ask for him at the tourist office – other people sell brincadores too but Trini, a popular tour guide, is known as the 'jumping bean king'. He sells them for 10 pesos a dozen, or about 100 pesos per litre (about 1200 brincadores). He can send them internationally; write (in English or Spanish) to José Trinidad Hurtado S, Apartado Postal 9, Alamos, Sonora, CP 85760, México. The brincadores are sent out from around July to September. If you get some jumping beans and they don't jump very much, close your hand around them to warm them up.

Interestingly, though Mexican jumping beans are sold as a curiosity in other parts of the world including the USA, Europe and the Far East, you almost never see them sold in other parts of Mexico. ■

Try the incredibly popular place at the top of Matamoros, across the stream bed and up the hill about a 15-minute walk from the town centre. There's no sign; everyone calls it simply *'Con Julia'* ('with Julia') or *'Allá con Julia'* ('over there with Julia') after the friendly cook who runs it. Cheap but delicious tortas, tostadas, tacos, carne asada and hamburgers are served every evening from around 6 to 11 pm or later, closing on Monday nights in summer. To find it, walk north of town to a fork on Matamoros, take the left fork, then go one block straight ahead; it's in a white house with tables set up under arches out front.

The restaurant-bars at Alamos's beautifully restored colonial hotels provide an elegant atmosphere for a fine meal. The bar-and-grill restaurant at the *Hotel Mansión de la Condesa Magdalena* is open for lunch and dinner every day, but only from October to April. Across the street, the *Posada Casa Encantada* B&B welcomes non-guests for breakfast, with bookings. At the *Hotel Casa de los Tesoros* you can dine in the air-con restaurant, on the courtyard or in the cosy bar. It's open every day from 7 am to 9.30 pm with Indian dances on Saturday nights in winter; there is live dinner music all other evenings in winter, Saturday only in summer. The *Top o' the Park* restaurant at the El Caracol trailer park, open Tuesday to Sunday from noon to 9 pm, has also won rave reviews.

There are several bakeries in town but one of the best is the *Panadería La Moderna*, on Calle Juárez just across the dry stream bed on the north edge of town. The best time to come is at about 1 pm, when the baked goods emerge from the outdoor oven.

Getting There & Away

Access to Alamos is via a paved road coming 53 km up into the foothills from Navojoa, on highway 15. Alamos's bus station is on the north side of the Plaza Alameda. Buses depart for Navojoa hourly from 6.30 am to

6.30 pm; the cost is 5 pesos for the 45-minute ride. Navojoa is served by all buses and trains coming up and down the coast.

Getting Around
There's a taxi stand on the east end of the Plaza Alameda, opposite the mercado. A ride in town costs 7 pesos.

AROUND ALAMOS
El Chalotón, a park about two km east of town, is a popular place to swim in the summer. About 10 km east of town, the **Arroyo de Cuchujaqui** has a delightful swimming hole, and people go there for fishing, camping and bird-watching, too. If you have no car you'll have to go by taxi or walk; taxis charge 50 pesos each way, and will return to pick you up at an appointed time. The **Presa El Mocuzari** reservoir is also good for swimming, camping and fishing, with abundant largemouth bass, bluegill and catfish. Take the turnoff on the Navojoa-Alamos road, about 20 km west of Alamos; the reservoir is about 12 km from the turnoff.

A few small historic towns near Alamos make interesting day excursions. Check out **Minas Nuevas**, about nine km from Alamos on the Navojoa-Alamos road; the bus to Navojoa will drop you there for about 1 peso. Other historic towns near Alamos include **La Aduana** and **Promontorios**. You can visit all these places on your own, or the tourist office can arrange for a guide to take you.

LOS MOCHIS
• *pop: 305,000*
Many travellers pass through Los Mochis, as it's the coastal terminus of the famous Copper Canyon (Chihuahua al Pacífico) railway. Topolobampo, 24 km south-west of the city, is the terminus of a ferry from La Paz, connecting Baja California to the mainland. The city is unremarkable otherwise, but it does have everything travellers may need.

Orientation & Information
It's difficult to get lost in Los Mochis – the streets are laid out on a grid. Avenida Gabriel Leyva, the main street through the city, runs south-west from highway 15 directly into the centre of town, changing names from Calzada López Mateos to Avenida Gabriel Leyva as it enters the city centre. Boulevard Castro is another major artery.

Tourist Office The Delegación de Turismo (☎ /fax (681) 2-66-40) on the ground floor of the large government building on Allende near the corner of Cuauhtémoc is open Monday to Friday from 8 am to 4 pm and 5 to 7 pm. They have a few brochures (in Spanish) about the state of Sinaloa, but if you need concrete information or tickets you're better off going somewhere else – to Viajes Flamingo, downstairs in the Hotel Santa Anita, for the Copper Canyon railway (see the Barranca del Cobre section later in this chapter), and to Viajes Paotam for the ferry to La Paz (see Getting There & Away in this section).

Money Banks are dotted around the centre; they're open Monday to Friday from 9 am to 1 pm. Casas de cambio are open longer hours. Servicios Multiples Rocha on the corner of Hidalgo and Ángel Flores is open Monday to Friday from 9 am to 7 pm, Saturday 8 am to 6 pm. The Casa de Cambio Rocha on Hidalgo between Zaragoza and Guillermo Prieto is open Monday to Saturday from 9 am to 2 pm and 4 to 7 pm. Or there's Dinámica de Cambio, on Hidalgo between Leyva and Ángel Flores, open Monday to Saturday from 9 am to 6.30 pm. The American Express agent is Viajes Araceli (☎ 2-20-84, 2-41-39) at Obregón 471A Pte between Leyva and Ángel Flores, open Monday to Friday from 8.30 am to 6.30 pm, Saturday 8.30 am to 2 pm.

Post & Telecommunications The post office, on Ordoñez between Zaragoza and Guillermo Prieto, is open Monday to Friday from 8 am to 7 pm, Saturday 8 am to 1 pm. A Lada caseta with telephone and fax is on Leyva between Obregón and Hidalgo, open every day from 8 am to 10 pm, with discounts in the evenings; another is on the

NORTH-WEST MEXICO

corner of Allende and Hidalgo, open Monday to Saturday from 8 am to 9 pm, Sunday 8 am to 6 pm, and there's another caseta a couple of doors down on Allende. Yet another is in the Transportes del Pacífico bus station, on Morelos between Leyva and Zaragoza. Ladatel phones are plentiful in the downtown area.

Laundry Lavamatic 2000 at Allende 218 Sur, between Juárez and Independencia, is open Monday to Saturday from 7 am to 7 pm, Sunday 7 am to 1 pm.

Places to Stay – bottom end

Camping The *Los Mochis-Copper Canyon RV Park* (☎ (681) 2-68-17), on Calzada López Mateos one km west of highway 15, has 140 spaces with full hook-ups at 36 pesos per space.

Hotels Los Mochis doesn't have many hotels in the budget range – the hotels seem to have got together and agreed to charge higher rates. The *Hotel Hidalgo* (☎ (681) 2-34-56) upstairs at Hidalgo 260 Pte between Zaragoza and Guillermo Prieto has singles/doubles at 50/65 pesos but the price is the only reason to stay there.

Places to Stay – middle

There are plenty of hotels in the middle price range. All those mentioned here are clean, with air-con, TV in the rooms, and hotel restaurants. The *Hotel Montecarlo* (☎ (681) 2-18-18, 2-13-44), on the corner of Independencia and Ángel Flores, has rooms around a sunny courtyard with a restaurant on one end and a bar on the other; singles/doubles are 75/92 pesos. The *Hotel América* (☎ (681) 2-13-55, 2-19-05, fax 2-59-83), at Allende 655 Sur between Castro and Cuauhtémoc, has singles/doubles at 75/90 pesos; rooms facing the rear are quieter. Both have enclosed parking at the back where you can leave a vehicle while you visit the Copper Canyon.

Similar hotels with similar prices, but without enclosed parking, are the *Hotel Lorena* (☎ (681) 2-02-39, 2-09-58; fax 2-45-

17), at Obregón 186 Pte on the corner of Guillermo Prieto, and the *Hotel Fenix* (☎ (681) 2-26-23/25, fax 5-89-48), at Ángel Flores 365 Sur between Independencia and Hidalgo. The *Hotel Beltran* (☎ /fax (681) 2-07-10), at Hidalgo 281 Pte on the corner of Zaragoza, is more worn around the edges but it's also a bit cheaper if you have two sharing a bed – rooms are 75 pesos with one double bed, 110 pesos with two beds.

Places to Stay – top end

The *Hotel Santa Anita* (☎ (681) 8-70-46, 8-71-36; fax 2-00-46), on the corner of Leyva and Hidalgo, has an English-speaking staff, air-con, restaurant, parking and singles/doubles at 242/264 pesos, with a 15% discount on your room rate if you buy your Copper Canyon train ticket from the Viajes Flamingo travel agency downstairs. A free bus for hotel guests departs daily at 5.15 am for the Copper Canyon train station. You can store a vehicle here while you visit the Copper Canyon.

Places to Eat

Two good seafood restaurants are *El Farallón* on the corner of Ángel Flores and Obregón, open every day from 8 am to 10 pm, and *Restaurant Henry* at Hidalgo 47 Pte between Allende and Guillermo Prieto, open every day from 9 am to 7.30 pm. Both are cool and pleasant, with powerful air-con. *El Taquito* on Leyva between Hidalgo and Independencia, with air-con, plastic booths and a varied bilingual menu, is open 24 hours a day. *España Restaurante* at Obregón 525 Pte between Ángel Flores and Guerrero, similar but with a little more class, is open every day from 7 am to 11 pm. There are plenty of places for an inexpensive taco or quesadilla; the air-con *Cabaña* on the corner of Allende and Obregón, open every day from 7.30 am to 1 am, is especially good.

Getting There & Away

Air The airport (☎ 5-29-50, 5-25-75) is about 12 km south-west of the city on the road to Topolobampo. Aeroméxico (☎ 5-25-70/80) has daily direct flights to Chihuahua,

North-West Mexico
Top: Pithaya cactus fruits (NK); Timber truck near Creel (PP)
Bottom: Fishing boats, Guaymas (PP); Cascada Cusárare (JL)

North-West Mexico
Top: Sonora Desert (JL); Looking over the Copper Canyon (JL)
Bottom: Children near Creel (PP); Landscape near Guaymas (PP)

Hermosillo, La Paz and Mazatlán; Aero California (☎ 5-22-50) has daily direct flights to Culiacán, Guadalajara, La Paz, Mexico City and Tijuana; and Aero Litoral (☎ 5-25-70) has direct flights to La Paz and Chihuahua, all with connections to other centres. The small airline Leo López has weekday flights to Chihuahua.

Bus Los Mochis is on the coastal highway 15; several major bus lines offer hourly buses heading both north and south, 24 hours a day. Each 1st-class bus line has its own terminal: Tres Estrellas de Oro is on the corner of Juárez and Degollado; Elite is a couple of doors down; Transportes del Pacífico is on Morelos between Zaragoza and Leyva; Transportes Norte de Sonora is next door but it only has 2nd-class buses.

Prices are the same on all the 1st-class bus lines, and their buses all go to the same places:

Guadalajara – 995 km, 16 hours (116 pesos)
Guaymas – 349 km, five hours (47 pesos)
Hermosillo – 460 km, seven hours (64 pesos)
Mazatlán – 427 km, six hours (53 pesos)
Mexico City (Terminal Norte) – 1583 km, 24 hours (197 pesos; 230 pesos by Elite)
Navojoa – 155 km, two hours (21 pesos)
Nogales – 742 km, 12 hours (98 pesos)
Tepic – 716 km, 12 hours (89 pesos)
Tijuana – 1455 km, 20 hours (169 pesos)

Second-class buses include:

El Fuerte – 78 km, two hours, 9 pesos; every half hour, 7.30 am to 7.30 pm, from Cuauhtémoc between Zaragoza and Guillermo Prieto
Sufragio/San Blas – 52 km, one hour, 4 pesos; every 20 minutes, 5 am to 8 pm, from the bus station on the corner of Zaragoza and Ordoñez
Topolobampo – 24 km, 40 minutes, 2.60 pesos; every 15 minutes, 5.45 am to 8 pm, from Cuauhtémoc between Zaragoza and Guillermo Prieto

Train The primera especial Estrella del Pacífico and segunda clase Burro trains

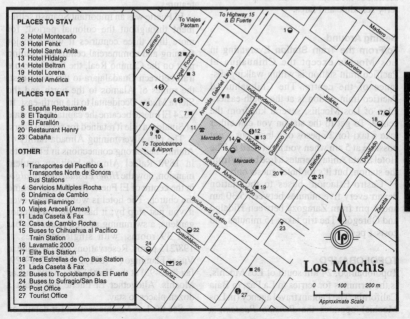

PLACES TO STAY
2 Hotel Montecarlo
3 Hotel Fenix
7 Hotel Santa Anita
13 Hotel Hidalgo
14 Hotel Beltran
19 Hotel Lorena
26 Hotel América

PLACES TO EAT
5 España Restaurante
8 El Taquito
9 El Farallón
20 Restaurant Henry
23 Cabaña

OTHER
1 Transportes del Pacífico & Transportes Norte de Sonora Bus Stations
4 Servicios Multiples Rocha
6 Dinámica de Cambio
7 Viajes Flamingo
10 Viajes Araceli (Amex)
11 Lada Caseta & Fax
12 Casa de Cambio Rocha
15 Buses to Chihuahua al Pacífico Train Station
16 Lavamatic 2000
17 Elite Bus Station
18 Tres Estrellas de Oro Bus Station
21 Lada Caseta & Fax
22 Buses to Topolobampo & El Fuerte
24 Buses to Sufragio/San Blas
25 Post Office
27 Tourist Office

To Viajes Paotam
To Highway 15 & El Fuerte
Madero
Guerrero
Angel Flores
Morelos
Avenida Gabriel Leyva
Independencia
Zaragoza
Juárez
Guillermo Prieto
Allende
Degollado
Zapata
Mercado
Hidalgo
Avenida Alvaro Obregón
Boulevard Castro
Cuauhtémoc
Ordoñez
To Topolobampo & Airport

Los Mochis
0   100   200 m
Approximate Scale

along the Pacific coast between Guadalajara and the US border do not stop in Los Mochis but in Sufragio/San Blas, about 52 km to the north-east. Tickets are sold at the station (☎ (681) 4-01-28/17). The Chihuahua al Pacífico train stops at this station and you can transfer there, but the connections are inconvenient – and often not on time. See the Guadalajara section of the Western Central Highlands chapter for schedules of the Pacific trains. Information and schedules for the Chihuahua al Pacífico (Copper Canyon) trains are given in the Barranca del Cobre section.

Ferry The Paotam travel agency (☎ (681) 5-82-62, ☎ /fax 5-19-14) at Rendón 517 Pte between Ángel Flores and Guerrero sells tickets for the ferry from Topolobampo to La Paz, and delivers them for free anywhere in Los Mochis. It's open Monday to Saturday from 8 am to 1 pm and 3 to 7 pm, Sunday and holidays 9 am to 1 pm. See the La Paz section of the Baja California chapter for the ferry schedule and fares.

Getting Around
To/From the Train Station Everything in Los Mochis except the Chihuahua al Pacífico train station is within walking distance of the centre. The Chihuahua al Pacífico train station is at the south-eastern edge of Los Mochis, several km from the centre. To get to the station you can either take a taxi for 25 pesos or a local bus – not possible at 5 am when you most need it. The Hotel Santa Anita operates a free bus to/from the station, but it's for hotel guests only.

'Castro-Estación' buses to the station depart every five minutes between 5.30 am and 8 pm from Zaragoza between Hidalgo and Obregón. The trip takes 15 minutes and costs 1 peso.

TOPOLOBAMPO
Topolobampo, 24 km south of Los Mochis, is the terminus for ferries to La Paz, in Baja California. The Paotam travel agency (in Los Mochis) operates the *Pensión Paotam*, a

European-style hostelry beside the ferry terminal. Rates are 50/100 pesos for singles/doubles, or 35 pesos per person in a large hostel-style room with 15 beds, all sharing common separate-sex bathrooms. There are plenty of places to eat in Topolobampo, and good beaches nearby.

Ferry tickets are sold at the Paotam travel agency in Los Mochis (see the Los Mochis section). In Topolobampo you can buy them at the ferry terminal (☎ (686) 2-01-41, fax 2-00-35) two hours before the ferry departs, or the day before; reservations by phone are accepted up to two weeks in advance.

EL FUERTE
• *pop: 30,000*
Founded in 1564 by the Spanish conqueror Francisco de Ibarra, El Fuerte (The Fort) is a picturesque Spanish colonial town notable for its colonial ambience and Spanish architecture; the **Palacio Municipal**, the **plaza**, the **church**, the **museum** and the **Hotel Posada del Hidalgo** are its most notable features.

El Fuerte was an important Spanish settlement throughout the colonial period; for more than three centuries it was a major farming and commercial centre and trading post on the Camino Real, the Spanish mule trail between Guadalajara to the south-east, the mines of Alamos to the north and the Sierra Madre Occidental to the north-east. In 1824 El Fuerte became the capital of the state of Sinaloa, a title it retained for several years.

The rich silver-mining Almada family of Alamos had strong connections in El Fuerte. In 1890 Rafael Almada built an opulent mansion, now the *Hotel Posada del Hidalgo*, in the centre of El Fuerte in the street behind the church. The hotel is worth seeing, even if you just stop by; it has beautiful interior gardens, a swimming pool, a restaurant/bar and 39 rooms, with singles/doubles at 198/215 pesos. Reservations can be made at Viajes Flamingo (☎ (681) 2-16-13, 2-19-29; fax 8-33-93) at the Hotel Santa Anita in Los Mochis. Altogether El Fuerte has about a dozen places to stay.

See the Los Mochis section for details on

getting to El Fuerte by bus, and the Barranca del Cobre section for details on getting there by train.

CULIACÁN
* *pop: 600,000*

The present capital of the state of Sinaloa, Culiacán, is equidistant from Los Mochis and Mazatlán – about 210 km (three hours' drive) from either place. Primarily a commercial, administrative and agricultural centre, the city has little to attract tourists. If you do spend time in Culiacán you could check out the 17th-century **cathedral**, the **Palacio Municipal**, the **Museo Regional de Sinaloa** in the Centro Cívico Constitución, and the **Malecón walkway** along the Río Tamazula and Río Humaya.

BARRANCA DEL COBRE (COPPER CANYON)

The Barranca del Cobre (Copper Canyon) is a natural wonder which actually consists of not one but 20 canyons. Together they are four times larger than Arizona's Grand Canyon and equally spectacular. The route of the famous Copper Canyon Railway includes several stops in the Barranca del Cobre.

Copper Canyon Railway

The Chihuahua al Pacífico railway between Los Mochis and Chihuahua, known in English as the Copper Canyon railway, is among Mexico's most scenic rail journeys. A considerable feat of engineering, it has 39 bridges and 86 tunnels along 655 km of railway line connecting the mountainous, arid interior of northern Mexico to the Pacific coast. It was opened in 1961 after taking many decades to build. The major link between Chihuahua and the coast, the line is used heavily by passengers and freight; the beauty of the landscape it traverses has made it one of the country's prime touristic excursions as well.

The Chihuahua al Pacífico railway operates two trains: the primera especial train which is faster, cleaner, more comfortable and air-con or heated, and the segunda clase which is more crowded, dirtier and has windows that let in dust and smoke. It takes about 13 hours to make the trip on the primera especial train, and about three hours longer (at least) on the segunda clase train, which stops frequently along the way. If you're heading towards Los Mochis and you want to see the sights, take the primera train, as the segunda, running later, passes much of the best scenery (between Los Mochis and Creel) after dark. If you're travelling only between Creel and Chihuahua you may prefer to take the bus, as the schedule is more convenient. If you're basically taking a side trip up from Los Mochis you can travel to Creel and back and see most of the sights.

Try to get a window seat on the right side of the carriage if you're going inland, on the left side if you're going to the coast. If you can't manage it, though, don't worry – often the passengers end up congregating in the vestibules between cars, hanging out the windows to take photos.

Sights along the Way Departing from Los Mochis as the sun rises, the train passes through flat, grey farmland and gradually begins to climb through fog-shrouded hills. The land takes on the bluish-white hue of dawn until the first rays of sunlight creep over the hilltops and colour everything pale yellow. Like fingers popping up from beneath the desert, dark pillars of cacti become visible.

About three hours from Los Mochis the train passes over the long Río Fuerte bridge and through the first of the 86 tunnels. It cuts through small canyons and hugs the sides of cliffs as it climbs higher and higher through the mountains of the Sierra Tarahumara, a subrange of the Sierra Madre Occidental. The trip becomes an exciting sequence of dramatic geological images – craggy cliffs, sheer canyon walls and the river bed far below. Seven hours out of Los Mochis, the train stops for 15 minutes at Divisadero for a good view of the Copper Canyon. Along the rest of the trip, the train runs through pine forests skirting the edge of the canyon, but not close enough to see down into it. Unless you make a trip into the 2300-metre-deep canyon, the

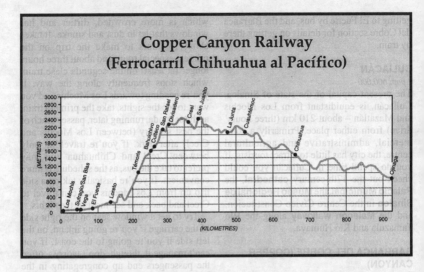

Copper Canyon Railway
(Ferrocarríl Chihuahua al Pacífico)

(KILOMETRES)

viewpoint at Divisadero is the only chance you'll get to see it. This will also probably be the first time you see some of the Tarahumara Indians who inhabit the canyon. The Tarahumara come up from the canyon to display and sell their handicrafts to visitors.

If you want to break your journey, Creel probably makes the best base in the Copper Canyon – it's only a small town but it has the most economical places to stay, plenty of tours and things to do (see the Creel section following). There are several other places to stay along the Chihuahua al Pacífico railway line, however. Stopping overnight at any of them gives you 24 hours before the train passes by again – time enough to explore.

See the earlier section for information on **El Fuerte,** an attractive colonial town. **Cerocahui,** a picturesque village at an altitude of 1630 metres, in a valley with apple and peach orchards and pine and madrone trees, is about 16 km (a 35-minute drive) from the Bahuichivo train stop. The **Posada Barrancas** train stop, 2220 metres high at the rim of the vast Copper Canyon, has magnificent views, trips into the canyon by foot, car or horseback, and three fine hotels.

All the trains stop at **Divisadero** for the

spectacular view of the Copper Canyon – but only for 15 minutes. The Hotel Divisadero Barrancas (see Places to Stay) will arrange guided tours into the canyon, but you can arrange a far better deal yourself with one of the Tarahumara Indians – many Tarahumara come to this train stop daily to sell handicrafts and food. You must have your own food for the tour; there are two restaurants, but no stores in Divisadero. Your guide will lead you down 1820 metres to the Río Urique. Carry enough water for the descent and be prepared for a change in climate from very cold – Divisadero is over 2460 metres high – to warm and humid near the river. Fall (autumn) is the best time to come because flash floods and suffocatingly high temperatures are a problem in summer.

Places to Stay
Cerocahui The *Hotel Misión,* opposite the Misión de Cerocahui church founded in 1690 by the Jesuit Padre Juan María de Salvatierra, has 31 comfortable rooms at 325/462 pesos for singles/doubles, including three meals a day. A variety of short and long excursions depart from the hotel by foot, vehicle and horseback. Reservations are

made at the Hotel Santa Anita in Los Mochis (see the Los Mochis section). A hotel bus provides free transport to/from the train.

Five km north of Cerocahui village, you can camp at the *Rancho del Oro* campground on the banks of the Arroyo del Ranchito river, a tranquil spot with a pleasant beach and swimming, good bird-watching (over 100 species), burial caves and archaeological sites a short walk away, and interesting excursions. Camping costs 30 pesos per tent; tents can be rented for 20 pesos if you don't have your own. Hot showers are available at the nearby *Hotel Paraíso del Oso*, which can also provide meals and other services. The camping ground is 12 km from the Bahuichivo train station; the bus costs 10 pesos.

Posada Barrancas Perched on the rim of the canyon with exceptional views from the private terraces of all the rooms, the *Posada Barrancas Mirador* has 32 luxury rooms and suites at 325/462 pesos for singles/doubles, including three meals a day. Right at the train stop and just a five-minute walk from the viewpoint, the *Rancho Posada* has 36 rooms at 193/231 pesos for singles/doubles, with breakfast included and a restaurant serving other meals. Reservations for both can be made at the Hotel Santa Anita in Los Mochis (see the Los Mochis section). The *Mansión Tarahumara* (☎ Chihuahua (14) 15-47-21, fax 16-54-44) is also known as El Castillo because it looks like a medieval stone castle; from May to September singles/doubles are 200/300 pesos, rising to 255/375 pesos from October to May.

Divisadero At the train stop, the *Hotel Divisadero Barrancas* (☎ Chihuahua (14) 10-33-30, 15-11-99; fax 15-65-75) has 52 rooms, all with that same magnificent view; singles/doubles are 210/310 pesos from May to September, 308/460 pesos from October to May, including two walking tours and three meals a day.

Getting There & Away
Tickets Primera especial tickets are available from the train stations, from travel agencies or by mail in advance.

The train station in Chihuahua (☎ (14) 15-77-56) sells primera especial tickets every day from 6 am to 2 pm; in Los Mochis the train station (☎ (681) 2-93-85) sells primera especial tickets Monday to Friday

---

Tarahumara Indians

More than 50,000 Tarahumara Indians live in the canyons of the Sierra Tarahumara (of which the Copper Canyon is only one). Many Tarahumara still live in caves and log cabins – a few of these dwellings can be seen near Creel – and subsist on very basic agriculture consisting mainly of maize and beans.

Although the Tarahumara are a large tribe, they have been one of the most isolated, and have therefore been able to maintain many of their traditions. One such tradition is the foot races for which the Tarahumara are famous, in which they run nonstop for 160 km or more through rough, often vertical terrain along the canyon sides, kicking a small wooden ball ahead of them. Indeed, running is so significant to the Tarahumara that in their own language they call themselves 'Rarámuri' – those who run fast. Traditionally the Tarahumara hunted by chasing down and exhausting deer, then driving them over cliffs to be impaled on wooden sticks. Another Tarahumara tradition is the *tesquinada*, the object of which is to consume copious amounts of potent *tesquino* or maize beer at raucous gatherings.

Catholic missionaries have made some progress improving living conditions for the Tarahumara, but they haven't been entirely successful in converting them to Catholicism. Many of the Tarahumara attend church services, but their ancestral gods are still worshipped, particularly Raiénari, the sun god and protector of men, and Mechá, the moon god and protector of women. Sorcerers are as important as Catholic priests and are the only members of the Tarahumara permitted to consume peyote, a hallucinogen derived from a small cactus. They often take peyote in order to perform a bizarre dance to cure the sick. ■

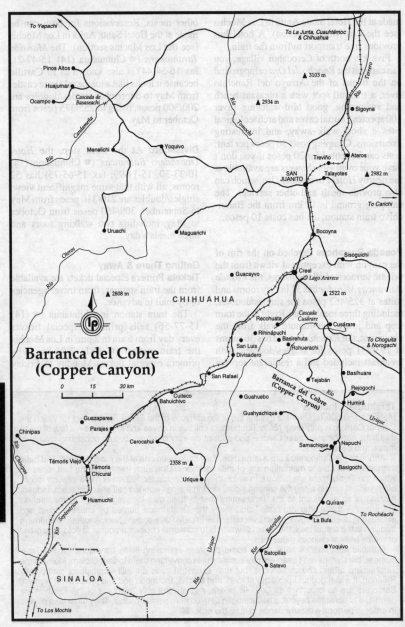

To Yepachi

Pinos Altos

Huajumar

Ocampo

Cascada de
Basaseachi

Río Candameña

Menelichi

Yoquivo

Uruachi

Maguarichi

Río Oteros

To La Junta, Cuauhtémoc
& Chihuahua

Río Terrero

3103 m

2934 m

Sigoyna

Río Tomochi

Treviño

Ataros

SAN
JUANITO

Talayotes

2982 m

To Carichi

Bocoyna

Sisoguichi

Guacayvo

Creel

Lago Arareco

2522 m

CHIHUAHUA

2808 m

Cascada
Cusárare

Recohuata

Cusárare

To Choguita
& Norogachi

Rihinápuchi

Basirehuta

San Luis

Rohuerachi

Divisadero

San Rafael

Tejabán

Basihuare

Río

Rejogochi

Humirá

Barranca del
Cobre
(Copper Canyon)

Río Urique

Barranca del Cobre
(Copper Canyon)

0   15   30 km

Guahuebo

Guahyachique

Cuiteco
Bahuichivo

Guazapares

Parajes

Chinipas

Cerocahui

Río Chinipas

Témoris Viejo

Témoris
Chicural

2358 m

Samachique

Napuchi

Basigochi

Huamuchil

Urique

Quírare

Río Septentrión

La Bufa

To Rochéachi

Río Batopilas

Yoquivo

Batopilas

Satevo

Río Urique

SINALOA

To Los Mochis

Copper Canyon Train – Los Mochis to Chihuahua

Station	Primera Especial Train No 73		Segunda Clase Train No 75	
	Departs	Fare from Los Mochis (pesos)	Departs	Fare from Los Mochis (pesos)
Los Mochis	6.00 am		7.00 am	
Sufragio/San Blas	6.43 am	16.50	7.55 am	3.00
El Fuerte	7.30 am	16.50	8.40 am	4.00
Loreto	8.10 am	21.50	10.30 am	6.00
Témoris	11.11 am	35.50	12.40 pm	10.00
Bahuichivo	12.12 pm	42.00	1.50 pm	12.00
Cuiteco	12.24 pm	43.00	2.00 pm	12.50
San Rafael	1.15 pm	47.00	2.40 pm	13.00
Posada Barrancas	1.30 pm	48.50	2.45 pm	13.50
Divisadero	1.35 pm	49.50	3.45 pm	14.00
Creel	3.14 pm	58.50	5.10 pm	16.00
San Juanito	4.51 pm	64.00	5.55 pm	18.00
La Junta	5.25 pm	77.50	7.35 pm	22.00
Cuauhtémoc	6.25 pm	85.50	8.50 pm	24.00
Chihuahua	8.50 pm	107.50	11.25 pm	29.50

Copper Canyon Train – Chihuahua to Los Mochis

Station	Primera Especial Train No 74		Segunda Clase Train No 76	
	Departs	Fare from Chihuahua (pesos)	Departs	Fare from Chihuahua (pesos)
Chihuahua	7.00 am		8.00 am	
Cuauhtémoc	9.15 am	22.50	10.25 am	6.50
La Junta	10.05 am	30.50	11.25 am	8.50
San Juanito	11.19 am	43.50	1.15 pm	12.00
Creel	12.26 pm	48.50	2.00 pm	13.50
Divisadero	1.45 pm	58.50	3.30 pm	16.00
Posada Barrancas	2.15 pm	59.00	3.35 pm	16.50
San Rafael	2.30 pm	61.00	4.15 pm	17.00
Cuiteco	3.20 pm	65.00	5.14 pm	18.00
Bahuichivo	3.32 pm	66.00	5.25 pm	18.50
Témoris	4.30 pm	72.50	6.35 pm	20.00
Loreto	5.30 pm	86.50	8.50 pm	24.00
El Fuerte	6.20 pm	93.50	9.42 pm	26.00
Sufragio/San Blas	7.54 pm	101.00	10.25 pm	28.00
Los Mochis	8.50 pm	107.50	11.25 pm	29.50

from 5 am to 1 pm, Saturday, Sunday and holidays from 5 to 9 am. Tickets for the segunda clase trains are sold an hour or two before the train departs.

The Viajes Flamingo travel agency (☎ (681) 2-16-13, 2-19-29; fax 8-33-93) on the ground floor of the Hotel Santa Anita on the corner of Leyva and Hidalgo in Los Mochis specialises in the Copper Canyon. They can send you a ticket (primera especial only), or you can pick it up there. They recommend making reservations at least one

month in advance for travel at Semana Santa, July, August or Christmas. At other times you can buy your ticket a day or two in advance, at about the same price as at the train stations.

Primera especial tickets can be purchased in advance by mail in the USA from Mexico by Train, PO Box 2782, Laredo, TX 78044 USA (☎ 1-800-321-1699); the cost is much higher if you do this (US$85 one way, US$150 return), but you are assured of getting a seat.

Schedule Check departure times carefully, as the train crosses a time zone at the border of Sinaloa and Chihuahua states. Previously the whole train ran on Central (Chihuahua) time, an hour later than Mountain (Sinaloa) time. In mid-1994 they seemed to be listing the Sinaloa train stops (Los Mochis, Sufragio/San Blas and El Fuerte) on Mountain (Sinaloa) time. We're doing the same here – we're using the time the train actually leaves each stop according to the appropriate time zone. Beware the old system, though, which may still be used; travellers daily show up for the primera especial train in Los Mochis just after it's left the station.

The schedule is shown on the previous page. Children aged five to 11 pay just over half fare; children under five years ride free. Trains tend to run late; cargo trains en route cause delays. The segunda clase train is virtually never on time, often arriving at the end of the line around 1 am.

From your carriage window, the Copper Canyon railway shows you spectacular scenery

CREEL
• *pop: 3000*

Creel, a pleasant small town surrounded by pine forests and interesting rock formations, is many travellers' favourite stop on the Copper Canyon railway. You can stock up on maps and staples and catch a bus to Batopilas, a village 140 km away deep in the heart of the canyon and Tarahumara country. Creel is also convenient for a number of other interesting day tours and hikes.

This is also a regional centre for the Tarahumara Indians, and you will see many of them in traditional dress here.

At an elevation of 2338 metres, Creel can be very cold, even snowy, especially in winter. In summer the cool air and the smell of pine from the town's lumber mill are a welcome relief from the heat of the tropical coastal lowlands or the deserts of northern Mexico.

Orientation & Information

Creel is a very small town, so it's virtually impossible to get lost. Just about everything you need is on López Mateos, the town's main street, which runs parallel to the train tracks one block to the east. Around the town plaza, which is between López Mateos and the tracks, are two churches, the post office, a bank, the town's most popular guesthouse, and the Artesanías Misíon (Mission Crafts) shop (see Things to Buy in this section). The train station is one block north of the plaza. Several hotels and restaurants and most of the town's other businesses are on López Mateos; across the tracks are a couple more hotels and restaurants and the bus station for buses to Chihuahua.

Creel has no formal tourist office but information about the town, the Copper Canyon and other things to see and do in the area is available from the travel agency, from the Artesanías Misíon shop and from most of the places to stay.

Money Banca Serfin on the plaza is open Monday to Friday from 9 am to 1.30 pm, changing money from 10 am to 1 pm.

Post & Telecommunications The post office in the Presidencia Municipal on the plaza is open Monday to Friday from 9 am to 1 pm and 3 to 6 pm, Saturday 9 am to 1 pm. A Lada caseta in the papelería (paper shop) beside the Farmacia Cristo Rey on López Mateos, half a block south of the plaza, is open every day from 9 am to 8 pm. Another Lada caseta is in the paper shop two doors from the Casa de Huéspedes Margarita, which is on López Mateos on the north-east corner of the plaza; it's open every day from 8.30 am to 1 pm and 3 to 8 pm.

Travel Agency Chihuahua al Pacífico Tours (☎ /fax (145) 6-02-24), on López Mateos half a block south of the plaza, offers tours, trekking, camping, mountain bike rental and other travel agency services.

Books & Maps A large map of Creel is posted on the outside wall of the Artesanías Misíon shop on the north side of the plaza. Maps of the surrounding area are posted on the window of the travel agency on López Mateos; they are sold there and at the paper shop beside the Farmacia Cristo Rey on López Mateos. Topographical maps of the canyon can be obtained from the Dirección General de Geografía del Territorio Nacional, San Antonio Abaz No 124, 5th floor, Mexico City, Mexico DF. The *San Jacinto No 6 13-1, Chihuahua* map is recommended. A general map of the Copper Canyon region can be ordered from the International Map Company, 5316 Santa Teresa, El Paso, Texas, USA. Decent topographical maps and the general map can be bought at the Artesanías Misíon shop on the plaza.

The Artesanías Misíon shop also sells a number of books about the Copper Canyon and the Tarahumara. One of the best books about the Tarahumara is *Tarahumara – Where Night is the Day of the Moon* by Bernard L Fontana, with colour photos by John P Schaefer (1990, Northland Publishing, PO Box N, Flagstaff, AZ 86002, USA). *National Parks of Northwest Mexico, Volume II* by Rick Fisher (Sunracer Publications, PO Box 40092, Tucson, AZ 85717, USA) is a good book about the trails in the Copper Canyon and other national parks in north-west Mexico.

Laundry The Lavandería Santa María at López Mateos 61 is open Monday to Friday from 9 am to 2 pm and 3 to 6 pm, Saturday 9 am to 2 pm.

Complejo Ecoturístico Arareko

An excellent local hike (or drive) is to the Complejo Ecoturístico Arareko, an area of Tarahumara communal land (ejido) with over 200 sq km of pine forest with waterfalls, hot springs, caves and other rock formations, deep canyons, farmlands, Tarahumara villages, Lago Arareco and more. Their office on López Mateos beside the Farmacia Cristo Rey, half a block south of the plaza, rents horses, bicycles and boats for excursions on Lago Arareco.

To get there from Creel, head south on López Mateos and veer left, passing the town cemetery on your left. About 1.5 km south of town there's a gate where an entrance fee is charged (10 pesos, children 5 pesos) and you're given a map and printed information about the ejido. Continue straight ahead; caves and farmlands will appear on both sides of the road before you eventually arrive at the small Tarahumara village of San Ignacio, where there's a 400-year-old mission church. You can also enter the ejido, on foot or by car, from Lago Arareco, which is seven km south of Creel on the road to Cusárare. The ejido also offers camping, a hostel and a hotel near the lake (see Places to Stay).

Trips & Tours

All of Creel's hotels offer tours of the surrounding area, with trips to canyons, rivers, hot springs, Lago Arareco and other places. All the trips require a minimum number of people, usually four or five; the easiest place to get a group together is often at the Casa de Huéspedes Margarita, but any hotel will organise a tour if there are four or five people wanting to go. Most hotels don't require that you be a guest in order to go on a tour. The Chihuahua al Pacífico Tours travel agency on López Mateos also organises tours. Prices vary depending on who you go with, but the trips are basically to the same places; the ones here are run by Margarita, Pensión Creel and Cabañas Berti's. If you have your own transport you can do many of these trips on your own. Popular tours include:

Lago Arareco An easy seven-km hike or drive from town along the road to Cusárare; hitchhiking is also relatively easy. A few caves inhabited by Tarahumaras can be seen along the way. At the lake there's an old log cabin that was used as a set for the filming of a Mexican movie, *El Refugio del Lobo* (Refuge of the Wolf). Two hours; 20 pesos per person.

Valle de los Monjes The Valley of the Monks is nine km away and is considered a day trip by horse. Horses and a guide can be hired from the Complejo Ecoturístico Arareko office on López Mateos, or ask at your hotel.

Cascada Cusárare The 30-metre-high Cusárare waterfall is 22 km south of Creel near the Tarahumara village of Cusárare. As you get near the town, look for a small roadside shrine and km marker on the right side of the road. Just past that is a small sign marking the road to the 'Cascada – Waterfall Hotel'. Follow that road to the right for three km, crossing the river three or four times. When the road ends, follow the trail to the top of the waterfall. The trail winds around to the bottom of the falls. Hitchhiking to the 'hotel' road is usually easy. The four to five-hour tour involves going 22 km by car, stopping at Lago Arareco on the way, then 2.5 km by foot to the waterfall. 40 pesos per person.

Recohuata Hot Springs The seven-hour trip begins with a 1½-hour truck ride and then a hike down 607 metres into the canyon to the hot springs. 40 pesos per person.

Cascada de Basaseachi Basaseachi Falls, 140 km north-west of Creel, is a high, dramatic waterfall, especially spectacular in the rainy season. It takes all day to visit the falls – a bumpy three-hour drive, then three hours walking down, half an hour at the waterfall, three hours walking up again, and a bumpy three-hour return ride – but if you're up for it, it's worth it. Nine hours; 80 pesos per person.

La Bufa The nine-hour tour to La Bufa, a canyon 1750 metres deep with a cool river at the bottom, takes you up and down through five spectacular canyons until you reach La Bufa, 105 km from Creel. Batopilas is two hours further along the same road; if you don't have two days to spare to visit Batopilas this tour to La Bufa lets you experience some of that spectacular scenery in one

day, with plenty of stops along the way. 80 pesos per person.

Divisadero It's a two-hour drive from Creel to Divisadero. If you are going to the coast on the Copper Canyon Railway you'll be stopping at Divisadero anyway, but only for 15 minutes. Divisadero is a four to five-hour day trip from Creel; 60 pesos per person.

Río Urique The seven-hour tour to this river, at the bottom of the spectacular Urique Canyon, passes several indigenous villages. 60 pesos per person.

Río Oteros The Río Oteros walk is considered a day hike; ask before you go.

Campos Menonitas An eight-hour excursion to the Mennonite country includes a tour of a Mennonite cheese factory (see the Central North Mexico chapter for more information on the Mennonites). 100 pesos per person.

Batopilas Several hotels offer two-day excursions to Batopilas (see further on in this chapter) for around 150 pesos per person.

Tour Guides For all of these tours as well as for more extensive trips into the canyons, you could also hire a guide from the office of the Complejo Ecoturístico Arareko, on López Mateos; the cost is around 20 pesos per day. Horses can also be hired here.

Places to Stay – bottom end

Camping & Cabins The *Pensión Creel* (☎ (145) 6-00-71, fax 6-02-00) at López Mateos 61, two blocks south of the plaza, has camping spaces at 15 pesos per night, and spacious, comfortable self-contained wooden cabins with private kitchen and bath at 45/90 pesos for singles/doubles, breakfast included. Some larger cabins have three bedrooms and could sleep a large group.

The *Complejo Ecoturístico Arareko* (☎ /fax (145) 6-01-26) has a campground on the north-east shore of Lago Arareco, seven km south of town, with barbecue pits, picnic areas, bathrooms and hot showers but no electricity. The cost is 10 pesos per person. They also operate the *Albergue de Batosárachi* a km south of Lago Arareco, with three rustic cabins with bunk beds or individual rooms, and hot showers; you can cook in the communal kitchen or arrange to have meals prepared. The cost is 35 pesos per person. They'll pick you up at the train or bus station if they know you're coming.

Guesthouses & Hotels The most popular place to stay in Creel is the *Casa de Huéspedes Margarita* (☎ /fax (145) 6-00-45) at López Mateos 11, on the north-east corner of the plaza between the two churches, with a variety of accommodation and prices. A bunk in the dorm room is 15 pesos with your own sleeping bag, 20 pesos with bedding, or 10 pesos for a mattress on the floor; private rooms are 40/70 pesos with shared/private bath. All of these prices include both breakfast and dinner. Margarita's is a great place to meet other travellers, as everyone gathers at the table to eat together – often in shifts, since the place is so popular.

Pensión Creel is probably the second most popular place to stay in Creel. (It's operated by the same people who run the other *Pensión Creel* – see Camping & Cabins.) It's on López Mateos about a km south of town, with 11 rooms around a stone courtyard, all sharing a common sitting room and kitchen where you can do your own cooking. The cost is 30 pesos per room for one or two people with breakfast included, 25 pesos without breakfast, with some larger rooms sleeping up to six people. A van provides transport to/from the train station. It's usually not as crowded as Margarita's. *Cabañas Berti's* (☎ (145) 6-00-86) at López Mateos 31 has 12 rooms, all with private bath, starting at 45/50 pesos for singles/ doubles. *Casa Valenzuela* at López Mateos 68 has simple rooms with shared or private bath at 25/50 pesos for singles/doubles.

Across the train tracks from the plaza, beside the Estrella Blanca bus station, the *Hotel Korachi* (☎ (145) 6-02-07) has simple rooms with bath at 40/60 pesos for singles/doubles. A block south, *La Posada de Creel* (☎ /fax (145) 6-01-42) has rooms with shared bath at 30 pesos per person, or rooms with private bath at 105 pesos.

Places to Stay – middle

The *Hotel Margarita Plaza Mexicana* (☎ /fax (145) 6-02-45), on Calle Chapultepec half a block from López Mateos, is operated by Margarita of the Casa de Huéspedes Margarita; it has a restaurant, bar and 26 rooms

around a pleasant courtyard at 80/100 pesos for singles/doubles. The *Motel Cascada Inn* (☎ (145) 6-02-53, fax 6-01-51) at López Mateos 49 has a covered swimming pool, a steakhouse and bar, parking spaces and 32 rooms at 152/166 pesos for singles/doubles.

The *Motel Parador de la Montaña* (☎ (145) 6-00-75, ☎ /fax 6-00-85) at López Mateos 44 is the luxury place to stay in Creel, with a restaurant, bar, parking and 50 large, comfortable rooms at 170/182 pesos for singles/doubles. The Complejo Ecoturístico Arareko (see Camping & Cabins) operates the luxury *Cabaña de Segórachi* on the south shore of Lago Arareco, seven km south of Creel, with a private boat launch and other amenities; the cost is 120 pesos per person.

Places to Eat

There are plenty of restaurants on López Mateos in the few blocks south of the plaza – stroll along and take your pick. *Restaurant Verónica* and *Restaurant Estela* are recommended by locals. *Caballo Bayo* sometimes has music in the evenings, as does the restaurant at *Margarita Plaza Mexicana* on Calle Chapultepec. *Restaurant Jorge's* is a simple place with good food; from the plaza, cross the train tracks, find Calle Cristo Rey, go one block away from the plaza and you'll see it on the corner.

Things to Buy

Several places around Creel sell Tarahumara handicrafts, including baskets, colourful dolls, wood carvings, violins, flutes, archery sets, pottery, clothing and more. The best place to buy them is at the Artesanías Misíon shop on the north side of the plaza; not only is the quality some of the best you'll find, but all the money earned at the shop goes to support the Catholic mission hospital which provides free medical care for the Tarahumara. The shop is open Monday to Saturday from 9.30 am to 1 pm and 3 to 6 pm, Sunday 9.30 am to 1 pm.

Getting There & Away

Bus The Estrella Blanca bus station, across the train tracks from the plaza, has buses to Chihuahua (276 km, 4½ hours; 33 pesos), passing through San Juanito (30 km, one hour; 7 pesos), La Junta (102 km, 2½ hours; 15 pesos) and Cuauhtémoc (170 km, three hours; 21 pesos) on the way. Departures are at 7, 8.30, 10 and 11.30 am, and 1, 2.30, 4 and 5.30 pm.

A bus to Batopilas (140 km, seven hours; 30 pesos) departs from the Novedades Fredy's shop on López Mateos, 1½ blocks south of the plaza. The bus leaves Creel at 7 am on Tuesday, Thursday and Saturday, leaving from Batopilas for the return trip at 4 am on Monday, Wednesday and Friday.

Train See the Barranca del Cobre section for schedules and information about the Copper Canyon train.

BATOPILAS

• *pop: 600* • *alt: 495 metres*

Batopilas, a serene 19th-century silver-mining village 140 km south of Creel, deep in the heart of the canyon country, is a great starting point for treks into the canyons. Even the journey to get there is a thrilling descent into the canyons, from an altitude of 2338 metres at Creel to 495 metres at Batopilas, with dramatic descents and climbs through several canyons along the way. Batopilas's climate is distinctly warmer and more tropical than Creel's; you descend from a vegetation zone of cool pine forest to a semitropical zone where mangoes, bananas and other tropical fruits are grown. Batopilas has a few small hotels and guesthouses where you can rent rooms, including the hotels *Batopilas, Samachique, Napuchi* and *Parador*.

Central North Mexico

This chapter includes much of the state of Chihuahua, the state of Durango and a small corner of Coahuila (Torreón). It covers a long-used travel route between what is now central Mexico and the USA. The route is along the high plains, parallel to the Sierra Madre, through flat or undulating country with occasional rocky ranges rising sharply from the plains. The mostly dry, sparsely populated rangeland is intersected by rivers which flow intermittently from the sierra, and appear as lines of green along the valleys. The irrigated areas are green oases where fruit, cotton and other crops are grown, and where most of the towns have been established.

There are a number of options for spectacular side trips across the mountains towards the Pacific coast. The best known is the Chihuahua al Pacífico railway via Creel and the Copper Canyon to Los Mochis (for details of this trip, see the North-West Mexico chapter).

CIUDAD JUÁREZ & EL PASO (Texas)
- *pop: Ciudad Juárez 789,500; El Paso 515,300*
- *alt: 1145 metres*

For many short-term visitors, the main attractions of Ciudad Juárez are cheap dental work, cheap shopping, under-21 drinking, and even more dubious pursuits. It's a grimy, noisy, but booming border town, inextricably linked with El Paso, which is not pretty either.

The two towns are a study in the unequal relationships 'across the line', but they stand on a travel route which was being used long before the conquistador Cabeza de Vaca found the 'paso del norte' in the 16th century. Modern travellers use the same crossroad, but most find that the ambience gets more pleasant as they get further away from the border.

The area can be insufferably hot in summer, and freezing cold and windy in winter, but between these extremes it is often warm, dry, sunny and very pleasant.

Central North Mexico

History

For Indians, Spanish explorers, missionaries and traders, the main north-south travel route followed the course of the Rio Grande, which broke through the low but rugged range of mountains at El Paso del Norte. In 1848, following the Mexican-American War, the river became the border between the US state of Texas and the Mexican state of Chihuahua.

In the 1860s the river changed course, shifting southward so that an additional couple of sq km came to be on the US side. The resulting border dispute was the subject of international arbitration in 1911, but wasn't resolved until 1963, when a treaty was signed which provided for engineering works to move the channel of the Rio Grande, and the transfer of some land to Mexico. This land is now the Parque Chamizal in Ciudad Juárez.

In the turbulent years of the Mexican Revolution (from 1910), Ciudad Juárez had a strategic importance beyond its small size. Pancho Villa stormed the town on 10 May 1911, enabling Madero's faction to force the resignation of the dictator Díaz. After Huerta's coup against Madero, Villa escaped to refuge in El Paso. In March 1913 he rode across the Rio Grande, with just eight followers, to begin the reconquest of Mexico. Within months he had recruited and equipped an army of thousands, El División del Norte, and in November he conquered Juárez for a second time – this time by loading his troops in a train, deceiving the defenders into thinking it was one of their own, and steaming into the middle of town in a new version of the Trojan horse tactic. Juárez was a vital strategic asset, being situated at the northern end of the railway which Villa employed to transport captured goods and cattle from other parts of Mexico, which were then smuggled into the USA and traded for munitions and supplies.

Juárez is now a major centre for *maquiladoras*, which provide a great deal of employment and have attracted many new arrivals, making Juárez Mexico's fourth-largest city by some accounts. Nevertheless, the US is still an economic magnet, and pressure along the border is immense, manifesting itself in illegal immigration and the smuggling of drugs from Mexico to the USA, and the smuggling of consumer goods from the USA to Mexico. On a short drive along El Paso's border highway you will see much evidence of illegal crossings, and the US border patrol in action trying to stem the inevitable tide of people.

Orientation

Ciudad Juárez and El Paso sprawl over a wide area on both sides of the Rio Grande, but most of the things of interest to travellers are concentrated in the central areas of the two towns – around El Paso's Stanton and Santa Fe Streets, which go over separate bridges and continue as Avenidas Lerdo and Juárez on the Mexican side of the border. You can walk across either bridge, but by car you must take Stanton St going south and Lerdo going north. Avenida Juárez, lined with shops, bars, restaurants and seedy hotels, is the most important tourist street in Ciudad Juárez and the one to follow if you are heading for the bus station or the centre of town. About five km east of Avenida Juárez, the Cordova Rd bridge ('The Bridge of the Americas') leads to a less congested part of Juárez, and to a bypass road which in turn leads directly to the main highway south to Chihuahua. Even further east, the new Zaragoza toll bridge entirely avoids both El Paso and Juárez.

Information

Tourist Office In Juárez you will find the government tourist office (☎ (16) 14-08-37) near the immigration checkpoint on Malecón between Juárez and Lerdo. Look for it in the basement of the grey, high-rise government building. The staff are quite helpful, and there is usually someone there who speaks English, but their city maps are pretty useless. The office is open Monday to Friday from 8 am to 8 pm, weekends to 3 pm.

The El Paso tourist office (☎ (915) 544-0062), just north of the Greyhound terminal on Civic Centre Plaza, opens every day from

8.30 am to 5 pm. They have lots of brochures on El Paso and surrounding attractions in the USA, but not much on Mexico. This office is the starting point for the El Paso-Juárez trolley (see Getting Around in this section).

Money In Juárez there are banks on Avenida 16 de Septiembre, open Monday to Friday from 9 am to 1 pm. In the afternoon, you can change cash in the souvenir shops along Juárez. Travellers' cheques are more difficult but the moneychanger at the bus station can change them.

If you are in El Paso outside banking hours, go to Valuta (☎ 544-1152) at 301 East Paisano, between El Paso Ave and Stanton St, which is always open; it changes cash and travellers' cheques to pesos and does credit card advances, money orders and faxes.

Post The Juárez post office is at the intersection of Lerdo and Ignacio Peña. Hours are from 8.30 am to 7.30 pm Monday to Friday; from 9 am to 1 pm on weekends.

Foreign Consulates The Mexican consulate in El Paso (☎ (915) 533-3644, 533-4082) is at 910 East San Antonio St and opens from 9 am to noon, Monday to Friday. In Juárez, the US consulate (☎ (16) 13-40-48) is at López Mateos Norte 924. For emergencies outside office hours, US citizens can call El Paso 525-6060.

If you don't intend to venture beyond the border zone or stay for more than 72 hours, you won't need a tourist card. Those moving deeper into Mexico can get one in El Paso from a Mexican immigration office (they are situated at the foot of the Stanton St bridge and on the Cordova bridge), or from the Mexican consulate. To enter the USA from Mexico you must be able to show proof of US or Canadian citizenship or residency, or have a passport with a US visa.

Car Insurance For liability and vehicle insurance cover in Mexico, try these companies in El Paso: International Gateway Insurance (☎ 1-800-933-9332; (915) 595-6544), at 1155 Larry Mahan Drive; Sanborns

(☎ (915) 779-3588), 440 Raynolds St; or AAA (☎ (915) 778-9521), 910 East San Antonio Ave.

Things to See
Ciudad Juárez is not the most charming town, and many of its attractions are pitched at those making day trips from El Paso. The emphasis is on shopping, bars, and 'instant Mexico' type developments. Nevertheless, the Plaza de Armas and a few of the old buildings around it are of interest.

The **Misión de Guadalupe** building was constructed between 1658 and 1668 and housed the original mission, the first established in the area. It's on the west side of the plaza, adjacent to the cathedral, which also dates from the seventeenth century.

East of the plaza, on the corner of Avenida Juárez and Avenida 16 de Septiembre, is the **Museo Histórico**, in the handsome old Aduana, the 1889 customs building. It houses exhibits covering the history of the region from the time of the Paquimé culture, through the colonial period, the struggle for independence and the revolution. It gives an excellent overview and has some interesting artefacts; all the written information is in Spanish but the maps are very descriptive. It's open from 10 am to 6 pm, Tuesday to Sunday; admission is free.

In the Plaza de las Américas (formerly called ProNaf), the **Museo de Arte** has modern and historical Mexican works, and is open from 11 am to 7 pm every day except Monday.

The **Parque Chamizal** is not a very attractive park, but it does provide some respite from the noise and fumes of the city. In the park is the Museo de Arte Prehispánica (also known by its old name, Museo Arqueológico), with exhibits from each Mexican state, though many are plastic replicas. It's open Monday to Saturday from 9 am to 2 pm, Sunday from 1 to 8 pm; admission is free.

Places to Stay – bottom end
Ciudad Juárez Bottom-end accommodation in Juárez consists of some very overpriced dives and none can really be recommended – many of the real cheapies prefer to rent

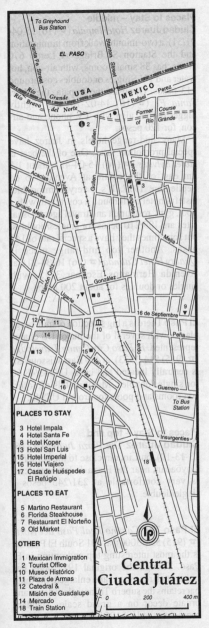

PLACES TO STAY

3 Hotel Impala
4 Hotel Santa Fe
8 Hotel Koper
13 Hotel San Luis
15 Hotel Imperial
16 Hotel Viajero
17 Casa de Huéspedes
   El Refúgio

PLACES TO EAT

5 Martino Restaurant
6 Florida Steakhouse
7 Restaurant El Norteño
9 Old Market

OTHER

1 Mexican Immigration
2 Tourist Office
10 Museo Histórico
11 Plaza de Armas
12 Catedral &
   Misión de Guadalupe
14 Mercado
18 Train Station

**Central
Ciudad Juárez**

0   200   400 m

their rooms by the hour. The cheapest is *Casa de Huéspedes El Refúgio*, on Mina near Corregidora, with singles/doubles for 20/25 pesos. The rooms are very basic and do not have bathrooms, but they don't smell too bad and the courtyard adds a touch of character.

Hotel Viajero, on Mina near the corner of Noche Triste directly in front of Mercado Hidalgo, is dingy. Rooms with grubby bathrooms cost 30 pesos for singles or doubles. A block or so south of the cathedral on Calle Mariscal, the *Hotel San Luis* has basic singles/doubles with bath from 30/40 pesos, but they are mostly grimy, gloomy and airless. At the south end of Avenida Juárez, the *Hotel Koper* is particularly unattractive at 50 pesos for a small, dark room.

The best value is the *Hotel Imperial* (☎ (16) 15-03-23, 15-03-83), at Guerrero 206 near the south end of Avenida Juárez, which offers singles/doubles with bathrooms for 60/70 pesos. It's a biggish place, and a bit worn, but with TV, phone and air-con it's quite OK, especially by Juárez standards.

El Paso The *Gardner Hotel* (☎ (915) 532-3661), at 311 East Franklin St near the intersection of Stanton St, is the top budget choice for those who may not want to stay overnight in Juárez. It has a hostel section, affiliated with American Youth Hostels, where accommodation in a four-bed dorm with shared bath costs US$12 for IYHF/AYH members only. There is a kitchen with excellent facilities, and a common room. For nonmembers, singles/doubles cost from US$27.50/35 plus 14% tax. There's no off-street parking.

The *Gateway Hotel* (☎ (915) 532-2611), with Mexican guests, management and style, is centrally located at 104 Stanton St near the San Antonio St corner. It has air-con singles and doubles for US$28 plus tax, and provides parking a block away for US$1.50.

Travellers with their own cars can look for a motel on the outskirts of town. There are plenty of budget places on North Mesa St – try the *Mesa Inn Hotel* (☎ (915) 532-7911) at No 4151; it costs US$26.16 for singles or doubles, including tax, and has a pool.

CENTRAL NORTH MEXICO

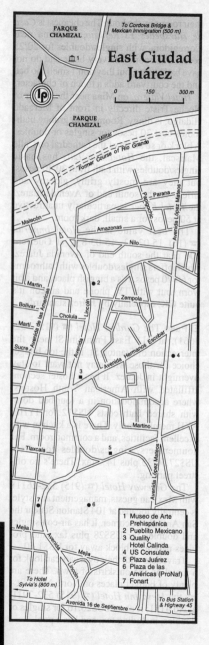

East Ciudad Juárez

0   150   300 m

PARQUE CHAMIZAL

To Cordova Bridge & Mexican Immigration (500 m)

PARQUE CHAMIZAL

Former Course of Río Grande

Militar

Parana

Amazonas

Nilo

Malecón

Avenida López Mateos

Padloooog

Martin

Zempola

Bolívar

Cholula

Martí

Avenida de las Américas

Avenida Lincoln

Sucre

Avenida Hermanos Escobar

Martino

Tlaxcala

Avenida López Mateos

Mejía

Mejía

Avenida Lincoln

To Hotel Sylvia's (800 m)

Avenida 16 de Septiembre

To Bus Station & Highway 45

1 Museo de Arte Prehispánica
2 Pueblito Mexicano
3 Quality Hotel Calinda
4 US Consulate
5 Plaza Juárez
6 Plaza de las Américas (ProNaf)
7 Fonart

Places to Stay – middle

Ciudad Juárez *Hotel Impala* (☎ (16) 15-04-91/31), a two-minute walk from immigration and the Stanton St Bridge at Lerdo 670 Norte, has 38 small rooms, with air-con, hot water and TV. Singles or doubles cost around 113 pesos. Opposite the Impala, the *Hotel Santa Fe* (☎ (16) 14-02-70) has slightly bigger rooms, also with TV, phone and air-con, for 120 pesos.

Many mid-range hotels in Juárez have special promotion rates. One of the best is *Hotel Sylvia's* (☎ (16) 15-04-42), about 1.5 km east of the centre at Avenida 16 de Septiembre 1977. It's a very comfortable, tasteful hotel built round a courtyard, with a pool, gym, restaurant and travel agent. Usual rates are 199/210 pesos for singles/doubles, but sometimes they have a special rate of 143 pesos. Another top mid-range place is *Quality Hotel Calinda* (☎ (16) 16-34-21), at Avenida Hermanos Escobar 3515, with singles or doubles for about 200 pesos.

El Paso There is a big selection of mid-range places, with several of the major US chains represented. *El Paso City Centre Travelodge* (☎ (915) 544-3333), at 409 East Missouri St, is centrally located and costs US$43/48.60 for singles/doubles. Many motels offer air-con rooms and pools for around US$40.

Places to Stay – top end

Ciudad Juárez The *Plaza Juárez* (☎ (16) 13-13-10), on Lincoln close to the corner of Coyoacán, near the Plaza de las Américas, is very comfortable at 231/245 pesos a single/double.

El Paso The *Camino Real Paso del Norte* (☎ (915) 534-3000), at 101 South El Paso St, is the most interesting top-end option in El Paso. Though the original 1912 hotel has been much renovated and enlarged, the main bar retains the superb Tiffany glass dome and ornate decor on a grand scale. Standard rooms start at US$105, plus tax.

Places to Eat

Ciudad Juárez There are cheap taquerías everywhere in Juárez, but exercise discretion if you are entering Mexico for the first time. It's best to build up some immunity to new bacilli for a few days before you become too adventurous with local fare.

A favourite among locals is *Restaurant El Norteño*, on Juárez just north of 16 de Septiembre (opposite Hotel Koper), where you can fill up on tacos or chicken and fries for around 10 pesos. For those willing to spend more money, there are lots of high-gloss eateries on Avenida Juárez Norte, like *Martino Restaurant* at 412, *Villa Española*, nearby where Juárez intersects Colón, and *Florida Steakhouse* at 301. Beside the *old market* you can have tacos at outdoor tables from 8 pesos, and other Mexican-style dishes for around 15 pesos.

El Paso Some cheap eating places can be found in the central area along San Antonio east of Stanton. *The Tap* bar and restaurant looks more like the former than the latter, but has substantial set lunches for US$3.75, and a steak dinner for US$6.75. The nearby diners, and *Kim's* Chinese place, are not expensive. There are a couple of places with excellent breakfast deals on Mills between Stanton and Kansas. Most of the many franchised fast-food outlets are further out of town.

Things to Buy

Juárez boasts some quality crafts amid its sea of junk, but at prices significantly higher than elsewhere in Mexico. Unless this is your last chance to buy a knick-knack for Aunt Tilly or a bottle of mezcal for Uncle Bob, don't waste your time shopping in Ciudad Juárez. The old Juárez market, east of the centre on Avenida 16 de Septiembre, has the biggest single collection of souvenir stalls, where you can be overwhelmed by tacky possibilities.

The Plaza de las Américas (formerly ProNaf) shopping centre was being redeveloped at the time of writing. Fonart, just to the west of it, has a good stock of handicrafts

from all over Mexico; prices seem high but they offer big discounts. If you want a very sanitised Mexican shopping experience, Pueblito Mexicano is a new shopping centre decorated in imitation of a traditional Mexican village, with a supermarket, restaurants and a number of speciality shops. It's on Avenida Lincoln, south of the Cordova bridge.

Getting There & Away

Air Ciudad Juárez airport (Aeropuerto Internacional Abraham González) is just to the east of highway 45, about 15 km south of the centre of town. There are direct flights to Mexico City, Aguascalientes, Mazatlán and Chicago. Flights to other major cities go via Chihuahua or Mexico City. It's probably cheaper to fly from the USA to Mexican cities on discounted fares than to buy tickets in Juárez. El Paso is also an important airline hub, with flights from most US cities and some European and Asian capitals.

Bus The Ciudad Juárez Central de Autobuses is new, big and a long way from town – for information on getting there, see the Getting Around section. Main destinations are:

Chihuahua – 376 km, five hours; frequent 1st-class (40 pesos) and 2nd-class buses
Mexico City (Terminal Norte) – 1830 km, 25 hours; 1st-class buses leave in the afternoon and evening (200 to 230 pesos); some deluxe buses (270 pesos)
Nuevo Casas Grandes – 315 km, four hours; 1st-class (30 pesos) and more frequent 2nd-class buses (20 pesos)

Direct buses also go to Durango (111 pesos), Mazatlán, Monterrey, San Luis Potosí (173 pesos), Saltillo, Tijuana, Zacatecas (15 hours; 150 pesos). Mexican buses going direct to US destinations (eg Albuquerque, US$20; Los Angeles, US$35; Denver, US$69) are cheaper than Greyhounds from El Paso.

The El Paso Greyhound bus station (☎ 542-1355 or 532-2365) is on Santa Fe St, just south of the Civic Center Plaza. There are several buses daily to many destinations including Los Angeles (15 hours, US$69),

Chicago (36 hours, US$102), New York (53 hours, US$150) and Miami (46 hours, US$150).

Train You can walk to Juárez's train station from the Mexican side of the Stanton St Bridge. Just keep walking straight along Lerdo for about 11 blocks (its name changes to Corona). The Ferrocarriles Nacionales station is at the intersection of Corona and Insurgentes.

Train No 8, El División del Norte, departs Ciudad Juárez at 10 pm daily for Mexico City (130/79 pesos for primera/segunda clase) via Chihuahua (23/15 pesos), Torreón, Zacatecas, Aguascalientes and Querétaro. There are no primera especial seats available, so it's a long, uncomfortable trip, and buses would be preferable. For more information, see Getting There & Away in the Mexico City chapter. There are no passenger trains to Nuevo Casas Grandes.

El Paso's Amtrak station (☎ 545-2247) is at 700 San Francisco St, three blocks west of Civic Center Plaza. Trains run three times a week on a number of routes, eg Los Angeles (16½ hours, US$65), Miami (about 54 hours, US$96), Chicago (US$81 one way) and New York (via Jacksonville, Florida; US$166). These are discounted, one-way fares.

Car Follow the signs to the Aeropuerto to reach highway 45, which goes south to Chihuahua. It's a good four-lane road, but somewhere along the way you will have to pay for it – there's at least one tollbooth, charging 13 pesos. The good but narrow road to Nuevo Casas Grandes branches west at a traffic circle just south of town. On either road you will be stopped for a check of your papers and vehicle permit after a few km.

Getting Around

Local buses to the Ciudad Juárez bus station leave from the corner of Guerrero and Corona. Catch a Ruta 1A bus marked 'Lomas' or 'Granjera' on the south-east corner of the intersection; it runs direct to the bus station (45 minutes; 1 peso). From the bus station,

local buses marked 'Centro' will drop you close to the cathedral – just get off at the end of the line. Taxis from the bus station to the city centre cost 26 pesos.

You can bypass Juárez altogether if you take one of the direct buses between the El Paso and Juárez bus stations – they leave every hour and take 45 minutes (US$5).

The El Paso-Juárez trolley starts and finishes at the El Paso Tourist Office, making a one-hour loop through Juárez with eight stops en route, all at places for eating, drinking or shopping. You can get off at any of them, and get on the next trolley an hour later. The trolley is actually a bus done up like one of El Paso's old street-cars. It's pretty much a tourist outing, though you can ride it on a one-way trip into Mexico for US$5.

OTHER BORDER CROSSINGS

Though El Paso-Juárez is the most important and frequently used route between Central North Mexico and the USA, there are some alternative crossing points.

Columbus (New Mexico)-Palomas

The small town of Palomas is about 150 km west of Juárez, and the border is open 24 hours a day. The Mexican customs station is 35 km south, at the junction of the road to Juárez. There's a motel and a cheapish hotel, and 2nd-class bus connections to Juárez and Nuevo Casas Grandes.

Columbus, on other side of the line, has a campground and a motel, but no public transport connections into the USA. It's known as the site of the only foreign invasion of the USA – Pancho Villa's gang sacked the town in 1916. The US government sent a 10,000-strong expeditionary force into Mexico in response, but it was unable to catch Villa. A museum in Columbus has some exhibits on the attack.

Presidio (Texas)-Ojinaga

This border crossing is 209 km north-east of Chihuahua, and little used by travellers. There are a few buses per day from Chihuahua, and one segundo clase train, but public transport connections into Texas from Presidio may not be good. Ojinaga has some cheap places to stay and eat.

CASAS GRANDES & NUEVO CASAS GRANDES

Nuevo Casas Grandes is a four-hour bus trip south-west of Ciudad Juárez, and you could make it to here for a quiet first night in Mexico. It's a peaceful, prosperous country town serving the surrounding farmlands. The substantial brick houses around the town, which look like they should be in the American mid-west, are homes of local Mennonites. The main reason to visit is to see the ruins of Paquimé, adjacent to the nearby village of Casas Grandes.

Orientation & Information

Most of the facilities visitors need are within a few blocks of 5 de Mayo and Constitución (the street with railway tracks down the middle). There are banks (ATMs at Banamex and Bancomer), a casa de cambio (next to the Hotel California) and a post office.

Paquimé Ruins

The 'Casas Grandes' (big houses) are a complex of adobe structures, partially excavated and restored so the networks of crumbled walls now resemble roofless mazes. The area is known as Paquimé, as were the people who lived here. The Paquimé civilisation was the major Indian trading settlement in northern Mexico between 900 and 1340 AD. Agriculture flourished, with irrigated maize crops and poultry kept in adobe cages for protection against the extremes of heat and cold.

The Paquimé structures are similar to Pueblo houses of the US south-west, with distinctive T-shaped door openings. Timber beams set into the walls supported roofs and upper floors, a couple of which have been reconstructed. The largest dwellings had up to three levels.

As the city grew, it was influenced through trade with southern Indian civilisations, particularly the Toltecs. Paquimé acquired some Toltec features, such as a ball court, of which

there are remnants. At its peak, the local population is estimated to have been around 10,000.

Despite fortifications, Paquimé was invaded, perhaps by Apaches, in 1340. The city was sacked, burned and abandoned, and its once-great structures were left alone for more than 600 years. The site was partially excavated in the late 1950s, and exposure to the elements led to erosion of the walls. They are now heavily restored, and some of the unique interior water systems and hidden cisterns have been rebuilt. Numerous mounds in the surrounding fields probably cover other ruins.

The Paquimé were great potters, and produced earthenware with striking red, brown or black geometric designs over a cream background. Other pieces are made of a black clay. Fine examples can be seen in Mexico City's Museo Nacional de Antropología, and the Museo Histórico in Ciudad Juárez.

To reach the site, take a bus from the centre of Nuevo Casas Grandes to (old) Casas Grandes – they run every half-hour during the day, and are marked 'Casas Grandes/Col Juárez'. The eight-km journey takes about 15 minutes. You will be let off at the main plaza of old Casas Grandes, which is quite picturesque, and signs direct you to the 10-minute walk to the ruins. This walk can be hot, so bring water and a hat. The site is managed by INAH; it's open from 10 am to 5 pm and admission costs 10 pesos.

Places to Stay

Most budget travellers stay at the basic *Hotel Juárez* (☎ (169) 4-02-33), at Obregón 110 close to the bus stops. It costs 30/50 pesos for singles/doubles, or 50 pesos with two beds. The showers are lukewarm trickles and there's no heating, but the owner is helpful and speaks English.

The *Hotel California* (☎ (169) 4-08-34), at Constitución 209, has clean air-con singles/doubles with bath at 85/95 pesos or 65/75 pesos for upstairs rooms.

Two mid-range motels are on Avenida Juárez as you come into town from the north.

Both have well-maintained air-con rooms with TVs and hot showers. The *Motel Piñon* (☎ (169) 4-06-55) costs 90/100 pesos for singles/doubles and has a restaurant and a pool (summer only). A block closer to town, the *Motel Paquimé* (☎ (169) 4-13-20, 4-47-20) has new rooms at 110/125 pesos a single/double, but the older rooms, around the courtyard, are nicer and better value at 85/95 pesos.

Top of the range is *Motel La Hacienda* (☎ (169) 4-10-48), 1.5 km further north of town, with a garden courtyard, swimming pool, tennis court and restaurant. Comfortable air-con rooms cost 159/176 pesos for singles/doubles.

Places to Eat

Nuevo Casas Grandes has a number of good, reasonably priced restaurants. The restaurant at *Motel Piñon*, *Denni's* and *Constantino* are all on Avenida Juárez, and serve good food in pleasant surroundings, but none of them are cheap. Probably the best budget eatery is *Café de la Esquina*, convenient to the bus depots at the intersection of 5 de Mayo and Obregón; it's clean with good food.

Getting There & Away

Buses run regularly to/from Ciudad Juárez (315 km, about four hours; 20 pesos) and Chihuahua (352 km, about 4½ hours; 41 pesos). Other buses go to Madera (four hours; 29 pesos; three per day), La Junta (on the Chihuahua al Pacífico railway), Cuauhtémoc and Creel. The road south, via Zaragoza and Gomez Farías, is very scenic. There are no passenger trains to Juárez, but enthusiasts can take very slow, uncomfortable 2nd-class trains to Madera (eight hours) and La Junta (12 hours or more).

AROUND NUEVO CASAS GRANDES

Trips in the areas west and south of Nuevo Casas Grandes take in some interesting little towns, cool forests and several archaeological sites. Most can be reached by bus, but to see the ancient rock carvings in the rugged **Arroyo los Monos** you will need a vehicle

with good clearance, and probably a local guide as well.

A good day trip could include the Mormon village of **Colonia Juárez**, the **Hacienda de San Diego** (a 1904 mansion owned by the Terrazas family, which controlled most of Chihuahua state until the revolution), and the village of **Mata Ortiz**. This village (originally called Pearson, after the railway engineer) is a centre for the production of ceramic pottery, using materials, techniques and decorative styles which are similar to those used by the ancient Paquimé culture. Juan Quezada is the best known of the Mata Ortiz potters.

Getting There & Away

A train goes to Mata Ortiz from Nuevo Casas Grandes at 10 am on Monday, Wednesday and Friday (time variable – about an hour; cost negligible – maybe two pesos), then you'll need to get a bus or lift to Colonia Juárez, from where there are regular buses back to Nuevo Casas Grandes.

MADERA

In the sierra south of Nuevo Casas Grandes, Madera (meaning wood, or timber) retains some forested areas despite the timber industry. The surrounding area has a number of archaeological sites, as well as some natural attractions. About 66 km west of the town, **Cueva Grande** has a waterfall cascading past its mouth, and inside the cave are some ancient dwellings resembling those of the Pueblo Indians in south-west USA.

More of these cliff dwellings can be seen at **Complejo Anasazi**, about 40 km west of Madera. In the same area is the **Puente Cogante** (suspension bridge) over the Río Huápoca, and some **thermal springs**. Several lakes and dams west and north of town are suitable for fishing.

Places to Stay

For budget accommodation, try *Hotel Maria* (☎ (157) 2-03-23) at 5 de Mayo 304, with singles/doubles/triples for 50/80/100 pesos. Much more expensive is *Motel Real del*

Bosque (☎ (157) 2-83-05), on the highway coming in from Chihuahua.

Getting There & Away

There are several buses a day to Madera from Nuevo Casas Grandes, Cuauhtémoc and Chihuahua. Six slow trains per week (three in each direction) run from Nuevo Casas Grandes to La Junta, stopping at Madera. Getting to the places of interest north and west of town is easiest with your own wheels, but your hotel should be able to help with transport.

CHIHUAHUA

• *pop: 800,000* • *alt: 1392 metres*

Chihuahua, capital city of the state of Chihuahua (Mexico's largest state), is comfortable and prosperous, with some fine colonial buildings in the centre and a sprawl of newer suburbs and industries around the edges. Most travellers stay here as an overnight stop on a journey to the north or south,

or at the start or finish of a trip on the Copper Canyon railway.

Chihuahua's main attraction is the museum of the Mexican revolution, in Pancho Villa's old house, Quinta Luz, but there are some other points of interest. The market is visited early in the morning by Mennonites and colourfully attired Tarahumara Indians. Lots of men wear cowboy hats and boots, reminding you that this is cattle country, as it has been since the days of the great haciendas. A non-attraction of Chihuahua is the tiny dog of that name, which you are most unlikely to see in the city.

History

Chihuahua, in the language of the indigenous Nahua people, means 'dry and sandy zone'. The first Spanish settlers were miners seeking silver. Franciscan and Jesuit missionaries Christianised the agrarian people of the area, but brutal treatment by the Spaniards led to rebellions by even the most tranquil tribes.

The city of Chihuahua gradually grew in size to administer the surrounding territory and to serve as a commercial centre for cattle and mining interests. In the War of Independence, rebel leader Miguel Hidalgo fled here, only to be betrayed, imprisoned by the Spaniards, and shot. President Benito Juárez made Chihuahua his headquarters for a while when forced to flee northward by the French troops of Emperor Maximilian. The city also served as a major garrison for cavalry guarding vulnerable settlements from the incessant raids of the fierce Apaches, until they were subdued by the legendary Mexican Indian fighter, Colonel Joaquín Terrazas.

The Díaz regime brought railways to Chihuahua, and helped consolidate the wealth and power of the huge cattle fiefdoms – the Terrazas family controlled estates as large as Belgium.

Pancho Villa, who had spent his early years as a bandit and cattle thief preying on the big properties, had settled in Chihuahua by 1910, running a peaceful and profitable, if not entirely legitimate, business trading in

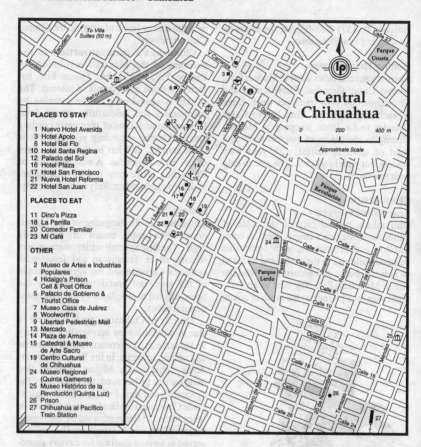

Central Chihuahua

0   200   400 m

Approximate Scale

PLACES TO STAY
1   Nuevo Hotel Avenida
3   Hotel Apolo
6   Hotel Bal Flo
10 Hotel Santa Regina
12 Palacio del Sol
16 Hotel Plaza
17 Hotel San Francisco
21 Nueva Hotel Reforma
22 Hotel San Juan

PLACES TO EAT
11 Dino's Pizza
18 La Parrilla
20 Comedor Familiar
23 Mi Café

OTHER
2   Museo de Artes e Industrias Populares
4   Hidalgo's Prison Cell & Post Office
5   Palacio de Gobierno & Tourist Office
7   Museo Casa de Juárez
8   Woolworth's
9   Libertad Pedestrian Mall
13 Mercado
14 Plaza de Armas
15 Catedral & Museo de Arte Sacro
19 Centro Cultural de Chihuahua
24 Museo Regional (Quinta Gameros)
25 Museo Histórico de la Revolución (Quinta Luz)
26 Prison
27 Chihuahua al Pacífico Train Station

horses and meat from dubious sources. He joined the revolution to depose Diáz, and his skills as a bandit, his local popularity, and his detailed knowledge of the country made him a successful guerrilla and general in the ensuing conflicts. His forces took the city of Chihuahua in 1913, and Villa established his headquarters here, had schools built and arranged other civic works.

Because of his association with the area Villa is a local hero. His old headquarters is a major attraction, and there is a statue of him at the intersection of Avenidas Universidad and División del Norte.

Orientation

Most areas of interest in Chihuahua are within a dozen or so blocks of the central Plaza de Armas – sometimes this means a longish walk, but taxis are expensive and the local bus system is difficult to decipher. The new bus station is a long way out of town.

Information

Tourist Office On the ground floor in the western corner of the Palacio de Gobierno, the tourist office (☎ (14) 10-10-77) is conveniently located and has helpful English-speaking staff. Open on weekdays from 9 am to 7 pm, they have quite a good city map and information about both the city and the state as a whole.

Money Most of the big banks are around the Plaza de Armas, and have ATMs. Banamex is two blocks north-west on Avenida Independencia. Usual banking hours are Monday to Friday from 9 am to 1 pm. Outside these times, you'll find casas de cambio in the streets behind the cathedral, but rates are not as good.

Post The main post office is on Juárez between Guerrero and Carranza (in the building above Hidalgo's cell). It's open Monday to Friday from 8 am to 7 pm, and Saturday from 9 am to 1 pm.

Cathedral

Chihuahua's cathedral, towering magnificently over the Plaza de Armas, has a marvellous baroque façade. Although construction began in 1717, continual raids by Indians postponed its completion until 1789. The interior is simpler, in Doric style, but with 16 Corinthian columns. On the south side is the entrance to the **Museo de Arte Sacro**, which houses religious paintings and objects from the colonial period.

Museo Histórico de la Revolución (Quinta Luz)

The museum of the Mexican Revolution is housed in the mansion and former headquarters of the revolutionary hero Pancho Villa, and is a must for history buffs. After his assassination in 1923, a number of his several wives filed claim for Villa's estate. Government investigations determined that Luz Corral de Villa was the generalissimo's legal spouse; the mansion was awarded to her and became known as Quinta Luz.

When Luz died in 1981, the government acquired the estate and transformed it into a museum. Inside are rooms with their original furnishings, a veritable arsenal of weaponry, and some exceptional photographs of the revolution and its principals. Unfortunately, the accompanying explanations are only in

Spanish. Parked in a courtyard is the black Dodge which Villa was driving when he was assassinated. It's carefully restored, except for the bullet holes.

You can walk to the museum from the city centre, or take a red city bus designated 'Avaloz y Juárez', running south on Ocampo. Get off at the corner of Mendez, cross the road and walk downhill on Mendez for two blocks. Quinta Luz will be on your left, with the entrance in Calle 10a. It's open daily from 9 am to 1 pm and 3 to 7 pm. Admission is 3 pesos.

Pancho Villa

Museo Regional (Quinta Gameros)

Manuel Gameros started building this mansion in 1907, and promised it to his fiancée as a wedding present. By the time it was finished, four years later, she had fallen in love with the architect and decided to marry him instead. The story goes that Gameros insisted on giving her the mansion anyway, for her wedding present as he had promised. Regardless of what this demonstrates about Latin attitudes to love and marriage, it's a gorgeous building with striking art nouveau decoration – the wood-carvings in the dining room are particularly exuberant. Upstairs, one room has Paquimé artefacts and another is made to resemble the inside of a Paquimé house – interesting, but out of place. Quinta Gameros is open Tuesday to Sunday from 10 am to 2 pm and 4 to 7 pm; admission is 5 pesos, or 2.50 pesos for students and children.

Palacio de Gobierno

This handsome 19th-century building is on Aldama between Carranza and Guerrero, facing the Plaza Hidalgo. The classic courtyard is surrounded by colonnades of arches, and the walls are covered with a mural by Aaron Piña Morales showing the history of Chihuahua – if you can't follow it, the tourist office in the western corner of the Palacio has a leaflet which helps a little. On one side of the courtyard is a small room with an eternal flame, which marks the place where Hidalgo was shot.

Hidalgo's Prison Cell

The cell in which Hidalgo was held prior to his execution is beneath the post office (a later construction), on Juárez behind the Palacio – look for the grimy eagle's head with the inscription 'Libertad' to find the entrance. There are a number of historic letters on display, and the cell contains Hidalgo's crucifix, pistol and other personal effects. Despite modern lighting, it still has a real dungeon ambience, and is quite moving if you have some imagination and a sense of history. It's open Tuesday to Sunday from 10 am to 2 pm and 4 to 7 pm; weekends from 10 am to 2 pm. Admission is 1 peso.

Museo Casa de Juárez

Home and office of Benito Juárez during the period of French occupation, the building exhibits documents and artefacts of the great reformer. It's open on weekdays from 9 am to 3 pm and 4 to 6 pm.

Museo de Artes e Industrias Populares

This is both a museum and a shop, specialising in Tarahumara Indian crafts, ponchos, sweaters and silver jewellery. It's at Reforma 5

near Independencia, and is open Tuesday to Saturday from 10 am to 1 pm and 4 to 7 pm.

Centro Cultura de Chihuahua

This small centre has a permanent exhibition of local archaeological artefacts, and sometimes interesting temporary exhibits as well. At Aldama 430, near Ocampo, it's open Tuesday to Sunday from 10 am to 2 pm and 4 to 7 pm, and is free.

Places to Stay – bottom end

There are a few cheapies in the blocks behind the cathedral – two of the best are on Victoria. *Hotel San Juan* (☎ (14) 10-26-83), at Victoria 823, is an older-style hotel with a courtyard and singles/doubles/triples at 30/40/60 pesos with heating and bathrooms. Another old place with style is *Nueva Hotel Reforma* (☎ (14) 12-58-08) at Victoria 814, with clean, spacious rooms with bath for 30/40/50 pesos. *Hotel Plaza* (☎ (14) 15-58-54), at Calle 4a No 206, right behind the cathedral, is pretty basic but cheap at 30/35 pesos a single/double, and you can find some more down-market options by heading down this street.

Places to Stay – middle

The *Hotel Bal Flo* (☎ (14) 16-03-00), at the intersection of Avenida Niños Héroes and Calle 5a No 702, has an underground car park and air-con rooms with bath for 130 pesos a double, but it's nothing special. The *Hotel Santa Regina* (☎ (14) 15-38-89) at Calle 3a No 107 is a better choice if you want a modern place near the centre. It's clean and has parking and is quite OK at 93/108 pesos a single/double. *Hotel Apolo* (☎ (14) 16-11-00), opposite the post office, has parking and a great-looking lobby, and ordinary singles/doubles/triples for 85/95/100 pesos. *Nuevo Hotel Avenida* (☎ (14) 15-28-91), across Carranza from the Apolo, is modern and comfortable with singles/doubles at 137/148 pesos, or 100/110 pesos on weekends.

For those with cars there are a number of motels on the main roads into town. Coming from the north, *Hotel Marrod* (☎ (14) 19-46-11) is on the right side, and offers comfortable air-con rooms with breakfast and all mod cons. Their special promotional price is 123 pesos a double.

Places to Stay – top end

The *San Francisco* (☎ (14) 16-75-50), at Victoria 504, is nearest the plaza, and costs 260/280 pesos a single/double. The highrise, deluxe *Palacio del Sol* (☎ (14) 16-60-00) on the corner of Avenida Niños Héroes and Independencia is also quite central and costs around 310 pesos for a room. For more luxuries at even higher prices you have to go a little further away from the centre, where *Hotel Casa Grande* (☎ (14) 19-66-33), at Avenida Tecnológico 4702, and the *Villa Suites* (☎ (14) 14-33-50), at Escudero 702, have enough room for tennis courts and swimming pools.

Places to Eat

As with accommodation, some of the best budget choices are along Avenida Victoria. Both the *Hotel San Juan* and the *Nueva Hotel Reforma* serve good cheap food in their restaurants – the San Juan has a more earthy atmosphere and is more popular. *Comedor Familiar*, at Victoria 830, serves a good breakfast, while *Mi Café* at Victoria 807 is more modern and more expensive but not bad value. A short walk towards the plaza from Mi Café, *La Parrilla*, at Victoria 420, is known for its barbecued meats in Argentine style, but seems pretty expensive and not well patronised. On the other side of Victoria, the restaurant at the *San Francisco* looks like one of the nicest around.

Dino's Pizza, just north of Independencia on Doblado, does a pretty good pizza at a moderate price. Another not-very-Mexican option is the cafe at *Woolworth's*, on the Libertad pedestrian mall, which is ultra-clean, medium-priced and does good coffee. The swankiest restaurants are along Juárez north-east of the centre near Avenida Colón, in an area called the Zona Dorada. At the other extreme, there are food stalls at the *market* which will do all the cheap tacos you can eat.

Entertainment

For bullfights, go on Sunday to the *Plaza de Toros* at the intersection of Canal and Cuauhtémoc. Some Saturdays and Sundays, you will find rodeos scheduled at the *Lienza Charro* in the western part of the town.

Getting There & Away

Air Chihuahua's airport has three flights daily to/from Mexico City and daily flights to Los Angeles and to main cities in northern Mexico.

Bus The new bus station has restaurants, luggage storage, a moneychanger (9 am to 9 pm weekdays, 9 am to 5 pm weekends) and a telephone office. Chihuahua is a major centre for buses in every direction. The ones mostly likely to be of interest to travellers are:

Ciudad Juárez – 376 km, five hours; several 1st-class buses (46 pesos) per hour, and frequent 2nd-class buses

Creel – 256 km, five hours; every two hours (32 pesos) by Estrella Blanca

Cuauhtémoc – 104 km, 1½ hours; frequent 1st-class (17 pesos) and 2nd-class buses

Durango – 709 km, 11 hours; frequent 1st-class buses (73 pesos)

Hidalgo del Parral – 301 km, 4½ hours; about six 2nd-class buses (25 pesos) per day

Mexico City (Terminal Norte) – 1412 km, 20 hours; many 1st-class buses (182 pesos) and some deluxe

Nuevo Casas Grandes – 352 km, 4½ to five hours; several a day (41 pesos)

Zacatecas – 832 km, 12½ hours; frequent 1st-class buses (104 pesos)

Other buses go to Acapulco, Aguascalientes, Guaymas, Hermosillo, Mazatlán, Ojinaga, Mexicali, Monterrey, Nogales, Nuevo Laredo, Saltillo, San Luis Potosí, Tampico, Torreón and Tijuana.

Train El División del Norte (Trains No 7 and 8) between Ciudad Juárez and Mexico City stop at Chihuahua at the Ferrocarriles Nacionales de México station on the north side of town. For train schedules, see Getting There & Away in the Mexico City chapter.

Chihuahua is also the north-eastern terminus of the Chihuahua al Pacífico line, for

---

The Mennonites

Founded by the Dutchman Menno Simonis in the 16th century, the Mennonite sect takes no oaths of loyalty other than to God, and eschews military service. Persecuted for their beliefs, the sect's members moved from Germany to Russia to Canada, and thousands settled in the tolerant, post-revolutionary Mexico of the 1920s.

In villages around Cuauhtémoc, you can see Mennonite men in baggy overalls and women in black dresses, driving their horse-drawn buggies and speaking their own dialect of old German. Traditionally they lead a spartan existence, speak little Spanish, and marry only among themselves, though some of the prosperous communities seem these days to be using tractors and driving cars. Their best known product is Mennonite cheese (queso Menonito), which is sold in many shops and sometimes peddled on the street. ∎

Barranca del Cobre (Copper Canyon) trains. These trains use the Chihuahua al Pacífico station, off Avenida Ocampo, nearly two km south-west of the Plaza de Armas. The air-con primera especial *vistatren* departs daily at 7 am on the 13½-hour run down through the canyon country to Los Mochis, near the Pacific coast (Tren 74; 107.50 pesos). The vistatren from the coast (Tren 73) arrives in Chihuahua at 8.50 pm. There is also a regular, far less comfortable segunda clase train which departs at 8 am and is scheduled to take about two hours longer (Tren 76; 29.50 pesos); it may be delayed, and not reach the most scenic area till after dark. For a description of the train journey and stops along the way, see the North-West Mexico chapter under Barranca del Cobre (Copper Canyon), following the Los Mochis section.

Getting Around

Airport buses collect passengers from the better city hotels – contact the nearest one even if you're not staying there.

The new bus station is way out to the east of town along Avenida Pacheco. To get there, catch a city bus marked 'Aeropuerto' or 'Central Camionera' from the corner of Avenidas Victoria and Ocampo.

For the Ferrocarriles Nacionales station, take a 'Granjas Colón' or 'Villa Colón' bus running from the centre, and ask the driver to let you know when you're there. For the Chihuahua al Pacífico station, take a 'Col Rosalía' or 'Avelos' bus and get out at the prison – it looks like a medieval castle – then walk behind the prison to the station.

There are local buses going throughout the city, but most places of interest to visitors are within walking distance of the centre. Taxis are unmetered so you have to bargain.

AROUND CHIHUAHUA

Cuauhtémoc

West of Chihuahua, this is a centre for the Mennonite population of northern Mexico. There are several decent places to stay in Cuauhtémoc, including the *Hotel del Norte* (cheap), the *Hotel Unión* (☎ (158) 2-11-14; mid-range) or the *Motel Tarahumara Inn* (☎ (158) 2-28-01; very good) amongst others.

Cuauhtémoc is 2½ hours by bus or 3½ hours by train west of Chihuahua, but you'll need a car or a tour operator to see the surrounding villages where the Mennonites actually live.

La Junta

The next town west of Cuauhtémoc, La Junta is the junction of the train line from Nuevo Casas Grandes and the Chihuahua al Pacífico line. This railway is the most popular route to/from the west coast, but it is possible to continue west by road to the spectacular Cascada de Basaseachi, Yepachi and, via a rough road, San Nicolás and on to Hermosillo (see the North-West Mexico chapter).

HIDALGO DEL PARRAL

• *pop: 130,000* • *alt: 1659 metres*

Founded as a mining settlement in 1631, the town took the 'Hidalgo' tag later, and is still commonly called just 'Parral'. In the 16th century, enslaved Indians mined the rich veins of silver, copper and lead. During the French intervention (1861-67) a fort on Parral's Cerro de la Cruz was occupied by French troops under orders from Emperor Maximilian.

Parral is now most famous as the place where Pancho Villa was murdered on 20 July 1923. A hero to the campesinos of the state of Chihuahua, Villa was buried in Parral, with 30,000 attending his funeral. A few years ago Villa's body (and Parral's major tourist attraction) was moved to Mexico City.

The building from which Villa was shot is now a library, with a small collection of Villa photos and memorabilia upstairs. Parral has churches from the 16th and 17th centuries, some quaint narrow streets and plazas, and a couple of old mansions and theatres. It's a pleasant enough town, and quite prosperous, but not a compelling attraction. Still, it's about the most interesting place to break a journey between Chihuahua and Durango.

Orientation

With its narrow, winding one-way streets, Parral can be confusing at first. A tourist map is available from the better hotels, and most of the places of interest are roughly in a line north of the river bed.

Places to Stay & Eat

The cheapest acceptable place is the *Hotel Fuentes* at Avenida Maclovia 79. It's central, basic but reasonably clean and charges 35/40 pesos for singles/doubles. *Hotel Acosta* (☎ (152) 2-06-57), at Agustín Barbachano 3, just off the Plaza Principal, is very clean and friendly at 50/60 pesos a single/double. *Hotel Adriana* (☎ (152) 2-25-70) is about the best in town, with clean, comfortable singles/doubles at 95/100 pesos, though some are quite dark. The *Motel El Camino Real* (☎ (152) 2-20-50) is a little more expensive, with a pool, but it's out near the bus station on Avenida Independencia.

There are some cheap food stalls and restaurants around and behind the market south of the Plaza Principal. On the central plaza (the

one with the cathedral), *El Pollo Rey* does great grilled chicken, while the nearby *Mariscos Esquinapa* has surprisingly tasty seafood.

Getting There & Away

The bus station on the south-east outskirts of town is most easily reached by taxi (about 5 or 6 pesos), or you can use the local bus. There are regular buses to Chihuahua (4½ hours; 25 pesos), Durango (45 pesos), and Valle de Allende (2nd class, 3.50 pesos). Several buses per day go to Mazatlán (94 pesos) and Mexico City (164 pesos).

AROUND HIDALGO DEL PARRAL

The road east to Ciudad Jiménez goes through dry, undulating country, but just south of this road the village of **Valle de Allende** is lush with trees and surrounded by green farmland. The stream through the valley is fed by mineral springs which start near **Ojo de Talamantes**, a few km west, where there's a small bathing area. It's not very deep, but it's safe for kids, and a cool and pretty place for a picnic, walking or camping – it costs a few pesos.

TORREÓN, GÓMEZ PALACIO & CIUDAD LERDO

• *pop: 700,000* • *alt: 1150 metres*

Of these three contiguous towns, Torreón is the largest, and is actually in the state of Coahuila. It was established in 1887 as a railway town, and continues as a centre for transport, as well as mining, smelting and other industries. On the other side of the Río Nazas, in Durango state, Lerdo dates from 1827 and has lots of trees and gardens, while Gómez Palacio, founded in 1899, is something of a commercial centre. Some of the surrounding land has been irrigated and grows wheat and cotton – the whole district, including the three towns, is known as La Laguna.

The 1910 battle for Torreón was Pancho Villa's first big victory in the Mexican Revolution, and it gave him control of the railways which radiate from the town. There were two more battles for Torreón in the ensuing struggles.

Orientation & Information

Torreón has few tourists, though it has an attractive central plaza and modern department stores nearby. There's a tourist office (☎ (17) 14-44-34) at Boulevard Miguel Alemán 250 Ote in Gómez Palacio, open on weekdays from 8.30 am to 3 pm, but it's not worth a special trip. Large scale maps are displayed on Torreón's main plaza and elsewhere – they show all the hotels and other things of interest to visitors.

Museo Regional de la Laguna

This museum has a small but interesting collection of pre-Hispanic artefacts from the region, and a selection of pieces from other parts of the country. It's on Avenida Juárez a couple of km east of the main plaza, and is open Tuesday to Sunday from 10 am to 4.30 pm; admission is 7 pesos (free on Sunday).

Places to Stay & Eat

There's a range of places near Torreón's main plaza. The cheapest, *Hotel Princesa* (☎ (17) 12-11-65) is at Morelos 1360, just to the west. An old-style place with rooms around a courtyard, it's basic, cleanish, and costs only 30 pesos a double. On the east side of the plaza, at Cepeda 273, the *Hotel Galicia* (☎ (17) 16-11-11) is a picture of faded elegance, with miles of tiles, stained glass and polished wood. It's run-down but clean, and a great place to stay at 50/60 pesos for singles/doubles, some better than others. The plushest place on the plaza, on the north side at Morelos 1280, is the eight-storey *Palacio Real* (☎ (17) 16-00-00), with rooms from 187/212 pesos, and an excellent restaurant.

For cheaper food, there's quite a good pizza shop on one side of the Hotel Galicia, and a juice bar on the other. There are other places to eat in the shopping area south of the plaza, getting cheaper as you go towards the market.

For motorists, there are motels on the access roads, like the *La Siesta* (☎ (17) 14-02-91) at Avenida Madero 320 in Gómez Palacio, (the road from the north), which is ordinary but acceptable at 70/85 pesos.

Getting There & Away

There are bus stations in both Torreón and Gómez Palacio, and long distance buses will stop at both, or will transfer you to the other without charge. The Torreón bus station is east of town; local buses along Boulevard Revolución take you to/from the main plaza. There are regular connections to Chihuahua (456 km, 6½ hours; 55 pesos), Durango (257 km, four hours – less if they take the toll road; 33 pesos), Mazatlán, Mexico City, Saltillo and Zacatecas (386 km, 5½ hours; 50 pesos) For details of the train connections to the north and south, see the Mexico City chapter. The tolls on the new highway to Durango cost 102 pesos for the whole trip; nearly all the traffic, including the buses, takes the slower and busier free road.

AROUND TORREÓN

The deserts north of La Laguna are starkly beautiful, with strange geological formations around **Dinamita**, and many semi-precious stones for gem hunters. It's easiest to get around with your own transport, but the tourist office in Gómez Palacio can arrange tours, and rental cars are available, though not cheap.

To reach the dusty old mining town of **Mapimí** from Gómez Palacio, go about 35 km north on highway 49 to Bermejillo, then 35 km west on highway 30. The town looks unchanged since Benito Juárez stayed here in the mid-19th century – the house where he stayed, near the north-west corner of the plaza, is now a small museum (closed Monday). East of town is the turnoff to the abandoned **Ojuela mine**, now a ruined ghost town. The spectacular 300-metre-long suspension bridge was built in 1892 and carried ore trains from the mine; its engineer later designed a better known suspension bridge in San Francisco.

At Ceballos, 87 km north of Gómez Palacio, a rough road goes east to the **Zona del Silencio**, so called because conditions here are said to prevent propagation of radio waves. Peppered with meteorites, it is also believed to be a UFO landing area. The surrounding **Bolsón de Mapimí** desert is a

Reserva Biosféra, dedicated to the study of the plants and animals of a very arid area, including a very rare land-based tortoise. This is a remote area with rough roads.

DURANGO
• *pop: 490,000* • *alt: 1912 metres*

Don't be too put off by the modernisation on the outskirts of the city – proceed immediately to Durango's delightful old Plaza de Armas, where you'll discover fine colonial architecture. The city was founded in 1523 by the conquistador Don Francisco de Ibarra, and named after the Spanish city of his birth. Just north of the city, Cerro del Mercado is one of the world's richest iron ore deposits, and was the basis of Durango's early importance, along with gold and silver from the Sierra Madre.

Other industries of the area include farming and grazing, timber and paper. Durango is also in the movie business, with a number of locations outside the city, especially for Westerns. A number of restaurants have movie or cowboy decor, and lots of shops sell cowboy boots, belts and hats. It's a fun town, and very friendly.

Orientation
Durango is a good town to walk around in, and most of the interesting places to see and stay are within a few blocks of the plaza. For some greenery, go to the extensive Parque Guadiana on the west side of town.

Information
Tourist Office The tourist office (☎ (18) 11-21-39) is at Hidalgo 408 between 5 de Febrero and Pino Suárez. The staff are friendly and helpful, and some of them speak English. Hours are from 9 am to 3 pm Monday to Friday.

Money For currency exchange you will find a Bancomer at the north-west corner of the Plaza de Armas. It's open Monday to Friday from 9 am to 1.30 pm, but come early to avoid a long wait. There are other banks nearby (with ATMs), and a casa de cambio next to the Hotel Roma which has longer hours and quicker service, but lower rates.

Post The post office is on Avenida 20 de Noviembre at the corner of Laureano Roncai, about 1.5 km east of the plaza. Hours are Monday to Friday from 8 am to 8 pm, Saturday from 8 am to 1 pm.

Telephone There are modern Ladatel phones in the plaza, and a Lada caseta just north on Martínez.

Walking Tour
The **Plaza de Armas** is attractive, especially on Sunday, when musicians perform on the bandstand and locals promenade. On the north side is the **cathedral**, with its imposing baroque façade, constructed from 1695 to 1750. Walk west on Avenida 20 de Noviembre and on your right you will see the elegant 19th-century **Teatro Ricardo Castro**, which houses temporary exhibitions and functions more as a cinema than a theatre.

Turn south on Martínez, past the **Teatro Victoria**, to another plaza. On its north side is the **Palacio de Gobierno**, built on the estate of a Spanish mine owner and expropriated by the government following the War of Independence. Inside are colourful murals depicting the history of the state. On the east side of the plaza is the **Universidad Juárez**. From there, walk east on 5 de Febrero to the **Casa del Conde de Suchil**, 17th-century home of the Spanish governor of Durango, the Conde de Suchil. Two blocks further east is the **Mercado de Goméz Palacio**, a good place for a snack and a rest.

Festivals
On 8 July, Feria Nacional, the celebration of Durango's founding, is one of the most exciting festivals in Mexico. The fiesta brings some of the country's most famous musicians, bands and dancers to the city, along with local industrial, agricultural and artistic exhibits. All hotels are booked in advance, so make a reservation.

Places to Stay – bottom end

The nicest places to stay are old colonial buildings around the Plaza de Armas. About the cheapest is the *Posada San Jorge* (☎ (18) 11-48-66), which is a few blocks up Constitución, with clean rooms around a pretty courtyard for only 40 pesos a single or double. *Hotel Posada Durán* (☎ (18) 11-24-12), situated just east of the Plaza de Armas at 20 de Noviembre 506, is great value, with a courtyard, fountain and spacious rooms for around 50/60 pesos a single/double. It's clean, well located and has a great atmosphere.

Parking is a problem in the middle of Durango, but the *Motel Ar-Vel* (☎ (18) 12-53-33) at Progreso 104 Sur is reasonably central and has a secure car park, and comfortable rooms with TV for 77 pesos a double, but none of the charm of the older places.

For less money (and less charm) but still near the centre of town, try *Hotel Gallo* (☎ (18) 11-52-90), at 5 de Febrero 117, near the corner of Progreso. It's clean, bright and cheap at 30/35 pesos a single/double. The *Hotel Reyes* (☎ (18) 11-50-50) at 20 de Noviembre 220 is pretty basic, but the manager is helpful and she speaks English. It's a multistorey place a good way east of

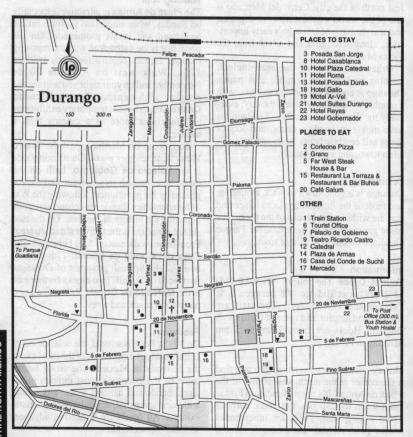

Durango

0   150   300 m

PLACES TO STAY
3   Posada San Jorge
8   Hotel Casablanca
10   Hotel Plaza Catedral
11   Hotel Roma
13   Hotel Posada Durán
18   Hotel Gallo
19   Motel Ar-Vel
21   Motel Suites Durango
22   Hotel Reyes
23   Hotel Gobernador

PLACES TO EAT
2   Corleone Pizza
4   Grano
5   Far West Steak
     House & Bar
15   Restaurant La Terraza &
     Restaurant & Bar Buhos
20   Café Salum

OTHER
1   Train Station
6   Tourist Office
7   Palacio de Gobierno
9   Teatro Ricardo Castro
12   Catedral
14   Plaza de Armas
16   Casa del Conde de Suchil
17   Mercado

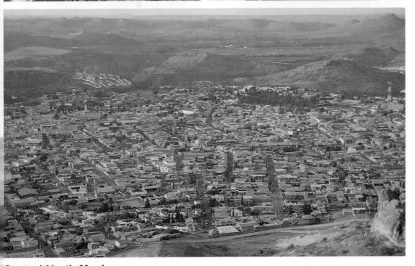

Central North Mexico
Top Left: Petroglyphs at Casas Grandes (JL)
Top Right: Roadside memorial (JL)
Bottom: View of Hidalgo del Parral (JL)

Central North Mexico
Top Left: Valle de Allende (JL)
Top Right: Church, Chihuahua (JL)
Bottom: Shopfront, Chihuahua (JL)

the plaza (look up to the 3rd floor for its sign), and it costs 39/46 pesos for singles/doubles.

Across the road from the bus station, *Hotel Karla* is like a set for a prison movie – a cell here costs 30 pesos. Much better value is the *CONADE youth hostel* (formerly CREA; (☎ (18) 17-22-16), a couple of hundred metres towards town on Heróico Colegio Militar, in the sports complex (Villa Juvenil Deportivo) behind the fence of orange bars. It costs 10 pesos per person in a spotless dorm, with a 20-peso deposit for linen. IYHA members get a discount.

Places to Stay – middle

For plush accommodation try the *Hotel Casablanca* (☎ (18) 11-35-99), only two blocks from the plaza at 20 de Noviembre 811. Large, well-appointed rooms with air-con and bath cost 99/114/142 for singles/doubles/triples. *Motel Suites Durango* (☎ (18) 11-55-80) at 5 de Febrero 103 Ote is similar in price, but not in style.

Hotel Plaza Catedral (☎ (18) 13-24-80) is another attractive colonial place with singles/doubles surrounding a courtyard, from 90/100 pesos to 120/150 pesos. It's next to the cathedral at Constitución 216 Sur. Also attractive, convenient and comfortable is the *Hotel Roma* (☎ (18) 12-01-22) at 20 de Noviembre No 705 Pte, at 82 pesos a double.

Places to Stay – top end

The *Hotel Gobernador* (☎ (18) 13-19-19), one km east of the plaza at 20 de Noviembre 257, is a modern building with colonial-style rooms, a swimming pool and an elegant restaurant. It's the best in town, with air-con singles or doubles with phones, TV and the works for 330 pesos.

Places to Eat

The best place to eat cheaply is at the market on 20 de Noviembre, four blocks east of the plaza. A few hole-in-the-wall taco places on Constitución, in the blocks north of the plaza, are good for breakfast or lunch. Further up this street, you'll find *Rincón Taurino*, *Gorditas Gabino* and *Corleone Pizza*, more or less side by side. The latter is more upscale, with movie posters and good pizzas. Two blocks west, on the corner of Negrete and Zaragoza, *Grano* is a vegetarian cafe and wholemeal bakery, and quite economical – it's open from 8 am but closes at 8 pm, so don't be late. *Café Salum*, on the corner of 5 de Febrero and Progreso, is clean and reasonably priced. The more expensive *Restaurant La Bohemia* (☎ 11-00-45), at Negrete 1314 Pte, serves good continental cuisine, and has a 20-peso comida corrida.

For eating with ambience, try the outdoor patio of *Restaurant La Terraza*, upstairs at 5 de Febrero overlooking the plaza. Breakfast costs from 5 to 14 pesos, sandwiches from 9 to 20 pesos, and for dinner, main courses and pizzas are from 15 to 30 pesos. The nearby *Restaurant & Bar Buhos* is also moderately expensive but has entertainment on most evenings. Another entertaining place to eat is the *Far West Steak House & Bar*, set up like an Old West saloon, complete with honky-tonk piano. The meals are expensive, but the decor is worth the price of a drink or two.

Getting There & Away

Bus There are good bus connections from Durango to many of the places which travellers want to go to. Most of these are quite long distances, so 2nd-class buses are not recommended. There are direct 1st-class buses to:

Chihuahua – 709 km, 11 hours; regular buses (74 pesos)

Guadalajara – 609 km, 9½ hours; several daily buses (74 pesos)

Hidalgo del Parral – 412 km, 6½ hours; several buses a day (45 pesos)

Mazatlán – 318 km, 6½ hours; a very scenic road so take a morning bus with Transportes del Norte (38 pesos)

Mexico City (Terminal Norte) – 903 km, 12 hours; several buses a day (115 pesos)

Torreón – 257 km, four hours (three on the toll road); regular buses (33 pesos)

Zacatecas – 290 km, 4½ hours; frequent buses (36 pesos)

Train The train to Torreón is cheap but very slow (11 hours) – for enthusiasts only. It leaves at 7 am. The once-grand train station is on the north side of town.

Getting Around

The Central Camionera is on the east side of town; a Ruta 2 white microbus from the other side of the bus station car park will get you to the plaza in comfort for 6.50 pesos, or you can buy a ticket for a taxi for 12 pesos. There are two local bus routes between the bus station and the main plaza – Ruta Amarillo and Ruta Azules. Buses marked 'Central Camionera' go to the bus station; those marked 'Centro' go to the main plaza. They are slow, crowded and cheap.

AROUND DURANGO
Movie Locations

The clear light and stark countryside make Durango a popular location for Hollywood movies. Around 120 have been shot in the area – mostly Westerns, including John Wayne vehicles like *Chisum*, *Big Jake* and *The War Wagon*. If you're into movies, it's fun to visit the 'sets' (that's what they're called).

Chupaderos is a dusty Mexican village

10 km north of Durango, with a few tacky façades on one intersection making a remarkably convincing Wild West town. Two km south of there, **Villa del Oeste** is a completely fake town, which is being done up as a tourist attraction with a saloon, café, stables and shops.

The Durango tourist office organises trips to the sets on weekends. Alternatively, take an Estrella Blanca bus from the bus station (3 pesos; every half-hour) to Chupaderos. It will drop you on the highway about 500 metres from the set. To get back to Durango just flag down any passing bus.

South of Durango is **Los Alamos**, a '1940s town' where *The Shadow Makers* made the first A-bomb. Other non-Western movies shot nearby include *Revenge*, *Dog Soldiers* and *Samson and Delilah*.

West of Durango

The road west of Durango to Mazatlán, on the coast, is particularly scenic, with a number of natural attractions on the way. In the area round **El Salto** you can trek to waterfalls, canyons and forests. The spectacular stretch of road about 160 km from Durango is called **El Espinazo del Diablo** (The Devil's Backbone).

North-East Mexico

This chapter covers the state of Nuevo León and most of the states of Tamaulipas and Coahuila – a huge area, stretching nearly 1000 km from north to south and 500 km from east to west. Many travellers enter Mexico at one of the five main border crossings from the USA, and take one of the several routes heading south to the Bajío region, central Mexico or the Gulf coast. But few travellers stay long in the region; most go through as quickly as they can to what is seen as the 'real' Mexico. This is not surprising, as north-east Mexico does not have impressive pre-Hispanic ruins, charming colonial towns, or pretty palm-fringed beaches. What it does have is a geography unlike anywhere else in Mexico, and an emerging culture which is unique in the world.

Geographically, the vast deserts of north-east Mexico are the southern extension of the Great Plains of North America, impressive for their stark, rugged beauty and sheer expanse. The Rio Grande, often called the Río Bravo del Norte in Mexico, is vital for irrigation in this arid region, and it has been developed as a resource by joint Mexican-US projects. In fact, it may have been over-developed, and attention is now being paid to environmental quality along the river. The coastal areas have remote beaches, lagoons and wetlands which are home to many types of marine life, and a winter stop-over for many migratory birds. In the south, the coastal environment extends into the lush, green, subtropical Huasteca country, west of Tampico. Going inland, numerous steep, winding roads climb to the eastern and northern edges of the Sierra Madre Oriental, offering spectacular scenery and a refreshing highland climate.

Culturally, north-east Mexico and the southern part of the USA is a frontier of epic proportions. It was here that the two great colonising movements, Spanish from the south and Anglo-Saxon from the north, confronted

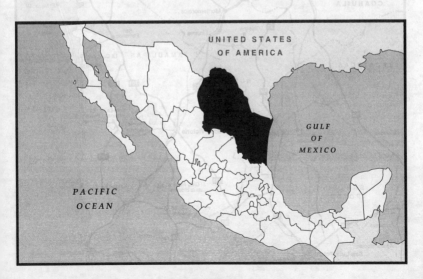

403

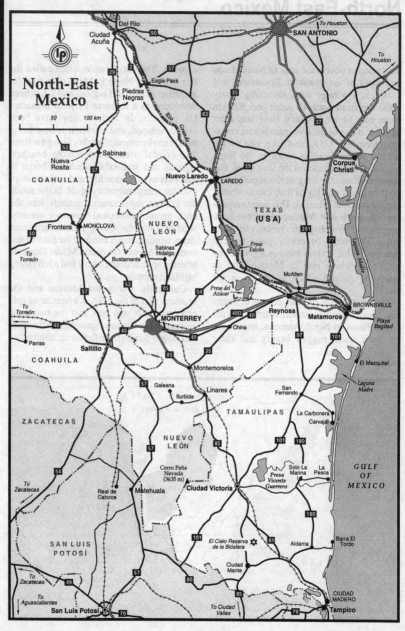

North-East Mexico

0   50   100 km

each other and displaced the native American nations. The war between Mexico and the USA (1845-47) was probably inevitable, and though it established the Rio Grande as the political border between the two countries, the cultural and economic boundaries remain much less distinct. There is so much Mexican influence in southern Texas that Spanish seems to be more widely spoken than English, while cities like Monterrey, capital of Nuevo León, are the most Americanised part of Mexico. Economically, the two sides of the river seem worlds apart, but money and resources surge back and forth across the line – much of the Texas economy depends on Mexican labour, while American investment is booming in maquiladoras in the border towns of northern Mexico.

If you're just looking for tourist attractions you may be disappointed in north-east Mexico, but if you want to see a fascinating, evolving region you should spend at least a few days here. This may be a window to the future of Mexico in the age of NAFTA – a place where Tex-Mex is more than a burrito, it's a way of life.

Tamaulipas

NUEVO LAREDO

• *pop: 300,000*

More foreign tourists enter Mexico through Nuevo Laredo than any other town on the north-east border. An excellent road runs south to Monterrey, which has good connections with central Mexico and the east and west coasts. Two international bridges cross the Rio Grande to Laredo, Texas, from where Interstate 35 goes north to San Antonio. A third international bridge crosses the border 20 km to the north-west, enabling motorists in a hurry to bypass Laredo and Nuevo Laredo altogether.

As border towns go, this pair is almost a classic example, and not unpleasant, though the heat can be unbearable. Nuevo Laredo has numerous restaurants, bars and souvenir shops catering to short-term visitors from the

USA – most of them accept US currency and quote prices in dollars. Many Mexican travellers pass through too, so there is also a fair selection of bottom-end places to stay and eat. 'Across the water', in Laredo, there are all-American supermarkets, motels and fast-food joints, as well as reliable phone and postal services, all staffed with Spanish-speaking workers.

History

The area was sparsely populated with nomadic Indian groups until Don Tomás Sánchez, a captain of the Spanish royal army, was given a grant of land at Laredo in 1775. The first settlers were ranchers, and missionaries passed through into the interior of Texas. In 1836, Texas seceded from Mexico and became an independent republic. From 1839 to 1841, the Rio Grande valley, and much of what is now north-eastern Mexico, declared itself a separate republic – the Republic of the Rio Grande, with its capital at Laredo.

The US annexation of Texas in 1845 precipitated the Mexican-American War, with the Rio Grande subsequently becoming the border between the USA and Mexico. A new Mexican town, called Nuevo Laredo, was established on the south side of the river and, with its predecessor on the US side, began its existence as a border town. Nuevo Laredo now collects more in tariffs and customs revenue than any other Mexican port of entry. It also has over 60 maquiladoras producing goods for the US market.

Orientation

There are two international bridges carrying vehicles and pedestrians between the two Laredos. Puente Internacional No 1 is the one to use if you're heading into Mexico – it has an immigration office at its southern end where you can get your tourist card (but you have to go to the aduana office in town to get a vehicle permit). This bridge brings you into Mexico at the north end of Guerrero, Nuevo Laredo's main street, which stretches for two km (one way going south). Heading north, signs direct traffic around the western side of the city, via Avenida López de Lara, to Puente Internacional No 1. Puente Internacional No 2 is for those who don't need a tourist card, and is often used by heavy vehicles. The city centre area spreads along either side of Guerrero for the first km from the bridge. Its main plaza, with a kiosk in the middle, the Palacio de Gobierno on the east side, and a few hotels and restaurants around it, is seven blocks along Guerrero from the bridge.

Street numbers on Guerrero indicate how far they are from the bridge: 109 would be in the block nearest the bridge, 509 in the fifth block south and so on. Other north-south streets, parallel to Guerrero, are numbered in the same way.

Nuevo Laredo's Central Camionera, the arrival and departure point for long-distance buses, is a long way away on the southern side of town. Local buses run between there, the town centre and the international bridges.

Information

Tourist Office There's a small tourist office (☎ (87) 12-01-04) near the immigration building, with a selection of leaflets on Nuevo Laredo and northern Mexico. It's open daily from 9 am to 2 pm, or sometimes to 6 pm (they're vague about the hours – welcome to Mexico).

Money Most casas de cambio will not change travellers' cheques – the Banamex/ Euromex casa de cambio on Guerrero is a notable exception. Most businesses will accept them if you want to buy something, and the main Mexican banks should change them. Businesses also accept cash dollars, but the exchange rate can be pretty low.

Post The post office is on Camargo, at the back of the government offices east of the plaza.

Foreign Consulate There's a US Consulate (☎ (87) 14-05-12) at Allende 3330, near the corner of Nayarit, on the south side of town. It doesn't issue US visas. It's open Monday to Friday from 8 am to noon and 1.30 to 4.30 pm, but US citizens can call a Laredo number

(☎ (08) 727-9661) if after-hours emergency assistance is required.

Immigration Mexican immigration is in the border post at the south end of the Puente Internacional No 1.

Vehicle Permits For a vehicle permit you have to go to the aduana office. To get there, go about 14 blocks south on Guerrero, turn right at Héroes de Nacataz and then go about nine blocks west to the corner of López de Lara, where you'll see a big car park on the right. Occasional blue-and-white signs point the way. The office is open daily from 9 am to 4 pm and should issue a permit without hassles if your papers are in order (see the Getting There & Away chapter). If you're leaving Mexico and need your vehicle permit cancelled, it's better to get it done at the Mexican checkpoints on the highways about 27 km from the border, which are more conveniently located and open 24 hours a day. Don't forget to do it, or the Mexican authorities might decide you've sold the car in Mexico and charge import duty and fines to your credit card.

Places to Stay

The cheap places cater to poorer Mexicans who are passing through, and they usually have small rooms with cleanish bathrooms, wobbly ceiling fans and not much else. *Hotel Sam's* (☎ (87) 12-59-32), at Hidalgo 2903, is run down but not too bad at only 25/35 pesos for one/two beds. *Hotel Texas* (☎ (87) 12-18-07), at Guerrero 837, is grimy but may be OK for 35/40 pesos.

Hotel Ajova, on Hidalgo half a block west of Guerrero, is modern though pretty shoddy with singles/doubles from 30/40 pesos, but it's about the cheapest place with air-con. The *Hotel la Llave* (☎ (87) 12-23-80), at Juárez 313, is just a few blocks from the international bridge and easy enough to find, though it's not well signposted. It costs 40/48 pesos for air-con singles/doubles. A little further up the scale is *Hotel Romanos* (☎ (87) 12-23-91), on Dr Mier just east of the plaza. Clean air-con rooms are 49/59 pesos with one/two beds; TV costs extra.

On the south side of the plaza, *Hotel Alameda* (☎ (87) 12-50-50), at González 2715, has air-con, parking, phone and TV. Single rooms are 65 pesos and pretty small, but doubles at 75 pesos are good value. *Hotel Fiesta* (☎ (87) 12-47-27), at Ocampo 559, is a clean, friendly place at around 70/88 pesos. The *Hotel Regis* (☎ (87) 12-90-35), at Pino Suárez 3013, is slightly more expensive at around 85/95 pesos but is very clean and offers air-con, phone, TV and parking.

Hotel Mesón Del Rey (☎ (87) 12-63-60), at

Guerrero 718 on the main plaza, has all the amenities and is comfortable and quite good value for 109/125 pesos. There are more expensive motels on the highway heading south, but if you want this sort of accommodation, you'd do better in Laredo on the US side.

Places to Eat

There are lots of eating possibilities, though the places on Guerrero for the first few blocks south of the bridge can be overpriced tourist joints. The side streets have cheaper eating places less geared to the tourist trade,

Nuevo Laredo

0   250   500 m

PLACES TO EAT
2 La Fittes Restaurant
9 Restaurant Principal
10 Café Quinto Patio
17 Restaurant Almanza

PLACES TO STAY
4 Hotel Fiesta
5 Hotel Sam's
6 Hotel Ajova
7 Hotel la Llave
8 Hotel Regis
11 Hotel Romanos
15 Hotel Mesón Del Rey
16 Hotel Texas
17 Hotel Alameda

OTHER
1 Mexican Border Post & Tourist Office
3 Mercado Juárez
12 Post Office
13 Town Bus Station
14 Plaza Hidalgo
18 Casa de Cambio Euromex
19 Train Station
20 Aduana Office (Vehicle Permits)

and the tourist restaurants offer better value as you go further south. One of the first attractive-looking places is the *Restaurant Principal* at Guerrero 624, with a substantial Mexican menu with antojitos from 10 to 15 pesos and meat dishes from 15 pesos; *cabrito* (roast kid) is around 34 pesos.

On the south side of the plaza, on the corner of Ocampo and González, is a small, cosy, family-run place, reasonably clean and not too expensive. It's called the *Café, Lonchería* or *Restaurant Almanza* (depending on which sign you read), and the menu includes fish (8 to 13 pesos), soups and breakfasts (8 pesos), and it's open from 7 am to midnight. The north side of the plaza has some small, plain cafés with standard Mexican fare, and a place selling pizzas for 13 pesos and up.

Two places very popular with locals lie a km or so down Guerrero from the international bridge. At Guerrero 2114, between Venezuela and Lincoln, *El Rancho* (☎ 14-87-53) is a not-so-poor person's taco-and-beer hall, offering a long list of different types of tacos. The *Río Mar* (☎ 12-91-94), at Guerrero 2403, is packed out at night with people tucking into mouth-watering seafood dishes starting at around 22 pesos.

Among Nuevo Laredo's classy eateries are *The Winery Pub & Grill* (☎ 12-08-95), at Matamoros 308, and *La Fittes* (☎ 2-22-08), on the corner of Matamoros and Victoria, which specialises in seafood.

Entertainment

Nuevo Laredo's horse and greyhound racing venue, the *Hipódromo-Galgódromo*, has been closed for a while but may reopen. In the meantime, punters can watch US and Mexican sports on satellite TV at the *Turf Club* on Dr Mier.

Nuevo Laredo holds an agricultural, livestock, industrial and cultural fair during the second week of September.

Things to Buy

If you're just setting out, the less you buy the better. But if you're on the way home, it's worth browsing around some of the shops and markets for the odd souvenir. There's a craft 'market' on the east side of Guerrero half a block north of the main plaza, another one on the west side of Guerrero half a block south of Hidalgo, and a small mall on the west side of Guerrero, between Hidalgo and Belden. There are also lots of individual shops along this northern section of Guerrero. There's a great deal of overpriced junk, but some first-quality work is available if you're prepared to look for it. Prices are a bit higher than in places further south, but not outrageously so, and with a bit of bargaining and cash payment, you may get 10% to 20% off the asking price.

Getting There & Away

Air Nuevo Laredo airport is off the Monterrey road, 14 km south of town. Mexicana has direct flights to/from Mexico City and Guadalajara. The Mexicana office (☎ 12-20-52, 2-22-11) is at Héroes de Nacataz 2335.

Bus Nuevo Laredo's bus station (Central Camionera) is about three km from the international bridge on the southern side of town. It has a left-luggage section and restaurant, and 1st and 2nd-class buses to every city in the northern half of Mexico. The main companies providing 1st-class services here are Transportes Frontera, Tres Estrellas de Oro, Transportes del Norte and Omnibus de México. Futura and Turistar provide deluxe services. For longer trips, 2nd-class buses are slow and not recommended. The most popular routes into Mexico include:

Ciudad Victoria – 512 km, seven hours; seven buses daily (57 pesos)
Matehuala – 518 km, seven hours (71 pesos)
Mexico City (Terminal Norte) – 1113 km, 16 hours; numerous buses (143 pesos) and some faster directos
Monterrey – 230 km, three hours; many buses (28 pesos)
Reynosa – 251 km, four hours (30 pesos)
Saltillo – 315 km, 4½ hours; lots of buses (42 pesos)
San Luis Potosí – 719 km, 11½ hours; hourly buses (92 pesos)
Tampico – 755 km, 12 hours; one bus daily (87 pesos)
Zacatecas – 658 km, nine hours; one bus daily (96 pesos)

There are also buses to Aguascalientes, Durango, Guadalajara and Querétaro. At the Transportes Frontera desk you can buy tickets directly to cities in Texas, including San Antonio, Houston and Dallas.

To/From Laredo, Texas There are buses from the Greyhound terminal in Laredo direct to cities in Mexico, including San Luis Potosí, Querétaro and Mexico City, but these are dearer than services from Nuevo Laredo. You can sometimes use these buses to go between Laredo and Nuevo Laredo bus stations, but you have to ask the driver – it's less hassle and often quicker just to walk over the international bridge ($US0.50 to walk over).

Train Nuevo Laredo train station is on Avenida César López de Lara, at the western end of Gutiérrez, 10 blocks from Guerrero. The level of service seems to get worse every year, and for speed, comfort and convenience, trains fall a long way behind the buses. The only passenger train now serving Nuevo Laredo is the Águila Azteca, train No 2, with 1st and 2nd-class seats, which departs at 6.55 pm for Monterrey (four to five hours; 30 pesos), Saltillo, San Luis Potosí, San Miguel de Allende, Querétaro and Mexico City (24 hours). Tickets go on sale at about 6 pm.

For trains from Mexico City to Nuevo Laredo, see Getting There & Away in the Mexico City chapter.

Car The route via Monterrey is the most direct way to central Mexico, the Pacific coast and/or the Gulf coast. An excellent toll road, highway 85D, goes south to Monterrey. It's fast but expensive – total tolls are 94 pesos. The alternative free road is longer and slower but passes through some towns on the way. Highway 2 is a mainly rural road which follows the Rio Grande south-east to Reynosa and Matamoros. To the USA, the bridge toll is 6 pesos.

Getting Around

Frequent city buses (1 peso) make getting around Nuevo Laredo simple enough. The easiest place to catch them is on the east side of the plaza, where all the buses seem to pass. Bus No 51 goes from there to the bus station, but you may be able to get one from closer to the bridge. For the train station from the city centre, catch a blue-and-white 'Arteaga González' bus. From the bus station there are local buses into town. A taxi from the bus station to the bridge will cost about 20 pesos.

REYNOSA

• *pop: 350,000* • *alt: 90 metres*

Reynosa was founded in 1749 as Villa de Nuestra Señora de Guadalupe de Reynosa, 20 km from its present location. Flooding forced the move to the present site in 1802. Reynosa was one of the first towns to rise up in the independence movement of 1810, but there is little of historical interest today.

Today, Reynosa is one of north-east Mexico's most important industrial towns, with oil refineries, petrochemical plants, cotton mills, distilleries and maquiladoras. Pipelines from here carry natural gas to Monterrey and into the USA. It's also the centre of a big cattle-raising, cotton, sugar cane and maize-growing area.

As a commercial border crossing, Reynosa is busier than Matamoros but less important than Nuevo Laredo. It has quite good road connections into Mexico and Texas, but most travellers will probably find one of the other crossings more direct and convenient. Across the Rio Grande, on the US side, is the small settlement of Hidalgo, with the bigger town of McAllen nine km away. The tourist trade is geared to short-term Texan visitors, with restaurants, nightclubs, bars and even bawdier diversions. Some handicrafts are available in the tourist markets, but the quality is generally low, while the prices are not.

Orientation

Reynosa's central streets are laid out on a grid pattern, between the Rio Grande and the Anzalduas Canal. The main plaza is on a rise a few blocks south-west of the international bridge, with a modern church, town hall, banks and hotels. Between the bridge and the centre lies the zona rosa, with restaurants, bars and nightclubs. Reynosa's industries have expanded so much on the south side of town that the 'central' area has more or less become the northern edge. If you're driving in from Mexico, follow the signs to the Puente Internacional, then go to the town centre if you want to. Avoid getting caught up in the maze of streets in the industrial zone south of the canal.

Information

Tourist Information The tourist information booth at the south end of the bridge has been vacated, but is evidently still used as a urinal. The Mexican customs and immigration building is being redeveloped and may incorporate a tourist office one day. Men on the street, sometimes with ID cards, will proffer assistance and information, but may expect a tip – often they are taxi drivers trying to generate business for themselves or their associates.

Money The customs building has a Bancomer which changes travellers' cheques. You can also change cash and cheques at Banamex, on Guerrero between Hidalgo and Juárez. The main banks have ATMs, some of which will dispense US dollars as well as pesos, and there are several casas de cambio. Some shops will change money at competitive rates.

Post The post office is on the corner of Díaz and Colón.

Customs & Immigration US immigration is at the north end of the international bridge. Mexican immigration is at the south end, and there's another immigration post in Reynosa bus station. Get a tourist card stamped at either post if you're proceeding beyond Reynosa deeper into Mexico. There's an aduana office which can issue temporary car import permits – ask at one of the immigration offices for the current location of this office.

Things to See & Do

Take a stroll around the main square and down Hidalgo, a pedestrian shopping strip, to the touristy craft market, Mercado Zaragoza. The zona rosa has tourist-oriented restaurants, bars and nightclubs, but it only comes to life on the nights when the young Texas crowd comes in. Much sleazier entertainment is offered at 'boys' town', a few km to the west and well served by taxi drivers.

Festival

Reynosa's major festival is that of Nuestra Señora de Guadalupe, on 12 December. Pilgrims start processions a week early and there are afternoon dance performances in front of the church.

Places to Stay

The best-value accommodation is found in a couple of places on Díaz, a few minutes' walk from the main square. The cheaper of the two, the *Hotel Nuevo León* (☎ (89) 22-13-10), on Díaz between Méndez and Madero, has quite sizeable, clean rooms with fans and private bathrooms at 40 pesos for a room with one bed, 50 to 60 pesos for bigger rooms. The *Hotel Rey*, a couple of doors down Díaz, has clean, bright rooms with air-con and TV at 65/75/85 pesos for singles/doubles/triples. It may not have a room if you arrive late.

On the west side of the main square, the somewhat run-down *Hotel Plaza* (☎ (89) 22-00-39) has rooms from 30/40 pesos. Nearby, the *Hotel San Carlos* (☎ (89) 2-12-80) is a step towards the luxury bracket, with clean, bright, air-con rooms with phone and TV from 100/110 pesos. It has its own restaurant and parking. Just south of the plaza, at Juárez 860, the pleasant *Hotel Savoy* (☎ (89) 22-00-67) has air-con rooms at 100/150 pesos.

The top downtown place is the *Hotel Astromundo* (☎ (89) 22-56-25) on Juárez between Guerrero and Méndez. It has clean, spacious rooms with TV, plus a swimming pool, parking facilities and a restaurant. Room prices are 110/140/160 pesos, with suites from 220 pesos. Other pricey places are the *Motel Engrey* (☎ (89) 23-17-30) and

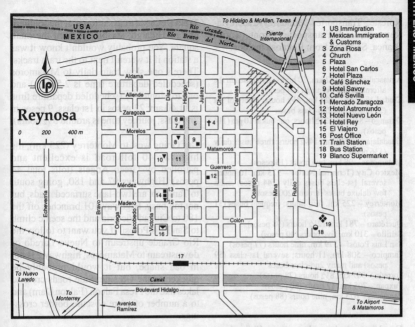

Reynosa

0   200   400 m

1	US Immigration
2	Mexican Immigration & Customs
3	Zona Rosa
4	Church
5	Plaza
6	Hotel San Carlos
7	Hotel Plaza
8	Café Sánchez
9	Hotel Savoy
10	Café Sevilla
11	Mercado Zaragoza
12	Hotel Astromundo
13	Hotel Nuevo León
14	Hotel Rey
15	El Viajero
16	Post Office
17	Train Station
18	Bus Station
19	Blanco Supermarket

the *Motel Virrey* (☎ (89) 23-10-50), both on highway 40 towards Monterrey.

There are a few places near the bus station, but it's not a very nice part of town. The *Hotel San Miguel* (☎ (89) 22-21-70), on Colón, has OK rooms from around 70 pesos.

Places to Eat

Places in the zona rosa have prices appropriate for the day-tripping Texans who make up a lot of their clientele, but they stay open late. The following places are nearer the centre and cater more to Mexicans. *El Viajero* (☎ 22-61-00) is at Díaz 520 Norte, just down the street from the hotels Nuevo León and Rey. It's friendly and comfortable, and decorated with Marilyn Monroe posters. The food is good and reasonably priced, with a comida corrida for 12 pesos.

Half a block from the main square, at Morelos 575, the clean and tidy *Café Sánchez* is popular with locals and has pretty good food – main courses from 12 to 24

pesos and snacks from 10 to 15 pesos. *Cafe Sevilla*, on the corner of Matamoros and Díaz, is more down-to-earth, and has a comida corrida for as little as 10 pesos.

Getting There & Away

Air Reynosa airport is eight km out of town, off the Matamoros road. There are daily Aeroméxico flights direct to Mexico City, and also flights to/from Guadalajara via Saltillo. The Aeroméxico office (☎ 22-11-15) is at Guerrero 1510, on the corner of Gil, about a km from the town centre.

Bus Both 1st and 2nd-class buses run to almost anywhere you'd want to go in Mexico, but avoid 2nd-class buses on long trips because they're so slow. The Central de Autobuses is on the south-eastern corner of the central grid, next to the big Blanco supermarket. First-class lines serving Reynosa are Transportes del Norte, ADO, Omnibus de México, Tres Estrellas de Oro, Transportes del

Noreste, Transportes Monterrey-Cadereyta-Reynosa, and Transportes Frontera and Blanca. Services from Reynosa include:

Aguascalientes – 747 km, 10 hours; five buses in the afternoon and evening (104 pesos)

Ciudad Victoria – 322 km, 4½ hours; plenty of 1st (39 pesos) and 2nd-class buses

Durango – 840 km, 13½ hours; one bus at 10 pm (114 pesos)

Guadalajara – 930 km, 14½ hours; three buses daily (136 pesos)

Matamoros – 98 km, two hours (13 pesos)

Mexico City (Terminal Norte) – 973 km, 16 hours; several 1st-class buses daily (144 pesos) and a few deluxe buses (around 200 pesos)

Monterrey – 225 km, four hours; frequent buses (31 pesos)

Querétaro – 781 km, 12½ hours (98 pesos)

Saltillo – 310 km, five hours (40 pesos)

San Luis Potosí – 579 km, nine hours (77 pesos)

Tampico – 508 km, 11 hours; several 1st-class (59 pesos) and many 2nd-class buses

Torreón – 587 km, 8½ hours (78 pesos)

Tuxpan – 705 km, 12 hours (80 pesos)

Zacatecas – 673 km, nine hours (88 pesos)

Good bus services also run to Chihuahua, Ciudad Juárez, Veracruz and Villahermosa, with 2nd-class services to local destinations. Some bus lines run direct to US cities including San Antonio, Houston and Dallas.

To/From McAllen, Texas The nearest Texas transport centre, McAllen, is nine km from the border. Valley Transit Company (VTC) runs buses both ways between McAllen and Reynosa bus stations for around 12 pesos one way, every 20 minutes between 6 am and 7 pm. There are three later services, with the last leaving Reynosa bus station at 11 pm. Transportes Monterrey-Cadereyta-Reynosa also runs between Reynosa's bus station and McAllen.

Coming from McAllen, if you don't want to go all the way to the Reynosa bus station, you can get off at the Greyhound office on the US side and walk over the international bridge to Reynosa. Leaving Mexico, you can walk over the bridge and pick up the buses at the same Greyhound office.

Train Reynosa train station is at the southern end of Hidalgo, six blocks from the main square. You probably wouldn't know it was a station if it weren't next to the train tracks. There's one slow train daily to Matamoros (scheduled departure time is 2.55 pm) and one to Monterrey (scheduled departure time is 11.40 am; 22 pesos in 1st class, 9 pesos in 2nd class; journey time is around 5½ hours).

Car Going west to Monterrey (225 km), the highway 40 toll road is excellent and patrolled by Green Angels (tolls total 44 pesos). Highways 97 and 180, going south to Tampico, are two-lane surfaced roads, but not too busy. Highway 101 branches off the 180 to Ciudad Victoria and the scenic climb to San Luis Potosí. If you want to follow the Rio Grande upstream to Nuevo Laredo or downstream to Matamoros, highway 2 is not in bad shape, but it would probably be quicker on the US side. Side roads cross to lakes like the Presa Falcón (Falcon Dam) and to a number of more obscure border crossings.

Getting Around

Battered microbuses rattle their way around Reynosa, providing cheap but uncomfortable transport. From the international bridge to the bus station, take No 14, or try to catch one of the Valley Transit Company or Transportes Monterrey-Cadereyta-Reynosa coaches from McAllen. If you walk up to the main plaza, catch the '17 Obrera' bus from Madero, on the corner of Díaz or Hidalgo. From the bus station to the centre, turn left out of the main entrance, walk to the end of the block, turn left again, and catch a '17 Obrera' on the next corner (Colón and Rubio).

MATAMOROS
• *pop: 470,000*

First settled during the Spanish colonisation of Tamaulipas in 1686, with the name Los Esteros Hermosas (The Beautiful Estuaries), it was renamed in 1793 after Father Mariano Matamoros. In 1846, Matamoros was the first Mexican city to be taken by US forces in the Mexican-American War, and Zachary Taylor then used it as a base for his attack on Monterrey. During the US Civil War, when sea routes to the Confederacy were blockaded, Matamoros trans-shipped cotton from Confederate Texas in exchange for supplies and war material.

Today, Matamoros is no historical monument, but there is more evidence of the past than in most border towns, and the town centre, with its church and plaza, looks typically Mexican. South of the central area is a broad circle of newer industrial zones. Apart from its maquiladoras, Matamoros is a commercial centre for a large agricultural hinterland – tanneries, cotton mills and distilleries are among its main industries.

Orientation

Matamoros lies across the Rio Grande from Brownsville, Texas. The river, which forms the international boundary, is spanned by a bridge with US border controls at the north end and Mexican border controls at the south. The Rio Grande is a disappointing trickle at this point, as most of its waters have been siphoned off upstream for irrigation.

From the southern end of the bridge, Álvaro Obregón winds around towards the town's central grid, 1.5 km to the south-west. The cheap accommodation is around Abasolo, a pedestrian street one block north of Plaza Hidalgo. Nearby are two markets with tourist-oriented crafts.

Yellow microbuses called 'maxi-taxis' link the border, the centre and the bus station. From the international bridge, walk south until you see a row of these vehicles; read the scrawl on their windscreens to find one going to the town centre or the bus station.

Information

Tourist Office The informal tourist office is in a shack on the right-hand side at the beginning of Obregón. What it lacks in written material it makes up for with the helpfulness of its staff, who are mostly English-speaking taxi drivers. They offer transport and guided tours for a price, but are happy to answer questions for nothing. Someone's usually

there from 8 am to 10 pm daily. If you need maps, brochures and printed giveaways, you may do better at the Brownsville Chamber of Commerce, on the right (east) side about 200 metres north of the bridge. Try also the Brownsville Information Centre on US highway 77/83, on the north-west side of town.

Money Matamoros has several banks (with ATMs) on Plaza Hidalgo and Calle 6, which will change cash or travellers' cheques. Often you get a better rate for cash dollars in the casas de cambio dotted around the central area. Casa de Cambio Astorga, on Calle 7 between Bravo and Matamoros, will change travellers' cheques.

In Brownsville, on the US side, there are casas de cambio on International Boulevard, the road running straight ahead from the north end of the international bridge. Some of them are open 24 hours a day.

Post & Telecommunications There is a post office at Calle 6 No 214, between Herrera and Iturbide, and another one in the bus station. There are plenty of Ladatel phones around, but most of them seem to reject cards.

Foreign Consulate The US Consulate (☎ (88) 16-72-70), at Calle 1 No 232, can issue visas but usually takes more than a day to do so. It's open weekdays from 8 to 10 am and 1 to 4 pm, but does not do visas on Wednesdays.

Customs & Immigration The Mexican border post waves most pedestrians through on the assumption that they're just there for a day's shopping or eating, but some cars will get the red light to be checked. If you're proceeding further south into Mexico than the border zone, get a tourist card and have it stamped before you leave Matamoros. And get a vehicle permit if you need one, otherwise you will be sent back from the checkpoint about 20 km down the road.

NORTH-EAST MEXICO *(vertical sidebar)*

Museums

Museo del Maíz Matamoros' main cultural attraction, the Museum of Maize, also called the Casa de Cultura, was closed in mid-1994 for what looked like a major refurbishment. Already an excellent museum, it will hopefully be even better when it reopens. Look for it on the corner of Calle 5 and Avenida Constitución, about seven blocks north of the main square.

Casa Mata This old fort, on the corner of Guatemala and Santos Degollado, was the scene of fighting in the Mexican-American War. It now contains some memorabilia of the Mexican revolution, a few Indian artefacts and some ill-assorted miscellanea. Entry is free. To reach this museum from Plaza Hidalgo, head east on Morelos as far as Calle 1, turn right, go five blocks to Santos Degollado, then two blocks to the left.

Playa Bagdad

Matamoros' beach was formerly known as Playa Lauro Villar (and also as Washington Beach) but it has recently adopted the name of Bagdad, a town at the mouth of the Rio Grande which prospered during the US Civil War but later succumbed to floods, hurricanes and military attacks. It's 37 km east of Matamoros on highway 2, and has a wide stretch of clean sand and a few beachside seafood restaurants. There are some mid-range motels along the road approaching the beach. 'Playa' buses go from the corner of Abasolo and Calle 11 in downtown Matamoros.

Places to Stay

There are one or two dingy places near the bus station, but better value is to be found on or near Abasolo. Bottom-end rooms are basic, but cheap enough at around 40 pesos a double. Mid-range accommodation, with air-con and parking, starts at around 80 pesos and is quite good value, but there's not much in between these levels.

The *Hotel México* (☎ (88) 12-08-56) at Abasolo 87, between Calles 8 and 9, charges 30/40 pesos for clean singles/doubles with bathroom and ceiling fan. Nearby, the *Hotel*

Majestic (☎ (88) 13-36-80), at Abasolo 89, is not quite as clean but has more character and some classic 1950s furnishings. It's a family-run place which also charges 30/40 pesos for rooms with private bath.

One block north of Abasolo, on the corner of Matamoros and Calle 6, the *Hotel Colonial* is friendly and has lots of clean rooms with the minimum comforts for 32/40 pesos. Check the room before you decide – some need maintenance and others are noisy, but it's not a bad place to stay.

Moving up the scale a little, the *Hotel Nieto* (☎ (88) 13-08-57), at Calle 10 No 1508, is an ordinary-looking 1960s-style hotel, with air-con, TV and parking, charging 88/110 pesos. *Hotel Roma* (☎ (88) 13-61-76, 16-05-73), on Calle 9 between Matamoros and Bravo, is quite central, modern, clean and friendly. It charges 95/110 pesos for smallish rooms with TV, telephone and carpeting. The *Hotel Ritz*, on Matamoros between Calles 6 and 7, is a lot classier with bigger rooms for 100/120 pesos.

Top places include the *Hotel Plaza* (☎ (88) 16-16-96), on the corner of Calle 9 and Bravo, which is tasteful and comfortable for 150/180 pesos. The best place is the *Gran Hotel Residencial* (☎ (88) 13-94-40) at Álvaro Obregón 249, with pleasant gardens and a swimming pool. The 120 air-con rooms with cable TV go for 190/250 pesos.

Places to Eat

Near the plaza, the clean *Café de México* (☎ 12-50-23), on González between Calles 6 and 7, is popular from morning to evening and the food isn't bad, with daily specials at 12 to 15 pesos with rice and salad. Another good option in the lower budget range is *Café y Restaurant Nuevo León*, on Calle 9 almost opposite Hotel Roma. It's very much a locals' place, with authentic food and atmosphere and no air-con; a filling comida corrida costs only 11 pesos.

Also popular, the *Cafetería 1916*, on Calle 6 between Matamoros and Abasolo, is less atmospheric, more comfortable, and a bit pricier with antojitos from 10 pesos and a comida corrida costing up to 18 pesos.

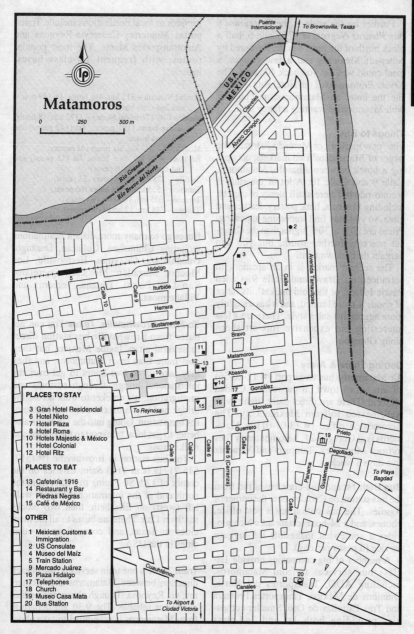

Matamoros

0   250   500 m

Río Grande
Río Bravo del Norte

USA
MEXICO

To Brownsville, Texas

Puente
Internacional

Claveles

Alvaro Obregón

Avenida Tamaulipas

Hidalgo
Iturbide
Herrera
Bustamente
Bravo
Matamoros
Abasolo
González
Morelos
Guerrero

Prieto
Degollado

To Playa
Bagdad

To Reynosa

Calle 10
Calle 9
Calle 11
Calle 8
Calle 7
Calle 6
Calle 5 (Carranza)
Calle 4

Panama
Guatemala
Calle 1

Cuauhtémoc
Canales

To Airport &
Ciudad Victoria

PLACES TO STAY

3 Gran Hotel Residencial
6 Hotel Nieto
7 Hotel Plaza
8 Hotel Roma
10 Hotels Majestic & México
11 Hotel Colonial
12 Hotel Ritz

PLACES TO EAT

13 Cafetería 1916
14 Restaurant y Bar
    Piedras Negras
15 Café de México

OTHER

1 Mexican Customs &
    Immigration
2 US Consulate
4 Museo del Maíz
5 Train Station
9 Mercado Juárez
16 Plaza Hidalgo
17 Telephones
18 Church
19 Museo Casa Mata
20 Bus Station

Further up the scale is the *Restaurant y Bar Piedras Negras*, at 175 Calle 6, half a block north of the main square. Favoured by better-off Mexicans and a few gringos, a meal could well set you back 40 pesos. The *Krysta Restaurant* of the Hotel Ritz is opposite the hotel on Matamoros, and popular with Matamorons wanting a fancy feed.

Things to Buy

The 'new market', or Mercado Juárez, is the larger of Matamoros' two markets, occupying a block between Abasolo, Matamoros, Calle 9 and Calle 10. A lot of the stuff is second-rate but there's still plenty of variety, including blankets, hats, pottery, leather and glass, so you may find something appealing. Prices are 20% to 30% higher than the cheapest markets further south, but you can bargain them down a bit.

The second market is in an arcade with entrances on Bravo and Calle 9. Called Pasaje Juárez, or the 'old market', its range of goods is more limited, and it has a slightly more aggressive sales style. There are a few interesting but expensive folk-art shops along Obregón.

Getting There & Away

Air Matamoros has an airport (☎ 12-20-56) 17 km out of town on the road to Ciudad Victoria. There are direct daily flights with Aeroméxico to/from Mexico City. The Aeroméxico office (☎ 13-07-01) in Matamoros is at Obregón 21. Aeromonterrey flies to/from Monterrey, Tampico and Veracruz five days a week.

Bus Both 1st and 2nd-class buses run from the bus station on Canales, near the corner of Aguiles. The bus station has a post office, phones, and a 24-hour restaurant which provides a somewhat makeshift left-luggage service (6 pesos per day).

A number of big companies provide 1st-class bus services to/from Matamoros, including ADO, Transportes del Norte, Omnibus de México, Transportes Frontera and Tres Estrellas de Oro. Smaller companies providing both 1st and 2nd-class

services to local destinations include Transportes Monterrey-Cadereyta-Reynosa and Autotransportes Mante. The most popular routes, with frequent 1st-class buses, include:

Ciudad Victoria – 312 km, 4½ hours; 1st (39 pesos) and 2nd-class buses
Mexico City (Terminal Norte) – 1172 km, 18 hours; deluxe buses (191 pesos), 1st (142 pesos) and 2nd-class buses
Monterrey – 243 km, six hours (42 pesos)
Reynosa – 98 km, two hours; 1st (13 pesos) and 2nd-class buses (10 pesos)
Saltillo – 328 km, seven hours (53 pesos)
Tampico – 555 km, eight hours (66 pesos)
Torreón – 605 km, 10 hours (90 pesos)
Tuxpan – 748 km, 12 hours (90 pesos)

Buses go to many more distant destinations including Chihuahua, Culiacán, Durango, Guadalajara, Guaymas, Hermosillo, Los Mochis, Mazatlán, Mexicali, Querétaro, San Luis Potosí, Tijuana, Veracruz and Villahermosa.

To/From Brownsville, Texas You can get buses from Brownsville bus station direct to several cities inside Mexico, but they cost more than from Matamoros, and they may take up to two hours to get over the international bridge, through customs and immigration. It's quicker to walk across the bridge and take a maxi-taxi to the Matamoros bus station. Going into the USA, it's also better to get local transport to the bridge and walk across.

The bus station in Brownsville (☎ (512) 546-7171) is at 1165 Saint Charles on the corner of 12th St. Facing the USA from the north end of the international bridge, walk left (west) on Elizabeth, then two blocks south on 12th. There are buses to all the main cities in Texas, and connections to other cities in the USA.

Train There's one train service a day in each direction between Matamoros and Monterrey, via Reynosa. Though cheap, it's neither quick nor reliable. The 9.30 am departure from Matamoros is scheduled to take about two hours to Reynosa and seven hours to Monterrey, but may take longer (1st class, 35 pesos; 2nd class, 15 pesos).

Car Driving across the bridge to/from Brownsville, Texas costs 6 pesos. The main routes into Mexico from Matamoros are highway 180 south to Tampico and the Gulf Coast, and highway 101 south-west to Ciudad Victoria and into the Bajío region. These are both two-lane roads, not very busy, in fair condition and free of heavy tolls. Officials at a checkpoint about 20 km to the south will want to see your tourist card and vehicle permit – if your papers are not in order you will be sent back to Matamoros. You can also go west to Monterrey via Reynosa.

Getting Around

Matamoros is served by small buses called maxi-taxis, which charge 1 peso to anywhere in town. You can stop them on almost any street corner. They usually have their destinations painted on the front windscreen: the town centre is 'Centro'; the bus station 'Central de Autobuses'; and the international bridge 'Puente Internacional'. Taxis from the border to the centre or the bus station cost about 16 pesos.

SOUTH OF MATAMOROS

Most of this 498-km road is 30 to 40 km inland from the coast, crossing several rivers but passing mainly through coastal lowlands where sugar cane is the main crop. For the first 183 km the route follows highway 101 towards Ciudad Victoria, then turns off along highway 180. There are basic hotels in San Fernando (137 km from Matamoros), Soto La Marina (269 km) and Aldama (381 km).

The landscape is generally unspectacular, but there are some more scenic stretches where the outliers of the Sierra Madre Oriental come close to the coast. Side roads go east to the coast at various points. Most of the coast faces lagoons which are separated from the Gulf of Mexico by narrow sand spits. The longest of the lagoons is the Laguna Madre, which extends hundreds of km up the coasts of Tamaulipas and Texas.

The lagoons, sand dunes and coastal wetlands support a unique ecosystem, with numerous bird species and excellent fishing. If you're interested in exploring this part of the coast of the Gulf of Mexico in detail, read Donald Schueler's excellent *Adventuring along the Gulf of Mexico* (San Francisco, Sierra Club Books), which gives full coverage of the ecology and wildlife.

El Mezquital

This is a small fishing village, with a light-house and beach, on the long thin spit of land that divides the Laguna Madre from the Gulf of Mexico. A road crosses marshland to reach El Mezquital, about 60 km off the highway, just south of Matamoros airport. Minibuses wait at the turnoff.

La Carbonera

This is a small, nondescript fishing village facing the lagoon. You might be able to get a boat out to the lagoon barrier island, where porpoises can sometimes be seen. Food is available, but there is no commercial accommodation. A road leads here from San Fernando (about 50 km). The only beach is at Carvajal, eight km south of La Carbonera.

La Pesca

Forty-eight km east from Soto La Marina is the fishing village of La Pesca, which has three hotels, a camping area and restaurants, and plans to develop itself into a major resort. It has a long, wide beach – Playa La Pesca – with shady palapas and seaside restaurants. There is quite good fishing in the estuary of the Río Soto La Marina, and in the Laguna de Morales. A fishing tournament for sea bass and other species takes place in November. Other attractions include hunting, and surfing on the beaches which face the Gulf of Mexico.

You can reach La Pesca by bus from Soto la Marina (one hour; 5 pesos) or Ciudad Victoria (19 pesos). The same buses continue to Playa La Pesca, about 15 minutes away. The last buses usually leave the beach for Soto la Marina at about 5.30 pm.

Barra El Tordo

A 44-km road goes east then north from Aldama, through the eastern fringes of the Sierra de Tamaulipas, to Barra El Tordo. It's another fishing village with a beach and good sport fishing, and is well known for its oyster harvest. Turtles spawn on the beaches between here and Altamira. There's one hotel, two restaurants and a campground.

CIUDAD VICTORIA

• *pop: 200,000* • *alt: 333 metres*

About 40 km north of the Tropic of Cancer, the capital of Tamaulipas state is a clean and pleasant city with just enough altitude to moderate the steamy heat of the coastal plains or the Rio Grande valley. It's around 320 km south of Matamoros and Reynosa, well served by buses in every direction, and a good spot to break a journey between central Mexico and the Texas border.

Orientation

Five highways converge at Ciudad Victoria, and a ring road allows through traffic to move between them without entering the city itself. The centre is a grid layout with one-way streets and a few pedestrian precincts. The north-south streets have both numbers (Calle Siete (7), Calle Ocho (8) etc) and names (Calle Díaz, Calle Tijerina etc).

Information

Tourist Office The tourist office (☎ (131) 2-70-02) is on the south side of town on the corner of Rosales and 5 de Mayo. It's open from 8.30 am to 3.30 pm, and sometimes later. The staff are friendly and quite helpful, but don't speak much English.

Things to See

Ciudad Victoria has no compelling tourist attractions, but there is the **Museo de Antropología e Historia**, run by the University of Tamaulipas. It has a collection of mammoth bones, Indian artefacts, colonial memorabilia and revolutionary photographs. The museum is on Calle Colón (Calle 10) just north of the Plaza Hidalgo, and is sup-

posedly open Monday to Friday from 9 am to 1 pm and 2 to 7 pm, but hours seem to be irregular.

Ciudad Victoria also has some interesting public buildings, like the **Palacio Gobierno** and the **Teatro Juárez**, both with large murals. There are several parks and a large public swimming pool. The Sierra Madre forms an impressive backdrop to the city, and highway 101, which climbs the slopes to San Luis Potosí, is incredibly scenic. Forty km north-east of Ciudad Victoria, **Presa Vicente Guerrero** is a huge reservoir which attracts Mexicans and US citizens for bass fishing and duck, goose and dove-hunting. The El Cielo Reserva de la Biósfera is about 100 km south and more easily reached from Ciudad Mante (see Ciudad Mante following).

Places to Stay & Eat

The *Hotel San Bernabe* (no phone), on the corner of Calle Colón and Matamoros, is about the cheapest place, with rooms from 30 pesos. *Hotel San Juan* (☎ (131) 2-79-93), on Calle Colón between Guerrero and Bravo, is better and slightly more expensive at 30/35 pesos for singles/doubles. *Hotel Los Monteros* (☎ (131) 2-03-00), on Plaza Hidalgo, is a lovely old colonial-style building. Rooms are spacious, clean and comfortable, with bath, phone and fan. There's a parking area behind, and it's a good deal with singles/doubles from 50/80 pesos. The *Hotel Condesa*, on Calle Tijerina between Hidalgo and Juárez, was being renovated at the time of writing, but should reopen as a good mid-range place.

The *Hotel Sierra Gorda* (☎ (131) 2-20-10), on the south side of Plaza Hidalgo, has an attractive colonial-looking lobby, and rooms with air-con, TV and phone for 143/179 pesos. The *Hotel Everest* (☎ (131) 2-40-50), on the west side of the same plaza, is an unashamedly modern place with all the usual comforts for 165/187 pesos. The *Hotel Santorín* (☎ (131) 2-80-66), at Calle Colón 349, is another modern place with exactly the same prices. Just south of town, on highway 85, the *Motel Las Fuentes* (☎ (131) 2-56-55) has all the mod cons plus a swimming pool, tennis courts and a children's playground.

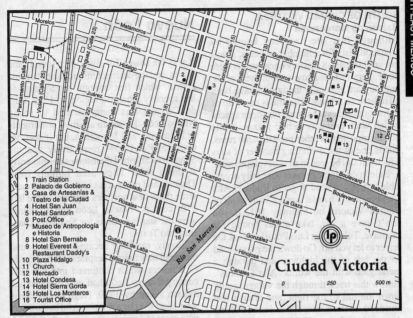

1 Train Station
2 Palacio de Gobierno
3 Casa de Artesanías &
   Teatro de la Ciudad
4 Hotel San Juan
5 Hotel Santorín
6 Post Office
7 Museo de Antropología
   e Historia
8 Hotel San Bernabe
9 Hotel Everest &
   Restaurant Daddy's
10 Plaza Hidalgo
11 Church
12 Mercado
13 Hotel Condesa
14 Hotel Sierra Gorda
15 Hotel Los Monteros
16 Tourist Office

Ciudad Victoria

Rooms in the 'Area Ejecutiva' cost 194/240 pesos, while those in the 'Area Comercial' are 145/168 pesos.

Restaurant Daddy's, in the Hotel Everest, looks like a 1960s American cafeteria, but the food is OK and reasonably priced. The restaurant in the *Hotel Los Monteros* has a lot more Mexican charm, slightly higher prices and quite good meals.

Getting There & Away

Air Ciudad Victoria has an airport, east of town off the Soto La Marina road. There are flights to Matamoros, Mexico City and Poza Rica with Aeroméxico (☎ 2-87-97, 2-97-40) and/or Aeromar (☎ 6-91-91).

Bus The bus station is near the ring road on the east side of town, and has a left-luggage service, post office and Ladatel phones. Buses (1st-class unless otherwise stated) go to many destinations including:

Ciudad Valles – 234 km, 3½ hours (29 pesos)
La Pesca – 172 km, three hours; 2nd-class buses (19 pesos)
Matamoros – 310 km, 4½ hours (39 pesos)
Mexico City (Terminal Norte) – 764 km, 11 hours (103 pesos), deluxe buses (139 pesos)
Monterrey – 288 km, four hours (33 pesos), deluxe buses (57 pesos)
Reynosa – 315 km, five hours (39 pesos)
San Luis Potosí – 348 km, 5½ hours (40 pesos)
Soto La Marina – 124 km, two hours; 2nd-class buses (16 pesos)
Tampico – 239 km, about 3½ hours (35 pesos)

Train From the old train station at the west side of town, slow segunda clase trains depart for Monterrey at 3 pm and Tampico at 2 pm.

Car From Ciudad Victoria, you can go south-east to Tampico for the Huasteca or the Gulf Coast, or take one of the steep but scenic roads onto the Sierra. For San Luis Potosí, take highway 101 to the south-west – a lovely route. For Mexico City, highway 85 south, via Ciudad Mante and Ciudad Valles, is the most direct.

SOUTH OF CIUDAD VICTORIA
Balcón de Montezuma

Although this site has been known by archaeologists for a number of years, it was not until late 1988 that any excavations were done. Very little is known about these ruins, but they are generally thought to have been a Huastec settlement. The site is made up of numerous circles set around two open spaces which were probably public plazas. While not as imposing as other pre-Hispanic ruins, this is one of the dwindling number of sites which can still be seen in an undeveloped state.

Balcón de Montezuma is not easily accessible – first you need to get to Ejido de Alta Cumbre, a tiny hamlet some 25 km south of Ciudad Victoria on highway 101. If you don't have a car, take a bus bound for Jaumave, Tula or San Luis Potosí and ask the driver to let you off. Go down the gravel road on the left of the highway and through a metal gate with the words 'Alta Cumbre'. Follow this track through the village, going down the hill to the right, and after a few hundred metres there's a faded 'Zona Arqueológica' sign. From there it's about four km down a 4WD track to the ruins.

Ciudad Mante

A town of about 80,000, Ciudad Mante is a centre for processing the sugar and cotton grown in the area. There are some cheap to mid-range hotels, motels and restaurants, and it's a quiet, clean place to stop for a night.

El Cielo Reserva de la Biósfera

A reserve of 1440 sq km, El Cielo covers a range of altitudes on the slopes of the Sierra, and is a transition zone between tropical, semi-desert and temperate ecosystems. It marks the northern limit for quite a number of tropical species of plant and animal.

The best access point for the reserve is the village of Gómez Farias, 14 km up a side road going west from the highway about 40 km north of Ciudad Mante. There's a sign on the left as you get to the plaza, and an office behind it which may have some information on weekdays. The reserve starts about two km down the rough track next to the sign.

Nuevo León

It was the search for silver (not found) and slaves, and the desire of missionaries to proselytise, which first brought the Spanish to this sparsely inhabited region. In 1579, Luis de Carvajal was commissioned to found Nuevo León. He set up abortive settlements in Monterrey and Monclova, but it was not until 1596 and 1644 respectively that the Spanish established themselves permanently at those sites. They used Indians from Tlaxcala and other areas to the south to help settle these new northern regions. In the late 17th century, Nuevo León and Coahuila were the starting points for Spanish expansion into Texas.

Slowly, ranching became viable around the small new towns, despite raids by hostile Chichimecs which continued into the 18th century. Nuevo León had an estimated 1.5 million sheep by 1710. Huge empty areas were taken over by a few powerful landowners who came to dominate the region. As the 19th century progressed and the railways arrived, ranching continued to expand, and industry developed, especially in Monterrey. By 1900, Nuevo León had 328,000 inhabitants.

MONTERREY

• pop: 2.18 million • alt: 540 metres

Monterrey, capital of Nuevo León, is Mexico's third-biggest city and its second-biggest industrial centre. It's perhaps the most Americanised city in Mexico, and parts of it, with leafy suburbs, 7-Eleven stores and giant air-con shopping malls, look just like suburbs in Texas or California. Industry and commerce drive Monterrey, and its pursuit of profit also seems more American than Mexican.

The central city area has been ambitiously remodelled, with a series of linked plazas and gardens, a pedestrian precinct on the west side and a historical zone on the east. Jagged mountains, including the distinctive saddle-shaped Cerro de la Silla (1740 metres), make a dramatic backdrop for the city, and provide opportunities for some worthwhile side trips into the northern Sierra – the surrounding country offers caves, canyons, lakes and waterfalls.

Most travellers bypass Monterrey in their haste to get to/from the 'real' Mexico, but the city is a fascinating mixture of old and new, industry and style, tradition and efficiency. There's a lot to see too, particularly if you like modern art and architecture. For budget travellers, Monterrey's disadvantage is that accommodation is expensive and the cheaper places are mainly in a seedy area near the bus station, which is a 20-minute ride from the city centre. The air pollution and the weather can be bad too, but you are just as likely to find fresh breezes, blue skies and clear, dry desert air.

History

There were three attempts to found a city here, the first in 1577. The second, in 1592, was by Luis de Carvajal and the third, in 1596, was by Diego de Montemayor. He christened his 34-person settlement Ciudad Metropolitana de Nuestra Señora de Monterrey, after the Conde de Monterrey who was viceroy of Mexico at the time.

Monterrey struggled as a remote northern outpost, but it slowly became the centre of a sheep-ranching area, and was often raided by the Chichimec Indians who lived in the region. Its importance grew with the colonisation of Tamaulipas in the mid-18th century, since it was on the trade route to the new settlements. In 1777, when Monterrey had about 4000 inhabitants, it became the seat of the new bishopric of Linares.

In 1824, Monterrey became the capital of the state of Nuevo León in newly independent Mexico. In the Mexican-American War, Monterrey was occupied by Zachary Taylor's troops – but only after three days of fierce fighting by the Mexicans. The city was occupied again in the 1860s by French troops, who were driven out by Benito Juárez's forces in 1866.

Monterrey's location close to the USA gave it advantages in trade and smuggling: in the American Civil War it was a staging post for cotton exports by the blockaded Confederates. Railway lines came in 1881, and tax exemptions for industry during the Porfiriato (1876-1910) attracted Mexican, US, British and French investment. Monterrey began to emerge as an industrial centre in the 1860s and by the early 20th century was one of Mexico's biggest cities; its population grew from 27,000 in 1853 to about 80,000 in 1910.

The city was the site of the first heavy industry in Latin America – the iron and steel works of the Compañía Fundidora de Fierro y Acero de Monterrey. In 1890, José Schneider founded the Cervecería Cuauhtémoc, which became Mexico's biggest brewery as well as manufacturing glass, cartons and bottle caps. Other industries produced furniture, clothes, cigarettes, soap, cement and bricks. Two intermarried families, the Garzas and the Sadas, came to dominate business and built a huge empire – the Monterrey Group – that owned many of the city's biggest companies.

After the 1940s, the spread of electricity enabled hundreds of new industries to set up. Little planning went into the city's growth, and the environment and the poor were mainly left to look after themselves, but education was promoted by the Garza and Sada families, and today Monterrey has four universities and a famous technological institute.

Economic success and distance from the national power centre have given Monterrey's citizens, called Regiomontanos, an independent point of view. Monterrey resents 'meddling' in its affairs by the central government, which in turn sometimes accuses the city of being too capitalistic or, worse, too friendly with the USA. Relations reached their lowest point under the left-leaning Mexican President Echeverría in the early 1970s. The Garzas and Sadas, perhaps in fear of wholesale nationalisation, broke the Monterrey Group into two parts – the Alfa Group and the VISA Group.

President López Portillo, Echeverría's successor, fostered better relations with the powers of Monterrey, and in the late 1970s the city was producing more than one-third of Mexico's exports. The economic crisis of the 1980s struck Monterrey hard. The Alfa Group went broke, the city government ran short of money, and a government-owned steel mill was closed. As the Mexican economy recovers, Monterrey seems well placed to profit from NAFTA, the free-trade agreement with the USA and Canada, and is destined to be a cornerstone in the evolving Tex-Mex economy.

Orientation

Central Monterrey focuses on the zona rosa, an extensive area of pedestrianised streets with the more expensive hotels, shops and restaurants. The eastern edge of the zona rosa meets the southern end of the Macro Plaza, a series of plazas and gardens studded with monuments and surrounded by imposing public buildings, many of them strikingly modern structures. A number of streets pass underneath the Macro Plaza, which has large car parks beneath it.

South of the city centre is the Río Santa Catarina, which cuts across the city from west to east – the dry river bed is used for sports grounds. The bus station is about 2.5 km north-west of the city centre, and the train station lies a few hundred metres north-west of the bus station. Most of the cheap accommodation is around the bus and train stations. Frequent, noisy buses run all over the city (see Getting Around), and a light rail metro system is being developed.

Streets in the city centre and bus station areas are on a grid pattern. The corner of Juárez and Aramberri, roughly halfway between the city centre and the bus station, is the centre of town as far as addresses are concerned. North of Aramberri, north-south streets have the suffix 'Norte' or 'Nte'; south of Aramberri, they have the suffix 'Sur'. West of Juárez, east-west streets have the suffix 'Poniente' or 'Pte'; east of Juárez, they have the suffix 'Oriente' or 'Ote'. Numbers get higher as they move further away from the intersection.

Information

Tourist Office Monterrey has a friendly, modern tourist office called Infotur (☎ (8) 345-08-70, 345-09-02), on the corner of Matamoros and Zaragoza, underneath the Macro Plaza. Staff speak fluent English, are knowledgeable about both Monterrey and the state of Nuevo León, and have lots of leaflets and maps of Monterrey. They can also tell you about cultural events and entertainment in the city. The office is open Tuesday to Sunday from 10 am to 5 pm.

Money Numerous city-centre banks will change cash, though some do not handle travellers' cheques, and they close at about 1.30 pm. Most of them have ATMs. There are a couple of casas de cambio on Ocampo, between Galeana and Juárez, which are usually open until 6 pm and on Saturday morning. Casa de Cambio Trebol, on Padre Mier between Escobedo and E Carranza, is open until 6 pm Monday to Friday and to 1 pm on Saturday and will change travellers' cheques. American Express (☎ 344-09-10) is at Padre Mier Pte 1424, on the corner of Bravo.

Post The central post office (☎ 342-40-03) is on Zaragoza between Washington and Cinco de Mayo, just north of the Macro Plaza. It's open from 9 am to 7 pm Monday to Friday and 9 am to 1 pm Saturday.

Foreign Consulates The US Consulate (☎ 345-21-20) is at Constitución Pte 411, not far from the city centre. The UK, Canada, France, Germany, Spain and the Netherlands also have consulates in Monterrey – Infotur has their addresses.

Macro Plaza

A city block wide and a km long, this great swath of urban open space is a controversial piece of urban redevelopment. Carved out in the 1980s by the demolition of several entire blocks of buildings, many regard it as a grandiose monument to Monterrey's ambition. Though work continues in some parts, the completed spaces are now softened by

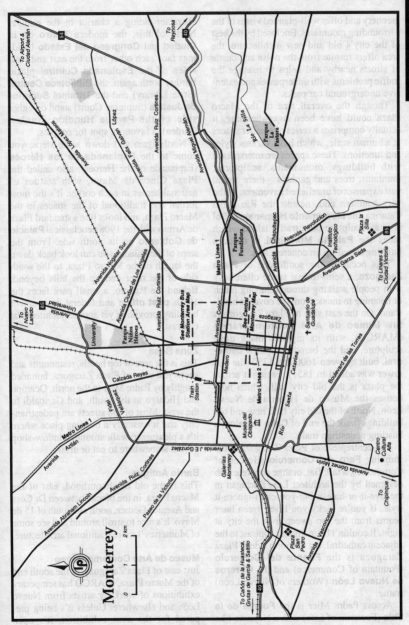

Monterrey

To Airport &
Ciudad Alemán

To Reynosa

54

40

Avenida Ruiz Cortines

Avenida Félix Galván

López

Avenida Miguel Nemón

Avenida Miguel Alemán

Avenida López Mateos

Parque
La Pastora

Río La Silla

Avenida Revolución

Plaza la
Silla

Avenida Chapultepec

Instituto
Tecnológico

Avenida Garza Sada

85

To Linares &
Ciudad Victoria

Metro Linea 1

Parque
Fundidora

Avenida Colón

See Monterrey Bus
Station Area Map

See Central
Monterrey Map

Zaragoza

Avenida Ruiz Cortines

Avenida Ciudad de los Ángeles

Avenida Nogalar Sur

To
Nuevo
Laredo

85

Avenida
Universidad

Parque
Niños
Héroes

University

Madero

Santa

Catarina

Santuario de
Guadalupe

Boulevard de las Torres

Calzada Reyes

Fidel
Velásquez

Train
Station

Metro Linea 2

Río

Santa

Catarina

Avenida
Aztlán

Metro Linea 1

Avenida J E González

Museo
del Obispado

Centro
Cultural
Alfa

To
Chipinque

Avenida Ruiz Cortines

Barrio Antiguo

Avenida Gómez Morín

Avenida Abraham Lincoln

Paseo de la Victoria

Galerías
Monterrey

Museo de Arte Contemporáneo

To Cañón de la Huasteca,
Grutas de García & Saltillo

Plaza
San Pedro

Avenida Vasconcelos

80

0   1   2 km

To
Chipinque

greenery and offer well-planned vistas of the surrounding mountains. Enclosed by the best of the city's old and new architecture, the area offers respite from the noise and bustle of streets nearby and helps to manage the traffic problems with underpasses and extensive underground car parks.

Though the overall size of the Macro Plaza could have been overwhelming, it actually comprises a series of smaller spaces at a human scale, which have various styles and functions. These spaces are interspersed with buildings, monuments, sculptures, fountains, trees and gardens – there are no vast expanses of unrelieved pavement. At the very southern end, nearest the Río Santa Catarina, the **Monumento Homenaje al Sol** is a tall sculpture on a traffic island which faces the **Palacio Municipal**, a modern building raised up on concrete legs.

This occupies the south side of **Plaza Zaragoza**, a semi-formal space often busy with people walking through, having lunch or listening to music from the covered bandstand. On the east side of Plaza Zaragoza is the **Museo de Arte Contemporáneo** (MARCO), with its gigantic black dove sculpture, and the baroque-façaded **cathedral**, built between 1600 and 1750 (the bell tower was added in 1851). Facing it across the plaza is the old city hall, which now houses the Museo de Historia de Nuevo León. North of the old city hall, new and old buildings flank the end of **Calle Morelos**, a bustling pedestrian mall.

The centrepiece of Plaza Zaragoza is the stunning **Faro del Comercio** (Beacon of Commerce), a tall, flat, orange concrete slab designed by the architect Luis Barragán in the love-it-or-hate-it-but-you-can't-ignore-it style. If you're lucky you'll see green laser beams from the top sweep over the city at night. It couldn't be in greater contrast to the adjacent cathedral. On the north side of Plaza Zaragoza is the **Fuente del Comercio** (Fountain of Commerce) and the **Obreros de Nuevo León** (Workers of Nuevo León) statue.

Across Padre Mier is the **Fuente de la Vida** (Fountain of Life) with a Neptune-like

character riding a chariot in the middle. North of this, the modern **Teatro de la Ciudad** and **Congreso del Estado** buildings face each other from the east and west sides of the **Esplanada Cultural** plaza. Further north again, the **Biblioteca Central** (State Library) and the **Tribunal Superior de Justica** (Supreme Court) stand on either side of the **Parque Hundido** (Sunken Garden), a favourite spot for couples.

North again and down some steps, you come to the **Esplanada de los Héroes** (Esplanade of the Heroes), also called the Plaza Cinco de Mayo, with statues of national heroes in each corner. It's the most formal and traditional of the spaces in the Macro Plaza, and looks like a standard Plaza de Armas with the 1908 neoclassical **Palacio de Gobierno** on its north side. From the steps of the Palacio you can look back down the length of the Macro Plaza, to the south side of the river and up the hills beyond. Behind the Palacio, a small park faces the 1930s **post office** and federal government building, providing yet another architectural contrast.

Zona Rosa

This is the area of top hotels, restaurants and shops just west of Plaza Zaragoza, bounded roughly by Padre Mier to the north, Ocampo and Hidalgo to the south, and Garibaldi to the west. Most of the streets are pedestrian-only and it's usually a bustling place where it's a pleasure to walk around, window-shop or find somewhere to eat or drink.

Barrio Antiguo

This is the old neighbourhood, east of the Macro Plaza, in the blocks between Dr Coss and Avenida Gómez, north and south of 15 de Mayo. It's nice to stroll around and see some of Monterrey's more traditional architecture.

Museo de Arte Contemporáneo

Just east of Plaza Zaragoza, at the south end of the Macro Plaza, MARCO has temporary exhibitions of work by artists from Nuevo León and elsewhere. Unless it's being prepared for the next exhibition, it's open

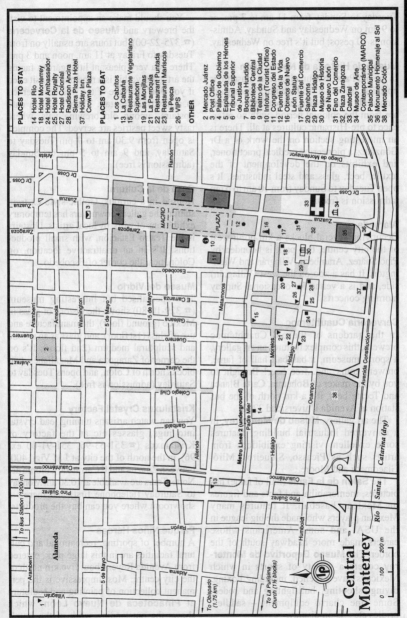

PLACES TO STAY

14 Hotel Río
18 Hotel Monterrey
24 Hotel Ambassador
25 Hotel Royalty
27 Hotel Colonial
28 Radisson Ancira
Sierra Plaza Hotel
37 Holiday Inn
Crowne Plaza

PLACES TO EAT

1 Los Cabritos
13 La Cabaña
15 Restaurante Vegetariano
Superbom
19 Las Monjitas
21 La Parroquia
22 Restaurant Puntada
23 Restaurant Mariscos
La Fresca
26 VIPS

OTHER

2 Mercado Juárez
3 Post Office
4 Palacio de Gobierno
5 Esplanada de los Héroes
6 Tribunal Superior
de Justicia
7 Bosque Hundido
8 Biblioteca Central
9 Teatro de la Ciudad
10 Infotur (Tourist Office)
11 Congreso del Estado
12 Fuente de la Vida
16 Obreros de Nuevo
León Statue
17 Fuente del Comercio
20 Sanborns
29 Plaza Hidalgo
30 Museo de Historia
de Nuevo León
31 Faro del Comercio
32 Plaza Zaragoza
33 Catedral
34 Museo de Arte
Contemporáneo (MARCO)
35 Palacio Municipal
36 Monumento Homenaje al Sol
38 Mercado Colón

Central
Monterrey

0   100   200 m

Tuesday to Sunday from 11 am to 7 pm, or to 9 pm on Wednesday and Sunday. Admission is 10 pesos, but it's free on Wednesday.

Museo de Historia de Nuevo León

In the old Palacio Municipal, this museum is upstairs around a 16th-century courtyard. Unusually for Mexico, its earliest exhibits are from the colonial period, with no reference to pre-Hispanic cultures at all. There is an interesting section on the work of a Dr González, a pioneering medical practitioner, and exhibits on the development of the textile, beer, glass and steel industries. It's open Tuesday to Sunday from 10 am to 6 pm (admission is free).

Alameda

Occupying several blocks a km north-west of the city centre, this park is bounded by Pino Suárez, Aramberri, Villagrán and Washington. It has a zoo on the west (Villagrán) side, and is a venue for occasional Sunday morning concerts.

Cervecería Cuauhtémoc

In the gardens of the old Cuauhtémoc brewery, this complex features an art gallery, a sports museum, a baseball hall of fame, brewery tours and...free beer! Brought to you by the maker of Bohemia, Carta Blanca and Tecate beer, it's a km north of the bus station at Avenida Universidad 2202.

The art gallery, **Museo de Monterrey**, in a converted industrial building, features some excellent visiting exhibitions from artists such as Picasso, Siqueiros, Miró, Giacometti and Moore.

The **Salon de la Fama** (hall of fame) has pictures, memorabilia and facts and figures on Mexican baseball. It features many Mexican players who made the big league in the USA, and some Americans whose careers made more headway south of the border. The **Museo Deportivo de Monterrey** covers a variety of sports in which Mexicans have excelled, including boxing, diving, shooting, bullfighting and rodeo. Some fine charro equipment – saddles, bridles etc – is on display.

You should make an appointment to visit the brewery and **Museo de la Cervecería** (☎ 375-22-00), but tours are usually on from Tuesday to Friday at 11 am, noon and 3 pm. There is a very pleasant little garden facing the art gallery; this is a nice place to sit even if you don't partake of the free beer, served in a handy little stall. There's also a café upstairs, among old brewing vats, where tasty sweet pastries are served. The complex is open from 9.30 am to 9 pm Tuesday to Saturday, and 9 am to 5 pm on Sunday (admission is free).

Casa de la Cultura

Housed in a curious, Gothic-style ex-train station, the gallery downstairs has temporary exhibitions of work by local artists. Upstairs is the Teatro Estación, with small productions. It's in an unattractive location, on Colón, near the corner of Escobedo.

Museo del Vidrio

This specialised but interesting museum (☎ 329-10-80) shows the history of glass in Mexico (ground floor), the manufacture and use of glass (1st floor), and glass as an artistic and sculptural medium (2nd floor). It's on the corner of Zaragoza and Magallanes, two blocks north of Colón, and opens Tuesday to Saturday (admission is free).

Kristaluxus Crystal Factory

You can watch artisans turning lead crystal into jugs, glasses etc at the factory of Kristaluxus (☎ 351-63-96, 351-91-00 ext 96), in the north of the city at J M Vigil 400, between Zuazua and E Carranza, Colonia del Norte. Tours are available at 10.30 am Monday to Saturday (telephone first) and there's a showroom where you can buy the products.

Parque Niños Héroes

A number of sporting, recreational and cultural facilities are in this large park, entered from Avenida Reyes about five km north of the city centre. Most impressive is the permanent collection of painting and sculpture at **Pinacoteca de Nuevo León**, which shows the outstanding work of the state's artists since colonial times. Their images of the desert landscape are particularly striking. A building next door shows temporary exhibitions, and also has some excellent work. These galleries are open from 11 am to 6 pm Tuesday to Sunday (admission is free).

The **Museo del Automovil** has a small collection of old cars, mainly of US origin, from the 1920s, 1930s and 1940s. It's next to the Pinacoteca, with the same hours and the same free admission.

At the **Museo de la Fauna y Ciencias Naturales,** you can see life-sized dioramas with stuffed wildlife in its 'natural' habitat, from Saharan Africa to the Arctic, with quite good labels and descriptions in Spanish. Kids will like it, and it's not *too* tacky, except for the moose's head hanging on the wall with its body and legs painted behind. It's open from 9 am to 7 pm Tuesday to Friday, and 10 am to 5.30 pm on weekends (admission is 3 pesos).

Iglesia de La Purísima

About a km west of the city centre, by a little park on the corner of Hidalgo and Peña, this church was designed by Enrique de la Mora and built in 1946. It's an interesting example of 'modern' architecture 50 years on. The main body of the church is supported by parabolic arches, and a squat rectangular school building has been added to the back. The statues on the sides of the church are of

Iglesia de La Purísima

the 12 apostles, each with a rectangular air-con unit next to him.

Museo del Obispado

The former bishop's palace *(obispado)*, on a hill 2.5 km west of the zona rosa along Matamoros, gives fine views over the city and surrounding mountains, smog permitting. Built in 1786-87, it served as a fort during the US attack on Monterrey in 1846, weathered the French intervention of the 1860s and confrontations between local Constitutionalists and the forces of Pancho Villa in the revolution years. It was also a yellow-fever hospital before becoming what it is now – a small historical museum with various colonial and revolutionary relics. It's open Tuesday to Sunday from 10 am to 5 pm and costs 10 pesos – don't feel too bad if you miss it.

Santuario de Guadalupe

This church is the strange pyramid you can see from the south end of the Macro Plaza. It looks like it was made from a gigantic piece of folded cardboard.

Instituto Tecnológico

The Technological Institute, in the south-east of the city on Avenida Garza Sada between Pernambuco and Avenida del Estado, is one of Mexico's best-regarded higher-education schools. It has some surprising architecture, like the building which appears to have been sliced apart, leaving the two halves toppling away from each other.

Parque La Pastora

Five km east of the centre, off Avenida Eloy Cavazos, this park has an open-air zoo, woodlands and rental-boat rides (admission is 5 pesos). Next to the park is the **Bosque Mágico**, a kids' amusement park open every day.

Colonia del Valle & Chipinque

Colonia del Valle, six km south-west of the centre, is one of Monterrey's most exclusive suburbs, with big houses on quiet tree-lined streets. The wealthiest people live further south, high up on the slopes of the Mesa de Chipinque, which rises to 835 metres above the city. It's like Monterrey's answer to Beverly Hills, with magnificent views of the city, the mountains and the desert. Colonia del Valle has a large mall and other areas of classy shops and restaurants in the streets off Calzada del Valle.

Mesa de Chipinque, several km up the hill from Colonia del Valle, offers woodland walks, fine views back over the city and the luxury Hotel Chipinque, where there are horses for hire. You need a taxi or your own vehicle to get there, since buses don't run beyond Colonia del Valle. It's open from 7 am to 7 pm. Vehicle entry is 10 pesos.

Centro Cultural Alfa

This cultural complex (☎ 378-58-19), sponsored by the Alfa industrial group, is in Colonia del Valle at Avenida Gómez Morin 1100, and is well worth the trip. The main building, which looks like a water tank tipping over, has floors devoted to computers, astronomy, physics, Mexican antiquities and temporary exhibitions. The scientific displays have lots of educational hands-on exhibits, and everything is well lit and carefully labelled (in Spanish only). In the centre of the building is the planetarium, which also functions as an Omnimax cinema.

Outside is the Jardín Cientifico, with more educational stuff, the Jardín Prehispanico, with replicas of some of the great archaeological finds, and an aviary. El Universo, a superb glass mural, was created by Rufino Tamayo for the headquarters of the Alfa group, but was considered so beautiful that a special building was constructed to display it to a wider audience. It's in the large building called the Pabellon (Pavilion), which resembles a covered wagon.

The complex is open from 3 to 9 pm Tuesday to Friday, 2 to 9 pm on Saturday and 11 am to 9 pm on Sunday. Admission is 10 pesos and parking 6 pesos. Special buses go every hour from the Alameda, and regular buses go to Colonia del Valle.

Festivals

Monterrey's festivals include:

Independence Anniversary Monterrey's biggest celebrations are held on 15 and 16 September, with a big parade on the 16th.

Spring Fair There are many festivities during the spring fair, which begins on Palm Sunday (the Sunday before Easter).

Nuestra Señora de Guadalupe Held on 12 December, but attracting thousands of pilgrims and worshippers several days before, this festival is centred on the Santuario de Guadalupe. The festival is also celebrated in a big way in Abasolo, a village about 25 km from Monterrey off the Monclova road, where there are pilgrimages, a fair, a parade of floats and horse riders, and folk-dancing.

Organised Tours

A company called Osetur (☎ (8) 347-15-33, 347-15-99) runs sightseeing and shopping tours to places in and around the city. Destinations covered depend on the day of the week but include the Macro Plaza, Cuauhtémoc brewery complex, Kristaluxus crystal factory, Galerías Monterrey shopping mall, and various craft shops. Tours outside the city include Centro Cultural Alfa, Grutas de García and Cola de Caballo. A basic morning city tour covers two or three destinations and costs around 30 pesos. Osetur is based in Colonia Loma Larga south of the Río Santa Catarina, but tours leave from the city centre on the corner of Escobedo and Ocampo. Telephone first or ask the tourist office where the tour goes on a particular day.

Places to Stay

Nearly all the cheaper hotels are within a few blocks of the bus and train stations. A room away from the noisy street is a definite plus. There's mid-range accommodation in this area and in the zona rosa, while the top-end places are nearly all in the zona rosa.

Places to Stay – bottom end

Some of the best accommodation can be found on Calle Amado Nervo, in the two blocks running south of the enormous bus station. The first place you come to, at Amado Nervo 1138, is the *Hotel Posada* (☎ (8) 372-39-08), which has clean rooms with fans, TV and plenty of hot water. Prices are 70/90 pesos for a single/double (TV extra). Some rooms on the upper floors have views over the city. In winter the rooms can be cold.

Half a block further down at Amado Nervo 1007, the *Hotel Nuevo León* (☎ (8) 374-19-00) is also clean and fairly modern, with parking and plenty of hot water. The interior rooms are pretty quiet for this part of town but they have very little light. It's 70 pesos for one or two people in one bed. The *Hotel Amado Nervo* (☎ (8) 375-46-32), at Amado Nervo 1110, has smaller, dingier rooms for 60/70 pesos, or 85 pesos with two beds. The *Hotel Virreyes* (☎ (8) 374-66-10), at Amado Nervo 902, has larger but tattier rooms with double beds for 50 pesos, 70 pesos with air-con.

If you arrive at the train station late at night, the nearest hotel is the *Hotel Estación*, at Victoria 1450, the street running straight ahead as you walk out of the southern exit road of the station. The location has nothing else going for it, and the newish rooms are very plain, but it's clean and tolerable at 60 pesos.

Places to Stay – middle
The middle range in Monterrey starts at around 90 pesos for a single. There are no great bargains in this range, but the comfort is a quantum leap up from the bottom-enders.

Bus Station Area The *Hotel Patricia* (☎ (8) 375-07-50) is at Madero Ote 123 between Juárez and Guerrero, and has parking and clean, quite pleasant, air-con rooms from 110 pesos. The *Hotel 5a Avenida* (Quinta Avenida) (☎ (8) 375-65-65), at Madero Ote 234 between Guerrero and Galeana, has secure parking and comfortable air-con rooms from 91/105 pesos, more with TV. It also has its own clean, modern restaurant.

Hotel Jandal (☎ (8) 372-46-06, 72-36-36), at Cuauhtémoc Nte 825 on the corner of Salazar, has comfortable, spotless, air-con singles/doubles with TV for 120/132 pesos; there's parking and a restaurant.

The best place in this area is the big *Fastos Hotel* (☎ (8) 372-32-50), over the road from the bus station at Colón Pte 956, on the corner of Villagrán. It's quite classy and comfortable. The hotel's 'económico' rooms, with air-con, TV and phone, are worth considering if there are three or four of you travelling together. They cost 195/195/233/280 pesos for one to four people.

East of the bus station, the *Hotel Son Mar* (☎ (8) 375-44-00), at Universidad Nte 1211 close to the corner of Colón, also has its own restaurant and parking, but is overpriced at 220 pesos for a single or double.

City Centre The very central location of the *Hotel Colonial* (☎ (8) 343-67-91), at Hidalgo Ote 475, makes it a tempting splurge. It has air-con, phone and TV, but smallish rooms at 134 pesos.

Other Areas Between the bus station and the city centre is the towering *Gran Hotel Yamallel* (☎ (8) 375-35-98), at Zaragoza Nte 912. Modern in style, it offers parking, phone, TV and a view over the city from the upper floors. Singles and doubles cost 121 pesos.

Places to Stay – top end
Downtown Monterrey has plenty of places for over 200 pesos. They mostly cater to business travellers and may give discounts on weekends. At all of them you can expect restaurants and bars, and carpeted rooms with air-con, TV and phone. For atmosphere, none rivals the *Radisson Ancira Sierra Plaza Hotel* (☎ (8) 345-75-75), on the corner of Escobedo and Plaza Hidalgo. It's been going since 1912, and it's said that Pancho Villa once rode into the lobby, which now has shops, a piano player, a restaurant and hovering waiters. Big rooms and plenty of old-fashioned elegance go for 286 pesos at weekends and 435 pesos during the week.

The 200-room *Hotel Monterrey* (☎ (8) 343-51-20), fronting onto the Plaza Zaragoza at Morelos Ote 574, has an electric band in its lobby bar and is one of the more popular top-end places. It charges 176 pesos at weekends and 242 pesos during the week for singles or doubles.

The enormous *Hotel Río* (☎ (8) 344-90-40, 344-95-10) occupies a whole block between Morelos and Padre Mier; its address is Padre Mier Pte 194. It has a swimming pool, and its 400 rooms cost from 220 pesos at weekends and 385 pesos during the week. The *Hotel Ambassador* (☎ (8) 342-20-40), on the corner of Hidalgo and E Carranza, has 241 rooms at 292 pesos at weekends and 383 pesos during the week. The *Holiday Inn Crowne Plaza* (☎ (8) 344-93-00), at Avenida Constitución Ote 300, is a huge 390-room place with blue-lit elevators gliding up and down above a cavernous restaurant/lounge where a rock band plays in the evenings. It is the most expensive place in town with rooms going for 302 pesos at weekends and a very international 418 pesos during the week.

Places to Eat

Monterrey abounds in *norteño* ('northern-style') ranch cooking, of which cabrito is perhaps the best-known dish: whole young goats are split open, flattened on racks and roasted before charcoal or wood fires. The best cabrito is tender and juicy, and tastes like spring lamb. It is not particularly cheap. Good steak, on the other hand, is very reasonable in Monterrey – a big, tender T-bone can cost as little as 15 pesos. Delicious sweets are another local speciality – try a *gloria*, made with milk, sugar and pecan nuts.

City Centre Every block of the zona rosa seems to have at least one restaurant or café. There's a wide range of prices and types of food, but real value for money is hard to come by at either end of the scale. The cheapest places of all are the comedores (basic cookshops) in the markets.

At Hidalgo 123 Ote, *Restaurant Puntada* has a long menu of Mexican items with nothing above 14 pesos, and is always packed. More expensive but with a pleasant atmosphere is *La Cabaña*, on Matamoros between Pino Suárez and Cuauhtémoc. It's a kind of large but comfortable log cabin where you can drink beer or eat soup, seafood, meat, or chicken enchiladas with mole sauce; the most expensive item on the menu is around 28 pesos.

Vegetarians will find a haven at *Restaurante Vegetariano Superbom* (☎ 45-26-63), upstairs on the corner of Padre Mier and Galeana. It does an excellent buffet lunch for 15 pesos, but closes at 5 pm and on weekends. Other vegetarian restaurants are on Escobedo, half a block north of Padre Mier, and on the corner of Ocampo and Cuauhtémoc.

For good international fare in a bizarre setting, try *Las Monjitas*, on Escobedo between Morelos and Plaza Hidalgo. You are served by waitresses dressed as nuns, as you sit in the cloisters and contemplate the wall paintings of smiling nuns preparing and serving food. Very generous main courses go for 10 to 20 pesos. Breakfast can cost as little as 8 pesos. The same menu, with serving sisters to boot, can be had at *La Parroquia*, nearby on the corner of Morelos and Galeana.

Bus Station Area Although a little on the expensive side, *El Pastor*, at Madero Pte 1067 on the corner of Alvárez, specialises in cabrito. They do a variety of different parts of the animal, usually char-grilled, at prices between 24 and 35 pesos. El Pastor is open from 11 am to 11 pm.

Fastory Restaurant, in the Fastos Hotel on Colón opposite the bus station, is a tidy modern place, open 24 hours, with Mexican and Western food. Spaghetti bolognese (no trimmings) costs 12 pesos, enchiladas 15 pesos and breakfasts up to 18 pesos. There's a *VIPS* on Pino Suárez, just north of Colón, where main courses cost 20 to 30 pesos and set breakfasts go from 10 to 18 pesos. The *Restaurant York*, in Hotel Quinta Avenida, is not as expensive as it looks, with main courses from around 18 pesos and an all-you-can-eat buffet lunch for 13.50 pesos.

Other Areas Near the alameda, *Los Cabritos*, on the corner of Aramberri and Villagrán, is another place specialising in cabrito. It's slightly dearer than El Pastor. Also popular in this part of town, but not cheap, is the *Café Lisboa*, on Aramberri on the north side of the park.

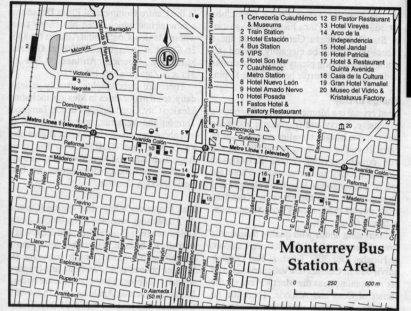

1	Cervecería Cuauhtémoc & Museums
2	Train Station
3	Hotel Estación
4	Bus Station
5	VIPS
6	Hotel Son Mar
7	Cuauhtémoc Metro Station
8	Hotel Nuevo León
9	Hotel Amado Nervo
10	Hotel Posada
11	Fastos Hotel & Fastory Restaurant
12	El Pastor Restaurant
13	Hotel Vireyes
14	Arco de la Independencia
15	Hotel Jandal
16	Hotel Patricia
17	Hotel & Restaurant Quinta Avenida
18	Casa de la Cultura
19	Gran Hotel Yamallel
20	Museo del Vidrio & Kristaluxus Factory

Monterrey Bus Station Area

0   250   500 m

Entertainment

Monterrey has numerous cinemas and an active cultural life including concerts, theatre and art exhibitions. The tourist office can tell you what's on, and posters are placed in strategic spots around town listing events. You might also come across some street theatre in the zona rosa.

There are Western-style rodeos every Sunday, and occasional charreadas where charros appear in all their finery to demonstrate their skills and horsemanship. Two better known charreada venues are in Guadalupe, on the eastern edge of the city, and Cryco, 35 km south by highway 85. Bullfights are held in the afternoons at the big covered *Plaza de Toros* at Universidad 2401 in the north of the city. September and October is the main bullfight season. The professional football (soccer) season is from about September to April, and the professional baseball season from March to August.

Monterrey's affluent younger set supports an active nightlife. The fashionable spots are always changing, so you might check at the tourist office for the current favourite. Places near the city centre include: *Fonda San Miguel* (☎ 342-09-02) at Morelos Ote 940, with live music on Thursday, Friday and Saturday; and *La Casa de Pancho Villa* (☎ 343-0345) at Padre Mier Pte 837, with Latin American music every night. There are more places in the expensive south-western suburbs, like *Kao's* (☎ 357-34-12) at Garza Sada 4502, *Black Jack* (☎ 333-77-64) at Ave Insurgentes 3987 in Vista Hermosa, and one

of the popular *Señor Frog's* nightclubs (☎ 363-23-38) at Plaza Fiesta San Agustín, in San Pedro Garza García. For all these places you should be elegantly dressed (no grunge here), bring plenty of cash for drinks and taxis, and not arrive before 10 or 11 pm.

Things to Buy

Lead crystal is a Monterrey speciality but it's expensive, heavy and fragile and about the last thing a budget traveller would want to carry. If you're returning to the USA by car you could consider it (see Kristaluxus Crystal Factory in this section). There are lots of leather goods, which are cheaper and more portable. Don't forget some of the delicious sweets made locally with sugar, milk, nuts and fruit.

Interesting shops with quality handicrafts from different parts of Mexico are Carápan, at Hidalgo Ote 305; Tikal, at Río Guadalquivir 319 in Colonia del Valle; and Casa de las Artesanías, near the Macro Plaza on the corner of Coss and Allende. There are no bargains, but some items are reasonably priced considering their quality.

The two main downtown markets, Mercado Colón and Mercado Juárez, are big, bustling places selling everyday items. The richer Regiomontanos, of which there are many, prefer to shop at one of the big air-con malls like Plaza la Silla, south of town on Eugenio Garza Sada; Plaza San Pedro, south-west in the suburb of San Pedro; or Galerías Monterrey, to the west of town near the intersection of Pablo González and José E González. It's worth visiting one of these shopping centres if you want to be cool (in the air-con of course!) or see the Mexican middle class en masse.

Getting There & Away

Air Aeroméxico (☎ 343-55-60) is on the corner of Padre Mier and Cuauhtémoc 812 Sur. The main Mexicana office (☎ 340-55-11) is at Hidalgo Pte 922, but there are several other offices. Aeromonterrey (☎ 356-56-61), a regional airline, is at Calzada San Pedro 500 in the Garza García district. Saro (☎ 342-35-97), at Hidalgo Pte

in the Centro Commercial Plaza Dorado, is a new airline which often has cheap fares within Mexico. Continental Airlines (☎ 333-26-82) is at Insurgentes 2500, in Galerías Monterrey. American Airlines (☎ 340-30-31) is at Zaragoza Sur 1300.

There are direct flights, usually at least daily, to all major cities in Mexico, including Mexico City, Guadalajara, Puebla, Tampico, Torreón and Veracruz, and connections to just about anywhere else. Direct flights also go to Chicago, Dallas, Houston, Los Angeles, Miami and New York. Connections to other international destinations are best made through Houston.

Bus Monterrey's huge bus station (Central de Autobuses) occupies three blocks along Colón between Pino Suárez and Reyes. It's a small city in itself, with ticket desks strung out along its whole length, restaurants, Ladatel phones and a 24-hour left-luggage service (12 pesos). First-class lines servicing Monterrey include Anáhuac (☎ 375-64-80), Omnibus de México (☎ 375-71-21), Transportes del Norte (☎ 375-42-80) and Tres Estrellas de Oro (☎ 374-24-10). Turistar and Futura provide deluxe services. Second-class services go to most places listed below and are slightly cheaper than the 1st-class fares shown, but can be a lot slower. Destinations of interest to travellers include:

Aguascalientes – 577 km, eight hours (98 pesos)
Chihuahua – 818 km, 11½ hours (98 pesos)
Ciudad Acuña – 492 km, seven hours (62 pesos)
Ciudad Valles – 512 km, 7½ hours (67 pesos)
Ciudad Victoria – 282 km, 4½ hours (36 pesos)
Durango – 615 km, 10 hours (76 pesos)
Guadalajara – 766 km, 10½ hours; 1st-class (88 pesos) and deluxe buses (150 pesos)
Matamoros – 323 km, six hours (42 pesos)
Matehuala – 340 km, five hours (41 pesos)
McAllen, Texas – 235 km, five hours (41 pesos)
Mexico City (Terminal Norte) – 966 km, 12 hours; 1st-class (115 pesos) and deluxe buses (153 pesos)
Nuevo Laredo – 220 km, three hours; 1st-class (38 pesos) and deluxe buses (48 pesos)
Querétaro – 745 km, 10 hours; 1st-class (86 pesos) and deluxe buses (129 pesos)
Reynosa – 225 km, four hours (31 pesos)
Saltillo – 85 km, 1½ hours (10 pesos)

North-East Mexico
Top Left: Charro displaying his roping skills (JL)
Top Right: Casa Madero winery, Parras (PP)
Bottom: Centro Cultural Alfa, Monterrey (JL)

North-East Mexico
Top Left: Taco stand (JL)
Top Right: Milk seller, Parras (PP)
Bottom: Iglesia del Santa Madero, Parras (JL)

San Luis Potosí – 541 km, six hours (66 pesos)
Tampico – 525 km, eight hours (67 pesos)
Torreón – 362 km, 5½ hours (43 pesos)
Zacatecas – 448 km, 6½ hours (53 pesos)

Train Monterrey train station (☎ (8) 375-46-04) is about half a km west of the bus station along Colón, then three blocks north on Nieto. Tickets and information for primera especial and coche dormitorio travel are only available from 8.30 am to 12.30 pm, and from 4 to 8 pm. Tickets for other services are sold in the hour or two before scheduled departure. Trains are always slower than buses and often delayed. Customer service on the railways is not good.

There are two trains daily to Mexico City. For timetable details, see the Mexico City Train section. El Regiomontano, train No 72, also known as the Pullman, has primera especial and coche dormitorio accommodation, and a dining car. It leaves Monterrey at 7.50 pm, reaching Mexico City at about 10 am and also stopping at Saltillo and San Luis Potosí. A primera especial ticket to Mexico City costs 114 pesos; a camarín costs 237/392 pesos for one/two people; an alcoba is 475 pesos for two, and up to 831 pesos for four people.

The Águila Azteca, train No 2, has no sleeping cars. It departs Monterrey at 11.30 pm, calls at Saltillo, San Luis Potosí, San Miguel de Allende and Querétaro, and reaches Mexico City at 7 pm. Fares on this train are 129 pesos for primera especial, 84 pesos for primera regular, and 40 pesos for segunda clase.

Only the northbound Águila Azteca, train No 1, from Mexico City continues past Monterrey to Nuevo Laredo – it is scheduled to leave Monterrey at 2.20 am and takes five hours to reach Nuevo Laredo (34 pesos primera especial, 22 pesos primera regular, 11 pesos segunda clase). El Tamaulipeco, train No 141, departs Monterrey at 10.30 am for Reynosa (2.40 pm) and Matamoros (arriving at 5.10 pm). In the other direction, train No 142 goes from Matamoros to Monterrey via Reynosa. It costs 43 pesos in primera especial.

There are also daily slow trains between Monterrey and Tampico (train No 172; departs 8 am, 11 hours) via Ciudad Victoria, and between Monterrey, Torreón and Durango (train No 175; departs 8.10 am).

Car Going to/from the US border there's an excellent toll road, highway 85D, to Nuevo Laredo (94 pesos) and another, highway 40D, to Reynosa (44 pesos).

A number of ring roads bypass Monterrey, especially between highway 85 from the north and highway 40 going west to Saltillo. Take the toll bypass and you won't see Monterrey at all. For any destination in north-west Mexico, head for Saltillo initially then go west via Torreón or south-west via Zacatecas.

The quickest route south to Mexico City (960 km) is via Saltillo and highway 57 to San Luis Potosí and Querétaro. It has heavy traffic but is mostly divided highway, except for some horrific two-lane stretches north and south of San Luis Potosí. The alternative routes south, on highway 85, pass through Linares, Ciudad Victoria and Ciudad Mante.

Car There is enough to see within a day's drive of Monterrey to make car rental worth considering. The big companies like Avis (☎ 369-08-34), Hertz (☎ 369-08-22) and Dollar (☎ 369-08-97) have branches at the international airport, and usually in town as well. You may get a cheaper deal with one of the smaller local outfits like Max (☎ 342-63-75) at Hidalgo Pte 480, Excellent (☎ 345-77-00) at Hidalgo 1612, or Renee (☎ 342-06-04) at Hidalgo Ote 418. Infotur has a long list of them.

Getting Around
To/From the Airport Monterrey airport is off the road to Ciudad Alemán (highway 54), north-east of the city, about 15 km from the city centre. There is no shuttle service to the airport. A taxi costs about 50 pesos.

Bus Buses (1 peso) go frequently to just about everywhere in Monterrey, but often by roundabout routes. A noticeboard at the east end of Morelos, facing the Macro Plaza, has maps showing all the bus routes. Infotur has the same maps and can help you find a bus to where you're going. Often the best idea is to ask at the front desk of your hotel before you go out. Many of the buses are privately owned and supplied by the large factories for their workers. The following routes might be useful:

Bus station to centre – Bus 17-Pio X and Bus 18, from the corner of Amado Nervo and Reforma, go to the edge of the zona rosa, then do a dogleg around it. For Macro Plaza, the best place to get off is the corner of Juárez and 15 de Mayo. For the zona rosa, get off on Pino Suárez on the corners of Padre Mier, Hidalgo or Ocampo.

Centre to bus station – No 39 (orange) can be picked up on Juárez on the corners of Ocampo, Hidalgo, Morelos or Padre Mier. It takes you to Colón. No 17-Pio X, going north from the corner of Cuauhtémoc and Padre Mier, also goes to Colón.

Bus station to Obispado, La Purísima and the city centre – No 1 from the corner of Amado Nervo and Reforma goes within a few blocks of the Obispado, passes La Purísima church, then goes along Ocampo to Zaragoza.

Centre to Obispado – No 4 from the corner of Padre Mier and Garibaldi goes west along Padre Mier. For the Obispado, get off when it turns left at Degollado, walk up the hill, turn left at the top of the steps, then take the first right (a 10-minute walk).

Centre or bus station to Cuauhtémoc brewery – No 1 ('San Nicolás-Tecnológico') goes up Juárez from the city centre and passes the corner of Cuauhtémoc and Colón (near the bus station) on its way up Universidad to the brewery. No 17 ('Universidad') goes north up Cuauhtémoc from Padre Mier to Colón, then on up Universidad to the brewery.

Cuauhtémoc Brewery to bus station and city centre – Nos 17 and 18 go south along Universidad, then right along Colón and left down Amado Nervo before heading towards the city centre.

Centre to Colonia del Valle/Garza García – 'San Pedro', from the corner of Hidalgo and Cuauhtémoc, goes to the big traffic circle in Colonia del Valle (where Gómez Morin, Vasconcelos and Calzada del Valle meet), then heads west along Vasconcelos.

Centre to Instituto Tecnológico – Take No 1 from the corner of Padre Mier and Pino Suárez.

Metro The first line of Monterrey's Metro opened in mid-1991. It is not yet of much interest to visitors as it only runs east to west in the north of the city, primarily going to outlying residential areas. Fares are about 1.20 pesos. A second line is expected to open soon. This new line will run from near the Cuauhtémoc brewery, past the bus station, and down to the Zona Rosa and the Macro Plaza, and will be very useful. The two lines will cross at the intersection of Colón and Cuauhtémoc, where the giant overhead Cuauhtémoc metro station is under construction.

AROUND MONTERREY

A number of sights near Monterrey are easily accessible in your own vehicle, and somewhat less accessible by bus. You might consider taking a tour to some of them, or renting a car between a few people.

Grutas de García

An illuminated, 2.5-km route leads through 16 chambers in this cave system high in the Sierra del Fraile, approached by a 700-metre ascent by funicular railway. The caves were formed about 50 million years ago and discovered by the parish priest in 1843. There are lots of stalactites and stalagmites, as well as petrified seashells. Each chamber has a different name such as 'The Eagle's Nest', 'Chamber of Clouds' and 'The Eighth Wonder'.

On Sunday a Transportes Monterrey-Saltillo bus leaves Monterrey bus station at 9, 10 and 11 am and at noon, returning in the afternoon (10 pesos for the return trip). On other days the same line runs buses every half an hour to Villa de García, nine km from the caves. To get there by car from Monterrey, take highway 40 towards Saltillo. After about 25 km a sign points the way to the caves – turn right and go another 18 km to the bottom of the funicular. This is a popular weekend outing, but the caves and funicular are open every day from 9 am to 5.30 pm. Entry is 20 pesos, including the funicular.

Cañón de la Huasteca

On the western edge of Monterrey, 16 km from the centre, this canyon is 300 metres deep and has some dramatic rock formations. There is a town at one end of it and a children's playground in the middle, which reduces its attraction as a wilderness area. Reach the mouth of the canyon by taking a 'Santa Catarina/Huasteca' bus from the corner of Padre Mier and Juárez, or Cuauhtémoc and Madero, in the centre of Monterrey. The same bus brings you back to the city centre. It's open daily from 8 am to 6 pm; entry is 7 pesos for a vehicle, 1 peso for a person.

The town of **Santa Catarina**, at the north end of the canyon, celebrates the festival of the Virgen de San Juan de Los Lagos with dances and fireworks from 10 to 15 August.

Cascadas Cola de Caballo

Horsetail Falls, a 25-metre waterfall, is six km up a rough road from El Cercado, a village 35 km south of the centre of Monterrey by highway 85. It has its share of hawkers and food stalls, but it's quite pretty and attracts a lot of picnickers. Walk up the valley beyond the falls to see the vegetation which flourishes on the slopes of the Sierra. The waterfall is on private land and open from 9 am to 5 pm Tuesday to Sunday; entry is 8 pesos. Horses and donkeys can be hired for the last km to the falls (15 pesos). Autobuses Monterrey-Villa de Santiago-El Cercado go to El Cercado from Monterrey bus station.

On the way to El Cercado you pass close to the **Rodrigo Gómez Dam**, known as La Boca – an artificial lake where Regiomontanos go swimming, sailing and water-skiing.

If you have your own vehicle, you can drive 33 km up a rough road from El Cercado to the **Laguna de Sánchez**, a mountain lake surrounded by pine forests.

NORTH OF MONTERREY

On the toll road to Nuevo Laredo, highway 85D, you'll see nothing but cactus, cattle and the occasional eagle. On the free road you pass the town of **Sabinas Hidalgo**, about halfway there; it has a few motels and restaurants. Forty km west of Sabinas Hidalgo are the **Grutas de Bustamente**, a series of underground chambers three km long. The caves are being developed for visitors.

SOUTH OF MONTERREY

You can go south-west from Monterrey to Saltillo, 95 km away by the excellent highway 40 (the main route towards Mexico City).

Going south-east on highway 85 towards Ciudad Victoria, you follow the edge of the Sierra through Mexico's most important citrus-growing area, centred on the towns of Allende, Montemorelos, Hualahuises and Linares. There are hotels in Montemorelos and Linares.

Sierra Madre Oriental

From Linares a scenic road (highway 58) heads west up into the Sierra Madre to the towns of Iturbide (44 km from Linares) and, with an eight-km northward detour, Galeana (72 km from Linares), climbing 1000 metres from the valley. Highway 58 continues west down on to the Altiplano Central, where it meets highway 57 between Saltillo and Matehuala, 98 km from Linares. It's superb up on the Sierra, with clear air, sparkling streams and unspoilt landscapes.

Iturbide This area has several caves, canyons and waterfalls. There's a hotel in town where you can hire horses to reach some of them. Nine km east of Iturbide, a giant bas-relief, *Los Altares*, by Nuevo León sculptor Federico Cantú, is cut into the cliff beside the road; it's dedicated to road builders.

Galeana High on a wheat-producing plateau, Galeana is a centre for handloomed wool shawls and blankets. The town celebrates the festival of San Pablo with fireworks and processions from 20 to 25 January. On the plaza, the *Hotel Magdalena* is OK for 25/35 pesos; the *Hotel Jardín* is not much better at 50/80 pesos. Nine km north (turn right at the Río San Lucas junction) is a 15-metre-high natural bridge called the **Puente de Dios**, over which a local road passes. For the best view, pull off onto the flat area to the left, just before the bridge. The 3635-metre peak of **Cerro Potosí**, one of the highest in the Sierra Madre Oriental, is 35 km west of Galeana.

Coahuila

The state of Coahuila is large, mostly desert and sparsely populated. The border crossings into Coahuila from Texas are less frequently used than those further south-east in Tamaulipas, because the road connections into Mexico and the USA are not as convenient for most travellers. The state capital, Saltillo, is definitely worth a visit, and the remoteness and the harsh, arid landscapes will appeal to some. For information about the west of the state, including the city of Torreón and the Zona del Silencio, see the Central North Mexico chapter.

The Spanish came to Coahuila in search of silver, slaves and souls, but stayed to establish sheep and cattle ranches which became viable despite raids by Chichimec Indians. A few big landowners came to dominate the area. In south-east Coahuila, one holding of 890 sq km was bought from the crown for 250 pesos in 1731, and grew to 58,700 sq km by 1771, becoming the Marquesado de Aguaya, protected by a private cavalry. The population remained sparse though – in 1800, Coahuila still had fewer than 7000 people.

After 1821, in the early years of independence, Coahuila and Texas were one state of the new Mexican republic, but Texas was lost after the Mexican-American War. As the 19th century progressed, ranching grew in importance, helped by the arrival of railways. By 1900, Coahuila had 297,000 inhabitants. In the 20th century, a steel foundry was established in Monclova, using coal mined near Sabinas, giving Coahuila a major industrial centre.

BORDER CROSSINGS

Ciudad Acuña
• *pop: 60,000*
Ciudad Acuña, across from the US town of Del Rio, is a fairly busy border crossing, open 24 hours a day. The **Presa de la Amistad** (Friendship Dam) is about 20 km upriver from Ciudad Acuña. A joint Mexican-US water management project, the artificial lake offers good fishing and boating facilities. From Ciudad Acuña to Saltillo it's an eight-hour bus ride, on quite good two-lane roads.

Piedras Negras
• *pop: 150,000*
The border crossing between Piedras Negras and the US town of Eagle Pass is a major commercial route, open 24 hours a day. Piedras Negras attracts quite a few short-term visitors from Texas. There's a craft shop in the old San Bernardino mission which features work from all over Mexico, and the casa de cultura has occasional displays of Mexican art, music and dance.

Highway 57 goes south-east to Allende, Sabinas and Monclova, and continues to Saltillo, about eight hours away by bus. Not recommended is the train (segunda clase only) which leaves Piedras Negras at 9.15 am, and is supposed to arrive in Saltillo at 6.55 pm.

MONCLOVA
• *pop: 250,000*
The Altos Hornos iron and steel works are one of the largest and most important in Mexico. The city also has a number of 17th and 18th-century buildings, and its Pape library and museum have a surprisingly good collection of Mexican and European artists. Highway 57 runs south to Saltillo, about 190 km away, or 2½ hours by bus; 25 km south of Monclova, highway 53 branches south-east to Monterrey (there are no fuel stations on this highway).

SALTILLO
• *pop: 600,000* • *alt: 1599 metres*
Set high in the arid Sierra Madre Oriental, Saltillo was founded in 1577 and is the oldest city in the north-east. It's on the main road and rail routes between the north-east border and central and western Mexico, and is a pleasant place to break a journey. Like Monterrey, it has excellent transport links with the rest of Mexico.

In the late 17th century, Saltillo was capital of an area that included Coahuila,

Nuevo León, Tamaulipas, Texas and 'all the land to the north which reaches towards the pole'. These days it has a quiet, central area with a small-town feel and some lovely colonial buildings, but there are extensive new suburbs and major industries on the city's outskirts. It's quite a prosperous city, and its pleasant climate and relaxed pace of life make it a popular place to stay.

History

The first mission to be established here was in 1591, as a centre for the education and religious conversion of the local Indian populations. Indians from Tlaxcala were brought to help the Spanish stabilise the area, and they set up a colony beside the Spanish one at Saltillo. The Tlaxcalans' skill on the treadle-loom and the abundance of wool in the area led to the development of a unique type of sarape, for which Saltillo became famous in the 18th and 19th centuries.

Capital of the state of Coahuila & Texas after Mexican independence, it was occupied by US troops under Zachary Taylor in 1846 during the Mexican-American War. At Buenavista, 10 km south of Saltillo, the 20,000-strong army of General Santa Anna was repulsed by Taylor's men in 1847, in the decisive battle for control of the north-east during that war.

President Benito Juárez came to Saltillo during his flight from the invading French forces in 1864, and the city was occupied again by foreign troops before being freed in 1866. During the Porfiriato, agriculture and ranching prospered in the area, and the coming of the railway helped trade and the first industries in the city, but Monterrey was by this time fast overtaking Saltillo in size and importance.

Saltillo's industrial development started with the processing of local primary products, including wheat and wool, and it is still a commercial and communications centre for a large livestock and agricultural area. In the postwar period it has expanded to include big automobile and petrochemical plants. Saltillo is still the capital of Coahuila, but it has been outgrown by the modern city of Torreón in the south-west of the state.

Orientation

Saltillo spreads out over quite a large area, but most of the interest for visitors is in the blocks around the two central plazas. Periférico Echeverría, a ring road, enables through traffic to bypass the inner-city area.

The Plaza de Armas is quite large and austere, and surrounded by fine colonial buildings, including the cathedral on the south-east side. Two main streets, Hidalgo and Juárez, meet at the plaza, at the western corner of the cathedral. This junction is a dividing point for Saltillo's street addresses; with your back to the main façade of the cathedral, up the hill on Hidalgo (to the left) is Sur (south), downhill to the right is Norte (or Nte, north), behind you is Oriente (or Ote, east), and in front of you is Poniente (or Pte, west). It's only approximate, however, as the street grid is not exactly north-south.

Two blocks away is the Plaza Acuña, with the market building on its north side. It's smaller, less formal and usually more lively than the Plaza de Armas. The Alameda Zaragoza is a large, shady public park, reached by going down Victoria from the west side of the Palacio Gobierno.

The bus station is in the south-west side of town, where Allende meets the periférico – a 15-minute bus ride away. The train station is a 20-minute walk west of the centre; from the west side of the alameda, turn left on E Carranza and walk three long blocks to the station on your right.

Information

Tourist Office Inconveniently located on the corner of Coss and Allende, about 1.5 km north of town, the tourist office (☎ (84) 12-40-50) sometimes gives out an excellent map but it's often out of stock. It's open from 9 am to about 5 pm Monday to Saturday.

Money You can change cash and travellers' cheques at the banks near the Plaza de Armas, all of which have ATMs. There are casas de cambio on Acuña and Aldama which stay open till 6 pm Monday to Friday, and 1 pm on Saturday.

Post & Telecommunications The post office, open Monday to Friday and on Saturday morning, is at Victoria Pte 223, a few doors from the Hotel Urdiñola. There are also postal facilities near the tourist office and at the bus station. There are Ladatel phones at the Café Victoria at Padre Flores 221, and also at the post office and bus station.

Plaza de Armas
In contrast to the bustling Plaza Acuña, the Plaza de Armas is spotlessly clean and relatively tranquil, with street vendors seemingly banished.

Cathedral Built between 1746 and 1801, the cathedral of Santiago dominates the plaza and has one of Mexico's finest Churrigueresque façades, with columns of elaborately carved pale grey stone. It's particularly splendid when lit up at night. Inside, the transepts are full of gilt ornamentation – look for the human figure perched on a ledge at the top of the dome. You can go up the smaller of the two towers if you ask the man in the religious goods shop underneath.

Palacio de Gobierno On the opposite side of the plaza is the state government headquarters. You are free to wander into the elegant building, which has a fountain in its inner courtyard.

Los Portales This is the colonnade under the arches on the north-east side of the plaza. It harbours a few café-restaurants and a video-games parlour.

Instituto Coahuilense de Cultura This art gallery is on the south-west side of the plaza. It puts on temporary exhibitions, changing every month or so; some are very good so it's worth looking in. It's open from 9 am to 7 pm Tuesday to Saturday, and it's free.

Alameda
The park, full of shady trees and pathways, has a children's playground and is a favourite spot for young couples. A pond at the southern end has an island shaped like a map of Mexico.

Museo de las Aves
This is a new museum devoted to the birds of Mexico. Most of the exhibits are birds stuffed and mounted in convincing dioramas of their natural habitat. There are special sections on nesting, territoriality, birdsongs, navigation, endangered species etc. Over 670 species of bird are displayed, along with bird skeletons, fossils and eggs. If you're even remotely interested in birds, and don't mind seeing them stuffed, this museum is definitely worth a visit. It's between Hidalgo and Allende, a few blocks south of the plaza, and is open from 10 am to 6 pm Tuesday to Saturday, 11 am to 6 pm on Sunday. Entry is 5 pesos for adults, 2 pesos for children and students and 10 pesos for families; it's free on Wednesdays.

Plaza México
Also known as the Fortín de Carlota (Carlota's Fortress), this spot in the south of the city offers the best views over Saltillo and the surrounding country. It's a 10-minute bus ride from the city centre (see Getting Around later in this section).

Festivals
Saltillo has some interesting festivals:

Día del Santo Cristo de la Capilla On 6 August, the Day of the Holy Christ of the Chapel brings dance groups from different parts of Coahuila to Saltillo to honour a holy image.
Feria Anual The city holds its annual fair in mid-August.
Feria de San Nicolás Tolentino On 10 September in Ramos Arizpe, about 10 km north of Saltillo on the Monterrey road, there are dances starting before dawn, and a parade at about 5 pm.

Places to Stay – bottom end
Hotel Hidalgo (☎ (84) 14-98-53), at Padre Flores 217, is very basic with shared bathrooms, but cheap at around 35 pesos. *Hotel*

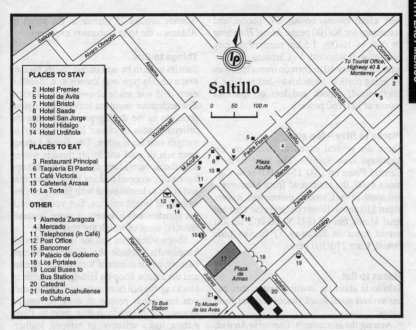

PLACES TO STAY

2 Hotel Premier
5 Hotel de Avila
7 Hotel Bristol
8 Hotel Saade
9 Hotel San Jorge
10 Hotel Hidalgo
14 Hotel Urdiñola

PLACES TO EAT

3 Restaurant Principal
6 Taquería El Pastor
11 Café Victoria
13 Cafetería Arcasa
16 La Torta

OTHER

1 Alameda Zaragoza
4 Mercado
11 Telephones (in Café)
12 Post Office
15 Bancomer
17 Palacio de Gobierno
18 Los Portales
19 Local Buses to Bus Station
20 Catedral
21 Instituto Coahuilense de Cultura

Saltillo

0   50   100 m

To Tourist Office,
Highway 40 &
Monterrey

Plaza
Acuña

Plaza
de
Armas

To Bus
Station

To Museo
de las Aves

De Avila (another sign calls it Hotel Jardín)
(☎ (84) 12-59-16), at Padre Flores 211 in the
north-west corner of Plaza Acuña, is not
much better, with singles/doubles at 40/50
pesos.

The *Hotel Bristol* (☎ (84) 10-15-02), on
Aldama Pte 405, is a definite improvement,
with clean, quiet rooms with bathrooms and
hot water, at 45/55 pesos. Better still is the
Hotel Saade (☎ (84) 12-91-20), with a range
of rooms from 65 pesos up to 85/100 pesos
with TV and phone.

There are two cheap hotels over the road
from the bus station. The *Hotel Central* is
comfortable enough, with singles/doubles
for 30/40 pesos. The *Hotel Siesta* is similar,
at 35/50 pesos, 20 pesos extra for TV. Opinions vary about which is better or worse.

Places to Stay – middle
A place which offers lots of character and
good value is the *Hotel Urdiñola* (☎ (84)
14-09-40), at Victoria Pte 207. There's a

sparkling white lobby with a wide stairway
that sweeps up to a stained-glass window.
Rooms face a long courtyard with trees and
a fountain. For big, clean rooms with TV, you
pay 85 pesos for one person, 95 pesos for
two. The hotel also has a pleasant, if not
cheap, dining room, helpful staff and car
parking just down the street. The only draw-
back is that they sometimes ask for a deposit
of more than a night's lodging when you
check in (any balance refundable).

The *Hotel Premier* (☎ (84) 12-10-50), at
Allende Nte 566, is comfortable enough but
without the atmosphere of the Urdiñola.
Singles/doubles are also 85/95 pesos. The
top downtown establishment is the *Hotel San
Jorge* (☎ (84) 12-22-22) at M Acuña Nte
240. It's modern and well maintained, with
a restaurant, rooftop swimming pool, and
clean, comfortable rooms with all the conve-
niences for 165/187 pesos a single/double.

A new place, across from the bus station,
is the *Hotel Saltillo* (☎ (84) 17-22-00), with

very clean rooms, colour TV, phone, and restaurant for 80/100 pesos. *Motel Huizache* (☎ (84) 16-10-00), 1.5 km north of the city centre at Boulevard V Carranza 1746 – where highway 40 to Torreón meets highway 57 going north to Monclova – has parking, a playground, a pool and lots of spacious rooms at 121/160 pesos.

Places to Stay – top end

There are several excellent motels on the highways near Saltillo. The *Best Western Eurotel Plaza* (☎ (84) 15-10-00) is at Carranza 4100, the main road from Monterrey, just south of the Carranza monument; it costs about 210 pesos. Even classier is the *Camino Real Motor Inn* (☎ (84) 30-00-00), six km out of town on highway 57 to San Luis Potosí, from 270/360 pesos.

Places to Eat

Saltillo is short on inviting restaurants but has several good snack places and fast-food joints.

Among the restaurants, *Cafetería Arcasa*, on Victoria next door to Hotel Urdiñola, does reasonable Mexican and Western food. A comida corrida costs around 18 pesos. For breakfast, egg dishes start at 6 pesos, and a meat dish for dinner will run at about 20 pesos. There's a selection of local and national newspapers to help you pass the time.

Restaurant Principal (☎ 14-33-84), at Allende Nte 710 four blocks down the hill from Plaza Acuña, specialises in cabrito, with various goat bits from 17 to 30 pesos. If neither of these places grabs you, try the more expensive restaurants in the hotels Urdiñola or San Jorge.

Pastelería y Cafetería Daisy Queen (☎ 13-33-49), at Allende Nte 515A, does cakes, fruit yoghurt, hamburgers etc. A package of hot dog, fries and a refresco costs 8.50 pesos. For tacos, try *Taquería El Pastor*, on Plaza Acuña on the corner of Aldama and Padre Flores. Delicious tacos al pastor (beefsteak) are 6 pesos for four, tacos de lengua (tongue) cost 8 pesos for four. For truly delicious sandwiches try *La Torta*, on

Allende around 75 metres to the south of Aldama – the torta Cubana is excellent.

Things to Buy

Saltillo used to be so famous for its sarapes that a certain type was known as a 'Saltillo' even if it was made elsewhere in Mexico. The technique involves leaving out colour fixatives in the dyeing process so that the different bands of colour *lloran* ('weep' or merge) into each other. The finest sarapes have silk or gold and silver threads woven into them. Nowadays the local workshops have sadly stopped making all-wool sarapes and seem to be obsessed with jarring combinations of bright colours. But you can still get ponchos and blankets in more 'natural' colours, some of which are pure wool.

Shops where you can see these and other handicrafts include the Silver & Sarape Factory, on the corner of Victoria and Acuña, and the Sarape Shop on Hidalgo, a couple of blocks up the hill from cathedral. In the latter you can watch people at work on treadle looms. The Mercado Juárez, next to Plaza Acuña, has a selection of sarapes, leatherwork and other souvenir stuff.

Getting There & Away

Air Aeroméxico (☎ 14-10-11), at Allende Nte 815, and TAESA have flights between Mexico City and Saltillo. The airport is 12 km north-east of town on highway 40; take a Ramos Arizpe bus (1 peso) or a taxi.

Bus Saltillo's modern bus station is on the periférico south-west of town. It has postal facilities, phones, and a left-luggage service (2 pesos per hour). First-class lines have their ticket desks to the right-hand end of the booking hall as you enter; 2nd class is to the left.

Lots of buses serve Saltillo but few start their journeys here. This means that on some buses, 2nd-class ones in particular, you often can't buy a ticket until the bus has arrived and they know how much room there is for new passengers. It also means that, on 2nd-class buses, you may have to stand for a while. Try to buy your tickets early and board the bus first or better still, take a 1st-class bus. The 1st-class lines include Transportes del Norte, Omnibus de México and Tres Estrellas de Oro. Anáhuac and Transportes Frontera have 1st and 2nd-class buses, while Linea Verde has 2nd-class buses only. Destinations include:

Aguascalientes – 492 km, 6½ hours; 1st (58 pesos) and 2nd-class buses (50 pesos)

Durango – 530 km, seven hours; 1st (65 pesos) and 2nd-class buses

Guadalajara – 681 km, nine to 11 hours; 1st (87 pesos) and 2nd-class buses (75 pesos); try to get a bus on a direct route, and avoid the ones that go via Aguascalientes

Matamoros – 408 km, seven hours; five 1st-class buses daily (51 pesos)

Matehuala – 261 km, four hours; 1st (30 pesos) and 2nd-class buses (27 pesos)

Mazatlán – 848 km, 10½ hours; deluxe (140 pesos) and 1st-class buses (103 pesos)

Mexico City (Terminal Norte) – 880 km, 11 hours; 1st (105 pesos) and 2nd-class buses (91 pesos)

Monterrey – 85 km, 1½ hours; frequent 1st-class buses (10 pesos)

Nuevo Laredo – 315 km, 4½ hours; nine 1st-class buses daily (51 pesos)

Parras – 160 km, 2½ hours; 2nd-class buses (16 pesos)

Reynosa – 310 km, five hours; five 1st-class buses daily (41 pesos)

San Luis Potosí – 455 km, five hours; 1st (52 pesos) and 2nd-class buses (43 pesos)

Tampico – 598 km, 10 hours; 1st-class buses at 7 and 10 pm (77 pesos)

Torreón – 277 km, 3½ hours; hourly de paso buses (33 pesos)

Zacatecas – 363 km, five hours; 1st (43 pesos) and 2nd-class buses

Buses also go to Chihuahua, Ciudad Acuña, Ciudad Juárez, Ciudad Victoria, Monclova, Querétaro and Tepic.

Train Saltillo train station (☎ 14-95-84) is just off E Carranza, south-west of the city centre. El Regiomontano (train No 71 or 72) is the best train; it has sleeping cars and a dining car and leaves at 10.15 pm for San Luis Potosí (5¾ hours away) and Mexico City (12 hours), and at 5.45 am for Monterrey (2½ hours).

The Águila Azteca (train Nos 1 and 2), with primera especial, primera regular and segunda clase seats, leaves Saltillo at 11.55

pm for Monterrey (2½ hours) and Nuevo Laredo (7½ hours); and at 2.35 am for San Luis Potosí (7½ hours), San Miguel Allende (10½ hours), Querétaro (12 hours) and Mexico City (16½ hours).

There are also trains to Piedras Negras at 8.15 am.

The station is open for ticket sales from 8 am to 2 pm. Fares to Mexico City are: primera especial, 101 pesos; primera regular, 55 pesos; segunda clase, 35 pesos. Sleeping accommodation costs 210 pesos for one person in a camarín, 419 pesos for an alcoba for two, and 734 pesos for an alcoba for four.

Car Saltillo is a junction of major roads in each direction. Highway 40 going north-east to Monterrey is a good four-lane road, and there are no tolls until you reach the Monterrey bypass. Going west to Torreón (277 km), highway 40D is an overpriced toll road (80 pesos) and most of it is two-lane. The alternative route, highway 40, is free and quite OK. Highway 57 goes north to Monclova and Piedras Negras and south to Mexico City (852 km). Outside Saltillo, it climbs to over 2000 metres, then descends gradually along the Altiplano Central to Matehuala (260 km) and San Luis Potosí (451 km) through barren but often spectacular country – there are still some dangerous two-lane stretches on this road. To the south-west, highway 54 crosses high, dry plains towards Zacatecas (363 km) and Guadalajara (680 km).

Getting Around

To reach the city centre from the bus station, go outside and turn right – minibus Nos 9 or 10 will take you to the centre for less than a peso. Get off at the cathedral or the main downtown bus stop on the corner of Allende and Treviño. To reach the bus station from the city centre, catch a No 9 on the corner of Aldama and Hidalgo.

From the train station, go out to the big road, E Carranza, turn left and walk three blocks, then turn right on Madero for one block to the alameda. Cross the park to Victoria and walk up the hill three or four blocks to the centre of town.

PARRAS

• *pop: 38,000* • *alt: 1580 metres*

This small town, 160 km west of Saltillo off the Torreón road, is an oasis in the Coahuilan desert. Underground streams carrying water from the Sierra come to the surface here as springs, supplying water to irrigate the grapevines for which the area is famous, and giving the town its full name – Parras de la Fuente. Parras was the birthplace of revolutionary leader Francisco Madero, and an obelisk on Calle Arizpe honours his memory.

Information

The Parras tourist office (☎ (842) 2-02-59) is on the roadside 4.5 km north of town. Open daily from 9 am to 5 pm, it has friendly, helpful staff and, if you're lucky, a map and some brochures.

Things to See & Do

The first winery in the Americas was established in Parras in 1597, a year before the town itself was founded. The winery, now called **Casa Madero**, is about two km north of town on the road going to the main highway. It's open every day from 9 am to 1 pm and 2 to 5 pm. Tours are conducted on the hour, and you can buy wine and brandy.

The town has an old aqueduct, some colonial buildings, and three *estanques* (large pools where water from the springs is stored) which are great for swimming. The **Iglesia del Santo Madero**, on the southern edge of town, sits on the plug of an extinct volcano. It's a good little climb, and there's an expansive view from the top.

Festival

The week-long grape fair, the Feria de la Uva, in early August, includes religious celebrations on Assumption Day and traditional

dances by descendants of early Tlaxcalan settlers.

Places to Stay

Hotels include *La Siesta* (☎ (842) 2-03-74), on Acuña, which is basic but OK at 35/40 pesos for one/two people. *Hotel Posada Bravo* (☎ (842) 2-13-09), at Nicolás Bravo 53, is better, though some rooms are very dark, at 40/70 pesos. On Zaragoza, a quiet street east of the centre, *Hotel Posada Santa María* (☎ (842) 2-01-00) is clean, friendly, and quite nice but just a little overpriced at 70/100 pesos.

The best place in town is *Hotel Posada Santa Isabel* (☎ (842) 2-05-72), at Madero 514, with comfortable rooms around a quiet garden for 100/120 pesos. *Hotel Rincón del Montero* (☎ (842) 2-05-40), a few km north of town, is a resort with golf, tennis, swimming and horse riding, which charges from 220 pesos for one or two people.

Places to Eat

Sweets made of sugar, nuts and milk are a local speciality – get some at one of the *dulcerías* (sweet shops) before you leave. There are quite a few cafés and restaurants with more substantial fare. *Restaurant Rincón del Recuerdo*, on Cayuso opposite the parish church, has a very nice atmosphere and good food, and is not too expensive.

Getting There & Away

Parras is easy to reach by car – at La Paila, about halfway between Saltillo and Torreón, turn off the highway and go 27 km south. Only 2nd-class buses go to Parras; there are nine daily from Saltillo (2½ hours, 16 pesos) and six daily from Torreón (also 16 pesos). A 1st-class bus might drop you at La Paila, from where you could get a local bus.

Central Pacific Coast

The central Pacific coast, stretching from Mazatlán to Acapulco, contains some of Mexico's principal beach resorts – Mazatlán, Puerto Vallarta, Zihuatanejo-Ixtapa and Acapulco – and some lesser-known but beautiful spots.

Coastal highways make travel easy up and down the coast, with frequent buses and easy driving, while several other highways connect the coast to the mountainous interior of the country. Due to the high volume of tourists, both national and international, air services to this region are also frequent and convenient.

MAZATLÁN
• *pop: 450,000*

Situated just 13 km south of the Tropic of Cancer, Mazatlán is Mexico's principal Pacific coastal fishing, shrimp and commercial port, as well as one of its prime Pacific beach resorts. Affectionately known as the 'Pearl of the Pacific', Mazatlán is famous for its beaches and its sportfishing, with over 7000 billfish (sailfish and marlin) tagged and released each year. Another of the city's distinctions is that El Faro, high on a peak at the south end of the city, is the second-highest lighthouse in the world; you can climb up to it for a magnificent 360-degree view of the city and coast. The sunset is especially beautiful in Mazatlán, as the sun sets behind three offshore islands which gradually change colour and fade into silhouettes, finally disappearing into the starry night.

Mazatlán has both 'old' and 'new' sections. The original city occupies a wide peninsula at the south end of town, with a newer tourist-oriented zone on the beaches arcing northward and a 17-km beachside boulevard passing fine beaches, hotels, restaurants, nightspots and other attractions.

The name Mazatlán means 'place of deer' in Nahuatl. In pre-Hispanic times it was populated by Totorames, who lived by hunting, gathering, fishing and agriculture. Though a

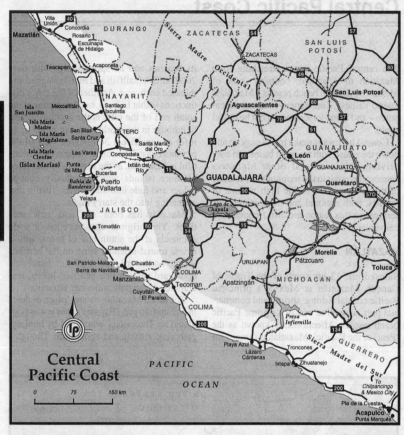

Central Pacific Coast

0   75   150 km

PACIFIC

OCEAN

group of 25 Spaniards led by Nuño de Guzmán officially founded a settlement here on Easter Sunday in 1531, almost three centuries elapsed before a permanent colony was established, in the early 1820s. During this time the Spanish referred to the area as 'Islas de Mazatlán' due to its many estuaries and lagoons, punctuated by hills.

Orientation

Old Mazatlán is concentrated on a wide peninsula at the southern end of the city, bound on the west by the Pacific Ocean and on the east by the Bahía Dársena. At the south end

of the peninsula are El Faro (the lighthouse), Mazatlán's sportfishing fleet, the terminal for ferries to La Paz, and Isla de la Piedra, which is not really an island but a long peninsula with a popular beach. On the east side are the shrimp, fishing and commercial docks, and the train station. The centre of the 'old' city is the cathedral, on the Plaza Principal.

A beachside boulevard runs along the Pacific side of the peninsula past Olas Altas, Mazatlán's first 'tourist' beach back in the 1950s, around some rocky outcrops and north around the wide arc of Playa del Norte to the Zona Dorada (Golden Zone), beginning at the traffic circle at Punta Las Gaviotas and heading a few blocks north. The Zona Dorada and the large hotels stretching north along the beaches comprise the city's major tourist zone.

Information

Tourist Office The Coordinación General de Turismo (☎ (69) 85-12-20/21, fax 85-12-22) in the large concrete Banco de México building at Paseo Olas Altas 1300, on the corner of Mariano Escobedo, has free maps and plenty of information; it's open Monday to Friday from 8 am to 7 pm. Two free twice-monthly bilingual tourist newspapers, *Pacific Pearl* and *La Puerta*, are available at the tourist office and at many places around the Zona Dorada.

Money Banks and casas de cambio are plentiful in both old and new Mazatlán. The banks will exchange money Monday to Friday from 9 am to noon; the casas de cambio are open at longer hours. If you plan to change money at the banks, get there early because long lines are common.

American Express (☎ 13-06-00) at Local 4 in the Plaza Balboa shopping centre, on Camarón Sábalo in the Zona Dorada, is open Monday to Friday from 9 am to 6 pm, Saturday 9 am to 1 pm.

Post & Telecommunications The main post office is on Juárez on the east side of the Plaza Principal; it's open Monday to Friday from 8 am to 7 pm, Saturday 9 am to 1 pm. Telecomm, with telegraph, telex, fax and coin telephones, is next door; it's open Monday to Friday from 8 am to 8 pm, Saturday and holidays 8 am to noon. Computel, with long-distance telephone and fax, is open 24 hours every day; it's at Aquiles Serdán 1512, one block east of the cathedral. Another 24-hour branch of Computel is in the central bus station, along with another post office and Telecomm office. Collect phone calls are not possible from the Computel offices but you can make them from Ladatel phones, which are plentiful around the city.

Foreign Consulates Foreign consulates in Mazatlán are usually open Monday to Friday from 9 am to 1 pm. They include:

Canada
  Hotel Playa Mazatlán, Zona Dorada (☎ 13-76-20)
France
  Jacarandas 6, Colonia Loma Linda (☎ 85-12-28, 82-85-52)
Germany
  Hotel Las Flores (☎ 13-51-00)
Netherlands
  Camarón Sábalo 6300 (☎ 13-51-55)
USA
  Rodolfo T Loaiza 202, opposite Hotel Playa Mazatlán, Zona Dorada (☎ 16-58-89, emergency ☎ 17-23-75)

Other consulates include those of Belgium, Italy, Denmark, Finland, Brazil and Paraguay; the tourist office has a complete list.

Emergency The Tourist Police (☎ 14-84-44) can help you with any problem you might have.

Things to See

The heart of 'old Mazatlán' is the large 19th-century **cathedral** at Juárez and 21 de Marzo, with its high twin yellow-and-blue towers and beautiful statues inside. It faces the **Plaza Principal**, with lush trees and a bandstand. The **Palacio Municipal** is on the west side of the plaza and the **mercado** is two blocks north on Juárez between Valle and Ocampo, behind the cathedral.

Two blocks west and two blocks south of the Plaza Principal, **Plazuela Machado** at Carnaval and Constitución is another historic plaza. The centre of a large historic area of Mazatlán that has been undergoing a massive renewal programme in recent years, the attractive plaza is surrounded by historic buildings. Half a block south of the plaza on the Carnaval walking street, the historic three-tiered **Teatro Angela Peralta**, built in 1865 and reopened in 1992 after a five-year restoration project, is open for viewing every day from 9 am to 6 pm; admission costs 3 pesos. Cultural events of all kinds are presented at the theatre (see Entertainment); check the kiosk at the front for announcements.

Four blocks towards Playa Olas Altas, the **Museo Arqueológico** at Sixto Osuna 76 is an interesting little archaeological museum, open Tuesday to Sunday from 10 am to 1 pm and 4 to 7 pm; admission is 6 pesos (children free). On Paseo Olas Altas are a couple of monuments: the **Escudo de Sinaloa y Mazatlán** (state and city shield) at the south end of the cove and the **Monumento al Venado** at the north end, representing Mazatlán's Nahuatl name meaning 'place of deer'. Around the rocky outcropping on the sea side of the **Cerro de la Nevería** are a couple of other monuments, including the

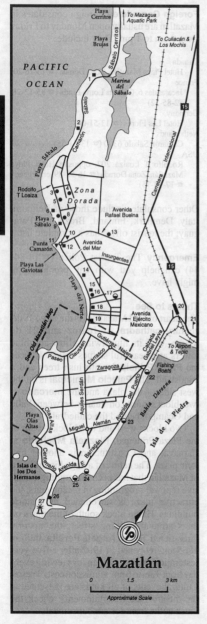

Mazatlán

0   1.5   3 km

Approximate Scale

PLACES TO STAY

1 Camino Real
2 El Cid Mega Resort
6 Hotel Playa Mazatlán
9 Hotel Los Sábalos
12 Hotel San Diego
14 Marco's Suites
15 Hotel del Sol
18 Hotel Sands
19 Hotel Aguamarina

PLACES TO EAT

3 No Name Café
10 McDonald's
11 Bora Bora
15 Señor Frog's

OTHER

3 Centro de Artesanías
4 Aleluya's Republic
5 Sea Shell City
7 Canadian Consulate
8 US Consulate
9 Joe's Oyster Bar
11 Valentino's Disco
13 Plaza de Toros
16 Acuario Mazatlán
17 Central Bus Station
20 Train Station
21 Club de Golf Campestre
22 Lanchas to Isla de la Piedra
23 Cruise Ship Docks
24 Lanchas to Isla de la Piedra
25 Ferry Terminal
26 Sportfishing Fleet (*Yate Fiesta*)
27 El Faro

Monumento a la Continuidad de la Vida (Monument to the Continuity of Life), with a human couple being led by a group of leaping dolphins. Also along here is the platform from where the **high divers** *(clavadistas)* dive into a crevasse with the ocean swells rising and falling inside, similar to the more famous high divers at La Quebrada in Acapulco; here it's a shorter dive and it can only be done when the water is high (there's no fixed schedule, as there is in Acapulco).

From Paseo Olas Altas the seafront road goes north around the rocky outcrops to Playa del Norte, and south around more rocky outcrops to **El Faro**, which at 157 metres above sea level is the second-highest lighthouse in the world (the highest is Gibraltar); you can climb the hill up to El Faro for a spectacular view of the city and coast. Mazatlán's sportfishing fleet, the ferry to La Paz and the *Yate Fiesta* are docked in the marina to your left (east) as you walk towards El Faro on the causeway, which was built in the 1930s to join the El Faro island to the mainland. Back north, beside the beach on Playa del Norte at the junction of Avenida del Mar and Avenida Gutiérrez Najera, the large **Monumento al Pescador** is another well-known symbol of Mazatlán.

North of the centre, a block inland from Playa del Norte, the **Acuario Mazatlán** on Avenida de los Deportes has 52 tanks with 150 species of fresh and saltwater fish and other creatures; sea lion and bird shows are presented four times daily. It's open every day from 9.30 am to 6.30 pm; admission is 18 pesos (children 8 pesos). In the Zona Dorada, the **Centro de Artesanías** on Rodolfo T Loaiza is a large complex with a wide variety of Mexican handicrafts; you can see some of the craftspeople at work in the rear patio. It's open Monday to Saturday from 9 am to 6 pm. Nearby, also on Rodolfo T Loaiza, **Sea Shell City**, with thousands of shells large and small, is open every day from 9 am to 8 pm. North of the city, past the marina (actually two marinas: the Marina El Cid and Marina del Sábalo), **Mazagua** is a family aquatic park with water toboggans, a

swimming pool with waves and other entertainment open every day from 9 am to dark.

Beaches Sixteen km of steadily improving beach go north from old Mazatlán and past the Zona Dorada. Nearest to the centre of town, **Playa Olas Altas** is a small beach in a small cove, where tourism began in Mazatlán in the 1950s.

Playa del Norte begins just north of old Mazatlán and arcs towards Punta Las Gaviotas, where a traffic circle and the anomalous white Valentino's disco complex on the rocky point mark the south end of the Zona Dorada. At this point the beach's name changes to **Playa Las Gaviotas**. As it continues through the Zona Dorada the name changes again, to **Playa Sábalo**. This is the serious tourist zone, with an army of tourists and an equal army of peddlers *(ambulantes)* selling everything from jewellery to hammocks. The beach becomes less populated as it continues past the marina and changes name again, first to **Playa Brujas** and then to **Playa Cerritos**. The Sábalo buses pass along all of these beaches, right up to Playas Brujas and Cerritos at the end of the line.

Activities

Boat Trips The island beach most visited by locals, **Isla de la Piedra** (Stone Island), is actually a long, thin peninsula whose tip is opposite El Faro, at the south end of the city. To get there, take a small boat across to the island from one of two docks – there's one near the intersection of Calzada Gabriel Leyva, Avenida del Puerto, Avenida Zaragoza and Calzada Gutiérrez Najera, and another at the extreme south end of the city, a block or two east of the ferry terminal. The boats operate every day, departing every 10 minutes from around 6 am to 6 pm; the cost is 3 pesos for the five-minute ride to the island. When you land, walk through the village to the far side of the island and a long, pale sandy beach bordered by coconut groves. The beach has several palapa restaurants, three of which hold dances on Sunday afternoon. A walk along the beach to your right (towards El Faro) brings you to another beach at **Isla Chivos**.

Other boat trips go to less crowded beaches on **Isla Venados**, the middle one of Mazatlán's three offshore islands (the other two are **Isla Lobos**, on the right if you're seeing them from the shore, and **Isla de Pájaros** on the left). Boats depart from the Aqua Sport Centre (☎ 13-33-33, ext 341) at the El Cid Resort on Avenida Camarón Sábalo every day at 10 am, noon and 2 pm, with the last boat returning at 4 pm; the cost is 50 pesos for the return trip, including snorkelling gear – the island is good for snorkelling and diving.

The *Yate Fiesta* (☎ 85-22-37, 81-71-54), also at the foot of El Faro, offers a daily three-hour cruise passing near the three offshore islands, the shrimp and fishing fleet docks, the white rocks, the sea lion colony (winter only), the beaches and more; the cost is 40 pesos per person. Bookings can be made directly or with travel agents.

Sports The Aqua Sport Centre at the El Cid Resort is the place to go for water sports, including scuba diving, water-skiing, jet skis, Hobie cats, parasailing, the 'banana', boogie boards and more. Jet skis, sailboats and boogie boards can also be hired at the Camino Real Hotel, north of El Cid. Surfing is popular at Punta Las Gaviotas and Playa Olas Altas; local surfers also head down the coast to San Blas for the 'world's longest wave'.

Mazatlán is famous for its sportfishing – especially for marlin, swordfish, sailfish, tuna and dorado (dolphinfish). The operator most often recommended is the Bill Heimpel Star Fleet (☎ (69) 82-38-78, 82-26-65; fax 82-51-55), with 35 years' experience and a fleet of 15 boats in the marina next to their office at the foot of El Faro; many other sportfishing operators also have offices along here. It's a good idea to make fishing reservations as far in advance as you can in the winter high season. Mazatlán is also popular for hunting; contact the Hermanos Aviles (☎ 81-60-60, 83-59-36).

On land, there's golf at the Club de Golf Campestre (☎ 80-02-02), south of town on highway 15, and at the El Cid Resort (☎ 83-

33-33), north of the centre. Tennis can be played at the Racquet Club Gaviotas (☎ 83-59-39, 81-31-86) in the Zona Dorada, the Club Deportiva Reforma (☎ 83-12-00/10) on Rafael Buelna, at the El Cid Resort and at almost any of the large hotels north of the centre.

Walking Mazatlán has many great places for walking. Besides 16 km of beautiful beaches, with a broad Malecón along the entire stretch of Playa del Norte offering a fine view of the three offshore islands, there's also the seafront road around the rocky outcrops on the north and south sides of the Olas Altas cove, the climb up the hill to El Faro and, to the south-east, the long, deserted beach of Isla de la Piedra.

Language Courses The Centro de Idiomas (☎ 82-20-53, fax 85-56-06) at Domínguez 1908 offers Spanish courses with a maximum of six students per class. You can begin any Monday and study for as many weeks as you like; registration is every Saturday morning from 9 am to noon. The weekly cost is 300/396 pesos for two/four hours of instruction daily, with discounts if you sign up for four weeks. Homestays can be arranged with a Mexican family; the cost is 390/450 pesos per week for a shared/individual room, including three meals a day (30 days' advance notice required).

Organised Tours

Marlin Tours (☎ 13-53-01, 14-26-90) offers a three-hour city tour (45 pesos); a high-country tour to the foothill villages of Concordia and Copala (107 pesos); a jungle tour to Teacapan, south of the city (137 pesos); and a tour to Rosario and Agua Caliente villages (76 pesos). Travel agents can arrange these and other tours.

Festivals & Annual Events

Celebrated with music, dancing, parades, other events and general revelling for the entire week leading up to Ash Wednesday in February or March, Carnaval (Mardi Gras) is celebrated in Mexico most flamboyantly in Veracruz and Mazatlán. The entire city goes on a week-long partying spree, with people pouring in from around the country for the festivities. Be sure to reserve a hotel room in advance, as the city fills up. On the morning of Ash Wednesday the party ends abruptly, and people go to church to receive ash marks on their foreheads for the first day of Lent. A Torneo de Pesca (fishing tournament) for sailfish, marlin and dorado is held around 1 June. On 12 December the day of the Virgen de Guadalupe is celebrated at the cathedral, with children brought to the cathedral in costumes.

Places to Stay – bottom end

Camping Mazatlán has a number of trailer parks, all of them on or near the beaches at the north end of town. Those listed with 's/n' means there is no street number in the address.

Las Palmas Trailer Park
> Avenida Camarón Sábalo 333 (☎ (69) 13-53-11, 13-64-24), 66 spaces

Mar Rosa Trailer Park
> Avenida Camarón Sábalo s/n (☎ (69) 13-61-87), 80 spaces

San Bartolo Trailer Park
> Avenida Camarón Sábalo s/n (☎ (69) 13-57-65), 40 spaces

Playa Escondida Bungalows & Trailer Park
> Calzada Sábalo Cerritos 999 (☎ (69) 88-00-77, fax 82-02-85), 236 spaces, 19 beachfront bungalows

Holiday Trailer Park
> Calzada Sábalo Cerritos s/n (☎ (69) 13-25-78), 234 spaces

Las Canoas Trailer Park
> Calzada Sábalo Cerritos s/n (☎ (69) 14-16-16), 60 spaces

Maravillas Trailer Park
> Calzada Sábalo Cerritos (☎ (69) 14-04-00), 26 spaces

La Posta Trailer Park
> Avenida Rafael Buelna (☎ (69) 83-53-10), 180 spaces

Hotels – old Mazatlán The *Hotel del Río* (☎ (69) 82-46-54), at Juárez 2410 on the corner of Quijano, has 30 rooms at 25/30 pesos for singles/doubles, 40 pesos for a family room. It's clean and friendly, and a very good deal. So is *Hotel Joncol's* (☎ (69)

81-21-31, 81-31-51) at B Domínguez 2701 Nte, a block from the beach, where clean, bright rooms with balconies are 40 pesos with fan, 60 pesos with air-con. The *Hotel San Jorge* (☎ (69) 81-36-95) on Aquiles Serdán on the corner of Gastelum, also a block from the beach, is old but clean, with 15 singles/doubles at 42/50 pesos.

The *Hotel Central* (☎ (69) 82-18-66), B Domínguez 2 Sur on the corner of Ángel Flores, four blocks from Playa Olas Altas and four blocks from the cathedral, has 67 clean rooms with air-con at 69/73 pesos for singles/doubles, 80 pesos for larger rooms. If you're at the end of your economic rope, the *Hotel México* (☎ (69) 81-38-06) at México 201 on the corner of Aquiles Serdán, a block from the beach, is very basic, but clean; the cost is 25 pesos per room.

The hotels on Playa Olas Altas, breathing the character and nostalgia of a simpler era, have been well maintained and refurbished. They are some of the most charming hotels in town. The *Hotel La Siesta* (☎ (69) 81-26-40) at Olas Altas 11, above the El Shrimp Bucket restaurant, has a courtyard full of tropical plants and the Bucket's tables. The 51 rooms are large and clean, with air-con, and some have balconies with a view over Olas Altas; singles/doubles are 60/75 pesos. The *Hotel Belmar* (☎ (69) 85-11-11/12, fax 81-34-28) at Olas Altas 166 Sur has a swimming pool, bar, parking and 150 rooms, 60 with private balconies overlooking Olas Altas beach, some with TV and air-con. All rooms are 60 pesos per night.

Hotels – Playa del Norte & Zona Dorada

Places on Avenida del Mar are opposite Playa del Norte, with frequent buses heading north and south. The *Hotel del Sol* (☎ (69) 85-11-03, fax 85-26-03) at Avenida del Mar 800, near the aquarium, has a swimming pool, parking and 21 rooms with air-con at 75 pesos; rooms with kitchen cost 110 pesos. *Marco's Suites* (☎ (69) 83-59-98) at Avenida del Mar 1234 has a swimming pool, parking and 12 rooms with kitchen and air-con at 60/100 pesos for two/four people. The *Hotel San Diego* (☎ (69) 83-57-03) at Avenida del

Mar and Rafael Buelna s/n, on the traffic circle near Valentino's Disco at the south end of the Zona Dorada, has 62 rooms with air-con and TV at 50 pesos. It's a noisy but convenient location, and the hotel offers parking.

Places to Stay – middle

Two good mid-range hotels are on Avenida del Mar, opposite Playa del Norte and convenient to buses. The *Hotel Sands* (☎ (69) 82-00-00, 82-06-00, toll-free 91-800-69-808; fax 82-10-25) at Avenida del Mar 1910 has a swimming pool, restaurant/bar, parking and 87 rooms, some with a sea view, with balcony, air-con, fan, satellite colour TV and refrigerator; singles/doubles are 88/110 pesos from May to November, 140 pesos from December to April. The *Aguamarina Hotel* (☎ (69) 81-70-80/85, fax 82-46-24) at Avenida del Mar 110, remodelled in 1994, is another good place, with a swimming pool, restaurant/bar, parking, travel agency and 125 rooms with air-con, cable TV and phone; regular rooms are 149 pesos, junior suites are 176 pesos.

Places to Stay – top end

Mazatlán has many luxurious top-end hotels on the beaches north of town. Most imposing is the 1000-room *El Cid Mega Resort* (☎ (69) 13-33-33, toll-free in the USA 1-800-525-1925; fax 14-31-11) on Avenida Camarón Sábalo s/n; rates range from 215 to 1980 pesos per night in the low season (mid-April to December), higher in winter. Another good choice is the *Camino Real* (☎ (69) 13-11-11, fax 14-03-11) at Punta del Sábalo s/n, with 169 rooms at 330/360 pesos with ocean/marina view. Air/hotel packages may make room rates cheaper; travel agents should have information on all of Mazatlán's big luxury hotels.

Places to Eat

Pastelería Panamá at Juárez 1702 on the corner of Canizales, diagonally opposite the rear of the cathedral, is a popular air-con restaurant, café and bakery open every day from 7 am to 10 pm; several other branches are found around town. *Restaurant Joncol's* at Ángel Flores 608, two blocks west of the Plaza Principal, is a simple air-con family restaurant with economical meals, including a comida corrida for 16 pesos; it's open every day from 7 am to 10.30 pm. *Restaurant Doney*, at Mariano Escobedo 610 at the intersection of 5 de Mayo, is an air-con restaurant with a covered patio serving tasty traditional Mexican food daily from 8 am to 10.30 pm.

For seafood, the *Restaurant Los Pelícanos*, on the corner of Paseo Claussen and Virgilio Uribe, is a tiny open-air thatched-roof place with some of the freshest, cheapest and tastiest seafood in Mazatlán: shrimp for 20 pesos, breaded fish fillet for 12 pesos, ceviche for 5 to 10 pesos, or a whole kilo of charcoal broiled fish (Pescado Zarandeado) for just 25 pesos. It has a great view of the entire arc of Playa del Norte, catches any sea breezes coming by, and is altogether a delightful place, open every day from 9 am to 6 pm. *Mariscos Camichin*, another seafood restaurant nearby at Paseo Claussen 97 on the corner of Nelson, is a popular open-air patio restaurant with a jolly crowd eating delicious seafood under cool shady trees; it's open every day from 10 am to 10 pm, with live music from 2 pm on.

The Plazuela Machado is a peaceful place to enjoy a meal or snack. In the daytime, the pleasant *La Casa de Ana* at Constitución 515 on the north side of the plaza serves vegetarian meals inside, or under trees on the sidewalk; a comida corrida costs 14 pesos. It's open Monday to Friday from 8 am to 5 pm, Sunday 8 am to 6 pm, with a Sunday buffet for 15 pesos. In the evening, *El Rincón de los Hartistas* at Constitución 517, serving tacos and other simple Mexican fare at sidewalk tables, is a popular gathering spot for artists and cultural types; say hello to Mirla and Rosa, the cheerful proprietresses. Next door, the *Café Pacífico* has sidewalk tables for enjoying a beer on the plaza. Or get a *raspado* (flavoured shaved ice) from *El Tunel*, opposite the Teatro Angela Peralta.

Olas Altas also has several good restaurants to choose from. *El Shrimp Bucket* at Olas Altas 11 is one of Mazatlán's best

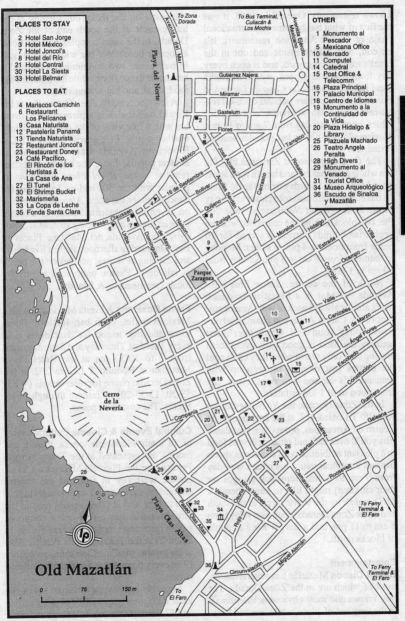

PLACES TO STAY
2 Hotel San Jorge
3 Hotel México
7 Hotel Joncol's
8 Hotel del Río
21 Hotel Central
30 Hotel La Siesta
33 Hotel Belmar

PLACES TO EAT
4 Mariscos Camichin
6 Restaurant
   Los Pelícanos
9 Casa Naturista
12 Pastelería Panamá
13 Tienda Naturista
22 Restaurant Joncol's
23 Restaurant Doney
24 Café Pacífico,
   El Rincón de los
   Hartistas &
   La Casa de Ana
27 El Tunel
30 El Shrimp Bucket
32 Marismeña
33 La Copa de Leche
35 Fonda Santa Clara

OTHER
1 Monumento al
   Pescador
5 Mexicana Office
10 Mercado
11 Computel
14 Catedral
15 Post Office &
   Telecomm
16 Plaza Principal
17 Palacio Municipal
18 Centro de Idiomas
19 Monumento a la
   Continuidad de
   la Vida
20 Plaza Hidalgo &
   Library
25 Plazuela Machado
26 Teatro Angela
   Peralta
28 High Divers
29 Monumento al
   Venado
31 Tourist Office
36 Museo Arqueológico
36 Escudo de Sinaloa
   y Mazatlán

Old Mazatlán

0   75   150 m

known restaurants. Opened in 1963, it was the first of what has become an international chain of Carlos Anderson restaurants. It's air-con, with tables inside and out in the hotel's tropical courtyard, and is open every day from 6 am to 11 pm, with a marimba band in high season. *La Copa de Leche* and *Fonda Santa Clara* are popular open-air restaurant/bars with sidewalk and interior tables, open every day from 7 am to 11 pm. *Marismeña* is a newer but popular seafood restaurant.

The *Casa Naturista* at Zaragoza 807 Pte is a wholegrain bakery and health food store, open Monday to Saturday from 8 am to 8 pm. Its baked goods are also sold closer to the city centre at the *Tienda Naturista* at Valle 208 Pte, one block behind the cathedral, where a vegetarian comida corrida is served for 10 pesos from noon to 4 pm; it's open Monday to Saturday from 8 am to 8 pm, Sunday from 10 am to 1 pm.

North of the centre, *Señor Frog's* on Avenida del Mar is a Mazatlán landmark that's almost always packed with Americans. Part of the Carlos Anderson chain, it advertises 'lousy food and warm beer', but actually the food is good (just overpriced) and the beer only warm when they can't cool the bottles fast enough to keep up with demand. It's air-con and open every day from noon until 1 am or later.

In the Zona Dorada, the *No Name Café* at Rodolfo T Loaiza 417, at the entrance to the Centro de Artesanías, boasts 'the best damn ribs you'll ever eat' and other delicious food in a pleasant ambience with an air-con sports bar and a tropical patio; it's open every day from 9 am to 2 am. Homesick gringos (or their children) might like to know there's a *McDonald's* by the traffic circle at the south end of the Zona Dorada, open every day from 8 am to 11 pm, and a *Burger King* a couple of blocks north.

Entertainment

Bars & Discos Mazatlán has several discos, most of which are in the Zona Dorada. The best known and most obvious is *Valentino's*, in the very out-of-place, white-washed fairy-tale castle on the rocky outcropping at the traffic circle at the south end of the Zona Dorada. In the same complex is *Bora Bora*, a popular beachfront bar with a sandy volleyball court, two swimming pools and a beachside dance floor, while the *Bali Hai* has food, drink and big-screen videos.

A few doors north, *Joe's Oyster Bar* at the Hotel Los Sábalos is a pleasant beachfront bar with a fine view of the offshore islands. Further north, *El Caracól* at the El Cid Resort on Avenida Camarón Sábalo is another popular disco. The beachside restaurant/bar at the *Hotel Playa Mazatlán* is popular with the 30s-and-up age group for dancing under the stars. *Aleluya's Republic* on Avenida Camarón Sábalo is another popular dining and dancing spot, as is *Señor Frog's* on Avenida del Mar (see Places to Eat). On Sunday afternoon there's live music and dancing at several palapas on the beach at Isla de la Piedra, patronised mostly by locals (see Beaches & Islands).

Fiesta Mexicana A Fiesta Mexicana, with a Mexican buffet, open bar, folkloric floorshow and live music for dancing is held every Tuesday, Thursday and Saturday night from 7 to 10.30 pm at the Hotel Playa Mazatlán at Rodolfo T Loaiza 202 in the Zona Dorada; phone for reservations (☎ 83-53-20, 13-53-20) or reserve through travel agents. The cost is 80 pesos.

Cultural Events & Cinema Cultural events of all kinds – concerts, opera, theatre and more – are presented at the Teatro Angela Peralta near the Plazuela Machado; a kiosk on the walkway in front of the theatre announces current and upcoming cultural events here and at other venues around the city. Mazatlán has a fine opera company, whose principals present operas (often in Spanish) at the Teatro Angela Peralta. Also at the theatre, the Cine Club sponsors quality films every Saturday at 5 or 6 pm; admission is free.

Mazatlán has several cinemas; check the local daily newspapers *El Sol del Pacífico* and *El Noroeste* for movie listings and other events. Films are often shown in English, with Spanish subtitles.

If you get a chance, try to hear a rousing traditional Banda Sinaloense – a loud, boisterous multipiece brass band unique to the state of Sinaloa and particularly Mazatlán – sometime during your visit.

Bullfights & Charreadas At the bullring on Rafael Buelna, inland from the Zona Dorada traffic circle, bullfights are held on Sunday at 4 pm from Christmas to Easter ; the Sábalo-Cocos bus will drop you there. Tickets are sold at the bullfight office (☎ 84-16-66) beside Valentino's disco on the traffic circle. Charreadas are held at the Lienzo charro ring in Colonia Juárez; contact the tourist office for dates.

Getting There & Away

Air The Mazatlán international airport is 20 km south of the city. Airlines serving this airport, and their direct flights (all with connections to other places), include:

Aero California
    Hotel El Cid, Local 30 & 31, Avenida Camarón Sábalo (☎ 13-20-42) – La Paz, Mexico City
Aeroméxico
    Avenida Camarón Sábalo 310, Local 1 & 2 (☎ 14-11-11, 14-16-21; airport 82-34-44) – Ciudad Juárez, Durango, Guadalajara, La Paz, León, Los Mochis, Mexico City, Tijuana, Torreón
Alaska Airlines
    Airport (☎ 85-27-30/31, toll-free reservations 95-800-426-0333) – Los Angeles, San Francisco
Aviación del Noroeste
    Avenida Camarón Sábalo 310, Local 12 (☎ 14-16-09/21, airport 82-48-94) – Ciudad Obregón, Culiacán, Durango, Hermosillo
Delta
    Airport (☎ 82-13-49, 81-06-09) – Los Angeles
Mexicana
    Paseo Claussen 101-B (☎ 82-77-22, airport 82-28-88) – Denver, Mexico City, Puerto Vallarta
Saro
    Avenida del Mar 1111, Local 5, beside Hotel Posada Don Pelayo (☎ 86-14-74) – Monterrey, Torreón
TAESA
    Centro Comercial Plaza San Ángel, Local 3 (in front of Banamex), Avenida Camarón Sábalo 353 (☎ 14-38-55/33) – Culiacán, Durango

Bus The central bus station (Central de Autobuses) is just off Avenida Ejército Mexicano on Avenida de los Deportes, about three blocks inland from the beach. The station has a cafeteria and left-luggage area, a post office, a Telecomm office with telegram, telex and fax, and a 24-hour Computel office with telephone and fax. First and 2nd-class bus lines operate from separate halls in the main terminal; buses to small towns nearby (Concordia, Copala, Rosario etc) operate from a smaller terminal behind the main terminal.

Buses from the 1st-class hall go north and south along the coast on highway 15, and inland over the mountains to Durango. They include:

Durango – 319 km, seven hours; nine daily by Transportes Chihuahuenses-Transportes del Norte (42 pesos)
Guadalajara – 569 km, eight hours; 19 daily by Transportes del Pacífico, 13 daily by Tres Estrellas de Oro-Elite (64 to 100 pesos)
Mexico City (Terminal Norte) – 1085 km, 18 hours; 11 daily by Transportes del Pacífico, five daily by Tres Estrellas de Oro-Elite (139 to 189 pesos)
Puerto Vallarta – 459 km, seven hours; once daily by Tres Estrellas de Oro-Elite (66 pesos), or take a bus to Tepic, from where buses depart frequently for Puerto Vallarta
Tepic – 290 km, 4½ to five hours; same as to Guadalajara (36 pesos)
Tijuana – 1882 km, 25 hours; 17 daily by Transportes del Pacífico, two daily by Tres Estrellas de Oro-Elite (226 pesos)

Buses from the 2nd-class hall go to all the places listed above, plus:

San Blás – 290 km, five hours; twice daily by Transportes Norte de Sonora, twice daily by Tres Estrellas de Oro-Elite (30 pesos)
Santiago Ixcuintla – 235 km, four hours; five daily by Transportes Norte de Sonora, once daily by Transportes del Pacífico (28 pesos)

Train The train station (☎ 84-67-10) is on the eastern outskirts of the city; tickets go on sale an hour before each departure. See the schedule in the Guadalajara section of the Western Central Highlands chapter.

Boat Ferries operate between Mazatlán and La Paz, Baja California. The ferry (trans-bordador) terminal (☎ (69) 81-70-20/21, toll-free 91-800-69-696) is at the south end of town; the office is open every day from 8 am to 2 pm. Tickets are sold the morning of departure, or several days in advance. See the La Paz section in the Baja California chapter for schedule and fare details.

Getting Around

To/From the Airport Colectivo vans and a bus, cheaper than taxis, operate from the airport to town, but not from town to the airport. A taxi to the airport costs 40 pesos.

Bus Local buses operate every day from around 5.30 am to 10.30 pm; the cost is 1.10 pesos. A good network of frequent buses provides convenient service to anywhere around the city you'd want to go. Routes include:

Sábalo – from the mercado to the beach via Juárez, then north on Avenida del Mar to the Zona Dorada and further north on Avenida Camarón Sábalo. Sábalo buses have mixed names (Sábalo-Centro, Sábalo-Cocos etc)
Playa Sur – south along Avenida Ejército Mexicano near the bus station and through the city, passing the mercado, then the ferry terminal and El Faro
Villa Galaxia – same route as the Playa Sur bus, but doesn't continue past the mercado
Insurgentes – south along Avenida Ejército Mexicano and through the city to the mercado, continuing on to the train station
Cerritos-Juárez – shuttles between the train station and the city centre

To get into the centre of Mazatlán from the bus terminal, go to Avenida Ejército Mexicano and catch an Insurgentes, Villa Galaxia, Playa Sur or any other bus going to your right if the bus terminal is behind you. Alternatively, you can walk a couple of blocks from the bus station to the beach and take a Sábalo-Centro bus heading south (left) to the centre.

Pulmonías & Taxis After buses, *pulmonías* are the cheapest way to get around Mazatlán. The word 'pulmonía' literally means 'pneumonia'; in Mazatlán it is also a small open-air vehicle similar to a golf cart. Taxis are the most expensive way to get around; look for those marked 'eco-taxi', which are cheaper. Pulmonías, taxis and eco-taxis are all plentiful around town. Be sure to agree on the price for the ride before you climb in; it never hurts to bargain.

Car & Motorbike Car-rental agencies include Aga (☎ 14-44-05, 13-40-77), Alal (☎ 16-45-89), Arrendadora Las Gaviotas (☎ 13-60-00, airport 82-40-00), Avis (☎ 14-00-40/50), Hertz (☎ 13-60-60, airport 85-08-45) and National (☎ 13-60-00, 13-61-00). As always, it pays to shop around for the best rates.

Several small companies hire small motorbikes for getting around town. Two places near the traffic circle in the Zona Dorada are Hot Wheels and Moto Rentas Nayeli (☎ 82-62-69). Both have the motorbikes lined up beside the road; similar line-ups with similar vehicles and prices can be seen along Avenida del Mar. You need a driver's licence to hire a bike; any type of licence will do.

AROUND MAZATLÁN

Several small, picturesque colonial towns in the Sierra Madre foothills make pleasant day trips from Mazatlán. **Concordia**, founded in 1565, has an 18th-century church with a baroque façade and elaborately decorated columns, and hot mineral springs nearby; the village is known for its manufacture of high-quality pottery and handcarved furniture. It's about a 45-minute drive east of Mazatlán; head south on highway 15 for 20 km to Villa Unión, turn inland on highway 40 (the highway to Durango) and go another 20 km to reach Concordia. **Copala**, 40 km past Concordia on highway 40, and also founded in 1565, was one of Mexico's first mining towns; it still has its colonial church (built in 1748), colonial houses and cobblestoned streets.

Rosario, 76 km south-east of Mazatlán on highway 15, is another colonial mining town, founded in 1655. Its most famous feature is the gold-leaf altar in its church, Nuestra Señora del Rosario. **Cosalá**, a beautiful colonial mining village in the mountains north of Mazatlán, was founded in 1550 and has a 17th-century church, a historical and mining museum in a colonial mansion on the plaza, and two simple but clean hotels. Various attractions nearby include **Vado Hondo**, a balneario with a large natural swimming pool and three waterfalls, 15 km from the town; **La Gruta México**, a large cave 18 km from the town; and the **Presa El Comedero** reservoir, 20 km from the town, with hired rowboats for fishing. To get to Cosalá, go north on highway 15 for 161 km to the turnoff (opposite the turnoff for La Cruz de Alota on the coast) and then go 54 km up into the mountains.

Buses to all these places depart from the small bus terminal at the rear of the main bus station in Mazatlán. Alternatively, there are tours (see Organised Tours in the Mazatlán section).

SANTIAGO IXCUINTLA

This town is mainly of interest as the jumping-off point for Mexcaltitán (see section following). It is not a tourist town but it does have the **Centro Huichol** (☎ (323) 5-11-71), a handicrafts centre where Huichol Indians make their distinctive arts and crafts, at Calle 20 de Noviembre 10 Pte on the outskirts of town towards Mexcaltitán. You can stop there to see them at work and buy their products. About 60 Huichols work there from October to June, but in summer most go to the mountains to plant crops. The centre is open every day from 9 am to 6 pm.

Getting There & Away

Turn off highway 15, 63 km north-west of Tepic, to get to Santiago Ixcuintla; the town is eight km west of the turnoff. Buses to Santiago leave frequently from Tepic and Mazatlán. Santiago Ixcuintla has two 2nd-class bus stations, Transportes del Pacífico and Transportes Norte de Sonora (TNS), a block apart. Services from these stations include:

La Batanga – 37 km, one hour; four daily by Transportes del Pacífico (5 pesos)

San Blás – 62 km, 1¼ hours; four daily by Transportes del Pacífico (8.50 pesos); buses also by TNS

Tepic – 70 km, one hour; every half-hour, 5 am to 7.45 pm, by Transportes del Pacífico (8 pesos); every half-hour, 5.30 am to 8.30 pm, by TNS (8 pesos)

MEXCALTITÁN

• *pop: 2000*

A small, ancient island village, Mexcaltitán is far from the tourist trail but a fascinating place to visit. Tourism has scarcely touched the island, though it does have a few facilities and a captivating small museum. To get there you must take a *lancha* (motorised wooden boat) through a large mangrove lagoon full of fish, shrimp and aquatic birds.

Mexcaltitán is sometimes called the 'Venice of Mexico' because the streets occasionally become flooded when the water level of the lagoon rises after heavy rains near the end of the rainy season, around September to November. At that time the high cement sidewalks turn the dirt streets into canals and all travel is done in canoes. If the water level rises very high, families may sleep in canoes tied to the posts in their houses, too!

Be sure to bring plenty of insect repellent, as the lagoon is a breeding ground for mosquitoes.

History

Mexcaltitán has a long, enthralling history. It is believed that this small island, originally called Aztlán, was the homeland of the Aztec people. From here (around 1116) they departed on a generations-long pilgrimage, eventually ending at Tenochtitlán in 1325, when the wandering Aztecs found the symbol that signified they had come to their 'promised land' – an eagle with a serpent in its claws, perched upon a cactus. Today this symbol of Mexico appears on the national flag.

Orientation & Information

The island is a small oval, about 350 metres from east to west, 400 metres from north to south, and about one km around the perimeter. At the centre of the island is a plaza with a gazebo in the centre, a church on the east side, the museum on the north side and a restaurant on the west side. The hotel is a block behind the museum.

All the telephones on the island go through one operator, who has a switchboard in the sitting room of her house. From outside the island, phone the switchboard (☎ (323) 2-02-11, 2-01-98) and ask for the extension you want.

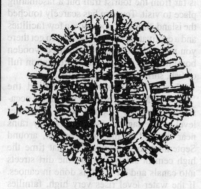

An aerial view of Mexcaltitán

Things to See & Do

The **Museo Aztlán del Origen** on the north side of the plaza is small but enchanting. Among the exhibits are ancient objects and a fascinating long scroll, the Codice Ruturini, telling the story of the peregrinations of the Aztec people, with notes in Spanish. The museum is open every day from 9 am to 1 pm and 3 to 6 pm; admission is free.

You can arrange for **boat trips** on the lagoon for bird-watching, fishing and sightseeing – every family has one or more boats.

The **billiards hall** beside the church provides about the only thing to do in the evening so it's naturally very popular.

Festivals

The Fiesta de San Pedro Apostol, patron saint of fishermen, is celebrated on 29 June with statues of St Peter and St Paul taken out into the lagoon in decorated lanchas for the blessing of the waters. Festivities start around 20 June and lead up to the big day.

Semana Santa is celebrated in a big way. On Good Friday a statue of Christ is put on a cross in the church, then taken down and carried through the streets. On the Día de Independencia on 16 September Father Hidalgo's Cry of Independence is re-enacted at the church on the plaza, with fiestas and celebrations.

Places to Stay & Eat

Mexcaltitán has one hotel and two restaurants. The *Hotel Parra* (☎ (323) 2-02-11, 2-01-98, ext 128) at Calle Venecia 5 is a simple place with eight rooms. Rooms with one double bed are 50 pesos, with two beds 70 pesos, with three beds 90 pesos, and with four beds (and air-con) 120 pesos.

Both of the island's restaurants specialise in seafood. The *Restaurant El Camarón* on the plaza, opposite the church, is open every day from around 9 am to 10 pm. The more attractive *Restaurant Alberca*, on stilts over the water, has a great view of the lagoon and catches any breezes coming by. It's open every day from around 8 am to 9 pm.

Getting There & Away

Getting to Mexcaltitán involves first getting to Santiago Ixcuintla (see the section earlier). From there, take a bus or colectivo taxi to La Batanga, a small wharf from where lanchas depart for Mexcaltitán. Taxis depart more frequently than buses.

Colectivo lanchas depart from La Batanga at 8 and 10.30 am, 12.20, 1, 4 and 5.30 pm for the 15-minute ride to Mexcaltitán; the cost is 2 pesos per person. Returning from the island to La Batanga, they depart at 7.45 and 10.15 am, 12.45, 2.45 and 5.15 pm. If you miss the colectivo lancha you can hire a whole lancha for 20 pesos. The lanchas connect with buses coming to/from Santiago Ixcuintla.

There is another way to reach Mexcaltitán that does not involve going through Santiago Ixcuintla, but through Tuxpan instead. However this route is less well made, isolated and dangerous.

SAN BLAS
• *pop: 8000*

The small fishing village of San Blas, 70 km north-west of Tepic, was an important Spanish port from the late 16th to the 19th century. The Spanish built a fortress here to protect their *naos* (trading galleons) from marauding British and French pirates. Today's visitors come to enjoy isolated beaches, exotic birds, a thick tropical jungle, estuaries and a navigable river. The town is known for its bird-watching opportunities and you can't help but notice a great many birds.

San Blas has the amenities of a small beach resort town – a few hotels, restaurants, grocery stores etc provide the essential needs. Its character remains principally that of a typical Mexican village, however, not that of a tourist town.

One suspects that the real reason the village hasn't been developed as a major resort is due to the proliferation of *jejenes* (sandflies), tiny gnat-like insects with huge appetites for human flesh that leave you with an indomitable itch. Abundant mosquitoes compete with the jejenes for your last drop of blood. Neither insect bothers you during the daylight hours, but around sunset they appear from nowhere to attack. Be sure to bring plenty of insect repellent and to accept a hotel room only if it has good window screens with no holes or tears.

Orientation
San Blas sits on a tongue of land bound on the west and south-west by El Pozo estuary, on the east by the San Cristóbal estuary, and on the south by Playa El Borrego and the Pacific Ocean. The only road into and out of the village is the 36-km paved road coming in from highway 15. Near San Blas, a coast road heads out around the Bahía Matanchén to Santa Cruz village and on to Puerto Vallarta.

Just west of the bridge over the San Cristóbal estuary, the road passes the Cerro de la Contaduría and the ruins of the old Spanish fortress. At the Pemex station, the road splits into three branches with the centre one, Juárez, becoming the main street of San Blas and leading to the village's small zócalo. Calle Batallón de San Blas runs along the western side of the zócalo and leads south to the beach; this could be considered the village's other main street. Everything in the village is within walking distance.

Information
Tourist Office The small Delegación Municipal de Turismo (☎ (321) 5-02-67, fax 5-00-01) at Juárez 65, half a block from the zócalo and roughly opposite the McDonald's restaurant, has free maps and information about the town. It's open Monday to Friday from 10 am to 2 pm and 6 to 8 pm. On weekends there's an information kiosk at the entrance to town.

Money The only place in town to change money is the Banamex bank on Juárez, about a block east of the zócalo. It's open Monday to Friday from 8 am to 2.30 pm but changes money only from 8 am to noon. It also has an ATM.

Post & Telecommunications The post office, on Sonora on the corner of Echeverría, is open Monday to Friday from 8 am to 1 pm and 3 to 5 pm, Saturday and holidays from 8 am to noon. Next door, SCT Telégrafos, with telegraph, telex and fax, is open Monday to Friday from 8 am to 2 pm.

A Lada caseta with telephone and fax at the south end of the zócalo, opposite the church, is open Monday to Saturday from 8.30 am to 3 pm and 5.30 to 10 pm, Sunday 8 am to 1 pm and 6 to 10 pm.

Travel Agency There's no official travel agency in San Blas, but Federico Rodríguez at the Posada Portola (see Hotels) reserves and sells air tickets and provides current information on the Mazatlán-La Paz ferry.

Things to See & Do
Beaches San Blas's attractions are its natural wonders – the surrounding beaches and jungles. The nearest beach is **Playa El Borrego** at the end of Calle Batallón de San Blas.

The best beaches are south-east of the village around the Bahía de Matanchén, starting with **Playa Las Islitas**, seven km from San Blas. A paved road that bears south from the road to highway 15 passes the dirt road to Playa Las Islitas and continues past the Oceanography School and through the village of Aticama, eight km from Playa Las Islitas. Between Playa Las Islitas and Aticama the beach is wonderfully isolated; it's very popular with surfers, who claim that the world's longest wave sweeps ashore here. Further on, **Playa Los Cocos** and **Playa Miramar**, also popular for surfing, have palapas under which you can lounge and drink the milk of a fresh coconut.

Boat Trips A boat trip through the jungle to the freshwater spring of **La Tovara** is one of the highlights of a visit to San Blas. Small boats (maximum of 10 passengers), departing from the embarcadero (jetty) to your left as you cross the bridge into town, go up the Estuario San Cristóbal to the spring, and beyond to visit the Cocodrilario (crocodile farm). A jungle full of exotic birds and lush, tropical plants and trees surrounds you. Bring your swimsuit to swim at La Tovara. The price is fixed at 100 pesos for one to four people, 20 pesos for each extra person, and the trip takes three hours. A shorter boat trip to La Tovara can be made from a point further up the river; this takes two hours and costs 80 pesos for one to four people, 15 pesos for each extra person.

A 4½ to five-hour bird-watching trip up the Estuario San Juan to the **Santuario de Aves** (Bird Sanctuary), leaving from the same embarcadero by the bridge, costs 240 pesos for one to four people, 50 pesos for each extra person. Other boat trips from San Blas include a trip to **Piedra Blanca** to visit the statue of the Virgin, to **Estero Casa Blanca** to gather clams, to **Isla del Rey**, which is just across from San Blas, and to **Playa del Rey**, a 20-km beach on the other side of Isla del Rey. Unfortunately it's not advisable for a woman to go to Playa del Rey alone.

You can make an interesting trip further afield to **Isla Isabel**, also called Isla María Isabelita, four hours north-west of San Blas by boat. The island is a bird-watcher's paradise, with colonies of many species, and there's a volcanic crater lake on the island. Isla Isabel is only about 1.5 km long and one km wide, with no facilities, so you must be prepared for self-sufficient camping. Permission is required to visit the island; the boatmen can arrange it.

Festivals & Annual Events
Every year on 31 January the anniversary of the death of Father José María Mercado is commemorated with a parade, a demonstration march by Mexican marines and fireworks in the zócalo. Mercado lived in San Blas in the early 19th century and helped Miguel Hidalgo with the independence movement by sending him a set of old Spanish cannons from the village.

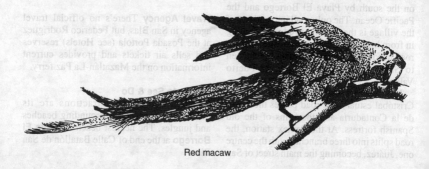

Red macaw

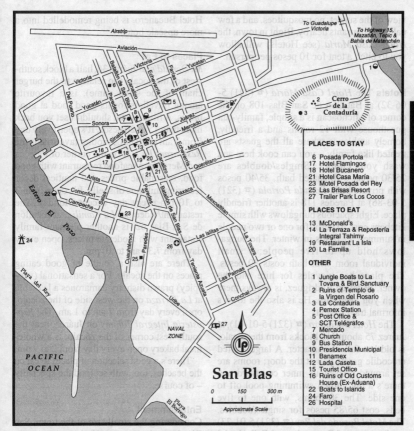

San Blas

0   150   300 m

Approximate Scale

PLACES TO STAY

6 Posada Portola
17 Hotel Flamingos
18 Hotel Bucanero
21 Hotel Casa María
23 Motel Posada del Rey
25 Las Brisas Resort
27 Trailer Park Los Cocos

PLACES TO EAT

13 McDonald's
14 La Terraza & Repostería
    Integral Tahimy
19 Restaurant La Isla
20 La Familia

OTHER

1 Jungle Boats to La
   Tovara & Bird Sanctuary
2 Ruins of Templo de
   la Virgen del Rosario
3 La Contaduría
4 Pemex Station
5 Post Office &
   SCT Telégrafos
7 Mercado
8 Church
9 Bus Station
10 Presidencia Municipal
11 Banamex
12 Lada Caseta
15 Tourist Office
16 Ruins of Old Customs
    House (Ex-Aduana)
22 Boats to Islands
24 Faro
26 Hospital

On 3 February, festivities for San Blas, the town's patron saint, are an extension of those begun on 31 January, with dance and musical presentations. Carnaval is celebrated the weekend before Ash Wednesday, while the Virgen de Fátima is honoured on 13 May. Día de la Marina is celebrated on 1 June with burro races on the beach, sporting events, dances and partying. Surfing competitions take place in summer; contact the tourist office for dates. A party called the Convivencia de la Fraternidad is put on by the tourist office on 27 December for all the foreign visitors in town.

Places to Stay

Considering its small size, San Blas has a fair selection of places to stay. Look at any room before you accept it and be sure that the window screens are without holes or tears.

Camping The *Trailer Park Los Cocos* (☎ (321) 5-00-55) is near Playa El Borrego, almost at the end of Calle Batallón de San Blas, in a grassy area with lots of trees. Beware of the mosquitoes that swarm at sunset. At Playa Los Cocos, about a 15-minute drive from town, the attractive beachfront *Playa Amor* trailer park has a fine view of the sunset, no mosquitoes, and a few palapa restaurants nearby. Right in town, the *Hotel Casa María* (see Hotels) will allow you to pitch a tent for 10 pesos per person.

Hotels The *Hotel Casa María* (☎ (321) 5-06-32) at Batallón de San Blas 108 on the corner of Michoacán is a simple, family-run guesthouse with 12 rooms and a friendly, homely ambience where all the guests are treated like family – you can cook here and wash your clothes. Singles/doubles are 25/30 pesos with shared bath, 35/40 pesos with private bath. *Posada Portola* (☎ (321) 5-03-86) at Paredes 118 is another friendly place. Eight spacious bungalows with simple kitchens cost 70 pesos for one or two people in summer, 77 pesos in winter. The bungalows hold up to five people; a small individual room with bath costs 30 pesos. The place has bicycles for hire and the owner, Federico Rodríguez, is always there when you need him. He is also the town's informal travel agent.

The *Hotel Bucanero* (☎ (321) 5-01-01), at Juárez 75 about 1½ blocks from the zócalo, is old but full of character. A large stuffed crocodile greets you at the door; rooms are set around a spacious inner courtyard and there's a big garden swimming pool off to one side. The 30 rooms, with one to five beds, cost 65/85 pesos for singles/doubles. The *Motel Posada del Rey* (☎ (321) 5-01-23) on the corner of Campeche and Callejón del Rey is a simple, clean, relatively modern place with a small swimming pool and a family ambience. Rooms cost 90 pesos with fan, 110 pesos with air-con.

The *Las Brisas Resort* (☎ (321) 5-01-12, 5-04-80; fax 5-03-08) at Paredes 106 Sur has a large garden, a swimming pool, an air-con restaurant/bar, and 42 large rooms with air-con, satellite TV and other luxuries. Singles/doubles are 180/210 pesos most of the year, 187/242 pesos in high season from 15 December to 15 April, with breakfast included. They also have some more expensive suites with kitchens. The *Hotel Flamingos* at Juárez 105 Pte, just past the

Hotel Bucanero, is being remodelled into a more upscale hotel.

Places to Eat
McDonald's, at Juárez 36, half a block south-west of the zócalo (no relation to the burger chain of the same name), is a favourite among travellers for its good food at good prices. A filling meal shouldn't set you back more than 15 or 20 pesos. It's open every day from 7 am to 10 pm. Another favourite is the *Restaurant La Isla* on the corner of Paredes and Mercado, a seafood restaurant with good food, reasonable prices and nautical decor featuring millions of shells. It's open from 2 to 10 pm every day except Monday. The restaurant/video bar *La Familia*, at Batallón de San Blas 62, is another pleasant family restaurant with moderate prices, open every day from 7.30 am to 10 pm.

There are also a couple of good eating places on the zócalo. For a sensational (very spicy) prawn dish, try camarones a la diabla at *La Terraza* on the west side of the zócalo, open every day from 7 am to 1 am. The *Repostería Integral Tahimy* on Juárez, near the south-west corner of the zócalo, is a whole-meal bakery open every day from 2 to 9 pm.

There's a good selection of places to eat on the beaches, too, with seafood the speciality – of course.

Entertainment
Considering the small size of the town, San Blas has quite an array of places to go to in the evening. For dancing there's the *Disco Lafitte* on Juárez beside the Hotel Bucanero; *Mike's Place* over McDonald's restaurant, also on Juárez; *Disco Fancy* on Canalizo, half a block back from the zócalo and bus station; and *El Herradero* on Batallón de San Blas. Pleasant bars include *El Mirador*, upstairs at the Motel Posada del Rey, and *El Coco Loco*, by the Trailer Park Los Cocos near Playa El Borrego.

Getting There & Away
The bus station is on the corner of Sinaloa and Canalizo, at the north-east corner of the zócalo. Buses depart for Tepic (1½ hours, 8

pesos, 12 daily), Puerto Vallarta (3½ hours, 22 pesos, two daily), Guadalajara (five hours, 38 pesos, one daily) and Mazatlán (five hours, 30 pesos, two daily).

Getting Around

Bicycles can be rented from the Posada Portola for 30 pesos per day, whether or not you're a guest there.

Buses to Santa Cruz, the village at the far end of Bahía de Matanchén, leave from the corner of Sinaloa and Paredes several times daily, with additional Sunday buses; the schedule is posted at the tourist office. The buses serve all the villages and beaches on Bahía de Matanchén, including Matanchén, Playa Las Islitas, Aticama, Playa Los Cocos and Playa Miramar. You can also take a taxi.

TEPIC

• *pop: 100,000*

Capital of the state of Nayarit, Tepic is the bustling small capital of a small state. It's the crossroads for highways 15 and 200, the two Pacific coast highways, and is where highway 15 turns inland towards Guadalajara and Mexico City.

Many travellers pass through the outskirts of Tepic by car, bus or train without stopping to visit. It doesn't take long to visit the city but there are a few things of interest, including a large neo-Gothic cathedral and several museums. Huichol Indians, who live in the mountains of Nayarit, can often be seen in town wearing colourful traditional clothing. Huichol artwork is sold in shops and in front of the cathedral, and displayed in museums. The climate in Tepic is noticeably cooler than on the coast.

Orientation

The Plaza Principal, with the large cathedral at the east end, is the heart of the city. Running south from the cathedral, Avenida México is the city's main street. Six blocks south of Plaza Principal is another plaza, Plaza Constituyentes. Along Avenida México between these two plazas are banks, the tourist office, restaurants, the state museum and other places of interest. The bus

and train stations are on the eastern and south-eastern outskirts of the city. Peripheral roads make it possible to drive or bus through Tepic without entering the city centre.

Information

Tourist Offices The Secretaría de Turismo (☎ (321) 2-95-45/6/7, fax 2-95-46) at Avenida México 34 Sur, with free maps and information on Tepic and the state of Nayarit, is open Monday to Friday from 9 am to 9 pm. Another tourist office, the Coordinación Consultiva Estatal de Turismo (☎ (321) 4-10-17, ☎ /fax 3-92-03) at the Ex-Convento de la Cruz at the foot of Avenida México, is open Monday to Friday from 9 am to 2 pm and 6 to 8 pm. If you're interested in the area and you can read Spanish, ask for the paperback *Estado de Nayarit Guía Turística*, a guidebook about Nayarit.

Money Banks and casas de cambio are found on Avenida México Nte between the two plazas.

Post & Telecommunications The post office, on Durango between Allende and Morelos, is open Monday to Friday from 8 am to 7 pm, Saturday 8 am to noon. Telecomm, with telegram, telex and fax, is at Avenida México 50 Nte, on the corner of Morelos; it's open Monday to Friday from 8 am to 7 pm (money wires/giros till 4 pm), Saturday 8 to 11 am. Long-distance telephone and fax services are available at the Cafetería Moderna at Hidalgo 61-4 Ote.

Post and Telecomm offices, and Ladatel phones, are also found in the bus station.

Things to See

The large **cathedral** on the Plaza Principal opposite the Palacio Municipal was dedicated in 1750; the towers were completed in 1885.

The 18th-century **Templo y Ex-Convento de la Cruz de Zacate** is at the end of Avenida México on the corner of Calzada del Ejército, about two km south of the cathedral. It was here in 1767 that Father Junipero Serra organised the expedition that resulted

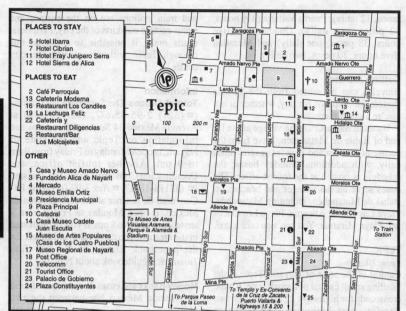

PLACES TO STAY

5   Hotel Ibarra
7   Hotel Cibrian
11 Hotel Fray Junípero Serra
12 Hotel Sierra de Alica

PLACES TO EAT

2   Café Parroquia
13 Cafetería Moderna
16 Restaurant Los Candiles
19 La Lechuga Feliz
22 Cafetería y
    Restaurant Diligencias
25 Restaurant/Bar
    Los Molcajetes

OTHER

1   Casa y Museo Amado Nervo
3   Fundación Alica de Nayarit
4   Mercado
6   Museo Emilia Ortiz
8   Presidencia Municipal
9   Plaza Principal
10 Catedral
14 Casa Museo Cadete
    Juan Escutia
15 Museo de Artes Populares
    (Casa de los Cuatro Pueblos)
17 Museo Regional de Nayarit
18 Post Office
20 Telecomm
21 Tourist Office
23 Palacio de Gobierno
24 Plaza Constituyentes

Tepic

in his founding of a chain of Spanish missions in the Californias; you can visit the room where he stayed. The church attached to the convent has a cross of age-old plants growing from the ground on one side, which is said to have appeared miraculously and to have lived on untended.

On Plaza Constituyentes, a few blocks south on Avenida México, the **Palacio de Gobierno** has murals inside. In the southwest section of the city is the large **Parque Paseo de la Loma**.

Cultural events are held at the **Fundación Alica de Nayarit** at Veracruz 256 Nte, half a block north of the Plaza Principal; you can stop by any time to find out the schedule and see the exhibit of antique furnishings and historical photos of Tepic. It's open Monday to Friday from 7 am to 2 pm and 4 to 7 pm, Saturday 7 am to 2 pm.

Museums The **Museo Regional de Nayarit** at Avenida México 91, with a variety of interesting exhibits, is worth a visit. It's open Monday to Friday from 9 am to 7 pm, Saturday 9 am to 3 pm; admission is 7 pesos, students and seniors are admitted free. The **Casa y Museo Amado Nervo** at Zacatecas 284 Nte celebrates the life of the poet Amado Nervo, who was born in this house in 1870. It's open Monday to Friday from 9 am to 2 pm and 4 to 7 pm, Saturday 10 am to 1 pm; admission is free.

Casa Museo Cadete Juan Escutia at Hidalgo 71 Ote was the home of Juan Escutia, one of Mexico's illustrious 'Niños Héroes', who died in 1847 at age 17 defending the Castillo de Chapultepec from US forces. It's open Tuesday to Friday from 9 am to 2 pm and 4 to 7 pm, Saturday and Sunday 10 am to 6 pm; admission is free.

Opposite, the **Museo de Artes Populares** at Hidalgo 60 Ote is also called the Casa de los Cuatro Pueblos. Contemporary popular arts of Nayarit's Huichol, Cora, Nahuatl and Tepehuano peoples are displayed and sold here, including clothing, yarn art, weaving, musical instruments, ceramics, beadwork and more. It's open Monday to Friday from 9 am to 2 pm and 4 to 7 pm, Saturday and Sunday 9 am to 2 pm; admission is free.

The **Museo de Artes Visuales Aramara** at Allende 329 Pte is another museum of visual arts. It's open Tuesday to Friday from 10 am to 2 pm and 4 to 8 pm; admission is free. The **Museo Emilia Ortiz**, at Lerdo de Tejada 192 Pte, honours the painter Emilia Ortiz and her work.

Festival

The Feria de la Mexicanidad, held from mid-November to early December, celebrates Mexican culture with all kinds of events.

Places to Stay

Camping About five km south of the Plaza Principal, the *Trailer Park Los Pinos* (☎ (321) 3-12-32) offers bungalows and spaces for trailers and tents. About 10 km south-east of the centre, the *KOA* campground (☎ (321) 3-31-13) has about 70 spaces.

Hotels The *Hotel Ibarra* (☎ /fax (321) 2-36-34, 2-32-97) at Durango 297 Nte is a fine place to stay, with 44 clean, bright rooms, a restaurant and enclosed parking. Singles/doubles are 68/80 pesos. The *Hotel Cibrian* (☎ (321) 2-86-98/99) at Amado Nervo 163 Pte is another good, clean hotel with similar prices.

In the block south of the cathedral, the *Hotel Sierra de Alica* (☎ (321) 2-03-25, fax 2-13-09) at Avenida México 180 Nte has 60 rooms at 90/100 pesos. Right on the Plaza Principal, the *Hotel Fray Junipero Serra* (☎ (321) 2-25-25, 2-22-11; fax 2-20-51) is luxurious but more expensive, with rooms at 155/175 pesos.

Two more economical hotels are behind the bus station; neither is luxurious, but both are clean and acceptable, and all rooms have private bath. The *Hotel Tepic* (☎ (321) 3-13-77) at República de Chile 438 has 82 small, clean singles/doubles at 32/35 pesos. In the

next block, the *Hotel Nayar* (☎ (321) 3-63-14) at Dr Martinez 430 has 47 large rooms at 25/32 pesos. Frequent local buses provide easy transport to the centre of town.

Places to Eat

On the north side of the Plaza Principal, the *Café Parroquia*, upstairs under the arches, is a popular gathering place open Monday to Saturday from 8 am to 9 pm.

Another popular gathering spot with good food at good prices is the *Cafetería y Restaurant Diligencias* at Avenida México 29 Sur, open Monday to Saturday from 7 am to 10 pm, Sunday 5 to 10 pm. The *Cafetería Moderna* at Hidalgo 61-4 Ote, another simple place, is open Monday to Saturday from 7 am to 9 pm, Sunday 7 am to 3 pm.

For good traditional Mexican food in a fancier atmosphere, try the *Restaurant/Bar Los Molcajetes* at Avenida México 133 Sur, open Monday to Saturday from 10 am to 1.30 am. The *Restaurant Los Candiles* at Avenida México 139 Nte, also with traditional Mexican food, is open every day from 7 am to 10.30 pm.

Vegetarians might like *La Lechuga Feliz*, a vegetarian restaurant on Morelos near the corner of Durango.

Getting There & Away

Air Tepic's airport is in Pantanal, about a 20 or 30-minute drive from Tepic, going towards Guadalajara. Aero California and Saro offer direct flights to Mexico City and Tijuana, and Aerolitoral has direct flights to Guadalajara, all with connections to other centres.

Bus The bus station is on the south-eastern outskirts of town; local buses marked 'Central' and 'Centro' make frequent connections between the bus station and the city centre. The bus station has a cafeteria, a left-luggage office, shops, a post office, a Lada caseta and a Telecomm office with fax, telegram and telex. Buses include:

Guadalajara – 279 km, 3½ to four hours; hourly or half-hourly 1st-class buses by Omnibus de México, Tres Estrellas de Oro, Autotransportes Transpacíficos and Transportes del Pacífico; nine daily by Elite (32 to 35 pesos).

Ixtlán del Río – 88 km, 1½ hours; same buses as to Guadalajara (11 pesos)

Mazatlán – 290 km, four to five hours; hourly or half-hourly 1st-class buses by Tres Estrellas de Oro, Autotransportes Transpacíficos, Transportes del Pacífico and Elite (32 to 36 pesos)

Mexico City (Terminal Norte) – 792 km, 12 hours; hourly 1st-class buses by Tres Estrellas de Oro (115 pesos); several 1st and 2nd-class buses daily by several other lines

Puerto Vallarta – 169 km, 3½ hours, all 2nd-class; 29 buses daily by Transportes del Pacífico (21 pesos); eight daily by Autotransportes Transpacíficos (21 pesos); seven daily by Tres Estrellas de Oro and Transportes Norte de Sonora (25 pesos)

San Blás – 70 km, 1½ hours; hourly, 6 am to 7 pm, by Autotransportes Transpacíficos (8 pesos)

Santiago Ixcuintla – 70 km, 1½ hours, all 2nd-class; buses every half-hour, 5 am to 10 pm, by Transportes del Pacífico (8 pesos); hourly, 5 am to 8 pm, by Transportes Norte de Sonora (8 pesos)

Train The train station (☎ 3-48-14/13) is on the eastern outskirts of town; local 'Estación' buses will take you there. Tickets are sold at the station every day from 10 am to 5.40 pm. See the Guadalajara section of the Western Central Highlands chapter for schedules.

Getting Around
Local buses operate from around 5 am to 8.30 or 9 pm; the cost is 0.60 pesos. Otherwise there are plenty of taxis; a ride in town costs 7 pesos.

AROUND TEPIC
Laguna Santa María del Oro
This idyllic lake surrounded by steep forested mountains is in a volcanic crater thought to be 100 to 200 metres deep. The clear, clean water takes on colours ranging from turquoise to slate. You can make a very pleasant walk around the lake on a footpath in about 1½ hours, seeing numerous birds and butterflies along the way. You can also climb to an abandoned gold mine or row on

the lake, or swim. A few small restaurants serve fresh lake fish.

The good *Koala Bungalows* (☎ (321) 4-05-09), owned and operated by Englishman Chris French, has bungalows, camping spaces for trailers or tents, and a restaurant.

To get to the lake, take the Santa María del Oro turnoff about 40 km from Tepic along the Guadalajara road; from the turnoff it's about 10 km to the village, then another eight km from the village to the lake. Buses to the village depart from the bus station in Tepic, then you'll have to taxi, walk or hitch to the lake.

Volcán Ceboruco
This extinct volcano, with several old craters, interesting plants and volcanic forms, has several short, interesting walks at the top. The 15-km cobblestoned road up the volcano passes lava fields and fumaroles (steam vents), with plenty of vegetation growing on the slopes. The road begins at the village of Jala, seven km off the highway from Tepic to Guadalajara; the turnoff is 76 km from Tepic, 12 km before you reach Ixtlán del Río.

Ixtlán del Río
The small town of Ixtlán del Río, 1½ hours (88 km) from Tepic on the road to Guadalajara, is unremarkable in itself, but Carlos Castaneda fans will remember that this is where Don Juan took Carlos in the book *Journey to Ixtlán*. You may see an occasional soul paying pilgrimage to the place, watching the plaza for crows. Outside Ixtlán is an archaeological site, **Los Toriles**, with an impressive round stone temple, the Templo a Quetzalcóatl. Any bus between Tepic and Guadalajara will drop you at Ixtlán.

Mirador del Águila
This lookout point on highway 15, about 11 km north-west of Tepic, offers a wide view over a lush jungle canyon; it's known for bird-watching in the early morning and late afternoon.

Central Pacific Coast
Top Left: Weaver, Puerto Vallarta (SW)
Top Right: Bus stop at Mismaloya, near Puerto Vallarta (NK)
Bottom: Mazatlán (PP)

Central Pacific Coast
Top: Woodcarver, Mazatlán (NK); Looking across to Acapulco from the fort (TW)
Bottom: Footbridges, Mexcaltitán (NK); La Quebrada divers, Acapulco (TW)

PUERTO VALLARTA

• *pop: 300,000*

Puerto Vallarta lies beside the Río Cuale between green palm-covered mountains and the sparkling blue Bahía de las Banderas (Bay of Flags). Formerly a quaint seaside village, Vallarta has now been transformed into a world-famous resort city with 750,000 visitors annually, accommodated in over 30,000 hotel rooms with more being built all the time. Some of the most beautiful beaches, secluded and romantic just a few years ago, are now dominated by giant luxury mega-resorts. Tourism – Vallarta's only industry – has also made it a bilingual city, where English is almost as commonly spoken as Spanish. Despite all this, though, the cobblestoned streets, lined with old-fashioned white adobe buildings with red tile roofs, still make Vallarta one of Mexico's most picturesque coastal cities.

Vallarta's attractions suit all tastes and pockets, with idyllic white-sand beaches, water sports and cruises, horse rides and tours, shopping, art galleries, abundant restaurants and an active nightlife.

History

Puerto Vallarta's history is not very long; the first recorded settlement here was in 1851, when the Sánchez family came and made their home by the mouth of the Río Cuale, which now divides the city. Farmers and fisherfolk

followed. By 1918, enough people lived around the Río Cuale to give the settlement a name on the map. The name Vallarta was chosen in honour of Ignacio Luis Vallarta, a former governor of the state of Jalisco. It was called Puerto (port) because farmers had been shipping their harvests by boat from a small port area north of the Río Cuale.

Tourists began to visit Vallarta in 1954 when Mexicana airlines started a promotional campaign and initiated the first flights here, landing on a dirt airstrip in Emiliano Zapata, an area which is now the centre of Vallarta. But it was not until a decade later, when John Huston chose the nearby deserted cove of Mismaloya for the shooting of the film version of Tennessee Williams' *The Night of the Iguana* in 1964, that the town was put on the international tourist map.

The paparazzi of Hollywood descended to report on every development of the romance between Richard Burton and Elizabeth Taylor for hungry scandalmongers, while Burton's co-star Ava Gardner also raised more than a few eyebrows, and Puerto Vallarta suddenly became world-famous with an aura of steamy tropical romance. Tour groups began arriving not long after the film crew left and they've been coming ever since.

Orientation

The town centre is around the Río Cuale, with the small Isla Cuale in the middle of the

---

Bahía de las Banderas

The Bahía de las Banderas is a very large bay – the seventh-largest in the world, with an area of about 34 km by 52 km, a 161-km shoreline and a probable depth of around 1800 metres, though depth-measuring instruments have never found the bottom. Supposedly the bay was formed by the sunken crater of a giant, extinct volcano. This is difficult to see when you're on land, but they say that if you fly around the perimeter of the bay, it's quite easy to see from a bird's-eye view.

The bay is teeming with life, but it has the unusual distinction of being virtually shark-free. This is because of the numerous dolphins inhabiting the bay, which bear their young here all year round. To protect their colony they mount a patrol at the bay's entrance, not allowing sharks to enter.

Pilot and grey whales also bear their young in the bay, but only from around February to April. If you're out on the bay in a boat you will probably see dolphins, and whales in season. Giant manta rays with four-metre 'wingspans' also inhabit the bay; it's said that if you're here during their mating season in April, you can see them from the Malecón, jumping up into the air. ■

river and two bridges allowing easy passage between the two sides of town. To the north of the city are the airport (10 km) and two recent developments: Marina Vallarta, a large yachting marina about a km south of the airport, and Nuevo Vallarta, further north around the bay, about 25 km from the city centre. Also north of the city are a host of giant luxury hotels fanning out along the shore, and some fine beaches. To the south of the city are more resorts and some of the most beautiful beaches in the area.

The heart of the city centre is the Plaza Principal, also called Plaza de Armas, sitting by the sea between Morelos and Juárez, the city's two principal thoroughfares. The crown-topped cathedral, called the Templo de Guadalupe, towers a block behind the plaza, while on the sea side of the plaza is an amphitheatre with arches that have become a symbol of the town. The wide seaside walkway known as the Malecón, stretching about 10 blocks north from the plaza, is lined with bars, restaurants, nightclubs and boutiques.

South of the river are bus stations, hotels, restaurants and the only two beaches in the city centre: Playa Olas Altas (poorly named, because it doesn't really have 'big waves') and Playa de los Muertos (Beach of the Dead), taking its strange name from a fierce fight there sometime in the distant past.

City traffic has been reduced dramatically by the opening of the *libramiento* or bypass road on the inland side of the city centre, diverting traffic away from the centre.

Information

Tourist Information The Delegación de Turismo (☎ (322) 2-02-42, 3-07-66; fax 2-02-43), in the municipal building on the north-east corner of the Plaza Principal, has free maps, bilingual tourist literature and friendly bilingual staff. It's open Monday to Friday from 9 am to 9 pm, Saturday 9 am to 1 pm.

Vallarta Today, a daily English-language newspaper for visitors and Vallarta's English-speaking community, is free at the tourist office. So too is *Puerto Vallarta Life-styles*, a glossy quarterly magazine. The *Puerto Vallarta Lifestyles* map, also free and the best map for the area, appears in smaller versions within the magazine.

Money Most businesses in Vallarta accept US dollars cash as readily as they accept pesos, though the rate of exchange they offer is usually less favourable than the banks, which offer the best rate. Many banks are found around the Plaza Principal; they are open Monday to Friday from 9 am to 1.30 pm but often have long queues. Banamex, on the south side of the plaza, has a separate currency exchange office, open Monday to Friday from 9 am to 1 pm.

A great number of casas de cambio are found around Vallarta; their rates differ so it may pay to shop around. Though their rates are less favourable than those of the banks, the difference often comes to only a few cents and the longer opening hours and faster service may make it worthwhile to change money here. Most are open every day from around 9 am to 7.30 pm, sometimes with a lunch break from 2 to 4 pm.

On the north side of the Río Cuale along the Malecón there are a number of casas de cambio. Two others are on Calle Rodríguez opposite the Mercado Municipal, and at Juárez 270 near the Plaza Principal. On the south side of the river, there's a casa de cambio on Vallarta between Madero and Aquiles Serdán beside the Hotel Posada Río Cuale, one at Insurgentes 140 near the corner of Aquiles Serdán, and another on Olas Altas.

American Express (☎ 4-68-76/77), in the Villa Vallarta commercial centre a few km north of the city, is open Monday to Friday from 9 am to 2.30 pm and 4 to 6 pm, Saturday 9 am to 1 pm.

Post & Telecommunications The post office on Mina, half a block from the Malecón, is open Monday to Friday from 8 am to 7.30 pm, Saturday 9 am to 1 pm, Sunday 9 am to noon. The Telecomm office, with telegram, telex and fax, is at Hidalgo 582 near the corner of Aldama. It's open

Monday to Friday from 9 am to 7 pm, Saturday 9 am to noon.

Vallarta has many Lada casetas, most on the south side of the Río Cuale. Those with both telephone and fax include Computel at Madero 296 near Constitución, and three offices of Larga Distancia: at Lázaro Cárdenas 267, opposite the Primera Plus bus station; at the Transportes del Pacífico bus station at Insurgentes 282; and at Lázaro Cárdenas 181, beside the Hotel Eloisa on Plaza Lázaro Cárdenas.

Foreign Consulates The US Consulate (☎ (322) 2-00-69, fax 3-00-74) is upstairs behind La Fuente del Puente restaurant; look up to the 2nd floor and you'll see the large American seal. It's open Monday to Friday from 9 am to 1 pm. The Canadian Consulate (☎ (322) 2-53-98, fax 2-35-17) at Hidalgo 226 is open Monday to Friday from 10 am to 2 pm.

Bookshops Books and magazines in English are available at the GR supermarket on the corner of Constitución and Aquiles Serdán. The Librería Limón at Carranza 310 sells used and new books and magazines in English. A Page in the Sun, on the corner of Olas Altas and Diéguez, buys and sells quality used books in English. Archie's Wok at Rodríguez 130 has an English book exchange.

Laundry Several laundries are south of the Río Cuale, including Lavandería Blanquita at Madero 407-A and Lavandería Cartagena at Madero 428. The Olas Altas area has the Lavandería Adriana at Rodolfo Gómez 142, the Lavandería Elsa at Olas Altas 385 and the Lavandería Acuarius at Púlpito 145, near the corner of Olas Altas.

Supermarket Conveniently located in the centre of town, the giant air-con Gutierrez Rizo ('GR') on the corner of Constitución and Aquiles Serdán on the south side of the river, has local merchandise as well as items imported from the USA, including magazines and paperbacks in English. It's open every day from 6.30 am to 10 pm.

Things to See & Do

Museo del Cuale This tiny museum on Isla Cuale, with a small collection of ancient objects and changing art exhibitions, is open Tuesday to Saturday from 10 am to 7 pm, Sunday 10 am to 3 pm; admission is free.

Art Galleries These have been sprouting like mushrooms in Puerto Vallarta in recent years. Some of the better known galleries include Arte Mágico Huichol at Corona 164 (there are many other interesting galleries in the same block), the Brooks de Gooyer gallery at Morelos 589, Galería Uno at Morelos 561, Galería Vallarta at Juárez 263, Galería Indígena at Juárez 270, the Sergio Bustamante gallery at Juárez 275, the Galería Pacífico at Insurgentes 109 on the south side of the Río Cuale, and the Galería Pyrámide at Basilio Badillo 272.

Beaches The two beaches in the city centre, **Playa Olas Altas** and **Playa de los Muertos**, on the south side of the Río Cuale, are the most popular, but many beautiful beaches are found outside the city. Southwards, accessible by minibuses plying highway 200 (the coastal highway) are Conchas Chinas, Estacas, Los Venados, Punta Negra, Garza Blanca, Playa Gemelas and Mismaloya.

Mismaloya, where John Huston directed *The Night of the Iguana*, is about 12 km south of town. The tiny cove, formerly deserted, is now dominated by condominium projects and the giant 303-room La Jolla de Mismaloya hotel, but the buildings used in the film still stand on the south side of the cove and you can walk up to them. For an adventurous excursion you can head inland along a riverside dirt road to Chino's Paraíso, two km upriver, or El Eden de Mismaloya, about five km further upriver (see Places to Eat). The film *Predator* was made at El Eden, accounting for the burned-out hull of a helicopter at the entrance; here you can also take jungle walks, see a small zoo and explore two waterfalls just a little upriver. Getting to these places is a hike if you don't have transport; you can hitch or take a taxi from

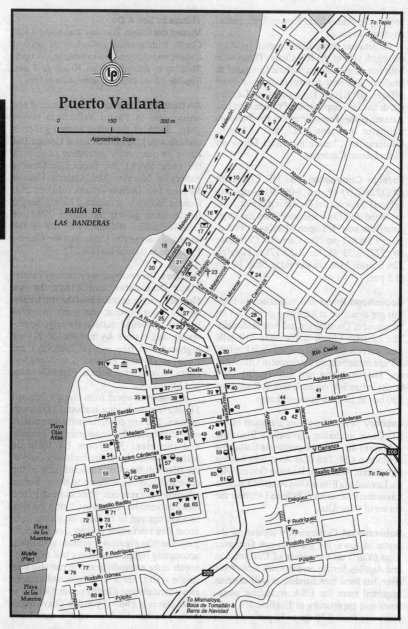

Puerto Vallarta

0   150   300 m

Approximate Scale

BAHÍA DE
LAS BANDERAS

To Tepic

To Tepic

To Mismaloya,
Boca de Tomatlán &
Barra de Navidad

PLACES TO STAY

1   Hotel Rosita
30 La Casa del Puente
35 Hotel Molino de Agua
36 Hotel Posada
    Río Cuale
41 Hotel Azteca
42 Hotel Villa del Mar
47 Hotel Hortencia
50 Estancia San Carlos
54 Hotel Eloisa
65 Hotel Mayo
70 Hotel Posada de Roger
71 Hotel Yazmín
72 Apartamentos Posada
    Olas Altas
78 Hotel San Marino
    Plaza

PLACES TO EAT

2   McDonald's
4   Woolworth's
    Restaurant
5   Carlos O'Brian's
6   Cenaduría Doña
    Raquel
7   Rito's Baci
8   Hard Rock Café
10 Tuti Fruti
12 Mr Tequila's Grill &
    The Mariachi House
13 Brazz
14 Café San Cristobal
16 Panadería Munguía
20 VIPS & Domino's Pizza
22 Kentucky Fried
    Chicken

24 Mi Casa Buffet
26 Chef Roger
30 La Fuente del Puente
31 Chico's Paradise II
33 Cuiza
34 Le Bistro Jazz Café
39 Panadería Munguía
40 Café Sierra
46 Pollo Giro
48 Fonda La China
    Poblana
49 La Iguana
62 The Pancake House
64 Café Eclair &
    Pizza Joe
66 Adobe Café
67 Pie in the Sky
69 El Tucan
71 Café de Olla
74 Rosa's Espresso
75 El Palomar de
    los Gonzáles
76 Las Tres Huastecas
77 Archie's Wok

OTHER

3   University of
    Guadalajara
9   Zoo
11 Seahorse Statue
15 Telecomm
17 Post Office
18 Arches & Outdoor
    Amphitheatre
19 Tourist Office
21 Plaza Principal
23 Templo de Guadalupe
25 Los Balcones

27 Canadian Consulate
28 Casa Kimberley
29 Mercado
30 US Consulate
32 Museo del Cuale
37 Sala Elizabeth Taylor
38 Gutierrez Rizo (GR)
    Supermarket
43 Lavandería Cartagena
44 Lavandería Blanquita
45 Cine Bahía
51 Transportes Cihuatlán
    Bus Station
52 Club Roxy
53 Paco Paco
55 Plaza Lázaro Cárdenas
56 Local Buses to
    Mismaloya & Boca
    de Tomatlán
57 Mariachi Loco
58 Servicios
    Coordinados,
    Primera Plus & ETN
    Bus Station
59 Transportes del
    Pacífico Bus Station
60 TNS Bus Station &
    Librería Limón
61 Tres Estrellas de Oro
    & Elite Bus Station
63 Gerardo's Party Pad
68 Cactus Disco
73 Lavandería Elsa
74 A Page in the Sun
79 Sí Señor & Lavandería
    Adriana
80 Lavandería Acuarius

Mismaloya. The walk back is downhill all the way and makes a pleasant stroll.

About four km past Mismaloya, **Boca de Tomatlán** is a peaceful, less commercialised seaside village in a small cove where the Río de Tomatlán meets the sea – a jungly place with quiet water, a beach and a number of restaurants.

Further around the south side of the bay are the more isolated beaches of Las Ánimas, Quimixto and Yelapa, accessible only by boat. **Playa de las Ánimas** (Beach of the Spirits), a lovely beach with a small fishing village and some palapa restaurants offering

fresh seafood, is said to be the most beautiful beach on the bay. **Quimixto**, not far from Las Ánimas, has a waterfall you can reach with a half-hour hike, or you can hire a pony on the beach to take you up.

Yelapa, furthest from town, is probably the most popular cruise destination; this picturesque cove is crowded with tourists, restaurants and parasailing operators. The charming village at Yelapa has a sizeable colony of US residents; you can find a place to stay if you ask around. Take a hike upriver to see the waterfalls.

Still more beaches are found around the

north side of the bay. Nearest Vallarta are the beaches in the Zona Hotelera: Camarones, Las Glorias, Los Tules, Las Palmas, Playa de Oro and, past the Marina, El Salado. Nuevo Vallarta also has beaches. Further on around the bay are Playa Flamingos, Bucerías, Destiladeras, Punta del Burro, Paraíso Escondido, El Anclote and Punta de Mita, at the northern boundary of the bay.

Cruises A host of cruises are available in Vallarta, with daytime, sunset and evening cruises, some including snorkelling stops at Los Arcos. The most popular are probably the cruises to Yelapa and Las Ánimas beaches. Sunset cruises are a good way to spend an evening. The tourist office or any travel agency can tell you what cruises are operating, details of where they go, what they offer (many include meals, an open bar, live music and dancing) and current prices.

If you just want to visit the beaches, a cheaper way to get there is by water taxi (see Getting Around).

Water Sports Snorkelling, scuba diving, deep-sea fishing, water-skiing, jet-skiing, windsurfing, sailing, parasailing, riding the 'banana' and just plain swimming are all popular in Vallarta. Most can be arranged on the beaches in front of any of the large hotels. The tourist office can help connect you with operators.

The most spectacular spots for snorkelling and diving are the National Underwater Park at **Los Arcos**, an island rock formation just north of Mismaloya, and the **Islas Marietas** at the entrance to the bay, with impressive reefs, underwater caves, tunnels, walls and opportunities to see dolphins, whales and giant manta rays.

Vallarta has a number of diving and snorkelling operators. *Chico's Dive Shop* (☎ 2-18-95, 2-54-39), on the Malecón at Paseo Díaz Ordaz 770-5, open Monday to Saturday from 9 am to 9 pm, offers several good diving and snorkelling trips as well as diving instruction.

Deep-sea fishing is popular all year, with a major international sailfish tournament each November. Prime catches are sailfish, marlin, tuna, red snapper and sea bass. The tourist office can recommend fishing operators for the type of trip you have in mind.

Sailfish

Golf & Tennis Golf and tennis are both popular sports at Vallarta. Golf courses north of the city include the exclusive Marina Vallarta Golf Club (☎ 1-01-71, 1-00-73) and the less exotic Los Flamingos Golf Club (☎ (329) 8-02-80). Another golf course is under construction in Nuevo Vallarta.

A favourite with tennis fans (or those who want to learn) is the John Newcombe Tennis Club (☎ 4-43-60) in the Zona Hotelera, also north of the city. Most of the large luxury hotels also have courts; phone them to reserve a court. Los Tules (☎ 4-45-60), the Sheraton Buganvilias (☎ 3-04-04), the Hotel Krystal (☎ 4-02-02) and the Marriott Hotel (☎ 1-04-04) all have courts available, and there are plenty of others.

Language Courses The University of Guadalajara's Foreign Student Study Centre has a branch in Puerto Vallarta, specialising in the teaching of Spanish. Classes begin every Monday and last for one week; you can study for as many weeks as you like. Classes are semi-intensive (two hours per day, 10 hours per week) or intensive (four hours per day, 20 hours per week); the cost is 20 pesos per hour for instruction, plus a one-time 75-peso registration fee. One university credit is given for each two weeks passed. Contact: University of Guadalajara Spanish Language School, Jesús Langarica 200 Penthouse, Puerto Vallarta, Jalisco, CP 48300, México (☎ (322) 3-00-43, fax 2-44-19).

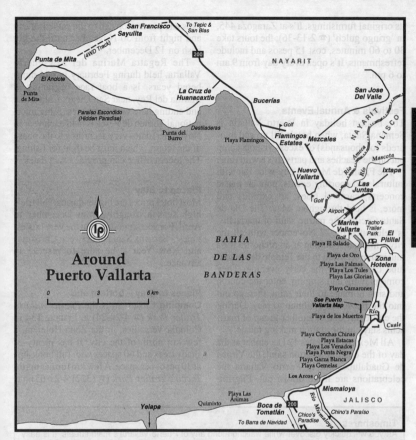

NAYARIT

To Tepic &
San Blas

San Francisco
Sayulita

Punta de Mita

El Anclote

(4WD Track)

Punta
de Mita

Paraíso Escondido
(Hidden Paradise)

La Cruz de
Huanacaxtle

Bucerías

San Jose
Del Valle

Destiladeras

Punta del
Burro

Playa Flamingos

Golf

Flamingos
Estates

Mezcales

Nuevo
Vallarta

Rio Ameca

Rio Ameca

NAYARIT

JALISCO

Mascota

Ixtapa

Las
Juntas

Golf

Airport

Marina
Vallarta

Tacho's
Trailer
Park

El
Pitillal

**Around
Puerto Vallarta**

BAHÍA
DE LAS
BANDERAS

Golf

Playa El Salado

Playa de Oro

Playa Las Palmas
Playa Los Tules
Playa Las Glorias

Zona
Hotelera

0   3   6 km

Playa Camarones

See Puerto
Vallarta Map

Río

Playa de los Muertos

Cuale

Río
Cuale

Playa Conchas Chinas
Playa Estacas
Playa Los Venados
Playa Punta Negra
Playa Garza Blanca
Playa Gemelas

Los Arcos

Mismaloya

JALISCO

Yelapa

Quimixto

Playa Las
Ánimas

Boca de
Tomatlán

200

Río Mismaloya

Chico's
Paradise

Chino's Paraíso

To Barra de Navidad

Organised Tours

The tourist office and travel agents can set you up with city tours, jungle tours, tropical tours, bicycle tours and horse riding tours.

Bike Mex Mountain Bike Adventures (☎ 3-16-80) and Sun Bike Tours Mountain Biking (☎ 2-00-80) both offer mountain bike tours with experienced bilingual guides, tailored to your level of fitness and experience.

The Rancho Amigo – Marco Polo (☎ 4-73-42), a small, personal and friendly horse riding enterprise, operates 3½ to four-hour rides up into the hills through isolated terrain which you can't get to any other way, for 75 pesos. Two larger operators are the Rancho El Charro (☎ 4-01-14) and the Rancho Ojo de Agua (☎ 4-82-40, 4-06-07). Horsemen along the beach charge around 30 pesos per hour for beach rides.

The Friendship Club offers two-hour tours of some of Puerto Vallarta's luxurious private homes, departing at 11 am on Thursday and Saturday from the Plaza Principal. Or you can take a tour of Casa Kimberley, the house that Richard Burton bought for Elizabeth Taylor back in the 1960s, still with its original furnishings. It's at Zaragoza 445, in 'gringo gulch' (☎ 2-13-36); the tours take 30 to 60 minutes, cost 15 pesos and include refreshments. It's open every day from 9 am to 6 pm.

Festivals & Annual Events

The busiest holiday in Puerto Vallarta is Semana Santa, when hotels fill up and hundreds (or thousands) of excess visitors camp out on the beaches and party. It's a wild time.

The Fiestas de Mayo, a city-wide fair with cultural and sporting events, popular music concerts, carnival rides, art exhibits and more, is held throughout May. The Día de Santa Cecilia, the patron saint of mariachis, is celebrated on 22 November with all the city's mariachis uniting as an orchestra for a musical procession to the Templo de Guadalupe cathedral in the early evening. They come playing and singing, enter the church and sing homage to their saint, then go out into the plaza and continue to play. During the entire day one or another group of mariachis stays in the church making music.

All Mexico celebrates 12 December as the day of the country's patron saint, the Virgen de Guadalupe, but in Puerto Vallarta the celebrations are more drawn out. Pilgrimages and processions go to the cathedral day and night from 30 November until the big bash on 12 December.

The Regatta Marina del Rey-Puerto Vallarta, held during February in odd-numbered years, is a boat race beginning at Marina del Rey, near San Diego, California, and ending here with festivities. A big international Torneo de Pesca is held each year in November; dates vary according to the phase of the moon, which must be right for fishing. The tourist office can provide exact dates.

Places to Stay

Most hotel prices are higher during Vallarta's high season, roughly from December to April. For accommodation at the very busiest times – Semana Santa or between Christmas and New Year – be sure to reserve in advance.

Places to Stay – bottom end

Camping Closest in is the *Puerto Vallarta Trailer Park* (☎ 4-24-24) at Francia 134 in Colonia Versailles, in the Zona Hotelera, a few km north of the city. It has plenty of shady trees and 60 spaces with full hook-ups at 30 pesos per space. A few km further north, *Tacho's Trailer Park* (☎ (322) 4-21-63) has

---

Timeshares

As you will quickly discover while walking along any of Puerto Vallarta's main streets, it is easy to arrange a free or greatly discounted cruise, dinner, jeep rental, horse ride or what-have-you by attending a timeshare presentation. On almost every block in the city there are at least two booths staffed by English-speaking hawkers with inviting smiles who try to coax you to their stands with sugary hellos and offers of jeeps or free tours.

Of course, there's a catch to the offers. You get one of the goodies mentioned in exchange for listening to a 90-minute breakfast presentation about the benefits of investing in one of Puerto Vallarta's burgeoning timeshare condominium projects, and then touring the project. You must be over 25 years old, in possession of a major credit card, and employed; many timeshare projects require that you be married as well, and that both husband and wife attend the presentation. Breakfast is free and they will pay the taxi fare from your hotel to the project. You are under no obligation to buy or sign anything.

Travellers give mixed reports about the presentations. Some say it's a painless enough way to get a cheap jeep, tour or cruise. Others are still angry days later when they've had to fend off the 'hard sell'. We won't recommend that you go or stay away – it's up to you. Just be wary of the seasoned professional salespeople who can sometimes come on very strong, and by all means, if you're thinking of buying, use your intelligence, keep your wits about you and be sure you understand the sneaky fine print in the contract. ■

a swimming pool and 120 spaces; the cost is 36 pesos per space, with weekly or monthly discounts.

Hotels The cheapest places to stay are found south of the Río Cuale, with most concentrated along Madero. All are basic but clean, with fan and private bath.

The *Hotel Villa del Mar* (☎ (322) 2-07-85) at Madero 440, on the corner of Jacarandas, has 50 rooms, many featuring private balconies with chairs and flowering plants; up on the roof are sitting areas with a view of the town. Rooms with balconies are 40/50 pesos for singles/doubles in high season, 34/42 pesos the rest of the year; interior rooms are about 10 pesos cheaper. Studio apartments with fully equipped kitchens are 50/60 pesos, or 1200 pesos by the month. The quality you get for the price makes this one of the best deals in Vallarta.

The 46-room *Hotel Azteca* (☎ (322) 2-27-50) at Madero 473 has clean singles/doubles at 28/36 pesos all year round, 54 pesos for rooms with kitchenettes. The *Hotel Hortencia* (☎ (322) 2-24-84) at Madero 336 has 18 rooms at 35/45 pesos. A number of other simple, cheap hotels are found along Madero in the four blocks between Vallarta and Jacarandas.

The *Hotel Yazmín* (☎ (322) 2-00-87), at Basilio Badillo 168, has rooms at 50/60 pesos all year round. The hotel is a favourite, clean and friendly, with courtyard gardens and a good, inexpensive restaurant next door. It is an excellent deal and just a block from Playa de los Muertos, the most popular beach in Vallarta.

Nearby, the *Apartamentos Olas Altas*, Olas Altas 356 on the corner of Basilio Badillo, seems an anomaly in this district of fancier places. It has six fully equipped apartments, with kitchens, that are quite basic and perhaps only a true beach bum would like them. However, the price is right at 30/40 pesos for singles/doubles, with discounts by the month.

The *Hotel Mayo* (☎ (322) 2-34-03) at Basilio Badillo 300 is an older hotel with a friendly family atmosphere. Regular rooms

are 35/45 pesos, cabañas are 55/65 pesos; one-bedroom apartments with kitchen are 55/65 pesos, two-bedroom apartments are 80 to 150 pesos. All room prices include accommodation for one or two children, and all are cheaper by the week or month. It's one of the only cheapies with enclosed parking.

Places to Stay – middle

The *Hotel Posada de Roger* (☎ (322) 2-08-36, 2-06-39; fax 3-04-82), at Basilio Badillo 237, is famous for its friendly atmosphere, cleanliness and security, and has a pleasant courtyard swimming pool plus a convivial restaurant/bar, El Tucan, where good breakfasts are served. Singles/doubles with ceiling fan are 55/65 pesos, with air-con 65/80 pesos; the air-con prices rise to 100/120 pesos from December to March.

The *Casa Corazón* (☎ /fax (322) 2-13-71; in the USA ☎ (505) 523-4666, 522-4684) at Amapas 328 is an attractive B&B guesthouse with spacious terraces overlooking Playa de los Muertos. Low-season rates are 30 to 75 pesos for singles, 45 to 90 pesos for doubles, rising to 90 to 180 pesos for singles and 105 to 180 pesos for doubles at peak periods. All prices include breakfast and they have a beachside restaurant, *Looney Tunes*, down the hill.

The *Hotel Eloisa* (☎ (322) 2-64-65, fax 2-35-20) at Lázaro Cárdenas 179, half a block from Playa Olas Altas, has a rooftop terrace with a children's pool and 75 bright, clean rooms with air-con and colour TV at 110/120 pesos for singles/doubles, a little higher from November to January.

Beside the beach at the north end of town, the *Hotel Rosita* (☎ /fax (322) 2-10-33, 2-21-71) at Paseo Díaz Ordaz 901 is a popular older hotel with a beachside swimming pool, restaurant and bar. Singles/doubles start at 80/91 pesos for regular rooms, higher for suites, but cheaper in the low season. All rooms have either a sea view or air-con.

The *Hotel Posada Río Cuale* (☎ (322) 2-04-50, 2-09-14), at Aquiles Serdán 242 on the corner of Vallarta, is a pleasant hotel with a swimming pool, a poolside restaurant/bar, and 21 rooms with air-con. Singles/doubles are 80/100 pesos most of the year, rising to 120/135 pesos from December to April.

A good deal for mid-range apartments is the *Estancia San Carlos* (☎ /fax (322) 2-53-27) at Constitución 210, with a courtyard swimming pool, covered parking and 24 clean, modern apartments with fully equipped kitchen, air-con, parabolic colour TV and private balcony. One-bedroom apartments are 100/130 pesos, two-bedroom apartments are 150/170 pesos, with discounts by the month. Prices are higher from November to April.

One of Vallarta's best kept secrets is the tiny *La Casa del Puente* (☎ (322) 2-07-49), tucked behind the Restaurant La Fuente del Puente beside the Río Cuale, with just one regular room with bath, a one-bedroom apartment and a two-bedroom apartment. Molly Muir, the owner, is a wonderful hostess and impromptu tour guide. Rates are very reasonable: the room/apartments are 66/116 pesos most of the year, and 106/215 from 15 December until the week after Easter.

Places to Stay – top end

If you can afford it, Puerto Vallarta has many beautiful places to stay at the upper end of the market. From April to mid-December, low-season discounts bring even some of the finest places down to a more affordable level.

One of Vallarta's best centrally located hotels is the *Hotel Molino de Agua* (☎ (322) 2-19-07/57, fax 2-60-56) at Vallarta 130, facing the beach on the south side of the Río Cuale. Though it's in the city centre, it's remarkably quiet and peaceful, with 65 cabins, rooms and suites set among tropical gardens covering two city blocks. Prices from 1 November to 30 April start at 195 pesos for cabins, higher for beachfront suites, with low-season discounts.

Top-end hotels line the beach at Playa de los Muertos. Typically they are high-rises with air-con, beachfront swimming pools and restaurants. For example, the *Hotel San Marino Plaza* (☎ (322) 2-30-50, 2-15-55; fax 2-24-31) at Rodolfo Gómez 111 has 162

rooms at 176 pesos from May to December, 250 pesos from mid-December to April.

Many giant Grand Tourism-category hotels, often with hundreds of rooms, are found along the beaches both to the north and south of town. Some of the most attractive are on the beaches south of town, including the *Camino Real, Costa Vida Vallarta* and *El Presidente*. In the Zona Hotelera are the *Sheraton Buganvilias, Qualton, Plaza Las Glorias, Krystal Vallarta, Continental Plaza, Fiesta Americana* and *Ramada Plaza*. Further north, in Marina Vallarta, are the *Marriott Casa Magna, Melia Vallarta, Bel-Air, Westin Regina, Vidafel* and *Velas Vallarta*. Still further north in Nuevo Vallarta are the *Sierra Radisson, Diamond Resorts* and *Jack Tar Village*. Travel agents can connect you with any of these places; they all do big business in foreign package tours.

Several elegant guesthouses provide a comfortable 'gay-friendly' ambience, including the *Casa de los Arcos* (☎ (322) 2-59-90), a luxurious mountainside villa overlooking the south part of town, and the *Casa Panorámica* (☎ (322) 2-36-56, in the USA (310) 396-7855 or 1-800-745-7805) at Km 1 on the highway to Mismaloya.

Places to Eat

Cafés & Coffee Houses The attractive *Café Sierra* coffee house and roastery at Insurgentes 109, overlooking the Río Cuale, is open every day from 8.30 am to 11 pm. *Café Eclair* at Basilio Badillo 269 is open Monday to Saturday from 7 am to 4 pm. *Rosa's Espresso* on the corner of Olas Altas and Diéguez shares space with *A Page in the Sun*, which has good-quality used books in English; it's open Monday to Saturday from 8 am to 9 pm. North of the river, the *Café San Cristobal* at Corona 272, 1½ blocks inland from the Malecón, is another good coffee house and roastery, open Monday to Saturday from 8 am to 10 pm.

Bakeries The *Panadería Munguía* at Juárez 467 is a good bakery, with everything from sweets to healthy wholegrain baked goods, open from 7 am to 9 pm every day. A smaller branch is on the corner of Insurgentes and Aquiles Serdán on the south side of the Río Cuale. *Pie in the Sky* at Basilio Badillo 278 is famous for its 'Beso', a rich triple chocolate brownie with a molten fudge centre and pecans top and bottom. It's open Monday to Saturday from 10 am to 8 pm.

Restaurants – south of the Río Cuale

There are some small, cheap, typical Mexican family-run restaurants along Madero. *Pollo Giro*, at Madero 350 on the corner of Insurgentes, is a clean, air-con restaurant which offers broiled chicken, open every day from 11 am to 11 pm. A few doors down Insurgentes at 222, the *Fonda La China Poblana* has typical Mexican food and an upstairs dining terrace, open 24 hours every day.

Many other restaurants south of the river are a step up in class; this being the city's main hotel district, most are heavily patronised by tourists.

Two restaurants a block apart on Basilio Badillo each claim to serve 'the best breakfast in Puerto Vallarta': *El Tucan*, connected to the Hotel Posada de Roger on the corner of Vallarta and Basilio Badillo, and *The Pancake House*, a block away at Basilio Badillo 289. We tried them both and couldn't decide which was best, but they are both great places for breakfast, with about 20 varieties of pancakes and waffles, plus treats like eggs Benedict, cheese blintzes and omelettes; eggs with hash browns, toast, butter and coffee come to around 10 pesos at either place. Both are open every day from 8 am to 2 pm. From December to April El Tucan serves dinner, too, and offers a bar, piano music, and nothing on the menu for over 30 pesos.

This block of Basilio Badillo has several other good restaurants. *Pizza Joe* at Basilio Badillo 269 is an Italian pizza and pasta house with tables on a rear patio beside a pool, fountains and romantic candlelight in the evening; it's open from 5 to 11 pm every day except Sunday. Opposite this, the popular *Puerto Nuevo* at Basilio Badillo 284 offers a platter of fresh seafood of the day,

from which you can make your selection; it's open every day from noon to 12.30 am. More expensive but also popular for its good food is the stylish, air-con *Adobe Café* at Basilio Badillo 300, open from 6 to 11 pm every day except Tuesday.

The *Café de Olla* at Basilio Badillo 168, beside the Hotel Yazmín, is a good find – a small, pleasant restaurant with good traditional Mexican food and an 'Old Mexico' atmosphere, open from 8 am to 10 pm every day except Tuesday.

One of Vallarta's best known restaurants is *Archie's Wok* at Francisca Rodríguez 130, half a block from the Playa de los Muertos pier. It was created by the former personal chef of film director John Huston. Archie's features wok specialities from many parts of Asia, with vegetarian or meat selections like gingery stir-fried vegetables (22 pesos) or fish sautéed in coconut milk and Thai red curry sauce (33 pesos). It's open from 2 to 11 pm every day except Sunday.

In the same neighbourhood, *Las Tres Huastecas*, on the corner of Olas Altas and Francisca Rodríguez, is a cheerful spot, with good food and moderate prices, open every day from 7 am to 8 pm.

El Palomar de los González at Aguacate 425 is a hillside restaurant with good food and an exceptional view over the city and bay, especially at sunset – a great place for a special night out, open every evening from 6 to 11 pm. Another elegant, peaceful spot is the garden restaurant of the *Hotel Molino de Agua*, on Vallarta just south of the Río Cuale, open every day from 7 am to 11 pm.

Restaurants – north of the Río Cuale

As in most Mexican towns, one of the cheapest places to eat is at the *Mercado Municipal* – only here in Vallarta the mercado is a lot cleaner and more pleasant. It's on the north side of the Río Cuale beside the inland bridge, and the upstairs floor has a number of simple restaurant stalls serving typical Mexican market foods. It's open every day from around 7 am to 11 pm.

Even more economical than the mercado is the *Mi Casa Buffet*, up the hill at Miramar

402 on the corner of Iturbide, where an 'all you can eat' buffet of soup, salad, rice, two main courses and dessert costs just 10 pesos. The tiny restaurant has only five tables; it's open Monday to Saturday from 2 to 9 pm, but it's a good idea to get there before 7 pm.

VIPS, beside the sea on the south side of the arches near the plaza, is a large air-con restaurant with a pleasant atmosphere, varied menu, reasonable prices, excellent service, valet parking and a fine view of the arches, the Malecón and the sea. It's open Sunday to Thursday from 7 am to 1 am, Friday and Saturday 24 hours.

The Malecón is lined with boutiques and restaurant/bars. Many have upstairs terraces with fine views of the bay. Prices are considerably higher than in other parts of the city. The *Hard Rock Café* and *Carlos O'Brian's* both serve expensive food but are nonetheless popular with visitors for their festive atmosphere in the evening. Various other places along the Malecón also have music and dancing.

Half a block off the Malecón, the *Cenaduría Doña Raquel* at Leona Vicario 131, serving inexpensive but delicious traditional Mexican food since 1968, is open every evening from 6 to 11.30 pm.

Also just off the Malecón, *Rito's Baci* at Domínguez 181 is a tiny Italian restaurant with excellent food, open every day from 1 pm to midnight. Phone for free delivery within the city (☎ 2-64-48).

The little *Tuti Fruti* on the corner of Morelos and Corona has stools to sit and enjoy fresh juices, fruit shakes, simple snacks or breakfasts. It's open Monday to Saturday from 8 am to 10 pm.

La Fuente del Puente on Insurgentes, at the north side of the bridge over the Río Cuale, is a pleasant open-air restaurant/bar with a traditional Mexican quartet every evening except Sunday. It's open Monday to Saturday from 7 am to 10.30 pm, Sunday 9 am to 4 pm.

Operated by a professional Swiss chef, *Chef Roger* at Rodríguez 267, near the mercado, is expensive but high-quality; it's open Monday to Saturday from 6.30 to 11 pm.

At the other end of the culinary spectrum, a few American fast-food chains have made it to Vallarta, including *McDonald's*, on the corner of Paseo Díaz Ordaz and 31 de Octubre, *Kentucky Fried Chicken*, facing the Plaza Principal on the corner of Juárez and Zaragoza, and *Domino's Pizza*, beside VIPS on the south side of the Malecón. All are air-con and open every day.

The *Woolworth's Restaurant* at Juárez and 31 de Octubre has air-con, 10 kinds of hamburgers served with French fries and salad (14 pesos) and an economical meal of the day, changing daily, with soup, main dish, rice and beans, bread and butter, a cold drink, dessert and coffee or tea, all for 7 to 12 pesos. It's open Monday to Saturday from 7 am to 10 pm, Sunday 7 am to 9 pm.

Restaurants – on Isla Cuale Restaurants on the Isla Cuale include the *Le Bistro Jazz Café* and *Chico's Paradise II*, both very beautiful but also expensive. You could always just drop in for a drink to enjoy the scenery.

Restaurants – Mismaloya Mismaloya has a couple of well-known restaurants: *Chino's Paraíso*, two km upriver from the beach, and *El Eden de Mismaloya*, about five km further upriver. Both are beautiful (but expensive) open-air restaurants with tables under palapas at spots where you can swim and stretch out in the sun on the boulders, and maybe see some metre-long iguanas doing the same. Both restaurants are open every day from around 11 am to 6 pm.

Entertainment

Dancing and drinking are Puerto Vallarta's main forms of night-time entertainment. Stroll down the Malecón in the evening and take your choice of everything from romantic open-air restaurant/bars to riotous revelling. A lot of people just stroll around; entertainment is often presented in the amphitheatre by the sea opposite the Plaza Principal. The softly lit Isla Cuale makes a beautiful, quiet, romantic haven for strolling in the evening.

Bars & Discos The *Hard Rock Cafe* along the Malecón has live rock music and dancing every night except Wednesday from around 10 pm to 2 am. The *Zoo* is another place with music and dancing. Or there's *Carlos O'Brian's*, a favourite drinking hole for fun-seeking, rabble-rousing gringos, with dancing into the wee hours.

On the south side of the river, *Sí Señor*, a bar/concert hall at Rodolfo Gómez near the corner of Olas Altas, has live rock, jazz, blues or soul bands every night from 10 pm to 2 am. *Club Roxy* at Vallarta 217, between Madero and Lázaro Cárdenas, also has live music.

For jazz fans, the classy *Le Bistro Jazz Café* on the Isla Cuale has over 1000 jazz CDs and a pleasant tropical atmosphere. *Cuiza*, also on Isla Cuale, calls itself an 'elegant cantina'.

Discos in Vallarta appear and disappear with some regularity. Still popular are *Cactus*, on the south side of the river on the corner of Vallarta and Francisca Rodríguez, and *Christine*, at the Hotel Krystal about seven km north of the city. *Elaine's*, beside the Jack Tar Hotel in Nuevo Vallarta, about 25 km north of the city, is another popular disco, open every night from around 10.30 pm till late.

There's evening entertainment of one kind or another at many of the large resort hotels. The *Camino Real* south of town gives a free concert, with free drinks and hors d'oeuvres, on the first Thursday of every month.

Puerto Vallarta has a relaxed, congenial gay scene. *Paco Paco* on the corner of Madero and Pino Suárez is the gay community's bar, with all the latest scoop on everything from gay guesthouses to horse rides; it's open every day from 3 pm to 3 am. *Los Balcones*, upstairs at Juárez 182 near the corner of Libertad, has a dance floor and lots of little candlelit balconies; it's open every night from around 9.30 pm. *Gerardo's Party Pad* at Carranza 268 has a swimming pool, outdoor garden and indoor dance floor; swim in the afternoon, relax in the piano bar in the early evening and dance from 10 pm on. The *Piano Bar* in front of the seahorse statue on the Malecón (no sign) is sleazy at best but it's the

only gay 'after hours' place in town; it doesn't get going until around 3 am and by that time maybe you're not too fussy anyway. The 'Blue Chairs' at the south end of Playa de los Muertos, beside the Looney Tunes restaurant, is a gay-friendly beach hangout.

Mariachis Traditional Mexican mariachi music can be enjoyed at several places around town. On the Malecón near the seahorse statue, the upstairs *Mr Tequila's Grill & the Mariachi House* has live mariachi music nightly from 8.30 to 11 pm. Nearby, on the corner of Morelos and Galeana, *Brazz* has live mariachi music nightly from 9.30 pm to midnight. After hours, the *Mariachi Loco* restaurant/bar on the corner of Lázaro Cárdenas and Vallarta has mariachis and other entertainment nightly from 10.30 pm on; it's open from 7 pm to 6 am.

Fiestas Mexicanas *La Iguana* at Lázaro Cárdenas 311 is an old Vallarta favourite, presenting a Fiesta Mexicana with traditional Mexican folkloric dances, mariachis, *ranchero* rope tricks, a piñata, bloodless cockfights, a huge Mexican buffet, an open bar and a dance band for dancing under the stars every Thursday and Sunday evening from 7 to 11.15 pm. At 85 pesos per person it's not cheap, but it's a truly delightful event.

Other Fiesta Mexicana nights are held at some of the giant luxury hotels around the area, including the *Hotel Krystal, Westin Regina, Sheraton Buganvilias* and *Costa Vida*. A weekly schedule is published in the *Vallarta Today* newspaper, or ask at the tourist office.

Cinemas Vallarta has several cinemas, including the *Cine Bahía* on Insurgentes near Madero, the smaller *Sala Elizabeth Taylor* just off Vallarta on the south side of the Río Cuale, the *Cine Vallarta* on Calle Uruguay opposite the Conasupo supermarket on Avenida México a few blocks north of the centre, and the *Cine Luz Maria* nearby at Avenida México 227. Often the films are shown in English with Spanish subtitles.

Other Entertainment Bullfights are held every Wednesday from January to March, starting at 5 pm, in the bullring across from the marina. The Chess Club gets together most evenings at around 7 or 8 pm in the lobby of the Hotel Cecattur on the corner of Hidalgo and Guerrero.

Things to Buy

Shops and boutiques in Puerto Vallarta sell just about every type of handicraft made in Mexico, but prices are higher here than elsewhere. Try the Mercado Municipal for haggling on everything from Taxco silver, sarapes and huarache sandals to wool wallhangings and blown glass. The mercado has over 150 shops and stalls; it's open Monday to Saturday from 9 am to 8 pm, Sunday 9 am to 2 pm. Many other shops line Rodríguez, facing the mercado.

Also, don't forget Vallarta's many superb art galleries, mentioned earlier.

Getting There & Away

Air Puerto Vallarta's international airport, on highway 200 about 10 km north of the city, is served by a number of national and international airlines. The following list includes details of direct flights, all with connections to other places:

Aeroméxico
    Plaza Genovesa, Locales 2 & 3 (☎ 4-27-77) – Aguascalientes, Guadalajara, León, Los Angeles, Mexico City, San Diego (California)
Alaska Airlines
    Airport (☎ 1-13-50/52) – Los Angeles, San Francisco, Seattle
American Airlines
    Airport (☎ 1-19-27) – Dallas
Continental
    Airport (☎ 1-10-25) – Houston
Delta
    Airport (☎ 1-19-19, 1-10-32) – Los Angeles
Mexicana
    Centro Comercial Villa Vallarta, Local G-18 (☎ 4-89-00, 4-61-65) – Chicago, Guadalajara, Los Angeles, Los Cabos, Mazatlán, Mexico City, San Francisco
TAESA
    Opposite airport (☎ 1-15-21/31) – Mexico City, New York

Bus Intercity bus lines operate from individual terminals on the south side of the Río Cuale. They include Tres Estrellas de Oro & Elite (☎ 3-11-17) on the corner of Basilio Badillo and Insurgentes, ETN, Primera Plus & Servicios Coordinados/Costalegre (☎ 3-29-99, 2-69-86) on Lázaro Cárdenas between Constitución and Vallarta, Transportes del Pacífico (☎ 2-10-15) at Insurgentes 282, Transportes Cihuatlán & Autocamiones del Pacífico (☎ 2-34-36) on the corner of Madero and Constitución, and Transportes Norte de Sonora (TNS) (☎ 2-16-50, 2-66-66) at Carranza 322. Plaza Lázaro Cárdenas at Playa Olas Altas is the departure hub for all of the bus lines. Services include:

Barra de Navidad – 210 km, 3½ to 5 hours; same buses as to Manzanillo
Guadalajara – 397 km, six to seven hours, all 1st-class; hourly buses, 7 am to 4 pm, and every half-hour, 10.30 pm to 1.30 am, by Elite and Tres Estrellas de Oro (60 pesos); 13 daily by ETN (80 pesos) and Primera Plus (63 pesos); seven daily by Transportes del Pacífico (60 pesos)
Manzanillo – 302 km, five to 6½ hours; two 1st-class buses (five hours, 38 pesos) and nine 2nd-class buses (6½ hours, 31 pesos) by Transportes Cihuatlán; three 2nd-class buses daily by Servicios Coordinados/Costalegre (6½ hours, 31 pesos); three 1st-class buses daily by Tres Estrellas de Oro (five hours, 35 pesos); two daily by Primera Plus (five hours, 38 pesos)
Mazatlán – 459 km, eight hours; three 1st-class buses daily by Tres Estrellas de Oro (61 pesos); two 2nd-class buses daily by TNS (54 pesos)
Mexico City (Terminal Norte) – 932 km, 14 to 15 hours, all 1st-class; four daily by Tres Estrellas de Oro and Elite (140 pesos); one daily by Transportes del Pacífico (140 pesos); one daily by ETN (195 pesos)
San Blás – 95 km, three hours; two 2nd-class buses daily by TNS (22 pesos)
San Patricio-Melaque – 205 km, 3½ to 5 hours; same buses as to Manzanillo
Tepic – 169 km, three to four hours, all 2nd-class; buses every half-hour, 4 am to 9.45 pm, by Transportes del Pacífico (22 pesos); seven daily by TNS (21 pesos)
Zihuatanejo – 707 km, 15 hours; three 1st-class buses daily by Tres Estrellas de Oro (95 pesos), continuing on to Acapulco (18 hours, 135 pesos)

Getting Around

To/From the Airport Colectivo vans operate from the airport to town, but not from town to the airport. The cheapest way to get to the airport is on a local bus, which costs 1 peso; the 'Aeropuerto', 'Juntas' and 'Ixtapa' buses stop outside the airport entrance. A taxi from the city centre costs around 20 pesos.

Bus Local buses operate every five minutes from 5 am to 11 pm on most routes and cost 1 peso. Plaza Lázaro Cárdenas at Playa Olas Altas is a major departure hub.

Northbound buses marked 'Hoteles', 'Aeropuerto', 'Ixtapa', 'Pitillal' and 'Juntas' pass through the city heading north to the airport, the Zona Hotelera and Marina Vallarta; the 'Hoteles', 'Pitillal' and 'Ixtapa' routes can take you to any of the large hotels north of the city.

Southbound 'Boca de Tomatlán' buses pass along the southern coastal highway through Mismaloya to Boca de Tomatlán. They operate every 10 minutes from 6 am to 9 pm and cost 1.20 pesos.

Taxi Taxi prices are regulated by zones; the cost for a ride is determined by how many zones you cross. A ride in town costs around 7 pesos; to the airport 20 pesos, to Mismaloya 35 pesos, or 60 pesos to Nuevo Vallarta.

Car & Motorbike Rental agencies in Puerto Vallarta include:

Alfa	☎ 2-01-01, 2-17-79
Amigo	☎ 4-68-80
Ansa	☎ 2-65-45
Auto Rentas Guadalajara	☎ 2-29-06
Avis	☎ 4-14-12, 4-32-12
Clover	☎ 4-49-10, 4-06-35
De Alba	☎ 2-35-76
Dollar	☎ 2-42-56
Fun	☎ 3-02-25
Hertz	☎ 4-00-56
Marina	☎ 4-77-87
National	☎ 2-05-15, 2-27-42
Odin	☎ 2-28-25, 2-03-61
Payless	☎ 1-10-11
Peso	☎ 4-44-45
Quick	☎ 2-14-42, 2-35-05

To hire a vehicle you must be at least 25 years of age, have a valid driver's licence (a foreign one will do) and a major credit card. If you don't have a credit card you'll have to pay a large cash deposit. It pays to shop around as rates vary widely.

Jeeps are the most popular vehicles. Discounts on jeeps are frequently offered as an inducement to attend timeshare presentations.

Motorbikes can be hired from Moto Gallo (☎ 2-16-72) at Basilio Badillo 324.

Boat In addition to taxis on land, Vallarta also has a water taxi departing from Los Muertos Pier and heading south around the bay with stops at Las Ánimas (25 minutes), Quimixto (30 minutes) and Yelapa (45 minutes); the cost is 25 pesos one way or 50 pesos return for any destination. The boat goes twice a day, at 10.30 and 11 am.

Cheaper water taxis to the same places depart from Boca de Tomatlán and Mismaloya, both south of town and easy to reach by local bus. A water taxi to Las Ánimas (15 minutes), Quimixto (20 minutes) and Yelapa (30 minutes) leaves Boca de Tomatlán daily at 10 am and 1 pm, more frequently if enough people want to make the trip; the cost is 10 pesos one way for any destination (double for return). Water taxis to these destinations also go from Mismaloya, but only once in the morning, at around 9.30 or 10 am; the cost is 10 pesos to Las Ánimas, 15 pesos to Quimixto and 20 pesos to Yelapa.

Another way to reach Yelapa is by the supply boat leaving at 11.30 am every day except Sunday from the beach just south of the Hotel Rosita; the cost is 20 pesos for the half-hour trip. The same boat departs Yelapa daily at 7.30 am for the trip to Vallarta.

Private yachts and lanchas can be hired from the south side of the Playa de los Muertos pier. They'll take you to any secluded beach around the bay; most have gear aboard for snorkelling and fishing trips. The cost is 75 pesos per hour for the whole boat, which holds seven to 10 people. Lanchas can also be hired privately at Mismaloya and Boca de Tomatlán, but they are expensive.

CHAMELA

The first major coastal town south of Puerto Vallarta is Chamela, 152 km away. The town is little more than a scattering of small settlements along the 11-km shore of the Bahía de Chamela. Much of this shore consists of fine, untouched beaches – perfect escapes, though tourism is slowly creeping in to alter the landscape.

From Chamela's Super Mercado, a km-long road leads to the beachfront *Villa Polinesia & Camping Club* (Guadalajara ☎ (36) 22-39-40, fax 25-90-10), with 12 villas, 35 Polynesian-style huts, and shaded trailer spaces with full hook-ups. The appropriately named *Motel Trailer Park* is just north of the turnoff to the Villa Polinesia.

SAN PATRICIO-MELAQUE

• *pop: 4600*

Known to locals as Melaque, the small beach resort town of San Patricio-Melaque on the lovely Bahía de Navidad is 60 km south-east of Chamela, just after highway 80 from Guadalajara merges with highway 200. Although it is a little larger than its twin resort town of Barra de Navidad two km along the beach to the south-east, it rarely appears on maps.

Two haciendas owned by foreigners, those of San Patricio (on the east side) and Melaque (on the west), used to stand side by side here, with the dividing line between them running where Calle López Mateos is today. Settlements gradually grew around the two haciendas, and eventually merged into one town, which preserves the names of both.

In addition to being a popular beach resort for Mexican families when school is out, and a watering hole for yachties from November to May, the town is famous for its week-long St Patrick's Day celebrations (Fiesta de San Patricio) in March.

Orientation

Everything in Melaque is within walking distance. Most of the hotels, restaurants and public services are concentrated on or near Gómez Farías, running beside the beach, and López Mateos, the street coming in from the highway. Building numbers on Gómez Farías are not consecutive, so refer to the map for locations. Barra de Navidad is accessible from Melaque via highway 200 (five km) or by walking down the beach (two km).

Information

Tourist Office The tourist office in Barra de Navidad serves both Barra de Navidad and Melaque.

Money The Casa de Cambio Melaque at Local 11 in the Pasaje Comercial Melaque, on Gómez Farías opposite the main bus station, changes cash and travellers' cheques Monday to Saturday from 9 am to 2 pm and 4 to 7 pm, Sunday 9 am to 2 pm. There are no banks in either San Patricio-Melaque or Barra de Navidad; the closest banks are in Cihuatlán, about 15 km away.

Post & Telecommunications The post office and SCT Telégrafos, the telegraph office, share a building on Orozco near the corner of Corona. It's open Monday to Friday from 9 am to 3 pm.

There are several Lada casetas. The one on Vallarta near the corner of Gómez Farías, behind the corner store, has both telephone and fax; another caseta with phone and fax is on Corona near the corner of Hidalgo. Casetas with telephone only include one on the west side of the plaza and another at Artesanías Javito on Gómez Farías, half a block east of the main bus station. There are Ladatel phones near the bus station.

Laundry The Lavandería Industrial Hotelera at Gómez Farías 26, in the block west of the main bus station, is open Monday to Saturday from 8 am to 4 pm.

Things to See & Do

This is a peaceful little beach town with not a lot to do – swimming, lazing or walking on the beach, watching the pelicans fishing at sunset down at the west end of the bay, or walking down the beach to Barra de Navidad are the main activities here. It's a great place simply to relax and take life easy.

Fiesta de San Patricio

St Patrick's Day is celebrated in a big way in this town, with week-long festivities leading up to 17 March – parties all day, domino competitions, bull races through the town every afternoon, and a fiesta with fireworks every night in the plaza. The 17th begins with a mass and the blessing of the fleet. It's held in the Los Pelícanos restaurant, which is a major partying centre for the foreigners in town; they have their own pie-eating contests and other events throughout the week.

Places to Stay

Room rates vary greatly depending on the season; the town fills up with tourists (mostly Mexican families) during the school holidays in July and August, in December and at Semana Santa, when prices are higher and it's best to reserve a room in advance. The rest of the time it's pretty quiet, and many of the hotels will give discounts. Bungalows – apartments with kitchens – are common in this town, making it easy to do your own cooking.

Places to Stay – bottom end & middle

Camping The *Playa Trailer Park* (☎ (335) 5-50-65) at Gómez Farías 250, right on the beach, has 45 spaces with full hook-ups at 20/35 pesos for one/two people in a tent, 35 pesos in a trailer, 5 pesos for each extra person. There's also an unofficial campground on a flat area by the beach at the west end of town; it has no water or other facilities, though you can buy water from a truck that comes by. Most of the beachside palapa restaurants nearby will let you have a free shower.

Hotels *Posada Clemens* (☎ (335) 5-51-79) at Gómez Farías 70 on the corner of Guzmán has 14 clean, simple rooms at 40/50 pesos for singles/doubles. The *Hotel Hidalgo* (☎ (335) 5-50-45) at Hidalgo 7 has 14 simple rooms at 45/54 pesos. The *Hotel Monterrey* (☎ (335) 5-50-04) at Gómez Farías 27, on the beach opposite the bus station, has a swimming pool, restaurant, parking and 22 rooms with singles at 60 to 70 pesos, doubles at 80 to 100 pesos most of the year, and

singles/doubles at 88/110 pesos from December to April.

The *Hotel de Legazpi* (☎ (335) 5-53-97) on Avenida Las Palmas, on the beach at the west end of town, has a swimming pool and 16 large, bright rooms, some with a sea view and balcony; singles/doubles are 80/100 pesos in low season. Nearby, at Legazpi 5, is a pleasant little family place with no name, new in 1994 and half a block from the beach. It has just five rooms with bath for 40 pesos per person; contact Rafael Gálvez or Evelia Moreno (☎ (335) 5-58-61) at Corona 95, or ask at the Restaurant Los Pelícanos nearby. The *Hotel Las Brisas* (☎ (335) 5-51-08) at Gómez Farías 9, also on the beach, has 28 rooms at 70/90 pesos for singles/doubles and eight bungalows with kitchen at 190 pesos.

Bungalows *Bungalows Quinta Lety* (☎ (335) 5-50-64) at Gómez Farías 111 has four two-bedroom bungalows at 50 or 60 pesos for one or two people, 125 pesos for four or five, with discounts when it's not busy. It's a good place for families, with a children's pool, table tennis and a handball and basketball court. *Bungalows Los Arcos* (☎ (335) 5-51-84) at Gómez Farías 2 has two and three-bedroom bungalows at 140 and 220 pesos.

Beside the beach, *Bungalows Las Hamacas* (☎ (335) 5-51-13) at Gómez Farías 97 has a small swimming pool, parking, a beachfront restaurant and 26 bungalows with singles/doubles at 80/100 pesos, larger bungalows at 216 pesos, with discounts when they're not busy. Also on the beach, the *Hotel Vista Hermosa* (☎ (335) 5-50-02) at Gómez Farías 23 opposite the bus station has a swimming pool, parking and 26 bungalows at 225 pesos for five people, 325 pesos for eight, plus 21 regular rooms at 80/100 pesos; it's free for children under 10.

Bungalows Villamar (☎ /fax (335) 5-50-05) at Hidalgo 1 is a pleasant place with five spacious garden bungalows, a children's pool and a raised terrace overlooking the beach. A studio bungalow is 45 pesos, two-bedroom bungalows are 65 pesos, with discounts for weekly or monthly stays.

San Patricio-Melaque

Approximate Scale

BAHÍA DE NAVIDAD

PLACES TO STAY

6 Posada Pablo de Tarso
7 Posada Clemens
8 Hotel Hidalgo
9 Bungalows Villamar
10 Playa Trailer Park
14 Hotel Monterrey
16 Hotel Vista Hermosa
17 Bungalows Quinta Lely
20 Hotel Las Brisas
21 Bungalows Las Hamacas
23 Bungalows Los Arcos
24 Club Náutico El Dorado
27 Casa Grande Hotel & Resort
28 Hotel de Legazpi
29 Rooms
33 Unofficial Campground

PLACES TO EAT

25 Restaurant/Bar El Dorado
30 Restaurant La Tesmiza
31 Restaurant Los Pelícanos
32 Restaurant Tropicana

OTHER

1 Lada Caseta
2 Church
3 Cine Tropical
4 Lada Caseta
5 Post Office & SCT Telégrafos
11 Tres Estrellas de
   Oro Bus Station
12 Lada Caseta (Artesanías Javito)
13 Main Bus Station
15 Casa de Cambio Melaque
18 Lavandería Industrial Hotelera
19 Costalegre Bus Station
22 Lada Caseta
26 Disco Tanga

English is spoken; it's popular with North American visitors.

Places to Stay – top end

The beachside *Club Náutico El Dorado* (☎ (335) 5-52-39, 5-57-66; fax 5-57-70) at Gómez Farías 1-A has a swimming pool, parking, a pleasant beachfront restaurant and 56 well-appointed rooms; singles/doubles are 149/187 pesos. The *Posada Pablo de Tarso* (☎ (335) 5-51-17, 5-52-68; fax 5-57-17) at Gómez Farías 408 is an attractive hotel with a large beachside pool and terrace. It has 12 bungalows (with kitchen) for six people

at 297 pesos and 14 suites (no kitchen) for four people at 190 pesos. The most expensive place in town is the giant 223-room *Casa Grande Hotel & Resort* (☎ (335) 5-50-01, 5-51-95; fax 5-53-82). The prices include all meals, an open bar and a host of daily activities; singles/doubles are 431/570 pesos, with one child accommodated free for each adult.

Places to Eat

A row of pleasant palm-thatched palapa restaurants stretches along the beach at the west end of town. The most popular with foreigners is the *Restaurant Los Pelícanos*, whose American-born owner/chef/author, the gregarious Philomena ('Phil') Garcia, provides a 'home away from home' for travellers and yachties. She dishes up delicious food in large portions every day from 9 am to 9 pm; you can also buy her cookbooks at the restaurant, in addition to the *Pelican's Pouch*, her informative little book about Mexico.

Other palapa restaurants along this stretch include the *Restaurant Tropicana* and the *Restaurant La Tesmiza*. A fancier beachside restaurant/bar is the *Restaurant/Bar El Dorado* at the Hotel Club Náutico, with a great view of the bay. It's open every day from 8 am to 11 pm. You can get a simple snack or light meal at many places around the plaza.

Entertainment
Disco Tanga on Gómez Farías, operated by the fancy Casa Grande Hotel & Resort, is the only one in town; it's open from 10 pm to 3 am every night in high season, Thursday to Sunday night in low season. The beachside *Restaurant/Bar El Dorado* at the Hotel Club Naútico has live music and dancing on weekend evenings. A movie house, the *Cine Tropical*, is on the south side of the plaza.

Getting There & Away
Air See the following Barra de Navidad Getting There & Away section for details of air services. The travel agent for flight arrangements is found in that town.

Bus Melaque has three bus stations. The main station is on the corner of Gómez Farías and Carranza. Buses departing from this station go to:

Barra de Navidad – five km, 10 minutes; every 15 minutes, 6 am to 10 pm (1 peso) or southbound long-distance buses
Guadalajara – 294 km; seven 1st-class (five hours, 44 pesos) and 14 2nd-class buses (6½ hours, 34 pesos) daily
Manzanillo – 97 km; six 1st-class buses daily (one hour, 9 pesos); 2nd-class buses hourly, 6 am to midnight (1½ hours, 7 pesos)

Puerto Vallarta – 205 km; two 1st-class (3½ hours, 31.50 pesos) and 12 2nd-class buses (five hours, 25 pesos) daily

The 1st-class Tres Estrellas de Oro bus station is on Gómez Farías, 1½ blocks east of the main bus station. Two buses go daily to Puerto Vallarta (3½ hours, 25 pesos), with one continuing up the coast all the way to Tijuana. Two more buses head south daily through Manzanillo (1¼ hours, 7 pesos) and Zihuatanejo to Acapulco. The Costalegre bus station is a block from the main station, on the corner of Carranza and Corona.

Taxi A taxi between San Patricio-Melaque and Barra de Navidad costs 15 pesos.

BARRA DE NAVIDAD
• *pop: 2200*
The beach resort town of Barra de Navidad is around the bay from San Patricio-Melaque – a two-km walk along the beach, or five km by road. The waves are bigger here than in Melaque – locals from Melaque often come over here for surfing, especially in January when the waves are best. The town is squeezed onto a sandbar between the Bahía de Navidad and the Laguna de Navidad.

Orientation
Legazpi, the main street, runs beside the beach. Veracruz, the town's other major street and the route to the highway, runs parallel to Legazpi before merging with it at the south end of town, which terminates in a fingerlike sandbar.

Information
Tourist Office The Delegación Regional de Turismo (☎ (335) 5-51-00, ☎ /fax 5-51-59) is in Bungalow 11 at Club Privado Las Palmas, at the north end of Legazpi. It's open Monday to Friday from 9 am to 7 pm, Saturday 9 am to 1 pm.

Money There are no banks in either Barra de Navidad or San Patricio-Melaque; for banks you must go to Cihuatlán, about 15 km away. You can change money at Vinos y Licores

Licorín on Legazpi near the south-west corner of the plaza, open every day from 9 am to 11 pm, and at Telmex, on Sinaloa between Legazpi and Veracruz, open every day from 9 am to 9 pm.

Post & Telecommunications The post office, on Guanajuato near the corner of Mazatlán, is open Monday to Friday from 8 am to 3 pm, Saturday 9 am to 1 pm. The telegraph office, SCT Telégrafos, is on the corner of Veracruz and Guanajuato, on the south-east corner of the plaza. It's open Monday to Friday from 9 am to 2.30 pm.

The Telmex Lada caseta on Sinaloa between Legazpi and Veracruz is open every day from 9 am to 9 pm. The mini-market on the corner of Legazpi and Sonora also has a caseta, open Monday to Saturday from 10 am to 9 pm, Sunday 10 am to 5 pm.

Travel Agency Isla de Navidad Tours (☎ 5-56-65/66, fax 5-56-67) at Veracruz 106, opposite the plaza, can make flight arrangements. It's open Monday to Saturday from 9 am to 8 pm.

Laundry Lavandería Jardín at Jalisco 71 is open Monday to Saturday from 9 am to 2 pm and 4 to 7 pm.

Activities
Boat Trips The beach, of course, is Barra de Navidad's prime attraction. Boating on the lagoon is also popular. The local boat operators' cooperative, the Sociedad Cooperativa de Servicios Turísticos Miguel López de Legazpi, at Veracruz 40 is open every day from 9 am to 6 pm, with a price list posted on the wall. Half-hour tours of the lagoon cost 40 pesos for a boat holding up to eight people; a 45-minute bay tour is 50 pesos for up to seven people. They also offer deep-sea fishing, snorkelling and diving trips, rides on the 'banana' and longer boat trips including a jungle boat trip or an all-day trip to Tenacatita.

The cooperative also does trips to the village of Colimilla across the lagoon; the return trip is 30 pesos for up to eight people.

Or you can go halfway down the block where colectivo boats to Colimilla operate every day from 6 am to 8 pm; the cost is 1.50 pesos per person (3 pesos return).

Fishing Tournaments National and international fishing tournaments are held annually for marlin, sailfish, tuna and dorado, with prizes that include boats and cars.

The most important, the Torneo Internacional de Pesca de Marlin, Pez Vela y Dorado por Equipos, is held for three days around January or February; dates vary slightly. The second most important tournament is the Torneo Internacional de Marlin Club de Pesca Barra de Navidad, held for three days during late May or early June, with another two-day tournament in early August. A tuna tournament is held in June or July. The final tournament of the year is held before Independence Day on 15 and 16 September.

Places to Stay – bottom end
Camping You can camp for free by the beach at the north end of town, but there are no facilities provided.

Hotels The *Posada Pacífico* (☎ (335) 5-53-59) at Mazatlán 136, on the corner of Michoacán, is probably the best deal in town, with 25 large, clean rooms at 40/50 pesos for singles/doubles. The *Hotel San Lorenzo* (☎ (335) 5-51-39) at Sinaloa 7 near the corner of Mazatlán has 24 rooms at the same price. The simple little *Casa de Huéspedes Caribe* (☎ (335) 5-52-37) at Sonora 15 has 11 rooms at 25 pesos per person, with discounts for stays of a week or more.

Places to Stay – middle
Barra de Navidad has a number of good mid-range places to stay. One of the best is the *Hotel Delfín* (☎ (335) 5-50-68, fax 5-60-20) at Morelos 23, opposite the lagoon, with 26 large, clean and pleasant rooms looking out onto wide walkways; from each room you can view the lagoon and the swimming pool below. It has an exercise and weights

room and an outdoor restaurant with a breakfast buffet for 15 pesos. Singles/doubles are 75/88 pesos from May to October, 88/96 pesos from November to April.

Over on Legazpi are several other good hotels right on the beach, including the *Hotel Bogavante* (☎ (335) 5-53-84, 5-61-20; fax 5-68-07) with regular rooms at 70/90 pesos, bungalows with kitchen starting at 150 pesos. Next door, the less attractive *Bungalows Karelia* has bungalows at 100 pesos. The *Hotel Tropical* (☎ (335) 5-50-20, fax 5-51-49) at Legazpi 96 is a fancier place with

rooms at 132/176 pesos. The *Hotel Barra de Navidad* (☎ (335) 5-51-22, fax 5-53-03) at Legazpi 250, with a restaurant/bar and a beachside swimming pool, has 60 rooms at 93/147 pesos.

The *Hotel Sands* (☎ /fax (335) 5-50-18) at Morelos 24 beside the lagoon has a swimming pool, a poolside restaurant/bar and 44 rooms at 70/88 pesos most of the year, 135 pesos from November to April, with more expensive suites and bungalows.

The *Bungalows Mar Vida* (☎ (335) 5-59-11, fax 5-53-49) at Mazatlán 168, run by an

PLACES TO STAY
2 Unofficial Camping on Beach
4 Bungalows Mar Vida
5 Posada Pacífico
6 Hotel Bogavante & Bungalows Karelia
12 Hotel Barra de Navidad
14 Hotel San Lorenzo
17 Hotel Delfín
18 Hotel Sands
19 Casa de Huéspedes Caribe
20 Hotel Tropical

PLACES TO EAT
16 Crepes y Café Ambar
22 Velero's & Restaurante Eloy
23 Nacho's
24 Restaurant/Bar Pacífico
26 El Manglito

OTHER
1 Tourist Office
3 Bus Station
7 Plaza
8 Travel Agency
9 Post Office
10 SCT Telégrafos
11 Vinos y Licores Licorín
13 Telmex
15 Lavandería Jardín
21 Mini-Market & Lada Caseta
25 Boats for Lagoon Tours
27 Boats to Colimilla

Barra de Navidad

BAHÍA DE NAVIDAD

LAGUNA DE NAVIDAD

To Highway 200 & San Patricio-Melaque

To San Patricio-Melaque (via beach)

0   100   200 m
Approximate Scale

American/Mexican couple, is a fine little guesthouse with a swimming pool and five studio apartments at 125 pesos.

Places to Eat

There are more restaurants in Barra de Navidad than you would expect from the size of the town. Several are on terraces overlooking the beach, with a beautiful view of the sunset. Several more are beside the lagoon, and still others are on Calle Veracruz, in the centre of town.

Beside the beach, *Nacho's* on Legazpi just south of Yucatán has good food. Next door, at Legazpi 206, the *Restaurant/Bar Pacífico* is run by some folks from Texas.

Beside the lagoon, *Velero's* on Veracruz is a good restaurant/bar with a fine view, open every day from noon to 10 pm. Nearby, also overlooking the lagoon, are the *Restaurante Eloy* and *El Manglito*.

One of the most pleasant restaurants in town is *Crepes y Café Ambar*, upstairs on the corner of Veracruz and Jalisco. It's a clean '50% vegetarian' restaurant with a fine atmosphere under a high palapa roof, good music and probably the best coffee in town. It's open every day except Thursday from 8 am to 3 pm and 5 to 11 pm, but only from November to April.

Entertainment

The one disco in town is *El Galeón*, at the Hotel Sands. It's naturally quite popular. The Hotel Sands's two-for-one happy hour, from 2 until 4 or 6 pm at the poolside bar, is also popular, especially since it includes the use of their lagoonside pool, but only in high season from November to April.

Getting There & Away

Air Barra de Navidad and Melaque are served by the Playa de Oro international airport, 38 km south-east on highway 200. To get there you must either take a taxi (half an hour, 60 pesos), or a bus 15 km to Cihuatlán and a cheaper taxi from there. Aeroméxico offers daily direct flights to Guadalajara and Mexicana offers daily

direct flights to Mexico City, both with connecting flights to many other places.

Bus The bus station is at Veracruz 228, near the corner of Nayarit. Buses include:

Guadalajara – 291 km; five 1st-class (five to 5½ hours, 44 pesos) and 13 2nd-class buses (seven hours, 34 pesos) daily

Manzanillo – 92 km; 1st-class (one hour, 9 pesos) and 2nd-class (1½ hours, 7 pesos) buses hourly from 8 am to 9 pm

Puerto Vallarta – 210 km; two 1st-class buses daily (3½ hours, 31.50 pesos); 2nd-class buses every two hours, 6 am to 11.30 pm (five hours, 25 pesos)

San Patricio-Melaque – five km, 10 minutes; every 15 minutes, 6 am to 10 pm (1 peso) or by northbound long-distance buses

Taxi A taxi between Barra de Navidad and San Patricio-Melaque costs 15 pesos.

MANZANILLO
• *pop: 93,000*

Manzanillo is a major port and industrial city, with a tangle of train tracks, shipping piers and traffic surrounded by stagnant marshes that locals call lagoons. Surprisingly, away from the centre and out around the Bahía de Manzanillo and Bahía de Santiago is an area known for its beaches – but you have to search for them. There's also deep-sea fishing, and good bird-watching in the lagoons and around the golf course.

Orientation

Manzanillo extends for 16 km from northwest to south-east. The resort hotels and finest beaches begin on Playa Azul across the Bahía de Manzanillo from Playa San Pedrito, the closest beach to the centre (about one km away). Farther around the bay is the Santiago peninsula, a rocky outcrop occupied by Las Hadas Resort and the beaches of La Audiencia, Santiago, Olas Altas and Miramar. Just west of Miramar is the Laguna Juluapan.

Central Manzanillo is bound by the Bahía de Manzanillo to the north, the Pacific Ocean to the west, and the Laguna de Cuyutlán to the south-east and south. Avenida Morelos,

CENTRAL PACIFIC COAST

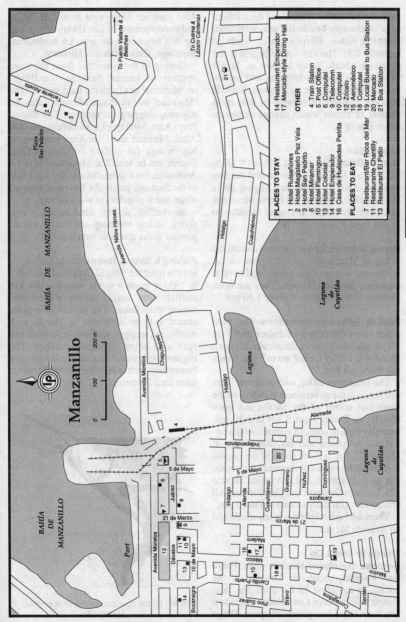

Manzanillo

0   100   200 m

BAHÍA DE MANZANILLO

Port

BAHÍA DE MANZANILLO

Playa San Pedro

To Puerto Vallarta & Beaches

To Colima & Lázaro Cárdenas

Teniente Azueta

Avenida Niños Heroes

Hidalgo

Cuauhtémoc

Laguna de Cuyutlán

Laguna de Cuyutlán

Laguna

Chapultepec

Avenida Morelos

Hidalgo

Alameda

Independencia

5 de Mayo

Hidalgo

Allende

Cuauhtémoc

Guerrero

Núñez

Domínguez

Zaragoza

21 de Marzo

Madero

México

Camillo Puerto

Bravo

Pino Suárez

Serdán

Consaglora

México

5 de Mayo

Juárez

21 de Marzo

Avenida Morelos

Dávalos

10 de Mayo

Bocanegra

PLACES TO STAY
1 Hotel Ruiseñores
2 Hotel Magisterio Pez Vela
3 Hotel San Pedrito
8 Hotel Miramar
9 Hotel Flamingos
14 Hotel Colonial
14 Hotel Emperador
16 Casa de Huéspedes Petrita

PLACES TO EAT
7 Restaurant/Bar Roca del Mar
11 Restaurante Chantilly
13 Restaurant El Patio

OTHER
4 Train Station
5 Post Office
6 Computel
9 Telecomm
10 Computel
15 Aeroméxico
18 Zócalo
18 Computel
19 Local Buses to Bus Station
20 Mercado
21 Bus Station

14 Restaurant Emperador
17 Mercado-style Dining Hall

the principal avenue, runs along the northern edge of the city beside the sea, west from Avenida Niños Héroes which leads to highway 200. The city centre begins at the plaza or zócalo (also known as Jardín Obregón) on Avenida Morelos, and continues southward with the major street, Avenida México, crossed from west to east by a number of streets which change names on either side of it.

Information
Tourist Office The tourist office (☎ (333) 3-22-77/64, fax 3-14-26) is around the bay in Playa Azul at Boulevard Miguel de la Madrid 4960, between the Fiesta Mexicana and Marbella hotels. It's open Monday to Friday from 8.30 am to 3 pm.

Money Many banks are scattered around the centre of Manzanillo, including one on the north-west corner of the zócalo and several others on Avenida México. They are open Monday to Friday from 9 am to 1.30 pm.

Post & Telecommunications The post office is on the corner of Juárez and 5 de Mayo, one block east of the zócalo. It's open Monday to Friday from 8 am to 7 pm, Saturday 9 am to 1 pm.

The Telecomm office, with telegram, telex and fax, is in the government building on the south-east corner of the zócalo. It's open Monday to Friday from 9 am to 5.30 pm, Saturday 9 am to noon. Computel, with long-distance telephone and fax, has offices at Madero 72, half a block south of the zócalo, at Avenida Morelos 144, between the zócalo and the train station, and at Avenida México 326, between Guerrero and Cuauhtémoc. All offices are open daily from 8 am to 10 pm.

There are Ladatel phones in the zócalo and on Avenida México.

Things to See & Do
Beaches The closest beach to town, **Playa San Pedrito**, about one km east of the zócalo, is too close to the port. The next closest beach, **Playa Las Brisas**, caters to a few hotels and has plenty of space. **Playa Azul** stretches north-west from Las Brisas and curves around to Las Hadas Resort and the best beaches in the area: **La Audiencia, Santiago, Olas Altas** and **Miramar**.

Getting to these beaches from the town centre is easy: take any 'Santiago', 'Las Brisas' or 'Miramar' bus from the train station. The 'Miramar' bus to Playa Miramar takes 40 minutes, stopping en route at Las Brisas, Playa Azul, Santiago, La Audiencia and Olas Altas. Miramar and Olas Altas have waves big enough for surfing or body-surfing. Boards can be rented at Miramar. Playa La Audiencia, on a quiet cove at the west side of the Santiago peninsula, has more tranquil water and is popular for water-skiing.

Snorkelling, diving, windsurfing, water-skiing, sailing and deep-sea fishing are all popular water sports around the bay.

Fishing & Sailing Tournaments Manzanillo calls itself the 'World Capital of Sailfish'; in 1957 it made a world record when 336 sailfish were caught during a three-day fishing tournament. The sailfish *(pez vela)* season is from November to March, with marlin, red snapper, sea bass, yellowtail and tuna also being important catches. The biggest international tournament is held each November, with a smaller national tournament each February.

Fishing for the spectacular marlin is popular at Manzanillo

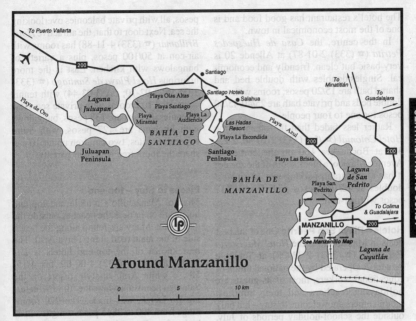

Around Manzanillo

During the first part of February a sailing tournament coming from San Diego, California, or Puerto Vallarta (in alternate years) ends with celebrations at the Las Hadas Resort.

Festivals

The Fiestas de Mayo, held from 1 to 10 May, celebrate Manzanillo's anniversary with sporting competitions and other events. The Fiesta de Nuestra Señora de Guadalupe is held from 1 to 12 December in honour of Mexico's patron saint.

Places to Stay

The best places to stay in central Manzanillo are within a block or two of the zócalo. This area is safe and clean. A few blocks south in the town centre there are a number of places to stay, but the area is comparatively dirty and squalid. Alternatively, you may prefer to stay at nearby Playa San Pedrito, not the best stretch of beach but convenient both to town and transport to the better beaches. On the

latter, hotels tend to be more expensive; four good, economical ones are found half an hour away by bus at Playa Santiago.

Places to Stay – bottom end & middle

Camping The *Trailer Park El Palmar* (☎ (333) 2-32-90) at Km 4.5 on the Manzanillo-Santiago road has 77 spaces with full hook-ups at 25 pesos.

Hotels – centre A few doors from the south-east corner of the zócalo, the *Hotel Miramar* (☎ (333) 2-10-08) at Juárez 122 has clean singles/doubles at 35/50 pesos. Half a block south of the zócalo, the *Hotel Flamingos* (☎ (333) 2-10-37) at Madero 72 has singles/doubles at 40/60 pesos. Half a block from the south-west corner of the zócalo, the clean but very basic *Hotel Emperador* (☎ (333) 2-23-74), at Dávalos 69, has singles at 30 to 35 pesos, doubles at 45 pesos; the rooms on the top floor are a little brighter than the rest.

The hotel's restaurant has good food and is one of the most economical in town.

In the centre, the *Casa de Huéspedes Petrita* (☎ (333) 2-01-87) at Allende 20 is very basic but clean, friendly and economical. Singles/doubles with double bed and shared bath are 15/20 pesos; rooms with two double beds and private bath are 25/40/45/50 pesos for one to four people.

Rather less faded than the others is the *Hotel Colonial* (☎ /fax (333) 2-10-80, 2-12-30) at Bocanegra 100 on the corner of Avenida México, a block south of the zócalo; it has a restaurant, parking and 38 singles/doubles at 78/104 pesos with fan, 91/117 pesos with air-con.

Hotels – Playa San Pedrito One of the best deals in Manzanillo is the *Hotel Magisterio Pez Vela* (☎ (333) 2-11-08) at Teniente Azueta 7. Operated by the national union of educational workers, most of its guests are holidaying teachers and their families, though others are welcome to stay – but only outside the school-holiday periods of July, August, Christmas and Easter. Right on the beach, it has 36 clean rooms around a swimming pool courtyard; singles/doubles are 30/50 pesos. A little further down Teniente Azueta, the similar *Hotel Ruiseñores* (☎ (333) 2-06-46, 2-24-24) has 71 singles/doubles at 55/80 pesos. Also similar is the *Hotel San Pedrito* (☎ (333) 2-05-35, fax 2-22-24) at Teniente Azueta 3, with singles/doubles at 50/80 pesos.

Hotels – Playa Santiago A 10 or 15-minute walk (or five-minute ride) from highway 200 and Santiago town, on a fine stretch of beach on the bluff at Playa Santiago, are four reasonably priced beachfront hotels. All have swimming pools and all except the Anita have restaurant/bars.

Cheapest of the lot is the *Hotel Anita* (☎ (333) 3-01-61) with 91 rooms at 25 pesos per person. Next door, the *Hotel Marlyn* (☎ (333) 2-06-32, 3-01-07) has regular rooms at 50/80 pesos for singles/doubles, and bungalows with kitchen for 200 to 350

pesos, all with private balconies overlooking the sea. Next door to that, the attractive *Hotel Brillamar* (☎ (333) 4-11-88) has rooms with air-con at 50/100 pesos, plus a variety of bungalows with kitchen. Last is the more luxurious *Hotel Playa de Santiago* (☎ (333) 3-00-55, 3-02-70; fax 3-03-44) with tennis courts and 105 rooms with private sea-view balconies. Rooms are 138 pesos, bungalows with kitchens are 127 pesos, with more expensive suites; two children under 10 can share the room free with their parents.

Places to Stay – top end

Most of Manzanillo's middle and top-end hotels are on or near the beaches outside the city centre. Many are found along the beach side of the main road along Playa Azul. The best known of the top-end hotels is *Las Hadas Resort* (☎ (333) 4-00-00, fax 4-19-50), a white Arabian-style resort on the Santiago peninsula where the film *10*, featuring Bo Derek, was made. The 220 rooms range from 490 to 2845 pesos a night – 25% higher from December to April.

A couple of newer top-end places are said to surpass even Las Hadas. The *Club Maeva* (☎ (333) 5-05-95/96, fax 5-03-95) at Playa Miramar, with 514 villas and rooms, is great for active types – the nightly cost of 400 pesos per person includes all you can eat and drink, water sports, good entertainment – the works. For a more relaxing time, the ultimate is the *Sierra Radisson Plaza* (☎ (333) 3-20-00, fax 3-22-72) on the Santiago peninsula near Las Hadas, where double rooms are 430 to 475 pesos.

More moderately priced, the *Hotel Villas La Audiencia* (☎ (333) 3-08-61, 3-06-83; fax 3-26-53) on the Santiago peninsula is good value in the top-end range, especially for families. All the villas come with kitchen, air-con and colour satellite TV, and there's a swimming pool and restaurant/bar. Villas with one/two/three bedrooms cost 205/260/315 pesos. Also more moderately priced and closer to town is the *Hotel La Posada* (☎ /fax (333) 3-18-99), at Lázaro Cárdenas 201 on Playa Azul, a friendly beachfront lodge with a swimming pool. The hotel is in a good position for snorkelling and windsurfing. Singles/doubles are 145/158 pesos most of the year, 220 pesos from 16 December to 30 April, breakfast included.

Places to Eat

Around the zócalo are a number of good places to eat. The *Restaurant/Bar Roca del Mar* on the east side of the zócalo has a pleasant atmosphere and is good for all meals. Among its specialities is a seafood comida corrida with seafood soup, rice, fish or shrimp and dessert, all for 14.50 pesos. It's open every day from 7 am to 10.30 pm. On the south side of the zócalo, the *Restaurante Chantilly* is a popular corner restaurant open from 7 am to 10 pm every day except Saturday.

Restaurant Emperador, on the ground floor of the Hotel Emperador at Dávalos 69, half a block west of the zócalo, is simple and small but it has good food at some of the most economical prices in Manzanillo, with a comida corrida, meat or seafood meals for 10 pesos, breakfast or enchiladas for just 5 pesos. It's open every day from 7 am to 10 pm.

Also good is *El Patio* at the Hotel Colonial, a block south of the zócalo on the corner of Avenida México and Bocanegra. Its comida corrida costs 15 pesos; dinners are more expensive. It's open Monday to Saturday from 8 am to 11 pm, with live music in the afternoon and evening (see Entertainment below).

A mercado-style dining hall on the corner of Madero and Cuauhtémoc is open every day from around 6 am to 10 pm, with a number of stalls to choose from.

Many more restaurants are spread out around the bay. *Carlos 'n Charlie's* on the highway at Playa Azul is a fun place with good food. *Savoy-2* on the plaza at Santiago is popular for its traditional Mexican food.

Entertainment

If you're here on a Sunday evening, stop by the zócalo, where everyone from toddlers to grandparents are out enjoying an ice cream,

the company and the balmy night air. This tradition, which has disappeared in many parts of Mexico, is still alive and well in Manzanillo. Sometimes a band plays in the gazebo to entertain the crowd.

A block south of the plaza, the restaurant/bar *El Patio* at the Hotel Colonial on the corner of Avenida México and Bocanegra features live music Monday to Saturday from 2.30 to 4.30 pm and from 8.30 to 10.30 pm.

The nightlife for tourists in Manzanillo is mostly spread out around the bay. The *Vog*, on the highway at Playa Azul, is a popular disco with a cover charge. Beside it, the *Bar de Felix* has no cover charge and many people like it better for dancing. *Teto's Bar* near the Hotel Fiesta Mexicana on Playa Azul is another popular dancing spot with live music. Also on Playa Azul, don't forget *Carlos 'n Charlie's*, one of the Carlos Anderson bar/restaurant chain which puts on a good time for tourists all over Mexico.

The luxurious *Club Maeva* on Playa Miramar has the *Disco Boom Boom* and the *Tropical Hut*. They also present theme entertainment several nights weekly, including a Mexican Fiesta night, a Tropical Latin night and a Best of Broadway night. All events last from 8 to 11.30 pm; the cost of 72 pesos per person includes a sumptuous theme buffet and open bar. Phone for reservations (☎ 3-05-96, ext 145).

Getting There & Away

Air Manzanillo is served by the Playa de Oro international airport, 45 km north-west of the city on highway 200. Aeroméxico offers daily direct flights to Guadalajara, while Mexicana offers daily direct flights to Mexico City, both with connections to many other places.

The Aeroméxico office (☎ 2-12-67, 2-17-11) is at Local 107, in the Centro Comercial on Avenida Carrillo Puerto between Allende and Cuauhtémoc; it's open Monday to Friday from 9 am to 7 pm, Saturday 9 am to 2 pm and 3 to 7 pm. Mexicana (☎ 3-23-23) only has an office at the airport, but their tickets are sold and serviced at the Aeroméxico office in town.

Bus The bus terminal, about 1.5 km east of the centre, has a restaurant, a luggage-storage area and a Lada caseta. Destinations include:

Armería – 45 km, 45 minutes; buses every 15 minutes, 4 am to 10.30 pm, by Sociedad Cooperativa de Autotransportes Colima, Armería, Cuyutlán, Manzanillo (4 pesos); every 20 minutes by Autotransportes del Sur de Jalisco (3 pesos)

Barra de Navidad – 92 km, 1½ hours; 26 daily by Auto Camiones del Pacífico (7 pesos)

Colima – 101 km, 1½ to two hours; 2nd-class buses every 15 minutes, 4 am to 10.30 pm, by Sociedad Cooperativa de Autotransportes Colima, Armería, Cuyutlán, Manzanillo (8 pesos); every 20 minutes, 2.15 am to 10 pm, by Autransportes del Sur de Jalisco (7 pesos); plus all the buses to Guadalajara (1¼ to 1½ hours, 1st-class 12.50 pesos, primera plus 17.50 pesos)

Guadalajara – 325 km, 4½ hours; 18 daily by Autobuses de Jalisco La Linea; 18 daily by Flecha Amarilla; 13 daily by Auto Camiones del Pacífico; 11 daily by Primera Plus (1st-class 44 pesos, primera plus 50 to 58 pesos)

Lázaro Cárdenas – 330 km, seven hours; three 1st-class buses daily by Tres Estrellas de Oro (41 pesos); six 2nd-class buses daily by Autotransportes del Sur de Jalisco (37 pesos)

Mexico City (Terminal Norte or Terminal Poniente) – 843 km, 12 hours; 'via corta' (short route) or via Morelia; three 1st-class buses daily by Tres Estrellas de Oro (108 or 128 pesos); three daily by Primera Plus (118 pesos); five 2nd-class buses daily by Autobuses de Occidente (87 pesos); six daily by Flecha Amarilla (87 or 115 pesos); two daily by Servicios Coordinados (87 pesos)

Puerto Vallarta – 302 km, five to six hours; two 1st-class buses daily by Auto Camiones del Pacífico, two daily by Tres Estrellas de Oro, one daily by Primera Plus (38 pesos); 11 2nd-class buses daily by Auto Camiones del Pacífico (31 pesos)

San Patricio-Melaque – 97 km, 1¾ hours; same as to Barra de Navidad

Train The train station is on Avenida Morelos, a couple of blocks east of the zócalo. The ticket office is open every day but only from 5 to 6 am, selling tickets for the one train of the day, the segunda clase Train 91, which departs at 6 am for Guadalajara (seven hours, 16 pesos) via Colima (two hours, 4.30 pesos). The schedule is posted on the wall at the station.

Getting Around
To/From the Airport Transportes Turísticos Benito Juárez (☎ 4-15-55) operates a door-to-door van to/from the airport. The cost is 20 pesos per person when there are three people or more, 50 pesos per person for one or two people. A taxi from the centre to the airport costs 50 pesos.

Bus Local buses heading around the bay to San Pedrito, Salahua, Santiago, Miramar and all the beaches along the way depart from in front of the train station or from the main bus station every 10 minutes from 5 am to 11.30 pm. The fare is 0.50 pesos to San Pedrito, 1.60 pesos to Playa Santiago and 2 pesos to Playa Miramar.

The 'Campos', 'Rocío' and 'Torres' local bus routes connect the centre with the bus station, stopping on the corner of Avenida México and Domínguez and at the mercado along the way. They operate daily from 6 am to 9.30 pm (0.70 pesos).

Taxi Taxis are plentiful around Manzanillo. From the centre of town it's 5 pesos to the bus station, 15 pesos to Playa Azul, 25 pesos to Playa Santiago, 30 pesos to Playa Miramar and 50 pesos to the airport. Agree on the price before you get into the cab.

CUYUTLÁN & PARAÍSO
• *pop: Cuyutlán 1865; Paraíso 200*
The small black-sand beach resort towns of Cuyutlán and Paraíso are south-east of Manzanillo off highway 200. Cuyutlán, the more developed of the two, is near the south-eastern end of the Laguna de Cuyutlán, about an hour from either Manzanillo or Colima. A paved road connects Cuyutlán with Paraíso, six km to the south-east.

Both towns have a few hotels and restaurants that are popular with Mexican families and seldom visited by norteamericanos. Beachfront accommodation consequently costs much less here.

In Cuyutlán most of the hotels and places to eat are near one another on the beach or about half a block back from it. If you arrive in town by bus you'll be let off on Calle

Hidalgo, on one side of the zócalo. Walk four blocks towards the sea on Hidalgo and you'll be right in the middle of the hotel and restaurant area beside the beach.

Aside from its long stretch of relatively isolated beach, Cuyutlán is also known for its 'green wave' in April and May, caused by little green phosphorescent critters.

Paraíso is a small fishing village, with a black-sand beach, three hotels, a number of simple thatched-roof seafood restaurants (*enramadas*) and some fishing boats.

Information

Neither Cuyutlán or Paraíso has a post office or banks; for these you'll have to go into Armería (see Getting There & Away). Both do have Lada casetas, however. Cuyutlán's caseta is on Calle Hidalgo, in the shop on the corner one block past the zócalo, heading away from the beach. In Paraíso it's in the restaurant opposite the beach and the bus stop.

Places to Stay

Cuyutlán To telephone the hotels from outside the town, you must dial the town caseta (☎ (332) 4-18-10); ask for the three-digit extension for the place you want and they will connect you.

At Christmas and Semana Santa, all the hotels fill up with Mexican families on holiday. If you come at these times you should reserve in advance. Most of the hotels require that you take three meals a day included in the price at these times; the cost for room and meals will be around 90 pesos per person.

Camping If you don't mind roughing it you can camp on the beach to the right of the hotels. A couple of simple thatch-roofed restaurants nearby have signs posted out front saying they rent showers and baths or '*cuartos con baño*' – simple rooms that may be only partitions in large halls behind the restaurants. These are the cheapest rooms in town.

Hotels As you come to the beach on Calle Hidalgo you'll reach the corner of Hidalgo and Calle Veracruz, the beachside road. On this corner are two of Cuyutlán's best budget hotels. The other hotels are a block or two to either side of this corner. The *Hotel Morelos* (☎ 107), on this corner at Hidalgo 185, has 48 clean, pleasant rooms with private bath and ceiling fan at 25 to 30 pesos per person. Opposite this, the *Hotel Fénix* (☎ 147) is another good place, with 18 rooms at 20 pesos per person. To your right is the *Hotel Tlaquepaque* (☎ 106) at Veracruz 30, with simple rooms at 30/40/50 pesos for singles/doubles/triples.

More stylish is the *Hotel El Bucanero* (☎ 102), on the beachfront behind the Hotel Fénix; the cost is 20/30 pesos per person for interior/sea-view rooms. Opposite this, also right on the beach, the large *Hotel Ceballos* (☎ 101) at Veracruz 10 is quite a bit more expensive. To the left of this at Veracruz 46, the *Hotel San Rafael* (☎ 108) has a swimming pool, a beachfront restaurant/bar and courtyard or sea-view rooms, all at 45 pesos per person.

Paraíso Of the three hotels, the fancy one is the *Hotel Paraíso* (cellular ☎ (332) 8-10-09; reservations in Colima ☎ (331) 2-47-87, 2-10-32), with a swimming pool, pleasant terraces, a seafood restaurant and 60 rooms at 85 pesos for up to two adults and two children. The *Posada & Enramada Valencia* (☎ (332) 4-28-50, 4-29-10), new in 1993, has 13 rooms with one/two beds at 60/80 pesos. Or there's the very basic *Enramada Los Equipales* (☎ (332) 4-29-10) with 10 rooms at 40 pesos each. Otherwise you could camp on the beach, or probably string up a hammock under one of the enramadas.

Places to Eat

Cuyutlán Several of the hotels have good seafood restaurants. The *El Bucanero* and the *Siete Mares*, attached respectively to the Hotel El Bucanero and the Hotel San Rafael, are attractive beachfront restaurant/bars. On the corner of Hidalgo and Veracruz, also sharing with hotels, are two of the town's most economical restaurants: the *Restaurante Morelos* and the *Restaurante Fénix*.

Both offer good-value meals at 12 pesos for breakfast or dinner, 14 pesos for a comida corrida. For a simple snack, stands on the beach sell seafood and cold drinks. Or you can grab a snack at one of the restaurants near the plaza.

Paraíso All the beachfront enramadas serve basically the same food at the same price. The classiest of the hotel restaurants is the poolside restaurant at the *Hotel Paraíso*, open every day from 8 am to 6 pm. Some enramadas stay open later, until around 9 pm.

Getting There & Away

Cuyutlán and Paraíso are connected to the rest of the world through Armería, a dusty town on highway 200 about 60 km southeast of Manzanillo and 45 km south-west of Colima. From Armería to Cuyutlán it's 17 km down a paved road passing through orchards and coconut plantations to the coast; a similar road runs eight km south-west from Armería to Paraíso.

To reach either place by bus involves going first to Armería and changing buses there. The Sociedad Cooperativo de Autotransportes Colima Manzanillo bus line, with an office and bus stop on Armería's main street, operates 2nd-class buses to Manzanillo every 15 minutes from 5 am to 11 pm (4 pesos, 45 minutes) and to Colima every half-hour from 5.40 am to 9.40 pm (4 pesos, 45 minutes). A couple of doors away, Flecha Amarilla has 2nd-class buses to Mexico City and Guadalajara.

Buses to Cuyutlán and Paraíso depart from the same stop in Armería, on the corner of Netzahualcóyotl (the main street) and 5 de Mayo, beside the Restaurant Camino Real, a couple of blocks from the long-distance bus stop. There are taxis but no buses between the two beaches; to go by bus from one to the other, you must return to Armería and change buses there.

Buses from Armería to Cuyutlán depart every half-hour from 6.30 am to 8 pm (2 pesos, 20 minutes). Buses to Paraíso depart every 45 minutes from 6 am to 7.30 pm (1.50 pesos, 15 minutes).

Taxis go from Armería to Cuyutlán (15 pesos), from Armería to Paraíso (10 pesos) and between Cuyutlán and Paraíso (15 pesos).

LÁZARO CÁRDENAS

• *pop: 135,000*

Lázaro Cárdenas is the largest city on the coast of Michoacán, one of Mexico's most beautiful states. The city is named after the reform-minded leader who served as governor of Michoacán from 1928 to 1932, and as president of Mexico from 1934 to 1940. In the late 1960s he encouraged President Díaz Ordaz to begin constructing a huge US$500-million Sicartsa iron and steel works and US$40-million port in the village of Melchor Ocampo. The project didn't get under way until after his death in 1970, during the administration of President Luis Echeverría (1970-76).

Echeverría renamed the village Lázaro Cárdenas and erected what became a slum city around the project, which by this time was slated to cost over US$1 billion. The resulting plant produced steel wire, which Mexico really didn't need, and was run with coal imported from Colombia. The plant cost much more than it could ever earn and greatly contributed to the 450% increase in Mexico's foreign debt, which was more than US$19 billion by 1976.

Today the plant continues to run, supposedly with injections of British capital, but more emphasis seems to have been placed on the city's burgeoning port facilities. While not as much of an eyesore as it was in the past, the city has nothing of real interest to travellers. Reasons to stop here are to stock up on food and water, change buses, and head for Playa Azul 24 km to the west.

Getting There & Away

Air Lázaro Cárdenas has an airport served by a variety of obscure airlines; there are connections to Mexico City by Aeromar, to Uruapan by Aerocuahonte, and to Guadalajara by Aerocuahonte and Tagsa. Tickets are sold at Chinameca Viajes (see Train).

Bus While the town itself is not of much

interest to travellers, Lázaro Cárdenas is a terminus for several bus routes, so you may need to change buses here if you're travelling in this part of the country.

Lázaro has two bus terminals, two blocks apart. The Galeana and Parhikuni bus lines (☎ 2-02-62, 2-30-06), with services northwest to Manzanillo and inland to Uruapan, Morelia and Mexico City, share a terminal at Avenida Lázaro Cárdenas 1810, on the corner of Calle Constitución de 1814. Avenida Lázaro Cárdenas is the city's main street and there are many hotels, restaurants and shops around this bus station.

The Estrella Blanca, Cuauhtémoc and Tres Estrellas de Oro bus lines (☎ 2-11-71) have buses south to Zihuatanejo, Acapulco, and then inland from Acapulco to Mexico City, with one route daily heading up the coast to Mazatlán and another to Tijuana. They share a separate terminal two blocks behind the Galeana terminal, at Calle Francisco Villa 164, half a block from Calle Constitución de 1814. Walk two blocks on Calle Constitución de 1814 to get from one terminal to the other.

Destinations from Lázaro Cárdenas include:

Acapulco – 311 km, six hours; 1st or 2nd-class buses every half-hour, 4 am to 6 pm, then hourly until midnight, from Estrella Blanca terminal (39 to 48 pesos)

Manzanillo – 330 km, six hours; six 2nd-class buses daily, from Galeana terminal (37 pesos)

Mexico City (Terminal Sur or Terminal Poniente) – 711 km; three 1st-class buses daily via Zihuatanejo, Acapulco, Chilpancingo, Iguala and Cuernavaca, from Estrella Blanca terminal (10 hours, 110 to 120 pesos); two 2nd-class buses daily via Uruapan and Morelia, from Galeana terminal (13 hours, 61 pesos)

Morelia – 406 km, eight hours; 23 daily, 1st and 2nd-class, from Galeana terminal (40 to 58 pesos)

Uruapan – 282 km, six hours; same buses as to Morelia (27 to 41 pesos)

Zihuatanejo – 72 km, two hours; same buses as to Acapulco (13 to 15 pesos)

Combis to Playa Azul, passing through La Mira, depart from a stop on Avenida Lázaro Cárdenas, opposite the Galeana bus terminal, every 10 minutes from 6 am to 9 pm. The 24-km trip takes about half an hour and costs 3 pesos.

Train If you're heading inland towards the mountains of Michoacán, the train from Lázaro Cárdenas to Uruapan, El Purépecha, makes a pleasant alternative to the bus. It takes six hours to reach Uruapan, the same as the bus, but it does not have to negotiate as many curves as the highway, making for a smoother trip. The train departs Lázaro Cárdenas every day at noon, arriving in Uruapan at around 6.15 pm. Seats cost 36 pesos in primera especial, 22 pesos in primera regular. The same train continues on from Uruapan to Pátzcuaro, Morelia, Toluca and Mexico City. See the schedule in the Mexico City section.

In Lázaro Cárdenas the train station is on the outskirts of town, several km from the centre. Tickets are sold at the station (☎ 16-39-65, 16-16-44) every day from 9 am to noon. They are also sold in town at Chinameca Viajes (☎ (753) 7-08-74, fax 2-49-44) at Javier Mina 178, about three blocks from the bus stations, which is a helpful travel agency open Monday to Friday from 8 am to 8 pm, Saturday 8 am to 7 pm.

The '44 Estación' local combi route, stopping on Avenida Lázaro Cárdenas outside the Galeana bus terminal, connects the bus and train stations; the cost is 1.50 pesos. A taxi between the bus and train stations costs 12 pesos.

PLAYA AZUL
• *pop: 3200*

Playa Azul is a small beach resort town backed by lagoons formed by a tributary of the Río Balsas. Although it mostly attracts Mexican families, foreign travellers are gradually being attracted by the beautiful beach and surfable waves. A strong undertow, however, makes swimming in the sea here extremely dangerous; also beware of stingrays lying on the sand. Swimming is good, however, at Barra de Pichi, on the coast a km or two east of Playa Azul, where there's a large lagoon with boat trips for seeing the plants, animals and birds.

Orientation & Information

Playa Azul is so small and everything is so close that there's little need for street names, since everyone knows where everything is – but just in case you want to know, there are four streets in town, all running parallel to the beach. The beachside street, usually called the Malecón, is technically named Calle Emiliano Zapata. The next street inland is Calle Venustiano Carranza; the next one is Francisco I Madero; and the fourth is Independencia.

A Pemex station *(la gasolinera)* on the corner of Independencia marks the beginning of town as you enter from the highway. This is a major landmark in the town, with buses and combis arriving and departing from here. The beach is three blocks straight ahead. A few blocks east (left as you face the sea) is a large plaza. Almost everything you need in the town is found somewhere between the plaza and the gasolinera. A long row of thatched-roof open-air restaurants *(enramadas)* stretches along the beach.

The post office, on Calle Francisco I Madero at a rear corner of the plaza, is open Monday to Friday from 9 am to 4 pm. A Lada caseta is on Calle Venustiano Carranza.

Things to See & Do

Since the beach is not safe for swimming, you may want to swim in one of the pools. The Balneario Playa Azul, on the Malecón behind the Hotel Playa Azul, has a large swimming pool, a big waterslide and a restaurant/bar. It's open every day from 10 am to 6 pm; admission is 10 pesos per person, but free to guests of the Hotel Playa Azul or its trailer park.

Both the Hotel Playa Azul and the Hotel María Teresa Jericó also have courtyard swimming pools with poolside restaurants (see Places to Eat).

There are swimming and boat trips at Barra de Pichi, a km or two down the beach.

Places to Stay

Camping If you have a hammock, you can string it up at one of the enramadas along the beach; ask permission from the family

running the restaurant, who probably won't mind, especially if you eat there once or twice. If you don't have your own hammock they may let you use one of theirs. There are public toilets and showers at a couple of the enramadas, and on the road running between the Pemex station and the beach.

The *Hotel Playa Azul* (read on) has a small trailer park with full hook-ups in the rear; the cost of 40 pesos per space includes free use of the balneario and the hotel's swimming pool.

Hotels & Bungalows The *Bungalows de la Curva* (☎ (753) 6-00-58) on Avenida Independencia, one block towards the beach from the Pemex station at the entrance to town, has a small swimming pool. Singles/doubles without kitchen are 50 pesos, rooms with kitchen for two or three people are 70 pesos, or larger rooms with kitchen are 100 pesos.

Next door, the *Hotel Delfín* (☎ (753) 6-00-07) on Calle Venustiano Carranza is a pleasant place with 25 clean, comfortable rooms around a small swimming pool courtyard with a restaurant; singles/doubles are 35/50 pesos. They also operate *Bungalows Delfín* on the west side of the plaza, with 10 bungalows at 60/100/120 pesos for two/four/six people.

Hotel María Isabel (☎ (753) 6-00-30/16), on Calle Francisco I Madero on the far side of the plaza, is a fine place to stay, with an attractive swimming pool and 30 large, clean rooms at 52/65 pesos for singles/doubles. The large, 73-room *Hotel Playa Azul* (☎ (753) 6-00-24/88, fax 6-00-92) on Calle Venustiano Carranza is the town's big luxury hotel, with rooms at various prices starting at 52/60 pesos. Another fine hotel is the *Hotel María Teresa Jericó* (☎ (753) 6-00-05, 6-01-30; fax 6-00-55) at Avenida Independencia 626, on the inland side of the plaza. It has a swimming pool and poolside restaurant/bar, parking, and 42 clean, comfortable rooms, all with air-con; singles/doubles are 88/110 pesos, with a 20% discount for stays of two days or more.

Places to Eat

Two small family restaurants, the *Restaurant Galdy* and the *Restaurant Familiar Martita*, both on the market street near Calle Madero, around the corner from the Hotel Playa Azul, are often recommended by locals – both serve good food at very economical prices and are open every day from 7 am to 11 pm.

The poolside restaurant/bar at the *Hotel Playa Azul* is a favourite with travellers; if you come here to eat, you can swim in the pool for free (minimum consumption 20 pesos per person). It's open every day from 7 am to 11 pm. The poolside restaurant/bar at the *Hotel María Teresa Jericó* runs on a similar system. The small poolside restaurant at the *Hotel Delfín* is also recommended by travellers.

Enramadas line the beachfront. All charge the same prices and serve basically the same selection of fresh seafood.

Getting There & Away

Combis run about every 10 minutes from 6 am to 9 pm from Lázaro Cárdenas (see under that listing). The combis enter Playa Azul and go down Calle Carranza, dropping you off anywhere along the way. In Playa Azul, catch the combis on Carranza, or at the Pemex station. The fare for the half-hour trip to Lázaro Cárdenas is 3 pesos.

Intercity buses do not pass through Playa Azul; they will drop you off at the highway junction in La Mira, seven km from Playa Azul.

A taxi from Lázaro Cárdenas to Playa Azul costs 50 pesos.

ZIHUATANEJO & IXTAPA

• *pop: Zihuatajeno 80,000; Ixtapa 12,000*

Not so long ago, Zihuatanejo ('see-wah-tah-NAY-ho') was a small fishing village and nearby Ixtapa ('ees-STOP-pah') was a coconut plantation. Then in 1970 Fonatur, the Mexican government tourism development organisation that built Cancún, decided that the Pacific coast needed a Cancún-like resort to bring more tourist dollars into Mexico.

Using market studies of American tourists, Fonatur chose Ixtapa, 210 km northwest of Acapulco, for its new resort complex. Proximity to the USA, an average temperature of 27°C, tropical vegetation and, most importantly, the quality of the beaches, were its criteria. Fonatur bought the coconut plantation, laid out streets, built reservoirs, strung electrical lines and invited the world's best known hotel chains to begin construction.

Today, Ixtapa is a string of impressive resort hotels spread out along the Bahía del Palmar; the Club Méditerranée and some fine beaches are farther west beyond Punta Ixtapa. The luxurious hotels, restaurants and shops of Ixtapa are expensive, and many travellers cringe at Ixtapa's artificial glitz created for the gringos.

Zihuatanejo, on the other hand, eight km away, though quite touristy, retains an easygoing coastal town ambience, and its setting on a small, beautiful bay with a number of fine beaches makes it a pleasant place to visit. Small-scale fishing is an important part of the town's economy; if you walk down on the beach near the pier in the early morning you can join the pelicans in greeting the returning fishermen and see the morning's catch.

Orientation

Though Zihuatanejo's suburbs are growing considerably, spreading out around the Bahía de Zihuatanejo and climbing the hills behind the town, the city centre is compact, with everything within a few square blocks.

Around
Zihuatanejo &
Ixtapa

0   2.5   5 km

Approximate Scale

It's difficult to get lost; there are only a few streets and the street names are clearly marked. Ixtapa, eight km away, is easily reached by frequent local buses or by taxi.

Information

Tourist Offices In Zihuatanejo the municipal Dirección de Turismo (☎ (753) 4-20-01/82, ext 120 or 121; fax 4-34-53), on Juan N Alvarez just north of the basketball court, is open Monday to Saturday from 9 am to 3 pm and 6 to 8 pm, handing out free maps and answering questions.

In Ixtapa the state-run Sefotur tourist information office (☎ (753) 3-19-67), officially called the Sub-Secretaría de Fomento Turístico del Estado de Guerrero, is near the tourist police station and opposite the Hotel Stouffer Presidente. It's open Monday to Friday from 9 am to 2 pm and 4 to 7 pm.

Zihuatanejo and Ixtapa both have many sidewalk kiosks and small offices set up with tourist information. They are actually in business to promote various time-share schemes in Ixtapa, but they will also provide free maps and answer any questions you may have. Then they'll try to encourage you to go for a free breakfast, cocktail or whatever at some new place in Ixtapa.

Money Zihuatanejo and Ixtapa both have a number of banks and casas de cambio where you can change US dollars and travellers' cheques. The banks give the best rate of exchange; they're open Monday to Friday from 9 am to 1.30 pm. The casas de cambio give a slightly less favourable rate but they're open longer, more convenient hours. In Zihuatajeno the Casa de Cambio Ballesteros on Galeana near the corner of Nicolás Bravo is open every day from 8 am to 9 pm.

American Express (☎ (743) 3-08-53, 3-21-21), in Ixtapa at the Hotel Westin Ixtapa, is open Monday to Saturday from 9 am to 2 pm and 4 to 6 pm.

Post & Telecommunications The post office in Zihuatanejo, situated in the north-west section of the town centre, is open Monday to Friday from 8 am to 8 pm, Saturday 9 am to 1 pm. Since it has been moved to this slightly inconvenient location, several other places in town, all of them near post boxes which are serviced daily, have started selling stamps. Among them are the Terminal Portuario building at the foot of the pier and a souvenir shop on Juan N Alvarez, roughly opposite the tourist office, with a post box beside it. In Ixtapa you can mail letters from any big hotel.

The Zihuatanejo Telecomm office, with Ladatel phones, telegram, telex and fax, is in the same building as the post office; it's open Monday to Friday from 9 am to 2 pm and 3 to 5 pm, Saturday 9 am to noon.

Long-distance telephone and fax are available at a number of Lada casetas in Zihuatanejo, including the Caseta Telefónica on the corner of Galeana and Pedro Ascencio, the Casa de Cambio Ballesteros on Galeana, near the corner of Nicolás Bravo, and the Terminal Portuario building at the foot of the pier.

Laundry Lavandería Super Clean, in Zihuatanejo at Catalina González 11 on the corner of Galeana, offers free delivery within Zihuatanejo (☎ 4-23-47); it's open Monday to Saturday from 8 am to 8 pm. Around the corner on Cuauhtémoc near the corner of González, the Tintorería y Lavandería Aldan does laundry and dry-cleaning.

Things to See

Museum At the north end of Paseo del Pescador in Zihuatanejo, the Museo Arqueológico de la Costa Grande houses exhibits on the culture and archaeology of the coastal areas of the state of Guerrero, plus changing exhibitions. It is open Tuesday to Sunday from 10 am to 6 pm; admission is 4 pesos.

Beaches Waves are gentle at all of the beaches on the Bahía de Zihuatanejo. If you want big ocean waves you'll have to go over to Ixtapa, which takes only a few minutes on the local bus.

On the Bahía de Zihuatanejo, **Playa Municipal**, right in front of town, is the least appealing for swimming. Standing on this beach you can see several other beaches spread around the bay, starting with Playa Madera just past the rocky point on your left, then the long, white stretch of Playa La Ropa past that, and finally, directly across the bay, Playa Las Gatas.

Playa Madera was formerly isolated from Playa Municipal by a couple of rocky points, but now a lighted walkway around the rocky sections has made it an easy five-minute walk from town.

Walk over the hill along the coast road for about another 20 minutes or so from Playa Madera and you reach the broad, two-km expanse of **Playa La Ropa**, bordered by palm trees and seafood restaurants. It's a pleasant walk, with the road rising up onto cliffs offering a fine view over the bay. About the most beautiful beach on the bay, La Ropa is great for swimming, parasailing, water-skiing, jet-skiing and the 'banana'.

Opposite Zihuatanejo, **Playa Las Gatas** is a protected beach, good for snorkelling and as a swimming spot for children. According to legend, Calzontzin, a Tarascan chief, built a stone barrier here in pre-Hispanic times to keep the waves down and prevent sea creatures from entering, making it a sort of private swimming pool. Coral growing on the rocks makes for good snorkelling. Shacks on the beach hire snorkelling gear for around 15 pesos per day.

Boats to Playa Las Gatas depart from the Zihuatanejo pier every 10 minutes from 8 am to 5 pm; the last boat leaves Las Gatas for the return trip at 5 pm. Tickets are sold at the ticket booth at the foot of the pier; save your ticket because you'll need it for the return trip. The cost is 8 pesos for the return trip (4 pesos one way). The return ticket is valid only on the day you buy it. Or you can reach Playa Las Gatas by walking around the bay along the rocks from Playa La Ropa; it isn't far but with all the scrambling up and down rocks it takes about 20 minutes. At the time of writing a road to Playa Las Gatas was being built, but no one knew when it would be completed.

Between Zihuatanejo and Ixtapa, **Playa Majahua** has only recently become accessible due to the construction of a new road designed to serve a new hotel zone there, similar to Ixtapa. The beach faces the open sea, so it has large waves and similar conditions to Ixtapa.

The big hotels in Ixtapa are lined up along **Playa del Palmar**, a long, broad stretch of white sand. Be very careful if you swim here: the large waves crash straight down and there's a powerful undertow. The west end of this beach, just before the entrance to the lagoon, is called **Playa Escolleras** by the locals and it's a favourite spot for surfing. Further west, past the marina, are three small beaches which are among the most beautiful in the area: **Playa San Juan, Playa Casa Blanca** and **Playa Cuatas**.

To the west, past Punta Ixtapa, are **Playa Quieta** and **Playa Linda**. From Playa Quieta boats run every 10 minutes to **Isla Ixtapa** just offshore, which has four more beaches, all with calm water and which are even better for snorkelling than Las Gatas. The cost is 8 pesos for the return-trip boat ride, which takes only about five minutes each way; the boats operate every day from 8 am to 5 pm, with the last boat back returning at 5 pm.

You can also reach Isla Ixtapa by taking a boat from the Zihuatanejo pier. It departs once a day (if there are eight people or more) at 11 or 11.30 am, departing the island at around 4 pm to be back in town at 5 pm. The trip takes about an hour from town; the return trip costs 22 pesos. Tickets are sold at the ticket office at the foot of the pier.

Activities
Most of the activities around Zihuatanejo are naturally oriented towards the sea. Swimming is good at Playa La Ropa, where you can also hire sailboards, sailboats and jet-skis, and arrange water-skiing, parasailing or a ride on the 'banana'.

Snorkelling & Scuba Diving Snorkelling is good at Playa Las Gatas and even better on Isla Ixtapa; snorkelling gear can be hired at either place for around 15 pesos per day. The same beaches also have diving operators, who will take you for a dive for around 135 pesos, or give you scuba lessons in the quiet water. The most professional scuba diving operation in Zihuatanejo is the NAUI-affiliated Zihuatanejo Scuba Center (☎ /fax (753) 4-21-47) at Cuauhtémoc 3, opposite Banamex, which has morning and afternoon dives every day; they have many diving photos on display and can answer any questions you may have about diving in this area. There is an abundance of species here due to a convergence of currents, and there is sometimes great visibility, up to 35 metres.

'Las Gatas' Were Not Cats ... & Other Tales of Zihuatanejo
Several places around Zihuatanejo and Ixtapa have names rooted in the distant past. The name 'Zihuatanejo' comes from the Nahuatl word 'Zihuatlán', meaning 'place of women'; the Spanish added the suffix '-ejo', meaning 'small'. 'Ixtapa', also from the Nahuatl dialect, means 'white place'; it was so named not only for its white sands but also for the white guano left by the sea birds on the rocky islands just offshore.

The beaches around the Bahía de Zihuatanejo also have historical names. Playa Madera (Wood Beach) got its name from the timber that was sent from here to various parts of the world; at one time there was also a shipyard here. The name of Playa La Ropa (Beach of the Clothes) commemorates an occasion when a Spanish galleon coming from the Philippines was wrecked in front of the bay, and its cargo of fine silks was washed up on this beach. Playa Las Gatas (Beach of the Cats) was not actually named for cats, but for the nurse sharks that inhabited the waters here in ancient times – harmless sharks without teeth, called 'cats' because of their whiskers. ∎

Sportfishing Sportfishing is also popular. Sailfish are caught here all year round; seasonal fish include blue or black marlin from March to May, roosterfish in September-October, wahoo in October, mahi mahi or dorado in November-December, and Spanish mackerel in December. Three fishermen's cooperatives, all with offices near the foot of the Zihuatanejo pier, can arrange deep-sea fishing trips or small game trips, all at the same prices: the Sociedad Cooperativa de Lanchas de Recreo y Pesca Deportiva del Muelle Teniente José Azueta (☎ /fax 4-20-56) at the foot of the pier; Servicios Turísticos Acuáticos de Zihuatanejo Ixtapa (☎ /fax 4-41-62) at Paseo del Pescador 6; and Sociedad Cooperativa Benito Juárez (☎ 4-37-58) at Paseo del Pescador 20-2. Or you can just walk along the pier and talk with the various fishermen, many of whom speak some English and frequently make fishing trips.

Other Sports Golf and tennis can be played at the Ixtapa Club de Golf Palma Real (☎ 3-10-62, 3-10-30) and at the Marina Ixtapa Golf Club (☎ 3-14-10), both in Ixtapa and both with 18 holes, tennis courts and swimming pools. There's a yacht club at Porto Ixtapa (☎ 3-11-31) beside the Ixtapa Marina. Rancho Playa Linda on Playa Linda, past Ixtapa, offers horse riding.

Cruises For cruises, the large *Tristar* trimaran (☎ 4-35-89) departs from a dock at Puerto Mio, about a 15-minute walk around the bay from Zihuatanejo. The Sail & Snorkel trip from 10 am to 2 pm goes outside the bay to Playa Manzanillo, a secluded white-sand beach said to offer the best snorkelling in the area, returning to the bay for some spinnaker fly fishing and a great party. The cost of 150 pesos (120 pesos in low season) includes snacks and an open bar. They also do a two-hour sunset cruise around the bay and out along the coast of Ixtapa for 100 pesos (90 pesos in low season). They're also thinking of starting trips to Isla Ixtapa. English, French and Spanish are all spoken.

Places to Stay
The reasonably priced places to stay are in Zihuatanejo; Ixtapa's big resort hotels are quite pricey, upwards of 450 pesos a night in the winter high season from mid-December to Easter, cheaper the rest of the year. If you want to stay in Ixtapa, you could arrange a package deal through a travel agent, including airfare from your home country.

During the high season many hotels in Zihuatanejo may be full, so phone ahead to reserve a hotel room; if you don't like what you get, you can always look for another room early the next day. The busiest times of all are Semana Santa and the week between Christmas and New Year; at these times you must reserve a room and be prepared to pay more. From around mid-April to mid-December, tourism is much slower; you can bargain for a discount and probably get it.

Places to Stay – bottom end
Camping Two small family-run campgrounds at Playa La Ropa offer spaces for trailers and tents. The *Trailer Park La Ropa*, beside the Mercado de Artesanías which is right on the beach, has spaces at 10 pesos per person, plus 20 pesos per space if you get power. Nearby, the *Trailer Park Los Cabañas* (☎ (753) 4-47-18), to the right of the dolphin fountain, has spaces at 10 pesos per person most of the year, 15 pesos from October to March; tents (10 pesos per day) and other camping accessories are available for hire. In Zihuatanejo, the *Villa Juvenil Zihuatanejo* (see Hostels) will allow you to pitch a tent for 7.50 pesos per person.

Hostel The cheapest place to stay in Zihuatanejo is the *Villa Juvenil Zihuatanejo* (☎ (753) 4-46-62), a 60-bed hostel on Paseo de las Salinas, about a 10-minute walk from town. The cost is 15 pesos per night for a bed in a clean single-sex dormitory with four to eight beds. No hostel card is needed, but if you have one there's a 10% discount. The main disadvantage is that it's next door to the town sewage treatment plant; it doesn't always smell the best. The hostel is open all day and evening.

Hotels Beside the beach in Zihuatanejo, next door to the larger Hotel Avila, the *Casa de Huéspedes La Playa* (☎ (753) 4-22-47) at Juan N Alvarez 6 is a small, simple guesthouse with just six rooms. It's one of the most economical places in town; from December to February it's often full with guests who return every year. English is spoken. A block from the beach, *Casa de Huéspedes Juve* (☎ (753) 4-26-69, fax 4-31-36) at Pedro Ascencio 3 is a basic place with 24 remodelled rooms at 25 pesos per person, and a few more basic rooms at 15 pesos per person.

The *Casa de Huéspedes Miriam* (☎ (753) 4-38-90) at Antonio Nava 8 is a simple but clean guesthouse with rooms at 30 pesos per person. *Hotel Lari's* (☎ (753) 4-21-14, 4-37-67) at Ignacio Altamirano 4 is a similar place, with off-street parking and rooms at 35 pesos per person.

The *Hotel Casa Aurora* (☎ (753) 4-30-46) at Nicolás Bravo 27 has rooms at 30/50 pesos per person in low/high seasons, 120 pesos with air-con; ask for one of the upstairs rooms. The *Hotel Casa Bravo* (☎ (753) 4-25-48) at Nicolás Bravo 11 has six clean, pleasant rooms at 50/60 pesos for singles/doubles.

The *Hotel Raúl Tres Marias* (☎ (753) 4-21-91, 4-25-91) at Calle La Noria 4, Colonia Lázaro Cárdenas, is just across the water from town, over a small footbridge. This is many budget travellers' favourite place to stay in Zihuatanejo; many of its 25 rooms open onto large terraces with flowers and views over town and the bay. Singles/doubles with cold-water bath are 40/60 pesos most of the year, 70/100 pesos from December to April.

Places to Stay – middle

Posada Citlali (☎ (753) 4-20-43) at Vicente Guerrero 3 is very pleasant, with terrace sitting areas and rooms around a courtyard filled with trees and plants. The rooms are comfortable and clean, with singles/doubles at 60/80 pesos most of the year, 70/90 pesos December to April.

The *Hotel Raúl Tres Marías Centro* (☎ (753) 4-29-77, fax 4-23-91) at Juan N Alvarez 52 has 17 simple but clean singles/doubles at 60/80 pesos with fan, 100/120 pesos with air-con. The *Hotel Imelda* (☎ (753) 4-76-62, ☎ /fax 4-31-99) at Catalina González 11 has a swimming pool, enclosed parking and clean rooms starting at 90 pesos, higher with air-con.

The *Hotel Avila* (☎ /fax (753) 4-20-10) at Calle Juan N Alvarez 8, right on the beach, has terraces overlooking the sea, private parking and large, clean rooms with air-con, fan, colour TV and other luxuries. Sea-view rooms are 140/160 pesos for singles/doubles, other rooms are 120/140 pesos, all 20 pesos higher in high season.

Apartments

The *Hotel Amueblados Valle* (☎ (753) 4-20-84, ☎ /fax 4-32-20) at Vicente Guerrero 14 is a good deal, with five large, airy one-bedroom apartments with everything you need, including fully equipped kitchens, at 80/100 pesos in low/high season and three two-bedroom apartments at 140/160 pesos in low/high season. If they're full (which they often are in high season), try the *Hotel Amueblados Isabel* (☎ (753) 4-36-61, fax 4-26-69) at Pedro Ascencio 11, with fully equipped two/three-bedroom apartments at 225/275 pesos, 75 pesos higher in July, August, at Christmas and Easter. Or ask Luis Valle at the Hotel Amueblados Valle about other apartments in town which may be cheaper, especially for longer stays.

Playa Madera

Playa Madera, only a five-minute walk from the centre of Zihuatanejo, has several good places to stay, most of them bungalows with fully equipped kitchens, all with large terraces offering fine views of the bay. Closest to town, *Bungalows Pacíficos* (☎ /fax (753) 4-21-12) on Calle Eva S de López Mateos, Cerro de la Madera, has six attractive bungalows with fully equipped kitchens at 150 pesos. Anita Hahner, the Swiss owner, is a gracious and helpful hostess who speaks English, Spanish, German and Swiss-German, and can help you find anything from good restaurants to good bird-watching spots.

At Calle Eva S de López Mateos 3, the

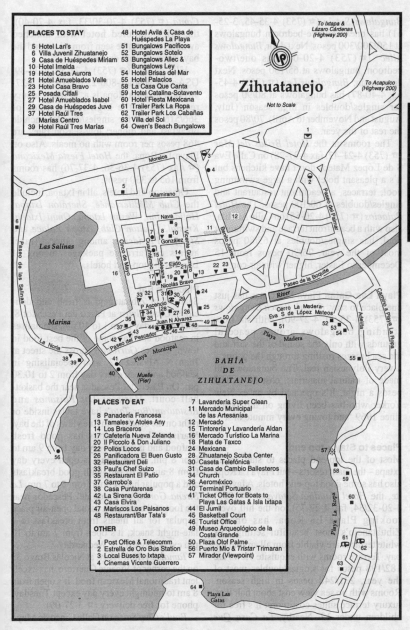

PLACES TO STAY

5 Hotel Lari's
6 Villa Juvenil Zihuatanejo
9 Casa de Huéspedes Miriam
10 Hotel Imelda
19 Hotel Casa Aurora
21 Hotel Amueblados Valle
23 Hotel Casa Bravo
25 Posada Citlali
27 Hotel Amueblados Isabel
29 Casa de Huéspedes Juve
37 Hotel Raúl Tres Marías Centro
39 Hotel Raúl Tres Marías
48 Hotel Avila & Casa de Huéspedes La Playa
51 Bungalows Pacíficos
52 Bungalows Sotelo
53 Bungalows Allec & Bungalows Ley
54 Hotel Brisas del Mar
55 Hotel Palacios
58 La Casa Que Canta
59 Hotel Catalina-Sotavento
60 Hotel Fiesta Mexicana
61 Trailer Park La Ropa
62 Trailer Park Los Cabañas
63 Villa del Sol
64 Owen's Beach Bungalows

Zihuatanejo

Not to Scale

To Ixtapa & Lázaro Cárdenas (Highway 200)

To Acapulco (Highway 200)

PLACES TO EAT

8 Panadería Francesa
13 Tamales y Atoles Any
14 Los Braceros
17 Cafetería Nueva Zelanda
20 Il Piccolo & Don Juliano
22 Pollos Locos
26 Panificadora El Buen Gusto
33 Paul's Chef Suizo
35 Restaurant El Patio
37 Garrobo's
42 Casa Puntarenas
42 La Sirena Gorda
43 Casa Elvira
47 Mariscos Los Paisanos
48 Restaurant/Bar Tata's

OTHER

1 Post Office & Telecomm
2 Estrella de Oro Bus Station
3 Local Buses to Ixtapa
4 Cinemas Vicente Guerrero
7 Lavandería Super Clean
11 Mercado Municipal de las Artesanías
12 Mercado
15 Tintorería y Lavandería Aldan
16 Mercado Turístico La Marina
18 Plata de Taxco
24 Mexicana
28 Zihuatanejo Scuba Center
30 Caseta Telefónica
31 Casa de Cambio Ballesteros
34 Church
36 Aeroméxico
40 Terminal Portuario
41 Ticket Office for Boats to Playa Las Gatas & Isla Ixtapa
44 El Jumil
45 Basketball Court
46 Tourist Office
49 Museo Arqueológico de la Costa Grande
50 Plaza Olof Palme
56 Puerto Mio & Tristar Trimaran
57 Mirador (Viewpoint)

Bungalows Sotelo (☎ (753) 4-35-45, 3-25-61) has one/two/three-bedroom bungalows at 150/200/300 pesos. Next door, *Bungalows Allec* (☎ (753) 4-20-02) has one/two-bedroom bungalows at 65/150 pesos. Next door again, *Bungalows Ley* (☎ (753) 4-45-63, 4-40-87) has bungalows at 80/90 pesos for singles/doubles in high season (July, August and November to April), 70/80 pesos the rest of the year.

The rooms at the *Hotel Brisas del Mar* (☎ (753) 4-21-42, fax 4-37-28) on Calle Eva S de López Mateos don't have kitchens but it's a pleasant hotel with a large swimming pool, terraces, a beachfront restaurant and singles/doubles at 60/100 pesos. The *Hotel Palacios* (☎ (753) 4-20-55) on Calle Adelita, also with a beachfront terrace and swimming pool, has singles/doubles at 65/80 pesos most of the year, 75/90 pesos from 15 December to Easter, higher with air-con.

Playa Las Gatas Playa Las Gatas has just one place to stay, *Owen's Beach Bungalows* (☎ (753) 4-35-90, 4-27-90), with six free-standing bungalows around peaceful grounds with only the sound of the surf and the sea breezes rustling through the palms – a very Polynesian feel. The bungalows, all made of natural materials, cost 80 to 100 pesos a night. It's operated by an ex-New Yorker who has been living on this beach since 1969 'and loving every minute of it'.

Places to Stay – top end
Most of the top-end places to stay are in Ixtapa – the giant resorts – but Playa La Ropa also has some good top-end hotels. A favourite, the *Hotel Catalina-Sotavento* (☎ (753) 4-20-32/34, fax 4-29-75), on the hill over-looking Playa La Ropa, has one of Zihuatanejo's most beautiful settings; its white terraces are visible from all around the bay. Terrace rooms with exquisite views are 182/198 pesos for singles/doubles most of the year, 231/248 pesos in high season. Rooms with no sea view cost about half that, luxury terrace suites cost more; it's free for children under 12. Nearby, *La Casa Que*

Canta (☎ (753) 4-70-30/33, fax 4-70-40), the brick-coloured hotel with thatched awnings that can be seen from all around the bay, is much more expensive.

Villa del Sol (☎ (753) 4-22-39, 4-32-39, USA and Canada 1-800-223-6510; fax 4-27-58) on Playa La Ropa is a 36-room luxury resort where the high-season rates of 366/516 pesos for singles/doubles include breakfast and dinner; low-season rates are 468 pesos per room with no meals. Also on Playa La Ropa, the *Hotel Fiesta Mexicana* (☎ /fax (753) 4-36-36, 4-37-76) has rooms from 165 to 330 pesos.

Other top-end hotels, all in Ixtapa, include the *Club Méditerranée, Sheraton Ixtapa, Holiday Inn, Westin Ixtapa, Omni Ixtapa, Krystal, Qualton Club, Ixtapa Palace* and *Stouffer Presidente*, among others. Travel agents can arrange packages at any of Ixtapa's big top-end hotels.

Places to Eat
Seafood in Zihuatanejo is fresh and delicious. *Casa Elvira* at Paseo del Pescador 8, open every day from 1 to 10 pm, specialises in seafood and has some of the best food in town, as does *Garrobo's* across the street at Juan N Alvarez 52, also specialising in seafood and open every day from 2 to 10.30 pm. On Paseo del Pescador near the basketball court, *Mariscos Los Paisanos* and *Restaurant/Bar Tata's* have tables inside or right on the beach, with fine views of the bay. Mariscos Los Paisanos has good fresh seafood and is open every day from 9 am to 6 or 8 pm, while Tata's is open every day from 8 am to 10 pm, with good breakfasts and a popular happy hour from 5 to 7 pm. *La Sirena Gorda*, on Paseo del Pescador near the foot of the pier, is a casual open-air place popular for all meals from breakfast to a late-night snack; it's open from 7 am to 10 pm every day except Wednesday.

Tamales y Atoles Any, at Nicolás Bravo 33 on the corner of Vicente Guerrero, has excellent traditional Mexican food. It's open from 8 am to midnight every day except Tuesday; phone for free delivery (☎ 3-27-09).

Paul's Chef Suizo on Calle Cinco de Mayo

between Ejido and Nicolás Bravo is a small patio restaurant with expensive but delicious food – 'the best food we had all year', some of our readers wrote to tell us. Swiss owner/chef Paul, who speaks English, German and Spanish, performs his culinary wizardry Monday to Saturday from 2 to 10 pm. Also on Calle Cinco de Mayo, beside the Catholic church on the corner of Pedro Ascencio, the *Restaurant El Patio* is another popular patio restaurant, open only in high season.

For Italian food there's the *Ristorante-Bar-Pizzeria Don Juliano* and the *Video Bar Il Piccolo*, next door to each other at Nicolás Bravo 22 near the corner of Vicente Guerrero. Don Juliano is open from 2 to 11 pm every day except Wednesday, Il Piccolo every day from 4 pm to midnight, closing on Monday in the low season.

For cappuccino and café fare, *Restaurant Deli* at Cuauhtémoc 12-B has some sidewalk tables, others inside and on the rear garden patio; it's open Monday to Saturday from 8 am to 11 pm. *Cafetería Nueva Zelanda* at Cuauhtémoc 23, stretching through the block to Galeana on the other side, is a clean, popular café open every day from 7.15 am to 10.30 or 11 pm; English and Spanish are spoken and you can get anything they have 'to go' *(para llevar)*.

Pollos Locos at Nicolás Bravo 15 is just an open-air place with simple folding tables and chairs, but it serves some of the best wood-grilled chicken on the coast; it's a popular place, open every day from 1 to 11 pm. *Los Braceros* at Ejido 21 is a similar popular spot, with a sidewalk grill where you can see the meat being cooked – their menu features a variety of meat and vegetable combinations and other tasty meat dishes. It's open daily from 4 pm to 1 am.

Casa Puntarenas on Calle La Noria, across the water from town over a small footbridge, is a simple family-run patio restaurant open for breakfast daily from 8.30 to 11 am and for dinner from 6.30 to 9 pm. The atmosphere is relaxed and enjoyable, and its reputation for serving large portions of good, inexpensive food keeps the family busy; it's open only from November to March.

Zihuatanejo has a couple of good bakeries: the *Panificadora El Buen Gusto* at Vicente Guerrero 8-A, open Monday to Saturday from 7.30 am to 10 pm, and the *Panadería Francesa* on the corner of Galeana and Catalina González, open every day from 7 am to 9 pm.

Playa La Ropa & Playa Las Gatas Playa La Ropa and Playa Las Gatas both have plenty of beachside restaurants specialising in seafood. On Playa La Ropa, *Rossy's* and *La Perla* are popular; on Playa Las Gatas, *Restaurante Oliverio* prepares good seafood.

Ixtapa Ixtapa has plenty of restaurants to choose from, in addition to all the big hotel restaurants. *Carlos 'n Charlie's, Señor Frog's, Señor-itto* and *Montmartre* are all popular for a good meal and a good time. *Casa Elvira* is a branch of the famous restaurant of the same name in Zihuatanejo.

Entertainment

The happy hour from 5 to 7 pm at *Restaurant/Bar Tata's*, right on the beach on Zihuatanejo's Playa Municipal, attracts a jolly sunset crowd; for more serious nightlife, head for Ixtapa. All of Ixtapa's big hotels have bars and nightclubs, and most also have discos. Probably the most popular disco is *Christine* at the Hotel Krystal; others include *Euforia* near the Posada Real Hotel and the *Magic Circus, Flash Le Club, Visage* and *Tropicana Night Club*, all in the Ixtapa shopping centre. The *Sanca Bar* at the Sheraton is popular for dancing, with Mexican music. Also popular in Ixtapa are *Carlos 'n Charlie's* and *Señor Frog's*, lively restaurant/bars with dancing, both in the Carlos Anderson chain.

Several of Ixtapa's big hotels hold Fiestas Mexicanas in the evening, with a Mexican buffet and open bar, and entertainment including Mexican folkloric dancing, mariachis, rope and cockfighting demonstrations, door prizes and dancing. The Sheraton has fiestas on Wednesday night from 7 to 10.30 pm all year round; in the high season several other hotels also have fiestas, including the

Krystal, Omni and Dorado Pacífico. Reservations can be made directly or through travel agents.

Things to Buy

Mexican handicrafts, including ceramics, wood carvings, huaraches, shells and shell crafts, silver from Taxco and masks from around the state of Guerrero, are available in Zihuatanejo and Ixtapa. In Ixtapa there's the Tourist Market; in Zihuatanejo check out the Mercado Turístico La Marina on Calle Cinco de Mayo, the Mercado Municipal de las Artesanías on González near Benito Juárez, and the many artesanías shops in the block west of the basketball court. One of these shops, El Jumil at Paseo del Pescador 9, specialises in authentic Guerrero masks; Guerrero is known for its variety of interesting masks and there are some museum- quality ones here, most costing around 50 to 70 pesos.

Several shops around Zihuatanejo sell silver from Taxco; Plata de Taxco on the corner of Cuauhtémoc and Nicolás Bravo has a large selection of quality items. Beach clothing is sold at a great many shops around Zihuatanejo. Large Pacific shells are sold at several shops, too, including a couple right on the beach on Zihuatanejo's Playa Municipal.

Getting There & Away

Air The Ixtapa/Zihuatanejo international airport is 19 km from Zihuatanejo, about two km off highway 200 heading towards Acapulco. Airlines serving this airport, and their direct flights, are listed below; all have connections to other centres.

Aeroméxico
    Juan N Alvarez 34, corner Calle Cinco de Mayo, Zihuatanejo (☎ 4-20-18/19/22); Airport (☎ 4-22-37, 4-26-34) – Guadalajara, Mexico City
Delta
    Airport (☎ 4-33-86) – Los Angeles
Mexicana
    Vicente Guerrero 15 near the corner of Nicolás Bravo, Zihuatanejo (☎ 4-22-08/9, 3-22-10); Hotel Dorado Pacífico, Ixtapa (☎ 3-22-08/9); Airport (☎ 4-22-27) – Guadalajara, León/El Bajío, Mexico City

Bus Estrella Blanca and Cuauhtémoc share a large bus terminal, the Central de Autobuses (☎ 4-34-77), on highway 200 about two km out of Zihuatanejo, heading towards Acapulco. Estrella de Oro (☎ 4-21-75) has its own small terminal, closer to town at Paseo del Palmar 54. Buses include:

Acapulco – 239 km, four hours; hourly buses, 6 am to 9.30 pm, by Estrella Blanca and Cuauhtémoc (33 pesos); three daily by Estrella de Oro (26 pesos), all 1st-class
Lázaro Cárdenas – 72 km, two hours; directo buses hourly, 6 am to 7.30 pm (15 pesos), and ordinario buses every half-hour, 8 am to 11 pm (13 pesos), by Cuauhtémoc; 11 1st-class buses daily by Estrella Blanca (15 pesos); two 1st-class buses daily by Estrella de Oro (14 pesos)
Mexico City (Terminal Sur) – 640 km, nine to 10 hours; seven buses daily by Cuauhtémoc and four buses daily by Estrella Blanca (90 to 125 pesos); six buses daily by Estrella de Oro (87 to 160 pesos)

Tres Estrellas de Oro has one bus daily going up the coast to Mazatlán, and another going up the coast all the way to Tijuana, both departing from the Central de Autobuses.

Getting Around

To/From the Airport Trans-Ixtapa (☎ 3-00-24/84) offers transport to/from the airport for 15 pesos per person. A taxi from Zihuatanejo to the airport costs 30 pesos.

Bus Local buses run frequently between Zihuatanejo and Ixtapa, departing every 15 minutes from around 6 am to 10 pm; the cost is 1 peso for the 15-minute ride. In Zihuatanejo the buses depart from the corner of Avenida Benito Juárez and Avenida Morelos. In Ixtapa the bus stops all along the main street, in front of all the large hotels. Some of these buses, marked 'Zihuatanejo-Ixtapa-Playa Linda', continue on through Ixtapa to Playa Linda, stopping near Playa Quieta on the way. They operate only from around 7 am to 6 pm, going hourly during the middle of the day but more frequently in the morning and late afternoon. The 'Correa' route goes to the Central de Autobuses, departing from the same bus stop as the buses to Ixtapa, every day from around 6 am to 9.30 pm; the cost is 1 peso.

Car & Motorbike Several car-rental companies serve Ixtapa/Zihuatanejo. These include:

Autos Hernandez	☎ 3-18-30
Avis	☎ 4-22-48, 4-29-32
Budget	☎ 4-48-37
Dollar	☎ 3-18-58, 4-23-14
Econo Rent	☎ 3-05-30
Hertz	☎ 4-22-55
National	☎ 3-00-18, 3-10-32
Quick	☎ 3-18-30

Several have offices at the airport. As always, it's best to phone around to compare prices.

Motorbikes can be hired in Zihuatanejo at Renta de Motos Michelle, Galeana 4 near the corner of Pedro Ascencio, and in Ixtapa at Renta Motos in the Centro Comercial Patios. At either place you must have current ID and a credit card or a 300-peso deposit; a driver's licence is not needed.

Taxi Taxis are plentiful in both Ixtapa and Zihuatanejo. Prices seem to be fixed; clarify the price you'll pay before setting off.

AROUND ZIHUATANEJO & IXTAPA
Troncones
About a 25-minute drive north-west of Zihuatanejo, Playa Troncones is a beach on the open sea with a number of beachfront seafood restaurants, a popular outing for Zihuatanejo families. Troncones Point, with a left-hand break, attracts surfers.

Dewey and Karolyn, a friendly, easy-going American couple from Seattle, operate a beachfront restaurant/bar (the *Burro Borracho*) and a couple of enjoyable places to stay on the beach. The Burro Borracho has three duplex bungalows (six units), all with relaxing hammocks on beachfront terraces; singles/doubles are 120/150 pesos. Also here are camping sites with full hook-ups at 30 to 45 pesos per space. They also operate the

Casa de la Tortuga (fax (753) 4-32-96), a pleasant guesthouse with singles from 75 to 120 pesos, doubles from 105 to 150 pesos, or you can rent the entire villa, which sleeps 10 people. All prices include breakfast; prices are 25% lower from 2 May to 30 November, and are always 'negotiable'. Activities include fishing, sea kayaking, surfing, horse riding (they have horses), hiking, bird and sea turtle watching (the sea turtles lay their eggs here in the sand on moonlit nights) and plenty more.

Getting There & Away To get to Troncones, head north-west from Zihuatanejo on highway 200, as if going to Lázaro Cárdenas; after about 40 km you'll come to the village of Buena Vista. The turnoff to Troncones is about six km further on; it's marked by signs for the Casa de la Tortuga and many restaurants, including the Burro Borracho, La Gaviota and Costa Brava. Troncones is three km from the turnoff; when the road meets the sea, the Burro Borracho is about 1.5 km to your left, the Casa de la Tortuga about 1.5 km to your right. Buses will let you off at the highway turnoff, but there are no buses all the way to Troncones. A taxi from Zihuatanejo costs 50 pesos.

Barra de Potosí
About a 40-minute drive from Zihuatanejo, Barra de Potosí is a popular area with a long, sandy, open sea beach, beautiful but dangerous for swimming, and another beach on a large (eight-sq-km) lagoon with good swimming and a number of seafood restaurants. If you want to stay over, check out the *Barra de Potosí Hotel & Resort* (☎ (753) 4-33-19) with a restaurant, bar and swimming pool.

Getting There & Away To get there, drive on highway 200 heading towards Acapulco; turn off at the town of Los Achotes, about 25 km from Zihuatanejo, and head for the sea, about another 10 km. You can take a local bus to Los Achotes from the bus stop on Ejido in the block east of the mercado in Zihuatanejo; take the bus heading to Petatlán, tell the driver you're going to Barra de Potosí and you'll be let off where you can meet a minibus going the rest of the way. The cost is about 6 pesos if you go by bus; a taxi from Zihuatanejo costs 80 pesos.

ACAPULCO
• pop: 1.5 million

Acapulco is the granddaddy of Mexican coastal resort cities. Tourism is the city's No 1 industry, and has been for decades; the name Acapulco evokes images of white-sand beaches, high-rise hotels, glittery nightlife and the divers at La Quebrada gracefully swan-diving into a narrow crevasse with the surf rising and falling inside.

With a population of well over a million, Acapulco is a fast-growing city of dual personalities. Around the curve of the Bahía de Acapulco stretches an arc of beautiful beaches, luxury hotels, discos, shopping plazas and restaurants with trilingual menus (many French Canadians come here). Just inland is a none-too-glamorous commercial centre with filthy streets, crowded sidewalks, congested traffic and long lines of loud, fuming buses choking passers-by.

Throughout the year you can expect average daytime temperatures of 27°C to 33°C and night-time temperatures of 21°C to 27°C. Afternoon showers are common from June to September, but quite rare the rest of the year.

Orientation

Acapulco is on a narrow coastal plain along the 11-km shore of the Bahía de Acapulco. Reached by highway 200 from the east and west and by highway 95 from the north, it is 400 km south of Mexico City and 242 km south-east of Zihuatanejo-Ixtapa.

For tourism purposes, Acapulco is divided into three parts: 'Acapulco Tradicionál' (Traditional Acapulco) in the west (old) part of the city, 'Acapulco Dorado' (Golden Acapulco) heading around the bay east from Playa Hornos, and 'Acapulco Diamante'

A Long & Illustrious History

The name 'Acapulco' is derived from ancient Nahuatl words meaning 'where the reeds stood' or 'place of giant reeds'. Archaeological finds show that when the Spaniards arrived, Indians had been living around the Bahía de Acapulco and the nearby bay of Puerto Marqués for about 2000 years, and had progressed from a hunting and gathering society to an agricultural one.

Spanish sailors discovered the Bay of Acapulco in 1512. Port and shipbuilding facilities were later established here because of the bay's substantial natural harbour.

In 1523 Hernán Cortés, Juan Rodríguez Villafuerte and merchant Juan de Sala joined forces to finance an overland trade route between Acapulco and Mexico City. This route, known as the 'Camino de Asia', was the principal trade route between Mexico City and the Pacific; the 'Camino de Europa', continuing on from Mexico City to Veracruz on the Caribbean coast, formed a link between the Orient and Spain.

Acapulco became the only port in the New World authorised to receive naos (Spanish trading galleons) from the Philippines and China. During the annual Acapulco Fair, lasting three to eight weeks after the galleons arrived from Manila each spring, traders converged on Acapulco from Mexico City, Manila and Peru.

By the 17th century, trade with the Orient was flourishing and Dutch and English pirate ships abounded in the Pacific and along the coastlines of Mexico and Baja California. To ward off the pirates, Fort San Diego was built atop a low hill overlooking the bay. It was not until the end of the 18th century that Spain permitted its American colonies to engage in free trade, ending the monopoly of the naos and the Manila-Acapulco route for trade with the Orient. The naos continued trading until the early 19th century when they were replaced by bigger and better sailing ships.

With independence, Mexico severed most of its trade links with Spain and its colonies, and Acapulco declined as a port city. It became relatively isolated from the rest of the world until a paved road was built in 1927 linking it with Mexico City. As Mexico City grew larger, its citizens began flocking to the Pacific coast for vacations. With a new international airport, Acapulco had become a booming resort by the 1950s, and has remained so ever since. ■

(Diamond Acapulco), a brand-new luxury tourist resort area being developed from the peninsula on the southern tip of Puerto Marqués stretching east about 10 km down Playa Revolcadero to the international airport. Pie de la Cuesta, a lagoon and beach area about 10 km west of Acapulco, is another attractive area where tourism is more low key (see the Around Acapulco section following).

At the western end of Acapulco, the Peninsula de las Playas juts south from central Acapulco. Just south of the Peninsula de las Playas is the popular Isla de la Roqueta and, nearby, the so-called 'underwater shrine', a submerged bronze statue of the Virgen de Guadalupe. From Playa Caleta on the southern edge of the peninsula, Avenida López Mateos climbs west and then north to Playa La Angosta and La Quebrada before curling east back towards the city centre.

Playa Caleta also marks the beginning of Avenida Costera Miguel Alemán (often known simply as 'La Costera'), Acapulco's principal bayside avenue. Most of Acapulco's major hotels, restaurants, discos and other points of interest are along or just off La Costera. From Playa Caleta, La Costera cuts north/north-west across the peninsula and then hugs the shore all the way around the bay to the Icacos naval base at the east end of the city. After passing the naval base, La Costera becomes La Carretera Escénica (The Scenic Highway) for nine km, at which point it intersects highway 200 on the left and the road to Puerto Marqués on the right. The airport is 2.5 km straight ahead.

As in most Spanish colonial cities, the heart of the old central district is the cathedral and its adjacent plaza. This plaza is called the zócalo, with the sea at one end and the church at the other.

Information

Tourist Offices The Secretaría de Fomento Turístico del Estado de Guerrero (☎ (74) 86-91-67, 84-31-40; fax 84-62-52), in a white office building on the ocean side at La Costera 187, hands out free city maps and plenty of printed information on Acapulco and the state of Guerrero, and answers any questions. It's open Monday to Friday from 9 am to 2 pm and 4 to 7 pm.

The Procuraduría del Turista (Tourist Assistance Bureau) (☎ (74) 84-44-16, 84-45-83), at La Costera 4455 near the sidewalk in front of the Acapulco convention centre, offers assistance for all manner of tourist needs, problems or complaints. It's open every day from 9 am to midnight.

Money You can change money at many places around Acapulco. The numerous banks give the best rates; they are open Monday to Friday from 9 am to 1 pm. The casas de cambio pay a lower rate; it is worth checking around the various places as rates vary. There are many casas de cambio all along La Costera and they are open longer, more convenient hours than the banks. Hotels will also change money, but their rates are usually not good.

American Express (☎ (74) 84-15-10, 84-52-00) at La Costera 709A, just east of the Diana statue, changes Amex travellers' cheques at the same rates as the banks, but is less crowded and is open more convenient hours: Monday to Friday from 9 am to 6 pm, Saturday 9 am to 1 pm.

Post & Telecommunications The main post office is at La Costera 125, in the Palacio Federal beside the Sanborns department store, a couple of blocks east of the zócalo. It's open Monday to Saturday from 8 am to 8 pm, Sunday 8 am to 1 pm. In the same building, the Telecomm office, with telex, telegram, money order and fax, is open Monday to Friday from 9 am to 8 pm, Saturday 9 am to noon.

Long-distance telephone calls can be made from Ladatel phones – plentiful throughout the city – or from Lada casetas (look for signs saying 'larga distancia'). Telephone and fax services are available on the west side of the zócalo at Tel-Plus at Hidalgo 6, which is open every day from 7 am to 10 pm, and at Caseta Alameda on Calle

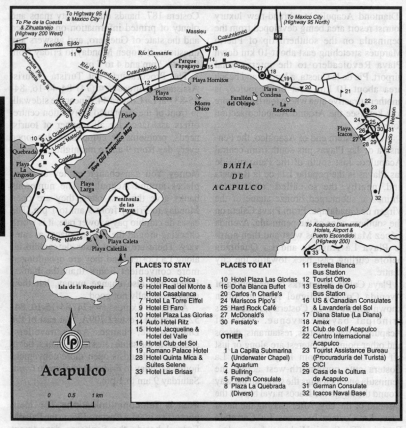

Acapulco

0   0.5   1 km

PLACES TO STAY
3 Hotel Boca Chica
6 Hotel Real del Monte &
   Hotel Casablanca
7 Hotel La Torre Eiffel
9 Hotel El Faro
10 Hotel Plaza Las Glorias
14 Auto Hotel Ritz
15 Hotel Jacqueline &
   Hotel del Valle
16 Hotel Club del Sol
19 Romano Palace Hotel
28 Hotel Quinta Mica &
   Suites Selene
33 Hotel Las Brisas

PLACES TO EAT
10 Hotel Plaza Las Glorias
16 Doña Blanca Buffet
20 Carlos 'n Charlie's
24 Mariscos Pipo's
25 Hard Rock Café
27 McDonald's
30 Fersato's

OTHER
1 La Capilla Submarina
   (Underwater Chapel)
2 Aquarium
4 Bullring
5 French Consulate
8 Plaza La Quebrada
   (Divers)

11 Estrella Blanca
   Bus Station
12 Tourist Office
13 Estrella de Oro
   Bus Station
16 US & Canadian Consulates
   & Lavandería del Sol
17 Diana Statue (La Diana)
18 Amex
21 Club de Golf Acapulco
22 Centro Internacional
   Acapulco
23 Tourist Assistance Bureau
   (Procuraduría del Turista)
26 CICI
29 Casa de la Cultura
   de Acapulco
31 German Consulate
32 Icacos Naval Base

La Paz. There are many other Lada casetas along La Costera. Collect calls can be made from any public phone.

Foreign Consulates The following consulates can be found in Acapulco:

Canada
    Hotel Club del Sol, La Costera & Reyes Católicas, Local No 9 (☎ (74) 85-66-00, ☎ /fax 85-66-21)
France
    Costa Grande 235, Fraccionamiento Las Playas (☎ (74) 82-33-94)

Germany
    Antón de Alaminos 26, Fraccionamiento Costa Azul (☎ (74) 84-18-60, 84-74-37; fax 84-38-10)
UK
    Hotel Las Brisas, Carretera Escénica 5255 (☎ (74) 84-66-05, 84-16-50; fax 84-14-95)
USA
    Hotel Club del Sol, La Costera & Reyes Católicas, Local No 8 (☎ (74) 85-66-00, ☎ /fax 85-72-07)

Other consulates in Acapulco include those of Austria, Finland, Holland, Italy, Norway, Panama, Spain and Sweden. The tourist offices have a complete list.

Bookshops The Super Super department store on La Costera opposite CICI has books in English, plus a few in German and French. Near the zócalo, Sanborns department store has a smaller collection of books in English.

Supermarkets The large Super Super, Comercial Mexicana, Gigante and Bodega combination supermarkets and discount department stores are along La Costera between the zócalo and Parque Papagayo; Super Super has another branch opposite CICI (the Centro Internacional de Convivencia Infantil).

Laundry Laundries in the centre include Lavandería y Tintorería Coral at Juárez 12, next door to hotel La Mama Hélène, Ghost Cleaners at José María Iglesias 9 and Lavandería América, up the hill at La Quebrada 830. On La Costera, Lavandería del Sol at the Club del Sol hotel is open Monday to Saturday from 9 am to 9 pm.

Emergency Locatel (☎ 81-11-00), operated by the state tourist office, is a 24-hour hotline for all types of emergencies. The Tourist Police can be contacted on ☎ 85-04-90.

Things to See

The five-sided **Fuerte de San Diego** was built in 1616 atop a hill just east of the zócalo to protect the naos (galleons) that conducted trade between the Philippines and México from marauding Dutch and English pirates. It must have done some good because this trade route lasted until the early 19th century. Apparently it was also strong enough to forestall independence leader Morelos's takeover of the city in 1812 for four months. The fort had to be rebuilt after a 1776 earthquake which damaged most of Acapulco. It remains basically unchanged today, and has been restored to top condition. The fort is now the home of the **Museo Histórico de Acapulco**, a museum with interesting historical exhibits. It's open Tuesday to Sunday from 10.30 am to 4.40 pm; admission is 13 pesos (free on Sunday and holidays, and free every day for children, students and seniors).

The famous **clavadistas of La Quebrada** have been amazing visitors to Acapulco ever since 1934, diving with graceful finesse from heights of 25 to 45 metres into a narrow crevasse with the ocean swells rising and falling inside. Not surprisingly, the divers pray at a small shrine before leaping over the edge. (So did Elvis Presley in the film *Fun in Acapulco*.) Diving times are daily at 12.45, 7.30, 8.30, 9.30 and 10.30 pm, with three divers leaping each time; admission is 5 pesos (children under 10 free). To get to La Quebrada you can either walk up the hill from the zócalo on Calle La Quebrada, or take a taxi. La Quebrada is also an excellent place to come and watch the sunset.

You can also get a great view of the divers from the restaurant/bar of the Plaza Las Glorias hotel. It costs 50 pesos to enter the bar while the diving's going on (the price includes two drinks); the view is even better from the restaurant (see Places to Eat).

The **Parque Papagayo** amusement park, with access to Playas Hornos and Hornitos, is a large park full of tropical trees. Its attractions, for both kids and adults, include a roller-skating rink, a lake with paddle boats, a children's train, mechanical rides and a hill from which there's an excellent view. To get up and down you can take a chair lift (*telesilla*) for 2 pesos; toboggan back down for 4 pesos. The chair lift and toboggan are open from 11 am to 7 pm daily, noon to 8 pm Sunday. The park is open weekdays from 6 am to 7 pm, weekends till 8 pm, with no admission charge. The mechanical rides section is open weekdays from 4 to 10.30 pm, or 11.30 pm on weekends.

The Centro Internacional de Convivencia Infantil (all it's ever called is **CICI**) is a family water-sports park on La Costera on the east side of Acapulco. Shows with dolphins, seals and divers are held several times daily; there's also a 30-metre-high water toboggan, a pool with artificial waves, a small tidepool aquarium and other kids' games. It's open every day from 10 am to 6 pm; admission is 30 pesos (25 pesos for children aged two to 10). Any local bus marked 'CICI', 'Base' or 'Puerto Marqués' will take you there.

The **Centro de Convenciones** (Acapulco Convention Centre; ☎ 84-70-50), also called the Centro Internacional Acapulco, is a large complex on the mountain side of La Costera, not far from CICI. The centre has a permanent craft gallery (Galería de Artesanías), temporary special exhibitions, a large plaza, theatres and concert halls. A Fiesta Mexicana is held several evenings each week (see Entertainment). Phone the centre to ask about current offerings, or stop by the information kiosk in front of the centre.

The **Casa de la Cultura** complex (☎ 84-23-90, 84-38-14 for schedules) is a group of buildings set around a garden at La Costera 4834, just east of CICI. An archaeological museum, an innovative art gallery and a handicrafts shop are all open Monday to Saturday from 10 am to 2 pm and 4 to 7 pm. Also here are an open-air theatre and an indoor auditorium.

Mágico Mundo Marino is an aquarium on a small point of land between Playas Caleta and Caletilla. Highlights include a sea lion show, the feeding of sharks and piranhas, swimming pools, water toboggans and an oceanographic museum. It's open every day from 9 am to 7 pm; admission is 20 pesos (15 pesos for children aged three to 12).

Out on the Isla de la Roqueta is a **zoo**, which also features telescopes and children's games, open every day except Tuesday from 10 am to 5 pm; admission is 3 pesos.

Beaches Visiting Acapulco's beaches tops most visitors' lists of things to do here. The beaches heading east around the bay from the zócalo – **Playas Hornos, Hornitos, Condesa** and **Icacos** – are the most popular. The high-rise hotel district begins on Playa Hornitos, at the eastern side of Parque Papagayo, and heads east from there. City buses constantly ply La Costera, the beachside avenue, making it easy to get up and down this long arc of beaches.

Playas Caleta and **Caletilla** are two small, protected beaches beside one another in a cove on the south side of the Peninsula de las Playas. They're especially popular for families with small children, as the water is

very calm. An aquarium on a tiny point of land separates the two beaches. Boats depart from here for **Isla de la Roqueta** just offshore, which has a zoo and another popular beach. Any bus marked 'Caleta' heading down La Costera will take you to these beaches.

Playa La Angosta is another beach in a tiny, protected cove on the south side of the peninsula. From the zócalo it takes about 20 minutes to walk there, or you can take any 'Caleta' bus and get off near the Hotel Avenida, on a corner of La Costera, from where the beach is just one short block to the west.

Activities
Water Sports Just about everything that can be done on, under and above the water is done at Acapulco. On the Bahía de Acapulco, water-skiing, jet-skiing, boating, the 'banana' and parasailing are all popular activities. The smaller Playas Caleta and Caletilla have all of these plus sailboats, fishing boats, motor boats, pedal boats, canoes, snorkelling gear, black inner tubes and bicycles for hire.

Scuba-diving trips and/or instruction can be arranged on Playa Caleta, on the Bahía de Acapulco, or by contacting any of several diving operators, including Aqua Mundo (☎ 82-10-41) at La Costera 100, Divers de México (☎ 82-18-77) on La Costera, Hermanos Arnold (☎ 82-18-77) at La Costera 205 and Mantarraya (☎ 82-69-56) at Gran Via Tropical 2.

Deep-sea fishing is another possibility; the cost is around 500 pesos for a five-hour trip. Phone Deep-Sea Fishing Acapulco (☎ 82-41-91/71, 84-86-71), Barracuda's Fleet (☎ 83-85-43, 82-52-56), ask on the beaches or at travel agencies, or just stroll along the Malecón near the zócalo and see which boats look likely.

Other Sports Acapulco has three golf courses: the Club de Golf Acapulco (☎ 84-48-24) on La Costera, a course at the Acapulco Princess Hotel (☎ 69-10-00) in Acapulco Diamante (near the airport) and another at the Pierre Marqués Hotel (☎ 84-

20-00), also in Acapulco Diamante. Another, the Campo de Golf de Playa Diamante, is under construction. For tennis, try the Club de Tenis Alfredo's at Avenida del Prado 29, the Club de Tenis Hyatt (☎ 84-12-25), the Villa Vera Racquet Club (☎ 84-03-33) or the Acapulco Princess Hotel. Acapulco also has gymnasiums, squash courts and facilities for other sports. The tourist office has information on sport in Acapulco.

Cruises Various boats and yachts offer cruises, departing from the Malecón near the zócalo. Cruises are available day and night; they range from multilevel boats with blaring salsa music and open bars to yachts offering quiet sunset cruises around the bay. All take basically the same route – they leave from the Malecón, go around the Peninsula de las Playas to Isla de la Roqueta, pass by to see the cliff divers at La Quebrada, cross over to Puerto Marqués, and then come back around the Bahía de Acapulco. The *Hawaiano* (☎ 82-21-99, 82-07-85), the *Bonanza* (☎ 83-18-03, 83-25-31), the *Yate Fiesta* (☎ 83-18-03, 83-25-31) and the large *Aca Tiki* catamaran (☎ 84-61-40, 84-67-86) are all popular; you can make reservations by calling them directly, through any travel agency or at most hotels.

From Playas Caleta and Caletilla a glass-bottomed boat departs for Isla de la Roqueta, giving you a view of the underwater sights and La Capilla Submarina (The Underwater Chapel), a submerged bronze statue of the Virgen de Guadalupe. The return trip takes about 45 minutes and costs 25 pesos. You can get off on the island and come back on a later boat if you like – the island has a beach, a zoo, and snorkelling and diving possibilities. It takes just eight minutes to reach the Isla de la Roqueta if you go straight there; the return-trip cost is 15 pesos.

Festivals
Probably the busiest time of the year for tourism in Acapulco is Semana Santa, when the city fills up with tourists and there's lots of action in the discos, on the beaches and all over town. A Tianguis Turístico held for one week in May features promotions relating to the tourist industry. Following the tianguis, the Festivales de Acapulco, also held for one week in May, features prominent Mexican and international entertainment at many venues around Acapulco.

The festival for Mexico's patron saint, the Virgen de Guadalupe, is celebrated all night on 11 December and all the following day, with processions accompanied by small marching bands, fireworks and folk dances in the streets, all converging on the cathedral in the zócalo, where children dressed in costumes are brought. It's a lesser version of the Mexico City festival. Expo-Acapulco, an industrial and commercial exposition, is held from 20 December to 7 January to encourage investment in Acapulco.

Places to Stay
Acapulco has a great number of hotels in all categories and over 30,000 hotel rooms, but its tourism is seasonal. High season is from the middle of December until the day after Easter, with another flurry of activity during the July and August school holidays; the rest of the year, tourism is much slower. Most hotels raise their rates during these times, when they can be as much as double the low-season price, though some do this for only part of the season. At other times of year you can often bargain for a better rate, especially if you plan to stay a while. If you come to Acapulco at Semana Santa or Christmas/ New Year, be sure to have hotel reservations or you may do a lot of searching for a room.

Places to Stay – bottom end
Most of Acapulco's budget hotels are concentrated around the zócalo area and on Calle La Quebrada, the street going up the hill from behind the cathedral to La Quebrada, where the divers do their stuff. There are many more hotels in this area, if all the ones listed here are full.

On La Quebrada, *Hotel Angelita* (☎ (74) 83-57-34) at No 37 is clean and popular, with singles/doubles at 30/50 pesos most of the year, 40/60 pesos in winter. Next door, the

Hotel Mariscal (☎ (74) 82-00-15) at No 35 has rooms at 20 pesos per person. The *Hotel Asturias* (☎ (74) 83-65-48) at No 45 is a popular place, very clean and well tended, with pleasant rooms on a courtyard with a small swimming pool; the cost is 30 pesos per person. Other hotels with swimming pools on La Quebrada are the *Hotel Coral* (☎ (74) 82-07-56) at No 56, with rooms at 25 pesos per person, and the *Hotel Casa Amparo* (☎ (74) 82-21-72) up the hill at No 69, with private parking and rooms at 30/50 pesos per person in summer/winter. If you're at the end of your economic rope, check out the *Casa de Huéspedes Aries* (☎ (74) 83-24-01) at No 30 and the *Casa de Huéspedes La Tía Conchita* (☎ (74) 82-18-82) next door at No 32; both have tiny rooms at 20 pesos per person all year round.

Up the hill at the top of La Quebrada is the Plaza La Quebrada, overlooking the sea where the cliff divers perform. The large parking lot here is a safe place to park a car (there are attendants) but it gets very busy and loud in the evening, when the divers are one of Acapulco's major attractions. The hotels here are somewhat cooler than places down the hill in town, since they catch the sea breezes. Perched on a hill above the plaza, *La Torre Eiffel* (☎ (74) 82-16-83) at Inalámbrica 110 has a small swimming pool and large balconies with sitting areas set up for a view of the sea. Its bright rooms cost 30 pesos per person most of the year, 50 pesos per person in April, July, August, November and December; bargain for a good rate here. Right on the plaza at La Quebrada 83, the *Hotel El Faro* (☎ (74) 82-13-65) has large rooms with balconies at 30/60 pesos for singles/doubles most of the year, 50/80 pesos in winter.

Budget hotels near the zócalo include the *Hotel Sutter* (☎ (74) 82-02-09) at Azueta 10 and the *Hotel Maria Antonieta* (☎ (74) 82-50-24) at Azueta 17, on opposite corners of Azueta and La Paz, both with rooms at 30 pesos per person.

Places to Stay – middle
In the zócalo area, a favourite with many travellers (especially those who speak French) is *La Mama Hélène* (☎ (74) 82-23-96, fax 83-86-97) at Benito Juárez 12, near the corner of Calle Felipe Valle. Hélène, the proprietress, comes from France, speaks English, French and Spanish, and does indeed treat her guests like a 'mama'. Though it's in the city centre, it has a quiet and pleasant atmosphere, with nicely decorated rooms and a courtyard with aquariums, table tennis, and tables where breakfast is served. The cost is 40 pesos per person all year round, breakfast extra.

Nearby, the *Hotel Misión* (☎ (74) 82-36-43, 82-20-76) at Felipe Valle 12 is a relaxing colonial-style place with rooms set around a lovely, shady courtyard (with plants, tiles and heavy Spanish furniture) where breakfast is served; singles/doubles are 45/80 pesos.

On the east side of Parque Papagayo, near La Costera and the popular Playa Hornitos, the *Hotel Jacqueline* (☎ (74) 85-93-38) at Gonsalo Gómez 6 has 10 air-con rooms at 90 pesos around a pleasant little garden, higher at busy times. Next door, the *Hotel del Valle* (☎ (74) 85-83-36/88) at Costera y Gonzálo G Espinosa 150 has a small swimming pool, kitchens, and rooms at 80/110 pesos with fan/air-con.

Also half a block from Playa Hornitos, the *Auto Hotel Ritz* (☎ (74) 85-80-23, fax 85-56-47) on Avenida Wilfrido Massieu (no number) is an attractive six-storey hotel with indoor parking; the rooms, all with air-con and large private balconies overlooking the swimming pool, cost 128 pesos.

Near the CICI water-sports park and Playa Icacos are a number of other hotels, including two with large apartments with swimming pool, parking, air-con and fully equipped kitchens: *Suites Selene* (☎ (74) 84-29-77) at Cristobal Colón 175, one door from the beach, with one/two-bedroom apartments at 154/330 pesos (higher at holidays), and *Hotel Quinta Mica* (☎ (74) 84-01-21/22) at Cristobal Colón 115 with apartments at 165 pesos all year round. The Super Super supermarket nearby is convenient for groceries.

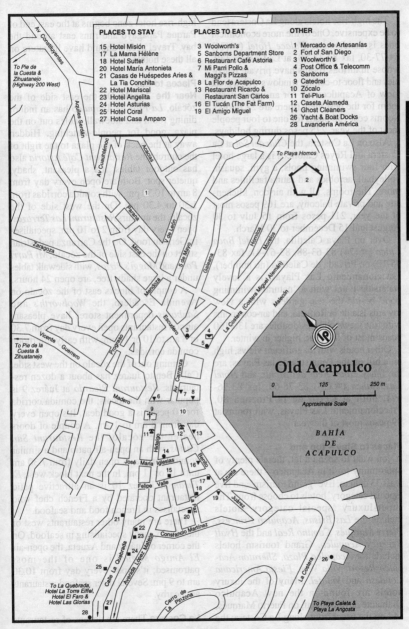

PLACES TO STAY

15 Hotel Misión
17 La Mama Hélène
18 Hotel Sutter
20 Hotel María Antonieta
21 Casas de Huéspedes Aries &
   La Tia Conchita
22 Hotel Mariscal
23 Hotel Angelita
24 Hotel Asturias
25 Hotel Coral
27 Hotel Casa Amparo

PLACES TO EAT

3 Woolworth's
5 Sanborns Department Store
6 Restaurant Café Astoria
7 Mi Parri Pollo &
  Maggi's Pizzas
8 La Flor de Acapulco
13 Restaurant Ricardo &
   Restaurant San Carlos
16 El Tucán (The Fat Farm)
19 El Amigo Miguel

OTHER

1 Mercado de Artesanías
2 Fort of San Diego
3 Woolworth's
4 Post Office & Telecomm
5 Sanborns
9 Catedral
10 Zócalo
11 Tel-Plus
12 Caseta Alameda
14 Ghost Cleaners
26 Yacht & Boat Docks
28 Lavandería América

To Pie de
la Cuesta &
Zihuatanejo
(Highway 200 West)

To Pie de la
Cuesta &
Zihuatanejo

Av Constituyentes

Aquiles Serdán

Av Cuauhtémoc

Acacias

Parana

Mina

V de León

5 de Mayo

Galeana

Zaragoza

Mendoza

Escudero

Vicente Guerrero

Progreso

Hornos

Morelos

La Costera (Costera Miguel Alemán)

Malecón

Madero

Av Carranza

Hidalgo

José María Iglesias

Felipe Valle

Azueta

Benito

Juárez

Constancio Martínez

Calle La Quebrada

Avenida López Mateos

La Costera

To La Quebrada,
Hotel La Torre Eiffel,
Hotel El Faro &
Hotel Las Glorias

Cerro de
La Pinzona

To Playa Caleta &
Playa La Angosta

To Playa Homos

Old Acapulco

0   125   250 m

Approximate Scale

**BAHÍA
DE
ACAPULCO**

The high-rise hotels along La Costera tend to be expensive. One of the more economical ones is the *Romano Palace Hotel* (☎ (74) 84-77-30, fax 84-13-50) at La Costera 130, whose luxurious rooms have private balconies and floor-to-ceiling windows with a great view of Acapulco; ask for an upper-storey room for the best view (there are 22 floors). Rooms cost 138 pesos for one to four people most of the year, 275 pesos during holidays.

Also on La Costera, the *Club del Sol* at La Costera and Reyes Católicos is a large hotel with four swimming pools, a gym, squash, volleyball, aerobics and sauna facilities and more. The rooms, all with air-con, kitchenette and private balcony, are 169 pesos most of the year, 211 pesos from 15 July to 30 August and 15 December to 30 March.

Over on Playa Caletilla, the *Hotel Boca Chica* (☎ (74) 83-63-88, 83-67-41; fax 83-95-13) on Privada de Caletilla (no number), Fraccionamiento Las Playas, is a lovely waterside hotel with a 'natural swimming pool' beside the sea, gardens with a view towards Isla de la Roqueta, and air-con rooms with fine views. Singles/doubles are 130/160 pesos most of the year, higher in winter.

Other hotels with magnificent views, high on a hill on the Peninsula de las Playas, are the fancy *Hotel Real del Monte* and *Hotel Casablanca* (☎ (74) 83-76-66, fax 83-76-67), both at Cerro de la Pinzona 80, Fraccionamiento Las Playas, with rooms at 99 pesos most of the year.

Places to Stay – top end

If you want to spend a lot, there's plenty of opportunity for it in Acapulco – there are at least 33 deluxe, five 'grand tourism' and five 'special category' hotels to choose from. The super-luxury 'special category' hotels include the *Las Brisas, Acapulco Princess, Pierre Marqués, Camino Real* and the *Hyatt Regency Acapulco*. Grand tourism hotels include the *Acapulco Plaza, Sheraton Acapulco Resort, Villa Vera, Fiesta Americana Condesa* and *Vidafel*. Many of the luxury hotels are found in the new Acapulco Diamante development, on Puerto Marqués, and on the beachfront along La Costera; the high-rise hotel zone begins at the east end of Parque Papagayo and runs east around the bay. Travel agents should have literature on all these hotels.

Places to Eat

Near the Zócalo On the east side of the zócalo, *La Flor de Acapulco* has an indoor dining room and sidewalk tables out on the plaza, good for people-watching. Hidden away at the back of the plaza to the right of the church, the *Restaurant Café Astoria* also has outdoor tables; it's a pleasant, shady, quieter spot. Both are open every day from 8 am to 10.30 pm, with comida corridas from 1.30 to 4.30 pm. On the west side of the zócalo, the upstairs *Restaurant Las Terrazas*, open every day from 2 to 10 pm, specialises in German food. On the Carranza pedestrian street on the east side of the zócalo, *Mi Parri Pollo* and *Maggi's Pizzas*, with sidewalk tables under a large shady tree, are open 24 hours.

A couple of blocks east of the zócalo on Avenida Escadero, the *Woolworth's* and *Sanborns* department stores have pleasant air-con restaurants open every day from 7.30 or 8 am to 10 or 11 pm, with early-afternoon comida corridas.

Coming out of the zócalo on the west side, Calle Benito Juárez has about a dozen restaurants. *Restaurant Ricardo* at Juárez 9 is popular with the locals; the comida corrida for 10 pesos is a good deal. It's open every day from 8 am to 1 am. A couple of doors nearer the zócalo, the *Restaurant San Carlos*, with an open-air patio and a similar comida corrida, is open daily from 7.30 am until 10 or 11 pm. In the next block west, *El Tucán* at Juárez 10 is an attractive patio restaurant operated by a French chef who specialises in French food and seafood.

There are many other restaurants west of the zócalo, many specialising in seafood. On the corner of Juárez and Azueta, the open-air *El Amigo Miguel* is one of the most patronised; it's open every day from 10.30 am to 9 pm. Several other seafood restaurants are nearby.

La Costera There are dozens of restaurants

as you head east down La Costera towards the big high-rise hotels. *Fersato's*, on La Costera opposite the Casa de la Cultura, near CICI, is a long-standing family establishment with delicious, reasonably priced Mexican food (a comida corrida is 13 pesos); it's open every day from 7 am to midnight. One block west of CICI, the famous (and much more expensive) *Hard Rock Cafe* is open every day from noon to 2 am. Another block west, *Mariscos Pipo's* is known for its good seafood; try a combination seafood plate for 25 pesos (small) or 30 pesos (large). It's open every day from 1 to 9.30 pm.

Back along La Costera, *Carlos 'n Charlie's* at La Costera 999, opposite Las Torres Gemelas, is one of the Carlos Anderson chain found throughout Mexico, with a fascinating collection of old photos covering every inch of wall space, rowdy music and a quirky bilingual menu. It's not cheap, but the Anderson restaurants always put on a good time for the tourists. It's open every day from 6 pm to midnight. Another Anderson restaurant, *Sr Frog's*, is on the Carretera Escénica on the east side of the Bahía de Acapulco, with a great view.

For cheaper fare on La Costera, the open-air *Doña Blanca Buffet* at the Club del Sol hotel features all-you-can-eat buffets from 9 am to noon (10.50 pesos) and from 1 to 5.30 pm (12.50 pesos).

Juice stands and restaurants in the *100% Natural* chain are found throughout Acapulco; there are many spread out along La Costera. Several of the US chain restaurants are also found on La Costera, including *Denny's, Big Boy* (both open 24 hours), *Shakey's Pizza, Domino's Pizza, Pizza Hut, Kentucky Fried Chicken* and *McDonald's*. The outdoor McDonald's behind the CICI water-sports complex, which can be entered separately from Calle Cristobal Colón, is right on the beach and has a great view of the Bahía de Acapulco.

Playa Caletilla There are many open-air seafood restaurants under the big trees lining the rear of Playa Caletilla.

La Quebrada For a splurge you could try the *Restaurant La Perla* at the Plaza Las Glorias Hotel on the Plaza La Quebrada; go in the evening when the divers are performing. This fancy restaurant offers a nightly buffet from 7 pm to midnight for 110 pesos per person, with dining on candlelit terraces under the stars, with a great view of the divers (☎ 83-12-60, 83-11-55 for reservations).

Entertainment

Nightclubs Acapulco's active nightlife rivals its beaches as the main attraction. Much of the nightlife revolves around the many discos and nightclubs, with new ones continually opening up to challenge the old. Most of the discos open around 10 pm and have a cover charge of around 50 pesos; some charge more to get in but have an open bar.

Extravaganzza and the *Palladium*, both in the Las Brisas area in the south-east part of the city, and *D'Paradisse* and *Salon Q* on La Costera, the latter with Latin rhythms and live music, were the newest raves at the time of writing.

Fantasy, also in the Las Brisas area, has a laser light show and disco dancing. *Baby'O* at La Costera and Horatio Nelson also has a laser light show and is supposedly one of the best discos in Acapulco, attracting a younger crowd. *Bey's Rock*, near Baby'O, has live rock bands, golden hits and the newest videos. The *News* disco and concert hall at La Costera 12, billing itself as 'one of the largest and most spectacular discos in the world', is another favourite, as is *Atrium*, a smaller disco at La Costera 30. *Disco Beach* is also popular, right on Playa Condesa. *Nina's* at La Costera 41 and *Cat's* at Juan de la Cosa 32, just off La Costera, specialise in live tropical music. *B&B* at Gran Via Tropical 5 in the Caleta area features hits of the 1950s to 1980s.

Don't forget the *Hard Rock Cafe*; the Acapulco branch of the famous chain, at La Costera 37 just west of CICI, is open every day from noon until 2 am, with live music nightly except Tuesday from 11 pm to 1.30 am.

Acapulco has an active gay scene and several predominantly gay bars and clubs.

Tequila's Le Club opposite Gigante is a popular gay disco; *New York* is another gay bar and is said to have some of the best music in Acapulco.

If you don't feel up to a disco, most of the big hotels along La Costera have bars with entertainment, be it quiet piano bars or live bands.

Bullfights These are held at the Plaza de Toros south-east of La Quebrada and north-west of Playas Caleta and Caletilla on Sunday at 5.30 pm; tickets are sold at the bullring from 4.30 pm. The traditional bullfighting season is from December to April (Christmas to Easter) but sometimes it ends earlier; travel agencies or the bullring ticket office (☎ 82-11-82, 83-95-61) will have details. The 'Caleta' bus passes near the bullring.

Other Entertainment Apart from the disco scene there are plenty of other things to do around Acapulco in the evening. At the Centro de Convenciones there's a Fiesta Mexicana every Wednesday and Friday night from 7 to 10.30 pm, featuring regional dances from many parts of Mexico, mariachis, the famous Papantla voladores and a rope performer; there's also a sumptuous Mexican buffet and open bar. The cost is 130 pesos per person; phone ☎ 84-70-50, ext 448/449 for reservations.

Other theatres at the Centro de Convenciones present plays, concerts, dance and other cultural performances, as does the Casa de la Cultura (☎ 84-23-90, 84-38-14); phone or stop by for current schedules.

Acapulco has several cinemas; there's one on the zócalo, a couple on La Costera, and several more around town. Current cinema listings are found in the *Novedades* and *Sol de Acapulco* newspapers.

Evening cruises are another possibility, and there are the spectacular cliff divers at La Quebrada. Or it's pleasant to sit at one of the sidewalk restaurants on the zócalo, feel the warm night air, and watch the activity in the plaza.

Things to Buy
Acapulco's main craft market, the 400-stall Mercado de Artesanías, is a few blocks east of the zócalo between Avenida Cuauhtémoc and Vicente de León. Paved and pleasant, it's a good place to get better deals on everything that you see in the hotel shops and on the beaches – sarapes, hammocks, silver jewellery, huaraches, clothing, T-shirts etc. Bargaining is definitely the rule. It's open every day from 9 am to 8 pm.

Getting There & Away
Air Acapulco has a busy international airport, with direct flights to/from the USA, including Oakland, Chicago and New York with TAESA, and Los Angeles with Delta. Most other flights connect through either Mexico City or Guadalajara, both short hops from Acapulco. Airlines serving Acapulco include:

Aeroméxico
    La Costera 286, beside Cine Playa Hornos (☎ 85-16-00/25)
Delta Airlines
    Airport (reservations toll-free ☎ 91-800-90-221)
Mexicana
    Torre Acapulco, La Costera 1252 (☎ (74) 84-68-90/37, 84-69-43)
TAESA
    Hotel Imperial, La Costera 251 (☎ (74) 86-45-76)

Bus Acapulco has two major long-distance bus stations. The Estrella de Oro terminal (☎ (74) 85-93-60, 85-87-05) is on the corner of Avenidas Cuauhtémoc and Wilfrido Massieu. The Base-Cine Río-Caleta local bus passes by this terminal; you can catch it opposite the Sanborns department store on La Costera, two blocks east of the zócalo. The Estrella Blanca terminal (☎ (74) 69-20-32/25) is at Avenida Ejido 47; any local bus marked 'Ejido' departing from opposite the Sanborns department store will get you there.

Both companies offer frequent services to Mexico City with various levels of luxury; journey durations depend on whether they use the new, faster autopista or the old federal highway. Both lines have buses to both the Terminal Sur and Terminal Norte in Mexico City. Services include:

Estrella Blanca – primera (65 pesos, 6½ hours), primera especial (77 pesos, 5½ hours), futura (85 pesos, five hours) and ejecutivo (110 pesos, five hours), with departures hourly from 6 am to 6.35 pm, hourly again from 8.45 pm to 2 am, and a bus at 4 am

Estrella de Oro – primera (65 pesos, six hours, three daily), plus (77 pesos, five hours, nine daily), crucero (80 pesos, five hours, four daily) and diamante (130 pesos, five hours, three daily)

Other destinations include:

Chilpancingo – 132 km, 1½ to two hours; every half-hour, 5 am to midnight, by Estrella Blanca (22 to 24 pesos); every half-hour from 6.30 am to 11.45 am, then at 2.30, 3.40, 4.30, 6.45 and 11 pm by Estrella de Oro (24 pesos)

Cuernavaca – 315 km, four to five hours; by Estrella Blanca, primera (51 pesos, five hours, four daily), primera especial (64 pesos, 4½ hours, two daily) and futura (70 pesos, four hours, two daily); by Estrella de Oro, plus (64 pesos, four hours, three daily)

Iguala – 231 km, three hours; hourly buses, 5.30 am to 2.15 pm (38 pesos) by Estrella Blanca; departures same as for Chilpancingo by Estrella de Oro (40 pesos)

Puerto Escondido – 370 km, seven hours; nine daily by Estrella Blanca (56 pesos)

Taxco – 266 km, 4½ to five hours; five daily by Estrella Blanca (40 pesos); three daily by Estrella de Oro (40 pesos)

Zihuatanejo – 239 km, four hours; hourly buses, 7.30 am to 4.30 pm, also 9 pm, by Estrella Blanca (33 pesos); three daily by Estrella de Oro (26 to 33 pesos)

Getting Around

To/From the Airport Acapulco's airport is 23 km south-east of the zócalo, beyond the junction for Puerto Marqués. If you arrive by air, buy a ticket for transport into town from one of the colectivo desks before you leave the terminal; they all cost the same – 18 pesos per person for a lift directly to your hotel. Taxis from the airport to the centre cost 107 pesos.

Leaving Acapulco, phone Transportación de Pasajeros (☎ 62-10-95/98), Transportación Turística (☎ 86-49-32/33) or Movil Aca (☎ 66-92-98/99) 24 hours in advance to reserve your transport back to the airport. They'll pick you up 90 minutes before your departure for domestic flights, two hours

ahead for international flights; the cost is 18 pesos. Taxis from the centre to the airport cost 60 pesos.

Bus Acapulco has a good city bus system, with buses going every few minutes to most places you'd want to go. They operate every day from 5 am to 11 pm and cost 1 peso. From the zócalo area, the bus stop opposite Sanborns department store on La Costera, two blocks east of the zócalo, is a good place to catch buses – it's the beginning of several bus routes so you can usually get a seat. The most useful city routes include:

Base-Caleta – from the Icacos Naval Base at the south-east end of Acapulco, along La Costera, past the zócalo to Playa Caleta

Base-Cine Río-Caleta – from the Icacos Naval Base, cuts inland from La Costera on Avenida Wilfrido Massieu to Avenida Cuauhtémoc, heads down Cuauhtémoc through the business district, turning back to La Costera just before reaching the zócalo, continuing west to Caleta

Puerto Marqués-Centro – from opposite Sanborns, along La Costera to Puerto Marqués

Zócalo-Playa Pie de la Cuesta – from opposite Sanborns, to Pie de la Cuesta. Buses marked 'Playa' or 'Luces' go all the way down the Pie de la Cuesta beach road; those marked 'San Ysidro' stop only at the entrance to Pie de la Cuesta

Car & Motorbike Many car-rental companies hire jeeps as well as cars; several have offices at the airport as well as in town, and/or offer free delivery to wherever you choose. As always, it's a good idea to shop around to compare prices. Rental companies include:

Autos Hernandez	☎ 85-86-99, 86-34-20
Avis	☎ 66-90-35
Bet Mer	☎ 66-95-09
Budget	☎ 81-05-92, 66-91-69
Dollar	☎ 66-90-35, 84-28-88
Economovil	☎ 84-18-19, 66-90-02
Fast	☎ 84-48-44, 84-10-04
Flash	☎ 85-66-22
Hertz	☎ 85-89-47, 85-69-42
Inter Renta	☎ 85-37-67, 85-85-58
National	☎ 84-82-34, 84-17-00
Quick	☎ 86-34-20, 66-91-60
Saad	☎ 84-34-45, 84-53-25
Sands	☎ 84-38-32

Motorbikes (50cc) can be hired from Acamotos Rent (☎ 84-05-67), under a sidewalk awning on La Costera outside CICI. You must have a driver's licence (a licence for cars will do) and a credit card is extremely helpful; otherwise you'll be asked for a large (1000-peso) deposit. It's open every day from 8 am to 8 pm.

Taxi Taxis are plentiful in Acapulco and taxi drivers are happy to take gringos for a ride, especially for fares higher than the official rates. Always agree on the fare before you climb into the cab; it never hurts to bargain with taxi drivers.

AROUND ACAPULCO
Pie de la Cuesta
About 10 km north-west of Acapulco, Pie de la Cuesta is a narrow peninsula two km long stretching between the ocean and the large, freshwater Laguna de Coyuca. It's a popular

alternative to Acapulco – it's quieter, cleaner, closer to nature and much more peaceful. However, swimming in the ocean at Pie de la Cuesta can be dangerous due to a riptide and the shape of the waves; each year a number of people are killed in the surf. Laguna de Coyuca, three times as large as the Bahía de Acapulco, is better for swimming, and also has water-skiing; in the lagoon are the islands of Montosa, Presido and a bird sanctuary called Pájaros.

Pie de la Cuesta has many beachside restaurants, specialising in seafood, and it's a great place for watching the sunset. There's no nightlife, so if you're looking for excitement you may be better off staying in Acapulco. Water-skiing is popular on the Laguna de Coyuca, where there are several water-ski clubs; the Club Elsa-Pito also hires out canoes, jet skis and other equipment. Boat trips on the lagoon are another popular activity; you can go across to the place where

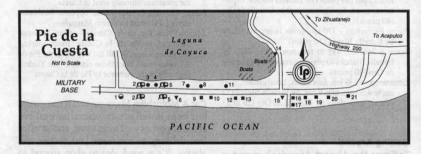

1	Buses to/from Acapulco	8	Club Náutico Cadena Ski	15	Restaurant/Bar El Zanate
2	Trailer Park Quinta Dora	9	Casa de Huéspedes Playa Leonor	16	Hotel Quinta Blanca
3	Sunset Lagoon Water Sports	10	Hotel & Restaurant Casa Blanca	17	Hotel Sunset, Racquet Club & Puesta del Sol
4	Club Elsa-Pito	11	Lago Mar Ski Club	18	Villa Nirvana
5	Acapulco Trailer Park & Mini-Super	12	Bungalows María Cristina	19	Hotel & Restaurant/Bar La Cabañita
6	Restaurant/Bar Tres Marías	13	Estacionamiento Juanita	20	Hotel & Restaurant Quinta Karla
7	Restaurant/Club de Ski Tres Marías	14	El Escondite/Steve's Hideout	21	Hotel & Restaurant Rocío

Sylvester Stallone filmed *Rambo*. Prices for boat trips are subject to negotiation and are set per boat rather than per person. You can also go horse riding on the beach.

Places to Stay Pie de la Cuesta is a good alternative to staying in Acapulco and, since there's only one road, you can easily check out what is on offer. There are some 14 hotels and two trailer parks spread along the two-km stretch of road between the beach and the lagoon. All the places to stay have private parking.

Camping Pie de la Cuesta has two clean, pleasant trailer parks at the far end of the road from the highway, near the end of the bus line coming from Acapulco: the *Trailer Park Quinta Dora* (☎ (74) 60-11-38) and the *Acapulco Trailer Park & Mini-Super* (☎ (74) 60-00-10). Both have full hook-ups and are good for both tents and trailers. Take a look at both parks and ask for prices before you choose your spot; they're only about a two-minute walk from each other but most campers have a distinct preference for one or the other. Both parks have camping areas on both the beach and lagoon sides of the road. The cost is around 30 pesos for trailers, 25 pesos for tents.

Hotels & Guesthouses The *Villa Nirvana* (☎ (74) 60-16-31) at Pie de la Cuesta 302, owned by a Canadian/Mexican couple, is one of the most attractive places on the beach, with just seven rooms set around a big garden with a beachside swimming pool. Singles/doubles are 50/70 pesos from May to October, 70/100 pesos from November to April. Nearby, the *Hotel Quinta Blanca* (☎ (74) 60-03-11) has a swimming pool, table tennis, and 25 rooms at 50 pesos all year round.

The *Hotel Sunset – Puesta del Sol & Racquet Club* (☎ (74) 60-04-12), about 50 metres from the coast road down a narrow lane, is right by the beach, and has a swimming pool, tennis court and restaurant/bar. Regular rooms are 75 pesos, large rooms with kitchen for up to seven people are 150 pesos, with

prices the same all year. *Quinta Karla*, also beside the beach and with a swimming pool, has rooms at 50 pesos all year.

On the beach side of the road are many smaller family-run guesthouses, all with beachfront restaurants. They include the *Hotel & Restaurant Rocío* (☎ (74) 60-10-08), where Félix López, the resident bartender, chef, guitarist and songster provides music and good times, and the *Hotel, Restaurant & Bar La Cabañita* (☎ (74) 60-00-52), with a swimming pool and hammocks overlooking the beach; at La Cabañita, rooms are 25 or 35 pesos per person.

Further along the road, *Bungalows María Cristina* (☎ (74) 60-02-62), run by a friendly family who speak English and Spanish, is a clean, well-tended, relaxing place with a bar-becue and hammocks overlooking the beach. Singles/doubles are 50/70 pesos from April to December, 100 pesos from December to April. Larger upstairs rooms with kitchens and sea views for up to five people cost 150/250 pesos in summer/winter. Next door, *Estacionamento Juanita* (☎ (74) 60-04-78) has singles/doubles at 35/50 pesos.

Still further along, the *Hotel & Restaurant Casa Blanca* (☎ (74) 60-03-24) is another clean, well-tended place on the beachfront, with a restaurant and a children's play area; singles/doubles are 30/60 pesos most of the year, higher in the high season. Nearby, the *Casa de Huéspedes Playa Leonor* (☎ (74) 60-03-48) has 10 rooms at 60 pesos from April to November, 90 pesos from November to April.

Places to Eat The restaurants at Pie de la Cuesta, most of which are attached to hotels and casas de huéspedes, are known for their fresh seafood. The *Restaurant El Zanate* beside the road is a small restaurant with good food; opposite this, on the shore of the lagoon with a terrace right over the water and a fine view, *El Escondite/Steve's Hideout* is an attractive place.

Most of the other restaurants are open-air places right beside the beach. The *Tres Marias* is known to have some of the best food in the area. The *Rocío, Quinta Karla, La Cabañita, Playa Leonor, Casa Blanca,*

Estacionamiento Juanita and the *Hotel Sunset – Puesta del Sol* hotels all have restaurants, as do some of the water-ski clubs.

Getting There & Away To get there from Acapulco, take a 'Playa Pie de la Cuesta' bus on La Costera opposite the post office (the one next to Sanborns, near the zócalo), on the bay side of the street. Buses go every 15 minutes from 6 am until around 8 pm; the cost is 1 peso for the 35-minute ride. Be sure to find out what time the last bus leaves Pie de la Cuesta for the return trip, unless you intend to stay the night. A taxi costs 35 pesos one way.

Other Destinations
About 18 km south-east of Acapulco, **Puerto Marqués** is a cove much smaller than the Bahía de Acapulco, with calm water. You get a magnificent view of the Bahía de Acapulco as the Carretera Escénica climbs south out of the city. The calm water at Puerto Marqués makes it a good place for water-skiing, sailing etc. Buses marked 'Puerto Marqués' depart from Acapulco's La Costera every 10 minutes from 5 am to 9 pm and cost 1 peso.

Past Puerto Marqués and heading out towards the airport, **Revolcadero** is the long, straight beach of the new Acapulco Diamante luxury tourism developments. The waves are large and surfing is popular here, especially in summer, but a strong undertow

makes swimming dangerous. Horse riding on the beach is another popular activity.

During Semana Santa, the Passion of Christ is acted out in the days before Easter in the town of **Treinta**, 30 km north-east of Acapulco; the Acapulco tourist office will have details.

CHILPANCINGO
• *pop: 136,200* • *alt: 1360 metres*
Chilpancingo, capital of the state of Guerrero, is a university city and agricultural centre on highway 95, about 130 km north of Acapulco and 270 km south of Mexico City. It's a rather nondescript place between two much more interesting destinations, Acapulco and Taxco.

Murals in the former **Palacio Municipal** showing the 1813 Congress of Chilpancingo are the only remaining signs of the city's important place in Mexico's history. In the spring of 1813, rebel leader José Maria Morelos y Pavón encircled Mexico City with his guerrilla army and then called for a congress to meet in Chilpancingo. The congress issued a Declaration of Independence and began to lay down the principles of a new constitution. Their achievements, however, were short-lived because Spanish troops broke the circle around Mexico City and recaptured most of Guerrero, including Chilpancingo. Morelos was tried for treason and executed by a firing squad.

Western Central Highlands

West of Mexico City lies an upland area of great geographical and cultural variety encompassing the inland parts of the states of Jalisco, Michoacán and Colima. (These states' narrow Pacific coastal plains, with some attractive resorts, big and small, are covered in the Central Pacific Coast chapter.) This region is off the really major tourist routes but has many very attractive destinations, among them the country's vibrant second city Guadalajara, capital of Jalisco; the fine capital of Michoacán, Morelia, and the spectacular El Rosario Monarch butterfly sanctuary to its east; the lovely colonial town of Pátzcuaro in the Michoacán highlands inhabited by Purépecha (Tarasco) Indians; and the volcano Paricutín, which rose in 1943 from the lush Michoacán country around Uruapan. Beyond these lie hundreds of km of little-visited back country, ripe for exploration.

An excellent companion guide if you're exploring this region is *Western Mexico – A Traveller's Treasury* by Tony Burton (Gua-dalajara, Editorial Agata, 1993), which covers lots of off-the-beaten-track places with plenty of interesting background. It's available in the region in most bookshops with English-language sections.

History

The Western Central Highlands were remote from Mexico's major pre-Hispanic empires, though a fairly advanced agricultural village society flourished in parts of the region as early as 200 BC. The major pre-Hispanic civilisation here was developed by the Tarascans or Purépecha of northern Michoacán in the 14th to 16th centuries AD, with its capital at Tzintzuntzan near Pátzcuaro. The zenith of the Tarascan empire coincided with the Aztec empire but the Tarascans always managed to fend off Aztec attacks, routing one particularly big Aztec invasion in 1479. West of the Tarascans – and occasionally at war with them – was the Chimalhuacán confederation of four Indian kingdoms, in

parts of what are now Jalisco, Colima and Nayarit states. (Jalisco takes its name – an Aztec word for 'sandy place' – from one of these kingdoms.) To the north were Chichimecs, seminomadic peoples regarded by the Aztecs as barbarians.

Colima, the leading Chimalhuacán kingdom, was conquered by the Spanish in 1523, but the region as a whole was not brought under Spanish control until the 1529-36 campaigns of Nuño de Guzmán, who tortured, killed and enslaved Indians all the way from Michoacán to Sinaloa in his pursuit of riches, territory and glory. Guzmán was appointed governor of most of the area he had conquered (which came to be called Nueva Galicia and retained some autonomy from the rest of New Spain until 1786), but eventually his misdeeds caught up with him and in 1538 he was sent back to Spain. A major Indian rebellion in Jalisco in 1540 set the region aflame in what's called the Mixtón War; this was not ended until the following year, by an army led by the Spanish viceroy himself. Guadalajara was established in its present location in 1542,

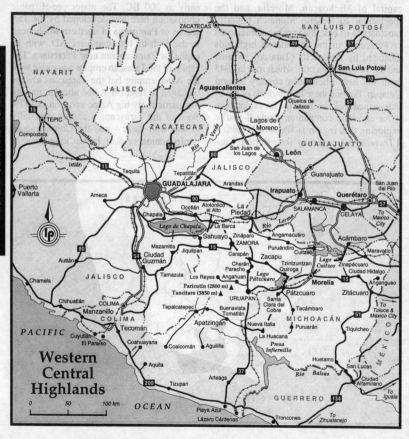

after three earlier settlements had been abandoned in the face of Indian attacks.

The region was slower to develop than mineral-rich areas like Zacatecas or Guanajuato, but ranching and agriculture grew, and Guadalajara, as 'capital of the west', was always one of Mexico's biggest cities. The church helped foster small industries and handicraft traditions to ease the poverty of Indians and others.

In the late 1920s Michoacán and above all Jalisco were hotbeds of the violent Cristero rebellion by Catholics against government antichurch policies. Later, the social reforms and concern for ordinary people shown by the popular Lázaro Cárdenas from Michoacán, as state governor from 1928 to 1932 then as national president from 1934 to 1940, did much to win favour for the post-revolutionary style of government.

Geography

The Western Central Highlands reach from the southern outliers of the Sierra Madre Occidental, in the north of Jalisco, to the western extremities of the Sierra Madre del Sur which rises behind the southern Pacific coast. In between, part of the Cordillera Neovolcánica sweeps east-west across the region. Between these main ranges lie assorted lesser hills and basins. Among the most rugged, sparsely populated expanses are the remote northern spur of Jalisco and the rather inaccessible ranges backing the Pacific coast. The few roads linking the coast and interior are spectacular.

Jalisco is Mexico's sixth-biggest state, at 80,836 sq km. Guadalajara lies towards the west end of an agriculturally productive basin stretching down from the state's north-east.

Michoacán (59,928 sq km) has the real highlands of the region – a big, green sweep above 2000 metres across the north of the state, strewn with the stumps of extinct and not-so-extinct volcanoes. The cordillera continues west into southern Jalisco and Colima, where the Volcán de Fuego de Colima (3960 metres) is Mexico's most active volcano.

The major rivers are the Lerma, flowing down from the east along the border of Michoacán and Jalisco into Lago de Chapala south of Guadalajara (Mexico's biggest lake at over 1100 sq km), and the Balsas, carrying almost all the runoff from the southern side of the Cordillera Neovolcánica.

Climate

The region is warm and pretty dry most of the year but has a distinct rainy season from June to September, when around 200 mm of rain falls each month in most areas. Where the land descends to lower altitudes – as at Uruapan in Michoacán, and around Colima city – temperature and humidity rise and the vegetation becomes lush and semi-tropical. Winter nights can get chilly at higher altitudes such as around Pátzcuaro.

Population & People

The region is home to over 10% of Mexico's people. Well over half of Jalisco's five million-plus people live in Guadalajara. Michoacán has 3.5 million people and Colima less than half a million.

The population is predominantly mestizo, with the 120,000 Purépecha of Michoacán and about 40,000 Huichol in isolated northern Jalisco forming the only significant Indian groups.

Guadalajara & Around

The city of Guadalajara itself is the major, unmissable attraction of inland Jalisco, but Lago de Chapala, 40 km south of the city, provides a pleasant change, with an idyllic climate that has attracted a large community of North American expatriates.

GUADALAJARA
• *pop: 4 million* • *alt: 1563 metres*
The second-largest city in Mexico, Guadalajara has a reputation as the nation's most 'Mexican' city. Many characteristically Mexican things and traditions were created here, including mariachi music, tequila, the Jarabe Tapatío or Mexican Hat Dance, the broad-rimmed sombrero hat, and charreadas.

Part of Guadalajara's appeal is that it has many of the attractions of Mexico City – fine museums and galleries, beautiful historic buildings, nightlife, culture, good places to stay and eat – but without all the capital's problems: Guadalajara may easily be western Mexico's biggest industrial centre but it's also a bright, modern, well-organised city where traffic flows fairly freely and pollution is not trapped by a ring of mountains. It is, too, probably Mexico's most musical city, with many lively venues and a big range of musical styles to be heard.

Excursions to the suburbs of Tlaquepaque and Tonalá, renowned for their arts and crafts, and further afield to Lago de Chapala, Mexico's largest lake, are also worthwhile. You'll never get bored in this city.

History

Guadalajara was established on its present site only after three settlements elsewhere had failed. Nuño de Guzmán founded the first Guadalajara in 1532 near Nochistlán in modern Zacatecas state with 63 Spanish families, naming it after his home city in Spain. But water was scarce, the land was hard to farm, and the local Indians were hostile. In 1533 Captain Juan de Oñate ordered the settlement moved to the old Indian village of Tonalá, today a suburb of Guadalajara. Guzmán, however, disliked Tonalá and in 1535 had it moved again to Tlacotán, just north-east of the modern city. In 1541 this settlement was destroyed by a confederation of local Indian tribes led by the chief Tenamaxtli. The colonists, however, escaped and picked a new site in the valley of Atemajac beside San Juan de Dios creek, which ran where Calzada Independencia is today. The new Guadalajara was founded by Captain Oñate on 14 February 1542, near where the Teatro Degollado now stands.

It finally prospered and in 1560 was declared the capital of Nueva Galicia province. Guadalajara quickly grew into one of New Spain's biggest, most important cities, the heart of a rich agricultural region and starting-point for Spanish expeditions and missions to the Philippines and western and northern New Spain. The Mexican independence movement leader Miguel Hidalgo set up a revolutionary government in Guadalajara in 1810 but was heavily defeated near the city in 1811, not long before his capture and execution in Chihuahua. The city was also the object of much fighting during the Reform War (1858-61), and between Constitutionalist and Villista armies in 1915 during the revolution.

Guadalajara had overtaken Puebla as Mexico's second-biggest city by the late 19th century. Its population has mushroomed since WW II and today it's a huge commercial, industrial and cultural centre and the communications hub for a big region.

Orientation

Guadalajara's giant twin-towered cathedral is at the heart of the city, surrounded by four lovely plazas in the four cardinal directions. The plaza east of the cathedral, Plaza de la Liberación, extends two blocks to the Teatro Degollado, another city landmark.

Behind the Teatro Degollado is the Plaza Tapatía, stretching half a km east to the Instituto Cultural Cabañas, another important historical edifice. Just south of Plaza Tapatía is the Mercado Libertad, a huge three-storey market covering an area of four city blocks.

Calzada Independencia, a major north-south central artery, runs south from the Mercado Libertad to Parque Agua Azul and the train and old bus stations, and north to the zoo, the Plaza de Toros and the Barranca de Oblatos canyon. Don't confuse Calzada Independencia with Calle Independencia, the east-west street one block north of the cathedral. In the centre, north-south streets change names at Hidalgo, the street running along the north side of the cathedral.

The long-distance bus station is the Nueva Central Camionera (New Bus Station), nine km south-east of the centre past the suburb Tlaquepaque.

About 25 blocks west of the cathedral, the north-south Avenida Chapultepec is the heart of Guadalajara's zona rosa, a stylish area with a number of fine restaurants and shops.

In the south-west of the city, Plaza del Sol on Avenida López Mateos is a huge modern shopping mall with restaurants, entertainment, and a number of hotels and motels nearby. A second line of Guadalajara's metro system, soon to open, will make reaching these areas much easier.

Guadalajara is 535 km north-west of Mexico City and 345 km east of Puerto Vallarta. Highways 15, 54, 70, 80 and 90 all converge here, combining temporarily to form the Periférico, a ring road around the city.

Information

Tourist Office The state tourist office (☎ (3) 658-22-22) is in Plaza Tapatía at Morelos 102, about 100 metres behind the Teatro Degollado, in an historic building called the Rincón del Diablo (Devil's Corner). It's open Monday to Friday from 9 am to 8 pm, Saturday and Sunday from 9 am to 1 pm. This is the place to come for free maps and information on Guadalajara and the state of Jalisco. English and a smattering of French are spoken. This office offers listings of cultural and other events happening every day around the city, information on anything you could want to know from local bus routes to retirement in Mexico. Ask for *Ver y Oír*, a monthly magazine listing cultural events in the city and environs, and *Let's Enjoy*, a bilingual monthly tourist magazine about the state of Jalisco. They also have a 'Teletur' service, where you can telephone the office to ask about anything you might need to know.

The state tourist office also operates a smaller information office in the Palacio de Gobierno, facing the Plaza de Armas just south of the cathedral, open Monday to Friday from 9 am to 3 pm and 6 to 8 pm, Saturday 9 am to 1 pm.

SECTUR (☎ (3) 614-86-65), the federal tourist office, is in Plaza Tapatía at Paseo Degollado 50, a block from the state office. It's open Monday to Friday from 9 am to 3 pm; it has information on travel in Mexico outside Jalisco.

Money Banks are plentiful in Guadalajara, and are open for currency exchange and other services Monday to Friday from 9 am to 1.30 pm. Many banks have ATMs. In addition many casas de cambio on López Cotilla in the three blocks between Corona and Molina offer good exchange rates. These are open longer hours than the banks; Casa de Cambio Libertad at López Cotilla 171 is open Monday to Saturday from 9 am to 7 pm, Sunday 11 am to 2 pm.

The American Express office and travel agency (☎ (3) 630-02-00, 615-89-10) is at Vallarta 2440, opposite Plaza Vallarta. It's open Monday to Friday from 9 am to 2 pm and 4 to 5 pm, Saturday 9 am to noon.

Post & Telecommunications The main post office is on Carranza, between Juan Manuel and Calle Independencia. It's open Monday to Friday from 8 am to 7 pm, Saturday and Sunday 9 am to 1 pm.

The Telecomm office, with telegram, telex and fax services, is in the Palacio Federal on Alcalde at Calle Hospital, opposite the Santuario church nine blocks north of the centre. It's open Monday to Friday from 9 am to 7 pm, Saturday 9 am to noon. There's a post office branch here too.

There are several Ladatel phones, some accepting coins, others credit cards or telephone cards, on Corona in the first few blocks south of the cathedral.

Telmex, the main Lada caseta, is at Donato Guerra 84 near the corner of Juárez. It's open every day from 7 am to 8.30 pm.

Computel, with long-distance telephone and fax services, has several offices around the city. There's one in the Edificio Mulbar on Corona opposite the Hotel Fenix, between Madero and López Cotilla; it's open Monday to Saturday from 7 am to 8.30 pm. Another is at 16 de Septiembre 599. Computel also has offices at the train station and at both the old and new bus stations.

Foreign Consulates Over 30 countries have consular offices in Guadalajara. The state tourist office has a complete list, or you can contact the Consular Association (☎ 616-06-29) for information. Consulates include:

Canada
    Hotel Fiesta Americana, Local 30, Aurelio
    Aceves 225 (☎ (3) 625-34-34)
France
    Avenida López Mateos 484 (☎ (3) 616-55-16)
Germany
    Corona 202 (☎ (3) 613-96-23)
Guatemala
    Mango 1440 (☎ (3) 611-15-03)
Netherlands
    Calzada Lázaro Cárdenas 601, Zona Industrial
    (☎ (3) 612-07-40)
UK
    Paulino Navarro 1165 esq Inglaterra (☎ (3) 611-
    16-78)
USA
    Calle Progreso 175 (☎ (3) 625-27-00)

Bookshops A fair selection of books and
magazines in English is available at the gift
shops of most major hotels. The Sandi Bookstore, Tepeyac 718, Colonia Chapalita, also
has a decent selection. Sanborns on the
corner of Juárez and 16 de Septiembre has
dozens of English-language magazines.

Useful Publications There are two weekly
English-language newspapers – the *Guadalajara Weekly*, really more of a broadsheet
for the visitor than a newspaper, and the
Guadalajara Reporter covering local and
national news plus lots of information about
what's on in the city.

The American-Canadian Club publishes a
newsletter, an information package on retirement in Mexico and a discount directory.
You can contact its office (Monday, Wednesday and Friday from 10 am to noon) in the
lobby of the Hotel Plaza del Sol on the corner
of Avenida López Mateos and Mariano
Otero, or phone them toll-free in the USA
(☎ 1-800-882-8215) or Canada (☎ 1-800-
368-0900).

MRTA (Mexico Retirement & Travel
Assistance) publishes the book *Guadalajara
– A Great Place to Visit or Retire* and an
excellent newsletter, the *MRTA Guadalajara/
Chapala Update*. You can pick up their
newsletter free at the state tourist office.
Their mailing address is PO Box 2190-23,
Henderson, NV 89009-7009, USA.

Their book and the interesting 60-page

Guadalajara Walking Tours are available at the
gift shops of most major hotels; in the centre,
try the Hotel Fenix or the Hotel Calinda Roma.

Cathedral

Guadalajara's huge twin-towered cathedral,
surrounded on all four sides by attractive
plazas, is its most famous symbol and most
conspicuous landmark. Begun in 1558 and
consecrated in 1616, it's almost as old as the
city. Up close you can see that it's a stylistic
hotchpotch: the exterior decorations, some
of which were completed long after the con-
secration, are in Churrigueresque, baroque,
neoclassical and other styles. The towers
date from 1848: they're much higher than the
originals, destroyed in an earthquake.

The interior includes 11 richly decorated
altars given to Guadalajara by King Ferdi-
nand VII of Spain (1784-1833), Gothic
vaults and Tuscany-style pillars. In the sacristy, which you can ask an attendant to open
for you, is *The Assumption of the Virgin*,
painted by Bartolomé Murillo in 1650.

Plaza de los Laureles & Presidencia Municipal

The Plaza de los Laureles is the plaza in front
of the west end of the cathedral. As its name
suggests, it's planted with laurels. On its
north side is the Presidencia Municipal (City
Hall), which though it appears much older
was actually built between 1949 and 1952.
Above its interior stairway is a mural depicting the founding of Guadalajara by Jaliscan
artist Gabriel Flores.

Plaza de Armas & Palacio de Gobierno

The Plaza de Armas, on the south side of the
cathedral, with the 18th-century Palacio de
Gobierno to its east, is a pleasant place to sit
and imagine how the city may have been in
colonial times. Free concerts of typical Jaliscan
music are held here on Thursday and Sunday
at 6.30 pm. They've been doing this since
1898 and haven't missed a performance yet.

The Palacio de Gobierno was finished in
1774 and, like the cathedral, was built in a
combination of styles – in this case, a strange
mix of simple, neoclassical features and

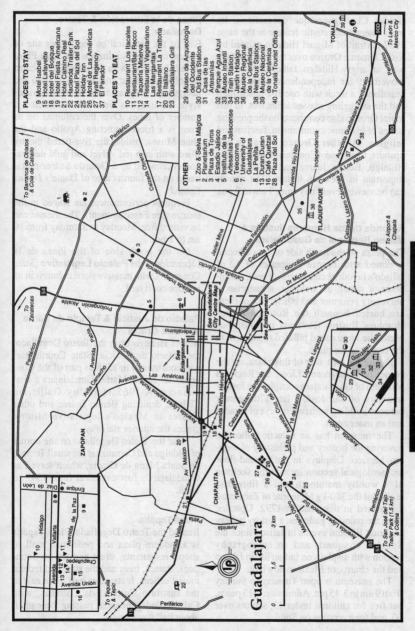

WESTERN CENTRAL HIGHLANDS

PLACES TO STAY

9 Motel Isabel
15 Hotel Lafayette
18 Hotel del Bosque
19 Hotel Fiesta Americana
21 Hotel Camino Real
22 Hacienda Trailer Park
24 Hotel Plaza del Sol
25 Motel de Las Américas
26 Hyatt Regency
37 El Parador

PLACES TO EAT

10 Restaurant Los Itacates
12 Restaurant/Bar Recco
14 Taquería Minerva
16 Restaurant Vegetariano
    Las Margaritas
17 Restaurant La Trattoria
20 El Italiano
23 Guadalajara Grill

OTHER

29 Museo de Arqueología
   del Occidente
30 Old Bus Station
31 Casa de las
   Artesanías
32 Parque Agua Azul
33 Museo Infantil
34 Tren Station
35 Jardín Hidalgo
36 Museo Regional
   de la Cerámica
38 New Bus Station
39 Museo Nacional
   de la Cerámica
40 Tonalá Tourist Office

1 Zoo & Selva Mágica
2 Planetarium
3 Plaza de Toros
4 Estadio Jalisco
5 Instituto de
  Artesanías Jaliscense
6 University of
  Guadalajara
7 Telecomm
8 La Peñita
13 Duran Duran
26 Café Quetzal
28 Plaza del Sol

To León &
Mexico City

To Barranca de Oblatos
& Cola de Caballo

To Zacatecas

To Tequila & Tepic

Guadalajara

To San José del Tajo
Trailer Park (1.5 km)

To Airport &
Chapala

To Tonalá

TONALÁ

TLAQUEPAQUE

CHAPALITA

ZAPOPAN

See Guadalajara
City Centre Map

See
Enlargement

See Enlargement

0   1.5   3 km

riotous Churrigueresque decorations. Its most interesting artistic feature is the huge 1937 portrait of Miguel Hidalgo painted by José Clemente Orozco over the interior stairway: an angry Hidalgo, father of Mexico's movement for independence from Spain, brandishes a torch with one fist raised high and the struggling masses at his feet. In this mural Orozco also comments on the pressing issues of his time: communism, fascism and religion. Another Orozco mural in the upstairs Congreso (Congress Hall) depicts Hidalgo, Benito Juárez and other figures important in Mexican history. The murals can be viewed every day from 9 am to 9 pm.

Rotonda de los Hombres Ilustres & Museo Regional de Guadalajara

The plaza on the north side of the cathedral is dotted with bronze sculptures of 12 of Jalisco's favourite characters – a poet, a composer, a writer, an architect, a historian, a university reformer and others. Six of them are buried beneath the Rotonda de los Hombres Ilustres (Rotunda of Illustrious Men), the large round pillared monument in the centre of the plaza.

Facing the east side of this plaza, on the corner of Hidalgo and Liceo, the Regional Museum of Guadalajara occupies the former seminary of San José, a late 17th-century baroque building with two storeys of arcades and an inner court.

The museum has an eclectic collection covering the history and prehistory of western Mexico. Displays in the ground-floor archaeological section include the skeleton of a woolly mammoth and a fibreglass replica of the 780-kg Meteorite of Zacatecas, discovered in that state in 1792. Upstairs, there are painting galleries, a history gallery covering life and events in Jalisco since the Spanish conquest, and an ethnography section with displays on Indian life in Jalisco and the charro, or Mexican cowboy.

The museum is open Tuesday to Sunday from 9 am to 3.45 pm. Admission is 13 pesos, but free for children under 13, seniors over 60, and for everyone on Sunday.

Plaza de la Liberación & Teatro Degollado

East of the cathedral on the former site of several colonial buildings is the large Plaza de la Liberación, with the impressive Teatro Degollado at its far end. Begun in 1856 and inaugurated 30 years later, the neoclassical-style theatre has been reconstructed a number of times. Over the columns on its front is a frieze depicting Apollo and the Nine Muses; inside, the five-tiered theatre filled with lush red velvet and gold decoration is crowned by a Gerardo Suárez mural based on the fourth canto of Dante's *Divine Comedy*.

Frequent performances are staged in the theatre (see Entertainment). The theatre can be visited free, Monday to Saturday from 10 am to 1 pm.

On the north side of the Plaza de la Liberación is the **Palacio Legislativo** (State Congress), with massive stone columns in its interior courtyard.

Palacio de Justicia & Templo de Santa María de Gracia

Across Hidalgo from the Teatro Degollado, the Palacio de Justicia (State Courthouse) was constructed in 1588 as part of the Convento de Santa María, Guadalajara's first nunnery. A 1965 mural by Guillermo Chávez, depicting Benito Juárez and other figures in Mexico's legislative history, graces the interior stairway.

Near the Teatro Degollado on the corner of Hidalgo and Carranza is the small Templo de Santa María de Gracia, which served as Guadalajara's first cathedral from 1549 to 1618.

Plaza Tapatía

Behind the Teatro Degollado, Plaza Tapatía is a modern plaza and pedestrian mall of shops, restaurants, street performers, fountains, statues, trees and the state and federal tourist offices. It stretches half a km east to the Instituto Cultural de Cabañas, with Calzada Independencia passing beneath it about halfway along.

Instituto Cultural de Cabañas

This huge neoclassical gem at the east end of Plaza Tapatía was constructed between 1805 and 1810 by Spanish architect Manuel Tolsá. Called the Hospicio Cabañas after its founder Bishop Don Juan Cruz Ruíz de Cabañas, it served as an orphanage for over 150 years until 1980, sometimes housing up to 3000 children at a time. It also occasionally served as an insane asylum, military barracks and jail. Miguel Hidalgo signed a proclamation against slavery here in 1811.

Between 1936 and 1939 José Clemente Orozco painted a series of murals in the main chapel that are regarded by many critics as his finest work. Most notable is *The Man of Fire* in the dome; 53 other dramatic frescos cover the walls and ceiling of the large chapel. Interpretations vary on what *The Man of Fire* means. A small book in English and Spanish, *The Murals of Orozco in the Cabañas Cultural Institute*, on sale at the main entrance, gives background information on the artist, the murals here, how they were executed and the story behind each one.

The Instituto Cultural Cabañas is a cultural institute containing a museum, a theatre and a school. All 23 courts and the chapel that Tolsá designed are intact; tours are given through them. The museum features a permanent exhibition of over 100 Orozco drawings and paintings, plus temporary exhibitions of painting, sculpture and engraving. The institute also hosts dance festivals, theatre performances, concerts and films.

The Instituto is open to the public Tuesday to Saturday from 10.15 am to 6 pm, Sunday 10.15 am to 3 pm. Admission is 5 pesos, except on Sunday when it's free.

Plazuela de los Mariachis

The Plazuela de los Mariachis, just south of the Mercado Libertad near the intersection of Javier Mina and Calzada Independencia Sur, is a small plaza known throughout Mexico for the mariachi bands that play here at all hours of the day and night. Several restaurants have tables out on the plaza and the mariachi bands come around and offer a song to the customers – for a price, of course. They get strumming hardest late at night.

Colonial Churches

Besides the cathedral and the Templo de Santa María de Gracia there are 13 other churches in the centre of Guadalajara, some of them impressively beautiful. The baroque **Templo de La Merced**, near the cathedral on the corner of Hidalgo and Pedro Loza, was built in 1650; inside are several fine large paintings, crystal chandeliers and lots of gold decoration.

The **Santuario de Nuestra Señora del Carmen**, facing the small plaza on the corner of Juárez and 8 de Julio, is another lovely church, with lots of gold decoration, old paintings, and murals in the dome.

On the corner of 16 de Septiembre and Miguel Blanco, the **Templo de Aranzazú**, built from 1749 to 1752, has three splendidly ornate Churrigueresque golden altars. Beside it is the older and less ornate **Templo de San Francisco**, built two centuries earlier in 1550.

Parque Agua Azul

About 20 blocks south of the centre, near the south end of Calzada Independencia Sur, Parque Agua Azul is a large verdant park offering pleasant relief from the city hubbub, with an orchid house, a butterfly house, an aviary, and a children's wading pool and playground. It's open Tuesday to Sunday from 10 am to 6 pm; admission is 3 pesos (children 1 peso). Bus No 60 heading south on Calzada Independencia will bring you here from the city centre.

The **Casa de las Artesanías de Jalisco** on the north side of the park, entered through a separate entrance on González Gallo, features handicrafts and arts from all over Jalisco, including ceramics, paintings, statues, textiles, wood and straw crafts, masks, furniture, Huichol yarn art and other items. Everything is for sale; prices are high but the quality can't be beaten. It's open Monday to Friday from 10 am to 7 pm, Saturday and Sunday 10 am to 4 pm; admission is free.

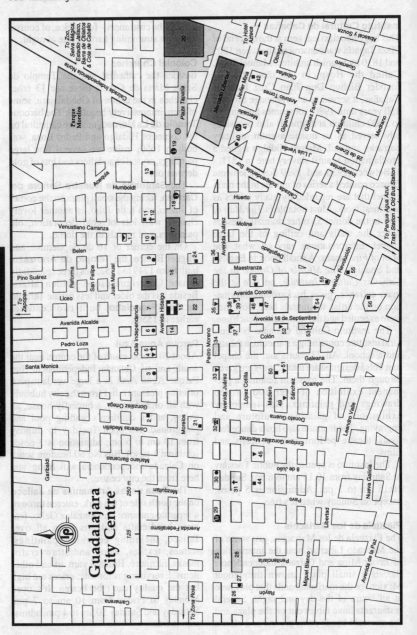

WESTERN CENTRAL HIGHLANDS

Guadalajara
City Centre

0   125   250 m

To Zona Rosa

PLACES TO STAY		38	Sanborns	18	State Tourist Office
		39	Restaurant La Chata	19	Federal Tourist Office
2	Hotel González	45	Villa Madrid		(SECTUR)
11	Hotel de Mendoza	49	Restaurant Acuarius	20	Instituto Cultural
13	Hotel Las Américas	51	Restaurant		de Cabañas
21	Hotel Internacional		Vegetariano	22	Plaza de Armas
24	Hotel Francés	52	Café/Restaurant	23	Palacio de Gobierno
26	Hotel del Parque		Málaga		& Tourist Information
36	Hotel Calinda Roma				Office
42	Hotel Ana Isabel		OTHER	25	Parque Revolución
43	Hotel México 70			27	Copenhagen 77
44	Posada de la Plata	1	Main Post Office	28	Parque Revolución
46	Hotel Fenix Best	3	Mercado Corona	29	Metro Station
	Western	5	Templo de la Merced	30	Ex-Convento del
47	Posada San Pablo	6	Presidencia Municipal		Carmen
48	Posada Regis	7	Rotonda de los	31	Santuario de Nuestra
50	Hotel Hamilton		Hombres Ilustres		Señora del Carmen
55	Hotel Aranzazú	8	Museo Regional	32	Telmex
56	Hotel Continental		de Guadalajara	34	Plaza de los Mártires
		9	Palacio Legislativo	40	Plazuela de los
PLACES TO EAT		10	Palacio de Justicia		Mariachis
		12	Templo de Santa	41	Metro Station
4	Restaurant La Terraza		María de Gracia	53	Templo de Aranzazú
33	Restaurant La Copa	14	Plaza de los Laureles	54	Templo de San
	de Leche	15	Catedral		Francisco
35	Café Madrid	16	Plaza de la Liberación		
37	Denny's	17	Teatro Degollado		

The collection of the **Museo de Arqueología del Occidente de México**, on Calzada Independencia Sur opposite the entrance to the park, includes some pre-Hispanic figurines and artefacts from Jalisco and the neighbouring states of Nayarit and Colima.

On the east side of the park is the **Museo Infantil** (Children's Museum), reached through a separate entrance on Dr R Michel near the corner of González Gallo. It features exhibits on geography, space (with a small planetarium dome), prehistoric animals and more, with several hands-on exhibits. It's open Monday to Friday from 9 am to 1 pm (free).

Universidad de Guadalajara

West of the centre, where Juárez meets Federalismo, is another shady park, **Parque Revolución**. Three blocks further west at Juárez 975 is one of the main buildings of the University of Guadalajara. Inside, the **Paraninfo** (theatre hall) contains large, powerful murals by José Clemente Orozco on the stage backdrop and dome.

Tequila Sauza Bottling Plant

The Tequila Sauza Bottling Plant is at Vallarta 3273, on the western outskirts of the city. Free tours of the plant – with free samples, of course – are offered Monday to Friday and holidays from 10 am to noon. Bus No 45 heading west on Madero will take you there.

Zoo, Selva Mágica & Planetarium

The zoo, the Selva Mágica amusement park and the planetarium are all near one another just off Calzada Independencia Norte on the northern outskirts of the city. Bus No 60 heading north on Calzada Independencia will drop you at the entrance monument, from where it's about a 10-minute walk to the actual entrances.

The Zoológico Guadalajara is a large zoo with over 500 animals on display. At one end is a view of the **Barranca de Huentitán**, similar to the view of the Barranca de Oblatos – it's all the same canyon. Other notable features are two pyramid-shaped aviaries, a herpetarium (snake house), a

WESTERN CENTRAL HIGHLANDS

children's petting zoo, and a train that will take you around the zoo if you don't feel like walking. The zoo is open Tuesday to Sunday from 10 am to 5 pm; admission is 7 pesos (children 5 pesos).

Beside the zoo is Selva Mágica, a children's amusement park with mechanical rides, a dolphin and seal show three times daily, and a trained bird show. It's open Tuesday to Sunday from 11 am until 7 pm; entrance is 5 pesos for adults or children. If you pay to visit the zoo, you can enter Selva Mágica free, but you'll have to pay something to see the animal shows.

About a five-minute walk from the zoo (turn left after 200 metres) is the planetarium, called the Centro de Ciencia y Tecnología. It has exhibits on astronomy, space, aeroplanes, the history of telephones, the body, and other science topics. Planetarium shows are held hourly from 10.30 am. It's open Tuesday to Sunday from 9 am to 7 pm; admission is 1 peso (free for children under 12), plus an extra 2.50 pesos for the planetarium show.

Barranca de Oblatos & Cascada Cola de Caballo

The Barranca de Oblatos is the same canyon you see from the zoo. Otherwise, you can take bus No 60 north on Calzada Independencia to **Parque Mirador**, a little past the entrance to the zoo, for a view of the 670-metre-deep canyon. The park is always open. This canyon rivals the Barranca del Cobre (Copper Canyon) in north-western Mexico for the title of 'Mexico's Grand Canyon', though the Barranca del Cobre is more spectacular.

Also in the canyon is the long Cola de Caballo (Horse Tail) waterfall. It flows all year but is most impressive in the rainy season. For a view of the falls take the Ixcatan bus from the Glorieta de la Normal, on Alcalde about 10 blocks north of the cathedral, and get off at Parque Dr Atl, from where there's a view of the falls.

Zapopan

About eight km from the city centre on the north-western edge of Guadalajara, Zapopan was an Indian village before the Spanish arrived and an important maize-producing village in colonial times. Its main attractions are its large basilica and the nearby Huichol museum.

The tourist office (☎ (3) 633-05-71) is upstairs in the Casa de la Cultura, a block north of the basilica at Vicente Guerrero 233. Staff give out maps of Zapopan and leaflets, in Spanish, detailing places of interest in and around the suburb. Hours are 9 am to 9 pm Monday to Friday and 9 am to 1 pm on Saturday.

The large **Basílica de Zapopan**, built in 1730, houses Nuestra Señora de Zapopan, a tiny statue visited by pilgrims from near and far. On 12 October during Guadalajara's Fiesta de Octubre the image, which has been visiting other churches in Jalisco, is taken from Guadalajara's cathedral and returned to its home in Zapopan amid throngs of people and much merrymaking. The image receives a new car each year for the procession, but the engine is never turned on; instead, the car is hauled along by ropes.

To the right of the basilica entrance the small **Museo Huichol** is a museum of Huichol Indian art with many colourful yarn paintings and other arts and crafts. Most of the items on display are for sale. Hours are Monday to Friday from 9 am to 1 pm and 4 to 7 pm, Saturday and Sunday 10 am to 1 pm (free).

Bus No 275 'Diagonal' heading north on 16 de Septiembre stops beside the basilica, about 20 minutes north of the city centre.

Tlaquepaque

About seven km south-east of downtown Guadalajara, Tlaquepaque ('tlah-keh-PAH-keh') also used to be a separate village, with an initial population of potters swelled by Guadalajara gentry who built luxurious homes here in the 19th century. More recently Tlaquepaque's many artisans decided to capitalise on their talents by cleaning and beefing up the central plaza, and renaming many of the shops (formerly large country homes) 'galleries' to attract tourist dollars. Fortunately, the throngs of crafts-hungry gringos who have descended on the place have not spoiled the refurbishment of central Tlaquepaque.

Many flowers, small benches and monuments grace the plaza. The shops are full of ceramics (including bizarre anthropomorphic monsters), papier mâché animals, bronze figures, handmade glassware, embroidered clothing, leather gear, carved wood, wrought iron and more, including many items from elsewhere. Many shops are closed on Sunday. The tourist office (☎ (3) 635-05-96) is next to the post office at Guillermo Prieto 80. Hours are 9 am to 8 pm daily.

Visit the **Museo Regional de la Cerámica y los Artes Populares de Jalisco** at Independencia 237 to get an idea of the best handicrafts available in Tlaquepaque. It's open Tuesday to Saturday from 10 to 4 pm, and Sunday 10 am to 1 pm (free). Also visit the glass factory across the street from the museum. There are some good restaurants, many attached to Tlaquepaque's 'galleries', serving up tasty Mexican food to live music – see the Places to Eat section following.

To get to Tlaquepaque, take local bus No 275A or 275B heading south on 16 de Septiembre. The trip takes around 30 minutes. After turning off Avenida Revolución, watch for a brick pedestrian bridge then a small traffic circle (glorieta). Get down here and on the left 's Independencia which will take you to the heart of Tlaquepaque.

Tonalá

The suburb of Tonalá, beyond Tlaquepaque, about 13 km south-east of the centre, is the poorer, less touristy relative of Tlaquepaque. The shops here call themselves 'factories', not galleries – an accurate description considering that many of them manufacture the glassware and ceramics found in Tlaquepaque and other parts of Guadalajara. On Thursday and Sunday most of the town becomes a huge street market that takes hours to explore. The best crafts are to be found in the 'factories', but you can pick up some good bargains at the market. Tonalá has several old churches of interest and holds a charreada every Saturday afternoon, after 5 pm.

The tourist office (☎ (3) 683-17-40) is at Tonaltecas 140, in the Casa de Artesanos. Staff give out free leaflets containing a map and information, in Spanish.

The **Museo Nacional de la Cerámica**, at Constitución 110 near the Presidencia Municipal, houses an eclectic array of pots from all over Mexico. It's open Tuesday to Saturday from 10 am to 5 pm, Sunday 10 am to 2 pm; admission is free.

Bus No 275 'Diagonal' heading south on 16 de Septiembre will take you to Tonalá, passing through Tlaquepaque on the way. The trip takes 45 minutes. As you enter Tonalá, get down on the corner of Avenidas Tonalá and Tonaltecas from where it's three blocks to the tourist office and about six blocks to the Plaza Principal; you'll pass through the market en route if it's a Thursday or Sunday.

Courses

The University of Guadalajara is the second-largest university in Mexico, with over 180,000 students. Its Foreign Student Study Centre offers 10 levels of intensive five-week Spanish-language courses ranging from beginners to advanced. It also offers courses in history, culture, politics, economics, literature, art and other subjects, all taught in Spanish, which can be taken in addition to or independently of the Spanish-language courses. Workshops in folkloric dance, guitar and singing, Mexican cuisine etc are also offered, as are special cultural events and excursions to other parts of Mexico.

The registration and basic tuition fees amount to 900 pesos for each five-week session of two hours per day. Lodging is arranged with local Mexican families at a cost of 1416 pesos for the session. The workshops and excursions are an optional expense.

For more specific information and an application form, write to Universidad de Guadalajara, Centro de Estudios para Extranjeros (☎ (3) 653-60-24, 653-21-50, fax 653-00-40), Calle Guanajuato 1047, Apartado Postal 1-2130, Guadalajara, Jalisco 44100, México.

Many universities in the USA, Canada, Europe, Japan and Latin America have relations with the University of Guadalajara, making it easy for you to get credits in your country of origin for courses taken here. The Departamento de Intercambio Académico (☎ (3) 626-40-48) at Juárez 975 has a complete list of these universities.

In the USA, the University of Arizona (☎ (602) 621-4729) also offers a summer programme in Guadalajara. Write to Guadalajara Summer School, Robert Nugent Building 205, University of Arizona, Tucson, Arizona 85721, USA.

Sports

There are plenty of opportunities for playing golf, tennis, squash and other sports in and around Guadalajara. Ask the state tourist office for details.

Organised Tours

Panoramex (☎ 610-50-57, 610-50-05), at Federalismo Sur 944, operates a variety of all-day tours with English, French and Spanish-speaking guides.

Tour No 1 (every day) visits some of the main sights of Guadalajara (cathedral, Teatro Degollado, Palacio de Gobierno, fountains, monuments etc) and Tlaquepaque; the cost is 75 pesos with lunch or 40 pesos without lunch.

Tour No 2 (every day), visiting the Lago de Chapala towns of Chapala, Ajijic and Jocotepec, costs 85 pesos with lunch or 50 pesos without lunch.

Tour No 3 (Monday, Wednesday, Friday) visits the Barranca de Oblatos, the Cola de Caballo waterfall, the Zapopan Basilica and Huichol art museum, and ends at Amatitán with a tour of one of the area's oldest tequila distilleries. The cost is 85 pesos with lunch or 45 pesos without lunch.

During holidays (Easter and the second half of December) there are free guided city walking tours (two and three hours) organised by the state tourist office.

Festivals

Several major festivals, in addition to a number of minor ones, are celebrated each year in Guadalajara and the towns nearby. They include:

Feria de Tonalá Annual handicrafts fair in Tonalá, specialising in ceramics; Semana Santa

Fiestas de Tlaquepaque Tlaquepaque's annual fiesta and handicrafts fair; mid-June to the first week of July

Fiestas de Octubre Beginning with an inaugural parade on the first Sunday in October, the October Fiestas, lasting all month, are Guadalajara's principal annual fair. There's continuous free entertainment every day from around noon to 10 pm in the fairgrounds at the Benito Juárez auditorium, plus livestock shows, art and other exhibitions, and sporting and cultural events around the city. On 12 October a religious element enters the festivities with a procession from the cathedral to Zapopan carrying the miniature image of the Virgin of Zapopan – see the Zapopan section above.

Places to Stay – bottom end

Camping Guadalajara has two trailer parks, both offering full hook-ups and spaces for tents, trailers and motor homes.

San José del Tajo trailer park (☎ (3) 686-14-95) is 15 km south-west of the city centre at Km 15 on Avenida López Mateos (highway 54/80), the start of the Colima road. Facilities include a swimming pool, tennis court, laundry and 200 sites; cost is 42 pesos per site, a little cheaper for tents.

Hacienda Trailer Park (☎ (3) 627-17-24, 627-18-43) is at Circunvalación Poniente 66, Ciudad Granja, 10 km west of the city centre, between Avenida Vallarta and the Periférico. Features include a swimming pool, billiards, laundry, barbecue, plenty of trees and 98 sites. Cost is 39 pesos for two people.

Hotels – central district The *Posada San Pablo* (☎ (3) 613-33-12) at Madero 218 is a friendly, family-run guesthouse with just seven rooms around an upstairs covered patio filled with plants, tables and some cheerful parakeets – the inside rooms are bigger and quieter. Many international travellers stay here; singles are 35 pesos, doubles 45 pesos (one bed), 55 pesos (two beds), plus 20 pesos key deposit.

Around the corner at Corona 171, *Posada*

Regis (☎ (3) 614-86-33) is an upstairs hotel in a converted 19th-century French-style mansion with high ceilings and ornate details. The 19 rooms with bath open onto a covered patio filled with plants, where economical meals are served; these rooms cost 80/100 pesos for singles/doubles. A few plainer but cheaper *económico* rooms at 35/60 pesos are up on the roof. Discounts are given for stays of a few days or more.

The *Posada de la Plata* (☎ (3) 614-91-46) at López Cotilla 619 is also popular, but its management a bit surly. The 12 rooms with high ceilings and large bathrooms open onto a covered central courtyard. Singles/doubles are around 30/40 pesos.

Hotel Las Américas (☎ (3) 613-96-22) at Hidalgo 76 opposite Plaza Tapatía, is one of the best deals for its price in Guadalajara – its only drawbacks are traffic noise in the streetfront rooms and a rather soulless atmosphere. The 49 rooms are clean and fairly modern, with TV, carpeting and large windows. The price of 50/55 pesos (66 pesos for a double with two beds) is cheap for what you get.

Hotel Hamilton (☎ (3) 614-67-26) at Madero 381 is simple but clean, with rooms at 35/45 pesos. *Hotel González* (☎ (3) 614-56-81) at González Ortega 77 is a basic but friendly family-run hotel, with 24 rooms at 32/40 pesos around an interior courtyard full of clotheslines which you are welcome to use.

The *Hotel Continental* (☎ (3) 614-11-17) at Corona 450 is a bit more upmarket, with parking, a restaurant and 124 fairly clean, comfortable, old-fashioned rooms. They have carpeting and telephone and cost 55/72 pesos with black-and-white TV, 71/88 pesos with colour TV.

Hotels – near Mercado Libertad Several other popular budget hotels are found along Javier Mina, opposite Mercado Libertad and near the Plazuela de los Mariachis. This part of town is not quite as pleasant as the centre and not as safe for walking at night. The hotels are large and can be noisy.

Hotel Ana Isabel (☎ (3) 617-79-20, 617-48-59), at Javier Mina 164, opposite the Mercado Libertad, is one of the best in this district. It has 50 small, clean rooms lined up along three floors of walkways draped with a few plants. Each has private bath and ceiling fan; singles/doubles cost 50/60 pesos.

Hotel México 70 (☎ (3) 617-99-78) at Javier Mina 230 has 80 simple but clean rooms with private bath, also at 50/60 pesos.

Hotel Azteca (☎ (3) 617-74-65, 617-74-66) at Javier Mina 315 has 70 fairly clean, pleasant, reasonably sized rooms on five floors around an interior well. There's a restaurant and parking too. All the rooms have a bath and ceiling fan. Cost is again 50/60 pesos, or 80 pesos for a two-bed double. For an extra 10 pesos you can get TV in your room.

Places to Stay – middle
Central District One of the centre's most attractive middle-range hotels is the *Hotel del Parque* (☎ (3) 625-28-00) at Juárez 845 near the Parque Revolución. It has a pleasant restaurant and lobby bar with sidewalk café tables, and 81 rooms in three price categories ranging from 72/95 pesos to 107/130 pesos, with a variety of possible amenities including colour TV, bathtubs and mini-bar.

Hotel Internacional (☎ (3) 613-03-30) at Moreno 570 has 112 carpeted rooms, some with colour TV, all at 95/120 pesos.

More expensive but also more luxurious is the historic *Hotel Francés* (☎ (3) 613-11-90, fax 658-28-31), the oldest hotel in Guadalajara, at Maestranza 35 near the Plaza de la Liberación. It was founded in 1610 as an inn, with rooms upstairs and horses kept in the arched stone courtyard (which is now an elegant lobby bar with a fountain and music). It has 52 good rooms of varying sizes at 145/165 pesos and eight suites at 188/234 pesos, all with tiled floors, colour satellite TV and ceiling fan, some with bathtub and shower. The exterior rooms have French doors opening onto small wrought-iron balconies, but the interior rooms are quieter.

The *Hotel Fenix Best Western* (☎ (3) 614-57-14, fax 613-40-05) at Corona 160 charges 176/198 pesos for big, bright, pleasant rooms (exterior ones have balconies).

Nueva Central Camionera *Hotel El Parador* (☎ (3) 659-01-42), at the new bus terminal, has two swimming pools and 377 basic but clean rooms with colour TV at 90 pesos. Its restaurant is reasonable if you have time to kill at the bus station.

Motels Avenida López Mateos, running north-south a couple of km west of the centre, is Guadalajara's 'motel row'. A good place is the *Hotel del Bosque* (☎ (3) 621-46-50, 621-47-00), at López Mateos Sur 265, just south of the Glorieta Minerva. It has an interior garden, swimming pool, restaurant and bar, and all 74 rooms have carpeting and satellite TV. Singles/doubles are 150/160 pesos; there are also suites with kitchens. The 'Par Vial' bus heading west on Calle Independencia will take you from the city centre to Glorieta Minerva.

The *Motel de Las Américas* (☎ (3) 631-44-15), at López Mateos Sur 2400, opposite the Plaza del Sol shopping mall, is a four-star motel with swimming pool, air conditioning and other amenities; its 101 rooms cost 135/168 pesos, 200 pesos with kitchen. There are plenty of other motels near the Plaza del Sol. Bus No 258 heading west on San Felipe will bring you here from the centre.

Another popular motel, cheaper and closer to the centre, is *Motel Isabel* (☎ (3) 626-26-30), at J Guadalupe Montenegro 1572, one block from Avenida de la Paz and about eight blocks towards the centre from Avenida Chapultepec. It has 50 rooms, a swimming pool, restaurant, bar and inside parking; singles/doubles cost 94/121 pesos.

Places to Stay – top end
The *Hotel de Mendoza* (☎ (3) 613-46-46, fax 613-73-10), at Carranza 16 on the north side of the Teatro Degollado, was built as the convent to the church of Santa María de Gracia, which is still standing on one side of it. Today, the convent has been refurbished into a four-star hotel, with 110 modern rooms and all the amenities – satellite colour TV, air conditioning, restaurant, bar, swimming pool and parking. Singles/doubles cost 220/242 pesos.

Other fine hotels in the centre include the *Hotel Calinda Roma* (☎ (3) 614-86-50, fax 613-05-57), Juárez 170, with 172 rooms at 198/231 pesos, plus a rooftop pool; and the *Hotel Vista Aranzazú* (☎ (3) 613-32-32, fax 614-50-45), Revolución 110, near the corner of Corona, with two towers and 500 rooms at 220/242 pesos.

Then there's the lovely *Hotel Lafayette* (☎ (3) 615-025-2, fax 630-11-12), at Avenida de la Paz 2055, just west of Avenida Chapultepec, in Guadalajara's plush zona rosa. It has 181 attractive rooms with carpeting, colour TV and air conditioning at 310 pesos for singles or doubles, down to 175 pesos in the winter.

Several large hotel chains also have top-class hotels in Guadalajara. They include the *Camino Real* (☎ (3) 647-80-00, 647-67-81) at Vallarta 5005 (330/450 pesos); the *Holiday Inn Crowne Plaza Guadalajara* (☎ (3) 634-10-34, 634-06-50) at López Mateos Sur 2500 (rooms 495 pesos); the *Hyatt Regency Guadalajara* (☎ (3) 622-66-88, 622-77-78) at López Mateos and Moctezuma (270/435 pesos); and the *Fiesta Americana Guadalajara* (☎ (3) 625-34-34, 625-48-48) at Aurelio Aceves 225 (rooms 441 pesos).

Places to Eat
Central District For good traditional Mexican food, try the *Restaurant La Chata* at Corona 126. The speciality of the house (and most expensive thing on the menu) is the Platillo Jalisciense, with a quarter chicken, potatoes, a sope, an enchilada and a flauta, all for 22 pesos. Enchiladas or chiles rellenos are around 15 pesos. It's not an elegant restaurant, but it's been there for over 50 years and when you taste the food you'll see why. It's open every day from 9 am to 10.30 pm.

Another favourite is the *Café Madrid* at Juárez 264, near the corner of Corona. It's a popular place open every day from 8 am to 10 pm, with good food, excellent coffee, and a comida corrida for 20 pesos. Wearing cropped white coats and black bow ties (an odd contrast with the lino floor and steel and plastic tables), the smiling waiters offer brisk, efficient service.

The *Restaurant La Terraza* on an upstairs terrace at Hidalgo 436, just off the Plaza de los Laureles, is another popular spot, especially in the evening when there's live music from 6 to 9 pm. It serves economical meals, with meat and chicken around 12 pesos, cheeseburgers 6 pesos, and a comida corrida for 11 pesos. It's open every day from noon to 10 pm.

For a more elegant meal, try the *Restaurant/Bar La Copa de Leche*, at Juárez 414. It's a bit more expensive, with main dishes around 25 to 30 pesos and a comida corrida for 26 pesos, but the atmosphere is pleasant both in the downstairs dining room and on the upstairs terrace, with romantic candlelight in the evening. It's open every day from 7.30 am until around 10 or 11 pm.

All the fancy hotels have classy restaurants. Check out the ones at the *Hotel Francés*, Maestranza 35, and the *Hotel de Mendoza*, Carranza 16, both historic city landmarks near the Teatro Degollado.

Restaurant Las Jaulas, in the Hotel Fenix at Corona 160 near the corner of López Cotilla, is open every day from 7 am to midnight. They have a daily breakfast buffet from 7 am to noon (27 pesos) and an ample afternoon buffet from 1 to 4 pm. The *Hotel Calinda Roma* restaurant at Juárez 170 does breakfast and lunch buffets (19 and 23 pesos) Monday to Saturday.

There's a *Denny's*, open 24 hours, at Juárez 305 on the corner of 16 de Septiembre, and a *Sanborns* on the opposite corner. The little *Cafe/Restaurant Málaga*, 2½ blocks south at 16 de Septiembre 210, is a good, inexpensive place for any meal. All mains are under 20 pesos, various salads and enchiladas are 13 pesos; breakfasts start at 8 pesos. It's open from 7 am to 10 pm daily.

The *Mercado Libertad* has hundreds of little restaurant stalls. They're probably the cheapest eats you'll find in the city, and they feed thousands of people a day. Sensitive stomachs, beware – the hygiene here is not always the best. Choose a stall that looks clean and busy.

Vegetarian The friendly *Restaurant Acuarius* at Sánchez 416 is a popular vegetarian restaurant and health food store, especially at lunchtime when the excellent, filling comida corrida is served (18.50 pesos). They also serve soya-based meals, yoghurt with fruits, and similar vegetarian fare; it's open every day except Sunday, from 9.30 am to 8 pm.

Restaurant Vegetariano at Sánchez 370B, one block east of the Acuarius, has a bakery with wholemeal breads, even croissants; its comida corrida is 17.50 pesos. Hours are Monday to Saturday from 8 am to 6 pm.

Villa Madrid at López Cotilla 223 is not an exclusively vegetarian restaurant but its tasty, good-value meals include vegetarian options like soyburgers, salad and fries (7.80 pesos), salads with cottage cheese or soya (18.50 pesos), or quesadillas (13.50 pesos). The fruit salads and licuados are tantalising. It's open daily from noon to 9 pm.

Near Avenida Chapultepec Just a 10-minute bus ride from the city centre, Guadalajara's zona rosa is a much quieter district, with some fine restaurants worth the trip to reach them. Catch the 'Par Vial' bus heading west on Calle Independencia and get off at Avenidas Chapultepec and Vallarta, 2.5 km from the cathedral.

Restaurant Los Itacates, at Chapultepec Norte 110, 4½ blocks north of Vallarta, is a pleasant restaurant/bar specialising in traditional food *de la vieja cocina Mexicana* (from the old Mexican kitchen) at surprisingly inexpensive prices. A quarter pollo adobado with two cheese enchiladas, potatoes, rice and tortillas is 15 pesos. There are tacos with 19 fillings to choose from at 2 pesos each. The ample breakfast buffet for 15 pesos, served every day from 8.30 am to noon, is a good deal. The restaurant is open every day from 8 am to 11 pm except Sunday, when it closes at 7 pm.

Restaurant/Bar Recco, at Libertad 1981, just east of Chapultepec two blocks south of Vallarta, is a more elegant restaurant specialising in European food, with main courses from around 24 to 40 pesos. It's open every day from 1 to 11.45 pm (Sunday 10 pm).

Restaurant Vegetariano Las Margaritas at López Cotilla 1477, just west of Chapultepec one block south of Vallarta, is a good vegetarian restaurant whose comida corrida at 14 pesos (18 pesos on Sunday) runs out fast; you have to show up at around noon to get it. Their menu includes 13 safe-to-eat salads, 17 hot or cold sandwiches, and a variety of juices; breakfasts are 12 to 14 pesos. It's open Monday to Saturday from 8 am to 8 pm, and Sunday 10 to 6 pm.

Taquería Minerva on the corner of Chapultepec and Vallarta is a bright place to drop in for a late snack – it's open till 1 am Thursday to Saturday, to midnight other nights. There's a variety of tacos costing around 2 pesos each.

Near Avenida López Mateos About 20 blocks west of Avenida Chapultepec, López Mateos is another large avenue with a number of better restaurants. Bus No 258 from Calle San Felipe in the city centre runs along López Mateos to, or near, all these restaurants (a 30 or 40 minute trip).

Restaurant La Trattoria at Niños Héroes 3051, one block east of López Mateos, is one of the finest Italian restaurants in Guadalajara, but it's not expensive. A salad bar is included in the price of all meals, which range from 18 pesos for pastas to 26 to 30 pesos for meat and seafood meals. It's open every day from 1 pm to midnight. *El Italiano* at Avenida México 3130, about a km beyond the intersection with López Mateos, is another excellent, but more expensive, Italian restaurant. Pastas are around 20 pesos (the spaghetti marinara, 22 pesos, is tasty); other mains, including chicken and seafood, are 28 to 35 pesos.

The *Guadalajara Grill*, López Mateos 3711 Sur, on the corner of Conchita about a km south of the Plaza del Sol, is also popular. It's a large, fun place with a lively atmosphere, good music, and dancing in the bar. Steaks or shrimps are 34 pesos, red snapper 30 pesos and chicken 25 pesos. It's open every day from 1.30 pm to midnight, and to 5 pm on Sunday.

Tlaquepaque Aside from the central, atmospheric but noisy *El Parian*, there are a number of other pleasant restaurant/bars. Several have lively mariachi bands in the afternoon and evening. *El Patio* at Independencia 186 has live music and dining in a fine garden patio. Seafood and meat mains go for around 30 pesos, quesadillas for 10 pesos. *Casa Fuerte* at Independencia 224 has a restaurant with live music, folk and Latin American, on Friday, Saturday and Sunday afternoons. *Restaurant Abajeño* at Juárez 231 has garden dining and a group of mariachis. The *No Name Restaurant* at Madero 80 is a favourite spot, with good food and live music in a lovely setting with parrots and peacocks. *Mariscos Progreso* at Progreso 80 specialises in seafood, which is served under the trees.

Entertainment

Guadalajara has something going on to fit any taste, from rodeos to classic films to some of the best mariachi music in Mexico. Above all, the city is in love with music of all kinds and live performers can be heard any night of the week at loads of popular venues.

Phone or stop by the state tourist office to check out their weekly schedule of events; the friendly bilingual staff will help you find something to suit your fancy. Their magazine *Ver y Oír* has listings of music and cultural events, film and video presentations, plays at a dozen different theatres, and exhibitions at the city's 35 or more galleries. The *Occidental* and *Informador* daily newspapers also have entertainment listings.

Cultural performances are held frequently at the *Teatro Degollado* (☎ 658-38-12) and the *Instituto Cultural Cabañas* (☎ 617-43-22), both right in the centre, and at the *Ex-Convento del Carmen* (☎ 614-71-84) at Juárez 638 and many other locations. Free concerts of *típico* Jaliscan music are held in the Plaza de Armas on Thursday and Sunday at 6.30 pm, always drawing a crowd.

Ballet Folklórico Every Sunday from 10 am to noon the Ballet Folklórico of the University of Guadalajara stages a magnificent performance at the Teatro Degollado. Tickets range from 10 pesos in the gallery to 50 pesos in the *luneta* (stalls); buy them at the theatre ticket office, which is open every day from 10 am to 1 pm and 4 to 7 pm. On a Wednesday night you might check out the Ballet Folklórico of the Instituto Cultural Cabañas, performing at 8.30 pm. Tickets are 15 pesos.

Philharmonic Orchestra The Filarmónica de Jalisco performs every Sunday at the Teatro Degollado from 12.30 to 2 pm, right after the Ballet Folklórico, and on Thursday nights at 8.30 pm. Tickets cost from 5 to 40 pesos and are sold at the theatre any day of the week.

Music – Cafés/Bars/Restaurants If you head out of the centre along Juárez and its westward continuation, Vallarta, you'll come across half a dozen or more music spots within three km of the cathedral. There's another concentration of lively nightlife venues on López Mateos, south of Vallarta, around the Plaza del Sol. (The westward 'Par Vial' bus on Calle Independencia travels all the way along Vallarta to Avenida Chapultepec and the zona rosa area. Bus No 258 west on San Felipe goes out to Plaza del Sol.)

Copenhagen 77 (☎ 625-28-03), on the west side of Parque Revolución on the corner of López Cotilla, about 700 metres west of the centre, has lively blues in its Bar Revolución nightly except Sunday from 8 pm to 1 am (no cover charge), and also 'gourmet jazz' in its restaurant the same nights from 8 pm to 12.30 am. They serve a good paella.

About 500 metres further west at Vallarta 1110 is *La Peñita* (☎ 625-58-63), a pleasant café-restaurant which presents Latin American music (often folk) from 9 pm most Thursday, Friday and Saturday nights. There was also a reggae/blues/bolero group playing on Wednesday when we last checked. It's an enjoyable place, also open as a restaurant from 11.30 am daily – you can ring to find out what music's coming up.

Another 900 metres to the west, *Duran Duran* on the corner of Vallarta and Marsella is a bright, busy bar/café presenting smooth rock or blues till midnight or 1 am Thursday to Saturday.

Three more blocks west then 2½ blocks south, at Avenida Unión 236, *Café Quetzal* (☎ 616-02-01) is a relaxed café presenting a different type of music just about every night of the week; on our last visit there was South American music on Monday and Thursday, ballads on Tuesday, blues on Wednesday, folk on Friday, canto nuevo on Saturday, and urban rock on Sunday! The cover charge is normally 5 pesos.

Other popular venues with varying schedules throughout the week include the Instituto Cultural Mexicano Norteamericano de Jalisco (☎ 625-58-38, 625-41-01) at Enrique Díaz de León 300; the Centro Cultural Centenario (☎ 626-95-42) at Cruz Verde 272 between Garibaldi and Reforma, and the Peña Cuicacalli (☎ 625-46-90) at Niños Héroes 1988 near Avenida Chapultepec.

Most of the large, fancy hotels offer music and entertainment. In the centre, the attractive lobby piano bar of the Hotel Francés, at Maestranza 35 near the Plaza de la Liberación, is especially popular with gringos.

Discos & Dance Halls The *Coco & Coco* dance hall next door to the Hotel Fenix at Corona 160 is a popular downtown place with salsa and other música tropical to get the feet moving. Cover charges range from nothing for women from Monday to Wednesday to 17 pesos for everyone on Saturday. *El Barón* is a dance-hall alternative across the street.

About half a km west of the centre along Juárez, *Bar Antillano's* is a more downmarket, but fun, dance hall with no cover charge and no minimum consumption.

The *Roxy Centro Cultural*, in a big converted theatre at Mezquitan 80, has live dance music, sometimes reggae, from Thursday to Saturday with a cover charge of 35 pesos.

Some of the most popular discos are *Daddy'O* at López Mateos 2185; *Osiris*, on Lázaro Cárdenas two blocks from the large Hotel Camino Real; and the disco in the Hotel Carlton on the corner of Niños Héroes and 16 de Septiembre.

Mariachi Bands To see and hear mariachi music in the place where it was born, head for the Plazuela de los Mariachis (see under that listing near the beginning of the Guadalajara section).

Cinemas Several cinemas show international films. Check *Ver y Oír*. Some of the best places to catch them are:

Alianza Francesa – López Cotilla 1199 (☎ 625-55-95)
Bellas Artes – Jesús García 720 (☎ 614-16-14)
Centro de Investigación y Enseñanza Cinematográficas – Vallarta 2181 (☎ 653-03-02)
Cine Charles Chaplin – López Mateos Norte 843 (☎ 641-54-07)
Cine Cinematógrafo – Vallarta 1102, on the corner of Argentina (☎ 625-05-14)
Cine-Teatro Cabañas – in the Instituto Cultural Cabañas (☎ 617-43-22)
Premier Cri Cri – Eulogio Parra 2233, on the corner of Avenida Las Américas
University of Guadalajara, Departamento de Video y TV – Hidalgo 1296 (☎ 625-57-23)

Rodeos, Bullfights & Cockfights Charreadas are held every Sunday in the rodeo ring behind Parque Agua Azul. Charros and charras come from all over Jalisco and Mexico to show off their skills.

The bullfighting season is September to January, but bullfights are not held every Sunday. There will be a couple for sure during the October Fiestas; the rest of the season they may be sporadic. Check with the tourist office. When bullfights are held, they're on Sunday at 4 pm in the Plaza de Toros at the northern end of Calzada Independencia; bus No 60 heading north on Calzada Independencia will take you there. Tickets can be bought in advance at the bullfight office, Avenida de la Paz 1271, on the corner of Federalismo (☎ 625-19-74) or, on the day of the fight, at the Plaza de Toros.

Cockfights are held regularly at the palenque (cockfighting arena) near Parque Agua Azul, and at the palenques in Tlaquepaque and Zapopan.

Football Fútbol (soccer) is one of Guadalajara's favourite sports. The city has four teams playing in the national primera división: Guadalajara (nicknamed las Chivas) which is the second most popular club in the country after América of Mexico City, Atlas (los Zorros), Universidad de Guadalajara (los Leones Negros) and Universidad Autónoma de Guadalajara (los Tecos). They play at stadiums around the city during the season from August/September to May. The tourist office keeps abreast of the matches, or you can phone the main Estadio Jalisco (☎ 637-05-63, 637-03-01) to ask about the games. Take bus No 60 heading north on Calzada Independencia to reach the stadium.

Things to Buy

Handicrafts from Jalisco, Michoacán and other Mexican states are available in Guadalajara. See the earlier Tlaquepaque and Tonalá sections for information on two craftmaking suburbs. The Casa de las Artesanías, at González Gallo on the north side of Parque Agua Azul about 20 blocks south of the centre, has a good selection; prices are high but the quality is excellent. It's open Monday to Friday from 10 am to 7 pm, Saturday 10 am to 4 pm, Sunday 11 am to 3 pm. Bus No 60 heading south on Calzada Independencia will drop you at the entrance to Parque Agua Azul.

The Instituto de la Artesanía Jaliscense at Alcalde 1221, about 20 blocks north of the centre, has a similar selection. It's open Monday to Saturday from 10 am to 5 pm; any bus heading north on 16 de Septiembre/Alcalde will take you there.

Mercado Libertad, right in the centre, is a giant general market with three floors of shops and stalls covering an area equivalent to four city blocks. It's open every day. On Sunday you can check out the huge El Baratillo market stretching for blocks in every direction, beginning about 15 blocks east of Mercado Libertad. Take the 'Par Vial' bus east along Hidalgo.

There are several good department stores in the centre. About seven km south-west of the centre, Plaza del Sol on López Mateos Sur offers exclusive shopping in air-con comfort.

Getting There & Away

Air Guadalajara's Aeropuerto Internacional Miguel Hidalgo (☎ 689-00-89) is 17 km south of the city centre, just off the highway to Chapala. It is a major airport served by a number of airlines, with direct flights to/from about a dozen North American and over 20 Mexican cities, and one-stop connections to many others.

There are over 100 travel agencies in Guadalajara where you can make flight arrangements; look in the telephone directory yellow pages under 'Agencias de Viajes'. Airlines are listed in the yellow pages under 'Aviación – Lineas de'. They include:

Aero California
    López Cotilla 1423 (☎ 626-19-62, 626-19-01)
Aeroméxico, Aerolitoral & Aeromar
    Corona 196, corner of Madero (☎ 669-02-02, 689-02-76)
Alaska Airlines
    Hotel Hyatt Regency, Plaza del Sol (☎ 621-53-06)
American Airlines
    Vallarta 2440 (☎ 630-03-49)
Continental
    Hotel Hyatt Regency, Plaza del Sol (☎ 647-66-75, 647-42-51)
Delta
    López Cotilla 1701 (☎ 630-35-30)
Mexicana
    Mariano Otero 2353 (☎ 647-22-22)
TAESA
    (☎ 616-54-74)
United Airlines
    (☎ 800-0-03-07)

Bus Guadalajara has two bus stations. The long-distance bus station, called the Nueva Central Camionera, or Nueva Central for short, is a huge modern terminal with seven separate buildings (*módulos*), nine km south-east of the centre past Tlaquepaque.

Each módulo is the base for a number of bus lines and has a 24-hour information kiosk which can tell you where to find other lines, or buses to a particular destination. These kiosks also provide tourist information – but watch out for their information on hotels; they may try to steer you towards expensive hotels which will give them commission.

Each módulo also has places to eat,

Ladatel coin and card phones, a Lada caseta, a guardería for leaving luggage, and fax service.

There are buses, often frequent, to just about everywhere in western, central and northern Mexico. Distances, travel times and typical 1st-class prices include:

Barra de Navidad – 291 km, six hours (44 pesos)
Colima – 220 km, 2½ to three hours (30 pesos)
Guanajuato – 300 km, five hours (37 pesos)
Mazatlán – 520 km, eight to nine hours (75 pesos)
Mexico City (Terminal Norte) – 535 km, seven to eight hours (80 pesos)
Morelia – 367 km, five hours (34 pesos)
Puerto Vallarta – 397 km, six to seven hours (60 pesos)
Querétaro – 348 km, five to six hours (53 pesos)
San Miguel de Allende – 380 km, six hours (57 pesos)
Tepic – 228 km, four hours (35 pesos)
Uruapan – 305 km, five hours (33 pesos)
Zacatecas – 320 km, five hours (45 pesos)

Bus tickets can be bought in the centre at the Agencia de Viajes MaCull (☎ 614-70-14, 614-70-15), López Cotilla 163, near the corner of Degollado. It's open Monday to Friday from 9 am to 2 pm and 4 to 7 pm, Saturday 9 am to 2 pm.

Guadalajara's other bus station is called the Vieja Central Camionera, Vieja Central, or Antigua Central (all meaning 'old bus station'). Before the new bus station was built, this was the only bus terminal. It's 1.5 km south of the cathedral, near Parque Agua Azul, occupying the block bounded between Avenida 5 de Febrero, Calle Los Ángeles, and Calle Dr R Michel (which is the southward continuation of Avenida Corona). The old bus station now serves as the terminal for destinations nearer Guadalajara. There are sets of ticket booths on both the Los Ángeles and 5 de Febrero sides. Buses go every half-hour, from 7 am to 8 pm, to Chapala (40 km, one hour, 4.50 pesos), Ajijic (47 km, 1¼ hours, 5.50 pesos) and Jocotepec (68 km, two hours, 7 pesos); and every 20 minutes, from 6 am to 9 pm, to Tequila (50 km, 1¾ hours, 6 pesos).

Train The Estación del Ferrocarril (☎ 650-08-26, 650-04-44, ext 462) is at the southern end of Calzada Independencia Sur, about 20 blocks from the centre.

Tickets for the Estrella del Pacífico and El Tapatío trains can be bought in advance at the station and at Agencia de Viajes MaCull (see Bus).

El Tapatío to Mexico City (train No 6) departs Guadalajara nightly at 9 pm, taking 11½ hours. This is one of Mexico's best trains and has coche dormitorio, primera especial and primera regular accommodation; a one-person camarín costs 161.35 pesos, a primera especial seat 80.65 pesos and a primera regular seat 40.30 pesos. At the station, tickets for El Tapatío are sold from 8 am to 8 pm. The corresponding train No 5 leaves Mexico City nightly at 8.30 pm.

The Estrella del Pacífico (train No 1, also referred to as Servicio Estrella) departs Guadalajara daily at 9.30 am for Mexicali on the US border. This train also pulls carriages bound for Nogales, which are separated at Benjamín Hill, north of Hermosillo in Sonora state. The Estrella del Pacífico has primera especial seating only. At the station, tickets for the Estrella del Pacífico are sold from 8 am to 1 pm. Its schedule (with fares from Guadalajara) is:

departs		pesos
Guadalajara	9.30 am	–
Tepic	1.35 pm	33
Mazatlán	6.30 pm	70
Culiacán	9.44 am	96
Sufragio	12.45 am	121
Navojoa	2.10 am	138
Ciudad Obregón	3.57 am	146
Empalme (Guaymas)	5.40 am	161
Hermosillo	7.45 am	177
Caborca	12.20 pm	207
Puerto Peñasco	2.10 pm	226
arrives		
Nogales	12.30 pm	209
Mexicali	5.55 pm	256

Times and fares from Mexicali for the southbound Estrella del Pacífico (train No 2) are:

departs		pesos
Mexicali	9 am	–
Puerto Peñasco	1.20 pm	30
Caborca	3.17 pm	48
Nogales	3.30 pm	–

Hermosillo	7.45 pm	78
Empalme (Guaymas)	9.55 pm	95
Ciudad Obregón	11.24 pm	111
Navojoa	1.15 am	120
Sufragio	2.15 am	136
Culiacán	5.26 am	160
Mazatlán	8.15 am	185
Tepic	1.30 pm	225
arrives		
Guadalajara	7.30 am	256

A segunda-clase train (No 3) following the same route departs Guadalajara daily at noon, but it's slower (supposedly 35 hours to Nogales, 44 hours to Mexicali), more crowded, dirtier and much less pleasant. Fares are just 70 pesos to Nogales, 97 pesos to Mexicali, but it's worth spending the extra money on the Estrella del Pacífico.

Segunda-clase train No 92 leaves Guadalajara daily at 9 am, reaching Colima (10 pesos) about 3 pm and Manzanillo (14 pesos) about 5 pm.

Car Guadalajara has over 30 car-rental agencies; they are listed in the telephone yellow pages under 'Automóviles – Renta de'. Several of the large US companies are represented in Guadalajara, but you may get a better deal from local companies. Many agencies will deliver the car to you at no extra cost. When we last checked with Avis, a VW Beetle with unlimited mileage cost 147.80 pesos per day, plus 39 pesos insurance and 10% tax. Agencies include:

Auto Rent de Guadalajara
    Federalismo Sur 542A (☎ 626-20-14, 689-04-32)
Avis
    Hotel Fiesta Americana, Aurelio Aceves 225 (☎ 615-53-18, 630-17-50)
Budget
    Niños Héroes 934 (☎ 613-00-27, 613-02-86)
Dollar
    Circunvalación Agustín Yañez 2557 (☎ 630-01-17, 616-50-23)
    Airport (☎ 689-0522)
Hertz
    Niños Héroes 9 (☎ 614-61-62, 614-61-39)
    Hotel Camino Real, Vallarta 5005 (☎ 647-80-00, ext 1054)
    Airport (☎ 689-01-56)

National
  Niños Héroes & Manzano (☎ 614-79-94)
  Airport (☎ 689-02-81)
Odin
  Avenida 16 de Septiembre 742 (☎ 614-71-20,
  614-86-84)
  Airport (☎ 689-05-05)
Quick Rent A Car
  Niños Héroes 954 (☎ 614-22-47, 614-60-52)
  Airport (☎ 689-05-02)

Getting Around

To/From the Airport 'Aeropuerto' combis
(No 625, 6 pesos) run between the airport
and city centre but only about once an hour.
Going to the airport, you can pick them up
on Juárez. Auto Transportaciones Aeropuerto (☎ 612-93-37, 612-93-39) run
colectivo combis between the airport and the
city (they'll pick you up at your hotel) but
charge 50 pesos to the centre for one to four
people, whereas a taxi costs 40 to 50 pesos,
depending on your bargaining power.

To/From the Bus & Train Stations To reach
the city centre from the new bus station, you
can take any 'Centro' or No 644 city bus
from the loop road within the station
(immediately outside your módulo). These
are not very frequent so it's often quicker to
walk out of the station between módulo 1 and
the Hotel El Parador and take any bus No
275, 275A or 275B going to the right (north)
along the road outside. These run every few
minutes from 5.30 am to 10.30 pm, and bring
you into the centre along Avenida 16 de
Septiembre, though they don't take the most
direct route along the way. For a taxi into
town, buy a ticket from the taxi taquilla in
any of the módulos: fares are regulated by
zones – to the centre (zona 3) it's 22 pesos in
daytime and 27 pesos at night, for up to four
people.

From the city to the new bus station, you
can take the frequent bus Nos 275, 275A and
275B southward on 16 de Septiembre, anywhere between the cathedral and Avenida
Revolución, though these tend to be crowded
(difficult if you have much baggage) and can
take half an hour or more to get there. Bus
No 644 heading east on the corner of Corona

and Avenida Revolución is less frequent but
takes a more direct route. A taxi should cost
20 to 25 pesos.

Bus No 60 south on Calzada Independencia will take you from the city centre to
both the old bus station and the train station.
No 616 and other buses run between the old
and new bus stations.

Bus & Combi Guadalajara has a good city
bus system. On the major routes, buses go
every five minutes or so every day, from 5.30
am to 10.30 pm; they cost between 0.70
pesos and 1.20 pesos depending on the age
of the bus. A few routes are served by
combis. The tourist office has a complete list
of the 140 bus routes in Guadalajara, and can
help you figure out how to get anywhere you
want to go.

Metro Two subway routes crisscross the city.
Stops are marked by a red and blue 'T'
symbol. Línea 1 runs north-south for 15 km
below Calzada del Federalismo, a few blocks
west of the centre, and Avenida Colón, going
all the way from the Periférico Norte to the
Periférico Sur. You can catch it at Parque
Revolución, on the corner of Avenida Juárez.
Línea 2 (due to operate from August 1994)
runs east-west for 10 km below Avenida
Juárez and will make getting to the zona rosa
and the west of the city much easier. Stops
include Mercado Libertad/San Juan de Dios,
the University of Guadalajara, Avenida
Chapultepec and Avenida López Mateos.
Línea 1 operates frequently every day from
6 am to 11 pm; the fare is 1 peso. Línea 2
should have the same frequency and fare.

Taxi Taxis are plentiful in the centre. They
are supposed to charge fixed rates, according
to distance. Typical fares from the centre are
around 12 pesos to the train station, old bus
station or Parque Azul; 20 pesos to the Plaza
del Sol, Tlaquepaque, the zoo or Zapopan;
25 pesos to the new bus station; 30 pesos to
Tonalá; and 40 pesos to the airport. Always
clarify the fare before you get into the cab.

LAGO DE CHAPALA

Mexico's largest lake, 40 km south of Guadalajara, is 85 km long and 28 km wide. It's a beautiful place ringed by hills and a very popular get-away spot from the city, though large areas of its surface are now clogged by *lirio* (water hyacinth), a fast-growing floating plant nourished by the fertilisers and soil washed into the lake. The near-perfect climate in the small northern lakeside towns of Chapala, Ajijic and Jocotepec has attracted one of the largest communities of North American expatriates in the world; estimates of numbers vary but 30,000 is frequently mentioned.

Getting There & Away

Chapala, Ajijic and Jocotepec are all easily reached by bus from Guadalajara (see Guadalajara Getting There & Away). There are also Chapala-Ajijic buses every 15 minutes (a 20-minute trip, 1.70 pesos), and Chapala-

Ajijic-Jocotepec buses every half-hour (50 minutes, 2 pesos), from about 7 am to 10 pm.

The scenic road along the south shore of the lake is an attractive alternative route to Michoacán if you're driving.

Chapala
• *pop: 20,000*

The largest of the settlements towards the western end of the lake, Chapala took off as a resort when President Porfirio Díaz holidayed here every year from 1904 to 1909. D H Lawrence wrote most of *The Plumed Serpent* in the private house at Calle Zaragoza 307; San Francisco church at the lake end of Avenida Madero, the main street, figures in the final pages of the book. Today Chapala is a small, laid-back place that only gets busy on weekends and holidays.

Orientation & Information From the bus station it's a 10-minute walk straight down

Avenida Madero to the lake. Hidalgo heads west off Madero a couple of hundred metres before the lake to become the road to Ajijic. All services can be found on Madero or Hidalgo. There's a helpful tourist office at Serdán 26, on the first street to the left off Hidalgo. Libros de Chapala, opposite the small plaza three blocks down Madero from the bus station, has a terrific range of North American magazines, plus some newspapers and books. The market is on the opposite (east) side of the same plaza.

Things to See & Do On the waterfront at the foot of Madero are a small park and a few craft stalls, some selling attractive, inexpensive weavings from Jocotepec. There's a covered crafts market, the **Mercado de Artesanías**, about 400 metres east along Paseo Ramón Corona from the end of Madero. The large lakeside **Parque La Cristiania**, entered from Calle Cristiania off Ramón Corona, has a big swimming pool, a playground and attractive picnic lawns.

From the embarcadero (jetty) at the foot of Madero you can take a lancha to the **Isla de los Alacranes** (Scorpion Island), six km east, which has some restaurants; or to **Isla de Mezcala**, also called Isla El Presidio, about 15 km east, which has ruins of a fort and other buildings constructed by Mexican independence fighters who heroically held out there from 1812 to 1816, repulsing several Spanish attempts to dislodge them and finally winning a full pardon from their enemies. An Alacranes trip, with 30 minutes on the island, costs 60 pesos per boat.

Places to Stay The long-established *Gran Hotel Nido* (☎ (376) 5-21-16) at Madero 202 near the waterfront has fairly pleasant, clean, sizeable singles/doubles for 60/70 pesos (70/80 pesos with TV), and a moderately clean pool.

Casa de Huéspedes Las Palmitas (☎ (376) 5-30-70) at Juárez 531, just south of the east side of the market, has dilapidated rooms with private bath for 30/40 pesos.

Villa Montecarlo (☎ (376) 5-22-16) at Hidalgo 296, one km west of the centre, has

grounds running down to the lake, a circular thermal swimming pool, and rooms at 140 pesos single or double.

Places to Eat Chapala's speciality is pescado blanco (whitefish), the same tender little creature as is found around Lago Pátzcuaro in Michoacán. Today it's as likely to come from fish farms as from Lago de Chapala, which suffers from overfishing and pollution. A restaurant portion is around 30 pesos or more.

The *Café Paris* and the *Restaurant Superior*, a couple of doors apart on the east side of Madero just north of Hidalgo, are both clean, popular places doing a good range of decent food at reasonable prices. The Paris has a four-course comida for 13 pesos. The *Gran Hotel Nido* has a slightly more expensive restaurant adorned with photos of old Chapala. There are also waterfront restaurants in both directions from the embarcadero, and a couple of cheaper places behind the market.

Ajijic
* *pop: 10,000*

Ajijic ('ah-hee-HEEK'), about seven km west of Chapala along the lakeside, is a beautiful, friendly little town of cobbled streets and prettily painted houses, home to a sizeable colony of Mexican and North American artists. It's fairly sleepy except during the nine-day Fiesta of San Andrés at the end of November, and over Easter, when a well-known re-enactment of Christ's trial and crucifixion is staged over three days.

Buses will drop you on the highway at the top of Colón, the main street, which leads six blocks to the lake. The chapel on the north side of the plaza, two blocks down, dates from at least the 18th century. There's a handful of galleries and some upmarket crafts shops on and off Colón.

Places to Stay & Eat *Pal Trailer Park* (☎ (376) 5-37-64), two km east of central Ajijic on the Ajijic-Chapala highway, has a swimming pool, laundry, and 110 sites with full hook-ups. Cost is 30 pesos a night for one or two people.

Apartments Suite Plaza Ajijic (☎ (376) 6-03-83), at Colón 33 on the plaza, has sizeable two-room suites with kitchen at 75 pesos a day for one or two people.

La Nueva Posada (☎ (376) 6-14-44) at Donato Guerra 9, by the lake three blocks east of Colón, is a beautiful small hotel run by a friendly Canadian family. It has 16 large, artistically decorated rooms, some with great lake views, mostly costing from 165/187 to 176/198 pesos for singles/doubles, including breakfast. There's also a nice pool, and an excellent restaurant spilling out into a fine lakeside garden: most meat or fish main dishes are 28 to 45 pesos, but there are cheaper daily specials.

Los Veleros, on the highway 1½ blocks east of Colón, is a cheaper restaurant with some of the best food in town – chicken, fish or steaks for 20 to 30 pesos, pasta for 14 to 16 pesos – plus happy hours and live music in the evenings.

The main cluster of cheaper cafés and small restaurants is around the plaza on Colón.

San Juan Cosalá

At San Juan Cosalá, 10 km west of Ajijic towards Jocotepec, there's a thermal water spa in an attractive lakeside setting, with its own natural geyser and several swimming pools. You can visit for the day or stay in the *Motel Balneario San Juan Cosalá* (☎ (376) 3-03-02) on the spot for 130/160 pesos.

Jocotepec

• *pop: 15,000*

Jocotepec ('ho-co-teh-PEC'), 21 km west of Chapala and a km or two from the lakeshore, is far less gringo-influenced than Chapala or Ajijic. It's a pleasant enough town but there's nothing very special to see or do except look for the attractive blankets, sarapes and wall hangings woven here, which are sold in shops on Calle Hidalgo. The main festival is the two-week Fiesta del Señor del Monte in early-mid January.

TEQUILA

The town of Tequila, 50 km north-west of Guadalajara, has been home to the liquor of the same name since the 17th century. Fields of agave, the cactus-like plant from which tequila is distilled, surround the town. You can almost get drunk just breathing the heavily scented air that drifts from the town's distilleries. The two largest distilleries – Sauza and Cuervo – offer public tours of their operations and, of course, free samples.

Tequila is on highway 15; it's easy to reach from either Guadalajara or towns to the north. Buses depart every 20 minutes from Guadalajara's old bus station (see Guadalajara Getting There & Away for details).

Inland Michoacán

Michoacán is a beautiful state with a number of fascinating destinations along the Cordillera Neovolcánica, the volcanic range which gives it both fertile soils and a striking mountainous landscape. In a 200-km stretch of the cordillera across the northern part of Michoacán are found the spectacular El Rosario Monarch butterfly sanctuary; the handsome state capital Morelia; the beautiful colonial town of Pátzcuaro, set near scenic Lago Pátzcuaro in Purépecha Indian country, with several interesting villages, archaeological sites, islands and other lakes nearby; the town of Uruapan, with a fine miniature tropical national park within the city boundaries; and the famous volcano Paricutín a short distance beyond Uruapan.

The territory inhabited by the state's 120,000 Purépecha (or Tarasco) Indians extends from around Lago Pátzcuaro to west of Uruapan. The Purépecha are direct descendants of the Tarascans, who developed western Mexico's most advanced pre-Hispanic civilisation, but their early origins are obscure and the Purépecha language has no established links to any other. The old Tarascans were noted potters and metalsmiths, and many Purépecha villages still specialise in particular handicrafts, which are among the most interesting in Mexico. The Purépecha also maintain some of the country's most vital religious traditions, with the Day of the Dead remembrances around Lago Pátzcuaro particularly famous.

The name Michoacán is an Aztec word meaning 'Place of the Masters of Fish' – still an apt description of the Lago Pátzcuaro area, although nowadays the traditional 'butterfly' nets are used on the lake as much to catch tourists' pesos as fish.

The more tropical coastal areas of Michoacán, reached by the spectacular highway 37 down through the hills from Uruapan, are covered in the Central Pacific Coast chapter.

MORELIA
• *pop: 428,500* • *alt: 1910 metres*
Morelia, the capital of Michoacán, lies in the north-eastern part of the state, 315 km west of Mexico City and 367 km south-east of Guadalajara. It's a lively city with a university, an active cultural scene and a number of language schools offering Spanish courses – a good place for an extended visit, as many foreigners have discovered.

Morelia was officially founded in 1541, although a Franciscan monastery had been in the area since 1537. New Spain's first viceroy, Antonio de Mendoza, named it Valladolid after the Spanish city of that name and encouraged families of Spanish nobility to move here. The families remained and maintained Valladolid as a very Spanish city, at least architecturally, until 1828.

By that time, New Spain had become the independent republic of Mexico. The state legislature changed the city's name to Morelia to honour one of its native sons, José Maria Morelos y Pavón, a key figure in Mexico's independence movement.

Today, with its downtown streets lined by colonial buildings, Morelia still looks as Spanish as it probably did before independence. City ordinances now require that all new construction in the centre be done colonial-style with arches, baroque façades and carved pink stone walls.

Orientation
Almost everything of interest is within walking distance of the zócalo, also called the Plaza Central, Plaza de los Mártires or Plaza de Armas. The large cathedral in the middle of the zócalo is a major landmark.

Avenida Madero, running along the north side of the zócalo, is the major downtown avenue: to the west it's called Madero Poniente, to the east Madero Oriente. Nine blocks east of the zócalo on Madero, the Fuente Tarasca (Tarascan Fountain) is another main landmark, marking a major intersection; it's here that you will enter Morelia city centre if you're driving in from Mexico City.

Information
Tourist Office The helpful Galería de Turismo (☎ (43) 13-26-54) is a block west of the zócalo on the corner of Madero Poniente and Nigromante, on an outside corner of the Palacio Clavijero. It has free maps and leaflets in Spanish and English on Morelia and Michoacán, plus a monthly calendar of films and cultural events in the city. Hours are Monday to Friday from 9 am to 9 pm, Saturday and Sunday 8 am to 8 pm.

The Dirección de Operación y Desarrollo Turístico (☎ (43) 13-26-54), in the courtyard of the Palacio Clavijero, also has tourist information. Hours are Monday to Friday from 9 am to 3 pm and 6 to 8 pm.

Money Banks are plentiful in the zócalo area, particularly on and around Madero. They give the best rates for changing money, but are only open from 9 am to 1.30 pm, Monday to Friday.

Casa de Cambio Michoacán, at Valladolid 22 near the south-east corner of the zócalo, changes US dollars and travellers' cheques Monday to Friday from 9 am to 6 pm, Saturday 9 am to 1 pm.

Casa de Cambio Majapara at Pino Suárez 166 on the corner of 20 de Noviembre changes US dollars cash and travellers' cheques and sells Thomas Cook travellers' cheques. It's open Monday to Friday from 9 am to 6.30 pm, Saturday 9 am to 2 pm.

Casa de Cambio Troca-Mex at Nigromante

WESTERN CENTRAL HIGHLANDS

132, near the corner of Melchor Ocampo, changes US dollars cash and travellers' cheques daily from 9 am to 2 pm and 4 to 6 pm.

Post & Telecommunications The main post office and the Telecomm office, which has telegram, telex, fax and giro services, are in the Palacio Federal at Madero Oriente 369 on the corner of Serapio Rendón, four blocks east of the zócalo. The post office is open Monday to Friday from 8 am to 7 pm, Saturday and Sunday 9 am to 1 pm. Telegram hours are Monday to Saturday, 9 am to 8 pm; telex and fax hours are Monday to Friday 9 am to 8 pm, Saturday 9 am to 1 pm.

Computel has Lada casetas, with fax service too, at the bus station (open 24 hours daily) and on Madero opposite the cathedral at Portal Galeana 157 (open daily, 7 am to 10 pm).

Laundry Lavandería Santo Niño, at Corregidora 787 on the corner of Nicolás Bravo, is open Monday to Friday from 8 am to 2 pm and 4 to 8 pm, Saturday from 8 am to 5 pm.

Cathedral

The cathedral dominating the zócalo took over a century to build, from 1640 to 1744. Architecturally, it is a combination of Herreresque, baroque and neoclassical styles. Its twin 70-metre towers, for instance, have classical Herreresque bases, baroque mid-sections and multicolumned neoclassical tops. Inside, much of the baroque relief work was replaced in the 19th century with more balanced and calculated neoclassical pieces. Fortunately, however, one of the cathedral's interior highlights was preserved: a sculpture of the Señor de la Sacristía made from dried maize and topped with a gold crown from the 16th-century Spanish King Philip II. There's also a large organ with 4600 pipes.

Museo Regional Michoacano & Palacio de Justicia

Just off the zócalo at Allende 305 and Abasolo is the Michoacán Regional Museum.

Housed in the late 18th-century baroque palace of Isidro Huarte, the museum displays a great variety of pre-Hispanic artefacts, colonial art and relics, contemporary paintings by local artists, and exhibits on the geology and fauna of the region. A highlight is the mural on the stairway by Mexican painter Alfredo Alce, divided in two halves portraying those who have had a positive (right half) and negative (left half) influence on Mexico.

The museum is open Tuesday to Saturday from 9 am to 7 pm, Sunday 9 am to 2 pm (closed Monday). Admission is 13 pesos, but free to those under 13 and over 60, and free to everyone on Sunday.

Across Abasolo from the museum, the Palacio de Justicia was built between 1682 and 1695 to serve as the city hall. Its façade is an eclectic but well-done mix of French and baroque styles. A dramatic mural by Agustín Cárdenas graces the courtyard.

Museo del Estado

The State Museum of Michoacán at Guillermo Prieto 176, on the corner of Santiago Tapia, is a good place to learn about this very interesting state. Downstairs is devoted to the history of Michoacán from prehistoric times to the first contact between the Tarascans and the Spanish. Upstairs, the story continues up to the present, with exhibits on many aspects of modern life in Michoacán including clothing, handicrafts and agriculture.

The museum is open daily from 9 am to 2 pm and 4 to 8 pm (on Saturday, Sunday and holidays it closes at 7 pm). Admission is free.

Free cultural events such as regional music, dance, artesanías etc are presented every Wednesday at 7.30 pm.

Morelos Sites

José Maria Morelos y Pavón, one of the most important figures in Mexico's struggle for independence from Spain, was born in the house on the corner of Corregidora and García Obeso on 30 September 1765. Two centuries later, it was declared a national monument and made into the **Museo Casa Natal de Morelos** (Morelos Birthplace

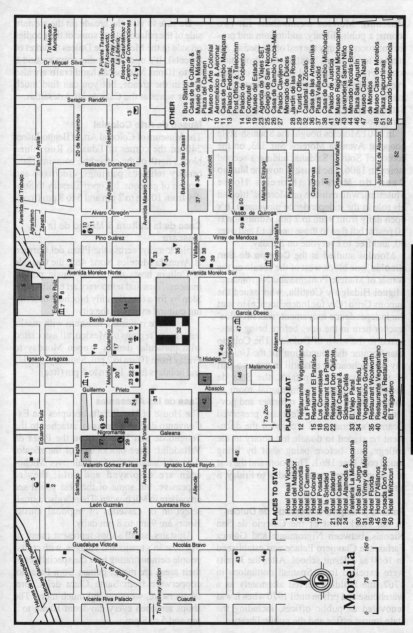

WESTERN CENTRAL HIGHLANDS

Morelia

OTHER
3   Bus Station
5   Casa de la Cultura &
    Museo de la Máscara
6   Plaza del Carmen
7   Museo de Arte Colonial
10 Aeroméxico & Aeromar
11 Casa de Cambio Majapara
13 Post Office & Telecomm
14 Palacio Federal
16 Palacio de Gobierno
19 Coepuliz
20 Museo del Estado
25 Agencia de Viajes SET
26 Colegio de San Nicolás
27 Palacio Clavijero &
    Mercado de Dulces
28 Jardín de las Rosas
29 Tourist Office
32 Catedral & Zócalo
36 Casa de las Artesanías
37 Plaza Valladolid
38 Casa de Cambio Michoacán
41 Palacio de Justicia
42 Museo Regional Michoacano
43 Lavandería Santo Niño
44 Mercado Nicolás Bravo
46 Plaza San Agustín
47 Museo Casa Natal
    de Morelos
48 Museo Casa de Morelos
51 Plaza Capuchinas
52 Mercado Independencia

PLACES TO EAT
12 Restaurante Vegetariano
    La Fuente
15 Restaurant El Paraíso
18 Los Comensales
20 Restaurant Las Palmas
21 Restaurant La Dulce,
    Café Catedral &
    Sidewalk Cafés
33 El Viejo Paral
34 Restaurant Hindu
    Vegetariano Govinda
35 Restaurante Vegetariano
40 Acuarius & Restaurant
    El Tragadero

PLACES TO STAY
1   Hotel Real Victoria
2   Hotel del Matador
4   Hotel Concordia
8   Hotel El Carmen
9   Hotel Posada
17 Hotel Posada
    de Cortés
21 Hotel Colonial
22 Hotel Casino
24 Hotel Alameda &
    Paletería La Michoacana
30 Hotel San Jorge
31 Hotel Virrey de Mendoza
39 Hotel Florida
45 Hotel D'Allanos
49 Posada Don Vasco
50 Hotel Mintzicuri

Museum). Morelos memorabilia fill two rooms; a public library, auditorium and projection room occupy the rest of the house. An eternal torch burns next to the projection room. Free international films and cultural events are held at the museum (see Entertainment). The museum is open Monday to Saturday from 9 am to 2 pm and 4 to 8 pm; admission is free.

In 1801 Morelos bought the Spanish-style house at Avenida Morelos Sur 323, on the corner of Soto y Saldaña, adding a second storey in 1806. The house is now the **Museo Casa de Morelos** (Morelos House Museum), with exhibits on Morelos' life and his role in the independence movement. It's open daily from 9 am to 7 pm. Admission is 10 pesos, but free to those under 13 and over 60, and free to everyone on Sunday.

Morelos studied at the **Colegio de San Nicolás**, one block west of the zócalo on the corner of Madero Poniente and Nigromante. Miguel Hidalgo y Costilla, who issued the famous Grito (Cry for Independence) to start the independence movement, was Morelos' teacher here in the days before being transferred to the town of Dolores. The Colegio later became the foundation for the University of Michoacán; it is still in use as a part of the university. Upstairs, the Sala de Melchor Ocampo is a memorial room to another Mexican hero, a reformer and governor of Michoacán. Here are preserved Ocampo's library and a copy of the document he signed to donate his library to the college, just before being shot by firing squad on 3 June 1861. This room and the rest of the college are open Monday to Friday, 8 am to 2 pm (free).

Palacio Clavijero & Mercado de Dulces

In the block west of the Colegio de San Nicolás, between Nigromante and Gómez Farías, the Clavijero Palace was established in 1660 as a Jesuit school. After the Jesuits were expelled from Spanish dominions in 1767, the building served alternately as a warehouse and prison until 1970 when it was renovated as public offices, including the state tourist office and the public library.

Be sure to visit the arcade on the western side of the palace to taste some of the goodies on sale in the Mercado de Dulces (Market of Sweets). It's open every day from around 8 am to 10 pm. Michoacán handicrafts are also sold in the arcade, but you can find much better wares at the Casa de las Artesanías.

Museo de Arte Colonial

The Museum of Colonial Art, at Benito Juárez 240 on the corner of Eduardo Ruiz, three blocks north of the cathedral, contains 18th-century religious paintings, crucifixes and models of galleons. It's open Tuesday to Sunday from 10 am to 2 pm and 5 to 8 pm (free).

Casa de la Cultura & Museo de la Máscara

A block away, across the Plaza del Carmen at Avenida Morelos Norte 485, the Casa de la Cultura hosts dance and music performances, films and temporary art exhibitions. Stop by for a free monthly brochure describing cultural events in the city.

Also here is a mask museum with masks from many regions of Mexico, all associated with particular dances – open Monday to Friday from 10 am to 2 pm, Saturday, Sunday and holidays from 10 am to 5 pm (free).

Casa de las Artesanías

The House of Handicrafts occupies the Ex-Convento de San Francisco, attached to the Templo de San Francisco on the Plaza de Valladolid, three blocks east of the zócalo. Arts and handicrafts from all over Michoacán are displayed and sold; they're expensive, but some of the best you'll see anywhere in Michoacán. There's also a small selection of cassettes of regional music. Hours are 9 am to 8 pm daily.

Upstairs, small shops represent many of Michoacán's towns and villages, with craftspeople demonstrating how the specialities of their areas are made: guitars from Paracho, copperware from Santa Clara del Cobre, lacquerware, weaving and much more. The shops are open every day from 10 am to 3 pm and 5 to 8 pm.

Fuente Tarasca, El Acueducto & Bosque Cuauhtémoc

The Tarascan Fountain at the end of Madero Oriente, nine blocks east of the zócalo, consists of a bevy of half-naked Tarascan women in stone, holding aloft a large basket of fruits and vegetables. It is a 1960s replacement of a fountain that mysteriously disappeared in 1940. The effect is strangely beautiful at night.

The aqueduct beginning at the Tarascan fountain extends south-east along Avenida Acueducto. Although it looks much older, the aqueduct was built between 1785 and 1788 to satisfy the city's growing water needs. With 253 arches stretching two km, it is an impressive sight, especially at night when spotlights illuminate the arches and the fountain.

The Bosque Cuauhtémoc, or Cuauhtémoc Forest, is a large park stretching south from Avenida Acueducto. In the park at Avenida Acueducto 18, a couple of blocks from the Tarascan fountain, is an interesting **Museo de Arte Contemporáneo**, open Tuesday to Sunday from 10 am to 2 pm and 4 to 8 pm, with changing exhibitions of modern art; admission is free.

On Plaza Morelos, about 100 metres north-east of Bosque Cuauhtémoc between Avenida Acueducto and the cobbled Calzada Fray Antonio de San Miguel, stands the **Estatua Ecuestre al Patriota Morelos**, a statue of Morelos on horseback trotting to battle. It was sculpted by the Italian Giuseppe Ingillieri between 1910 and 1913.

Centro de Convenciones

The Centro de Convenciones complex has several places of interest in extensive park-like grounds about 1.5 km south of the Bosque Cuauhtémoc on Calzada Ventura Puente. You can reach it on the yellow route combi ('Ruta Amarilla') heading east on Santiago Tapia-20 de Noviembre. This route stops running at 9 pm.

The **Planetario de Morelia**, with 164 projectors and a cupola 20 metres in diameter, presents one-hour programmes on Friday and Saturday at 7 pm, and Sunday at 6.30

pm. On Sunday at 5 pm there's a separate family programme (minimum age five). Admission is 5 pesos.

The **Orquidario**, or orchid house, is open Monday to Friday from 10 am to 6 pm, Saturday and Sunday 10 am to 3 pm and 4 to 6 pm. They sell entrance tickets for 1, 3 and 5 pesos; you choose how much of a donation you want to make. The large, modern **Teatro Morelos** is also in the complex.

Parque Zoológico Benito Juárez

The Benito Juárez Zoo is three km south of the zócalo on Calzada Juárez, which is an extension of Nigromante and Galeana. It's a pleasant zoo with many animals, a lake with rowing boats for hire, a small train, picnic areas and a playground – open every day except Tuesday from 10 am to 6 pm.

The maroon combi route ('Ruta Guinda'), heading south on Nigromante from the stop on the east side of the Palacio Clavijero near the zócalo, will drop you at the zoo entrance.

Markets

Three large mercados are within 10 blocks or so of the zócalo: Mercado Nicolás Bravo on Nicolás Bravo between Corregidora and Guerrero; Mercado Independencia on the corner of Vicente Santa Maria and Ana Maria Gallaga; and Mercado Municipal Revolución on the corner of Revolución and Plan de Ayala.

Language Courses

There are several language schools offering intensive courses in Spanish. Most central is the Centro Cultural de Lenguas (☎ /fax (43) 12-05-89) at Madero Oriente 560. Courses here run from two to four weeks, five hours daily with three hours of classroom work and the rest of the time spent on workshops related to Mexican history, literature and culture. You can take the language studies only for 570 pesos for the first week, less for subsequent weeks, or the full programme for 930 pesos for the first week, less for further weeks. One-to-one tuition is 30 pesos per hour. Living with Mexican families is encouraged – cost 40 pesos per day – and organised by the school.

WESTERN CENTRAL HIGHLANDS

The Baden-Powell Institute (☎ (43) 12-40-70) at Alzate 565, three blocks south of Madero Oriente, is a smaller school offering courses in Spanish language and Mexican politics and culture – mostly on a one-to-one basis, though group classes can be arranged. One-to-one classes cost 25 pesos per hour, less after you notch up 80 hours. Accommodation with a Mexican family is 36 pesos per day, including three meals.

Centro Mexicano Internacional (☎ (43) 12-45-96) in a large colonial building at Calzada Fray Antonio 173, near the aqueduct, offers courses in Spanish language and Mexican culture etc for 735 pesos for the first week, 585 pesos for additional weeks. You can start any week of the year. Classes run for six hours daily in groups of no more than five students. Living with a Mexican family costs 42 pesos a day. Mailing address is Apartado Postal No 56, Morelia, Michoacán 58000.

Tours

The Dirección de Operación y Desarrollo Turístico (☎ 13-26-54) in the Palacio Clavijero offers free walking tours of the historical city centre any time five or more people want to go; all you need do is phone in advance to schedule it.

Agencia de Viajes SET on Madero, opposite the zócalo, between the Hotel Valladolid and Hotel Casino, arranges guided three-hour city tours, on foot or by van (35 pesos per person). There are also day tours for 100 pesos or more to Uruapan; Parque Nacional Los Azufres, a national park in a volcanic area about 100 km east of Morelia with pine forests, lakes, geysers and a hot sulphur pool; and, from November to March, to El Rosario Monarch Butterfly sanctuary (see the Santuario de Mariposas El Rosario section for how to get there independently).

Festivals

Morelia's many annual festivals include:

Feria de Morelia Morelia's major annual fair, with exhibits of handicrafts, agriculture and livestock from all over Michoacán, plus cultural events, regional dances, bullfights and fiestas. The *Feria*

de Órgano, an international organ festival during the first two weeks of May, is part of the celebrations, and the anniversary of the founding of Morelia in 1541 is celebrated on 18 May with fireworks, exhibitions of historical photos and more; 29 April to 20 May

Festival Internacional de Música International Music Festival; final week of July and first week of August

Morelos' Birthday This is celebrated with a parade and events similar to those for the city's anniversary; 30 September

Día de la Virgen de Guadalupe The day of the Virgen de Guadalupe is celebrated on 12 December at the Templo de San Diego. From 27 October to 12 December, typical Mexican foods are sold on the pedestrian street Calzada Fray Antonio de San Miguel which runs roughly parallel with the aqueduct.

Feria Navideña Christmas Fair, with traditional Christmas items, foods, handicrafts and manufactured goods from Michoacán; from approximately 1 December to 6 January

Places to Stay – bottom end

The cheapest place to stay in Morelia is the CONADE youth hostel, *Villa Juvenil* (☎ (43) 13-31-77), in the INJUDE sports complex on the corner of Oaxaca and Chiapas, a 15 or 20-minute walk south-west of the zócalo. The hostel is clean, with four beds (two bunks) and a locker in each room, and separate men's and women's areas. Cost is 11 pesos per bunk. In the sports complex are a swimming pool, a gym and several sports fields.

There are a number of good inexpensive hotels within a few blocks of the zócalo, including a couple near the bus station. *Hotel del Matador* (☎ (43) 12-46-49), at Eduardo Ruíz 531 opposite the bus station door, has 57 clean rooms with private bath and windows admitting light and air. Singles/doubles are 60/70 pesos.

Hotel Concordia (☎ (43) 12-30-52/54) at Gómez Farías 328, on the east side of the bus station, also charges 60/70 pesos. The rooms facing the street are the best, with little balconies and a whole wall of windows; the interior rooms are quieter but a bit dark.

A few blocks away, *Hotel El Carmen* (☎ (43) 12-17-25) is at Eduardo Ruiz 63, between Juárez and Morelos, facing the small Plaza del Carmen. The rooms opening onto the plaza are quite pleasant, with small balconies; interior rooms have no windows. Singles are 30 or 40 pesos, doubles 70 or 80 pesos.

Around the corner, two blocks from the zócalo, the *Hotel Colonial* (☎ (43) 12-18-97) at 20 de Noviembre 15, on the corner of Avenida Morelos Norte, is a colonial-style hotel with 25 rooms at 40/70 pesos. Street-facing rooms are good – large, with high beamed ceilings and small balconies – but this is a busy corner with much traffic noise; the interior rooms are quieter.

Posada Don Vasco (☎ (43) 12-14-84) at Vasco de Quiroga 232 is a colonial-style hotel with rooms arranged around a courtyard with sitting areas and plants. It has a variety of rooms, some quite pleasant; all have carpet, phone and private bath (hot water 6.30 am to 2 pm). Most are 45/57 pesos but there are some cheaper ones at 25/30 pesos. Don't be put off by the one or two unsmiling desk staff. The hotel restaurant is popular and cheap.

Opposite the Don Vasco, *Hotel Mintzicuri* (☎ (43) 12-06-64) at Vasco de Quiroga 227 has 37 small, clean rooms, all with carpet and phone, around a courtyard with parking spaces. Singles/doubles are 53/77 pesos; they have a restaurant, and Turkish baths too!

Four blocks west of the zócalo, *Hotel San Jorge* (☎ (43) 12-46-10) at Madero Poniente 719, on the corner of Guadalupe Victoria, has large, clean rooms with ample windows opening onto the interior walkway; cost is 42/50 pesos.

Places to Stay – middle

Two blocks south-west of the zócalo, *Hotel D'Atilanos* (☎ (43) 12-01-21) at Corregidora 465, on the corner of Ignacio Rayón, is a colonial-style hotel with 27 large rooms, all with colour TV and phone, arranged around a lovely covered courtyard. Singles/doubles are 65/90 pesos.

Hotel Florida (☎ (43) 12-18-19) is half a block south of the zócalo at Avenida Morelos Sur 161. It's a clean, modern place where all rooms have colour TV, carpet, and phone;

most rooms have good ventilation, and those facing the street catch the afternoon sun. Cost is 66/88 pesos.

On the north side of the zócalo, the *Hotel Casino* (☎ (43) 13-10-03) at Portal Hidalgo 229 has 48 clean, comfortable rooms, all with carpet, phone and colour TV. Those facing the street have small balconies overlooking the zócalo; the interior rooms open onto a covered courtyard with a popular restaurant on the ground floor. Rates are 114/143 pesos.

In the same block, the *Hotel Catedral* (☎ (43) 13-07-83, fax 13-04-67) at Zaragoza 37, opposite the cathedral, is another attractive colonial-style hotel with comfortable rooms around a covered courtyard. The normal rate, 190/200 pesos, seems high, but sometimes prices go down as low as 120/140 pesos.

Hotel Real Victoria (☎ (43) 13-23-00, 13-25-11) at Guadalupe Victoria 245 is a modern hotel with 110 clean, pleasant rooms, all with colour TV and carpet, at 115/160 pesos. There's enclosed parking and a restaurant on the ground floor of the covered courtyard.

Places to Stay – top end

On the north-west corner of the zócalo, the *Hotel Virrey de Mendoza* (☎ (43) 12-06-33, 12-49-40) at Portal Matamoros 16 is the converted mansion of Antonio de Mendoza, the first viceroy of Mexico. The 52 rooms are elegantly furnished with antiques, crystal chandeliers and so on. Interior rooms cost 198 pesos, those with balconies over the street are 264 pesos, and suites are from 350 to 500 pesos.

Another good choice is the *Hotel Posada de la Soledad* (☎ (43) 12-18-88) at Zaragoza 90, on the corner of Ocampo. Built around 1700, it has been a carriage house, a convent and a private mansion. It has 50 standard rooms at 165/200 pesos, plus nine suites.

Back on the north-west corner of the zócalo, the *Hotel Alameda* (☎ (451) 2-20-23, fax 3-87-27) at Madero Poniente 313 is a more modern, attractive, 116-room hotel. Rooms in the older section are 182/203 pesos; in the new section they're 259/289 pesos, suites 404 pesos. There's a popular restaurant and bar, too.

Places to Eat

Morelia has a variety of good, economical restaurants to choose from. But it can be difficult to get breakfast before 8.30 am despite advertised earlier opening times! Opposite the front doors of the cathedral, at Portal Galeana 103 on the corner of Madero and Benito Juárez, *Restaurant El Paraíso* is a reasonable, basic restaurant with moderate prices for all meals. The comida corrida is 10 to 12 pesos; they also have a variety of breakfast combinations and a typical à la carte menu. It's open every day from 7.30 am to 11 pm.

In the next block west along Madero, opposite the zócalo, is a row of restaurants and sidewalk cafés, open every day from around 8 am to 10 pm. The *Café Catedral* is a popular spot, as is the *Restaurant Don Quijote*, the restaurant of the Hotel Casino, with tables both inside and out on the sidewalk. The sidewalk tables are popular all day and evening for coffee and people-watching. Prices are higher here with breakfasts around 10 pesos, the menu del día 20 pesos, beers 5 pesos.

Half a block off the zócalo, at Madero Poniente 327, the *Paletería La Michoacana* makes good fruit drinks and ice cream, good for taking to the zócalo and sitting on a bench under a tree. It's open every day from 8 am to 9 pm. Another good juice bar/café is *El Viejo Paral* on the south side of Madero Oriente, just east of the cathedral. It's clean with attentive service and a homely touch to food presentation. A tasty breakfast costs 7 pesos.

On the south side of the zócalo, Hidalgo is a shopping street blocked off to traffic. *Restaurant El Tragadero* at Hidalgo 63, half a block from the zócalo, is a family-run, basic restaurant that's good for all meals; it's open from 8 am to 10 pm Monday to Saturday, 8 am to 8 pm on Sunday. The comida corrida is 14 pesos. Unfortunately, the TV is on all the time.

Restaurante Woolworth is a pleasant-enough clean cafeteria in a converted former church on Virrey de Mendoza, half a block south of Madero. Breakfasts start at 8 pesos. It's open from 8 am to 9 pm Monday to Saturday, 9 am to 8 pm on Sunday.

A block north of the zócalo, *Restaurant Las Palmas* at Melchor Ocampo 215 serves up filling meals in an ordinary setting. A big breakfast of juice, eggs, coffee, tortillas and bread goes for 9 pesos. You won't need lunch! *Los Comensales*, 1½ blocks north of the zócalo, is more upscale with tables in a covered courtyard – good if you're fed up with street noise. There's lots of seafood with pescado blanco at 35 pesos, or paella, steaks and other meat dishes at 25 pesos. There are cheaper vegetarian dishes and snacks too. Hours are 8 am to 10 pm daily.

For real cheap eats, there are several restaurants near the bus station, open daily from around 7 am to midnight; a comida corrida might cost as little as 5 pesos here. Or there's a row of cheap eating stalls with tables under the covered arches running around three sides of the Plaza San Agustín, one block south of the zócalo; they're open every day from around 3 or 4 pm until around 1 am.

For a splash-out meal, try the *Meson San Diego* at Calzada Fray Antonio de San Miguel 344, the charming cobblestoned, tree-lined street behind the aqueduct. It's open Tuesday to Saturday from 2 to 11 pm, Sunday 2 to 6 pm. The café in the *Casa de la Cultura* is worth a visit.

Vegetarian On the east side of the zócalo at Morelos Sur 39, *Restaurant Hindu Vegetariano Govinda* is a quiet, attractive restaurant serving a selection of breakfasts, vegetarian burgers and comida corrida combos for 9 to 11 pesos. It's open Monday to Saturday from 9 am to 5 pm, closed Sunday.

South of the zócalo at Hidalgo 75, *Restaurante Vegetariano Acuarius* is open 9 am to 5 pm every day, serving breakfasts for 9 pesos and a good comida corrida for 11 pesos. It's in a pleasant covered courtyard.

Queen of Morelia's vegetarian restaurants is the popular *Restaurante Vegetariano La*

Fuente, five blocks east of the zócalo at Madero Oriente 493-B. It's open daily from 1 to 6 pm, serving a delicious and filling comida corrida for 15 pesos, with selections changing daily. A guitarist entertains at lunch time.

Entertainment

Being a university town as well as the capital of one of Mexico's most interesting states, Morelia has a lively cultural life. Stop by the tourist office and the Casa de la Cultura for their free monthly calendars listing films and cultural events around Morelia.

Morelia's two daily newspapers *El Sol de Morelia* and *La Voz de Michoacán* have cultural sections with events notices and theatre and cinema ads. There are several cinemas around the centre.

There are regular band concerts in both the zócalo (Sunday) and the Jardín de las Rosas on the corner of Gómez Farías and Santiago Tapia, and frequent organ recitals in the cathedral.

International film series are presented by various cine clubs, with admission often free. Venues are the *Museo Regional Michoacano*, the *Museo Casa Natal de Morelos* (both several times a week), the *Casa de la Cultura* and *La Librería* – see below.

The Museo Casa Natal de Morelos also presents free talks and other cultural events at its Viernes Culturales, on Friday at 7 pm.

Regional dances, music, stories and exhibitions from the state of Michoacán are presented every Wednesday at 7.30 pm at the *Museo del Estado*.

La Librería, a bookstore and coffee house at Calzada Fray Antonio de San Miguel 284, a couple of blocks east of the Tarascan fountain, has a pleasant university atmosphere, a cine club showing international films on Saturday at 7.30 pm, and live music on Sunday at 7.30 pm. There's no charge for any of their events; just have a coffee, tea or a cake from the café.

An interesting bar popular with students is *Bombay Jungle Bar* on Bocanegra near the corner of Avenida Acueducto. There's sometimes live music. For higher cultural entertainment, Morelia also has a number of discos, including *Club XO*, the *Canta Bar* (formerly *Bambalina's*), the *Bol-Morelia*, *Las Moras*, *Inchátiro*, *Los Quinqués*, and the *Factory* (in the Hotel Presidente). You can expect to pay a cover charge of at least 20 pesos at most of these places.

Getting There & Away

Air The Francisco J Múgica airport is 27 km from Morelia, on the Morelia-Zinapécuaro highway. There are plenty of connections to other Mexican and some North American cities. Wagon Lits Viajes next to the Hotel Alameda is a very central agency for air tickets.

Mexicana (☎ 13-80-85), in the lobby of the Gran Hotel, Centro de Convenciones, has daily direct flights to/from San Francisco, Chicago, Los Angeles, Guadalajara and Zacatecas. Aeroméxico and Aeromar (☎ 13-05-55), on the corner of Pino Suárez and 20 de Noviembre, and TAESA (☎ 13-40-50), at Plaza de Rebollones, opposite the north-west end of the aqueduct, have daily flights to/from Mexico City. TAESA also serves Tijuana and Zacatecas. Aero Sudpacífico (☎ 15-24-13) flies most days to Uruapan, Lázaro Cárdenas, Mexico City and Guadalajara. Aerolitoral (☎ 13-68-33) has daily direct flights to/from Guadalajara.

Bus Morelia's Central Camionera is conveniently located just a few blocks north-west of the zócalo, on Eduardo Ruíz between Valentín Gomez Farías and León Guzmán. In the bus station are a 24-hour Computel Lada caseta with fax service, several cafeterias, and places where you can store your luggage. Daily departures include:

Angangueo – 175 km, four hours; 2nd-class buses at 2.55 and 4.20 pm by Autobuses de Occidente via Zitácuaro (15 pesos); or take a bus to Zitácuaro then a local bus to Angangueo

Guadalajara – 367 km, five hours; eight deluxe buses by ETN (57 pesos) and five by Primera Plus (45 pesos); 12 1st-class buses by Autobuses de Jalisco (34.50 pesos) and eight by Servicios Coordinados (34 pesos); 2nd-class buses by Autobuses de Occidente and Flecha Amarilla (29 pesos)

Guanajuato – 176 km, four hours; eight 2nd-class buses by Flecha Amarilla (16.50 pesos)

Lázaro Cárdenas – 406 km, seven to eight hours; hourly 2nd-class buses by Galeana (36 pesos)

León – 197 km, 3½ to four hours; 15 deluxe buses by Primera Plus (26.50 pesos); six 1st-class by Servicios Coordinados (22 pesos); 2nd-class buses every 20 minutes, 4 am to 10.30 pm, by Flecha Amarilla (18.50 pesos)

Mexico City (Terminal Poniente or Terminal Norte) – 310 km, four to five hours; 25 deluxe buses by ETN (65 or 70 pesos) and five by Primera Plus (47 pesos); hourly 1st-class buses by Herradura de Plata (40 or 47 pesos); 2nd-class buses every 20 minutes, 24 hours, by Autobuses de Occidente (34 pesos)

Pátzcuaro – 62 km, one hour; 2nd-class buses every 10 minutes, 6 am to 7.30 pm, by Galeana, and every 30 minutes, 4.15 am to 10.30 pm, by Flecha Amarilla (6 pesos)

Querétaro – 259 km, three to four hours; a few deluxe and 1st-class buses by Primera Plus, Elite and Servicios Coordinados (19 to 24 pesos); 2nd-class Mexico City-bound buses every 30 minutes, 5.15 am to 11.30 pm, by Flecha Amarilla (17 pesos)

Uruapan – 124 km, two hours; five deluxe buses by Primera Plus (17 pesos) and two by ETN (22 pesos); two 1st-class buses each by Elite (17 pesos) and Servicios Coordinados (14 pesos); 11 2nd-class buses by Flecha Amarilla (12 pesos)

Zitácuaro – 150 km, 2½ to three hours; 1st-class bus at 10.30 am by Tres Estrellas de Oro (17 pesos); 2nd-class buses every 20 minutes by Autobuses de Occidente (13 pesos), others by Transportes Frontera and Autobuses México-Toluca-Zinacantepec (14 pesos)

Train The Estación del Ferrocarril (☎ 16-39-65) is on Avenida Periodismo, on the south-west outskirts of the city, about a 15-minute combi ride from the centre – see Getting Around. The ticket office is open Monday to Saturday from 5.30 to 6 am, 11 am to noon, 5 to 6 pm, and 10 to 11 pm.

El Purépecha, with primera especial and primera regular seating, departs for Mexico City (train No 32) at 10.55 pm and for Pátzcuaro, Uruapan and Lázaro Cárdenas (train No 31) at 5.30 am. See the Mexico City train section for further timetable information. Fares from Morelia (primera regular/primera especial) include Mexico City 24.45/46 pesos; Uruapan 9.25/17.50 pesos; Lázaro Cárdenas 28.40/53.40 pesos.

There's also a segunda-clase train to Pátzcuaro and Uruapan at 5.30 pm and to Mexico City at 10.30 am.

Getting Around

A Zinapécuaro bus will get you to/from the airport. A taxi costs 45 to 50 pesos. There's an airport taxi service; telephone 15-63-53, or 15-06-46 or 13-10-43.

Around town, local combis – white Volkswagen vans – operate frequently from 6 am to 9 pm and cost 0.80 pesos. Their routes are designated by the colour of their stripe: Ruta Roja, red; Ruta Amarilla, yellow; Ruta Guinda, maroon; Ruta Azul, blue; Ruta Verde, green. A few routes operate until 10 pm. The only difficulty is getting them to slow down and stop!

Ruta Azul and Ruta Verde combis will drop you at the rail station – pick them up heading south on García Obeso. Local buses marked 'Indeco' or 'Magisterio' also run between the station and the centre.

Taxis are plentiful in the centre; the average taxi ride costs around 5 pesos. To the rail station costs 7 pesos, to the Centro de Convenciones 5 pesos.

SANTUARIO DE MARIPOSAS EL ROSARIO

In the easternmost part of Michoacán, near the border of México state, is the El Rosario Monarch Butterfly (*Mariposa monarca*) Sanctuary. Somewhere from 35 million to hundreds of millions of Monarch butterflies come here every year to breed, arriving around the end of October or beginning of November and departing again around the beginning or middle of April for their long migration back to the USA and southern Canada. When they are present, there are so many butterflies in the sanctuary that they cover the trees, turning them a flaming orange; it's a spectacular sight.

The sanctuary is open every day during the season the butterflies are present. The entrance fee of 10 pesos includes a guide (of course he/she expects a 'tip') who takes you through the sanctuary, explaining the butterflies' life cycle and so on. You can stay in the sanctuary as long as you like, but it only takes a couple of hours to tour it. It's a good idea to get there in the morning, when the butterflies are up in the trees. As the day warms up, they begin to flutter around and then come down onto the ground where it's more humid, and there are so many that you can't avoid crushing some as you walk.

The sanctuary is quite off the beaten track, but not too difficult to reach.

A newly-hatched Monarch butterfly

Getting There & Away

Second-class Autobuses de Occidente buses leave Morelia at 2.55 and 4.20 pm for Angangueo (175 km, four hours, 15 pesos), and there are four daily 1st-class buses of the México-Toluca-Zinacántepec y Ramales line to Angangueo from Mexico City's Terminal Poniente (190 km, four hours, 23 pesos). Many other buses go to Zitácuaro, from where plenty of local buses make the 45-minute uphill journey to Angangueo. For buses to Zitácuaro from Morelia, see the Morelia Getting There & Away section; from Mexico City (Terminal Poniente), there are 25 daily 1st-class buses by Vía 2000, and buses every 20 minutes by Autobuses de Occidente, both 19 pesos. A new Central Camionera should by now be completed in the dusty bus yard behind Zitácuaro's main street.

Camionetas, or vans, depart from the main road in Angangueo for the rugged nine-km, one-hour trip to the Monarch sanctuary. It's about another 15-minute walk from the parking place to the sanctuary. You have to hire the whole van, so the more people pitching in to share the cost, the better. Cost for the 10-person van is around 120 to 180 pesos (depending on your bargaining power) for the return trip, including waiting while you visit the sanctuary. The occasional independent operator might charge less. You'll have the best chance of finding other travellers to share the ride on weekends, but there are usually a few travellers around even during the week.

To walk from Angangueo to the sanctuary is a steep uphill journey taking around three hours. The track to the sanctuary is the continuation of Matamoros so the Hotel Parakata is a useful starting point. After about an hour, you'll come to a statue of the Virgin of Guadalupe; turn left here then stay on the middle track and don't deviate until you get to the entrance to the sanctuary, where there are usually stalls and people milling about.

Another alternative is to visit the sanctuary from the town of Ocampo, on the Zitácuaro-Angangueo road 15 km from the sanctuary. Ocampo is not as attractive as Angangueo but it's easier on your car if you're driving. There are places to stay in Ocampo, and camionetas going from there to the sanctuary. If you walk, it's less strenuous, though longer, than from Angangueo.

Angangueo

The main starting point for visits to the sanctuary is the pretty mountain village of Angangueo, a former mining town with a population of about 3000 souls, about 25 km north of Zitácuaro, a regional commercial centre on highway 15 from Mexico City to Morelia.

In Angangueo you can enjoy strolling around, seeing the two churches and the Monument to the Miner, with a good view over the town.

Places to Stay & Eat Angangueo has several places to stay, including the *Hotel Parakata* at Matamoros 7, with a small sign on the main road about a km before the village centre; singles/doubles with private bath and hot water cost 50/60 pesos. On the main street between Matamoros and the two churches are the *Casa Huéspedes El Paso de la Monarca* and the *Casa Huéspedes Juárez*. The Monarca has rooms set in a tiered garden with views of the hills; cost with private bath is 25/50 pesos. Rooms at the Juárez were being renovated when we last checked, but they're centred on a pretty, rose-filled courtyard; cost is 30 pesos. The *Hotel Albergue Don Bruno* on Morelos, the main road, a few hundred metres before Matamoros as you come into town, is more expensive with good rooms at 80/105 pesos.

The *Restaurant La Margarita* beside the Hotel Albergue Don Bruno is a good place to eat, or there's a restaurant at the Hotel Parakata. Early in the morning, you can sip a delicious spiced coffee prepared by a woman who sits next to a brazier set up in the church grounds.

PÁTZCUARO
• *pop: 60,000* • *alt: 2175 metres*

Pátzcuaro is a beautiful highland town in the heart of Purépecha Indian country, with some very stately small-scale colonial architecture. The centre of town lies 3.5 km from the south-east shore of Lago Pátzcuaro, almost equidistant between Morelia and Uruapan (both are about 60 km away on the good highway 14). Mexican tourists come in large numbers over Christmas and New Year, for Semana Santa and for the area's famous Day of the Dead celebrations on 1 and 2 November. It can get quite chilly in this mountainous area in winter – bring at least a warm sweater.

History
The Tarascans, ancestors of today's Purépecha who live around Lago Pátzcuaro and in areas to the west, emerged around Lago Pátzcuaro about the 14th century. They may have originated as semi-barbaric Chichi-

mecs from further north, but their language has no established links with any other tongue (although linguists have suggested connections with various languages including Zuni, spoken in the American south-west, and Quechua, spoken in Peru). The Spanish supposedly began calling them Tarascos because the Indians often used a word that sounded like *tarasco*.

Pátzcuaro was the Tarascan capital from probably about 1325 to 1400. Then, on the death of the powerful king Tariácuri, the Tarascan state became a three-part league comprising Pátzcuaro, Tzintzuntzan and Ihuatzio, the last two both on the east side of the lake. First Ihuatzio dominated, then Tzintzuntzan. The league repulsed Aztec attacks and the Spanish first came to the area in 1522, when they received a friendly reception. They then came back in 1529 under Nuño de Guzmán, the conquistador of legendary cruelty.

Guzmán's inhumanity to the Indians was so severe that the Catholic church and the colonial government sent Vasco de Quiroga, a respected judge and churchman from Mexico City, to straighten out the mess he had left. Quiroga, who arrived in 1536, established a bishopric (based initially at Tzintzuntzan, then from 1540 at Pátzcuaro) and pioneered Indian village co-operatives based on the humanistic ideas of Sir Thomas More's *Utopia*. To avoid Indian dependence on Spanish mining lords and landowners, Quiroga successfully encouraged education and agricultural self-sufficiency in the villages around Lago Pátzcuaro, with all villagers contributing equally to the community. He also helped each village develop its own craft speciality. The Utopian communities declined after his death in 1565 but the craft tradition continues to this day. Not surprisingly, Tata Vascu, as the Indians called him, is much venerated for his work; streets, plazas, restaurants and hotels in Michoacán are named after him.

Orientation
Pátzcuaro has a handsome, compact core of lovely colonial buildings and some less

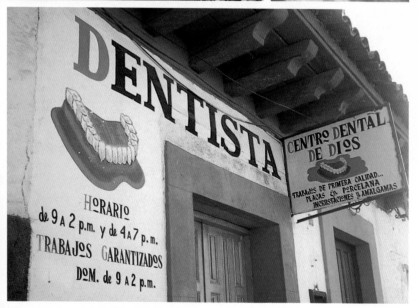

Western Central Highlands
Top Left: Selling limes in the market, Pátzcuaro (PP)
Top Right: Parque Nacional Eduardo Ruiz, Uruapan (JN)
Bottom: 'God's Dental Centre', Pátzcuaro (JN)

Western Central Highlands
Top Left: Baby-sitting donkey, Real de Catorce (PP)
Top Right: Catedral, Guadalajara (JL)
Bottom: Mural of Miguel Hidalgo, Palacio de Gobierno, Guadalajara (PP)

beautiful outlying areas stretching as far as the lakeside, 3.5 km north of the centre. Central Pátzcuaro focuses on the beautiful, wide Plaza Vasco de Quiroga and the smaller but busier Plaza Gertrudis Bocanegra, one block north, with the town market on its west side. The town centre is fairly flat, with just a few gentle hills.

Calle Ahumada heads north from Plaza Vasco de Quiroga to the Morelia-Uruapan highway three km away, changing its name first to Avenida Lázaro Cárdenas then to Avenida de las Américas along the way (these last two names are sometimes used interchangeably). Lago Pátzcuaro is half a km north of the highway.

The bus station is on a ring road on the south-west side of town, one km from the centre.

Information

Tourist Office The Delegación Estatal de Turismo (☎ (454) 2-12-14) is just off the north-west corner of Plaza Vasco de Quiroga, at Calle Ibarra 2, Interior 4. The office gives out free maps, can help you find a hotel room or anything else you might need, and provides information on the state of Michoacán. Hours are Monday to Friday 9 am to 2 pm and 4 to 7 pm, Saturday and Sunday 9 am to 2 pm. On major festival days they stay open until 9 pm.

Money You can change cash dollars or travellers' cheques at several banks on the two main plazas or Calle Dr Mendoza which links them. Some will only exchange between 10 am and noon. Banamex at Dr Mendoza 16 has an ATM. Numismática del Lago at Iturbe 30 changes cash dollars at rates slightly worse than the banks, from 10 am to 2 pm and 4 to 7 pm Monday to Wednesday, and 10 am to 1 pm Friday to Sunday.

Post & Telecommunications The post office is at Obregón 13, half a block north of Plaza Gertrudis Bocanegra. It's open Monday to Friday from 8 am to 7 pm, Saturday 9 am to 1 pm.

The Telecomm office at Títere 15 offers

telegram and fax services Monday to Friday from 9 am to 1 pm and 3 to 5 pm, Saturday from 9 am to 2 pm. Aeroflash on Iturbe also has a public fax service.

There's a Lada caseta in the upstairs lobby of the Hotel San Agustín, on the west side of Plaza Gertrudis Bocanegra, open every day from 8.30 am to 10 pm. The Computel Lada caseta in the lobby of the Teatro Emperador Caltzontzin, on the north side of the same plaza, is more expensive. The bus station also has a Lada caseta, open from 7 am to 8.45 pm.

Laundry The Lavandería Automática at Terán 14, 1½ blocks west of Plaza Vasco de Quiroga, is open Monday to Saturday from 9 am to 2 pm and 4 to 8 pm. Cost for washing, drying and folding 3 kg of laundry is 12 pesos.

Plaza Vasco de Quiroga

Pátzcuaro's large, peaceful main plaza is one of the loveliest in Mexico. A tall statue of Bishop Vasco de Quiroga gazes benignly down from the central fountain. The plaza is surrounded by trees and lined by a number of arched 17th-century mansions now used as hotels, restaurants and shops – all in pleasing proportion to the dimensions of the plaza itself.

One of the finest buildings is **La Casa del Gigante** at Portal Matamoros 40 on the east side of the plaza. Built in 1663, it takes its name from a giant statue of a man in the interior courtyard. Today it's a private home and not open to the public.

Another old mansion, the **Palacio de Huitzimengari** on the north side of the plaza, said to have belonged to the last Tarascan emperor, now houses a few unexceptional craft stalls as well as a Purépecha cultural organisation.

Casa de los Once Patios

The House of the 11 Courtyards, 1½ blocks south-east of Plaza Vasco de Quiroga on the cobbled Calle de la Madrigal de las Altas Torres, is a fine rambling building constructed as a Dominican convent in the 1740s. Earlier, one of Mexico's first hospitals, founded by Vasco de Quiroga, had stood on the site. Today the house is a warren of small artesanías shops, each specialising in a particular craft of Michoacán. Copperware from Santa Clara del Cobre, straw goods from Tzintzuntzan, musical instruments from Paracho, as well as gold-leaf-decorated lacquerware, handpainted ceramics and attractive textiles can be found. The shops are open every day from around 10 am to 7 pm.

Around Plaza Gertrudis Bocanegra

Pátzcuaro's second main plaza is named after a local heroine who was shot by firing squad in the town in 1818 for her support of the independence movement. Her statue adorns the centre of the plaza.

The plaza bustles with the activity of the town's **mercado**, stretching away from its west side. The busiest market days are Sunday, Monday and Friday. You can find everything from fruit, vegetables and fresh Lago Pátzcuaro fish to herbal medicines, crafts and clothing, including the region's distinctive striped shawls, sarapes and *peruanas* (a kind of sarape-shawl worn by women).

The **Biblioteca Gertrudis Bocanegra** (Gertrudis Bocanegra Library) occupies the 16th-century former San Agustín church on the north side of the plaza. A large, colourful Juan O'Gorman mural covering the rear wall depicts the history of Michoacán from pre-Hispanic times to the 1910 revolution. A great selection of books in English at the back is testimony to the large number of gringos passing through. The library is open Monday to Friday from 9 am to 2 pm and 4 to 7 pm, Saturday from 9 am to 2 pm.

A small **Mercado de Artesanías** stands next to the library. Crafts sold here include grotesque Tocuaro masks, carved wooden forks and knives from Zirahuén, and pottery. Bargaining is the rule though prices are already low.

On the other (west) side of the library, the **Teatro Emperador Caltzontzin** was a convent until it was converted to a theatre in 1936. Movies and occasional cultural events are presented here. Murals in the main

upstairs hall colourfully remind movie-goers of various epochs in Michoacán's history, including the meeting of Tarascan King Tangahxuan II and the Spanish conquistador Cristóbal de Olid near Pátzcuaro in 1522.

Basílica de Nuestra Señora de la Salud

Two blocks east of the south end of Plaza Gertrudis Bocanegra, the basilica was intended by Vasco de Quiroga as the centrepiece of his Michoacán community, a cathedral big enough for 30,000 worshippers, but the existing basilica, finished in the 19th century, is only the central nave of the original design. Quiroga's tomb, the Mausoleo de Don Vasco, is just to the left inside the main west doors.

Behind the altar at the east end stands a much-revered figure of the Virgin, Nuestra Señora de la Salud (Our Lady of Health). The image was made in the 16th century, on Quiroga's request, by Tarascan Indians from a corn cob and honey paste called *tatzingue*. Soon the Indians began to receive miraculous healings, and Quiroga had the words 'Salus Infirmorum' (Healer of the Sick) inscribed at the figure's feet. Ever since, pilgrims have come from all over Mexico to ask this Virgin for a miracle. Many make their way on their knees across the plaza, into the church and along its nave. You can walk up the stairs behind the image to see the many small tin representations of hands, feet, legs and so on that pilgrims have offered to the Virgin, now arranged into a sort of mosaic.

Museo Regional de Pátzcuaro & Casa de la Cultura

One block south of the basilica on the corner of Calle Enseñanza and Calle Alcantarillas, the Pátzcuaro Regional Museum is in the former Colegio de San Nicolás Obispo, a college founded in the 16th century by Vasco de Quiroga. This comprehensive museum of Michoacán arts and crafts includes delicate white lace rebozos from Aranza, handpainted ceramics from Santa Fe de la Laguna and copperware from Santa Clara del Cobre. One room is set up as a typical Michoacán kitchen with a tremendous brick oven.

The museum is open Tuesday to Saturday from 9 am to 7 pm, Sunday from 9 am to 3 pm (closed Monday). Admission is 13 pesos.

Opposite the museum on Alcantarillas is a large building constructed in the 16th century as a Jesuit college. Plans to restore it as a cultural centre have been in the works for several years. Attached to it is the 16th-century Iglesia de la Compañia.

Other Churches

If you like old churches, Pátzcuaro has several others of interest, including El Sagrario, San Juan de Dios, San Francisco and El Santuario. All are shown on the map.

El Estribo

El Estribo, a lookout point on a hill three or four km west of the town centre, offers a magnificent view of the entire Lago Pátzcuaro area. It takes up to an hour to walk there; in a vehicle, it takes only a few minutes. Either way, you can reach it by taking Calle Ponce de León from the southwest corner of Plaza Vasco de Quiroga and following the signs.

Festivals

Pastorelas These dramatisations of the journey of the shepherds to see the infant Jesus are staged in Plaza Vasco de Quiroga on several evenings around Christmas. *Pastorelas indígenas*, on the same theme but including mask dances, enacting the struggle of angels against devils trying to hinder the shepherds, are held in eight villages around Lago Pátzcuaro on different days between 26 December and 2 February. Rodeos and other events may accompany them. The tourist office can provide details.

Semana Santa The week leading up to Easter is full of events in Pátzcuaro and the villages around the lake, including Palm Sunday processions in several places; *Viacrucis* processions enacting Christ's journey to Calvary, and the crucifixion itself, on Good Friday (usually in the morning); candlelit processions in silence on Good Friday evening; and a ceremonial burning of Judas on Easter Sunday evening in the Plaza Vasco de Quiroga. There are many local variations: again the tourist office can provide details.

Día de los Muertos The Day of the Dead attracts visitors to the Pátzcuaro region from all over Mexico and beyond. What's special locally is the magical quality and pre-Hispanic undertones of the Purépecha villagers' celebrations, with special altars of flowers (chiefly marigolds, which have had ceremonial importance since before Spanish times) built in graveyards, and candlelit vigils there by the women from midnight on the night of 1-2 November. Best known – to the point where sightseers almost overwhelm the place – are the events on Isla Janitzio in the lake, with traditional dances and a parade of decorated canoes on the evening of 1 November. The story goes that the souls of Mintzita and Itzihuapa, a pair of Purépecha royal lovers at the heart of a legend of sunken treasure involving, as usual, the cruelty of Nuño de Guzmán, make their way to the graveyard of the island church on this night.

There are also picturesque ceremonies in many other villages including Tzintzuntzan, Ihuatzio, Jarácuaro and Tzurumútaro. The Pátzcuaro tourist office, and special information booths at strategic points around the town, can provide plenty of information. Many more events – including craft markets, traditional and contemporary dances, exhibitions and concerts – are held in Pátzcuaro and the villages around the Day of the Dead. In Jarácuaro local dance groups and musicians stage a traditional contest of their skills in the village square on the evening of 1 November.

Nuestra Señora de la Salud The high point of a two-week feria in honour of the Virgin of Health in the first half of December is a colourful procession to the basilica on 8 December. Traditional dances, including Los Reboceros, Los Moros, Los Viejitos, Los Panaderos and Los Mojigangas, are performed.

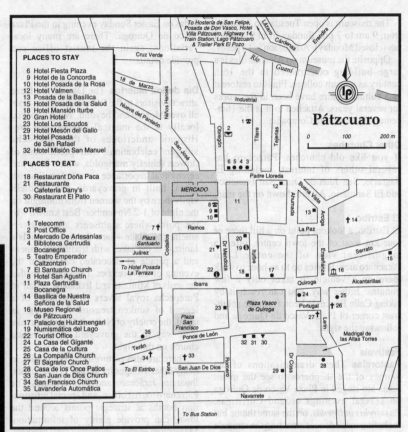

PLACES TO STAY
6 Hotel Fiesta Plaza
9 Hotel de la Concordia
10 Hotel Posada de la Rosa
12 Hotel Valmen
13 Posada de la Basílica
15 Hotel Posada de la Salud
16 Hotel Mansión Iturbe
20 Gran Hotel
23 Hotel Los Escudos
29 Hotel Mesón del Gallo
31 Hotel Posada
   de San Rafael
32 Hotel Misión San Manuel

PLACES TO EAT
18 Restaurant Doña Paca
21 Restaurante
   Cafetería Dany's
30 Restaurant El Patio

OTHER
1 Telecomm
2 Post Office
3 Mercado De Artesanías
4 Biblioteca Gertrudis
  Bocanegra
5 Teatro Emperador
  Caltzontzin
7 El Santuario Church
8 Hotel San Agustín
11 Plaza Gertrudis
   Bocanegra
14 Basílica de Nuestra
   Señora de la Salud
17 Museo Regional
   de Pátzcuaro
18 Palacio de Huitzimengari
19 Numismática del Lago
22 Tourist Office
24 La Casa del Gigante
25 Casa de la Cultura
26 La Compañía Church
27 El Sagrario Church
28 Casa de los Once Patios
33 San Juan De Dios Church
34 San Francisco Church
35 Lavandería Automática

Pátzcuaro

Places to Stay – bottom end

Camping The *Hotel Villa Pátzcuaro* (☎ (454) 2-07-67) at Avenida de las Américas 506, 2.5 km north of the town centre on the road to the lake, has a small trailer park in pleasant grounds. Two people with a vehicle pay about 30 pesos for a space with full hook-ups. There's a lawn area for tents, plus a small kitchen with a fireplace, and showers. Campers can use the hotel's swimming pool.

A bit nearer town on the same road, the top-end *Posada de Don Vasco* (☎ (454) 2-02-27, fax 2-02-62) has a trailer park with 25 spaces with full hook-ups, costing 50 pesos

a space, plus room for tents. It's only open at busy tourist periods, however. Guests can use the hotel's facilities.

Trailer Park El Pozo (☎ (454) 2-09-37) is on the lakeside, just off the Pátzcuaro-Morelia highway, one km east of its junction with Avenida de las Américas. Watch carefully for the sign pointing across the train tracks to the site, which has 20 places with full hook-ups, hot showers and a dock. Cost is 25 pesos per person.

Hotels *Hotel Valmen* (☎ (454) 2-11-61) at Padre Lloreda 34, on the corner of Ahumada one block east of Plaza Gertrudis Bocanegra, is one of the best deals in Pátzcuaro if you don't mind a 10 pm curfew (there's not much to do in Pátzcuaro after that time anyway). All the 16 large, spotless rooms have private bathrooms with steaming hot water, and most are arranged around a covered patio, with large exterior windows. Singles/doubles are just 20/40 pesos.

Hotel Posada de la Salud (☎ (454) 2-00-58) at Serrato 9, half a block behind the basilica, is a well-kept little place with 15 clean, pleasant rooms at 35/55 pesos looking onto a grassy courtyard.

Three long blocks west of the central plazas, *Hotel Posada La Terraza* (☎ (454) 2-10-27) at Juárez 46 is a small family-run hotel with just 11 rooms. There's a long front garden, an upstairs enclosed terrace with a bit of a view, and they offer breakfast if you like. Rooms, all with private bath and 24-hour hot water, are 25 pesos a person. A couple of larger rooms sleep up to seven people.

The *Gran Hotel* (☎ (454) 2-04-43) at Plaza Gertrudis Bocanegra 6 is about the best of several bottom-end places on this plaza. Smallish but clean, quite pleasantly furnished rooms, modernised not long ago, are 35/65 pesos. The hotel is on the south side of the plaza. On the west side of the plaza at Portal Juárez 31, *Hotel de la Concordia* (☎ (454) 2-00-03), has plain but clean, modernised rooms around two courtyards at 40/70 pesos. It's popular with Mexican families. Next door at Portal Juárez 29, entered through a shop, *Hotel Posada de la Rosa* (☎ (454) 2-08-11) is cheaper but more basic. The rooms, along an upstairs patio, all have two beds: cost per room is 30 pesos with clean shared bath, or 40 pesos with private bath.

The pleasant *Hotel Villa Pátzcuaro* (☎ (454) 2-07-67) at Avenida de las Américas 506 is set back from the road to the lake, about 2.5 km from the centre of town. The 12 cosy rooms all have fireplaces. Singles/doubles are 55/70 pesos. There's a swimming pool. It's most convenient if you have a vehicle, but local buses to the lake or town pass by every few minutes.

Places to Stay – middle
Several of the 17th-century mansions around Plaza Vasco de Quiroga have been turned into elegant colonial-style hotels, all with restaurants. The most attractive is the *Hotel Los Escudos* (☎ (454) 2-01-38) at Portal Hidalgo 73, on the west side of the plaza. Most of the 30 rooms have colonial paintings on the walls and all have carpeting, private bath and colour satellite TV; some also have fireplaces. They're set around two lovely patios full of plants, and cost 70/100 pesos for singles/doubles, or 120 pesos for a two-bed double.

On the north side of Plaza Vasco de Quiroga, *Hotel Mansión Iturbe* (☎ (454) 2-03-68) at Portal Morelos 59 is a former mansion still retaining its colonial elegance, with 12 good, big, wood-beamed, carpeted rooms. In peak seasons they cost 120 pesos for one or two people; at other times they're 80/100 pesos for singles/doubles. On the south side of Plaza Vasco de Quiroga, *Hotel Misión San Manuel* (☎ (454) 2-13-13) at Portal Aldama 12 is a former monastery building with 42 rooms. Some have a fireplace, all have carpeting, painted tile bathrooms and beamed ceilings. Cost is 81/104 pesos (146 pesos for a two-bed double).

Nearby at Portal Aldama 18, the *Hotel Posada de San Rafael* (☎ (454) 2-07-70) has 103 smaller, more basic rooms, with carpeting but no fireplaces. They cost 105/130 pesos in the *sección remodelada* (which means they have TV and newer carpets and mattresses), and 85/100 pesos elsewhere.

One block south of Plaza Vasco de Quiroga, *Hotel Mesón del Gallo* (☎ (454) 2-14-74, ☎ /fax 2-15-11), at Dr Coss 20, is less historic than some of the hotels on the plaza, but has a swimming pool, a pleasant restaurant, a lawn and garden area and a bar. The 20 singles/doubles are 74/95 pesos.

Hotel Fiesta Plaza (☎ (454) 2-25-15) at Plaza Gertrudis Bocanegra 24 is a modern place in colonial style with 60 pleasant, medium-sized rooms on three floors around two courtyards. Singles/doubles, with TV, are 140/160 pesos.

Away from the plazas, *Posada de la Basílica* (☎ (454) 2-11-08), opposite the basilica at Arciga 6, has 11 pleasant, sizeable rooms around an open courtyard which has views over the red-tiled roofs of town; singles/doubles are 60/80 pesos. Wood for fires is provided. The *Hostería de San Felipe* (☎ (454) 2-12-98) is out of the centre, on Avenida Lázaro Cárdenas two km north of the central plazas, but it's quite good value at 80/100 pesos for sizeable, modern rooms with fireplaces. There's a restaurant too.

Places to Stay – top end

Posada de Don Vasco (☎ (454) 2-02-27, fax 2-02-62), about 2.5 km north of the centre at Avenida de las Américas 450, is the most expensive place in town at 317 pesos single or double. It has 101 comfortable though not huge rooms (those in the newer blocks at the back are bigger and brighter), plus a tennis court, swimming pool, a games room with tenpin bowling, restaurant, bar, and so on.

Places to Eat

While you're in Pátzcuaro, try a couple of the town's typical foods. Most famous is the pescado blanco (whitefish), a small, tender fish traditionally caught on Lago Pátzcuaro by fishermen in canoes with large 'butterfly' nets (mariposas) – though equally likely to come from fish farms nowadays. A serving is likely to cost at least 30 pesos in a restaurant. Other specialities include corundas (tamales with a pork, beans and cream filling), and sopa Tarasca, a hearty tomato-based soup with bits of crisp tortilla, dried chile and cream on top.

All the colonial mansion hotels on Plaza Vasco de Quiroga have restaurants. One of the most popular and pleasant is the one in the *Hotel Los Escudos*, which has attractive decor and good food at moderate prices, with most meat or fish main dishes in the 13 to 22 peso range. It's open every day from 8 am to 10 pm. *Restaurant El Patio* at Portal Aldama 9 on the south side of the plaza is another good, busy place with moderate prices, open the same hours. *Restaurant Doña Paca* in the Hotel Mansión Iturbe is a good quiet place

to sit back with a coffee, cake or a drink. It has one or two tables outside on the street.

Restaurante Cafetería Dany's at Dr Mendoza 30, less than a block north of Plaza Vasco de Quiroga, is a popular, clean and friendly little place serving fish, meats and snacks at reasonable prices. The four-course 17-peso comida corrida is tasty and satisfying. Dany's is open from 8 am to 10 pm.

The restaurant at the *Gran Hotel*, nearby on Plaza Gertrudis Bocanegra, also serves good food, from 8 am to 8 pm. The breakfasts are decent value by Pátzcuaro standards, and the coffee is strong, with a free refill. There's a filling comida corrida for 20 pesos from 1.30 to 7.30 pm.

In the evenings you can fill up for 10 pesos on large plates of pechuga (chicken breast), vegetables and tortillas at the sit-down food stalls outside the market on Plaza Gertrudis Bocanegra. Your mound of food starts off tastily but gets a bit soggy towards the bottom! Good, warming ponche (fruit punch) is sold here too at 1.50 pesos a cup.

For a good view over town and lake, try the restaurant at the *Posada de la Basílica*, which is only open for breakfast and lunch. It has woven tablecloths and heavy Michoacán ceramic plates. There's a four-course comida for 20 pesos.

An inexpensive place to try local fish is beside the embarcadero on the lake, where the boats depart for Janitzio. A row of simple open-air restaurants all charge the same – 27 pesos for pescado blanco, 15 for mojarra, and 9 pesos for portions of charales (also called charalitos) – tiny fish, not quite as long as your finger, which are eaten whole. You can choose your fish and they'll fry it up on the spot.

Entertainment

The Pátzcuaro area has a number of traditional regional dances, complete with music, costumes and masks. To see most of them you have to be present at a festival when they're performed, but one of the most delightful dances, the Danza de los Viejitos (Dance of the Old Men), is presented twice weekly at the *Posada de Don Vasco* hotel.

The costumed dancers, wearing comical masks of grinning *viejitos* with long grey hair, hooked noses, rosy cheeks and no teeth, enter hobbling on skinny canes. Their dance gets more and more animated, with wooden sandals clacking on the floor, until finally they hobble off again, looking as if they can barely make it to the door.

This dance is performed along with other musical entertainment at 8 pm every Wednesday and Saturday in the hotel's Salón Tolimán. There's no charge for the performance; a 45-peso buffet dinner is served but you may be able to get away with just a drink or two. You should reserve a table (☎ 2-02-27) on the day of the performance, or one day before.

The *Teatro Emperador Caltzontzin* on Plaza Gertrudis Bocanegra hosts occasional performances of theatre, music and dance in addition to the usual fare of cinema in small-town Mexico – F-grade kung fu movies and the like.

Otherwise, there's not much to do around Pátzcuaro in the evening except eat or drink in one of the restaurants. Except at holiday times, the town seems to close up with a thud around 9.30 pm.

Things to Buy

Good places to find Michoacán crafts include the Casa de los Once Patios, and the main market and the Mercado de Artesanías, both on Plaza Gertrudis Bocanegra. See the earlier sections on those places. One useful buy for cool Pátzcuaro nights can be a woolly poncho, available for 30 to 50 pesos. Attractive table-cloths in bright check patterns cost around 40 to 80 pesos, depending on size and quality.

On Friday mornings a ceramics market, with pottery from different villages, is held in Plaza San Francisco, one block west of Plaza Vasco de Quiroga.

Getting There & Away

Bus Pátzcuaro's Central Camionera is on the south-west outskirts of town, on the ring road called Avenida Circunvalación or El Libramiento. It has a cafeteria, a guarda

equipaje where you can store your luggage and a Lada caseta. Buses from Pátzcuaro (2nd-class unless stated) include:

Erongarícuaro – 18 km, 30 minutes; every 20 minutes, 7 am to 8 pm, by Autobuses de Occidente (2 pesos)

Guadalajara – 347 km, six hours; one 1st-class bus each by Servicios Coordinados (28.50 pesos) and Vía 2000 (31 pesos); two 2nd-class nightly by Flecha Amarilla

Lázaro Cárdenas – 342 km, seven hours; about half-hourly, 6 am to 6.30 pm, by Galeana (32 pesos)

Mexico City (Terminal Poniente) – 370 km, 6½ hours; 29 daily by Herradura de Plata (1st-class 54 pesos, 2nd-class 48 pesos); hourly by Flecha Amarilla

Morelia – 62 km, one hour; 1st-class buses at least half-hourly, 7 am to 12.30 am, by Parhikuni or Herradura de Plata (7 pesos); 2nd-class every 15 minutes, 5.30 am to 8.30 pm, by Galeana (6.50 pesos)

Quiroga – 22 km, 30 minutes; every 15 minutes, 5.50 am to 8.45 pm, by Galeana (5 pesos)

Santa Clara del Cobre – 20 km, 30 minutes; every 40 minutes, 5.45 am to 8.25 pm, by Galeana (5 pesos)

Tzintzuntzan – 15 km, 20 minutes; same buses as to Quiroga (3 pesos)

Uruapan – 62 km, one hour; buses every 15 minutes, 6 am to 9 pm, by Galeana (6 pesos)

Zirahuén – 20 km, 30 minutes; buses at 9 am, 3 pm and 9.40 pm by Flecha Amarilla (5 pesos)

Train The Estación del Ferrocarril (☎ 2-08-03) is three km north of the town centre, on the road to the lake, just north of the highway to Uruapan. The main train is El Purépecha, running between Mexico City and Lázaro Cárdenas. It's scheduled to depart Pátzcuaro at 6.45 am westbound (train No 31) and 9 pm eastbound (No 32). See the Mexico City Train section for further timetable information. Fares (primera regular/primera especial) from Pátzcuaro on this train include: Mexico City 28.75/54.10 pesos; Morelia 2.10/4 pesos; Uruapan 2.60/4.95 pesos; Lázaro Cárdenas 24.15/45.35 pesos.

There's also a slower 2nd-class train running just between Mexico City and Uruapan. It departs Pátzcuaro at 6.45 pm westbound (train No 29) and 9 am eastbound (train No 30).

WESTERN CENTRAL HIGHLANDS

Getting Around

'Centro' buses and colectivos (minibuses), from the yard to your right when you walk out of the bus station, will take you to Plaza Gertrudis Bocanegra. Returning to the bus station, catch a 'Central' vehicle from Plaza Gertrudis Bocanegra – colectivos stop on the north side of the plaza, buses on the west side. For the train station and the lakeside embarcadero where boats leave for Janitzio, 'Lago' buses and colectivos go from the north-east corner of Plaza Gertrudis Bocanegra – but always check with the driver because some 'Lago' vehicles here are actually going in another direction. Returning to town from the station or embarcadero, you'll be dropped at Plaza Gertrudis Bocanegra. Buses cost 0.80 pesos, colectivos 1 peso; they run from around 6 am to 10 pm.

AROUND PÁTZCUARO

There are many interesting day or half-day trips from Pátzcuaro. All the following places can be reached or nearly reached by public transport – details of bus services to most of them are given in the Pátzcuaro section.

Isla Janitzio

Janitzio, the largest island in Lago Pátzcuaro, is worth a visit, though it's heavily devoted to tourism and on weekends and holidays it gets overrun by Mexican day-trippers. The 20-minute launch trip from Pátzcuaro offers views of villages along the shore while local fishermen demonstrate the use of their famous butterfly-shaped fishing nets from conveniently placed canoes. They then paddle alongside your launch holding out trays for your coins.

You can see the island in an hour or two. It has an abundance of fish restaurants and cheap souvenir shops, a few kids begging, and a giant 40-metre statue of the independence hero Jose María Morelos on its highest point. Inside the statue is a set of murals depicting Morelos' life; for 1 peso you can climb up inside all the way to his raised fist, from which there's a terrific view.

Getting There & Away

Launches to Janitzio go every day from around 7 am to 6 pm from two *muelles* (jetties) on the lakeside 3.5 km north of central Pátzcuaro. They leave whenever they fill up, which may be frequently or not, depending when you go. From the Muelle General, about half a km past the train station on Avenida de las Américas, launches cost 8 pesos for the return trip. From the less busy Muelle San Pedrito, about half a km further on (a sign points to it at an intersection about 200 metres before the Muelle General), the cost is 6 pesos. You can go back on any boat returning to your departure point, when you're ready.

Buses and colectivos marked 'Lago' run frequently to the lakeside from Plaza Gertrudis Bocanegra in the town.

Ihuatzio

Ihuatzio, about 14 km from Pátzcuaro near the eastern shore of Lago Pátzcuaro, was capital of the Tarascan league after Pátzcuaro but before Tzintzuntzan. Buses run to this village from Plaza Gertrudis Bocanegra in Pátzcuaro. There's an extensive archaeological site, only part excavated. The main feature is an open ceremonial space about 200 metres long with two quite large pyramids at its west end. The unexcavated areas, not officially open to the public, include walled causeways and a round-based building thought to have been an observatory. The site is open daily, 10 am to 3 pm.

Tzintzuntzan

• *pop: 2650* • *alt: 2050 metres*

The interesting little town of Tzintzuntzan ('tseen-TSOON-tsahn') is 15 km from Pátzcuaro near the north-eastern corner of Lago Pátzcuaro. It has impressive buildings from both the pre-Hispanic Tarascan empire and the early Spanish missionary period, plus modern handicrafts on sale.

Tzintzuntzan is a Purépecha name meaning Place of Hummingbirds. It was the capital of the Tarascan League at the time of invasions by the Aztecs in the late 15th century (which were repulsed) and the Spanish in the 1520s. The Purépecha chief came to peaceable terms with Cristóbal de Olid, leader of the first Spanish expedition in 1522, but this did not satisfy the rapacious Nuño de Guzmán, who arrived in 1529 or 1530 and reportedly had the chief burned alive in his quest for gold.

Vasco de Quiroga established his first base here when he reached Michoacán in the mid-1530s, and Tzintzuntzan became the headquarters of the Franciscan monks who followed him, although the town declined in importance after he shifted his base to Pátzcuaro in 1540.

Just along the main street from the ex-convento, craftspeople sell a variety of straw goods, the local speciality, and other Michoacán artesanías. You can reach the lakeshore by continuing straight down this street for about one km.

Las Yácatas The centrepiece of pre-Hispanic Tzintzuntzan is an impressive group of five round-based temples, known as yácatas, on a large terrace of carefully fitted stone blocks. They stand on the hillside just above

Lago Pátzcuaro

0   2.5   5 km

To Zamora

San Jerónimo Purenchécuaro

San Andrés Tziróndaro

Chupícuaro

Santa Fe De La Laguna

To Morelia

Quiroga

Lago Pátzcuaro

Opongio

Tzintzuntzan

Isla de Pacanda

Puacuaro

Isla Yuñuén

Napizaro

Isla Tecuén

San Pedro Cucuchucho

Erongarícuaro

Isla Janitzio

Sanabría

San Francisco Uricho

Jarácuaro

Ihuatzio

Arocutín

Muelle San Pedrito

Tocuaro

Isla Uranden Morelos

San Pedro Pareo

Tzurumútaro

Nocupetaro

San Bartolo Pareo

Tzentzénguaro

Huecorio

Muelle General

To Morelia

Santa Ana Chapitiro

Train Station

Pátzcuaro

To Zirahuén, Tingambato & Uruapan

Bus Station

To Santa Clara del Cobre

the town, on the east side of the road from Pátzcuaro. There are good views from this elevated location. It's about a 700-metre walk to the site entrance from the centre of the town. Also at the site are a few other structures and a small museum. Opening hours are 9 am to 6 pm daily; admission is 10 pesos.

Ex-Convento de San Francisco On the west side of the main street, Avenida Lázaro Cárdenas, is a complex of religious buildings built partly with stones from las Yácatas, which the Spanish wrecked. Here Franciscan monks began the Spanish missionary effort in Michoacán in the 16th century. The olive trees in the large, peaceful churchyard are said to have been brought from Spain and planted by Vasco de Quiroga.

Straight ahead as you walk into the churchyard is the still-functioning Templo de San Francisco, built for the monks' own use. Inside, half-way along its north side, is the Capilla del Señor del Rescate (Chapel of the Saviour), with a much-revered painting of Christ which is the focus of a week-long festival in February. The cloister of the old monastery, adjoining the church, contains the parish offices and some old but very weathered murals. On the north side of the churchyard stands the church built for the Indians, the Templo de Nuestra Señora de la Salud, with a holy image of El Cristo de Goznes (The Christ of Hinges). In the enclosed yard beside this church is an old open chapel, the Capilla Abierta de la Concepción.

Quiroga
• *pop: 12,000* • *alt: 2074 metres*
The town of Quiroga, 10 km north-east of Tzintzuntzan at the junction of highway 15 between Morelia and Zamora, has existed since pre-Hispanic times. Today it's named after Vasco de Quiroga, who was responsible for many of the buildings and handicrafts here. Quiroga is known for its brightly painted wooden products, leatherwork, and for wool sweaters and sarapes. These and

many other Michoacán artesanías are sold in the town.

On the first Sunday in July, the Fiesta de la Preciosa Sangre de Cristo (Festival of the Precious Blood of Christ) is celebrated with a long torchlight procession, led by a group carrying an image of Christ crafted from a paste of corn cobs and honey.

Buses run west out of Quiroga to Erongarícuaro about every 1½ hours, making it possible to do a full circuit of Lago Pátzcuaro by bus. Ask carefully about departure points, as they're rather confusing.

Erongarícuaro
• *pop: 2500*
On the south-west edge of Lago Pátzcuaro, a pretty 16 km trip from Pátzcuaro, Erongarícuaro – often just called 'Eronga' – is one of the oldest settlements on the lake. It's just a peaceful little town where you can enjoy strolling along streets still lined with old Spanish-style houses. About all there is to focus on is the plaza, the church a block away, and the old seminary attached to the church.

On 6 January, the Fiesta de los Reyes Magos (Festival of the Three Kings) is celebrated with music, dances and much festivity.

Santa Clara del Cobre
• *pop: 10,000*
Santa Clara del Cobre (also called Villa Escalante), 20 km south of Pátzcuaro, was a big copper-mining centre from about 1553 onwards. Though the mines no longer operate, the town still specialises in copper artisanry, with over 50 workshops making a variety of copper goods. There's a copper museum too, next to the main plaza.

The Feria del Cobre (Copper Fair) is held for one week in August; exact dates change each year.

Zirahuén
• *pop: 2200*
Smaller than Lago Pátzcuaro, the blue lake beside the small colonial town of Zirahuén, 20 km from Pátzcuaro off the road to Uruapan, makes a peaceful spot for a day trip

or for camping. Buses to Zirahuén are infrequent: alternatively, you could take an Uruapan bus, get off at the Zirahuén turnoff and walk the remaining five km.

Tingambato
• *pop: 5400*

At Tingambato, a small village about 40 km from Pátzcuaro on the road to Uruapan, are ruins of an ancient ceremonial centre of about 450 to 900 AD, showing Teotihuacán influence and dating from well before the Tarascan empire. They include a ball court (rare in western Mexico), temple pyramids, and an underground tomb where a skeleton and 32 skulls were found. A blue sign with a white pyramid points to the site from the highway, about one km away.

URUAPAN
• *pop: 220,000* • *alt: 1650 metres)*

When the Spanish monk Fray Juan de San Miguel arrived here in 1533, he was so impressed with the Río Cupatitzio and lush vegetation surrounding it that he named the area Uruapan ('oo-roo-AH-pahn'), which translates roughly as 'Fruit and Flowers' or 'Eternal Spring'. Uruapan is 500 metres lower in altitude than Pátzcuaro, and much warmer. The vegetation becomes noticeably more tropical on the 62-km trip between the two places.

Fray Juan had a large market square, hospital and chapel built, and arranged streets in an orderly chequerboard pattern. Under Spanish rule Uruapan quickly grew into a productive agricultural centre and today it's renowned for its high-quality avocados and fruit. Its craftspeople are famed for their handpainted cedar lacquerware, particularly trays and boxes.

Uruapan is a larger, untidier place than Pátzcuaro, with far less colonial ambience, but still looks attractive with its red-tile roofs in a lush hillside setting. A beautiful miniature national park, the Parque Nacional Eduardo Ruiz, lies within the city, only a few minutes' walk from the centre. Uruapan is also the best base for visiting the remarkable volcano Paricutín, 35 km west.

Orientation
The city slopes down from north to south, with the Río Cupatitzio running down its west side. Most of the streets are still arranged in the grid pattern laid down in the 1530s. Apart from the bus station in the north-east of town, and the train station in the east, everything of interest to travellers is within walking distance of the 300-metre-long main plaza. This is actually three joined plazas named, from east to west, El Jardín Morelos, La Pérgola Municipal, and El Jardín de los Mártires de Uruapan. A colonial church stands at either end of the north side of the plaza.

Most streets change their names at this central plaza. The busy street along the south side of the plaza is called Emilio Carranza to the west and Obregón to the east. Further east, it changes again to Sarabia, which intersects Paseo Lázaro Cárdenas, the main road south to the coast.

Information
Tourist Office The Delegación de Turismo (☎ (452) 4-06-33) is in office 204 of the Centro Comercial Uruapan at Calle 5 de Febrero 23, almost a block south of the east end of the central plaza. The staff give out a map of Uruapan, and brochures about Michoacán in English and Spanish, and are helpful with questions. It's open Monday to Saturday, 9 am to 2 pm and 4 to 7 pm, and Sunday from 9 am to 2 pm.

Money There are several banks near the central plaza, especially on Cupatitzio in the first two blocks south of the plaza. Most are open 9 am to 2 pm Monday to Friday but have shorter hours for foreign exchange. It's worth comparing their rates before you part with your dollars. Banca Serfin at Cupatitzio 13 does foreign exchange from 9.30 am to 12.30 pm – longer than most. Many of these banks have ATMs. Centro Cambiario de Divisas Hispanimex, at Portal Matamoros 19 towards the east end of the south side of the central plaza, and Compra y Venta de Dólares, on Cupatitzio 1½ blocks south of the plaza, will change your dollars (cash or travellers' cheques) Monday to Saturday from 9 am to 2 pm, also 4 to 7 pm Monday to Friday – but at worse rates than the banks.

Post & Telecommunications The main post office is at Reforma 13 just west of 5 de Febrero, three blocks south of the central plaza. It's open Monday to Friday from 8 am to 7 pm, Saturday 9 am to 1 pm.

The Telecomm office on Ocampo, half a block north of the west end of the central plaza, has a Ladatel credit card phone and telegram and fax services. It's open Monday to Friday from 9 am to 8 pm, Saturday from 9 am to noon. There are a dozen or more Lada casetas on and around the central plaza – look for the 'Teléfono Público' signs. You may find lower charges at some of those just off the plaza. The caseta in the Regalos Uruapan shop, on 5 de Febrero in the first block south of the plaza, is open 9 am to 8 pm Monday to Saturday, 9 am to 2 pm Sunday. The bus station also has a Lada caseta and a telegraph office.

Museo Regional Huatapera
For a quick overview of Michoacán crafts, visit the Museo Regional Huatapera, adjoining the Iglesia de la Inmaculada on the north-east corner of the central plaza. The fine museum building, erected in 1533, was the first hospital in the Americas. The carving around the door facing the plaza, and around the windows, is similar to the Moorish-style work on the church at Angahuan near Paricutín volcano. The museum is open Tuesday to Sunday, 9.30 am to 1.30 pm and 3.30 to 6 pm; admission is free.

Parque Nacional Eduardo Ruiz
This lovely tropical park, also called Parque Nacional Barranca del Cupatitzio, is about 600 metres west of the central plaza. It consists of the gushing headwaters of the Río Cupatitzio and its lushly vegetated banks for a km or so downstream. It's a beautiful, shady place with waterfalls, bridges, a trout farm, playground and paved paths for easy strolling. Boys dive into one or two of the river's deeper pools and ask for coins afterwards.

The main entrance is on Calzada La Quinta at the end of Calle Independencia. If you don't want to walk there, take a 'Parque' bus up Independencia from Ocampo. The park is open every day from 8 am to 6 pm (admission 1 peso): maps and leaflets on its history are on sale at the ticket kiosk.

Festivals
Uruapan's festivals include:

Semana Santa Palm Sunday is marked by a procession through the city streets. Figures and crosses woven from palm fronds are sold after the procession. There's also a ceramics contest, with a week-long Michoacán handicrafts exhibition and market filling up the central plaza. Prices get lower as the week goes on.

San Francisco St Francis, the patron saint of Uruapan, is honoured with colourful festivities and the Canácuas dance by women; 4 October

Festival de Coros y Danzas The Choir & Dance Festival, held some years, is a contest of Purépecha dance and musical groups; three days around 24 October

Feria del Aguacate The Avocado Fair is a big event with bullfights, cockfights, concerts and agricultural, industrial and handicraft exhibitions; two weeks in November (exact dates vary; check with the tourist office)

Places to Stay – bottom end
Camping *Trailer Park La Joyita* (☎ (452) 3-03-64) is at Estocolmo 22, 1½ blocks east of Paseo Lázaro Cárdenas at the southern end of town. It's a small park with full hookups for 10 trailers, a lawn area for tents, a barbecue and 24-hour hot water in the showers. Cost for two people and a vehicle is 30 pesos. Local buses marked 'FOVISSSTE' operate frequently between here and Calle Cupatitzio, 1½ blocks south of the central plaza.

Hotels The *Hotel del Parque* (☎ (452) 4-38-45) at Independencia 124, 6½ blocks west of the central plaza and half a block from the Parque Nacional Eduardo Ruiz, is easily the most pleasant of Uruapan's cheapies. Singles/doubles are 25/40 pesos in clean rooms with tile floors, Japanese-design bedspreads, private bath and 24-hour hot water. The owner speaks good English. There's a rear patio area, and enclosed parking.

Second choice is the *Hotel Mi Solar* (☎ (452) 4-09-12) at Delgado 10, two blocks north of the central plaza, with 20 slightly run-down rooms around two open courtyards. They have private bathrooms and cost 30/40 pesos.

On the east side of the central plaza is a trio of other cheapies, best of which is the *Hotel Capri* (no phone), Portal Santos Degollado 12. It has 24-hour hot water and its rooms, at 25/30 pesos (40 pesos for two beds), are bigger and mostly brighter than those at the *Hotel Moderno* (☎ (452) 4-02-12) or the *Hotel Oseguera* (☎ (452) 3-98-56) down the block. The Moderno charges 25/30 pesos and the Oseguera 30/40 pesos.

Places to Stay – middle

Uruapan has several attractive places in this range. *Hotel Villa de Flores* (☎ (452) 4-28-00) at Emilio Carranza 15, 1½ blocks west of the central plaza, is a well-kept colonial-style hotel whose clean, comfortable rooms, with private bath, open onto pleasant courtyards with plants. Singles/doubles are 65/75 pesos. The two-bed rooms on the rear courtyard are particularly good, being newer and brighter than the others. The hotel has a restaurant too.

On the south side of the central plaza itself, *Hotel Regis* (☎ (452) 3-58-44), Portal Carrillo 12, has brightly decorated, mostly well-lit, rooms for 63/72 pesos, plus its own restaurant and parking. *Hotel Concordia* (☎ (452) 3-04-00), next door at Portal Carrillo 8, is a comfortable, modern hotel with 63 large, spotless rooms, all with colour TV and carpeting. It also has parking, a restaurant/bar, and laundry service. Singles/doubles are 96/120 pesos.

Half a block south of the central plaza, *Nuevo Hotel Alameda* (☎ (452) 3-41-00) at 5 de Febrero 11 is another good middle-range hotel, with clean, comfortable if plain rooms for 70/85 pesos with colour TV. There's parking too.

Hotel El Tarasco (☎ (452) 4-15-00), half

a block north of the central plaza at Independencia 2, is a step up in quality, with 65 large, bright and attractive rooms at 136/170 pesos, plus a restaurant and a large swimming pool. There are good views from the upper floors.

Hotel Plaza Uruapan (☎ (452) 3-37-00) at Ocampo 64 on the west side of the central plaza is also quite luxurious, though there's a big difference between the interior rooms with no outlook and some of the large exterior ones, which have great views from floor-to-ceiling windows. Singles/doubles are 132/162 pesos. In off-peak periods, some of the big exterior rooms may be let as singles.

If you have a vehicle, you might like the *Motel Pie de la Sierra* (☎ (452) 4-25-10), four km north of the town centre on highway 37 towards Paracho and Carapán. At the foot of the mountains, as its name says, it has large, well-kept grounds, a swimming pool, games room, a pleasant restaurant/bar, and 72 attractive rooms with fireplace, colour TV, private terraces and mountain views. Rates are 90/114 pesos.

Places to Stay – top end

The hacienda-style *Hotel Mansión del Cupatitzio* (☎ (452) 3-21-00, fax 4-67-72), at the north end of the Parque Nacional Eduardo Ruíz on Calzada Fray Juan de San Miguel, is one of the best hotels in Uruapan. Its restaurant overlooks the Rodilla del Diablo pool where the Río Cupatitzio begins. The hotel has a large swimming pool, grounds, laundry etc; singles/doubles range from 150/180 pesos to 200/220 pesos.

Places to Eat

One of the best places is the tiny, cheap *Cocina Económica Mary* at Independencia 57, 3½ blocks west of the central plaza. Open from about 8.30 am to 5.30 pm, Monday to Saturday, this family-run place serves a really good 10-peso home-style comida corrida of sopa followed by a choice of several guisados (main courses) – which might range from bistek ranchero or fish to ensalada de nopales (cactus-ear salad) – plus

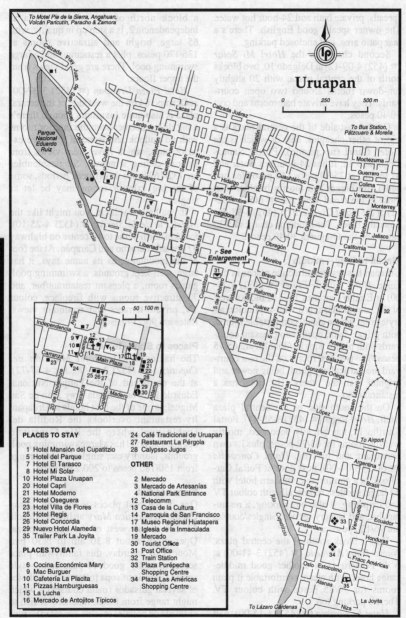

WESTERN CENTRAL HIGHLANDS

To Motel Pie de la Sierra, Angahuan,
Volcán Paricutín, Paracho & Zamora

Calzada Fray Juan de San Miguel

Calzada La Quinta

Parque
Nacional
Eduardo
Ruiz

Río Cupatitzio

Uruapan

0   250   500 m

Calzada Juárez

Lacas

Lerdo de Tejada

Revolución
Culver City
Carrillo Puerto
Serdán
Ayala
Delgado

Calzada Juárez

Nervo
Constitución
Romero
Cuauhtémoc

To Bus Station,
Pátzcuaro & Morelia

Moctezuma

Guerrero

Pino Suárez

Independencia

Emilio Carranza

Madero

Libertad

20 de Noviembre

Ocampo

García

Ortiz

16 de Septiembre

Corregidora

Hidalgo

Tejeda
Guadalupe Victoria

Colima

Veracruz

Monterrey

Yucatán
Sinaloa
Michoacán

Jalisco

California

Sarabia

Obregón

Morelos

Bravo

Reforma

Juárez

Villa
Acapulco
Hidalteros
Galeana

Américas

Alvarado

Arteaga

Salazar

32

**See
Enlargement**

Cupatitzio
5 de Febrero
Aldama
Dr Silva

Vergel

Las Flores

5 de Mayo

Pérez Coronado

Mendoza

González Ortega

Paseo Lázaro Cárdenas

Púrpechas

López

To Airport

Lisboa

Argentina

Paris

Brasil

Amsterdam

Ecuador

Honduras

Fracc Américas

Oslo   Estocolmo

Atenas

La Joyita

To Lázaro Cárdenas

Niza

To Airport

Río Cupatitzio

33 Plaza Purépecha

34 Plaza Las Américas

35

0   50 100 m

Independencia
Ayala
Delgado

7   8

Carranza
9   12 13
10 11   14 15   16
17
18
19
20
21
22

Main Plaza

25 26 27
28
29
30

20 de Noviembre
Ocampo
Cupatitzio
Madero

23

24

PLACES TO STAY

1 Hotel Mansión del Cupatitzio
5 Hotel del Parque
7 Hotel El Tarasco
8 Hotel Mi Solar
10 Hotel Plaza Uruapan
20 Hotel Capri
21 Hotel Moderno
22 Hotel Oseguera
23 Hotel Villa de Flores
25 Hotel Regis
26 Hotel Concordia
29 Nuevo Hotel Alameda
35 Trailer Park La Joyita

PLACES TO EAT

6 Cocina Económica Mary
9 Mac Burguer
10 Cafetería La Placita
11 Pizzas Hamburguesas
15 La Lucha
16 Mercado de Antojitos Típicos

24 Café Tradicional de Uruapan
27 Restaurant La Pérgola
28 Calypsso Jugos

OTHER

2 Mercado
3 Mercado de Artesanías
4 National Park Entrance
12 Telecomm
13 Casa de la Cultura
14 Parroquia de San Francisco
17 Museo Regional Huatapera
18 Iglesia de la Inmaculada
19 Mercado
30 Tourist Office
31 Post Office
32 Train Station
33 Plaza Purépecha
   Shopping Centre
34 Plaza Las Américas
   Shopping Centre

a refresco or a generous jug of fresh agua de fruta. You can also get a breakfast of excellent huevos a la Mexicana and café con leche for 10 pesos.

Pizzas Hamburguesas at Emilio Carranza 8, a few steps west of the central plaza, does good, filling pizzas with generous toppings from 8 am to 10.30 pm daily. The chica size at 15 pesos is plenty for one person. There are tacos, quesadillas, burritos and other snacks too.

Mac Burguer at Independencia 7, half a block west of Ocampo, is a reasonable little place for tacos (4.50 pesos for an order of three), tortas, burritos or a Mac Burguer (10 pesos with bacon, cheese and fries). Juices and licuados are available too.

Calypsso Jugos at Obregón 2A, just off the south-east corner of the central plaza, is an inexpensive juice and licuado bar also offering snacks like tortas or yoghurt and fruit. It serves a 9-peso breakfast of fruit or juice, eggs and coffee from 7 am.

The classier *Cafetería La Placita*, beneath the Hotel Plaza Uruapan on the west side of the central plaza, has a good range of excellent food with chicken or meat main dishes mostly in the 20 to 30 pesos bracket. There are various antojitos for 7.50 to 19 pesos, or fruit salad, yoghurt and granola for 8 pesos. It's open 7 am to 11 pm daily.

Several of the hotel restaurants are worth considering. The *Hotel Concordia* and the *Hotel El Tarasco* both serve ample four-course comidas corridas for 18 to 20 pesos. The *Restaurant La Pérgola* at Portal Carrillo 4 on the south side of the central plaza, open daily from 8 am to 11.30 pm, is fairly popular, though its comida corrida is ordinary.

Uruapan also has a couple of excellent cafés for enjoying good, strong coffee amid carved wooden furniture. One is *La Lucha*, half a block north of the central plaza on the small street García Ortiz. It's open every day from 9 am to 2 pm and 4 to 9 pm. The other is the *Café Tradicional de Uruapan* at Emilio Carranza 5B, half a block west of the central plaza. It's more expensive, but with a large selection of coffees to choose from – open

daily from 8.30 am to 2 pm and 4 to 10 pm. They also serve breakfasts and desserts.

The *Mercado de Antojitos Típicos*, on Corregidora one short block north of the central plaza, is a cheap place to sample local food, with about 40 food stalls serving up Michoacán dishes every day from around 6 am to midnight. Pick a stall that looks popular.

Entertainment

Uruapan is not exactly New York City for nightlife, but besides lingering over coffee at a good café or going to church you might find one or two other things to do in the evening. The tourist office has information on what's on.

The Casa de la Cultura on García Ortiz, half a block north of the central plaza, hosts exhibitions, occasional concerts and so on.

The Hotel Plaza Uruapan on the west side of the central plaza has a bar, disco and live entertainment on weekends. Several of the other better-class hotels near the central plaza also have bars. Or there are a few cinemas in town.

Things to Buy

Local crafts such as lacquered trays and boxes can be bought at the Mercado de Artesanías, on Calzada La Quinta opposite the entrance to the Parque Nacional Eduardo Ruiz. A few shops nearby on Independencia sell the same sorts of thing. But easily the best selection of handicrafts, quality stuff from all around Mexico, is sold in the artesanías shop in the Hotel Mansión del Cupatitzio. The town market, which stretches over half a km up Constitución from the central plaza to Calzada Juárez, is worth a browse too. Fruit and vegetables are concentrated near the top.

Getting There & Away

Air Aeromar (☎ 3-50-50 at the airport) flies daily except Sunday to/from Mexico City via Morelia. Aerosudpacífico (☎ 4-53-55) and Aerocuahonte both fly twice daily, Monday to Saturday, to/from Lázaro Cárdenas, and once or twice a day (except Sunday) to/from

Guadalajara. A helpful travel agent for booking flights is Excursiones y Turismo (☎ 4-12-50) in office 214 at 5 de Febrero 23, the same building as the tourist office.

Bus The Central Camionera is about three km north-east of central Uruapan on the highway to Pátzcuaro and Morelia. It has a post office, telegraph and fax office, Lada caseta, a guardería for leaving luggage, cafeterias and a few shops. Daily buses run all over central and northern Mexico, including:

Colima – 400 km, six hours; two buses each by Vía 2000 Plus (deluxe, 51 pesos) and Vía 2000 (1st-class, 38 or 44 pesos)

Guadalajara – 305 km, five hours, via La Barca; six deluxe buses each by ETN (54 pesos) and Primera Plus (38 pesos), and four by La Línea Plus (38 pesos); six 1st-class each by La Línea and Servicios Coordinados (33 pesos); for the more scenic route around the south side of Lago de Chapala, you need to change to local buses at Zamora

Lázaro Cárdenas – 280 km, six hours; six buses by Parhikuni (42 pesos deluxe, 31 pesos 1st-class); three deluxe buses by La Línea Plus (42 pesos); two 1st-class by Tres Estrellas de Oro (30 pesos); hourly 2nd-class buses, 24 hours, by Galeana (26 pesos)

Mexico City (Terminal Poniente or Terminal Norte) – 430 km, six hours; six deluxe buses by ETN (85 pesos) and four by Primera Plus (67 pesos); five 1st-class by Vía 2000 Plus (67 pesos)

Morelia – 125 km, two hours; buses every 15 or 20 minutes until 11 pm by Parhikuni (19 pesos deluxe, 16 pesos 1st-class); three deluxe buses by ETN (24 pesos) and five by Primera Plus (19 pesos); 2nd-class buses every 20 minutes with Galeana Ruta Paraíso (13 pesos)

Pátzcuaro – 62 km, one hour; 2nd-class buses every 15 minutes with Galeana Ruta Paraíso (6 pesos)

Train The Estación del Ferrocarril (☎ 4-09-81) is about 1.5 km east of the centre on Paseo Lázaro Cárdenas at the east end of Calle Américas.

El Purépecha, running between Mexico City and Lázaro Cárdenas, is scheduled to depart Uruapan eastbound (train No 32) at 6.10 pm, and southbound (train No 31) at 9 am. Tickets for this train are sold from 10 am to noon, and 4 to 7 pm. Fares (primera regular/primera especial) are 33.70/63.35

pesos to Mexico City, 9.25/17.50 pesos to Morelia, 2.60/4.95 pesos to Pátzcuaro, and 20/36 pesos to Lázaro Cárdenas. See the Mexico City Train section for schedules.

There's also a slower 2nd-class train, No 30, from Uruapan to Mexico City, departing at 6.35 am.

Car Viajes Cupatitzio in the Hotel El Tarasco, Viajes Tzitzi in the Hotel Plaza Uruapan, and Excursiones y Turismo (☎ 4-12-50) in office 214 at 5 de Febrero 23, are all travel agencies offering cars to rent.

Getting Around
To/From the Airport The airport is on Avenida Latinoamericana about eight km south-east of the city centre, a 15-minute drive. A taxi costs about 8 pesos.

Bus Local buses marked 'Centro' run from the door of the bus station to the central plaza. If you want a taxi, buy a ticket (6 to 8 pesos anywhere in town) from the taquilla in the station. On the return trip catch a 'Central Camionera' or 'Central' bus on the south side of the central plaza.

From the train station, take a 'Centro' bus west along Calle Américas to the central plaza. Heading from the centre of town to the station, a 'Quinta' bus from outside La Pérgola restaurant on the central plaza will drop you on Paseo Lázaro Cárdenas three short blocks south of the station.

The local buses run every day from around 6 am to 9 pm; they cost 0.60 or 0.80 pesos, depending on how clapped-out they are.

AROUND URUAPAN
Cascada de Tzaráracua
Ten km south of Uruapan just off highway 37, the Río Cupatitzio cascades 30 metres into a couple of pools surrounded by lush vegetation. Two km farther upstream there's another beautiful waterfall, the smaller Tzararacuita. 'Tzaráracua' buses depart about every half-hour on Saturday, Sunday and holidays – when the falls get crowds of visitors – from the middle of the south side of Uruapan's central plaza. Other days these

buses go only every couple of hours, so it's better to take an Autotransportes Galeana bus heading for Nueva Italia from Uruapan bus station: these depart every 20 minutes and will drop you at Tzaráracua. The buses stop at a car park, from where it's a steep descent of about one km to the main fall. Often there are horses available for about 10 pesos for the return trip.

Paracho
• *pop: 14,350*

Paracho, 40 km north of Uruapan on highway 37, is a small Purépecha town famous for its handmade guitars. It's worth visiting if you want to buy an instrument or watch some of the world's best guitar-makers at work. The local artisans are also known for their high-quality violins, cellos, and other woodcrafts, including furniture. There are many shops selling all these crafts. The liveliest time to come is during the annual Feria Nacional de la Guitarra (National Guitar Fair), a big week-long splurge of music, dance, exhibitions, markets and cockfights in early August.

Most buses from Uruapan bus station to Zamora will stop in Paracho. Auto-transportes Galeana (2nd-class) has the most frequent service, leaving every 15 minutes for the one-hour trip (4 pesos).

Volcán Paricutín

In the afternoon of 20 February 1943, a Purépecha Indian farmer, Dionisio Pulido, was ploughing his cornfield about 35 km west of Uruapan when the ground began shaking, swelling and emitting steam, dust, sparks and hot ash. The farmer, it's said, tried at first to cover the moving earth, but when that proved impossible, it seemed best to keep a distance. A volcano started to rise from the spot. Within about a year it had risen 410 metres above the surrounding land and its lava had engulfed the Purépecha villages of San Salvador Paricutín and San Juan Parangaricutiro. The villagers had plenty of time to move away as the lava flow was so gradual.

The volcano continued to spit lava and fire

until 1952. Today its large, black cone stands mute, emitting gentle wisps of steam. Near the edge of the 20-sq-km lava field, the top of San Juan's church protrudes eerily from the sea of black solidified lava – the only visible trace of the two buried villages.

Visiting the Area An excursion to Paricutín from Uruapan makes a spectacular trip. It's not a particularly high mountain – the much bigger Tancítaro (3850 metres) towers to its south – but it's certainly memorable and fairly easy of access.

If you want to do it in one day from Uruapan, as most people do, start early. It's advisable to stock up on snacks and water before leaving Uruapan. First you have to reach the Purépecha village of Angahuan, 32 km from Uruapan on the road to Los Reyes, which branches west off highway 37 about 15 km north of Uruapan. Galeana 2nd-class buses leave Uruapan bus station for Los Reyes hourly from 5.30 am to 7.30 pm. On the 45-minute ride to Angahuan (4.50 pesos) you pass the now-forested stumps of a dozen or two older volcanoes. There are buses back

Volcán Paricutín erupting

from Angahuan to Uruapan up until at least 7.30 pm.

From Angahuan you have various options. (Local guides with ponies wait where the buses stop on the main road, about half a km from the village centre. They have to be gently fended off if you don't want one. If you do want one, you must bargain over the price.) The quickest, easiest option is just to visit the Centro Turístico de Angahuan, a small, low-key accommodation place, often just called 'Las Cabañas', on the edge of the village. Here there is a mirador (lookout point) with good views over the lava field, the protruding San Juan church tower, and the volcano itself. There's also a restaurant and a small exhibition on the volcano and its history. To reach Las Cabañas from the bus stop on the main road, walk into the village centre, turn right at the main plaza, then left after a couple of hundred yards by a building with a TV satellite dish, opposite a shoe shop. From here the track leads straight to Las Cabañas, about 15 minutes' walk.

San Juan church is a half-hour walk down from Las Cabañas. The path is through woods with a few confusing forks, so you need a good sense of direction if you don't have a guide. You can also reach the church direct from the village without visiting Las Cabañas, but again the route is not obvious – a walking guide from the bus stop costs about 15 pesos.

Reaching the Cone A much more exciting option is to go to the top of the volcano. You can do this on foot or by pony. For walkers, a path marked with splashes of white paint crosses the lava field from Las Cabañas to the cone. It takes around three hours – mostly fairly flat but rough going across the moon-scape-like field of jagged solidified lava, with a half-hour ascent of the dusty cone at the end. Coming down takes a bit less time. A walking guide for this route costs 20 to 30 pesos.

Renting a pony and guide to the cone costs around 60 pesos for one person, 90 or 100 pesos for two. The guide will ask for a tip at the end too. The ride is two to three hours

each way, depending on how fast you go. The route skirts the edge of the lava field to the foot of the cone, then you have a half-hour scramble to the top on foot. You can detour to San Juan church on the way up or the way back.

The cone is a spectacular place with wisps of steam issuing from the crater and the still-warm earth around the rim. You can return to the horses in two exhilarating minutes by running down a steep dust slope.

Angahuan Angahuan itself is worth a stop on your way through. It's a typical Purépecha village with characteristic wooden houses, dusty streets, little electricity, and loudspeakers booming out announcements in the Purépecha language. On the main plaza is the 16th-century Iglesia de Santiago Apostol, with some fine carving around its door, done by a Moorish stonemason who accompanied the early Spanish missionaries here. Around to the right of the church, a couple of doors back from the plaza, there's an interesting modern wooden door, carved with the story of Paricutín.

Festival days in Angahuan are the Fiesta de San Isidro Labrador on 15 May, with a weaving contest, and the Fiesta de Santiago Apostol on 25 July, with handicraft displays, music, contests and games.

Places to Stay & Eat The *Centro Turístico de Angahuan* has eight clean cabañas (cabins) of various sizes, each with a living room and fireplace, plus a trailer park and campsite, and a restaurant with decent regional food. The smallest cabaña, for two people, costs 20 pesos a night; a six-person cabaña is 90 pesos; others sleep up to 24 people. You can make reservations by calling Angahuan's public telephone office on (452) 5-03-83, or through the tourist office in Uruapan.

Local guides may be able to offer you accommodation in a village house at around 10 pesos per person (meals extra). There are one or two small restaurants and shops around the village centre.

ZAMORA

• *pop: 110,000*

Zamora, about 150 km west of Morelia, 115 km north-west of Uruapan and 190 km south-east of Guadalajara, is the centre for a rich agricultural region known for its strawberries. You'll probably pass this way if you're travelling between Michoacán and Jalisco. It's a pleasant town to stroll around in, founded in 1574, with a curious unfinished cathedral, the **Catedral Inconclusa**. Fifteen km south-east of Zamora, a short distance off highway 15 at Tangancícuaro, is the clear, spring-fed, tree-shaded **Lago de Camécuaro**, a lovely spot for drivers to stop for a swim and picnic. If you need to spend the night in Zamora, there's a range of hotels to choose from. The bus station is on the outskirts of town. Primera Plus runs six deluxe buses a day from Uruapan (2½ hours, 17 pesos) and Galeana has 2nd-class service every 15 minutes.

Inland Colima

The tiny (5191 sq km) state of Colima ranges from towering volcanoes on its northern fringes to tropical lagoons near the Pacific coast. The climate is equally diverse with heat and humidity along the coast and cooler temperatures in the highlands. This section deals with the upland three-quarters of the state: the narrow coastal plain, with the beach resorts of Manzanillo, Cuyutlán and Paraíso, is covered in the Central Pacific Coast chapter.

Colima, the state capital, is a small and little-touristed but pleasant and interesting semi-tropical city. Overlooking it from the north are two spectacular volcanoes – the active, constantly steaming Volcán de Fuego de Colima (3960 metres) and the extinct snow-capped Volcán Nevado de Colima (4330 metres). Both can be reached relatively easily if you have a taste for adventure and a not-too-tight budget.

Colima state's most important agricultural products are coconuts, lemons, bananas and other fruits. The largest part of the industrial sector is mining, with one of Mexico's richest iron deposits near Minatitlán.

History

Pre-Hispanic Colima was remote from the major ancient cultures of Mexico. Seaborne contacts with more distant places may have been more important and there's even a legend that one king of Colima, Ix, had regular treasure-bearing visitors from China.

Colima certainly produced some remarkable pottery, which has been found in over 250 sites, mainly tombs, dating from roughly 200 BC to 800 AD around the small state. It includes a variety of human figures, often quite comical and admirably expressive of emotion and movement. Best known are the rotund figures of hairless dogs, known as Izcuintlis, a totem of the indigenous peoples who lived here. In some ancient Mexican cultures dogs were buried with their owners as they were believed able to carry the dead to paradise. The dogs also had a more mundane function: the reason they are always fat is that they were force-fed as an important part of the indigenous diet!

Archaeologists have inferred that the makers of this pottery lived in small agricultural settlements spread around the state. The type of grave in which much of the pottery was found, the shaft tomb, does not occur in Mexico outside the four western states of Colima, Michoacán, Jalisco and Nayarit, but it does occur in Panama and South America, which suggests possible seaborne contacts with places much further south.

When the Spanish reached Mexico, Colima was the leading force in the four-kingdom Chimalhuacán Indian confederation that dominated Colima and areas of Jalisco and Nayarit beyond the ambit of the Tarascans (Purépecha) of Michoacán. Two Spanish expeditions were defeated by the Colimans before Gonzalo de Sandoval, one of Cortés's chief lieutenants, conquered them in 1523. The same year he founded the town of Colima – the third Spanish town in New Spain, after Veracruz and Mexico City. The town was moved to its present site, from

WESTERN CENTRAL HIGHLANDS

its unhealthy original location at Caxitlán, in 1527.

The Spanish practically destroyed the indigenous people's way of life, displacing their authorities, their religions, and their cultures with their centuries-old roots.

COLIMA
• *pop: 145,000* • *alt: 492 metres*

Colima lives at the mercy of the forces of nature. Volcán de Fuego de Colima, clearly visible 25 km to the north (along with the taller but extinct Nevado de Colima), has erupted nine times in the past four centuries and is expected to do so again by the year 2010. Even more dangerous, the city has been hit by a series of violent earthquakes over the centuries – the most recent major one was in 1941 – which is why, although Colima was the first Spanish city in western Mexico, there are few colonial buildings left today.

Today it's a pleasant, small-scale city, graced by palm trees, lying on a fertile plain surrounded by hills and mountains. Not many tourists come here, but there are a number of interesting things to see and do in town and in the surrounding farmland. Though only 45 km from the coast, Colima is at a higher elevation and, consequently, is cooler and less humid. The rainy months are July to September.

Orientation
Central Colima spreads around three plazas, with the Plaza Principal (also known as the Jardín Libertad) at the centre of things. The Jardín Quintero lies a block east, behind the cathedral, and three blocks further east is the Jardín Núñez. Street names change at the Plaza Principal.

The shiny modern main bus terminal is about two km east of the centre, beside the Guadalajara-Manzanillo road.

Information
Tourist Office The state tourist office (☎ (331) 2-43-60, ☎ /fax 2-83-60) is at Portal Hidalgo 20 on the west side of the Plaza Principal. Look for the big 'Turismo'

sign over the door. The office is open Monday to Friday from 8.30 am to 3 pm and 5 to 9 pm, Saturday and Sunday 9 am to 1.30 pm, and has free maps, brochures and information on the city and state of Colima.

Money There are a number of banks around the centre where you can change money; they are open Monday to Friday from 9 am to 1 or 1.30 pm. Banamex on Hidalgo a block east of the cathedral has an ATM.

Majapara Casa de Cambio at the southwest corner of Jardín Núñez gives a rate similar to the banks and is open better hours: Monday to Friday from 9 am to 2 pm and 4.30 to 6.30 pm, Saturday 9 am to 2 pm.

Post & Telecommunications The post office is at Madero 247 at the north-east corner of Jardín Núñez – open Monday to Friday 8 am to 7 pm, Saturday 8 am to noon.

The Telecomm office, with telegram, telex and fax services, is one door to the left of the post office. It's open Monday to Friday from 9 am to 8 pm, Saturday 9 am to 1 pm.

Several Ladatel coin and card phones are dotted along Madero between the Plaza Principal and Jardín Núñez. There are also three Computel offices with Lada casetas. Those at Morelos 236, facing Jardín Núñez, and at Medellín 55 near the corner of Hidalgo, have fax service too; the one at the bus station has telephone only. All three are open every day from 7 am to 10 pm.

Laundry Lavandería Victoria at Victoria 131 between Ocampo and De la Vega, a blue building with no sign out front, charges 2 pesos for washing 3 kg of laundry if you do it yourself, 3 pesos if you drop it off to be washed only, or 6 pesos for wash, dry and fold. It's open Monday to Saturday from 7 am to 2 pm and 3 to 8 pm.

Around Plaza Principal
The **Cathedral**, the Santa Iglesia, on the east side of the Plaza Principal, has been rebuilt several times since the Spanish first erected a cathedral here in 1527. The most recent

reconstruction dates from just after the 1941 earthquake.

Next to the cathedral is the **Palacio de Gobierno**, built between 1884 and 1904. Local artist Jorge Chávez Carrillo painted the murals on the stairway, depicting Mexican history from the Spanish conquest to independence, to celebrate the 200th anniversary of the birth of independence hero Miguel Hidalgo, who was once parish priest of Colima.

The **Museo de Historia de Colima**, on the south side of the plaza, is worth a visit to see its ceramic vessels and figurines, mostly people and Izcuintli dogs, unearthed in Colima state. There are also permanent displays of masks, textiles, costumes, basketry, shellwork from the Colima coast, and temporary exhibits. The museum is open Tuesday to Sunday from 10 am to 2 pm and 4 to 8 pm; admission is free. Next door is the **Sala de Exposiciones de la Universidad de Colima**, with changing art exhibitions; it's open the same hours as the museum (free).

The **Teatro Hidalgo** on the corner of Degollado and Independencia, one block south of the Plaza Principal, was built in neoclassical style between 1871 and 1883 on a site originally donated to the city by Miguel Hidalgo. The theatre was destroyed by the earthquakes of 1932 and 1941, with reconstruction undertaken in 1942.

Casa de la Cultura & Museo de las Culturas de Occidente

This large, modern cultural centre for the state of Colima is at the intersection of Calzada Galván and Ejército Nacional, a little over one km north-east of the centre.

The chief attraction is the **Museo de las Culturas de Occidente** (Museum of Western Cultures), fronting Ejército Nacional. Here in a well-lit building are exhibited hundreds of pre-Hispanic ceramic vessels and figurines from Colima state, with explanations in Spanish. Most famous and impressive are the human figures and fat Izcuintli dogs, but there's a wide variety of other figures including musical instruments,

mammals, reptiles, fish and birds, some of which still exist in the area and others which have now disappeared. The museum is open Tuesday to Sunday from 9 am to 7 pm (free).

The site's administrative building (☎ 2-31-55, 2-84-31), open every day from 9 am to 9 pm, has a permanent exhibition of the renowned Colima modernistic painter Alfonso Michel (1897-1957) and sometimes high-quality temporary art exhibits. The 800-seat **Teatro Casa de la Cultura** adjoins this building. There's a café on the ground floor of the **Edificio de Talleres** (Workshops Building) next door. Also on the site is the **Biblioteca Central del Estado**, the state library. Half a block away, the Cine Teatro USI presents cultural film series.

Museo Universitario de Culturas Populares

The University Museum of Popular Cultures is in the Instituto Universitario de Bellas Artes (IUBA), on the corner of 27 de Septiembre and Manuel Gallardo, about 900 metres north of the Plaza Principal. It displays folk art from Colima and other states, with a particularly good section of costumes and masks used in traditional dances in Colima. Other exhibits include textiles, ceramics, musical instruments and furniture. Hours are Monday to Saturday from 9 am to 2 pm and 4 to 7 pm; holidays 9 am to 2 pm; Sunday closed. Admission is free.

Also at IUBA is the interesting **Taller de Reproducciones**, just inside the gate and to your right, where you can see the process of reproducing ancient Coliman ceramic figures. In the museum foyer is a shop with inexpensive handicrafts from Colima and elsewhere, including Izcuintli dogs and other figures made in the Taller de Reproducciones.

Parks

The **Parque Regional Metropolitano** on Degollado, a few blocks south-west of the centre, has a small zoo, a swimming pool, an open-air theatre and a forest section with an artificial lake and rowing boats.

Parque Piedra Lisa, east of the centre on Calzada Galván, is named after its famous

Sliding Stone, which you'll see when you enter the park from the traffic circle at the intersection of Calzada Galván and Aldama. Legend says that visitors who slide on this stone will return to Colima some day.

Festivals

A number of colourful masked dances are enacted at fiestas in Colima state: the Museo Universitario de Culturas Populares has a good display of the costumes and information on their where, when and why. The following festivals take place in or very near Colima city.

Ferias Charro-Taurinas San Felipe de Jesús This festival, celebrated in honour of the Virgen de la Candelaria (whose day is 2 February), takes place in Villa de Álvarez, about five km north of the city centre. Each day of the festival except Tuesday and Friday, a large group rides from Colima's cathedral to Villa de Álvarez preceded by giant *mojigangos*, figures of the village's mayor and wife, followed by musical groups. When they arrive at Villa de Álvarez the celebrations continue with food, music, dancing, rodeos and bullfights; late January and early February

Feria de Todos los Santos Also called the Feria de Colima, the Colima state fair includes agricultural and handicraft exhibitions, cultural events, funfairs and bullfights; late October and early November

Día de la Virgen de Guadalupe Women and children dress in pretty regional costume to pay homage at the Virgin's altar in the cathedral. In the evenings the Jardín Quintero behind the cathedral fills with busy food stalls; around 1 to 12 December

Places to Stay – bottom end

If you're on a tight budget there are two places to try. One is the little family-run *Casa de Huéspedes* (☎ (331) 2-34-67) at Morelos 265, near the south-east corner of Jardín Núñez. It has 12 guest rooms; those with common bath cost 20/30 pesos for singles/doubles, those with private bath 25/40 pesos. If you arrive early in the day your room might not be cleaned until evening, but the people are friendly. There's a small interior garden full of flowers and plants.

The other cheapie is the *Hotel Núñez* (☎ (331) 2-70-30) nearby at Juárez 88, on the west side of Jardín Núñez. It's an old, basic place, but tolerable for a night or two. The 32 rooms around two courtyards have no windows, so they tend to be stuffy, but they have fans and are kept clean. Rooms with shared baths (which are OK) cost 25 pesos: there are also rooms with private bath at 40 pesos, though these are mostly on the noisier first courtyard.

A big step up in quality is the *Hotel La Merced* (☎ (331) 2-69-69) at Hidalgo 188, half a block west of Jardín Núñez. This is a recently opened small hotel in a modernised old building. All rooms have private bath and fan, and most are around an open courtyard. Singles are 50 pesos, doubles 60 pesos with one bed, 70 pesos with two beds. The rooms are cool and pleasant and have good showers. Those with two beds are a very good size.

Hotel Flamingos (☎ (331) 2-25-25, 2-25-26) at Avenida Rey Colimán 18, half a block south of Jardín Núñez, has the same prices but less character. Its 56 clean, modern rooms with bath and fan all have full-wall windows and balconies, good for catching the breeze. Those on the upper floors offer a bit of a view over the town and the surrounding mountains; those on the side away from the street are much quieter. There's a restaurant on the ground floor.

Places to Stay – middle

Hotel Ceballos (☎ (331) 2-44-44, fax 2-06-45) at Portal Medellín 12, on the north side of the Plaza Principal, is a stately building, dating from 1880, which has been the home of three state governors. Many of the 63 clean, pleasant high-ceilinged rooms have French windows opening on small balconies. Most have air-con and cost 125 pesos for one or two people. A few with fan are 70 pesos.

More modern is the *Hotel América* (☎ (331) 2-74-88, 2-95-96, fax 4-44-25) at Morelos 162, half a block west of Jardín Núñez. Its 75 rooms, all air-con, come with high wood-beamed ceilings, colour TV etc; facilities also include steam baths, swimming pool, restaurant, laundry and parking. Rates are 170 pesos for one or two people.

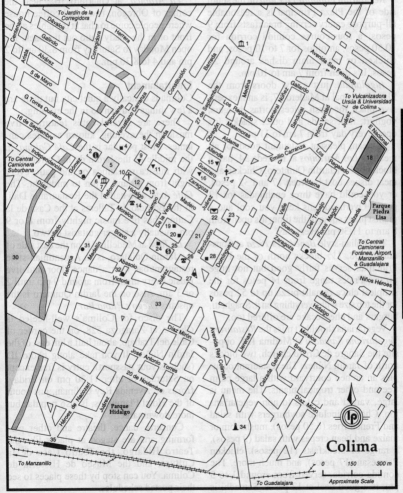

PLACES TO STAY

4 Hotel Ceballos
19 Hotel La Merced
20 Hotel Núñez
24 Hotel América
27 Hotel Flamingos
28 Casa de Huéspedes

PLACES TO EAT

6 Restaurant Familiar La Plata
8 Benedetti's Pizza
9 Jugolandia
11 Los Naranjos
15 Restaurant Vegetariano Samadhi
16 La Arábica
23 Centro de Nutrición Lakshmi

OTHER

1 Museo Universitario de Culturas Populares
2 Tourist Office
3 Teatro Hidalgo
5 Plaza Principal (Jardín Libertad)
7 Museo de Historia de Colima
10 Catedral & Palacio de Gobierno
12 Jardín Quintero
13 La Taba
14 Computel
17 Sangre de Cristo Church
18 Casa de la Cultura & Museo de las Culturas de Occidente
21 Jardín Núñez
22 Post Office & Telecomm
25 Majapara Casa de Cambio
26 Computel
29 Cheers Disco
30 Parque Regional Metropolitano
31 Mercado Constitución
32 Lavandería Victoria
33 Jardín Juárez
34 Monument to Rey Colimán
35 Train Station

Colima

0   150   300 m

Approximate Scale

To Jardín de la Corregidora
To Central Camionera Suburbana
To Vulcanizadora Ursúa & Universidad de Colima
Parque Piedra Lisa
To Central Camionera Foránea, Airport, Manzanillo & Guadalajara
Parque Hidalgo
To Manzanillo
To Guadalajara

Places to Eat

For a simple meal or snack there are many small restaurants and cafés around the Plaza Principal. Some offer cold drinks, ice cream and frozen paletas (ice lollies), welcome in this warm climate; *Nevería La Flor de Michoacán* on one corner of the plaza has a good selection, and it's open every day from 8 am to 10 pm.

Restaurant Familiar La Plata on the south side of the Plaza Principal is a reasonable all-purpose eatery serving breakfasts from 9 pesos, a four-course comida corrida for 10.50 pesos, antojitos for 7 to 10 pesos, and chicken or meat main dishes around 20 pesos. It's open from 7 am to 10 pm.

Jugolandia, just a few doors from the Plaza Principal at Madero 17, is an inexpensive place for fresh juices, tortas, burgers, yoghurt, fruit salads and other snacks. It's open every day from 7 am to 11 pm.

A clean, pleasant restaurant good for all meals is *Los Naranjos* at Barreda 34, half a block north of Jardín Quintero. Chicken and meat dishes cost between 17 and 32 pesos, or you could have three enchiladas for 12 pesos. Overhead fans keep you cool and a pianist plays some of the time; it's open from 8 am to 11.30 pm every day.

The Italian-style *Benedetti's Pizza* at Constitución 58, 1½ blocks north of the Plaza Principal, serves fairly good but not huge pizzas. Prices range from 14 pesos for the simplest chica (small) pizza up to 52 pesos for the top size with everything on it. Spaghetti, burgers and cheesecake are offered too.

Vegetarians shouldn't miss the *Restaurant Vegetariano Samadhi* at Medina 125, opposite the Sangre de Cristo church, two blocks north of Jardín Núñez. The restaurant occupies an arched courtyard with a large palm tree and other tropical plants. The menu is large, varied and caters to non-vegetarians too. Choices include soyburgers with salad and French fries (6.50 pesos), mushroom or maize and bean crepes with salad (9 pesos), a range of breakfasts (12 pesos), chicken Parmesan (17 pesos), and much more. The comida corrida, served from around 1 to 3 pm, is a good deal at 12 pesos. Samadhi is

open from 8 am to 10 pm every day, except Thursday when it closes at 5 pm.

Centro de Nutrición Lakshmi is also near Jardín Núñez, at Madero 265. It includes a wholegrain bakery, a section with vitamins and health products, and a restaurant section serving soyburgers, flavoured yoghurts and fruit salads. It's open Monday to Saturday from 8.30 am to 9.30 pm, Sunday 6 to 9.30 pm.

La Arábica, at Guerrero 162, near the corner of Obregón, is a small coffee house where people come to chat at the tables at the front or in the shady patio out the back. It's open Monday to Saturday from 8.30 am to 2 pm and 4 to 8.30 pm.

Entertainment

Colima is basically a quiet city but there are a few things you can do in the evening.

There are several cafés featuring live music in the evening, known as cafés cantantes. Most popular is the *Café Colima*, in the middle of the Jardín de la Corregidora, with música romántica on the patio every night from around 9 pm to midnight. The *Café Arte*, also called the Restaurante Dali, in the Edificio de Talleres at the Casa de la Cultura has live music nightly from 8 or 9 pm – usually a singer-guitarist or two.

La Taba at Medellín 11, on the east side of the Jardín Quintero, is an Argentinian-style restaurant/bar with a dance floor and live music every night from around 9 pm until 2 or 3 am. Also on the Jardín Quintero is the upstairs *Diego's Piano Bar*.

The disco for Colima's well-heeled is *Cheers*, at Zaragoza 528, on the corner of Calle del Trabajo, about half a km east of the Jardín Núñez. If you take along photo ID (such as your passport), entry is free except on Saturday or after 11.30 pm on Friday. *Horus* on Avenida Rey Colimán, just south of the Hotel Flamingos, is also popular but more downmarket.

Concerts, dance, theatre and other performing arts are staged at places like the Teatro Hidalgo, the Teatro Casa de la Cultura, and the Museo de Historia de Colima. You can stop by these places to see their posted schedules.

Things to Buy

Tienda de Artesanías DIF, a block north of the Plaza Principal on the corner of Constitución and Zaragoza, has a good range of Colima handicrafts including attractive reproductions of Izcuintli dogs (39 pesos for small ones, 90 pesos for larger ones or a dancing pair). Izcuintlis and other artesanías are also sold at the Museo Universitario de Culturas Populares.

The main market is the Mercado Constitución, on Calle Reforma three blocks south of the Plaza Principal.

Getting There & Away

Air Aeromar (☎ 3-13-40 at the airport) and Aero California both fly daily to/from Mexico City, with onward connections. Aero California also has daily flights to/from Tijuana. Avitesa travel agency (☎ 2-19-84, 2-69-70, fax 2-69-80) on the corner of Constitución and Zaragoza, a block north of the Plaza Principal, can make flight arrangements, and they speak English. They're open Monday to Friday from 8.30 am to 7 pm, Saturday 9 am to 2 pm.

Bus Colima has two bus stations. The main long-distance terminal is the Central Camionera Foránea, two km from the centre at the meeting of Avenida Niños Héroes and the city's eastern by-pass. At the station are Ladatel credit card and telephone card phones, a Lada caseta, a pharmacy, and various restaurants and snack shops. Daily departures from here include:

Guadalajara – 220 km, 2½ to three hours; several deluxe buses each by ETN, La Línea Plus and Primera Plus (35 to 45 pesos); several 1st-class each by La Línea, Omnibus de México, Servicos Coordinados and Tres Estrellas de Oro (27 to 33 pesos)

Manzanillo – 101 km, 1½ hours; several deluxe buses each by ETN, La Línea Plus and Primera Plus (14 to 20 pesos); several 1st-class each by La Línea, Servicos Coordinados and Tres Estrellas de Oro (11 or 12 pesos); 54 2nd-class via Tecomán and Armería (two hours) by Autotransportes del Sur de Jalisco (7.50 pesos)

Mexico City (Terminal Norte) – 740 km, 11 hours; a few deluxe buses by ETN, Tres Estrellas de Oro and Primera Plus (102 to 155 pesos); a few 1st-class by Servicios Coordinados, Tres Estrellas de Oro and Omnibus de México (83 to 96 pesos); seven 2nd-class by Autobuses de Occidente (77 pesos)

There's also frequent service to Ciudad Guzmán and 10 buses a day to Morelia by various companies, one to Melaque by Tres Estrellas de Oro (1st-class), and three to Lázaro Cárdenas and one to Uruapan by Autobuses de Occidente (2nd-class).

The second bus station is the Central Camionera Suburbana, also known as the Terminal Suburbana, about 1.5 km south-west of the Plaza Principal on the Carretera a Coquimatlán. This is the place to come for buses to Comala and other places close to Colima, and for 2nd-class Autobuses Colima-Manzanillo which goes to Manzanillo every 30 minutes (8 pesos, 1½ hours), Tecomán every 15 minutes (3.50 pesos) and Armería every 30 minutes (4 pesos).

Train The Estación del Ferrocarril (☎ 2-92-50) is about 10 blocks south of the Jardín Quintero down Medellín. There's one daily 2nd-class train in each direction. Train No 91, departing at 8 am, takes about five hours to Guadalajara (12 pesos). Train No 92, departing at 3 pm, takes two hours to Manzanillo (4.30 pesos).

Tickets go on sale half an hour before the actual arrival of the train. Schedules may vary; check at the station.

Getting Around

To/From the Airport Colima's airport is near Cuauhtémoc, about 12 km north-east of the city centre off the highway to Guadalajara. A taxi to/from the centre is about 25 pesos.

Bus & Taxi Local buses (0.80 pesos) run every day from 6 am to 9.30 pm. Ruta 4A and Ruta 5 buses from the main bus station will take you to the city centre: returning to the bus station you can catch Ruta 4A on 5 de Mayo or Zaragoza, or Ruta 5 on Bravo south of the Jardín Núñez. To reach the

Central Camionera Suburbana, take a Ruta 2 or Ruta 4 bus west along Morelos.

Taxis are plentiful. The maximum fare around the city – from the bus station into town, for example – is 4 pesos.

AROUND COLIMA
Comala

A small, picturesque, whitewashed town of 8000 people nine km north of Colima, Comala is known for its fine handicrafts, especially carved wood furniture, and as a popular weekend outing from Colima. On Sunday and Monday there are markets to browse in.

You can see Comala furniture being made at the Sociedad Cooperativa Artesanías Pueblo Blanco, which is renowned for its colonial-style handcarved furniture, wood paintings and ironwork. The centre is one km south of town, just off the road to Colima: it's open Monday to Friday from 9 am to 6 pm, Saturday 9 am to 2 pm.

There's a simple but beautiful church on the plaza, which has a fine white gazebo and trees blooming with brilliant yellow flowers. Under the arches along one side of the plaza are some attractive sidewalk cafés, open from 11 am or noon to 6 pm, with a delightful tradition: when you order something to drink, they bring you all the *botanas* (snacks of regional food) you can eat. Many people come to Comala just to enjoy these restaurants. There are more restaurants on the Colima road at the edge of Comala.

Comala buses leave Colima's Central Camionera Suburbana about every 10 minutes; fare is 1.50 pesos for the 15-minute ride. In Comala, the buses back to Colima depart from the plaza.

Suchitlán

The Indian village of Suchitlán, eight km north-east of Comala, is famous for its animal masks. These are carved in the village and worn by the dancers in the traditional Danza de los Morenos which takes place here during Semana Santa. The dance commemorates a legend that dancing animals enabled the Marys to rescue Christ's body by distracting the Roman guards. Masks and other crafts are sold in Suchitlán's Sunday tianguis. There are several restaurants in the village. There are buses to Suchitlán from the Central Camionera Suburbana in Colima.

San Antonio & La María

About 15 km north of Suchitlán the paved road ends at the Ex-Hacienda de San Antonio, a 19th-century coffee finca now converted to an elegant hotel, with large grounds crossed by a stone aqueduct, and fine views of the Volcán de Fuego de Colima towering some 10 km to the north.

A gravel road continues from San Antonio to La María, about 10 minutes' drive to the east. There's a lovely lake, the Laguna La María, here, which is a popular weekend picnic and camping spot, and a few cabins with equipped kitchens costing 84 to 96 pesos for four to six people. You can book the cabins at the Avitesa travel agency in Colima (see Getting There & Away – Air in the Colima section).

A few buses run daily from Colima's Central Camionera Suburbana to San Antonio – those saying 'La Becerra' or 'Zapotitlán' will probably go there, but check. From San Antonio you must walk to La María if you don't have a vehicle.

Volcán de Fuego de Colima & Nevado de Colima

These two dramatic mountains overlook Colima from the north. The nearer, the steaming Volcán de Fuego de Colima (3960 metres), is about 30 km from the city as the crow flies. Most of the Volcán de Fuego, including its crater, and all of the more northerly and higher, but extinct, Nevado de Colima (4330 metres) are in Jalisco state. If you have the time and energy and a taste for a bit of adventure, either mountain would make a great trip from Colima.

The Volcán de Fuego de Colima is Mexico's most active volcano, having erupted about 30 times in the past four centuries. Its activity appears to come in cycles lasting 40 to 70 years. A major eruption in 1913 spelled the end of one cycle of activity, but another

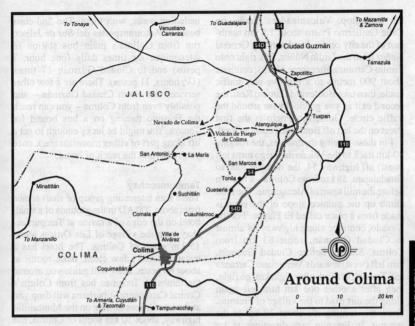

began in the 1960s and is still going on. Vulcanologists at Colima University expect an explosive eruption by about 2010.

Ascending the Volcanoes Pine forests cover most of the Nevado but peter out at a lower altitude on the Volcán de Fuego. Most of the year it's possible to get within a couple of hours' walk of the summit of either mountain by vehicle. The track up the Nevado is rough but reckoned to be passable for an ordinary car unless the weather has been particularly wet. The Volcán de Fuego track is in poor condition and impassable even for 4WD vehicles after the July to September/October rains: it's also closed when the volcano is considered dangerous. The Colima tourist office can advise on this. The nearest you can get by bus is about 40 km from the summit of Nevado de Colima or about 30 km from the top of Volcán de Fuego de Colima.

Both peaks are usually snowcapped from December or January to March or April, which makes the final ascent on foot more difficult. The snow may reach a depth of eight metres on the Nevado in December and January.

One possible way of getting up on the volcanoes would be to ask the Departamento de Volcanología in the Rectoría building at the Universidad de Colima (about three km north-east of the city centre): they may have a research vehicle going up the volcanoes that could take you along. Alternatively, if you can afford it, Señor Melchor Ursúa (☎ 2-58-58, 2-03-77), the head of the Colima fire brigade, can provide transport to within a couple of hours' walk of either summit. He'll charge around 500 pesos for a day trip for up to about five people. The drive is 2½ to three hours each way for either mountain; the final ascent on foot then takes about two hours in each case, and the descent about 30 minutes. Señor Ursúa can also rent camping equipment and provide food. During working hours he can normally be found at his workshop, Vulcanizadora Ursúa, on Calle Guillermo Prieto about 1.5 km northeast of the city centre: head north up General Núñez from the Jardín Núñez, fork right onto Emilio Carranza after three blocks, continue about 900 metres to a big five-way traffic circle, then take Boulevard Camino Real, the second exit as you go clockwise around the traffic circle. Guillermo Prieto is the first street on the left off Boulevard Camino Real.

For those driving themselves, the roughly 30-km track to the Volcán de Fuego turns left (west) off highway 54, the non-toll road to Guadalajara, 58 km from Colima – a few km before the mill town of Atenquique. The final climb up the pumice slope of the cone is made from a place called El Playón. For the Nevado, continue along highway 54 almost to Ciudad Guzmán, some 83 km from Colima. Shortly before Ciudad Guzmán, turn left (west) towards Venustiano Carranza and Tonaya; at a fork after eight km, go right, then after another one km turn left again along the dirt road to the village of Fresnito. From this turning it's about 30 km to the summit. In Fresnito, ask directions to La Joya, which is a climbers' cabin on the upper slopes of the Nevado, or Las Antena, a TV transmitting station where the track ends and the final ascent on foot begins, a couple of km past La Joya.

Getting There & Away Those planning to walk up the volcanoes should plan on at least one night up there and take all supplies,

including water, with them. The 2nd-class buses of Autotransportes del Sur de Jalisco run from Colima's main bus station to Atenquique six times daily (one hour, 7 pesos) and to Ciudad Guzmán 17 times (1½ hours, 11 pesos). There are a few other services too. From Ciudad Guzmán – and possibly even from Colima – you can reach the Fresnito turning on a bus bound for Tonaya. You might be lucky enough to get a lift along part of either mountain track once you're beyond the reach of buses.

Tampumacchay

There's an interesting group of shaft tombs from about 200 AD in the grounds of a small hotel on the edge of a ravine at Tampumacchay, near the village of Los Ortices about 15 km south of Colima. The hotel has a restaurant and a few clean, basic rooms at about 80 pesos. Staff will guide you around the tombs. A Tecomán bus from Colima's Central Camionera Suburbana will drop you at the Los Ortices turning on the Manzanillo highway, about 10 km south of Colima, but then you'll have to walk about five km to the hotel unless you happen upon a taxi.

Minatitlán

Minatitlán is an iron-ore mining town 55 km west of Colima. It's on a scenic route through the mountains from Colima to the coast that drivers might consider as an alternative to the main toll road.

Northern Central Highlands

North-west from Mexico City stretches a fairly dry, temperate upland region comprising the southern part of the Altiplano Central between the Sierra Madre Occidental and the Sierra Madre Oriental. This was where the Spanish found most of the silver and other precious metals that were so central to their colonial ambitions in Mexico – and where they built some of the country's most magnificent cities from the great fortunes that silver brought them. The most spectacular of these are Guanajuato and Zacatecas, which along with Potosí in Bolivia were the major silver-producing centres of the Americas. San Miguel de Allende, Querétaro and San Luis Potosí also have a wealth of colonial architecture. Today most of these cities are still of moderate size and have lively arts and entertainment scenes.

This region is less visited than some others south of the capital but highly rewarding if you do come. Overland travellers from the north may well pass through in any case. The distances are not huge and the landscape between the cities is always impressive, with vistas to mountains near or far. The land becomes steadily more fertile as you move south from Zacatecas and San Luis Potosí to the area around Guanajuato and Querétaro known as the Bajío, which has long been one of Mexico's major agricultural zones.

The Bajío is also known to Mexicans as La Cuna de la Independencia (The Cradle of Independence), for it was here that the movement for independence from Spain began in 1810. The town of Dolores Hidalgo, where the uprising started, and nearby places like San Miguel de Allende, Querétaro and Guanajuato are full of key sites from this historic movement.

Before the Spanish reached Mexico, the Northern Central Highlands were inhabited by fierce semi-nomadic Chichimec tribes, who mostly remained outside the ambit of the main pre-Hispanic cultures. They resisted Spanish conquest longer than any

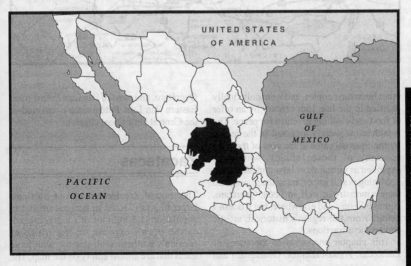

589

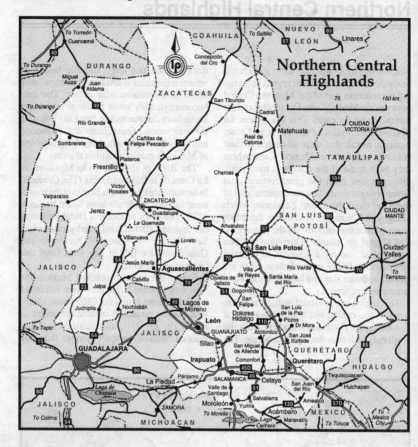

Northern Central Highlands

other Mexican peoples, and were only finally pacified in the late 16th century by an offer of food and clothing in return for peace. The wealth subsequently amassed in the region by the Spanish came at the cost of the lives of many of these Indians, who were exploited as virtual slave labour in the mines.

Mining is still important in the region, and there's industry as well, in León, Querétaro, Aguascalientes and elsewhere, but it doesn't detract from the region's historical, artistic and scenic attractions.

This chapter encompasses the states of Zacatecas, Aguascalientes, Guanajuato and

Querétaro, and most of San Luis Potosí state. Eastern San Luis Potosí state is covered in the Central Gulf Coast chapter.

Zacatecas

The state of Zacatecas is one of Mexico's larger in area (73,252 sq km) but smaller in population (1.3 million). It's a dry, rugged, cactus-strewn expanse on the fringe of Mexico's northern semi-deserts, with large tracts that are almost empty on the map. The fact that it has any significant population at all is largely due to the mineral wealth the Spanish discovered here, centred mainly around the capital city Zacatecas. Today there are still over 100 mines of various kinds in the state, and it remains Mexico's biggest silver producer.

ZACATECAS

• *pop: 195,000* • *alt: 2445 metres*

If you've come from the north, welcome to the first of Mexico's justly fabled silver cities. If you've been visiting more southerly silver cities like Guanajuato, don't hesitate to journey a few hours further, as Zacatecas is particularly beautiful and fascinating.

Some of Mexico's finest colonial buildings, including perhaps its most stunning cathedral, all built from the riches of the local silver mines, cluster along narrow, winding streets at the foot of a spectacular rock-topped hill called Cerro de la Bufa. Set amid dry, arid country, this historic city has much to detain you, from trips into an old silver mine to some excellent museums and the ascent of la Bufa itself by teleférico. A state capital and university city, Zacatecas is surprisingly sophisticated for its size – and it's all the more to be appreciated for its off-centre location and consequent lack of tourists.

History

Before the Spanish arrived, the area was inhabited by Zacateco Indians, one of the wild northern tribes known to the Aztecs as Chichimecs. Indians in the region had mined mineral deposits centuries before the Spanish arrived, and it's said that the silver rush here was started by an Indian giving a piece of the fabled metal to a conquistador.

The Spaniards founded a settlement and starting mining operations, virtually enslaving many Indians in the process, in 1548. Caravan after caravan of silver was sent off to Mexico City. While some treasure-laden wagons were raided by the Indians, enough silver reached its destination to create fabulously wealthy silver barons. Agriculture and ranching developed to serve the rapidly growing town.

In the first quarter of the 18th century, Zacatecas' mines were producing 20% of New Spain's silver. At this time too the city became an important base for missionaries spreading Catholicism to north-western New Spain – as far as the modern south-western states of the USA.

In the 19th century political events somewhat diminished the flow of silver as various forces fought to control the city. In 1871, Benito Juárez decisively defeated local rebels here. Although silver production later improved under Porfirio Díaz, the revolution disrupted it. Here in 1914 Pancho Villa, through brilliant tactics, defeated a stronghold of 12,000 soldiers loyal to the unpopular President Victoriano Huerta.

After the revolution, Zacatecas continued to thrive due to silver. To this day it remains a mining centre, with the 200-year-old El Bote mine still productive.

Orientation

The city centre lies in a valley between Cerro de la Bufa, with its strange rocky cap, to the north-east, and the smaller Cerro del Grillo to the north-west. Most places of interest and places to stay are within walking distance of each other. There are two key streets in the central area. One is Avenida Hidalgo, running roughly north-south, with the cathedral towards its north end. The other is Avenida Juárez, running roughly east-west across the south end of Avenida Hidalgo. When you get lost, as you inevitably will, just ask the way back to one of these two streets. Avenida Hidalgo becomes Avenida González Ortega at its intersection with Juárez.

Information

Tourist Office The tourist office (☎ (492) 4-03-93, 4-05-52) is easy to find; it's opposite the cathedral at Avenida Hidalgo 601. Some of the helpful staff speak English and they have plenty of brochures on Zacatecas' attractions (although these are in Spanish). The office is open daily from 8 am to 8 pm.

Money There are several banks on Hidalgo between the cathedral and Juárez. You may find the best exchange rates at Multibanco Comermex next to the Teatro Calderón. Banks are open Monday to Friday, 9 am to 1.30 pm, though some have more limited hours for currency exchange. Banamex on Hidalgo opposite the Café Zas has an ATM.

Post & Telecommunications The post office is at Allende 111, just east of Hidalgo. Its hours are Monday to Friday from 8 am to 7 pm and Saturday 9 am to noon.

The Telecomm office on Hidalgo on the corner of Juárez, open Monday to Friday 9 am to 8 pm and Saturday 9 am to 12.30 pm, offers a public fax service. There's also a fax service in the bus station.

There are Ladatel coin and credit-card phones at the entrance to the Mercado González Ortega, and Lada casetas in the bus station and the Casa Jaquez shop on Avenida Hidalgo almost opposite the Café Zas.

Laundry Lavandería El Indio Triste at Hidalgo 824, opposite the corner of Villalpando, does a service wash for 4.20 pesos per kg.

Cathedral
Zacatecas' pink stone cathedral is a real masterpiece of Mexican architecture. Built chiefly between 1729 and 1752, it's one of the ultimate expressions of Mexican baroque, created just before baroque edged into its final Churrigueresque phase. In this city of affluent silver barons no expense was spared. The highlight is the stupendous main façade facing Avenida Hidalgo, the whole of which is encrusted with amazingly detailed yet harmonious carving. This façade has been interpreted as a giant symbol of the tabernacle, the receptacle for the wafer and wine which confer the communion with God that is at the heart of Catholic worship. A tiny figure of an angel holding a tabernacle can be seen at the heart of the design, on the keystone at the top of the round central window. Above this, at the centre of the third tier, is Christ, and above Christ is God. The other main statues are the 12 apostles, while

a smaller figure of the Virgin Mary stands immediately above the centre of the doorway.

The south and north façades, though simpler, are also very fine. The central sculpture on the southern façade is of La Virgen de los Zacatecas, the city's patroness. The north façade shows Christ crucified, attended by the Virgin Mary and St John.

The interior of the cathedral is today disarmingly plain compared to the exterior, though it was once adorned with elaborate gold and silver ornaments and festooned with tapestries and paintings. This wealth was plundered in the course of Zacatecas' turbulent history.

Plaza de Armas
The open space on the north side of the cathedral is called the Plaza de Armas. The **Palacio de Gobierno** on the plaza's east side was built in the 18th century for a family of colonial gentry, and acquired by the state in the 19th century. In the turret of its main staircase is a mural of the history of Zacatecas state, painted in 1970 by Antonio Rodríguez.

The fine white-painted **Palacio de la Mala Noche** on the west side of the plaza, built in the late 18th century for the owner of the Mala Noche mine near Zacatecas, houses state government offices.

Mercado González Ortega
South of the cathedral, between Hidalgo and Tacuba, is the impressive iron-columned 1880s building which used to hold Zacatecas' main market. It replaced earlier market sites on and near the same spot. In the 1980s the upper level of the market, entered from Hidalgo, was renovated into an upscale shopping centre complete with restaurants.

Teatro Calderón
Also dating from the Porfiriato period is the Teatro Calderón, across Avenida Hidalgo from the south end of the Mercado González Ortega. This lovely theatre, built in the 1890s, is as busy as ever staging plays, concerts, films and art exhibitions.

Northern Central Highlands
Top: Statue of Pancho Villa (JL)
Bottom: Shopping in Zacatecas (JL)
Right: Boy, Real de Catorce (PP)

Northern Central Highlands
Top: On the road to Real de Catorce (PP)
Bottom: Guanajuato balconies (PP)

Templo de Santo Domingo

Santo Domingo Church dominates the Plazuela de Santo Domingo, reached from the Plaza de Armas by a narrow lane called Callejón de Veyna. The church is in a more sober baroque style than the cathedral. Inside, however, are some fine gilded altars and paintings, and a graceful horseshoe staircase. Built by the Jesuits in the 1740s, the church was taken over by Dominican monks when the Jesuits were expelled from New Spain in 1767, and became the city's second most important church (after the cathedral).

Museo Pedro Coronel

The Pedro Coronel Museum is housed in a 17th-century former Jesuit college beside Santo Domingo. Pedro Coronel (1923-85) was an affluent Zacatecan artist who bequeathed to his home town this collection of his own art and of artefacts from all over the world. Coronel amassed art from Asia, Africa, and ancient Mexico, Rome, Greece and Egypt as well as works by Hogarth, Goya, Picasso, Roualt, Chagall, Kandinsky and Miró. It all adds up to one of provincial Mexico's best art museums – open from 10 am to 2 pm and 4 to 7 pm on Monday, Tuesday, Wednesday, Friday and Saturday, and 10 am to 5 pm on Sunday (closed Thursday). But, unfortunately for those who would like to linger over some of the exhibits, visits are only by guided tour in Spanish. The cost is 10 pesos.

Calle Dr Hierro & Calle Miguel Auza

Calle Dr Hierro, leading south from Plazuela de Santo Domingo, and its continuation Calle Miguel Auza, are quiet, narrow streets. About 150 metres from Plazuela de Santo Domingo is the **Casa de Moneda**, which housed the Zacatecas mint (Mexico's second biggest) during the 19th century. A further 100 metres south is the **Ex-Templo de San Agustín**, built as a church for Augustinian monks in the 17th century. During the anticlerical movement of the 19th century, the church was turned into a casino. Then, in 1882, it was bought by American Presbyterian missionaries who destroyed its 'too-Catholic' main façade, now a blank white wall. In the 20th century the church returned to Catholic use and its adjoining ex-monastery is now the seat of the Zacatecas bishopric. The church's finest feature is the plateresque carving of the conversion of St Augustine over the north doorway.

The street ends at **Jardín Juárez**, a tiny rectangle of park with the Rectoría, or administrative headquarters, of the Universidad Autónoma de Zacatecas in a neoclassical building on its west side.

Mina El Edén

El Edén Mine, once one of Mexico's richest mines, is a 'must' for visitors to Zacatecas because of the dramatic insight it gives into the source of wealth in this region – and the terrible price paid for it. Digging for fabulous hoards of silver, gold, iron, copper and zinc, enslaved Indians, including many children, worked under horrific conditions. At one time up to five a day died from accidents or illness.

El Edén was worked from 1586 until the 1950s. Today the third of its seven levels is kept open for visitors. The lower levels are flooded. A miniature train runs you deep inside the Cerro del Grillo, the hill in which the mine is located, then guides – some of whom speak a little English – lead you along floodlit walkways past deep shafts and over subterranean pools. It is easy to see why so many miners lost their lives to accidents and diseases like silicosis and tuberculosis.

To reach the mine, walk west along Avenida Juárez and stay on it after its name changes to Avenida Torreón at the Alameda park. Turn right immediately after the big hospital above the park. You can take a Ruta 7 bus up Avenida Juárez from the corner of Avenida Hidalgo. Mine tours leave every few minutes from noon to 7.30 pm, Tuesday to Sunday; closed Monday. Cost is 10 pesos. The guides here are paid a very low wage. Some are students working their way through college, and a generous tip may be in order.

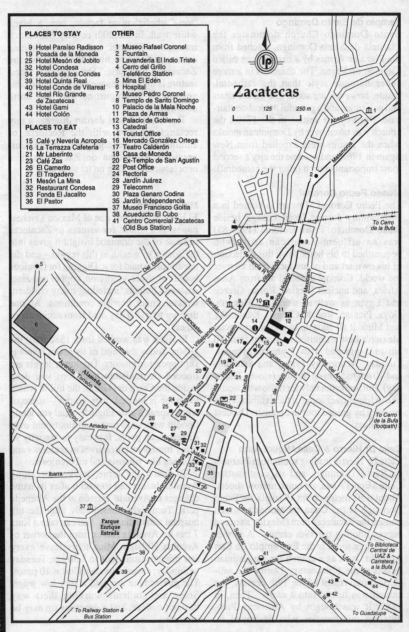

PLACES TO STAY

9 Hotel Paraíso Radisson
19 Posada de la Moneda
25 Hotel Mesón de Jobito
32 Hotel Condesa
34 Posada de los Condes
39 Hotel Quinta Real
40 Hotel Conde de Villareal
42 Hotel Río Grande de Zacatecas
43 Hotel Gami
44 Hotel Colón

PLACES TO EAT

15 Café y Nevería Acropolis
16 La Terrazza Cafetería
21 Mr Laberinto
23 Café Zas
26 El Carnerito
27 El Tragadero
31 Mesón La Mina
32 Restaurant Condesa
33 Fonda El Jacalito
36 El Pastor

OTHER

1 Museo Rafael Coronel
2 Fountain
3 Lavandería El Indio Triste
4 Cerro del Grillo Teleférico Station
5 Mina El Edén
6 Hospital
7 Museo Pedro Coronel
8 Templo de Santo Domingo
10 Palacio de la Mala Noche
11 Plaza de Armas
12 Palacio de Gobierno
13 Catedral
14 Tourist Office
16 Mercado González Ortega
17 Teatro Calderón
18 Casa de Moneda
20 Ex-Templo de San Agustín
22 Post Office
24 Rectoría
28 Jardín Juárez
29 Telecomm
30 Plaza Genaro Codina
37 Jardín Independencia
38 Museo Francisco Goitia
39 Acueducto El Cubo
41 Centro Comercial Zacatecas (Old Bus Station)

Zacatecas

0   125   250 m

To Cerro de la Bufa

To Cerro de la Bufa (footpath)

To Biblioteca Central de UAZ & Carretera a la Bufa

To Railway Station & Bus Station

Parque Enrique Estrada

To Guadalupe

Teleférico

The most exhilarating ride in Zacatecas, and the easiest way to reach the Cerro de la Bufa, is the teleférico which crosses high above the city from the Cerro del Grillo. Just walk to the left from the exit of El Edén mine and you'll reach the teleférico's Cerro del Grillo station after a couple of minutes. Alternatively, Ruta 7 buses from the bus station run up Avenida González Ortega then west along Avenida Juárez and Avenida Torreón to the teleférico; or you can climb the steps of Callejón de García Rojas, which lead straight up to the teleférico from the north end of Villalpando. The Swiss-built teleférico operates every 15 minutes from noon to 7.30 pm daily, except when winds exceed 60 kph. The trip takes seven minutes and costs 4 pesos one way.

Cerro de la Bufa

Cerro de la Bufa is the rock-topped hill which overlooks and dominates Zacatecas from the north-east. The most appealing of the many explanations for its name is that *bufa* is an old Spanish word for wineskin, which is certainly what the rocky formation atop the hill looks like. The views from the top are superb and there's an interesting group of monuments, a chapel and a museum up there.

An exciting and convenient way to ascend la Bufa is by the teleférico from near the El Edén mine exit. More strenuously, you can walk up it (start by going up Calle del Ángel at the rear, east, end of the cathedral). There's also a road, Carretera a la Bufa, which begins beside the university library on Avenida López Velarde. All three routes bring you out near the group of monuments, chapel and museum. Just above the teleférico station is a meteorological observatory.

The **Museo de la Toma de Zacatecas** commemorates the 1914 battle fought on the slopes of la Bufa in which the revolutionary División del Norte, led by Francisco 'Pancho' Villa and Felipe Ángeles, defeated the forces of President Victoriano Huerta. This gave the revolutionaries control of Zacatecas, which was the gateway to Mexico City, in this war to depose the unpopular Huerta. The museum is open Tuesday to Sunday, 10 am to 4 pm. Admission is 5 pesos.

La Capilla de la Virgen del Patrocinio, adjacent to the museum, is named after the patron saint of miners and thus also of Zacatecas. Above the altar of this 18th-century chapel is an image of the Virgin said to be capable of healing the sick. Thousands of pilgrims make their way to this chapel each year during the weeks either side of 8 September, when the image is carried to the cathedral.

Just east of the museum and chapel stand three imposing equestrian **statues** of the victors of the battle of Zacatecas – Villa, Ángeles and Pánfilo Natera. A path behind the Villa and Natera statues leads to the rocky **summit of la Bufa**, where there are marvellous views over the city and away to mountain ranges stretching far into the distance on all sides. The hill is topped by a metal cross which is illuminated at night.

A path along the foot of the rocky hilltop, starting to the right of the statues, leads to the **Mausoleo de los Hombres Ilustres de Zacatecas**, with the tombs of Zacatecan heroes from 1841 to the present day.

You can return to the city by the teleférico or by a footpath leading downhill from the statues.

Museo Rafael Coronel

The Rafael Coronel Museum, imaginatively housed in the ruins of the lovely 16th-century ex-Convento de San Francisco in the north of the city, contains Mexican folk art collected by the Zacatecan artist Rafael Coronel, brother of Pedro Coronel and son-in-law of Diego Rivera. The highlight is the colourful display of over 2000 masks used in traditional dances and rituals. This is probably the biggest mask collection in the country. Also to be seen are pottery, puppets, pre-Hispanic objects, and drawings and sketches by Rivera. To reach the museum follow Hidalgo about 800 metres north from the cathedral to a fountain where the street forks. Follow the right fork, Calle Matamoros, for 400 metres, and the museum will be on the left. Opening hours are 10 am to 2 pm and 4 to 7 pm Thursday to Tuesday, closed Wednesday. Entry costs 10 pesos.

Museo Francisco Goitia

The Francisco Goitia Museum displays work by six major Zacatecan artists of the 20th century. Set in a fine former governor's mansion at Enrique Estrada 102, above the pleasant Parque Enrique Estrada in the south of the city's central area, it's well worth visiting. Francisco Goitia (1882-1960) himself did some particularly good paintings of Indians. There's also a very striking Goitia self-portrait in the museum. Other artists represented include Pedro and Rafael Coronel.

The museum's hours are 10 am to 1.30 pm and 5 to 7.30 pm Tuesday to Sunday, closed Monday. Admission is free. To reach it, go south up Avenida González Ortega from the corner of Avenida Hidalgo and Avenida Juárez, till you come to the Parque Enrique Estrada on the right, crossed by part of an early 19th-century aqueduct named El Cubo. Turn right along the edge of the park and follow this street to the museum.

Festivals

La Morisma Held usually on the last Friday, Saturday and Sunday in August, this festival includes the most spectacular of the mock battles staged at Mexican fiestas to act out the triumph of Christians over Moors (Muslims) in old Spain. Rival 'armies' parade through the city streets in the mornings then, accompanied by bands of musicians, enact two traditional battle sequences around midday and in the afternoon over the area between Lomas de Bracho in the north-east of the city and the Cerro de la Bufa. One sequence portrays a conflict between Emperor Charlemagne and Almirante Balám, king of Alexandria. The other deals with a 16th-century Moorish rebellion led by Argel Osmán. Each develops over the three days, culminating in the victory of the Christians on the Sunday. Church services and other ceremonies also form part of the celebrations.

Feria de Zacatecas Zacatecas stages its annual feria from about 5 to 21 September. Renowned matadors are imported to fight the famous bulls bred in this region; charreadas, concerts, plays and agricultural and craft shows are staged; and on 8 September the image of La Virgen del Patrocinio is carried to the cathedral from its chapel on the Cerro de la Bufa.

Places to Stay – bottom end

Zacatecas' cheap lodgings are in extreme contrast to the stately beauty of its colonial architecture.

The *Hotel Conde de Villareal* (☎ (492) 2-12-00) is as good a bet as any thanks to its central location, at Zamora 303 just south of Jardín Independencia, and friendly management. Prices are good at 30/35 pesos for singles/doubles (40 pesos for a twin). Rooms have private bath but those at the back are dark and those at the front receive traffic noise. There are plans to improve some rooms.

The cheapest hotel worth considering is the *Hotel Río Grande de Zacatecas* (☎ (492) 2-53-49) at Calzada de la Paz 513. This is a very bare and basic but clean place on a hillside about 1.25 km south of the cathedral. Smallish rooms, with private bath, cost 25/31 pesos (37 pesos for a twin). Some rooms have great views of la Bufa but also traffic noise. Calzada de la Paz is a small street almost opposite the old bus station on Avenida López Mateos. The hotel is 250 metres up the street.

A similar distance from the centre at López Mateos 106 or López Velarde 508 – depending which entrance you use – the *Hotel Colón* (☎ (492) 2-04-64) has medium-sized rooms, a bit fusty, at 54/64 pesos with bathroom. The hotel is sandwiched between two busy, noisy streets. The *Hotel Gami* (☎ (492) 2-80-05) nearby at López Mateos 309 is barer but reasonably clean rooms at 56/66 pesos (85 pesos for a double with two beds).

Places to Stay – middle

The *Hotel Condesa* (☎ (492) 2-11-60), centrally located at Avenida Juárez 5 near the corner of Avenida Hidalgo, is good value. Agreeable singles/doubles with private bath cost 80/95 pesos. The hotel is being attractively renovated, from the top down, so go for a room on one of the already-completed floors. The rooms are built around a central well with a plastic roof. Nearly all have exterior windows. There's a decent restaurant, open 7 am to 11 pm, on the ground floor.

The *Posada de los Condes* (☎ (492) 2-10-93), across the street from the Condesa at Juárez 107, is a colonial monument over three centuries old but a recent modernisation has removed most evidence of its age from the interior. Rooms, though not big, are pleasant and well kept, with TV and phone. They cost 90/110 pesos.

Another fair choice is the *Posada de la Moneda* (☎ (492) 2-08-81), a block south of the cathedral at Avenida Hidalgo 413. Pleasant rooms with TV, bath, and Huichol yarn paintings on the walls, are ranged along wide corridors. They cost 100/125 pesos.

Places to Stay – top end

The *Hotel Paraíso Radisson* (☎ (492) 2-61-83, fax 2-62-45) is superbly located in a modernised colonial building at Hidalgo 703 on the Plaza de Armas. The 115 air-con rooms and suites are attractively furnished and equipped with TV and mini-bars. There's a good restaurant and a central fountain courtyard. Rooms cost 310 pesos single or double.

The *Hotel Mesón de Jobito* (☎ /fax (492) 4-17-22), centrally but peacefully situated at Jardín Juárez 143, is another lovely old building with 31 finely decorated rooms and suites from 330 to 440 pesos. It has a restaurant and bar.

The top place is the classy *Hotel Quinta Real* (☎ (492) 2-91-04, fax 2-84-40), about 1.5 km south of the cathedral just off Avenida González Ortega. It's spectacularly constructed around Zacatecas' former main bullring, with the arches of the fine old El Cubo aqueduct running across the front of the hotel. Large, very comfortable rooms are yours for around 550 pesos.

Places to Eat

There are several good places on Avenida Hidalgo and Avenida Juárez. For expensive top-class meals, make your way to the restaurants of the Quinta Real, Paraíso Radisson or Mesón de Jobito hotels.

Avenida Hidalgo The *Café y Nevería Acropolis*, on Hidalgo immediately south of the cathedral, is the main city-centre meeting place, busy from 8.30 am to 10 pm with a range of customers from students to middle-class families. It's not especially cheap, with breakfasts at 15 to 17 pesos or a moderately sized cappuccino at 5 pesos, but there's a big choice of all sorts of snacks, light meals and drinks.

The Mercado González Ortega, next door to the Café Acropolis, harbours *La Terrazza Cafetería*, on the upper level entered from Hidalgo, with open-air tables looking down on Calle Tacuba.

Some of the best value in the city centre is found at *Mr Laberinto* at Hidalgo 342 half a block south of the Mercado González Ortega, a popular restaurant serving tasty, well presented food in bright, pleasant surroundings. Pollo a la parrilla (grilled chicken with vegetables) is excellent at 16 pesos. Meat dishes are around 20 pesos.

Café Zas towards the south end of Hidalgo at No 201, is a clean, friendly place serving decent breakfasts from 10 to 15 pesos, antojitos from 6 to 15 pesos, and chicken or meat dishes from 15 to 30 pesos. It's open until 10 pm.

Avenida Juárez The friendly *El Pastor* at Independencia 214 on the south side of Jardín Independencia, just off the east end of Juárez, is busy from 8 am to 9 pm serving up economical charcoal-roasted chicken dishes – with crisps and a bit of salad for 8 pesos, with mole and rice for 12 pesos. A sign out front commemorates this building as the birthplace, in 1668, of the first journalist in America.

Several eateries on Juárez between Jardín Independencia and Avenida Hidalgo offer adequate if unspectacular Mexican fare, with antojitos in the 10 to 18 peso range, chicken and meat dishes for 15 to 25 pesos, and breakfasts around 15 pesos. *Mesón La Mina* at Juárez 15, *Restaurant Condesa* next door, and *Fonda El Jacalito* across the street all fall into this bracket. Mesón La Mina also serves superior meat filetes for 31 to 34 pesos.

El Tragadero on Juárez in the block west of the Hidalgo intersection is a good-value Mexican eatery. To order, tick your choices on a list where most items are priced between 8 and 15 pesos. Alambre con queso (slices of grilled meat with cheese) is a good choice at 11 pesos. There are also generous serves of guacamole at 5 pesos, and beer at 2.50 pesos. *El Carnerito* in the same block, at Juárez 105, serves an economical comida corrida for 13.50 pesos.

Entertainment

The exotically situated disco in the *Mina El Edén* functions Thursday to Sunday, 9 pm to 3 am. It's aimed as much at tourists (Mexican and foreign) as at locals, and entry costs around 35 pesos, with drinks extra. Numbers are limited, so it's a good idea to reserve a table. The only sure way of doing this seems to be to go to the mine during the day and ask to speak with someone who knows about the disco.

Disco El Elefante Blanco next to the Cerro del Grillo teleférico station has a more local flavour, a young crowd, and romantic views over the city. It's open 9 pm to 2 am Thursday to Saturday.

There are a few live music places on Juárez between Hidalgo and Villalpando which look promising but struggle to get going most nights. You might be lucky. They include the bars *Mi Canto* and *La Cueva*, and the restaurant *La Toma*.

Paraíso, a slightly smart bar in the south-west corner of the Mercado González Ortega on Hidalgo, is pretty busy most nights. A beer is 6.50 pesos, a cocktail 11 pesos, and there's food too. The *Nueva España* bar, across the little plaza outside the Paraíso, and the video bar of *Mr Laberinto* restaurant down the street, are a bit cheaper.

Things to Buy

Zacatecas is known for its fine leatherwork and colourful sarapes. You can bargain at the shops around the Plaza Genaro Codina and in the indoor market between there and Calle Allende.

Getting There & Away

Air Mexicana flies direct daily to/from Los Angeles, Ontario (California), Mexico City, León, Morelia and Tijuana, to/from Chicago and San Luis Potosí four days a week, and to/from Denver twice a week. Its office (☎ 2-74-29) is at Avenida Hidalgo 406. TAESA flies direct to/from Chicago three times weekly, and direct to Oakland four times weekly. Oakland-Zacatecas requires an overnight connection in Guadalajara. TAESA also flies to/from Ciudad Juárez, Mexico City, Morelia and Tijuana. Its office (☎ 2-00-50) is at Avenida Hidalgo 305-1.

Bus Zacatecas bus station is on the south-west edge of town, about three km from the centre. Many buses from here are de paso. The station has a left-luggage room which is open from 7 am to 10 pm, Lada casetas and a fax office. Daily services from Zacatecas include:

Aguascalientes – 130 km, two hours; three deluxe buses by Futura (22 pesos); six 1st-class by Transportes Chihuahuaenses (16 pesos); 30 2nd-class by Estrella Blanca (14 pesos)

Durango – 290 km, 4½ hours; two deluxe buses by Futura (47 pesos); 11 1st-class by Omnibus de México (34 pesos); 17 2nd-class by Estrella Blanca and 11 by Camiones de los Altos (31 pesos)

Fresnillo – 60 km, one hour; 2nd-class buses every 30 minutes by both Estrella Blanca and Camiones de los Altos (7 pesos)

Guadalajara – 320 km, five hours; a few deluxe buses by Turistar Ejecutivo (76 pesos) and Futura (66 pesos); frequent 1st-class buses by Estrella Blanca, Rojo de los Altos and Omnibus de México (42 to 48 pesos); 26 2nd-class buses by Camiones de los Altos (31 pesos)

Guanajuato – 310 km, five hours; 1st-class bus at 6 am by Omnibus de México (44 pesos); otherwise change at León

León – 250 km, four hours; 10 1st-class buses by Transportes Chihuahuaenses (32 pesos)

Mexico City (Terminal Norte) – 615 km, eight to nine hours; a few deluxe buses by Turistar Ejecutivo (120 pesos) and Futura (93 pesos); three 1st-class by Transportes Chihuahuaenses (79 pesos), nine by Omnibus de México (72 pesos); 16 2nd-class by Estrella Blanca (69 pesos)

Monterrey – 450 km, six hours; a few deluxe buses by Turistar Ejecutivo (85 pesos) and Futura (75 pesos); four 1st-class by Transportes del Norte (53 pesos); 14 2nd-class by Estrella Blanca and 13 by Rojo de los Altos (46 pesos)

San Luis Potosí – 190 km, three hours; nine 1st-class buses by Omnibus de México (24 pesos); hourly 2nd-class buses by Estrella Blanca (20 pesos)

There are also frequent buses to Torreón and several a day to Chihuahua, Ciudad Juárez, Saltillo, Nuevo Laredo and Matamoros.

Train The 'División del Norte' train between Mexico City and Ciudad Juárez stops at Zacatecas at 9.50 am northbound (train No 7) and 8.15 pm southbound (train No 8). Primera regular fares are 84 pesos to Ciudad Juárez, 60 pesos to Chihuahua, 28 pesos to Torreón, 8 pesos to Aguascalientes and 46.30 pesos to Mexico City. See the Mexico City train section for further timetable details.

Zacatecas station is on Avenida González Ortega, about 1.25 km south of Avenida Juárez. Tickets are sold from about one hour before the trains arrive.

Car Budget (☎ 2-94-58) has an office next to the Hotel Colón on Avenida López Mateos. Numero Uno Autorentas (☎ 2-34-07) at Avenida López Mateos 305A offers large discounts for guests of several hotels including the Condesa and Posada de los Condes.

Getting Around
To/From the Airport Zacatecas airport is about 20 km north of the city. For airport transport for about 25 pesos, call ☎ 2-59-46.

City Transport The Ruta 8 bus from the bus and rail stations runs right to the cathedral in the city centre. Heading out to the bus and rail stations from the centre, catch this bus going south on Villalpando or from Jardín

Independencia. The Ruta 7 bus from the bus and rail stations runs to the junction of Avenida González Ortega and Avenida Juárez in the centre, then heads west along Juárez and winds around to the teleférico station on Cerro del Grillo. Bus fares are 0.80 pesos.

AROUND ZACATECAS
Guadalupe
This small town, about 10 km east of the Zacatecas city centre, has a major museum of colonial art – the **Museo y Templo de Guadalupe**. It's housed in a historic ex-monastery next to a still-working church, and is worth the trip if you have any interest in colonial history, art or architecture.

The monastery, the ex-Convento de Guadalupe, was established by Franciscan monks in the early 18th century as a Colegio Apostólica de Propaganda Fide (Apostolic College for the Propagation of the Faith). It was a base for missionary work in northern New Spain and had a strong academic tradition and renowned library. It was closed in the 1850s. The building now houses the Museo de Guadalupe, one of Mexico's best collections of colonial art, with many works by Miguel Cabrera, Juan Correa, Antonio Torres and Cristóbal Villalpando. Visitors can also see part of its library and step into the choir on the upper floor of the monastery church (templo), with fine carved and painted chairs. From the choir you can look down into the beautifully decorated 19th-century Capilla de Napoles on the church's north side. Museum hours are Tuesday to Sunday, 10 am to 4.30 pm; admission is 13 pesos. The ground level of the church, also with a view into the Capilla de Napoles, can be visited free. There's some fine baroque carving on the church's exterior.

Next door to the Museo de Guadalupe is the embryonic **Museo Regional de Zacatecas**, with a small collection of old carriages and cars – free and worth a look.

The town holds its annual **feria** from 3 to 13 December, coinciding with the build-up to 12 December, the Day of the Virgin of Guadalupe.

Getting There & Away From Zacatecas, Transportes de Guadalupe buses run to Guadalupe every few minutes from the old bus station, now called the Centro Comercial Zacatecas, on the corner of López Mateos and Salazar. The fare is 0.80 pesos for a 20-minute ride. Get off at a small plaza in the middle of Guadalupe where a 'Museo Convento' sign points to the right, along Calle Madero. Walk about 250 metres along Madero to a sizeable plaza, called Jardín Juárez. The museums are on the left side of the plaza. To return to Zacatecas, you can pick up the bus where you got off it.

FRESNILLO
• *pop: 75,000*

Fresnillo is an unexciting town 60 km north of Zacatecas on the road to Torreón and Durango. The main reason to stop here is the Santuario de Plateros, one of Mexico's most-visited shrines, five km north-east of the town in the village of Plateros.

Orientation

Fresnillo bus station is on Calle Ebano, about one km north-east of the town centre. If you need to go into town for a meal or a room, you'll find it's a higgledy-piggledy place with three main plazas. The most pleasant of the three is the Jardín Madero with the colonial church of Nuestra Señora de la Purificación on its north side. Three blocks west, along Avenida Juárez, is the Jardín Obalisco with a theatre on its north side. Between these two, Avenida Hidalgo heads two blocks south off Juárez to the Jardín Hidalgo.

Santuario de Plateros

A visit to Plateros gives quite an insight into Mexican Catholicism. The goal of the pilgrims who flock here every day of the year is El Santo Niño de Atocha. This quaint image of the infant Jesus, holding a staff and basket and wearing a colonial pilgrim's feathered hat, resides on the altar of the Santuario de Plateros, an 18th-century church. The avenue approaching the church is lined with stalls selling a vast array of gaudy religious imagery and other souvenirs. The Santo Niño is credited with all manner of wonders and a series of rooms to the right of the church entrance is lined with thousands of little retablos depicting his miracles.

Buses of the Fresnillo-Plateros line run from Fresnillo bus station to Plateros every 30 minutes from 6.50 am to 6.20 pm. Ruta 6 city buses also run to Plateros from Calle Emiliano Zapata, 2½ blocks east of the Jardín Madero. Fare is 1.60 pesos on either service.

Places to Stay & Eat

The fairly modern *Hotel Lirmar* (☎ (493) 2-45-98) at Durango 400 on the corner of Ebano, just outside the bus station, has reasonable singles/doubles with private bath for 50/60 pesos.

In town, the *Hotel Maya* (☎ (493) 2-03-51) at Calle Ensaye 9, one block south of Avenida Juárez and one block west of Avenida Hidalgo, has nice bright rooms with bathroom and TV for 38/45 pesos. *Hotel Del Fresno* (☎ (493) 2-11-20) at Avenida Hidalgo 411 facing Jardín Hidalgo, and the pleasant *Hotel Casa Blanca* (☎ (493) 2-12-88) at Calle García Salinas 503, three blocks east of Jardín Hidalgo, both have comfortable rooms at 132/154 pesos.

El Molinito on Jardín Hidalgo is a bright, clean, busy restaurant serving a good-value three-course comida for 12 pesos, or à la carte main courses for about the same price.

Getting There & Away

Fresnillo is well served by long-distance buses, though many are de paso. There are frequent 1st and 2nd-class buses to Durango (230 km, 3½ hours, 23 to 26 pesos), Torreón (330 km, five hours, 38 to 42 pesos) and Zacatecas (60 km, one hour, 7 pesos), as well as many buses to Aguascalientes, Chihuahua, Mexico City, Guadalajara, San Luis Potosí and elsewhere.

Getting Around

Ruta 4 'Central-Centro' buses run between Calle Ebano, outside the bus station, and the town centre. Leaving town, you can pick them up on the south side of Jardín Madero.

JEREZ
• *pop: 35,000*

A small country town 30 km south-west of Zacatecas, Jerez has some surprisingly fine 18th and 19th-century buildings which testify to the wealth that silver brought to even the lesser towns of the Zacatecas region. Jerez holds a lively Easter feria, lasting about 10 days from Good Friday, with charreadas, cockfights and other activities.

Information
There's a tourist office next to the Teatro Hinojosa on Jardín Juárez but it opens erratically. Promotora de Divisas Real de Ángeles, open daily on the corner of Calle Las Flores and Calle de la Bizarra Capital, two blocks south of the central plaza, Jardín Páez, changes travellers' cheques and cash. The post office and the Telecomm office, with a fax service, are side by side on Calle de la Bizarra Capital. There's a Lada caseta at Alvaro Obregón 20B, half a block north of Jardín Páez.

Things to See
The 18th-century **Parroquia de la Inmaculada Concepción** and the 19th-century **Santuario de la Soledad** both have fine stone carving. To find them go one block south from the south-east corner of the main plaza, Jardín Páez, then one block east for the parroquia, or one block west for the santuario. Just past the santuario, on the north side of the little Jardín Hidalgo, is a beautiful little 19th-century theatre, the **Teatro Hinojosa**.

Places to Stay & Eat
Hotel Plaza (☎ (494) 5-20-63) on the south side of Jardín Páez has small, bare, clean singles/doubles with bathroom for 30/35 pesos, or 40/45 pesos with TV. The 'hot' water may be a long time coming. The hotel's restaurant is OK – a quarter chicken with fries, beans, greens and tortillas is yours for 8 pesos.

The *Hotel Del Jardín*, on the west side of

the same plaza, has similar room prices to the Hotel Plaza.

Restaurant La Luz, a block west of Jardín Páez along Emilio Carranza, is a good little family-run eating place – actually the front room of a family house – where you can get a good bistek with beans, salsa, tortillas and a beer for around 16 pesos.

Things to Buy
Fine leatherwork can be found at shops like Zapatería Lo Legalidad on Luis Moya half a block south of Jardín Páez, or La Palma, which specialises in charrería gear, one block east and half a block north of Jardín Páez. There's a craft market, open erratically, on Calle Hidalgo half a block south of the Jardín Hidalgo.

The market is two blocks east of Jardín Páez along Calzada Suave Patria.

Getting There & Away
The turning to Jerez is at Malpaso, on the Zacatecas-Guadalajara road 23 km south of Zacatecas. The Zacatecas-Jerez line runs 2nd-class buses from Zacatecas bus station to Jerez every 30 minutes from 5 am to 10 pm for 6 pesos. There are also services by Omnibus de México and Rojo de los Altos. Jerez bus station is on the east side of town, about one km from the centre along Calzada Suave Patria. 'Centro-Central' buses run to/from the centre for 0.60 pesos. There are also several buses a day to/from Guadalajara (33 pesos) and Fresnillo (7 pesos).

LA QUEMADA
The ruins of La Quemada stand on a hill in a broad valley about 55 km south of Zacatecas, one km east of the Zacatecas-Guadalajara road. They're also known as Chicomostoc, because they were once thought to be the place of that name where the Aztecs halted during their legendary wanderings towards the Valley of Mexico. The ruins' fine, rather isolated setting makes them well worth the trip from Zacatecas if you have time.

La Quemada was inhabited between about 300 and 1200 AD and early in that period was part of a regional trade network linked to Teotihuacán. Fortifications at the site suggest that La Quemada later tried to dominate trade in this part of Mexico, while traces of a big fire indicate that its final downfall was violent.

Some of the ruins can be seen up on the hill to the left as you approach from the Zacatecas-Guadalajara road. The nearest main structure to the site entrance is the Salón de las Columnas (Hall of the Columns) which was probably a ceremonial hall. A bit further up the hill are a ball court, a steep offerings pyramid, and an equally steep staircase leading towards the upper levels of the site. From the upper levels of the main hill a path leads westward to a spur hilltop with the remains of a cluster of buildings called the Citadel. A stone wall thought to have been built for defensive purposes in the later stages of La Quemada stretches across the slopes north of here.

The site is open daily from 10 am to 5 pm. Entrance is 13 pesos, free on Sunday.

Getting There & Away

From Zacatecas bus station, take an Omnibus de México or Camiones de los Altos bus heading to Villanueva. Each company has six or seven daily services. Some buses heading for Guadalajara may also stop at La Quemada. The fare is 7 pesos. Tell the conductor you want 'Las Ruinas' and

you'll be dropped at the Restaurant Las Siete Cuevas at the start of the one-km paved approach road to the site. Returning to Zacatecas, you may have to wait a while before a bus shows up.

Aguascalientes

The state of Aguascalientes, bordered on the south by Jalisco and surrounded on its other sides by Zacatecas, is one of Mexico's smallest and was originally part of Zacatecas; according to history, a kiss planted on the lips of dictator Santa Anna by the attractive wife of a prominent local politician brought about the creation of a separate Aguascalientes state.

Aguascalientes is primarily an agricultural state, with maize, beans, chiles, fruits and grains grown on its fertile lands. Livestock is also important and the state's ranches raise famous bulls for bullfights all over Mexico as well as cattle for meat and hides. Industry is concentrated in and around the capital city, Aguascalientes.

AGUASCALIENTES
• *pop: 520,000* • *alt: 1800 metres*

Aguascalientes ('Hot Waters'), named after its hot springs, is a prosperous industrial city with just enough colonial legacies to justify a brief visit.

Crunch, Munch

November must be the high season for crickets in the La Quemada area. The approach road to the site, as I walked along it in that warm, dry month, was carpeted with the creatures – big, fat, juicy ones. Vehicles had inevitably squashed hundreds of them. And the presence of so many fresh corpses had brought thousands more crickets out from the undergrowth for a feast on this source of juicy, immobile nourishment. Many other crickets were in the mood to sate other bodily urges, and were climbing on the backs of the chomping cannibals to procreate. All this produced great heaving mounds of living and dead crickets dotted all the way along the road to the site, and it was impossible to avoid crunching them underfoot if I lifted my eyes from the road to take in the landscape or look for the ruins up on the hill. Happily these crickets were either not of the flying variety or were too sated to do anything but crawl.

For some reason the ruins site itself was cricket-free and I was able to forget all about them as I climbed up level with the soaring eagles and cut red tuna – cactus fruit – to eat as I surveyed the fine views from the top of this thousand-year-old settlement.

John Noble

History

Before the Spanish invasion, indigenous people built a labyrinth of catacombs which made the first Spaniards arriving here dub Aguascalientes La Ciudad Perforada – the perforated city. Archaeologists have no explanation for the tunnels, which are off limits to visitors.

Pedro de Alvarado, sent by Cortés to subdue the tribes in this region in 1522, was driven back by fierce Chichimec Indians. A small garrison was founded here in 1575 to protect silver convoys from Zacatecas to Mexico City and outlying miners and cattle drovers. Eventually, as the Chichimecs were pacified, the springs at Ojo Caliente served as the basis for the growth of a town; a large tank beside the springs helped irrigate local farms where fruits, vegetables and grains were cultivated.

Today, more than half of the state's population lives in the city, where industry, textiles, and trade from the region's ranches, vineyards and orchards provide employment.

Orientation

Aguascalientes is flat and easy to get around. The centre of town is the Plaza de la Patria, formerly the Plaza de Armas. On this plaza are the cathedral and the Palacio de Gobierno. Many hotels, restaurants, sites of interest and shops are within a few blocks of the plaza. Avenida López Mateos, the main east-west artery across the central part of the city, is a couple of blocks south of the Plaza de la Patria. The bus and train stations, both on the outskirts of town, are served by frequent local buses.

Information

Tourist Office The Delegación de Turismo del Estado de Aguascalientes (☎ (49) 15-11-55) is on the ground floor of the Palacio de Gobierno on the Plaza de la Patria. Open Monday to Friday from 8.30 am to 3 pm and 5 to 7 pm, and Saturday 8.30 am to 3 pm, it gives out free city maps and information on the city and state of Aguascalientes.

Money Multibanco Comermex on the east side of the Plaza de la Patria exchanges cash and travellers' cheques from 9 am to noon, Monday to Friday. Operadora Internacional del Centro, half a block east of the plaza on Montoro, has worse exchange rates but longer hours – 9 am to 2 pm and 4 to 6.30 pm Monday to Friday, 9.30 am to 1.30 pm Saturday. Banca Serfin on the south side of López Mateos Poniente, just west of Galeana, has an ATM.

Post & Telecommunications The post office is at Hospitalidad 108, a couple of blocks north-east of the Plaza de la Patria. It's open Monday to Friday from 8 am to 7 pm, Saturday 9 am to 1 pm. A Lada caseta, open daily from 8 am to 10 pm, is above the Tortas Estilo México restaurant on the south-east corner of the Plaza de la Patria. The main Telecomm office, with telegram and fax service, is at Galeana 102, a block from the Plaza de la Patria – open Monday to Friday from 8 am to 8 pm, Saturday 9 am to noon. Ladatel coin and card phones can be found in the bus station.

Plaza de la Patria

The 18th-century baroque **cathedral** is more magnificent on the inside than the outside. Over the altar at the east end of the south aisle is a painting of the Virgin of Guadalupe by Miguel Cabrera. There are more Cabrera works in the cathedral's own *pinacoteca* (picture gallery) – ask one of the priests to let you in.

Facing the south side of the cathedral is the **Teatro Morelos**, the scene of the 1914 Convention of Aguascalientes, in which revolutionary factions led by Pancho Villa, Venustiano Carranza and Emiliano Zapata tried unsuccessfully to patch up their differences. Busts of these three plus Alvario Obregón stand in the foyer.

The red and pink stone **Palacio de Gobierno** on the south side of the plaza is the most noteworthy colonial building in Aguascalientes. Once the mansion of the colonial baron, the Marqués de Guadalupe, it dates from 1665 and has a striking courtyard of arches and pillars. A mural painted in

1992 by the Chilean Osvaldo Barra on the wall just inside the courtyard depicts the 1914 convention, pointing out that some of its ideas were crystallised in Mexico's still-current 1917 constitution – including the eight-hour working day enshrined in Article 123. Barra, whose mentor was Diego Rivera, also painted the mural on the far (south) wall of the courtyard, a compendium of the historic and economic forces that forged Aguascalientes.

Museums & Churches

The **Museo Regional de Historia** at Avenida Carranza 110, one block west of the cathedral, was designed as a family home by Refugio Reyes, the self-taught architect who also designed San Antonio church. It's open Tuesday to Sunday from 10 am to 2 pm and 5 to 8.30 pm; admission is 5 pesos, free on Sunday and holidays. The **Museo de Arte Contemporaneo** is at Juan de Montoro 222, 1½ blocks east of the Plaza de la Patria – open Tuesday to Sunday from 10 am to 2 pm and 5 to 8 pm (free).

The most interesting Aguascalientes museum is the **Museo José Guadalupe Posada** in the former convent of the Templo del Encino on the Jardín Francisco, on Díaz de León about 450 metres south of Avenida López Mateos Oriente. Posada (1852-1913), a native of Aguascalientes, was in many ways the founder of modern Mexican art. His satirical cartoons and engravings during the Porfiriato dictatorship broadened the audience of art, drew attention to social decay, and inspired later artists like Diego Rivera. Posada's hallmark was the *calavera* (skull or skeleton). The museum has a large collection of his work and also shows temporary art exhibitions. It's open Tuesday to Sunday from 10 am to 2 pm and 4 to 8 pm; admission is free. The **Templo del Encino** beside the museum contains a black statue of Jesus which some believe is growing. When it eventually reaches an adjacent column, a worldwide calamity is anticipated.

The **Museo de Aguascalientes**, in a beautiful turn-of-the-century building at Zaragoza 505 near the corner of Pedro Parga,

houses a permanent exhibition of the art of Saturnino Herran, born in Aguascalientes in 1887, plus temporary exhibitions. It's open Tuesday to Sunday from 10 am to 2 pm and 4.30 to 7.30 pm; admission is free. Opposite this museum is the **Templo de San Antonio**, a crazy-quilt of architectural styles built at the turn of the century by the local self-taught architect Refugio Reyes. The interior is highly ornate, with huge round paintings and intricate decoration highlighted in gold.

Expo Plaza & Around

One km west of the Plaza de la Patria along López Mateos or Nieto, Expo Plaza is a modern shopping and entertainment focus for the city, with a wide pedestrian boulevard leading to a big new bullring, the Plaza de Toros Monumental. There are many restaurants along Calle Arturo Pani, which leads two blocks north from the Hotel Fiesta Americana to the 18th-century Templo de San Marcos and the Jardín de San Marcos, a shady walled park. The Palenque de Gallos in the Casino de la Feria building on Pani is the city's cockfighting arena. The old bullring, the Plaza de Toros San Marcos, is just north of the Jardín San Marcos. The Expo Plaza area is the hub of the annual Feria de San Marcos.

Thermal Springs

It's no surprise that there are hot springs in a town called Aguascalientes. The best known are at the **Centro Deportivo Ojo Caliente** on the eastern edge of the city at the end of Avenida López Mateos. Several bus routes from the city centre go to Ojo Caliente, including No 19 which you can pick up heading east on Juan de Montoro from Morelos, and Nos 16, 26 and 27. Entrance is 8 pesos a day. The large pool, and some other smaller pools, have warmish water; the hot water is in private pools, which rent for 55 or 65 pesos an hour for up to seven people. In the large park-like grounds are tennis, volleyball and squash courts. Hours are 7 am to 7 pm every day. Returning to the city centre, bus No 12 will take you along López

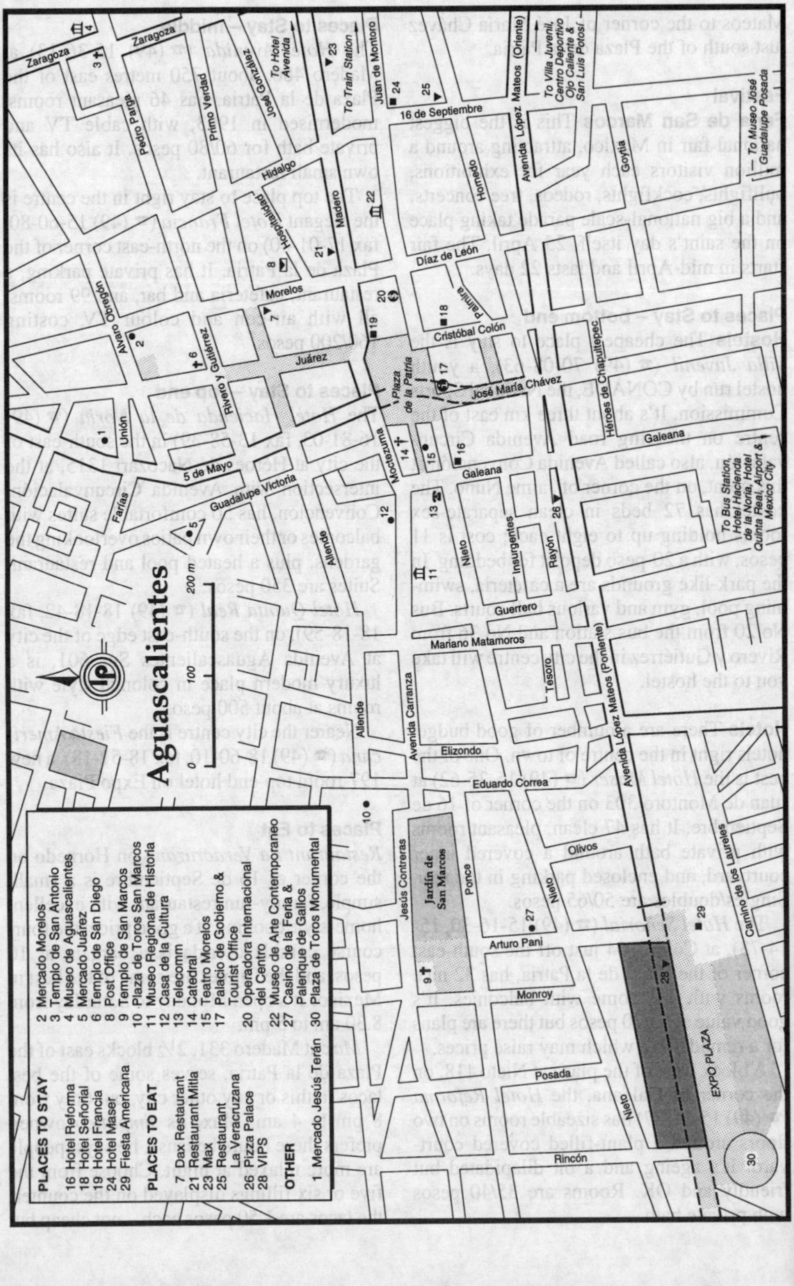

Aguascalientes

PLACES TO STAY
16 Hotel Reforma
18 Hotel Señorial
19 Hotel Francia
24 Hotel Maser
29 Fiesta Americana

PLACES TO EAT
7 Dax Restaurant
21 Restaurant Mitla
23 Max
25 Restaurant La Veracruzana
26 Pizza Palace
28 VIPS

OTHER
1 Mercado Jesús Terán
2 Mercado Morelos
3 Templo de San Antonio
4 Museo de Aguascalientes
5 Mercado Juárez
6 Templo de San Diego
8 Post Office
9 Templo de San Marcos
10 Plaza de Toros San Marcos
11 Museo Regional de Historia
12 Casa de la Cultura
13 Catedral
14 Telecomm
15 Teatro Morelos
17 Palacio de Gobierno & Tourist Office
20 Operadora Internacional del Centro
22 Museo de Arte Contemporaneo
27 Casino de la Feria & Palenque de Gallos
30 Plaza de Toros Monumental

Mateos to the corner of José María Chávez just south of the Plaza de la Patria.

Festival

Feria de San Marcos This is the biggest national fair in Mexico, attracting around a million visitors each year for exhibitions, bullfights, cockfights, rodeos, free concerts, and a big national-scale parade taking place on the saint's day itself, 25 April. The fair starts in mid-April and lasts 22 days.

Places to Stay – bottom end

Hostels The cheapest place to stay is the *Villa Juvenil* (☎ (49) 70-08-63), a youth hostel run by CONADE, the National Sports Commission. It's about three km east of the centre on the ring road Avenida Circunvalación, also called Avenida Convención at this point, on the corner of Jaime Nuno. The hostel has 72 beds in clean separate-sex rooms holding up to eight each; cost is 11 pesos, with a 20-peso deposit for bedding. In the park-like grounds are a cafeteria, swimming pool, gym and various ball courts. Bus No 20 from the bus station and No 36 from Rivero y Gutiérrez in the city centre will take you to the hostel.

Hotels There are a number of good budget hotels right in the centre of town. One of the best is the *Hotel Maser* (☎ (49) 15-35-62) at Juan de Montoro 303 on the corner of 16 de Septiembre. It has 47 clean, pleasant rooms with private bath around a covered inner courtyard, and enclosed parking in the rear. Singles/doubles are 50/65 pesos.

The *Hotel Señorial* (☎ (49) 15-16-30, 15-14-73), at Colón 104 just off the south-east corner of the Plaza de la Patria, has 32 nice rooms with TV, some with balconies. It's good value at 55/70 pesos but there are plans for a remodelling which may raise prices.

A block west of the plaza at Nieto 118, on the corner of Galeana, the *Hotel Reforma* (☎ (49) 15-11-07) has sizeable rooms on two floors around a plant-filled covered courtyard. It's ageing and a bit dilapidated but friendly and OK. Rooms are 35/40 pesos with private bath.

Places to Stay – middle

The *Hotel Avenida* (☎ (49) 15-36-13) at Madero 486, about 750 metres east of the Plaza de la Patria, has 46 pleasant rooms, modernised in 1993, with cable TV and private bath for 60/80 pesos. It also has its own small restaurant.

The top place to stay right in the centre is the elegant *Hotel Francia* (☎ (49) 15-60-80, fax 17-01-40) on the north-east corner of the Plaza de la Patria. It has private parking, a restaurant, cafeteria and bar, and 99 rooms, all with air-con and colour TV, costing 160/200 pesos.

Places to Stay – top end

The *Hotel Hacienda de la Noria* (☎ (49) 16-81-03, fax 13-58-39) in the south-east of the city at Héroes de Nacozari 1315, at the intersection with Avenida Circunvalación/ Convención, has 50 comfortable suites with balconies or their own patios overlooking the gardens, plus a heated pool and restaurant. Suites are 350 pesos.

Hotel Quinta Real (☎ (49) 18-18-42, fax 18-18-59), on the south-east edge of the city at Avenida Aguascalientes Sur 601, is a luxury modern place in colonial style with rooms at about 500 pesos.

Nearer the city centre is the *Fiesta Americana* (☎ (49) 18-60-10, fax 18-51-18), a new 197-room top-end hotel on Expo Plaza.

Places to Eat

Restaurant La Veracruzana on Hornedo on the corner of 16 de Septiembre is a small, simple, family-run restaurant with excellent home-style cooking at a good price: the four-course comida corrida is a bargain at 10 pesos, and the frijoles are some of the best in Mexico! It's open Monday to Saturday from 8.30 am to 5 pm.

Max at Madero 331, 2½ blocks east of the Plaza de la Patria, serves some of the best tacos in this or any other city, but only from 8 pm to 4 am. Max, its *simpático* owner, prefers these hours because, he says, people are more relaxed at night. Choose from the five or six fillings displayed on the counter: the tacos are 1.50 pesos each – not cheap but so tasty that it's very hard to resist when Max inquires: '¿Otro taquito, señor?'.

The *Restaurant Mitla* at Madero 220 is large, clean and pleasant, with a wide variety of dishes on the menu. The four-course comida corrida is 18 pesos, enchiladas 13 pesos, and meat, chicken or seafood dishes from 17 to 34 pesos. The Mitla is open every day from 8 am to 11.30 pm.

Pizza Palace at López Mateos Poniente 207 near the corner of Galeana is a small family-run restaurant with a useful 12.50-peso all-you-can-eat buffet of pizza, spaghetti, hamburguesas, salads and fruit every day from noon to 5.30 pm. It's open from 11 am to 1 pm. *Pizza Par* two doors west has a similar, slightly cheaper, deal from noon to 6 pm.

The cool, modern *Dax Restaurant-Video Bar* at Allende 229 on the corner of Morelos serves good food – antojitos 8 to 15 pesos, main meals 25 to 30 pesos. It's open from 8 am to 1 am daily and you can breakfast here too.

There are several more eateries in the Dax price range on Calle Arturo Pani in the Expo Plaza area, and a branch of the reliable chain restaurant *VIPS* in the Expo Plaza building itself.

The top place to eat in the city centre is the smart *Villa Andrea* restaurant in the Hotel Francia, where you'll be served by tuxedo-clad waiters to the sound of a tinkling piano.

There are several markets selling fresh produce a few blocks north of the Plaza de la Patria: Mercado Juárez, Mercado Jesús Terán and Mercado Morelos.

Entertainment

The *Casa de la Cultura*, housed in a fine 17th-century building on Avenida Carranza just west of Galeana, hosts art exhibitions, concerts, theatre, dance and other cultural events. Stop in to look at their schedule.

The *Teatro Morelos* on the Plaza de la Patria and the *Teatro de Aguascalientes* on the corner of José María Chávez and Avenida Aguascalientes, in the south of the city, both stage a variety of cultural events.

Free concerts, dance and theatre are presented some Sunday lunchtimes in the courtyard of the Museo José Guadalupe Posada.

Aguascalientes' top discos are *El Cabús* (☎ 73-04-32) in the fancy Hotel Las Trojes about 20 km (15 minutes) from the centre on the highway to Zacatecas, and *Meneos* (☎ 13-32-70) in the Centro Comercial El Dorado on Avenida Las Américas, about seven km south of the centre.

Getting There & Away

Air The Jesús Terán airport is 22 km from Aguascalientes on the road to Mexico City. Aeroméxico (☎ 17-02-52), at Madero 474, flies direct daily to/from Mexico City and Tijuana, and three times a week to/from Los Angeles and Puerto Vallarta. Aerolitoral (☎ 18-10-17 at the airport) flies daily to/from McAllen (Texas), Monterrey and Guadalajara. Aero California (☎ 17-23-10) at Juan de Montoro 203, and TAESA, at the airport, also have flights.

A convenient travel agency for flight tickets is Wagons-Lits Viajes (☎ 15-59-73, fax 15-38-70) in the lobby of the Hotel Francia.

Bus The bus station (Central Camionera) is about two km south of the centre on Avenida Circunvalación Sur, also called Avenida Convención, on the corner of Quinta Avenida. It has a post office, long-distance telephones, fax and telegram services, a cafeteria, and a guarda equipaje for storing luggage.

Daily services from Aguascalientes include:

Guadalajara – 250 km, 3½ to four hours; several deluxe buses each by ETN (52 pesos), Primera Plus (33 pesos) and Expreso Futura (34 pesos); frequent 1st-class by Omnibus de México (30 pesos); hourly 2nd-class by Rojo de los Altos (25 pesos)

Guanajuato – 184 km, three hours; one de paso 1st-class bus by Omnibus de México (20 pesos); four 2nd-class by Flecha Amarilla (19 pesos)

Mexico City (Terminal Norte) – 468 km, 6½ to seven hours; over 25 deluxe buses by Primera Plus, Expreso Futura or ETN (77 to 100 pesos); about 20 1st-class by Omnibus de México (66 pesos)

San Luis Potosí – 168 km, three hours; eight deluxe buses by Expreso Futura (25 pesos); 13 2nd-class buses by Estrella Blanca (18 pesos)

Zacatecas – 130 km, two hours; 17 1st-class buses by Omnibus de México (15 pesos); 2nd-class buses every half-hour by Rojo de los Altos (14 pesos)

There are also services (mostly frequent) to Chihuahua, Ciudad Juárez, León, Monterrey, Morelia, San Miguel de Allende and Torreón.

Train The station is about two km east of the centre, on Jardín del Ferrocarril, a few metres north of Avenida Alameda, the eastward continuation of Juan de Montoro. The ticket office is open Monday to Saturday from noon to 1.30 pm and 8 to 10.40 pm, and Sunday and holidays from 6 to 9 am and 9 to 10.40 pm.

The 'División del Norte' train between Mexico City and Ciudad Juárez stops at Aguascalientes at 6.50 am northbound (train No 7) and 10.40 pm southbound (train No 8). Primera regular fares are 8 pesos to Zacatecas and 38.70 pesos to Mexico City. See the Mexico City train section for further details.

A slow 2nd-class train, No 13 northbound (departing 9.15 pm) and No 14 southbound (7.50 am), also operates on the Mexico City-Ciudad Juárez route. There's also a 2nd-class train to/from San Luis Potosí (five hours), No 351 eastbound (departing Aguascalientes 8.20 am) and No 352 westbound.

Getting Around

Most places of interest are within easy walking distance of the centre. City buses run every day from 6 am to 10 pm; fares (0.70 or 0.90 pesos) are posted in the cab.

Bus Nos 3, 4, 9 and 13 run from the bus station to the city centre. Get off at the first stop after the tunnel under the Plaza de la Patria: this will be on 5 de Mayo or Rivero y Gutiérrez. From the city centre to the bus station, take any 'Central' bus on Moctezuma opposite the north side of the cathedral.

For the train station take bus No 17 or 19, or any other 'Estación' bus, east along Juan de Montoro from the corner of Morelos. From the station to the centre take any 'Centro' bus west along Avenida Alameda.

A taxi from the centre to the bus or train stations costs around 6 pesos, to the airport about 40 pesos.

San Luis Potosí

The state of San Luis Potosí ('poh-toh-SEE') has two of the most interesting destinations on the way south from Mexico's north-east border: the mountain ghost town of Real de Catorce and the city of San Luis Potosí itself, steeped in history and the first major colonial town reached on this route into Mexico.

The state is mostly high (average altitude around 2000 metres) and dry, with little rainfall. The exception is its eastern corner, which drops into a tropical valley (see Tampico & the Huasteca in the Central Gulf Coast chapter for coverage of this area).

Before the Spanish conquest of Mexico in 1521, western San Luis Potosí was inhabited by warlike hunters and collectors known as Guachichiles (the Aztec word for sparrows), from their custom of wearing little but loincloths and sometimes pointed bonnets resembling sparrows.

A couple of Christian missions entered the south-west of the state in the 1570s and 1580s, but it was the discovery of silver in the Cerro de San Pedro hills that really awakened Spanish interest. San Luis Potosí city was founded near these deposits in 1592. Cattle ranchers moved into the area in the 1590s too. Indians from further south – Tlaxcalans, Tarascans and Otomíes – were brought to work the mines and haciendas.

In the 18th century the area was noted for maltreatment of Indians, partly because a number of parishes were transferred from the hands of the Franciscans, who did their best to protect the Indians, into the control of the secular (non-monk) clergy. In 1767 there was an uprising sparked by the appalling conditions in the mines and discontent over the expulsion from all Spanish territory of the Jesuits, who ran the best schools in Mexico and managed their estates relatively well.

Under Spanish reforms in 1786, San Luis Potosí city became the administrative centre for a huge area covering the modern states of San Luis Potosí, Tamaulipas, Nuevo León, Coahuila and Texas. But such power lasted only until Mexican independence: in 1824 the state of San Luis Potosí was formed with its present area.

Today it's a fairly rich state; its silver mines, mostly in the northern area, are some of the richest in the country, and gold, copper, zinc and other minerals are also produced. Other major sources of wealth are agriculture (maize, beans, wheat and cotton), livestock and industry, which is mainly concentrated in the capital city.

SAN LUIS POTOSÍ
• *pop: 680,000* • *alt: 1860 metres*

The capital of San Luis Potosí state is the first major colonial city on the way south from Mexico's north-east border. It has played important roles in Mexican history, first as a silver-producing centre, later as host to governments-in-exile and revolutionaries. Today its main importance is as a regional capital and centre of industry, including brewing, textiles and metal foundries. San Luis is less spectacular and scruffier than Zacatecas, which is on an alternative route south from the USA, but its colonial heart has been preserved from industry, and its plazas, churches, museums, markets, cafés and restaurants all make it well worth some of your time if you're passing this way. It has a university and a fairly active cultural life.

History
Founded in 1592, 20 km west of the silver deposits in the Cerro de San Pedro hills, San Luis is named Potosí after the immensely rich Bolivian silver town of that name, which the Spanish hoped it would rival.

Yields from the mines started to decline in the 1620s, but the city was well enough established as a ranching centre to ensure its continued importance. It remained the major

city of north-eastern Mexico until overtaken by Monterrey at the start of the 20th century.

Known in the 19th century for its lavish houses and luxury goods imported from the USA and Europe, San Luis was twice the seat of President Benito Juárez' government during the French intervention of the 1860s. A national liberal convention here in 1901 was the first gathering in opposition to the dictatorial President Porfirio Díaz. In 1910 Díaz jailed Francisco Madero, his liberal opponent in that year's presidential election, in San Luis. Bailed out after the election, Madero here hatched his Plan de San Luis Potosí – a strategy to depose Díaz – and announced it in San Antonio, Texas, in October 1910. The plan declared the recent election illegal, named Madero provisional president and designated 20 November as the day for Mexico to rise in revolt.

Orientation
Central San Luis Potosí is a flat, compact area, stretching about 600 metres from the Alameda park in the east to the Plaza de los Fundadores and Plaza San Francisco in the west. Within this triangle lie two more main plazas, the Plaza del Carmen and the Plaza de Armas. Hotels and restaurants are mainly in this central area, with most cheaper lodgings close to the Alameda, near the train station. The bus station is on the eastern edge of the city, about 1.75 km past the Alameda. A scattered zona rosa, with a bit of nightlife and some upscale restaurants and shops, stretches some three km west from the Plaza de los Fundadores along Avenida Carranza.

Information
Tourist Office The state Dirección General de Turismo (☎ (48) 12-30-68, 12-99-43, fax 12-67-69) is at Avenida Carranza 325, next door to the Hotel Panorama half a block west of the Plaza de los Fundadores. It's open Monday to Friday from 9 am to 8 pm, Saturday 9 am to 1 pm and 4 to 8 pm. Brochures given out here suggest lots of ideas for those who want to get off the beaten track in San Luis Potosí state.

Money Numerous banks around the Plaza de Armas and Plaza de los Fundadores change cash and travellers' cheques; they're open Monday to Friday from 9 am to 1.30 pm but some only exchange currency until noon. Some have ATMs.

American Express (☎ (48) 17-60-04) at Avenida Carranza 1077, a little over one km west of the Plaza de los Fundadores, is open Monday to Friday from 9 am to 2 pm and 4 to 6 pm, Saturday 10 am to 1 pm. It sells travellers' cheques and will replace lost or stolen ones, but cannot change cheques to pesos.

Post The main post office is at Morelos 235 between Ortega and Salazar, three blocks north and one block east of the Plaza de Armas. It's open Monday to Friday from 8 am to 7 pm, Saturday 9 am to 1 pm.

Telecommunications The Telecomm office, with fax, telegram and telex services, is at Escobedo 200 on the south side of the Plaza del Carmen, at the west end of the Museo Nacional de la Máscara building. It's open Monday to Friday from 9 am to 8 pm, Saturday 9 am to noon.

There are Ladatel card and coin phones on Hidalgo in the three or four blocks north of the Plaza de Armas, and more in the bus station. Computel at Universidad 700 on the south side of the Alameda has a Lada caseta and fax service, open every day from 7 am to 9 pm. Another Computel branch at Avenida Carranza 360B, half a block west of the Plaza de los Fundadores, has the same services and hours but closes on Sunday.

Foreign Consulate There's a US consular agency (☎ (48) 12-64-44, 17-25-57) in the Instituto Mexicano-Norteamericano at Avenida Carranza 1430, two km west of the Plaza de los Fundadores; it's open Monday to Friday from 9 am to noon.

Laundry Lavandería Automática at Avenida Carranza 1093, 1.25 km west of the Plaza de los Fundadores, is open daily from 8 am to 8 pm. A load of washing costs 9.30 pesos if you drop it off or 6.50 pesos if you do it yourself.

Plaza de Armas & Around

Also known as Jardín Hidalgo, the Plaza de Armas is the city's central square, popular for chatting and watching the world go by. It's fairly quiet as traffic is channelled away from it.

The three-nave baroque **cathedral**, built between 1660 and 1730, is on the east side of the plaza. Originally it had just one tower; the northern one was added this century. The marble apostles on the façade are replicas of statues in the San Juan de Letran Basilica in Rome. The interior, remodelled in the 19th century, has a Gothic feel, with sweeping arches carved in pink stone; the leaf motif on the arches is repeated in blue and gold on the ceiling.

Beside the cathedral, on its north side, the 19th-century **Palacio Municipal** is a stocky building with powerful stone arches. Finished in 1838, it was the home of Bishop Ignacio Montes de Oca from 1892 to 1915, when it was turned over to the city. In the rear of the patio is a stone fountain carved with the heads of three lions; the city's coat of arms in stained glass overlooks the double staircase.

The **Palacio de Gobierno** lines the west side of the plaza. It was built between 1798 and 1816. Numerous important Mexicans have lodged here, including presidents Iturbide and Santa Anna, but its most illustrious occupant was Benito Juárez – first in 1863 when he was fleeing from invading French forces, then in 1867 when he confirmed the death sentence on the French puppet emperor Maximilian. In the Sala Juárez, one of the upstairs rooms that Juárez occupied, are life-size models of Juárez and, kneeling before him, Princess Ines de Salm Salm, an American who had married into Maximilian's family and came to San Luis in June 1867 to make one last plea for his life. The Sala Juárez is open Monday to Saturday from 9 am to 2.30 pm; admission is free.

Plaza de los Fundadores & Around

The busy Founders' Plaza, also called Plaza Juárez, is where the city started. On the north side is a large building housing the offices of

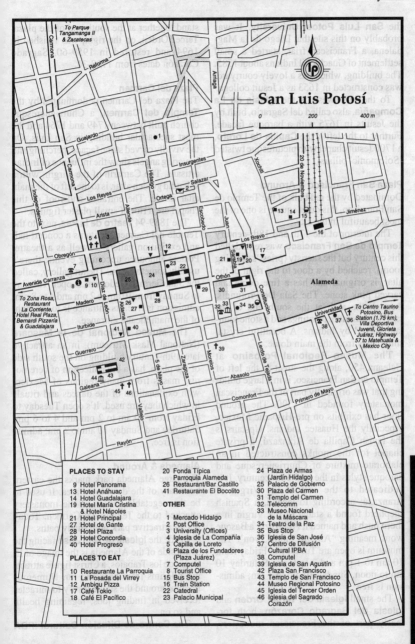

San Luis Potosí

0   200   400 m

PLACES TO STAY

9   Hotel Panorama
13 Hotel Anáhuac
14 Hotel Guadalajara
19 Hotel María Cristina
    & Hotel Nápoles
21 Hotel Principal
27 Hotel de Gante
28 Hotel Plaza
29 Hotel Concordia
40 Hotel Progreso

PLACES TO EAT

10 Restaurante La Parroquia
11 La Posada del Virrey
12 Ambigu Pizza
17 Café Tokio
18 Café El Pacífico

20 Fonda Típica
    Parroquia Alameda
26 Restaurant/Bar Castillo
41 Restaurante El Bocolito

OTHER

1   Mercado Hidalgo
2   Post Office
3   University (Offices)
4   Iglesia de La Compañía
5   Capilla de Loreto
6   Plaza de los Fundadores
    (Plaza Juárez)
7   Computel
8   Tourist Office
15 Bus Stop
16 Train Station
22 Catedral
23 Palacio Municipal

24 Plaza de Armas
    (Jardín Hidalgo)
25 Palacio de Gobierno
30 Plaza del Carmen
31 Templo del Carmen
32 Telecomm
33 Museo Nacional
    de la Máscara
34 Teatro de la Paz
35 Bus Stop
36 Iglesia de San José
37 Centro de Difusión
    Cultural IPBA
38 Computel
39 Iglesia de San Agustín
42 Plaza San Francisco
43 Templo de San Francisco
44 Museo Regional Potosino
45 Iglesia del Tercer Orden
46 Iglesia del Sagrado
    Corazón

NORTHERN CENTRAL HIGHLANDS

the **San Luis Potosí University**. It was probably on this site that Diego de la Magdalena, a Franciscan friar, started a small settlement of Guachichil Indians about 1585. The building, which has a lovely courtyard, was constructed in 1653 as a Jesuit college.

To the left (west) is the **Iglesia de La Compañía**, also called del Sagrario, built by the Jesuits in 1675 with a baroque façade. Further to the left is the **Capilla de Loreto**, a 1700 Jesuit chapel with picturesque twisted 'Solomonic' pillars.

Plaza San Francisco & Around

Dominated by the red bulk of the Templo de San Francisco, this quiet square is one of the most beautiful in the city.

The interior of the 17th and 18th-century **Templo de San Francisco** was remodelled this century but the sacristy (priest's dressing room), reached by a door to the right of the altar, is original and has a fine dome and carved pink stone. The Sala De Profundis, through the arch at the south end of the sacristy, has more paintings and a stone fountain carved by Indians. A beautiful crystal ship hangs from the main dome.

The **Museo Regional Potosino** at Galeana 450, along the street to the left of Templo de San Francisco, is in a large building that was originally part of the Franciscan monastery founded in 1590. The ground floor has exhibits on pre-Hispanic Mexico, especially the Huastec Indians. Upstairs is the lavish Capilla de Aranzazú, a private chapel for the monks constructed in an elaborate mixture of Churrigueresque and baroque styles in the mid-18th century. It is dedicated to the cult of the Virgin of Aranzazú; according to legend, a Spanish shepherd found a statue of the Virgin in a thorn bush and named it Aranzazú, a Basque word meaning 'Among thorns, you'. The museum is open are Tuesday to Friday from 10 am to 1 pm and 3 to 6 pm, Saturday 10 am to noon, Sunday 10 am to 1 pm; admission is free.

The small **Iglesia del Tercer Orden** and **Iglesia del Sagrado Corazón**, both formerly part of the Franciscan monastery, stand together at the south end of the plaza. Tercer Orden, on the right, was finished in 1694 and restored in 1959-60. Sagrado Corazón dates from 1728-31.

Plaza del Carmen

The Plaza del Carmen is dominated by the **Templo del Carmen**, a Churrigueresque church built between 1749 and 1764 and the most spectacular building in San Luis. On the vividly carved stone façade, perching and hovering angels show the influence of Indian artisans. The Camarín of the Virgin, with a splendid golden altar, is to the left of the main altar inside. The entrance and roof of this chapel are a riot of small plaster figures.

The 1889-94 **Teatro de la Paz**, next to the Templo del Carmen, contains a concert hall and exhibition gallery as well as a theatre. Posters announce upcoming events; there's usually something on. The art gallery, called the Sala Germán Gedovius, is open Tuesday to Sunday from 10 am to 2 pm and 4 to 8 pm; admission is free. Its entrance is to the right of the main theatre entrance.

The **Museo Nacional de la Máscara** (National Mask Museum), in an attractive late-19th-century building on the south side of the plaza, has a big collection of ceremonial masks from many regions of Mexico, with explanations of the dances and rituals in which they are used. It's open Tuesday to Friday from 10 am to 2 pm and 4 to 6 pm, Saturday and Sunday 10 am to 2 pm; admission is free.

Alameda & Around

The large Alameda park marks the eastern boundary of the downtown area. It used to be the vegetable garden of the monastery attached to the Templo del Carmen. Today it's an attractive park with shady paths.

Inside the **Iglesia de San José** facing the south side of the Alameda is the image of El Señor de los Trabajos, a Christ figure attracting pilgrims from near and far. Numerous retablos around the statue testify to miracles received in finding jobs, regaining health and so on.

The **Centro de Difusión Cultural IPBA**

is a cultural centre sponsored by the Instituto Potosino de Bellas Artes (Potosino Institute of Fine Arts), in a large modernistic building facing the south side of the Alameda. Inside are art galleries with changing exhibitions, and a theatre. The galleries are open Tuesday to Saturday from 10 am to 2 pm and 5 to 8 pm, Sunday 10 am to 2 pm and 6 to 8 pm; admission is free.

On Avenida Universidad, just over the railway bridge east of the Alameda, is the **Centro Taurino Potosino**, with the Plaza de Toros and, just along the street, a bullfighting museum with intricately decorated matador suits and capes, historical posters and photos, stuffed bulls' heads and more. The museum is open Tuesday to Saturday from 11 am to 2 pm and 5 to 8 pm, and Sunday 11 am to 2 pm; admission is free.

Casa de la Cultura

About 2.5 km west of the Plaza de los Fundadores at Avenida Carranza 1815, the Casa de la Cultura occupies a fine early-20th-century neoclassical building in landscaped grounds. It has a permanent collection of pre-Hispanic and colonial art. A busy programme of concerts, theatre, art exhibitions and other cultural events is held here; the schedule is posted at the entrance. Regular opening hours are Tuesday to Friday 10 am to 2 pm and 4 to 6 pm, Saturday 10 am to 2 pm and 6 to 8 pm, and Sunday from 10 am to 2 pm.

Parks

Two or three km south-west of the centre, the giant 333-hectare **Parque Tangamanga I** has a history museum, planetarium, outdoor theatre, funfair, two lakes, sports fields and hectares of green open spaces. To get there, take a southbound 'Perimetral' bus from the west end of the Alameda.

Two or three km north of the centre is the newer **Parque Tangamanga II**, another big park with sports fields and green open spaces. A 'Perimetral' bus heading north on Avenida 20 de Noviembre behind the train station will take you there.

Festivals

Among San Luis's many festivals are the following:

Semana Santa The week before Easter is celebrated with concerts, exhibitions and other activities. On Good Friday morning Christ's passion is re-enacted in the barrio of San Juan de Guadalupe, followed by a silent procession through the city.

Festival de Arte Primavera Potosina The Spring Arts Festival, normally held in the last two weeks of May, presents concerts, art exhibitions, theatre, dance, films and more, with national and international artists. Check with the tourist office for exact dates.

Festival Nacional de Danza This national festival of contemporary dance is held in the last two weeks of July.

Feria Nacional Potosina The San Luis Potosí National Fair isn't held every year but is normally in the last two weeks of August when it takes place. It's a festival of cultural and popular events including concerts, bullfights, rodeos, cockfights and sports events, and livestock and agriculture shows.

San Luis Rey On 25 August, day of San Luis Rey de Francia (St Louis, King of France), the city's patron saint, various events are organised including a large parade with floats.

Places to Stay – bottom end

Camping The *Motel El Mezquite* (☎ (48) 12-03-65) is 13.5 km north of the city centre on highway 57 to Matehuala. It has a trailer park with a swimming pool and 50 trailer spaces with full hook-ups; the cost for a vehicle and two people is 30 pesos. There are rooms here, too, at 65/75 pesos for singles/doubles.

Hostel San Luis' youth hostel is the *Villa Deportiva Juvenil* (☎ (48) 18-16-17) on Avenida Diagonal Sur, 1½ blocks north of the bus station and just before the big Glorieta Juárez intersection. From the exit of the bus station's 2nd-class hall, turn right, walk to the main road, then go 1½ blocks left. From the 1st-class hall, go left and walk 1½ blocks.

Separate-sex dorms sleep four to a room; cost is 11 pesos a night. In the grounds are various sports facilities. The office is open daily from 6 am to 11 pm.

Hotels There are three very central hotels in this range, plus others a short distance west of the train station.

Hotel Plaza (☎ (48) 12-46-31) at Jardín Hidalgo 22, on the south side of the Plaza de Armas, is in an 18th-century building. The 32 singles/doubles have private bathrooms and cost 45/55 pesos. The few at the front, overlooking the plaza, are the best. The others open onto two upstairs patios, but are dark, dilapidated and rather airless.

The *Hotel de Gante* (☎ (48) 12-14-92/93) at 5 de Mayo 140, half a block south of the Plaza de Armas, is much better. Large, bright, comfortable rooms with sizeable bathrooms and TV cost 61/65 pesos.

Hotel Progreso (☎ (48) 12-03-66) nearby at Aldama 415 is another older place, with classical-looking 1920s statues of ladies overlooking the staircase and lobby. In its day it was probably a classy place. Some of the 51 largeish, high-ceilinged rooms have been modernised, others haven't, but either way the price is 48/53 pesos. There are a couple of superior modernised doubles with TV for 85 pesos.

The *Hotel Anáhuac* (☎ (48) 12-65-04/05, fax 14-49-04) at Xochitl 140, one block west and one north of the train station, has 43 sizeable, bright rooms for 48/56 pesos, plus a restaurant and parking facilities.

The *Hotel Guadalajara* (☎ (48) 12-46-12) at Jiménez 253, on the small plaza between the station and the Hotel Anáhuac, has enclosed parking and 33 clean, comfortable rooms with ample windows, colour TV and fan. Cost is 60 pesos single, 65 pesos for a one-bed double, 70 pesos for two beds.

Hotel Principal (☎ (48) 12-07-84) at Juan Sarabia 145, three blocks west of the station, has small, dark rooms, but it's tolerably clean. The 18 rooms have private baths and cost 30/40 pesos.

Places to Stay – middle

Hotel María Cristina (☎ (48) 12-94-08, fax 12-88-23) and *Hotel Nápoles* (☎ (48) 12-84-18), side by side on Juan Sarabia, a short block north-west of the Alameda, are twins in price – 99/110 pesos for singles/doubles –

and very similar in quality. The nine-storey María Cristina (at Juan Sarabia 110) has nice, comfortable, bright rooms with satellite colour TV, carpet and fan. The Nápoles (Juan Sarabia 120) has comfortable, modern rooms with the same facilities. Both hotels have parking and their own restaurants.

Slightly more central and also at the same price, the *Hotel Concordia* (☎ (48) 12-06-66, fax 12-69-79), on the corner of Othón and Morelos, is an older hotel but in a modern style; its 94 rooms all have colour TV, carpeting and other amenities. Choose an exterior room if you can, as the interior ones can be a bit musty. There's parking and an inexpensive restaurant.

There are also two middle-range hotels near the bus station. Opposite the station's 2nd-class hall, at José Guadalupe Torres 158, is the *Hotel Arizona* (☎ (48) 18-18-48, fax 22-21-82). It's clean and modern, with 92 rooms at 99/110 pesos (again), but seems a bit overpriced. Half a block west and two short blocks north, at Avenida de las Torres 290, the *Hotel Central* (☎ (48) 12-14-44) is cheaper at 75/95 pesos but pleasant enough. The 70 clean rooms have colour TV, carpet and ample windows. It has its own restaurant and parking.

Motels on highway 57, heading out of San Luis towards Mexico City, include the *Motel Cactus* (☎ (48) 22-02-92) charging 135 pesos for a single or one-bed double; and *Motel Sand's* (☎ (48) 18-24-13), charging 100/125 pesos.

Places to Stay – top end

Near the south-west corner of the Plaza de los Fundadores, the *Hotel Panorama* (☎ (48) 12-17-77, fax 12-45-91) at Avenida Carranza 315 is a luxury 10-storey, four-star hotel. All 126 rooms have full-wall windows and most on the south side have private balconies overlooking the swimming pool. Singles/doubles are 180/210 pesos. The hotel has a good 10th-floor restaurant, a piano bar and one of the city's best discos.

About 700 metres further west at Avenida Carranza 890, the *Hotel Real Plaza* (☎ 14-60-55, fax 14-66-39) is another modern four-star hotel with every amenity, and the same prices as the Panorama.

On highway 57 to Mexico City, about 500 metres past the Glorieta Juárez intersection on the eastern edge of the city, the *Hotel Real de Minas* (☎ (48) 18-26-16, fax 18-69-15) has 178 rooms in landscaped grounds at 200/230 pesos. The *Hotel María Dolores* (☎ (48) 22-18-82, fax 22-06-02), also top-end, is across the road.

Places to Eat

Around Plaza de Armas *Ambigu Pizza*, a bright little café at the north-east corner of the Plaza de Armas, serves up quick chicken and fries for 10 to 20 pesos and respectable pizzas from 20 to 42 pesos. *La Posada del Virrey* on the north side of the same plaza is a fancier restaurant in a former home of Spanish viceroys, built in 1736. It has an attractive covered courtyard with live music at lunchtime. You can come for meals or just for coffee and desserts like banana split or cheesecake; it's open every day from 7 am to midnight. Meat and seafood dinners are 16 to 26 pesos.

Restaurant/Bar Castillo at Madero 145, half a block west of the Plaza de Armas, is a cheaper spot for dining or just hanging out over coffee. At breakfast, the egg choices are generous, coming with beans and salad for 6 pesos. It's open every day, 8 am to 11 pm.

Restaurante La Parroquia on the south side of the Plaza de los Fundadores is a large, clean, popular place with fairly generous portions. The four-course comida corrida is 14 pesos, many à la carte main dishes are 16 to 18 pesos. It's open every day from 7 am to midnight.

The friendly *Restaurante El Bocolito* on the north-east corner of Plaza San Francisco serves up huge platters with names like gringa, sarape and mula india, which are combinations of meats fried up with herbs, onion, chile, tomato and green pepper, often with melted cheese on top. These cost 14 to 16 pesos. Tacos and cheap breakfasts are served too. It's open every day from 8.30 am to 10.30 pm and is a cooperative venture of

the Casas José Martí, benefiting young Indian students.

Worth considering for a special lunch or dinner is the *Sky Room* restaurant up on the 10th floor of the Hotel Panorama at Avenida Carranza 315. It serves an array of international dishes and its full-wall windows offer a great view over the entire city. There's music for dancing every night from 9 pm to 2 am, except Sunday night when there's a pianist.

Alameda Area *Café Tokio* at Othón 415, facing the north-west corner of the Alameda, is a large, clean, air-con restaurant good for all meals; the comida corrida is 17.50 pesos, antojitos (enchiladas, tacos, etc) 9.50 to 14.50 pesos, meat and seafood meals 14 to 26 pesos. It's open every day from 7 am to midnight.

Café El Pacífico on the corner of Los Bravo and Constitución is a similar place with a similar menu and prices, open 24 hours a day. Also in the same price range is the *Fonda Típica Parroquia Alameda* on the corner of Constitución and Othón, a cheerful place with brightly painted chairs and tables, a big range of breakfasts, live music Friday and Saturday nights, and open all night on Friday and Saturday.

Zona Rosa One of San Luis' most attractive eateries is the *Restaurant La Corriente* at Avenida Carranza 700, 400 metres west of the Plaza de los Fundadores. This fancy plant-filled courtyard restaurant specialises in regional ranch-style food. A good four-course comida corrida is served for 15 pesos Monday to Saturday. A la carte main dishes are 25 to 35 pesos, antojitos (served from 7 pm only) are 12 to 15 pesos. The Corriente is open every day from 8 am to midnight; there's music in the evenings.

About the brightest atmosphere of any eatery in San Luis is at *Bernardi Pizzeria*, 2.25 km west of the Plaza de los Fundadores at Avenida Carranza 1670. A young, happy crowd enjoys live music in the evenings and good pizzas at reasonable prices: the mediana size, enough for two or three people, costs 28 to 40 pesos. It's open daily.

Entertainment

San Luis has quite an active entertainment scene. Ask in the tourist office for what's on and keep your eyes on posters. The Teatro de la Paz has something on most nights; concerts, theatre, exhibitions and other events are also presented at places like the Centro de Difusión Cultural IPBA, the Casa de la Cultura, and the Teatro de la Ciudad in Parque Tangamanga I. *Guiarte* schedules posted at some of these places give full listings of what's on.

Chanok is a lively little rock music club at Avenida Carranza 1519, two km west of the Plaza de los Fundadores, open Thursday to Saturday evenings. Also worth a look is the *Dali Video-Bar* at Avenida Carranza 1145, about 750 metres back towards the centre. Two of the best discos are *La Jaula* in the Hotel Panorama (entry 25 pesos), and the *Disco Oasis*, usually open Thursday to Saturday nights and popular with students, in the Hotel María Dolores.

Things to Buy

A few handicraft shops are dotted around town. Probably best is the Consejo Estatal para la Cultura y las Artes, next to the Templo San Francisco, but there's little local stuff available. The main area of shops is between the Plaza de Armas and the Mercado Hidalgo, four blocks north.

Getting There & Away

Air The airport is 23 km north of the city, on highway 57 towards Matehuala. A handy travel agency for making flight arrangements is Solymar (☎ /fax 14-71-87) at Avenida Carranza 713, 400 metres west of the Plaza de los Fundadores. Mexicana (☎ 17-89-20) at Avenida Carranza 2325 flies direct to/from Mexico City daily, and Chicago daily via either Monterrey or Zacatecas. Aeromar flies direct to/from Mexico City several times daily and San Antonio (Texas) three times weekly. Aerolitoral flies direct to/from Guadalajara, Querétaro, Tampico, Monterrey and San Antonio daily. Aeromar and Aerolitoral share the Aeroméxico office (☎ 17-79-36) at Avenida Carranza 1160.

Bus The bus station (Central de Autobuses) is on the eastern outskirts of the city, on the corner of Avenida Diagonal Sur and José Guadalupe Torres, just south of the big Glorieta Juárez intersection. San Luis Potosí is a major hub of bus transport and the terminal has separate departure halls for 1st, 2nd and 3rd-class buses. The ticket counters outside each hall correspond roughly to these classes. The station has Ladatel coin and card phones (in the 1st-class hall), a guardería de equipaje for storing luggage (opposite the 3rd-class ticket counters, open 7 am to 9 pm), a restaurant, a post office and a Telecomm office with fax and telegram service.

Daily departures include:

Aguascalientes – 168 km, three hours; hourly deluxe buses by Expreso Futura (25 pesos); 10 2nd-class by Estrella Blanca (18 pesos)

Guadalajara – 354 km, five to six hours; seven deluxe buses by ETN (69 pesos); three 1st-class by Servicios Coordinados (43 pesos) and four by Transportes Frontera (40 pesos); nine 2nd-class by Omnibus de Oriente

Guanajuato – 210 km, four hours; seven 2nd-class buses by Flecha Amarilla (23 pesos)

Matehuala – 191 km, 2½ hours; hourly 1st-class buses by Autobuses Blancos Saltillo-Torreón (22 pesos); hourly de paso buses by Transportes Frontera (22 pesos 1st-class, 19 pesos 2nd-class)

Mexico City (Terminal Norte) – 400 km, five to six hours; 17 deluxe buses each by ETN (80 pesos) and Expreso Futura (62 pesos); 11 to 17 1st-class each by Transportes Frontera, Omnibus de México, Transportes del Norte and Transportes Chihuahuaenses (52 or 53 pesos)

Monterrey – 537 km, six to seven hours; seven deluxe buses by Expreso Futura (78 pesos); hourly 1st-class buses by Autobuses Blancos Saltillo-Torreón (70 pesos) and seven daily by Transportes del Norte (61 pesos); 15 or more 2nd-class buses by Estrella Blanca (53 pesos)

Querétaro – 200 km, 2½ to three hours; deluxe buses by Expreso Futura and ETN (32 to 36 pesos); frequent 1st-class buses by Autobuses Blancos Saltillo-Torreón, Omnibus de México and Transportes del Norte (24 to 27 pesos); 15 2nd-class by Flecha Amarilla (22 pesos)

San Miguel de Allende – 153 km, three hours; eight 2nd-class buses by Flecha Amarilla (19.50 pesos)

Zacatecas – 190 km, three hours; two deluxe buses by Expreso Futura (26 pesos); seven 1st-class by Transportes Chihuahuaenses (22 pesos); eight 2nd-class by Estrella Blanca (18 pesos)

There are also many buses to Ciudad Juárez, Ciudad Valles, Ciudad Victoria, Chihuahua, Dolores Hidalgo, Morelia, Saltillo, Tampico and Torreón, and several a day to Ciudad Acuña, León, Matamoros, Nuevo Laredo, Piedas Negras and Reynosa.

Train The Estación del Ferrocarril is on the north side of the Alameda. The main trains through San Luis Potosí are El Regiomontano, train Nos 71 and 72, running between Mexico City and Monterrey with primera especial and coche dormitorio accommodation; and train Nos 1 and 2 between Mexico City and Nuevo Laredo, with primera regular and primera especial seats. See the Mexico City Getting There & Away section for timetables.

Tickets for El Regiomontano are sold only between 11 am and 12.30 pm. Tickets for other trains go on sale one hour before departure. Fares on El Regiomontano (primera especial/one-person camarín) are 53.55/111.10 pesos to Mexico City and 61/126 pesos to Monterrey. Fares on train Nos 1 and 2 (primera regular/primera especial) are 29.10/44.75 pesos to Mexico City, 11/18 pesos to San Miguel de Allende and 48/80 pesos to Nuevo Laredo.

There are also 2nd-class trains to/from Aguascalientes (five hours), leaving San Luis at noon, and Tampico (six hours), leaving San Luis at 8 am.

The trains are often late, and schedules are subject to change. Check the current schedules at the station.

Car Rental agencies include Budget (☎ 11-10-92) at Avenida Carranza 1160A, Dollar (☎ 22-14-11) in the Hotel María Dolores, and Robinson (☎ 17-68-86) at Avenida Carranza 1529.

Getting Around

To/From the Airport Taxi Aéreo (☎ 12-21-22) runs a colectivo to/from the airport for 42 pesos per person, but for two or more people a taxi (about the same price) is cheaper for the half-hour trip.

Bus City buses run every day from 5.30 am to around 10 pm; they cost 0.50 or 0.80 pesos, seemingly dependent on how clapped-out they are. To reach the centre from the bus station, walk left from the exit of the 2nd-class hall and take any 'Centro' bus from the first corner. A convenient place to get off is Avenida 20 de Noviembre, the first stop past the Alameda. Returning from the city to the bus station, take a 'Central' bus southbound on Constitución on the west side of the Alameda.

For places along Avenida Carranza, pick up a 'Morales' bus in front of the train station or anywhere on Carranza west of Avenida Reforma, 400 metres west of the Plaza de los Fundadores.

SANTA MARÍA DEL RÍO
• *pop: 9600*

Forty-seven km south of San Luis Potosí, just off the highway to Mexico City, this small town is known for its excellent handmade rebozos and inlaid woodwork. The rebozos are usually made of synthetic silk thread called *artisela*, in less garish colours than in many Mexican textile centres. You can see and buy them at the Escuela del Rebozo (Rebozo School) on the central Plaza Hidalgo, and in a few private workshops. A Rebozo Fair is held each year in the first half of August. There's a motel and restaurant, the *Puesta del Sol* (☎ (485) 3-00-59), at the entrance to Santa María from the highway. Autobuses Rojos and Autobuses Potosinos companies both run frequent 3rd-class buses to Santa María from San Luis Potosí for 4 pesos.

GOGORRÓN

The Balneario de Gogorrón is the major hot-springs resort in the San Luis area; its waters reach 42°C and are allegedly beneficial for rheumatism and arthritis. It's 56 km south of the city on the Villa de Reyes-San Felipe road, which branches south-west off the main Mexico City road. Facilities include four large swimming pools, two children's pools, private Roman baths, large green areas, basketball and volleyball courts and horse riding. The resort is open every day from 9 am to 6 pm; cost for day use is 15 pesos (children 12 pesos).

If you want to stay over, accommodation is available in comfortable bungalows. With three meals a day, the cost for two adults is 245 pesos in smaller bungalows, 340 pesos in large ones. A stay without meals is about half-price. All the bungalows have private Roman baths.

You can get more information and make reservations at the Gogorrón office (☎ (48) 12-15-50, 12-36-36), in office 52 at Othón 100, San Luis Potosí, on the Plaza de Armas. It's open Monday to Friday from 9 am to 8 pm, Saturday 9 am to 2 pm.

Getting There & Away
Gogorrón can easily be visited on a day trip from San Luis. From the bus station, Autobuses Rojos runs hourly to Gogorrón for 5 pesos, or you could take a Flecha Amarilla bus heading for San Felipe. It takes about an hour to reach Gogorrón and the bus will drop you off right at the gate.

MATEHUALA
• *pop: 60,000* • *alt: 1600 metres*
The only town of any size on highway 57 between Saltillo and San Luis Potosí, Matehuala ('ma-te-WAL-a') is unremarkable but quite a pleasant and prosperous place high on the Altiplano Central. Matehuala was founded in the 17th century, and its central streets have a colonial air. Most travellers just use it to get to Real de Catorce, but the town has attracted long-term visitors from time to time. It's a friendly place – strangers will talk to you in the plaza.

Orientation
Central Matehuala lies between two plazas about 400 metres apart: the shady Plaza de Armas with a kiosk in the middle, and the bustling Placita del Rey to the north, with a large concrete church. Cheaper hotels and the town's restaurants are in this area; motels are on highway 57 which bypasses the town to the east.

The bus station is just off the highway,

about two km south of the centre. To walk to the centre from the bus station, turn left out of the entrance, then go straight along the road (5 de Mayo) for about 1.5 km until you reach the corner of Guerrero, where you turn left. Guerrero ends after a few blocks when it meets Morelos. The Plaza de Armas is a few metres to the left along Morelos.

Festivals
Matehuala has two main festivals:

Fiesta del Cristo de Matehuala Held in the first two
  weeks of January, the festival includes religious
  ceremonies and processions, fireworks, folk
  dances, rodeos and cockfights. The main day is
  6 January.
Founding of Matehuala From 8 to 16 July a feria
  celebrates the founding of the town.

Places to Stay
In Town The place with the most atmosphere is the *Hotel Matehuala* (☎ (488) 2-06-80) on the corner of Bustamante and Hidalgo. The departure point for buses to Real de Catorce is close. The hotel has a large central courtyard with rooms on two levels around it. Rooms are basic, but the place has a pleasant atmosphere and friendly staff. Singles/doubles are 40/45 pesos. Rooms away from the street are much quieter.

Elsewhere, the *Hotel Alamo* (☎ (488) 2-00-17) on Guerrero near the Morelos end is adequate, with singles/doubles at 25/35 pesos. The *Hotel María Esther* is a family-run place where singles/doubles with private bath, TV and car parking cost only 46/50 pesos. It's on Madero – go north along Hidalgo, past the church, and turn right at the traffic lights.

On the Highway Several 60s-style motels dot highway 57 as it passes Matehuala to the east. They include, in north-south order, the *Hacienda* (☎ (488) 2-00-65) where singles/doubles are 90/110 pesos; *Las Palmas* (☎ (488) 2-00-02), with a camping area, which is slightly more expensive; and *El Dorado* (☎ (488) 2-01-74) with rooms at 92/114 pesos. All three have their own restaurants.

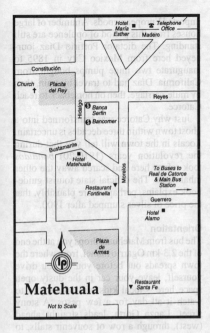

Matehuala

Not to Scale

Places to Eat

Restaurant Santa Fe, on the Plaza de Armas, is clean, friendly and reasonably priced, and serves generous portions of good plain food – tasty tacos are 1.60 pesos; meat dishes around 20 pesos. A comida corrida is around 14 pesos. It's also a good place for a cheap breakfast.

Restaurant Fontinella (☎ 2-02-93), at Morelos 618 around the corner from the Hotel Matehuala, does a reasonable-value four-course comida corrida plus coffee for 14 pesos, and has good regional dishes.

Getting There & Away

Bus From the central de autobuses there are fairly frequent services north and south, but Matehuala is mid-route for most buses so you can usually buy tickets only when the bus arrives.

Companies passing through Matehuala are Transportes del Norte (1st class), Autobuses Anáhuac (1st and 2nd class),

Transportes Frontera (1st and 2nd class) and Transportes Tamaulipas (2nd class). There are frequent buses to main destinations including:

Mexico City (Terminal Norte) – 585 km, eight hours; some 1st-class directo (76 pesos) buses, and many 2nd class de paso (66 pesos)
Monterrey – 340 km, 5 hours; 1st-class (41 pesos) and 2nd-class (35 pesos)
Nuevo Laredo – 518 km, eight hours; three 1st-class buses per day (75 pesos)
Querétaro – 393 km, five hours; 1st-class (48 pesos) and 2nd-class (42 pesos)
Saltillo – 261 km, four hours; 1st-class (30 pesos) and 2nd-class (25 pesos)
San Luis Potosí – 191 km, 1½ hours; 1st-class (25 pesos) and 2nd-class (20 pesos)

Buses also go to Real de Catorce (see the Getting Around section following), Guanajuato and Reynosa.

Getting Around

Beige buses marked 'Centro' run from the bus station to the town centre but aren't very frequent; buses marked 'Central' go the other way. It's often quicker to walk (25 minutes).

Buses for Real de Catorce leave at 8 and 10 am, noon, 2 pm and 6 pm from Guerrero, a little way to the east of the Hotel Alamo and on the other side of the road. One-way fare is 7.20 pesos. It's a good idea to buy your ticket early – an hour before departure time.

REAL DE CATORCE

• *pop: 1000* • *alt: 2756 metres*

This is a place with a touch of magic. High in an offshoot of the Sierra Madre Oriental, Real de Catorce was a wealthy and important silver-mining town of 40,000 people until early this century. Thirty km west of Matehuala and reached by a road tunnel through former mine shafts, the town lies in a narrow valley at a high elevation, with spectacular views westward to the plain below.

A few years ago it was almost deserted, its paved streets lined with decaying or boarded-up stone houses, its mint a ruin, and only a few hundred people eking out an existence from old mine workings or from visiting pilgrims. Pilgrims still come to pay homage to the figure of Saint Francis of Assisi in the town's church, and the festival of San Francisco, on 4 October, attracts between 100,000 and 200,000 people between 25 September and 12 October. Recently, Real has begun to attract trendier residents – wealthy Mexicans and gringos looking for an unusual retreat, and a few Europeans setting up hotels and restaurants. Film makers use the town and the surrounding hills, and some artists have settled here too. Old buildings are being restored, and the town may well become another Taxco or San Miguel de Allende.

The Huichol Indians, who live 400 km away on the Durango-Nayarit-Jalisco-Zacatecas borders, believe that their peyote and maize gods live here. Every May or June they make a pilgrimage to the hills around Catorce, known to them as Wírikuta, for rituals involving peyote. This hallucinogenic cactus has great cultural and religious significance, and its indiscriminate use by foreigners is regarded as obnoxious and offensive.

You can visit Real de Catorce for a day trip from Matehuala, but it's worth staying for a few days to explore the surrounding hills and soak up the atmosphere.

History

The name Real de Catorce literally means 'Royal of 14': the '14' probably comes from 14 soldiers killed by Indians in the area about 1700. The town was founded in the mid-18th century and the church was built between 1783 and 1817.

The mines had their ups and downs: during the independence war years (1810-21) some of the shafts were flooded and in 1821-22 an Englishman called Robert Phillips made a year-long journey from London to Catorce bringing a 'steam machine' for pumping the water from the mines.

Real de Catorce reached its peak in the late 19th century when it was producing an estimated US$3 million in silver a year, and had a theatre, a bull ring and shops selling imported European goods. A number of large houses from this period of opulence are still standing. The dictator Porfirio Díaz journeyed here from Mexico City in 1895 to inaugurate two mine pumps bought from California. Díaz had to travel by train, then by mule-carriage, then on horseback to reach Catorce.

Just why Catorce was transformed into a ghost town within three decades is uncertain. Locals in the town will tell you that during the revolution years (1910-20) *bandidos* took refuge here and scared away the other inhabitants. The official state tourist guidebook explains, perhaps more plausibly, that the price of silver slumped after 1900.

Orientation

The bus from Matehuala drops you at the end of the 2.3-km Ogarrio tunnel, from where the town spreads out before you. If you drive yourself, leave your car in the dusty open space here – local kids will hassle you to watch it all day for a few pesos. A stony street, Lanza Gorta, leads straight ahead (west), through a row of souvenir stalls, to the church at the centre of town. There's one public phone in town, on the north side of the plaza near the church.

Parroquia

The parish church is quite an impressive neoclassical building but it's the reputedly miraculous image of St Francis of Assisi on one of the side altars that is the attraction for thousands of Mexican pilgrims. A cult has grown up this century around the statue, whose help is sought in solving problems. Some believe it can cleanse their sins.

In a separate area in the back of the church are walls covered with retablos. These usually have a naive depiction of some life-threatening situation from which St Francis has rescued the victim, and include a brief description of the incident and some words of prayer and gratitude. Car accidents and medical operations are common themes. Retablos have become much sought after by collectors, and are sometimes seen in antique or souvenir shops. Many of those on sale have been stolen from old churches, which must be very bad karma.

Casa de la Moneda

Opposite the façade of the church, the old mint (literally House of Money), which is in bad repair, is being used as a craft centre and may be due for restoration. Coins were minted here for a few years in the 1860s.

Plaza Hidalgo

Further west along Lanza Gorta, past the church and mint, you reach some steps going up from the right side of the street to this small plaza, terraced into the hillside. The plaza was constructed in 1888 with a fountain in the middle; the kiosk you see now replaced the fountain in 1927. Around the plaza are a few pleasant restaurants and a place to rent ponies.

Palenque de Gallos & Plaza de Toros

A block or so north-west of the plaza lies a monument to the town's heyday – a cock-fighting ring built like a Roman amphitheatre. It was restored in the 1970s and now hosts occasional theatre or dance performances. It's normally locked, but someone at the mint may have a key to let you in. Further up the hill on Calle Zaragoza you reach the edge of the town. Here you'll find the Panteón (graveyard), which is worth a look, and the bullring (Plaza de Toros), which has recently been restored.

Museum

On Lanza Gorta, facing the side of the church, is a small museum containing photos, documents and other junk rescued from the crumbling town, including an ancient, rusting car, said to be the first to reach Catorce. It's open from 10 am to 5 pm Thursday to Saturday, and admission costs 1 peso.

Places to Stay & Eat

Real de Catorce has cheap casas de huéspedes which cater mainly to pilgrims, and some attractive mid-range places in restored buildings.

On Lanza Gorta between the bus stop and the church, Casa de Huéspedes La Providencia has basic singles or doubles for 30 pesos, some with views down the valley. The attached restaurant does an excellent comida corrida for around 13 pesos. For rock-bottom accommodation, you may be able to rent a room from Doña Celia. Her place is behind a blue door, the second one on the left of the church. The rooms are small, with zero luxuries and a shared bathroom, for 15 pesos a single or double.

El Real, up the hill to the right off Lanza Gorta one block after the church, is an old house restored to provide a few quite comfortable bedrooms at 70 pesos a double, and there's an attractive restaurant serving Italian and other food. There's another branch, El Real II, up the hill from the church. On the far side of town, on Zaragoza, is the Quinta La Puesta Del Sol, with little old-world charm but a superb view down the valley to the west. Rooms with TV and private bath cost 100 pesos on weekends, 80 pesos during the week, or a special price of 60 pesos if they really want to rent a room.

The best place is El Corral de Conde (☎ (488) 2-37-33), with six very comfortable rooms in a tastefully restored old house. They speak French and charge 150 pesos including breakfast.

El Cactus Café, on Plaza Juárez, does a basic comida corrida from about 14 pesos, but for a bit more money, and with a bit of advance notice, the Italian chef here could make you something really special. Try some excellent minestrone (about 8 pesos) or creamy lasagne (12 pesos).

Getting There & Away

Bus Five buses a day make the journey from Matehuala to Real de Catorce and back. One-way fare is 7.20 pesos and the journey takes at least 1¼ hours. In Matehuala the buses leave at 8 and 10 am, noon, 2 and 6 pm, and it's advisable to get your ticket early – an hour before departure. You can buy return tickets.

Train Estación de Catorce is at the bottom of

the hill, down a very rough road about 17 km west of town. Very slow segunda clase trains go to Saltillo and San Luis Potosí – strictly for campesinos and rail enthusiasts.

Car From highway 57, turn off to Cedral, 27 km away on a mostly paved road. From Matehuala you can take a back road to Cedral, and avoid going out onto the highway. After Cedral, turn south to reach Catorce on what must be one of the longest cobblestone streets in the world. It's a slow but spectacular drive, up a steep mountainside, past various abandoned buildings. The Ogarrio tunnel, part of the old mine, is only wide enough for one vehicle; men stationed at each end with telephones control traffic and collect a 5-peso toll as you go in. You may have to wait up to 20 minutes for traffic in the opposite direction to pass. If it's really busy, you may have to leave your car at the tunnel entrance and continue to Catorce on a minibus.

Guanajuato

The state of Guanajuato was historically one of Mexico's richest. After silver was found in Zacatecas, Spanish prospectors combed the rugged lands north of Mexico City and were rewarded by discoveries of silver, gold, iron, lead, zinc and tin.

For two centuries 30% to 40% of the world's silver was mined in Guanajuato. Silver barons in Guanajuato city lived opulent lives at the expense of Indians who worked the mines, first as slave labour and then as wage slaves.

Eventually the growing well-heeled criollo class of Guanajuato and Querétaro began to resent the dominance and arrogance of the Spanish-born in the colony. After the occupation of much of Spain by Napoleon Bonaparte's troops in 1808 and subsequent political confusion in Mexico, some provincial criollos began – while meeting as 'literary societies' – to draw up plans for rebellion.

The house of a member of one such group in Querétaro was raided on 13 September 1810. Three days later a colleague, parish priest Miguel Hidalgo, declared independence in Dolores, Guanajuato. After Dolores, San Miguel de Allende was the first town to fall to the rebels, Celaya the second, Guanajuato the third. Guanajuato state is proud to have given birth to Mexico's most glorious moment and is visited almost as a place of pilgrimage by people from far and wide. Today Guanajuato has some important industrial centres like León (famous for its shoes and other leather goods), Salamanca (which has a big oil refinery), Celaya and Irapuato. It's also a fertile agricultural state, producing grains, vegetables and fruit – most famously the strawberries grown around Irapuato – and still an important source of silver, gold and fluorspar.

GUANAJUATO

• *pop: 100,000* • *alt: 2017 metres*

Guanajuato is a city crammed onto the steep slopes of a ravine, with underground tunnels acting as streets. This impossible topography was settled in 1559 because the silver and gold mines found here were among the richest in the world. Many of the colonial structures built from this wealth remain intact, making Guanajuato a living monument to a prosperous, turbulent past.

But it's not only the past that resounds from Guanajuato's narrow cobbled streets. The University of Guanajuato, known for its arts programmes, attracts 15,000 students each year, giving the city a youthfulness, vibrancy and cultural life just as attractive as the colonial architecture and exotic setting. The city's cultural side peaks during the Festival Internacional Cervantino, usually held in October each year.

History

One of the hemisphere's richest veins of silver was uncovered in 1558 at La Valenciana Mine, five km north of Guanajuato. For 250 years, the excavation of what is now the periphery above the city produced 20% of the world's silver. Colonial barons benefiting from this mineral treasure were infuriated when King Charles III of Spain slashed their share of the wealth in 1765. The king's 1767 decree banishing Jesuits from Spanish dominions further alienated both the wealthy barons and the poor Indian miners who gave allegiance to the Jesuits.

This anger found a focus in the War of Independence. In 1810 the priest and rebel leader Miguel Hidalgo, whose Grito (Cry for Independence) in nearby Dolores set off Mexico's independence movement, took Guanajuato with the assistance of its citizenry – the first military victory of the independence rebellion. When the Spaniards eventually retook the city they retaliated by conducting the infamous 'lottery of death', in which names of Guanajuato citizens were drawn at random and the unlucky 'winners' were tortured and hanged.

Independence was eventually won, freeing the silver barons to amass further wealth with which mansions, churches and theatres were built, ensuring that Guanajuato would become one of Mexico's most handsome cities.

Orientation

Guanajuato's central area is quite compact, with only a few major streets. The main street, running roughly west-east, is called Juárez from the Mercado Hidalgo to the Basilica on Plaza de la Paz, then Obregón from the Basilica to the Jardín de la Unión, the city's main plaza, then Sopeña as it continues east.

Roughly parallel to Juárez and Obregón is another long street, running west-east from the Alhóndiga to the university, and going through the names 28 de Septiembre, Galarza, Positos and Lascuraín de Retana along the way. Hidalgo, parallelling Sopeña, is another important street. Once you know these streets you can't get lost in the centre. You can, however, have a great time getting lost among the city's *callejones* – the maze of narrow, crooked alleys winding up the hills from the centre.

Another twist on getting around the city is that several of the major roadways are under the ground. These are only used by vehicular traffic, however. Many were created along the dried-up bed of Río Guanajuato, which was diverted elsewhere after it flooded the city in 1905.

Information

Tourist Office The state-run tourist office (☎ (473) 2-15-74, 2-00-86), in a courtyard at Plaza de la Paz 14 almost opposite the Basilica, has a large 'Información Turística' sign. The friendly staff give out free city maps and brochures about the city and state of Guanajuato in Spanish and English; they also sell larger, more detailed maps (3 pesos). The office is open Monday to Friday from 8.30 am to 7.30 pm, Saturday and Sunday 10 am to 2 pm.

Another branch of the tourist office is in the bus station. It's open Tuesday to Sunday from 10 am to 3 pm.

Money There are a number of banks on Plaza de la Paz and Juárez, open Monday to Friday from 9 am to 1.30 pm. When these are closed, some of the larger hotels will change money at slightly less favourable rates.

Post The main post office is at the eastern end of Lascuraín de Retana, opposite the Templo de la Compañía. It's open Monday to Friday from 9 am to 8 pm, Saturday 9 am to 1 pm. There's another post office in the bus station, open Monday to Friday, 9 am to 4 pm.

Telecommunications The Telecomm office at Sopeña 1, beside the Teatro Juárez and opposite the Jardín de la Unión, has telegram, telex and fax services. It's open Monday to Friday from 9 am to 8 pm, Saturday 9 am to noon.

There are Ladatel coin and card phones in an alley off the south side of Obregón in the centre. The Lada caseta in the bus station is open 24 hours every day. Another in the Miscelanea Unión shop at Hidalgo 18, just east of the Jardín de la Unión, is open daily from 9.30 am to 4 pm and 6 to 10 pm. The Lonchería Pípila, at Alonso 14 in the same block as the Casa Kloster, also has a Lada caseta which is open daily.

Laundry Lavandería Automática Internacional has two branches where you can drop off your laundry or do it yourself. One is at the eastern end of the centre at Manuel Doblado 28, on the corner of Hidalgo. The other is in the west of the town at Alhóndiga 35A. Both are open Monday to Saturday from 9 am to 2 pm and 4 to 8 pm.

Jardín de la Unión & Other Plazas
Pretty Jardín de la Unión, surrounded by cafés and shaded by trees, is the social heart of the city. People congregate here in the late afternoons and evenings, with guitarists serenading everyone.

The steps of **Plazuela de los Ángeles** on Juárez are a popular congregating spot for students, with the Callejón del Beso just a few steps away. Further west on Juárez is the **Jardín de la Reforma**; just off this is **Plaza San Roque**, where *entremeses* (theatrical sketches) are performed during the Cervantino festival; and nearby is the pleasant **Plazuela San Fernando**.

Plaza de la Paz, in front of the Basilica, is surrounded by the former homes of wealthy silver lords. **Plaza Alhóndiga**, on the corner of 28 de Septiembre and 5 de Mayo in front of the Alhóndiga, is quite bare.

Teatro Juárez & Other Theatres
Opposite the Jardín de la Unión stands the magnificent Teatro Juárez, built between 1873 and 1903. It was inaugurated by the dictator Porfirio Díaz, whose lavish yet refined tastes are reflected in the interior. The outside is festooned with columns, lampposts and statues; inside the impression is Moorish, with the bar and lobby gleaming with carved wood, stained glass and precious metals.

The theatre can be visited from 9 am to 1 pm and 4 to 6 pm daily except Monday; admission is 5 pesos, cameras extra. Performances are held here during the Cervantino festival and at other times; check for the current schedule.

The **Teatro Principal**, on Hidalgo near the other end of the Jardín de la Unión, and the **Teatro Cervantes**, at the eastern end of Hidalgo, are not as spectacular as Teatro Juárez but they have more frequent performances. Statues of Don Quijote and Sancho Panza grace the courtyard of the Teatro Cervantes.

Basilica & Other Churches
The Basílica de Nuestra Señora de Guanajuato, on Plaza de la Paz, one block west of the Jardín de la Unión, contains a jewel-covered image of the Virgin, patroness of Guanajuato. The wooden statue was supposedly hidden from the Moors in a cave in Spain for 800 years. Philip II of Spain gave it to Guanajuato in thanks for riches which accrued to the Crown.

Other fine colonial churches include the **Iglesia de San Diego**, opposite the Jardín de la Unión, the **Templo de San Francisco** on Sopeña, and the large **Templo de la Compañía de Jesús**, completed in 1747 for the Jesuit seminary whose buildings are now occupied by the University of Guanajuato.

Universidad de Guanajuato
The University of Guanajuato, whose green ramparts are visible above much of the city, is on Lascuraín de Retana one block up the hill from the Basilica. It is considered one of Mexico's finest schools for music and theatre, and also has a Spanish language programme for foreign students. The buildings originally housed a large Jesuit seminary.

The university houses three art galleries – the Salas de Exposiciones Hermenegildo Bustos and Polivalente on the ground floor of the main building, and the Sala de Exposiciones El Atrio under the front courtyard of La Compañia church next door. On the 4th floor of the university building is the Museo de Historia Natural Alfredo Dugés, honouring one of the university's foremost naturalists. The extensive collection of preserved and stuffed animals, birds, reptiles and insects includes some strange specimens such as a two-headed goat.

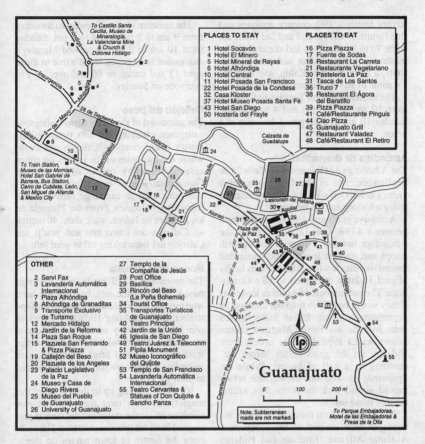

PLACES TO STAY

1 Hotel Socavón
4 Hotel El Minero
5 Hotel Mineral de Rayas
6 Hotel Alhóndiga
10 Hotel Central
11 Hotel Posada San Francisco
22 Hotel Posada de la Condesa
32 Casa Kloster
37 Hotel Museo Posada Santa Fé
43 Hotel San Diego
50 Hostería del Frayle

PLACES TO EAT

16 Pizza Piazza
17 Fuente de Sodas
18 Restaurant La Carreta
21 Restaurante Vegetariano
30 Pastelería La Paz
31 Tasca de Los Santos
36 Truco 7
38 Restaurant El Ágora del Baratillo
39 Pizza Piazza
41 Café/Restaurante Pinguis
44 Ciao Pizza
45 Guanajuato Grill
47 Restaurant Valadez
48 Café/Restaurant El Retiro

OTHER

2 Servi Fax
3 Lavandería Automática Internacional
7 Plaza Alhóndiga
8 Alhóndiga de Granaditas
9 Transporte Exclusivo de Turismo
12 Mercado Hidalgo
13 Jardín de la Reforma
14 Plaza San Roque
15 Plazuela San Fernando & Pizza Piazza
19 Callejón del Beso
20 Plazuela de los Angeles
23 Palacio Legislativo de la Paz
24 Museo y Casa de Diego Rivera
25 Museo del Pueblo de Guanajuato
26 University of Guanajuato
27 Templo de la Compañía de Jesús
28 Post Office
29 Basílica
33 Rincón del Beso (La Peña Bohemia)
34 Tourist Office
35 Transportes Turísticos de Guanajuato
40 Teatro Principal
42 Jardín de la Unión
46 Iglesia de San Diego
49 Teatro Juárez & Telecomm
51 Pípila Monument
52 Museo Iconográfico del Quijote
53 Templo de San Francisco
54 Lavandería Automática Internacional
55 Teatro Cervantes & Statues of Don Quijote & Sancho Panza

Note: Subterranean roads are not marked.

Guanajuato

0   100   200 m

To Parque Embajadoras,
Motel de las Embajadoras &
Presa de la Olla

Museo del Pueblo de Guanajuato

Opposite the university at Positos 7 is the Museo del Pueblo de Guanajuato, an art museum with a collection ranging from colonial to modern times. The museum occupies the former mansion of the Marqueses de San Juan de Rayas who owned the San Juan de Rayas mine, built in 1696. The private church in the courtyard contains a powerful mural by Chávez Morado. The museum is open Tuesday to Saturday from 10 am to 2 pm and 4 to 6 pm, Sunday from 10 am to 3.30 pm (closed Monday). Admission is 5 pesos (free for those up to age 11 and over 60).

Museo y Casa de Diego Rivera

The birthplace of Diego Rivera, today a museum honouring the painter, is at Positos 46 between the university and the Alhóndiga. Rivera was born in this house on 8 December 1886, together with a twin brother who died at the age of two; the family moved to Mexico City when he was six years old.

In conservative Guanajuato, where Catholic influence prevails, the Marxist Rivera was *persona non grata* for years. The city now honours its once blacklisted son with a small collection of his work in the house where he was born. The 1st floor contains the

Rivera family's 19th-century antiques and fine furniture. On the 2nd and 3rd floors are some 70 to 80 paintings and sketches by the master, including Indian and peasant portraits, a nude of Frida Kahlo, and sketches for some of Rivera's memorable murals.

The museum is open Tuesday to Saturday from 10 am to 1.30 pm and 4 to 6.30 pm, Sunday 10 am to 2.30 pm. Admission is 5 pesos.

Alhóndiga de Granaditas

The Alhóndiga de Granaditas on Calle 28 de Septiembre, site of the first major rebel victory in Mexico's War of Independence, is today a history and art museum.

A massive grain-and-seed storehouse built between 1798 and 1808, in 1810 the Alhóndiga became a fortress for Spanish troops and royalist leaders who barricaded themselves inside when 20,000 rebels led by Miguel Hidalgo attempted to take Guanajuato. The outnumbered Spaniards looked as if they would be able to hold out until, on 28 September, a young Indian miner named Juan José de los Reyes Martínez (better known as El Pípila), under orders from Hidalgo, set the gates ablaze before succumbing to a hail of bullets. While the Spaniards choked on smoke, the rebels moved in and took the Alhóndiga, killing most of those inside.

The Spaniards later took their revenge: the heads of four leaders of the rebellion – Aldama, Allende, Jiménez and Hidalgo himself, who was executed in Chihuahua – were hung outside the Alhóndiga from 1811 to 1821. The long black hooks that held the metal cages in which the heads hung may still be seen at the top of the four outer corners of the building. For a century from 1864 the Alhóndiga was used as a prison. It became a museum in 1967. Historical sections cover Guanajuato's pre-Hispanic past, its great flood of 1905, and modern times. There's also a fine art gallery housing a permanent collection and temporary exhibits. Don't miss José Chávez Morado's dramatic murals of Guanajuato's history on the staircases.

The museum is open Tuesday to Saturday from 9 am to 2 pm and 4 to 6 pm, Sunday from 10 am to 2.30 pm (closed Monday). Admission is 13 pesos, but it's free to those aged 13 and under, or 60 and over, and to everyone on Sunday.

Callejón del Beso

The narrowest of the many narrow alleys, or callejones, climbing the hills from Guanajuato's main streets is Callejón del Beso, where the balconies of the houses on either side of the alley practically touch. In Guanajuatan legend, lovers living on opposite sides used to exchange furtive kisses from these balconies. From the Plazuela de los Ángeles on Juárez, walk about 40 metres up Callejón del Patrocinio and you'll see Callejón del Beso taking off to your left.

Monumento al Pípila

The monument to El Pípila, with its torch raised high over the city, honours the hero who torched the Alhóndiga gates on 28 September 1810, enabling Hidalgo's forces to win the first victory of the independence movement. At the base of the statue is the inscription 'Aun hay otras Alhóndigas por incendiar' ('There are still other Alhóndigas to burn').

It's worth coming up to the statue for the magnificent view over the city; you can climb up inside the statue but the view is just as good from the terraces at its feet. The walk from the centre of town passes up steep, picturesque lanes. One possible route is to walk east on Sopeña from Jardín de la Unión, then turn right on Callejón de Calvario (you'll see the 'Al Pípila' sign). Another ascent, unmarked, goes uphill from the small plaza on Alonso. If the climb is too much for you, the 'Pípila-ISSSTE' bus heading west on Juárez will let you off right by the statue.

Museo Iconográfico del Quijote

This excellent museum at Manuel Doblado 1, on the tiny plaza in front of the Templo de San Francisco, holds an impressive collection of art relating to Don Quijote de la Mancha. Exhibits range from room-sized murals to a tiny painting on an eggshell, with dozens more paintings, statues, figurines, tapestries, and even a collection of postage stamps from several countries honouring the famous hero of Spanish literature. The museum is open Tuesday to Saturday from 10 am to 6.30 pm, Sunday 10 am to 2.30 pm; admission is free.

Ex-Hacienda San Gabriel de Barrera

Built at the end of the 17th century, the Ex-Hacienda San Gabriel de Barrera was the grand hacienda of Captain Gabriel de Barrera, whose family was descended from the first Count of Valenciana of the famous La Valenciana mine. Opened as a museum in 1979, the hacienda has been magnificently restored with period European furniture and art; in the chapel is an ornate gold-covered altar.

The large grounds, originally devoted to processing ore from La Valenciana mine, were converted in 1945 to beautiful terraced gardens with pavilions, pools, fountains and footpaths – a lovely and tranquil retreat from the city.

The museum, about two km west of the city centre, is open every day from 9 am to 6 pm. Admission is 5 pesos, plus 3 pesos for a camera or 5 pesos for a video camera. Frequent 'Central de Autobuses' buses heading west on Juárez will drop you a few hundred metres before the hacienda, then you have to brave the highway traffic – there is a ditch-like footpath. Say you want to get off at the Ex-Hacienda San Gabriel when you board the bus.

Museo de las Mómias

The famous Museum of the Mummies, at the cemetery on the western outskirts of town, is a quintessential example of Mexico's obsession with death. Visitors from far and wide come to see scores of corpses disinterred from the public cemetery.

The first remains were dug up in 1865, when it was necessary to remove some bodies to make room for more. What the authorities uncovered were not skeletons but flesh mummified in grotesque forms and facial expressions. The mineral content of the soil and extremely dry atmospheric conditions had combined to preserve the bodies in this unique way.

Today over 100 mummies are on display in the museum, including the first mummy to be discovered, the smallest mummy in the world, a pregnant mummy and plenty more. Since space is still tight in the cemetery, bodies whose relatives don't want to pay around 200 pesos to keep them there in perpetuity continue to be exhumed to make room for newcomers – and mummies are still being found. It takes only five or six years for a body to become mummified here, though only 1% or 2% of the bodies exhumed have turned into 'display quality' mummies. The others are cremated.

The museum is open every day from 9 am to 6 pm; admission is 5 pesos, plus 2 pesos for a camera or 5 pesos for a video camera. To get there take any 'Mómias' or 'Panteón' bus heading west on Juárez.

Museo de Mineralogía

The Mineralogy Museum at the university's Escuela de Minas campus, overlooking the town a km or two from the centre on the road to La Valenciana, is among the world's foremost mineralogy museums. Over 20,000 specimens from around the world include some extremely rare minerals, some found only in the Guanajuato area. The museum is open Monday to Friday from 8 am to 3 pm (free). To get there, take a 'Presa-San Javier' bus heading west on Juárez and ask to get off at the Escuela de Minas.

Mina & Templo La Valenciana

For 250 years La Valenciana mine, on a hill overlooking Guanajuato about five km north of the centre, produced 20% of the world's silver, in addition to quantities of gold.

Shut down after the revolution, it reopened in 1968 and is once again in operation, now cooperatively run. The mine still yields silver, gold, nickel and lead and can be visited any day from around 8 am to 7 pm; admission is 2 pesos. Any day except Sunday you can see the earth being extracted and miners descending an immense main shaft, nine metres wide and 500 metres deep.

Near the mine is the magnificent Templo La Valenciana, also called the Church of San Cayetano. One legend says that the Spaniard who started the mine promised San Cayetano that if it made him rich, he would build a church to honour the saint; another legend says that the silver baron of La Valenciana, Conde de Rul, tried to atone for exploiting the miners by building the ultimate in Churrigueresque churches.

Whatever the motive, ground was broken in 1765, and the church was completed in 1788. La Valenciana's façade is spectacular and its interior dazzling with ornate golden altars, filigree carvings and giant paintings. It's open from around 9 am to 7 pm, every day except Monday.

To get to La Valenciana, take a 'Valenciana' local bus (0.80 pesos) departing every half-hour from 5 de Mayo in front of the Plaza Alhóndiga. Get off at the church; the mine is about 300 metres down the dirt road opposite the church.

Presa de la Olla

In the hills at the east end of the city are two scenic reservoirs, Presa de la Olla and Presa de San Renovato, with a green park between them and a lighthouse on the hill above. It's a popular family park on Sunday, when you can bring a picnic and hire small rowing boats. The rest of the week it's quiet and peaceful. Any eastbound 'Presa' bus, from the underground stop down the steps at the south-west corner of the Jardín de la Unión, will take you there.

Language Courses

Guanajuato is a university town and it has an excellent atmosphere for studying Spanish.

The most flexible programme is offered by the Instituto Falcón (☎ (473) 2-36-94), whose mailing address is Mexiamora 42, 36000 Guanajuato, Gto, Mexico. Classes have a maximum of six students, there are weekend recreational trips and registration is every Saturday morning. Fifty-five minutes' one-to-one instruction daily costs 105 pesos

a week: two small-group sessions daily cost 165 pesos a week; five sessions daily cost 300 pesos a week. The institute can help to arrange for students to live with local Mexican families; in 1993 the average daily cost of this was 48 pesos.

The University of Guanajuato offers summer courses for foreigners in Spanish, Mexican and Latin American culture. The cost is 1650 pesos for a four-week period; classes begin early in June and early in July with registration in February and March. The university can help you arrange to stay with local Mexican families. For information you can write to Centro de Idiomas, Universidad de Guanajuato (☎ (473) 2-72-53, fax 2-26-62), Lascuraín de Retana No 5, 36000 Guanajuato, Gto, México, or contact the universities of Chicago, Illinois, Indiana, Iowa, Michigan, Minnesota, Northwestern, Purdue or Wisconsin in the USA.

The university also offers a six-semester language course to foreigners: semesters begin in January and July and last 19 weeks with classes of 1½ hours per day. Students must register in person six months beforehand. Cost is 721 pesos per semester.

Organised Tours

At least two companies offer tours in Spanish of several of Guanajuato's major sights. You can reach all the same places on local buses, but if your time is limited a tour may be useful.

Transporte Exclusivo de Turismo (☎ 2-59-68) has a kiosk on the corner of Juárez and 5 de Mayo. Their Guanajuato Colonial tour includes the mummies, La Valenciana mine and church, the Pípila monument and the Panoramic Highway with a view over the town. Another tour goes to Cristo Rey. Both these trips go three times daily, last 3½ hours, and cost 20 pesos. Other tours go farther away and cost more.

Transportes Turísticos de Guanajuato (☎ 2-21-34, 2-28-38) has an office below the front courtyard of the Basilica. Their city tours go to much the same places, also for 20 pesos. Both companies do night tours (five hours, 50 pesos) taking in Guanajuato's views and nightspots and the *callejoneadas* – see the Entertainment section below.

Festivals

Fiestas de San Juan y Presa de la Olla The Fiestas de San Juan are celebrated at the Presa de la Olla park from 15 to 24 June. The 24th is the big blowout bash for the saint's day itself, with dances, music, fireworks and picnics. On the first Monday in July, everyone comes back to the park for another big party celebrating the opening of the dam's floodgates.

Fiesta de la Virgen de Guanajuato This festival, celebrated on 8 August, commemorates the date when Philip II gave the jewelled wooden Virgin now adorning the Basilica to the people of Guanajuato.

Festival Internacional Cervantino Guanajuato's arts festival is dedicated to the Spanish writer Miguel Cervantes, author of *Don Quijote*. It has grown from entremeses from Cervantes' work performed by students in the 1950s to one of the foremost arts extravaganzas in Latin America. Music, dance and theatre groups converge on Guanajuato from around the world, performing work which nowadays may have nothing whatever to do with Cervantes. The festival lasts two to three weeks and is usually held in October. If your visit to Mexico coincides with it, don't miss it.

Tickets and hotels should be booked in advance. Tickets normally go on sale around the beginning of October. In Guanajuato they're sold on the left side of the Juárez Theatre (not in the theatre ticket office); in Mexico City they can be bought at the FIC office at Alvaro Obregón 273, Colonia Roma (☎ (5) 514-7365), or from Ticketmaster (☎ (5) 325-90-00).

While some events are held in Teatro Juárez and other theatres, the most spectacular of entremeses, with galloping horses and medieval costumes, are performed in the ancient setting of the Plazuela San Roque and in the Plaza Alhóndiga.

Places to Stay – bottom end

The top budget choice is *Casa Kloster* (☎ (473) 2-00-88) at Alonso 32, a short block down an alley from the Basilica. Birds and flowers grace the sunny courtyard, and the well-cared-for rooms with shared bath are clean and comfortable. Cost is 30 pesos per person, 40 pesos in the larger rooms. Many European travellers congregate here and it's a relaxed, friendly place. It fills up early in the day.

A distant second choice for rock-bottom lodging is the *Hotel Posada de la Condesa* (☎ (473) 2-14-62), at Plaza de la Paz 60, also near the Basilica. It has plenty of rooms, all with private bath and 24-hour hot water, but is a bit tired and run-down, though the rooms are kept clean enough. Some rooms are large and even have little balconies over the street, others are claustrophobic with no ventilation. All cost 30/40 pesos for a single/double.

In the area around the Mercado Hidalgo are several other relatively cheap hotels, including the *Hotel Central*, *Hotel Granaditas*, *Hotel Posada San Francisco*, *Hotel Juárez* and *Posada Hidalgo*, but none is as cheap or as good as the Casa Kloster or even the Posada de la Condesa. The Hotel Central is friendly enough and the rooms, at 45/75 pesos, tolerable.

Places to Stay – middle

There are several medium-priced hotels around Plaza Alhóndiga and on Alhóndiga, the street heading north from the plaza. The *Hotel Alhóndiga* (☎ (473) 2-05-25) at Insurgencia 49, visible from the plaza, has clean, comfortable rooms with colour TV, and some with small private balconies; there's also a restaurant, a sitting area and enclosed parking. Singles/doubles are 70/80 pesos.

Around the corner at Alhóndiga 7 is the *Hotel Mineral de Rayas* (☎ (473) 2-19-67, 2-37-49). Rooms are dark and damp and have seen better days; some have tiny balconies over a side street. We found it noisy here at night. Rooms are 70/80 pesos.

A little further along Alhóndiga at No 12A, the *Hotel El Minero* (☎ (473) 2-52-51) is a reasonable place with small, comfortable rooms, all with TV, and many with balconies over the street, also at 70/80 pesos.

Further along at Alhóndiga 41A, the *Hotel Socavón* (☎ (473) 2-48-85, 2-66-66) is an attractive, well-kept hostelry with rooms around a courtyard. All have copper washbasins, painted tiles in the bathrooms, colour TV, and plenty of windows; cost is 80/90 pesos. There's a restaurant/bar on the 2nd floor.

Near the Jardín de la Unión at Sopeña 3, the *Hostería del Frayle* (☎ (473) 2-11-79) is very attractive. All the rooms have high wood-beamed ceilings and colour TV; though it's right in the centre of town, the building's thick adobe walls keep it quiet. Rooms here are 165/198 pesos.

Only a five-minute bus ride east of the centre is the *Motel de las Embajadoras* (☎ (473) 2-00-81) beside Parque Embajadoras on the corner of Embajadoras and Paseo Madero. It has an elegant but inexpensive restaurant/bar, plenty of parking space, and a lovely courtyard full of plants, trees and birds. All rooms have colour TV and are clean, comfortable and well-kept; they cost 165/200 pesos. An 'Embajadoras' or 'Presa' bus heading east underneath the Jardín de la Unión (see the earlier Presa de la Olla section) will take you there.

The *Castillo Santa Cecilia* (☎ (473) 2-04-77/85, fax 2-01-53) on the road to La Valenciana mine at Carretera Valenciana Km 1, built of stone and resembling a castle, is known for both its luxurious accommodation and excellent restaurant. Rooms are 170 pesos for one or two people in the low season, 210 pesos in the high season (Easter and during the Cervantino festival); there are also suites.

Places to Stay – top end
There are two old favourites right on the Jardín de la Unión. The *Hotel San Diego* (☎ (473) 2-13-00/21, fax 2-56-26) at Jardín de la Unión 1, near Teatro Juárez, has 52 elegant rooms and two suites, a 2nd-floor restaurant overlooking the plaza, and a large roof terrace. Singles range from 150 to 200 pesos, doubles from 180 to 270 pesos.

At the other end of the Jardín de la Unión, *Hotel Museo Posada Santa Fé* (☎ (473) 2-00-84, fax 2-46-53) is a sumptuous hotel in an elegant 19th-century mansion. Rooms are 242/287 pesos; suites are more expensive. On the ground floor is an expensive restaurant with some tables out on the plaza.

Hotel San Gabriel de Barrera (☎ (473) 2-39-80, fax 2-74-60), in the west of the city beside the Ex-Hacienda San Gabriel de Barrera at Km 2.5 on the Camino Antigua a Marfil, has a restaurant, bar, swimming pool, tennis courts and 139 luxury rooms at 220/247 pesos.

Places to Eat
There are a number of good, inexpensive restaurants around the Jardín de la Unión and the Basilica. Two popular standbys are *Restaurant Valadez*, opposite the Teatro Juárez on the corner of the Jardín de la Unión, and the *Café/Restaurant El Retiro*, a few doors down at Sopeña 12. Both are open every day from 8 am to 11 pm, serving a comida corrida for 14 pesos in the early afternoon.

Also at this end of the Jardín de la Unión, the *Hotel San Diego* has an elegant upstairs restaurant with several balcony tables overlooking the plaza. It's rather expensive, with main meals at around 30 pesos, but you can get a good breakfast special for 12 to 20 pesos.

At the far end of the Jardín, the *Café/Restaurante Pinguis* has no sign out front, but it's one of the most popular places in town for its good prices – there are sandwiches and tortas for 2 or 3 pesos, and the comida corrida is only 10 pesos. It's open every day from 8.30 am to 9.30 pm.

Just beyond this end of the plaza is the pleasant *Restaurant El Ágora del Baratillo* in a courtyard setting on the corner of Hidalgo. Breakfasts cost 8 to 11 pesos and the comida corrida is 14 pesos. It's open Monday to Saturday, 8 am to 9 pm.

Pizza Piazza has a branch at Hidalgo 14, just off the Jardín de la Unión; another on the Plazuela de San Fernando; and another at Juárez 69A. All are open every day from 2 to 11 pm and have a relaxed student atmosphere and good pizza, at good prices of around 16 pesos for the chica size (enough for one or two people) or 22 pesos mediana (two to four people).

Also popular with students is *Ciao Pizza* on Alonso just a few doors down from the Casa Kloster. It's open from 1 to 11 pm Monday to Friday, 1 pm to midnight on weekends.

One of our favourites near the Basilica is *Truco 7*, at Truco 7. A small, intimate, artsy café-restaurant-gallery, it has great atmosphere and delicious food at reasonable prices, with a variety of breakfast specials and a comida corrida for 13.50 pesos. Background music includes jazz, blues, and classical. It's open Monday to Friday from 9 am to midnight, weekends 11 am to midnight.

On the plaza in front of the Basilica, *Tasca de Los Santos* is a busy café-restaurant with a few outdoor tables. Also near the Basilica, *Pastelería La Paz* at Aguilar 53 is a large bakery and pastry shop, open every day from 7 am to 10 pm.

For delicious chicken try the *Restaurant La Carreta* at Juárez 96, heading down towards the Mercado Hidalgo. Served with large portions of rice and salad, a quarter chicken costs 7 pesos, a half chicken 12.50 pesos, to take away or eat there. It's open every day from 8 am to 9.30 pm.

A few doors away at Juárez 120, *Fuente de Sodas* is good for a quick inexpensive juice, licuado, fruit salad or torta. Nearby at Callejón de Culixto 20, off Plazuela de los Ángeles, *Restaurante Vegetariano* is a peaceful place with good food including wholesome breakfasts and a tasty comida corrida (12 pesos) served from 2 pm. It's open from 8 am to 6 pm Monday to Saturday.

For one of the best value comidas in town head for the restaurant of the *Hostal Cantarranas* on Hidalgo. The tasty, filling five-course menú del día here costs just 13.50 pesos. There's à la carte fare too.

Entertainment

Every evening, the Jardín de la Unión comes alive with students and others congregating there; the cafés along one side of the plaza are popular for having a drink, people-watching and listening to the strolling musicians. The state band and other bands give free concerts in the gazebo on Tuesday and Thursday evenings from around 7 to 8 pm and on Sunday afternoons from around noon to 2 pm.

On Friday, Saturday and Sunday evenings at around 8 or 8.30 pm, *callejoneadas* (or *estudiantinas*) depart from in front of San Diego church on the Jardín de la Unión. The callejoneada tradition is said to come from Spain. A group of songsters and musicians, dressed in traditional costumes, starts up the music in front of the church, a crowd gathers, and the whole mob takes off winding around through the ancient alleyways of the city, playing and singing heartily, taking along a burro laden with wine. It's good fun and one of Guanajuato's most enjoyable traditions. There's no cost except for the wine you drink, around 15 to 20 pesos for a carafe. Tour companies and others try to sell you tickets for the callejoneadas, but you don't need them!

The *Rincón del Beso*, at Alonso 21A not far from the Jardín de la Unión, is also affectionately known as La Peña Bohemia since it's a rather Bohemian club. Live music starts nightly around 10.30 pm. Often the whole club joins in singing; they stay open as long as there are people there wanting to party, often all night long. There's no cover charge, though the drinks are a bit expensive.

Guanajuato has three fine theatres, the *Teatro Juárez*, the *Teatro Principal and the Teatro Cervantes*, none far from the Jardín de la Unión. Check their posters to see what's on – though events at magnificent Teatro Juárez are sporadic. International films are sometimes shown at the Teatro Principal and Teatro Cervantes.

With its youthful population, Guanajuato has plenty of bars and discos. The *Guanajuato Grill* at Alonso 4 is a popular late-night restaurant/bar. *La Lonja* in the Jardín de la Unión has a 'happy hour' in the early evening. Some of the most popular discos are the *Galería* in the San Javier district, *Sancho's* in the Mineral de Cata district, and *Jav's* in Las Pastitas park in the west of the city. All are a short taxi ride from the city centre.

Getting There & Away
Air Guanajuato is served by León airport, which is about 12 km before León on the Guanajuato-León road and about 40 km from Guanajuato. See the León section for flight information. In Guanajuato you can buy air tickets from travel agencies like Viajes Frausto Guanajuato (☎ 2-35-80, fax 2-66-20) at Obregón 10, between the Jardín de la Unión and the Basilica or Viajes Georama (☎ 2-59-09, 2-51-01, fax 2-19-54) at Plaza de la Paz 34, in front of the Basilica.

Bus Guanajuato's Central de Autobuses is on the south-western outskirts of town. It has a post office, Lada caseta, tourist information office, restaurant and left-luggage office. Daily departures include:

Dolores Hidalgo – 54 km, one hour; one deluxe bus by Primera Plus (9 pesos); 2nd-class buses every 20 minutes, 6.20 am to 10.30 pm, by Flecha Amarilla (4.50 pesos)
Guadalajara – 300 km, five hours; five deluxe buses by Primera Plus (42 pesos); a few 1st-class by Tres Estrellas de Oro (38 pesos) and Servicios Coordinados (36 pesos); 10 2nd-class by Flecha Amarilla
León – 56 km, one hour; five deluxe buses by Primera Plus (9 pesos); a few 1st-class by Servicios Coordinados and by Omnibus de México (8 pesos); 2nd-class buses every few minutes, 6 am to 10.30 pm, by Flecha Amarilla or Azteca de Oro (both 6 pesos)
Mexico City (Terminal Norte) – 355 km, 4½ hours; two deluxe buses by ETN (70 pesos) and four by Primera Plus (56 pesos); eight 1st-class by Estrella Blanca (57 pesos)
San Luis Potosí – 210 km, four hours; one 1st-class bus each by Tres Estrellas de Oro (27 pesos) and Omnibus de México (25 pesos); two 2nd-class by Flecha Amarilla (22 pesos)
San Miguel de Allende – 82 km, 1½ to two hours; three deluxe buses by Primera Plus (13.50 pesos); one 1st-class by Tres Estrellas de Oro (12 pesos); seven 2nd-class by Flecha Amarilla (9.50 pesos)

There are also frequent 2nd-class Flecha Amarilla buses to Celaya, and a few to Morelia, Querétaro and Aguascalientes.

Train The Estación del Ferrocarril (☎ 2-10-35, 2-03-06) is on Calle Tepetapa on the west side of town. The Constitucionalista train runs daily to/from Mexico City, departing Mexico City at 7 am and Guanajuato at 2.25 pm. The trip takes 6½ to seven hours with several stops – much slower than a bus. The fare to Mexico City in primera especial, the only class available, is 50.35 pesos.

Getting Around
To/From the Airport A taxi from Guanajuato to León airport costs around 100 pesos. A cheaper alternative is to take a bus to Silao, about 15 km before the airport, and a taxi from there. SITSA travel agency at Hidalgo 6 in Guanajuato has an airport transport service.

Bus & Taxi City buses run from around 5 am to 10 pm; fare is 0.80 pesos. 'Central de Autobuses' buses run frequently between the bus station and the city centre up to midnight. From the centre, you can catch them heading west on Juárez, or on the north side of the Basilica.

Many of Guanajuato's principal sights are in the city centre, within easy walking distance. Useful buses for outlying sights are mentioned in the relevant sections. The tourist office near the Basilica is very helpful with bus information.

Taxis are plentiful in the centre. Cost for a ride in the centre is around 6 pesos; between the centre and the bus station is around 10 pesos, more if the traffic is heavy.

AROUND GUANAJUATO
Cerro de Cubilete & Cristo Rey
Cristo Rey (Christ the King) is a 20-metre bronze statue of Jesus erected in 1950 on the summit of the Cerro de Cubilete about 15 km west of Guanajuato, said to be the exact geographical centre of Mexico. For religious Mexicans, there is a significance in having Jesus at the heart of their country – the statue is a popular attraction for Mexicans visiting Guanajuato.

Tour companies offer 3½-hour trips to the statue (see Organised Tours above), but you can go on your own for only 5 pesos each way by an Autobuses Vasallo de Cristo bus from the bus station; they depart every day at 6, 7, 9, 10 and 11 am, 12.30, 2, 4 and 6 pm, with additional buses on weekends and holidays. From the bus station it is possible to see the statue up on the hill in the distance.

LEÓN
• *pop: 950,000* • *alt: 1854 metres*

The industrial city of León, 56 km west of Guanajuato, is a big bus interchange point and a likeable enough place if you need to stay a few hours or a night. It's famous for its shoes, saddles and other leather goods; other products include steel, textiles and soap.

Things to See & Do
The wide **Plaza Principal** is a pleasant, traffic-free space at the heart of the city, with one or two old buildings around it, such as the Casa Municipal and Parroquia del Sagrario on the west side. Beside the parroquia is a smaller plaza with the **Museo de la Ciudad de León** under one of its arcades, and a block north of here on the corner of Obregón and Hidalgo is the big twin-towered baroque **Basílica** (cathedral). Take a look at some of the dozens of shoe shops around the centre or anywhere in town – there's an enormous range of footwear at good prices. The central market is on the corner of Comonfort and Belisario Domínguez, two blocks south and two blocks west of the Plaza Principal.

Places to Stay & Eat
There are many economical hotels near the bus station on Calle La Luz (walk to the right from the station's main exit: La Luz is the first cross-street). In the centre, pick from *Hotel Fundadores* (☎ (47) 16-17-27) at Ortiz de Dominguez 220, 2½ blocks west of the Plaza Principal, with singles/doubles at 50/60 pesos; *Hotel Rex* (☎ (47) 14-24-15) on 5 de Febrero, one block south and half a block east of the Plaza Principal, with 120 bright rooms at 80/90 or 90/105 pesos; the smart *Hotel León* (☎ (47) 14-10-50) at

Madero 113, half a block east of the Plaza Principal, with a stylish restaurant, charging 130 pesos single or double; or the *Hotel Condesa* (☎ (47) 13-11-20) at Portal Bravo 14 on the east side of the Plaza Principal, with very comfortable rooms at 160/205 pesos including a buffet breakfast. The Condesa's busy restaurant does a good four-course comida for 25 pesos or light dishes for 12 to 15 pesos. More expensive top-end hotels are on Boulevard López Mateos.

Cafetería Rex, on Pino Suárez 1½ short blocks south of the Plaza Principal, does a cheap comida for 14 pesos. *Refresquería El Pasaje* in the alley off the north side of the Plaza Principal is popular for cheap tacos, tortas and other snacks.

Getting There & Away
Air León airport, sometimes known as the Bajío airport, is about 12 km from town along the Mexico City road. Airlines serving it include Aerolitoral, Aeroméxico, Continental, Mexicana, TAESA and Saro. Flights include daily direct services to/from Guadalajara, Mexico City, Monterrey, Tijuana and Zacatecas. Continental has daily flights to/from Houston with connections to/from 10 major US cities. Aeroméxico has daily Los Angeles flights and Mexicana flies to/from Chicago and San Antonio, Texas.

Bus There's good service to/from just about everywhere in northern and western Mexico from the Central de Autobuses on Boulevard Hilario Medina, just north of Boulevard López Mateos towards the eastern edge of town. Over 60 deluxe buses a day go to Mexico City and 28 to Guadalajara. To Guanajuato, Flecha Amarilla runs 2nd-class buses every 30 minutes from 5.20 am to 10.40 pm (one hour, 6 pesos); there are also a few better buses by ETN, Primera Plus and Servicios Coordinados. Primera Plus runs three daily deluxe buses to San Miguel de Allende (2¼ hours, 21.50 pesos).

Train León is served by the División del Norte train between Mexico City and Ciudad

Juárez – see the Train section in the Mexico City chapter for details.

Getting Around

'Centro' buses (0.80 pesos), directly across the street from the bus station main exit, go to the city centre. Returning to the bus station catch a 'Central' bus east along López Mateos, two blocks north of the Plaza Principal.

DOLORES HIDALGO

• *pop: 40,000*

This is where the Mexican independence movement began in earnest. At 5 am on 16 September 1810, Miguel Hidalgo, the parish priest, rang the bells to summon people to church earlier than usual and issued the Grito de Dolores, whose precise words have been lost to history but which boiled down to 'Viva Our Lady of Guadalupe! Death to bad government and the gachupines!'

Gachupines was the derisive name for Mexico's Spanish overlords, against whom a powder-keg of resentment finally exploded in this small town. Hidalgo, Ignacio Allende and other conspirators, alerted to the discovery of their plans for an uprising in Querétaro, decided to launch their rebellion immediately from Dolores.

After the Grito they went to the lavish Spanish house on the plaza, today called the Casa de Visitas, and took prisoner the local representative of the Spanish viceroy and the Spanish tax collector. They freed the prisoners in the town jail and, at the head of a growing band of criollos, mestizos and Indians, set off for San Miguel on a campaign that would bring their own deaths within a few months but ultimately led to the independence of Mexico.

Today Hidalgo is Mexico's most revered hero, rivalled only by Benito Juárez in the number of streets, plazas and statues dedicated to him throughout the country. Dolores was renamed in his honour in 1824. Visiting Dolores has acquired pilgrimage status for Mexicans. If you're interested in the country's history, it's well worth a trip, and easily reached from Guanajuato or San Miguel de Allende.

Orientation & Information

Everything of interest is within a couple of blocks of the Plaza Principal.

Tourist Office The Delegación de Turismo is on the north side of the Plaza Principal in the Presidencia Municipal building to the left of the church. The staff can answer, in Spanish, any questions about the town. The office is open Monday to Friday from 10 am to 3 pm and 5 to 8 pm, Saturday and Sunday 10 am to 6 pm.

Money Cash and travellers' cheques can be changed at Bancomer on the north-west corner of the Plaza Principal Monday to Friday from 9 am to 1.30 pm. Outside these hours, you can change cash, dollars only, at the Hotel Posada Las Campanas.

Post & Telecommunications The post and Telecomm offices are in the same building at Puebla 22 on the corner of Veracruz, not far from the Plaza Principal. The post office is open Monday to Friday from 8 am to 7 pm, Saturday 8 am to noon. The Telecomm office, with telegram, telex and fax services, is open Monday to Friday from 9 am to 1 pm and 3 to 6 pm, Saturday 8 am to noon.

There are Lada casetas in the post office, the Restaurant Plaza and the Hotel Posada Las Campanas. The latter is open 24 hours every day. There's also a caseta plus fax service at the bus station, open daily from 7 am to 11 pm.

Plaza Principal & Around

The **Parroquia de Nuestra Señora de Dolores**, the church where Hidalgo issued the Grito, is on the north side of the plaza. It has a fine 18th-century Churrigueresque façade; inside, it's fairly plain. Some say that Hidalgo uttered his famous words from the pulpit, others that he spoke at the church door to the people gathered outside. The church is open every day from 6 am to 2 pm and from 4 to 8 pm. Don't enter wearing shorts!

To the left of the church is the **Presidencia Municipal**, which has two colourful murals on the independence theme. The

Miguel Hidalgo

The balding, visionary head of Father Miguel Hidalgo y Costilla is familiar to anyone who's looked at Mexican murals, statues or books on the country. He was, it seems, a genuine rebel idealist, who had already sacrificed his own career at least once before that fateful day in 1810. And he launched the independence movement clearly aware of the risks to his own life.

Born on 8 May 1753, son of a criollo hacienda manager in Guanajuato, he studied at the College of San Nicolás Obispo in Valladolid (now Morelia), won a bachelor's degree and was ordained as a priest in 1778. Returning to teach at his old college, he eventually became rector. But he was no orthodox cleric: Hidalgo questioned the virgin birth and the infallibility of the pope, he read banned books, gambled, danced and had a mistress.

In 1800 he was brought before the Inquisition. Nothing was proved, but a few years later in 1804 he found himself transferred as priest to the hick town of Dolores.

Hidalgo's years in Dolores show that he was interested in the economic and cultural as well as the religious welfare of the local people. Somewhat in the tradition of Don Vasco de Quiroga of Michoacán, founder of the College of San Nicolás where Hidalgo had studied, he started new industries in the town such as tile, ceramics and pottery-making (still practised in the town today), plus the production of silk and the growing of vines. He also started a music band.

When Hidalgo met Ignacio Allende from San Miguel, he became caught up in the criollo discontent with the Spanish stranglehold on Mexico. His standing among the mestizos and Indians of his parish was vital in broadening the base of the rebellion that followed.

On 13 October 1810, shortly after his Cry for Independence, he was formally excommunicated for 'heresy, apostasy and sedition'. He answered by proclaiming that he never would have been excommunicated if it had not been for his call for the independence of Mexico, and that, furthermore, the Spanish were not truly Catholic in any religious sense of the word, but only for political purposes, specifically to rape, pillage and exploit Mexico. A few days later, on 19 October, Hidalgo dictated his first edict calling for the abolition of slavery in Mexico.

Hidalgo led his growing forces from Dolores to San Miguel, Celaya and Guanajuato, north to Zacatecas, south almost to Mexico City, and west to Guadalajara. But then, pushed northwards, their numbers dwindled and on 30 July 1811, having been captured by the Spanish, Hidalgo was shot by firing squad in Chihuahua. His head was returned to the city of Guanajuato, where his army had scored its first major victory, and hung in a cage for 10 years on an outer corner of the Alhóndiga de Granaditas building, along with the heads of Allende, Aldama and Jiménez. Rather than intimidating its people, this lurid display kept the memory, the goal and the example of the heroic martyrs fresh in everyone's mind. ∎

plaza contains a huge **statue of Hidalgo** and a tree which, according to a plaque beneath it, is a **sapling of the Tree of the Noche Triste**, under which Cortés is said to have wept when his men were driven out of Tenochtitlán in 1520.

The **Casa de Visitas** on the west side of the plaza was the residence of Don Nicolás Fernández del Rincón and Don Ignacio Díaz de la Cortina, the two representatives of Spanish rule in Dolores. On 16 September 1810 they became the first two prisoners of the independence movement. Today, this is where visiting Mexican presidents and other dignitaries stay when they come to Dolores for ceremonies. It's open to visitors every day from 9.30 am to 2 pm and 4 to 6 pm; admission is free.

Museo de la Independencia Nacional

Half a block west of the Plaza Principal at Zacatecas 6, this museum has few relics but plenty of information on the independence movement and its background. It charts the appalling decline in New Spain's Indian population between 1519 (an estimated 25 million) and 1605 (one million), and lists 23 Indian rebellions before 1800 as well as several criollo conspiracies in the years leading up to 1810. There are vivid paintings, quotations, and some details on the heroic last 10 months of Hidalgo's life. The museum is open Monday to Friday from 9 am to 2 pm and 4 to 7 pm, Saturday and Sunday 9 am to 3 pm; admission is 2 pesos.

Museo Casa de Hidalgo

This house, where Hidalgo lived and where (with Ignacio Allende and Juan de Aldama) he decided in the early hours of 16 September 1810 to launch the uprising, is something

of a national shrine. One large room is devoted to a big collection of memorials, wreaths and homages to Hidalgo. Other rooms contain replicas of Hidalgo's furniture and documents of the independence movement including the order for Hidalgo's excommunication. Also on view are ceramics made in the workshop Hidalgo founded, and a door from the jail where he set the prisoners free.

The house is on the corner of Hidalgo and Morelos, one block south of the Plaza Principal. It's open Tuesday to Saturday from 10 am to 6 pm, Sunday from 10 am to 5 pm (closed Monday). Admission is 13 pesos, free on Sunday.

Festival

Día de la Independencia Dolores is the scene of major celebrations of the independence anniversary on 15 and 16 September, with the Mexican president often officiating.

Dolores Hidalgo

0   150   300 m

1 Posada Dolores
2 Museo de la Independencia Nacional
3 Mercado
4 Casa de Visitas
5 Presidencia Municipal & Tourist Office
6 Parroquia de Nuestra Señora de Dolores
7 Hotel El Caudillo
8 Posada Cocomacán
9 Restaurant El Delfín
10 El Patio Restaurant Bar & Grill
11 Restaurant Plaza
12 Fruti y Yoghurt
13 Museo Casa de Hidalgo
14 Herradura de Plata Bus Station
15 Primera Plus & Flecha Amarilla Bus Station
16 Post Office & Telecomm
17 Hotel Posada Las Campanas

Places to Stay

Most visitors stay here just long enough to see the church and museums and eat an ice cream on the plaza. If you want to stay over, though, there are a few choices.

Most economical is the *Posada Dolores* (☎ (468) 2-06-42) at Yucatán 8, one block west of the Plaza Principal. This simple, friendly, clean casa de huéspedes has singles/doubles with shared bath for 20/30 pesos, and rooms with private bath for 40 pesos.

On the east side of the Plaza Principal is the fancier *Posada Cocomacán* (☎ (468) 2-00-18); its 50 rooms have private bath, windows for good ventilation, and parquet floors; they cost 60/70 pesos. *Hotel El Caudillo* (☎ (468) 2-01-98, 2-04-65) at Querétaro 8, opposite the right side of the church, has 32 rooms that are carpeted and clean enough, but small and stuffy, for 60/70 pesos.

Hotel Posada Las Campanas (☎ (468) 2-04-27, 2-14-24) at Guerrero 15, 2½ blocks east of the Plaza Principal, has 40 well-kept rooms, all with private bath, carpet and TV, at 110/120 pesos.

Places to Eat

Dolores is famous not only for its historical attractions but also for its ice cream. On the south-west corner of the Plaza Principal you can get ice cream cones in a variety of unusual flavours including mole, chicharrón, avocado, maize, cheese, honey and any of about 20 tropical fruit flavours.

You can grab a torta or a snack at many small eateries on and near the plaza, including *Fruti y Yoghurt* on Hidalgo just south of the square. On the south side of the plaza, opposite the church, the *Restaurant Plaza* is a good family restaurant with breakfasts, enchiladas and other antojitos at around 6 pesos. The comida corrida and other meals are around 18 to 21 pesos; they also serve pizza. Hours are Monday to Saturday from 8 am to 9 pm, Sunday 8 am to 5 pm.

The restaurant/bar at the *Hotel El Caudillo* is a bit more upscale. The comida here is 20 pesos, but you can get a good breakfast for 11 pesos, or enchiladas, soup or sandwiches

from 3 to 12 pesos. They're open from 8 am to 11 pm. *Posada Cocomacán* has a comida for 15 pesos. Almost next door, *El Patio Restaurant Bar & Grille* does a Sunday buffet comida for 18.50 pesos.

For seafood try the *Restaurant El Delfín* at Veracruz 2, one block east of the Plaza Principal. It's a pleasant family seafood restaurant open every day from 9 am to 7 pm. Fare includes fish dishes at 19 pesos, seafood soup at 12.50 pesos and shrimps at 27 pesos.

Things to Buy

Ceramics, pottery and Talavera tiles have been the special handicrafts of Dolores ever since Padre Hidalgo founded the town's first ceramics workshop in the early 19th century. A number of shops sell these and other crafts. The mercado is worth a look to get a feel for the town.

Getting There & Away

Primera Plus (deluxe) and Flecha Amarilla and Herradura de Plata (2nd-class) are the bus lines serving Dolores Hidalgo. The Primera Plus and Flecha Amarilla bus station is on Calle Hidalgo, 2½ blocks south of the Plaza Principal. Herradura de Plata is on the corner of Chiapas and Chihuahua, around the corner. Daily departures include:

Guanajuato – 54 km, one hour; Flecha Amarilla buses every half-hour, 5.20 am to 9 pm (4.50 pesos)

Mexico City (Terminal Norte) – 470 km, five hours; Herradura de Plata buses every half-hour, 4.40 am to 6.20 pm, and at 11.15 and 11.50 pm, and 16 Flecha Amarilla buses (all 35 pesos)

San Miguel de Allende – 43 km, one hour; Flecha Amarilla buses every 20 minutes, 4.30 am to 10.30 pm; same buses as to Mexico City by Herradura de Plata (all 4 pesos)

There's also frequent service to Querétaro and around 10 Flecha Amarilla buses daily to San Luis Potosí.

SAN MIGUEL DE ALLENDE

• *pop: 80,000* • *alt: 1840 metres*

A colonial town in a beautiful setting, San Miguel has become known for its large colony of North Americans. Starting around the 1940s, when David Alfaro Siqueiros was giving mural-painting courses at the Escuela de Bellas Artes, the town began attracting artists of every persuasion from Mexico and the USA. Over the decades, many painters, sculptors, writers, poets, textile artists and every other creative type from Mexico as well as North America have come to San Miguel. Neal Cassady, hero of Jack Kerouac's *On the Road*, died here in February 1968, walking on the railroad tracks towards Celaya.

Once San Miguel was entrenched on the gringo circuit, it naturally lost some of its bohemian character. Today the town is home to several thousand foreigners, many of them middle-class retirees, others who return annually for the winter months. You can easily visit San Miguel and speak no Spanish at all. There are ample tourist facilities but less in the budget range than in some places in Mexico.

The physical beauty of San Miguel stems from the hillside setting of its many lovely old buildings and cobbled streets, which afford vistas over the plains and distant hills. To protect its charm, the Mexican government has declared the entire town a national monument. San Miguel has a very agreeable climate and superbly clear light, which is one reason it still attracts artists.

San Miguel is a well-known place for foreigners to learn Spanish. Nearly all visitors find it easy to feel at home. For the Mexicans' part, they are inordinately addicted to the festivals which make the place even more colourful.

San Miguel's peak tourist period is from mid-December to the end of March, with a flurry again during the North American summer months, June to August.

History

The area around San Miguel supported irrigation-based agriculture as early as 200 BC. The town itself, so the story goes, owes its founding to a few hot dogs. These hounds were dearly loved by a courageous barefoot Franciscan friar, Fray Juan de San Miguel, who started a mission near an often-dry river

five km from the present town in 1542. One day the dogs wandered off from the mission, to be found later reclining at the spring called El Chorro in the south of the present town. This site was so much better than the original that the mission was moved.

San Miguel was then the most northerly Spanish settlement in central Mexico. Tarascan and Tlaxcalan Indians, allies of the Spanish, were brought to help pacify the local Otomí and Chichimecs. Even so, San Miguel barely survived the fierce Chichimec resistance until 1555, when a Spanish garrison was established here to protect the new road from Mexico City to the silver centre of Zacatecas. Spanish ranchers and crop growers settled in the area and San Miguel grew into a thriving commercial centre known for its sarapes and other textiles, knives and horse tackle, and home to some of the wealthy Guanajuato silver barons.

San Miguel's favourite son, Ignacio Allende, was born here in 1779. He became a fervent believer in the need for Mexican independence and one of the leaders of a Querétaro-based conspiracy which set 8 December 1810 as the date for armed uprising. When the plan was discovered by the authorities in Querétaro on 13 September, a messenger rushed to San Miguel and gave the news to Juan de Aldama, another conspirator. Aldama sped north to Dolores where, in the early hours of 16 September, he found Allende at the house of the priest Miguel Hidalgo, also one of the coterie.

A few hours later Hidalgo proclaimed rebellion from his church. By the same evening, San Miguel was in rebel hands, its local regiment having joined forces with the band of insurgent criollos, mestizos and Indians arriving from Dolores. The Spanish population of San Miguel was locked up and Allende was only partly able to restrain the rebels from looting the town. After initial successes, Allende, Hidalgo and other rebel leaders were captured in 1811 in Chihuahua. Allende was executed almost immediately, Hidalgo four months later. It was not until 1821 that Mexico finally achieved independence.

In 1826 San Miguel was renamed San Miguel de Allende. It began to take on its current character with the founding of the Escuela de Bellas Artes in 1938 and the Instituto Allende in 1951, both of which attracted many foreign students.

Orientation

The Plaza Principal, called the Jardín, is the focal point of the town. The Gothic-like spires of the parroquia on the south side of the plaza can be seen from far and wide. The town slopes up from west to east.

The central area is small and straightforwardly laid out. Most places of interest are within easy walking distance of the Jardín. Most streets change names at the Jardín. Canal/San Francisco, on its north side, and Umarán/Correo, on the south side, are the main streets of the central area. The bus station is about one km west of the Jardín on Canal; the train station is at the end of Canal, one km further on.

Information

Tourist Office The tourist office (☎ (415) 2-17-47) is on the south-east corner of the Jardín, in a glassed-in office behind some tables of the La Terraza restaurant. They have maps of the town (1 peso), printed brochures in English and Spanish, and can answer questions in both languages. Hours are Monday to Friday from 10 am to 2.45 pm and 5 to 7 pm, Saturday 10 am to 1 pm, and Sunday 10 am to noon.

Money There are several banks on Calle San Francisco in the couple of blocks east of the Jardín, and another on the Jardín itself, on the west side. These have the best rates for changing money; they're open Monday to Friday 9 am to noon for currency exchange. Some also have ATMs.

Deserve Casa de Moneda (☎ 2-50-50) in the lobby of the Posada San Francisco, on the north-west corner of the Jardín, changes cash and travellers' cheques at only slightly less favourable rates than the banks, and it's less crowded. It's open Monday to Saturday, 9 am to 7 pm. There are also reasonable rates

at Deal at Correo 15, opposite the Telégrafos office, and at Juárez 27 near the corner of Mesones. Both branches are open from 9 am to 1.45 pm and 4 to 5.45 pm Monday to Friday, and 9 am to 1.45 pm Saturday.

American Express (☎ 2-18-56, 2-16-95) is at Hidalgo 1A, half a block north of the Jardín – open Monday to Friday, 9 am to 2 pm and 4 to 6.30 pm.

Post & Telecommunications The post office is one block east of the Jardín, on the corner of Correo and Calle de la Corregidora. It's open Monday to Friday from 8 am to 7 pm, Saturday 9 am to 1 pm. One door down Correo is a Mexpost express mail office. The Telégrafos office at Correo 16, two doors from the post office, has telegram, telex and fax services and a Ladatel coin telephone. Hours are Monday to Friday from 9 am to 1 pm and 3 to 6 pm, Saturday 9 am to noon.

You can also make long-distance telephone calls at several Lada casetas. One is upstairs on the corner of Correo and Recreo; it's open every day except Monday, 10 am to 2.30 pm and 5 to 10 pm. Another, El Toro, is at Hernández Macías 58A opposite the Hotel Sautto (open every day from 9 am to 2 pm and 3 to 8 pm). There's also a caseta in the bus station, open every day from 7 am to 11 pm.

La Conexión (☎ 2-16-87 & 2-15-99) at Aldama 1 offers a 24-hour fax and phone message service, mailboxes and more.

Foreign Consulate The US Consulate (☎ (415) 2-23-57; in emergencies 2-00-68 or 2-09-80) is at Local 6 in the Plaza Colonial, on the corner of Canal and Hernández Macías. Hours are Monday and Wednesday from 9 am to 1 pm and 4 to 7 pm, Tuesday and Thursday from 4 to 7 pm, and at other times by appointment.

Bookshops & Libraries The Biblioteca Pública (Public Library) at Insurgentes 25 has an excellent collection of books in English and Spanish on Mexico, plus novels and other books in English, and a large selection of used books in English for sale at cheap prices; it's open Monday to Saturday from 10 am to 2 pm and 4 to 7 pm. El Colibrí bookshop, at Diez de Sollano 30, 1½ blocks south of the plaza, has new books and magazines in English, plus a few in Spanish, French and German; hours are the same.

Newspapers & Notice Boards The expatriate community puts out a weekly English-language newspaper, *Atención San Miguel* (2 pesos); its office is in the Biblioteca Pública. It's full of what's on plus lots of small ads offering rooms, apartments or houses to sell, rent or exchange; furniture sales; house-sitter jobs; classes in yoga, Spanish, art or dance; and so on. You can buy it at the Biblioteca Pública, the supermarket on the north side of the Jardín and elsewhere. The same sorts of things are advertised on notice boards in the Biblioteca Pública, the supermarket on the Jardín, the language schools, hotels, restaurants such as Casa Mexas at Canal 15, and (for what's-on information) the Escuela de Bellas Artes.

Laundry ATL Lavandería Automática at Local J in the Pasaje Allende mall, Mesones 5, charges 13 pesos for a full load if you drop it off, less if you do it yourself. It's open Monday to Saturday from 8 am to 2 pm and 4 to 7 pm. Lava Mágica at Pila Seca 5 has similar rates.

Colonial Buildings
Parroquia The pink 'sugar-candy' pointed towers of the parroquia dominate the Jardín. These strange soaring pinnacles were designed by an untutored local Indian, Zeferino Gutiérrez, in the late 19th century. He reputedly instructed the builders by scratching plans in the sand with a stick. Most of the rest of the church dates from the late 17th century. The crypt contains the remains of a 19th-century Mexican president, Anastasio Bustamante. In the chapel to the left of the main altar is a much-revered image of the Cristo de la Conquista (Christ of the Conquest), made by Indians in Pátzcuaro from cornstalks and orchid bulbs, probably in the 16th century.

The church to the left of the parroquia is

San Rafael, founded in 1742, which has undergone Gothic-type alterations.

Museo Histórico de San Miguel de Allende To the right of the parroquia on Cuna de Allende stands the house where Ignacio Allende was born, now a museum. Exhibits relate the interesting history of the San Miguel area, with special exhibits on Allende and the independence movement. An inscription on the façade says '*Hic natus ubique notus*' – Latin for 'Here born, everywhere known'. Another plaque points out that the more famous independence hero, Miguel Hidalgo, only joined the movement after being invited by Allende.

The museum is open Tuesday to Sunday from 10 am to 3.30 pm (free). It also hosts changing art exhibitions.

Casa del Mayorazgo de Canal This house of the Canal family is one of the most imposing of San Miguel's old residences. The entrance is at Canal 4 and it stretches above the arcade on the west side of the Jardín. It's a neoclassical building with some late baroque touches. The house was undergoing substantial renovations when we were last in town but should now have resumed its programme of art exhibitions, movies and free tours for groups. It's open Tuesday to Friday from 9 am to 1.30 pm and 4 to 6 pm, Saturday and Sunday 10 am to 5 pm.

Iglesia de San Francisco This church on the north side of a small garden on the corner of San Francisco and Juárez has an elaborate late-18th-century Churrigueresque façade. An image of San Francisco de Assisi is at the top.

Tercer Orden This chapel on the west side of the same garden was built in the early 18th century and like the San Francisco church was part of a Franciscan monastery complex. The main façade shows San Francisco and symbols of the Franciscan order.

Oratorio de San Felipe Neri This multi-towered and domed church, built in the early

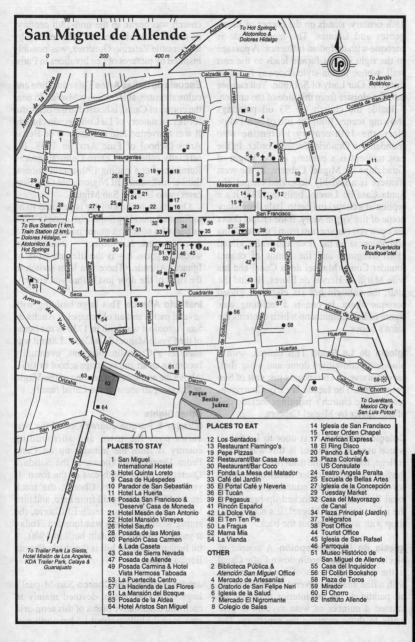

San Miguel de Allende

To Hot Springs,
Atotonilco &
Dolores Hidalgo

To Jardín
Botánico

To Bus Station (1 km),
Train Station (2 km),
Dolores Hidalgo, —
Atotonilco &
Hot Springs

To La Puertecita
Boutique'otel

To Querétaro,
Mexico City &
San Luis Potosí

To Trailer Park La Siesta,
Hotel Misión de Los Angeles,
KDA Trailer Park, Celaya &
Guanajuato

Parque
Benito
Juárez

PLACES TO STAY

1 San Miguel
International Hostel
3 Hotel Quinta Loreto
5 Casa de Huéspedes
10 Parador de San Sebastián
11 Hotel La Huerta
16 Posada San Francisco &
'Deserve' Casa de Moneda
21 Hotel Mesón de San Antonio
22 Hotel Mansión Virreyes
26 Hotel Sautto
28 Posada de las Monjas
40 Pensión Casa Carmen
& Lada Caseta
43 Casa de Sierra Nevada
47 Posada de Allende
49 Posada Carmina & Hotel
Vista Hermosa Taboada
53 La Puertecita Centro
57 La Hacienda de Las Flores
61 La Mansión del Bosque
63 Posada de la Aldea
64 Hotel Aristos San Miguel

PLACES TO EAT

12 Los Sentados
13 Restaurant Flamingo's
19 Pepe Pizzas
22 Restaurant/Bar Casa Mexas
30 Restaurant/Bar Coco
31 Fonda La Mesa del Matador
33 Café del Jardín
35 El Portal Café y Nevería
36 El Tucán
39 El Pegasus
41 Rincón Español
42 La Dolce Vita
48 El Ten Ten Pie
50 La Fragua
52 Mama Mia
54 La Vianda

OTHER

2 Biblioteca Pública &
Atención San Miguel Office
4 Mercado de Artesanías
5 Oratorio de San Felipe Neri
6 Iglesia de la Salud
7 Mercado El Nigromante
8 Colegio de Sales
14 Iglesia de San Francisco
15 Tercer Orden Chapel
17 American Express
18 El Ring Disco
20 Pancho & Lefty's
23 Plaza Colonial &
US Consulate
24 Teatro Angela Peralta
25 Escuela de Bellas Artes
27 Iglesia de la Concepción
32 Casa del Mayorazgo
de Canal
34 Plaza Principal (Jardín)
37 Telégrafos
38 Post Office
44 Tourist Office
45 Iglesia de San Rafael
46 Parroquia
51 Museo Histórico de
San Miguel de Allende
55 Casa del Inquisidor
56 El Colibrí Bookshop
58 Plaza de Toros
59 Mirador
60 El Chorro
62 Instituto Allende

18th century, stands on the corner of Insurgentes and Llamas. The main façade is baroque with an Indian influence. A passage to the right of this façade leads to the east wall, whose Indian-style doorway holds an image of Our Lady of Solitude. You can see into the cloister from this side of the church.

Inside the church are 33 oil paintings showing scenes from the life of San Felipe Neri, the 16th-century Florentine who founded the Oratorio Catholic order. In the east transept is a painting of the Virgin of Guadalupe by Miguel Cabrera. In the west transept is a lavishly decorated chapel, the Santa Casa de Loreto, built in 1735. It's a replica of a chapel in Loreto, Italy, legendary home of the Virgin Mary. If the chapel doors are open you can see tiles from Puebla, China and Valencia on the floor and walls, gilded cloth hangings and the tombs of chapel founder Conde Manuel de la Canal and his wife María de Hervas de Flores. Behind the altar, the camarín has six elaborate gilded baroque altars. In one is a reclining wax figure of San Columbano which contains the saint's bones.

Iglesia de La Salud This church, with a blue-and-yellow-tiled dome and a big shell carved above its entrance, is just east of San Felipe Neri. The façade is early Churrigueresque. The church's paintings include one of San Javier by Miguel Cabrera.

Colegio de Sales Next door to La Salud, which used to be part of it, this was once a college, founded in the mid-18th century by the San Felipe Neri order. Many of the 1810 revolutionaries were educated here. The local Spaniards were locked up here when the rebels took San Miguel. It's now a craft shop with workshops out the back.

Iglesia de La Concepción A couple of blocks west of the Jardín down Calle Canal is the splendid church of La Concepción, with a fine altar and several magnificent old oil paintings. On the interior doorway are painted a number of wise sayings to give pause to those entering the sanctuary. The

church was begun in the mid-18th century; its dome, added in the late 19th century by the versatile Zeferino Gutiérrez, was possibly inspired by pictures of Les Invalides in Paris.

Escuela de Bellas Artes This education and cultural centre, at Hernández Macías 75 near the corner of Canal, is housed in the beautiful former monastery of La Concepción church. It was converted into the Escuela de Bellas Artes (School of Fine Arts) in 1938. It's officially called the Centro Cultural Ignacio Ramírez, after a leading 19th-century liberal thinker nicknamed El Nigromante (The Sorcerer) who lived in San Miguel.

One room in the cloister is devoted to an unfinished mural by Siqueiros, done in 1948 as part of a course in mural painting for US war veterans. Its subject – though you wouldn't guess it – is the life and work of Ignacio Allende. (There is a light switch to the right of the door just before you enter!)

Instituto Allende This large building with several patios and an old chapel at Ancha de San Antonio 4 was built in 1736 as the home of the Conde Manuel de la Canal. Later it was used as a Carmelite convent, eventually becoming an art and language school in 1951. Above the entrance is a carving of the Virgin of Loreto, patroness of the Canal family.

Other Sights

Mirador & Parque Juárez One of the best views over the town and surrounding country is from the mirador up on Calle Pedro Vargas, also known as the Salida a Querétaro, in the south-east of the town. If you take Callejón del Chorro, the track leading directly downhill from here, and turn left at the bottom, you reach El Chorro, the spring where the town was founded. Today it gushes out of a fountain built in 1960. A bit further down the hill is the shady Parque Benito Juárez.

Jardín Botánico El Charco San Miguel's large botanical garden, devoted mainly to cacti and other native plants of this semi-arid area, is on the hilltop about 1.5 km north-east of the town centre. Though only a few years old and still being developed, it's a lovely place for a walk, particularly in the early morning or late afternoon. Pathways range along the slope above a reservoir and above a deep canyon into which the reservoir flows. Admission is free and the garden is open daily, roughly during daylight hours.

The direct approach is to walk uphill from the Mercado El Nigromante along Homobono and Cuesta de San José, then fork left up Montitlan past the Balcones housing development, and keep walking another few minutes along the track ahead at the top. If the gate here is shut, follow the fence around to the right to another entrance. Alternatively, a two-km vehicle track leads north from the Gigante shopping centre which is 2.5 km east of the centre on the Querétaro road. Gigante can be reached on 'Gigante' buses heading west along the north side of the Jardín. Or take a taxi all the way to the gardens.

Activities

Walking Tours A House & Garden tour, visiting some of the lovely houses and gardens in San Miguel which are otherwise closed to the public, starts at 12.15 pm every Sunday from the Biblioteca Pública. Tickets are on sale from 11 am. Cost is around 25 pesos for the 1½ to two-hour tour, with four different houses visited each week.

Every Friday morning groups form in the Jardín at 9 am for a two-hour walking tour of the town. The cost is 20 pesos with proceeds helping to provide medical care for underprivileged children in San Miguel.

The Travel Institute of San Miguel (☎ 2-00-78, fax 2-01-21) at Cuna de Allende 11 conducts two-hour historical walking tours of central San Miguel for 30 pesos, plus a variety of other tours. Stop by for a brochure.

Swimming Several hotel pools are open to outsiders, including the clean pools of the Posada de la Aldea (10 pesos) and the Hotel Aristos (15 pesos). Don't miss the balnearios in the surrounding countryside – see the Around San Miguel section.

Courses

San Miguel has an excellent atmosphere for developing your artistic inclinations. There are many easy-to-join courses which demand only enthusiasm. Language courses, group or private, are also numerous. Most courses run almost year-round with just a three-week break in December.

Instituto Allende (☎ /fax (415) 2-01-90), in an old mansion on Ancha de San Antonio, offers courses in fine arts, crafts and Spanish. Art and craft courses can be joined at any time, usually involve nine hours' attendance a week and cost 300 to 630 pesos a month. Spanish courses begin about every four weeks and range from conversational (50 minutes, five days a week, 315 pesos for four weeks) to total impact (individual tuition, three to six hours a day, five days a week, 1620 to 2835 pesos for four weeks). Write to Instituto Allende, San Miguel de Allende, Guanajuato 37700, Mexico for details.

The Academía Hispano Americana (☎ (415) 2-03-49, ☎ /fax 2-23-33) at Mesones 4 runs courses in Spanish language and Latin American culture at 1200 pesos for a four-week session, or two weeks for 750 pesos. The cultural courses are taught in elementary Spanish. Language classes on a one-to-one basis, for any period you like, are also available at 30 pesos an hour. The school can arrange for you to live with a Mexican family for about 1350 pesos a month, meals included, or help with other living arrangements.

La Casa de la Luna at Cuadrante 2 begins small-group Spanish classes every Monday. Two hours daily costs 150 pesos a week or 540 pesos a month; four hours daily is 270 pesos a week or 960 pesos a month.

The San Miguel International Hostel at Organos 34 may be able to help with Spanish tuition at cheaper rates.

The Escuela de Bellas Artes (☎ (415) 2-02-89) is at Hernández Macías 75 on the corner of Canal in a beautiful ex-monastery. Courses in art, dance, crafts and music are usually given in Spanish and cost 210 pesos a month; each class is nine hours a week. Registration is at the beginning of each month. Some classes are not held in July, and there are no classes in August.

Festivals

Being so well endowed with churches and patron saints (it has six), San Miguel has a multitude of festivals every month. You'll probably learn of some by word of mouth – or the sound of fireworks – while you're there. Specifically local events include:

Blessing of the Animals This happens in several churches, including the parroquia, on 17 January.

Allende's Birthday On 21 January various official events celebrate this occasion.

Cristo de la Conquista This image in the parroquia is fêted on the first Friday in March, with scores of dancers in elaborate pre-Hispanic costumes and plumed headdresses in front of the parroquia.

Semana Santa Two weekends before Easter pilgrims carry an image of the Señor de la Columna (Lord of the Column) from Atotonilco, 14 km north, to the church of San Juan de Dios in San Miguel on Saturday night or Sunday morning. During Semana Santa itself, the many activities include the lavish Procesión del Santo Intierro on Good Friday and the burning or exploding of images of Judas on Easter Day.

Fiesta de la Santa Cruz This unusual festival happens on the last weekend in May at Valle del Maíz, two km from the centre of town. Oxen are dressed in lime necklaces and painted tortillas, and their yokes festooned with flowers and fruit. One beast carries two boxes of 'treasure' (bread and sugar) and is surrounded by characters in bizarre costumes on horses or donkeys. A mock battle between 'Indians' and 'Federales' follows, with a wizard appearing to heal the 'wounded' and raise the 'dead'. This rather solemn festival has its roots in the 16th century; sensitivity is recommended if you want to observe it.

Corpus Christi This moveable feast in June features dances by children in front of the parroquia. One is called Los Hortelanos (The Gardeners).

Chamber Music Festival The Escuela de Bellas Artes sponsors an annual Chamber Music Festival in the first two weeks of August.

San Miguel Arcángel Celebrations honouring the town's chief patron saint are held on the saint's day, 29 September (or on the weekend after, if the 29th falls on a weekday). There are cockfights, bullfights and bull-running in the streets, but the hub of a general town party is provided by traditional dancers from several states who meet at Cruz del Cuarto, on the road to the train station. Wearing bells, feather headdresses, scarlet cloaks

and masks, groups walk in procession to the parroquia carrying flower offerings called *xuchiles*, some playing armadillo-shell lutes. The roots of these events probably go back to pre-Hispanic times. Dances continue over a few days and include the Danza Guerrero in front of the parroquia, which represents the Spanish conquest of the Chichimecs.

San Miguel Music Festival This largely classical music festival presents an almost daily programme with Mexican and international performers throughout the second half of December. Most concerts are at the fine Teatra Angela Peralta, built in 1910, on the corner of Mesones and Hernández Macías.

Places to Stay

Some of the better-value places are often full; book ahead if you can, especially during the high season from December to March and during the summer.

Many hotels give discounts for long-term guests. If you're planning to stay a while in San Miguel, there are houses, apartments and rooms to rent: check the newspapers, notice boards and estate agents. You could expect to pay 1200 to 1500 pesos a month for a decent two-bedroom house. House-sitting is another possibility.

Places to Stay – bottom end

Camping *Lago Dorado KDA Trailer Park* (☎ (415) 2-23-01, fax 2-36-86) beside the reservoir five km south of town, has a swimming pool, lounge, laundromat and 60 spaces with full hook-ups, plus 40 more spaces without hook-ups. Cost is 30 pesos for one or two people, less for longer stays. From town, take the Celaya road, then after three km turn right at the Hotel Misión de los Ángeles and continue another two km towards the lake, crossing the train tracks. The mailing address is Apartado Postal 523, San Miguel de Allende, Guanajuato 37700.

Trailer Park La Siesta (☎ (415) 2-02-07) is in the grounds of the Motel La Siesta, on the Celaya road two km south of town. It has 62 spaces with full hook-ups; amenities are minimal. Cost is 30 pesos for one or two people. The postal address is Apartado Postal 72.

Hostel The friendly *San Miguel International Hostel* (☎ (415) 2-06-74) at Organos 34 is in a pleasant colonial-style house, with a gurgling fountain in a courtyard full of flowers and trees. Beds in separate-sex dorms are 19.50 pesos (15 pesos with a hostel card); there are also a few singles/doubles with private bath at 36/45 pesos. Free coffee, tea and continental breakfast are included; kitchen use costs 5 pesos extra per day, with staples like rice, beans, spaghetti and spices provided. There are laundry facilities and the hostel has a splendid view from its rooftop.

Hotels Half a block from the Jardín at Cuna de Allende 10, the *Posada de Allende* (☎ (415) 2-06-98) looks a little old and worn; its five rooms, all with private bath and some with balconies over the street, cost 50/60 pesos for singles/doubles.

There are three good choices in the low-price bracket on or near Mesones. The *Casa de Huéspedes* (☎ (415) 2-13-78) at Mesones 27 is a clean, pleasant upstairs hostelry whose rooftop terrace has a good view. All six rooms have private bath. They cost 40/70 pesos, slightly more with a kitchenette. Ask about discounts for longer stays. Many European travellers stay here.

Further up the hill at Mesones 7, the *Parador de San Sebastián* (☎ (415) 2-07-07) is quiet and attractive, with 24 rooms, all with fireplace and private bath, arranged around an arched courtyard full of plants. Rooms are 60/75 pesos.

Hotel La Huerta (☎ (415) 2-08-81, 2-03-60) is a bit further up the hill, off Calle Aparicio, the eastward continuation of Mesones. It's a good place if you enjoy peace and quiet, as there are many trees, birds, and a running stream which you can hear at night (along with the dogs and roosters). At 40/50 pesos this is one of San Miguel's cheapest places.

West of the Jardín, the *Hotel Sautto* (☎ (415) 2-00-51/52) at Hernández Macías 59 has 25 rooms, about half with fireplaces, around lovely grounds with plenty of sitting areas and a swimming pool that's filled in the

summer. There is also an Italian restaurant. Rooms are 65/75 pesos, with discounts for longer stays.

Places to Stay – middle
San Miguel is brimming with good places in the middle range. Just off the Jardín at Cuna de Allende 7, *Posada Carmina* (☎ (415) 2-04-58) is a former colonial mansion with 10 large, attractive rooms at 116/125 pesos, and a pleasant restaurant/bar in the courtyard. In the same block at No 11 is the similar *Hotel Vista Hermosa Taboada* (☎ (415) 2-00-68, 2-04-37), whose 18 rooms with fireplace and carpet are 94 pesos.

Half a block from the Jardín at Canal 19, the *Hotel Mansión Virreyes* (☎ (415) 2-08-51, fax 2-38-65) is another colonial place with 22 rooms around two courtyards, and a restaurant/bar in the rear patio. Rooms are 75/95 pesos.

Nearby, the *Hotel Mesón de San Antonio* (☎ (415) 2-05-80, 2-28-97) at Mesones 80 has four rooms from 95 to 155 pesos single or double and seven townhouse-style suites from 120 to 175 pesos, around an attractive courtyard with a lawn and small swimming pool.

Further down Canal at No 37, *Posada de las Monjas* (☎ (415) 2-01-71) is a beautiful hotel in a former monastery. The 65 rooms are comfortable and well decorated and the bathrooms all have slate floors and hand-painted tiles. There are terraces with a great view over the valley, and a restaurant, bar, laundry and parking. The larger rooms with fireplaces and plenty of sun cost 90/180 pesos. Smaller rooms are 70/125 pesos.

Pensión Casa Carmen (☎ (415) 2-08-44) at Correo 31 is an old colonial home whose 11 rooms, all with high-beamed ceilings, are set around a pleasant courtyard with a fountain, orange trees and flowers. The price of 105/165 pesos includes a delicious breakfast and lunch, served in a communal dining room. Reserve well in advance for the high seasons.

Hotel Quinta Loreto (☎ (415) 2-00-42, fax 2-36-16) at Calle Loreto 15 is another long-time favourite. The 38 rooms are simple but pleasant, set around large grounds with a swimming pool, tennis courts and plenty of parking space. The restaurant is good. Rooms are 70/85 pesos per night, with a 10% discount for a stay of a week or longer. Reserve well ahead!

Posada San Francisco (☎ /fax (415) 2-24-25, 2-00-72) at Plaza Principal 2 (right on the Jardín) is another popular hotel, with rooms at 150/180 pesos.

Yet another popular place is *La Mansión del Bosque* (☎ (415) 2-02-77), at Aldama 65, opposite Parque Benito Juárez. All 23 rooms are different and comfortable with good furniture and original art. Most have both tub and shower, and some also have fireplaces. During the winter high season rates are 108 to 156 pesos single, 204 to 216 pesos double and include both breakfast and dinner. The rest of the year, prices are lower. Reserve well in advance. The address is Apartado Postal 206, San Miguel de Allende, Guanajuato 37700.

Opposite the Instituto Allende, on Ancha de San Antonio, is the attractive *Posada de la Aldea* (☎ (415) 2-10-22, 2-12-96), whose 66 large rooms cost 150/180 pesos.

Places to Stay – top end

The elegant *Casa de Sierra Nevada* (☎ (415) 2-04-15, 2-18-95, fax 2-23-37) at Hospicio 35 was converted from four colonial mansions. It has three rooms at 225/300 pesos and 17 suites from 300 to 570 pesos.

La Hacienda De Las Flores (☎ (415) 2-18-08, fax 2-18-59), at Hospicio 16, has wonderful views from its upstairs rooms and verandahs. Rooms cost from 240/264 to 291/315 pesos in the high season, slightly less in the low season.

La Puertecita Boutique'otel (☎ (415) 2-21-18, 2-22-50, fax 2-04-24) at Santo Domingo 75, about one km uphill from the post office, is another luxury place with nine suites costing from 513 to 825 pesos. It has a cheaper sibling hotel closer to the centre, *La Puertecita Centro* at Cerrada de Pila Seca 2, where rooms are 180 to 210 pesos, less by the week.

Behind the Instituto Allende is the *Hotel Aristos San Miguel* (☎ (415) 2-03-92, fax 2-16-31) at Ancha de San Antonio 30, with 56 rooms and four suites, all with outdoor terraces, around a large garden with tennis courts and a swimming pool. Rooms cost 246 pesos for one or two people, suites more.

Places to Eat

San Miguel has loads of places to eat covering an array of international cuisines. Most are pretty good but you need to find one to suit your pocket as the bill can easily mount up.

Inexpensive For quick cheap eats, there are some excellent panaderías (bakeries). Try *La Colmena Panadería* at Reloj 21, half a block north of the Jardín; it has several varieties of wholegrain bread and rolls, and tasty tuna or cheese empanadas. *Genesis Tienda Naturista* at Reloj 34B bakes its own wholewheat and pitta breads, and cakes, almost daily; it's closed on Wednesday. Also good is *Panadería La Espiga* at Insurgentes 119, in front of the International Hostel.

The food stalls on the east side of the Jardín offer cheap, tasty Mexican fare such as fried chicken with vegetables, tortillas, salsa and pickles for around 6 pesos. There's more to choose from on Sunday and holidays.

Just a couple of doors from the north-east corner of the Jardín, *El Tucán* at San Francisco 2 makes good hot tortas for 3 to 4.50 pesos. They also serve economical hamburgers, omelettes, quesadillas, enchiladas, licuados and juices. Open every day, 9 am to 10 pm.

Nearby, *Restaurant Flamingo's* at Juárez 15 is a small family-run place. Chickens turn on a spit out front. The comida corrida (13 pesos), served from 1 to 4 pm, and a huge mug of café con leche (2 pesos) are good deals. It's open daily from 9 am to 10.30 pm.

Around the corner, *Los Sentados* at Mesones 42 is a snack-bar serving large jugos (4 pesos), tortas, tacos and sandwiches (each 3 pesos), and excellent tropical fruit salads with granola (7 pesos).

La Vianda down at Zacateros 50 is always busy with both Mexicans and foreigners, particularly on Sunday. Its plentiful comida corrida (13 pesos) is varied daily. Open Wednesday to Monday 11.30 am to 10 pm.

Restaurant/Bar Coco on the corner of Umarán and Hernández Macías opens early for economical breakfasts – 6 pesos for eggs, bacon, beans, bread, juice and coffee.

Mid-Range & Expensive Several European-style places around the Jardín do good coffee, cakes, snacks and light meals. They're open from around 9 or 10 am to 10 pm. They include *El Portal Café y Neveria* at the south-east corner of the Jardín and the *Café Del Jardín* at the south-west corner. *La Dolce Vita* at Recreo 11 is another of this type.

An excellent lunch spot is the friendly, family-run *El Pegasus* on Corregidora opposite the post office. Try their fancy sandwiches such as smoked turkey (9.50 pesos) or smoked salmon with cream cheese (18.50 pesos).

Some of the best food in town is found at the little *Fonda La Mesa del Matador* at Hernández Macías 76, between Canal and Umarán. Spaghetti a la Mesa, prepared at your table with shrimp and wine, is 17 pesos. A T-bone steak, mixed grill, or pollo suprema Parmesana (sliced chicken breast dipped in Parmesan cheese and fried, served with vegetables and fries) is 22 pesos. They're open every day from 8 am to 11 pm.

Mama Mia at Umarán 8, in a pleasant, cool courtyard half a block from the Jardín, is a favourite with foreigners, not only for its food but for the live South American music nightly from around 8 pm to midnight. Many of their dishes are quite expensive (meats and seafoods 30 to 40 pesos, pastas 25 pesos) but their breakfasts from 5 to 9 pesos are a better deal. They're open every day from 8 am to 12.30 am.

Another popular courtyard restaurant/bar with live music nightly is *La Fragua* at Cuna de Allende 3, just off the Jardín. It's open daily from noon until at least midnight. A few doors further away from the centre, the *Posada Carmina* at Cuna de Allende 7 also has a popular courtyard restaurant, particularly busy for Sunday lunch – menú del día

18 pesos. It's open from 8 am to 9.30 pm. On the corner of Cuna de Allende and Cuadrante, the little *El Ten Ten Pie* serves up home-style cooking with excellent chile sauces. Try the cheese and mushroom tacos – 4.50 pesos for a small serve.

Rincón Español at Correo 29 has a comida corrida for 15 pesos served the whole time it's open: 1 to 11 pm Monday to Thursday, until 2 am Friday to Sunday. Their other dishes, Spanish specialities, are more expensive. There's a Flamenco dinner show on weekends – see Entertainment.

A popular place with the foreign set is the pleasant restaurant of the *Hotel Quinta Loreto* at Calle Loreto 15. The ample comida corrida for 19.50 pesos, served with soup, salad and spaghetti, features selections like roast beef and orange chicken. The restaurant is open every day from 8 to 10.30 am and 1.30 to 5 pm.

Casa Mexas at Canal 15 is on the expensive side but it's a fun restaurant/bar with Tex-Mex specialities and Texas-size portions. In the back is a bar with a big-screen TV and, further back, a billiards room. It's open daily from noon to 11 pm.

Pepe Pizzas (☎ 2-18-32) at Hidalgo 26, 1½ blocks north of the Jardín, open daily from 1 to 11 pm, is a good pizza parlour which does home deliveries for no extra cost. A medium-sized vegetarian pizza (27 pesos) is enough for two people. It's open from 1 to 11 pm.

Entertainment

San Miguel has a thriving entertainment scene. Keep an eye on the notice boards and *Atención San Miguel* to find out what's on. Some events are held in English.

Villa Jacaranda at Aldama 53 has a Cine Bar showing recent releases of North American movies. Entry is 15 pesos and includes a drink and popcorn. The *Casa del Mayorazgo de Canal* may be showing free films on Friday, Saturday and Sunday afternoons. Or try the back room of *Casa Mexas* at Canal 15; their satellite dish brings movies in English to a large screen TV. If the movies are no good, you could always go in the back and play billiards.

Mama Mia restaurant at Umarán 8, half a block from the Jardín, has live South American music every night from around 8 pm to midnight. There's also a wine bar at the front and a downstairs venue for live music – the action here starts around 10 pm on weekend nights in the low season with additional nights in the tourist seasons (cover charge is 10 pesos on an ordinary night). *La Fragua*, just off the Jardín at Calle Cuna de Allende 3, is another courtyard restaurant/bar with live music.

El Buen Café on the corner of Jesús and Cuadrante has live music and sing-along sessions on Friday and Saturday nights from about 6 pm until midnight.

The *Rincón Español* at Correo 29, one block from the Jardín, presents a Flamenco dinner show on Friday at 9.30 pm, Saturday at 9.30 and 11.15 pm, and Sunday at 3 pm.

If you're more in the mood for doing the dancing yourself, *Pancho & Lefty's* at Mesones 99 attracts a young crowd with live and disco music from around 10 pm to 3 am, Wednesday to Saturday. There's usually a cover charge of around 20 pesos and 'two for one' drinks for much of the night.

Restaurant/Bar Coco at Hernández Macías 85 on the corner of Umarán is a laid-back place with live blues, rock or reggae, starting around 10.30 pm nightly. It offers 'two for one' beers from 6 to 8 pm.

San Miguel has several discos. Central and popular is *El Ring* at Hidalgo 25, open Tuesday to Sunday from 10 pm to 4 am (cover charge around 30 pesos). It also has live music on Wednesday, Thursday and Friday nights. Other discos include *Laberinto's* at Ancha de San Antonio 7 near the Instituto Allende (open Tuesday to Sunday 10 pm to 3 am), and *Eduardo's* on Calle Pedro Vargas, about 100 metres past El Mirador on the Querétaro road.

On the more cultural side, the Escuela de Bellas Artes hosts a variety of events including art exhibitions, concerts, readings and theatre; check its notice board for the current schedule. The Escuela de Bellas Artes, the Instituto Allende and the Casa del Mayorazgo de Canal all stage art exhibitions year-round. Galería San Miguel on the north side of the Jardín and Galería Atenea at Cuna de Allende 15, one block behind the parroquia, are two of the best and most established commercial galleries. Many others are advertised in *Atención San Miguel*.

For a great concert of birds in the trees, be in the Jardín at sunset. The birds make a racket calling to one another from all the trees, while below them the people gather to socialise, doing much the same.

Things to Buy

San Miguel has one of the biggest and best concentrations of craft shops in Mexico, selling folk art and handicrafts from all over the country. Prices are not low, but quality is high and the range of goods available is enormous. Casa Maxwell on Calle Canal, a few doors down from the plaza, is one place with a huge range; there are many, many more within a few blocks, especially on Canal, San Francisco and Zacateros. Local crafts include tinware, wrought iron, silver, brass, leather and textiles. Most of these are traditions going back to the 18th century. The Mercado de Artesanías, with a number of small handicraft stalls, is in an alleyway running between Colegio and Loreto. However, its wares are of lower quality than those in San Miguel's smart shops.

San Miguel has several regular markets. The daily Mercado El Nigromante is on Colegio, behind the Colegio de Sales; stalls with fruits, vegetables and assorted other goods stretch along Colegio. The town's biggest market takes place on Tuesday: walk west down Canal from the Jardín for about six blocks and you'll run into it. There is a supermarket on the north side of the Jardín.

Getting There & Away

Air The nearest airport is at León: see the León section for flight information. Otherwise you can fly into Mexico City. One place you can buy air tickets in San Miguel is American Express, at Hidalgo 1A (☎ 2-18-56, 2-16-95).

Bus San Miguel has a modern Central de Autobuses on Canal, about one km west of the centre of town. Tickets for Primera Plus long-distance buses can also be bought at Transporte Turístico on Diez de Sollano just off Correo. Daily buses from San Miguel include:

Celaya – 52 km, 1¼ hours; 2nd-class buses every 15 minutes, 5 am to 9.30 pm, by Flecha Amarilla (5.50 pesos)

Dolores Hidalgo – 43 km, one hour; 2nd-class buses every 10 or 20 minutes, 6 am to midnight, by Flecha Amarilla or Herradura de Plata (4 pesos)

Guadalajara – 380 km, six hours; two deluxe buses by Primera Plus (57 pesos)

Guanajuato – 82 km, one to 1½ hours; two deluxe buses by Primera Plus (13.50 pesos); one 1st-class by Omnibus de México (14 pesos); eight 2nd-class by Flecha Amarilla (9.50 pesos)

León – 138 km, 2¼ hours; two deluxe buses by Primera Plus (21.50 pesos)

Mexico City (Terminal Norte) – 280 km, 3¼ to four hours; four deluxe buses by Primera Plus (41 pesos); three 1st-class nonstop by Herradura de Plata (41.70 pesos); 2nd-class semi-directo buses at least every half-hour, 5 am to 7.30 pm, by Herradura de Plata or Flecha Amarilla (31 pesos)

Querétaro – 60 km, one hour; frequent 2nd-class buses, 5 am to 9 pm, by Herradura de Plata and Flecha Amarilla (7.50 pesos)

Other services include a few Flecha Amarilla buses to San Luis Potosí and Aguascalientes.

Train The Estación del Ferrocarril (☎ 2-00-07) is at the end of Calle Canal, about two km west of the centre. Train Nos 1 and 2, between Mexico City and Nuevo Laredo, stop at San Miguel; see the Train section in the Mexico City chapter for the schedule – though the trains are frequently late. Tickets go on sale 30 minutes before departure. The trains have primera especial, primera regular and segunda clase seats. Primera especial costs 35 pesos to Mexico City, 18 pesos to San Luis Potosí, 69 pesos to Monterrey and 96 pesos to Nuevo Laredo.

Car There are two car-rental agencies in town. Gama (☎ (415) 2-08-15) at Hidalgo 3 rents VW sedans (their cheapest cars) for 87 pesos a day plus 0.60 pesos per km, or 207

pesos a day with unlimited km, both plus 10% tax. You should book at least a week ahead during the winter season (December to March). Office hours are 9 am to 2 pm Monday to Friday and 9 am to 2 pm Saturday. Dollar Rent-A-Car (☎ (415) 2-01-98) out front of the Hotel Real de Minas on Ancha de San Antonio charges similar rates.

Getting Around

To/From the Airports American Express (☎ (415) 2-18-56, 2-16-95) at Hidalgo 1A offers combis, holding up to six people, to/from León and Mexico City airports. Rates for the vehicle are 285 pesos to León (1½ hours) and 510 pesos to Mexico City (four hours). The Travel Institute (☎ (415) 2-00-78 ext 4) at Cuna de Allende 11 offers vans holding up to five people for 255 pesos to León airport, or 555 pesos to Mexico City airport.

Bus Local buses run every day from 7 am to 9 pm and cost 0.80 pesos. 'Central Estación' buses go every few minutes from the train and bus stations to the town centre. Coming into town these go up Insurgentes, wind through the town a bit and terminate on the corner of Mesones and Colegio. Heading out from the centre, you can pick one up on Canal.

Taxi San Miguel has many taxis. Between the centre and the bus station costs 5 pesos; to the train station it's 7 or 8 pesos. Sometimes you have to bargain.

AROUND SAN MIGUEL
Hot Springs
There are several balnearios at hot springs near San Miguel, on or near the highway to Dolores Hidalgo. All have swimming pools with mineral waters (good for the skin) and pleasant surroundings.

Taboada Most popular is Taboada, eight km north of San Miguel and then three km west along a signposted side-road. It has a large lawn area and three swimming pools: one Olympic-size with warm water, and two smaller ones that get quite hot. It's open from 10 am to 6 pm every day except Tuesday; entry is 15 pesos. There's a small kiosk and bar for drinks and snacks.

A taxi costs around 25 to 30 pesos each way. You can ask the driver to return for you at an appointed time. Buses to Nigromante (hourly) or Xote (a few daily) from the corner of Insurgentes and Loreto in San Miguel will get you most of the way to Taboada: you must get off where the bus turns off the Taboada side-road and walk the remaining one km or so to the hot springs. Or take any bus heading for Dolores Hidalgo from the Central de Autobuses, get off at the Taboada turnoff and walk or hitchhike the rest of the way – about three km.

Santa Veronica This balneario is right beside the highway to Dolores Hidalgo, at the Taboada turnoff, eight km from San Miguel. It has a large Olympic-size swimming pool with water a bit cooler than at Taboada. It's open from 9 am to 6 pm every day except Friday; admission is 12 pesos. Any bus heading for Dolores Hidalgo will drop you there.

Parador del Cortijo Nine km from San Miguel on the Dolores Hidalgo road, Parador del Cortijo (☎ (415) 2-17-00, 2-07-58) is a natural health centre offering a number of services. It costs 15 pesos to swim in the hotel-size thermal pool, or 90 pesos for a full-day health programme with swimming, sauna, jacuzzi, a thermal mud wrap, massage and lunch. They clean the pool on Tuesday or Wednesday; phone to find out which day or to ask about their programmes. The centre is clearly signposted on the road; any bus to Dolores Hidalgo will drop you there.

Escondido Place This balneario has two warm outdoor pools and three connected indoor pools, each progressively hotter, with pretty stained-glass windows above. The indoor pools are open daily, the outdoor ones only on weekends. Entry is 15 pesos. The grounds have plenty of space for picnicking and there's a small kiosk for drinks and snacks. Take any bus heading for Dolores Hidalgo and get off just before the Parador del Cortijo. Escondido Place is clearly signposted on the highway but from here it's about a km down a dirt road.

Atotonilco
Turn off the Dolores Hidalgo highway at the Parador del Cortijo, continue on past it about one km and you come to the hamlet of Atotonilco, dominated by the Santuario founded in 1740 as a spiritual retreat. Here Ignacio Allende was married in 1802; eight years later he returned with Miguel Hidalgo and the band of independence rebels en route from Dolores to San Miguel, to take the shrine's banner of the Virgin of Guadalupe as their flag.

Today Atotonilco is a goal of pilgrims and penitents from all over Mexico, and the starting point of an important and solemn procession two weekends before Easter, in which the image of the Señor de la Columna is carried to the church of San Juan de Dios in San Miguel. Inside, the sanctuary has six chapels and is vibrant with statues, folk murals and other paintings. Indian dances are held here on the third Sunday in July.

Pozos
Once a flourishing silver and copper-mining centre, Pozos is now more or less a ghost town. A couple of thousand people live on among abandoned houses and mine workings in what, 90 or so years ago, was a town of about 50,000. Some of them make a living from textile handicrafts. If you've got time to spare, Pozos might make a side trip from San Miguel de Allende or Querétaro.

To get to Pozos from San Miguel de Allende by bus involves a trip of two or three hours on three different buses: first to Dolores Hidalgo, then to San Luis de la Paz, and from there 11 km south to Pozos. From San Miguel with your own vehicle, you can take the Querétaro road, turn left off it after four km towards Dr Mora, follow that road for 35 km crossing highway 57 on the way, and proceed left at a crossroads from which Pozos is 14 km away.

Querétaro

Querétaro is primarily an agricultural and livestock-raising state, with industry developing around Querétaro city and in certain other places, notably San Juan del Río. The state also turns out opals, mercury, zinc and lead. Many visitors never get past Querétaro city, with its fine colonial architecture, active cultural life and rich history, but the towns of San Juan del Río and, particularly, Tequisquiapan are also interesting to visit.

QUERÉTARO

• *pop: 454,000* • *alt: 1762 metres*

Querétaro's museums, monuments and colonial architecture are less spectacular than those of Guanajuato and Zacatecas, but the city still warrants a visit, especially if you're interested in Mexico's history, in which it has played an important role.

History

First settled by Otomí Indians, who in the 15th century became absorbed into the Aztec empire, Querétaro was conquered by the Spaniards in 1531. Franciscan monks used the settlement as a base for missions to what is now the US south-west as well as around Mexico. In the early 19th century Querétaro became a centre of intrigue among disaffected criollos plotting to free Mexico from Spanish rule. Conspirators, including Miguel Hidalgo, met secretly at the house of Doña Josefa Ortiz (La Corregidora), wife of a former *corregidor* (administrator) of Querétaro.

When the conspiracy was discovered, the story goes, Doña Josefa was locked in a room in her house (now the Palacio de Gobierno) but managed to whisper to a co-conspirator, Ignacio Pérez, through a keyhole that their colleagues were in jeopardy. He galloped off to inform another conspirator in San Miguel de Allende, who in turn carried the news to Dolores Hidalgo, where on 16 September 1810 Padre Hidalgo gave his famous Grito,

a cry to arms initiating the War of Independence.

In 1867, Emperor Maximilian surrendered to Benito Juárez' General Escobedo at Querétaro after a near-100-day siege and it was here that the ill-fated Maximilian was executed by firing squad.

In 1917, the Mexican constitution – still the basis of Mexico's law – was drawn up by the 'Constitutionalist' faction of revolutionaries in Querétaro. Mexico's ruling party, the PNR (ancestor of the PRI), was organised in Querétaro in 1929.

Orientation

The heart of the city is the Plaza Principal, called Jardín Obregón. Running along its east side, by the church of San Francisco, is Corregidora, the main avenue of the downtown area. Three blocks south of the centre on Corregidora is the large, green Parque Alameda; the bus station faces the south side of this park. The centre is laid out in a grid and everything of interest is within walking distance.

Other important central plazas are the Plaza de la Corregidora just off the north-east corner of Jardín Obregón, and the Plaza de la Independencia, a block east of Jardín Obregón.

Information

Tourist Office The tourist office (☎ (42) 14-56-23, 13-85-11) is at Pasteur Sur 17, on the south-east corner of the Plaza de la Independencia. Guided walking tours of the city centre (10 pesos) leave here every day at 10.30 am, lasting around 1½ to 2½ hours. The office gives out free maps and information on both the city and state of Querétaro. Hours are Monday to Friday from 9 am to 2 pm and 5 to 8 pm, Saturday and Sunday 9 am to 4 pm.

Money There are several banks on and near the Jardín Obregón, especially on Corregidora Norte, heading north out of the plaza. They are open Monday to Friday from 9 am to 1.30 pm.

Cash and travellers' cheques can also be

changed at the Casa de Cambio de Querétaro, in the large building at Madero 6 on the south side of the Jardín Obregón. It's open Monday to Thursday from 9 am to 3 pm, Friday 9 am to 1.30 pm. Outside these hours some of the larger hotels may change money, but their rates are less favourable.

Post & Telecommunications The main post office is at Arteaga Poniente 7, between Juárez and Allende. It's open Monday to Friday from 8 am to 7 pm, Saturday 9 am to noon.

The Telecomm office, with telegram, telex and fax services, is at Allende Norte 4. Opening hours are Monday to Friday from 9 am to 8 pm, Saturday from 9 am to 1 pm. There's a Lada caseta at 5 de Mayo 33, the pedestrian street heading east off Jardín Obregón beside San Francisco church. It's open daily from 7.30 am to 10 pm. Another caseta, open 24 hours every day, is at the bus station.

Templo de San Francisco
The magnificent Church of San Francisco is situated on the Jardín Obregón, on the corner of Corregidora and 5 de Mayo. Its dome's pretty coloured tiles were brought from Spain in 1540, around the time construction on the church began. Inside are some fine religious paintings from the 17th to 19th centuries.

Museo Regional
The Regional Museum is beside the Templo de San Francisco. The ground floor holds artefacts and exhibits on pre-Hispanic Mexico and archaeological sites in Querétaro state, the early Spanish occupation of the area, and the state's various Indian groups.

Upstairs are exhibits on Querétaro's role in the independence movement, the post-independence history of Mexico and Querétaro, and much religious art. Included are the table where the Treaty of Guadalupe Hidalgo was signed, and the desk of the tribunal that sentenced Maximilian to death.

The museum is housed in part of what was once a huge monastery and seminary (to which the Iglesia de San Francisco was attached). Begun in 1540, by 1567 the seminary was the seat of the Franciscan province of San Pedro y San Pablo de Michoacán. Building continued on and off until at least 1727, which explains the mixture of architectural styles. The tower was the highest vantage point in the city and in the 1860s the monastery was used as a fort both by imperialists supporting Maximilian and by the forces who finally defeated Maximilian in 1867.

The museum is open from 10 am to 6 pm Wednesday to Saturday, 10 am to 3.30 pm Tuesday and Sunday, closed Monday. Admission is 12 pesos, but free on Sunday, and always free to those under 13, over 60, and to students with a student card.

Museo de Arte de Querétaro
Querétaro's Museum of Art at Allende Sur 14 occupies the former monastery to which the adjacent Church of San Agustín was attached. Built in 1728-32, it's a splendid example of baroque architecture, with angels, gargoyles, statues and other ornamental details all over the building but particularly in the interior courtyard.

The museum is very well organised and well displayed. If you can read Spanish, the explanations accompanying the exhibits add up to an illustrated course in art history. On the ground floor are displays of 16th and 17th-century European painting, tracing interesting influences, for example from Flemish to Spanish to Mexican art; 19th and 20th-century Mexican paintings; a collection of 20th-century Querétaro artists; and a salon for temporary exhibits. The top floor has a photographic display on the history of the monastery and rooms with art from 16th-century mannerism to 18th-century baroque. The museum is open Tuesday to Sunday from 11 am to 7 pm (closed Monday). Admission is 5 pesos, but free for those under 12 and over 60, and free for everyone on Tuesday.

Teatro de la República
One block north of the Jardín Obregón, on

the corner of Juárez and Angela Peralta, the Teatro de la República was where a tribunal met in 1867 to decide the fate of Emperor Maximilian. Mexico's constitution, still in use today, was signed here on 31 January 1917. The stage backdrop lists the names of its signatories and the states they represented. In 1929, politicians met in the theatre to organise Mexico's ruling party, the PNR (now the PRI).

The theatre is open Monday to Friday from 10 am to 2 pm and 6 to 9 pm, Saturday 10 am to 1 pm (closed Sunday), and admission is free. Cultural events are presented here from time to time.

Casa de la Corregidora (Palacio de Gobierno)

The Casa de la Corregidora, Doña Josefa Ortiz' home, where she informed Ignacio Pérez of the plans to arrest the independence conspirators, sits on the north side of the Plaza de la Independencia. Today the building is the Palacio de Gobierno, the state government building.

The room where Doña Josefa was locked up is not marked, but it's the large room upstairs over the entrance to the building. It is now used as the governor's conference room.

The building can be visited any day from around 7 am to 9 pm; guards on duty will let you in.

Convento de la Santa Cruz

About 10 minutes' walk east from the centre of Querétaro is one of the city's most interesting sights, the Convento de la Santa Cruz, on Plaza de los Fundadores. This monastery was built between 1654 and about 1815 on the site of a battle in which a miraculous appearance of St James had led Otomí Indians to surrender to the conquistadors and Christianity. Emperor Maximilian had his headquarters here while under siege in Querétaro from February to May 1867. After his surrender and subsequent death-sentence, he was jailed here while he awaited the firing squad. Today the monastery is used as a religious school.

A guide will provide insight into the Convento's history and artefacts including an ingenious water system and unique colonial ways of cooking and refrigeration. The guide will also relate several of the Convento's miracles, including the legendary growth of a tree from a walking stick stuck in the earth by a pious friar in 1697. The thorns of the tree form a cross.

The Convento is open Monday to Friday from 9 am to 2 pm and 4 to 6 pm, Saturday and Sunday from 11 am to 6 pm. There's no admission fee, but your guide will request a donation to the convent at the end of your tour. Tours are given in English or Spanish.

Mirador & Mausoleo de la Corregidora

Walk down the sidewalk to the left of the Convento de la Santa Cruz and you come to a mirador with a view of Querétaro's aqueduct whose 76 towering arches stretch along Avenida de los Arcos. Built in 1726-28, the aqueduct still brings water about 12 km to the city.

Across the street is the tomb of Doña Josefa Ortiz (La Corregidora) and her husband, Miguel Domínguez de Alemán. Behind the tomb is a shrine with photos, lithographs, documents and a tribute to Doña Josefa's life.

Other Sights

One block west of Jardín Obregón on the corner of Madero and Allende is the **Fuente de Neptuno** (Neptune Fountain), designed by the noted Mexican neoclassical architect Eduardo Tresguerras in 1797. The adjacent **Templo de Santa Clara** has an ornate baroque interior.

Two blocks further along Madero, past the Jardín Guerrero, is the **Archivo Histórico del Estado** at No 70. In 1917 this was the provisional National Palace when a Mexican government was established in Querétaro. On the corner of Madero and Ocampo is the rather plain 18th-century **cathedral**.

At the intersection of Arteaga and Montes stands the **Templo de Santa Rosa de Viterbos** with its pagoda-like bell tower and impressively gilded and marbled interior.

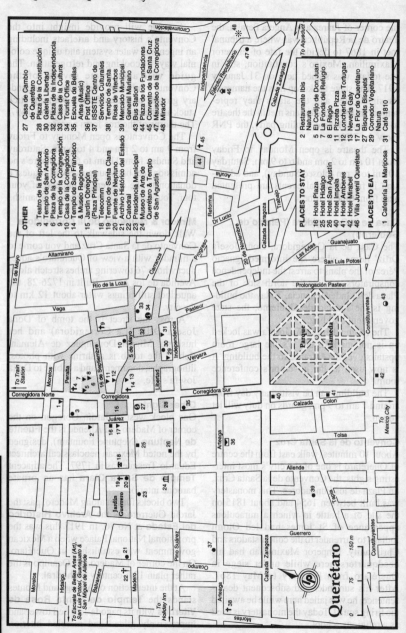

OTHER

3 Teatro de la República
4 Templo de San Antonio
6 Plaza de la Corregidora
9 Templo de la Congregación
14 Casa de la Corregidora
14 Templo San Francisco & Museo Regional
15 Jardín Obregón (Plaza Principal)
18 Telecomm
19 Templo de Santa Clara
20 Fuente de Neptuno
21 Archivo Histórico del Estado
22 Catedral
23 Presidencia Municipal
24 Museo de Arte de Querétaro & Templo de San Agustín
27 Casa de Cambio de Querétaro
28 Plaza de la Constitución
30 Galería Libertad
32 Plaza de la Independencia
33 Casa de la Cultura
34 Tourist Office
35 Escuela de Bellas Artes (Music)
36 Post Office
37 ISSSTE Centro de Servicios Culturales
38 Templo de Santa Rosa de Viterbos
39 Mercado Municipal General Mariano
43 Bus Station
44 Plaza de los Fundadores
45 Convento de la Santa Cruz
47 Mausoleo de la Corregidora
48 Mirador

PLACES TO STAY

16 Hotel Plaza
25 Hotel Hidalgo
26 Hotel San Agustín
40 Hotel Impala
41 Hotel Amberes
42 Hotel Mirabel
46 Villa Juvenil Querétaro

PLACES TO EAT

1 Cafetería La Mariposa
2 Restaurante Ibis Natura
5 El Cortijo de Don Juan
8 La Fonda del Refugio
11 Pizzetta Pizza
12 Lonchería las Tortugas
13 Nevería Galy
17 La Flor de Querétaro
27 Bisquets Bisquets
29 Comedor Vegetariano Natura
31 Café 1810

Tresguerras remodelled the church with what some say is the first four-sided clock built in the New World.

Other notable colonial churches include **San Antonio** on the corner of Corregidora Norte and Angela Peralta, with two large pipe organs, elaborate crystal chandeliers, gilt red wallpaper and several oil paintings; and the **Templo de la Congregación** on the corner of Pasteur Norte and 16 de Septiembre, with some beautiful stained-glass windows and a splendid pipe organ.

Parque Alameda

Opposite the bus station and not far from the city centre, the large Alameda park, shady and green, is a popular place for picnics, jogging, roller skating, strolling and generally just taking it easy.

Cerro de las Campanas

At the west end of the city, a good 35-minute walk from the centre, is the Cerro de las Campanas (Hill of the Bells), the site of Maximilian's execution by firing squad. The emperor's family constructed a chapel on the spot. Near it is a statue of Benito Juárez. You can get there from the Jardín Obregón on a 'Ruta R' bus going north on Corregidora. Get off at the Centro Universitaria.

Festival

Querétaro holds its major annual festival, the Exposición Ganadera, Agrícola e Industrial (the state fair), during the entire second week of December.

Places to Stay – bottom end

The *Villa Juvenil Querétaro* youth hostel (☎ (42) 14-30-50) is on Ejército Republicano between the Convento de la Santa Cruz and the Mausoleo de la Corregidora. It has 72 beds, with four people to a room in separate-sex dorms, costing 11 pesos a night. The office is open from 7 am to 11 pm.

On the west side of the Jardín Obregón, the *Hotel Plaza* (☎ (42) 12-11-38) at Juárez Norte 23 is a great place to stay in the budget category. All its 29 rooms are tidy and comfortable, with windows opening on the interior courtyard or French doors opening on small balconies facing the plaza, offering plenty of light, air and noise. Singles/doubles are 55/70 pesos, rooms with two double beds 75 pesos.

Hotel Hidalgo (☎ (42) 12-00-81), owned and managed by an Englishman, is just a few doors off the Jardín Obregón at Madero 11 Poniente, between Juárez and Allende. Rooms are 40/55 pesos; some large ones can hold up to seven people, at around 15 pesos for each extra person. Some upper-floor rooms have small balconies overlooking the pedestrian street. There's parking in the courtyard, and an economical restaurant open from 8 am to 10 pm.

Back-to-back with the Hotel Hidalgo, the *Hotel San Agustín* (☎ (42) 12-11-95, 12-39-19) at Pino Suárez 12 is a modern-style place, not luxurious but OK; all 35 rooms have colour TV. They cost 65/70 pesos. Rooms facing the street are the best, with a whole wall of windows and a balcony large enough for sitting out.

Places to Stay – middle

Hotel Impala (☎ (42) 12-25-70, 12-26-20, fax 12-45-15), on the corner of Corregidora Sur and Zaragoza, opposite the Parque Alameda (the official address is Colón 1), is a modern four-storey hotel whose 102 rooms all have colour TV and carpet. Some have a view of the park, but beware traffic noise as it's a very busy corner; the interior rooms are bright enough and quieter. Singles/doubles are 80/95 pesos, rooms with two double beds 120 pesos.

Hotel Amberes (☎ (42) 12-86-04, fax 12-88-32) at Corregidora Sur 188, also opposite the park, is similar, with rooms at 100/125 pesos.

Hotel Mirabel (☎ (42) 14-39-29, 14-35-35, fax 14-35-85), at Constituyentes Oriente 2, on the corner of Corregidora, to your left as you leave the bus station, is a step up in luxury. Its 171 modern rooms, costing 140/160 pesos, all have colour TV and air-con, and some have a view over the park.

Places to Stay – top end

The *Hotel Jurica Querétaro* (☎ (42) 18-00-22, fax 18-01-36), a converted 17th-century hacienda, is about eight km north of the centre on Calle Paseo Jurica, Fraccionamiento Jurica (Km 229 on highway 57). It offers swimming, tennis, squash, riding, soccer, volleyball, billiards, table tennis, a discothèque, a bar and two restaurants as well as singles/doubles at 261/348 pesos.

The *Holiday Inn* (☎ (42) 16-02-02, fax 16-89-02), 2.5 km west of the city centre on Carretera Constitución (highway 57), just south of Avenida Pino Suárez, charges 294 pesos for one or two people. It has a swimming pool, tennis courts, miniature golf, a bar, cafeteria and restaurant.

Places to Eat

La Flor de Querétaro, at Juárez Norte 5 on the west side of the Jardín Obregón, is a good, basic restaurant with reasonable prices, open every day from 7.30 am to 10.30 pm. On the south side of the Jardín Obregón, in the rear of the large building at Madero 6, *Bisquets Bisquets* is a small, friendly restaurant with good food at good prices, open every day from 7.30 am to 10 pm.

Vegetarians and natural food fans will like the pleasant, popular *Restaurante Ibis Natura* at Juárez Norte 47, half a block north of the Jardín Obregón. It's open every day from 8 am to 9.30 pm. The comida corrida for 13.75 pesos is an excellent deal; so are the soyburgers with mushrooms and cheese at 5.75 pesos. *Comedor Vegetariano Natura* at Vergara 7, just off the pedestrian street to the right of the Templo de San Francisco, is another good vegetarian restaurant; it's open from 8 am to 9 pm Monday to Saturday.

Plaza de la Corregidora, off the north-east corner of the Jardín Obregón, has a number of romantic sidewalk cafés and restaurant/bars: *El Cortijo de Don Juan*, *El Regio*, the *Fonda del Refugio* and *Pizzeta Pizza*.

Nevería Galy at 5 de Mayo 8, off the Jardín Obregón, is a Querétaro institution known for its homemade ice cream. Specialities include lemon ice cream with mineral water, or cola, or red wine. Opposite, *Lonchería las Tortugas* is very popular for take-out food.

A pleasant place for dessert and coffee is *Cafetería La Mariposa* at Angela Peralta 7, near the corner of Corregidora Norte one block north of the Jardín Obregón. This bright, ice-cream-parlour-like restaurant is entered through the ice cream and sweets shop to one side; it serves basic Mexican meals at good prices, and there's an Italian espresso machine in the back.

Café 1810 is a more expensive restaurant/bar with some outdoor tables facing the south side of the pleasant, quiet and green Plaza de la Independencia.

Entertainment

Querétaro has cultural activities befitting a state capital and university city. You can pick up a calendar of events from the tourist office. Sit in the Jardín Obregón Sunday evenings to watch local families enjoying concerts; the state band performs every Sunday from around 6 to 8 pm, sometimes with dancers.

Other outdoor music can be enjoyed at the less central Jardín de los Platitos, on Juárez at Avenida Universidad. Mariachis, ranchera groups and others start tuning up every evening around dusk and go on until the wee hours, with people requesting their favourite tunes.

The Casa de la Cultura (☎ 12-56-14) at 5 de Mayo 40 on the corner of Carranza sponsors concerts, dance, theatre, art exhibitions and other events, as does the ISSSTE Centro de Servicios Culturales (☎ 12-73-69) at Arteaga 70. Stop by during office hours to pick up their monthly schedules.

Querétaro University's Escuela de Bellas Artes (☎ 16-90-22) has three branches with regular events. The main campus is on Hidalgo between Avenida Tecnológico and Régules. Art exhibitions of one kind or another are usually going on. The music campus (☎ 12-05-70), on the corner of Independencia and Juárez Sur, presents free classical concerts every Thursday at 7 pm. On Saturday and Sunday at 6 pm they have concerts in the Jardín Guerrero.

The Galería Libertad at Libertad 56, on the south side of the Plaza de la Independencia, hosts some excellent changing art exhibitions; it's open every day from 8 am to 8 pm.

Querétaro's most popular discos are *Qiu* at Monte Sinia 102; *La Opera* at Circuito Jardín Sur 1; *JBJ Disco* at Boulevard Zona Dorada 109 in Fraccionamiento Los Arcos; and *Tiffani's* at Zaragoza Poniente 67. All except Tiffani's have live music.

Getting There & Away

Air Aeromar (☎ 24-13-33 at the airport) flies to/from Mexico City six days a week. Aerolitoral (☎ 14-57-88 at the airport) flies to/from Guadalajara, San Luis Potosí, Monterrey and San Antonio (Texas) daily.

Bus Querétaro is a hub for bus transport going in many directions; the big, busy Central Camionera is on Constituyentes opposite the Parque Alameda, one km south of the Jardín Obregón. It has restaurants, shops, a guarda equipaje for storing luggage, and a 24-hour Lada caseta. Daily departures include:

Guadalajara – 348 km, five to six hours; eight deluxe buses by Primera Plus (61 pesos) and six by ETN (69 pesos); 12 1st-class by Omnibus de México (53 pesos) and four by Servicios Coordinados (46 pesos)

Guanajuato – 133 km, 2½ hours; two 1st-class buses by Omnibus de México (22.50 pesos); four 2nd-class by Frontera (20.50 pesos); or take one of the frequent buses to Irapuato, from where buses leave for Guanajuato every few minutes

Mexico City (Terminal Norte) – 220 km, 2½ to three hours; buses by every line in the terminal, including deluxe buses every half-hour, 5 am to 11 pm, by ETN (43 pesos); seven deluxe by Primera Plus (33 pesos); 11 1st-class by Estrella Blanca (33 pesos) and 13 by Servicios Coordinados (28 pesos)

Morelia – 195 km, three to four hours; three deluxe buses by Primera Plus (26 pesos); three 1st-class by Estrella Blanca (21.50 pesos); hourly 2nd-class buses, 6 am to 9 pm, by Flecha Amarilla

San Juan del Río – 52 km, 45 minutes; 2nd-class buses every few minutes by Flecha Roja, Herradura de Plata, Flecha Amarilla and Amealcenses (4.50 pesos)

San Luis Potosí – 204 km, 2½ hours; many buses including three deluxe by ETN (36 pesos) and two by Primera Plus (32 pesos); several 1st-class by Omnibus de México, Servicios Coordinados and Chihuahuaenses (25 to 27 pesos); 2nd-class buses hourly, 7.30 am to 11.30 pm, by Flecha Amarilla (22 pesos)

San Miguel de Allende – 60 km, one hour; two 1st-class buses by Omnibus de México (8 pesos); frequent 2nd-class buses by Herradura de Plata and Flecha Amarilla (7.50 pesos)

Tequisquiapan – 72 km, 1½ hours; hourly 2nd-class buses, 7 am to 7 pm, by Flecha Azul (6.50 pesos)

Train The Estación del Ferrocarril (☎ 12-17-03) is on Avenida Héroes de Nacozari at the intersection of Calle Cuauhtémoc Norte, about a km north of the centre. The ticket office is open every day from 9 to 10.30 am and from noon to 5.30 pm. Tickets for Saturday, Sunday or holiday trips on the División del Norte train must be bought in advance.

Querétaro is served by the Constitucionalista train between Mexico City and Guanajuato, the División del Norte between Mexico City and Ciudad Juárez and Train Nos 1 and 2 between Mexico City and Nuevo Laredo. See the Mexico City Train section for details of these trains' schedules and other stops.

Fares on the Constitucionalista (primera especial only) are 30.40 pesos to Mexico City and 19.90 pesos to Guanajuato. On the División del Norte (primera regular) it's 16.20 pesos to Mexico City and 114.40 pesos to Ciudad Juárez. Train Nos 1 and 2 have both primera especial and primera regular seats: primera especial is 24.90 pesos to Mexico City, 10.80 pesos to San Miguel de Allende.

Getting Around

Querétaro is a compact city and you will easily reach most major sights on foot. The airport is an eight-km taxi ride north-east of the city centre.

The local buses, called *urbanos*, run from 6 am until 9 or 10 pm and cost 0.80 pesos. There are buses to the centre from the bus and train stations; going from the centre to the train station, catch 'Ruta 13' going north on Corregidora. The northbound buses on Corregidora stop outside San Francisco church on the Jardín Obregón.

SAN JUAN DEL RÍO

• *pop: 61,650*

Just east of highway 57, 56 km south of Querétaro and 170 km north of Mexico City, San Juan del Río has a pleasant colonial centre, produces good wine and cheese, and is something of a craft centre. It's known particularly for its gems and jewellery– a business based on local opals but also including the polishing and setting of stones from elsewhere.

Orientation & Information

The centre of town is about one km east of highway 57; the bus station is beside the highway. Avenida Hidalgo is the main road between the two and its intersection with Avenida Juárez, overlooked by El Santuario church, is the town's principal intersection and commercial area. Many opal and lapidary shops, hotels and restaurants are near this intersection, especially on Juárez. The central Plaza de los Fundadores is one block further past this intersection on Hidalgo; its two colonial churches are called La Parroquia and El Templo.

The tourist office is in the Centro Histórico y Cultural at Juárez 30 Oriente, near the Hidalgo intersection. Open daily 9 am to noon and 4 to 7 pm, it gives out free maps and information about the town.

Museo de la Santa Veracruz

The town museum is in the lovely ex-convent of the colonial church of La Santa Veracruz. From the Hidalgo/Juárez intersection, walk one block back towards the highway on Hidalgo, go left up the hill on Calle F de Tapia for a block or two , and turn right onto the street marked by a large arrow pointing to 'Museo'. The church and museum are a block or two further on. The museum – entered around behind the church – holds exhibits on the archaeology, ethnography, geography and history of the area. It is open Tuesday to Friday from 9.30 am to 2 pm and 4 to 6 pm; Saturday, Sunday and holidays from 10.30 am to 2 pm.

Places to Stay – bottom end

Hotel Layseca (☎ (467) 2-01-10) at Juárez 9 Oriente, half a block from Hidalgo, is a pleasant hotel in a well-kept colonial building with enclosed parking. Its 23 clean rooms with high wood-beamed ceilings and private bath open onto an arched courtyard filled with plants and flowers. Singles are 50 or 60 pesos, doubles 60 to 80 pesos.

Opposite this is the *Hotel La Estancia* (☎ (467) 2-00-38, 2-09-30) at Juárez 20 Oriente, with 42 modern, clean rooms and enclosed parking. The rooms facing the street have French doors opening onto tiny balconies; singles/doubles are 60/77 pesos.

If both these are full, try the *Hotel Jalisco* (☎ (467) 2-04-25) at Hidalgo 15 Sur, a block or two towards the highway from the Juárez intersection. The rooms cost 40 pesos and are basic but clean.

Places to Stay – middle & top end

The *Hotel Colonial* (☎ (467) 2-29-85) is at Juárez 28 & 30 Poniente, 1½ blocks west of the main intersection. It has a swimming pool, parking and 55 rooms with air-con, carpet and satellite TV; some also have private poolside terraces. Its pleasant restaurant occupies a courtyard covered with stained glass, with a gurgling fountain off to one side. Singles/doubles are 120/180 pesos; suites with fridge are dearer.

Two resort-hotels in old haciendas to the west of town are used mainly by people from Mexico City for a spot of relaxation. The *Hotel Estancia de San Juan* (☎ (467) 2-01-55) at highway 57, Km 172, has tennis, volleyball, a swimming pool and horse riding; singles/doubles are 150/171 pesos. The luxurious five-star *Hotel La Mansión Galindo* (☎ (467) 2-00-50, fax 2-01-00) at Carretera Amealco, Km 5, has a swimming pool, horses, golf and every other amenity; its 163 rooms cost around 390/420 pesos.

Places to Eat

There are a number of pleasant restaurants, from cheap ones to high class, on Juárez near the corner of Hidalgo, and around the Plaza de los Fundadores.

Getting There & Away

Bus The bus station, beside highway 57, has a cafeteria, a guarda equipaje, and a Lada caseta open daily from 7 am to 11 pm. Local buses run frequently between the centre and the bus station, costing 0.80 pesos, or you can walk in about 15 minutes. Daily buses from San Juan del Río include:

Mexico City (Terminal Norte) – 170 km, two hours; seven deluxe buses by ETN (33 pesos); frequent 1st-class by Omnibus de México and Tres Estrellas de Oro (22 pesos); many 2nd-class by Herradura de Plata, Flecha Roja and Flecha Amarilla (20 pesos)

Querétaro – 56 km, 45 minutes; 1st-class buses hourly, 8 am to 5 pm, by Omnibus de México (6.20 pesos); frequent 2nd-class buses by Amealcenses, Flecha Amarilla, Flecha Roja and Herradura de Plata (4.50 pesos)

San Miguel de Allende – 116 km, two hours; frequent 2nd-class buses by Herradura de Plata (12 pesos)

Tequisquiapan – 26 km, 25 minutes; 2nd-class buses at least every 15 minutes, 6 am to 10 pm, with Flecha Blanca or Flecha Roja (2 pesos)

Train El Constitucionalista, which runs between Guanajuato and Mexico City, stops at San Juan del Río. See the Mexico City Train section for schedules. The fare to Mexico City is 23.70 pesos (primera especial). The train station is on the northern outskirts of town.

TEQUISQUIAPAN
• *pop: 19,230*

This small town ('teh-kees-kee-AP-an') 26 km north-east of San Juan del Río is a quaint, pleasant retreat from Mexico City or Querétaro. It used to be known for its thermal spring waters – some of Mexico's presidents in earlier times came here to ease their aches and tensions – but the development of a couple of large industries in the area has drained off the hot water. Nonetheless there are still some delightful cool-water pools.

One pleasure of 'Tequis' is simply strolling the brick-paved Spanish streets lined with brilliant purple bougainvillea. The town is also a thriving crafts centre, with interesting goods in both the main market and the Mercado de Artesanías.

Orientation

The central Plaza Tequisquiapan is overlooked by the Church of Santa Maria de la Asunción. Around the plaza are many little restaurants and artesanías shops. The market and the Mercado de Artesanías beside it are one block from the plaza, through a couple of little lanes. The large, verdant Parque La Pila, and many hotels and restaurants, are within a couple of blocks of this area.

The bus station is on the outskirts of the town; local buses coming from the station into town will let you off between the Mercado de Artesanías and the main market. The plaza is one block straight ahead.

Information

The tourist office is at Morelos 23, about a block from the central plaza. It has a brightly coloured sign out front and helpful staff. It's open Tuesday to Sunday, 10 am to 6 pm, with free maps of the town, brochures and information on Tequisquiapan and the state of Querétaro. The post office is next door.

Balnearios

The large, cool pool at the Hotel Neptuno, at Avenida Juárez Oriente 5 just around the corner from the main market, makes a pleasant place for a swim. It's open Saturday and Sunday from 8 am to 6 pm; entrance is 15 pesos per person.

The Hotel El Relox at Morelos 8, just down the block from the Mercado de Artesanías, also has a large pool but if you're not a guest you have to rent a room for the day to be able to use the pool. However, you should be able to arrange a single room price even if you are two or more people (see Places to Stay – top end). There are also private indoor pools, costing 20 and 40 pesos an hour at the weekend, less during the week.

Organised Tours

Tequisquiapan Tours (☎ 3-13-62/02, fax 3-16-61) at Callejón 20 de Noviembre 2A in the centre operates a variety of tours of the local area. The Posada Los Arcos also organises tours for guests and non-guests.

Festivals

Tequisquiapan's festivals include:

Festival Turístico Artesanal This festival, during Semana Santa, features displays of traditional handicrafts from all over Querétaro state.

Feria del Queso y del Vino The Wine and Cheese Fair, held for two weeks in June or July, is the big bash of the year, attracting celebrants from far and wide for tastings, music and other events. Dates are changeable; check with the tourist office.

Día de la Santa Maria de la Asunción Religious celebrations for Tequisquiapan's patron saint are held from 13 to 17 August; the saint's day is 15 August.

Places to Stay – bottom end

Tequisquiapan has few good budget hotels, but an exception is the *Posada Mejia* (☎ (467) 3-02-36), run by a friendly and hospitable family at Guillermo Prieto 17, on the corner of 16 de Septiembre. The 16 rooms are simple but clean and pleasant, arranged around a grassy courtyard with trees and roses. Cost is 35 pesos per person.

Places to Stay – middle

Posada Los Arcos (☎ (467) 3-05-66) at Moctezuma 12 has a small restaurant and nine rooms, each with two double beds, around a fountain courtyard. Singles/doubles are 50/96 pesos.

Posada San Francisco (☎ (467) 3-02-31) at Moctezuma 2, on the corner of Madero, is a pleasant family hotel with a communal sitting room, a dining room, and a large enclosed garden whose swimming pool is overlooked by a statue of a ruminating nymph. The 11 rooms cost 77 pesos per person, or 120 pesos with three meals included. The *Hotel/Balneario Neptuno* (☎ (467) 3-02-24) is at Avenida Juárez Oriente 5, just down the block from the central plaza; rooms are 150 pesos and it has a large pool.

Places to Stay – top end

Right on the central plaza, *Hotel La Plaza* (☎ (467) 3-02-89, 3-00-56) has a swimming pool, restaurant, bar and parking, and 17 rooms from 110 to 330 pesos. Facing the central plaza, *Hotel Maridelfi* (☎ (467) 3-00-52, 3-10-29) is a lovely, luxurious hotel popular with wealthy Mexican families. Three meals a day are included in the price of 170 pesos per person.

The *Hotel/Balneario El Relox* (☎ (467) 3-00-06/66) near the Mercado de Artesanías has 110 singles/doubles at 180/240 pesos, including dinner. (There is a 30% discount from Monday to Thursday). It has a large outdoor pool and two indoor pools – see Balnearios. Similarly priced, the *Posada del Virrey* (☎ (467) 3-02-39, 3-09-02) at Guillermo Prieto Norte 9, on the corner of 16 de Septiembre, has 22 rooms and a pool.

Places to Eat

There are many restaurants in all price categories around the centre of town. The cheapest place for a good meal or snack is the rear of the main market, where many clean little *fondas* (food stalls) have tables under awnings in the patio. They're open every day from around 8 am to 8 pm.

The restaurant at the *Hotel Maridelfi* on the plaza is good but a little expensive with the comida corrida at 28 pesos. Another good but expensive place for a night out is *El Patio de Tequisquiapan* beside the Hotel El Relox, near the Mercado de Artesanías. Their speciality is Sonora beef, with steak dinners and the comida corrida each at around 29 pesos. They have a dance floor with live music on Saturday nights – cover charge 20 pesos.

Getting There & Away

Bus Tequisquiapan bus station is a vacant lot on the south-west edge of town. Local buses (0.80 pesos) run frequently between here and the Mercado de Artesanías, one block from the central plaza. Buses from Tequisquiapan are all 2nd-class. They include:

Mexico City (Terminal Norte) – 196 km, 2¾ hours; every half-hour, 6 am to 8 pm, by Flecha Amarilla (21 pesos)

Querétaro – 82 km, one hour; hourly, 7.30 am to 6.30 pm, by Flecha Azul (6.50 pesos)

San Juan del Río – 26 km, 25 minutes; every 10 minutes, 6 am to 8.30 pm, by Flecha Amarilla (2 pesos)

Central Gulf Coast

The route from north-east to south-east Mexico lies along the hot coastal plain between the Gulf of Mexico and the country's central mountains. Veracruz is the most appealing of the coastal cities – a popular holiday resort for Mexicans, with a famously festive atmosphere and the country's most riotous annual Carnaval. A number of cities lie inland, in the foothills of the Sierra Madre. Xalapa, the capital of Veracruz state, and Córdoba are the most attractive of them.

This chapter covers the coast and hinterland from Tampico-Ciudad Madero to Coatzacoalcos in far south-east Veracruz state – just over 600 km as the crow flies but over 800 by highway 180, following the curve of the coast. It's an area with a fascinating prehistory but only one major archaeological site – El Tajín, near Papantla, which shouldn't be missed as you travel through.

Southern Veracruz was the Olmec heart-land, but there's little to see there now. The best collections of Olmec artefacts – including several of the mighty 'Olmec heads' of sculpted basalt – are in the Museo de Antropología in Xalapa, and at Parque-Museo La Venta in Villahermosa (see the Tabasco & Chiapas chapter). The Xalapa museum has by far the best archaeological collection from the Gulf Coast as a whole.

HISTORY
Olmec
The first great centre of Central America's earliest civilisation, and Mexico's ancestral culture, the Olmec, flourished from about 1200 to 900 BC at San Lorenzo, in the hot, wet far south of Veracruz state. After this centre fell, La Venta in neighbouring Tabasco was the main Olmec centre until it too was violently destroyed in about 400 BC. Olmec culture lingered, influenced gradually from elsewhere, for another 400 years or so at Tres Zapotes, in Veracruz.

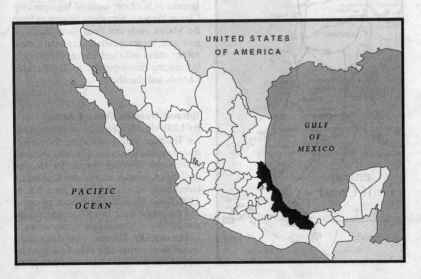

Central Gulf Coast

0   40   80 km

Classic Veracruz

In the Classic period (300-900 AD), the centres of civilisation on the Gulf Coast moved west and northwards. In central and northern Veracruz, a number of power centres arose which were politically independent but shared religion and culture. Together they're known as the Classic Veracruz civilisation. Their hallmark is a unique style of carving, with pairs of parallel lines curved and interwoven. The style often appears on three types of mysterious carved stone objects; these objects are probably connected with the important ritual ball game. They are the U-shaped *yugo*, probably representing a wooden or leather belt worn in the game; the long, paddle-like *palma*; and the flat *hacha*, shaped a little like an axehead. The last two are thought to represent items attached to the front of the belt, and are often carved in human or animal forms. Hachas may also have been court markers.

The most important Classic Veracruz centre, El Tajín, was at its height from about 600 to 900 AD and contains at least 11 ball courts. Other main centres were Las Higueras near Vega de Alatorre, close to the coast south of Nautla, and El Zapotal near Ignacio de la Llave, south of Veracruz city. Classic Veracruz sites show influences from the Mayan lands and from Teotihuacán; in their turn, Veracruz cultures exported cotton, rubber, cacao and vanilla to central Mexico, influencing developments in Teotihuacán, Cholula and elsewhere.

Totonac, Huastec, Toltec & Aztec

By 1200 AD, when El Tajín was abandoned, the Totonacs were establishing themselves from Tuxpan in the north to beyond Veracruz in the south. North of Tuxpan, the Huastec civilisation, another web of small, probably independent states, flourished from 800 to 1200. It was Mexico's chief cotton producer and the people built many ceremonial sites and developed great skill in stone carving.

The warlike Toltecs, who dominated central Mexico in the early Postclassic age, also moved into the Gulf Coast area, occupying the Huastec centre Castillo de Teayo for some time between 900 and 1200. There's Toltec influence too at Zempoala, a Totonac site near Veracruz city. In the mid-15th century, the Aztecs subdued most of the Totonac and Huastec areas, exacting tribute of goods and sacrificial victims, and maintaining garrisons to control revolts.

Colonial Era

When Cortés arrived on the Gulf Coast in April 1519, he was able to make the Totonacs of Zempoala his first allies against the Aztecs – he told them to imprison five Aztec tribute collectors and promised to protect them against reprisals. Cortés set up his first settlement, Villa Rica de la Vera Cruz (Rich Town of the True Cross), north of modern Veracruz city, and a second one at La Antigua, where he scuttled his ships before advancing to Tenochtitlán, the Aztec capital. In May 1520 he returned to Zempoala and defeated the rival Spanish expedition sent to arrest him.

All the Gulf Coast was in Spanish hands by 1523. The Indian population was devastated by a combination of diseases, particularly recently introduced ones like smallpox. Veracruz harbour became an essential link in trade and communication with Spain, and was vital for anyone trying to conquer or govern Mexico, but the hot, damp climate, tropical diseases and the threat of pirate attacks inhibited the growth of Spanish settlements.

19th & 20th Centuries

The population of Veracruz city actually shrank in the first half of the 19th century. Under dictator Porfirio Díaz, Mexico's first railway linked Veracruz to Mexico City in 1872, and some industries started to develop.

In 1901 oil was discovered in the Tampico area, which by the 1920s was producing a quarter of the world's oil. That proportion declined, but new oilfields were discovered in southern Veracruz, and by the 1980s the Gulf Coast had well over half Mexico's petroleum reserves and refining capacity.

GEOGRAPHY & CLIMATE

More than 40 rivers run from the inland mountains to the central Gulf Coast, mostly passing through an attractive, well-watered, hilly landscape. In the north there is an undulating coastal plain, while in the south-east there are more low-lying areas, prone to flooding, with marshes and jungles which extend into Tabasco.

It's warm and humid most of the time: hotter along the coast, wetter in the foothills, hottest and wettest of all in the low-lying south-east. Two-thirds or more of the rain falls between June and September. The city of Veracruz receives about 1650 mm of rain a year, with temperatures well over 30°C from April to October and falling into the teens at night only from December to February. Tuxpan and Tampico, on the north coast, are a bit drier, a little hotter in summer and a fraction cooler in winter. Coatzacoalcos in the south-east gets 3000 mm of rain a year.

PEOPLE

Veracruz, with over six million people, is Mexico's third most populous state. Large numbers of African slaves were shipped to the Gulf Coast in the 16th century, and their descendants, plus more recent immigrants from Cuba, contribute a visible African element to the population and culture. Of the region's nearly half a million Indians, the most numerous are the roughly 150,000 Totonacs (see the El Tajín section) and 150,000 Huastecs (see below).

Tampico & the Huasteca

The fertile, often beautiful Huasteca ('wass-TEK-a') region is inland from Tampico, where the coastal plain meets the fringes of the Sierra Madre Oriental. Spread over southern Tamaulipas, eastern San Luis Potosí and northern Veracruz, the region is named after the Huastec people who have lived here for about 3000 years. If you're heading south-east, a couple of routes go through the Huasteca to the Central Gulf

The Huastecs

The Huastec language is classified as one of the Mayance family, along with the languages of the Yucatán Maya – possibly stemming from a single tongue once spoken all down the Gulf Coast. One suggestion is that the Huastec language split from the rest of the family in about 900 BC, when the Olmec culture arose in the intervening area. The central-Mexican feathered serpent god Quetzalcóatl was probably of Huastec origin.

The Huastecs' greatest period was roughly 800 to 1200 AD. Under a number of independent rulers, they built many ceremonial centres, practised phallic fertility rites and expanded as far west as north-east Querétaro and Hidalgo. They developed great skill in pottery and in carving stone and shells. The two most interesting Huastec sites to visit are Tamuín and Castillo de Teayo (see the Around Tuxpan section), though neither is spectacular.

After the Spanish conquest, slavery and imported diseases cut the Huastec population from an estimated one million to probably under 100,000 during the 16th century. Rebellions began and continued into the 19th century. Today, about 150,000 Huastecs live in the Huasteca, mostly between Ciudad Valles and Tamazunchale, and east of Tantoyuca. Many of the women still wear quechquémitls, colourfully embroidered with traditional trees of life, animals, flowers and two-armed crosses. Huastecs still practise land fertility ceremonies, particularly dances. ■

Coast. Going west from the coast to the Bajío region or Mexico City, there are four steep, winding routes which climb onto the Sierra – from Ciudad Valles, Xilitla, Tamazunchale or Huejutla.

TAMPICO-CIUDAD MADERO

• pop: 600,000

Sweaty, smelly, seedy but jolly Tampico, a few km upstream from the mouth of the Río Pánuco, detains few travellers. Somewhat faded since its 1920s heyday, it's still Mexico's busiest port, a tropical place where bars and cantinas stay open late. (But if tropical port atmosphere is what you're after, head on down to Veracruz city, which has it in spades.) Hotel prices are slightly inflated by the oil business, but reasonable-value accommodation is available, as well as good seafood. Ciudad Madero, between Tampico and the coast, is the processing centre for the country's oldest oilfields, and has a wide sandy beach.

History

In 1523 Cortés defeated the native Huastec Indians and founded a colony called San Estéban, now Pánuco, 30 km upriver from Tampico. In the next few years he prevailed not only over the rebellious Huastecs, but also over Spanish rivals including Nuño de Guzmán, who was appointed royal governor

of the Pánuco area in 1527. De Guzmán concentrated on pillage and slaughter in western Mexico, and organised slave raids north of the Pánuco, but was eventually sent back to Spain.

In the 1530s, a mission was established in Tampico, in order to convert the Huastecs to Christianity. The town was destroyed by pirates in 1684 but was refounded in 1823 by families from Altamira, to the north. After 1901, when oil was discovered in the area, Tampico suddenly became the world's biggest oil port: rough, tough and booming. The oil and its profits were under foreign control until 1938 when the industry was nationalised by President Lázaro Cárdenas, following a strike by Tampico oil workers.

Mexico's 1970s and 1980s oil boom took place further down the coast, but the Tampico-Ciudad Madero area remains important. Pipelines and barge fleets bring oil from fields north and south, onshore and offshore, to its refineries and harbour, and Ciudad Madero is the headquarters of the powerful oil workers' union, the STPRM.

Orientation

Tampico is in a marshy region near the mouth of the Río Pánuco, surrounded by several lakes including Laguna del Chairel, which is used for recreation, and the unattractive Laguna del Carpintero, which isn't. You'll cross a number of smaller estuarine rivers as you approach the city from the north or the west. Going south, the spectacular Puente Tampico (Tampico Bridge) crosses the Río Pánuco to Veracruz state.

Downtown Tampico (*el centro*) centres on two plazas. One is the zócalo or Plaza de Armas, with the 20th-century cathedral on its north side and the Hotel Inglaterra on its south side. One block south and one east is the Plaza de la Libertad, which was being redeveloped at the time of writing. Hotels and restaurants of all grades are within a few

blocks of these two plazas. Down a gentle hill south of either plaza you come to a smelly, sleazy area containing the market, train station and riverside docks – it doesn't feel very safe at night around here. Tampico's bus station is in the north of the city, north of the swampy Laguna del Carpintero. Colectivos will take you to the city centre from there for 1 peso. The centre of Ciudad Madero is a few km north-east of central Tampico, and its industrial zones extend east to Playa Miramar, on the Gulf of Mexico.

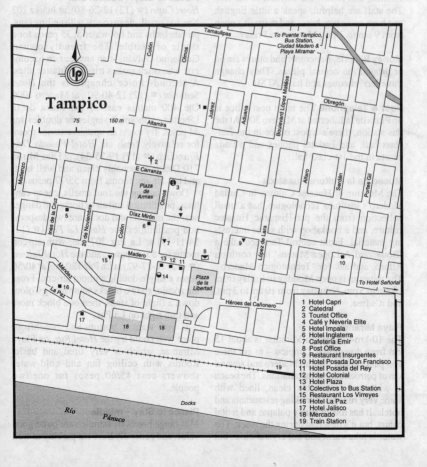

1 Hotel Capri
2 Catedral
3 Tourist Office
4 Café y Nevería Elite
5 Hotel Impala
6 Hotel Inglaterra
7 Cafetería Emir
8 Post Office
9 Restaurant Insurgentes
10 Hotel Posada Don Francisco
11 Hotel Posada del Rey
12 Hotel Colonial
13 Hotel Plaza
14 Colectivos to Bus Station
15 Restaurant Los Virreyes
16 Hotel La Paz
17 Hotel Jalisco
18 Mercado
19 Train Station

Addresses on east-west streets usually have the suffix Ote (east) or Pte (west), while those on north-south streets are Nte (north) or Sur (south). The dividing point between east, west, north and south is the junction of Colón and Carranza at the north-west corner of the zócalo.

Information

Tourist Office Tampico's tourist office (☎ (12) 12-00-07) is on the zócalo, upstairs at Olmos Sur 101, but it's not conspicuous. Go up one flight of stairs beside Helados Chantal, and follow the corridor to the left. The staff are helpful, speak a little English and have some brochures and maps. It's open from 9 am to 7 pm, Monday to Friday.

Money Banorte, Bancomer and others are on or around the central plazas. They change travellers' cheques and have ATMs.

Post & Telephone The main post office is on Plaza de la Libertad at Madero 309. At the bus station, there's a post office in the 2nd-class hall, and Ladatel phones and a Lada caseta in the 1st-class hall.

Museo de la Cultura Huasteca

The Museum of Huastec Culture, in Ciudad Madero's Instituto Tecnológico, has a small collection from the pre-Hispanic Huastec culture, and a bookshop with some interesting material. From central Tampico take a 'Boulevard A López Mateos' bus north on Alfaro, and ask for 'Tecnológico Madero'. The museum is open Monday to Friday from 10 am to 5 pm, Saturday from 10 am to 3 pm, and it's free.

Playa Miramar

The 10-km-long Playa Miramar is about 15 km from downtown Tampico – to get there you pass central Ciudad Madero and several km of petrochemical installations. The beach is wide and reasonably clean, lined with some very run-down looking restaurants and hotels. It has lots of shady palapas and rental chairs, but it's deserted during the week. The water is lukewarm and not crystal-clear, but

it's clean enough. From central Tampico, take a 'Playa' bus or colectivo.

Festivals

Semana Santa brings numerous activities to Playa Miramar, such as regattas, fishing and windsurfing competitions, sand-sculpture contests, music, dancing and bonfires. The anniversary of Tampico's 1823 refounding is celebrated on 12 April, with a procession from Altamira which passes through Tampico's zócalo.

Places to Stay – bottom end

Hotel Capri (☎ (12) 12-26-80), at Juárez 202 Nte, has small, clean rooms with ceiling fans, private baths and hot water at 35 pesos for a single or double. The friendly owner, Guillermo Galván, is an amateur archaeologist who often makes trips to Huastec sites. A second-choice cheapie is the *Hotel Señorial* (☎ (12) 12-40-90), at Madero 1006 Ote 400 metres east of the Plaza de la Libertad, with small singles or doubles for 44 pesos. Try to get an upstairs exterior room, for relatively fresh air. *Hotel Posada Don Francisco* (☎ (12) 19-25-34), at Díaz Mirón 710 Ote, is reasonably clean and well kept, and has air-con rooms from 55/77 pesos.

Down among the foul smells, cheap cantinas, prostitution and air of nocturnal danger near the markets and docks are two desperation possibilities: the *Hotel La Paz* (☎ (12) 14-11-19) at La Paz 307 Pte, with air-con rooms for 55/75 pesos; and the *Hotel Jalisco* (☎ (12) 12-27-92) at La Paz 120 Pte, at 40/50 pesos a single/double without air-con. From the zócalo, go two blocks south along Colón, down a flight of steps, then one block more and turn right on La Paz.

If you want a bottom-end beachfront place, you could try the *Hotel Ritz*, on Playa Miramar, which is very tired and basic. Rooms with ceiling fan and cold-water showers cost 45/60 pesos for one/two people.

Places to Stay – middle

Mid-range hotels in Tampico are quite good value, and generally have car parking as well as air-con rooms with carpet, cable TV and phone. The *Hotel Plaza* (☎ (12) 14-16-78), at Madero 204 Ote on the corner of Olmos, has clean, comfortable, sizeable rooms with air-con for 80/90 pesos. The *Hotel Posada del Rey* (☎ (12) 14-11-55), on the same block at Madero 218 Ote, charges 85/102 pesos for air-con rooms with a double bed; 118 pesos for two-bed rooms. Between these two, and superior to both, is the *Hotel Colonial* (☎ (12) 12-76-76) at Madero 210 Ote, with clean, tasteful, air-con, modern rooms. They normally cost 185/200 pesos, but the owner sometimes gives 50% discounts for cash, making this place a bargain at 87/110 pesos. The *Hotel Impala* (☎ (12) 12-09-90), at Díaz Mirón 220 Pte, 1½ blocks west of the zócalo, is also comfortable and good value at 85/110 pesos.

Places to Stay – top end

The top downtown place is the *Hotel Inglaterra* (☎ (12) 12-56-78) on the zócalo at Díaz Mirón Ote 116, with 120 comfortable air-con singles or doubles at 242 pesos, its own good restaurant and a small pool. If you arrive in Tampico by air, this hotel will give you a free ride from the airport.

Out towards the airport, at Avenida Hidalgo 2000, the *Hotel Camino Real* (☎ (12) 13-88-11) is Tampico's most luxurious hotel, with rooms and bungalows facing a tropical garden-courtyard, and a large pool. Prices start at around 396 pesos.

Places to Eat

Tampico is no gourmet paradise, but the seafood can be good. A local speciality is carne asada Tampiqueña (grilled meat Tampico-style), beefsteak marinated in garlic, oil and oregano and usually served with guacamole, strips of chile and totopos (maize chips).

The best downtown restaurants are probably in the big hotels like the Inglaterra. The clean, air-con *Restaurant Los Virreyes*, on the corner of Colón and Madero, a block from the zócalo, is open from 8 am to 10 pm and serves pretty good food, including a buffet comida corrida for 14 pesos. Seafood (including crab) is mostly in the 20-peso

bracket, meat dishes are 15 to 25 pesos and breakfasts are 8 to 12 pesos. A seafood specialist is the busy *Café y Nevería Elite*, on Díaz Mirón half a block east of the zócalo, where you can get two stuffed crabs for 20 pesos, snapper for 25 pesos or a set breakfast from 9 to 23 pesos.

The *Cafetería Emir*, at Olmos 107 Sur half a block south of the zócalo, has wobbly tables and loud music, and is popular with locals. Quesadillas and enchiladas cost around 14 pesos, meat dishes from 20 to 27 pesos and fish around 16 pesos. The *Restaurant Insurgentes*, on Díaz Mirón between Aduana and López de Lara, is OK too, with antojitos from 6 to 10 pesos, meat dishes at 18 pesos and fish at 24 pesos.

Getting There & Away

Air There are flights every day to/from Mexico City, Monterrey, Veracruz, San Luis Potosí and McAllen (Texas) with Mexicana (☎ (12) 13-96-00), whose office is at Avenida Universidad 700-1; the staff also do bookings for Aeromonterrey. Aero Litoral (☎ (12) 28-08-57) flies to/from Monterrey, Veracruz and Villahermosa. Saro (☎ (12) 28-03-90) offers some of the cheapest fares to Mexico City.

Bus Tampico bus station is out on Calle Zapotal, about four km north of the city centre. First-class ticket sales and departures are from the right side of the bus station as you enter, 2nd-class on the left. The 1st-class side has left-luggage facilities and Ladatel phones. There are connections to most main towns north of Mexico City and down the Gulf Coast – 1st-class buses are much quicker; 2nd-class buses have more frequent departures but are recommended only for short trips. The main destinations include:

Matamoros – 500 km, eight hours; about 12 1st-class buses daily by various companies (66 pesos) and numerous 2nd-class buses

Mexico City (Terminal Norte) – 515 km, 9½ hours; one deluxe overnight bus by UNO (111 pesos), frequent 1st-class buses by ADO (76 pesos) and other companies and numerous 2nd-class buses (72 pesos)

Monterrey – 585 km, eight hours; 10 1st-class buses daily (75 pesos) and regular 2nd-class buses

Nuevo Laredo – 820 km, 12 hours; four 1st-class (105 pesos) and seven 2nd-class buses daily

Pachuca – 380 km, nine hours; one or two 1st-class (58 pesos) and a few 2nd-class buses daily

Poza Rica – 250 km, five hours; one deluxe (65 pesos), several 1st-class (34 pesos) and frequent 2nd-class (31 pesos) buses daily

San Luis Potosí – 410 km, seven hours; one deluxe (75 pesos), seven 1st-class (44 pesos) and several 2nd-class buses daily

Tuxpan – 180 km, four hours; 11 1st-class (29 pesos) and frequent 2nd-class buses daily

Veracruz – 505 km, 10 hours; one deluxe (125 pesos) and 12 1st-class buses daily (85 pesos) daily

Long-distance 1st-class buses also go to Reynosa, Soto la Marina, Villahermosa and Xalapa, while towns in the Huasteca are mostly served by 2nd-class buses – these include Ciudad Valles (2½ hours; 10 to 15 pesos), Tamazunchale (27 pesos) and Huejutla.

Train Slow segunda clase trains go to Monterrey via Ciudad Victoria (departing 7.45 am), and to San Luis Potosí (departing 8 am).

Car Highway 180 is in patchy condition for much of the 95-km stretch between Altamira and Aldama, north of Tampico. Heading south out of Tampico, the highway soars over the Pánuco River on the Puente Tampico bridge; the toll is 10 pesos. Between here and Tuxpan there are more stretches of poor, bumpy road.

Getting Around

To/From the Airport Tampico airport is about 15 km north of the city centre. Transporte Terrestre (☎ 28-45-88) runs colectivo combis from arriving flights to anywhere in Tampico-Ciudad Madero for 10 pesos per person, but only operates a taxi service (about 30 pesos from the centre) going *to* the airport. 'Aviación Boulevard' colectivos going to the left from the road outside the airport terminal will take you to López de Lara in central Tampico for 1 peso. 'Aviación' buses running north on Alfaro from central Tampico go to the airport.

To/From the Bus Station & Beach The city's colectivo taxis are large, old American cars, usually bright yellow, with the destinations painted on the doors. They wait outside the bus station to take you to the city centre (1 peso). From the city centre to the bus station, take a 'Perimetral' or 'Perimetral-CC' colectivo from Olmos, a block south of the zócalo. 'Playa' buses or colectivos north on Alfaro will reach Playa Miramar.

CIUDAD VALLES
• *pop: 220,000*

Ciudad Valles ('VAH-yes'), sometimes just called Valles, lies on highway 85, the Pan-American, a little over halfway from Monterrey to Mexico City, at the junction of the highway from Tampico to San Luis Potosí. It's a convenient overnight stop for motorists. Commerce in cattle and coffee are among the most important activities.

Orientation
The main plaza is about seven blocks west of highway 85; the Central de Autobuses is on the highway at the southern edge of town.

Museo Regional Huasteco
On the corner of Rotarios and Artes, the museum has a collection of Huastec artefacts, and is open from 10 am to 6 pm on weekdays.

Places to Stay
Two adequate places are the *Hotel Rex* (☎ (138) 2-33-35) at Hidalgo 418, 3½ blocks from the plaza, and the *Hotel Piña* (☎ (138) 2-01-83) at Juárez 210, a little closer to the plaza (Juárez is parallel to Hidalgo, one block north). Both are clean and unspectacular with moderately sized singles from 60 to 85 pesos and doubles from 77 to 95 pesos, depending on whether you want TV and/or air-con.

One km north of the town along highway 85, the *Hotel Valles* (☎ (138) 2-00-50) is a luxurious motel with good, large air-con rooms from around 145/190 pesos. It has a big swimming pool and a 25-site campground/trailer park where full hook-ups cost around 30 pesos.

Places to Eat

Pizza Bella Napoli, next to the Hotel Piña at Juárez 210, does good spaghetti (8 to 10 pesos) and pizza (12 to 45 pesos). For Mexican food, including comida corrida, try the *Restaurant Malibu* at Hidalgo 109, a few doors from the central plaza. Hotel Valles has a steakhouse, the *Restaurant Del Bosque*, in its grounds.

Getting There & Away

Bus There are fairly frequent but mainly 2nd-class buses to most places in north-east Mexico. Few are locales. Departures include:

Matamoros – 545 km, 10 hours; several 2nd-class buses daily (52 pesos)

Mexico City (Terminal Norte) – 465 km, 10 hours; four 1st-class buses daily (47 pesos) and hourly 2nd-class buses

Monterrey – 520 km, nine hours; half a dozen 1st-class (67 pesos) and 2nd-class buses daily

San Luis Potosí – 270 km, 4½ hours; two 1st-class buses daily (30 pesos) and frequent 2nd-class buses

Tampico – 140 km, 2½ hours; several 1st-class buses daily (19 pesos) and frequent 2nd-class buses

There are also buses to Pachuca, Ciudad Victoria (26 pesos) and Tamazunchale.

Car Highway 70, west to San Luis Potosí (270 km), is spectacular as it rises across the Sierra Madre to the Altiplano Central. It's a twisting road, and you can get stuck behind slow trucks and buses, so don't count on doing it in a hurry. Highway 110, east to Tampico, is in poor condition, but it's straighter. Going south, highway 85 goes to Tamazunchale in the heart of the Huasteca. You can continue past Tamazunchale to Huejutla, and make a circle of the Huasteca back to Tampico.

TAMUÍN

The important Huastec ceremonial centre of Tamuín flourished from about 700 to 1200 AD – the ruins are not spectacular but this is one of the few Huastec sites worth visiting at all. The site is seven km from the town of Tamuín, 30 km east of Ciudad Valles on

highway 110 (the Tampico road). About one km east of the town, turn south from the highway down a road marked 'San Vincente'. Continue for 5.5 km to a small sign indicating the 'zona arqueológica'; from there it's about an 800-metre walk to the ruins. Frequent buses between Tampico and Ciudad Valles go through Tamuín. The rest of the way you must walk or take a taxi.

The only cleared part of the 170,000-sq-metre site is a plaza with platforms made of river stones on all four sides. A low bench with two conical altars, extending from the east side of a small platform in the middle of the plaza, bears the remains of frescos (probably 8th or 9th century) which may represent priests of Quetzalcóatl.

TANCANHUITZ

The small town of Tancanhuitz, also called Ciudad Santos, is in the heart of the area inhabited by modern-day Huastecs. It's in a narrow, tree-covered valley 52 km south of Ciudad Valles, three km east of highway 85. A lively market takes place on Sunday. There are pre-Hispanic Huastec remains near **Tampamolón**, a few km east.

Tancanhuitz, and also Aquismón (see below), are centres for the festivals of San Miguel Arcángel on 28 and 29 September and the Virgen de Guadalupe on 12 December. Huastec dances performed then include Las Varitas (The Little Twigs) and Zacamson (Small Music), which imitate the movements of wild creatures.

AQUISMÓN

The Huastec village of Aquismón, up a side road a few km west of highway 85, holds its market on Saturday. The Zacamson dance, a speciality around Aquismón, has in its full version more than 75 parts, danced at different times of the day and night. At festivals it is accompanied by much drinking of sugarcane alcohol.

In the wild country nearby, not accessible by vehicle, is the 105-metre **Cascada de Tamul**, which is 300 metres wide when in flood, and the **Sótano de las Golondrinas** (Pit of the Swallows), a 300-metre-deep hole which is home to tens of thousands of swallows and parakeets, and a challenge for serious speleologists.

XILITLA

On the slopes of the Sierra at 1000 metres, this small town has a 16th-century church and mission, a temperate climate and lots of rain. Two nearby attractions are the **Cueva del Salitre**, with stalactites etc, and the **Castillo de Sir Edward James**, the architectural folly of an eccentric English aristocrat. Xilitla is 21 km west of highway 85, up highway 120 – one of the least travelled routes between the Huasteca and the Sierra.

TAMAZUNCHALE

• *pop: 65,000*

Quaint Tamazunchale, 95 km south of Ciudad Valles on highway 85, is in a low-lying area of tropical vegetation with exuberant bird and butterfly life. The Sunday market is colourful, but has little in the way of Huastecan handicrafts. For the Day of the Dead (2 November), the people spread carpets of confetti and marigold petals on the streets. There's no bus station as such, but buses pull in at various company offices on Avenida 20 de Noviembre, which also has a few hotels and restaurants. *Hotel San Carlos* (☎ (136) 6-01-21) is only 33/44/55 pesos, or 10 pesos extra with TV; *Hotel González* (☎ (136) 2-01-36) is a bit better quality at 42/50 pesos.

South-east of Tamazunchale, highway 85 climbs steeply to Ixmiquilpan, then continues to Pachuca and Mexico City. This is about the most direct route from the Huasteca to Mexico City, and the most used. It's another steep but scenic route up onto the Sierra Madre, and you can encounter mist and fog, so start early for the best chance of clear conditions.

HUEJUTLA

• *pop: 40,000*

On the northern edge of Hidalgo state, but still in the semitropical lowlands, Huejutla has a fortress-monastery dating from the 16th century, when this area was frontier territory and subject to Indian attacks. The big Sunday market in the square attracts many Nahua Indians from outlying villages. For accommodation try the *Hotel Posada Huejutla* (☎ (129) 6-03-00), at Morelos 32, or the *Hotel Fayad* (☎ (129) 6-00-40), on the corner of Hidalgo and Morelos, where air-con rooms with TV cost 55/66 pesos.

SOUTH OF HUEJUTLA

Highway 105 mostly goes through lush, green, undulating farmland from Tampico, but south of Huejutla it climbs gradually into the beautiful Sierra Madre Oriental. It's a tortuous, sometimes foggy and in parts poorly surfaced route to Pachuca. On the way, there are old monasteries at **Molango** and **Zacualtipán**. In Molango try the *Hotel Plaza* at Plaza de la República 27.

The highway then leaves the forested Sierra Madre and drops several hundred metres to **Metzquititlán** (300 km) in the fertile Río Tulancingo Valley. The village of **Metztitlán**, 23 km north-west up the valley by paved road, has a reasonably well-preserved monastery. It was the centre of an Otomí Indian state which the Aztecs couldn't conquer. After another 100 km, and an 800-metre climb up from the Tulancingo valley, you reach Atotonilco el Grande, 34 km from Pachuca (see the Around Mexico City chapter for information about places near Pachuca).

Northern Veracruz

South of Tampico you enter the state of Veracruz, whose northern half is mostly rolling plains, lying between the coast and the southern end of the Sierra Madre Oriental. The Laguna de Tamiahua stretches 90 km along the coast, separated from the Gulf of Mexico by a series of sandbars and islands, with isolated beaches and opportunities for fishing, bird-watching and diving. The major archaeological attraction is the site of El Tajín, usually reached from Papantla.

TUXPAN

• *pop: 75,000*

Tuxpan ('TOOKS-pahn'; sometimes spelled Tuxpam) is a fishing town and minor oil port near the mouth of the Río Tuxpan, 310 km north of Veracruz city and 190 km south of Tampico. The town itself has a wide, tropical river, pleasant little parks, decent-value hotels and a beach 12 km away. On holidays and weekends it attracts Mexican families and students, and though it's not an idyllic seaside resort, it is a more agreeable place to break a journey than Tampico.

Orientation

The town centre is on the north bank of the Río Tuxpan, spreading five or six blocks west (upstream) from the high toll bridge which spans the river. The riverfront road, Boulevard Jesús Reyes Heroles, passes under the bridge and continues 12 km east to the beach at Playa Norte. A block inland from Heroles is Avenida Juárez, with many hotels. Parque Reforma, at its west end, functions as a zócalo and is crowded in the cool of the evening.

Information

There's a helpful tourist office (☎ (783) 4-01-77) in the Palacio Municipal on Juárez, open daily. There is a bunch of Ladatel phones in Parque Reforma, with a Banamex (ATM) nearby. Banca Serfin and Bancomer, on Juárez, also have ATMs. The Hotel Plaza will change travellers' cheques outside business hours. The post office is at Morelos 12. There's a scuba-diving and water-sports operation a few km east of town on the road to Playa Norte.

Museums

On the west side of Parque Reforma is a small **Museo Arqueológico** with Totonac and Huastec artefacts (open from 9 am to 5 pm, Tuesday to Saturday; free admission).

The **Museo Histórico de la Amistad México-Cuba** (Mexican-Cuban Friendship Museum), on the south side of the river, commemorates Fidel Castro's 1956 stay in Tuxpan, planning and preparing the Cuban revolution. It has a not-very-interesting collection of B&W photos, posters and a map of his Cuban campaign. Beside the museum stands a replica of the wooden *Granma*, in which Castro and 82 comrades sailed to Cuba to launch the revolution. The museum is open daily from 9 am to 2 pm and 4 to 7 pm, and it's free, but a donation is requested. To reach it, take one of the small boats across the river (0.50 pesos), walk two or three blocks inland to Obregón, then turn right. The museum is at the end of Obregón, just before you reach the river again.

Playa Norte

Tuxpan's beach is a wide strip of sand stretching 20 km north from the mouth of the Río Tuxpan, 12 km east of the town. Its beauty has been diminished by a new power station two km north of the river mouth, but the water and sand are reasonably clean and, apart from holidays and weekends, it's almost empty. A line of palapas serve seafood and sell souvenirs. Local buses marked 'Playa' leave every 10 minutes or so from the south side of Heroles, and drop you at the south end of the beach (25 minutes; 2 pesos). On the way back they do a quick tour of the town centre before leaving you on Heroles near the end of Rodríguez.

Festivals

A big fishing tournament brings hundreds of visitors to Tuxpan in late June or early July, and festivities for the Assumption on 15 August continue for a week with folk-dancing contests, bullfights and fireworks. The Totonac voladores (flyers; see the El Tajín section) usually perform.

Places to Stay

The recently renovated *Hotel Posada El Campanario* (☎ (783) 4-08-55), at 5 de Febrero 9, has clean singles/doubles with private bath and fan for 50/60 pesos, 60/70 pesos with TV. Though rooms at *Hotel El Huasteco* (☎ (783) 4-18-59), Morelos 41, are somewhat small and dark, they're all air-con and the place is clean and friendly, so it's quite good value at 42/46 pesos. About

CENTRAL GULF COA.

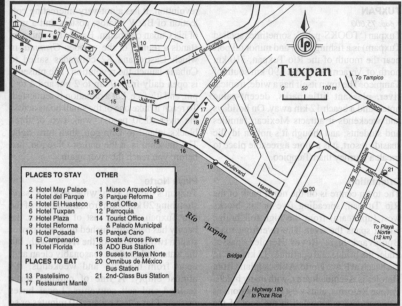

Tuxpan

To Tampico

0   50   100 m

Río Tuxpan

To Playa
Norte
(12 km)

Bridge

Highway 180
to Poza Rica

PLACES TO STAY

2   Hotel May Palace
4   Hotel del Parque
5   Hotel El Huasteco
6   Hotel Tuxpan
7   Hotel Plaza
9   Hotel Reforma
10   Hotel Posada
     El Campanario
11   Hotel Florida

PLACES TO EAT

13   Pastelisimo
17   Restaurant Mante

OTHER

1   Museo Arqueológico
3   Parque Reforma
8   Post Office
12   Parroquia
14   Tourist Office
     & Palacio Municipal
15   Parque Cano
16   Boats Across River
18   ADO Bus Station
19   Buses to Playa Norte
20   Omnibus de México
     Bus Station
21   2nd-Class Bus Station

the cheapest in town is the *Hotel Tuxpan* (☎ (783) 4-41-10), on the corner of Juárez and Mina, with 30 rooms (fan only) at 40/45 pesos, but it's a bit grimy and the rooms overlooking the street are noisy, while the others are dark. *Hotel del Parque* (☎ (783) 4-08-12) is on the east side of the bustling Parque Reforma and may also be noisy, but it's basically clean, and cheap at 45 pesos for singles or doubles with fan.

The upper front rooms of the 77-room *Hotel Florida* (☎ (783) 4-02-22) at Juárez 23 have superb river views. They're big and clean, though some beds are saggy. Rooms with fan cost 60/90 pesos; with air-con and TV they're 100/130 pesos. There are wide balconies/sitting areas and a lift.

The *Hotel Plaza* (☎ (783) 4-07-38) at Juárez 39 has clean, air-con but characterless rooms for 80/100 pesos with TV and phone. The most comfortable place in the town centre is the *Hotel Reforma* (☎ (783) 4-02-10) at Juárez 25, with air-con, phone and TV,

and bigger rooms than the Plaza's, at 118/140/162 for singles/doubles/triples. There's a pleasant covered courtyard with a fountain. The *Hotel May Palace* is a smart-looking new place, almost completed on the south side of Parque Reforma. There are more mid-range places, aimed at motorists, on Adolfo López Mateos as it loops around the north side of town towards the Tampico highway. A couple of top-end places, like the *Hotel Tajín* (☎ (783) 4-22-60), on the south side of the river, cater for business travellers and conventions.

Hotel Playa Azul is almost on the beach at Playa Norte, and quite cheap at 60/70 pesos. *Río Paraíso* (☎ (783) 4-60-78) is halfway between the town and the beach but is more comfortable, and costs around 90/100 pesos.

Places to Eat

The restaurants of the hotels *Florida* and *Plaza*, and *Antonio's* in the Hotel Reforma, all on Juárez, serve some of the best fare in town, with a bias towards seafood. Of course you pay for the clean, orderly surroundings. The popular Hotel Florida restaurant is particularly quick and helpful, with comida corrida at 20 pesos. Antonio's is the fanciest and most expensive.

There are other eateries on Juárez, and several bakeries towards the east end. *Restaurant Mante*, on Rodríguez opposite the end of Juárez, is cheap, popular and friendly with a range of dishes from antojitos (6 pesos) and seafood cocktails (12 to 16 pesos) to carne Tampiqueña (strips of beef with fried bananas, small tortillas, guacamole, frijoles, salad and cheese; 20 pesos).

Pastelisimo, on Parque Cano between Juárez and the waterfront, is clean and inviting for cakes and coffee. There is a pleasant cluster of places in the middle of Parque Reforma serving fresh fruit, juice and ice cream. The road to the beach passes several seafood restaurants and on the beach itself is a line of cheap palapa seafood joints, where you typically pay 8 pesos for fish soup, 22 to 25 pesos for a fresh fish and 15 pesos for a large shrimp cocktail or octopus with rice.

Getting There & Away

Book 1st-class buses out of Tuxpan as far ahead as possible, as there's a limited number of seats for passengers boarding here. You might have to get a 2nd-class bus to Poza Rica, and a 1st-class one from there. The ADO (1st-class) station is on Rodríguez, half a block north of the river. Omnibus de México (also 1st class) is under the bridge on the north side of the river. The 2nd-class bus station is on the corner of Constitución and Alemán, two blocks east of the bridge. Departures include:

Matamoros – 680 km, 12 hours; one or two 1st-class buses daily by ADO (90 pesos), plus one or two 2nd-class buses
Mexico City (Terminal Norte) – 355 km, six hours; eight 1st-class buses daily by ADO and three by Omnibus de México (39 pesos)
Papantla – 90 km, 1¼ hours; four 1st-class buses daily by ADO (8.50 pesos)
Poza Rica – 60 km, one hour; about 10 1st-class buses

daily by ADO (6 pesos) and 2nd-class buses every 10 minutes
Tampico – 180 km, four hours; four 1st-class buses daily by ADO (29 pesos) and two by Omnibus de México; 2nd-class buses about half-hourly
Veracruz – 320 km, six hours; four 1st-class buses daily by ADO (53 pesos)
Villahermosa – 995 km, 14 hours; two 1st-class buses daily by ADO (108 pesos)
Xalapa – 350 km, 6½ hours; three 1st-class buses daily by ADO (44 pesos)

AROUND TUXPAN
Tamiahua

Tamiahua, 43 km north from Tuxpan by paved road, is at the southern end of Laguna de Tamiahua. It has a few seafood shack-restaurants and you can rent launches for fishing or trips to the lagoon's barrier island. Omnibus de México has 1st-class buses from Tuxpan to Tamiahua at 6 and 11 am and 1 pm each day for 3 pesos.

Castillo de Teayo

This small town, 23 km up a bumpy road west off highway 180 (the turning's 44 km from Tuxpan, 15 km from Poza Rica), was from about 800 AD one of the southernmost points of the Huastec civilisation. Beside its main plaza is a steep, 13-metre-high restored pyramid topped by a small temple. It's in Toltec style and was probably built during Toltec domination of the area some time between 900 and 1200.

Around the base of the pyramid are some stone sculptures found in the area, thought to be the work of both the Huastecs and the Aztecs. The Aztecs controlled the area briefly before the Spanish conquest.

POZA RICA

The dirty, noisy oil city of Poza Rica is at the junction of highway 180, from Tampico to Veracruz, and highway 130, which climbs up to Pachuca. You might find yourself changing buses here, though it's not an attractive place to stay. If you're stuck here overnight, there are quite a few hotels – *Poza Rica Inn* on the Papantla road is probably the best; *Los Arcos* and *Fénix* are more basic places close to the bus station.

Getting There & Away

The main Poza Rica bus station has some 1st-class departures, but most are from ADO, which is in an adjoining building. There are regular ADO buses daily to/from the following destinations:

Mexico City (Terminal Norte) – 260 km, five hours; 38 pesos
Pachuca – 209 km, four hours; 23 pesos
Tampico – 250 km, five hours; 33 pesos
Tuxpan – 60 km, one hour; 6 pesos
Veracruz – 250 km, five hours; 45 pesos
Xalapa – 285 km, five to six hours; 40 pesos

To Papantla there are ADO buses about every hour (25 km, 30 minutes; 2.50 pesos) and 2nd-class buses every 15 minutes with Transportes Papantla (1.50 pesos). You can also fly to Poza Rica from Tampico several days a week with Litoral.

To/From El Tajín If you're in Poza Rica early enough, you can go directly to El Tajín on Transportes Papantla's hourly buses to Coyutla (about 2 pesos) and have plenty of time to explore the site. Buses to El Chote, Agua Dulce or San Andrés, by Autotransportes Coatzintla and other 2nd-class companies, should also get you to El Tajín. Ask for 'Desviación El Tajín' (El Tajín turning).

POZA RICA TO PACHUCA

The 200-km Poza Rica-Pachuca road, highway 130, is the direct approach to Mexico City from the northern part of Veracruz state. It climbs into the Sierra Madre across the semitropical north of Puebla state into Hidalgo – a very scenic but often misty route; you should try to do it early in the morning to give yourself the best chance to enjoy it. The area's population has a high proportion of Nahua and Totonac Indians.

Huauchinango, roughly halfway between Poza Rica and Pachuca, is the centre of a flower-growing area. You'll also find embroidered textiles in the busy Saturday market. A week-long flower festival, including traditional dances, focuses on the third Friday in Lent. At **Xicotepec**, 22 km northeast of Huauchinango, *Mi Ranchito* is a very

nice budget place to stay. **Acaxochitlán**, about 25 km west of Huauchinango, has an interesting Sunday market; specialities include fruit wine and preserved fruit. The Nahua women here often wear richly embroidered blouses.

The traditional Nahua village of **Pahuatlán** is the source of many of the cloths woven with multicoloured designs of animals and plants. It is reached from a turning north off highway 130 about 10 km past Acaxochitlán. A spectacular 27-km dirt road winds several hundred metres down to the village, which holds a sizeable Sunday market. There's at least one hotel here, and a restaurant. About half an hour's drive beyond Pahuatlán is **San Pablito**, a traditional Otomí village, where colourfully embroidered blouses abound.

Highway 130 climbs steeply to Tulancingo, in the state of Hidalgo – see the Around Mexico City chapter for details on the rest of this route to Pachuca.

PAPANTLA

• *pop: 97,000 • alt: 290 metres*

Set on a hillside among the outliers of the southern Sierra Madre Oriental, Papantla is an interesting base for visiting El Tajín. It's a scruffy town, though the central zócalo is quite pleasant, especially on Sunday evenings when half the town is out and voladores perform beside the cathedral. Some Totonacs still wear traditional costume here: the men sport baggy white shirts and trousers, the women embroidered blouses and quechquémitls. The Corpus Christi festival, in late May and early June, is the big annual event, and a celebration of Totonac culture.

Orientation

Papantla lies on highway 180, which runs south-east from Poza Rica. The centre of town is uphill (south) from the main road. To get to the centre from the ADO bus station, turn left as you go out, and walk a couple of hundred metres west along the main road, until you reach Calle 20 de Noviembre (there's a Pemex station on the south-west corner). Turn left and go up 20 de Noviembre

The Totonacs

Approximately 260,000 Totonacs survive in modern Mexico, mostly living between Tecolutla on the Veracruz coast and the southern Sierra Madre Oriental in northern Puebla. Roman Catholicism is superimposed on their more ancient beliefs, with traditional customs stronger in the mountain areas. The chief Totonac deities are their ancestors, the sun (which is also the maize god) and St John (also the lord of water and thunder). Venus and the moon are identified with Qotiti, the devil, who rules the kingdom of the dead beneath the earth. Some Totonacs apparently believe that the world is flat, the sky is a dome and the sun travels beneath the earth at night. The Feast of the Holy Cross (3 May) coincides with ceremonies for fertility of the earth and the creation of new seeds. ■

(it's quite steep) until you get to Calle Enríquez, the downhill boundary of the zócalo. From the Transportes Papantla bus terminal, on the east side of Calle 20 de Noviembre halfway down the hill, just turn left and walk uphill to the zócalo.

Zócalo

The zócalo, officially called Parque Téllez, is on a slope with the cathedral high above its south side. Beneath the cathedral a 50-metre-long mural faces the square, depicting Totonac and Veracruz history. A serpent stretches along most of the mural, linking a pre-Hispanic stone carver, El Tajín's Pyramid of the Niches, voladores and an oil rig. Inside the Palacio Municipal are copies of carvings from the southern ball court at El Tajín.

Volador Monument

At the top of the hill, above the cathedral, towers a 1988 statue of a volador musician playing his pipe as preparation for the four flyers to launch themselves into space. A red light adorns one of his fingers to warn off passing aircraft. Take the street heading uphill from the corner of the cathedral yard to reach the statue. Inscriptions around its base give an explanation of the voladores' ritual.

Festivals

For the last week or so of May and the first couple of days of June, Papantla is thronged for the parades, dances and other cultural events of Corpus Christi. Voladores perform specially, maybe two or three times a day. The main procession is on the first Sunday. Other dances you might catch are Los

Negritos, Los Huehues (The Old Men) and Los Quetzalines.

Places to Stay

The *Hotel Tajín* (☎ (784) 2-06-44) at Nuñez 104 – a blue building a few metres uphill from the left end of the zócalo mural – has singles/doubles with fan for 65/79 pesos, or with air-con for 93/108 pesos; rooms with two beds are from 93 to 120 pesos. The rooms vary a lot in outlook – those at the front are blessed with balconies looking over the town – but all are clean, sizeable and in good shape.

The cheaper *Hotel Pulido* (☎ (784) 2-10-79) at Enríquez 205, 250 metres east from the downhill (north) side of the zócalo, has smaller and dirtier rooms around a central parking area. It's quite friendly, though. Singles/doubles with one bed cost 40/50 pesos; it's 60 pesos for two beds.

The modern *Hotel Premier* (☎ (784) 2-00-80), on the north side of the zócalo at Enríquez 103, has large, clean, comfortable singles/doubles with air-con for 114/125 pesos, and suites up to 285 pesos.

Places to Eat

Papantla food is strictly Mexican, with an emphasis on meat in this cattle-raising area. The restaurant of the *Hotel Tajín* is adequate but not cheap, with various beefsteak fillets at around 20 pesos. There are a number of places on Enríquez, on the downhill (north) side of the zócalo. The *Restaurant Sorrento* at Enríquez 105, on the north-east corner, is very ordinary and not overwhelmingly clean, but it has a cheap comida corrida for only 8 pesos. The fanciest place is the *Restaurante*

Enríquez, in the Hotel Premier, with air-con, tablecloths, TV and black-tie waiters. Meat and fish dishes are around 20 pesos and up, while set breakfasts run from 9 to 15 pesos. In between these two, in price and position, is the *Plaza Pardo* which has some mediocre main courses from 10 to 15 pesos, but specialises in yummy milk shakes (around 7 pesos) and fruit drinks (from 3 pesos).

Things to Buy

The Hidalgo market, at the north-west corner of the zócalo, has Totonac costumes (some quite pretty), good baskets and vanilla. Papantla is Mexico's leading vanilla-growing centre and you can buy it in extract form, in the original pods or in *figuras* – pods woven into the shape of flowers, insects etc. The Juárez market, at the south-west corner opposite the cathedral, mainly sells food.

Getting There & Away

Few long-distance buses stop here and there's no service at all to/from Tampico (change at Tuxpan or Poza Rica). Try to book your bus out of Papantla as soon as you arrive, but even this is difficult as most buses are de paso. If desperate, consider going to Poza Rica and getting one of the much more frequent buses from there. ADO at Juárez 207 is the only 1st-class line serving Papantla. The unappealing 2nd-class alternative is Transportes Papantla on Calle 20 de Noviembre, with slow, old vehicles. See the Orientation section earlier for directions to/from the terminals. Departures from Papantla include:

Mexico City (Terminal Norte) – 290 km, 5½ hours; four 1st-class buses daily by ADO (36 pesos)
Poza Rica – 25 km, 30 minutes; eight 1st-class buses daily by ADO (2.50 pesos) and 2nd-class buses about every 15 minutes by Transportes Papantla (1.50 pesos)
Tuxpan – 90 km, 1¼ hours; three 1st-class buses daily by ADO (8.50 pesos)
Veracruz – 230 km, five hours; five 1st-class buses daily by ADO (43 pesos) and five 2nd-class buses by Transportes Papantla
Xalapa – 260 km, 5½ hours; five 1st-class buses daily by ADO (35 pesos) and two 2nd-class buses by Transportes Papantla

To/From El Tajín White microbuses go on the hour to El Tajín from 16 de Septiembre, the street on the south (uphill) side of the cathedral (about 30 minutes; 2 pesos). Alternatively, you can do the trip in two stages by getting a bus from the same stop to the village of El Chote, then any of the frequent buses going west (to the right) from El Chote to the El Tajín turning. Other buses from Papantla to El Chote leave from the Transportes Papantla terminal.

EL TAJÍN

Among hills covered in tropical vegetation a few km from Papantla, El Tajín ('el ta-HEEN') is Totonac for thunder, lightning or hurricane – all of which can happen here in summer. The ancient Totonacs may have occupied El Tajín in its later stages, but most of it was built before the Totonacs became important. It is the highest achievement of Classic Veracruz civilisation, about which little is known.

El Tajín was first occupied about 100 AD, but most of what's visible was built around 600 or 700. It was at its peak of activity and importance from about 600 to 900 – seemingly a town as well as a ceremonial centre. Around 1200 it was abandoned, possibly after attacks by Chichimecs, and lay unknown to the Spaniards until about 1785, when an official came upon it while looking for illegal tobacco plantings.

Among El Tajín's special features are rows of square niches on the sides of buildings, a huge number (at least 11) of ball courts, and sculptures showing human sacrifice connected with the ball game. The Mexican archaeologist who did much of the excavation here, José García Payón, believed that El Tajín's niches and stone mosaics symbolised day and night, light and dark, and life and death in a universe composed of pairs of opposites, though this interpretation is not universally accepted. Despite extensive reconstruction of the pyramids and plazas in 1991, El Tajín retains an aura of mystery and has a more 'lost in the jungle' feel than many of the more famous sites.

Voladores

The voladores rite – a sort of slow-motion quadruple bungee jump – starts with five men in colourful costumes climbing to the top of a pole. Four sit on the edges of a small square, arrange their ropes and then rotate the square to wind the ropes around the pole. The fifth man dances, bangs a drum and plays a whistle while standing on a tiny platform above them. Suddenly he stops and the others launch themselves backwards into thin air. Upside down, arms outstretched, they revolve gracefully round the pole and descend slowly to the ground as their ropes unwind.

This ancient ceremony is packed with symbolism. One interpretation is that it's a fertility rite and the flyers are macaw-men who make invocations to the four corners of the universe before falling to the ground, bringing with them the sun and rain. It is also said that each flyer circles the pole 13 times, giving a total of 52 revolutions, which is not only the number of weeks in the modern year but was an important number in pre-Hispanic Mexico, which had two calendars – one corresponding to the 365-day solar year, the other to a ritual year of 260 days – with a day in one calendar coinciding with a day in the other calendar every 52 solar years.

While it's in a way sad to see a sacred act turned into a show for tourists, the feat is dangerous and spectacular, and the people who do it say they need the money because they have no land. ■

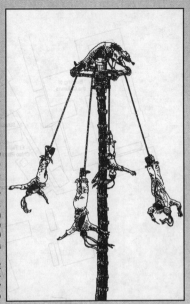

Information

The site is open daily from 9 am to 5 pm and entry costs 13 pesos, but it's free on Sunday and for those under 13 or over 60. The whole site covers about 10 sq km. Two main parts have been cleared: the lower area where the Pyramid of the Niches stands and, uphill, a group of buildings known as El Tajín Chico (Little El Tajín). Interpretive signs near the main structures provide background information in Spanish, English, German, French and Totonac. The new visitors' centre has a restaurant, souvenir shops, a place to leave bags, an information desk and an interesting little museum with a good model of the whole site. Outside there's a car park, bus stop and stalls selling food, drinks and handicrafts. You can get extremely hot walking around the site, so it's best to get there as early as you can.

Totonac Voladores

Totonac Indians carry out the exciting voladores rite most days from a 20-metre-high steel pole beside the visitors' centre. Performances are usually around noon, and before they start a Totonac in traditional dress requests donations from the audience (5 pesos per person). If there's a big enough crowd to make it worthwhile, they may fly two or three times a day.

Lower Plaza

Inside the site, after the unremarkable Plaza del Arroyo, you reach the Lower Plaza, part of El Tajín's main ceremonial centre, with a low platform in the middle. A statue on the first level of Structure 5, a pyramid on the plaza's west side, represents either a thunder-and-rain god, who was especially important at El Tajín, or Mictlantecuhtli, a death god.

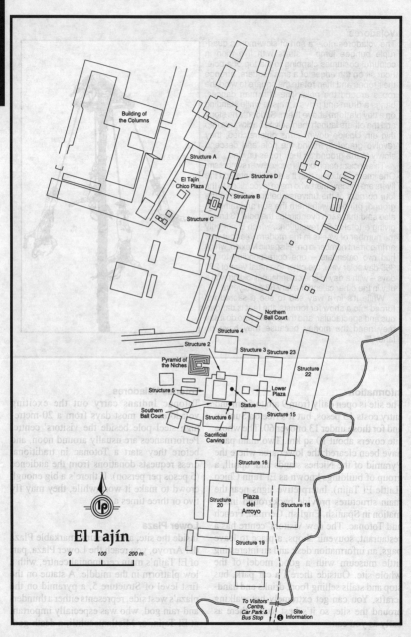

All the structures around this plaza were probably topped by small temples, and some were decorated with red or blue paint.

Southern Ball Court

The 60-metre-long ball court between Structures 5 and 6 is one of Mexico's most famous because of six sculptures, dating from about 1150, on its walls.

North Corners The panel on the north-east corner (immediately on the right as you enter the court from the Lower Plaza) is the easiest to make out. Three ballplayers wearing knee-pads are in the centre. One has his arms held by the second while the third is about to plunge a knife into his chest in a ritual post-ball-game sacrifice. A skeletal death god on the left and a presiding figure on the right look on. Another death god hovers over the victim. The panel at the far (north-west) end of the same wall is thought to represent a ceremony which preceded the ball game. Two players face each other, one with crossed arms, the other holding a dagger. Speech symbols emerge from their mouths. To their right is a figure with the mask of a coyote – the animal which conducted sacrificial victims to the next world. The death god is on the right.

South Corners The south-west panel seems to show the initiation of a young man into a band of warriors associated with the eagle. A central figure lies on a table; to the left another holds a bell. Above is an eagle-masked figure, possibly a priest. On the south-east panel one man offers a bunch of spears or arrows to another, possibly part of the same ceremony.

Central Panels These are devoted to the ceremonial drinking of the cactus-beer pulque. In the northern central panel, a figure holding a drinking vessel signals to another leaning on a pulque container. Quetzalcóatl sits cross-legged beside Tláloc, the fanged god of water and lightning. On the south panel Tláloc, squatting, passes a gourd to someone in a fish mask who appears to be in

a pulque vat. On the left is the maguey plant, from which pulque is made. Maguey is not native to this part of Mexico, which points to influences from central Mexico (possibly Toltec) at this late stage of El Tajín.

Pyramid of the Niches

The Pyramid of the Niches, 35 metres square, is just off the Lower Plaza, by the north-west corner of Structure 5. The six lower levels, each surrounded by rows of

Geometric detail of the stairway,
Pyramid of the Niches

small square niches, climb to a height of 18 metres. The wide staircase on the east side was a late addition, built over some of the niches. Archaeologists believe that there were originally 365 niches, suggesting that the building may have been used as a kind of religious calendar. The insides of the niches were painted red, and their frames blue. The only similar building known is a seven-level niched pyramid at Yohualichán near Cuetzalán, 50 km south-west of El Tajín; this was probably an earlier site.

El Tajín Chico

The path north towards El Tajín Chico passes the Northern Ball Court, smaller and earlier than the southern one, but also with carvings on its sides. Many of the buildings of El Tajín Chico have geometric stone mosaic patterns known as Greco (Greek), which resemble later decorations in Mitla (Oaxaca).

The main buildings, probably 9th century, are on the east and north sides of El Tajín Chico Plaza. Structure C, on the east side, with three levels and a staircase facing the plaza, was originally painted blue. Next to it, Structure B was probably living quarters for priests or officials. Structure D, behind Structure B and off the plaza, has a large lozenge-design mosaic and a passage underneath it.

On the north side of the plaza, Structure A has a façade like a Mayan roofcomb, with a stairway leading up through an arch in the middle. This 'corbelled' arch, with the two sides jutting closer and closer to each other until they are joined at the top by a single slab, is typical of Mayan architecture – yet another element in this mixture of pre-Hispanic cultures.

Uphill to the north-west of El Tajín Chico Plaza is the as yet unreconstructed Building of the Columns – one of the site's most important buildings. It originally had an open patio inside and adjoining structures stretching over the hillside to cover an area of nearly 200 by 100 metres. Parts of the columns have been reassembled and are displayed in the museum at the visitors' centre.

Getting There & Away

There are frequent local buses to El Tajín from both Papantla and Poza Rica – see the sections on those towns for details. To return, catch a local bus from the area next to the car park.

SOUTH OF PAPANTLA

Highway 180 runs close to the coast for most of the 230 km from Papantla to Veracruz city. Swimmers should watch out for undertow on this coast.

Tecolutla & the Costa Esmeralda

At Gutiérrez Zamora, 30 km east of Papantla, a side road goes to Tecolutla, 11 km north-east from highway 180 at the mouth of the Río Tecolutla. It's a minor seaside resort with a palm-fringed beach and a few hotels. There are ADO and Transportes Papantla buses to/from Papantla.

The Costa Esmeralda (Emerald Coast) is the 20-km strip between La Guadalupe (20 km south-east of Gutiérrez Zamora) and Nautla. Numerous hotels, holiday homes, restaurants and at least three trailer parks line the strip between highway and beach. It's a popular summer spot, but very quiet most of the year. **Nautla**, a small fishing town, has a handful of cheap but respectable hotels and a long beach where you can eat seafood.

Laguna Verde & Villa Rica

Mexico's controversial first nuclear power station is at Laguna Verde, about 80 km north of Veracruz city, on the coastal side of highway 180. The first unit came into operation in 1989. When the second unit is running, the station is planned to generate 4% of Mexico's electricity. The fishing village of Villa Rica, 69 km north of Veracruz, is where Cortés probably founded the first Spanish settlement in Mexico. There are traces of a fort and a church on the Cerro de la Cantera. The nearby Totonac tombs of **Quiahuiztlán** are spectacularly situated on a hill overlooking the coast.

Central Veracruz

Highway 180 follows the coast past the ruins of Zempoala to Cardel, where highway 140 branches west to Xalapa, the pleasant state capital surrounded by picturesque countryside. The bustling port city of Veracruz is 35 km south of Cardel, beyond which highway 150 branches south and west to Córdoba, Fortín de las Flores and Orizaba, in the foothills of the Sierra Madre.

ZEMPOALA

The pre-Hispanic Totonac town of Zempoala (or Cempoala) holds a key place in the story of the Spanish conquest of Mexico. Its ruins stand in a modern town of the same name 42 km north of Veracruz city, three km west of highway 180. The turnoff is by a Pemex station, eight km north of Cardel. Voladores perform at the ruins most Saturdays and Sundays from around noon to 2 pm.

The site is attractive, with lines of palms, and mountains in the background. Most of the buildings are faced with smooth, rounded river-bed stones and are constructed as a series of narrow platforms. Their typical feature is battlement-like 'teeth' called *almenas*.

History

Zempoala became an important Totonac centre after about 1200 AD, and may have been the leader of a 'federation' of southern Totonac states. It fell subject to the Aztecs in the mid-15th century and many of the buildings are in Aztec style. The town had a system of defensive walls, underground water and drainage pipes and, in May 1519 when the Spanish came, about 30,000 people. As Cortés approached the town, one of his scouts reported back that its buildings were made of silver – but it was only white plaster or paint shining in the sun.

Zempoala's portly chief, Chicomacatl, known to history as 'the fat cacique' from a description by Bernal Díaz del Castillo, struck an alliance with Cortés for protection against the Aztecs. But his hospitality didn't stop the Spanish from smashing his gods' statues and lecturing the Zempoalans on the virtues of Christianity. Zempoalan carriers went with the Spaniards when they set off for Tenochtitlán in August 1519. The following

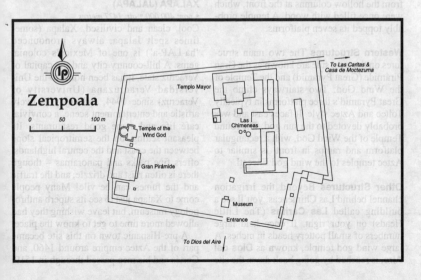

Zempoala

0   50   100 m

To Las Caritas &
Casa de Moctezuma

Templo Mayor

Las
Chimeneas

Temple of the
Wind God

Gran Pirámide

Museum

Entrance

To Dios del Aire

year, it was at Zempoala that Cortés defeated the expedition of Pánfilo de Narváez, sent by the governor of Cuba to arrest him.

By the 17th century Zempoala had virtually ceased to exist. Its population, devastated by new diseases, was down to eight families and soon afterwards the town was abandoned. The present town dates from 1832.

Zempoala Ruins

The main ruins are at the end of a short track to the right as you enter Zempoala, where a sign says 'Bienvenidos a Cempoala'. They're open daily from 9 am to 6 pm. Entrance is 10 pesos except on Sunday, when it's free.

Templo Mayor The Main Temple is an 11-metre-high, 13-platform pyramid on a base 65 by 40 metres. Originally it was plastered and painted. A wide staircase ascends to the remains of a three-room shrine on top. This was probably Pánfilo de Narváez' headquarters in 1520, which Cortés's men captured by setting fire to the thatched roof of the shrine.

Las Chimeneas (The Chimneys) This is where Cortés and his men were lodged on their first visit to Zempoala. Its name comes from the hollow columns at the front, which were once filled with wood. A temple probably topped its seven platforms.

Western Structures The two main structures on the west side are known as the Gran Pirámide (Great Pyramid) and the Temple of the Wind God. Two stairways climb the Great Pyramid's three platforms in typically Toltec and Aztec style. It faces east and was probably devoted to the sun god. The round Temple of the Wind God, with a rectangular platform and ramps in front, is similar to Aztec temples to the wind god Ehecatl.

Other Structures Beyond the irrigation channel behind Las Chimeneas, you'll see a building called **Las Caritas** (The Little Heads) on your right. It once held large numbers of small pottery heads in niches. A large wind god temple, known as **Dios del Aire**, is reached by going back down the site

entrance road, straight on over the main road and then around the corner to the right.

Getting There & Away

Zempoala is most easily approached from Cardel, which is a stop for most buses on highway 180. From Veracruz bus station the very frequent buses to Cardel cost 6 pesos by 1st-class ADO or 3 pesos by 2nd-class AU. From the bus stop at Cardel frequent green-and-white colectivo taxis (2 pesos) and some buses run to Zempoala. Total journey time from Veracruz to Zempoala is about one hour.

AROUND ZEMPOALA

The main town in the area is **Cardel** (also called José Cardel), which most people only pass through on the way to the ruins (see above), but you can stay here – try the *Hotel Plaza* for around 52/75 pesos. **Chachalacas** is on the coast a few km north-east from Cardel. There's a beach with seafood restaurants, and you can use the swimming pool at the upscale *Chachalacas Hotel*. North of the Zempoala turnoff, **Paso de Doña Juana** is on the coastal side of the highway and has a campground, trailer park and youth hostel.

XALAPA (JALAPA)

• *pop: 400,000* • *alt: 1427 metres*

Cool, clean and civilised, Xalapa (sometimes spelt Jalapa, always pronounced 'ha-LAP-a') is one of Mexico's colonial gems. A hill-country city and the capital of Veracruz state, it has been home to the Universidad Veracruzana (University of Veracruz) since 1944, and enjoys a lively artistic and entertainment scene, a convivial café life and some good restaurants. Its pleasant setting, on the semitropical slope between the coast and the central highlands, offers fine parks and panoramas – though there is often mist and drizzle, and the traffic and the fumes can be vile! Many people come to Xalapa just to see its superb anthropology museum, but leave wishing they had allowed more time to get to know the place.

A pre-Hispanic town on this site became part of the Aztec empire around 1460, and Cortés and his men passed through in 1519.

The Spanish town didn't take off until the annual trade fair of Spanish goods was first held here in 1720 (it ran until 1777). Today Xalapa is a commercial hub for the coffee and tobacco grown on the slopes, and well known for its flowers.

Orientation

The city centre is on a hillside with the plaza, Parque Juárez, more or less in the middle of things. Xalapa's cathedral is on Enríquez, just east of Parque Juárez, while many of the hotels and restaurants are on Enríquez and Zaragoza, also east of Parque Juárez. The bus station is two km east of the centre, and the must-see anthropology museum is a few km north.

Information

Tourist Office The tourist information kiosk in the bus station always seems to be closed. Try instead the Dirección de Turismo del Estado (State Tourism Directorate; ☎ (28) 18-72-24) at Manuel Avila Camacho 191, two km north-west from the centre, which has lots of good printed information about Xalapa and the state of Veracruz. Some English is spoken and the staff can be helpful. The office is open from 9 am to 9 pm Monday to Friday and 9 am to 1 pm Saturday.

Money Banca Serfin, Bancomer and Banamex are all on Enríquez; they all have ATMs, but Bancomer won't change travellers' cheques. Casa de Cambio Jalapa, at Gutiérrez Zamora 36, has slightly lower rates but is open longer hours – Monday to Friday from 9 am to 1.30 pm and 4 to 6.30 pm.

Post & Telecommunications The main post office, open from 8 am to 7 pm Monday to Friday and 9 am to 1 pm Saturday, is on the corner of Gutiérrez Zamora and Diego Leño. Next door on Gutiérrez Zamora is the Centro de Servicios Integrados de Telecomunicaciones, with public fax, telex and telegram services. It's open from 9 am to 8 pm Monday to Friday and 9 am to 1 pm Saturday. There's a clutch of Ladatel phones on the wall of the Palacio de Gobierno, on Enríquez facing Dr Lucio.

City Centre

Parque Juárez is the central garden, with its elevated south side like a terrace overlooking the town below. The arched portales of the **Palacio Municipal** are on its north side and the **Palacio de Gobierno**, the seat of the Veracruz state government, is on its east side. The Palacio de Gobierno has a fine **mural** by José Chávez Moreno depicting the history of justice – it's above the stairway on the east side of the building. Facing the Palacio de Gobierno across Enríquez is the 1772 **catedral**, from where Revolución and Dr Lucio both lead up to the bustling area around and above the mercado. Coming down from there you can descend steps from Dr Lucio to Madero and return to Enríquez by older little streets like Callejón Diamante.

Museo de Antropología

The Museo de Antropología de la Universidad Veracruzana, devoted to the archaeology of Veracruz state, is one of the best museums in Mexico. Its large collection includes no fewer than seven huge Olmec heads, and its spacious layout is a textbook example of museum design.

The museum is a long, low grey building with a fountain outside, on the west side of Avenida Xalapa four km north-west of the city centre. Take a 'Tesorería-Centro-SEP' or 'Museo' bus west from the Restaurant Terraza Jardín on Enríquez (1.50 pesos). Buses marked 'Centro' will return you to the centre. Buses can be infrequent or full, so a taxi may be worth the 4-peso fare. The museum is open from 10 am to 5 pm daily except Monday; admission is 8 pesos (free on Sunday). It has an excellent bookshop.

The exhibits are in a series of galleries and courtyards descending a gentle slope. You reach the Olmec material, from southern Veracruz, first, and the El Tajín display, from northern Veracruz, is near the bottom. The largest Olmec head here, from San Lorenzo, is 2.7 metres high. Another San Lorenzo head is pocked with hundreds of small holes, thought to be a deliberate mutilation at the time of San Lorenzo's fall. Apart from many more fine Olmec carvings, other museum

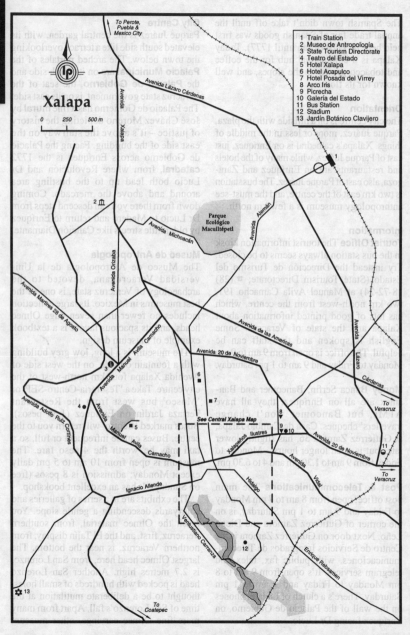

Xalapa

0   250   500 m

To Perote,
Puebla &
Mexico City

1   Train Station
2   Museo de Antropología
3   State Tourism Directorate
4   Teatro del Estado
5   Hotel Xalapa
6   Hotel Acapulco
7   Hotel Posada del Virrey
8   Arco Iris
9   Picrecha
10 Galería del Estado
11 Bus Station
12 Stadium
13 Jardín Botánico Clavijero

Avenida Lázaro Cárdenas

Xalapa

Avenida

Avenida Michoacán

Parque
Ecológico
Macuiltépetl

Avenida Orizaba

Avenida Ateman

Avenida Martínez 28 de Agosto

Avenida Manuel Avila Camacho

Avenida de las Américas

Avenida 20 de Noviembre

Avenida Adolfo Ruíz Cortines

Avenida Manuel Avila Camacho

See Central Xalapa Map

Xalapeños Ilustres

Avenida 20 de Noviembre

Avenida Lázaro Cárdenas

Cárdenas

To
Veracruz

To
Veracruz

Avenida Vidal

Ignacio Allende

Hidalgo

Venustiano Carranza

Enrique Rebsamen

To
Coatepec

13

12

highlights include an array of beautiful yugos and hachas from central Veracruz, murals from the Classic Veracruz centre Las Higueras and a collection of huge Classic-period pottery figures from El Zapotal.

Huge Olmec head at the Museo de Antropología, Xalapa

Galería del Estado

The Veracruz state art gallery is in a fine renovated colonial building on Xalapeños Ilustres a km east of the centre, just past Arteaga. It houses some excellent temporary exhibitions – contact the tourist office to find out what's on.

Parks

Just south of Parque Juárez is **Parque Paseo de los Lagos**, winding a km along either side of a lake. At its northern end is the Casa de Artesanías, with a small collection of local handicrafts on sale. **Parque Ecológico Macuiltépetl**, in the north of the city, occupies the highest ground in Xalapa – the thickly treed cap of an old volcano. The park is 800 metres east of Avenida Xalapa along Michoacán; the turning is about 200 metres south of the anthropology museum. Paths spiral to the top where there are good views.

South-west of town, the **Jardín Botánico Clavijero** is also attractive.

Places to Stay – bottom end

Xalapa has a good range of budget lodgings. The central *Hotel Limón* (☎ (28) 17-22-07) at Revolución 8 has small, tiled rooms and a tiled courtyard with a fountain. Clean rooms with private bath and hot water cost 28 pesos for singles, 32 pesos for doubles with one bed and 40 pesos with two. A km up the hill from the centre, the *Hotel Acapulco* (☎ (28) 15-16-41), on Julian Carrillo between Revolución and Dr Lucio, has bare, basic but clean, well-kept rooms with private baths, for 30/40 pesos.

The *Hotel Continental* (☎ (28) 17-35-30) at Gutiérrez Zamora 4 is an old, friendly, shabby place with a roofed courtyard and big rooms. Some are much better than others and traffic noise at the front is hideous. Most are bare and mildly decayed but kept clean enough. All have private baths but hot water is very erratic. Singles/doubles are 34/39 pesos, or 43 pesos with two beds.

The best rooms in the bottom end – good, clean and spacious, with hot water – are at the *Hotel Principal* (☎ (28) 17-64-00), also central at Zaragoza 28. Singles or doubles with one bed cost 45 pesos, with two beds 50 pesos. Beware of noise in street-side rooms.

Places to Stay – middle

The large *Hotel Salmones* (☎ (28) 17-54-31) at Zaragoza 24 has a small garden, big lobby, restaurant and rooms with carpets, phones and TV. Singles/doubles are 60/70 pesos. The *Hotel Posada del Virrey* (☎ (28) 18-61-00) at Dr Lucio 142, about 700 metres uphill from the centre, is a comfortable, modern hotel with TV in rooms, a bar and restaurant. Moderately sized rooms are not bad value at 75/85 pesos, or 95 pesos with two beds.

The number-one downtown hotel is the 114-room *Hotel María Victoria* (☎ (28) 18-60-11) at Zaragoza 6. Very clean though not huge rooms with phone, TV and air-con or heating cost 120 to 140 pesos a single and 140 to 170 pesos a double. There's a restaurant and a bar with entertainment too. An

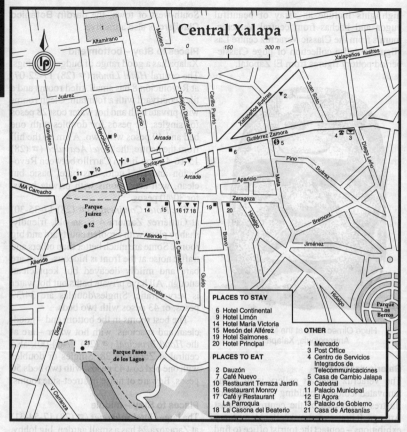

Central Xalapa

PLACES TO STAY

6 Hotel Continental
9 Hotel Limón
14 Hotel María Victoria
15 Mesón del Alférez
19 Hotel Salmones
20 Hotel Principal

PLACES TO EAT

2 Dauzón
7 Café Nuevo
10 Restaurant Terraza Jardín
16 Restaurant Monroy
17 Café y Restaurant
    La Parroquia
18 La Casona del Beaterio

OTHER

1 Mercado
3 Post Office
4 Centro de Servicios
   Integrados de
   Telecommunications
5 Casa de Cambio Jalapa
8 Catedral
11 Palacio Municipal
12 El Agora
13 Palacio de Gobierno
21 Casa de Artesanías

interesting place with a bit of character is the *Mesón del Alférez* (☎ (28) 18-63-51), also on Zaragoza, with a variety of rooms in a renovated building from 90 to 190 pesos.

Places to Stay – top end

The top place in town is the modern, 200-room *Hotel Xalapa* (☎ (28) 18-22-22), a km west of the centre on Victoria 1½ blocks uphill from Manuel Avila Camacho. The central part is built around a swimming pool and there are bars, a restaurant and a good cafeteria. Rooms are air-con and cost 242 pesos for one or two people.

Places to Eat

The best place to soak up the city's ambience – and enjoy good, solid fare served by efficient waiters – is the *Café y Restaurant La Parroquia* at Zaragoza 18. Anyone and everyone meets, eats and drinks here between 7.30 am and 10.30 pm, and even if you squeeze breathlessly in at 10.25 pm you'll still be served one of the set dinners – say vegetable soup and chicken and chips for 26 pesos – without a quibble. There's a range of set breakfasts from 8 to 24 pesos; other snacks and meals cost from 8 to 30 pesos.

Next door at Zaragoza 20, *La Casona del*

Beaterio has an even more inviting ambience in its pretty courtyard or in several rooms decorated with hundreds of photos of old Xalapa. The long menu of reliable choices includes yoghurt with honey (4.50 pesos), spaghetti (9 to 15 pesos), crepes (11 to 14 pesos), enchiladas (11 to 15 pesos) and meat dishes (22 to 34 pesos). The five-course comida corrida is a bargain at 14 pesos.

Also on Zaragoza, the clean *Restaurant Monroy* concentrates on antojitos and has a four-course comida corrida for 13 pesos. The *Aries Restaurant* in the Hotel María Victoria further along the street is open 24 hours. Good for late-night coffee or snacks is the *Café Nuevo* on Enríquez, open till 12.30 am, with antojitos from 5 to 9 pesos and breakfasts from 7 to 10 pesos. A plate of sweet pastries comes with Nescafé con leche – you pay for what you eat.

The big, bright *Restaurant Terraza Jardín* on Enríquez overlooking the Parque Juárez does a four-course comida for 10 pesos, and breakfasts from 7 to 13 pesos. A number of places on Dr Lucio, just up from Enríquez, offer quick, cheap, stand-up snacks. There are plenty of good bakeries and cake shops, including several branches of *Dauzón*. The one on Xalapeños Ilustres between Mata and Soto has a café at the back where you can sample cakes, pies and strudels (2.50 to 6 pesos) or down a full breakfast for around 8 pesos.

A km east of the city centre but well worth the walk for its candlelit, mildly bohemian atmosphere and good Italian and Mexican food at reasonable prices is *Picrecha*, on the corner of Xalapeños Ilustres and Arteaga. For vegetarian fare, walk up Arteaga to *Arco Iris*.

Entertainment

El Agora, an arts centre under the Parque Juárez containing a cinema, theatre and gallery, is the focus of Xalapa's busy arts scene. It's open from 8.30 am to 9 pm daily except Monday and has a bookshop and café. Look here, or on the noticeboard in the Café La Parroquia on Zaragoza, for news of what's on in town, including theatre, exhibitions and all kinds of music. The *Teatro del Estado Ignacio de la Llave* (state theatre), on the corner of Manuel Avila Camacho and De la Llave, stages performances by the Orquesta Sinfónica de Xalapa and the Ballet Folklórico of the Universidad Veracruzana.

Getting There & Away

Bus Xalapa's gleaming, modern, well-organised bus station, two km east of the city centre, is known as CAXA (Central de Autobuses de Xalapa). Departures include:

Cardel – 72 km, 1½ hours; frequent buses by ADO (9 pesos)

Mexico City (TAPO) – 315 km, five hours; three deluxe buses daily by UNO (85 pesos) and 24 1st-class buses daily by ADO (40 pesos)

Papantla – 260 km, 5½ hours; 10 1st-class buses daily by ADO (35 pesos)

Puebla – 185 km, 3¼ hours; 12 1st-class buses daily by ADO (24 pesos) and 16 2nd-class directo buses by AU (20 pesos)

Tampico – 540 km, 11 hours; one 1st-class bus daily by ADO (76 pesos)

Veracruz – 100 km, two hours; 1st-class buses by ADO every 20 or 30 minutes from 5.30 am to 10 pm (15 pesos) and frequent 2nd-class buses (10 pesos)

Villahermosa – 575 km, nine hours; four 1st-class buses daily by ADO (69 pesos)

Other places served by ADO include Acayucan, Campeche, Catemaco, Córdoba, Fortín de las Flores, Mérida, Orizaba, Poza Rica, San Andrés Tuxtla and Santiago Tuxtla. AU goes to Salina Cruz. ADO charges slightly more for services using Mercedes Benz buses. For some destinations, it may be better to go to Veracruz first.

Car Xalapa is 185 km from Puebla by highway 140, which may be rough after Perote. The Xalapa-Veracruz road is better, but it's not all divided highway. From the northern Gulf Coast, it's easiest to follow highway 180 along the coast to Cardel, then turn inland; the inland road via Martínez de la Torre is scenic but slow.

Car-rental firms in Xalapa include Renta Car Xalapa (☎ 14-11-61), at Lázaro Cárdenas 696, and Automoviles Sanches (☎ 17-70-46) – they both charge over 275 pesos per day.

Getting Around

For buses from the bus station to the city centre, follow the signs to the taxi rank, then continue downhill (south) to the big road, Avenida 20 de Noviembre. Turn right to the bus stop, from where any microbus or bus marked 'Centro' will take you within a short walk of Parque Juárez for about a peso. A taxi ticket from the bus station to the centre is 5 pesos, or walk down to 20 de Noviembre and hail one on the street. To return to the bus station from the city centre, take a 'CAXA' bus east along Zaragoza.

AROUND XALAPA

The countryside around Xalapa is scenic, with mountains, caves and waterfalls. There are hot springs at **El Carrizal**, south of the Veracruz road 44 km from town. Spelunkers can check the caves at El Volcanillo and Acajete. **Hacienda Lencero**, 10 km from town, dates from the period of French rule and has original furniture and a small museum.

Parque Nacional Cofre de Perote

The 4274-metre-high Cofre de Perote volcano is south-west of Xalapa. A rough dirt road (initially Calle Allende) from the town of Perote, 50 km west of Xalapa on highway 140, climbs 1900 metres in 24 km to just below the summit.

Coatepec & Xico

Coatepec, a colonial town 15 km south of Xalapa, is known for its locally grown coffee and orchids. The María Cristina orchid garden, on the main square, is open daily. Xico is another pretty colonial village, eight km south of Coatepec. Accommodation and meals are available in both towns – *Doña Nena*, in Xico, is recommended for typical local food. The 40-metre Texolo waterfall is a pleasant two-km walk from Xico.

Buses go about every 15 minutes to Coatepec or Xico from Avenida Allende, about a km west of central Xalapa.

LA ANTIGUA

A km east of the coastal highway 150, and 23 km north of Veracruz, this riverside village is where Cortés is thought to have scuttled his ships. It is the site of one of the Spanish settlements that preceded Veracruz, and boasts a house that was supposedly occupied by Cortés, and the very early Ermita del Rosario church, probably dating from 1523. Small seafood restaurants are popular with day-trippers from Veracruz.

VERACRUZ

• *pop: 1 million*

Often referred to as Puerto Veracruz (to distinguish it from the state of which it is *not* the capital), this is one of the most festive Mexican cities, with a hedonistic, tropical port atmosphere, a zócalo that becomes a party every evening and the biggest annual Carnaval between Rio de Janeiro and New Orleans. Its people, known as Jarochos, are good-humoured and relaxed. Unfortunately, the seaside here is neither clean nor attractive, though people from Mexico City flood down here at weekends and holiday times. At Christmas, Carnaval (the week before Ash Wednesday) and Semana Santa, the city and nearby beaches are jam-packed with visitors. You need to book accommodation and transport in advance for these times.

Historically, Veracruz was Mexico's main gateway to the outside world, from the day Cortés landed here until the coming of the aeroplane. Invaders and pirates, incoming and exiled rulers, settlers, silver and slaves – all came and went to make the city a linchpin in Mexico's history, second to none except the capital. Before the Spanish, the area was occupied by Totonacs, with influences from Toltecs and Aztecs which can be seen at Zempoala 42 km to the north (see the previous Zempoala section).

History

The Spanish Cortés made his first landing here at an island two km offshore, where he found the remains of human sacrifices and which he named Isla de los Sacrificios. Anchoring off the island of San Juan de Ulúa on Good Friday, 21 April 1519, Cortés made his first contact with Moctezuma's envoys. The harbour here immediately became the

Central Gulf Coast
Top: Hat seller, Tlacotalpan (JL); Rainforest, near Catemaco (JL)
Bottom: Olmec head, Museo de Antropología, Xalapa (JL); Church, Catemaco (JL)

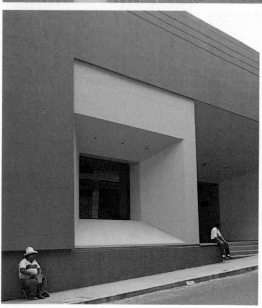

Central Gulf Coast
Top: Modern mural, Papantla (JL)
Bottom Left: Modern architecture, Córdoba (JL)
Bottom Right: Voladores, El Tajín (JN)

Spaniards' most important anchorage, but Cortés's first settlement appears to have been at Villa Rica, 69 km north. In 1525 the settlement moved to La Antigua, between Veracruz and Zempoala, before being established on the present site of Veracruz in 1598.

Until 1760 Veracruz was the only port allowed to handle trade with Spain. Tent cities blossomed for trade fairs when the annual fleet from Spain arrived, but because of frequent seaborne raids and an unhealthy coastal climate, with malaria and yellow fever rampant, Veracruz never became one of Mexico's biggest cities.

In 1567 nine English ships under John Hawkins sailed into Veracruz harbour, with the intention of selling slaves in defiance of the Spanish trade monopoly. They were trapped by a Spanish fleet and only two ships escaped. One of them, however, carried Francis Drake, who went on to harry the Spanish endlessly in a long career as a sort of licensed pirate. The most vicious pirate attack of all came in 1683, when the Frenchman Laurent de Gaff, with 600 men, held the 5000 inhabitants of Veracruz captive in the city's churches, with little food or water. They killed any who tried to escape, piled the Plaza de Armas with loot, got drunk, raped many of the women, threatened to explode the church unless the people revealed their secret stashes, and left a few days later 600,000 pesos richer.

19th Century In 1838 General Antonio López de Santa Anna, fresh from his rout by the Americans two years earlier, fled Veracruz in his underwear under bombardment from a French fleet in the 'Pastry War' (an attack pursuant to various damages claims

against Mexico, including those of a French pastry cook whose restaurant had been wrecked by unruly Mexican officers). But the general replied heroically, driving the invaders out and losing his left leg in the process.

When the 10,000-strong army of Winfield Scott attacked Veracruz in 1847 in the Mexican-American War, over 1000 Mexicans, including many civilians, were killed in a week-long bombardment before the city surrendered.

In 1859, during Mexico's internal Reform War, Benito Juárez' Veracruz-based liberal government promulgated the reform laws that nationalised church property and put education into secular hands. In 1861 when Juárez, having won the war, announced that Mexico couldn't pay its foreign debts, a joint French-Spanish-British force occupied Veracruz. The British and Spanish planned only to take over the customs house and recover what Mexico owed them, but Napoleon III of France intended to conquer Mexico. Realising this, the British and Spanish went home, while the French marched inland to begin their five-year intervention.

Mexico's first railway was built between Veracruz and Mexico City in 1872, and, under the dictatorship of Porfirio Díaz, investment poured into the city.

20th Century In 1914, during the civil war that followed Díaz's departure in the 1910-11 revolution, US troops occupied Veracruz to stop a delivery of German arms to the conservative dictator Victoriano Huerta. The Mexican casualties caused by the intervention alienated even Huerta's opponents. Later in the civil war, Veracruz was for a while the capital of the reformist Constitutionalist faction led by Venustiano Carranza.

Orientation

The centre of the city's action is the Plaza de Armas, or zócalo – site of the cathedral, the Palacio Municipal, and numerous cafés and restaurants. The harbour is 250 metres east, with San Juan de Ulúa fort on its far side. Boulevard Manuel Avila Camacho follows

---

The Heroic City
Veracruz is now officially titled 'Four Times Heroic', in reference to the final expulsion of the Spanish in 1825, the triumph over the French in the Pastry War and the resistance to the Americans in 1847 and 1914. ∎

the coast to the south, past the naval and fishing vessels to a series of dirty beaches. About 700 metres south of the zócalo along Independencia is Parque Zamora, a multiple road junction with a wide green area in the middle. Near here is the main market. The 1st and 2nd-class bus stations are two km south of Parque Zamora along Díaz Mirón.

Information

Tourist Office The city and state tourist office (☎ (29) 32-19-99) is on the ground floor of the Palacio Municipal, on the zócalo, open from 9 am to 9 pm daily. Staff are well informed (even about city buses) and some speak English.

Money Banamex and Bancomer, both on Independencia one block north of the zócalo, have ATMs and change travellers' cheques on weekday mornings. Casa de Cambio Puebla, at Juárez 112, gives rates almost as good as the banks and is open longer hours – from 9 am to 6 pm Monday to Friday.

The American Express representative, Viajes Olymar (☎ (29) 31-31-69), at Camacho 2221 next to the Hostal de Cortés hotel, is open from 9 am to 1 pm and 4 to 6 pm Monday to Friday and 9 am to noon Saturday, but will not exchange travellers' cheques.

Post & Telecommunications The main post office at Plaza de la República 213, a five-minute walk north of the zócalo, is open from 8 am to 8 pm Monday to Friday and 9 am to 1 pm Saturday.

The telégrafos office next door to the main post office has public fax, telegram and telex services, and is open from 9 am to 8 pm Monday to Friday and 9 am to noon Saturday. There are Ladatel phones, including one for credit cards, on the zócalo, but they work erratically.

Foreign Consulates The US consulate (☎ (29) 31-01-42) is at Victimas del 25 de Junio 384, east of Parque Zamora. The tourist office has details of at least 14 other consulates in the city, including several European countries.

Zócalo

The Veracruz zócalo, also called the Plaza de Armas, Plaza Lerdo and Plaza de la Constitución, is the hub of the city for Jarochos and visitors alike. It's a fine-looking place with palm trees, a fountain, the 17th-century Palacio Municipal on one side and an 18th-century cathedral, also known as the parroquia, on another.

Each evening, as the sweat cools off Veracruz bodies, the zócalo becomes a swirling, multifaceted party. From one of the cafés under the portales along the north side you might witness, in two blinks, a Mexico City couple celebrating their anniversary with wild, energetic dancing, prostitutes meeting Korean sailors, a holidaying middle-class couple trying to control their children, a politician making a campaign speech and a vendor hawking leaping foam-rubber lizards – all to the accompaniment of half a dozen groups of wandering mariachis, marimba-players, trumpeters and guitarists vying to be heard above each other and trying to find some café customers who'll pay for personal serenades. The anarchy increases as the evening progresses and more and more alcohol is consumed, reaching a crescendo somewhere between midnight and 2 am. Some evenings there's formal entertainment too, in the shape of visiting musicians or dancers on a temporary stage.

You can watch the show for nothing from the paths and benches around the zócalo, but it's not too expensive to enjoy a drink in the portales. A beer is about 5 pesos; mixed drinks are from 7 to 10 pesos, and they're generous with the booze. Places at the east end, east of the plaza proper, are a bit cheaper and just as noisy.

Harbour

Veracruz harbour, about 250 metres east of the city centre, is still busy, though oil ports like Tampico and Coatzacoalcos now handle greater tonnages. Stroll along Insurgentes (also called Paseo del Malecón) and view the ships and cranes across the water. In front of the Faro Carranza lighthouse (see Museums below), the Mexican Navy goes through an elaborate parade early each morning. On the corner of the Malecón and Camacho are monuments to the city's defenders against the Americans in 1914 and to all sailors who gave their lives to the sea. Boats from the Malecón offer one-hour harbour tours for 12 to 15 pesos per person.

San Juan de Ulúa

This fortress protecting Veracruz harbour was once an island but is now linked to the mainland by a causeway across the north side of the harbour. In 1518 the Spaniard Juan de Grijalva landed here during an exploratory voyage from Cuba and found four priests at a shrine to Tezcatlipoca, the Aztec smoking mirror god. The next year Cortés also landed here and it became the main entry point for Spanish newcomers to Mexico. The Franciscan chapel is thought to have been built in 1524 and the first fortifications in the 1530s, but what we see now mostly dates from 1552-1779.

The fortress has also acted as a prison – most notoriously under Porfirio Díaz who reserved three damp, stinking cells called El Purgatorio, La Gloria and El Infierno (Purgatory, Heaven and Hell) in the central part of the fortress, Fuerte San José (San José Fort), for political prisoners. Many inmates died of yellow fever or tuberculosis. Díaz himself left for exile from San Juan de Ulúa, but didn't savour one of his own dungeons.

Today San Juan de Ulúa is an empty ruin of passageways, battlements, bridges and stairways, which you can wander around between 9 am and 4.30 pm Tuesday to Sunday (entry 13 pesos, except Sunday and holidays when it's free). Guided tours are available in Spanish.

To get there, take a 'San Juan de Ulúa' bus (0.80 pesos) from the east side of Plaza de la República. The last bus back to town leaves at 6 pm.

Museo Histórico de la Revolución

On Insurgentes, near the waterfront, stands the Faro Carranza, a substantial yellow building incorporating a lighthouse, some navy offices and the Museo Histórico de la Revolución. The small museum is devoted to the revolutionary hero Venustiano Carranza, whose government-in-exile was based in Veracruz for a time. The 1917 Mexican constitution was formulated here, and the museum has exhibits on Carranza's life, political struggles and assassination. The museum is open from 9 am to 6 pm Tuesday to Saturday. Entry is free, and there is an explanatory booklet available in English.

Baluarte de Santiago

Of the nine forts which once surmounted Veracruz' defensive wall, the Baluarte (bastion) de Santiago on the corner of Canal and 16 de Septiembre is the only survivor. It was built in 1526. Inside, Las Joyas del Pescador is a small exhibition of pre-Hispanic gold jewellery similar to that found by a fisherman in Veracruz harbour in 1976. Some of the pieces are gorgeous, but it's an expensive visit at 13 pesos. The exhibit is open daily from 10 am to 4.30 pm, but you can walk around the outside of the fort at any time.

Museo de la Ciudad de Veracruz

The Veracruz City Museum, on the corner of Zaragoza and Morales, has fascinating displays on the city's early history (particularly slavery), though exhibits on contemporary customs and Carnaval are not as good. Hours are from 9 am to 4 pm Monday to Saturday and 9 am to 2.30 pm Sunday. Entry is 3 pesos.

Beaches & Lagoons

Few people venture into the grubby water at Playa de Hornos or Playa Villa del Mar, both south of the city centre. Cleaner beaches are five km south of the city at **Costa de Oro** and seven km south at **Mocambo**, where people do go in the water (though few put their heads under). If you really want to swim, pay 12 pesos to use the tree-shaded Olympic pool behind Mocambo beach.

Further south, the road goes to **Boca del Río**, with popular seafood restaurants. Over the bridge, the coast road continues to **Mandinga**, 21 km from Veracruz, where you can hire a boat to explore the lagoons.

1	San Juan de Ulúa
2	Hotel Royalty
3	Hotel Acapulco
4	Bus Stations
5	Hostal de Cortés
6	Hotel Villa del Mar
7	Torremar Resort
8	Hotel Playa Paraíso
9	Expover
10	Hotel Mocambo
11	Hotel Posada de Cortés

Diving

The beaches near Veracruz may not look inviting, but there is quite good scuba diving on the reefs around the offshore islands, and at least one accessible wreck. Part of the area has been designated an underwater 'natural park'. Two dive-boat operators are Curacao, Boulevard Avila Camacho in Boca del Río, and La Tienda SoBuca in Antón Lizardo.

Carnaval

Veracruz breaks into a nine-day party before Ash Wednesday (February or March) each year. Starting the previous Tuesday, brilliantly colourful parades wind through the city every day, beginning with one devoted to the 'burning of bad humour' and ending with the 'funeral of Juan Carnaval'. Other organised events include fireworks, dances, music (plenty of salsa and samba), children's parades and handicrafts, food and folklore shows. Informally, everyone's hell-bent on having as good a time as possible, and a festive atmosphere takes over the whole city. It's easy to pick up a programme of events when you're there.

Places to Stay

Hotel prices in Veracruz are reasonable, but in the peak times of mid-November to mid-January, Carnaval, Semana Santa and mid-June to early September, some places may charge higher rates than shown here. The most interesting area to stay is around the zócalo, where there are some budget hotels. Some of the seafront hotels can offer good value too. The cheapest places are near the bus stations, while expensive resort hotels are in the beach suburb of Mocambo, seven km south of the centre.

Places to Stay – bottom end

In the cheapest city hotels you might not get hot water.

Zócalo On the corner of Lerdo, just east of the zócalo but with the entrance around the corner on Morelos, the *Hotel Sevilla* (☎ (29) 32-42-46) has spacious rooms with ceiling fan, TV and bath for 45/50 pesos. They're pretty clean but can be noisy. Further up Morelos are the very basic *Casa de Huéspedes La Tabasqueña* (☎ (29) 32-05-60), with airless rooms in the cell-block style for 35/50 pesos for one or two people, and the newer, cleaner *Hotel Mexico* (☎ (29) 32-05-12), with lots of brown tiles and quiet, dark rooms with TV for 50/80 pesos. *Hotel Concha Dorada* (☎ (29) 31-31-21) at Lerdo 77 has clean, small, hot rooms with fan and private bath for 60/65 pesos, or larger air-con ones with a balcony over the zócalo for 70/80 pesos, or 100 pesos with two beds. Rooms facing the zócalo are noisy, but others are quiet.

Other cheap hotels are grouped a couple of blocks south-east of the zócalo. The *Hotel Santo Domingo* (☎ (29) 32-82-85) at Serdán 451 has small, sometimes grimy rooms with fan and private bath for 44/55 pesos. The older *Hotel Amparo* (☎ (29) 32-27-38) across the street at Serdán 482 is a basic but clean place with spartan tiled floors, uniformly lime-green walls and blue-and-white striped bedspreads. The small rooms with fan and private bath are 35/40 pesos. The slightly bigger, though worn, rooms in the nearby *Hotel Santillana* (☎ (29) 32-31-16) at Landero y Cos 209 have the same colour scheme and cost 50 pesos a single, 60 pesos a double with one bed and 75 pesos a double with two beds. They're reasonably clean and have TV and fan.

City Seafront For a budget place directly across the street from salt water, try the *Hotel Villa Rica* (☎ (29) 32-48-54) at Camacho 7, with small, tidy, fan-cooled rooms at 50/60 pesos. The *Hotel Royalty* (☎ (29) 36-10-41) on the corner of Camacho and Abasolo has no-frills but clean, balconied rooms for 60/70 a single/double with fan and 100/120 with air-con. There are particularly good views, both out to sea and inland, from its upper floors.

Bus Station Area The best deal is just over a km from the bus stations but worth the effort. It's the *Hotel Acapulco* (☎ (29) 32-92-87) at Uribe 1327, just west of Díaz Mirón

nine blocks north of the bus stations. Very clean, fairly bright, fan-cooled rooms of a reasonable size go for 40/50 pesos, and the staff are friendly.

There are a few places close to the bus stations, convenient if you're just passing through or have an early bus. They all tend to be noisy. The *Hotel Central* (☎ (29) 37-22-22), half a block north of the 1st-class bus station at Díaz Mirón 1612, is clean and very busy, with fan-cooled rooms at 50/60 pesos, 100 pesos with two beds and up to 150 pesos for big rooms with air-con.

The *Hotel Rosa Mar* (☎ (29) 37-07-47) at Lafragua 1100, opposite the 2nd-class bus station, is clean enough, but not very welcoming. Fan-cooled rooms with private bath cost 40 pesos a single, 50 pesos a double with one bed and 60 pesos a double with two beds. *Hotel Azteca* (☎ (29) 37-42-41) at 22 de Marzo 218 on the corner of Orizaba, a block east from the 2nd-class bus station, is a green building with a small courtyard and a friendly owner. Rooms have one bed, fan and private bath, which could be cleaner, for 40/50 pesos. *Hotel Impala* (☎ (29) 37-01-69), east of the bus station at Orizaba 650, has air-con, TV and phones and is probably better value at 50/65 pesos.

Places to Stay – middle
Zócalo Right on the zócalo there's a choice of three middle-range hotels. The 180-room *Hotel Colonial* (☎ (29) 32-01-93) at Lerdo 117 has an indoor pool and tiled terraces on the 5th and 6th floors overlooking the square. Prices start at 95/125 pesos for singles/doubles – interior rooms are dark but quiet and quite comfortable; rooms at the back are lighter. Rooms at the front with balconies over the zócalo are noisier and more expensive. All have air-con and TV, but they vary in value, so check out the room before you check in.

The *Hotel Prendes* (☎ (29) 31-02-41) on the corner of Lerdo and Independencia has comfortable rooms with air-con, phone, TV and, if you're lucky, a window and balcony for 90 pesos, and suites up to 120 pesos. The

Gran Hotel Diligencias (☎ (29) 31-22-41), on the west side of the zócalo at Independencia 1115, has 134 clean, modern, air-con rooms from 99 pesos for singles or doubles.

Just off the zócalo at Lerdo 20, on the corner of Landero y Cos, the *Hotel Oriente* (☎ (29) 31-24-90) has clean but not very big air-con rooms at 88/110 pesos. Outside rooms have balconies, more light and more noise.

South-east from the zócalo, on a quiet street looking across to the Baluarte de Santiago, the *Hotel Baluarte* (☎ (29) 32-52-22) at Canal 265, on the corner of 16 de Septiembre, is excellent value for its clean, modern, well-kept rooms – with TV and air-con – at 88/99 pesos.

City Seafront On the corner of Camacho and Figueroa, the big and busy *Hotel Mar y Tierra* (☎ (29) 31-38-66) has both an older front section with rooms at 76/108 pesos and a rear extension at 110/142 pesos. All rooms have air-con, TV and carpet, but some are better than others so look before you choose.

The *Hotel Villa del Mar* (☎ (29) 31-33-66) at Camacho 2707 opposite Playa Villa del Mar, 2.5 km south of the zócalo, is good value if you can get a room away from the noisy road. There's a good open-air pool, and the rooms, all air-con, are in both a central block and garden bungalows. Few have a sea view owing to buildings on the other side of the road, but at least it's a breezy location. The rooms cost 176 pesos for singles or doubles.

Mocambo A short walk from the beach, the little *Hotel Posada de Cortés* (☎ (29) 37-96-88) has 'junior suites' (clean, pleasant, moderately sized, air-con rooms with one double bed) for 120 pesos and 'bungalows' (larger rooms, which can hold four people) for 200 pesos. A garden and small pool are at the centre of things. The hotel faces the inland side of Carretera Veracruz-Boca del Río – the entrance is from the first street on the right a couple of hundred metres south of the traffic circle by the Hotel Mocambo.

Places to Stay – top end

Zócalo & Harbour The most central top-end place is the fully modernised *Hotel Veracruz* (☎ (29) 31-22-33, toll-free 800-2-92-33) on the corner of Independencia and Lerdo overlooking the zócalo, where carpeted, well-decorated, air-con rooms, some with balconies, cost from 290 pesos and up. There's a rooftop pool with a great view. The *Hotel Emporio* (☎ (29) 32-75-20, toll-free 800-2-90-19) towers over the harbour on the corner of Insurgentes and Xicoténcatl. An outside lift soars above three swimming pools to a roof garden. The 200 rooms and suites, some with views, range upward from 'standard' air-con singles/doubles (which are comfortable but could be bigger) at 260/290 pesos.

City Seafront The *Hostal de Cortés* (☎ (29) 32-00-65, toll-free 800-2-98-00), on the corner of Camacho and Las Casas, facing Playa de Hornos, is the first top-end hotel on the way south down the coast. It's a modern place with about 100 air-con rooms, some with sea-view balconies, and a pool. Rooms are 320 pesos including breakfast.

Mocambo The *Hotel Mocambo* (☎ (29) 22-02-05, toll-free 800-2-90-01), on Carretera Veracruz-Mocambo seven km south of the city centre, is a venerable luxury hotel – once the best in Veracruz and only ever-so-slightly faded – with over 100 rooms, fine terraced gardens and three sizeable pools (two indoors). The rooms are all a good size, with air-con, TV and a variety of outlooks. Doubles are 265 pesos with one bed, 275 pesos with two. Playa Mocambo is a minute's walk from the foot of the gardens.

The *Hotel Playa Paraíso* (☎ (29) 21-86-00, toll-free 800-2-90-10), at Ruíz Cortínes 3500 in Mocambo, has 34 air-con rooms and suites for 280/310/345 pesos. The eight-storey *Torremar Resort* (☎ (29) 21-34-66, toll-free 800-2-99-00), at Ruíz Cortínes 4300, has hundreds of rooms at 380/398 pesos for singles/doubles and junior suites at 520 pesos. Both places have pools, gardens and a private beach.

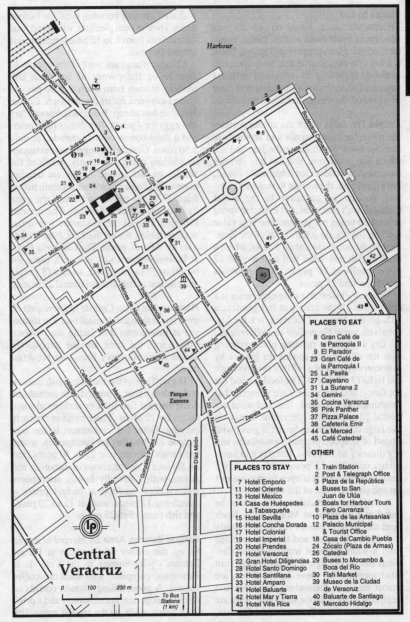

Central Veracruz

0   100   200 m

To Bus
Stations
(1 km)

PLACES TO STAY

7 Hotel Emporio
11 Hotel Oriente
13 Hotel Mexico
14 Casa de Huéspedes
    La Tabasqueña
15 Hotel Sevilla
16 Hotel Concha Dorada
17 Hotel Colonial
19 Hotel Imperial
20 Hotel Prendes
21 Hotel Veracruz
22 Gran Hotel Diligencias
28 Hotel Santo Domingo
32 Hotel Santillana
33 Hotel Amparo
41 Hotel Baluarte
42 Hotel Mar y Tierra
43 Hotel Villa Rica

PLACES TO EAT

8 Gran Café de
   la Parroquia II
9 El Parador
23 Gran Café de
   la Parroquia I
25 La Paella
27 Cayetano
31 La Suriana 2
34 Gemini
35 Cocina Veracruz
36 Pink Panther
37 Pizza Palace
38 Cafetería Emir
44 La Merced
45 Café Catedral

OTHER

1 Train Station
2 Post & Telegraph Office
3 Plaza de la República
4 Buses to San
   Juan de Ulúa
5 Boats for Harbour Tours
6 Faro Carranza
10 Plaza de las Artesanías
12 Palacio Municipal
   & Tourist Office
18 Casa de Cambio Puebla
24 Zócalo (Plaza de Armas)
26 Catedral
29 Buses to Mocambo &
   Boca del Río
30 Fish Market
39 Museo de la Ciudad
   de Veracruz
40 Baluarte de Santiago
46 Mercado Hidalgo

Places to Eat

Veracruzana sauce, found on fish all over Mexico, is made from onions, garlic, tomatoes, olives, green peppers and spices. There is a risk of contracting cholera from uncooked seafood, including ceviche and ostiones naturales (oysters), so unfortunately both these items are off the menus at seafood restaurants.

Zócalo The cafés under the zócalo portales are more for beer, tequila and atmosphere than for food. Stroll along the line and see which one grabs you. You can buy shrimps from passing vendors to nibble while you sit. For a meal here, the air-con *Restaurant Colonial*, beside the entrance to the Hotel Colonial, isn't bad value, but expect to spend at least 30 pesos per person. The best value food on the zócalo itself is out of the limelight on the south side, at *La Paella*, where a meal of fish and salad will cost around 17 pesos, paella is 20 pesos and the comida corrida around 15 pesos.

Veracruz's essential eating experience is a few metres off the zócalo at Independencia 105, on the corner of Zamora. It's the big, convivial, noisy *Gran Café de la Parroquia*, the city's favourite meeting place, echoing with the clinking of spoons on glasses by customers in need of a refill of the good café con leche (2.50 pesos). The food is good but not fancy, and the waiters are energetic but sometimes overworked: fish and meat are around 20 to 24 pesos (the ración de pavo is five large slabs of turkey breast in gravy with a bowl of jalapeño peppers), enchiladas and egg dishes 7 to 10 pesos. Burgers and sandwiches cost 7 to 13 pesos and a beer is 5 pesos. The Parroquia is open from 6 am to 1 am and packed most of the time.

A different Veracruz tradition can be found at *Cayetano*, at Molina 88 a block from the zócalo, famous for its deliciously cool juices, licuados and nieves concocted from a wide range of tropical fruits. Creations like mondongo de frutas, a large fruit salad topped with nieve for 12 pesos, are almost meals in themselves. Licuados con leche cost 6 pesos. In the same little plaza are two versions of the *Restaurant La Gaviota*,

with staff running between them for various items. They're both pleasant, with good food – breakfasts from 8 to 12 pesos, main meals around 20 pesos.

Cheaper places are west of the zócalo. *El Jarocho* on the corner of Emparán and Madero, is open from 8 am to 6.30 pm and always crowded for its cheap lunch. *Cocina Veracruz* has cheap, basic, wholesome fare like eggs for 4 pesos, fish dishes for 8 pesos and a three-course comida corrida for only 5.50 pesos. *Gemini* is a vegetarian restaurant on Madero doing lunch only. South of the zócalo, on and around Arista, are trendier places. The *Pizza Palace* has medium pizzas from 23 to 38 pesos, and there are some hamburger places nearby. The quaint Callejon Héroes de Nacozari has quiet outdoor tables, where the *Pink Panther* has a set meal for 11 pesos. The *Cafetería Emir*, at Independencia 1520, is a slick place for breakfast (7 to 12 pesos), snacks (8 pesos) and chicken or fish dishes (around 22 pesos).

Harbour The *Gran Café de la Parroquia II*, even larger than the original near the zócalo, sits at Insurgentes 340 facing the harbour. The menu's the same and the atmosphere almost as jovial. Navy brass hats breakfast here.

The top floor of the municipal fish market, on Landero y Cos, is packed with comedores doing bargain fish fillet or shrimps al mojo de ajo for 12 pesos. These close in the early evening. Other fish restaurants in the area include *El Parador*, on Insurgentes, where most main courses cost 25 to 30 pesos, and *La Suriana 2*, on the corner of Zaragoza and Arista, with a friendly family atmosphere and excellent seafood at budget prices – cocteles at 12 pesos, soup at 12 to 20 pesos and fish from 15 to 25 pesos.

Parque Zamora Area *La Merced* at Rayón 81 on the corner of Clavijero is Parque Zamora's jolly answer to the Café de la Parroquia, complete with clinking coffee spoons. A good, filling comida corrida of chicken soup, rice, bread, sweets and a drink is 14 pesos, while on the regular menu, fish and meat courses are mostly 20 to 25 pesos and antojitos around 6 to 9 pesos. The nearby *Café Catedral*, at Ocampo 202 in Pasaje Castillo, half a block west of Independencia, is a similar but slightly more subdued place with the same sort of prices.

Down the Coast Restaurants at Mocambo beach tend to be overpriced and nothing special. The coffee shop at the *Hotel Mocambo* has some atmosphere and does a good breakfast.

A seafood meal in the rivermouth village of Boca del Río, 10 km south of Veracruz centre, is an indispensable part of a visit to Veracruz for many Mexicans – and a long Sunday lunch is the favourite way to do it. *Pardiño's* at Zamora 40 in the centre of the village is the biggest and best-known restaurant, but there are several more by the riverside.

Mandinga, about eight km further along the coast from Boca del Río, is also known for its seafood (especially prawns) and has a clutch of small restaurants.

Entertainment

A café seat under the zócalo portales is a ringside ticket to the best entertainment in town, but if you hanker for something more formal, the tourist office has information on exhibitions, concerts and other cultural events. There are several cinemas, including two on Arista, and quite a few nightclubs and discos, mostly near the waterfront – *Carlos & Charlie's, Club 21* (young), *Freeday* (new) and *Ocean* (flashy and expensive) all get going after 11.30 pm.

Things to Buy

The Plaza de las Artesanías on the corner of Insurgentes and Landero y Cos, and the line of stalls across the street, are devoted more to seaside souvenirs than genuine artisanry. But if you need a sailor cap or a '*Veracruz – Ciudad Del Amor*' T-shirt, drop by. Ordinary Jarochos shop for their daily needs at the Mercado Hidalgo, a block south-west of

Parque Zamora between Cortés and Soto. Shops are on Independencia and the streets to its west.

Getting There & Away

Air Mexicana (☎ 32-22-42) flies four times daily to/from Mexico City (45 minutes; 292 to 350 pesos). Its Veracruz office is at 5 de Mayo 1266, on the corner of Serdán, downtown. Saro has cheap flights to/from Mexico City twice a week – Viajes Ahinco (☎ 31-43-48) in the Hotel Veracruz sells its tickets, along with those of the Veracruz-based airline Litoral and other lines. To get the cheap fares you have to book and pay eight days ahead.

Litoral flies to/from Villahermosa (one hour; 137 pesos), Poza Rica (30 minutes) and Tampico (one hour) usually twice daily. Its own ticket office (☎ 31-52-32) is in the Hostal de Cortés hotel on Camacho facing Playa de Hornos. Aeromonterrey flies to/from Tampico five days a week (394 pesos).

Aerocaribe flies daily to/from Mérida or Cancún (2½ to 3½ hours) via Minatitlán and/or Villahermosa. Its office (☎ 37-02-60) is at Camacho 2983 between Bolívar and Valencia, about 3.5 km south of the zócalo. Aeromar flies to/from Uruapan, Morelia and other central Mexico cities. For Aeroméxico reservations, call ☎ 35-08-33.

Bus Veracruz is a major hub, with good services up and down the coast and inland along the Puebla-Mexico City corridor. The 1st and 2nd-class bus stations (Centrales de Autobuses) are back-to-back between Díaz Mirón and Lafragua, two km south of Parque Zamora and 2.75 km south of the zócalo. The 1st-class side (almost exclusive to ADO) fronts Díaz Mirón on the corner of Xalapa. The 2nd-class side is at the rear, entered from Lafragua.

Note that tickets for AU's ordinario buses are sold not in the main 2nd-class ticket hall but from a separate taquilla by the 2nd-class platforms. Try to avoid the slow, uncomfortable buses of Transportes Los Tuxtlas for all but short hops. Departures (all 1st-class are by ADO; their Mercedes Benz buses cost slightly more) include:

Acayucan – 250 km, five hours; 12 1st-class buses daily (26 pesos)

Catemaco – 165 km, three hours; eight 1st-class buses daily (20 pesos); a few 2nd-class directo buses daily by AU and Transportes Los Tuxtlas; 2nd-class ordinario buses every 10 minutes by Transportes Los Tuxtlas

Córdoba – 125 km, two hours; 12 1st-class buses daily (17 to 19 pesos) and 22 directo 2nd-class buses daily by AU

Mexico City (TAPO) – 430 km; five deluxe buses per day by UNO (5½ hours, 98 pesos) and 20 1st-class buses per day by ADO (six hours, 59 pesos)

Oaxaca – 460 km, 8½ hours via Teotitlán del Camino, departs 7.15 am (62 pesos); 540 km, 10½ hours via Huajuapan de León, departs 8.15 pm (62 pesos); one 2nd-class directo bus via Teotitlán del Camino by AU; two 2nd-class buses daily via Tuxtepec by Cuenca (tickets sold in the 1st-class station)

Orizaba – 150 km, 2¼ hours; 18 1st-class buses daily (20 pesos) and 21 2nd-class directo buses by AU

Papantla – 230 km, five hours; 1st-class Mercedes Benz buses go daily (49 pesos)

Poza Rica – 250 km, 5½ hours; 14 1st-class buses daily (41 to 46 pesos)

Puebla – 300 km, five hours; one deluxe bus daily by UNO, 10 1st-class buses (41 pesos) and 19 2nd-class directo buses daily by AU

San Andrés Tuxtla – 155 km, 2¾ hours; about 30 1st-class buses daily (18 pesos)

Santiago Tuxtla – 140 km, 2½ hours; 16 1st-class buses daily (17 pesos) and 2nd-class buses every 10 minutes by Transportes Los Tuxtlas

Tampico – 500 km, 10 hours; deluxe UNO bus at 9 pm (118 pesos) and 13 1st-class buses daily (79 to 87 pesos)

Tuxpan – 320 km, six hours; four 1st-class buses daily (53 pesos)

Tuxtla Gutiérrez – 750 km, 14 hours; one 1st-class bus daily (76 pesos)

Villahermosa – 475 km, eight hours; 11 1st-class buses daily (56 to 62 pesos)

Xalapa – 100 km, two hours; frequent 1st-class buses from 3 am to 10 pm (15 pesos) and 2nd-class buses every 15 minutes by AU

Buses also go to Campeche, Cancún, Chetumal, Matamoros, Mérida and Salina Cruz.

Train The overnight sleeper between Veracruz and Mexico City, El Jarocho, is slower and dearer than a bus but you get more chance of sleep. It leaves Mexico City at 9.15 pm, or Veracruz at 9.30 pm, and passes through Córdoba, Fortín de las Flores and Orizaba. The full trip is supposed to take 10 hours but allow for a couple of hours' delay. A camarín to or from Mexico City costs 115 pesos for one person, 190 pesos for two people; an alcoba for two is 230 pesos, a primera especial seat 54 pesos. Book as far ahead as you can. There are two other daily trains to Mexico City which have only segunda clase seats at 17 pesos: Tren 52 departs at 8 am and goes via Córdoba; Tren 101 comes through from Tapachula (so could be very late), theoretically arriving at 6 am and departing for Mexico City via Xalapa at 7.25 am.

Incurable railway buffs could take train No 102 to Tapachula, 885 km away on the Chiapas-Guatemala border. The daily service, segunda clase only, costs 40.50 pesos, departs at 9 pm and takes an alleged 22 hours 25 minutes. Down the line in Chiapas, station staff say these trains can turn up any time of day or night.

Veracruz station is at the north end of Plaza de la República, a five-minute walk from the zócalo. The ticket office is open Monday to Saturday from 6 to 9 am, 9.30 to 11 am and 4 to 9 pm; Sunday and holidays from 6 to 10 am and 6 to 9 pm.

Car From Veracruz, highway 180 goes north and south along the coast, with regular tollbooths charging 5 to 7 pesos. Highway 140 goes north-west to Xalapa, and highway 150 goes south then west to Córdoba; both continue to Puebla.

Car-rental agencies in Veracruz include Auto Rentas Fast (☎ (29) 36-14-16) at Lerdo 245; Autos Laurencio (☎ (29) 32-70-60) at Serdán 3 in the Hotel Emporio building; Avis (☎ (29) 32-98-34) at Collado 241; Budget (☎ (29) 31-21-39) at Díaz Mirón 1123 (on the corner of Alacio Pérez); Dollar (☎ (29) 32-00-65) in the Hostal de Cortés hotel; Hertz (☎ (29) 32-40-21) at Autover, Serdán 14; and National (☎ (29) 31-17-56) at Díaz Mirón 1036.

Getting Around

To/From the Airport Veracruz airport (☎ (29) 34-90-08) is about 11 km south-west of town near highway 140. Transportación Aeropuerto (☎ 32-35-20) at Hidalgo 826 runs an airport colectivo (8 pesos) and taxi (35 pesos) service. It will pick you up from your hotel.

To/From the Bus Stations For the city centre, take a bus marked 'Díaz Mirón X Madero' (1 peso) from in front of the Hotel Central, on Díaz Mirón half a block north of the 1st-class bus station. The bus goes to Parque Zamora then up Madero. For the zócalo, get off on the corner of Madero and Lerdo and turn right. Returning to the bus stations, pick up the same bus going south on 5 de Mayo. From the booth outside the 1st-class bus station a taxi ticket to the zócalo costs 5.50 pesos; the hustlers inside the bus station will charge from 7 pesos upwards.

To/From Mocambo, Boca del Río & Mandinga Bus 'Mocambo – Boca del Río' (2.50 pesos), every few minutes from the corner of Zaragoza and Serdán near the zócalo, goes to Parque Zamora then down the seafront Boulevard Camacho to Mocambo (15 minutes; get off at Expover exhibition hall on Calzada Mocambo and walk down the street left of the Hotel Mocambo to the beach) and Boca del Río (25 minutes).

AU ordinario 'Antón Lizardo' buses from the 2nd-class bus station, every 20 minutes from 6 am to 8.45 pm, stop at Boca del Río and Mandinga. The last one back to town leaves around 8 pm. The less frequent directo buses to Antón Lizardo stop at Boca del Río only.

CÓRDOBA

• *pop: 150,000* • *alt: 924 metres*

Córdoba ('CORR-do-ba'), 126 km from Veracruz in the foothills of Mexico's central mountains, has a long colonial history and a pleasant centre, and the verdant, dramatic hill country around the town is enticing.

History

Córdoba was founded in 1618 by 30 Spanish families to stop escaped black slaves attacking travellers between Mexico City and the coast. It's known as La Ciudad de los Treinta Caballeros (City of the 30 Knights). Today it's a prosperous commercial and processing centre for sugar cane, coffee and tobacco from the surrounding hillsides and fruit from the lowlands.

Orientation

Everything of interest is within a few blocks of the central Plaza de Armas. La Parroquia de la Inmaculada Concepción is at the plaza's south-east end, while its north-east side is lined by 18th-century portales and a string of busy outdoor cafés. The new bus station is three km south-east of the plaza. Streets running north-west to south-east are called Avenidas; Calles are at right angles to Avenidas.

Information

The Cámara Nacional de Comercio, Servicios y Turismo (☎ (271) 2-11-47) at 308 Calle 5, between Avenidas 3 and 5, can give some information, though it's not really a tourist office. It's open from 9 am to 1 pm and 4 to 7 pm Monday to Friday and 9 am to 1 pm Saturday.

The post office is at 3 Avenida 3, just north-west of the Plaza de Armas. The main banks (with ATMs) are around the plaza and will change travellers' cheques in the morning. A casa de cambio on Avenida 3, just south-east of the plaza, is open from 9 am to 2 pm and 4 to 7 pm Monday to Friday and 10 am to 1 pm Saturday.

The market is bounded by Calles 7 and 9 and Avenidas 8 and 10. Shops are in the blocks south and east of the Plaza de Armas.

Ex-Hotel Zevallos

This is not a hotel but the former home, built in 1687, of the Condes (Counts) of Zevallos. It's on the north-east side of the Plaza de Armas, behind the portales.

Plaques in the courtyard record that Juan O'Donojú and Agustín de Iturbide met here

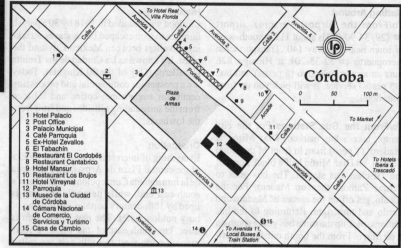

Córdoba

0   50   100 m

1 Hotel Palacio
2 Post Office
3 Palacio Municipal
4 Café Parroquia
5 Ex-Hotel Zevallos
6 El Tabachín
7 Restaurant El Cordobés
8 Restaurant Cantabrico
9 Hotel Mansur
10 Restaurant Los Brujos
11 Hotel Virreynal
12 Parroquia
13 Museo de la Ciudad
    de Córdoba
14 Cámara Nacional
    de Comercio,
    Servicios y Turismo
15 Casa de Cambio

after Mass on 24 August 1821 and agreed on
terms for Mexico's independence from
Spain. O'Donojú, the new viceroy, had con-
cluded it was useless for Spain to try to cling
to its colony; Iturbide was the leader of the
anti-imperial forces, a former royalist
general who had changed sides. Contrary to
the Plan de Iguala, in which Iturbide and
Vicente Guerrero had proposed a European
monarch as Mexican head of state, O'Donojú
and Iturbide agreed that a Mexican could
hold that office. Iturbide went on to a brief
reign as Emperor Agustín I.

Other Things to See
The big late-18th-century church in the Plaza
de Armas, **La Parroquia de la Inmaculada
Concepción**, has famously loud bells. The
Museo de la Ciudad de Córdoba, in a
17th-century house at 303 Calle 3, has a
small, well-displayed collection including a
Classic Veracruz palma and some beautifully
made personal ornaments.

Places to Stay
Hotel Mansur (☎ (271) 2-60-00), on the
Plaza de Armas at 301 Avenida 1, is well kept
with an elegant lobby and singles/doubles

with TV, phone and air-con from 70/80
pesos. The *Hotel Virreynal* (☎ (271) 2-23-
77), on the corner of Avenida 1 and Calle 5,
is an old-style place with clean, spacious
rooms with tiled floors, private bath and fan
for 60/70/80 pesos.

The *Hotel Iberia* (☎ (271) 2-13-01), at
919 Avenida 2 (two blocks downhill from the
Virreynal, then one block to the left and half
a block to the right), has small, modern
rooms around a courtyard with trees for
40/50 pesos with TV and fan. Next door at
909 Avenida 2, the *Hotel Trescadó* (☎ (271)
2-23-66) is very bare and basic, but has
parking and costs only 20 pesos for singles,
25 to 35 pesos for doubles.

The *Hotel Palacio* (☎ (271) 2-21-88), on
the corner of Avenida 3 and Calle 2, has big,
pleasant, air-con rooms with TV for 99/120
pesos. The *Hotel Real Villa Florida* (☎ (271)
4-66-66) at 3002 Avenida 1, 1.5 km north-
west of the centre where Avenida 1 meets
highway 150, has tasteful, modern, air-con
rooms for 198/253 pesos, attractive gardens
and a restaurant.

Places to Eat
The Plaza de Armas portales are lined with

cafés and restaurants where you can dine and drink the local coffee in a variety of ways. Prices seem to be highest at the northern end, starting with the *Café Parroquia*. Further down, *El Tabachín* makes a speciality of freshwater prawns (langostinos). The long menu at the *Restaurant El Cordobés* includes meat fillets (28 pesos), spaghetti (12 to 16 pesos) and seafood cocktails (15 to 19 pesos). Its five-course comida corrida is good value at 18 pesos. Down the road, the *Hotel Virreynal* is popular at breakfast and also for its excellent comida corrida.

Just off the Plaza de Armas, the *Restaurant Cantabrico* at 11 Calle 3 is a more expensive but tasteful place with piped music and plenty of choice of antojitos, fish and meat. *Restaurant Los Brujos* at 306 Avenida 2 (down an arcade next to Telas Parasina on Avenida 1) is much cheaper, with set breakfasts and a bargain comida corrida. For a treat, try the *Restaurant Las Fuentes* at the Hotel Palacio, which serves good Italian-Mexican meals and some Lebanese dishes and seafood. Prices are a little upscale, but it's still good value.

Getting There & Away

Bus Many buses from Córdoba are de paso, which usually means waiting around the bus station till they come in to see whether you can get on, though ADO has a new communication system which lets them sell some seats before the bus arrives. On AU (2nd-class) buses it may mean standing-room only if you do get on.

The new bus station, with 1st-class (ADO and Cristóbal Colón) and 2nd-class (AU) services, is at Avenida Privada 4, about three km south-east of the plaza. To get to the centre take a local bus marked 'centro' or buy a taxi ticket (4 pesos). To Fortín de las Flores and Orizaba, it's more convenient to take a local bus from Avenida 11 than to go out to the Córdoba bus station. Long-distance buses from Córdoba include:

Mexico City (TAPO) – 305 km, 4½ hours; deluxe buses at 6 am and 4 pm by UNO (70 pesos); frequent 1st-class buses by ADO and Cristóbal

Colón (45 pesos); 2nd-class buses (11 locales, 16 de paso) daily (38 pesos)

Oaxaca – 317 km, seven hours; two 1st-class buses daily by ADO and one with Cristóbal Colón (50 pesos); one 2nd-class evening departure (35 pesos)

Puebla – 175 km, three hours; 17 1st-class buses daily, including nine locales, by ADO (29 pesos); 42 2nd-class buses daily including seven locales (23 pesos)

Veracruz – 125 km, two hours; 20 1st-class buses daily, including 10 locales, by ADO (19 pesos); frequent 2nd-class buses (15 pesos)

Xalapa – 200 km, 3½ hours; 11 1st-class buses daily by ADO (14 pesos)

Train The El Jarocho night sleeper between Mexico City and Veracruz (see the previous Veracruz section) stops at Córdoba. Eastward, it is scheduled to leave Córdoba at 4.45 am; westward, at 11.35 pm. A camarín from Mexico City costs 87 pesos for one person. The station is on the corner of Avenida 11 and Calle 33 in the south part of the town.

Car The toll autopista 150D from Puebla bypasses Fortín de las Flores and Orizaba. Highway 150 from Veracruz continues west from Córdoba through those towns to Tehuacán.

FORTÍN DE LAS FLORES

• **pop: 16,000** • **alt: 970 metres**

Fortín ('forr-TEEN') de las Flores is seven km west of Córdoba – the two places nearly run into each other. The local industry is the *viveros* (nurseries) producing flowers for export, but if you expect to see streets and plazas dripping with blossoms you may be disappointed. From April to June is the main season, but most of the colour is confined to commercial nurseries and private gardens. There's a week-long flower festival at the end of April and start of May. Year-round, Fortín is a weekend retreat for the Mexico City middle class.

Fortín has a big open plaza, the Parque Principal, with the Palacio Municipal in the middle and a cathedral at the south end.

Places to Stay & Eat

The *Hotel Bugambilia* (☎ (271) 3-05-22), two blocks east of the Parque Central on the corner of Avenida 1 and Calle 7, has ordinary singles/doubles with private bath but no fan for 35/40 pesos.

Hotel Fortín de las Flores (☎ (271) 3-00-55, 3-01-08), on Avenida 2 between Calles 5 and 7, one block north and 1½ blocks east of the north-east corner of the Parque Central, is a good middle-range hotel with gardens, swimming pool, bar and restaurant. Pleasant rooms cost 143 pesos for one or two people.

The *Hotel Posada Loma* (☎ (271) 3-03-03) is one km from the plaza, above the road to Córdoba. The rooms are in bungalows in big gardens and start at 110 pesos. Facilities include a swimming pool and a squash court.

There are a few restaurants along Calle 1, both on the Parque Central and north of it.

Getting There & Away

Bus From Córdoba, there are frequent buses marked 'Fortín' going north-west along Avenida 11 (15 minutes; 1.70 pesos). They arrive and depart from Calle 1 Sur, on the west side of the plaza.

The ADO (1st-class) bus office is on the corner of Avenida 2 and Calle 6, three blocks west of the plaza along Avenida 1, then one block north. There are seven buses daily to Mexico City (44 pesos), eight to Veracruz (18 pesos), five to Puebla (25 pesos) and three to Xalapa (13 pesos). They are all de paso, but some seats can be purchased in advance.

Train Fortín is on the Mexico City-Veracruz route, 30 minutes west of Córdoba. The station is two blocks north of the plaza.

ORIZABA

• *pop: 175,000* • *alt: 1219 metres*

Orizaba, 16 km west of Córdoba, was founded by the Spanish to guard the Veracruz-Mexico City road. It retains a few colonial buildings and church domes, though much was lost in the 1973 earthquake. An industrial centre in the late 19th century, its factories were early centres of the unrest that led to the unseating of dictator Porfirio Díaz. Today it has a big brewery and cement, textile and chemical industries. The surrounding mountains are scenic, and hot springs in the area have been developed as balnearios.

Orientation

The central plaza, Parque del Castillo, has the Parroquia de San Miguel on its north side. Madero, running down the west side of the plaza, and Avenidas Pte 7/Ote 6 are the busiest streets.

Information

There's a tourist office in the Palacio Municipal, open from 10 am to 1.30 pm and 5 to 7 pm Monday to Friday, and 10 am to 1 pm Saturday. The post office is on the corner of Sur 7 and Ote 2. There are banks with ATMs a block south of the plaza.

Things to See

The bizarre-looking iron and steel **Palacio Municipal**, off the north-west corner of Parque del Castillo, was the Belgian pavilion at the Paris International Exhibition in the late 19th century. Orizaba bought it for 105,000 pesos and had it dismantled, shipped across to Mexico and reassembled.

San Miguel, the big parish church on the north side of Parque del Castillo, is mainly 17th century in style with several towers and some Puebla-style tiles. The 18th-century **La Concordia** and **El Carmen** churches have Churrigueresque façades.

The **Centro Educativo Obrero** (Workers' Education Centre), on Colón between the Parque del Castillo and the Alameda park, has a 1926 mural by Orozco.

Places to Stay

Orizaba's best bottom-end value is the *Hotel Arenas* (☎ (272) 5-23-61) at 169 Norte 2, half a block south of Ote 5. It's family-run and friendly, with a tropical courtyard garden. Clean singles/doubles with bath are 30/40 pesos, or 45 pesos with two beds. The *Hotel San Cristóbal* (☎ (272) 5-11-40), at 243

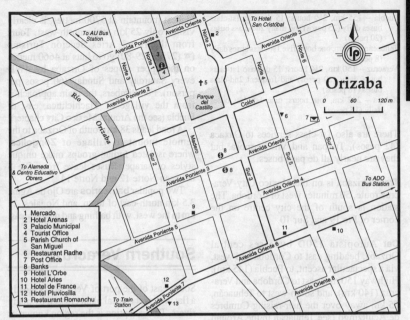

1 Mercado
2 Hotel Arenas
3 Palacio Municipal
4 Tourist Office
5 Parish Church of
   San Miguel
6 Restaurant Radhe
7 Post Office
8 Banks
9 Hotel L'Orbe
10 Hotel Aries
11 Hotel de France
12 Hotel Pluviosilla
13 Restaurant Romanchu

Norte 4, half a block north of Ote 5, has clean rooms with bath for 35 pesos a single or double.

Middle-range places include the *Hotel L'Orbe* (☎ (272) 5-50-33), at 33 Pte 5, with air-con rooms with TV from 80/100 pesos. The *Hotel Pluviosilla* (☎ (272) 5-52-65) at 163 Pte 7 has car parking and rooms for 66/68 pesos. The *Hotel Aries* (☎ (272) 5-35-20) at 265 Ote 6 is close to the bus station and not bad value at 67/82 pesos, but the *Hotel de France* at 186 Ote 6 may have more character.

Places to Eat

Most restaurants are along Madero, Sur 3 and Pte 7/Ote 6; they usually close by 8.30 pm. One of the best is the *Restaurant Romanchu* opposite the Hotel Pluviosilla on Pte 7. Hotels with restaurants include *L'Orbe*, with an 18-peso comida corrida, the *Pluviosilla*, with breakfasts from 8 to 15 pesos, and the *Aries*, with moderately tasty pizza from 18 to 30 pesos. *Restaurant*

Radhe, on Sur 5, does very good, moderately priced vegetarian food.

Getting There & Away

Bus The local buses from Fortín or Córdoba stop four blocks north and six blocks east of the centre, around Ote 9 and Norte 14A. The AU (2nd-class) station is at 425 Zaragoza Pte, north-west of the centre. To reach the town centre from here, turn left outside the station, cross the bridge, take the first fork right and head for the church domes.

The 1st-class ADO bus station is at 577 Ote 6 between Sur 11 and Sur 13. Most long-distance buses from Orizaba are de paso. Outbound services include:

Mexico City (TAPO) – 285 km, four hours; deluxe
  UNO buses at 6 am and 4.30 pm (66 pesos); ADO
  GL service (50 pesos); four local and 18 de paso
  1st-class buses daily by ADO (44 pesos); about
  40 2nd-class buses daily (35 pesos)

Puebla – 155 km, 2½ hours; 15 de paso 1st-class buses daily (25 pesos) and many 2nd-class buses (20 pesos)

Tehuacán – 65 km, one hour; five 1st-class buses daily (8 pesos)

Veracruz – 150 km, 2¼ hours; 15 de paso 1st-class buses daily (20 pesos) and frequent 2nd-class buses (18 pesos)

Xalapa – 242 km, four hours; nine 1st-class buses daily (15 pesos)

There are also 1st-class services to Oaxaca (42 pesos), Tuxpan and Villahermosa, but they are nearly all de paso buses.

Train Orizaba is on the Mexico City-Veracruz route, 50 minutes west of Córdoba. The station is south of the city centre on the corner of Pte 19 and Sur 10.

Car Autopista 150D bypasses central Orizaba, heading east to Córdoba and west, via a spectacular ascent, to Puebla (145 km). Highway 150 runs east to Córdoba and Veracruz (140 km), and south-west to Tehuacán, 65 km away over the hair-raising Cumbres de Acultzingo (see Tehuacán in the Around Mexico City chapter).

AROUND ORIZABA

Looming over the Alameda park west of town, **Cerro del Barrego** offers brilliant views if you get to the top very early, before the mist rolls in. **Pico de Orizaba**, Mexico's

Pico de Orizaba

highest mountain at 5700 metres, is clearly visible only 25 km to the north-west. Tours from the Hotel Aries Sección Turismo (☎ (272) 6-29-80) go to huts at 4660 metres on the upper slopes of Orizaba by 4WD every Saturday and Sunday (60 pesos per person). For climbers, the main approach is from the village of Tlachichuca, east of Puebla (see the Around Mexico City chapter).

A road leads 38 km south of Orizaba to the remote mountain village of **Zongolica**, where isolated Indian groups make unique styles of sarape. Buses leave from Ote 3 between Norte 12 and Norte 14.

Two popular **balnearios** are Ojo de Agua, 3.5 km north-east of town, and Nogales, 12 km to the west, with bathing and picnic areas.

Southern Veracruz

South-east of the port of Veracruz is mostly a flat, hot, wet coastal plain crossed by many rivers. The exception is the region known as Los Tuxtlas ('TOOKS-tlahs'), around the towns of Santiago Tuxtla and San Andrés Tuxtla, which is hilly, green and fertile with several lakes and waterfalls, and a quiet coastline. Los Tuxtlas is one of the most agreeable and climatically comfortable parts of Veracruz, and attracts Mexican vacationers to the small lakeside resort of Catemaco.

Los Tuxtlas is also the western fringe of the ancient Olmec heartland, with interesting Olmec museums at Santiago Tuxtla and nearby Tres Zapotes. The basalt for the huge Olmec heads was quarried from Cerro Cintepec in the east of the Sierra de los Tuxtlas and then transported, probably by roller and raft, to San Lorenzo, 60 km to the south.

ALVARADO

• *pop: 60,000*

The busy fishing town of Alvarado, 67 km down highway 180 from Veracruz city, stands on a spit of land separating the Gulf from the Laguna de Alvarado, which is the meeting point of several rivers including the Papaloapan. The channel from the lagoon to

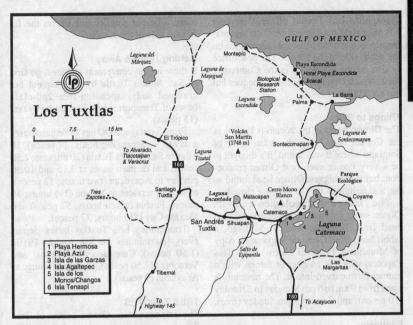

GULF OF MEXICO

Los Tuxtlas

0   7.5   15 km

To Alvarado,
Tlacotalpan
& Veracruz

Laguna del
Márquez

Laguna de
Majagual

Montepío

Playa Escondida
Hotel Playa Escondida
Jicacal

Biological
Research
Station

Laguna
Escondida

La Palma

La Barra

El Trópico

Volcán
San Martín
(1748 m)

Laguna de
Sontecomapan

Sontecomapan

Laguna
Tizatal

Santiago
Tuxtla

Laguna
Encantada

Cerro Mono
Blanco

Parque
Ecológico

Coyame

Tres
Zapotes

Matacapan

San Andrés
Tuxtla

Sihuapan

Catemaco

Laguna
Catemaco

Salto de
Eyipantla

Las
Margaritas

Tibernal

To
Highway 145

To Acayucan

1 Playa Hermosa
2 Playa Azul
3 Isla de las Garzas
4 Isla Agaltepec
5 Isla de los
   Monos/Changos
6 Isla Tenaspi

the sea is crossed by a long toll bridge east
of the town (7 pesos per car).

Alvarado has a few hotels and restaurants,
as well as post and telephone offices. Carnaval celebrations here start immediately after
the Veracruz Carnaval finishes. You can hire
boats for trips on the lagoons or up the river
to Tlacotalpan (about two hours).

TLACOTALPAN
• pop: 15,000
A very quiet old town beside the wide Río
Papaloapan, 10 km south of highway 180,
Tlacotalpan has some pretty streets,
churches, plazas and colourful houses. The
Museo Salvador Ferrando, open daily
except Monday (3 pesos), has some 19th-
century furniture and artefacts. You can rent
boats for river trips. Tlacotalpan's lively
Candelaria festival, in late January and early
February, features bull-running in the streets
and an image of the Virgin floating down the
river followed by a flotilla of small boats.

There are two small hotels – the *Posada
Doña Lala* (☎ (288) 4-25-80), with pleasant
rooms starting at 88/110 pesos, and the *Hotel
Reforma*, from 90 pesos. Some restaurants
are along the riverfront, others near the plazas.

Highway 175 (narrow in parts) goes from
Tlacotalpan up the Papaloapan Valley to Tuxtepec, then twists and turns over the mountains
to Oaxaca (320 km from Tlacotalpan).

SANTIAGO TUXTLA
• pop: 11,000 • alt: 285 metres
Santiago, founded in 1525, is a pretty valley
town in the rolling green foothills of the
volcanic Sierra de los Tuxtlas. It's a pleasant
stopover, and worth visiting for the Olmec
remains and museums in the town and at Tres
Zapotes, 23 km away.

Orientation & Information
ADO buses arriving in Santiago drop you
where Calle Morelos runs off the highway.
Go south down Morelos a little, and the

Transportes Los Tuxtlas office is on your left; turn right here (west) on Calle Ayuntamiento to reach the Museo Arqueológico on the south side of the zócalo. The post office is also on the zócalo, as is the Comermex bank, which changes travellers' cheques but has no ATM.

Things to See

The **Olmec head** in the zócalo is known as the Cobata head, after the estate west of Santiago where it was found. It's thought to be a very late or even post-Olmec production, but is the biggest Olmec head found so far, and unique in that its eyes are closed.

The **Museo Arqueológico** exhibits Olmec stone carvings, including a colossal head from Nestepec west of Santiago, a rabbit head from Cerro de Vigía and a copy of Monument F or 'El Negro' from Tres Zapotes, which is an altar or throne with a human form carved into it. The museum is open from 9 am to 6 pm Monday to Saturday (10 pesos), and 9 am to 3 pm Sunday (free).

Festivals

Santiago celebrates the festivals of San Juan (24 June) and Santiago Apóstol (St James, 25 July) with processions and dances including the Liseres, in which the participants wear jaguar costumes.

Places to Stay & Eat

The family-run *Hotel Morelos* (☎ (244) 7-04-04) has Morelos 12 as its address but its entrance is actually on Obregón, which runs off Morelos almost opposite the Transportes Los Tuxtlas bus station. Rooms cost 30/50/60 pesos, and have fans and private bath with hot water but aren't very big. Some are brighter than others.

The modern *Hotel Castellanos* (☎ (244) 7-02-00), in a circular building on the north side of the zócalo, is amazingly good for a small-town hotel, with a clean swimming pool and 48 bright, clean, panoramic, air-con rooms of varying sizes. Singles/doubles are 80/100 pesos. Its pleasant restaurant is good value, with egg dishes at 8 pesos, meat or chicken 10 to 15 pesos and seafood a bit

more. Cheaper eateries line up on the far (south) side of the zócalo.

Getting There & Away

If there are no convenient services, go first to San Andrés Tuxtla by the frequent but cramped and suspension-free 2nd-class buses of Transportes Los Tuxtlas, or by taxi (15 pesos).

From Santiago, ADO has 14 de paso buses a day to Veracruz (2½ hours; 17 pesos), 18 a day to San Andrés Tuxtla (20 minutes; 2.50 pesos) and de paso buses at 3.15 and 10.30 pm day to Acayucan (two hours; 12 pesos), as well as services to Xalapa (3½ hours; 30 pesos), Puebla (seven hours; 57 pesos) and Mexico City (8½ hours; 77 pesos).

Transportes Los Tuxtlas buses depart every few minutes for San Andrés Tuxtla (1.50 pesos), Catemaco (2.50 pesos) and Veracruz (12.50 pesos), and about hourly to Acayucan (9 pesos).

TRES ZAPOTES

The important late Olmec centre of Tres Zapotes is now just a series of mounds in maize fields, but many interesting finds are displayed at the museum in the village of Tres Zapotes, 23 km west of Santiago Tuxtla.

History

Tres Zapotes was probably first occupied while the great Olmec centre of La Venta (Tabasco) still flourished. It carried on after the destruction of La Venta (about 400 BC) in what archaeologists regard as an 'epi-Olmec' phase, when the spark had gone out of Olmec culture and other civilisations – notably Izapa – were also leaving their mark here. Most of the finds are from this later period.

At Tres Zapotes in 1939, Matthew Stirling, the first great Olmec excavator, unearthed part of a chunk of basalt with an epi-Olmec were-jaguar carving on one side and, on the other, a series of bars and dots apparently giving part of a date in the Mayan Long Count dating system. Stirling decoded the date as 3 September 32 BC – which would mean that the Olmecs had preceded the Maya, who until then were believed to have been Mexico's earliest civilisation. Much controversy followed but other finds over the next decades supported Stirling's discovery. In 1969 a local farmer came across the rest of the stone, now called Stele C, which bore the missing part of Stirling's date.

Museum

Tres Zapotes' museum is open daily from 9 am to 5 pm. Entry is 7 pesos (free on Sunday and holidays). The objects are arranged on a cross-shaped platform. On the far side is the Tres Zapotes head, dating from about 100 BC, which was the first Olmec head to be discovered in modern times; it was found by a hacienda worker in 1858. Opposite the head, the biggest piece is Stele A, with three human figures in the mouth of a jaguar. This originally stood on its end. To the right of Stele A are what may have been a sculpture of a captive with hands tied behind its back ('fingers' are visible at the base) and another piece with a toad carved on one side and a skull on the other. Beyond Stele A is an altar or throne carved with the upturned face of a woman, and beyond that, in the corner, the less interesting part of the famous Stele C (the part with the date is in the Museo Nacional de Antropología but there's a photo of it on the wall here). The museum attendant is happy to answer questions (in Spanish).

The site these objects came from is about a km away, though there's little to see. Walk back past the Sitio Olmeca taxi stand, turn left at the end of the road past the small village square and go over the bridge and along the road.

Getting There & Away

The road to Tres Zapotes goes south-west from Santiago Tuxtla (a 'Zona Arqueológica' sign points the way from highway 180). Eight km down this road, you fork right onto a decent dirt track for the last 15 km to Tres Zapotes village. It comes out at a T-junction next to a taxi stand called Sitio Olmeca. From here you walk to the left, then turn left again to reach the museum.

Transportes Los Tuxtlas runs buses to Tres Zapotes from San Andrés Tuxtla (one hour)

via Santiago Tuxtla (30 minutes), supposedly every 1½ hours from 5.30 am to 2.30 pm, but the schedule is unreliable. The last buses back supposedly leave Tres Zapotes at 1.30 and 3.30 pm.

The alternative is to take a green-and-white taxi from Santiago Tuxtla, for 4 pesos if it's going colectivo or 20 pesos if you have it all to yourself. Taxis leave from the Sitio Puente Real, on the far side of the pedestrian bridge at the foot of Zaragoza, the street going downhill beside the Santiago Tuxtla museum.

SAN ANDRÉS TUXTLA
• pop: 80,000 • alt: 365 metres

San Andrés is in the centre of the Los Tuxtlas area, surrounded by attractive countryside producing maize, bananas, beans, sugar cane, fruit and cattle; and tobacco, which is turned into cigars (puros) in the town. There are some scenic attractions nearby, including the dormant San Martín volcano, 1748 metres high.

Orientation & Information

The ADO (1st-class) bus station is a km north-west of the plaza on Juárez, which runs downhill to the centre. The AU (2nd-class) bus station is also on Juárez, closer to the town centre. The cathedral overlooks the north of the plaza, with the Palacio Municipal on the west side, and a Banamex on the south side which changes travellers' cheques and has an ATM. Most places to stay and eat are within a few blocks of the plaza, and the market is three blocks west. The post office is on Lafragua: head down 20 de Noviembre directly across the plaza from the Palacio Municipal and follow it around to the left.

Things to See

The **Laguna Encantada** (Enchanted Lagoon), a lake with the odd habit of rising in dry weather and falling when it rains, occupies a small volcanic crater three km north-east of San Andrés. A dirt road goes there but there are no buses.

Twelve km from San Andrés, a 242-step staircase leads down to the 50-metre-high,

40-metre-wide **Salto de Eyipantla** waterfall. Transportes Los Tuxtlas buses (2 pesos) run about half-hourly to Eyipantla, taking 40 minutes. The route follows highway 180 east for four km to Sihuapan, then turns right down a dirt road.

At Cerro del Gallo near **Matacapan**, just east of Sihuapan, is an early Classic (300-600 AD) pyramid in Teotihuacán style. It may have been on the route to Kaminaljuyú in Guatemala, the farthest-flung Teotihuacán outpost.

Places to Stay

For the cheapest hotels turn left when you hit the plaza from Juárez, then take the second right, Pino Suárez. The *Hotel Catedral* (☎ (294) 2-02-37), on the corner of Pino Suárez and Bocanegra, has clean singles/doubles with fan, private bath and 24-hour hot water for 22/27 pesos, or 33 pesos with two beds. A bit further up the street, the *Hotel Figueroa* (☎ (294) 2-02-57) has helpful staff and clean rooms with private bath for 20 to 25 pesos, plus 5 pesos for parking – some rooms are better than others.

Hotel San Andrés (☎ (294) 2-04-22), at Madero 6 (turn right when you hit the zócalo from Juárez), is fair value, with friendly staff and 31 clean rooms with TV and private bath at 55/70 pesos with fan, or 75/80 pesos with air-con. Some have balconies.

The two top places in town are the 48-room *Hotel Del Parque* (☎ (294) 2-01-98), at Madero 5 on the zócalo, and the *Hotel De Los Pérez* (☎ (294) 2-07-77), at Rascón 2, down the street beside the Del Parque. The newer De Los Pérez is preferable for its clean, sizeable, modern, air-con rooms with TV from 80/100 pesos for singles/doubles. The Del Parque's rooms, also air-con and with TV, are lighter but a little faded, for 75/100 pesos.

Places to Eat

Cafe Winni's, just down Madero from the plaza, has soup at 4 pesos, eggs at 5 pesos, antojitos to 10 pesos and substantial main courses from 12 to 20 pesos. The two *Mariscos Chazaro* places, at Madero 12 just along from the Hotel San Andrés and also on the back street behind the Hotel De Los Pérez, have excellent, fresh seafood dishes like sopa de mariscos and seafood cocktails from 15 to 18 pesos.

The *Hotel Del Parque* restaurant is the social centre of town; its service is professional but the food is nothing inspired (egg dishes 7 pesos; meat, seafood or chicken 20 to 25 pesos). For vaguely Westernised, slightly expensive fare, visit the *Cafetería California* at Rascón 2, beneath the Hotel De Los Pérez. You'll get a respectable burger for 10 to 14 pesos, carrot or other juices for 4 pesos.

Things to Buy

The Santa Lucia factory at Boulevard 5 de Febrero 10 (highway 180), about 200 metres from the top of Juárez, has short, long, fat and thin cigars at factory prices. Even if you don't want to buy, the sights and smells of cigar-making are interesting.

Getting There & Away

Bus San Andrés is the transport centre for Los Tuxtlas, with fairly good bus services in every direction – though many are de paso, with limited seats, so try to book ahead. Transportes Los Tuxtlas buses – old, dirty and slow but often the quickest way of getting to local destinations – leave from the corner of Cabada and Rafael Solana Norte, a block north of the market; they skirt the north side of town on Boulevard 5 de Febrero (highway 180), and you can get on or off at most intersections. Departures from the San Andrés bus stations include:

Acayucan – 95 km, 1½ hours; 20 1st-class buses daily (11 pesos)

Campeche – 770 km, 12½ hours; two 1st-class buses per day (92 pesos)

Catemaco – 12 km, 20 minutes; 2nd-class buses by Transportes Los Tuxtlas every few minutes

Mérida – 1020 km, 15 hours; two 1st-class buses daily (114 pesos)

Mexico City (TAPO) – 550 km, nine hours; ADO deluxe bus at 11 pm (89 pesos) and five 1st-class buses daily (76 pesos)

Puebla – 420 km, seven hours; two 1st-class buses daily (61 pesos)

Santiago Tuxtla – 14 km, 20 minutes; 18 1st-class buses daily (2.50 pesos) and 2nd-class buses by Transportes Los Tuxtlas every few minutes (1.50 pesos)

Veracruz – 155 km, 2¾ hours; 28 1st-class buses daily (19 to 21 pesos)

Villahermosa – 320 km, six hours; seven 1st-class buses daily (39 pesos)

Taxi A taxi to/from Catemaco or Santiago Tuxtla costs about 15 pesos.

CATEMACO
• *pop: 25,000* • *alt: 370 metres*

This small, scruffy town on the western shore of beautiful Laguna Catemaco makes most of its living from fishing and from Mexican tourists who flood in during July and August, and for Christmas, New Year and Semana Santa. The rest of the year it's a quiet, economical place to visit. The annual convention of *brujos* (witch doctors), held on Cerro Mono Blanco (White Monkey Hill) north of Catemaco on the first Friday in March, is becoming more a tourist event than a supernatural one.

Orientation & Information
Catemaco is small and slopes gently down to the lake shore. There is no tourist office. The post office is on Mantilla, just south of the Hotel Los Arcos.

You can change cash and travellers' cheques on weekdays before 11.30 pm at Multibanco Comermex on the zócalo. At a pinch, try at the Hotel Los Arcos, which gives low rates but is open longer hours.

Laguna Catemaco
The lake, surrounded by volcanic hills, is roughly oval and 16 km long. Streams flowing into the lake are the source of Catemaco and Coyame mineral water. **El Tegal** is a grotto topped with a blue cross where the Virgin is believed to have appeared in the 19th century. Further on is **Playa Hermosa**, less a beach than a narrow strip of grey sand where people swim in the slightly murky water, and **Playa Azul**, with an upscale hotel and the trendiest nightspot.

These can be visited in an easy walk east of Catemaco.

The lake has several islands; on the largest, Tenaspi, Olmec sculpture has been found. **Isla de los Monos** (or Isla de los Changos – Monkey Island) has around 60 red-cheeked *Macaca arctoides* monkeys, originally from Thailand. They belong to the University of Veracruz, which uses them for research purposes. Despite pleas from the university for the animals to be left alone, boat operators bring food for them so that tourists can get close-up pictures.

Further around the north shore is the **Parque Ecológico**, where a small piece of rainforest has been preserved. A guided walk in Spanish (5 pesos) on a path through the reserve includes the chance to sample mineral water and test the cosmetic benefits of smearing black mud on your face. Not-so-wild-life includes toucan, monkey, tortoise, pecari (peccary) and mapache (raccoon) enclosures. It's quite interesting, but a bit contrived, like a movie set – *The Last Eden* was filmed here. You can reach the park by road, or by boat.

Festivals
The pretty domed and towered Iglesia del Carmen in Catemaco's zócalo is a pilgrimage centre for a couple of days leading up to 16 July.

Places to Stay
Catemaco has accommodation in all price ranges, but add 30% to 50% at peak periods.

Places to Stay – bottom end
Camping *Restaurant Solotepec* at Playa Hermosa, 1.5 km east of town along the road around the lake, has a small camping area/trailer park close to the water.

Hotels The *Hotel Julita* at Avenida Playa 10, near the waterfront just down from the zócalo, has a few basic but adequate rooms with fan and private bath for 25/40 pesos. The *Hotel Acuario* (☎ (294) 3-04-18), on the zócalo on the corner of Carranza and Boettinger, is good value with comfortable

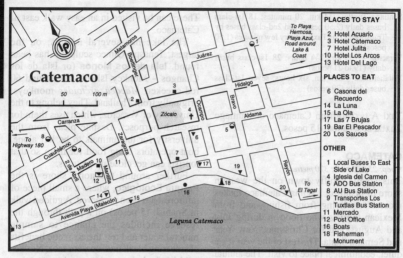

Catemaco

0   50   100 m

To Highway 180

To El Tegal

Laguna Catemaco

PLACES TO STAY
2   Hotel Acuario
3   Hotel Catemaco
7   Hotel Julita
10 Hotel Los Arcos
13 Hotel Del Lago

PLACES TO EAT
6   Casona del Recuerdo
14 La Luna
15 La Ola
17 Las 7 Brujas
19 Bar El Pescador
20 Los Sauces

OTHER
1   Local Buses to East Side of Lake
4   Iglesia del Carmen
5   ADO Bus Station
8   AU Bus Station
9   Transportes Los Tuxtlas Bus Station
11 Mercado
12 Post Office
16 Boats
18 Fisherman Monument

single/double/two-bed rooms with private bath at 20/40/50 pesos. Some rooms are better than others.

Places to Stay – middle

Hotel Los Arcos (☎ (294) 3-00-03), at Madero 7 on the corner of Mantilla, has helpful staff and clean, bright rooms with fans, private baths and wide balconies at 70/80 pesos. The *Hotel Catemaco* (☎ (294) 3-00-45), on the north side of the zócalo, has a restaurant, video bar, small pool and rooms with air-con and TV for 80/90 pesos. The lakefront *Hotel Del Lago* (☎ (294) 3-01-60), on Avenida Playa on the corner of Abasolo, has good, clean, if not very big air-con rooms with TV for 100/150 pesos. There's a restaurant and small pool.

The *Hotel Playa Azul* (☎ (294) 3-00-01), 2.5 km east of town by the lake, has 80 bright, clean, modern rooms, half of them air-con, in single-storey blocks around a garden. Singles/doubles are 150/170 pesos, and there is also a restaurant, volleyball court, boat rental and disco (in season). The lakeside *Hotel La Finca* (☎ (294) 3-03-22), two km out of town on the Acayucan road, has 36 rooms with air-con, balconies and

lake views at 170/190 pesos. A taxi to either place from town costs around 5 pesos.

Places to Eat

The lake provides the specialities here, among them the tegogolo, a lake snail reputed to be an aphrodisiac and best eaten in a sauce of chile, tomato, onion and lime; chipalchole, a soup with shrimp or crab claws; mojarra, a type of perch; and anguilas (eels). Tachogobi is a hot sauce sometimes served on mojarra; eels may come with raisins and hot chile. Many eating places can be depressingly empty out of season, and tend to close early.

The *Hotel Julita* has a good, economical restaurant with filling soups and meat and fish dishes from 18 to 20 pesos. Further east, *Las 7 Brujas* is in an interesting round building and stays open late. The lakeside *Bar El Pescador* and the cheaper *Los Sauces* are also popular restaurants. *La Ola* is a waterfront place west of the centre, with a nice outlook and cool breezes, but the food is not great value. *La Luna*, across the road, may be better.

Near the plaza, the *Hotel Catemaco* restaurant serves quite good food – spaghetti is

15 pesos, chicken and meat dishes 18 to 35 pesos, mojarra en tachogobi 16 pesos. The *Casona del Recuerdo* has delightful balcony tables, friendly service and tasty seafood for 15 to 20 pesos, and its comida corrida is good value at about 12 pesos.

Getting There & Away

Relatively few long-distance buses reach Catemaco, so you may have to travel via San Andrés Tuxtla, 12 km west on highway 180, or Acayucan, 80 km south, and then take more frequent but less comfortable local buses to/from Catemaco. The only 1st-class bus company is ADO, on the corner of Aldama and Bravo. The 2nd-class AU buses go from 2 de Abril just off Carranza. Transportes Los Tuxtlas is on Cuauhtémoc near the corner of 2 de Abril. Departures from Catemaco include:

Acayucan – 80 km, 1¼ hours; 1st-class buses at 4 pm and 9 pm (9 pesos); four 2nd-class buses daily by AU (7 pesos); Transportes Los Tuxtlas buses about every half hour

Mexico City (TAPO) – 565 km, nine hours; 1st-class bus at 9 pm daily (76 pesos) and four 2nd-class buses by AU

San Andrés Tuxtla – 12 km, 20 minutes; four 1st-class buses daily (1.50 pesos); eight 2nd-class buses daily by AU; Transportes Los Tuxtlas buses every few minutes (1.30 pesos)

Santiago Tuxtla – 25 km, 40 minutes; four 1st-class buses daily (3 pesos) and Transportes Los Tuxtlas buses every few minutes (2.50 pesos)

Veracruz – 165 km, three hours; about eight 1st-class buses daily (20 pesos) and frequent Transportes Los Tuxtlas buses (14 pesos)

Villahermosa – 310 km, 5½ hours; one 1st-class bus daily (37 pesos)

Getting Around

Bus To explore the villages and country east of the lake, where the mountain Santa Marta stands out, take a local bus going to Las Margaritas. They leave every hour or two from the corner of Juárez and Rayón.

Boat Boats do trips on the lake from the moorings just down from the zócalo. The posted price for a trip around the lake's main attractions with up to six people is 125 pesos, or 25 pesos per person if you go as an individual.

THE COAST NEAR CATEMACO

About four km north-east of Catemaco there's a fork: the road right follows the lake around past Coyame; the road left is sealed and scenic as it goes over the hills to **Sontecomapan**, 15 km from Catemaco. There's a basic hotel here, and a couple of restaurants, and you can hire boats for trips on the lagoon. After Sontecomapan the road is much rougher as it continues to a little-visited stretch of the Gulf Coast. This is mainly ranchland – horses are a common form of transport – and green hills roll right down to the shore. Be warned that people camping on beaches here have been robbed.

About eight km from Sontecomapan, near La Palma, an even rougher track goes right to El Real and La Barra, near the mouth of the lagoon. There are isolated beaches but no facilities. About five km past La Palma, a sign points down another rough side road to Playa Escondida. This takes you past the long grey-sand beach of **Jicacal**, with a small, poor fishing village and one restaurant, then up to a forested headland where the *Hotel Playa Escondida* stands, two or three km from the main 'road'. This unassuming establishment has basic rooms (shower but no hot water) for 40/50 pesos, great views and a small restaurant. **Playa Escondida** itself is another km down a steep path from the hotel.

Back on the 'road' you pass a biological research station next to one of the few tracts of unspoiled rainforest left on the Gulf Coast. Station staff may be able to point you to paths through the forest. A turnoff here leads to pretty Laguna Escondida, hidden in the mountains. The end of the road is at **Montepío**, where there's a nice beach at the rivermouth, a couple of places to eat and the *Posada San José*, with six comfortable rooms for 45/65 pesos.

Getting There & Away

Every half-hour or so between 6 am and 3 or 4 pm, *camionetas* (pick-up trucks with hard benches in the back and crammed seats in the cab) go from Catemaco to Montepío. The 35-km trip, with numerous stops, takes 1½ hours and costs 8 pesos. They leave from the corner of Revolución and the Playa Azul road – from the north-east corner of the plaza, walk five blocks east and six blocks north, and look for vehicles congregating.

ACAYUCAN

Acayucan is a road-junction town where highway 180 (between Veracruz and Villahermosa) meets highway 185 (which goes south across the Isthmus of Tehuantepec to the Pacific coast). You may have to change buses here but try to avoid it – most buses are de paso, the 1st-class bus station is not a great setup (no left-luggage storage) and the 2nd-class buses go from offices scattered in surrounding streets. The town itself has nothing of interest, but archaeology fans might want to seek out the Olmec site of San Lorenzo, 35 km to the south-east.

Orientation & Information

The bus stations are on the east side of town – to reach the central plaza, walk uphill through (or past) the market to Avenida Miguel Hidalgo, turn left and walk six blocks. The plaza has a modern church on the east side and the town hall on the west. Bancomer and Banamex, both near the plaza, have ATMs and change travellers' cheques.

Places to Stay & Eat

The *Hotel Ritz* (☎ (924) 5-00-24), between the bus stations and the central plaza at Hidalgo 7, is hardly ritzy, with grubby singles/doubles at 30/40 pesos. On the south side of the plaza, the *Hotel Joalicia* (☎ (924) 5-08-77) is good value with clean, sizeable rooms for 35/45 pesos with fan, and from 60 pesos with air-con. The restaurant isn't bad either. The top place is the *Hotel Kinaku* (☎ (924) 5-04-10) at Ocampo Sur 7, a block east of the plaza, where spacious, comfortable rooms with air-con and TV cost 115/137 pesos, and the restaurant, open from 7 am to 11 pm, is the smartest place in town. The *La Parrilla* restaurant, on the plaza, has tasty snacks from 4 to 10 pesos and substantial main courses at about 20 pesos.

Getting There & Away

Most 1st-class buses are de paso, so you usually have to wait till a bus comes in before you can get a ticket out. Departures include:

Catemaco – 80 km, 1¼ hours; two 1st-class buses daily by ADO (9 pesos); seven 2nd-class buses daily by AU (7 pesos); frequent Transportes Los Tuxtlas buses

Juchitán – 195 km, three hours; six 1st-class buses daily by Cristóbal Colón (27 pesos) and 2nd-class buses by Sur

Mexico City (TAPO) – 750 km, 11 hours; deluxe buses by Cristóbal Colón (100 pesos); nine 1st-class buses daily (81 to 89 pesos); 2nd-class buses by AU

San Andrés Tuxtla – 95 km, 1½ hours; 15 1st-class buses daily by ADO (12 pesos); several 2nd-class buses daily by AU; frequent buses by Transportes Los Tuxtlas

Santiago Tuxtla – 110 km, two hours; two 1st-class buses daily by ADO (13 pesos) and hourly Transportes Los Tuxtlas buses

Tapachula – 550 km, nine hours; a few 1st-class buses daily by Cristóbal Colón (57 pesos) and 2nd-class buses by Sur (47 pesos)

Tuxtla Gutiérrez – 500 km, eight hours; one 1st-class bus each daily by Cristóbal Colón and ADO (55 pesos)

Veracruz – 250 km, five hours; about 15 1st-class buses daily (33 pesos)

Villahermosa – 225 km, 3½ hours; several 1st-class buses daily (30 pesos) and 2nd-class buses by AU

SAN LORENZO

The first of the two great Olmec ceremonial centres, which flourished from about 1200 to 900 BC, is about 35 km south-east of Acayucan. The extraordinary main structure is a platform about 50 metres high, 1.25 km long and 700 metres wide, with ridges jutting from its sides which may have been meant to produce a bird or animal-shaped ground plan.

Eight Olmec heads have been found here, and other large stone objects have been detected underground, but most of the main finds are in museums elsewhere. Some very heavy stone thrones, with figures of rulers carved in the side, were also found. Tools made from the black volcanic glass, obsidian, were imported from Guatemala or the highlands of Mexico, and basalt for the heads and thrones was transported from the Sierra de los

Tuxtlas. Such wide contacts, and the organisation involved in building the site, show how powerful the rulers of San Lorenzo were. Other features include an elaborate stone-pipe drainage system, and evidence of cannibalism. During its dramatic destruction, which occurred around 900 BC, most of the big carvings were mutilated, dragged on to the ridges and covered with earth.

Getting There & Away

From Acayucan take a bus to Texistepec (south of the Minatitlán road), then another to San Lorenzo, a total journey of 1½ to two hours. San Lorenzo proper is three km south-west of the village of Tenochtitlán. Finds

have also been made at Tenochtitlán and at Potrero Nuevo, three km south-east of San Lorenzo.

MINATITLÁN & COATZACOALCOS

These two towns, 50 and 70 km respectively east of Acayucan, are now bypassed by highway 180. They mushroomed into transport and refining centres of nearly half a million people each in the oil boom of the late 1970s. The area is an industrial wilderness, though Coatzacoalcos retains a pleasant central plaza, and the bridge over the Río Coatzacoalcos is impressive. There are plenty of hotels here for the oil people but nothing to make anyone else want to stay.

Oaxaca State

The rugged southern state of Oaxaca ('wa-HA-ka') reaches to within just 250 km of Mexico City but, divided from central Mexico by ranks of hard-to-penetrate mountains, remains a whole world away in atmosphere. It enjoys a slower, sunnier existence and a somehow magical quality that has something to do with the rocky dry landscape, the remoteness, the bright southern light, the sparse population, and the high proportion of Indians, who are the driving force behind Oaxaca state's especially fine handicrafts.

Oaxaca city has become a big travel destination, but remains beautiful, lively, artistic and colonial. Around the city, in the Central Valleys of Oaxaca, are thriving village markets and spectacular ruins of pre-Hispanic Indian towns like Monte Albán and Yagul. On the Oaxaca coast, Mexico's newest mega-resort is growing up on the lovely Bahías de Huatulco. Puerto Escondido and Puerto Ángel are older beach spots which will probably always remain small-scale and more laid-back.

There's also enough Indian-inhabited back country, as far from Oaxaca city in culture and travelling time as Oaxaca is from Mexico City, to offer a lifetime's exploring – though initially you may get a cautious reception since the people have been driven to these retreats by centuries of conflict.

HISTORY
Zapotecs & Mixtecs
Pre-Hispanic Oaxaca traded with other parts of Mexico, but until the Aztecs arrived in the 15th century Oaxaca's cultures were left more or less undisturbed, to reach heights rivalling those of central Mexico.

The three Central Valleys have always been the hub of life in Oaxaca. Building began at the hilltop site of Monte Albán, near the meeting of the three valleys, about 500 BC. This became the centre of the Zapotec culture, which extended its control over the

Central Valleys and other parts of Oaxaca by conquest and peaked between 250 and 750 AD. Monte Albán grew into a town of perhaps 25,000 people, but declined suddenly, and by about 750 AD, along with many other Zapotec sites in the Central Valleys, was deserted.

From about 1200 those that remained came under the growing dominance of the Mixtecs, renowned potters and metalsmiths from the north-west uplands of modern Oaxaca. Mixtec and Zapotec cultures became entangled in the Central Valleys before they fell, like the north-west, to the Aztecs in the mid-15th and early 16th centuries, and became tribute-payers.

Colonial Era

The Spaniards received a very hostile reception in Oaxaca, sending at least four expeditions before founding the city of Oaxaca in 1529. Cortés donated large parts of the Central Valleys to himself and was officially named Marqués del Valle de Oaxaca. The Indian population slumped disastrously. The Central Valleys, which had about 150,000 Indians in 1568, had only 40,000 to 50,000 just 70 years later. Rebellions continued into the 20th century but the different Indian peoples rarely united to form a serious threat.

Juárez & Díaz

Benito Juárez, the great reforming leader on the liberal side in mid-19th-century Mexico, was a Zapotec. He served two terms as Oaxaca state governor, opening new village schools and cutting bureaucracy, between 1848 and his election as national president in 1861.

Juárez appointed Porfirio Díaz, son of a Oaxaca horse trainer, as state governor in 1862. Díaz, rebelling against Juárez' presidency in 1871, went onto control Mexico with an iron fist from 1877 to 1910. While his rule kept the peace and brought the country into the industrial age, it fostered corruption, repression, foreign ownership of resources and, eventually, the revolution. In Valle Nacional in northern Oaxaca, for instance, tobacco planters set up virtual slave plantations, most of whose 15,000 workers, according to the American writer J K Turner who visited them, had to be replaced annually because of deaths from disease, beating or starvation.

20th Century

During the Mexican Revolution a group of *jefes serranos* (leaders from the hills) won control of Oaxaca state in 1913 and decided to dissociate Oaxaca from the national factions, declaring self-government. Though Oaxaca city was taken by the liberal Constitutionalists in 1916, the jefes serranos carried on fighting and in 1920 they allied with Alvaro Obregón to help depose the national Constitutionalist government.

About 300 ejidos were set up in the 1930s, but land ownership is still a source of friction today. With little industry, Oaxaca is one of Mexico's poorest states, many peasants being forced to seek work in the big cities or the USA; the situation is made worse in some areas by deforestation and erosion. An EZLN uprising in Chiapas in 1994 led to rumours of a similar revolutionary movement in Oaxaca. Tourism is increasingly useful as a contribution to the economy, particularly in Oaxaca city and some places on the coast.

GEOGRAPHY & CLIMATE

At 94,000 sq km, Oaxaca is Mexico's fifth-biggest state. Its western two-thirds are rugged and mountainous; the eastern part of the state lies on the hot, low-lying Isthmus of Tehuantepec, Mexico's narrow 'waist'. Oaxaca also has a thin plain along the Pacific coast, and a low-lying north-central region bordering Veracruz.

The western mountains are basically two ranges. The Sierra Madre del Sur (average height 2000 metres) enters Oaxaca from the west and stretches along the coast. The Sierra Madre de Oaxaca (average height 2500 metres) runs down from Mexico's central volcanic belt. The two ranges meet roughly in the centre of the state. Between them, converging at the city of Oaxaca, lie the three

OAXACA STATE

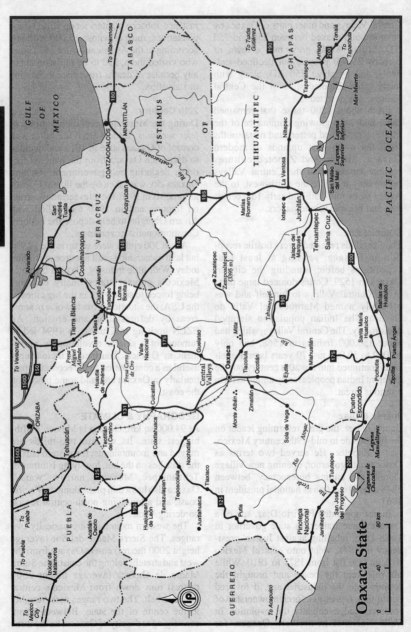

OAXACA STATE

Oaxaca State

Central Valleys. The highest peak is Zempoaltépetl (3395 metres) near Zacatepec.

The Central Valleys are warm and dry. Temperatures range from the low teens on winter nights to the low 30s (°C) during the day in summer. Most of the annual 600 mm of rain falls from June to September. On the coast and in the low-lying areas it's hotter and a bit wetter.

PEOPLE

Oaxaca's population of 3.02 million includes about a million Indians of at least 14 different peoples. Each people has its own language with perhaps three-quarters of Oaxaca Indians speaking Spanish. Some Indian ways are buckling under the pressure of change – colourful costumes, for instance, are seen less and less in Oaxaca city and the coastal resorts – but there's a strong Indian presence noticeable in handicrafts, markets and festivals as well as dress.

Indian land and housing are often the poorest in the state. Typically they own land communally and share work. Indian groups' relations with each other, and with the mestizos who dominate property, business and politics, are often strained. When Indian organisations campaign for land rights, the reaction of the powers-that-be can be literally murderous.

Some 500,000 Zapotecs live mainly in and around the Central Valleys and on the Isthmus of Tehuantepec. You're sure to come into contact with them, though you may not realise it since there are few obvious signs to identify them. Most are farmers, though they're also involved in trading their produce, which includes handicrafts and mezcal. Many have to emigrate temporarily for work.

The Mixtecs are Oaxaca's other major Indian people. Some 500,000 of them are spread around the mountainous borders of Oaxaca, Guerrero and Puebla, with over two-thirds in western Oaxaca. The two other most numerous Indian peoples are the 100,000 or so Mazatecs in the far north, who retain much of their traditional dress and belief in a magical and ritual world; and the 80,000 Mixes in the isolated highlands north-east of the Central Valleys.

Another group you may well see in Oaxaca city, since the women, wearing bright red huipiles, populate craft markets there, are the Triquis from western Oaxaca. They are perhaps only 12,000 strong.

Oaxaca City

• pop: 220,000 • alt: 1550 metres

The state's capital and only sizeable city is a Spanish-built place of narrow, straight streets liberally sprinkled with lovely colonial buildings. What's special is its atmosphere – at once relaxed and energetic, remote and cosmopolitan. The dry mountain heat, the city's manageable scale, its old buildings, plazas and cafés help slow the pace of life. At the same time the meeting here of diverse Oaxacan, Mexican and international cultures creates a current of excitement. There's rarely a dull moment in Oaxaca. Head for the zócalo to get a first taste of the atmosphere.

Experiencing Oaxaca is a matter of giving yourself time to ramble and see what markets, handicrafts, cafés and festivities you come across. There are also many fascinating places within day-trip distance in the Central Valleys, notably the ruins at Monte Albán, Mitla, Yagul and Cuilapan, and the village markets and craft centres.

Accommodation in Oaxaca is relatively inexpensive. Foreign and Mexican tourists are numerous, but Oaxaca accommodates them with minimal impact. The unwelcome changes that have come to the city – notably the traffic in parts of the centre – are part of changes in Mexican life in general.

History

The Aztecs' settlement here was called Huaxyacac (Place of Gourds), from which 'Oaxaca' is derived. The first Spanish settlement was 1.5 km north-east of the modern centre, but after several Indian uprisings, a new town was laid out around the existing zócalo in 1529. First called Antequera (after a city in Andalucía, Spain) its name was

OAXACA STATE

changed to Oaxaca in 1532. It quickly became the most important town in southern Mexico. The religious orders based here played a big part in pacifying the region's Indians by relatively humane conduct.

Eighteenth-century Oaxaca grew rich on exports of cochineal, a red dye from tiny insects. The boom ended in 1783 when the Spanish crown banned debt slavery, by which many of the 30,000 peasants producing cochineal were bound to traders in the city. But Oaxaca continued to thrive as a textile centre: by 1796 it was probably the third-biggest city in New Spain, with about 20,000 people (including 600 clergy) and 800 cotton looms. The city's elite was opposed to the 19th-century independence movement.

An earthquake in 1854 destroyed much of the city. Under the presidency of Porfirio Díaz Oaxaca began to grow again; in the 1890s its population passed 30,000. During the revolution, the Establishment was again conservative. The decade of turmoil cut the population from over 35,000 to under 28,000. An earthquake in 1931 left 70% of the city uninhabitable. Its major expansion has come in the past two decades, with tourism and other new industries encouraging migration from the countryside.

Orientation

The centre of Oaxaca is the zócalo and the adjoining Alameda plaza in front of the cathedral. Streets in the central area usually change their names when they pass the north-east corner of the cathedral. Calle Alcalá, running north from this corner to the Iglesia de Santo Domingo, a famous Oaxaca landmark, is mostly pedestrian-only.

In general the few blocks north of the zócalo are smarter, cleaner and less traffic-infested than those to the south, especially the south-west, where cheap hotels and some markets congregate.

Highway 190 from Mexico City winds around the slopes of the Cerro del Fortín in the north-west of the city, then runs eastward across the north of the city as Calzada Niños Héroes de Chapultepec. The 1st-class bus

station is beside this road, a 1.75-km walk north-east of the zócalo. The 2nd-class bus station is almost a km west of the centre, near the main market.

Information

The *Oaxaca Times*, a free monthly paper for tourists in English, is useful. You can pick it up at Plaza Alcalá on the corner of Alcalá and Bravo.

Tourist Offices Oaxaca has two major tourist offices. It depends who's on duty but the information from the Palacio Municipal office (☎ (951) 6-01-23), on the corner of García Vigil and Independencia facing the Alameda, is perhaps more reliable than that from the state tourist office (☎ (951) 6-48-28) on the corner of 5 de Mayo and Morelos. The Palacio Municipal office is open from 9 am to 3 pm and 6 to 8 pm daily; the state tourist office is open from 8 am to 8 pm daily.

Money Most banks open from 9 am to 1 pm Monday to Friday, with foreign exchange closing at 11.30 am, but bank queues are long and slow. Unless you can use an ATM (Bancomer at García Vigil 202 and Banamex at Hidalgo 821, both about a block from the zócalo, have them), the lower rates of exchange at casas de cambio are a bargain for the time they save – but beware of attempts to short-change you. Two near the zócalo are Interdisa, a few steps up Valdivieso from the north-east corner of the zócalo, are open from 8 am to 8 pm Monday to Saturday and 9 am to 5 pm Sunday, and La Estrella at Alcalá 201, is open from 9 am to 8 pm, Monday to Saturday only.

The American Express representative is Viajes Micsa (☎ 6-27-00) at Valdivieso 2.

Post & Telecommunications The main post office, open Monday to Friday from 8 am to 7 pm and Saturday 9 am to 1 pm, is on the Alameda, beside Independencia. Viajes Micsa (see Money, above) runs an American Express client mail service.

You can send and receive telegrams and faxes at the Telégrafos office on Independencia, next door to the post office and open the same hours.

There are Ladatel phones outside the Telmex office at Morelos 103 and at the north-west and south-west corners of the zócalo; one of those at the north-west corner takes credit cards. Computel offices, with Lada casetas and fax service, are in the 2nd-class bus station and on Trujano between J P García and 20 de Noviembre. The latter is open daily from 7 am to midnight.

Foreign Consulates The US consular agent (☎ (951) 4-30-54), open Monday to Friday from 9 am to 2 pm, is at Alcalá 201. You can find the Canadian (☎ (951) 3-37-77), Italian (☎ (951) 5-31-15), German and British representatives (both ☎ (951) 6-56-00) all at Hidalgo 817/5. The French representative (☎ (951) 6-35-22) is at Guerrero 101.

Laundry Superlavandería Hidalgo on the corner of Hidalgo and J P García, and Lavandería Automatica at 20 de Noviembre 605, both charge 15.50 pesos for a same-day service wash of up to 3.5 kg. Opening hours are 9 am to 8 pm Monday to Saturday.

Bookshops & Libraries The best Spanish bookshop is Proveedora Escolar on the corner of Reforma and Independencia. Its local history, archaeology and anthropology section, upstairs, is excellent. But you'll find more English books in Librería Universitaria, at Guerrero 108 just off the zócalo, or El Desvan bookshop at 5 de Mayo 408-5. The regional and Rufino Tamayo museums also sell books.

The Biblioteca Circulante de Oaxaca (Oaxaca Lending Library) at Alcalá 305 has quite a big collection of books and magazines in English and Spanish, many of them on Oaxaca and Mexico. It's open from 10 am to 1 pm and 4 to 7 pm Monday to Friday and 10 am to 1 pm on Saturday. For a joining fee of 50 pesos plus a 50-peso deposit, you can borrow books. The library also has a useful bulletin board advertising accommodation etc. The Museo de Arte Contemporáneo de Oaxaca at Alcalá 202 has an excellent

Spanish-language arts library which visitors can consult. The city's public library is also on Alcalá, on the corner of Morelos.

Zócalo & Alameda

The zócalo is the geographical and social heart of Oaxaca. Shady, traffic-free and lined with cafés and restaurants, it's the perfect place to relax and watch the city go by. The adjacent Alameda, also traffic-free but without the cafés, is another popular local gathering place.

The south side of the zócalo is occupied by the **Palacio de Gobierno**, whose stairway has a mural depicting Oaxacan history. Its centre panel is devoted mainly to the 19th-century reformers, notably Juárez (shown with his wife Margarita) and Morelos. Porfirio Díaz appears below in blue. At bottom right, Guerrero's death at Cuilapan is shown. The left wall shows ancient Mitla while the right wall is dominated by women, notably Juana Inés de la Cruz, the 17th-century nun and love poet.

Oaxaca's **cathedral**, begun in 1553 and finished (after several earthquakes) in the 18th century, stands on the north side of the zócalo, partly behind the Hotel Marqués del Valle. Its main (west) façade on the Alameda has some fine baroque carving.

Buildings near the Zócalo

Colonial churches with fine carved façades are **La Compañía** (by the south-west corner of the zócalo) and the popular **San Juan de Dios** on the corner of Aldama and 20 de Noviembre. San Juan de Dios, which dates from 1526 and is the oldest church in Oaxaca, has canvases by the famous 18th-century Oaxacan artist Miguel Cabrera. Carvings on **San Agustín**, on Guerrero 1½ blocks east of the zócalo, show scenes from the saint's life. The 1903 **Teatro Macedonio Alcalá** on the corner of 5 de Mayo and Independencia is in the French style fashionable under Porfirio Díaz. It has a marble stairway and a five-tier auditorium holding 1300 people. The 17th-century baroque **Templo de San Felipe Neri**, two blocks west of the cathedral on Independencia, is

OAXACA STATE

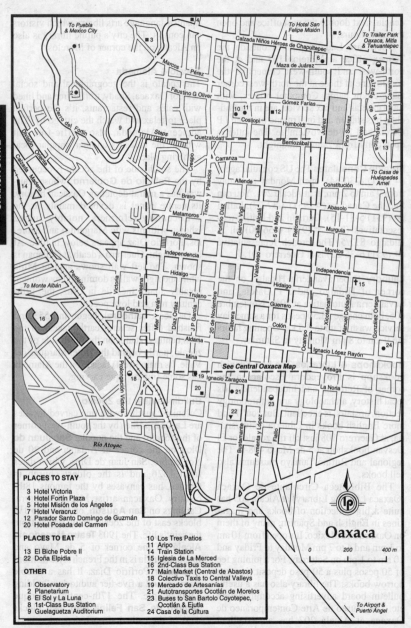

Oaxaca

0   200   400 m

PLACES TO STAY

3 Hotel Victoria
4 Hotel Fortín Plaza
5 Hotel Misión de los Ángeles
7 Hotel Veracruz
12 Parador Santo Domingo de Guzmán
20 Hotel Posada del Carmen

PLACES TO EAT

13 El Biche Pobre II
22 Doña Elpidia

OTHER

1 Observatory
2 Planetarium
6 El Sol y La Luna
8 1st-Class Bus Station
9 Guelaguetza Auditorium
10 Los Tres Patios
11 Aripo
14 Train Station
15 Iglesia de La Merced
16 2nd-Class Bus Station
17 Main Market (Central de Abastos)
18 Colectivo Taxis to Central Valleys
19 Mercado de Artesanías
21 Autotransportes Ocotlán de Morelos
23 Buses to San Bartolo Coyotepec,
    Ocotlán & Ejutla
24 Casa de la Cultura

To Airport &
Puerto Ángel

Oaxaca State
Top Left: Pre-Hispanic sculpture, Oaxaca city (PW)
Top Right: Cemetery, Puerto Ángel (DT)
Bottom: Façade, Oaxaca city (PW)

Oaxaca State
Top: Monastery church, Coixtlahuaca (JN); Playa del Panteón, Puerto Ángel (JN)
Bottom: Panel at Monte Albán (TW); Iglesia de Santo Domingo, Oaxaca city (PW)

where Benito Juárez and Margarita Maza, daughter of the family for whom his sister had been a servant, were married in 1843.

Calle Alcalá

Alcalá has been closed to traffic, and its stone buildings cleaned up and restored, to make a fine walking route from the city centre to the Iglesia de Santo Domingo. Tourist-oriented shops and restaurants are dotted along the street but are in keeping with its colonial appearance.

The **Museo de Arte Contemporáneo de Oaxaca** is housed in the fine colonial Casa de Cortés at Alcalá 202. Permanent displays include the work of five famous Oaxacan artists – the great Rufino Tamayo, a Oaxaca-born Zapotec whose colours often seem suffused with the bright light of this southern region, along with Francisco Gutiérrez, Rodolfo Nieto, Francisco Toledo and Rodolfo Morales. There are also temporary exhibitions, other cultural events, a good library, and a pleasant courtyard café out the back. The museum is open from 10.30 am to 8 pm, Wednesday to Monday. Entrance is by donation.

Iglesia de Santo Domingo

Santo Domingo, four blocks north of the cathedral, is the most splendid of Oaxaca's churches. Built mainly between 1570 and the early 17th century, it was the church of the city's Dominican monastery. The finest artisans were brought from Puebla and elsewhere to help create it. Like other large buildings in this earthquake-prone region, it has immensely thick stone walls. During the 19th-century wars and anticlerical movements it was used as a stable.

Amid the fine carving on the baroque façade, the figure holding a church is Santo Domingo de Guzmán, the 13th-century Spanish monk who founded the Dominican order, with its emphasis on study and teaching of the holy writ, and strict vows of poverty, chastity and obedience. In Mexico the Dominicans gave the Indians some protection from the worst excesses of other colonists.

The church is usually locked from 1 to 4 pm. The interior, lavishly ornamented in gilded and coloured stucco, has a magically warm glow during candlelit evening masses. Just inside the main door, on the ceiling, is an elaborate family tree of Santo Domingo de Guzmán. The 18th-century Capilla de la Virgen del Rosario (Rosary Chapel) on the south side is a profusion of yet more gilt.

Museo Regional de Oaxaca

The highlight of the Museo Regional de Oaxaca, housed in the beautiful green stone cloister attached to Santo Domingo, is the Mixtec treasure from Tomb Seven at Monte Albán. This and other archaeological sections make most sense if you visit them after seeing some sites in the Central Valleys. All explanatory matter is in Spanish and there are no on-the-spot guides. The museum is open from 10 am to 6 pm Tuesday to Saturday, 10 am to 5 pm on Sunday. Entry is 13 pesos (free on Sunday and holidays).

The Mixtec trove – on the museum's lower floor – dates from the mid-14th century when the Mixtecs reused an old Zapotec tomb at Monte Albán to bury one of their kings and his sacrificed servants. With the bodies they placed a hoard of beautifully worked silver, turquoise, coral, jade, amber, jet, pearls, finely carved jaguar and eagle bone, and above all, gold. It was discovered in 1932 by Alfonso Caso. Other sections of the museum cover the history of Oaxaca state since the Spanish conquest, the state's Indian peoples, its archaeology and the history of the Dominican order.

Centro Cultural Santo Domingo

In 1993 former monastery buildings and land behind Santo Domingo, which had been in military use for over a century, were handed over to the Oaxaca state government. The site is being turned into a cultural centre with a Oaxacan botanical garden, a regional plastic arts school and added space for the regional museum.

Instituto de Artes Gráficas de Oaxaca

The Graphic Arts Institute at Alcalá 507, almost opposite Santo Domingo, has changing exhibitions of graphic art in a beautiful

OAXACA STATE

Benito Juárez

Juárez trained for the priesthood but abandoned it for law. He worked as a lawyer for poor villagers and became a member of the Oaxaca city council, then of the Oaxaca state government. From 1848 to 1852 he was the Oaxaca state governor, pursuing liberal policies such as opening schools and cutting bureaucracy. Exiled by the conservative national government in 1853, Juárez returned to Mexico in the 1855 Revolution of Ayutla, which ousted General Santa Anna, and became justice minister in a new liberal national government. His Ley (Law) Juárez, transferring the trials of soldiers and priests charged with civil crimes to ordinary civil courts, was the first of the Reform laws which sought to break the power of the Church. They provoked the Reform War of 1858 to 1861 in which the liberals, after setbacks, defeated the conservatives.

Juárez was elected national president in 1861 but had only been in office a few months when the French, supported by many conservatives and clergy, invaded Mexico and forced him into exile again. In 1866, with US support, he returned and ousted the French and their puppet emperor Maximilian. One of his main political achievements was to make primary education theoretically free and compulsory. He died in 1872, a year after being elected to his fourth presidential term. Countless statues and streets, schools and plazas named after him preserve his memory, and his maxim *El respeto al derecho ajeno es la paz* (Respect for the rights of others is peace) is widely quoted. ■

colonial house donated by the artist Francisco Toledo. Opening hours are 10.30 am to 8 pm daily except Tuesday. Donations are requested when you enter.

Museo Casa de Juárez

The Juárez House Museum, at García Vigil 609 opposite the Templo del Carmen Alto, is where Benito Juárez found work as a boy. A Zapotec with only a few words of Spanish, he came to Oaxaca in 1818 from the village of Guelatao, 60 km to the north. His employer Antonio Salanueva, a bookbinder, spotted the boy's potential and helped pay for an education he otherwise might not have received.

The house shows how the early-19th-century Oaxaca middle class lived. The binding workshop is preserved, along with pictures and a death mask of Juárez, some of his correspondence and other documents. The house was closed for restoration when we were last in town. Check for current opening hours with the tourist office.

Museo Rufino Tamayo

This museum in a fine old house at Morelos 503, donated to Oaxaca by the artist Rufino Tamayo, focuses on the aesthetic qualities of pre-Hispanic artefacts and is arranged to trace artistic developments in the pre-conquest era. It's strong on the Preclassic era and lesser known civilisations like Veracruz. Hours are from 10 am to 2 pm and 4 to 7 pm Monday and Wednesday to Saturday, 10 am to 3 pm Sunday. Admission is 10 pesos.

Basílica de La Soledad

The 17th-century La Soledad church, five blocks west of the Alameda along Independencia, is much revered because it contains the image of Oaxaca's patron saint, the Virgen de la Soledad (Virgin of Solitude). The church, with a rich baroque façade, stands where the image is said to have miraculously appeared in a donkey-pack. Today the image is adorned with a two-kg gold crown, 600 diamonds and a huge pearl. The adjoining convent buildings contain a religious museum.

Cerro del Fortín

This wooded hill overlooking the city from the north-west is a great place to escape the city noise and smells, with fine views and pleasant walking. From the large open-air Guelaguetza auditorium just above the highway that winds around the middle slopes, a quiet road leads up to the Cerro del Fortín observatory, with a track branching to the Nundehui planetarium. On foot you can reach the hill by the Escalera del Fortín, a long stairway climbing up from Crespo. It's about two km, uphill all the way, from the zócalo to the observatory. Beyond the observatory, a foot trail leads to the top of the hill, marked by a cross, 20 to 30 minutes' walk further up.

Language Courses

Language students we have met from the Instituto Cultural Oaxaca (☎ (951) 5-34-04), at Juárez 909 on the corner of Calzada Niños Héroes de Chapultepec, seemed to have a good time and make friends as well as improve their Spanish, though some recent students have expressed less satisfaction. Twelve four-week courses, with six hours' tuition (including craft workshops) five days a week, are run each year but it's usually possible to start any Monday. The fee for four weeks is 1200 pesos. The classes have been accepted for credit by some US universities. For more information, write to Lic. Lucero Topete, Instituto Cultural Oaxaca, Apartado Postal 340, Oaxaca, Oaxaca 68000.

The Instituto de Comunicación y Cultura (☎ (951) 6-34-43), upstairs in the Plaza Alcalá at Alcalá 307 on the corner of Bravo, offers three hours' small-class tuition, Monday to Friday, for 300 pesos a week or 1050 pesos a month. Classes can start any Monday. Other places to ask about classes are the Language Centre of the University of Oaxaca on Burgoa, between Armenta y López and Bustamante, and the Biblioteca Circulante de Oaxaca at Alcalá 305. Private tutors are fairly easy to find.

Schools can usually arrange family or hotel accommodation for students. Staying with a family costs between 35 and 60 pesos a night, depending on how many meals are provided.

Organised Tours

If you're short of time, several companies offer day tours in the city and Central Valleys. Three with a wide choice of itineraries are Viajes Turísticos Mitla (☎ 4-31-52), in the Hotel Mesón del Ángel at Mina 518, Viajes Xochitlán (☎ 4-36-64), in Plaza San Cristóbal at Bravo 210, and Turismo El Convento de Oaxaca (☎ 6-18-06, extension 112) in the Hotel Stouffer Presidente.

Festivals

Guelaguetza The Guelaguetza, a brilliant feast of folk dance, takes place in a big amphitheatre on Cerro del Fortín, usually on the first two Mondays after 16 July. Thousands of people flock into the city and a festive atmosphere builds for days beforehand. Hotel rooms quickly fill. On the appointed days the whole hill comes alive with hawkers, food stalls and picnickers.

From about 10 am to 1 pm magnificently costumed dancers from the seven regions of Oaxaca perform a succession of dignified, lively and even comical traditional dances to live music, tossing generous offerings of local produce to the crowd as they finish. Excitement climaxes with the incredibly colourful pineapple dance by women of the Papaloapan region and the final stately, prancing Zapotec feather dance (Danza de las Plumas), by men wearing glorious feather headdresses, which symbolically re-enacts the Spanish conquest of Mexico.

Seating in the auditorium, which holds perhaps 10,000, is divided into four areas *(palcos)*. For the two nearest the stage, tickets (165 or 115 pesos) go on sale 15 days in advance from the 5 de Mayo tourist office or other outlets in town. These tickets guarantee a seat but you should still arrive by 9 am if you want one of the better ones. The two larger rear palcos are free and fill up early: you need to be in by 8.30 am to ensure a seat and by 10 am you'll be lucky to get even standing room. For all areas take a hat

---

Origins of the Guelaguetza

The pre-Hispanic Zapotecs, Mixtecs and Aztecs of the Central Valleys held a festival in the same place at the same time of year in honour of their maize gods. Christian priests replaced this with the feast of the Virgen del Carmen (16 July), before such semi-pagan goings-on were abolished altogether in 1882. But people continued to make pilgrimages and have picnics on the hill on the two Mondays following 16 July. Celebrations in something like their present form began in the 1930s and the purpose-built amphitheatre was opened in 1974.

The only time the Guelaguetza is not held on the first two Mondays after 16 July is when 18 July (the anniversary of Benito Juárez' death) falls on a Monday, in which case Guelaguetza is celebrated on 25 July and 1 August. ■

---

and something to drink as you'll be sitting under the naked sun for hours.

Virgen del Carmen The streets around the Templo del Carmen Alto on García Vigil become a big fairground for a week or more before the day of the Virgen del Carmen on 16 July. The nights are lit by processions and fireworks.

Blessing of Animals Pets are dressed up and taken to Iglesia de La Merced about 5 pm on 31 August.

Virgen de la Soledad The city's patron saint's day, 18 December, and the two previous nights see processions and traditional dances focused on La Soledad church.

Noche de los Rábanos (Night of the Radishes) Amazing figures carved from radishes are displayed in the zócalo on 23 December. You're supposed to eat *buñuelos* (a type of crisp pancake) and throw your bowl in the air afterwards.

Places to Stay – bottom end
Most places in this range are in the noisy, crowded streets south and west of the zócalo, but several of the better deals are to be found on the other sides of town. Streetside rooms everywhere are likely to be noisy.

Camping The large, fairly shady *Trailer Park Oaxaca* (☎ (951) 5-27-96) is 3.5 km north-east of the centre on the corner of Violetas and Heroica Escuela Naval Militar. The rate for a vehicle with all hook-ups and

one/two people is 30 pesos. Turn north up Calzada Manuel Ruiz off Calzada Niños Héroes de Chapultepec, five blocks east of the 1st-class bus station, and go seven blocks. Ruiz becomes Violetas.

South of the Zócalo *El Pasador* backpackers' hostel (☎ (951) 6-12-87), at Fiallo 305, two blocks east and half a block south of the zócalo, is the cheapest place to stay in town. It's not glamorous and is a bit cramped but clean enough and the staff are young and friendly. There are around 30 beds in one large and three smaller dormitories (18 pesos per person) plus three double rooms (20 pesos per person). Kitchen and laundry facilities are available and there's a big dining table in the small courtyard. There's hot water only in the mornings. A 5-peso fee is charged for daytime use of the facilities. The hostel has a few mountain bikes for rent at 15 pesos per day.

One of the better cheap hotels is the *Hotel Aurora* (☎ (951) 6-41-45), at Bustamante 212, with singles/doubles at 30/40 pesos. Bathrooms are shared but the rooms, around a wide single-storey courtyard, are large, cool and tidy. The management is friendly.

The friendly *Hotel Pasaje* (☎ (951) 6-42-13), at Mina 302, half a block west of the 20 de Noviembre market, is a travellers' favourite. Small but very clean rooms with private bath are 35/40 pesos.

The *Hotel Vallarta* (☎ (951) 6-49-67) at Díaz Ordaz 309 is well kept, clean and bright, charging 40/50 pesos.

Calle 20 de Noviembre has several hotels, typically consisting of a long, narrow courtyard flanked by three-storey rows of box-like rooms. The *Hotel Chayo* (☎ (951) 6-41-12) at No 508 opposite the 20 de Noviembre market and the *Hotel Típico* (☎ (951) 6-41-11), a block beyond at No 612, both charge 43/53 pesos for clean rooms with private bathrooms. Better is the *Hotel Posada del Carmen*, a block further out at No 712, which has spruced-up paintwork and furnishings, and friendly staff. Rooms are 40/50 pesos.

North of the Zócalo The eccentric *Hotel Pombo* (☎ (951) 6-26-73), at Morelos 601, a block north of the Alameda, is a rambling place with 50 very varied rooms and nearly always some vacancies. It's spartan, and clean if you don't look too closely. The best rooms are quite spacious and bright. In some you are given woodshavings wrapped in newspaper to make a fire to warm the water. Singles/doubles with private bath cost around 40/50 pesos. With shared bath they're mostly older, damp, enclosed and only a little cheaper.

Not bad value for its very central position is the *Hotel Central* (☎ (951) 6-59-71) at 20 de Noviembre 104, with adequately clean, smallish rooms, mostly around an untidy little roofed courtyard, for 35/40 pesos (44 pesos double with two beds).

On Plazuela Labastida, four blocks north of the zócalo, the friendly *Posada Margarita* is a good family-run place with a surprising view of the towers of the Iglesia de Santo Domingo. The clean if rather dark rooms have private baths and vary in size, costing 40/50 pesos.

Places to Stay – middle
The middle range has some good-value hotels with prices kept low by competition. For the best, reservations are advisable.

Around the Zócalo One good place is the *Hotel Las Rosas* (☎ (951) 4-22-17) at Trujano 112, half a block west of the zócalo. The entrance is up a flight of stairs and the well-kept rooms, with private baths, are on two levels around a pleasant courtyard.

Singles/doubles are 66/88 pesos and there's a TV lounge, a place to wash clothes on the roof, and tea and coffee available in the lobby.

The *Hotel Real de Antequera* (☎ (951) 6-46-35) at Hidalgo 807, half a block east of the zócalo, has a wide stone staircase up from the courtyard café to the rooms, which are clean, medium-sized and have TV. Everything is roofed over, which retains the heat. The price is 75/90 pesos.

The *Hotel Monte Albán* (☎ (951) 6-27-77), faces the cathedral at Alameda de León 1. It's about 400 years old with a pillared courtyard-restaurant (unfortunately covered), where folk-dance shows take place nightly. Rooms are on two floors around this and cost 88/110 pesos. Those at the front are bigger but the whole place is comfortable and has a colonial atmosphere.

The *Hotel Gala* (☎ (951) 4-22-51) at Bustamante 103, half a block south of the zócalo, is a modernised 1930s building with sizeable, comfortable, well-decorated rooms and good tiled bathrooms. Prices are 138/165 pesos.

The *Hotel Señorial* (☎ (951) 6-39-33), on the zócalo at Portal de Flores 6, has over 100 rooms ranging from small, dark, interior ones which are poor value at 110/125 pesos, to bigger, airier ones with lots of daylight for 150/162 pesos. The best are generally on the top floor. All are clean and have TV. There's a good restaurant.

South of the Zócalo The *Hotel Trebol* (☎ (951) 6-12-56), almost hidden opposite the Juárez market on the corner of Las Casas and Cabrera, has sizeable, bright, clean, well-furnished rooms around a modern courtyard for 100 pesos, with private bath.

The *Hotel Rivera* (☎ (951) 6-38-04) at 20 de Noviembre 502 on the corner of Aldama has big, clean, bare singles/doubles for 70/90 pesos, but also offhand staff and echoing corridors. It's a fallback if everywhere else is full.

North of the Zócalo The *Hotel Veracruz* (☎ (951) 5-05-11) at Boulevard Niños

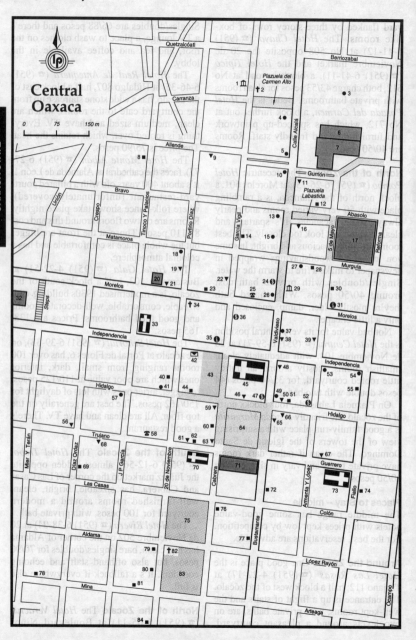

Central Oaxaca

0   75   150 m

OAXACA STATE

PLACES TO STAY

8	Hotel Las Golondrinas
12	Posada Margarita
14	Hotel Calesa Real
17	Hotel Stouffer Presidente
23	Hotel Pombo
28	Hotel Parador Plaza
30	Hotel Principal
40	Hotel Central
44	Hotel Monte Albán
51	Hotel Real de Antequera
55	Posada San Pablo
60	Hotel Señorial
62	Hotel Las Rosas
69	Hotel Vallarta
72	Hotel Gala
74	El Pasador
76	Hotel Trebol
77	Hotel Aurora
78	Hotel Mesón del Angel
79	Hotel Rivera
80	Hotel Chayo
81	Hotel Pasaje
84	Hotel Típico

PLACES TO EAT

9	Candela
11	Pizzería Alfredo da Roma
16	El Topil
19	Restauran La Flor de Loto del Sureste
21	Restauran Flor de Loto
22	Cafetería Bamby

38	Quicklys
39	Restaurant Santa Fe
46	El Marqués
48	El Sagrario
50	El Mesón
56	Cafetería Alex
59	La Casa de la Abuela
61	Cafetería Chip's
63	Café-Bar Del Jardín & El Asador Vasco
65	Restaurants Antequera & Amarantos
66	La Piñata
67	Restaurant Del Vitral
68	Restaurant Flami

OTHER

1	Museo Casa de Juárez
2	Templo & Ex-Convento del Carmen Alto
3	Centro Cultural Santo Domingo
4	Instituto de Artes Gráficas
5	Aeromorelos
6	Museo Regional
7	Iglesia de Santo Domingo
10	Palacio Santo Domingo
13	Plaza Alcalá
15	Biblioteca Circulante
18	Eclipse
20	Museo Rufino Tamayo
24	Casa de Cambio La Estrella & US Consulate
25	Telmex
26	La Mano Mágica
27	Casa Cantera

29	Museo de Arte Contemporáneo
31	State Tourist Office
32	Basílica de la Soledad
33	Templo de San Felipe Neri
34	Templo del Carmen Bajo
35	Palacio Municipal Tourist Office
36	Bancomer
37	Yalalag
41	Aeroméxico
42	Post & Telégrafos Office
43	Alameda
45	Catedral
47	Casa de Cambio Interdisa
49	Viajes Micsa/Amex
52	Banamex
53	Teatro Macedonia Alcalá
54	Mexicana
57	Superlavandería Hidalgo
58	Computel
64	Zócalo
70	Iglesia de La Compañía
71	Palacio de Gobierno
73	Iglesia de San Agustín
75	Mercado Juárez
78	Viajes Turisticos Mitla & Buses to Monte Albán
82	Iglesia de San Juan de Dios
83	20 de Noviembre Mercado

Héroes 1020 is next door to the 1st-class bus station and worth a look if you want a room quickly after a long bus ride. Pleasantly decorated, sizeable doubles cost 88 pesos. Big bottles of purified water are placed in the corridors and there's a restaurant.

Within 10 minutes of the 1st-class bus station, in a quiet cobbled neighbourhood 20 minutes' walk from the city centre, the family-run *Casa de Huéspedes Arnel* (☎ (951) 5-28-56) is geared up for backpackers and deservedly popular. The small but

very clean rooms are on two storeys around a big, jungly, parrot-inhabited courtyard. Singles/doubles/triples with private bath cost 50/85/102 pesos; rooms with shared bath are cheaper. There's 24-hour hot water and clothes-washing facilities. Food is available and you can book here for buses to the coast. Casa Arnel is at Aldama 404 on the corner of Hidalgo in Colonia Jalatlaco, 1.5 km north-east of the zócalo.

The excellent *Hotel Las Golondrinas* (☎ (951) 6-87-26, ☎ /fax 4-21-26) is at

Tinoco y Palacios 411, 4½ blocks north and two west of the zócalo. An oasis of calm, lovingly tended by friendly owners and staff, Las Golondrinas (The Swallows) has about 18 rooms opening onto a trio of lovely plant-strewn little courtyards. Rooms vary: none is vast but all are individually planned, tastefully decorated, and immaculately clean. Good breakfasts are served from 8 to 10 am. Singles/doubles/triples with private bath are 65/85/100 pesos which, for the doubles in particular, is good value.

A long-established travellers' favourite still providing good rooms at a reasonable price is the *Hotel Principal* (☎ (951) 6-25-35), 3½ blocks north-east of the zócalo at 5 de Mayo 208. It's well kept, with large old rooms opening on a sunny, peaceful courtyard. Doubles are 82 pesos. Only a couple of the 16 or so rooms are offered as singles (66 pesos) but several will function as triples (99 pesos). A few rooms in the less attractive rear courtyard are smaller than others.

The *Hotel Calesa Real* (☎ (951) 6-55-44) at García Vigil 306, 1½ blocks north of the Alameda, is prettily tiled and very clean but the rooms, with fan and TV, are mostly windowless, and small for 198 pesos, single or double. There's a swimming pool. A block and a half east, the *Hotel Parador Plaza* (☎ (951) 4-20-27) at Murguía 104 has been attractively modernised and brightened up, but some of the rooms lack natural light. Singles/doubles are 138/165 pesos.

Apartments *Posada San Pablo* (☎ (951) 6-49-14), two blocks east of the zócalo at Fiallo 102, once part of a convent, has 20 or so clean, stone-walled rooms facing a colonial courtyard. They're well kept – though short of natural light – and are billed as apartments since each has a cooker, fridge and private bath. The cost is 105/132 pesos a day.

The spacious, clean, well-furnished, modern apartments of *Parador Santo Domingo de Guzmán* (☎ (951) 5-98-52) are at Alcalá 804, 8½ blocks north of the zócalo. Each has a bedroom with two double beds, a sitting room, a bathroom and a well-equipped kitchen. There's hotel-style room service with

clean sheets daily. You can rent by the day at 116/143/159 pesos for singles/doubles/triples or by the week at 711/868/966 pesos.

To rent your own apartment or house, check the ads in the *Oaxaca Times* and the noticeboards in the Instituto Cultural Oaxaca language school, the Biblioteca Circulante de Oaxaca, or Cafetería Chip's.

Places to Stay – top end

The *Hotel Stouffer Presidente* (☎ (951) 6-06-11), at 5 de Mayo 300, four blocks north-east of the zócalo, is Oaxaca's ultimate hotel for colonial atmosphere. The entire 16th-century convent of Santa Catalina was converted to create it in the 1970s: the old chapel is a banquet hall, one of the courtyards contains a swimming pool, and the bar is lined with books on otherworldly devotion. Thick stone walls – some still bearing original frescos – keep the place cool. There are 91 varied, well-decorated rooms costing 483 pesos single or double. If you can, choose one upstairs and away from the street and the noises and smells of the kitchens.

Other top hotels are in the north of the city, well out of the centre. The modern six-storey *Hotel Fortín Plaza* (☎ (951) 5-77-77) is at Venus 118, immediately above highway 190 as it winds down from Cerro del Fortín, about 1.25 km from the centre. Its ambience is low-key and pleasant, with tile and marble decor. The rooms are bright and fairly spacious, with balconies. Those at the front have views over the city. The hotel is used by both tour groups and individual travellers. Singles/doubles are 209/253 pesos.

The 164-room *Hotel Misión de los Ángeles* (☎ (951) 5-15-00), just north of highway 190 at Calzada Porfirio Díaz 102 (about a km east of the Fortín Plaza), has over 100 large, comfortable rooms among tropical gardens, plus tennis courts and a pool. Rates are 237/297 pesos.

Calzada Porfirio Díaz also leads to *Hotel San Felipe Misión* (☎ (951) 5-01-00), three or four km further north at Jalisco 15 in Fraccionamiento San Felipe del Agua, which has 154 balconied rooms, more gardens, and a pool. The price is 193/241 pesos. There's a golf course close by. A shuttle bus runs between this hotel and the city centre; a taxi is about 10 pesos.

The *Hotel Victoria* (☎ (951) 5-26-33) stands above highway 190 on the lower slopes of the Cerro del Fortín. Many of the 150 large rooms and suites look over the city and the hotel has an Olympic pool set in big gardens. Its restaurant gets good reports, too. Standard doubles cost 330 pesos. The walk to the city centre is 20 to 30 minutes. The hotel also runs a shuttle bus to the city in the morning, returning in the evening.

Places to Eat

Specialities Probably the two best places specialising in Oaxaqueño food, at opposite ends of the price spectrum, are El Biche Pobre II and La Casa de la Abuela – both open only for lunch, which can begin as late as 5 pm.

El Biche Pobre II is at Calzada de la República 600, 1.5 km north-east of the zócalo. It's open from 1 to 6.30 pm daily and is an informal, friendly place with about a dozen tables, some long enough to stage lunch for a whole extended Mexican family. For an introduction to Oaxacan food you can't do better than order a 15-peso botana surtida (assortment of snacks). This brings you a dozen tasty little items which add up

to a meal. Individual main dishes, several of which are al horno (baked in the oven), are mostly around 10 to 12 pesos.

La Casa de la Abuela (☎ 6-35-44) is a lot more expensive, its cuisine more delicate, and its location much more central, upstairs at Hidalgo 616 on the north-west corner of the zócalo. It's open from 1 to 6.30 pm daily except Friday. The equivalent of a botana surtida here is the parrillada Oaxaqueña, with six items for 42 pesos. Meat and chicken dishes are mostly about 32 pesos. The delicious chiles rellenos de picadillo (18 pesos) are about half a meal.

Cheap Oaxaqueño meals can be found in the 20 de Noviembre market a couple of blocks south of the zócalo. Many of the small comedores here serve up local specialities, with a main dish typically costing 8 pesos. The busiest will usually be the best. Many of the comedores stay open till early evening but their fare is freshest earlier in the day.

Other restaurants where you can find some Oaxacan specialities include Doña Elpidia, the Santa Fe and El Topil (see the following sections).

Zócalo All the cafés and restaurants beneath the zócalo arches are great places to watch the life of Oaxaca but the fare and service vary widely. We like the *Café Bar Del Jardín*

Cocina Oaxaqueña

Good Oaxaqueño cooking is spicily delicious, though it offers limited choice for vegetarians. (Many restaurants in Oaxaca city and the beach spots, though, still offer vegetarians more choice than is usual in Mexico.) Some Oaxaca specialities include:

Amarillo con pollo – chicken in a yellow cumin and chile sauce
Chapulines – grasshoppers fried, often with onion and garlic; high in protein and good with a squeeze of lime
Coloradito – pork or chicken in a red chile and tomato sauce
Mole Oaxaqueño or *Mole negro* – dark sauce made from chiles, bananas, chocolate, pepper and cinnamon, usually served with chicken
Picadillo – spicy minced or shredded pork, often used for the stuffing in chiles rellenos
Tamale Oaxaqueño – tamale with a mole Oaxaqueño and (usually) chicken filling
Quesillo – Oaxacan stringy cheese
Verde con espinazo – pork back in a green sauce made from beans, chiles, parsley and epazote (goosefoot or wild spinach) ■

at the south-west corner, which is always bustling and a favourite with locals. When you get a table, you can linger over a coffee (the best around the zócalo) or beer – or eat a snack or meal from the long menu of Oaxacan and international food. The omelettes at 9 pesos are big and excellent while the fruit salad, yoghurt and granola (8 pesos) appears in a small glass bowl.

The *Antequera* on the east side of the zócalo serves up a menú del día for 15 pesos and a botana Oaxaqueña for 25 pesos per person. Almost next door, the *Amarantos* does breakfasts from 8 to 15 pesos.

El Marqués under the arches on the north side of the zócalo does good exotic breakfasts such as *potosinos* (11 pesos) – scrambled eggs with onions, hot peppers and tomatoes wrapped in a tortilla, topped with red mole sauce, the whole sitting in mole negro. Other meals cost around 18 pesos.

El Asador Vasco (☎ 6-97-19) above the Del Jardín at the zócalo's south-west corner, serves good, if not cheap, Basque, Mexican and international food, but the staff look down their noses if you order one dish between two people, and when they bring the bill they like to point out that service is not included. Evening diners are serenaded by musicians who deposit a tambourine inscribed 'Thank you for your tip' beside your elbow. Main dishes are mostly in the 30 to 40 pesos bracket and portions of some are on the mean side. Steaks and brochetas (kebabs) are among the best choices. For a table overlooking the zócalo, book earlier in the day.

The *Restaurant Señorial* in the Hotel Señorial on the west side of the zócalo efficiently serves up good-value fare in a large, pleasant dining room. A breakfast of juice, eggs, bacon, coffee and assorted bread rolls is 13 pesos.

You can eat as well at *El Mesón*, at Hidalgo 805 just off the north-east corner of the zócalo, as anywhere on the square itself. A wide selection of tasty, mainly charcoal-grilled Mexican food is prepared at ranges in the centre of the restaurant, and at lunchtime there's a good 14-peso all-you-can-eat buffet

of meat and bean dishes, rice, fruit, salad and corn. If you're not having the buffet, you tick off your order on a printed list – and if you don't understand what the items are, the waiters will patiently try to explain. Tacos and quesadillas are specialities but they don't come cheap at between 5 and 14 pesos for a serve of two. Alambres and tacos razas con queso (bean tacos with cheese) are both delicious. *La Piñata* across the street does an even cheaper lunch – 9 pesos for its four-course comida.

A few metres from the opposite corner of the zócalo, on Trujano, *Cafetería Chip's* looks on its last legs but serves up probably the best café con leche in Oaxaca for 2 pesos, big orange juices for 3 pesos, and a variety of excellent-value snacks from torta vegetariana (an avocado, cheese, tomato and lettuce roll) for 3.60 pesos, to ensalada supersónica (a mound of fruit salad, honey, yoghurt and granola) for 4.50 pesos. It's open from 9 am to 9 pm.

South of the Zócalo The clean, lively *Cafetería Alex*, at Díaz Ordaz 218 on the corner of Trujano, is well worth finding for great-value breakfasts, served from 7 am to noon daily, or an inexpensive lunch or dinner up to 9 pm any day except Sunday. One breakfast possibility, for 9 pesos, is juice, scrambled eggs with potato and bacon or cheese, frijoles, bread or tortillas and coffee. Portions are generous. Later in the day choose from soups (5 pesos), chicken and fries (11 pesos), an order of enchiladas or tacos for 12 pesos, or the comida corrida for 10 pesos. There's usually a mixed Mexican and gringo crowd and service is friendly and quick.

Restaurant Flami at Trujano 301, an extensive, busy place with mainly Mexican customers, does a decent four-course carnivore's comida – soup, rice, choice of three lean meat courses and flan for 10 pesos. *Doña Elpidia* at Cabrera 413, 5½ blocks south of the zócalo, has been serving up one of Oaxaca's most substantial and carefully prepared comidas for decades. Open lunchtime only, it's in a shabby part of town with just a shabby 'Restaurant' sign outside, but inside you enter a large, green, birdsong-filled courtyard. The six-course meal, for 18 pesos, usually starts with a botana and proceeds to dessert by way of soup, rice and a couple of skilfully seasoned meat dishes. They can accommodate vegetarians, too.

At Guerrero 201, just off Armenta y López, the *Restaurant Del Vitral* (☎ 6-31-24) is Oaxaca's most elegant eatery. Upstairs in an imposing town mansion, its ambience is that of pre-revolutionary privilege, with smooth, efficient staff. The cuisine is 'Oaxaca Meets Europe'. You might try the lemony grasshoppers for starters and order flambé steak in mustard sauce to ensure a taste treat to follow. Without wine or any other drink, you're looking at 60 pesos or more for dinner. The Del Vitral is open from lunchtime to 11.30 pm.

North of the Zócalo *El Sagrario* at Valdivieso 120, half a block north of the zócalo, is a popular pizzeria/restaurant/bar serving Mexican, Italian and international food. Main dishes are 15 to 35 pesos but there's a 16-peso all-you-can-eat buffet served from 1 to 5 pm daily and good live Latin American music with no cover charge in the evenings.

Quicklys, at Alcalá 101, 1½ blocks from the zócalo, is a good standby for a reliable and inexpensive, if bland, feed. Parrilladas – big grilled vegetable and rice platters topped with melted cheese and served with tortillas and guacamole – are guaranteed to fill you for 11 to 17 pesos. Some varieties have meat too. You can also choose from a variety of burgers (including vegetarian ones) with fries, or an order of six tacos, for around 10 pesos.

Just off Alcalá 2½ blocks further up, in Plazuela Labastida, *El Topil* serves individualistic Oaxacan and Mexican dishes which have the touch of home cooking. Tasajó (a slab of pounded beef) with guacamole and vegetables is one speciality for 20 pesos, and there's a range of soups – garbanzo (chickpea, 9 pesos) is delicious – plus some good antojitos. Nube especial is a big queso

fundido with raw vegetable salad and guacamole for 23 pesos. The menú del día is 15 pesos.

Pizzeria Alfredo da Roma, at Alcalá 400, just below the Iglesia de Santo Domingo, has reasonable Italian food. Pastas are mainly in the 15-peso range, while pizzas come in over 20 combinations and four sizes. Lei-lui, for two people, are mostly around 26 pesos – the shrimp is recommended. There are salads too, and you can rinse it all down with sangría or wine.

For a breakfast splurge, the all-you-can-eat buffet in the *Hotel Stouffer Presidente* at 5 de Mayo 300 costs 38 pesos. The Sunday lunch buffet from 1 to 5 pm costs 45 pesos.

If you're near Santo Domingo between 1 and 6 pm, you could do little better than eat at *Candela*, 1½ blocks west of the church at Allende 211. The building looks like a private house but inside there's a large dining room with a short menu of tasty, inexpensive Mexican dishes, which you can eat in or take away. We have tried spaghetti marinara, verduras al vapor (steamed vegetables), chiles rellenos (all around 12 pesos) and filete pescado a la crema (15 pesos), all of which were delicious. In the evenings, when Candela becomes a live music venue, food quality sinks.

The bright, sparkling clean *Cafetería Bamby* at García Vigil 205, 2½ blocks north of the zócalo, is open from 8 am to 10 pm daily except Sunday and serves up sizeable portions of plain but good Mexican and gringo food – salads 7 to 8 pesos, spaghetti 8 to 10 pesos, chicken and meats 15 to 20 pesos. There's also a fair four-course comida corrida for 15 pesos. The Bamby bakery, just down the street on the corner of Morelos, is a convenient stop for bolillos and pan integral.

There are two vegetarian possibilities near the noisy corner of Morelos and Porfirio Díaz, three blocks north-west of the zócalo. The purist vegetarian *Restauran la Flor de Loto del Sureste* at Porfirio Díaz 217B is good for soups and juices (including carrot and beetroot) at 3.50 to 5 pesos. The main dishes we have tried were small, but the bread's good and the four-course daily menú especial is reasonable value for 12 pesos. There are also breakfast deals. The *Restauran Flor de Loto* at Morelos 509, just up Morelos from the corner, is generally better value. It's a fairly successful stab at pleasing a range of gringo palates. For vegetarians, the crepas de verduras (vegetable pancakes) and verduras al gratin (vegetables with melted cheese) are both good at 12 pesos. For carnivores there are good chicken and meat dishes around 16 pesos, pasta or burgers for 9 to 11 pesos. The 15-peso comida corrida, with veggie options, is a real meal.

The three-floor *Restaurant Santa Fe* at 5 de Mayo 103, one block east and 1½ blocks north from the zócalo, is clean, reliable and popular with tourists, but hardly inspired. The menu combines Oaxacan tamales, mole or enchiladas (14 to 20 pesos) with other Mexican and some gringo dishes (steaks mostly 20 to 28 pesos).

A little further east, *Panificadora La Luna* at Independencia 1105, half a block past Juárez, must be the city's most varied bakery, with good croissants and several types of pan integral on offer.

Entertainment

Oaxaca has a lively entertainment scene, thanks mainly to its student and tourist population. Pick up the monthly programme of cultural events from the Palacio Municipal tourist office. To start with there's live music – usually marimbas or a brass band – Sunday lunchtimes and most nights in the zócalo.

Near the zócalo, *El Sagrario* at Valdivieso 120 has good Latin American music nightly in its downstairs bar overlooked by the 1st-floor restaurant. There's no cover charge. *El Sol y La Luna* at Maza de Juárez 409, a brisk 20-minute walk north of the zócalo, has live bands or solo guitarists in a pleasant, plant-filled covered courtyard from 7 or 8 pm until late every night except Sunday. The cover charge is 10 pesos. Food is available but expensive, with pastas at 15 pesos, steaks 35 pesos and one-person pizzas 25 pesos.

Candela, at Allende 211, 1½ blocks west of the Iglesia de Santo Domingo, has live music every night except Monday – mainly

salsa and rumba, sometimes with a rock band as support. You sit at tables, restaurant-style, but though Candela *is* also a restaurant you can stick to drinks only. The music goes from about 8.30 pm to about 1 am and the cover charge is 15 pesos. It's popular with students, especially on Friday and Saturday.

Los Tres Patios at Cosijopí 208, three blocks north of Candela, is a relaxed, friendly place with good jazz from 10 pm to 1.30 am Tuesday to Saturday. The cover charge is 10 pesos. Snacks and light meals are available from 10 to 20 pesos.

The *Hotel Monte Albán* stages *danzas folklóricas* at 8.30 pm nightly in its courtyard. The 1½-hour show is the same every night – worthwhile if you don't get any other chance to see Oaxacan dance. Tickets are 15 pesos and it's advisable to book a day ahead. Also good is the lively mini-Guelaguetza staged nightly at the *Casa Cantera*, Murguía 102. A range of Oaxacan dances is performed in colourful costume with live music. The charge is 25 pesos and food and drinks are available.

Oaxaca's best discos are attached to the expensive hotels in the north of town. Two of the most popular are *Yonkee* at the Hotel San Felipe Misión (you'll need a taxi to get there) and the *Victoria* at the Hotel Victoria (great views from the bar). There's also *Kaftan's* at the Hotel Misión de los Ángeles. Opening times and charges vary, but expect all three to be open at least Tuesday to Saturday from about 10 pm to 2 am. On Saturday you pay about 30 pesos entry at any of them, but often less on other nights. *Eclipse* at Porfirio Diaz 219, on the corner of Matamoros, is a disco closer to the centre, open Friday to Sunday nights and with a cover charge of 35 pesos.

The Casa de la Cultura Oaxaqueña, in an ex-monastery east of the zócalo at González Ortega 403 between Colón and Rayón, runs an almost daily programme of exhibitions, concerts, dance, theatre, classes etc.

Cineclub Maco at the Museo de Arte Contemporáneo, Alcalá 202, shows foreign and Mexican films, usually from Friday to Sunday at 6.30 pm; admission is free. Find the current programme in the museum's library.

Craft, art and photo exhibitions, open-air or street theatre, dance, music and talks are likely to pop up anywhere in Oaxaca any time.

Things to Buy

The state of Oaxaca has one of Mexico's richest, most inventive folk-art scenes and the city is the chief clearing-house for its products. In general, the best work is found in the tourist shops along Alcalá, García Vigil and nearby streets north of the zócalo, with the very best in just a handful of places. But prices are lower in the markets. Oaxaca crafts are not necessarily dearer in the city than in the villages where they are made.

Though many traditional techniques remain – the backstrap loom is used alongside the pedal loom, and pottery is turned by hand – that doesn't stop new forms appearing in response to the now international market for these products. The brightly painted copal wood animals which have become the rage in recent years developed from toys that Oaxacans had been carving for their children for centuries. The three villages where most of them are carved, San Martín Tilcajete, Arrazola and La Unión Tejalapan, have become relatively rich.

Crafts to look out for include the distinctive black pottery from the village of San Bartolo Coyotepec; blankets and rugs from Teotitlán del Valle; huipiles and other Indian clothing from anywhere (those from Yalalag and the Triqui Indians are among the prettiest); and stamped and coloured tin from Oaxaca itself, which has been a boom business ever since someone thought of making Christmas decorations from the stuff.

In jewellery, a Oaxaca speciality is gold earring replicas of the Mixtec treasure from Monte Albán – the best pairs cost around 1500 pesos. Silver and precious-stone jewellery are also sold here – the best shops are on Alcalá – but most prices are a bit higher than in Mexico City or Taxco. In the markets you'll also find lots of leather, bags, hats, textiles, shoes and clothes – not necessarily local.

Markets The vast main market, the Central de Abastos (Supplies Centre), is in the west of town next to the 2nd-class bus station. Saturday is the big day, but the place is a hive of activity any day. You can find almost anything if you look for it long enough. Each type of goods has a section to itself – so you'll find 20 or so woven-basket sellers here, a couple of dozen pottery stalls there, and so on. The care that goes into the displays of food, particularly vegetables, would put any Western shop-window to shame. Every bunch of chiles becomes a work of art. In addition to the everyday items that Oaxacans buy and sell here, there are some handicrafts. There are also medicinal herbs and numerous things whose identity you can only discover by asking.

Nearer the city centre are various more specialised markets. The indoor Juárez market, a block south of the zócalo, concentrates on food (more expensive than the Central de Abastos) but there are also flowers and a fair range of handicrafts. The 20 de Noviembre market, in the next block south, is mainly taken over by comedores but there are a few craft stalls on its west and south sides.

The official Mercado de Artesanías, on the corner of Zaragoza and J P García, a block south-west of the 20 de Noviembre market, gets few customers because it's a bit off the beaten track. So vendors seize on anyone who looks interested and you may pick up some bargains. It's strong on rugs and other textiles.

Two smaller street craft markets function every day in plazas off Alcalá. In Plazuela Labastida you'll find jewellery, carved animals and belts, while Plazuela del Carmen Alto is the place for weavings, embroideries, rugs and other textiles. Triqui women weave at backstrap looms here.

Shops The highest quality crafts are found in about 10 shops. Yalalag at Alcalá 104, near the corner of Independencia, is one, dealing in fine goods from Oaxaca and further afield and specialising in pottery and textiles. Further from the centre, Aripo at García Vigil

809 is run by the state government. Different rooms are devoted to different crafts – table cloths, clothing, pottery, tin, woodwork etc; much of this is among the best you'll find in Oaxaca. Weavers work at treadle looms in a back room and the shop is open Sunday morning as well as from 9 am to 7 pm every other day. Other good shops include Fonart on the corner of García Vigil and Bravo, Artesanías Chimalli at García Vigil 513 (good for stamped tin), La Mano Mágica at Alcalá 203 (also with some excellent contemporary art), and El Cactus at Alcalá 401 (blankets and rugs). There are several smart, expensive shops selling beautiful crafts on 5 de Mayo opposite Hotel Stouffer Presidente. Casa Brena at Pino Suárez 700 out towards the 1st-class bus station focuses on ceramics and costumes. Nearly all these shops will mail things home for you if you want.

For jewellery, the Bodega del Fraile on the corner of Allende and Alcalá has stunning pieces.

The Oaxaca area is one of Mexico's chief mezcal brewing zones and several shops south-west of the zócalo sell nothing but mezcal, in a variety of strange vessels. Try Mezcal Perla del Valle and El Rey de Mezcales, both on Aldama between J P García and Díaz Ordaz.

Getting There & Away

Air Mexicana, Aeroméxico and Aviacsa between them fly direct to/from Mexico City (one hour, around 235 pesos) nine times daily. Aeroméxico also has direct flights to/from Guadalajara, Monterrey and Tijuana daily.

Aerocaribe flies daily to/from Cancún (4½ hours) via Tuxtla Gutiérrez, Villahermosa and Mérida (518 pesos). Aviacsa flies daily to/from Mérida via Tuxtla Gutiérrez continuing onto Cancún on three days and Villahermosa on four days.

At least two airlines make the spectacular half-hour hop over the Sierra Madre del Sur to/from the Oaxaca coast. Aeromorelos flies daily to/from Puerto Escondido and Bahías de Huatulco (both 243 to 290 pesos one way, depending on season). Aerovega uses a five-

seater plane and stops daily at Puerto Escondido (210 pesos) between Oaxaca and Bahías de Huatulco (250 pesos).

Airline offices in Oaxaca include: Aerocaribe (☎ 5-63-73) at the Hotel Misión de los Ángeles; Aeroméxico (☎ 6-37-65) at Hidalgo 513; Aeromorelos (☎ 6-09-74) at Alcalá 501B, opposite the Iglesia de Santo Domingo; Aerovega (☎ 6-27-77) at Alameda de León 1; Aviacsa (☎ 3-18-09) at the Hotel Misión de los Ángeles; and Mexicana (☎ 6-84-14) at Fiallo 102. Useful travel agents for air tickets are Viajes Micsa (☎ 6-27-00), at Valdivieso 2 just off the zócalo, Centroamericana de Viajes (☎ 6-29-76) on the west side of the zócalo, and Viajes Turísticos Mitla (☎ 6-61-75) in the Hotel Mesón del Ángel at Mina 518.

Bus Reaching Oaxaca from any direction involves several hours' travel through twisting, isolated mountain stretches. Most buses from Mexico City and Puebla come through the La Cañada area via Teotitlán del Camino, a route known as the Vía Corta; a smoother but slower route is via Huajuapan de León.

Oaxaca has a number of bus stations and ticket offices. The main 1st-class bus station, used by all ADO and Cristóbal Colón buses, is at Calzada Niños Héroes de Chapultepec 1036, 1.5 km north-east of the zócalo. The main 2nd-class bus station, swarming with hundreds of people and dozens of bus companies, is about 900 metres west of the zócalo along Trujano or Las Casas. All 2nd-class buses mentioned in the details that follow use the 2nd-class bus station unless noted (the main exceptions concern buses to the Oaxaca coast).

It's advisable to book in advance for some of the less frequent services out of Oaxaca, such as the single daily bus to San Cristóbal de Las Casas and the better buses to the coast. Cristóbal Colón has a city centre booking office at 20 de Noviembre 204A.

Take special care with your belongings on buses to the coast – apart from theft from luggage racks, there are tales of travellers losing bags in a sudden crush that happens when people are getting on these buses.

Daily buses from Oaxaca include:

Bahías de Huatulco – see Santa Cruz Huatulco

Mexico City (mostly to Terminal Oriente; a few to Terminal Sur or Terminal Norte) – 500 km, nine hours via Teotitlán del Camino; 580 km, 11 hours via Huajuapan de León; most buses overnight; eight deluxe ('GL') buses by ADO (72 pesos) and four ('Plus') by Cristóbal Colón (66 pesos); frequent 1st-class buses by ADO (58 to 64 pesos) and eight by Cristóbal Colón (61 pesos)

Pochutla – 240 km, six hours; three 2nd-class directo buses by Transportes Turísticos (32 pesos, tickets and departure from the Hotel Mesón del Ángel at Mina 518, also bookable at Centroamericana de Viajes travel agency on the zócalo) and one by Autotransportes Turísticos Aragul (25 pesos, tickets at the Hotel Trebol); seven 2nd-class ordinario buses by Estrella del Valle/Oaxaca Pacífico; one deluxe (Plus) bus (29 pesos) and two 1st-class (23 pesos) by Cristóbal Colón via Salina Cruz (8½ hours)

Puebla – 370 km, seven hours via Teotitlán del Camino; 450 km, nine hours via Huajuapan de León; two deluxe (GL) buses by ADO (55 pesos) and one (Plus) by Cristóbal Colón (52 pesos); five 1st-class buses by ADO (40.50 pesos) and two by Cristóbal Colón (45 pesos)

Puerto Escondido – 310 km, seven hours; one overnight 2nd-class directo ('Star Service') bus by Estrella del Valle/Oaxaca Pacífico (42.50 pesos); two 2nd-class directo buses by Transportes Turísticos (32 pesos, tickets and departure from the Hotel Mesón del Ángel at Mina 518, also bookable at Centroamericana de Viajes travel agency on the zócalo) and one by Autotransportes Turísticos Aragul (30 pesos, tickets at the Hotel Trebol); seven 2nd-class ordinario buses by Estrella del Valle/Oaxaca Pacífico (30.50 pesos); two 1st-class buses by Cristóbal Colón via Salina Cruz (10 hours, 30 pesos)

San Cristóbal de las Casas – 630 km, 12 hours; one 1st-class bus by Cristóbal Colón (58 pesos)

Santa Cruz Huatulco – 275 km, seven hours; one overnight 2nd-class directo bus ('Star Service', 38.50 pesos) and two 2nd-class ordinario buses (28.50 pesos) by Estrella del Valle/Oaxaca Pacífico; one overnight deluxe (Plus) bus by Cristóbal Colón via Salina Cruz (7½ hours, 34 pesos)

Tehuantepec – 250 km, 4½ hours; one deluxe (Plus) bus (30 pesos) and nine 1st-class (24 pesos) by Cristóbal Colón; 16 2nd-class by Transportes Oaxaca-Istmo (21 pesos)

Tuxtla Gutiérrez – 550 km, 10 hours; one deluxe (Plus) bus (65 pesos) and four 1st-class (51 or 57 pesos) by Cristóbal Colón; four 2nd-class buses

each by Fletes y Pasajes (FYPSA) and Transportes Oaxaca-Istmo (45 pesos)

Veracruz – 460 km, 8½ to 10 hours; one deluxe (Plus) overnight bus by Cristóbal Colón (60 pesos); two 1st-class by ADO (54 pesos); two 2nd-class by Cuenca del Papaloapan from the 1st-class bus station (33 pesos)

Villahermosa – 700 km, 12 hours; one 1st-class bus each by ADO (71.50 pesos) and Cristóbal Colón (67.50 pesos)

There's also fairly frequent 1st and 2nd-class service to Juchitán; a few 1st-class buses to Salina Cruz; two 1st-class and a few 2nd-class to Tonalá and Tapachula; and a few 1st and 2nd-class to Acayucan.

Information on buses to the Central Valleys, the Mixteca and Northern Oaxaca state is given in the sections on the relevant places.

Train *El Oaxaqueño* is a reasonable way of travelling between Mexico City and Oaxaca if you don't mind its lack of sleeping accommodation and even the occasional absence of primera especial coaches. Though much slower than the buses, the train takes a more scenic route. See the Mexico City Getting There & Away section for schedules and fares. In practice the train often arrives three or so hours late, which means that southbound, you spend the morning daylight hours winding through the spectacular Sierra Madre de Oaxaca; northbound you spend them passing by a series of volcanoes on the approach to the capital. Tickets are sold at Oaxaca station from 2 to 6.30 pm: queues can be long late in the afternoon.

Oaxaca station is on Calzada Madero (the westward continuation of Independencia) about two km west of the zócalo.

Car Budget (☎ 6-06-11) in the Hotel Stouffer Presidente, Dollar (☎ 6-63-29) at Matamoros 100, and Hertz (☎ 6-24-34) at Plazuela Labastida 115 all have uniquely confusing ways of quoting car rental prices. Once you've clawed your way through their intricacies you generally pay around a total of 300 pesos plus petrol for a day with unlimited km in a VW sedan. Bigger cars go up to about twice that.

Getting Around

To/From the Airport Oaxaca airport is about six km south of the city off the road to Ocotlán and Pochutla. Tickets for the yellow combi colectivos which meet incoming flights are sold at the airport's Transporte Terrestre desk. These will take you anywhere in the city centre for 8 pesos. If you have a lot of baggage they may charge you double. A taxi costs about 30 pesos – or you could walk the half-km to the main road and pick up one of the frequent buses that pass.

You can book Transporte Terrestre from the city to the airport by visiting or phoning the office (☎ 4-43-50) at Alameda de León 1-6, next to the Hotel Monte Albán. Its hours are 9 am to 2 pm and 5 to 8 pm, Monday to Saturday. Buses going to San Bartolo Coyotepec or Ocotlán (see the Central Valleys section) will stop at the airport approach road.

City Transport Most points of importance in the city are within walking distance of each other. You can walk from the bus stations too, and even the train station if you like, but there are transport alternatives.

City buses cost from 0.70 to 1.40 pesos depending on how modern and comfortable they are. From the 1st-class bus station to the centre, take any 'Centro' bus heading left (west) outside the station, or going south down Juárez 300 metres west of the station. All go within a few blocks of the zócalo. A 'Gigante' bus going north up Reforma will take you from the centre back to the 1st-class bus station. An 'Etapa Blanco Juárez Colón' bus up Reforma will take you to the corner of Juárez, 300 metres away.

Buses between the 2nd-class bus station and the city centre – in both directions – pass slowly along crowded streets and it may be as quick to walk. 'Centro' buses from outside the station head towards the centre along Trujano. Going out to the bus station, catch a 'Central' bus west along Mina anywhere between Fiallo and 20 de Noviembre.

From the train station to the centre, take a 'Centro' bus but get off when it turns left and uphill on Crespo, three blocks before the cathedral.

A taxi to the zócalo costs around 10 pesos from the 1st-class bus station or the train station, around 8 pesos from the 2nd-class bus station.

Central Valleys

Three valleys radiate from the city of Oaxaca: the Valle de Tlacolula stretching 50 km east, the Valle de Etla reaching about 40 km north, and the Valle de Zimatlán stretching about 100 km south to Miahuatlán, beyond which the land rises before falling away to the coast.

In these Central Valleys (Valles Centrales), all within day-trip distance of Oaxaca city, you'll find pre-Hispanic ruins, craft villages and lively country markets, one or more of which is held every day except Saturday. The ancient Zapotec capital Monte Albán stands on its dramatic hilltop site just nine km west of Oaxaca, strategically placed at the hub of all three valleys. (The people of the valleys are still mostly Zapotec today.) East of the city, ancient Mitla, with its mosaic-like stonework, is almost as well known as Monte Albán, while the ruins of Yagul are arguably the region's most dramatic, and the Tlacolula market one of its busiest. The weavers of Teotitlán del Valle are among Mexico's most famous artisans. To the south are the beautiful old monastery at Cuilapan, the renowned potters of San Bartolo Coyotepec and more busy markets at Zaachila and Ocotlán.

Orientation

Most of the places east of Oaxaca in what follows are on or within walking distance of the Oaxaca-Mitla road. South from Oaxaca, highway 175 goes through San Bartolo Coyotepec, Ocotlán, Ejutla and Miahuatlán on its way to Pochutla and the Pacific coast. A separate road goes to Cuilapan and Zaachila. Monte Albán is at the end of a short road south-west from Oaxaca.

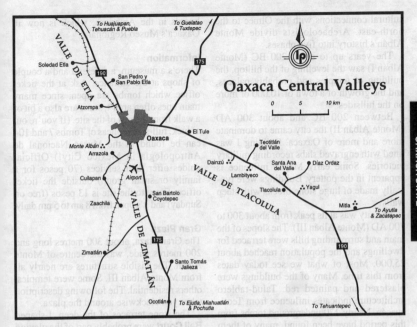

Oaxaca Central Valleys

0   5   10 km

OAXACA STATE

Market Days

The markets are at their busiest in the morning and start to wind down in early afternoon. Here are the details:

Sunday – Tlacolula (east of Oaxaca)
Monday – Miahuatlán (south)
Tuesday – Soledad Etla (north)
Wednesday – Zimatlán (south) and San Pedro y San Pablo Etla (north)
Thursday – Zaachila and Ejutla (both south)
Friday – Ocotlán (south)

Getting There & Away

Transportes Oaxaca-Istmo's buses to Mitla, every few minutes from Gate 9 of the 2nd-class bus station in Oaxaca, will drop you wherever you want along the Oaxaca-Mitla road. Further detail of bus services is given where useful under individual places.

A good alternative to buses, costing two to three times as much, is a colectivo taxi. These run to El Tule, Teotitlán del Valle, Tlacolula, Cuilapan, Zaachila, San Bartolo Coyotepec and Ocotlán from Prolongación Victoria by the Central de Abastos (the main market) in Oaxaca. They leave when they're full (five or six people).

MONTE ALBÁN

The ancient Zapotec capital Monte Albán ('MON-teh al-BAN' – White Mountain) stands on a flattened hilltop 400 metres above the valley floor, nine km west of Oaxaca. Monte Albán's hilltop position, with views over the hills and valleys for many km around, makes it spectacular even if you're bored by old stones. Try to take a torch/flashlight so that you can look in the tombs and tunnels.

History

The site was first occupied some time between 800 and 400 BC, probably by Zapotecs from the outset. One theory is that it was established as a governing and religious centre for the newly united Central Valleys. Some of its founders probably had cultural connections with the Olmec to the north-east. Archaeologists divide Monte Albán's history into five phases.

The years up to about 200 BC (Monte Albán I) saw the levelling of the hilltop, the building of temples and probably palaces, and the growth of a town of 10,000 or more on the hillsides.

Between 200 BC and about 300 AD (Monte Albán II) the city came to dominate more and more of Oaxaca. Building J was lined with engraved slabs recording military victories. Some early Mayan influence is apparent in the pottery. Buildings were typically made of huge stone blocks with steep walls.

The city was at its peak from about 300 to 700 AD (Monte Albán III). The slopes of the main and surrounding hills were terraced for dwellings and the population reached about 25,000. Most of what we see today dates from this time. Many of the buildings were plastered and painted red. Talud-tablero architecture indicates influence from Teotihuacán. Nearly 170 underground tombs from this period have been found, many of them elaborate and decorated with frescos. Monte Albán was the centre of a highly organised, priest-dominated society. There was extensive irrigation and at least 200 other settlements and ceremonial centres were established in the Central Valleys. Monte Albán's people ate tortillas, corn dough, beans, squash, chile, avocado and other plants, plus sometimes deer, rabbit and dog. In the dry season water was probably carried up to them from the valley.

Between about 700 and 950 AD (Monte Albán IV) the place was abandoned, perhaps because supplying its growth was now beyond the Central Valleys' resources. Monte Albán gradually fell into ruin and Zapotec life centred instead on other places in the Central Valleys.

The period from 950 to 1521 (Monte Albán V) saw minimal life at Monte Albán, except that Mixtecs arriving in the Central Valleys between 1100 and 1350 reused old tombs here to bury their own dignitaries. In Tomb 7 they left one of the richest treasure

hoards in the Americas, which is now in Oaxaca's Museo Regional.

Information

There's a museum, a cafeteria and a couple of shops at the entrance. Ask at the ticket office which tombs are open, since many main ones often aren't; some are also a bit of a walk from the rest of the site. (If you're out of luck, full-size replicas of Tombs 7 and 104 can be found in the Museo Nacional de Antropología in Mexico City!) Official guides offer their services (70 pesos for a family or small group) outside the ticket office. Entry to the site is 13 pesos (free on Sunday) and it's open from 8 am to 5 pm daily.

Gran Plaza

The Gran Plaza, about 300 metres long and 200 metres wide, was the centre of Monte Albán. The visible structures are nearly all from Monte Albán III. Some were temples, others residential. The following description takes you clockwise around the plaza.

The stone terraces of the deep, I-shaped **Ball Court** were probably part of the playing area, not stands for spectators. The round stone in the middle may have been used for bouncing the ball at the start of the game.

A small pillared temple stood on top of the pyramidal **Building P**. From the altar in front of the pyramid came a well-known jade bat-god mask, probably from Monte Albán II and now in the Museo Nacional de Antropología.

The **Palace** has a broad stairway. Under the inner patio on top was found a cross-shaped tomb, probably from Monte Albán IV, constructed after the site had been largely abandoned.

The big **South Platform**, with its wide staircase, is good for a panorama of the plaza. Two or three hundred metres south-east is a big structure called **Building Seven Deer**, from an inscription on its entrance lintel.

Building J, an arrowhead-shaped Monte Albán II building, riddled with tunnels and inner staircases, stands at an angle of 45° to the other Gran Plaza structures and is believed to have been an observatory.

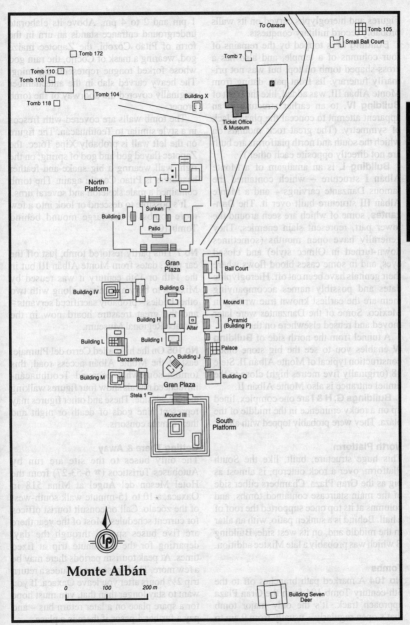

To Oaxaca

Tomb 105

Small Ball Court

Tomb 172

Tomb 7

Tomb 110
Tomb 103

Tomb 118

Tomb 104

Building X

Ticket Office
& Museum

North Platform

Sunken Patio

Building B

Gran Plaza

Ball Court

Building IV

Building G

Mound II

North Platform

Building H

Altar

Pyramid
(Building P)

Building L

Building I

Palace

Danzantes

Building J

Building M

Building Q

Gran Plaza

Stela 1

Mound III

South Platform

Building Seven
Deer

Monte Albán

0   100   200 m

Figures and hieroglyphs carved on its walls probably record military conquests.

Building M is topped by the remains of four columns of a temple, and also has a cross-shaped tomb on top, but was not primarily funerary. Its front part, dating from Monte Albán III, was added, like the front of **Building IV**, to an earlier structure in an apparent attempt to conceal the plaza's lack of symmetry. (The great rock mounds on which the south and north platforms are built are not directly opposite each other.)

Building L is an amalgam of a Monte Albán I structure – which contained the famous Danzante carvings – and a Monte Albán III structure built over it. The **Danzantes**, some of which are seen around the lower part, represent slain enemies. They generally have open mouths (sometimes down-turned in Olmec style) and closed eyes, and in some cases blood flows where their genitals have been cut off. Hieroglyphic dates and possibly names accompanying them are the earliest known true writing in Mexico. Some of the Danzantes were later moved and reused elsewhere on the site.

A tunnel from the north side of **Building IV** enables you to see the big stone block construction typical of Monte Albán II. Stele 18 (originally five metres high) close to the tunnel entrance is also Monte Albán II.

Buildings G, H & I are one complex, lined up on a rocky eminence in the middle of the plaza. They were probably topped with altars.

North Platform

This huge structure, built, like the South Platform, over a rock outcrop, is almost as big as the Gran Plaza. Chambers either side of the main staircase contained tombs, and columns at its top once supported the roof of a hall. Behind is a sunken patio, with an altar in the middle and, on its west side, Building B which was probably a late Mixtec addition.

Tombs

No 104 A marked path branches off to the 5th-century Tomb 104 from the Gran Plaza approach track. It's the only major tomb that's open regularly – usually from 9 am to

1 pm and 2 to 4 pm. Above its elaborate underground entrance stands an urn in the form of Pitao Cozobi, the Zapotec maize god, wearing a mask of Cocijo, the rain god whose forked tongue represents lightning. The heavy carved slab in the antechamber originally covered the doorway of the tomb proper.

The tomb walls are covered with frescos in a style similar to Teotihuacán. The figure on the left wall is probably Xipe Tótec, the Zapotec flayed god and god of spring; on the right wall wearing a big snake-and-feather headdress is Pitao Cozobi again. The tomb contained a male skeleton and several urns.

It's possible to descend or look into a few more tombs in the large mound behind Tomb 104.

No 7 This partly restored tomb, just off the car park, dates from Monte Albán III but in the 14th or 15th century it was reused by Mixtecs to bury a dignitary along with two other bodies – probably sacrificed servants – and the great treasure hoard now in the Oaxaca Regional Museum.

No 105 On the hill called Cerro del Plumaje, east of the Monte Albán access road, this tomb's somewhat decayed Teotihuacán-influenced murals show four figures walking along each side. These and other figures may represent nine gods of death or night and their female consorts.

Getting There & Away

The only buses to the site are run by Autobuses Turísticos (☎ 6-53-27) from the Hotel Mesón del Ángel at Mina 518 in Oaxaca, a 10 to 15-minute walk south-west of the zócalo. Call or consult tourist offices for current schedules. Most of the year there are five buses spaced through the day, departing for the 20-minute trip at fixed times. At peak tourism periods there may be a few more. The 8-peso fare includes a return trip 2½ hours after you leave Oaxaca. If you want to stay longer than that, you must hope for a spare place on a later return bus – and pay a further 4 pesos if there is a place.

A taxi from Oaxaca to Monte Albán costs 20 to 25 pesos but coming down you may have to pay more. Other possibilities are hitching (don't leave it too late to come down) or a city bus from Trujano, outside Oaxaca's 2nd-class bus station, to Colonia Monte Albán suburb, about two km below the site on the road up from Oaxaca.

EL TULE

A vast *ahuehuete* tree (a type of cypress) in the churchyard at El Tule, 10 km from Oaxaca along the Mitla road, is claimed to have the biggest girth of any tree in the Americas. It's 42 metres round but its age as much as its size is what makes it important to local people: it's officially reckoned to be 2000 years old but may be 3000. The tree, protected by a fence, stands right by the road, so you might get a glimpse from the bus if you don't want to get off. The annual Feria del Árbol (Fair of the Tree) is on the second Monday in October.

El Tule's vast *ahuehuete* tree

DAINZÚ

Twenty-one km from Oaxaca along the Mitla road, a track leads a km south across a hillside to the small but interesting ruins of Dainzú, open daily from 8 am to 5.30 pm (7 pesos except on Sunday and holidays).

Dainzú has remains from 300 BC or earlier to 1000 AD.

To the left as you approach is the pyramid-like Building A, 50 metres long and eight metres high, built about 300 BC. Along its bottom wall are a number of engravings from the same date or earlier, similar to the Monte Albán Danzantes. They nearly all show ball players – with masks or protective headgear, protective handgear and a ball in the right hand. Behind the ball-players' wall, steps descend to a tomb, converted from a stairway about the 7th century AD.

Among the ruins below Building A are, to the right as you look down, a sunken tomb with its entrance carved in the form of a crouching jaguar and, to the left, a half-restored ball court from about 1000 AD. Between the two is a big building with many rooms. At the top of the hill behind the main part of the site are more carvings in natural rock similar to the ballplayers, but it's a stiff climb and you'd probably need a guide to find them.

TEOTITLÁN DEL VALLE

One of Mexico's most famous weaving villages is four km north along a paved road from the Oaxaca-Mitla road, about 26 km from Oaxaca. The turning is signposted. Blankets, rugs and sarapes wave at you from almost every second house as you enter Teotitlán del Valle, and signs point to the central *mercado de artesanías*, where there are hundreds more on sale in an enormous variety of designs – from Zapotec gods and Mitla-style geometric patterns through birds and fish to imitations of paintings by Picasso, Miró and Escher.

The weaving tradition here goes back to pre-Hispanic times. Teotitlán even had to pay tribute to the Aztecs in the form of cloth. Quality is still very high in many cases and traditional dyes made from cochineal, indigo, or even wood, moss or leaves are still sometimes used. Rugs with more muted colours are less likely to have been made with synthetic dyes than some of the more garish offerings. Prices for Teotitlán products are not necessarily lower than in

Oaxaca, but there's probably a bigger choice here. The very best work may be tucked away in weavers' houses; if you show interest you will probably be asked in to see someone's techniques and merchandise.

Teotitlán celebrates the fiesta of the Virgen de la Natividad on 3 April with the Feather Dance.

Eat at the restaurant attached to the Arnolfe Mendoza shop. The food is some of the very best Oaxaqueño fare you'll find anywhere. People come to Teotitlán specially to eat here. Several courses beginning with a hit of mezcal will cost you 40 pesos.

Getting There & Away

Buses of Autotransportes Valle del Norte run 10 times daily to Teotitlán (2 pesos) from Gate 29 of Oaxaca's 2nd-class bus station: the last one back from the village is about 7.30 pm. Alternatively use a colectivo taxi, or a Oaxaca-Mitla bus and walk or hitch from the main road.

LAMBITYECO

The small archaeological site of Lambityeco lies on the south side of the Mitla road, 29 km from Oaxaca. About 600-800 AD (around Monte Albán's decline) Lambityeco seems to have become a sizeable Zapotec place of about 3000 people. Its people may then have moved to Yagul, a more defensible site in a time of turmoil.

The chief interest lies in two patios. In the first, immediately left of the main pyramid beside the car park, are two carved stone friezes on either side of a small altar. Each shows a bearded man holding a bone (symbol of hereditary rights) and a woman with Zapotec hairstyle. Both couples, plus a third shown in stucco on a tomb in the patio, are thought to have occupied the building and ruled Lambityeco in the 7th century.

The second patio has two reconstructed heads of the rain god Cocijo. In one, a huge feather-like headdress, spreading above his stern face, forms itself into the face of a jaguar. Lambityeco is open from 8 am to 5.30 pm daily (7 pesos, free on Sunday and holidays).

TLACOLULA

Four km beyond Lambityeco and 33 km from Oaxaca, this town of about 20,000 people holds one of the Central Valleys' major markets every Sunday, with a strong Indian presence. The area around and behind the church becomes a packed throng. Teotitlán blankets are among the goods sold. An extra-big market is held on the second Sunday in October. Buses from Oaxaca cost 2 pesos.

The church was one of several founded in Oaxaca by Dominican monks. Inside, the domed chapel of Santo Cristo is a riot of golden, Indian-influenced decoration comparable with the Rosary Chapel in Santo Domingo, Oaxaca. Martyrs can be seen carrying their heads under their arms. The chapel gate and the pulpit are fine colonial wrought-iron work.

SANTA ANA DEL VALLE

A turn north off the main road at Tlacolula, towards Díaz Ordaz, brings you after about a km to a junction. Here, if you go left, you enter Santa Ana del Valle, another village with a textile tradition going back to before the Spaniards. Today it produces woollen blankets, sarapes and bags. Natural dyes have not entirely disappeared and traditional designs – flowers, birds, geometric patterns – are still in use. Prices in the co-operatively run textile market are considerably lower than in Teotitlán del Valle or the Oaxaca shops. Santa Ana also has a small museum covering archaeology, history and traditional textile methods, including the preparation of cactus and cochineal dyes. There's also a richly decorated 18th-century church. Minibuses run frequently from Tlacolula to the village.

YAGUL

The ruins of Yagul are finely sited on a cactus-covered hill, with good views around sunset, 1.5 km by paved road north from the Oaxaca-Mitla road. The signposted turnoff is 35 km (2.25 pesos by bus) from Oaxaca. The site is open from 8 am to 5.30 pm daily (7 pesos, free on Sunday and holidays). The attendants usually have some excuse not to open the interesting tombs: you may be luckier if you visit at a quiet time, and not too late in the day.

Yagul became a leading Central Valleys settlement some time after the decline of Monte Albán. Most of what's visible is from after 900 AD. Yagul was probably Zapotec, with Mixtec influence in the period from which the main structures date.

The **Patio of the Triple Tomb** was surrounded by four temples. On the east side is a stone-carved animal, probably a jaguar.

Next to the central platform is the entrance to one of several underground triple tombs at Yagul. Steps go down to a tiny court, with three tombs off it. Carvings in the court are in Mitla style. The largest tomb, to the left, has stone heads flanking its entrance.

The beautifully restored **Ball Court** is the largest known in the Central Valleys. To its west, on the edge of the hill, is **Patio 1**, with the narrow **Council Hall** along its north side. Behind the council hall is a pathway with Mitla-style stone mosaics.

The labyrinthine **Palace of the Six**

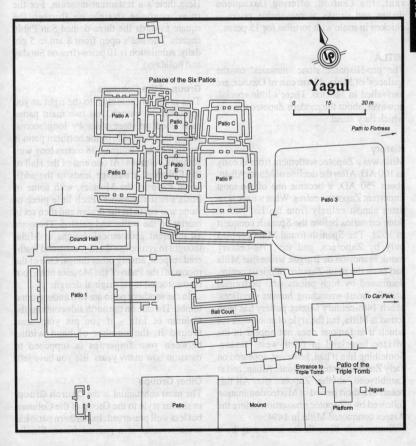

Palace of the Six Patios

Yagul

0   15   30 m

Path to Fortress

Patio A
Patio B
Patio C
Patio D
Patio E
Patio F
Patio 3

Council Hall

Patio 1

Ball Court

To Car Park

Entrance to Triple Tomb

Patio of the Triple Tomb

Patio

Mound

Platform

Jaguar

Patios was probably the leader's residence. Mitla-style structures were built over earlier Zapotec ones. The walls were faced with cut stone, plastered and painted red.

It's well worth ascending the **Fortress**, the huge rock which towers above the ruins. The path passes **Tomb 28**, made of cut stone. A few steps lead down to it and you can look in. From the top of the fortress the views are great. On the north side is a sheer drop of 100 metres or more. There are overgrown ruins of several structures up here.

Halfway along the Yagul road from the main road is a big, shady palapa-style restaurant, the *Centeotl*, offering Oaxaqueño dishes and drinks at reasonable prices – chicken in mole with tortillas for 15 pesos.

MITLA

The pre-Hispanic stone 'mosaics' on the 'palaces' of Mitla, 42 km east of Oaxaca, are unrivalled in Mexico. There's little special, however, about the modern Zapotec town in which they stand.

History

Mitla was a Zapotec settlement from as early as 100 AD. After the decline of Monte Albán, about 750 AD, it became one of the most important Zapotec centres. What we see now dates almost entirely from the last two or three centuries before the Spanish conquest in 1521. The Spanish found Mitla peopled only by Zapotecs, and the 17th-century monk Francisco de Burgoa wrote that Mitla had been the main Zapotec religious centre, dominated by high priests who performed literally heart-wrenching human sacrifices. Much 14th-century Mixtec pottery has been found at Mitla, but the style of stonework for which it is famous does not appear in the Mixtec heartland in north-west Oaxaca. Something like it had, however, appeared on early Zapotec pottery at Monte Albán, and at Lambityeco, another Zapotec site. All this points to a short period of Mixtec domination followed by a Zapotec reassertion before the Aztecs conquered Mitla in 1494.

Somewhere beneath the town may be a great undiscovered tomb of Zapotec kings and heroes; Burgoa wrote that Spanish priests found it but sealed it up.

It's thought that each of the groups of buildings we see at Mitla today was reserved for specific occupants – one for the high priest, one for lesser priests, one for the king, one for his officials, etc.

Orientation & Information

If you tell the bus conductor from Oaxaca that you're heading for *las ruinas*, you'll be dropped at a junction at the entry to the town, where you go left up to the central plaza. Here there's a restaurant-museum. For the ruins, continue straight on through the square towards the three-domed San Pablo church. The site's open from 8 am to 5 pm daily. Admission is 10 pesos (free on Sunday and holidays).

Group of the Columns

This group of buildings, to the right as you approach the church, has two main patios each lined on three sides by long rooms. Along the north side of the northern patio is the Hall of the Columns, 38 metres long with six thick columns. At one end of the Hall of the Columns, a passage leads to the additional Patio of the Mosaics, with some of Mitla's best stonework. Each little piece of stone was cut to fit the design and then set in mortar on the walls, and painted. There are 14 different geometrical designs at Mitla, thought to symbolise the sky, earth and feathered serpent, among other things. One of the rooms off the Patio of the Mosaics has a roof reconstructed to its original design.

In the southern patio are two underground tombs. The one on the north side contains the Column of Life – if you put your arms around it, the number of hand widths between your fingertips is supposed to measure how many years' life you have left.

Other Groups

The most substantial is the **Church Group**, in similar style to the Group of the Columns but less well preserved. Its northern patio has some remains of a painted frieze. Similar

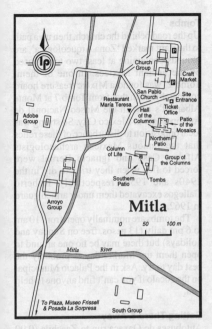

Mitla

0   50   100 m

To Plaza, Museo Frissell & Posada La Sorpresa

paintings once adorned many Mitla buildings. The church was built on top of one patio in 1590.

The **Arroyo Group** is the most substantial of the other, unexcavated, groups. The remains of forts, tombs and other structures are scattered over the country for many km around.

Museum

The Museo Frissell (open from 9 am to 5 pm daily, free) in the Posada La Sorpresa has a sizeable collection of small archaeological pieces.

Places to Stay & Eat

Posada La Sorpresa at Independencia 40 off the town plaza no longer has rooms, but still serves very good breakfasts (13 pesos) and lunches (26 pesos) at tables around a lovely courtyard. The modernish but fading *Hotel La Zapoteca* at 5 de Febrero 8, between the plaza and the ruins, has singles/doubles with

private bath for 45/65 pesos around an untidy courtyard; breakfasts here cost 6 pesos, lunch or dinner 12 pesos. The basic *Hotel Mitla* at Independencia 12, across the road from La Sorpresa, charges 30/40 pesos, also with bath. *Restaurant María Teresa*, near the church, has good food at reasonable prices.

Things to Buy

Mitla's streets are spattered with shops selling mezcal and textiles – embroidered dresses, rebozos, table cloths, rugs, hammocks, much of it made in Mitla. There's a craft market next to the ruins, with the same sort of stuff. Some striped rebozos are an original Mitla design.

Getting There & Away

The last four km to Mitla are along a side road east off highway 190. Bus fare from Oaxaca is 2.50 pesos. The last bus back to Oaxaca is at 8 pm.

MIXE REGION

Beyond Mitla is the isolated country of the Mixe Indians, about 80,000 of whom are spread through the mountains towards the Isthmus of Tehuantepec. The Mixe are among the least modernised, and most shy and self-contained, of Oaxaca's Indians. Two of their main settlements are **Ayutla** (population 4000, market day Sunday), about 30 km east of Mitla, and **Zacatepec** (population 3000, market day Wednesday), a further 40 km north-east beneath Zempoaltépetl, Oaxaca's highest peak.

Four Fletes y Pasajes (FYPSA) buses run daily to Ayutla, and one to Zacatepec, from Oaxaca's 2nd-class bus station. Only parts of the road from Mitla are paved.

CUILAPAN

Shortly before the Spanish conquest Cuilapan, 12 km south of Oaxaca, was a Mixtec town of over 10,000 people. Today it's one of the few Mixtec enclaves in the Central Valleys. The attraction is the ruins of its big, beautiful, historic **Dominican monastery** (open daily from 10 am to 6 pm, entry

13 pesos). Probably begun in 1555, its pale stone seems almost to grow out of the land.

In 1831 the Mexican independence hero Vicente Guerrero was executed at the monastery by soldiers supporting the rebel conservative Anastasio Bustamante, who had just thrown the liberal Guerrero out of the presidency. Guerrero had booked passage on a ship out of Acapulco but its captain handed him over to the authorities for 50,000 pieces of gold. Guerrero was transported to Cuilapan to die.

From the entrance you first reach the long, low, elegant, roofless capilla abierta. Beyond is part of the original monastery church. Around its right-hand end you reach the two-storey Renaissance-style cloister. The rear rooms on its ground floor have some 16th and 17th-century murals. A painting of Guerrero hangs in the room where he was held. Outside, a monument stands on the spot where he was shot.

The closed part of the church is said to contain the Christian tombs of Juana Donají (daughter of Cocijo-eza, the last Zapotec king of Zaachila) and her Mixtec husband.

Getting There & Away
Autobuses de Oaxaca run to Cuilapan (0.80 pesos) from gate 27 of Oaxaca's 2nd-class bus station every 10 minutes. They stop right by the monastery.

ZAACHILA
The part-Mixtec, part-Zapotec village of Zaachila, six km beyond Cuilapan, has a busy Thursday market in its main plaza. At Carnaval time Zaachila is the scene of a mock-battle in which masked *curas* (priests) defend themselves with crosses and buckets of water from whip-wielding *diablos* (devils). Zaachila was a Zapotec capital from about 1400 to the Spanish conquest but was controlled for some of that period by Mixtecs. Its last Zapotec king, Cocijo-eza, became a Christian with the name Juan Cortés and died in 1523. Six pre-Hispanic monoliths and the village church stand on the main square.

Tombs
Up the road behind the church, then up a path to the right marked 'Zona Arqueológica', are mounds containing at least two tombs used by the ancient Mixtecs. In one of them, Tomb 2, was found a Mixtec treasure hoard comparable with that from Tomb 7 at Monte Albán. It's now in the Museo Nacional de Antropología in Mexico City. So strong was local opposition to disturbance of these relics that the famous Mexican archaeologists Alfonso Caso and Ignacio Bernal were forced to flee when they tried to dig in the 1940s and 1950s respectively. Roberto Gallegos excavated them under armed guard in 1962.

The tombs are nominally open from 10 am to 6 pm daily (13 pesos, free on Sunday and holidays) but there may be no one around to open them up. Market day is probably the best day to try. Ask in the Palacio Municipal on the zócalo if you can't find anyone to help you.

Getting There & Away
Autobuses de Oaxaca run to Zaachila (0.90 pesos) from gate 27 of Oaxaca's 2nd-class bus station every 10 minutes. From Zaachila bus station, walk up the main street to the main square.

SAN BARTOLO COYOTEPEC
All the polished, black, surprisingly light pottery you see in Oaxaca comes from San Bartolo Coyotepec, a small village about 12 km south of the city on highway 175. Look out for the roadside sign to the alfarería of Doña Rosa, east of the road. Several village families make and sell the blackware but it was Rosa Valente Nieto Real who invented the method of burnishing it with quartz stones for the distinctive shine. She died in 1979, but her family carries on and gives skilful demonstrations on Friday from about 9 am to 2 pm. The pieces are handmoulded by an age-old technique in which two saucers play the part of a potter's wheel, then fired in pit kilns. They go black because of the iron oxide in the local clay and because smoke is trapped in the kiln.

The village saint's day, 24 August, is celebrated with dances, including the Feather Dance.

Getting There & Away

Buses run to San Bartolo (1 peso) every 15 or 30 minutes from a small terminal 500 metres south of the Oaxaca zócalo, on Armenta y López just south of La Noria.

SANTO TOMÁS JALIEZA

This little Zapotec village just east of highway 175, about 25 km south of Oaxaca, holds a textiles market on Friday to coincide with market day in Ocotlán. Its cotton waist-sashes have pretty animal or plant designs. You can see people weaving on the spot and the quality of the textiles is good. A colectivo taxi from Ocotlán costs 1 peso per person.

OCOTLÁN

The big, bustling Friday market at Ocotlán, 35 km from Oaxaca, goes back to pre-Hispanic days. Local specialities include reed baskets, and there's other merchandise from around the Central Valleys.

Getting There & Away

Autotransportes Ocotlán de Morelos microbuses run to Ocotlán from a small terminal on Cabrera, four blocks south of the Oaxaca zócalo, every 10 minutes. There are also buses every 15 or 30 minutes from another terminal on Armenta y López just south of La Noria. The ride is about 45 minutes and the bus fare 1.70 pesos.

EJUTLA

Some 60 km from Oaxaca down highway 175, Ejutla has a Thursday market and is known for its engraved knives, machetes and swords – and for its mezcal, reputedly the finest in Oaxaca. There are buses (3.20 pesos) every 15 or 30 minutes from the small terminal on Armenta y López just south of La Noria in Oaxaca.

Mixteca Alta & Mixteca Baja

Oaxaca's Mixteca (land of the Mixtecs) comprises three adjoining areas in the west of the state. The north-west borderlands around Huajuapan de León are part of the Mixteca Baja (Low Mixteca) which stretches across into Puebla state at 1000 to 1700 metres. The Mixteca Alta (High Mixteca) is the rugged area between the Mixteca Baja and the Oaxaca Central Valleys, mostly above 2000 metres. The Mixteca de la Costa is a remote south-western zone stretching back up into the hills from the coast (see the later West of Puerto Escondido section).

The Mixteca has been the heartland of the Mixtec people for at least 1200 years. It was from the Mixteca Alta in about the 12th century that Mixtec dominion began to spread to the Oaxaca Central Valleys and the Tehuantepec area. Famed as workers of gold and precious stones, the Mixtecs also developed a fine painted pottery known as Mixteca-Puebla which, it is said, was the only type the Aztec emperor Moctezuma would eat from. The Mixteca Alta and Baja were subjugated by the Aztecs in the 15th century.

Today much of the Mixteca is over-farmed and deforested, and politics and business are dominated by mestizos. Many Mixtecs have to emigrate for work. Foreign visitors are rather a rarity in this area.

Things to See

The 16th-century Dominican monasteries in the Mixteca Alta villages of Yanhuitlán, Coixtlahuaca and Teposcolula are among colonial Mexico's finest architecture, their restrained stonework fusing medieval, plateresque, Renaissance and Indian styles.

Yanhuitlán, the most easily reached, towers beside highway 190, 120 km from Oaxaca. It was designed to withstand earthquakes and serve as a defensive refuge. The cloister has an interesting little museum of

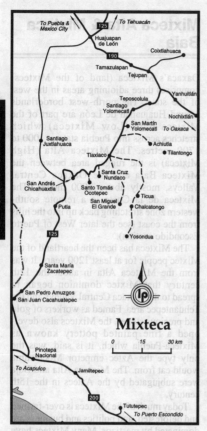

To Puebla & Mexico City
To Tehuacán
Huajuapan de León
Coixtlahuaca
Tamazulapan
Tejupan
Yanhuitlán
Teposcolula
Santiago Yolomecatl
Nochixtlán
San Martín Yolomecatl
To Oaxaca
Santiago Juxtlahuaca
Achiutla
Tlaxiaco
Tilantongo
Santa Cruz Nundaco
San Andrés Chicahuaxtla
Santo Tomás Ocotepec
Ticua
San Miguel El Grande
Putla
Chalcatongo
Yosondua
Santa María Zacatepec
San Pedro Amuzgos
San Juan Cacahuatepec

Mixteca

0   15   30 km

Pinotepa Nacional
To Acapulco
Jamiltepec
Tututepec
To Puerto Escondido

items from the monastery (open daily from 10 am to 6 pm, 13 pesos). The church contains valuable works of art and is usually locked. Ask the museum caretaker to open it. A fine Mudéjar timber roof supports the choir.

The monastery in **Coixtlahuaca**, 22 km north-east of highway 190 by a paved road, is if anything more beautiful than Yanhuitlán's. The turnoff, 142 km from Oaxaca, is at Tejupan, which has its own giant 16th-century Dominican church. Colectivo taxis wait at Tejupan to take people to Coixtlahuaca. Beside the monastery church stands its graceful, ruined capilla abierta. Enlist the

caretaker of the cloister museum to open the church itself, which has a lovely rib-vaulted roof with carved keystones. Coixtlahuaca holds a big procession, rodeo and firework show on 27 December for the feast of San Juan Evangelista.

Teposcolula lies on highway 125, 13 km south of highway 190. The monastery is beside the main plaza, which borders the road through the town. Its stately capilla abierta of three open bays is immediately north of the west end of the monastery church. The church itself is a replacement for the 16th-century original, which was probably destroyed by an earthquake. The cloister is a museum (open from 10 am to 6 pm daily, 13 pesos).

Tlaxiaco, 43 km south of Teposcolula on highway 125, was known before the revolution as Paris Chiquita (Little Paris), for the quantities of French luxuries like clothes and wine imported for its few rich land and mill-owning families. Today the only signs of that elegance are the portales around the main plaza and a few large houses with courtyards. The church two blocks south of the plaza, originally part of a 16th-century monastery, has a Gothic vault and a plateresque façade. The market area is off the south-east corner of the zócalo – Saturday is the main day.

South of Tlaxiaco, highway 125 – paved all the way – winds through the Sierra Madre del Sur to Pinotepa Nacional on the coastal highway 200. The only sizeable place on the way is **Putla**, 95 km from Tlaxiaco. Before Putla is **San Andrés Chicahuaxtla** in the small territory of the Triqui Indians. The Spaniards found the Triqui rebellious and nearly impossible to Christianise. Even today Triqui witch doctors reputedly carry out cures in churches after services, and a history of conflict between Triquis and mestizos or Mixtecs continues over land rights. The Amuzgo Indians of **San Pedro Amuzgos**, 73 km south of Putla, are known for their fine huipiles.

Places to Stay & Eat
You can visit the Mixteca Alta or Baja in a long day-trip from Oaxaca, but there are also

basic hotels in Nochixtlán, Yanhuitlán, Coixtlahuaca and Putla, and better ones in Tlaxiaco and Huajuapan de León. In Tlaxiaco, the *Hotel Del Portal* (☎ (955) 2-01-54) on the plaza has big clean singles/doubles with private bath around a pleasant courtyard for 46/60 pesos. *Casa Habitación San Michell* on Independencia is the other of the town's better places, charging a few pesos less. The *Hotel Colón* (☎ (955) 2-00-13), one block east of the plaza on the corner of Colón and Hidalgo, charges around 25 pesos with private bath, 15 pesos with shared bath.

Tlaxiaco's best food is at the *Cafe Uni-Nuu* next to the Hotel Del Portal, with comida corrida at 12 pesos plus a wide-ranging menu on which shrimps are about 25 pesos and most other main courses 12 pesos, and great coffee.

Getting There & Away

Huajuapan and Yanhuitlán, on highway 190 from Oaxaca to Mexico City or Puebla, are served by several 1st-class and numerous 2nd-class buses daily. Yanhuitlán is 2½ hours from Oaxaca for 14 pesos 1st-class. For Teposcolula, Tlaxiaco and other places on highway 125, there are a couple of 1st-class Cristóbal Colón buses from Oaxaca daily, plus half a dozen 2nd-class Fletes y Pasajes (FYPSA) buses. Or you can take any bus to the junction of highway 190 and highway 125, from where minibuses go down highway 125. Some Cristóbal Colón and Fletes y Pasajes buses run from Tlaxiaco to Putla and Pinotepa Nacional. There are buses from Mexico City's Terminal Oriente (TAPO) to several Mixteca towns.

Northern Oaxaca

TUXTEPEC & GUELATAO

On the Papaloapan River, 128 km from Alvarado on the Veracruz coast, **Tuxtepec** is the 'capital' of a low-lying area of northern Oaxaca which in culture and topography is akin to Veracruz. Highway 175 winds 210 km through the mountains from Oaxaca, so Tuxtepec is on a possible coast-to-coast route. It has several moderately priced hotels and is served by 1st-class and 2nd-class buses from many towns in Oaxaca and Veracruz.

On the way to Tuxtepec, 74 km from Oaxaca, is **Guelatao**, birthplace of Benito Juárez. There's a mausoleum with his remains, at least two statues of him, a museum devoted to him (open Tuesday to Saturday, 10 am to 2 pm and 4 to 6 pm, 13 pesos), and more memorabilia in the Palacio Municipal. In **Ixtlán**, a km north of Guelatao on highway 175, is the 16th-century church where he was baptised. Buses leave Oaxaca's 2nd-class bus station five times daily for Guelatao (6 pesos, 2½ hours), run by – yes – the Benito Juárez bus company.

HUAUTLA DE JIMÉNEZ

The hallucinogenic mushrooms (*hongos*) used for spiritual renewal by the Mazatec Indians of Huautla de Jiménez once acted as a magnet to young Mexicans and travellers. Now outsiders trickle in, mainly in rainy June, July and August, when los hongos appear. (Out of season they can still be obtained, preserved in honey.) Locals disapprove of mushroom-taking just for thrills, but it's OK if aimed at 'cleaning the mind' under the direction of a 'guide' or *curandero*.

Places to Stay & Eat

There's a cheap *Casa de Huéspedes* at Juárez 19, not far from the market. It's also possible to rent rooms or cabins from families for 7 pesos or so. *Restaurant Karina* on Juárez does good basic food and its friendly owner will talk about mushroom traditions.

Getting There & Away

Huautla is 67 km east into the hills from Teotitlán del Camino, which is on highway 131 between Oaxaca and Tehuacán. Fletes y Pasajes (FYPSA) runs four buses a day from Oaxaca's 2nd-class bus station, taking about six hours for 24 pesos.

Oaxaca Coast

A laid-back stint on the Oaxaca coast is the perfect complement to the inland attractions of Oaxaca city and the Central Valleys. Though flights and newly paved roads have brought this isolated, rather special stretch of coast closer to the rest of Mexico in the last 20 years, and turned the two fishing villages of Puerto Escondido and Puerto Ángel into minor resorts, they remain small-scale and relaxed – Puerto Ángel especially so. Puerto Escondido has famous surf, while near Puerto Ángel is one of Mexico's great budget travellers' beaches, Zipolite. Further east a huge new resort is being systematically developed on the beautiful Bahías de Huatulco.

Getting There & Away

Air There are daily flights to Puerto Escondido and Huatulco from both Oaxaca and Mexico City – see the relevant town/city sections.

Bus There are buses to Puerto Escondido, Pochutla and Huatulco from Oaxaca, Acapulco and places as far east as San Cristóbal de Las Casas. For Puerto Ángel, get to Pochutla then take a local bus or taxi. If you're travelling from Chiapas to this coast, or vice-versa, and can't get a convenient through bus, the alternative is to get a bus to Juchitán or Salina Cruz then another bus on from there. More detail on services is given in the city/town sections.

Car The Acapulco-Salina Cruz coastal highway 200 heads along this coast linking Puerto Escondido, Pochutla (13 km north of Puerto Ángel) and the Bahías de Huatulco. From Oaxaca, highway 175 (all paved) winds 240 km down through the spectacular Sierra Madre del Sur to meet highway 200 at Pochutla. Highway 125, all paved, runs down through the remote west of the state, linking the Oaxaca-Mexico City highway 190 to highway 200 at Pinotepa Nacional.

Dangers & Annoyances

The Oaxaca coast, a rather impoverished region apart from its few tourist honey-pots, has more than its fair share of crime against tourists. Be on your guard against theft in Puerto Escondido and the Puerto Ángel-Zipolite area. Some thieves even brandish knives or guns. One traveller couple wrote to tell us of a far more horrifying incident: while driving a hire-car along the isolated Huatulco-Salina Cruz stretch of highway 200, they were forced off the road by another vehicle and taken to an empty building, where he was tied up and she was raped.

PUERTO ESCONDIDO

• *pop: 35,000*

A haunt of surfers since long before paved roads reached this part of Oaxaca, Puerto Escondido (Hidden Port) is more resort than fishing village now, but remains small and reasonably cheap. Scattered across a hillside above the ocean, it has few paved streets and hasn't made it onto the package holiday map. There are several beaches, a range of reasonable accommodation, cafés and restaurants, and a spot of nightlife.

Puerto Escondido is hotter and much more humid than the highlands of Oaxaca. Any breath of breeze can be at a premium and you're more likely to get one up the hill a bit, rather than down at sea level. The wettest months are May, June, early July and September. At these times tourism slumps and Puerto Escondido puts on its worst face in other ways too – you may encounter resentment towards tourists, and crime against tourists, never to be dismissed here, seems to increase.

Orientation

The town rises above a small, south-facing bay (the Bahía Principal). Highway 200 runs across the hill halfway up, dividing the upper town where the locals live and work – and buses arrive – from the lower, tourism-dominated part. Avenida Pérez Gasga, partly pedestrianised, is the heart of the lower town, with cafés, restaurants, shops and some hotels. The west end of Pérez Gasga winds up the slope to meet the highway at a crossroads known simply as El Crucero.

The Bahía Principal curves around, at its east end, to the long Playa Zicatela – good for surfing but dangerous for swimming – which is backed by several newer, mostly bottom-end and middle-range, places to stay. Other beaches line a series of bays to the west.

Information

Tourist Office Puerto Escondido's tourist office (☎ (958) 2-01-75) is located about as inconveniently as possible, a long uphill walk from town on the road to the airport, opposite the corner of 3a Norte. It's a couple of palm-thatched buildings with a 'Sedetur Representación de Turismo' sign, open Monday to Friday from 9 am to 2 pm and 5 to 8 pm, Saturday 9 am to 1 pm.

Money Bancomer is on Pérez Gasga opposite the hotel Rincón del Pacífico, and Banamex is a little way up the hill on Pérez Gasga on the corner of Calle Unión. Both change dollars and travellers' cheques from 9 am to noon, Monday to Friday (queues are generally shorter at Banamex), and have ATMs too. There are also a few casas de cambio – all called 'Money Exchange' – giving worse rates than the banks but open longer hours, typically 9 am to 2 pm and 4 to 7 pm, Monday to Saturday. Two are on the pedestrianised part of Pérez Gasga; a third is on Playa Zicatela next to Bungalows Acuario.

Post & Telecommunications The post office is a 20 or 30-minute uphill walk from the seafront, a blue building on Oaxaca on the corner of 7a Norte. You can take a 'Mercado' bus or colectivo taxi up Oaxaca to save your legs. It opens from 8 am to 7 pm Monday to Friday, and 9 am to 1 pm Saturday. The Telecomm office next door has telegram and fax service – open Monday to Friday from 9 am to 1 pm and 3 to 7 pm, Saturday 9 am to noon.

There's a Ladatel credit-card phone in front of the Farmacia Cortés on Pérez Gasga, and a Lada caseta, with fax service too, across the street next to the money exchange.

Laundry You can wash and dry 8 kg of clothes for 12 pesos at Lavamática del Centro on Pérez Gasga, a little uphill from the Hotel Nayar. Service wash is an extra 6 pesos.

Dangers & Annoyances Stories of knife-point robberies, bashings with bags of stones, even stabbings, were rife a few years ago. One reader even told us of her knife-point mugging on a sparsely populated Playa Bacocho at 1 pm. When last in town, we noticed a slight easing of the problem. Steps have been taken to make the popular Playa Zicatela, once renowned for muggings, safer – more street lighting and police patrols on Calle del Morro, the road that parallels the beach. But you should definitely stick to well-lit areas at night and to populated places by day to avoid any threat. Alternatively, catch a taxi.

Beaches

Bahía Principal The main town beach is long enough to accommodate a few restaurants at its west end, a small fishing fleet in the middle, sun-worshippers at the east end (known as Playa Marinero), and occasional flights of pelicans winging in, inches above the waves. A few hawkers wander up and down offering textiles and necklaces. The smelly water entering the bay at times from the inaptly named Laguna Agua Dulce will put you off dipping anywhere other than Playa Marinero, but don't get too close to the rocks there.

Zicatela The waters of Zicatela, beyond the rocky outcrop at the east end of Playa Marinero, have a literally lethal undertow and are for strong-swimming surfers only – though landlubbers can still enjoy the sand and the acrobatics of the board-riders on the 'Mexican Pipeline'. It is said that drownings here have ceased since lifeguards began to patrol the beach.

Las Olas cabañas rents surfboards for 30 pesos a day. Rockaway has surfboards, snorkel gear and beach umbrellas for hire. After dark, Zicatela is a renowned haunt of muggers.

Puerto Angelito The sheltered bay of Puerto Angelito, about a km west of the Bahía Principal as the crow flies, has two small beaches separated by a few rocks which you can walk across. You can rent snorkel gear at the small restaurant. On weekends and holidays Puerto Angelito can get as busy as the Bahía Principal.

Lanchas from in front of the Palmas de Cortés on Bahía Principal will take you to Puerto Angelito for about 10 pesos per person return. The boat returns at an agreed pick-up time. By land, go west along highway 200 for a few hundred metres from El Crucero. A sign points left down to Puerto Angelito. On the way down, fork left at the Pepsi sign – altogether a 30 to 40-minute walk from Avenida Pérez Gasga. A taxi from town costs about 7 pesos.

Carrizalillo The small cove of Carrizalillo, just west of Puerto Angelito, is rockier but OK for swimming, with a little beach. Lanchas from the Bahía Principal will bring you here too. A path down from the Puerto Escondido Trailer Park reaches the cove.

Bacocho This long, straight beach, on the open ocean just west of the Hotel Posada Real, has a dangerous undertow. In the past there have been muggings of tourists who leave the safety of numbers.

Diving

Jorgé Pere Bravo (☎ 2-00-47) of Aventura Submarina can provide diving gear and will act as a guide on diving trips. Apparently the San Andreas faultline begins somewhere straight out to sea from Zicatela!

Organised Tours

Several tour companies on Pérez Gasga run trips to places along the coast to the west – see the West of Puerto Escondido section – and to Huatulco, generally with a stop at Puerto Ángel (80 to 90 pesos per person). There are also horse-riding outings to Atotonilco hot springs, north of San José Manialtepec 20 km west of Puerto Escondido (90 pesos), and trips to the mountain

town of Nopalá, with a visit to a coffee plantation (100 pesos).

Festivals

Semana Santa is the big week for local partying. The Oaxaca state surf carnival is held at this time. An international surfing competition is held sometime in August. The national surfing title, competed for from November 17 to 20, coincides with the Puerto Escondido fiesta which includes a Guelaguetza, beauty contests, free drinks, food etc.

Places to Stay – bottom end

In the peak tourist season – Christmas to April – the most popular places may be full (this applies in all price ranges). Your best chance, if you haven't booked ahead, is to ask at about 9 or 10 am. Prices given here are for this high season: at other times they will be 20% to 50% lower in most places.

Camping/Trailer Parks *Puerto Escondido Trailer Park* (☎ (958) 2-00-77), about 1.5 km west of the town, occupies a large open area on the clifftop above Playa Carrizalillo. Water and electrical hook-ups are included at 25 to 30 pesos for two people. The best road approach is Avenida Guelatao, through the Fraccionamiento Bacocho area off highway 200 in the far west of the town.

Neptuno on the Bahía Principal has a grassy area for camping, with electrical hook-ups, and a big central fireplace. The communal toilets are grubby. The cost is 10 pesos per person. The *Palmas de Cortés* campground/trailer park next door has more shade but less space, charging 15 pesos per person and 20 pesos per vehicle, with showers, electrical hook-ups and fireplaces.

Elva's Place is a pleasant small campsite at Zicatela. It's next to Bruno's restaurant, on a thin strip of land leading up to a few cheap, basic cabañas. Small coconut palms provide a little shade. The cost is 25 pesos for one or two people.

Beyond Zicatela, at Playa Barra de Colotepec, *Campamento Ecológico Ayuda Las Tortugas* provides more camping if you're

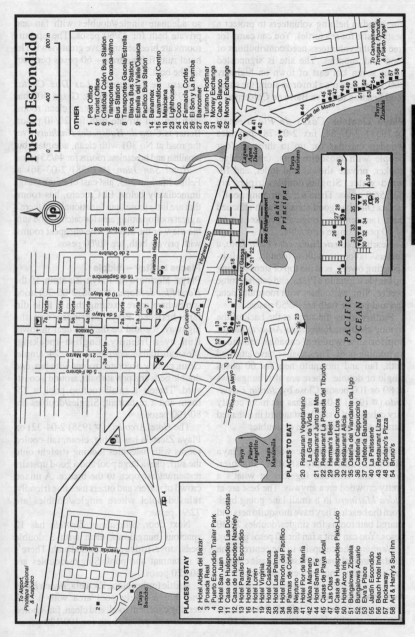

Puerto Escondido

OTHER

1 Post Office
5 Tourist Office
6 Cristóbal Colón Bus Station
7 Transportes Oaxaca-Istmo Bus Station
8 Trans Stortes Gacela/Estrella Blanca Bus Station
9 Estrella del Valle/Oaxaca Pacífico Bus Station
14 Banamex
15 Lavamática del Centro
18 Mexicana
23 Lighthouse
24 Coco
25 Farmacia Cortés
26 El Son y La Rumba
27 Bancomer
28 Turismo Rodimar
31 Money Exchange
46 Cabo Blanco
52 Money Exchange

PLACES TO STAY

2 Hotel Aldea del Bazar
3 Posada Real
4 Puerto Escondido Trailer Park
10 Hotel San Juan
11 Casa de Huéspedes Las Dos Costas
12 Casa de Huéspedes Naxhiely
13 Hotel Paraíso Escondido
16 Hotel Nayar
17 Hotel Loren
19 Hotel Virginia
28 Hotel Casablanca
33 Hotel Las Palmas
34 Hotel Rincón del Pacífico
38 Palmas de Cortés
39 Neptuno
41 Hotel Flor de María
42 Aldea Marinero
44 Hotel Santa Fe
45 Casas de Playa Acali
47 Las Olas
49 Casa de Huéspedes Pako-Lolo
50 Hotel Arco Iris
51 Bungalows Zicatela
52 Bungalows Acuario
53 Elva's Place
55 Jardín Escondido
56 Beach Hotel Inés
57 Rockaway
58 Art & Harry's Surf Inn

PLACES TO EAT

20 Restauran Vegetariano - La Gota de Vida
21 Restaurant Junto al Mar
22 Restaurant La Posada del Tiburón
29 Herman's Best
30 Restaurant Los Crotos
32 Restaurant Alicia
35 Osteria del Viandante da Ugo
36 Cafetería Cappuccino
37 Cafetería Bananas
40 La Patisserie
43 Restaurant Liza's
48 Cipriano's Pizza
54 Bruno's

To Airport,
Pinotepa Nacional
& Acapulco

Playa Bacocho

Playa Angelito

Playa Manzanilla

Playa Marinero

Bahía Principal

Laguna
Agua Dulce

Calle del Morro

Playa Zicatela

PACIFIC OCEAN

To Campamento
Tortugas, Pochutla,
& Puerto Ángel

See Enlargement

Highway 200

El Crucero

Oaxaca

21 de Marzo

5 de Febrero

3a Norte

2a Norte

1a Norte

5 de Mayo

10 de Mayo

16 de Septiembre

2 de Octubre

20 de Noviembre

Avenida Hidalgo

Avenida Pérez Gasga

Primero de Mayo

Avenida Guelatao

7a Norte
6a Norte
5a Norte
4a Norte
3a Norte
2a Norte
1a Norte

800 m
400
0

interested in helping volunteers to protect a nesting site for sea turtles. You can camp for free but the volunteers need contributions of food and supplies. The site is signposted about seven km east of town on highway 200. From here it's a km or so along the small road heading to Playa Barra de Colotepec.

Playa Zicatela *Casas de Playa Acali* (☎ (958) 2-07-54, fax 2-02-78) provides wooden cabañas for up to three or four people with mosquito nets, fans, fridge, cooker, private shower and toilet, and filtered water. Singles/doubles/triples are 60/75/90 pesos. There's a swimming pool.

Las Olas has good cabañas with attached bath, fan, screens, fridge and cooker for 65 or 70 pesos single or double.

Nearby, *Casa de Huéspedes Pako-Lolo*, a surfers' favourite with a friendly English-speaking owner, is at the top of steps leading up beside Cipriano's Pizza, and catches some breeze. Singles/doubles with mosquito nets, fan and private bath are 40/50 pesos.

Further along the strip, at the back of the money changer, *Bungalows Acuario* has 12 comfortable wooden cabañas around a swimming pool. The cabañas have attached bath, fan and mosquito nets for 60 pesos single or double. There are also bungalows at 80 or 100 pesos. Close by, *Jardín Escondido* (☎ (958) 2-03-48) has yet more comfy airy cabañas of a similar standard in a shaded garden at 66 pesos single or double.

Bahía Principal The cabañas on Playa Marinero are mostly smaller, shabbier, dirtier and crowded together in what's a pretty crowded area anyway. The best are at *Aldea Marinero* in a small lane going back from the beach. They have mosquito nets and shared bathrooms for singles/doubles 20/30 pesos. You can rent a fan for 50 pesos per day.

Neptuno, the campsite in the centre of the Bahía Principal, has some small, basic cabañas (no nets, a few mosquitoes) for 20 pesos.

Avenida Pérez Gasga *Hotel Virginia* on Alfaro, a track leading left off Pérez Gasga 400 metres uphill beyond the mall, has 10 or

so adequate singles/doubles with fan and private bath for 45/60 pesos. The upstairs rooms are breezier and have great views. The hotel runs fishing trips – 60 pesos per hour for the boat.

Casa de Huéspedes Las Dos Costas (☎ (958) 2-01-59) at Pérez Gasga 302 has bare, shabby, only moderately clean rooms with fan and private bath for 20/40 pesos. Better is *Casa de Huéspedes Naxhiely* over the road at No 301 with clean, adequate but smallish and breezeless rooms for 44/55 pesos.

Hotel San Juan (☎ (958) 2-03-36) at Felipe Marklin 503, just east of Pérez Gasga immediately below El Crucero, has rooms that are little more than functional, but there's a great rooftop sitting area for catching the sun, the view or the breeze. The cheapest rooms, with private bath, are 40/60 pesos.

Places to Stay – middle
Playa Marinero & Playa Zicatela If the *Hotel Flor de María* (☎ (958) 2-05-36) stood somewhere more exciting than a little dirt lane between Playa Marinero and the highway, it could be the best deal in town. Run by a friendly, English-speaking, Mexican-Italian couple, it has 24 ample, clean, prettily decorated rooms with fan, two double beds and private bath, around a courtyard. There's a small rooftop pool, a TV room and a restaurant. Singles/doubles are 80/100 pesos.

The *Hotel Arco Iris* (☎ (958) 2-04-32) on Playa Zicatela has 20 big, clean, fan-cooled rooms with balconies looking straight onto the surf, plus a large pool and a good upstairs restaurant/bar open to the breeze. A mixed crowd of surfers and others uses this friendly, relaxed hotel where singles/doubles are 72/91 pesos.

Next door, *Bungalows Zicatela* has 12 spacious bungalows, each with 3 double beds, stove, fridge and attached bath. There's a restaurant and pool. Singles/doubles are 50/120 pesos.

A little further along Zicatela, *Beach Hotel Inés* has a lovely pool area with a café serving excellent food, and clean, fan-cooled rooms with private bath for 100/120 pesos.

Nearby, *Rockaway* (☎ (958) 2-06-68) has good single/double/triple cabañas around a pool for 60/90/120 pesos.

Art & Harry's Surf Inn, just beyond Rockaway, has pleasant rooms with private bath, hot water, fans and mosquito screens for 80 pesos, single or double. Most rooms face the beach and a couple have an extra sitting area.

Avenida Pérez Gasga *Hotel Rincón del Pacífico* (☎ (958) 2-00-56) on the pedestrianised part of Avenida Pérez Gasga, has 20-odd big-windowed, fan-cooled rooms around a palmy courtyard, and its own café/restaurant on the beach. Though slightly dilapidated, it has cheery, helpful staff and fairly well-kept rooms at 90 pesos single or double. *Hotel Las Palmas* (☎ (958) 2-00-56) next door is similar but in our experience less friendly, and the rooms, though slightly bigger, are dearer at 100/120 pesos. Streetside rooms in both places may be assailed by loud late-night music from outside.

In some ways a better bet than either is the friendly *Hotel Casablanca* (☎ (958) 2-01-68) across the street at Pérez Gasga 905. It faces the street, not the beach – but since there's no traffic that's no hardship, except for the late-night music. It has 19 or so good, large, modern rooms, with fans, big bathrooms and, on the street side, balconies. Singles/doubles/triples are 80/90/100 pesos. There's a pool.

A minute uphill from the Pérez Gasga mall is the *Hotel Loren* (☎ (958) 2-00-57) charging 60/80 pesos for bare, no-frills, but good-sized rooms. All have fans, hot water and balconies – but not all catch a sea view. The management is friendly.

Slightly higher up the street, the similar *Hotel Nayar* (☎ (958) 2-03-19) gets a good breeze in its wide sitting areas/walkways. Its 36 rooms have fans (air-con 20 pesos extra), hot water and small balconies; some have sea views. Singles/doubles are 72/91 pesos. Both the Loren and the Nayar have swimming pools.

Top place in this part of town is the *Hotel Paraíso Escondido* (☎ (958) 2-04-44) on little Calle Unión, which shortcuts the bend

in Pérez Gasga. It's a rambling, old-fashioned whitewash-and-blue-paint place on several levels with lots of tile, pottery and stone sculpture decoration. There's an attractive restaurant/bar/pool area. The 24 clean though moderately sized rooms have air-con. Some have stained-glass window-panes. The cost is 150/180 pesos.

Places to Stay – top end
Beside the rocky outcrop that divides Playa Marinero from Playa Zicatela, *Hotel Santa Fe* (☎ (958) 2-01-70) has 40 varied rooms attractively set around small terraces and a palm-fringed pool. The stairways are tiled and there's a lovely airy restaurant/bar overlooking Playa Zicatela. Rooms vary in size and outlook, but good design – with tiles again cleverly used – makes most of them agreeable. Many have air-conditioning as well as a fan. Singles/doubles are 186/216 pesos. There are also several appealing bungalows complete with kitchen at 225 or 255 pesos. The hotel's postal address is Apartado Postal 96, Puerto Escondido.

Hotel Posada Real (☎ (958) 2-01-33, fax 2-01-92), part of the Best Western group, is about 2.5 km west of town at Boulevard Benito Juárez 11 in the still-being-developed Fraccionamiento Bacocho, off highway 200. It has 100 air-conditioned rooms with balconies in three four-storey buildings, and big palm-shaded gardens, on a headland overlooking Playa Bacocho. There's a pool, three bars (one on the beach) and two restaurants. Rooms are between 210 and 300 pesos, depending on the season. You can book in Mexico City (☎ (5) 208-72-84).

The *Hotel Aldea del Bazar* (☎ (958) 2-05-08) at Boulevard Benito Juárez 7, also above Playa Bacocho, is a big, plush new place in eye-catching modern Moorish style. Singles/doubles are 275/330 pesos and there are all the top-end facilities including a fine pool in extensive gardens.

Places to Eat
Puerto Escondido's restaurants and cafés are mostly simple, semi-open-air places.

Avenida Pérez Gasga There's a clutch of reasonably priced restaurants serving what we have always found to be fresh seafood around the west end of the Pérez Gasga mall. Several open onto the beach so you can check their current popularity from the sands in front. *Restaurant Junto Al Mar* and *Restaurant La Posada del Tiburón*, which has minor airs, both serve up a good meal. Most fish dishes – such as a whole juicy snapper (huachinango) with rice or fries and a little salad – go for 10 to 22 pesos in either place. The Junto Al Mar's flavoursome fish soup is almost a meal in itself, with whole large chunks of tender fish, for 22 pesos. This end of Pérez Gasga is sometimes afflicted by drain smells, so check wind direction!

Just beyond this west end of the mall, *Restauran Vegetariano – La Gota de Vida* serves up some tasty fare. Breakfasts and tortas are 10 pesos, salads 5 to 12 pesos. They have plenty tofu and tempeh – try the torta de tempeh con salsa barbacoa, a delicious tempeh burger served on grainy bread with salad and a spicy tomato sauce.

Around the middle of the mall, neighbouring the Hotel Las Palmas, little *Restaurant Alicia* is good value with cocktails and excellent fish dishes from 10 to 18 pesos. It also has some cheap breakfasts. Towards the east end of the mall, *Ostería del Viandante da Ugo* is an Italian-run Italian restaurant, and a good one at that – though standards seem to slip a little when *il signor* isn't present in person. There's a range of pasta dishes and one-person pizzas from 9 to 22 pesos, and some good salads around 8 to 16 pesos (including avocado and octopus). *Cafetería Cappuccino*, almost next door, serves probably the best coffee in town, plus good bowls of yoghurt, fruit salad and granola, decent crepas and more substantial mains including fish for around 20 pesos.

Just beyond the east end of the mall, you can enjoy cheap, tasty home cooking and the jolly humour of the cook/owner at *Herman's Best*. There are only seven tables and you might have to wait but it's worth it. For 10 pesos, he dishes up fried fish, chicken or pork with rice, frijoles, salad and huge tortillas.

Playa Marinero & Plaza Zicatela Good wholegrain and banana breads, croissants and pastries are made and sold at a tiny bakery, *La Patisserie*, just up from the Hotel Flor de María on the little lane leading back from Playa Marinero. Attached is a small fan-cooled palapa-style café offering good breakfasts and snacks, and bottomless cups of coffee. It's open from 7 am to 7 pm daily, closed Sunday in the off-season.

The *Hotel Santa Fe* restaurant, spacious and open to the breezes on a raised platform looking down Playa Zicatela, has a touch of flair in its cuisine, with some tasty seafood and vegetarian fare (but be ready for your choice to be unavailable). It's out of the budget range, though, with fish and seafood dishes mostly from 27 to 40 pesos, and antojitos, pasta, and tofu and soyburger offerings mostly 10 to 22 pesos.

Along Zicatela, *Cipriano's Pizza* does the best pizza we've found in town, with a thin crisp base and lots of good cheese, baked in a brick oven by a friendly family. There's a range of pizza toppings and the only size available, costing 14 to 18 pesos, is enough for two. They do cheap breakfasts too.

Beyond Cipriano's, the *Hotel Arco Iris* restaurant, with a good upper-storey position, serves a tasty mix of Mexican and international fare to satisfy the surfers in this part of town. Pasta and antojitos go for around 10 pesos, fish and meat courses for 15 to 30 pesos (though you'll probably need, say, a vegetable salad to really fill up).

Halfway down the Zicatela strip, *Bruno's* serves up cheap tasty meals and snacks including two-for-one burgers, and some nights even two-for-one meals. It offers a variety of cuisines, including Thai and Japanese, with mains around 15 pesos and healthy breakfasts from 5 to 9 pesos.

Many Zicatela hostelries have cooking facilities and there are at least four grocery stores.

Entertainment
Many Puerto Escondido evenings start at the happy hours – usually lasting from about 6 to 9 pm – in café-bars like *Coco*, *Bananas*,

Babalu or *Hotel Las Palmas* on Pérez Gasga, or *Restaurant Liza's* on Playa Marinero, or *Cabo Blanco* on Playa Zicatela. Then there are usually at least a couple of places with live music into the early hours – on our last visit *El Son y La Rumba* just up from the Pérez Gasga mall had an excellent Mexican salsa/samba band, while *Coco* thumped along to a gringo blues/reggae/rock trio. *Cinema Club Ariel* at Zicatela shows films in Spanish, English or French most nights.

Getting There & Away
Air See the Oaxaca city section for details of flights between Puerto Escondido and Oaxaca, and Oaxaca ticket offices.

Mexicana flies nonstop direct to/from Mexico City (one hour, one way 338 pesos) five days a week. Aeromorelos flies to/from Bahías de Huatulco on Wednesday. Mexicana's office (☎ 2-08-89) is on Pérez Gasga beside the Hotel Rocamar. Mexicana handles Aeromorelos tickets too, and there's also an Aeromorelos office (☎ 2-06-53) at the airport. Aerovega (☎ 2-01-51) has an office on Pérez Gasga. Turismo Rodimar (☎ 2-07-34) and Viajes Erikson (☎ 2-08-49), both on Pérez Gasga, also sell air tickets.

Bus The 2nd-class Estrella Blanca/Transportes Gacela, Transportes Oaxaca-Istmo, and Estrella del Valle/Oaxaca Pacífico bus terminals are all on Avenida Hidalgo, in the upper part of town: turn right (east) two blocks uphill from El Crucero. Estrella Blanca/Transportes Gacela directo services are almost up to 1st-class standard. Cristóbal Colón (1st-class) is on highway 200, two blocks west of El Crucero.

It's advisable to book ahead for some of the better and more limited services, such as the 'Turismo' buses to Oaxaca and Cristóbal Colón buses. Daily departures from Puerto Escondido include:

Acapulco – 370 km, seven hours; 10 directo buses (56 pesos) and 13 ordinario (46 pesos) by Estrella Blanca/Transportes Gacela
Bahías de Huatulco – see Santa Cruz Huatulco

Mexico City (Terminal Sur) – 790 km, 15 hours; one deluxe bus (125 pesos) and one 1st-class (118 pesos) by Turistar from the Estrella Blanca/Transportes Gacela terminal
Oaxaca – 310 km, seven hours; directo 'Turismo' buses at 8 am and 10.30 pm by Estrella del Valle/Oaxaca Pacífico (42.50 pesos); 2nd-class directo bus by Autotransportes Turísticos Aragul at 9.30 pm from Transportes Oaxaca-Istmo terminal (30 pesos); several ordinario buses by Estrella del Valle/Oaxaca Pacífico (30.50 pesos); two Cristóbal Colón buses via Salina Cruz (10 hours, 30 pesos)
Pochutla – 72 km, 1½ hours; 15 Estrella Blanca/Transportes Gacela buses (9 pesos directo, 7 pesos ordinario) and four by Transportes Oaxaca-Istmo
Salina Cruz – 250 km, five hours; three Cristóbal Colón buses (25 pesos); seven Estrella Blanca/Transportes Gacela buses (35 pesos directo, 27 pesos ordinario) and four by Transportes Oaxaca-Istmo
Santa Cruz Huatulco – 110 km, 2½ hours; two Cristóbal Colón buses (11 pesos); 15 Estrella Blanca/Transportes Gacela buses (16 pesos directo, 11 pesos ordinario) and four by Transportes Oaxaca-Istmo.

There are also two Cristóbal Colón buses to Tehuantepec, Juchitan, Tuxtla Gutiérrez and San Cristóbal de Las Casas.

Car Budget has an office in the Hotel Posada Real at Bacocho.

Getting Around
To/From the Airport The airport is about four km west of the town centre on the north side of highway 200. For two or three people, a taxi is probably the cheapest way into town if you can find one and agree on a reasonable price (10 to 15 pesos).

Otherwise, colectivo combis (6 pesos per person) meet incoming flights and will drop you anywhere in town. You can book them to take you back to the airport at the travel agents on Pérez Gasga. There should be no problem finding a taxi to go out to the airport for a reasonable fare.

Taxi & Lancha Taxis wait by the barriers at the ends of Pérez Gasga's pedestrian strip. Along with lanchas to some beaches, taxis are the only transport between the central

Pérez Gasga/Bahía Principal area and the outlying beaches if you don't want – or think it's unsafe – to walk. The standard taxi fare to Playa Zicatela is 7 pesos, Puerto Angelito 10 pesos. See Beaches for lancha details.

Bicycle Las Olas at Zicatela has bicycles for rent at 50 pesos a day.

WEST OF PUERTO ESCONDIDO
Highway 200, heading towards Pinotepa Nacional and Acapulco, passes through a coastal region with lagoons, pristine beaches and prolific bird, plant and marine life. The people are of mixed ancestry. In addition to the indigenous Mixtecs and the Spanish input, there are descendants of African slaves who escaped here from the Spaniards, of itinerant Asians, and of Chileans shipwrecked on their way to the California gold rushes. The latter inspired a local folk music known as la Chilena.

Getting There & Away
Tours from Puerto Escondido are the easiest way to reach the main natural attractions of the region. There are also frequent Estrella Blanca/Transportes Gacela buses from Pochutla and Puerto Escondido along highway 200. The 145-km trip from Puerto Escondido to Pinotepa Nacional takes 2½ hours and costs 19 pesos directo or 15 pesos ordinario.

Manialtepec
The jungle and the 12 km-long mangrove-surrounded lagoon here, 18 km from Puerto Escondido, are the haunt of mainly nocturnal mammals like raccoon and badger, and birds that include fishing eagles, herons, pelicans, ibis and egrets, most of them best spotted early in the morning. Tropical aquatic plants are a further attraction. You can get here by road then find a local boat operator to take you out on the lagoon. Colectivo boats cost 25 pesos per person while a boat to rent costs 150 pesos for two hours. Along the lagoon's shore, there are restaurants, some with space for camping.

Hidden Voyages Ecotours, run by knowl-edgeable Canadian ornithologist Michael Malone and operated through Turismo Rodimar on Pérez Gasga in Puerto Escondido, charges 100 pesos for its highly recommended early-morning or sunset tours to Manialtepec. Other bird-spotting tours with an English-speaking guide cost 80 pesos with Turismo Rodimar, or with Ana Márquez, found at the Hotel Rincón del Pacífico.

Chacahua
The area around the coastal lagoons of Chacahua and La Pastoría forms the Parque Nacional Lagunas de Chacahua. A four-km road leads south from highway 200, about 60 km out of Puerto Escondido, to Zapotalito on the edge of La Pastoría. This is the departure point for tours of the lagoons in lanchas operated by a local tourism cooperative – the cost is 20 pesos per person or 200 pesos for a whole boat for two hours. Mangrove-fringed islands in the lagoons harbour ibis, roseate spoonbills, black orchids, mahogany trees, alligators and turtles. The tours stop for a swim at Cerro Hermoso beach or the beach near Chacahua fishing village at the western extremity of the park. The village, which has an alligator farm and a hotel, is connected by a rough road (impassable in the wet season) to San José del Progreso, 30 km away on highway 200, about 80 km from Puerto Escondido.

Local buses run direct between Zapotalito and Rio Grande, about 15 km east on highway 200. Alternatively you could take a bus to the Chacahua sign on highway 200 – from there to Zapotalito, it's a long, hot walk, or an expensive taxi, or you could try hitching.

Easier is an all-day guided tour from Puerto Escondido, with the same operators as for Manialtepec. The cost is 90 to 120 pesos per person.

Tututepec
Tututepec, nine km north of the village of Santa Rosa about 75 km along highway 200 from Puerto Escondido, was the capital of a southern Mixtec kingdom which fought off

the Aztecs in the 15th century. Apparently a Mixtecan king still lives here. The town is in an archaeological zone; remains include stone carvings of a jaguar and a telamon. There's also a 17th-century church.

Jamiltepec

The mainly Mixtec town of Jamiltepec, 105 km from Puerto Escondido, has a Sunday market. Local craft specialities are shoes, Mixtecan clothes and pottery.

Pinotepa Nacional

The biggest town between Puerto Escondido and Acapulco has a high Mixtec population, a Sunday market, and several places to stay, of which the best is probably the *Hotel Carmona* (☎ (954) 3-22-22) at Porfirio Díaz 510. There's also the *Hotel Tropical* (☎ (954) 3-20-10) at Pte 3 on the corner of Progreso.

Pinotepa de Don Luis, one of the most traditional Mixtec villages, is about 15 km north-east of Pinotepa Nacional. Its main fiesta is for the Assumption (15 August, dances and horse races). North of Pinotepa Nacional is Amuzgo Indian country, where the women make and wear beautiful embroidered huipiles.

A few Cristóbal Colón and Fletes y Pasajes (FYPSA) buses take highway 125 north from Pinotepa Nacional to Tlaxiaco, 212 km away (see the Mixteca Baja & Mixteca Alta section). Some continue to Oaxaca.

POCHUTLA

Pochutla is the crossroads town where highway 175 from Oaxaca, 240 km north, meets the coastal highway 200. It's the nearest long-distance bus stop to Puerto Ángel, 13 km south.

Orientation

Highway 175 passes through Pochutla as Cárdenas, the narrow north-south main street. The Hotel Izala, on the corner of Juárez, marks the approximate mid-point of Cárdenas. The main square, Plaza de la Constitución, is a block along Juárez. The market is on Allende, east of Cárdenas two

blocks north of the Izala. Bus stations cluster on Cárdenas half to one km south of the Izala. Highway 175 meets highway 200 about 1.5 km south of the bus stations.

Information

Bancomer on Cárdenas at Allende changes travellers' cheques and US dollars from 9 to 11 am, Monday to Friday. Multibanco Comermex on Cárdenas half a block north of the Izala changes travellers' cheques only, at the same times. The Hotel Izala will often change money too. The nearest other banks are at Huatulco.

The post office is on Avenida Progreso behind the east side of the Plaza de la Constitución. The Telecomm office, with telegram and fax service, is on Juárez. Both are open Monday to Friday from 9 am to 1 pm and 3 to 6 pm, Saturday 9 am to noon.

Places to Stay & Eat

The *Hotel Izala* (☎ (958) 4-01-15) at Cárdenas 59 has reasonable rooms at 30 pesos single with fan, 55 or 60 pesos double with fan and TV, or 80 pesos double with air-con and TV. The *Hotel Pochutla* (☎ (958) 4-00-33), one block north and half a block east of the Izala at Madero 102, has 32 clean singles/doubles with fan for 45/54 pesos. The *Hotel Santa Cruz* (☎ (958) 4-01-16) at Cárdenas 88, just a block north of most of the bus stations, has more basic but clean enough rooms with fan and private bath for 25/30 pesos.

There are a few decent eateries on the west side of the Plaza de la Constitución. Other possibilities are *Restaurante Los Arcos* and *Maldonal's* facing each other across Cárdenas a block north of the Hotel Izala. A breakfast of eggs at Maldonal's is 8 pesos. The market has some cheap food stalls.

Getting There & Away

Bus The three main bus stations, in north-south order down Cárdenas, are Transportes Gacela (2nd-class) on the west side of the street, Estrella del Valle/Oaxaca Pacífico (2nd-class) on the east side, and Cristóbal

Colón (1st-class) on the west side. Daily buses from Pochutla include:

Acapulco – 440 km, eight hours; eight directo buses (66 pesos) and eight ordinario (53 pesos) by Transportes Gacela

Bahías de Huatulco – see Santa Cruz Huatulco

Mexico City – 860 km, 16 hours; two 1st-class afternoon buses (128 pesos) from the Transportes Gacela station

Oaxaca – 240 km, six hours; one directo 'Star Service' bus at 11 pm (32 pesos) and 12 semi-directo or ordinario buses (21.50 pesos), all by Estrella del Valle/Oaxaca Pacífico; one 2nd-class directo bus by Transportes Aragul at 10.30 pm (25 pesos, ticket office two blocks north of Transportes Gacela); three Cristóbal Colón buses via Salina Cruz (8½ hours, 23 pesos)

Puerto Ángel – 13 km, 20 minutes; buses every 20 minutes, 6 am to 8 pm, by Estrella del Valle/Oaxaca Pacífico (1 peso); also Transportes Pochutla microbuses (1 peso) from yard opposite Transportes Gacela station

Puerto Escondido – 72 km, 1½ hours; three Cristóbal Colón buses (7 pesos); about 15 Transportes Gacela buses (9 pesos directo, 7 pesos ordinario)

Salina Cruz – 180 km, 3½ hours; three Cristóbal Colón buses (18.50 pesos); three directo buses (25 pesos) and two ordinario (21 pesos) by Transportes Gacela; four 2nd-class buses by Transportes Oaxaca-Istmo from the Estrella del Valle/Oaxaca Pacífico station

San Cristóbal de Las Casas – 570 km, 11½ hours; two Cristóbal Colón buses (56 pesos)

Santa Cruz Huatulco – 35 km, one hour; 20 buses by Transportes Gacela, 8.30 am to 10.15 pm (5 or 6 pesos); Transportes Pochutla microbuses about every 15 minutes until 6 or 7 pm from yard opposite Transportes Gacela

Tuxtla Gutiérrez – 490 km, 9½ hours; two Cristóbal Colón buses (48 pesos)

Zipolite – 17 km, 30 minutes; same buses as to Puerto Ángel (2 pesos)

There are also two daily Cristóbal Colón buses to Tehuantepec and Juchitán.

Colectivo/Taxi Taxis wait on Cárdenas between the Transportes Gacela and Estrella del Valle/Oaxaca Pacífico bus stations. Up to about 8 pm they depart fairly often on a colectivo (shared) basis to Puerto Ángel, for 2.50 pesos per person. A whole taxi costs 12 to 15 pesos.

PUERTO ÁNGEL

Puerto Ángel ('PWERR-toh ANN-hell') is a fishing-village and travellers' haven straggling around a little bay between two rocky headlands. There are beaches within the bay, and others within a few km either side of the village – including the famous Zipolite, four km west.

Twenty years ago access to Puerto Ángel from Oaxaca was only by unpaved road over the Sierra Madre del Sur. Now paved roads lead from Oaxaca, Salina Cruz and Acapulco, or you can fly to Huatulco or Puerto Escondido, an hour or two away by bus. But Puerto Ángel remains a sleepy place where small-scale tourism has made little impact on the pace of life. More laid-back than Puerto Escondido, it has a number of good, cheap places to stay and eat – and it's very easy to travel out to Zipolite for the day.

Puerto Ángel gets pretty hot and any breath of wind can be a big bonus. May is usually the hottest month and most rain falls between June and September.

Orientation

The paved road from Pochutla, 13 km north, emerges at the east end of the small Bahía de Puerto Ángel, where you can see most of the village. The road winds around the back of the bay, over an often-dry creek bed, up a hill, then forks – right to Zipolite, left down to Playa del Panteón.

Information

The post, telegraph and tourist offices are side by side on Avenida Principal near the pier at the east end of Bahía de Puerto Ángel. The first two are open Monday to Friday from 9 am to 3 pm. The nearest bank is in Pochutla but several hostelries and restaurants will change cash or travellers' cheques at their own rates. There's a Lada caseta in a little café on Vasconcelos just up from the Hotel Soraya – check the cost *before* you call.

Theft can be a problem in the Puerto Ángel area, especially Zipolite and the Puerto Ángel-Zipolite road at night. Even gunpoint robberies are not unknown.

Beaches

Playa del Panteón The little beach on the west side of Bahía de Puerto Ángel is shallow and calm and its waters are cleaner than those near the pier across the bay. You can swim out to the rocky islet on the right. You can rent snorkelling gear from one of the handful of café-restaurants here – or get a fisher to take you for a boat trip from here (ask at King Creole restaurant) or from the pier on the other side of the bay.

Estacahuite Half a km from Puerto Ángel up the road to Pochutla, a sign points right along a path to this beach '500 metres' away. In fact it's 700 metres, but it's worth it to reach three tiny sandy bays, all good for snorkelling – but watch out for jellyfish. Two small shack restaurants serve good, reasonably priced seafood or spaghetti. At least one of them has a snorkel to rent.

Universidad del Mar

The University of the Sea, opened in 1992, stands on a hilltop about one km out of Puerto Ángel off the road to Zipolite. Marine biology and tourism administration are taught, and there's research into conservation and development of marine resources. Projects include the supply of larvae to prawn farms along the coast, and protection of the purple sea snail *(caracol púrpura)*, source of a dye used to colour local textiles.

Places to Stay

Some of Puerto Ángel's best accommodation is run by Mexican-North American or Mexican-European couples who have settled here. Places with an elevated position are more likely to catch any breeze. Mosquito screens are a big plus too. Some places have a water shortage; there's usually enough to wash yourself but not always your

Puerto Ángel

0   100   200 m

1 La Buena Vista
2 Pensión Puesta del Sol
3 Beto's
4 Casa de Huéspedes El Capy
5 Posada Loxicha
6 Posada Cañon Devata
7 Hotel Cabaña
8 Restaurants
9 Casa de Huéspedes Gundy y Tomás
10 Naval Base
11 Bus Stop
12 Villa Florencia
13 El Almendro
14 Beach Restaurants
15 Posada Rincón Sabroso
16 Lada Caseta
17 Hotel Soraya
18 Taxi Stand
19 Tourist, Post & Telegraph Offices

To Universidad del Mar, Zipolite & Mazunte

Arroyo

Calle del Tajo

Calle Palo Bello

Footpath

Boulevard Virgilio Uribe

Vasconcelos

Avenida Principal

To Estacahuite & Pochutla

Beach

Playa del Panteón

Bahía de Puerto Ángel

Islet

Pier

clothes. What follows is in east-to-west order.

The *Hotel Soraya* on Vasconcelos overlooking the pier lacks atmosphere but its rooms, with private bath and fan, are clean, and most have balcony access and good views. Singles/doubles are 60/70 pesos.

The little *Posada Rincón Sabroso* is up a flight of steps to the right as you start to wind your way around the bay. It has friendly young owners and a handful of clean, fancooled rooms along a greenery-shaded terrace, with a hammock outside each. They have private bathrooms but there's water for only a few hours a day. Singles/doubles are 40/50 pesos. There's a restaurant. *El Almendro*, in a shady garden up a little lane a few metres past the Rincón Sabroso steps, has similarly clean rooms, but they're mostly a bit smaller and darker. The cost is 30/50 pesos, but 60 pesos for some doubles. There are also a couple of bungalows with a shared kitchen for longer term rent. Ask about Spanish language classes here if you're interested.

Owned by the same people as El Almendro, *Casa de Huéspedes Gundy y Tomás* has a variety of rooms, ranging from doubles with clean shared bathroom for 35 pesos, to doubles with fan and private bath for 60 pesos. All have mosquito nets or screens. The cheaper ones are mostly higher up and feel airier. You can also hang or rent an open-air hammock for 10 pesos. Good food, including home-made bread and vegetable juices, is available and there are pleasant sitting areas.

To reach the excellent *La Buena Vista*, turn right along the creek, then go a short way up the first track on the left. There are a dozen big rooms here, kept very clean, all with private bathrooms and opening onto breezy balconies. They have fans and mosquito screens. Prices range from about 60 to 75 pesos per room depending on the time of year. There's an airy terrace restaurant with really good food, too.

The German-owned *Pensión Puesta del Sol* is up to the right past the creek. Rooms are sizeable and clean and have fans and screens. With shared bath, singles/doubles go for 35/45 pesos; with private bath, singles are 40 or 50 pesos, doubles 50 or 60 pesos. There's also a suite with a terrace at doubles/triples 70/80 pesos. Food is available in the morning and evening. The owner can organise boat trips.

Up a steep path on the right as the road descends to Playa del Panteón, *Posada Loxicha* has just a few basic rooms for 28/30 pesos or hammocks for 10 pesos. There's a very clean restaurant serving cheap meals and the view is gorgeous. Next door, *Casa de Huéspedes El Capy* has a few clean, cool but smallish rooms with fan, private bath and mostly good views for 25/30 pesos or 35/45 pesos. It has a good restaurant too.

At Playa del Panteón on the corner where the road turns right is the bigger *Hotel Cabaña* with clean, comfortable rooms at 70 and 80 pesos centred on a small, plant-filled patio.

Further along this road and up some steps to the right, the friendly *Posada Cañon Devata* has a variety of attractive accommodation scattered among the foliage on a quiet hillside. This is a good place to stay if you're seeking a quiet retreat (there are morning yoga sessions if you're interested), and snorkel gear and boat trips are available. Dinner (usually wholefood/vegetarian) is served at long tables in a lovely palm-roofed, open-sided dining room. Rooms range from comfortable singles/doubles with fans and private bathrooms at 50/60 pesos, to a two-room, four-bed unit at 90 pesos for two people, 10 pesos for each extra adult. The owners have reafforested the whole canyon since their arrival, and installed compost toilets. The posada is closed in May and June.

Places to Eat

La Buena Vista's excellent restaurant is open at breakfast and in the evenings only (closed Sunday). Set on an airy terrace overlooking the bay, it offers both Mexican and North American fare from hot cakes to delicious chiles rellenos at 15 pesos. The menu is selective but varied enough to please anyone, and the food is very well prepared. Another speciality is the tamales, with vegetarian or chicken and mole fillings, for 12 pesos. You don't have to be staying at La Buena Vista to eat here.

Nonresidents can also eat in the relaxed palapa restaurant at the *Posada Cañon Devata*, where a good dinner (usually vegetarian) of soup, main course and salad is served for 18 pesos. Book earlier in the day. From about 7.30 am to 4 pm you can get things like yoghurt with granola and bananas, sandwiches, enchiladas, or soyburgers on home-made bread for around 8 pesos.

There are numerous places to eat on the main town beach and the main street, Boulevard Virgilio Uribe. They're fairly economical – breakfast around 9 pesos, a big plate of spaghetti for 9 to 12 pesos, fish around 15 pesos, shrimps about 20 pesos – but none is very well frequented. Some of them are good for a sunset beer. The *Villa Florencia* Italian restaurant in front of the Farmacia usually manages good pasta for around 18 pesos, good cappuccinos, as well as pizza, seafood and Mexican fare. The restaurants on the more popular Playa del Panteón offer fish, rice and salad for around 20 pesos, or shrimps for about 28 pesos. Be careful about the freshness of seafood in the low season.

Two small restaurants on the road towards Playa del Panteón have reasonable food. At *Beto's* a tasty fish filete – which could be Veracruzana, al mojo de ajo, or natural – goes for just 10 pesos, or there's a variety of salads for 6.50 pesos. Chicken and meat dishes are 12 to 18 pesos. Beto's is open from late afternoon only. Also good is the terrace restaurant – cool in the evenings – of *Casa de Huéspedes El Capy*, where snapper (Veracruzana or in garlic sauce) is 15 pesos, shrimps 18 pesos, guacamole 5 pesos, papas fritas 5 pesos. There are decent breakfasts, too, for 6 to 8 pesos.

Getting There & Away
To reach Puerto Ángel you first have to get to Pochutla, 13 km north. There are buses to Pochutla from Oaxaca, Puerto Escondido, Acapulco, Huatulco and elsewhere, even San Cristóbal de Las Casas – see Pochutla and other town sections for details.

Frequent buses and colectivo taxis run up to about 8 pm between Pochutla and Puerto Ángel (see the Pochutla section). After that, you need a taxi, which may be 15 to 20 pesos at night. The main bus stop in Puerto Ángel is on the main street near the naval base.

ZIPOLITE
The two-km stretch of palm-fringed pale sand called Zipolite, beginning three km west of Puerto Ángel, is fabled as southern Mexico's ultimate place to lie back in a hammock and do as little as you like, in as little as you like, for almost as little as you like.

In recent years the fisherfolk's shacks, comedores and budget places to stay here have filled almost the whole length of the beach, and Zipolite has become much busier – but it's still a great place to take it easy and you may end up staying far longer than you planned. Its magic stems from pounding sea and sun, open-air sleeping, strange rocket-like palm huts on rocky pinnacles and, for some, the drug scene. There are even one or two small beachside discos now. (*Zipolipa's*, about 200 metres towards Puerto Ángel from the Zipolite bus stop, is the most active of these.)

Beware of the Zipolite surf: it's fraught with riptides, changing currents, a strong undertow, and can be deadly. There are no life-saving facilities and visitors drown most years. Locals rarely swim here. Particularly from about May to August, going in deeper than your knees can be risking your life. Keep away from the rocks at both ends of the beach. If you do get swept out, your best hope is to swim calmly parallel to the shore to get clear of the current pulling you outward.

Theft is a problem at Zipolite, and it's not advisable to walk along the Puerto Ángel-Zipolite road after dark. Also take care with drugs – if you buy any, be careful who you buy them from.

Nudity is nowadays more common up the far, west, end of the beach.

Places to Stay

Nearly all the palm shacks and other abodes along the beach rent small rooms or have hammock space for travellers. Pick one whose owner will look after, and preferably lock up, your things for you. The normal price for a rented hammock is 5 pesos a night, or you can sling your own for 4 pesos. Rooms cost 10 to 25 pesos, depending on size and whether shower, fan or mosquito net are available.

Among the more substantial places are *Lola's*, at the east end of the beach (nearest Puerto Ángel), and *Lyoban*, a bit further along, which is one of the few with two storeys. The upstairs catches more breeze. *Tao Zipolite*, towards the west end, has three storeys, showers and mosquito nets. Lyoban and Tao Zipolite both ask 15 pesos a person.

One of the most popular places is *Lo Cosmico*, with cabañas around a tall rock outcrop near the west end of the beach. A hammock in a cabaña here is 15 pesos, a hammock on a breezy terrace 7.50 pesos. A friendly, casual atmosphere prevails. On top of the rock are the rocket-shaped huts of the friendly Mexican-Swiss couple who own the place. Good food is served in the open-air restaurant here.

The long-established *Shambhala Posada*, more commonly known as *Casa Gloria* after its North American owner, is on the hill at the far end of the beach – with great views back along it. It offers hammocks for 10 pesos, small cabañas with bed and mosquito net for 25 pesos, or larger cabañas for 35 pesos.

Places to Eat

Few places at Zipolite have free drinking water. There are a dozen or two basic comedores – many also renting rooms or hammock space – along the beach, where a typical plate of fish, rice and salad costs around 10 pesos. Some offer spaghetti or other variations at similar prices.

A few places have greater choice and even formal menus. *Restaurante-Bar La Chaza*, about halfway along the beach, is one – a breakfast of eggs is 5 pesos; fish and other seafood dishes including prawns are up to 25 pesos.

Towards the west end of the beach are grouped three of the larger, most organised eateries. Their popularity testifies to their higher quality. The first, *Posada San Cristóbal*, does respectable huachinango or prawns for 20 pesos, spaghetti for 7 pesos or a tuna filete for 10 pesos. There's even cappuccino.

Lo Cosmico, on the rocks near the west end of the beach, has good food, especially its delicious crepas at 7 or 8 pesos, and its salads.

Getting There & Away

The road from Puerto Ángel to Zipolite is paved all the way. Buses and microbuses run every few minutes from Pochutla (see that section) through Puerto Ángel to Zipolite, from about 6 am to 8 pm. Fare is 1 peso from Puerto Ángel, 2 pesos from Pochutla. The Zipolite bus stop is behind the buildings about halfway along the beach. The Sitio Zipolite taxi stand is 200 metres back towards Puerto Ángel from the bus stop.

BEYOND ZIPOLITE

The handsome coast west of Zipolite is Mexico's major sea-turtle habitat and egg-laying ground. It was also, until recently, the scene of a gruesome turtle industry, with on occasions as many as 2000 turtles being slaughtered in a single day. Today the village of Mazunte, five km from Zipolite, is the scene of an interesting project aimed both at saving the turtles and providing an alternative income for the people.

San Agustinillo

The long San Agustinillo beach, beginning beyond the headland at the west end of Zipolite, is another in the Zipolite mould – but almost empty. There are footpaths over the headland from behind Casa Gloria, or you can follow the road past the Zipolite bus stop. The road loops inland at first but then comes back close behind San Agustinillo beach.

There are a couple of accommodation options atop the steep slope backing the beach, among them the Italian-owned *Posada Rancho Cerro Largo*, a small group of cabañas also reachable from the road. You're certainly right away from it all here. A couple more places, and a few comedores, are in San Agustinillo settlement at the end of the beach, four km from the middle of Zipolite. Also here are the remains of the slaughterhouse which was the centre of the local turtle industry. Beyond it, a rocky headland divides San Agustinillo from the next beach, Mazunte.

Mazunte

Mazunte village, one km along the road beyond San Agustinillo settlement, has another fine beach curving around to Punta Cometa, the headland at its west end. Mazunte is the home of most of the families who used to live off the turtle industry. When exploitation of turtles was banned throughout Mexico in 1990, following a disastrous slump in the turtle population, the villagers' livelihood was threatened despite a continuing illicit trade in turtle eggs. Many turned to slash-and-burn agriculture, endangering the nearby forests, an important bird habitat.

In 1992, with the backing of a Mexico City-based environmental group, Ecosolar, Mazunte declared itself a Reserva Ecológica Campesina, aimed at preserving the local environment while creating a sustainable village lifestyle. Projects include garbage separation and nutrition education. Tourism is a key element. Mazunte now has the publicly funded **Centro Mexicano de la Tortuga**, beside the road as you enter the village. This is intended to be a kind of aquarium-showcase for Mexico's many marine and freshwater turtle species (six of the world's seven marine turtles lay on Mexican beaches): when we last checked the new building still stood unused, with the turtles kept in tanks around the back, but it should be fully operational by the time you visit.

Another Mazunte attraction is lancha trips with local fishers to see turtles and dolphins out at sea. These are possible almost year-round: early afternoon is said to be the best

time. An hour's trip for up to 10 people costs 60 to 100 pesos. To organise it, ask at the house behind the Agencia Municipal on Mazunte's plaza (a short distance past the Centro Mexicano de la Tortuga). You could also approach fishers direct at Mazunte beach or San Agustinillo village.

Mazunte villagers also offer accommodation to visitors – ask at the house behind the Agencia Municipal. A hammock and one meal is 30 pesos, a hammock and three meals 60 pesos. A bed is 10 pesos extra. There are also places for camping, and a few comedores on Mazunte beach.

West of Mazunte stretches more fine coast, with reportedly an interesting wetland area some 10 to 20 km away.

Getting There & Away

Buses from Puerto Ángel run no further than Zipolite, but the walk over the headland from Zipolite and along San Agustinillo beach is good. Alternatively you can take a taxi from Puerto Ángel or Zipolite (Puerto Ángel to Mazunte is 25 pesos). The road from Puerto Ángel and Zipolite is paved till shortly before San Agustinillo village. It then continues as dirt to Mazunte and beyond.

BAHÍAS DE HUATULCO

Mexico's newest coastal resort is taking shape along a series of picturesque sandy bays, the Bahías de Huatulco ('wah-TOOL-koh'), some 35 km east of Pochutla and 140 km west of Salina Cruz. Though Huatulco has been slighted by some as 'another Cancún', in fact lessons from other modern Mexican resorts appear to have been taken to heart here. Six storeys is the maximum building height, effective sewage treatment has been installed, and discrete, limited-scale developments are separated by tracts of unspoiled shoreline. At this early stage of its growth, Huatulco is an enjoyable, relatively uncrowded resort to visit, with a succession of lovely beaches lapped by beautiful water and backed by forest.

Eventually, by the year 2010, Huatulco is planned to have 30,000 hotel rooms and a population of 300,000. It's oddly fascinating to witness tangled forest becoming instant modern city before your eyes.

Until the 1980s this barely peopled coast had just one small fishing village and was known to only a few outsiders as a great place for a quiet swim in translucent waters, and good fresh seafood. During the early years of development some locals complained of official pressure and trickery over compensation.

Orientation

A divided road leads a few km down from highway 200 to La Crucecita, the functional service town for the resort, with the bus stations, market, shops, the only cheap accommodation and most of the better-value restaurants. One km south of La Crúcecita, on Bahía de Santa Cruz, is Santa Cruz Huatulco, site of the original village, with some middle-range hotels and the harbour. The other bays are strung along the coast about 10 km in each direction from Santa Cruz. From west to east, they are San Agustín, Chachacual, Cacaluta, Maguey y Organo, Santa Cruz, Chahué, Tangolunda (site of the major developments to date) and Conejos.

Huatulco airport is on the north side of highway 200, 12 km west of the turning to La Crucecita and Santa Cruz Huatulco.

Information

Tourist Offices The small Información Turística kiosk on Avenida Guamuchil, just off La Crucecita's Plaza Principal, is helpful with information and has a rudimentary map. The main tourist office (☎ (958) 1-03-88) is at Tangolunda, about 250 metres west of the Holiday Inn Crowne Plaza – open from 9 am to 2 pm and 4 to 7 pm daily.

Money Banamex and Bancomer on Santa Cruz Huatulco's main street, Boulevard Santa Cruz, change cash and travellers' cheques from 10 am to noon, Monday to Friday. Both have ATMs.

Post & Telecommunications There are Ladatel credit card and telephone card phones on the south side of the Plaza Principal at La Crucecita, and a Lada caseta with fax half a block away at Bugambilias 505. La Crucecita's post office and Telecomm office (which has telegram and fax services) are together on Boulevard Chahué, 400 metres east of the Plaza Principal. They're open Monday to Friday from 9 am to 1 pm and 3 to 7 pm, Saturday 9 am to noon.

Beaches

The beaches are the thing. Santa Cruz Huatulco has a small one, **Playa Santa Cruz**, kept pretty clean, with a few moderate-value eateries, but it's far inferior to most other Huatulco beaches. Lanchas will whisk you out to these from Santa Cruz Huatulco harbour beside Boulevard Santa Cruz. The network of roads that is being built around the area reaches some beaches, and a taxi is much cheaper (if less fun) than a lancha. But if you're in the mood for a lancha, tickets are sold at a hut beside the harbour. They'll drop you off and pick you up any time up to 5 pm. Rates for a return trip for up to 10 people include: Playa La Entrega, 33 pesos; Bahía Maguey y Organo, 77 pesos; Bahía Conejos, 132 pesos. There's also a six-hour boat tour, with an hour or two on three different beaches, at 10.45 am daily. The 75-peso price includes drinks, food and use of snorkel gear.

You can rent **snorkels** at Santa Cruz Huatulco harbour and Playa La Entrega, among other places, for 15 pesos a day.

Playa La Entrega lies towards the outer edge of Bahía Santa Cruz, a five-minute lancha trip. It's a moderately busy 300-metre-long beach with beautifully clear, calm water, also reachable by a circuitous track from Santa Cruz Huatulco. There's no building here. La Entrega means 'the Handover': here in 1831 the Mexican independence hero Vicente Guerrero was delivered to his enemies by an Italian sea captain who had betrayed him for 50,000 pieces of gold. Guerrero was taken to Cuilapan, near Oaxaca, and shot.

The bays west of Bahía Santa Cruz are so far undeveloped and roads to them, where

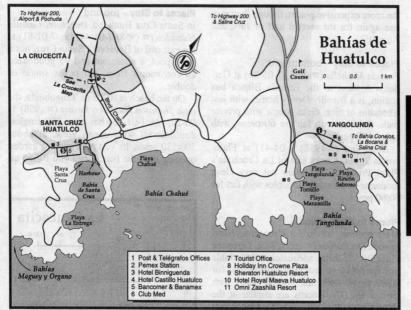

Bahías de Huatulco

0   0.5   1 km

1 Post & Telégrafos Offices	7 Tourist Office
2 Pemex Station	8 Holiday Inn Crowne Plaza
3 Hotel Binniguenda	9 Sheraton Huatulco Resort
4 Hotel Castillo Huatulco	10 Hotel Royal Maeva Huatulco
5 Bancomer & Banamex	11 Omni Zaashila Resort
6 Club Med	

they exist at all, are mostly rough tracks. Bahía Maguey y Organo has two good beaches, **Playa Maguey** and **Playa Organo**, separated by a small headland, with clear calm waters good for snorkelling. **Bahía Cacaluta**, inaccessible by land, has a beach about one km long and is protected by an island, though the sea is relatively strong. **Playa La India** on Bahía Chachagual, also inaccessible by land, is one of Huatulco's most beautiful. **Bahía San Agustín's** beach is said to be reachable by a 14-km track down from highway 200. There are one or two seafood comedores here, and good snorkelling.

East from La Crucecita and Santa Cruz Huatulco, a paved road runs to Bahía Chahué, Bahía Tangolunda and Bahía Conejos, continuing to join highway 200 a few km further on. **Bahía Chahué** is the scene of a marina development. **Bahía Tangolunda**, four km from Santa Cruz, is the site of the major top-end hotel developments to date. There's nothing to stop anyone using

the sands in front of the hotels. Tangolunda has an 18-hole golf course too. Three km further on is the long, somewhat exposed sweep of **Playa Punta Arena** on Bahía Conejos. Around a headland, at the east end of Bahía Conejos, is the more attractive, sheltered **Playa Conejos**, unreachable by road. Bahía Conejos is scheduled for eventual development.

Two to three km beyond Bahía Conejos the road runs down to the coast again at **La Bocana**, a handful of seafood comedores at the mouth of a small river, with another long beach stretching to the east.

Travel agencies in La Crucecita and several of the hotels offer **tours** of Huatulco bays, or to Puerto Ángel, Oaxaca, Monte Albán and so on.

Places to Stay

In the off-peak season – from shortly after Easter to shortly before Christmas – one-third is slashed off many prices, especially at the more expensive places, though they may rise again for the second half of July, and August.

Places to Stay – bottom end

Posada Michelle (☎ (958) 7-05-35) at Gardenia 8, next to the Estrella Blanca bus station, is a friendly family home, with just a handful of nice, clean rooms with private bath. Doubles with fan are 60 pesos, with air-con 70 pesos.

Hotel Inn (☎ (958) 7-04-41) at Flamboyan 2, two blocks east of La Crucecita's Plaza Principal, has plain but very clean moderate-sized singles/doubles with fan for 50/60 pesos.

Places to Stay – middle

Most options are in La Crucecita. *Hotel Posada Del Parque* (☎ (958) 7-02-19) on the Plaza Principal has adequately comfortable but moderate-sized singles/doubles for 80/90 pesos with fan, 90/100 pesos with air-con and TV. Rooms are similar at the *Hotel Grifer* (☎ (958) 7-00-48), a block east of the plaza on the corner of Guamúchil and Carrizal. Singles or doubles are 80 pesos, with TV and air-con.

The small *Hotel Suites Begonias* (☎ (958) 7-00-18) on Bugambilias just off the southeast corner of the plaza has slightly more comfortable rooms with TV, opening onto upstairs walkways, at 120/150 pesos.

The pink *Hotel Flamboyant* (☎ (958) 7-01-21, 7-01-13) on the north-west corner of the plaza has a pleasant interior courtyard, air-conditioned rooms at 250 pesos single or double, and its own restaurant.

In Santa Cruz Huatulco, the pleasant *Hotel Binniguenda* (☎ (958) 7-00-77) at the west end of Boulevard Santa Cruz, about 500 metres past the harbour, is Huatulco's oldest hotel, dating from 1987! It has colonial-style decor, a garden-courtyard, pool, restaurant, coffee shop, and 74 air-con rooms at 182 pesos a single or double.

The Flamboyant and the Binniguenda share a beach club on Bahía Chahué with the Hotel Castillo Huatulco. Free transport is provided.

Places to Stay – top end

In Santa Cruz Huatulco, the *Hotel Castillo Huatulco* (☎ (958) 7-01-44, fax 7-01-81) at the east end of Boulevard Santa Cruz, has a good pool, a restaurant and 95 good-sized air-con rooms from 286 pesos single or double.

On the beach at Bahía de Tangolunda, the pink *Sheraton Huatulco Resort* (☎ (958) 1-00-22, fax 1-01-13) has over 300 singles/doubles, all with ocean view, at about 500/530 pesos. Its vast pool sits in a garden opening onto the beach, and you'll find all

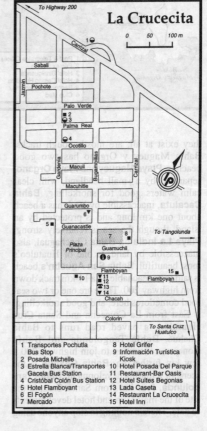

La Crucecita

To Highway 200

Carrizal

0   50   100 m

Sabali

Jazmin

Pochote

Palo Verde

■ 2
● 3

Palma Real

● 4

Ocotillo

Gardenia

Macuil

Bugambilias

Carrizal

Macuhitle

Guarumbo

6 ▼

5 ■

Guanacastle

7 ■ 8

To Tangolunda

Plaza
Principal

Guamuchil

● 9

Información

Flamboyan

■ 10

▼ 11
■ 12
☎ 13
▼ 14

Flamboyan

15 ■

Chacah

Colorin

To Santa Cruz
Huatulco

1 Transportes Pochutla Bus Stop	8 Hotel Grifer
2 Posada Michelle	9 Información Turística Kiosk
3 Estrella Blanca/Transportes Gacela Bus Station	10 Hotel Posada Del Parque
4 Cristóbal Colón Bus Station	11 Restaurant-Bar Oasis
5 Hotel Flamboyant	12 Hotel Suites Begonias
6 El Fogón	13 Lada Caseta
7 Mercado	14 Restaurant La Crucecita
	15 Hotel Inn

the amenities you'd expect in this price bracket – restaurants, bars, tennis, fitness centre, water sports, shops. Next door is the *Hotel Royal Maeva Huatulco* (☎ (958) 1-00-00, fax 1-02-20), with 268 rooms where the all-inclusive rate of around 650/850 pesos includes meals, drinks, entertainment, water sports and other activities. A little further around the bay, the *Omni Zaashila Resort* (☎ /fax (958) 7-00-80) boasts 65 swimming pools, many of them private, as well as the usual top-end amenities. The 120 rooms and 64 suites cost from about 600 to 1000 pesos.

Holiday Inn Crowne Plaza (☎ (958) 1-00-44, fax 1-02-21), a pink complex climbing the hillside at Boulevard Juárez 8, Tangolunda, is back from the beach but has its own beach club next to the Sheraton, plus restaurants, tennis and so on. It's cheaper than the beachfront places at 300/370 pesos for singles/doubles.

The biggest *Club Med* (☎ (958) 1-00-33, toll-free in the USA 800-258-2633) in the Americas stands in 20-hectare grounds on the west side of Tangolunda Bay, reached by its own 500-metre approach road.

Places to Eat

La Crucecita *Restaurant-Bar Oasis* on the south-east corner of the Plaza Principal has good, moderately priced fare from tortas at 4 to 8 pesos to filete de pescado at 18 pesos or steaks at 28 pesos. *Restaurant La Crucecita* on the corner of Bugambilias and Chacah, a block from the plaza, open from 7 am to 10 pm, does well-priced breakfasts as well as good-value meat, chicken or seafood dishes from 15 to 25 pesos. Its sincronizadas a la Mexicana (10 pesos) are a good antojito.

El Fogón, a block the other way along from the plaza, is a cheaper, sweatier place with carne asada and other good grilled meat choices for 12 pesos, or three tacos for 5 or 6 pesos. The Flamboyant and Posada Del Parque hotels have restaurants too.

Elsewhere There are several eateries on Playa Santa Cruz but value is disappointing. The restaurants of the Binniguenda and Castillo Huatulco hotels are better but dearer.

At Tangolunda all the big hotels have a choice of expensive bars, coffee shops and restaurants – the *Casa Real* in the Sheraton is said to be about the classiest of all. There are also a few independent restaurants, medium to expensive in price, along Tangolunda's two streets, including a pizzeria.

The seafood comedores at La Bocana will cook you up a tasty grilled fish with fries or salad for 12 to 20 pesos.

Getting There & Away

Air The airport is known as both Huatulco and Bahías de Huatulco, so look for both names in timetables. Mexicana flies three times daily, and Aeroméxico once, to/from Mexico City (400 pesos). Mexicana also has flights to/from Los Angeles.

Aeromorelos flies direct to/from Oaxaca (243 to 290 pesos) daily, and Puerto Escondido (135 pesos) on Wednesday.

Travel agencies in La Crucecita and several of the big hotels sell air tickets. Mexicana's office (☎ 7-02-23) is in the Hotel Castillo Huatulco at Santa Cruz Huatulco. Aeroméxico (☎ 1-03-36) and Aeromorelos (☎ 1-04-44) are both at the airport.

Bus The bus stations for Bahías de Huatulco are in La Crucecita. Most buses coming here are marked 'Santa Cruz Huatulco' but they still terminate in La Crucecita. Make sure your bus is *not* heading to Santa María Huatulco, which is a long way away.

The main bus stations are on Gardenia, which leads north off La Crucecita's Plaza Principal. Estrella Blanca/Transportes Gacela (2nd-class) is on the corner of Palma Real, five blocks from the plaza. Cristóbal Colón (1st-class) is a block nearer the plaza on the corner of Ocotillo. Most Cristóbal Colón buses are de paso. Transportes Gacela's directo services are quick and fairly comfortable. Daily departures include:

Acapulco – 495 km, nine hours; nine directo buses (72 pesos) and eight ordinario (58 pesos) by Gacela

Mexico City (Terminal Sur or Terminal Oriente) –
900 km, 17 hours; two Cristóbal Colón buses via
Salina Cruz (111 or 121.50 pesos); one Gacela
'Plus' service via Acapulco (132 pesos)

Oaxaca – 400 km, 7½ hours; one overnight deluxe
Cristóbal Colón Plus bus via Salina Cruz (34
pesos)

Puerto Escondido – 105 km, two hours; two Cristóbal
Colón buses (11 pesos); 20 by Gacela (16 pesos
directo, 11 pesos ordinario)

Pochutla – 35 km, one hour; four Cristóbal Colón
buses (5 pesos); 20 by Gacela (6 pesos directo, 5
pesos ordinario); Transportes Pochutla
microbuses about every 15 minutes up to about
7 pm from the main road opposite the north end
of Bugambilias

Salina Cruz – 140 km, 2½ hours; four Cristóbal
Colón buses (14 pesos); five by Gacela (20 pesos
directo, 16 pesos ordinario)

There are also two Cristóbal Colón buses to
Tehuantepec, Juchitán, Tuxtla Gutiérrez and
San Cristóbal de Las Casas.

Car There are rental desks at the airport and
in several hotels, including Budget at the
Hotel Flamboyant in La Crucecita. Dollar in
the Sheraton at Tangolunda was offering any
car for 280 pesos a day with unlimited km
and air-con.

Getting Around

To/From the Airport Transporte Terrestre
provides colectivo combis for about 20 pesos
per person. Get tickets at their airport kiosk.
A taxi is about 50 pesos.

Bus Local microbuses run every 15 minutes
or so till about 8 pm between La Crucecita,
Santa Cruz Huatulco and Tangolunda. In La
Crucecita they stop on Gardenia, opposite
the bus stations, and on Guamuchil just over
a block from the Plaza Principal. In Santa
Cruz Huatulco they stop by the harbour, and
in Tangolunda at the junction outside the
Hotel Royal Maeva.

Taxi Taxis are common. You can get a three
or four-km trip such as La Crucecita or Santa
Cruz Huatulco to Tangolunda for around 8
pesos with a little bargaining.

Isthmus of Tehuantepec

Eastern Oaxaca is the southern half of the
200 km-wide Isthmus of Tehuantepec ('teh-
wan-teh-PECK'), Mexico's narrowest point.
This is sweaty, flat, unpretty country. Of its
three towns, Tehuantepec is the most appealing but you may find yourself changing
buses in Salina Cruz or Juchitán, each with
a sizeable share of Oaxaca's limited industry.
If you do spend a night or two here you'll
probably be agreeably surprised by the
people's liveliness and friendliness.

Fifteen km east of Juchitán, around La
Ventosa where highway 185 to Acayucan
diverges from highway 190 to Chiapas,
strong winds sweep down from the north and
sometimes blow high vehicles off the road.

History & People

In 1496 the isthmus Zapotecs repulsed the
Aztecs from the fortress of Guiengola near
Tehuantepec, and the isthmus never became
part of the Aztec Empire. Later there was
strong resistance to the Spanish here, notably
from 1524 to 1527 (by an alliance of
Zapotecs, Mixes, Zoques and Chontals) and
in the 1660 Tehuantepec rebellion.

Isthmus women are noticeably more open
and confident than women in most of Mexico.
They're physically well-built and take a
leading role in business and politics. They're
also famous for their costumes. Many older
women still wear embroidered huipiles and
voluminous printed skirts. For fiestas, Tehuantepec and Juchitán women turn out in velvet or
sateen huipiles, skirts embroidered with fan-
tastically colourful silk flowers, and a variety
of odd headgear. They also deck themselves
in gold and silver jewellery, a sign of wealth.
Many isthmus fiestas feature the *Tirada* (or
Regada) de Frutas in which women climb
on roofs and throw fruit on the men below.

TEHUANTEPEC

• *pop: 50,000*

Tehuantepec is a friendly town where there's
often a fiesta going on in one of the barrios.

Orientation & Information

The Oaxaca-Tuxtla Gutiérrez highway 190 meets highway 185, from Salina Cruz, just west of Tehuantepec then skirts the north edge of the town. Tehuantepec's bus stations, collectively known as 'Terminal', are just off highway 190 on the north-east side of town, about 1.5 km from the centre. Local buses from Salina Cruz also stop, more conveniently, where highway 190 passes the end of 5 de Mayo, opposite the Posada Colonial, only a minute's walk from the central plaza. To reach the plaza from the bus stations on foot, follow Avenida Héroes, the street leading towards town, till it ends at a T-junction, then go right along Guerrero for four blocks to another T-junction, then one block left along Hidalgo.

Banca Serfin on the central plaza has an ATM. The dark, smelly, almost medieval market is on the west side of the plaza and the post and telegraph offices are on the north side.

Ex-Convento de Santo Domingo

This former religious complex on the south side of the central plaza, built in the 1540s and 1550s, has been rescued from ruin by being converted into the town's Casa de la Cultura. The side facing the plaza, now the town hall, was completely rebuilt in the 19th century. The original appearance can be appreciated on the side away from the plaza.

Guiengola

The hillside Zapotec stronghold of Guiengola, where the Aztecs were defeated in 1496, is north of the Oaxaca road from a turning about 11 km out of Tehuantepec. A sign points to 'Ruínas Guiengola 7' just past the 240-km marker. The site is open daily from 10 am to 6 pm and you can see the remains of two pyramids, a ball court, a 64-room complex known as El Palacio, and a thick defensive wall. There are fine views over the isthmus.

Festivals

The Vela Guiexoba (Jasmine Vigil) festival in the third week of May includes parades in regional dress and a tirada de frutas. Each

Tehuantepec barrio also holds its own fiesta, for several days around its saint's day, with tiradas de frutas and lots of marimba music. Barrios with fiestas include:

Lieza – San Sebastián, 22 January
Guichiveri & Atotonilco – San Juan, 24 June
Vishana – San Pedro, 30 June
Santa María, San Jacinto & Santa Cruz – Assumption, 15 August
Laborio – Birth of the Virgin Mary, 10 September
San Jerónimo & Cerrito – San Miguel, 1 October

Places to Stay

Hotel Donají (☎ (971) 5-00-64) at Juárez 10, two blocks south of the east side of the central plaza, has clean rooms with private bath (intermittent hot water) on two upper floors with open-air walkways. Singles/doubles with fan are 43/55 pesos (66 pesos with two beds), with air-con 71/99 pesos. *Hotel Oasis* (☎ (971) 5-00-08) at Ocampo 8 on the corner of Romero, one block south of the west side of the plaza, has slightly smaller fan-cooled rooms, also clean, for 35/45 pesos (55 pesos with two beds). Those on the upper floors are airiest.

Casa de Huéspedes Istmo at Hidalgo 31, about 150 metres north of the post office, has a big courtyard but small, only tolerably clean rooms for 25/35 pesos with shared bath, or 50 pesos double with private bath.

Places to Eat

Mariscos Rafa on the north side of the plaza is a little seafood restaurant doing excellent fish dishes, or shrimps several ways, for around 20 pesos, and seafood cocktails for 9 to 25 pesos. The aguacate relleno de camarones (avocado stuffed with shrimps) is a meal in itself at 15 pesos. At *Cafe Colonial* at Romero 66, 1½ blocks south of the west side of the plaza, generous chicken and meat dishes cost 15 to 20 pesos, or there are antojitos for 11 to 16 pesos.

In the evenings tables are set up around the plaza for cheap open-air eating.

Getting There & Away

See the Orientation & Information section above for where to find the bus stations. The

OAXACA STATE

250-km trip from Oaxaca takes 4½ hours in a 1st-class bus. You're winding downhill for the middle 160 km – spot the dead vehicles on the slopes below.

Cristóbal Colón (1st-class) runs eight daily buses to Oaxaca (24 to 30 pesos), four to Tuxtla Gutiérrez (28 pesos, five hours), two each to Santa Cruz Huatulco (16 pesos, three hours) and Pochutla (20 pesos, four hours), and one each to Puerto Escondido (27 pesos, five hours) and San Cristóbal de Las Casas (30 pesos, 7½ hours). There's also service to Acayucan, Mexico City, Tonalá, Tapachula, Veracruz and Villahermosa. Most of these buses are de paso, often in the wee hours. Sur (2nd-class) has a few buses to Oaxaca, Tapachula and Acayucan. Transportes Oaxaca-Istmo (2nd-class), 50 metres east along the highway from Cristóbal Colón, has hourly buses to Oaxaca around the clock, plus a few buses to Santa Cruz Huatulco, Pochutla and Puerto Escondido, Tonalá and Tapachula.

Across the street from Cristóbal Colón are local buses to Juchitán (25 km, 2 pesos) and Salina Cruz (15 km, 1.50 pesos). They go at least every half-hour, taking half an hour to either place.

Getting Around

Taxis (4 pesos), colectivos and 'Centro-Terminal' buses all run between the central plaza and the bus stations in daylight hours. From the centre to the bus stations, buses start at the north-west corner of the plaza.

A curious form of local transport is the *motocarro* – a kind of three-wheel buggy in which the driver sits on a front seat while the passenger stands behind on a platform.

SALINA CRUZ

• *pop: 62,000*

When a railway was built across the isthmus at the turn of the century, Salina Cruz became an important port. But a lack of major oil finds and the cutting of the Panama Canal further south soon ended its prosperity. In recent years it has developed again as an oil pipeline terminal, with a big refinery. It's a windy city with a bit of a Wild West feel today.

Orientation

Highway 200 from Puerto Escondido and Pochutla meets the Salina Cruz-Tehuantepec road, highway 185, on the northern edge of Salina Cruz, about two km from the town centre. Bus stations lie on or just off Avenida Ferrocarril, which runs south from this junction to the town centre: Sur and Estrella Blanca are on Obrero Mundial, off Avenida Ferrocarril nearly halfway to the centre; Cristóbal Colón is on Primero de Mayo, off Avenida Ferrocarril two blocks past Obrero.

If bus connections work out right, you may not need to venture into the centre at all. Avenida Ferrocarril becomes Avenida Tampico as it nears the centre, passing a block west of the wide, windy plaza, which is to the left.

Information

Banca Serfin and Banamex on Guaymas, an east-west street a block or two north of the plaza, both have ATMs. Eco on the west side of the plaza is a 24-hour Lada caseta with fax. The market is on the north-east corner of the plaza.

Places to Stay

Half a block north of the east side of the plaza at 5 de Mayo 43, the *Hotel Magda* (☎ (971) 4-01-07) has ordinary but reasonably clean singles/doubles with fans for 32/40 pesos. It can get noisy. *Hotel Posada del Jardín* (☎ (971) 4-01-62) at Camacho 108, a couple of blocks north of the west side of the plaza, has basic rooms around a leafy little courtyard for 30/40 pesos with fan, private bath and hot water.

At 5 de Mayo 520, 1½ blocks south of the east side of the plaza, *Hotel Altagracia* has clean air-con rooms for 100/115 pesos (negotiable), a small restaurant and friendly management. The *Hotel Bugambilias*, a couple of blocks north of the plaza at 5 de Mayo 24, has air-con rooms for 100 pesos single or double.

Places to Eat

The clean, modern *Restaurant El Lugar*, upstairs at the south-east corner of the main plaza, has a mixed menu of decently prepared food from egg dishes or hamburguesas at 6 to 9 pesos to fish, seafood or steaks at 15 to 24 pesos. It's open from 7.15 am to midnight. At the north-east corner of the plaza *La Jaiba Loca* is a big, echoing place offering octopus and prawns done in a variety of ways for 12 to 20 pesos.

Getting There & Away

Air Aeromar (☎ (971) 4-23-66) flies direct to/from Mexico City daily.

Bus Frequent buses to Tehuantepec (30 minutes, 1.50 pesos) and Juchitán (one hour, 3.50 pesos) leave from various central points and go up Avenidas Tampico and Ferrocarril. You can catch them on Tampico, about four blocks from the central plaza, or on Avenida Ferrocarril outside the long-distance bus stations (see Orientation for the locations of these).

Cristóbal Colón runs deluxe and 1st-class buses; the other lines are all 2nd-class (although Estrella Blanca has some quick directo services in comfortable buses which it calls 1st-class). Departures include:

Bahías de Huatulco – see Santa Cruz Huatulco
Oaxaca – 265 km, five hours; six Cristóbal Colón buses (26 to 32 pesos)
Pochutla – 175 km, 3½ hours; five Cristóbal Colón buses (18.50 pesos) and six by Estrella Blanca (21 to 25 pesos)
Puerto Escondido – 250 km, five hours; three Cristóbal Colón buses (25 pesos) and six by Estrella Blanca (27 to 35 pesos)
San Cristóbal de Las Casas – 390 km, eight hours; one Cristóbal Colón bus (38 pesos)
Santa Cruz Huatulco – 140 km, 2½ hours; three Cristóbal Colón buses (14 pesos) and six by Estrella Blanca (15 to 19 pesos)
Tuxtla Gutiérrez – 310 km, six hours; two Cristóbal Colón buses (30 pesos)

Cristóbal Colón and Sur run to Tonalá and Tapachula. Other Cristóbal Colón buses go to Acayucan, Mexico City, Veracruz and Villahermosa. Estrella Blanca has service to Acapulco, Zihuatanejo and even Tijuana.

Getting Around

'Centro' buses and microbuses (0.70 pesos) run along Avenida Ferrocarril from the bus stations to the town centre. Going out to the bus stations, catch a 'Cabaña' or 'Deportivo' bus from the south-west corner of the main plaza.

JUCHITÁN
• *pop: 66,500*

A friendly town visited by few gringos, Juchitán has cultural similarities to Tehuantepec. For most travellers it serves just as a bus junction.

Orientation & Information

Prolongación 16 de Septiembre leads into Juchitán from a busy crossroads on highway 190 on the north edge of town. The main bus terminal is about 100 metres along Prolongación 16 de Septiembre, on the right. This street continues past the Hotel La Mansión, then curves to the right and divides into 5 de Septiembre (the right fork) and 16 de Septiembre (left). These two streets run parallel to emerge as opposite sides of the central plaza, Jardín Juárez, after seven blocks.

There are several banks on and near Jardín Juárez, some with ATMs. A Lada caseta with fax service is in the Sur section of the main bus terminal.

Things to See & Do

The **Jardín Juárez** is a lively central square. A busy **market** spills into the streets from its indoor area behind the Palacio Municipal on one side of the plaza. It's a good place to look for hammocks, which are made locally.

Juchitán's **Casa de la Cultura**, a block along Juárez from Jardín Juárez (in the opposite direction to the market), then half a block to the left on Colón, has an art collection with works by leading 20th century Mexican artists such as Rufino Tamayo and José Luis Cuevas, and a good archaeological collection. It's housed around a big patio beside the 19th century Iglesia de San Vicente Ferrer.

OAXACA STATE

Festivals

Juchitán holds 26 annual *velas* (vigils), single-night fiestas in honour of saints with lots of eating, drinking and dancing. Most take place between April and September. The biggest is the Vela de San Vicente Ferrer, the town's patron saint, on the first Saturday of the second half of May, which rounds off a week of lesser velas. It features bull-running in the streets, processions and tiradas de frutas.

Places to Stay & Eat

Hotel Malla, upstairs in the Cristóbal Colón bus station, has cool, tolerably clean rooms with private bathrooms for 38.50 pesos a double. *Gran Hotel Santo Domingo* by the highway 190 crossroads is a step up, with air-con singles/doubles at 93.50/126.50 pesos. *Hotel La Mansión* (☎ (971) 2-10-55) at Prolongación 16 de Septiembre 11, two blocks into town from the main bus station, has air-con rooms for 85/95 pesos, and a restaurant. *Hotel Gonzanelly* (☎ (971) 2-03-88), further along at 16 de Septiembre 70, has bare but clean and sizeable rooms with private bath for 45/58 pesos with fan, or 55/66 pesos with air con. *Hotel Don Alex*, three blocks nearer the town centre at 16 de Septiembre 48, has similar prices.

Restaurant La Oaxaqueña at the highway 190 crossroads, near the bus stations, does good carne asada for 10 pesos. There are five or six other meat and fish dishes available. *Café Colón*, at the rear of the petrol station across the road, is a smarter alternative with bow-tied waiters and wine. There are restaurants in the *Gran Hotel Santo Domingo* and *Hotel La Mansión*, and a few small places around the town centre.

Getting There & Away

Bus Cristóbal Colón (1st-class) and Sur and AU (both 2nd-class) use the main terminal on Prolongación 16 de Septiembre just off highway 190. Frequent local buses to Tehuantepec (30 minutes, 2 pesos) and Salina Cruz (one hour, 3.50 pesos) stop across the street. Fletes y Pasajes (2nd-class) uses its own FYPSA terminal, separated from the main one by a Pemex station. Many long-distance buses are de paso and leave in the middle of the night. At busy times you may have to wait a few hours before getting a place. Daily departures include:

Acayucan – 195 km, three hours; three Cristóbal Colón buses (19 pesos) and eight Sur locales (18 pesos)

Bahías de Huatulco – see Santa Cruz Huatulco

Oaxaca – 275 km, five hours; seven Cristóbal Colón buses (26.50 to 34.50 pesos), six by Sur (26 pesos) and 18 by Fletes y Pasajes (23 pesos)

Pochutla – 215 km, 4½ hours; two Cristóbal Colón buses (22.50 pesos)

Puerto Escondido – 285 km, six hours; one Cristóbal Colón night bus (29.50 pesos)

San Cristóbal de Las Casas – 335 km, seven hours; two Cristóbal Colón buses (33.50 pesos)

Santa Cruz Huatulco – 180 km, 3½ hours; three Cristóbal Colón buses (18.50 pesos)

Tapachula – 390 km, six hours; four Cristóbal Colón buses (38 pesos), six by Sur (37 pesos) and four by Fletes y Pasajes

Tuxtla Gutiérrez – 250 km, five hours; seven Cristóbal Colón buses (25.50 to 32 pesos) and four by Fletes y Pasajes (23 pesos)

For Tonalá take a Tapachula bus. Cristóbal Colón and AU run buses to Mexico City, Veracruz and Puebla. Cristóbal Colón also goes to Villahermosa.

Tabasco & Chiapas

Just east of the Isthmus of Tehuantepec – Mexico's narrow 'waist' – lie the states of Tabasco and Chiapas. Their differences define them: Chiapas is rich in potential but poor in reality, whereas Tabasco is an oil-rich boomland. Chiapas is mostly mountainous and volcanic, with forests of oak and pine (although there are some low-lying parts), while Tabasco is low, well-watered and humid, and mostly covered in equatorial rainforest. Chiapas' indigenous history is Mayan, Tabasco's is Olmec and Totonac.

Despite their differences, Tabasco and Chiapas form a geographical whole. Separated from the cosmopolitan centres of Mexico City to the west and Mérida to the east, the Tabascan capital city of Villahermosa and the Chiapan capital of Tuxtla Gutiérrez generate their own isthmian society. Sharing frontage on the mighty Río Usumacinta and a border with Guatemala, they share a cross-border history of cultural exchange and conquest.

Tabasco

Tabasco is the low-lying coastal area to the north of Chiapas, kept fertile by huge rivers which slice through the state on their way to the Gulf of Mexico. It was in this unlikely country that the Olmecs developed Mesoamerica's first great civilisation. Besides its cultural wealth, Tabasco is noted for its mineral riches, particularly petroleum, which in recent years have brought great prosperity.

History
This land was once the Olmec heartland, home to the first great Mesoamerican civilisation (1200-400 BC), whose religion, art, astronomy and architecture would deeply influence the civilisations that followed. La Venta, the second great Olmec centre (after San Lorenzo, Veracruz) was in

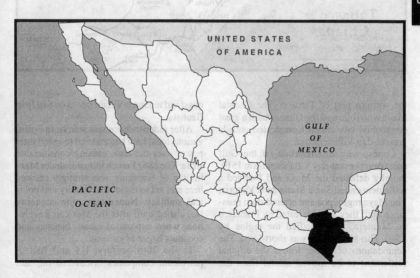

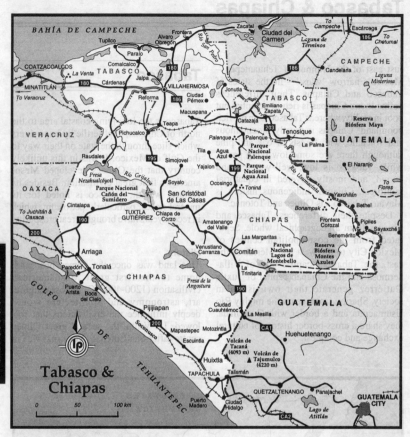

Tabasco & Chiapas

0   50   100 km

the western part of Tabasco. The Chontal Maya who followed the Olmecs built a great ceremonial city called Comalcalco outside present-day Villahermosa.

Cortés, who disembarked on the Gulf coast near present-day Villahermosa in 1519, initially defeated the Maya and founded a settlement called Santa María de la Victoria. The Maya regrouped and offered stern resistance until they were defeated by Francisco de Montejo, who pacified the region by 1540. This tranquillity was short-lived. The depredations of pirates forced the original settlement to be moved inland from the coast and renamed Villahermosa de San Juan Bautista.

After independence was won from Spain, various local land barons tried to assert their power over the area, causing considerable strife. The 1863 French intrusion under Maximilian of Hapsburg was strongly resisted here and led to regional solidarity and political stability. Nonetheless, the economy languished until after the Mexican Revolution, when exports of cacao, bananas and coconuts began to increase.

In the 20th century, US and British petroleum companies discovered oil, and

Tabasco's economy began to revolve around the liquid fuel. During the 1970s Villahermosa became an oil boom town and profits from the state's export of agricultural crops added to the good times. This new-found prosperity has brought a feeling of sophistication that cuts right through the tropical heat, stamping Tabasco as different from neighbouring Chiapas and Campeche.

Geography & Climate

Tabasco's topography changes from flat land near the seaside to undulating hills as you near Chiapas. Due to heavy rainfall – about 150 cm annually – there is much swampland and lush tropical foliage. Outside Villahermosa, the state is rather sparsely populated for Mexico, with a little more than a million people inhabiting about 25,000 sq km.

Be prepared for sticky humidity in this tropical zone. Much of the substantial rainfall here occurs between May and October. Outside of Villahermosa, it can be quite bug-infested (particularly near the rivers), so bring repellent.

VILLAHERMOSA

• *pop: 250,000*

Once just a way-station on the long, sweltering road from central Mexico to the savannas of Yucatán, Villahermosa was anything but a 'beautiful city' as its name implies. Its situation on the banks of the Río Grijalva was pleasant enough, but its lowland location meant it was bathed in tropical heat and humidity every day of every year.

Today, courtesy of the Tabasco oil boom, Villahermosa is indeed a beautiful city with wide, tree-shaded boulevards, sprawling parks, fancy hotels (for the oilies) and excellent cultural institutions.

If you want to see everything here, you will have to stay at least one night. The open-air Olmec archaeological museum, called the Parque-Museo La Venta, is one of Mexico's great archaeological exhibits, and it will take you most of a morning to take in its wonderful sights. The excellent Museo Regional de Antropología deserves at least

an hour or two. And just a short bus ride from the city are the ruins of ancient Comalcalco.

Orientation

Villahermosa is a sprawling city, and you will find yourself walking some considerable distances – in the sticky heat – and occasionally hopping on a minibus (combi) or taking a taxi.

Bottom and mid-range hotel and restaurant choices are mostly in the older commercial centre of the city, which stretches from the Plaza de Armas, between Independencia and Guerrero, and Parque Juárez, bound by streets named Zaragoza, Madero and Juárez. This section has been renovated in recent years and is known, because of those renovations, as the Zona Remodelada or, more poetically, as the Zona de la Luz. The zona is a lively place, busy with shoppers.

Top-end hotels are on and off the main highway which passes through the city, named Avenida Ruiz Cortines. The Parque-Museo La Venta is also on Avenida Ruiz Cortines, several hundred metres north-west of the intersection with Paseo Tabasco.

The Central Camionera de Primera Clase, sometimes called the ADO terminal (☎ (93) 12-89-00) is on Javier Mina, three long blocks south of Avenida Ruiz Cortines and about 12 blocks north of the city centre. The Central de Autobuses de Tabasco (2nd-class bus station) is on Avenida Ruiz Cortines near a traffic circle marked by a statue of a fisherman; the station is one block east of Javier Mina, five long blocks north of the 1st-class station, and about 16 long blocks from the centre.

Villahermosa's Rovirosa airport (☎ (93) 12-75-55) is 13 km east of the centre on highway 180, on the other side of the bridge across the Río Grijalva.

Information

Tourist Office The large, glitzy main Tabasco state tourist office (☎ (93) 16-36-23, fax 16-28-90) is in the governmental development known as Tabasco 2000, at Paseo Tabasco 1504, half a km north-west of

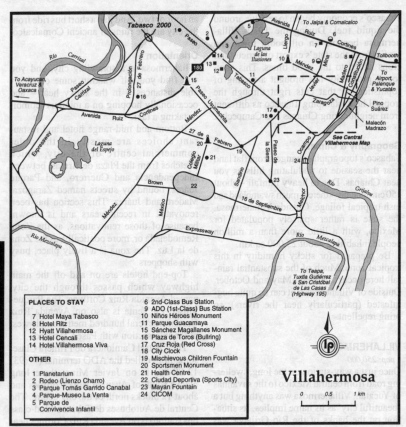

PLACES TO STAY
7 Hotel Maya Tabasco
8 Hotel Ritz
12 Hyatt Villahermosa
13 Hotel Cencali
14 Hotel Villahermosa Viva

OTHER
1 Planetarium
2 Rodeo (Lienzo Charro)
3 Parque Tomás Garrido Canabal
4 Parque-Museo La Venta
5 Parque de
    Convivencia Infantil
6 2nd-Class Bus Station
9 ADO (1st-Class) Bus Station
10 Niños Héroes Monument
11 Parque Guacamaya
15 Sánchez Magallanes Monument
16 Plaza de Toros (Bullring)
17 Cruz Roja (Red Cross)
18 City Clock
19 Mischievous Children Fountain
20 Sportsmen Monument
21 Health Centre
22 Ciudad Deportiva (Sports City)
23 Mayan Fountain
24 CICOM

Villahermosa

0   0.5   1 km

the intersection with Ruiz Cortines. It's not very accessible except by car. Hours are from 8.30 am to 4 pm Monday to Friday. The federal SECTUR office (☎ 16-28-91) is here as well. It's interesting that the tourist office is in an area convenient to bureaucrats but inconvenient to tourists.

Money There are at least eight banks within a five-block area of the Zona Remodelada, bound by Aldama, Zaragoza, Madero and Reforma. Many have cajeros automáticos (ATMs). Banamex (☎ (93) 12-89-94) at 27 de Febrero and Madero, has a cajero

automático connected to Plus System's network. Bancomer (☎ (93) 12-37-00) is at the intersection of Zaragoza and Juárez. Banking hours are 9 am to 1.30 pm.

Post & Telecommunications There's a small post office at the ADO bus station. The main post office (☎ (93)12-10-40), is on Saenz 131 on the corner of Lerdo de Tejada in the Zona Remodelada. Postal hours are from 8 am to 5.30 pm Monday to Friday, from 9 am to noon Saturday, closed Sunday. The telegraph office (☎ (93)12-24-94) is near the post office at Lerdo de Tejada 601.

Medical Services Unidad Medico Guerro Urgencias (☎ (93)14-56-97/8), on 5 de Mayo 44 at Lerdo de Tejada, is open 24 hours.

Laundry Super Lavandería Rex (☎ (93) 12-08-15), Madero 705 at Méndez, facing Restaurant Mexicanito, is open from 8 am to 8 pm Monday to Saturday. A three-kg load costs 28 pesos for three-hour service.

Acua Lavandería, next to the river on the corner of Madero and Reforma, is open every day except Sunday; they charge 4 pesos per kg for two-day service, 6 pesos per kg for same-day service; they do not have self-service.

Parque-Museo La Venta
The Olmec city of La Venta, built on an island where the Río Tonalá runs into the Gulf some 129 km west of Villahermosa, was originally constructed in about 1500 BC, and flourished from 800 BC to 200 AD.

Danish archaeologist Frans Blom did the initial excavation in 1925, and work was continued by Tulane and California universities. M W Sterling is credited with having discovered, in the early 1940s, five massive heads sculpted from basalt.

When petroleum excavation threatened the site, the most significant finds were moved to Villahermosa and arranged as the Parque-Museo La Venta, a museum without walls in a lush green setting that enables you to picture these sculptures in their original Olmec city setting.

The park is a maze of paths with numbered artefacts set amid jungle foliage. Three colossal Olmec heads, intriguingly African in their facial composition, were moved to the park. The largest weighs over 24 tonnes and stands more than two metres tall. It is a mystery how, originally, the Olmecs managed to move the basalt heads as well as religious statues some 100 km without the use of the wheel.

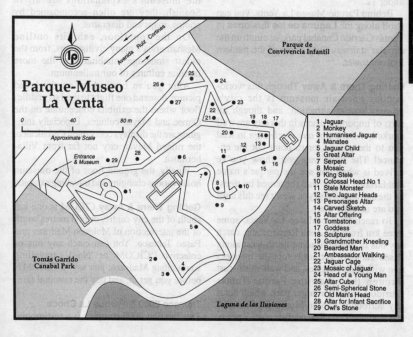

Parque-Museo La Venta

0   40   80 m
Approximate Scale

Avenida Ruiz Cortines

Parque de Convivencia Infantil

Entrance & Museum

Tomás Garrido Canabal Park

Laguna de las Ilusiones

1 Jaguar
2 Monkey
3 Humanised Jaguar
4 Manatee
5 Jaguar Child
6 Great Altar
7 Serpent
8 Mosaic
9 King Stele
10 Colossal Head No 1
11 Stele Monster
12 Two Jaguar Heads
13 Personages Altar
14 Carved Sketch
15 Altar Offering
16 Tombstone
17 Goddess
18 Sculpture
19 Grandmother Kneeling
20 Bearded Man
21 Ambassador Walking
22 Jaguar Cage
23 Mosaic of Jaguar
24 Head of a Young Man
25 Altar Cube
26 Semi-Spherical Stone
27 Old Man's Head
28 Altar for Infant Sacrifice
29 Owl's Stone

As well as the heads, you will see intricately carved stelae and sculptures of manatees, monkeys and, of course, the jaguar, the totemic animal of the Olmecs.

Parque-Museo La Venta (☎ (93) 15-22-28) is open from 8 am to 4 pm, closed Monday; entry is 7 pesos. Bring repellent as the mosquitoes can be vicious.

A small swarm of guides will approach you outside the gate and offer one hour tours for 45 to 60 pesos (one to five people). To prearrange a tour in English, Italian or French, call Luis Carlos García's guide service at ☎ (93) 53-11-52. A guide is perhaps the best way to see the park as the signage is cryptic and map brochures usually nonexistent.

On the north-east side of Parque-Museo La Venta is the **Parque de Convivencia Infantil**, the city's children's park. Playgrounds, a small zoo and an aviary keep the kids happy here daily except Monday from 9 am to 5 pm. Admission costs a small amount for adults, but is free for children under 12.

Behind Parque-Museo La Venta, you can stroll along the **Laguna de las Ilusiones** in Tomás Garrido Canabal park, or climb up the circular stairway (200 steps) of the modern lookout tower.

Getting There & Away Though this world-famous open-air museum is the city's primary tourist attraction, and though all sorts of important places in this city are well marked, *there is not one single sign* to lead you to the parque, or to point out the entrance! The only way you know you've arrived is when you see the parque's name emblazoned on the wall (obscured by trees) by the entrance – and you won't see this until you are actually there.

To reach Parque-Museo La Venta, some three km from the Zona Remodelada, catch any bus or combi heading north-west along Paseo Tabasco, get out before the intersection with Ruiz Cortines, and walk north-east through the sprawling Parque Tomás Garrido Canabal, a larger park which actually surrounds Parque-Museo La Venta. A taxi from the Zona Remodelada costs 7 pesos.

CICOM & Museo Regional de Antropología

The Center for Investigation of the Cultures of the Olmecs & Maya (CICOM) is a complex of buildings on the bank of the Río Grijalva, one km south of the Zona Remodelada. The centrepiece of the complex is the Museo Regional de Antropología Carlos Pellicer Cámara, dedicated to the scholar and poet responsible for the preservation of the Olmec artefacts in the Parque-Museo La Venta. Besides the museum, the complex holds a theatre, research centre, an arts centre and other buildings.

The Anthropology Museum (☎ (93) 12-32-02) is open daily except Monday from 10 am to 3.30 pm; admission is 10 pesos.

Just inside the front door is a massive Olmec head, one of those wonders from La Venta. The best way to proceed with your tour of the museum is to turn left, take the lift to the 2nd (top) floor (3rd floor American-style) and work your way down. Although the museum's explanations are all in Spanish, they are often accompanied by photos, maps and diagrams.

On the top floor, exhibits outline Mesoamerica's many civilisations, from the oldest stone-age inhabitants to the more familiar cultures of our millennium.

After you've brushed up on the broad picture, descend one flight to the 1st (middle) floor where the exhibits concentrate on the Olmec and Mayan cultures. Especially intriguing are the displays concerning Comalcalco, the ruined Mayan city not far from Villahermosa.

Finally, the ground floor of the museum holds various changing and travelling exhibits.

Getting There & Away CICOM is one km south of the city centre, or 600 metres south of the intersection of Malecón Madrazo and Paseo Tabasco. You can catch any bus or colectivo ('CICOM' or 'No 1') travelling south along Madrazo; just say 'a CICOM?' before you get in, and pay the nominal fare.

Tabasco 2000 & Parque La Choca

The Tabasco 2000 complex is a testimonial

to the prosperity the oil boom brought to Villahermosa, with its modern Palacio Municipal, chic boutiques in a gleaming mall, a convention centre and pretty fountains. There's also a planetarium, where Spanish-language Omnimax cinema shows are presented from Tuesday to Friday. If you are coming from the city centre, take a 'Tabasco 2000' bus along Paseo Tabasco.

Parque La Choca, just beyond the Tabasco 2000 complex, is the site of a state fair, complete with livestock exhibitions and a craft festival in late April. It is also a pleasant place to picnic, has a swimming pool and is open Monday to Saturday from 7 am to 9 pm.

Yumká

Yumká (☎/fax (93)13-23-90), 18 km east of the city (near the airport), is Villahermosa's attempt at ecotourism, a one-sq-km Nature Interpretive Center boasting spider monkeys, antelopes, wildebeests, zebras, giraffes, elephants, white rhinos, water buffaloes, ostriches, camels, caged jaguars, and maybe a crocodile. Though some metal fences partition the park, most animals are free to roam.

Named for the dwarf who looks after the jungle, the Yumká reserve is split into three sections: you begin with a half-hour stroll through the jungle, followed by an Asian and African Savanna tour by tractor-pulled trolley and finish up with a boat trip on the large lagoon. The obligatory guided tour takes 1½ to 2 hours. It's hardly a Kenya game drive, but if you fancy a dose of open space, greenery and a glimpse of the animal kingdom, go.

Yumká is open every day from 9 am to 5.30 pm. Admission costs 18 pesos. Drinks and snacks are available at the front gate.

Getting There & Away On weekends, shuttles go between the Parque-Museo La Venta car park and Yumká every thirty minutes from 10 am to 4 pm. On weekdays, there are supposedly combis to Yumká from Parque La Paz on Madero, yet I could find only taxis, charging 50 pesos for the ride.

Places to Stay – bottom end

Camping It might be possible to set up a tent or caravan/trailer at the *Ciudad Deportiva* in the southern part of the city. Ask at the fieldhouse adjacent to the Olympic Stadium during the day. The Tamolte bus runs out here. There's trailer parking also at Parque La Choca on Paseo Tabasco, north-west of Tabasco 2000, but no tents are allowed.

Hotels Most inexpensive hotels are in the Zona Remodelada, but there is one relatively cheap choice near the 1st-class bus station. Keep street noise in mind when choosing accommodation.

Hotel Palomino (☎ (93) 12-84-31) is on Javier Mina at Pedro Fuentes, across from the main entrance to the ADO (1st-class) bus station. Its location lets it get away with charging 70 pesos for a basic room (with fan and shower). It's sometimes noisy and you may be put on the 4th or 5th floor, which can be lethal if you arrive late in a semi-liquid state.

On Lerdo de Tejada, between Juárez and Madero, is a row of three small, plain and cheap hotels. *Hotel San Miguel* (☎ (93) 12-15-00), in the mall off Madero at Lerdo 315, is perhaps the best of the lot, renting its plain rooms for 45/60 pesos a single/double, or 80 pesos with air-con. *Hotel Tabasco* (☎ (93) 12-00-77), Lerdo 317, is a step down in quality, but will do for 40 pesos a double. *Hotel Oviedo* (☎ (93) 12-14-55) at Lerdo 303, the worst of the lot, charges 34/39/52 pesos for mediocre singles/doubles/triples.

Hotel Oriente (☎ (93) 12-01-21), Madero 425 near Lerdo, is simple and clean, and has its own good, cheap little restaurant on the ground floor. Rooms with private shower and ceiling fan go for 40/50 pesos a single/double.

For budget air-con rooms, try the *Hotel San Francisco* (☎ (93) 12-31-98), at Madero 604 between Zaragoza and María del Carmen. A lift does away with the sweaty hike upstairs. It's not bad for the price: 60/65/70 pesos a single/double/triple with fan and private bath; another 5 or 10 pesos per room for air-con.

TABASCO & CHIAPAS

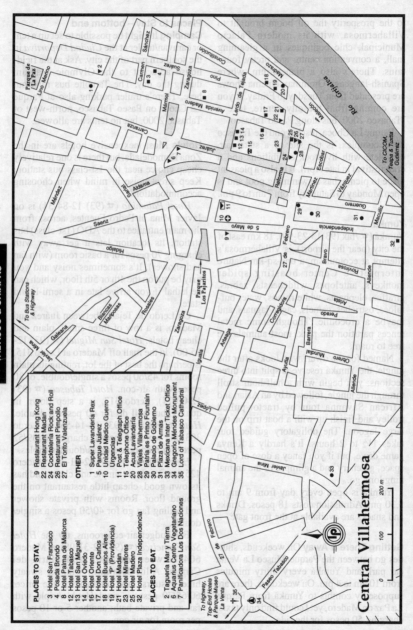

PLACES TO STAY

3 Hotel San Francisco
4 Posada Brondo
8 Hotel Palma de Mallorca
12 Hotel Tabasco
13 Hotel San Miguel
14 Hotel Oviedo
16 Hotel Oriente
17 Hotel Don Carlos
18 Hotel Buenos Aires
19 Hotel 'P' (Providencia)
21 Hotel Miraflores
23 Hotel Madan
25 Hotel Madero
32 Hotel Plaza Independencia

PLACES TO EAT

2 Taguería Mar y Tierra
6 Aquarius Centro Vegetariano
7 Panificadora Los Dos Naciones

OTHER

9 Restaurant Hong Kong
22 Restaurant Madan
24 Cocktelería Rock and Roll
26 Restaurant Pimpollo
27 El Torito Valenzuela

1 Super Lavandería Rex
5 Parque Juárez
10 Unidad Medico Guerro Urgencias
11 Post & Telegraph Office
15 Telephone Office
20 Acua Lavandería
28 Viajes Villahermosa
29 Patria es Primo Fountain
30 Palacio de Gobierno
31 Plaza de Armas
33 Mexicana Inter Ticket Office
34 Gregorio Méndes Monument
35 Lord of Tabasco Cathedral

Central Villahermosa

0   100   200 m

Hotel Palma de Mallorca (☎ (93) 12-01-44/5), Madero 510 between Lerdo de Tejada and Zaragoza, is slightly more comfortable, but hardly what you'd call special. Rooms with ceiling fan rent for 65/75 pesos a single/double, or 10 pesos more with air-con.

Hotel Madero (☎ (93) 12-05-16), Madero 301 between Reforma and 27 de Febrero, is in an old building with some character, but the rooms are soulless and prison-like at 45/55/65 pesos a single/double/triple with ceiling fan and private shower. Air-con costs 10 pesos per room more.

The cheapest beds are on Constitución. *Hotel Providencia* (☎ (93) 12-82-62), Constitución 210, between Lerdo and Reforma, has tiny rooms, and even tinier baths that are often acceptably clean; it's certainly well priced at 28 pesos per room. To find the hotel, look for the odd sign saying 'Hotel P', with an eye peering from a triangle. A few doors north of the Hotel Providencia, *Hotel Buenos Aires* (☎ (93) 12-15-55), Constitución 216, offers dispiriting rooms for slightly more.

Posada Brondo (☎ (93) 12-59-61), Pino Suárez 209 between Carmen Sánchez and Mármol, has white, bright, clean rooms with TV and shower for 54 pesos. For 65 pesos you get a room with a small couch, refrigerator, and perhaps a balcony. The lobby has good maps of Villahermosa and Tabasco.

Places to Stay – middle

Mid-range hotels are also in the Zona Remodelada. The *Hotel Miraflores* (☎ (93) 12-00-22/54), Reforma 304 just west of Madero, has a restaurant, terrace café, several bars, a car-rental office, and nicely appointed air-con rooms with bath for 145/160/175 pesos a single/double/triple.

Hotel Madan (☎ (93) 12-16-50), Pino Suárez 105 just north of Reforma, has 20 nice, modern air-con rooms with bath. The hotel entrance is at the eastern end of the building on Pino Suárez; the western end on Madero houses the restaurant (see Places to Eat later in this section). Rooms cost 105/115/125 pesos a single/double/triple.

Hotel Don Carlos (☎ (93) 12-24-92, fax 12-46-22), Madero 418 between Reforma and Lerdo, has air-con rooms with private baths, TV and telephones for 160 pesos a single or double, 175 pesos a triple. Though the lobby is lavish with mirrors and marble, the hotel has seen better days: many of the guestrooms are musty and the furniture is somewhat creaky.

Hotel Plaza Independencia (☎ (93) 12-12-99, fax 14-47-24), Independencia 123 near the Plaza de Armas, is a pleasant air-con hotel with TVs, private baths, and balconies (try for a room on an upper floor). A restaurant, bar, small pool and car park add to the hotel's appeal. Prices are 155/165/185 pesos a single/double/triple.

For a moderately priced hotel near the bus stations, try the *Hotel Ritz* (☎ (93) 12-16-11), Madero 1013. This modernised three-storey building is one block south of Ruiz Cortines (highway 180) and about five blocks east of both the 1st and 2nd-class bus stations. Air-con rooms with private baths are 155/165 pesos a single/double.

Places to Stay – top end

Three of the best hotels are near the intersection of Paseo Tabasco and Avenida Ruiz Cortines (highway 180), a pleasant 10-minute walk from Parque-Museo La Venta.

Poshest is the 211-room *Hyatt Villahermosa* (☎ (93) 13-44-44, fax 15-12-35), south-west off Paseo Tabasco on the Laguna de las Ilusiones, south-east of Avenida Ruiz Cortines, with all the expected luxury services at 500 pesos a double.

The *Villahermosa Viva* (☎ (93)15-00-00, fax 15-30-73), at the intersection of Paseo Tabasco and Avenida Ruiz Cortines (highway 180), is a two-storey motel-style white stucco building surrounding a large swimming pool. Comfortable rooms cost 325 pesos.

Another good option is the *Hotel Cencali* (☎ (93)15-19-96/97/99, fax 15-66-00), Calle Juárez off Paseo Tabasco, next to the Hyatt (this is a different Calle Juárez from the one in the city centre!). The Cencali has tropical foliage, grassy lawns, a good restaurant, clean swimming pool, and pleasant modern air-con rooms with TV for 280 pesos.

Holiday Inn Villahermosa (☎ (93)16-44-00, toll-free in Mexico 800-00-90-99; fax 16-44-99), Paseo Tabasco 1407 in the Tabasco 2000 complex, is Villahermosa's newest luxury lodging, a modern slab-like building with comfortable rooms for 500 pesos.

Hotel Maya Tabasco (☎ (93) 12-11-11, fax 14-44-66) is a cool, safe haven four blocks north of the ADO bus station, a block west of the 2nd-class bus station and near the intersection of Javier Mina and Ruiz Cortines. Air-con rooms come with TV (satellite hook-ups) for 275 pesos, single or double.

Places to Eat

Inexpensive There are a number of good cheap eateries clustered around the 1st-class bus station on Javier Mina, but the main strip for cheap eateries is Avenida Madero. The pedestrian streets of the Zona Remodelada (Lerdo, Juárez, Reforma, Aldama) also have lots of snack and fast-food shops. Coffee drinkers beware! Most cheap places give you a cup of lukewarm water and a jar of instant coffee (sometimes decaf). If you need a quick early-morning shot of the good stuff, try *KFC* at Juárez 420, near Reforma.

El Torito Valenzuela, 27 de Febrero 202 at Madero, open from 8 am to midnight, is the most popular and convenient cheap taquería. Tacos made with various ingredients cost 1.50 to 2 pesos apiece. Similarly varied *tortas* (sandwiches) go for twice as much. With its corner location, you can watch the busy street life as you munch.

Restaurant Pimpollo, on Madero between Reforma and 27 de Febrero, has quick service and a comida corrida for 15 pesos.

Near Parque Juárez, *Aquarius Centro Vegetariano*, Zaragoza 513 between Aldama and Juárez, is open daily except Sunday from 9 am to 9 pm. Granola, yoghurt and honey (5.50 pesos), a soyaburger (6 pesos), or its special sandwich (alfalfa, tomatoes, onions, avocado, cheese and beans on grain bread for 9 pesos) can be enjoyed at the counter or in the patio courtyard. They also sell whole-wheat baked goods and vitamins.

Taquería Mar y Tierra, Madero 704 north of Méndez, is a tidy little lonchería serving good tacos at decent prices.

Always packed in the late afternoon is *Cocktelería Rock and Roll*, on Reforma just east of Juárez, across from the Hotel Miraflores. Always full of Mexican families, it specialises in seafood cocktails and ceviches (fish, tomato sauce, lettuce, onions and a lemon squeeze) with crackers for 20 pesos.

At the Parque Los Pajaritos (Park of the Little Parrots), Zaragoza and 5 de Mayo, are two antojito stands where tacos are 1 peso and tortas less than 3 pesos. The food is OK, but it's the natural shade, big trees and the enormous cage of colourful birds that makes this park a relaxing snack stop. Somehow the breeze finds its way here and the fountain's quiet roar drowns out most city sounds.

If you're eating or drinking on the run, try *Jugos*, next to the Hotel San Miguel on Lerdo, for licuados or heaped fruit platters (4 pesos), or the *Panificadora y Pastelería* on Mármol facing the Parque Juárez, for sweet rolls, bread and pastries. Another useful bakery is the *Panificadora Los Dos Naciones*, on the corner of Juárez and Zaragoza.

Mid-Range Madero and Constitución have a number of suitable mid-range places to dine. *Restaurant Madan*, on Madero just north of Reforma, is bright, modern and has air-con, with a genuine espresso machine hissing in one corner. A full meal costs about 35 pesos, although you can have the comida corrida or a hamburger and beer for half that price. Opening hours are 8 am to 11.30 pm every day.

Restaurant Hong Kong, 5 de Mayo 433, just off the Parque Los Pajaritos, is a fine Chinese restaurant on an upper floor with a six-page menu and oriental decor. A full meal with wonton soup and roast or steamed duck might cost 40 pesos.

Besides the dining rooms of the luxury hotels, there are several garden restaurants along Paseo Tabasco between the river and Avenida Ruiz Cortines. You may want to coordinate a visit at the Museo Regional de

Antropología with lunch at the *Restaurant Los Tulipanes* in the CICOM complex, open from noon to 8 pm everyday. Seafood and steaks are their specialities and cost between 35 and 50 pesos. There is a pianist every afternoon and a Sunday buffet for 55 pesos.

Entertainment

Teatro Esperanza Iris at the CICOM complex offers folkloric dance, theatre or comedy from Wednesday to Saturday at 7 and 9.30 pm. Ask at the tourist office or your hotel for details.

The planetarium at *Tabasco 2000* has Omnimax cinema shows. (See Tabasco 2000 & Parque La Choca previously in this section.)

Discos can be found in the *Villahermosa Viva, Hyatt, Cencali* and *Maya Tabasco* luxury hotels; they're open every evening except Sunday and Monday from about 10 pm on. The cover charge is about 30 pesos. For other cultural goings-on, call the Instituto de la Cultura (☎ 12-79-47) or check their bulletin of events distributed to the museums and bigger hotels.

Getting There & Away

Air Villahermosa's Rovirosa airport (☎ (93) 12-75-55) is 13 km east of the centre on highway 180, on the other side of the bridge across the Río Grijalva.

Aerocaribe (☎ (93) 16-31-32), operated through the Mexicana office (☎ (93) 12-83-49), Avenida de Los Rios 105, Tabasco 2000, flies daily to Mérida (1½ hours, 465 pesos), Tuxtla (40 minutes, 294 pesos), Oaxaca (two hours, 531 pesos) and Cancún (three hours, 600 pesos). Mexicana has three flights to Mexico City (1½ hours, 540 pesos).

Aviacsa (☎ 14-57-77), at Francisco Javier Mina 1025-D, has four flights a week to Mérida (425 pesos) and Cancún (460 pesos). They fly daily to Oaxaca (488 pesos), Tuxtla (265 pesos) and Mexico City (500 pesos).

Aeroméxico (☎ (93) 21-15-28) at Avenida Carlos Pellicer Cámara 511, Plaza CICOM 2, has three flights a day to Mexico City (540 pesos). Aerolitoral (☎ (93) 14-36-14, fax 14-36-13), an Aeroméxico feeder airline based in Monterrey, services Villahermosa, Vera-

cruz, Tampico and Monterrey. Tickets are issued by Aeroméxico.

Viajes Villahermosa Travel Agency (☎ (93) 12-54-56, fax 14-37-21), at 27 de Febrero 207, between Juárez and Madero, sells international and domestic tickets; the staff speak English and can arrange excursions. Hours are Monday to Friday from 9 am to 7 pm, and Saturday from 9 am to 1 pm.

Bus The ADO bus station, Javier Mina 297, has a small post office and a selection of little eating places. You can leave your luggage in the station for 2 pesos per hour.

The two main 1st-class companies are ADO and Cristóbal Colón; UNO, the expensive deluxe line, has buses to central Mexico. Villahermosa is an important transportation point, but many buses serving it are de paso, so buy your onward ticket as far in advance as possible.

All of the listings below are daily 1st-class:

Campeche – 450 km, seven hours; 12 ADO buses (55 pesos)

Cancún – 915 km, 14 hours; five ADO evening buses (130 pesos)

Chetumal – 575 km, nine hours; a 10.45 pm Cristóbal Colón Plus (80 pesos); eight ADO buses (75 pesos)

Comalcalco – 53 km, 1½ hours; two Cristóbal Colón buses (14 pesos)

La Venta – 140 km, two hours; eight ADO buses (17.50 pesos)

Mérida – 700 km, 10 hours; 11 ADO buses (66 pesos); one evening UNO bus (49 pesos)

Mexico City (TAPO) – 820 km, 14 hours; 22 ADO buses (130 pesos); two Cristóbal Colón buses; and three evening UNO buses

Oaxaca – 700 km, 13 hours; two ADO buses (95 pesos); two Cristóbal Colón buses

Palenque – 150 km, 2½ hours; 10 ADO buses (23 pesos), or take a Campeche-bound bus as far as Catazajá (Palenque junction) (18 pesos)

San Cristóbal de Las Casas – 308 km, eight hours; all buses via Tuxtla by Cristóbal Colón

Tenosique – 290 km, four hours; 12 ADO buses (31 pesos)

Tuxtla Gutiérrez – 294 km, six hours; eight Cristóbal Colón buses daily (32 pesos); an evening Plus bus for slightly more

Veracruz – 475 km, eight hours; 24 ADO buses daily (58 pesos); one evening UNO bus for more

The 2nd-class Central de Autobuses de Tabasco bus station is on the north side of Avenida Ruiz Cortines (highway 180), just east of the intersection with Javier Mina. It's about five blocks from the 1st-class bus station as the crow flies. Use one of the pedestrian overpasses to cross the highway.

A number of smaller companies serve local destinations within the state of Tabasco, but there are also 2nd-class buses run by Autobuses Unidos to Acayucan (four daily, 23.40 pesos), Veracruz (one daily, 54 pesos), stopping along the way at Catemaco (23 pesos), and to Mexico City (three daily, 75 pesos). Buses to La Venta depart four times daily for 15 pesos.

Train The nearest station is 58 km away at Teapa.

Car Dollar Rent A Car (☎ (93) 13-32-69, fax 16-01-63) is in the Holiday Inn Villahermosa at Paseo Tabasco 1407; Hertz (☎ (93)12-11-11) is in the Hotel Maya Tabasco at Avenida Ruiz Cortines 907.

Getting Around

To/From the Airport Transporte Terrestre minibuses charge 20 pesos per person for the trip into town; a taxi costs 48 pesos. The 13-km trip takes about 20 minutes to the centre and 25 to 30 minutes to the top-end hotels. Buy your tickets from a counter in the terminal. From town to the airport, a taxi is your only choice. Check to see if Yumká is running shuttles to/from town. If so, they may drop you at the airport entrance.

To/From the Bus Terminals From the ADO bus station, it's generally about a 15 to 20-minute walk to the recommended hotels. Figure around 6 pesos in the cheaper VW Beetle taxis for almost any ride in the city. Local bus fares are only a few cents.

As you exit the front of the ADO station, go left for two blocks to the corner of Mina and Zozaya, where buses stop en route to the Zona Remodelada and Madero, the main thoroughfare. If you are walking, go out the ADO station's front door, cross Mina and

follow Lino Merino five blocks to Parque de la Paz on Madero, and turn right.

Bus & Minibus A dozen municipal (SEATA) bus routes link the centro with outlying areas of the city; the green and white minibuses and combis are more useful than the larger city buses. The minibuses travel tortuous, twisting routes, but it is easy enough to get where you want as they bear the names of major landmarks scrawled in their windscreens. Catch a 'Palacio Mpal' minibus along Paseo Tabasco to get to Tabasco 2000 and the tourist office; 'Chedraui' for the big department stores on Javier Mina, 1½ blocks from the ADO station and 'Centro' to get to the Zona Remodelada.

COMALCALCO RUINS

Comalcalco flourished during the Mayan Late Classic period between 500 and 900 AD, when the region's agricultural productivity prompted population expansion. The principal crop which brought Indian peasants from Palenque to this region was the cacao bean, which the Comalcalcans traded with other Mayan settlements. It is still the chief cash crop.

Comalcalco is open daily from 9 am to 5 pm; admission costs 9 pesos.

Resembling Palenque in architecture and sculpture, Comalcalco is unique because it is built of bricks made from clay, sand and – ingeniously – oyster shells. Mortar was made with lime from the oyster shells.

As you enter the ruins, the substantial structure to your left may surprise you, as the pyramid's bricks look remarkably like the bricks used in construction today. Look on the right-hand side for remains of the stucco sculptures which once covered the pyramid. In the northern section of the Acropolis are remains of fine stucco carvings.

Although the west side of the Acropolis once held a crypt comparable to that of Palenque's Pakal, the tomb was vandalised centuries ago and the sarcophagus stolen. Continue up the hill to the Palace, and from this elevation enjoy the breeze while you gaze down on unexcavated mounds.

Getting There & Away
The 55-km journey takes about an hour. ADO operates buses daily at 12.30 and 8.30 pm for 15 pesos. Ask the driver to take you to *'las ruinas'*.

RÍO USUMACINTA
The mighty Río Usumacinta snakes its way north-west along the border between Mexico and Guatemala. A journey along the Río Usumacinta today reveals dense rainforest, thrilling bird and animal life, and ruined cities such as Bonampak and Yaxchilán (see the Chiapas section). You can visit these ruins by air if time is short and money plentiful, but a journey by car and boat is cheaper and much more exciting.

You can also use a tributary of the Usumacinta as your water-road into El Petén, Guatemala's vast jungle province, with its stupendous ruins at Tikal. There are three routes through the jungle between Mexico and Tikal, Guatemala. (See the following Palenque and Yaxchilán sections for details.)

Chiapas

Mexico's southernmost state has enormous variety. At the centre of Chiapas is San Cristóbal de Las Casas, a cool, tranquil hill-country colonial town surrounded by mysterious, very traditional Indian villages. Two hours' drive west – and nearly 1600 metres lower – the surprisingly modern state capital, Tuxtla Gutiérrez, has probably Mexico's best zoo, devoted entirely to Chiapas' varied fauna. Only a few km from Tuxtla is the 1000-metre-deep Sumidero Canyon, through which you can take an awesome boat ride.

Three hours' drive south-east of San Cristóbal, near the border with Guatemala, with which Chiapas has always had much in common, is the lovely Montebello Lakes region. Chiapas also has a steamy Pacific coast, where Puerto Arista, near Tonalá, is a very laid-back beach spot.

About four hours north of San Cristóbal are the Agua Azul waterfalls, among Mexico's most spectacular. A little further on are the ruins of Palenque, one of the most beautiful of all ancient Mayan sites. Further east are the other fine Chiapas Mayan sites of Yaxchilán and Bonampak, both deep in the Lacandón jungle, one of Mexico's largest areas of tropical rainforest. You can even go from Palenque to Flores and Tikal in Guatemala's El Petén.

History
Pre-Hispanic civilisations straddled the Chiapas-Guatemala border, and for most of the colonial era Chiapas was governed from Guatemala.

Pre-Hispanic Central and coastal Chiapas came under the influence of the Olmecs, who flourished on the Gulf Coast from about 1200 to 400 BC. Izapa, in the southern corner of Chiapas near Tapachula, was the centre of a culture which peaked around 200 BC to 200 AD and is thought to be a link between the Olmec and the Maya.

During the Classic era (approximately 300-900 AD), coastal and central Chiapas were relative backwaters, but low-lying, jungle-covered eastern Chiapas gave rise to two important Mayan city-states, Palenque and Yaxchilán, which both flourished in the 7th and 8th centuries. Toniná and Chinkultic were lesser Mayan centres.

After the Classic Mayan collapse, highland Chiapas and Guatemala came to be divided among a number of often warring kingdoms, many with cultures descended from the Maya but some also with rulers claiming central Mexican Toltec ancestry. Coastal Chiapas, a rich source of cacao, from which chocolate is made, was conquered by the Aztecs at the end of the 15th century and became their most distant province, under the name Xoconochco (from which its present name, Soconusco, is derived).

Spanish Era Central Chiapas didn't come under effective Spanish control until the 1528 expedition of Diego de Mazariegos, who defeated the dominant, warlike Chiapa Indians, many of whom jumped to their death in Sumidero Canyon rather than be captured. Outlying areas of Chiapas were subdued in the 1530s and 1540s, though the Spaniards never gained control of the Lacandón forest, which remained a Mayan refuge.

Soconusco and inland Chiapas were administered separately, both from Guatemala, for most of the Spanish era, which meant that they lacked supervision for long periods and there was little check on colonists' excesses against the Indians. New diseases were brought by the Spaniards and one epidemic in 1544 killed about half the Indians of Chiapas.

The only light in the Indians' darkness was the work of some Spanish church figures, among them the Dominican monks. Preeminent was Bartolomé de Las Casas (1474-1566), appointed the first bishop of

Chiapas in 1545. Las Casas had come to the Caribbean as an ordinary colonist, but in 1510 he entered the Dominican order and spent the rest of his life fighting for Indian rights in the new colonies. His achievements, including partly observed laws reducing compulsory labour (1543) and banning Indian (but not black) slavery (1550), earned him the hostility of the colonists but the affection of the Indians.

19th & 20th Centuries In 1821, with the end of Spanish rule over Mexico and Central America, Mexico's new emperor, Agustín Iturbide, invited Spain's former Central American provinces (including Chiapas) to unite with Mexico. But Iturbide was soon overthrown, and when the Mexican congress was dissolved in 1823, the United Provinces of Central America declared their independence. A small military force under General Vicente Filísola, sent from Mexico City by Iturbide to preserve order in Guatemala City, returned home by way of Chiapas. Filísola used his power to bring Chiapas into the Mexican union, which it joined in 1824 after holding a referendum.

Permanent union with Mexico has not solved Chiapas' problems, however. Though quite rich in natural resources and economic potential, a succession of governors sent out from Mexico City, along with local landowners, have maintained an almost feudal control over the state – particularly in the highlands. Periodic uprisings and protests by the local indigenous peoples have borne witness to bad government, but the world took little notice until 1 January 1994, when a group calling itself the Zapatista National Liberation Army briefly occupied San Cristóbal de Las Casas and nearby towns by military force. With world press attention riveted on Chiapas, the Mexican government was forced to take vigorous measures to restore order and to meet the rebels' demands. Whether the Zapatista rebellion is the one which will bring Chiapas better government and better times, or is just another in the state's long history of rebellions, remains to be seen.

Bartolomé de Las Casas

The Zapatistas

'If all 14 of Chiapas' volcanoes had erupted during the past 18 years, they wouldn't have caused as much destruction as have the last seven calamities which we have had as governors...'

– Señora Concepción Villafuerte Blanco, directora of San Cristóbal's newspaper El Tiempo

On 1 January 1994, an armed peasant group calling itself the Zapatista National Liberation Army (Ejército Zapatista de Liberación Nacional, or EZLN) attacked and sacked government offices in San Cristóbal, Ocosingo and a few smaller towns in the area. Government troops evicted the Zapatistas within a few days, with about 150 people killed (fighting was particularly savage in Ocosingo). The rebels retreated to the Lacandón jungle, having succeeded in drawing the attention of the world's media to the situation in Chiapas. There they stayed at a remote forest base for over a year, encircled but not engaged by government forces, while a succession of attempts to negotiate came to nothing.

Rebel Zapatista leader Subcomandante Marcos, who has become a cult hero for some Mexicans

The EZLN's goal was to overturn the hold of Chiapas's wealthy minority on land, resources and power in the state, which had left many Indians and other peasants impoverished and lacking in education, health care and civil rights. It was often commented that the Mexican Revolution of 1910-20 never really happened in Chiapas. Though the Zapatistas were militarily far outnumbered, they attracted support and sympathy from many Mexicans, and their leader, a masked figure known only as Subcomandante Marcos, became something of a cult figure for many who resented the country's political stagnation.

The rebellion also provoked a social upheaval in Chiapas. Throughout 1994, while Marcos waged a propaganda war from his jungle hideout, demanding widespread reforms of the Mexican political and judicial systems, peasants took over hundreds of farms and ranches around the state. The evicted landowners focused much of their wrath on Samuel Ruiz García, Bishop of San Cristóbal, who follows in the Bartolomé de Las Casas tradition of support for the poor, and has earned the nickname El Obispo Rojo (The Red Bishop) from his enemies.

When Eduardo Robledo of the governing PRI was declared victor in the 1994 state governorship election, rival candidate Amado Amandano, of the leftist PRD party (Partido de la Revolución Democrática), claimed he had been robbed of victory by fraud. He declared himself head of a parallel state government, lending his support to villagers who evicted PRI officials from local government buildings.

In February 1995, the national government abruptly gave up on its attempts to negotiate with the Zapatistas and sent in the army to 'arrest' Marcos and other EZLN leaders. The timing of this – in the wake of a currency crisis which left Mexico desperately seeking a massive investment bailout – seems hardly coincidental. The Zapatistas had been perceived, somewhat debatably, as a threat to Mexico's national stability and economic prospects.

Marcos – whom the government had now 'unmasked' as a former university lecturer from Tampico called Rafael Sebastián Guillén Vicente – and most of his followers escaped the army, fleeing into yet more remote regions, accompanied by thousands of peasants. Whatever the eventual fate of Marcos and the EZLN, they have set off a chain of events which has surely rid Chiapas of the 'forgotten state' label for a long time. ■

TABASCO & CHIAPAS

Geography & Climate

Chiapas' 74,000 sq km fall into five distinct bands, all roughly parallel to the Pacific coast. The highest rainfall in all of them occurs from May to October.

The hot, fertile coastal plain, 15 to 35-km wide, called the Soconusco, receives quite heavy rainfall from June to October, especially in July and August.

Rising from the Soconusco is the Sierra Madre de Chiapas mountain range, mostly between 1000 and 2500 metres but higher in the south where the Tacaná volcano on the Guatemalan border reaches 4092 metres. The Sierra Madre continues into Guatemala, throwing up several more volcanoes.

Inland from the Sierra Madre is the wide, warm, fairly dry Río Grijalva valley, also called the Central Depression of Chiapas, 500 to 1000 metres high. The state capital, Tuxtla Gutiérrez, lies in the west of this valley.

Next come the Chiapas highlands, known to locals simply as Los Altos, mostly 2000 to 3000 metres high and stretching into Guatemala. San Cristóbal de Las Casas, in the

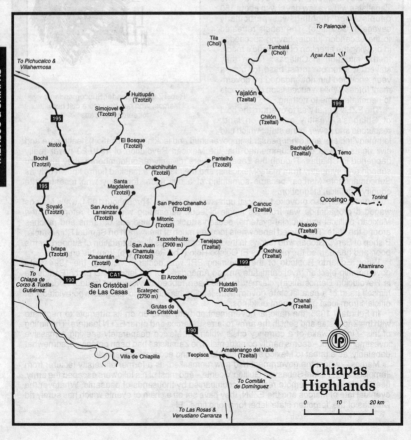

Chiapas Highlands

small Jovel valley in the middle of these uplands, is cool with temperatures between high single figures and the low 20s (°C) year-round. Rainfall in San Cristóbal is negligible from November to April, but about 110 cm falls in the other half of the year. The Chichonal volcano at the north-west end of these highlands erupted in 1981.

The north and east of the state include one of Mexico's few remaining areas of tropical rainforest, shrinking but still extensive at around 10,000 sq km. Its eastern portion is known as the Selva Lacandona.

Economy

Chiapas has little industry but is second only to Veracruz among Mexican states in value of agricultural output, producing more coffee and bananas than any other state. The fertile Soconusco and adjacent slopes are the richest part of Chiapas and the source of much of the coffee and bananas. Tapachula is the commercial hub of the Soconusco.

Chiapas has other sources of wealth. Oil was found in north-west Chiapas in the 1970s. The Río Grijalva, which flows through the centre of the state, generates more electricity than any other river in Mexico at huge dams like La Angostura, Chicoasén and Nezahualcóyotl. Most Chiapans, however, are very poor, and wealth is concentrated in a small oligarchy. Ironically, in this electricity-rich state, less than half the homes have electricity.

People

Of Chiapas' approximately 3.2 million people, an estimated 700,000 are Indians, descendants of the peoples who were here before the Spaniards came, including outlying Mayan groups. The Indians are 2nd-class citizens in economic and political terms, with the least productive land in the state. Some have emigrated into the eastern jungle to clear new land, or to cities further afield in search of jobs.

Despite these problems, traditional festivals, costumes, craft, religious practices and separate languages help Indian self-respect survive. Indians remain suspicious of outsiders, and are often resentful of interference – especially in their religious practices. Many particularly dislike having their photos taken, so ask if you're in any doubt. Nevertheless they may also be friendly and polite if you treat them with due respect. Spanish is no more than a second language to them.

Indian Peoples The Indian people that travellers are most likely to come into contact with are the 296,000 or so Tzotzils around San Cristóbal de Las Casas. Tzotzil textiles are among the most varied, colourful and elaborately worked in Mexico. You may also encounter the Tzeltals, another strongly traditional people, about 334,000 strong, who inhabit the region just east of San Cristóbal.

Other Chiapas Indians include about 80,000 Chols on the north side of the Chiapas highlands and the low-lying areas beyond, east and west of Palenque; an estimated 20,000 Mexican Mames near the Guatemalan border between Tapachula and Ciudad Cuauhtémoc, including some on the slopes of Tacaná (many more Mames – around 300,000 – are Guatemalans); and the Zoques, some 25,000 of whom used to inhabit western Chiapas, but were dispersed by the 1981 Chichonal eruption. Some have moved back to the area and there are hopes that the damage is not irreversible.

There are still a few hundred Lacandóns, the last true inheritors of ancient Mayan traditions, in the eastern Chiapas rainforest, with a language related to Yucatán Maya which they call 'Maya'. The past four decades have wrought more changes in Lacandón life than the previous four centuries: 100,000 land-hungry settlers have arrived in the forest, and North American missionaries have succeeded in converting some Lacandóns to Christianity.

TUXTLA GUTIÉRREZ

• *pop: 300,000* • *alt: 532 metres*

Many travellers simply change buses in Chiapas' state capital as they head straight through to San Cristóbal de Las Casas. However, if you're not in a hurry, this clean, surprisingly lively and prosperous modern city has several things worth stopping for – among them probably Mexico's best zoo (devoted solely to the fauna of Chiapas), and easy access to exhilarating motor-boat trips through the 1000-metre-deep Sumidero Canyon, though both these trips could also be made in a long day from San Cristóbal de Las Casas.

Tuxtla Gutiérrez is towards the west end of Chiapas' hot, very humid central valley. Its name comes from the Nahuatl *tuchtlan*, 'where rabbits abound', and from Joaquín Miguel Gutiérrez, a leading light in Chiapas' early 19th-century campaign not to be part of Guatemala. It was unimportant until it became the state capital in 1892.

Orientation

The centre of Tuxtla Gutiérrez is the large Plaza Cívica or zócalo, with the cathedral on its south side. The main east-west artery, here called Avenida Central, runs across the zócalo in front of the cathedral. As it enters the city from the west the same road is Boulevard Dr Belisario Domínguez; to the east it becomes Boulevard Ángel Albino Corzo.

The Cristóbal Colón bus station is two blocks west of the zócalo's north-west corner. The main 2nd-class bus station, Autotransportes Tuxtla Gutiérrez (ATG), is on 3 Sur Ote just west of 7 Ote Sur – from the south-east corner of the cathedral that's four blocks east, one south, one more east and one south.

Most hotels, places to eat and services are within a few blocks of the zócalo, but the tourist office and some middle and top-end hotels are in the west of the city on Boulevard Dr Belisario Domínguez.

The central point for Tuxtla's street-naming system is the corner of Avenida Central and Calle Central beside the cathedral. East-west streets are called Avenidas – 1 Sur, 2 Sur etc as you move south from Avenida Central, and 1 Norte, 2 Norte etc moving north. North-south streets are Calles – 1 Pte, 2 Pte and so on to the west of Calle Central; 1 Ote, 2 Ote etc to the east. It all gets a bit complicated with the addition (some-

times) of secondary names: each Avenida is divided into a Pte part (west of Calle Central) and an Ote part (east of Calle Central) – thus 1 Sur Ote is the eastern half of Avenida 1 Sur. Likewise Calles have Norte and Sur parts: 1 Pte Norte is the northern half of Calle 1 Pte.

Information

Tourist Office The Chiapas tourist office (☎ (961) 3-51-86) is 1.75 km west of the zócalo, on the ground floor of the Edificio Plaza de las Instituciones, the building beside Bancomer opposite the Hotel Bonampak. The staff are helpful, but don't speak much English, and the office is open 9 am to 8 pm every day.

Money Banamex, on the corner of 1 Pte and 1 Sur, and Bancomer, on the corner of Avenida Central Pte and 2 Pte, do foreign exchange from 10 am to noon Monday to Friday.

Post & Telecommunications The main offices are on a pedestrians-only block of 1 Norte Ote, just off the east side of the zócalo. The post office is open from 8 am to 6 or 7 pm Monday to Saturday for all services, and from 9 am to 1 pm Sunday for stamps only. Tuxtla's postal code is 29000.

Telegram, telex and fax services are available from 9 am to 8 pm Monday to Friday and 9 am to 5 pm Saturday.

There are Ladatel phones on the west side of the zócalo, in the Cristóbal Colón bus station, and by the Choco Centro shop behind the east end of the cathedral. One of those outside Choco Centro takes credit cards.

Laundry Gaily II at 1 Sur Pte 575, between 4 and 5 Pte Sur, charges 12 pesos for a four-kg load if you wash, 21 pesos if they wash. Hours are daily except Sunday from 8 am to 2 pm and 4 to 8 pm.

Plazas

Tuxtla's lively zócalo, the **Plaza Cívica**, occupies two blocks, with the modern San Marcos cathedral facing it across Avenida

TABASCO & CHIAPAS

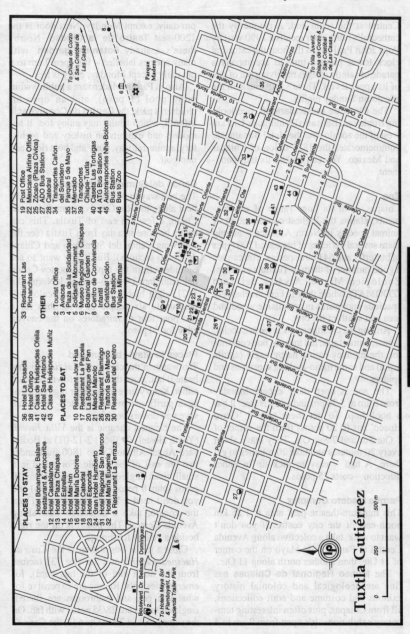

PLACES TO STAY

1 Hotel Bonampak, Balam Restaurant & Aerocaribe
12 Hotel Casablanca
13 Hotel Plaza Chiapas
14 Hotel Estrellas
15 Hotel Mar-Inn
16 Hotel María Dolores
18 Hotel Catedral
24 Hotel Española
31 Gran Hotel Humberto
32 Hotel María Eugenia & Restaurant La Terraza
36 Hotel La Posada
38 Hotel Olimpo
41 Casa de Huéspedes Ofelia
42 Hotel San Antonio
43 Casa de Huéspedes Muñiz

PLACES TO EAT

10 Restaurant Jow Hua
17 Restaurant La Parcela
20 La Boutique del Pan
21 Mesón Manolo
26 Restaurant Flamingo
29 Trattoria San Marco
30 Restaurant del Centro
33 Restaurant Las Pichanchas

OTHER

2 Tourist Office
3 Aviacsa
4 Agencia la Solidaridad
5 Solidarity Monument
6 Museo Regional de Chiapas
7 Botanical Garden
8 Centro de Convivencia Infantil
9 Cristóbal Colón Bus Station
11 Viajes Miramar
19 Post Office
22 Mexicana Airline Office
25 Zócalo (Plaza Cívica)
27 ADO Bus Station
28 Catedral
34 Transportes Cañón del Sumidero
35 Parque 5 de Mayo
37 Mercado
39 Transportes Chiapa-Tuxtla
40 Caseta Las Tortugas
44 ATG Bus Station
45 Autotransportes Nha-Bolom Bus Station
46 Bus to Zoo

Tuxtla Gutiérrez

0   250   500 m

Central at the south end. A plaque by the cathedral's north door recalls a 1990 visit by Pope John Paul II. On the hour the cathedral clock tower plays a tune to accompany a parade of saintly images revolving out of one of its upper levels. There's live music in the zócalo on Sunday nights.

The **Plaza de la Solidaridad**, overlooking Boulevard Belisario Domínguez 1.75 km west of the zócalo near the Hotel Bonampak, commemorates the 1824 union of Chiapas and Mexico. You can ascend its tall monument.

Zoo

Chiapas, with its huge range of environments, claims the highest concentration of animal species in North America – among them several varieties of big cats, 1200 types of butterfly and 641 bird species. You can see a good number of them in Tuxtla's excellent Zoológico Miguel Alvárez del Toro (ZOOMAT), where they're kept in relatively spacious enclosures in an hillside woodland area just south of the city.

Among the creatures you'll see are ocelot, jaguar, puma, tapir, red macaw, boa constrictor, the monkey-eating harpy eagle (aguila arpia) and some mean-looking scorpions and spiders.

The zoo is open daily except Monday from 8 am to 5.30 pm and entry is free. It has a bookshop. To get there take a 'Cerro Hueco' bus (0.20 pesos) from the corner of 1 Ote Sur and 7 Sur Ote. They leave about every 20 minutes and take 20 minutes to get there. A taxi – easy to pick up in either direction – costs 25 pesos.

Parque Madero Complex

This museum-theatre-park area is 1.25 km north-east of the city centre. If you don't want to walk, take a colectivo along Avenida Central to Parque 5 de Mayo on the corner of 11 Ote, then another north along 11 Ote.

The **Museo Regional de Chiapas** has fine archaeological and colonial history exhibits and costume and craft collections, all from Chiapas, plus often interesting temporary exhibitions. It's open from 9 am to 4

pm daily, except Monday. Next door is the 1200-seat **Teatro de la Ciudad**. Nearby there's a shady **botanical garden**, with many species labelled – it's open 9 am to 6 pm daily except Monday; entry is free.

Also in Parque Madero are a public swimming pool (1 peso), and an open-air children's park, the **Centro de Convivencia Infantil**, which adults may enjoy too. It has models and exhibits on history and prehistory, a mini-railway, pony and boat rides and minigolf.

Cañón del Sumidero Lookouts

The best way to see Sumidero Canyon is by boat along the Río Grijalva from Chiapa de Corzo, a few km east of Tuxtla. This can easily be done in a day from Tuxtla (see the following Cañón del Sumidero and Chiapa de Corzo sections). But if you want to see Sumidero from the top, Transportes Cañon del Sumidero (☎ 2-06-49), at 1 Norte Ote 1121, eight blocks east of the zócalo, will take up to six people in a minibus for a two-hour tour of miradores on the canyon edge for 50 pesos.

Places to Stay – bottom end

Tap water in the cheapies is *al tiempo* (not heated) but, since this is a hot town, not cold either. Keep your eye open for big bottles of agua purificada in lobbies etc – these can save you dollars on drinks.

The cleanest cheapie is the *Villa Juvenil* (Youth Hostel) (☎ (961) 2-12-01) at Boulevard Ángel Albino Corzo 1800, just under two km east of the zócalo. For a bed in a small, clean single-sex dormitory you pay 10 pesos (plus 6 pesos deposit for sheets) and you don't need a Youth Hostel card. From the zócalo, take a colectivo east along Avenida Central. The hostel is on the right beside a yellow footbridge.

Closest to the bus station is the *Casa de Huéspedes Muñiz* at 2 Sur Ote 733 (across from the north end of the bus yard), for emergencies only. Rooms are expensive for what you get, and bathrooms are shared; singles/doubles are 28/35 pesos with fan. On the same block at 2 Sur Ote 643, the *Casa de*

Huéspedes Ofelia (☎ (961) 2-73-46) has no sign but '643' is visible above its doorway if you look hard. Rooms are fanless but clean and cost 18/26 pesos for a single/double. An average room at Hotel La Posada (☎ (961) 2-29-32), 1 Sur Ote 555, costs 16/22 pesos for shared bathroom and 75 pesos for a large triple with bath.

Closer to the city centre, and slightly more expensive are the hotels on 2 Norte Ote, near the north-east corner of the zócalo. Hotel Casablanca (☎ (961) 1-03-05), half a block off the zócalo at 2 Norte Ote 251, is exceptionally clean and tidy for the price; rooms with shared bath are 18/36 pesos a single/double; with fan and private shower 36/48/60 pesos. On 2 Norte Ote 229, at 2 Ote Norte, is the similarly-priced Hotel Plaza Chiapas (☎ (961) 3-83-65). Its fancy lobby is modern and rooms are a bit better than at neighbouring hotels (and a bit larger).

Across the street, Hotel María Dolores and Hotel Estrellas (☎ (961) 2-38-27), at 2 Ote Norte 304 and 322, have indifferent rooms for 28/38/48 pesos. The Hotel Mar-Inn (☎ (961) 2-57-83), at 2 Norte Ote 347, with wide plant-lined walkways and a roof that seems to trap humidity, has 60 well-used rooms for 55 pesos a double.

The Hotel San Antonio (☎ (961) 2-27-13) at 2 Sur Ote 540 is an amicable modern building with a small courtyard and clean rooms for 33/44/55 pesos a single/double/triple. It's good, but a bit more expensive than the hotels to the north. Surprisingly, the rambling Hotel Olimpo (☎ (961) 2-02-95), at 3 Sur Ote 215, charges the same rates for small, muggy rooms, but it's clean and with bath.

For the travelling foursome who enjoy space, check out the Hotel Catedral (☎ (961) 3-08-24) at 1 Norte Ote 367, between 3 Ote Sur and the post office. They have enormous quadruples – two large rooms with a double bed in each and partitioned by a hallway. Bathroom, fan, hot water and cleanliness are included for 58 pesos a double.

Hotel Regional San Marcos (☎ (961) 3-19-40, fax 3-18-87)), 2 Ote Sur 176, at Avenida 1 Sur one block from the zócalo, is reasonable value at 65/75/85 pesos a single/double/triple for a moderately sized clean room; attached baths are prettified with tiles.

Places to Stay – middle

Hotel Esponda (☎ (961) 3-67-84), 1 Pte Nte 142, a block from the zócalo, has middling fan-cooled rooms with big bathrooms for 70/85/110 pesos a single/double/triple.

Gran Hotel Humberto, Avenida Central Pte 180 at 1 Pte Nte, a block west of the zócalo, has bright, spotless rooms with air-con, TV, phone and vast showers. Rooms are 120/150/180 pesos a single/double/triple.

The best city-centre hotel is Hotel María Eugenia (☎ (961) 3-37-67, fax 3-28-60), Avenida Central Ote 507, at 4 Ote, three blocks east of the zócalo. The hotel has attractive air-con rooms for 170/190/225 pesos, tax included, and a nice restaurant named La Terraza.

Hotel Bonampak (☎ (961) 3-20-50), Belisario Domínguez 180, 1.75 km west of the zócalo, is among the city's oldest 'luxury' hotels. Rooms in the main block and on the grounds (in bungalows) are 200/225 pesos a single/double. A pool, tennis and jai alai court, and a bar add to its attractiveness. There's a copy of Chiapas' famous Bonampak prisoner mural in the lobby which is more vivid than the original.

About 1.25 km further west is Hotel Maya Sol (☎ (961) 5-06-34), Belisario Domínguez 1380, set back from the busy road and draped in greenery; attractive air-con rooms go for 165/200 pesos; and there's a coffee shop, restaurant and pool.

Places to Stay – top end

Tuxtla's most luxurious hostelry is the Hotel Flamboyant (☎ (961) 5-08-88, fax 5-00-87), Belisario Domínguez Km 1081, four km west of the zócalo. The Disco Sheik (get it?) out front looks like a mosque. Rooms are priced at 350 pesos.

Places to Eat

Every fourth doorway in Tuxtla is a taco/torta shop. The cheapest quick bite you'll find is at one of the taco joints in the

TABASCO & CHIAPAS

pedestrian alley on your right as you exit the ATG station. The going rate is 1 peso a taco, but the taco fumes are likely to inspire vegetarian thinking.

Among the prettiest, fanciest panaderías is *La Boutique del Pan*, 2 Pte Nte 173, two blocks west and around a corner from the zócalo.

Enjoy pizza at the *Trattoria San Marco*, which has tables under red and white awnings. Twenty varieties of pizzas come in five sizes for 16 to 50 pesos, sandwiches on baguettes, salads and papas relleñas (potatoes with filling) are about 12, and they serve sweet, savoury crepas from 7 am to midnight every day. Next door, *Café Plaza* has a simpler menu, but good breakfasts (yoghurt, fruit, cereal and coffee) for 10 pesos, and plenty of open-air tables.

If you're looking for a big meal at a little price, try *Restaurant del Centro* on 2 Ote Sur just north of the Hotel Regional San Marcos, where a five-course comida corrida is 10 pesos. There are even a few outdoor tables. The tidy *Restaurant La Parcela*, at 2 Ote Norte 250 behind the Post Office, serves hotcakes, huevos or seven tacos for under 8 pesos, or a four-course comida corrida for 10 pesos. It's open every day, including Sunday.

Mesón Manolo, half a block west of the zócalo on Avenida Central Pte, has a steady stream of customers; menu options are a huevos rancheros breakfast for 8 pesos, tacos or quesadillas for 9.50 pesos, or meaty dishes for 12 to 20 pesos.

It's worth making the short trek six blocks east to the *Restaurant Las Pichanchas* (☎ 2-53-51) at Avenida Central Ote 857 (look for a sign with a black pot on a pink background and the words 'Sientase Chiapaneco'). This open-air, plant-filled courtyard restaurant has a long menu of local specialities. Try the chipilín, a cheese-and-cream soup on a maize base, and for dessert, chimbos, made from egg yolks and cinnamon. In between you could go for any of six types of tamales, vegetarian salads (beetroot and carrot), or more substantially, a steak. Full meals cost from 25 to 50 pesos. There is live marimba music most days from 2.30 to 5.30 pm and

8.30 to 11.30 pm, and Chiapas folk dances most evenings from 10.30 to 11.30 pm. Las Pichanchas is open every day from 8 am to midnight.

The *Restaurant Flamingo*, down a passage at 1 Pte Sur 17, is a quiet, slightly superior place with air-con. An order of three tacos or enchiladas is 14 pesos, and meat and fish dishes are 25 to 35 pesos.

As for a good comida corrida (26 pesos), one of the best for the money is served in the air-con environs of the *Restaurant La Terraza* of the Hotel María Eugenia 4 Avenida Ote Nte at Avenida Central Ote, three blocks east of the zócalo. Main course dishes are priced from 18 to 22 pesos; the restaurant is open on Sunday.

Restaurant Jow-Hua, 1 Norte Pte 217, 1½ blocks from the zócalo (around the corner from the Hotel Esponda), has a Cantonese comida corrida for 30 to 55 pesos.

Entertainment
There's live music in the zócalo Sunday nights. If it's dancing you're after, Tuxtla's best disco is *Colors* in the Hotel Arecas at Belisario Domínguez Km 1080, just west of the Hotel Flamboyant. Friday is the busiest night – drinks are 6 pesos and entry is about 25 pesos. You can also look for live music in the hotels. *Disco Sheik* at the Hotel Flamboyant is reputed to be fun, as is the singles bar in the *Hotel Bonampak*.

Things to Buy
The Casa de las Artesanías de Chiapas, next to the tourist information desk in the Edificio Plaza de las Instituciones, beside Bancomer opposite the Hotel Bonampak, has a good selling display of Chiapas craft – it's open from 9 am to 2 pm and 5 to 8 pm Monday to Saturday.

Tuxtla's main market spreads round Calle Central Sur, two to three blocks south of the cathedral.

Getting There & Away
Air Mexicana and Aviacsa fly nonstop to/from Mexico City (400 pesos, 1½ hours) at least three times daily. Aviacsa and Aero-

caribe fly nonstop to/from Oaxaca (300 pesos, one hour) daily, and direct to Cancún (500 pesos, three hours) via Villahermosa (200 pesos, 35 minutes) and/or Mérida (440 pesos, 1¼ hours) daily. Aviacsa also flies daily to/from Tapachula (200 pesos, 45 minutes). Sometimes promotional fares are lower than these – be sure to ask.

Tuxtla has two airports. Aeropuerto San Juan, 35 km west on highway 190, handles bigger jets, at present used only by Mexicana. Aviacsa and Aerocaribe use Aeropuerto Terán (TGZ), two km south of highway 190 from a signposted turning about five km west of the zócalo.

Mexicana (☎ 1-14-90) is at Avenida Central Pte 206, a block west of the zócalo. Aerocaribe (☎ 2-20-32, fax 2-20-53) is at the same address (Mexicana owns Aerocaribe). Aviacsa (☎ 2-68-80, fax 3-50-29) is at Avenida Central Pte 1144, 1.25 km west of the zócalo.

Bus Omnibus Cristóbal Colón, on the corner of 2 Norte Ote and 2 Pte Norte, two blocks north-west of the zócalo, is the major 1st-class bus line serving Tuxtla Gutiérrez. There is no place to leave your luggage in the bus station itself, but several *juguería* (juice bars) across the street (at No 259, for example) will guard it for you at a cost of 2 pesos.

ADO, on the corner of 5 Sur Pte and 9 Pte Sur, about 1.25 km west of the zócalo then five blocks south, has a limited number of services. The ageing 2nd-class buses of Autotransportes Tuxtla Gutiérrez congregate in a yard on 3 Sur Ote, half a block west of 7 Ote Sur, nearly a km south-east of the zócalo. Much newer 2nd-class buses are used on the San Cristóbal run by Autotransportes Nha-Bolom from 8 Ote Sur 330, two blocks east then half a block north of Autotransportes Tuxtla Gutiérrez. Departures from Tuxtla include:

Chiapa de Corzo – 12 km, 20 minutes; Transportes Chiapa-Tuxtla microbuses leave 3 Ote Sur, near the corner of 3 Sur Ote, every few minutes from 5 am to 7 pm (3 pesos)

Ciudad Cuauhtémoc (Guatemalan border) – 255 km, four hours; two morning Cristóbal Colón 1st-class buses (28 pesos); an-early morning ATG directo 2nd-class bus

Comitán – 170 km, 3½ hours; hourly Cristóbal Colón 1st-class buses from 5.30 am to 7 pm (19 pesos); 15 ATG 2nd-class buses daily

Mérida – 995 km, 16 hours; one deluxe Cristóbal Colón Plus bus daily (120 pesos); a lunch-time 2nd-class bus by ATG

Mexico City (TAPO) – 1000 km, 19 hours; two deluxe Cristóbal Colón Plus buses daily (150 pesos); eight Cristóbal Colón 1st-class buses daily; and five ADO buses (140 pesos)

Oaxaca – 550 km, 10 hours; one Cristóbal Colón morning 1st-class bus (75 pesos); an evening ADO 1st-class bus (60 pesos); three ATG 2nd-class buses daily

Palenque – 295 km, eight hours; about six Cristóbal Colón buses daily in various classes (28 to 40 pesos); seven more ATG buses; and a few ADO buses

Salina Cruz – 300 km, six hours; two Cristóbal Colón 1st-class buses daily (40 pesos)

San Cristóbal de Las Casas – 85 km, 1¾ to two hours; Cristóbal Colón buses at least every half-hour from 5 am to 9.15 pm (10 to 15 pesos) depending upon class of service; 2nd-class ATG buses and Autotransportes Nha-Bolom every half-hour until 6 pm

Tapachula – 405 km, seven hours; six Cristóbal Colón 1st-class buses daily (45 to 50 pesos); six ATG buses for less

Veracruz – 750 km, 14 hours; evening Cristóbal Colón 1st-class buses daily (75 pesos); ADO buses four days a week (70 pesos)

Villahermosa – 295 km, six hours; seven Cristóbal Colón buses daily (34 to 40 pesos); four ATG buses for less

Colectivos The quickest way to/from San Cristóbal de Las Casas is a colectivo taxi which does the trip in 1¼ hours for 18 pesos per person. Drivers wait outside the bus stations, especially Autotransportes Tuxtla Gutiérrez, and sometimes at Aeropuerto Terán. They leave when they have enough passengers.

Car Rental companies include Budget (☎ (961) 5-13-82) at Boulevard Belisario Domínguez 2510; Dollar (☎ (961) 2-89-32) at 5 Norte Pte 2260; Gabriel Rent-a-Car (☎ (961) 2-07-57) at Belisario Domínguez 780, 500 metres west of the Hotel Bonampak; and Hertz in the Hotel Bonampak.

TABASCO & CHIAPAS

Getting Around

To/From the Airport Transporte Terrestre combis (☎ 2-15-54) run to/from Aeropuerto San Juan for the Mexicana flights to/from Mexico City. The fare is 15 pesos per person. They'll drop you anywhere in the city. Going out to the airport you can board at the Gran Hotel Humberto two hours before take-off, or they'll collect you anywhere else in the city if you telephone at least two hours before you need to be picked up. For Aeropuerto Terán you need a taxi – 15 pesos to/from the city centre.

Chevy Suburban vans shuttle between Tuxtla Gutiérrez's Aeropuerto Teran and San Cristóbal for 40 pesos per person.

Local Transport All colectivo combis (1 peso) on Boulevard Belisario Domínguez-Avenida Central-Boulevard Albino Corzo run at least as far as the tourist office and Hotel Bonampak in the west, and 11 Ote in the east. Their official stops are marked by blue 'Ascenso'/'Descenso' signs but they'll sometimes stop for you elsewhere. Taxis are abundant and rides within the city usually cost around 20 pesos.

TUXTLA GUTIÉRREZ TO VILLAHERMOSA

After travelling 50 km from Tuxtla Gutiérrez on highway 190 (beyond Chiapa de Corzo; see the following section), you come to the junction with highway 195. Go straight on to San Cristóbal de Las Casas (34 km), or turn left (north) to Villahermosa on highway 195 (264 km).

The village of **Bochil** (population 13,000), 94 km from Tuxtla Gutiérrez and at an altitude of 1272 metres, is inhabited by Tzotzil Maya. It has two hotels: the tidy *Hotel Juárez* on the main road, and the more modest *Hotel María Isabel* set back a bit from the road. There's also a Pemex fuel station, the only one for many kilometres.

Five km before the Teapa turnoff, on the right-hand (east) side, is the **Balneario El Azufre** (Sulphur Baths); the origin of the name is immediately obvious once you descend into the valley to cross a stream and

the stink of sulphur rises to meet you. The highway bypasses Teapa to the west, 60 km from Villahermosa. The train to Mérida passes through Teapa.

CHIAPA DE CORZO

• *pop: 32,000* • *alt: 500 metres*

Chiapa de Corzo, 12 km east of Tuxtla Gutiérrez, is a little colonial town on the Río Grijalva. It is the starting point for trips to Sumidero Canyon.

History

Chiapa de Corzo has been occupied almost continuously since about 1500 BC. Its sequence of cultures – in a crossroads area where Olmec, Monte Albán, Mayan and Teotihuacán influences were all felt – makes it invaluable to archaeologists trying to trace pre-Hispanic cultural developments.

In the couple of centuries before the Spaniards arrived, the warlike Chiapa – the dominant people in western Chiapas at the time – had their capital, Nandalumí, a couple of km downstream from present-day Chiapa de Corzo, on the opposite bank of the river near the canyon mouth. When the Spaniards under Diego de Mazariegos arrived in 1528 to occupy the area, the Chiapa, realising defeat was inevitable, apparently hurled themselves by the hundreds – men, women and children – to death in the canyon rather than surrender.

Mazariegos then founded a settlement which he called Chiapa de los Indios here, but a month later shifted his base to a second new settlement, Villa Real de Chiapa (now San Cristóbal de Las Casas), where the climate and the Indians were less hostile.

In 1863, Chiapa was the scene of the decisive battle for Chiapas between liberals supporting president Benito Juárez and pro-church conservatives supporting the French invasion of Mexico. The conservatives had taken San Cristóbal de Las Casas but were defeated by forces from Chiapa and Tuxtla Gutiérrez, organised by the liberal state governor Ángel Albino Corzo and led by Salvador Urbina. The name of Corzo, who was born and died here, was given to the town in 1888, making it Chiapa de Corzo.

Orientation & Information

Chiapa de Corzo's large, slightly sloping zócalo is called Plaza General Ángel Albino Corzo. Buses stop on 21 de Octubre, the street running east from the top end of the zócalo. For boats into the canyon, walk down the west side of the zócalo (5 de Febrero) and go straight on for a couple of blocks to the embarcadero on the river front.

There's a post office on the way down, opposite the large church. Bancomer on La Mexicanidad (the east side of the zócalo) will change foreign cash and travellers' cheques. The market is on La Mexicanidad opposite the east end of the church. There are a few artesanías shops around the zócalo.

Things to See

The fine eight-sided **Spanish Fountain**, called La Pila, towards the bottom of the zócalo, was built in 1562 and is said to have been inspired by the Spanish crown. A block beyond the bottom of the zócalo, the large **Templo de Santo Domingo** is mid-16th century also. One of its towers has an enormous gold, silver and copper bell of famed sonority, made in 1576 (one of the earliest in Latin America).

On the west side of the zócalo is an interesting little **Museo de Laca** (Lacquer Museum) dedicated to the craft of lacquered wooden objects or *jícaras* (gourds), of which Chiapa de Corzo is a centre. Hours are from 9 am to 7 pm Tuesday to Sunday and from 9 am to 1 pm and 4 to 7 pm Monday; admission is free.

The staircase of the **Palacio Municipal**, on La Mexicanidad, has a mural of local history and a map of the 1863 battle.

Festivals

Some of Mexico's most colourful and curious fiestas, together known as the Fiesta de Enero, happen in Chiapa de Corzo every January.

From 9 January, young men dressed as women and known as Las Chuntá dance through the streets nightly – a custom said to derive from a distribution of food to the poor by the maids of a rich woman of colonial times, Doña María de Angulo.

Processions and dances of the bizarre Parachicos – men with wooden masks and ixtle 'hair', representing Spanish conquistadors – take place in daylight hours on 15, 17 and 20 January. They too are said, in part, to go back to the same Doña María de Angulo. A curandero who cured her crippled son allegedly advised her to provide entertainment for the boy *(para el chico)* in his convalescence, so she instructed some of her servants to shake maracas for him.

There's a musical parade on 19 January, then on the night of 21 January there's the Combate Naval – an hour-long mock battle on the river, enacted by people in canoes, with spectacular fireworks. The celebrations usually close with another parade and general merrymaking on 22 or 23 January. Women wear colourful, exquisitely worked dresses.

Places to Stay

There are plenty of places to stay in Tuxtla Gutiérrez – see the previous section for details.

Places to Eat

There are several restaurants by the embarcadero but more appealing is the friendly *Restaurant Jardines de Chiapa*, in a garden off the La Mexicanidad side of the zócalo. *Restaurant Los Corredores*, on the corner of Avenida Francesca and 5 de Febrero, serves a coffee, egg, toast and fruit breakfast for 7 pesos, or seafood options of pescado frito (fried fish), pescado or camarones empanizado (breaded fish or shrimp) for 20 pesos.

El Campanario is half a block off the zócalo (off La Mexicanidad) on Coronel Urbina. There is an international menu, a beautiful garden, winsome staff and good seafood for 20 to 28 pesos.

Getting There & Away

To/From Tuxtla Gutiérrez Transportes Chiapa-Tuxtla microbuses run every few minutes up to about 7 pm between 3 Ote Sur, near the corner of 3 Sur Ote in Tuxtla, and a yard on 21 de Octubre, half a block east of the Chiapa de Corzo zócalo. The fare for the 12-km, 20-minute trip is 3 pesos.

To/From San Cristóbal de Las Casas

Most Cristóbal Colón and Autotransportes Tuxtla Gutiérrez buses running between Tuxtla and San Cristóbal stop in Chiapa at offices on 21 de Octubre. Cristóbal Colón's is a white building a block from the zócalo, and ATG is at No 284, three-quarters of a block further up on the opposite side. Conductors don't always announce that you've reached Chiapa de Corzo, so keep alert.

CAÑÓN DEL SUMIDERO

Sumidero Canyon is a daunting fissure in the countryside a few km east of Tuxtla Gutiérrez, with the Río Grijalva or Río Grande de Chiapas flowing north through it. When the Chicoasén dam was completed at its north end in 1981, the canyon became a long, thin reservoir. Fast passenger launches speed along its 35-km length between near-sheer walls 900 to 1200 metres high. This two to three-hour trip can cost as little as 20 pesos – a bargain for a crocodile's-eye view of some of Mexico's most awesome scenery.

Highway 190, heading east from Tuxtla towards San Cristóbal, crosses the canyon mouth about 10 km from central Tuxtla, shortly before Chiapa de Corzo.

Fast, open fibreglass launches leave from the embarcadero on the Río Grijalva at Chiapa de Corzo, operating between roughly 7 am and 4 pm. A round trip of an hour each way and maybe a half-hour stop at the far end costs 200 pesos for a boat that will hold eight to 10 people (about 20 to 25 pesos each). If you don't have enough others with you, wait until more people come along, and share a boat with them. Around 11 am or noon is the busiest time. The launches travel pretty fast so take a layer or two of warm clothing – and something to shield you from the sun. Boat operators are often happy to stop for lunch at one of the small restaurants near the Chicoasén hydroelectric dam at the far end

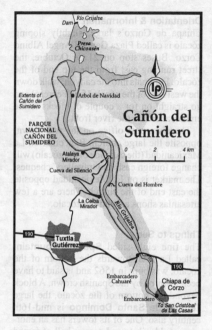

Cañón del Sumidero

for no extra cost as they'll get a free meal if they bring the restaurant custom.

It's about 35 km from Chiapa de Corzo to the dam. Soon after you pass under highway 190 the sides of the canyon reach an amazing 1000 metres above you. Along the way you'll see a variety of bird life – herons, egrets, cormorants, vultures, kingfishers – plus probably a crocodile or two. The boat operators will point out a few odd formations of rock or vegetation, including one cliff face covered in thick, hanging moss resembling a gigantic Christmas tree.

At the end of the canyon, the fast, brown river opens out behind the dam. The water beneath you is 260 metres deep.

SAN CRISTÓBAL DE LAS CASAS

• *pop: 70,000* • *alt: 2100 metres*

The road from Tuxtla seems to climb endlessly into the clouds before descending into the small valley of Jovel where lies San Cristóbal (cris-TOH-bal), a beautiful colonial town in a temperate, pine-clad mountain valley.

In the early weeks of January 1994, world attention was riveted on San Cristóbal as the Zapatista National Liberation Army, representing Mexico's (and especially Chiapas') oppressed Indians, seized the town by force of arms. Though the rebellion was suppressed by the Mexican army within a matter of weeks, it sent shock waves through the country, and attracted increased attention to the plight of Mexico's oppressed indigenous peoples. At the time of writing, an uneasy peace has returned to the region. The Mexican government has promised redress of grievances and the Zapatistas and the local Indians are waiting, restlessly, to see these promises fulfilled.

San Cristóbal generously rewards those who have the time to get acquainted with it, being endlessly intriguing to explore, surrounded by fascinating Indian villages, and endowed with abundant good-value accommodation, food to suit all tastes, and easy-to-find good company.

As long as the threat of renewed rebellion hangs over the town, it's a good idea to check on current conditions with your consulate before you visit. Most probably you will find a tranquil town when you come, with an increased military presence, but going about its daily business normally. Restrict your travel to the town proper, the more frequently visited nearby villages, and the major highways.

History

The Mayan ancestors of the Tzotzil and Tzeltal Indians of the San Cristóbal area may have moved to these highlands after the collapse of lowland Mayan civilisation in places like Yaxchilán and Palenque over 1000 years ago.

The Spaniards, who arrived in 1524, needed to use force only in neighbouring Chamula. Settlers arrived four years later when Diego de Mazariegos founded San Cristóbal as their regional headquarters. In the early days the Spaniards, perhaps 200 in number, occupied the area around the zócalo, known as El Recinto. Outside this were areas

for Indian allies who had accompanied the Spaniards; Aztecs, Tlaxcalans and Oaxacans settled in the Mexicanos, Tlaxcala and San Antonio barrios, Guatemalans in San Diego and Cuxtitali. A sixth barrio, El Cerrillo, was founded by freed Tzotzil slaves in 1549. The outlying villages were taken as encomiendas and, later, haciendas by the Spaniards.

For most of the colonial era San Cristóbal's Spanish citizens made their fortunes – usually from wheat – at the cost of the Indians, who lost their lands, and suffered diseases, taxes and forced labour. Early on, the church gave the Indians some protection against colonist excesses. Dominican monks arrived in Chiapas in 1545 and made San Cristóbal their main base. Bartolomé de Las Casas (after whom the town is now named), appointed bishop of Chiapas that year, and Juan de Zapata y Sandoval, bishop from 1613 to 1621, are both fondly remembered.

San Cristóbal was state capital from 1824, when Chiapas joined independent Mexico, to 1892, when Tuxtla Gutiérrez took over.

One day in 1867, at a place called Tzajalhemel, a Chamula girl named Agustina Gómez Checheb found three pieces of obsidian which seemed to talk. She entrusted them to a local Indian official, Pedro Díaz Cuzcat, who said they woke him at night with their noise inside a wooden box. Tzajalhemel became an Indian pilgrimage centre where Agustina and Díaz would interpret the 'oracles' of the stones. Díaz baptised 12 Indians as saints of the cult, which soon won more followers than the Catholic Church in many Indian villages north of San Cristóbal. This alarmed the church and civil authorities and in December 1868, the pair were imprisoned in San Cristóbal.

Enter the revolutionary Ignacio Fernández Galindo. Identifying himself with San Salvador or the Tzotzil god Cul Salik, he came from San Cristóbal to rouse the Chamulas to win back their lands and stop burdensome taxes. In June 1869, the schoolmaster and Catholic priest in Chamula were murdered and the rebels went through the countryside killing more mestizos. At San Cristóbal, they successfully demanded the release of Agustina and Díaz but were persuaded to leave Galindo and his wife as hostages.

When the hostages were not released, Díaz, joined by many Tzotzils, attacked San Cristóbal, but the authorities had time to gather reinforcements and the rebels were beaten. Galindo was sentenced to death; other rebels were shot or deported to remote parts of Mexico. Díaz survived to lead a short-lived uprising of hacienda servants in 1870.

Misrule in Chiapas continued into the 20th century, and indeed right up to our own times. The Zapatista rebellion of 1 January 1994 (described at the beginning of this section) is just the latest in a long line of protests by Chiapas' indigenous peoples against bad government – and often persecution – by local potentates and those appointed from Mexico City. It remains to be seen whether Coletos (residents of San Cristóbal) will be able to live in harmony, peace and justice.

Orientation

San Cristóbal is easy to walk around, with straight streets rambling up and down several gentle hills. The Pan-American Highway passes across the south side of town, with the main bus stations just off its north side. From these terminals, you walk north (slightly uphill) to the zócalo (Plaza 31 de Marzo), which has the cathedral on its north side. From the Cristóbal Colón terminal it's six blocks up Insurgentes to the zócalo; from Autotransportes Tuxtla Gutiérrez it's five blocks up Allende, then two to the right along Mazariegos.

Places to stay and eat are scattered all around town, but there are concentrations on Insurgentes, and also Real de Guadalupe and Madero which lead east from the zócalo.

Information

Tourist Office San Cristóbal's helpful tourist office (☎ (967) 8-04-14) is in the north end of the Palacio Municipal, on the west side of the zócalo. Hours are from 8 am to 8 pm Monday to Saturday and 9 am to 2 pm Sunday. The notice board in front is plastered with fliers detailing current happenings; there's a message board inside and they will hold mail.

There is also a little tourist information kiosk in front of the Cristóbal Colón bus station which is staffed – so it seems – on sunny days.

Money Several banks on and near the zócalo exchange foreign currency only from 9 to 11 am. It's quicker and easier to use their ATMs. You can also change cash or travellers' cheques at Casa de Cambio Lacantún (☎ (967) 8-25-87), Real de Guadalupe 12-A, half a block from the zócalo, where rates are only about 50 centavos per dollar worse than at the banks. The minimum transaction is US$50 and hours are 8.30 am to 2 pm and 4 to 8 pm Monday to Saturday, 9 am to 1 pm Sunday.

Post & Telecommunications The post office (☎ (967) 8-07-65) is on the corner of Cuauhtémoc and Crescencio Rosas, one block west and one south of the zócalo. It's open from 8 am to 7 pm Monday to Friday, 9 am to 1 pm Saturday, Sunday and holidays. San Cristóbal's postal code is 29200. For telegrams, go to Diego de Mazariegos 29, 2½ blocks west of the zócalo.

There are Ladatel phones on the west side of the zócalo and in the Cristóbal Colón and ATG bus stations. Sexto Sol, half a block east of the zócalo on Real de Guadalupe 24-D, can place calls and send faxes for you.

Bookshops & Libraries La Pared, in the Centro Cultural El Puente, Real de Guadalupe 55, has a large selection of used books in English and Spanish, mostly paperbacks which you can buy, sell, trade or rent. Also check out Susana Sanders' Good Books, Real de Guadalupe 53, next door to El Puente, with used books in English and Spanish; closed Sunday.

Librería Chilam Balam has a good selection of history and anthropology books, and some novels and guidebooks in English, German, and French. Their larger shop is on Utrilla 33 at Dr Navarro (diagonally opposite

Templo de La Caridad); a smaller shop is on Insurgentes 18 at León. Librería Soluna, at Real de Guadalupe 13-B, less than a block east of the zócalo, has a decent English section.

The 14,000 books at Na Bolom comprise one of the world's biggest collections on the Maya, and includes many other aspects of Chiapas and Central America. Those interested can use the library from 9 am to 1 pm Tuesday to Saturday.

Laundry Lavasec, at Crescencio Rosas 12 just north of Hermanos Domínguez, open from 8 am to 6 pm Monday to Saturday, will wash and dry three kg for 11 pesos, and has same-day service if you drop it off by 10 am. Lavasor has a drop-off/pick-up shop on Real de Guadalupe 26, between Utrilla and Juárez. Same-day service costs 10 pesos for four kg; hours are 8 am to 10 pm daily. Lavanderia Orve, on Juárez south of Real de Guadalupe, is open daily except Sunday from 8 am to 8 pm. Another place is Lavanderia Automática Mixtli, on Real de Mexicanos 1½ blocks west of the Templo de Santo Domingo.

Main Plaza

Officially called Plaza 31 de Marzo, this old Spanish centre of town was used for markets until early this century. Today it is a fine place to sit, watch the town life happen around you, or enjoy a meal in the central kiosk.

The cathedral, on the north side, was begun in 1528 but completely rebuilt in 1693. Its gold-leaf interior has a baroque pulpit and altarpiece.

The Hotel Santa Clara, on the south-east corner, was the house of Diego de Mazariegos, the Spanish conqueror of Chiapas. It's one of the few non-ecclesiastical examples of the Plateresque style in Mexico.

Templo de Santo Domingo

North-west of the centre, opposite the corner of Lázaro Cárdenas and Real de Mexicanos, Santo Domingo is the most beautiful of San Cristóbal's many churches – especially when its pink façade is floodlit at night. The church and the adjoining monastery were built from 1547 to 1560. The church's baroque façade was added in the 17th century. There's plenty of gold inside, especially on the ornate pulpit. Chamulan women conduct a daily craft market around the Templo de Santo Domingo and Templo de La Caridad (built in 1712) immediately to its south.

Weavers' Cooperatives

Sna Jolobil (a Tzotzil name meaning Weavers' House) is on Lázaro Cárdenas 42 across from the Templo de Santo Domingo, and **J'pas Joloviletic** is on Utrilla 43, just past the Templo de La Caridad. Sna Jolobil has 650 women in its organisation, J'pas Joloviletic about 850, all backstrap-loom weavers from 20 nearby Tzotzil and Tzeltal

Weaver with backstrap loom

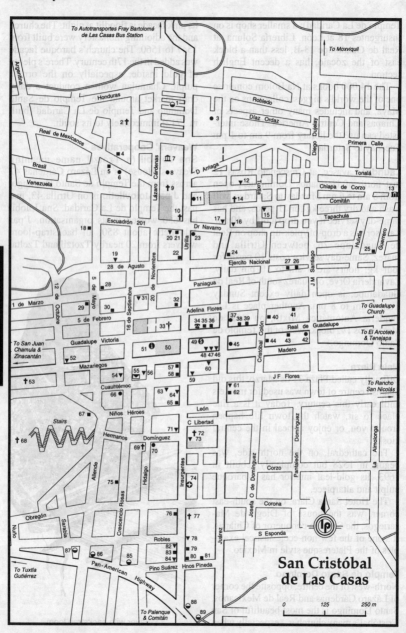

To Autotransportes Fray Bartolomé
de Las Casas Bus Station

To Moxviquil

Argentina

Honduras

Robledo

Díaz Ordaz

Dujelay

Primera Calle

Real de Mexicanos

Diego

Tonalá

Brasil

Chiapa de Corzo

Venezuela

Comitán

Tapachula

Escuadrón 201

Dr Navarro

Huixtla

Guerrero

28 de Agosto

Ejercito Nacional

5 de Mayo

Paniagua

J M Santiago

1 de Marzo

Adelina Flores

To Guadalupe
Church

5 de Febrero

Real de Guadalupe

To El Arcotete
& Tanejapa

Guadalupe

Victoria

Madero

To San Juan
Chamula &
Zinacantán

Mazariegos

J F Flores

To Rancho
San Nicolás

Cuauhtémoc

León

Niños Héroes

C Libertad

Stairs

Hermanos

Domínguez

Allende

Hidalgo

Insurgentes

Corzo

Pantaleón

La Almolonga

Crescencio Rosas

Corona

Obregón

Josefa O de Domínguez

Sarabia

Nuño

Pan-American

Juárez

S Esponda

To Tuxtla
Gutiérrez

Robles

Pino Suárez

Hnos Pineda

To Palenque
& Comitán

Highway

12 de Octubre

16 de Septiembre

20 de Noviembre

Lázaro Cárdenas

Utrilla

Cristóbal Colón

**San Cristóbal
de Las Casas**

D Ariaga

0   125   250 m

PLACES TO STAY

4	Posada El Candil
5	Casa de Gladys
18	Hotel Parador Mexicanos
21	Hotel Posada Caridad
22	Hotel Casa Mexicano
24	Posada El Cerrillo
25	Hotel Rincón del Arco
26	La Posadita
27	Posada Jovel
28	Posada Adrianita
29	Posada del Sol
30	Hotel El Paraíso
32	Hotel Posada Diego de Mazariegos
35	Hotel Real del Valle
36	Hotel San Martín
38	Posada Santiago
39	Casa de Huéspedes Margarita & Restaurant
40	Hotel Don Quijote
41	Hotel Casavieja
43	Posada Casa Real
44	Posada Virginia
57	Hotel Santa Clara
58	Posada San Cristóbal
62	Hotel Villa Real
65	Hotel Fray Bartolomé de Las Casas
67	Posada Los Morales
75	Hotel Arrecife del Coral
76	Posada Lucella
79	Posada Lupita
80	Hotel Capri
81	Posada Vallarta
83	Posada Insurgentes

PLACES TO EAT

12	Pizzas El Punto
15	El Zorro
16	La Casa del Pan
17	La Parrilla
19	Jardín de Cantón
20	Restaurant Las Estrellas
31	Café-Restaurant El Teatro
46	Restaurant Flamingo
47	Restaurant París México
48	Restaurant Fulano's
52	El Taquito
54	El Circo Restaurant
56	La Galería
59	Restaurant La Misión del Fraile
60	Restaurant Langosta
61	Comedor Familiar Normita II
63	Cafetería San Cristóbal
64	Restaurante Tuluc
71	Madre Tierra Restaurant & Panadería
73	Los Merenderos Cookshops
78	Cafetería & Lonchería Palenque
82	Restaurant Chamula
84	Tikal Restaurant

OTHER

1	Combis to San Juan Chamula, Zinacantán & Tenejapa
2	Church
3	Market
6	Lavandería Automática Mixtli
7	City Museum
8	Sna Jolobil Gallery
9	Santo Domingo Church
10	La Caridad Church
11	J'pas Joloviletic
13	Na Bolom
14	Church
23	Librería Chilam Balam
33	Cathedral
34	Sexto Sol
37	Casa de las Imagenes
42	Centro Cultural El Puente
45	Lavanderia Orve
49	Casa de Cambio Lacantún
50	Zócalo (Plaza 31 de Marzo)
51	Tourist Office
53	La Merced Church
55	Post Office
66	Centro de Investigaciones Ecológicas del Sureste
68	Hill & Church of San Cristóbal
69	El Carmen Church
70	Bellas Artes Auditorium
72	San Francisco Church
74	Hospital
77	Santa Lucía Church
85	Transportes Lacandonia Bus Station
86	Colectivos to Tuxtla Gutiérrez
87	ATG Bus Station
88	Cristóbal Colón Bus Station
89	Autotransportes Nha-Bolom Bus Station

TABASCO & CHIAPAS

villages. The co-ops were founded to foster this important folk art for income and to preserve Indian identity and tradition. The weavers aim to revive forgotten techniques and designs, and to continue to develop dyes from plants, dirt and tree bark.

Each Chiapas highland village has its own distinctive dress – see box on page 806 for more information.

Sna Jolobil is open daily except Sunday from 9 am to 2 pm and 4 to 6 pm; J'pas Joloviletic is open from 9 am to 1 pm and 4 to 7 pm Monday to Saturday, and Sunday 9 am to 1 pm. In both showrooms you can see huipiles, shawls, sashes, ponchos and hats. Prices range from a few dollars for smaller items up to US$500 for the finest huipiles and ceremonial garments.

City Museum

The Museo de Arqueología, Etnografía, Historia y Arte, next to the Templo de Santo

Traditional Highland Dress

Each Chiapas highland village has its own distinctive dress. In San Juan Chamula, men traditionally wear loose homespun tunics of white wool; cargo-holders – those charged with responsibility for important religious and ceremonial duties – wear black ones. The men of Zinacantan wear very distinctive red-and-white striped tunics (which appear pink), and flat, round, ribboned palm hats. Unmarried men's hats have longer, wider ribbons.

Women's costumes are more elaborately decorated than men's. Most of the seemingly abstract designs on these costumes are in fact stylised snakes, frogs, butterflies, birds, saints and other natural and supernatural beings. Some motifs have religious-magical functions: scorpions, for example, can be a symbolic request for rain, since scorpions are believed to attract lightning.

Some designs have pre-Hispanic origins: for instance the rhombus shape on some huipiles from San Andrés Larraínzar is also found on the garments shown on Lintel 24 at Yaxchilán. The shape represents the old Maya universe, in which the earth was cube-shaped and the sky had four corners.

Other costumes are of more recent origin: the typical men's ensemble from Chamula – long-sleeved shirt, wool tunic, belt and long trousers – stems from the Spaniards, who objected to the relative nudity of the loincloth and cloak that Chamulan men used to wear.

The sacredness of traditional costume is shown by the dressing of saints' images in old and revered garments at festival times. ■

Domingo, deals mainly with the history of San Cristóbal. All explanatory material is in Spanish. Hours are from 10 am to 5 pm Monday to Saturday and entry is 3 pesos.

Lacandón man

Templo del Carmen & Bellas Artes

El Carmen Church stands on the corner of Hidalgo and Hermanos Domínguez. Formerly part of a nunnery (built in 1597), it has a distinctive tower (built in 1680) resting on an arch, erected to replace one destroyed by floods 28 years earlier. Next door is the Casa de Cultura, containing an art gallery, library and the Bellas Artes auditorium.

Na Bolom

A visit to Na Bolom, a house on Guerrero 33 on the corner of Chiapa de Corzo, six blocks north of Real de Guadalupe, is one of San Cristóbal's most fascinating experiences. For many years it was the home of Danish archaeologist Frans Blom, who died in 1963, and his wife the Swiss anthropologist and photographer Gertrude (Trudy) Duby-Blom, who died in December, 1993 at age 92.

The couple shared a passion for Chiapas and particularly for its Indians. While Frans explored, surveyed and dug at ancient Mayan sites including Toniná, Chinkultic and Moxviquil, Trudy devoted much of her life to studying the tiny Lacandón Indian population of eastern Chiapas. She worked for the Lacandóns' wellbeing, but also attracted criticism for shielding the Lacandóns too zealously from change.

The house, whose name is Tzotzil for Jaguar House as well as a play on the owners' name, is full of photographs, archaeological and anthropological relics and books, a treasure-trove for anyone with an interest in Chiapas. Visits are by informal guided tours, conducted in English and Spanish, Tuesday through Sunday at 4.30 pm (admission is 10 pesos). Following the tour, a lengthy film is shown on the Lacandón and Trudy Blom's work.

Guest rooms are rented to those particularly interested in the Lacandón Maya and the Bloms' work. The cost is 180 pesos a double; reserve in advance if possible.

Centro Cultural El Puente

El Puente (☎ /fax (967) 8-22-50), on Real de Guadalupe 55, 2½ blocks east of the zócalo, is an information and cultural centre buzzing with locals, artists and interested travellers, open daily except Sunday from 8 am to 10 pm. El Puente has a gallery with continual exhibitions and a media room busy nightly with films, lectures, music or theatre (English or Spanish). The Centro's Café El Puente serves vegetarian meals.

Market

The flavour of outlying Indian villages can be sampled at San Cristóbal's busy market, between Utrilla and Belisario Domínguez, eight blocks north of the zócalo, open till late afternoon daily except Sunday. Many of the traders are Indian villagers for whom buying and selling is the main reason to come to town.

The Indians generally keep their distance from the mestizo population, the result of centuries of exploitation. But they can be friendly and good-humoured (and hard bargainers!).

San Cristóbal & Guadalupe

The most prominent of the several small hills over which San Cristóbal undulates are the Cerro de San Cristóbal in the south-west quarter of town, reached by steps up from Allende, and the Cerro de Guadalupe, seven blocks east of the zócalo along Real de Gua-

dalupe. Both are crowned by churches and afford good views. There's an amazing crucifixion sculpture made entirely of vehicle number plates behind the Templo de San Cristóbal; but there have been reports of attempted rapes here too.

Grutas de San Cristóbal

The grutas are in fact a single long cavern nine km south-east of San Cristóbal; among lovely pine woods, they are a five-minute walk south of the Pan-American Highway. The first 350 metres or so of the cave have a wooden walkway and are lit. You can enter for 3 pesos from 9 am to 5 pm daily. To get there take an ATG bus west and ask for 'Las Grutas' (1 peso). Camping is allowed, and there are horses for hire.

Huitepec Ecological Reserve & Pro-Natura

The Reserva Ecológica Huitepec is a two-km interpretative nature trail on the slopes of Cerro Huitepec, about 3.5 km out of San Cristóbal on the Chamula road. The ascent, rising through various vegetation types to rare cloud forests, takes about 45 minutes. It's open daily except Monday from 9 am to 4 pm.

Pro-Natura, an independent organisation staffed by volunteers and funded by donations, offers tours for 7 pesos. Its office is at Maria Adelina Flores 2 (☎ (967) 8-40-69).

Activities

Horse Riding Various travel agencies and hotels can arrange rides to surrounding villages or the caves. Try to find out about the animals before you commit yourself: are they horses or just ponies, fiery or docile, fast or slow? Will there be a guide?

Casa Margarita, Posada Jovel and Posada Del Sol charge about 55 pesos for a three to five-hour ride. José Hernández (☎ (967) 8-10-65) at Elías Calles 10 (a dirt road two blocks north-west of Na Bolom), off Huixtla just north of Chiapa de Corzo, hires horses cheaper at 42 pesos a ride. The Rancho San Nicolás campground (☎ (967) 8-18-73) also provides mounts.

Cycling Gante, at 5 de Mayo 10-B near 5 de Febrero, rents mountain bikes for 20 pesos a day; included in the price is a lock, key and map. It's a good way to explore the city and surrounding country.

Organised Tours

Travel agencies, hotels and individuals offer tours to nearby Indian villages. They rarely go anywhere you couldn't reach under your own steam, though they may be able to offer information or combinations of destinations that you couldn't manage easily.

Some of the most interesting tours are the small groups (three to eight people) led by Mercedes Hernández Gómez, a fluent English speaker who grew up in San Juan Chamula. You can find Mercedes near the kiosk in the zócalo at 9 am, twirling a colourful umbrella. Tours are 35 pesos and generally last 5 to 6 hours, travelling by public bus and foot. We have also had good reports of the tours led by Alex and Raul, who you can find in front of the main cathedral next to the zócalo daily at 9.30 am. They offer similar tours for the same price, but also give city tours. If you want to prearrange a special tour you can call them at (☎ (967) 8-37-41).

Travel agencies in San Cristóbal offer day trips further afield for those who are short of time. Average prices (with four people) are: Indian Villages (five hours, 60 pesos); Cañón del Sumidero (eight hours, 100 pesos); Lagos de Montebello-Chincultik ruins-Amatenango Del Valle (nine hours, 90 pesos); Palenque ruins-Agua Azul-Misol-Ha (13 hours, 135 pesos); and Toniná (six hours, 95 pesos).

Travel agencies include:

Sexto Sol (☎ /fax (967) 8-43-53) Real de Guadalupe 24-D, half a block east of the zócalo
Viajes Blanquita (☎ /fax (967) 8-03-80) in Centro Cultural El Puente, Real de Guadalupe 55, 2½ blocks east of the zócalo
Viajes Pakal (☎ /fax (967) 8-28-19), on the corner of Hidalgo and Cuauhtémoc

Language Courses

Centro Bilingüe, a language school, has two offices. Spanish classes are given in Centro Cultural El Puente (☎ /fax (967) 8-37-23) on Real de Guadalupe 55, and English is taught at Insurgentes 57 (☎ (967) 8-41-57).

One-on-one lessons are 25 pesos per hour, three-on-one lessons are 18 pesos per person per hour.

Homestay programmes offer 15 hours of instruction (three hours per day, five days a week), at least three hours of homework every day, homestay for a full week (seven days, double occupancy) and include three meals a day (every day except Sunday). A homestay with one-on-one instruction is 600 pesos, three-on-one is 475 pesos per week. If you study for more than one week, it's a bit cheaper. For 375 pesos you can sign up for 'lunch/breakfast with Spanish', a five-day programme which includes a meal and three hours of lessons each day.

Festivals

In spring, Semana Santa, with processions on Good Friday and the burning of 'Judas' figures on Holy Saturday, is followed by the Feria de la Primavera y de la Paz (Spring & Peace Fair) with more parades, bullfights and so on. Sometimes the celebrations for the anniversary of the town's founding (31 March) fall in the midst of it all too!

Also look out for events marking the feast of San Cristóbal (17 to 25 July), the anniversary of Chiapas joining Mexico in 1824 (14 September), National Independence Day (15 and 16 September), the Day of the Dead (2 November), the Feast of the Virgin of Guadalupe (10 to 12 December) and preparations for Christmas (16 to 24 December).

Places to Stay – bottom end

Camping The *Rancho San Nicolás* campground and trailer park (☎ (967) 8-00-57) is two km east of the zócalo: go east along León for a km after it becomes a dirt track. It's a friendly place with a grassy lawn, apple trees, horses grazing and hot showers. The cost is 10 pesos per person in a tent, 20 pesos in a cabin, 17 to 25 pesos per person in a caravan or camper with full hook-ups.

Hotels & Casas de Huéspedes Several cheap hostelries are dotted along Insurgentes, the street leading from the Cristóbal Colón bus station to the zócalo. Many are dingy and uncared for; most charge a premium because they're close to the bus stations. Better deals can be found along Real de Guadalupe, which heads east off the zócalo.

Insurgentes A block and a half up from the Cristóbal Colón bus station, *Hotel Capri* (☎ (967) 8-30-18, fax 8-00-15), Insurgentes 54, has modern, clean and fairly quiet rooms round a narrow flowery courtyard for 55/65/75 pesos a single/double/triple. Don't confuse it with Posada Capri, a block down on the other side of the street.

The friendly *Posada Vallarta* (☎ (967) 8-04-65), half a block east off Insurgentes at Hermanos Pineda 10 (the first street to the right as you go up Insurgentes) has clean and newish rooms with private baths and balconies for 50/60/70 pesos a single/double/ triple.

Posada Insurgentes (☎ (967) 8-24-35), Insurgentes 73, 1½ blocks north of the bus station, has unadorned but clean rooms, shared baths and caged macaws in the courtyard for 35/40 pesos a single/double.

Just opposite at Insurgentes 46, *Posada Lupita* is plain but with a cheery courtyard. Rates, however, are high for what you get – 40 pesos a double – because it's near the bus station.

Posada Lucella (☎ (967) 8-09-56), Insurgentes 55, directly across from the Templo de Santa Lucia, has OK doubles for 35 pesos, 45 pesos with private bath.

Hotel Fray Bartolomé de Las Casas (☎ (967) 8-09-32, fax 8-35-10), Niños Héroes 2 at Insurgentes, two blocks south of the zócalo, has cleanliness, character and a variety of spacious rooms for 60 pesos a double.

Posada San Cristóbal (☎ (967) 8-19-07), Insurgentes 3 at Cuauhtémoc, a block south of the zócalo, has airy, colourful rooms, set around a pleasant courtyard. It's an excellent, convenient choice for 50/60/70/80 pesos a single/double/triple/quad with bath.

Real de Guadalupe *Posada Santiago* (☎ (967) 8-00-24), Real de Guadalupe 32 near Colón, is a friendly, decent place where carpeted, ordinary double rooms with private baths are 60 pesos. *Casa de Huéspedes Margarita* (☎ (967) 8-09-57), Real de Guadalupe 34, 1½ blocks east of the zócalo, has long been popular. There's a great courtyard, a good restaurant and rooms with shared baths for 32/40/48 pesos a single/double/triple. The Margarita will hold mail for you.

Posada Virginia (☎ (967) 8-11-16), Cristóbal Colón 1, between Real de Guadalupe and Madero, is tidy, with a friendly, efficient señora and even a few parking spaces. Double rooms cost 55 pesos.

On Real de Guadalupe, next to El Puente, is *Posada Casa Real*. It is a humble and clean establishment and costs 18 pesos a bed.

Hotel Real del Valle (☎ (967) 8-06-80, fax 8-39-55), Real de Guadalupe 14, is good, clean, central, with a nice courtyard and rooms costing 62 pesos a double. The nearby *Hotel San Martin* (☎ (967) 8-05-33), Real de Guadalupe 16, is similarly pleasant, but better value at 42/52/68 pesos a single/double/triple. There's a laundry here as well.

Other Areas Undoubtedly the best deal in town is at *Bed and Breakfast Madero 83* (☎ (967) 8-04-40), Madero 83, five blocks east of the zócalo. Clean dorm beds (12 pesos), singles (18 pesos), and rooms with private baths (28 to 36 pesos) all include breakfast of egg, beans, tortilla and coffee. For a small charge you can use the kitchen.

Posada Jovel (☎ (967) 8-17-34) at Paniagua 28 between Cristóbal Colón and Santiago, attracts backpackers with its friendly owners and atmosphere and prices of 25/35 pesos with shared bath, 30/45 pesos with private bath. They also serve a nice breakfast. If the Jovel is full, try next door at *La Posadita*, Paniagua 30; rooms are off a bright courtyard and cost 6.50/8 pesos for a single/double with private bath.

Hotel Villa Real (☎ (967) 8-29-30), Juárez 8, is on a busy street, but has a quiet back courtyard with good twin-bedded rooms priced at 55 pesos with shower.

Posada El Cerrillo (☎ (967) 8-12-83), Belisario Domínguez 27 just north of

TABASCO & CHIAPAS

Ejercito Nacional, is somewhat out of the way, but offers excellent value. It's charming, clean, friendly and priced at 40/45/55 a single/double/triple with two double beds. It's worth the walk.

Posada Adrianita, 5 de Mayo at Primero de Marzo, three blocks north-west of the zócalo, is new, nice, quiet and offers good value at 35 pesos a double without bath.

Posada Del Sol (☎ (967) 8-04-95), on Primera de Marzo 22 at 5 de Mayo, three blocks west of the zócalo, has caged birds, 1970s decor and dangling light bulbs; the asking price is 30/35/50 pesos a single/double/triple with shared bathroom, 50/60 pesos a single/double with private bath.

Posada El Candil (☎ (967) 8-27-55), Real de Mexicanos 7, 1½ blocks west of the Templo de Santo Domingo, has bright, clean, simple (stark, really) rooms with shared baths for 18 pesos a single, 30 pesos a double. The nearby *Casa de Gladys* is a colonial house with a purplish courtyard, hanging hammocks and peace posters. Rooms cost 30 to 35 pesos a double; coffee and pure water are free.

Hotel Posada Caridad, Escuadrón 201 across from La Caridad park, has standard rooms and a good central location. Rooms are average, prices good: 30/35 pesos a double without/with shower.

Posada Los Morales (☎ (967) 8-14-72), Allende 17, has a dozen bare whitewashed two-person bungalows for 60 pesos per bungalow. The location is superb: the bungalows are built on a slope in a maze of gardens. Each has a fireplace, bathroom and gas stove. Some bungalows are cleaner and brighter than others, so check out a few.

Places to Stay – middle

Hotel Parador Mexicanos (☎ (967) 8-15-15, fax 8-00-55), 5 de Mayo 38, just south of Escuadrón 201, has big, comfortable, tidy colonial-style rooms flanking its garden-cum-drive, at the end of which is a tennis court. A lobby lounge, restaurant and pleasant verandas make it excellent value at 85/100/135/160 pesos for a single/double/triple/quad.

Hotel El Paraíso (☎ (937) 8-08-85), 5 de Febrero 19, three blocks west of the zócalo, has a cheery courtyard with leather deck chairs. It's an amiable atmosphere with fine rooms (90/135/155 pesos a single/double/triple) and an attached restaurant-bar serving Swiss and Mexican dishes.

Hotel Arrecife de Coral (☎ (967) 8-21-25), Crescencio Rosas 29, between Hermanos Domínguez and Obregón, reminds one of an American motel with its several buildings set amid grassy lawns. The 50 quiet, modern rooms on two floors have baths, TVs and phones, and cost 135/165/200/235 pesos a single/double/ triple/quad.

Hotel Don Quijote (☎ (967) 8-09-02, fax 8-03-46), Cristóbal Colón 7, between Real de Guadalupe and Adelina Flores, is among the brightest and newest in the area. Colourful maps and traditional costumes embellish the walls; rooms and the upstairs restaurant are pleasing, and it has a laundry service, travel service and free morning coffee. Rooms offer great value at 70/85/100 pesos a single/double/triple.

Hotel Casavieja (☎ (967) 8-03-85, fax 8-52-23), Adelina Flores 27, between Colón and Dujelay, is new but colonial in style, attractive and comfortable, with very friendly management. Rooms are arranged around grassy, flowered courtyards; there's a tidy restaurant. Rates are good at 135/165/200 pesos a single/double/triple.

Hotel Rincón del Arco (☎ (967) 8-13-13, fax 8-15-68) is in San Cristóbal's oldest neighbourhood, 2½ blocks from Na Bolom on Ejercito National 66 at Guerrero. Rooms, priced at 135/165 pesos a single/double, have ceramic fireplaces, telephones and TV. The 2nd-storey balconies have fabulous city views. The restaurant serves three meals a day and entertains with nightly marimba.

Back in the 16th century, the *Hotel Santa Clara* (☎ (967) 8-08-71), Avenida Insurgentes 1 (the south-east corner of the zócalo), served as the home to Diego de Mazariegos, the Spanish conqueror of Chiapas. Amenities here include sizeable, comfortable rooms, a pleasant courtyard brightened by caged red macaws, a restaurant, a bar/lounge and heated pool. Rooms cost 125/150/175 pesos a single/double/triple.

Places to Stay – top end

The 34-room *Hotel Casa Mexicano* (☎ (967) 8-06-98, fax 8-26-27), 28 de Agusto 1 at Utrilla, with its starlit garden, fountains, plants, and traditional art and sculptures, exudes colonial charm. Rooms are agreeable, have views of the courtyard and cost 215/240 pesos; suites with jacuzzi are 300 pesos. This is the most charming and pleasant hotel in San Cristóbal.

Hotel Posada Diego de Mazariegos (☎ (967) 8-07-25, fax 8-34-42), 5 de Febrero 1, occupies two fine old buildings on Utrilla, one block north of the zócalo. Rooms are tastefully furnished and most have fireplaces and TVs. The hotel has a restaurant, bar and a few shops. Rates are 210/240/265 pesos a single/double/triple.

Places to Eat

The cheapest meals are from the *cookshops* in a complex called Los Merenderos, just south of the Templo de San Francisco on Insurgentes. Pick items that look fresh and hot to be safe. A full meal can be had for 7 pesos or less.

A perennially popular eatery is *Restaurant Tuluc* at Insurgentes 5, 1½ blocks south of the zócalo. The Tuluc scores with its 6.15 am opening time for early breakfasts (around 9 pesos), efficient service, good food and value-for-money prices. Their filling, delicious four-course comida corrida costs just 18 pesos.

Madre Tierra Restaurant (Mother Earth), Insurgentes 19 at Hermanos Domínguez, is a vegetarian's oasis in the land of carnes and aves. The menu is eclectic and appetising with filling soups, wholemeal sandwiches, brown-rice dishes, pasta, pizzas and salads. Most everything on the menu is between 6 and 14 pesos; the three-course menú del dia costs 25 pesos, coffee or tea included. Excellent whole-wheat bread is served with all meals. The *Panadería Madre Tierra* next door is a wholefood bakery selling breads,

muffins, cookies, cakes, quiches, pizzas and frozen yoghurt.

Upstairs at Hidalgo 3, a few doors from the zócalo, *La Galería* has perhaps the most restful ambience in town with soft music wafting through the green courtyard. Built in 1540, this building was inhabited at various times by Diego de Mazariegos, Francisco de Montejo and various bishops of Chiapas. Today, bow-tied waiters will serve you breakfast, luncheon soups and salads, or a 20-peso, three-course dinner based on beef filet in mushroom sauce. English movies are shown nightly in the video bar, and there's often folk, salsa or Mexican music in the courtyard.

The *Casa Margarita*, at Real de Guadalupe 34, is a popular, pricey little restaurant with a reliable mixture of Western, Mexican and vegetarian options. Most meals are between 14 and 24 pesos.

La Casa del Pan, at Dr Navarro 10, serves a 'feel-great breakfast' of fruit, granola, yoghurt, muffins and organic coffee, and a veggie comida corrida of soup, rice, beans, quesadilla, beverage and dessert, each for 18 pesos. You may dine in the calming courtyard or the inside restaurant where they sell a variety of tasty grain breads, bagels, brownies and cookies. It's open daily except Monday from 7 am to 10 pm.

Café El Puente, in the Centro Cultural El Puente at Real de Guadalupe 55, serves a delicious waffle breakfast, a peanut butter-honey-banana-raisin sandwich, vegetable soup with warm wheat bread, or brown rice with salad, each for under 10 pesos. Though prices seem a bit high, El Puente is ideal for a leisurely café mocha or a cup of tea.

Probably the best coffee in town, and good cakes too, is served in the little *Cafetería San Cristóbal*, on Cuauhtémoc just off Insurgentes. The clientele is mainly Mexican men who bring along chess sets and newspapers to relax.

Restaurant Las Estrellas, Escuadrón 201 6B, across from La Caridad park, serves pesto dishes, veggie quiches and rice plates for 6 pesos or less, and pasta with garlic bread or pizza for 10 pesos. It's good for a

TABASCO & CHIAPAS

cheap lunch near the Indian craft market at the Templo de Santo Domingo. Service is friendly and fast.

Bus Station Area *Tikal Restaurant*, less than a block north of the Cristóbal Colón bus station on Insurgentes, is the most pleasant in the neighbourhood with its Guatemalan decor, quiet music and rack of *National Geographic* magazines. They serve generous kinds of spaghetti (such as Genovesa, with cheese, nutmeg and spinach), and good guacamole with totopos, all at 2.50 pesos. Meat dishes and burgers are a bit more.

Cafetería & Lonchería Palenque, at Insurgentes 40, serves orthodox Mexican fare in a cheerful atmosphere: sandwiches for 3 to 6 pesos, main courses for twice as much. *Restaurant Chamula*, Insurgentes 69, is a narrow, dark slot but has good meat, chicken and enchilada plates, or a comida corrida for 14 pesos.

International Dining Under a yin/yang signpost at 28 de Agosto 19, between 5 de Mayo and 16 de Septiembre, is the entrance to *Jardín de Cantón*, a Chinese restaurant that opens into a jungle garden lavishly decorated with Chinese lamps, gourds, bamboo, hundreds of plants in tin containers and an enormous tree. Order chop suey, lo mein, or vegetable and tofu dishes for about 18 pesos, or fried rice for 7 pesos. There is a vegetarian comida corrida for 20 pesos. It is open daily except Sunday from 1.30 pm to 9 pm.

Restaurant París México at Madero 20, one block east of the zócalo, is an arty little café serving French and Mexican specials daily for 18 pesos, crepas for 10 pesos and great coffee.

El Circo Restaurant at Crescencio Rosas 7, half a block from the zócalo, specialises in Italian food. Under its circus roof, you can sample ravioli, lasagne, pesto tagliolini, or pasta with four cheeses for 20 pesos, and top it off with tiramisu and an espresso. El Circo is open from 1 pm to 11 pm, and has live music Wednesday through to Saturday; its closed Sunday.

Café-Restaurant El Teatro, upstairs at Primero de Marzo 8, near 16 de Septiembre, is among the few top-ranking restaurants in town. The menu, based on French and Italian cuisine, lists chateaubriand, crêpes, fresh pasta, pizzas and desserts. Expect to spend 20 to 40 pesos for a full dinner here.

Mexican One block south of the zócalo, *Restaurant La Misión del Fraile*, Insurgentes 10 on the corner of J F Flores, is a long, high-beamed, tile-roofed room with colonial mountain town ambience. Try the tasty anafres (sizzling cheese or meat platters, 40 pesos for two), or mole Jovel (chicken in rich brown sauce, 16 pesos).

At the humbler *El Taquito*, on the corner of Diego de Mazariegos and 12 de Octubre, tacos are half the price and still good. You can also enjoy filete al queso a la parrilla (grilled meat filet with a cheese topping) for 17 pesos, or fruit cocktail with granola and honey for 7 pesos.

La Parrilla on the corner of Belisario Domínguez and Dr Navarro, open Sunday to Friday from 6.30 pm to midnight, serves excellent carnes and quesos al carbón (char-grilled meats and cheese). A dinner, drink and dessert will cost about 33 pesos.

The *Comedor Familiar Normita II*, on the corner of J F Flores and Juárez, has been around a while. It's been painted and spruced up (hence the II). The cooking remains local, good and cheap. Pozole, a rich meal-in-a-bowl soup of maize, cabbage, pork, radishes and onions costs 7 or 9 pesos, and a plato típico coleto, a local mixed grill with pork sausage, chops, frijoles and guacamole, costs 18 pesos. There is cheaper, plainer fare as well.

El Zorro, on Comitán, three blocks east of the Templo de La Caridad, is an attractive, casual Mexican restaurant. A small bar and grill take up the front room, and a pleasant restaurant is at the back. Breakfasts cost 6 pesos and up, with the comida corrida at around 25 pesos or so. The hours are 8 am to 3 pm and 5 pm to midnight; there's live music many nights.

Restaurant Flamingo, *Restaurant Fulano's* and *Restaurant Langosta* are all on

Madero. Flamingo and Fulano's are respectable, with similar menus and fair prices: spaghetti and salads are about 9 pesos, pizzas and main dishes are twice that. Langosta distinguishes itself with shish kebab, rice and beans for 25 pesos and live marimba music many days after 2 pm.

Entertainment

San Cristóbal is an early-to-bed town, and conversation in cafés, restaurants or rooms will most likely occupy many of your evenings. However, there are films, cultural events, concerts and rowdy music scenes to be relished if you are so motivated. Check the notice boards in front of the tourist office and in El Puente for scheduled events.

Centro Cultural El Puente, on Real de Guadalupe 55, has cultural programmes, films, concerts or conferences nightly.

The *Casa de las Imagenes*, at Belisario Domínguez 11, just north of Real de Guadalupe, is an art gallery-cum-bookshop-cum-café with a cinema showing interesting international films.

There are fairly regular musical and theatrical performances at the *Casa de Cultura/ Bellas Artes* on the corner of Hidalgo and Hermanos Domínguez.

A handful of restaurants have regular live music. *La Galería* has a piano bar, occasional folk music, and a video bar showing English-language movies nightly. *El Circo* has folk or Latin American music Wednesday and Thursday, and reggae/salsa on Friday and Saturday nights after 9 pm. *Casa Margarita* and *El Zorro* occasionally have live shows.

San Cristóbal's *Cinema Santa Clara* is at 16 de Septiembre 3, near 28 de Agusto. Nightly films and Saturday matinees are 7 pesos. There are two discos – *Crystal* and *Princess* – on opposite sides of the Pan-American Highway, about half a km in the direction of Comitán from the bottom of Insurgentes.

Things to Buy

Chiapas' Indian crafts are justifiably famous and there are now hosts of shops in San Cristóbal selling them. The heaviest concentrations are along Real de Guadalupe (where prices go down as you go away from the zócalo) and Utrilla (towards the market end). La Galería, at Hidalgo 3, has beautiful and expensive craftwork.

Textiles – huipiles, rebozos, blankets – are the outstanding items, for Tzotzil weavers are some of the most skilled and inventive in Mexico (see the Weavers' Cooperatives section earlier). Indian women also sell textiles in the park around Santo Domingo. You'll also find some Guatemalan Indian textiles and plenty of the appealing and inexpensive pottery from Amatenango del Valle (animals, pots, jugs etc) in San Cristóbal. Leather is another local speciality.

You can even buy black ski-mask hooded Subcomandante Marcos dolls – effigies of the popular leader of the Zapatista Liberation Army.

Always bargain unless prices are labelled (though there's no harm in trying even then), and don't imagine that local people are any softer than anyone else when it comes to commercial transactions.

Getting There & Away

Air Scheduled flights come no nearer than Tuxtla Gutiérrez. There's an Aviacsa office at Pasaje Mazariegos 16, just off the first block of Real de Guadalupe. Travel agencies can make bookings on other airlines.

Chevy Suburban vans shuttle between Tuxtla Gutiérrez's Aeropuerto Teran and San Cristóbal for 40 pesos per person. Buy your ticket at the Aviacsa ticket office (☎ 8-44-41, fax 8-43-84), Calle Real de Guadalupe 7.

Bus A new Central de Autobuses is planned in the south of the town but for the moment each company has its own terminal.

Each bus company serving San Cristóbal has various classes of service which it may call 2nd, 1st and deluxe, or by proprietary names. Usually price is a surer determinant of comfort and speed than class: the more you pay, the higher the comfort and quicker the trip.

Omnibus Cristóbal Colón is at the junction of Insurgentes and the Pan-American Highway; the sign on the terminal reads 'Rápidos del Sur', a Colón subsidiary. There is no place to leave your luggage, but shops nearby on Insurgentes will hold it for a small fee. Look for signs reading 'Se Reciben Equipaje', or words to that effect.

Autotransportes Tuxtla Gutiérrez is on Allende half a block north of the Pan-American Highway. The terminal is not visible from the highway: walk up the little street opposite the Chevrolet dealership, north-west of the Supermercado Jovel, south-east of the Policia Federal de Caminos. Andres Caso is on the Pan-American Highway between Hidalgo and Crescencio Rosas (1½ blocks west of Cristóbal Colón); Autotransportes Nha Bolom is on the Pan-American Highway half a block east of Cristóbal Colón; Autotransportes de Pasaje Rapidos de San Cristóbal is just south-east of Na Bolom; and Transportes Fray Bartolomé de Las Casas is on Avenida Salomon González Blanco, the continuation of Utrilla, 300 metres north of the market.

For transport to highland villages near San Cristóbal, see the Around San Cristóbal de Las Casas section. Bus departures from San Cristóbal include:

Chetumal – 700 km, 13 hours; one Cristóbal Colón Maya de Oro (deluxe) bus at 7 pm (100 pesos), which continues to Cancún (160 pesos from San Cristóbal)

Chiapa de Corzo – 70 km, 1½ hours; ATG 2nd-class buses (7.75 pesos) every half-hour; many buses to Tuxtla stop at Chiapa

Ciudad Cuauhtémoc (Guatemalan border) – 165 km, three hours; four Cristóbal Colón 1st-class buses (20 pesos); nine ATG 2nd-class buses (12 pesos); and several Andres Caso buses. Take an early bus if you hope to get any distance into Guatemala the same day

Comitán – 83 km, 1½ hours; hourly Cristóbal Colón 1st-class buses (11 pesos) from 6 am to 9 pm; four ATG 2nd-class buses (8 pesos); other Andres Caso buses

Mérida – 770 km, 15 hours; one Cristóbal Colón deluxe bus at 8 pm (112 pesos); one ATG Plus (deluxe) at 6 pm (105 pesos)

Mexico City (TAPO) – 1085 km, 21 hours; two Cristóbal Colón deluxe buses (160 pesos); three ATG 1st-class buses (135 to 155 pesos)

Oaxaca – 718 km, 12 hours; one Cristóbal Colón 1st-class bus (73 pesos) at 5 pm

Ocosingo – 108 km, three hours; three Cristóbal Colón 1st-class buses (12 pesos); several ATG 1st-class buses (10 pesos)

Palenque – 190 km, 4¼ to five hours; eight Cristóbal Colón 1st-class and deluxe buses (22 to 28 pesos); six ATG 2nd-class buses (18 pesos)

Tapachula – 350 km, eight hours; 15 Cristóbal Colón 1st-class buses (via Tuxtla, 50 pesos); three ATG 2nd-class buses (38 pesos).

Tuxtla Gutiérrez – 85 km, two hours; hourly Cristóbal Colón 1st-class buses (10 pesos) from 6 am to 9.30 pm, plus several deluxe services; ATG and Nha-Bolom have a dozen 2nd-class buses each (7 pesos) from 5.45 am to 7.30 pm

Villahermosa – 300 km, eight hours; Cristóbal Colón 1st-class buses (39 pesos) at noon and 8.15 pm

Colectivo The quickest way to/from Tuxtla Gutiérrez is a colectivo taxi, which costs 18 pesos per person and takes 1¼ hours. In San Cristóbal they wait on the corner of Allende and the Pan-American Highway, and leave when full.

Car The only car-rental agency is Budget (☎ 8-18-71), at Auto Rentas Yaxchilán at Diego de Mazariegos 36, 2½ blocks from the zócalo. Opening hours are from 8 am to 2 pm and 3 to 8 pm Monday to Saturday and from 8 am to noon and 5 to 7 pm Sunday. At busy periods you may need to book your car a few days in advance. The cheapest, a VW sedan, is around 135 pesos a day, taxes included.

Getting Around
Most people walk around San Cristóbal. See the following section for details of day trips from the town.

AROUND SAN CRISTÓBAL DE LAS CASAS

Visiting the Indian villages around San Cristóbal is among the most interesting things to do here.

Warning

Robbery Armed robbers have discovered that it's easy and profitable to hold up tourists walking between villages. Don't walk from village to village. Instead, take a horse, bus or taxi.

Photography In some villages, particularly those nearest San Cristóbal, you may be greeted with wariness, the result of centuries of oppression and the desire to preserve traditions from interference. Cameras are at best tolerated – and sometimes not even that. The San Cristóbal tourist office displays a sign stating that photography is banned in the church and during festivals at Chamula, and banned completely at Zinacantán. You may well put yourself in physical danger if you take photos without permission. If in any doubt at all, ask before taking a picture.

People

The Tzotzils and Tzeltals of highland Chiapas – descendants of the ancient Maya – are among Mexico's most traditional Indians, with some distinctly pre-Hispanic elements in their nominally Catholic religious life, and Spanish very much a second language. Their costume, too, marks them as the inheritors of ancient Mayan traditions.

The 150,000 or so Tzotzils occupy an area about 50 km from east to west and 100 km from north to south, with San Cristóbal at its centre. Tzeltal territory is of a similar size and shape, immediately east of the Tzotzil area. Most of the people live in the hills outside the villages, which are primarily market and ceremonial centres.

Most of these Indians are poor. Many men from San Juan Chamula and Mitontic, for instance, have to spend half the year away from home working on Soconusco coffee plantations. Some Tzotzil have moved to the Lacandón forest in search of land. Despite long repression, the Tzotzils' and Tzeltals' relatively large numbers have enabled them to maintain their group pride. Tzotzils and Tzeltals figured prominently in the Zapatista rebellion of January 1994.

Markets & Festivals

The villages' weekly markets are nearly always on Sunday. Proceedings start very early and wind down by lunch time.

Festivals often give the most interesting insight into Indian life, and there are plenty of them. Apart from fiestas for a village's patron and other saints, occasions like Carnaval (for which Chamula is famous), Semana Santa, the Day of the Dead (2 November) and the day of the Virgin of Guadalupe (12 December) are celebrated almost everywhere.

Getting There & Away

Remember, don't walk to or between the following villages because of the threat of robbery. Ride.

There are paved roads to San Juan Chamula, Zinacantán, Amatenango del Valle and most of the way to Tenejapa. Reaching the other villages mentioned involves long stretches of pretty rough dirt track, but buses make it along them and so can a VW sedan (slowly).

Bus and colectivo schedules are geared to getting villagers into town early and back home not too late.

Combis to the villages nearest San Cristóbal leave from the north-western corner of San Cristóbal market, between Utrilla and Cárdenas. They depart for San Juan Chamula and Zinacantán every 20 minutes or so up to about 5 pm; the fare is 2.50 pesos. For Tenejapa they leave about half-hourly, take an hour and cost 4 pesos. Return services from Tenejapa start getting scarce after noon.

To get to Amatenango del Valle, take a Comitán bus (see Getting There & Away in the San Cristóbal de Las Casas section). The fare is 4 pesos.

Transportes Fray Bartolomé de Las Casas (see also Getting There & Away in the San Cristóbal de Las Casas section) runs buses to

---

Ceremonial Brotherhoods

Traditional religious brotherhoods still exist in the indigenous villages of the Chiapan highlands. In the past these fraternal organisations were the governing bodies of Mayan society, and though they still exercise limited civil powers in some Guatemalan highland towns and villages, their functions are mostly ceremonial in Chiapas.

Members of the brotherhoods – which are all male – take turns discharging the obligations of *cargos* (charges or duties). These duties normally last for one year, and include caring for the images of saints in the churches, and the masks and costumes used in religious ceremonies. Other cargos entail organising and paying for the ceremonies, celebrations and fiestas which mark the many saints' days throughout the year.

Taking on a cargo is an honour and a burden. Only fairly prosperous villagers can afford the considerable expense of discharging a cargo; and by burdening the prosperous ones with the costs, village society ensures that the financial success of some works to the benefit of all.

Among the Tzotzils, senior cargo-holders called *mayordomos* are responsible for the care of saints' images; the *alféreces* organise and pay for fiestas; *capitanes* dance and ride horses at fiestas. After having successfully carried out the duties of a cargo several times, members enter the ranks of the *Principales*, or Village Elders.

Women are generally restricted to domestic work, including weaving. ■

Chenalhó (4 pesos, 2½ hours) four times daily, and to San Andrés Larraínzar (3.75 pesos, 2½ hours) at 2 pm. The return bus from San Andrés leaves at 7 am.

San Juan Chamula

The Chamulans put up strong resistance to the Spaniards in 1524 and launched a famous rebellion in 1869. Today they are one of the most numerous Tzotzil groups – 40,000-strong – and their village 10 km north-west of San Cristóbal is the centre for some unique religious practices. A big sign at the entrance to the village says it is strictly forbidden to take photos in the church or anywhere rituals are being performed.

From dawn on Sunday, people stream into town from the hills for the weekly market, and to go to church. The church stands on the far side of the main plaza. A sign on its door tells visitors to ask at the 'tourist office', also on the plaza, for tickets (3 pesos) to enter. Inside the church, the rows of burning candles, the thick clouds of incense, the chanting worshippers kneeling with their faces to the pine needle-carpeted floor make a powerful impression. Saints' images are surrounded with mirrors and dressed in holy garments.

Chamulans believe Christ rose from the cross to become the sun. Christian festivals are interwoven with older ones: the pre-Lent Carnaval celebrations, which are among the most important and last several days in February or March, also mark the five 'lost' days of the ancient Mayan Long Count calendar, which divided time into 20-day periods (18 of these make 360 days, which leaves five more to complete a full year). Other festivals include ceremonies for San Sebastián (mid to late January); Semana Santa; San Juan, the village's patron saint (22-25 June); and the annual change of cargos (30 December-1 January).

On such occasions a strong alcoholic brew called *posh* is drunk and you may see groups of ceremonially attired men, carrying flags and moving slowly round in tight, chanting circles. At Carnaval, troops of strolling minstrels called *mash* wander the roads strumming guitars and wearing sunglasses (even when it's raining) and tall pointed hats.

Cargo holders wear black tunics instead of the usual white ones.

Zinacantán

• pop: 15,000

The road to this Tzotzil village, 11 km north-west of San Cristóbal, forks left off the Chamula road, then goes down into a valley. Photos are banned altogether here.

The men wear very distinctive red-and-white striped tunics (which appear pink), and flat, round, ribboned palm hats. Unmarried men's hats have longer, wider ribbons. A market is usually held only at fiesta times. The most important celebrations are for the patron saint, San Lorenzo, between 8 and 11 August, and San Sebastián (January).

Zinacantecos venerate the geranium which, along with pine branches, is offered in rituals to bring a wide range of benefits. Zinacantán has two churches. The crosses dotting the Zinacantán countryside mostly mark entrances to the abodes of the important ancestor gods or the Señor de la Tierra (Earth Lord), all of whom have to be kept happy with offerings at the appropriate times.

Tenejapa

Tenejapa is a Tzeltal village 28 km north-east of San Cristóbal, in a pretty valley with a river running through it. There are about 20,000 Tenejapanecos in the surrounding area. A quite busy market fills the main street (round behind the church) early on Sunday mornings. Cargo-holders wear wide, colourfully beribboned hats, and chains of silver coins round their necks. Women wear brightly brocaded or embroidered huipiles.

Tenejapa has a few comedores in the main street and one basic posada, the *Hotel Molina*, but it's not always open. The main festival is for the patron saint, San Ildefonso, on 23 January.

Amatenango del Valle

The women of this Tzeltal village, by the Pan-American Highway 37 km south-east of San Cristóbal, are renowned potters. Amatenango pottery is still fired by the pre-Hispanic method of burning a wood fire around the pieces, rather than putting them in a kiln. In addition to the pots, bowls, urns, jugs and plates that the village has turned out for generations, young girls in the last 15 years or so have made animalitos, which find a ready market with tourists. These are small, appealing and cheap, if fragile. If you visit the village, expect to be surrounded within minutes by girls selling them.

The women wear white huipiles embroidered with red and yellow, wide red belts and blue skirts. Amatenango's patron saint, San Francisco, is fêted on 4 October.

Other Villages

Intrepid Mayaphiles might want to make visits to some more remote villages.

San Andrés Larraínzar is a hilltop Tzotzil and mestizo village 28 km northwest of San Cristóbal (18 km beyond San Juan Chamula). A turnoff uphill to the left, 10 km after San Juan Chamula, leads through spectacular mountain scenery to San Andrés. The patron saint's day is 30 November. A weekly Sunday market is held and the people seem less reserved towards outsiders than those of other villages. People from Santa Magdalena, another Tzotzil village a few km north, attend the San Andrés market; their ceremonial huipiles are among the finest of all Chiapas Indian garments.

The plaza at **Mitontic**, a small Tzotzil village a few hundred metres left of the Chenalhó road, 23 km beyond San Juan Chamula, has both a picturesque, ruined 16th-century church and a more modern working one. The patron saint, San Miguel, is honoured from 5 to 8 May.

San Pedro Chenalhó is a Tzotzil village in a valley with a stream running through it; it's 1500 metres high, 27 km beyond and quite a descent from Chamula. It's the centre for about 14,000 people in the surrounding area. There's a weekly Sunday market. The main fiestas are for San Pedro (27 to 30 June), San Sebastián (16 to 22 January) and Carnaval.

Huixtán, 32 km from San Cristóbal on the Palenque road, is the centre for roughly 12,000 Tzotzils, as it was in pre-Hispanic times. Huixtán has a 16th-century church. **Oxchuc**, 20 km beyond Huixtán, is a small Tzeltal and mestizo town dominated by the large colonial church of San Tomás.

SAN CRISTÓBAL TO PALENQUE

The 210-km journey – 12 km south-east down the Pan-American Highway from San Cristóbal, then north on highway 199 – takes

TABASCO & CHIAPAS

you from cool, misty highlands to steaming lowland jungle, and is dotted with interesting stopovers. Ocosingo, 100 km from San Cristóbal, is the jumping-off point for the little-known Mayan ruins at Toniná. The turnoff for the superb cascades of Agua Azul is about 50 km beyond Ocosingo. Another beautiful waterfall, Misol-Ha, with a good swimming hole, is two km off the road 40 km after the Agua Azul turning.

Ocosingo
• *pop: 20,000*

Ocosingo is a small mestizo and Tzeltal valley town on the San Cristóbal-Palenque road. Some 14 km east of the town are the ruins of the Mayan city of Toniná. These are impressive and becoming more so as new excavations progress.

During the Zapatista uprising of January 1994, the town suffered many deaths and casualties in the fighting. At the time of writing it is still a sensitive area, and you should enquire in advance at the tourist office in San Cristóbal or Palenque before planning to spend much time here.

Orientation & Information Ocosingo spreads downhill to the east of the main road. Avenida Central runs straight down from the main road to the zócalo. Most of the bus stations are on Avenida 1 Norte, parallel to Avenida Central a block north.

To orient yourself on the zócalo, remember that the church is on the east side and the Hotel Central on the north side. The large market is three blocks east along Avenida 1 Sur Ote from the church.

None of the banks in town will change cash or travellers' cheques, though this may change if Ocosingo edges on to the tourist map.

Places to Stay *Hotel Central* (☎ (967) 3-00-39), Avenida Central 1, on the north side of the zócalo, has simple, clean rooms with fan and bath for 40/60/80 pesos a single/double/triple.

Hotel Margarita (☎ (967) 3-02-80) on Calle 1 Pte Norte, one block north-west of

Hotel Central, charges 60 pesos a double. It's nothing elaborate but nicer than most hotels in town; rooms have fan and bath and there is a comfortable lobby downstairs and a restaurant upstairs.

Posada Agua Azul, at 1 Ote Sur 127, two blocks south of the church, has medium-size, average rooms around a courtyard which harbours a few tightly caged anteaters, hawks and macaws. Rooms cost 36/60 pesos a single/double.

At the really cheap end there's *Hospedaje La Palma*, on the corner of Calle 2 Pte and Avenida 1 Norte Pte, just down the hill from the ATG bus station. It's a clean, family-run place. Singles/doubles are 16/30 pesos with shared bathrooms. *Hospedaje San José* (☎ (967) 3-00-39), Calle 1 Ote 6, half a block north of the north-east corner of the zócalo, has small, dark, but clean rooms for 25/40 pesos a single/double.

Places to Eat Ocosingo is famous for its queso amarillo (yellow cheese), which comes in three-layered one-kg balls. The two outside layers are like chewy Gruyère, while the middle is creamy.

Restaurant La Montura has a prime location on the north side of the plaza, with tables on the Hotel Central's veranda as well as indoors. It has a large menu and is good for breakfast (fruit, eggs, bread and coffee for 10 pesos), lunch or dinner (comida corrida for 20 pesos, or a plate of tacos for 8 pesos). They'll make you some sandwiches if you want to take a picnic to the Toniná ruins.

Restaurant Los Portales, Avenida Central 19, facing the north-east corner of the zócalo, is a homey, old-fashioned place. Several matronly señoras will mother you here, offering traditional meals for 11 to 20 pesos. The Portales proves an interesting contrast to the neighbouring *Restaurant Los Arcos*, which is more modern, but not nearly so pleasant. On the opposite side of the zócalo, *Restaurant & Pizzería Troje* features the famous queso amarillo. Quesadillas are cheap (7 pesos), and pizzas of different sizes and sorts go for 10 to 30 pesos.

Restaurant Maya, two blocks west of the

zócalo on Avenida Central, is a tidy, bright little eatery featuring platos fuertes (main-course lunch or dinner platters) for 11 pesos; fruit salads and antojitos are less. The *Restaurant San Cristóbal*, Avenida Central 22, near the Town Hall, is a simple lonchería where you have to ask what's cooking the day you visit. Nothing on the menu is more than 12 pesos.

Pesebres Steak House, on Calle 1 Pte Nte above Hotel Margarita, has a nice breeze, super views and good dishes. If you're feeling carnivorous, order prime rib or filet mignon for 26 pesos; if not, Mexican dishes and salads will cost you less than 15 pesos.

Restaurant Rahsa, two blocks south-west of the zócalo on Avenida 3 Sur Ote, is set down a walkway, beside a courtyard, and provides the nicest dining atmosphere in Ocosingo. The restaurant has tall chairs, fresh flowers and fancy folded napkins on each table and a big wooden barrel of tequila in front of its wine rack. They serve seafood specialities baked in cognac and lemon for 26 pesos, a spinach salad for 10 pesos and flavoured local dishes for about 16 pesos.

Getting There & Away The Autotransportes Tuxtla Gutiérrez terminal is on Avenida 1 Norte, one block from the Palenque-San Cristóbal road. Autotransportes Fray Bartolomé de Las Casas is on the far side of the main road at the top of Avenida 1 Norte. They have a mixture of modern microbuses and decrepit big buses. Autotransportes Ocosingo is on the corner of Avenida Central and the main road. Quickest are the combis which shuttle to Palenque and San Cristóbal. They leave when full from the top of Avenida Central and charge 9 pesos.

Agua Azul Crucero – 40 km, one hour; numerous buses (10 pesos), any of which will drop you here
Palenque – 82 km, 1½ hours; five ATG 1st-class buses (18 pesos); two Autotransportes Fray Bartolomé de Las Casas 2nd-class buses (15 pesos)
San Cristóbal – 108 km, 2½ hours; two Cristóbal Colón 1st-class buses (11 pesos); six ATG 2nd-class buses (8 pesos); six Autotransportes Fray Bartolomé de Las Casas 2nd-class buses (7 pesos)
Tuxtla Gutiérrez – 193 km, 4½ hours; seven ATG 1st-class buses (14 pesos); five Autotransportes Ocosingo 2nd-class buses (8 pesos)
Villahermosa – 232 km, six hours; two ATG 2nd-class buses (11 pesos)

Toniná

The Mayan ruins at Toniná, 14 km east of Ocosingo, are relatively hard to reach and don't compare with Palenque for beauty or importance, but form a sizeable, interesting site with some big structures on terraces cut from a hillside. Recent excavations have reduced Toniná's 'lost in the jungle' feel, but have revealed and explained much more of this impressive site. The ruins are open daily from 9 am to 4 pm daily and cost 10 pesos. The house opposite the ticket office sells refrescos.

Toniná was probably a city-state independent of both Palenque and Yaxchilán, though it declined at the same time as they did, around 800 AD. Dates found at the site range from 500 to 800 AD, and like Palenque and Yaxchilán, it peaked in the last 100 years or so of that period.

The caretaker may be willing to go round the site with you, which can be helpful as there are few signs. If you have already visited Palenque or Yaxchilán, imagine a similar splendour here. Many of the stone facings and interior walls were covered in coloured paint or frescos.

The track goes past the small museum, which holds quite a number of good stone carvings – statues, bas-reliefs, altars, calendar stones – then over a stream and up to a flat area from which rises the terraced hill supporting the main structures. As you face this hillside, behind you in a field are an overgrown outlying pyramid and the main ball court. The flat area contains a small ball court and fragments of limestone carvings. Some appear to show prisoners holding out offerings, with glyphs on the reverse sides.

The most interesting area of the terraced hillside is the right-hand end of its third and fourth levels. The stone facing of the wall rising from the third to fourth levels has a zigzag x-shape, which may represent Quetzalcóatl and is also a flight of steps. To the right of the base of this are the remains of a tomb, with steps leading up to an altar. Behind and above the tomb and altar is a rambling complex of chambers, passageways and stairways, believed to have been Toniná's administrative hub.

Over towards the centre of the hillside are remains of the central stairway, which went much of the way up the hillside. One level higher than the top of the zigzag wall is a grave covered in tin sheeting, which you can lift to see a stone coffin beneath. Here were found the bodies of a ruler and two others. To the left on the same level is a shrine to Chac, the rain god. To the right at the foot of a crumbling temple is a carving of the earth god, labelled *monstruo de la tierra*. Higher again and to the left are two more mounds. The left-hand one, the pyramid of life and death, may have supported the ruler's dwelling. At the very top of the hill rise two more tall pyramid-temple mounds.

Getting There & Away The track from Ocosingo is dirt and in parts rough, but crosses pleasant, flat ranchland with lots of colourful birds.

In your own vehicle, follow Calle 1 Ote south from Ocosingo Church. Before long it curves left and you pass a cemetery on the right. At the fork a couple of km further on, go left. At the next fork, the site is signposted to the right. Finally, a sign marks the entry track to Toniná at Rancho Guadalupe on the left. From here it's another km to the site itself.

Otherwise, you have the options of a taxi (about 70 pesos for the round trip with an hour at the ruins), hitching (maybe six vehicles an hour pass Toniná), or a passenger truck from Ocosingo market (several a day, most frequent from late morning, about 4 pesos) or a bus of Carga Mixta Ocosingo from their yard near the market. There appear to be two or three buses to Guadalupe (near the ruins) and back each day. The ride costs 4 pesos and takes about 45 minutes. The Rancho Guadalupe sometimes puts people up for the night or allows them to camp.

For minibus day trips to Toniná with English-speaking guides, ask at the Casa Margarita in San Cristóbal de Las Casas. A 10 or 12-hour trip costs about 90 pesos per person.

Agua Azul

Just over 60 km from Palenque and 4.5 km off the highway, scores of dazzling white waterfalls thunder into turquoise pools surrounded by jungle. The Agua Azul cascades are among the wonders of Mexico.

On holidays the site is thronged with local families; at other times you will have few companions. Admission is 7 pesos per car, 3 pesos per person (on foot). Note that the beautiful colour which gives the place its name is often evident only in April and May. Silt clouds the waters in other months.

The temptation to swim is great but take extreme care – the current is deceptively fast and there are many invisible submerged hazards like rocks and dead trees. Use your judgement to identify slower, safer areas. Drownings are all too common, as memorials to foreign travellers and others who have died here show. During the height of the rainy season, the waters can turn muddy with brown silt.

A vehicle track leads down from highway 199 to a section of the falls with a car park, a collection of comedores and, nearby, a small village.

The falls stretch some distance upstream and downstream. Upstream, a trail takes you over some swaying, less-than-stable foot bridges and up through jungle.

Warning An experienced female traveller walking alone above the falls here reported that she was attacked, escaping only through a strategically aimed kick to the groin. Several travellers have also reported thefts at Agua Azul, even at gunpoint, so take care.

Places to Stay & Eat There are a few spots to hang your hammock or pitch a tent, but if you are looking for a decent bed, go back to Palenque. *Camping Agua Azul*, near the entrance, and *Restaurant Agua Azul*, next to the car park, rent hammocks and hammock space for a few dollars. You can leave your backpacks at Restaurant Agua Azul for 4 pesos per day. You'll find more solace and scenery if you camp upstream. Just follow the trail up the left bank.

A five to ten-minute walk will bring you to *Camping Casablanca*. It's far from elegant but you can hang your hammock (8 pesos) or rent one (12 pesos) in its big hollow barn. Owner Geronimo guides three-hour (five-km) hikes around the cascades for 20 pesos per person.

If you can gather another five minutes of walking energy, you'll find more pleasant camping at *José Antonio's*. It's the yellow house with white furniture and a Coca-Cola sign in front, a stone's throw from the water. There's a grassy lawn for tents, a palapa for hammocks, palm trees for atmosphere, and you're just steps away from safe swimming. A night here will cost you about 7 pesos.

There are several restaurants and food stalls next to the car park, but the food is overpriced and average. You would be much better off packing a picnic from Palenque.

Getting There & Away The Agua Azul junction, or *crucero*, on highway 199 is 45 km south of Palenque, 40 km north of Ocosingo, and 248 km north-east of San Cristóbal (3½ hours by bus). The 4.5-km walk from the crucero to the falls is OK on the way down, but the sweltering heat makes it hard on the uphill trip back out. If you want to take the risk, hitching is possible but don't rely on it.

An easy way of visiting Agua Azul and Misol-Ha (see following section) is as a day trip from Palenque with transport laid on. Several travel agencies in Palenque offer such trips, lasting about seven hours with typically three hours at Agua Azul and a half-hour at Misol-Ha, for 28 pesos per person including entrance fees. Colectivos Chambalu and Colectivos Palenque in Palenque charge 20 pesos for the 6½-hour trip. (For a list of Palenque travel agencies, see Organised Tours in the Palenque section.) A round-trip taxi tour from Palenque to Agua Azul, with a one-hour wait, costs around 200 pesos.

Alternatively you can travel by 2nd-class bus to the crucero and trust your legs and luck from there. Any bus between Palenque and San Cristóbal or Ocosingo will drop you there. The trip is about four hours from San Cristóbal (15 pesos), one hour from Ocosingo (10 pesos), and 1¼ hours from Palenque (6 pesos). Booking ahead on these buses is often not possible, and catching a bus from the crucero when you leave almost certainly means standing on the bus, to start with at least. Again, hitching is possible, but don't count on it.

Misol-Ha

About 20 km from Palenque, a waterfall drops nearly 35 metres into a beautiful, wide pool that's safe for swimming. The Misol-Ha (or Misol-Ja) cascade and its jungle surroundings are spectacular enough to be the setting for an Arnold Schwarzenegger epic.

The waterfall is 1.5 km west by dirt road off highway 199 and the turning is signposted. To enter you pay 7 pesos per car, or 2 pesos per visitor.

Near the waterfall, though out of sight from it, are a café, and some self-catering cabins. Camping is allowed in a small area near the waterfall.

See Agua Azul for information on getting to/from Misol-Ha. Buses stop at the Misol-Ha junction (crucero) just as they do at the Agua Azul crucero. A round-trip taxi tour from Palenque, with a one-hour wait, costs 100 pesos.

PALENQUE
• *pop: 70,000* • *alt: 80 metres*
Surrounded by emerald jungle, Palenque's setting is superb and its Mayan architecture and decoration are exquisite.

History
The name Palenque ('palisade' in Spanish) is modern and has no relation to the city's ancient name, which is uncertain. It could be Nachan (City of Snakes), Chocan (Sculptured Snake), Culhuacán, Huehuetlapalla, Xhembobel Moyos, Ototium...no one knows for sure.

Evidence from pottery fragments indicates that Palenque was first occupied more than 1500 years ago. It flourished from 600 to 800 AD, and what a glorious two centuries they were! The city first rose to prominence under Pakal, a club-footed king who reigned from 615 to 683 AD. Archaeologists have determined that Pakal is represented by hieroglyphics of sun and shield. He lived to a ripe old age, possibly 80 to 100 years.

During Pakal's reign, many plazas and buildings, including the superlative Temple of Inscriptions, were constructed within the 20 sq km of the city. The structures were characterised by mansard roofs and very fine stucco bas-reliefs. Hieroglyphic texts at Palenque state that Pakal's reign was predicted thousands of years prior to his ascension and would be celebrated far into the future.

Pakal was succeeded by his son Chan-Balum, symbolised in hieroglyphics by the jaguar and the serpent. Chan-Balum continued Palenque's political and economic expansion as well as the development of its art and architecture. He completed his father's crypt in the Temple of the Inscriptions and presided over the construction of the Plaza of the Sun temples, placing sizeable narrative stone stelae within each. One can see the influence of Palenque's architecture in the ruins of the Mayan city of Tikal in Guatemala's Petén region, and in the pyramids of Comalcalco near Villahermosa.

Not long after Chan-Balum's death, Palenque started on a precipitous decline. Whether this was due to ecological catastrophe, civil strife or invasion has been disputed, but after the 10th century Palenque was largely abandoned. Situated in an area receiving the heaviest rainfall in Mexico, the ruins were overgrown with vegetation and lay undiscovered until the latter half of the 18th century.

Orientation

There are two Palenques: the town and the archaeological zone, 6.5 km apart.

Coming south from the Catazajá junction on highway 186, it's 20 km to the village of Pakal-Na, which has Palenque's train station; Palenque town is several km farther south. Buses and minibuses run between Catazajá and Palenque town fairly frequently in the morning and afternoon. A taxi from Catazajá to Palenque town costs 35 pesos.

Coming north-east from Tuxtla Gutiérrez, San Cristóbal and Agua Azul, you pass the Hotel Nututum, and shortly after join the town-to-ruins road. Turn right for the town.

As you approach Palenque, you come to a fork in the road marked by a huge statue of a Mayan chieftain's head (King Pakal?). East of the statue is the area called La Cañada. Continue past the statue for Palenque town (one km).

Though most hotels and restaurants are in the town centre, the campgrounds and several middle and top-end hotels and restaurants are along the road to the ruins. There are also a few good hotels and restaurants at La Cañada, just to the left of the Mayan statue as you ride south from the highway.

Though relatively small, Palenque town is spread out. From the Mayan statue at its western limit to the Hotel Misión Palenque at the eastern end is about two km. But most of the bus offices are clustered a few hundred metres east of the Mayan statue past the Pemex fuel station on the way into town, and the walk to most hotels is 800 metres or less.

The main road from the Mayan statue into town is Avenida Juárez, which ends at the town's main square, known as simply el parque (the park). Juárez is also the centre of the commercial district.

It's always sweltering in Palenque, and there's rarely any breeze.

Information

Tourist Office Located in the Casa de la Cultura building on the corner of 20 de Noviembre and Jiménez, the tourist office (☎ (934) 5-08-28) has English-speaking staff, reliable town and transit information and a few maps. Office doors are open Monday to Saturday from 8 am to 2 pm and 5 to 8 pm.

Money Bancomer, 1½ blocks west of the park on Juárez, changes money between 10 and 11.30 am Monday to Friday. Banamex, 2½ blocks west of the park, does the exchange from 10.30 am to noon Monday to Friday. Some hotels, restaurants, travel agencies and exchange shops in town will also change money, though at less favourable rates. The banks will probably have ATMs soon.

Post & Telecommunications The post office, just off the park on the left side of the Palacio Municipal is open from 9 am to 1 pm and 3 to 5 pm Monday to Friday and from 9 am to 1 pm Saturday.

You can place long-distance telephone calls from the ADO bus station. Person-to-person or collect calls are subject to a 6-peso fee. There are a few Lada casetas on Juárez, near the banks. They offer a bit more privacy, and charge about 14 pesos per minute and 33 pesos per fax worldwide.

Bookshops Papelería y Novedades del Centro (☎ (943) 5-07-77), at Independencia 18 and Nicolás, is a small paper/bookshop attached to a café. Shelves hold a few English guidebooks, some Mayan literature and maps of Chiapas. There is a random magazine selection but you can find recent news sources or a copy of *Rolling Stone* magazine.

Medical Services Palenque has a Hospital General across from the Pemex station near the Mayan statue, a Centro de Salud Urbano (Urban Health Centre) next door, and various pharmacies. The Farmacia & Clinica Santa Fe, on Hidalgo at Javier Mina two blocks east of the park, is on call 24 hours a day.

Laundry Lavandería USA Clean is across Avenida Juárez from the ATG bus station. There's another laundry on the corner of Independencia and 5 de Mayo, open daily except Sunday from 9 am to 2 pm and from 4 to 8 pm.

Palenque Ruins

The archaeological zone of Palenque is in a much larger reserve, the Parque Nacional Palenque. A new Visitors Centre at the entrance to the park holds a museum and other services.

Only 34 of Palenque's nearly 500 buildings have been excavated. As you explore the ruins, try to picture the grey edifices as bright red; at the peak of Palenque's power, the entire city was painted vermilion. Everything you see here was achieved without metal tools, pack animals or the wheel.

One of the prime times to visit the site is just after it opens, when a humid haze rises and wraps the ancient temples in a mysterious mist. The effect is best in the winter when the days are shorter.

The archaeological site is open from 8 am to 5 pm daily; the crypt in the Temple of Inscriptions – not to be missed – is only open from 10 am to 4 pm; the museum is open from 10 am to 5 pm. Admission to the site costs 18 pesos; parking in the car park by the gate costs 2 pesos. There is no additional charge for entry to the crypt or the museum. Drinks, snacks and souvenirs are for sale in stands facing the car park.

Temple of Inscriptions After you enter the enclosure and walk along the path, look for a small stone structure on the left-hand side. This is the tomb of Alberto Ruz Lhuillier, the tireless archaeologist who revealed many of Palenque's mysteries between 1945 and 1952.

The magnificent pyramid on the right is the tallest and most prominent of Palenque's buildings. Constructed on eight levels, it has a central staircase rising some 23 metres to a temple which crowns the structure; it once had a tall roofcomb as well. Between the doorways are stucco panels with reliefs of noble figures. On the temple's rear wall are three panels with a long inscription in Mayan hieroglyphs which gives the temple its name. The inscription, dedicated in 692 AD, recounts the history of Palenque and of the temple.

Ascend the 69 steep steps to the top, both for a magnificent vista of Palenque and the

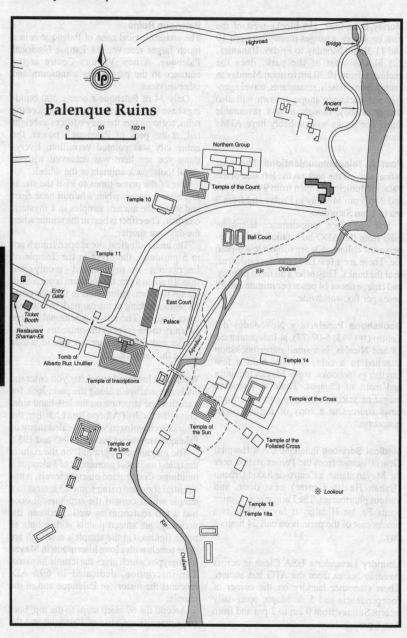

Palenque Ruins

0 50 100 m

Highroad

Bridge

Ancient Road

Northern Group

Temple of the Count

Temple 10

Ball Court

Río Otulum

Temple 11

Entry Gate

East Court

Palace

Ticket Booth

Restaurant Shaman-Ek

Tomb of Alberto Ruz Lhuillier

Temple of Inscriptions

Temple 14

Temple of the Cross

Temple of the Sun

Temple of the Foliated Cross

Temple of the Lion

Río Otulum

✳ Lookout

Temple 18

Temple 18a

surrounding jungle and for access to stairs down to the tomb of Pakal (open from 10 am to 4 pm). This crypt lay undiscovered until 1952 when Ruz Lhuillier, who had been excavating the staircase, found a sealed stone passageway in which were seated several skeletons. These victims of religious sacrifice were intended to serve Pakal in death and were buried with clay pots, jewellery and tools for his journey to the next world.

Although Pakal's jewel-bedecked skeleton and jade mosaic death mask were taken to Mexico City and the tomb re-created in the Museo Nacional de Antropología, the stone sarcophagus lid remains here. (The priceless death mask was stolen from the museum in 1985.) The carved stone slab protecting the sarcophagus includes the image of Pakal encircled by serpents, mythical monsters, the sun god and glyphs recounting Pakal's reign. Carved on the wall are the nine lords of the underworld. Between the crypt and the staircase, a snake-like hollow ventilation tube connected Pakal to the realm of the living.

This was the first crypt found in Mayan pyramids, and it gave rise to wild speculation linking the Maya with Egypt. Evidence of a few other pyramid crypts has been found, but nothing as elaborate as this.

Palace Diagonally opposite the Temple of Inscriptions, lying in the centre of Palenque's park, is the Palace, an unusual and significant structure harbouring a maze of courtyards, corridors and rooms. If you walk up to the tower (restored in 1955), you will see fine stucco reliefs on the walls. Palenque's stucco figures of royalty and prominent priests are superb. Using a mixture derived from clay and tree bark to make the stucco dry more slowly, Mayan sculptors were able to create intricate details. Archaeologists and artists alike say that the carved stonework of Palenque's ruins stands unparalleled among Mayan sites in Mexico.

On the northern interior wall are imposing monster masks. Archaeologists and astronomers believe that the tower was constructed so that Mayan royalty and the priest class could observe the sun falling directly into the Temple of the Inscriptions during the 22 December winter solstice. Some archaeologists believe that like the sun, Pakal was deified and that the Maya thought he would also rise again.

Within the tower's courtyard, you will see a singular well-preserved stone known as the Oval Tablet. Engraved on it is the image of Zac-Kuk, Pakal's mother, handing her son the ruler's ceremonial headdress. She ruled as regent for three years until Pakal was sufficiently mature (aged 12½ years) to rule on his own.

In the northern section of the palace are some interesting carved stucco figures, on the piers facing the stairs. Within the courtyard, nine substantial stone figures are shown kneeling, possibly awaiting sacrifice or rendering tribute.

Stucco head found in the Temple of Inscriptions

Rediscovery of Palenque

It is said that Hernán Cortés came within 40 km of the ruins without any awareness of them. In 1773, Mayan hunters told a Spanish priest that stone palaces lay in the jungle. Father Ordoñez y Aguilar led an expedition to Palenque and wrote a book claiming that the city was the capital of an Atlantis-like civilisation.

An expedition led by Captain Antonio del Río set out in 1787 to explore Palenque. Although his report was then locked up in the Guatemalan archives, a translation of it was made by a British resident of Guatemala who was sufficiently intrigued to have it published in England in 1822. This led a host of adventurers to brave malaria in their search for the hidden city.

Among the most colourful of these adventurers was the eccentric Count de Waldeck who, in his 60s, lived atop one of the pyramids for two years (1831-33). He wrote a book complete with fraudulent drawings which made the city resemble great Mediterranean civilisations, causing all the more interest in Palenque. In Europe, Palenque's fame grew and it was mythologised as a lost Atlantis or an extension of ancient Egypt.

Finally, in 1837, John L Stephens reached Palenque with artist Frederick Catherwood. Stephens wrote insightfully about the six pyramids he started to excavate and the city's aqueduct system. His was the first truly scientific investigation and paved the way for research by other serious scholars. ■

There is much to explore in the subterranean passageways and courtyards of the palace. In the eastern patio stand three-metre-tall statues of warriors thought to be worshipping a god.

Temples of the Cross Although Pakal had only the Temple of Inscriptions dedicated to him during his 68-year reign, Chan-Balum had three buildings dedicated to him, known today as the Temples of the Cross. Follow the path leading between the Palace and the Temple of Inscriptions, cross the Río Otolum (a mere stream; the name means Place of Fallen Stones) and climb the slope to the Temple of the Sun, on the right. The temple's decoration includes narrative inscriptions dating from 642 AD, replete with scenes of offerings to Pakal, the sun-shield king. The Temple of the Sun has the best preserved roofcomb of all the buildings at Palenque.

The smaller, less well-preserved Temple XIV next door also has tablets showing ritual offerings – a common scene in Palenque. Here a woman makes an offering to a 'dancing man' believed to be Chan-Balum.

Follow the path a few more metres to the largest of the buildings in this group, the Temple of the Cross, restored in 1990. Inside are sculpted narrative stones; some tablets have been taken from this relatively poorly

preserved temple to the Museo Nacional de Antropología in Mexico City. One archaeologist suggests that Chan-Balum may be buried under this temple, as the symbolism of its decoration is similar to that on the sarcophagus lid of Pakal. One particularly fine stucco carving shows a priest smoking a sacred pipe.

To the right of the Temple of the Sun, seemingly cut out from the jungle hillside, stands the Temple of the Foliated Cross. Here, the deterioration of the façade lets you appreciate the architectural composition, with the arches fully exposed. A well-preserved tablet carving shows a king with a sun-shield (most likely Pakal) emblazoned on his chest, corn growing from his shoulder blades and the sacred quetzal bird atop his head. One interpretation of this tablet is that it depicts the Mayan reverence for the life force of the god of maize.

Other Ruins North of the Palace is the Northern Group, unrestored, and the ruins of a ball court. Crazy Count de Waldeck lived in one of the temples of the Northern Group – Temple of the Count, constructed in 647 AD under Pakal.

Getting There & Away Colectivos Chambalu, on the corner of Hidalgo and Allende, and Colectivos Palenque, on the corner of Allende and 20 de Noviembre, operate combis between Palenque town and the ruins. The service runs every 15 minutes (or when seats are full) from 6 am to 6 pm daily. The minibuses will stop to pick you up anywhere along the town-to-ruins road, which makes it especially handy for campers. The fare is 1.50 pesos. A taxi charges 17 pesos between Palenque town and the ruins.

Organised Tours

Several companies in Palenque town operate transport and tour services to Palenque ruins, Agua Azul and Misol-Ha, Bonampak and Yaxchilán, and La Palma (for the boat to Flores in Guatemala), usually offering similar features at similar prices. Often there is a minimum number of passengers required for the minibus to go. Agencies include:

Amfitriones Turísticos de Chiapas, on Allende between Avenida Juárez and Hidalgo (☎ (934) 5-02-10, fax 5-03-56)
Colectivos Chambalu, on the corner of Hidalgo and Allende (☎ (934) 5-08-67)
Colectivos Palenque, on the corner of Allende and 20 de Noviembre
Shivalva Viajes Mayas, Merle Green 1A, La Cañada (☎ (934) 5-04-11, fax 5-03-92)
Viajes Aventura Maya, on Avenida Juárez, across from Banamex (☎ (934) 5-07-98)
Viajes Misol-Ha, on Avenida Juárez 48 at Aldama (☎ (934) 5-09-11, fax 5-04-88)
Viajes Pakal-Kin, 5 de Mayo 7, half a block west of the park (☎ (934) 5-11-80)
Viajes Shumb'al, 5 de Mayo 105, in the Kashlan Hotel (☎ (934) 5-20-80, fax 5-03-90)
Viajes Toniná, Juárez 105, near Allende (☎ (934) 5-09-02)
YAX-HA, Juárez 123, next to Banamex (☎ (934) 5-07-98, fax 5-07-67)

Places to Stay

Hotels here are not very well maintained and service is lackadaisical, but the magnificent ruins nevertheless draw crowds of tourists.

Places to Stay – bottom end

Camping Campers can string a hammock or pitch a tent at the *Camping Mayabell*, on the southern side of the road to the ruins, within the national park boundaries. The Mayabell charges 7.50 pesos (per person or car). They've got toilets, showers, some shade, full hookups, snacks and drinks for sale, and there is a waterfall nearby. Mayabell is only two km from the ruins, though the walk is all uphill.

Camping María del Mar, three km from the ruins on the opposite side of the road, is similar but with less shade at the same price.

It's also possible to camp by the river on the *Hotel Nututum's* grounds, 3.5 km along the road from Palenque to San Cristóbal de Las Casas. The fee is 10 pesos per person, 9 pesos per vehicle. A taxi from Palenque town to Nututum costs 12 pesos.

Hotels Hotels in town are cheaper than those on the road to the ruins, with the notable exception of the campgrounds.

Hotel La Croix (☎ (934) 5-00-14), Hidalgo 10, on the north side of the park, has a pretty courtyard with potted tropical plants and adequate rooms with fan and bath. Rooms cost 44/53 pesos a single/double. La Croix is usually full by mid-afternoon.

Rock-bottom options are on Hidalgo, west of the park. *Posada San Francisco*, Hidalgo 113 between Allende and Aldama, isn't bad for the price: basic doubles are 40 pesos. *Casa de Huéspedes León*, between Abasolo and Independencia, is worse but cheaper at 24/30 pesos for a single/double. Much nicer is *Hotel Naj K'in*, Hidalgo 72, two blocks west of the park, a recently remodelled family-run place with middling rooms, nice private bathrooms, hot water and fans. Rooms are 45/60/80 pesos a single/double/triple.

Hotel Santa Elena, near the hospital, has breezy, pleasant, mahogany-panelled rooms with fan and shower for 55 pesos. There are great rooftop views here. Also fairly near the ATG and Figueroa bus stations is *Posada Santo Domingo* (☎ (934) 5-01-36), at 20 de Noviembre 119. They charge 35 pesos for reasonably quiet, acceptable doubles with fan and private shower.

Posada Charito (☎ (934) 5-01-21), 20 de Noviembre 15, two blocks south-west of the park, is quiet, but recent years have been hard on it. For 35 pesos you get a well-worn, cell-like double with a shower and ceiling fan.

TABASCO & CHIAPAS

Canek Youth Hostel, on 20 de Noviembre (across from Posada Charito), was obviously built as shops, but now serves as guest quarters. The shops/rooms are big, with two to three beds each, louvred windows, and wooden lockers big enough for the biggest backpack, plus private toilet and sink. All three floors have single-sex communal showers. Beds are 23 pesos apiece.

Hotel Avenida (☎ (934) 5-01-16), at Juárez 183 opposite the ATG bus station, lets you hear every thunderous unmuffled bus. In addition to lack of sleep (and hot water), you may have to contend with broken bathroom fixtures, but the camaraderie here is worth it to some. Singles/doubles cost 35/50 pesos.

The quiet and friendly *Posada San Antonio*, three blocks north of the park on Independencia 42 at Velasco Suárez, has clean, indifferent rooms round a courtyard filled with plants and the family's laundry. Showers are cold. Singles/doubles/triples are 30/40/50 pesos.

Posada Shalom (☎ (934) 5-09-44), Juárez 156 between Allende and Aldama, is new, clean and friendly, with excellent prices of 40/55 pesos a single/double with private bath and ceiling fan.

To find *Posada Bonampak* (☎ (934) 5-09-25), walk north (down the hill towards the market) on Allende. Just after Reforma, take a right onto Avenida Dr Belisario Domínguez; a few doors up on the left is Posada Bonampak. No frills here, but rooms are well kept and bathrooms are nicely tiled. The back door opens into the jungle ravine. Doubles are 44 pesos.

The *Hotel Regional* (☎ (934) 5-01-83), Juárez at Aldama, has adequate rooms with shower and fan around a small plant-filled courtyard priced at 40/60/75 pesos. Also on Juárez, half a block west of the park, is *Hotel Misol-Ha* (☎ (934) 5-00-92), with serviceable, clean and bare rooms going for 45/55/70 pesos, private shower and fan included.

La Posada (☎ (934) 5-04-37), behind Hotel Maya Tulipanes in La Cañada, is a quiet backpackers' hangout with a courtyard/lawn, table tennis and a lobby wall covered with messages of peace, passion and travel. Average rooms with bath are 45/56 pesos a single/double.

Places to Stay – middle
Town Centre The *Hotel Kashlan* (☎ (934) 5-02-97, fax 5-03-09), Avenida 5 de Mayo 105 at Allende, is clean and near the bus stations. The Kashlan (Mayan for 'gringo', more or less) offers its rooms with ceiling fan and shower for 65/85 pesos a single/double. A sign at the reception explains that those small animals on the walls of your room are *cuijas* (geckos), harmless lizards which eat insects. You'll see cuijas on your walls through the Mexican tropics.

The *Hotel Palenque* (☎ (934) 5-01-88, fax 5-00-39), Avenida 5 de Mayo 15 at Independencia, is old but boasts a convenient location, pretty gardens and a small and sometimes presentably clean swimming pool. It's popular with cattle ranchers and local families. Doubles are 70 pesos with fan, 85 pesos with air-con.

Hotel Chan-Kah (☎ (934) 5-03-18, fax 5-04-89), above the restaurant of the same name, is on the corner of Juárez and Independencia overlooking the park. Lots of extras here: a lift, insect screens, two double beds and a TV in each room, little balconies and frequent live music in the bar. Doubles are 135 pesos with fan, 165 pesos with air-con.

Around the corner near the park on Juárez, the *Hotel Casa de Pakal* has 14 small rooms with air-con and private bath. If you must have electric coolness, you will pay 120 pesos a double.

La Cañada La Cañada is the forested area north-east of the Mayan statue, a 10 to 15-minute walk from Palenque centre.

When archaeologists were excavating and restoring the Palenque ruins, they lodged at the *Hotel La Cañada* (☎ (934) 5-01-02) at the east end of Calle Merle Green (the unpaved main street, also called Calle Cañada), a group of cottages surrounded by jungle. Their hosts were the Morales family. Decades have passed, the Morales family has grown, and now various scions own the other hotels in this area as well. The Cañada's older rooms are nothing special, but okay for 55/65/80 pesos a single/double/triple with bath and ceiling fan; newer rooms with two double beds and air-con are much nicer at 75/90/120 pesos. The Cañada's good thatch-roofed restaurant is still the eatery of choice in this neighbourhood.

Sharing some of La Cañada's advantages and its ownership by the Morales family is the nearby *Hotel Maya Tulipanes* (☎ (934) 5-02-01, fax 5-10-04), Calle Cañada 6. Rooms come with ceiling fan (80 pesos a double), air-con (105 pesos a double) or air-con and TV (140 pesos a double). There is a small pool and a nice restaurant.

Across the road is *Hotel Xibalbas* (☎ (934) 5-04-11, fax 5-03-92), Calle Merle Green 1A, which has attractive rooms above Shivalva Travel Agency and in the modern A-frame next door. The tidy if plain rooms (some with bathtubs, all with showers) look into the forest and cost 70/90/120 pesos a single/double/triple.

Hotel Chablis (☎ (934) 5-04-46), near Hotel La Cañada, has a traditional Mexican restaurant, video bar and appealing rooms with air-con at prices similar to the Xibalbas.

Readers with their own cars might want to consider staying at the *Hotel El Paraíso* (☎ (934) 5-00-45), Carretera a las Ruinas Km 2.5, which, as the address indicates, is 2.5 km along the road to the ruins, on the right-hand side. Large, airy, clean, air-con rooms with two double beds and gleaming tiled bathrooms cost 150 pesos.

Places to Stay – top end

The *Hotel Misión Palenque Park Plaza* (☎ (934) 5-04-44, fax 5-03-00), Rancho San Martín de Porres, Palenque, Chiapas 29960, at the far eastern end of town along Avenida Hidalgo, has aesthetic air-con rooms with a decor of wood, stone and stucco; it also has well-kept gardens, a pool, and a restaurant-bar. Rates are 345 pesos a double. The hotel's minibus shuttles guests to the ruins.

The most attractive and interesting lodgings in Palenque are at *Chan-Kah* (☎ (934) 5-11-00, fax 5-04-89), three km from town on the road to the ruins. Handsome wood-and-stone modern cottages have a Mayan accent; the palapa-topped restaurant, enormous stone-bound pool, the lush jungle gardens and other accoutrements are lavish, but sparsely populated. Perhaps the reason is the high price (300 pesos a double), the remoteness from town (a 12-peso taxi ride) and the lack of air-con.

South of town, 3.5 km on the road to San Cristóbal, is the *Hotel Nututum* (☎ (934) 5-01-00, fax 5-01-61), overlooking the Río Usumacinta just to the left of the road. The modern motel-style buildings are nicely arranged in spacious jungle gardens shaded by palm trees. Large air-con rooms with bath cost 250 pesos a double. You can also pitch your tent or park your camper here for 10 pesos per person and 9 pesos per vehicle. A swim in the hotel's river balneario costs 1 peso.

Hotel Plaza Palenque (☎ (934) 5-05-55, fax 5-03-95), a Best Western hotel 500 metres north of the Mayan statue, has a pleasant but generic atmosphere, with 100 air-con rooms surrounding a garden and swimming pool, and a disco, bar and restaurant. Doubles are 280 pesos.

Places to Eat

Inexpensive The cheapest fare in Palenque is at the open-air cookshops on Abasolo (a pedestrian step-street) between Juárez and 5 de Mayo. Next cheapest comes from the taquerías along the eastern side of the park, in front of the church. Try *Los Faroles* or *Refresquería Deportista* for a plate of tacos at 6 to 10 pesos.

Restaurant Artemio's is a family-run place on the corner of Jiménez and Hidalgo, to the left of the church. Everything on the menu seems to cost between 10 and 20 pesos whether it be filet, chicken, or traditional Mexican antojitos.

Sooner or later you'll probably drop into the *Restaurant Maya*, on the corner of Independencia and Hidalgo on the northwest corner of the park. This has been a popular meeting place for travellers as well as locals 'since 1958', so the menu says. The food is típico and the hours long (7 am to 11

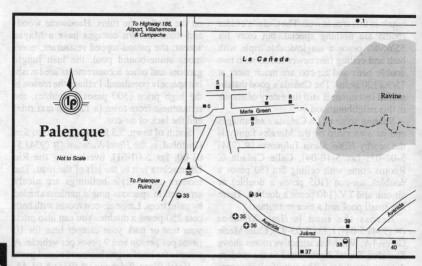

To Highway 186,
Airport, Villahermosa
& Campeche

La Cañada

Ravine

Palenque

Not to Scale

Merle Green

To Palenque
Ruins

Avenida

Juárez

Avenida

PLACES TO STAY		16	Hotel La Croix	56	Canek Youth Hostel
		18	Hotel Misión Palenque	59	Posada Charito
2	Posada San Antonio		Park Plaza		
3	Posada Bonampak	20	Hotel Naj K'in	**PLACES TO EAT**	
5	La Posada	28	Hotel Misol-Ha		
6	Hotel Maya Tulipanes	30	Hotel Casa de Pakal	12	Restaurant Virgos
7	Hotel Chablis	31	Hotel & Restaurant	15	Restaurant Artemio's
8	Hotel La Cañada		Chan-Kah	19	Restaurant Maya
9	Hotel Xibalbas &	37	Hotel Santa Elena	21	Pizzería Palenque
	Shivalvas Viajes	39	Hotel Avenida	24	Restaurant Paisanos
	Maya	40	Posada Santo Domingo	41	Restaurant La
10	Posada San Francisco	45	Hotel Kashlan		Francesca
11	Casa de Huéspedes	46	Hotel Regional	43	Restaurant Ixchel
	León	53	Hotel Palenque	44	Restaurant Girasoles

pm). Prices range from 16 to 35 pesos for a full meal; the comida corrida costs 16 pesos.

Park side, *Los Portales*, on the corner of 20 de Noviembre and Independencia (look for green polka-dotted pillars), has a breezy terrace dining area, views of a valley, a typical menu, and prices just a bit too high. Breakfast and antojitos go for about 12 pesos, and thirst-quenching fruit shakes for 7 pesos. Service is slow but friendly.

Avenida Juárez has lots of small, inexpensive restaurants. *Restaurant Paisanos*, on

Juárez between Aldama and Allende, is a tidy, cheaper workers' place where everything seems to cost about 11 pesos. The nearby *Restaurant El Herradero* is similar.

Pizzería Palenque, on Juárez at Allende, has surprisingly good pizzas ranging in price from a small cheese (18 pesos) to a large combination (48 pesos). *Pizzería Romanos*, 5 de Mayo 63 at Aldama, has pizza, privacy and promptness (20-minute service guaranteed). With just two tables, you can enjoy pasta (11 pesos), lasagne or eggplant parme-

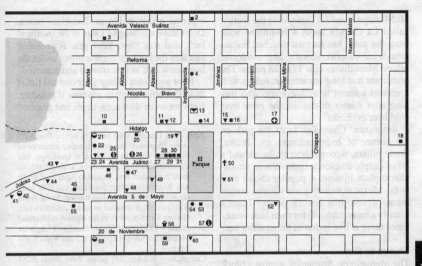

48	Pizzería Romanos	17	Farmacia & Clinica	36	Centro de Salud Urbano
49	Cookshops		Santa Fe (24 hours)		(Clinic)
51	Taquerías	21	Colectivos Chambalu	38	ATG Bus Station
52	'Restaurant Row'	22	Amfitriones Turísticos	42	ADO (1st-class)
60	Los Portales		de Chiapas		Bus Station
		25	Banamex	47	Farmacia Principal
OTHER		26	Bancomer	50	Church
		27	Mercado de Artesanías	54	Casa de la Cultura
1	Market	29	Farmacia Centro	55	Lavandería USA Clean
4	Papelería y Novedade	32	Maya Head Statue		Automática
	del Centro	33	Cristóbal Colón	57	Tourist Office
13	Post Office &		Bus Station	58	Colectivos Palenque
	Telegraph Office	34	Pemex Fuel Station		
14	Palacio Municipal	35	Hospital General		

san (22 pesos), or one of their 14 pizza varieties in a cosy, pleasant atmosphere.

One block west of the park, *Restaurant Virgos*, Hidalgo 4, offers open-air dining one flight up overlooking the street. White pillars, a red-tile roof, plants and (sometimes) marimba music set the scene, while Caesar salads for two or Espagueti Virgo (spaghetti smothered with cheese) will please the palate for under 18 pesos.

'Restaurant Row' is the name we give to 5 de Mayo at Mina, where there are six food

places in a row. Beside the cheap restaurants *Cenaduria, Capricornio* and *Shisho's*, there is a fruiterer and an ice cream shop.

There's a cluster of eating options around the bus stations. *Los Caminantes* has a patio restaurant overlooking the ravine, standard fare and prices, but nice atmosphere. *Restaurant Ixchel*, on Juárez across the street from ADO, serves cheap, good and quick breakfasts and antojitos. *Girasoles* and *La Francesca*, though close, are subject to horrific noise and fumes from idling buses.

Mid-Range *Hotel La Cañada*, in the section called La Cañada about a 10-minute walk from the park, has its own thatched restaurant with careful service and moderate prices. Most dishes cost 17 to 28 pesos. The restaurant has long attracted travellers with a serious interest in archaeology, who stay long after dinner discussing the ruins over cold beer or drinks.

Restaurant Chan-Kah faces the park on the corner of Independencia and Juárez. Stone pillars, wrought-iron grillwork and a bit of jungle ambience make this an atmospheric place to dine. A popular choice here is the Mexican variety plate with an assortment of antojitos for 18 pesos. There's usually a menu turistico for even less. Sometimes there is live music in the upstairs bar.

Things to Buy

The Mercado de Artesanías, almost a block west of the park on Juárez, carries leather products, textiles, batiks and clothing. The prices are fair (though you can bargain) and it's possible to browse peacefully. The mercado is open every day from 9 am to 2 pm, and 5 to 9 pm. If you're hammock hunting, bargain with the vendors on Juárez.

Getting There & Away

Air There is a small airstrip north of town, used mostly for air taxi and charter flights. Occasionally there is a short-hop service to/from Tuxtla Gutiérrez. Check with the tourist office or a travel agency in Palenque.

Bus The bus stations are all fairly close to one another, mostly between the Mayan statue and the centre of town. ADO is at the confluence of Avenida Juárez and 5 de Mayo. Autotransportes Tuxtla Gutiérrez, west of ADO, has a left-luggage room for 1 peso per piece per day. Transportes Figueroa is just to the west of ATG. Autobuses Lagos de Montebello is behind the Hotel Maya Tulipanes in La Cañada. Omnibus Cristóbal Colón is south-west of the Mayan statue at the beginning of the road to the ruins.

There is less thievery on the bus than on the train, but some bus passengers have reported goods stolen on 2nd-class buses. Don't leave anything of value in the overhead rack, and stay alert. Your gear is probably safest in the luggage compartment under the bus, but watch as it is stowed and removed.

It's a good idea to buy your onward ticket from Palenque a day in advance if possible. Here are some distances, times and prices:

Agua Azul Crucero – 60 km, 1¼ hours; five ATG buses (6 pesos); the same number courtesy of Figueroa. These buses go on to Ocosingo, San Cristóbal and Tuxtla Gutiérrez; seats are sold to those passengers first. Tickets to Agua Azul go on sale 30 minutes before departure, and if all seats are sold, you must stand all the way to the Agua Azul turnoff. It is easier to take a colectivo (see Getting There & Away in the Agua Azul section)

Bonampak – 152 km, six hours; Autobuses Lagos de Montebello buses (19 pesos) at 3 am, 9 am, 6 and 8 pm

Campeche – 362 km, 5½ hours; three direct ADO 1st-class buses (50 pesos) at 8 am, 8 and 10 pm; one Cristóbal Colón 1st-class bus (46 pesos) at 2 pm. You can also catch a bus or combi, or hitch-hike the 27 km north to Catazajá, on the main Villahermosa-Escárcega highway, and catch one of the buses which pass every hour or two

Catazajá – 27 km, 30 minutes; six ADO 1st-class buses (4.50 pesos); numerous minibuses as well

Chetumal – 487 km, seven hours; one ADO 1st-class bus (65 pesos) at 8.30 pm; another Cristóbal Colón 1st-class bus

La Palma (for Guatemala boat) – 175 km, four hours; 10.30 am bus (20 pesos)

Mérida – 556 km, 11 hours; three ADO 1st-class buses (75 to 90 pesos) at 8 am, 8 and 10 pm; a Cristóbal Colón 1st-class (74 pesos) at 1 am

Mexico City (TAPO) – 1020 km, 16 hours; one ADO 1st-class bus (150 pesos) at 6 pm; a 6 pm bus courtesy of Cristóbal Colón

Misol-Ha – 47 km, one hour; five ATG 2nd-class buses (3.50 pesos); the same courtesy of Figueroa. (See Agua Azul Crucero, above)

Ocosingo – 85 km, two hours; six ATG 1st-class buses (18 pesos); two Autobuses Fray Bartolomé de Las Casas buses; two Cristóbal Colón morning buses (20 pesos)

San Cristóbal de Las Casas – 190 km, 5½ hours uphill from Palenque, 4½ hours downhill; three Cristóbal Colón buses (28 pesos); six ATG 2nd-class buses (22 pesos) and several 1st-class buses

Tuxtla Gutiérrez – 275 km, 7½ hours; three Cristóbal Colón 1st-class buses (40 pesos); three ATG and Figoerua 2nd-class buses each (32 pesos)

Villahermosa – 150 km, 2½ hours; seven ADO 1st-class buses (22 pesos)

Boat If you're coming from Guatemala's Petén department, you can go by bus from Flores to El Naranjo, then by boat down the Río San Pedro to La Palma, then by bus to Tenosique and Palenque.

Buses to El Naranjo depart from the Flores market daily at 5 am and 12.30 pm on the rough, bumpy 125-km, six-hour, US$4.50 ride. From El Naranjo you must catch a boat on the river and cruise for about four hours to the border town of La Palma. From La Palma you can go by bus to Tenosique (1½ hours), then by bus or combi to Emiliano Zapata (40 km, one hour), and from there by bus or combi to Palenque.

Travel agencies in Palenque offer to get you from Palenque to La Palma by minibus in time to catch a special 9 am boat to El Naranjo, and then the bus to Flores, arriving there around 7 pm the same day. The cost is about US$55 per person. Though somewhat more expensive than doing it yourself, it is faster, surer and more convenient, and avoids a dreary overnight in spartan accommodation in El Naranjo.

BONAMPAK & YAXCHILÁN RUINS

The ruins of Bonampak – famous for frescos – and the great ancient city of Yaxchilán are accessible on camping excursions from Palenque, or by chartering an aircraft from Palenque, San Cristóbal or Tenosique.

The frescos at Bonampak have deteriorated greatly since they were discovered and do not provide the expected thrill. Go instead to look at the site, and then examine copies of the murals in books or in the Museo Nacional de Antropología in Mexico City. The site at Yaxchilán is more rewarding, and the trek through the jungle and across the Usumacinta is a thrill in itself.

Bonampak and Yaxchilán have neither food nor water, so make certain you are well supplied if you come on your own. It's bug-infested in these parts – bring insect repellent. Don't leave your gear unattended, as thefts have been reported on previous trips. Finally, carry a torch to see dark parts of the ruins better and for any camping emergencies.

Bonampak

Lying about 155 km south-east of Palenque near the Guatemalan frontier, Bonampak was hidden from the outside world by dense jungle until 1946. A young WW II conscientious objector named Charles Frey fled the draft and somehow wound up here in the Lacandonian rainforest. He was virtually adopted by local Indians and shown what the Indians told him was a sacred site of their ancestors. Impressed by what he saw, Frey enthusiastically revealed his findings to Mexican officials and archaeological expeditions were mounted. Frey died in 1949 trying to save an expedition member from drowning in the turbulent Usumacinta.

The ruins of Bonampak lie around a rectangular plaza. Only the southern edifices of the plaza are preserved; the rest is little more than heaps of stone. It was the frescos of a temple in the Southern Group, today designated Building 1, that excited Frey and the archaeologists who followed. They saw three rooms covered with paintings depicting ancient Mayan ways. Painted in profile are warriors decked with quetzal feathers, kings and royal families, priests, shamans,

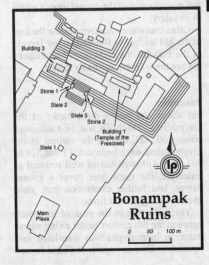

Bonampak Ruins

0   50   100 m

dancers, musicians and war captives. The details of costumes themselves reveal much about Mayan life and the murals are complete with glyphs.

The murals' original colours were brown, green and vermilion, with the figures outlined in black. Unfortunately, 12 centuries of weather deterioration were accelerated when the first expedition attempted to clean the murals with kerosene. On the positive side, some restoration has been undertaken and reproductions installed for comparison. Generally, the murals are so difficult to decipher that you may wonder what all the fuss was about. If you look closely (or view the reproductions) though, you may think you are looking at artwork from ancient Egypt.

Some of the murals depict the victory of the Maya over the Olmecs. One panel shows dancing at a celebration, another prisoners waiting to be sacrificed, and a third the giving of thanks to the gods for victory.

To best see what these faded frescos originally looked like, inspect the Bonampak mural reproductions in the Museo Nacional de Antropología in Mexico City, or the ones at the Museo Regional de Antropología Carlos Pellicer Cámara in Villahermosa. Tuxtla Gutiérrez's Hotel Bonampak has a full reproduction of the central room's mural in its lobby.

Other than some narrative stelae at the foot of the hill leading to Building 1, the Temple of the Frescos, the eight other buildings of the Southern Group are badly ruined.

Yaxchilán

Set above the jungle-thick banks of the Usumacinta, Yaxchilán was first inhabited about 200 AD, though the earliest hieroglyphs found have been dated from 514 to 807 AD. Although not as well restored as Palenque, the ruins here cover a greater extent, and further excavation may yield even more significant finds.

Yaxchilán rose to the peak of its prominence in the 8th century under a king whose name in hieroglyphs was translated into Spanish as Escudo Jaguar, or Shield Jaguar.

His shield-and-jaguar symbol appears on many of the site's buildings and stelae. The city's power expanded under Escudo Jaguar's son, Pájaro Jaguar, or Bird Jaguar (752-70). His hieroglyph consists of a small jungle cat with feathers on the back and a bird superimposed on the head.

Building 33 on the south-western side of the plaza has some fine religious carvings over the northern doorways, and a roofcomb which retains most of its original beauty. At the front base of the temple are narrative carvings of a ball game.

The central plaza holds statues of crocodiles and jaguars. A lintel in Building 20 shows a dead man's spirit emerging from the mouth of a man speaking about him, and stelae of Maya making offerings to the gods. In front of Building 20 are exceptional stelae featuring Mayan royalty.

Be certain to walk to Yaxchilán's highest temples, which are still covered with trees and are not visible from the plaza. Building 41 is the tallest of these, and the view from its top is one of the highlights of a visit to Yaxchilán. Some tour guides do not want to make the effort to show you Building 41 – insist on it!

Organised Tours

Combi & Boat Tours Various travel agencies in Palenque run two-day road and river tours to Bonampak and Yaxchilán; see Organised Tours in the Palenque section.

The rate for a two-day tour by land to Yaxchilán and Bonampak is 300 pesos, including transportation and all meals. A minivan takes you within 10 km of Bonampak and you walk the rest of the way. Tents are provided for overnight stays. The next morning, you are driven to the Río Usumacinta, where an outboard motor boat takes you for an hour through the jungle to Yaxchilán.

There are also one-day tours to Bonampak for 100 to 150 pesos, or to Yaxchilán and back for 150 to 200 pesos.

Viajes Pakal in Palenque offers the following two-day trip for 275 pesos per person (if five or six people sign up); 350 pesos per

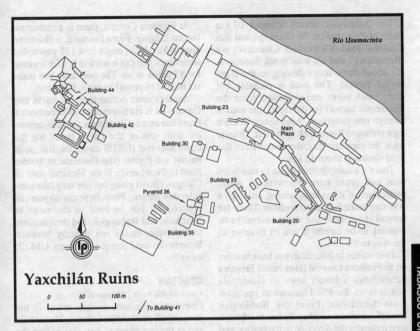

Yaxchilán Ruins

0   50   100 m

To Building 41

person (if three or four); or 650 pesos per person (if two). You drive from Palenque to the Lacandón settlement of Caribal Lacanjá by car, take a two-hour walk to Bonampak (stay 1½ to two hours), walk back to Caribal Lacanjá and camp or sleep in a Lacandón house. Next morning, travel by car to Frontera Echeverría, then boat along the Río Usumacinta to Yaxchilán, stay three hours, and then return to Palenque by boat and car.

Getting There & Away

Air Those with more money than time can charter a small plane to Bonampak and Yaxchilán from Palenque, San Cristóbal, Comitán or Tenosique. For current information on the travel agencies operating these flights, ask at the tourist office in each town.

In Palenque, Amfitriones Turísticos de Chiapas (☎ (934) 5-02-10), on Allende between Avenida Juárez and Hidalgo, can give you details on air tours, as can Viajes Shivalva (☎ (934) 5-04-11, fax 5-03-92),

Fraccionamiento La Cañada, Avenida Merle Green 1A. The cost is about 450 pesos per person.

In San Cristóbal de Las Casas, flights and tours to Yaxchilán and Bonampak can be arranged through Viajes Pakal (☎ (967) 8-28-18/19), on the corner of Hidalgo and Cuauhtémoc, or Amfitriones Turísticos in the Hotel Posada Diego de Mazariegos. The flight gives you a scheduled total of 3½ hours at the two sites.

Car Despite what you may hear, it is possible to drive to Bonampak and the trip doesn't even require 4WD – although the local car-rental company might not be too pleased if they knew where you were intending to take their VW Beetle. A full tank of fuel might just get you from Palenque to Bonampak, Yaxchilán and back, but you'd be better off buying a plastic container and carrying some additional fuel. The round trip is a bit over 300 km.

The Bonampak turnoff is about 10 km south of Palenque on the Ocosingo and San Cristóbal road. It's marked 'Chancalá', not 'Bonampak', and it's wise to ask directions. It's about three hours driving to the Bonampak turnoff. The road is passable but dusty, with rocks and potholes. After the Bonampak turnoff (to the right), the road is a rough one-lane track. After about 10 km a sign indicates Bonampak to the left. Despite what the sign may say, the distance for this final stretch is about 15 km.

There's a campground close to this junction and from here it's wise to walk, particularly if it has been raining, although a VW can make it in good weather. There are several streambeds and shaky bridges to be crossed, so be careful if you try to drive all the way to the site.

To continue to Yaxchilán you have to drive on to Frontera Corozal (also called Frontera Echeverría), a border town to Guatemala which is on the Río Usumacinta upstream from Yaxchilán. From the Bonampak turnoff, continue another 20 km to where a sign indicates the direction to the border, and from there you travel along another 30 km of rough track.

Boat Boats to the ruins at Yaxchilán can be hired from Corozal; you might be asked for around 135 pesos for a complete boat but should be able to knock that down. Yaxchilán is about 20 km downstream, and while you get there quite fast, the return trip against the swift current can take over two hours. Come prepared for the fierce sun.

To/From Guatemala You can reach Corozal and Yaxchilán by bus and boat from Flores, Petén, Guatemala. Buses run daily from Flores via El Subín crossroads to the hamlet of Bethel (four hours, US$3), on the Río Usumacinta. Frequent cargo boats make the two-hour trip downriver to Frontera Corozal (Echeverría) in Mexico, charging a few dollars for the voyage; the voyage upriver from Corozal to Bethel takes longer. A hired boat might cost US$15 (50 pesos). There are no services in Bethel except a small shop.

At Frontera Corozal, there is a restaurant but no lodging. From Frontera, a chartered boat to Yaxchilán might cost 175 pesos, but sometimes you can hitch a ride with a group for 35 pesos or so. The one daily bus takes six hours (16 pesos) to reach Palenque.

Another route connecting Yaxchilán and Guatemala is via Sayaxché and Benemerito. From Sayaxché, Guatemala, you can negotiate with one of the cargo boats for the eight-hour trip (US$8) down the Río de la Pasión via Pipiles (the Guatemalan border post) to Benemerito, in the Mexican state of Chiapas. (Boats going upriver may take considerably longer.) From Benemerito you can proceed by bus or boat to the ruins at Yaxchilán and Bonampak, and then onward to Palenque. Buses run directly between Benemerito and Palenque (10 hours, US$12) as well.

COMITÁN
• *pop: 84,000 • alt: 1630 metres*

Comitán, a pleasant enough town, is the jumping-off point for the Lagos de Montebello and is the last place of any size before the Guatemalan border at Ciudad Cuauhtémoc.

The first Spanish settlement in the area, San Cristóbal de los Llanos, was set up in 1527. Today the town is officially called Comitán de Domínguez, after Belisario Domínguez, a local doctor who was also a national senator during the presidency of Victoriano Huerta. Domínguez had the cheek to speak out in the senate in 1913 against Huerta's record of political murders and was himself murdered for his pains.

Orientation
The wide, attractive zócalo is bound by Avenida Central on its west side and Calle 1 Sur on the south. The 1st-class Cristóbal Colón bus station is on the Pan-American Highway about 20 minutes' walk from the centre. To reach the zócalo, turn left out of the bus station along the highway, take the first right (downhill along 4 Sur Pte but it's not marked), go six blocks (up and down hills – and the first two blocks are long), then turn left on to Avenida Central Sur and go three blocks.

The 2nd-class Autotransportes Tuxtla Gutiérrez is at 4 Sur Pte 55, between Avenida 3 and Avenida 4 Pte Sur; for the zócalo go left out of the entrance on 4 Sur Pte for 3½ blocks and at Avenida Central Sur go three blocks north.

Information

Tourist Office There's a tourist office (☎ (963) 2-00-26) in the Palacio Municipal on the north side of the zócalo, open from 9 am to 8 pm Monday to Saturday and from 9 am to 2 pm Sunday.

Money Bancomer is on the south-east corner of the zócalo. Banamex is a block south on the corner of 2 Sur Ote and 1 Ote Sur.

Post & Telecommunications The post office (open from 8 am to 7 pm Monday to Friday and 8 am to 1 pm Saturday) is on Avenida Central Sur between 2 and 3 Sur,

1½ blocks south of the zócalo. There's a Ladatel phone at the south-west corner of the zócalo, and a Lada caseta on 2 Sur Pte, half a block west of Avenida Central Sur.

Foreign Consulate The Guatemalan Consulate (☎ 2-26-69) is at 2 Pte Nte 28, open from 8 am to 1 pm and 2.30 to 4.30 pm Monday to Friday. Visas normally take about a half-hour to process and the fee depends upon your nationality.

Things to See

On the east side of the zócalo, the **Templo de Santo Domingo** dates from the 16th century. The adjacent **Casa de la Cultura**, on the south-east corner of the zócalo, includes an exhibition gallery, auditorium and museum.

The family home of martyr-hero Belisario Domínguez, at Avenida Central Sur 29, half a block south of the zócalo, has been turned

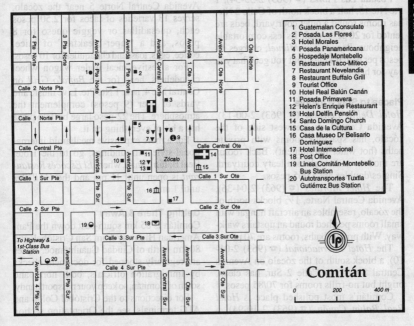

1 Guatemalan Consulate
2 Posada Las Flores
3 Hotel Morales
4 Posada Panamericana
5 Hospedaje Montebello
6 Restaurant Taco-Miteco
7 Restaurant Nevelandia
8 Restaurant Buffalo Grill
9 Tourist Office
10 Hotel Real Balún Canán
11 Posada Primavera
12 Helen's Enrique Restaurant
13 Hotel Delfín Pensión
14 Santo Domingo Church
15 Casa de la Cultura
16 Casa Museo Dr Belisario Domínguez
17 Hotel Internacional
18 Post Office
19 Linea Comitán-Montebello Bus Station
20 Autotransportes Tuxtla Gutiérrez Bus Station

Comitán

0   200   400 m

TABASCO & CHIAPAS

into a **museum** that provides an interesting insight into medical practices and the life of the professional classes in turn-of-the-century Comitán. It's open from 10 am to 6.45 pm Tuesday to Saturday, and 9 am to 12.45 pm Sunday; admission is 2 pesos.

Places to Stay – bottom end

Comitán has several cheap posadas with small, often dingy rooms, most of them OK for a night. *Posada Primavera*, Calle Central Pte 4, only a few steps west of the zócalo, charges 20 pesos per bed for rooms with sinks, but without bath or windows; doubles are 28 pesos. The *Hospedaje Montebello* (☎ (963) 2-17-70), a block further at Calle 1 Norte Pte 10, has acceptable rooms around a courtyard for 18/35 pesos a single/double. *Posada Panamericana*, on the corner of Calle Central Pte and Avenida 1 Pte Nte, has dark downstairs cubicles for 16 pesos a single, and upstairs there are brighter, breezier rooms for 30 pesos.

Posada Las Flores (☎ (963) 2-33-34), 1 Pte Nte 15, half a block north of Calle 2 Nte, has rooms round a quiet courtyard; beds are rented for 20 pesos each. Its less comfortable neighbour, *Posada San Miguel*, charges 14 pesos per bed; it's clean but you get what you pay for here.

Places to Stay – middle

Hotel Delfín Pensión (☎ (963) 2-00-13), Avenida Central on the west side of the zócalo, has spacious rooms with private baths (hot water intermittent). Back rooms are modern and overlook a leafy courtyard. Singles/doubles are 55/65 pesos.

The *Hotel Morales* (☎ (963) 2-04-36), Avenida Central Norte, 1½ blocks north of the zócalo, resembles an aircraft hangar with small rooms perched round an upstairs walkway. With private baths, rooms are 70 pesos.

The *Hotel Internacional* (☎ (963) 2-01-10), a block south of the zócalo on Avenida Central Sur 16 at Calle 2 Sur, has clean, bright but no-frills rooms for 70/85 pesos.

Comitán's most polished place is *Hotel Real Balún Canán* (☎ (963) 2-10-94), a block west of the zócalo at Avenida 1 Pte Sur 7. Prints of Frederick Catherwood's 1844 drawings of Mayan ruins decorate the stairs and the small rooms are comfortable with TV and phone. The rate is 160 pesos a double.

Places to Eat

Several reasonable cafés line the west side of the zócalo. Prime among them is *Helen's Enrique Restaurant*, in front of the Hotel Delfín. With a porch and pretensions to decor, Helen's serves buttered biscuits with beans and cheese for 11 pesos, antojitos, fried chicken, pizza, or huevos rancheros for a bit more. Main dishes cost between 12 and 25 pesos. *Restaurant Acuario*, *Restaurant Yuly* and *Restaurant Vicks*, in the same row, are more basic and cheaper.

Restaurant Nevelandia, on the north-west corner of the zócalo, has tacos for 1.50 to 2.50 pesos, antojitos, spaghetti and burgers for around 10 pesos, and meat dishes typically for 22 pesos.

The friendly, colourful *Taco-Miteco*, on Avenida Central Norte 5 near the zócalo, serves 13 varieties of tacos for 2.50 pesos each, quesadillas or veggie queso for 8 pesos, and a 'super-breakfast' of juice, coffee, eggs, toast and chilaquiles for 10 pesos.

For a festive meal under wagon wheel chandeliers, head for the *Buffalo Grill* on Central Nte 4, near 1 Nte Pte. Live music and yards of beer (9 pesos) complement the atmosphere. The 22-peso large buffalo pizza has a bit of everything on it.

For a more expensive meal amid international-style surroundings, go to the Hotel Real Balún Canán, where *El Escocés Restaurant* is open until 11 pm and the *Grill Bar* until 1 am.

Getting There & Away

Comitán is 85 km south-east down the Pan-American Highway from San Cristóbal, and 80 km north of Ciudad Cuauhtémoc. Buses are regularly stopped for document checks by immigration officials, both north and south of Comitán, so keep your passport handy.

For directions to the Cristóbal Colón and ATG terminals, see the Orientation section above. Linea Comitán-Montebello serves Lagos de Montebello from Avenida 2 Pte Sur 17-B between Calles 2 and 3 Sur Pte, two blocks west and 1½ blocks south of the zócalo.

Destinations include:

Ciudad Cuauhtémoc (Guatemalan border) – 80 km, 1½ hours; three Cristóbal Colón 1st-class buses (9 pesos); six ATG 2nd-class buses (7.50 pesos)
Mexico City (TAPO) – 1168 km, 21½ hours; one 1st-class bus (145 pesos); one Cristóbal Colón 1st-class Plus (175 pesos)
Palenque – 275 km, seven hours; one Linea Comitán-Montebello morning bus (18 pesos); more courtesy of San Cristóbal
San Cristóbal de Las Casas – 83 km, 1½ hours; hourly Cristóbal Colón buses from 6 am to 9 pm (11 pesos); four ATG buses (8 pesos); others courtesy of Andres Caso
Tapachula – 260 km, seven hours (via Motozintla); two ATG 2nd-class buses (20 pesos)
Tuxtla Gutiérrez – 170 km, 3½ hours; nine Cristóbal Colón 1st-class buses (20 pesos); three ATG 2nd-class buses (15 pesos)

LAGOS DE MONTEBELLO

The temperate forest along the Guatemalan border south-east of Comitán is dotted with about 60 small lakes – the Lagos or Lagunas de Montebello. The area is beautiful, refreshing, not hard to reach, and quiet. The many little-used vehicle tracks through the forest provide some excellent walks. Some Mexican weekenders come down here in their cars, but the rest of the time you'll probably see only resident villagers and a small handful of visitors. There are two very basic hostelries and a campground. At one edge of the lake district are the rarely visited Mayan ruins of Chinkultic. A number of Guatemalan refugee camps are in and around the lakes area.

Orientation

The paved road to Montebello turns east off the Pan-American Highway 16 km to the south of Comitán, just before the town of La

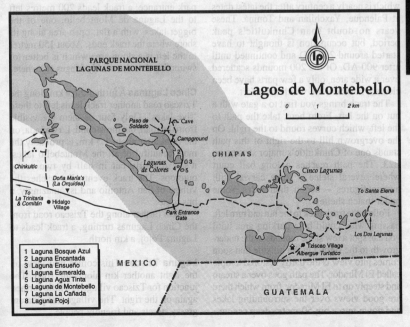

Lagos de Montebello

PARQUE NACIONAL
LAGUNAS DE MONTEBELLO

0   1   2 km

Paso de Soldado   Cave
Campground

CHIAPAS

Chinkultic

Lagunas de Colores

Cinco Lagunas

To Santa Elena

Doña María's (La Orquidea)

To La Trinitaria & Comitán   Hidalgo Village

Park Entrance Gate

Los Dos Lagunas

1 Laguna Bosque Azul
2 Laguna Encantada
3 Laguna Ensueño
4 Laguna Esmeralda
5 Laguna Agua Tinta
6 Laguna de Montebello
7 Laguna La Cañada
8 Laguna Pojoj

Tziscao Village
Albergue Turístico

MEXICO

GUATEMALA

Trinitaria. Running first through flat ranch-land, it passes Chinkultic after 30 km, entering the forest and the Parque Nacional de Montebello five km further on. At the park entrance (no fee) the road splits. The paved section continues three km ahead (north) to the Lagunas de Colores, where it dead-ends at two small houses 50 metres from Laguna Bosque Azul. To the right (east) from the park entrance, a dirt road leads to turnings for several more lakes and to the village and lake of Tziscao (nine km).

Chinkultic

These dramatically sited ruins lie two km along a track north off the La Trinitaria to Montebello road, 30 km from the Pan-American Highway. A sign 'Chinkultic 3' marks the turning. Doña María at La Orquidea restaurant, a km further along the road, has a map and book on Chinkultic.

Chinkultic was on the far western edge of the ancient Mayan area. Dates carved here extend from 591 to 897 AD – the last of which is nearly a century after the latest dates at Palenque, Yaxchilán and Toniná. These years no doubt span Chinkultic's peak period, but occupation is thought to have started around 200 AD and continued until after 900 AD. Of the 200 mounds scattered over a wide area, only a few parts have been cleared, but these are worth the effort.

The track brings you first to a gate with a hut on the left. From here, take the path to the left, which curves round to the right. On the overgrown hill to the right of this path stands one of Chinkultic's major structures, E23. The path reaches a long ball court where several stelae – some carved with human figures – lie on their sides, some under thatch shelters.

Follow the track back to the hut and turn left, passing what could be a parking area until you can spot a few stone mounds in the undergrowth to the right. On the hillside that soon comes into view is the partly restored temple called El Mirador. The path goes over a stream and steeply up to El Mirador, from which there are good views over the surrounding lakes and down into a big 50-metre-deep cenote.

The Lakes

Lagunas de Colores The paved road straight on from the park entrance leads through the Lagunas de Colores, so called because their colours range from turquoise to deep green. The first of these, on the right after about two km, is Laguna Agua Tinta. Then on the left come Laguna Esmeralda followed by Laguna Encantada, with Laguna Ensueño on the right opposite Encantada. The fifth and biggest is Laguna Bosque Azul, on the left where the road ends.

Two paths lead on from the end of the road. Straight ahead for 800 metres will bring you to the gruta – a cave shrine where locals make offerings (take a torch with you). To the left, you reach Paso de Soldado, a picnic site beside a small river after 300 metres. The track goes on; an old man sitting beside it once told us it reaches a place called Ojo de Agua after '1.5 leagues'.

Laguna de Montebello About three km along the dirt road towards Tziscao from the park entrance, a track leads 200 metres left to the Laguna de Montebello, one of the bigger lakes, with a flat, open area along its shore where the track ends. About 150 metres to the left is a stony area which is better for swimming than the muddy fringes elsewhere.

Cinco Lagunas A further three km along the Tziscao road another track leads left to these 'five lakes'. Only four of them are visible from the road, but the second, La Cañada, on the right after about 1.5 km, is probably the most beautiful of all the Montebello lakes; it's also nearly cut in half by two rocky outcrops. The track eventually reaches the village of San Antonio and is, amazingly, a bus route.

A km further along the Tziscao road from the Cinco Lagunas turning, a track leads to Laguna Pojoj, a km north.

Laguna Tziscao This comes into view on the right another km along the road. The junction for Tziscao village is a little further, again on the right. The village has pleasant grassy streets and friendly people.

Beyond Tziscao The road continues five km to **Las Dos Lagunas** on the eastern edge of the national park, then to Santa Elena village, about 30 km from Tziscao. Yet remoter villages lie north of Santa Elena; *Backpacking in Mexico & Central America* (see Books in the Facts for the Visitor chapter) describes a 10-day hike through these villages and plenty of jungle to the Palenque-Bonampak road, 45 km from Bonampak. Buses certainly go from Comitán to Santa Elena; trucks or buses may now go beyond it.

Places to Stay & Eat
Half a km past the Chinkultic turnoff, you can camp or rent a little cabin at *La Orquidea*, a small restaurant on the left of the road. The owner, Señora María Domínguez de Castellanos, better known as Doña María, has helped Guatemalan refugees by buying a nearby farm and turning it over to them. For the cabins, which have electric light but no running water, you pay 10 pesos per person. Meals are a bit less.

Inside the national park, camping is officially allowed only at Laguna Bosque Azul (no fee), the last and biggest of the Lagunas de Colores, where the paved road ends. There are toilets and water here. *Bosque Azul Restaurant*, at the Laguna Bosque Azul car park, serves eggs (7.50 pesos), chiles rellenos or meaty dishes (14 pesos), and drinks, chips and fruit. Outside the restaurant, local cowboys wait, eager to guide you (by horse) to the caves (11 pesos).

Tziscao village has a hostel – the *Albergue Turístico* – where you pay 10 pesos per person for a dormitory bunk or a wooden cabaña, or camp for 4 pesos. The hostel lies on the shore of one of the most beautiful lakes – you can rent a rowing boat – and Guatemala is just a few hundred metres away. Entering the village, turn right beside a corner store soon after you come level with a small church on the hill, and follow the track down towards the lake, then round to the left. The señora will cook up eggs, frijoles and tortillas (7.50 pesos) and there's a fridge full of refrescos. The toilets always seem to be in permanent need of a good clean.

Getting There & Away
It's possible to make a whirlwind tour of Chinkultic and the lakes in a day from San Cristóbal – either by public transport or tour (see Organised Tours in the San Cristóbal de Las Casas section) – but if you prefer a pace that enables you to absorb something of your surroundings, it's better to stay in the lakes or at least at Comitán.

Buses and combis to the Lagos de Montebello go from the yard of Linea Comitán-Montebello at 2 Pte Sur 17B in Comitán. One or other leaves every 20 or 30 minutes up to about 5 pm. They have a number of different destinations so make sure you get one that's going your way.

Most people head initially for Chinkultic, Doña María's (La Orquidea), Lagunas de Colores, Laguna de Montebello or Tziscao. The last vehicle to Tziscao (1¼ hours, 8 pesos) leaves about 2 pm. By combi it's 45 minutes (5 pesos) to Doña María's, the same price to the Chinkultic turnoff or Lagunas de Colores.

The last combi back to Comitán leaves Lagunas de Colores about 4.30 pm.

There's a steady trickle of vehicles through the lakes area, making hitching possible sometimes.

MOTOZINTLA
The small town of Motozintla lies in a deep valley in the Sierra Madre 70 km south-west of Ciudad Cuauhtémoc. A good road leads to it from the Pan-American Highway a few km north of Ciudad Cuauhtémoc, then continues down to Huixtla on the Chiapas coast near Tapachula – a spectacular, unusual trip. Be sure to carry your passport as there are immigration checks along the way. About half a dozen buses of Autotransportes San Francisco Motozintla cover the route daily on their seven-hour Tapachula-Comitán (and vice versa) run, calling at Ciudad Cuauhtémoc.

CIUDAD CUAUHTÉMOC
This 'city' is just a few houses and a comedor or two, but it's the last/first place in Mexico

on the Pan-American Highway. Comitán is 80 km north, San Cristóbal 165 km. Ciudad Cuauhtémoc is the Mexican border post; the Guatemalan one is three km south at La Mesilla. There are taxis (8 pesos), combis and trucks (2.50 pesos) running between the border posts.

Travellers have reported that those who need Guatemalan visas can get them at La Mesilla, but check the latest situation and if in doubt, get your paperwork sorted out in advance at the Guatemalan Consulate in Comitán or the embassy in Mexico City.

There's no bank at this border. Individual moneychangers operate but may give fewer quetzals than a bank would. You should use up all your local money before you get to the border, as the rate of exchange for peso-quetzal transactions is much worse than that for changing dollars.

Getting There & Away

Cristóbal Colón runs two 1st-class buses daily each way between Ciudad Cuauhtémoc and Comitán (9 pesos, 1½ hours), San Cristóbal de Las Casas (20 pesos, three hours) and Tuxtla Gutiérrez (24 pesos, five hours). At the time of writing, departures from the border are at 6 am, 12.30 and 3.30 pm. But it's often easier to use one of the 20 or so daily 2nd-class buses of Autotransportes Tuxtla Gutiérrez or Autotransportes San Francisco Motozintla, between Ciudad Cuauhtémoc and Comitán, and another bus to/from Comitán.

Guatemalan buses depart La Mesilla for main points inside Guatemala such as Huehuetenango, Quetzaltenango (Xela) and Guatemala City. Both Lake Atitlán and Chichicastenango lie off the Huehuetenango-Guatemala City road and if you want to reach them in one day you should be through the border by about 11 am. Before boarding a bus, try to find out when it's leaving and when it reaches your destination. This could save you several hours. For full information on travelling in Guatemala, get a copy of Lonely Planet's *Guatemala, Belize & Yucatán: La Ruta Maya*.

THE SOCONUSCO

The Soconusco is Chiapas' hot, fertile coastal plain, 15 to 35 km wide. Its climate is hot and humid all year round, with plenty of rain from June to October. The steep mountainsides of the Sierra Madre de Chiapas, sweeping up from the coast, provide an excellent climate for the cultivation of coffee, bananas and other crops. Though far less interesting than other parts of Chiapas, the Soconusco has its high points, which you might want to inspect if you're heading through on your way to/from Guatemala.

Arriaga

● *pop: 40,000* ● *alt: 40 metres*

Arriaga, where the Juchitán-Tapachula road meets the Tuxtla Gutiérrez-Tapachula road, has a few suitable lodgings and restaurants, but no good reason for you to stop.

For some reason, quite a few buses end their runs in Arriaga. Happily, the same number start their runs here. The new Central de Autobuses houses all the 1st and 2nd-class buses serving Arriaga. Destinations include:

Juchitán – 135 km, two hours; three Cristóbal Colón 1st-class (12 pesos); many Sur and Fletes y Pasajes/Transportes Oaxaca-Istmo 2nd-class buses (10 pesos)

Mexico City (TAPO) – 900 km, 16 hours; one Cristóbal Colón afternoon 1st-class bus (130 pesos); a Plus (deluxe, 160 pesos) at 6.30 pm; several Fletes Y Pasajes/Transportes Oaxaca-Istmo 2nd-class buses (110 pesos)

Oaxaca – 400 km, seven hours; one Cristóbal Colón 1st-class bus (50 pesos) at 10 pm; a few Sur and Fletes Y Pasajes/Transportes Oaxaca-Istmo 2nd-class buses (44 pesos)

Salina Cruz – 175 km, three hours; several Cristóbal Colón and Sur 1st-class buses (25 pesos)

San Cristóbal de Las Casas – 240 km, five hours; Cristóbal Colón 1st-class buses (25 pesos) every 30 minutes (via Tuxtla); and ATG buses (23 pesos)

Tapachula – 245 km, 3½ hours; seven Cristóbal Colón 1st-class buses (30 pesos); several others courtesy of Sur and ATG

Tonalá – 23 km, 30 minutes; Transportes-Arriaga-Tonalá microbuses every few minutes (3 pesos)

Tuxtla Gutiérrez – 155 km, three hours; Cristóbal Colón 1st-class buses (75 pesos) every hour; ATG 2nd-class buses (63 pesos)

Tonalá

- *pop: 25,000* • *alt: 40 metres*

Twenty-three km south-east of Arriaga on highway 200, Tonalá is the jumping-off point for the laid-back beach spot of Puerto Arista. A tall pre-Hispanic stele in the Tonalá zócalo appears to depict Tláloc, the central Mexican rain god. There's a small regional museum at Hidalgo 77, with some archaeological pieces found in the region.

Orientation & Information

Highway 200 runs north-south through the middle of Tonalá under the name Avenida Hidalgo, forming the west side of the zócalo. Bus stations are several blocks from the centre, at each end of the town on this road.

The tourist office (☎ (966) 3-01-01) is on the ground floor of the Palacio Municipal (look for its clock), on the Hidalgo side of the zócalo. It's open from 9 am to 3 pm and 6 to 8 pm Monday to Friday, and 9 am to 2 pm Saturday.

Tonalá has no great accommodation deals. If you're heading for Puerto Arista, go straight there if you can.

Puerto Arista

Puerto Arista, 18 km south-west of Tonalá, is a km or so of palm shacks and a few more substantial buildings in the middle of a 30-km grey sand beach, where the food's mostly fish, you get through a lot of refrescos, and nothing else happens except the crashing of the Pacific waves...until the weekend, when a few hundred Chiapanecos cruise in from the towns.

Usually, the most action you'll see is when an occasional fishing boat puts out to sea, or a piglet breaks into a trot if a dog gathers the energy to bark at it. The temperature's mostly sweltering if you stray more than a few yards from the shore, and it's humid in summer.

The sea is clean but don't go in more than knee-deep: there's an undertow, and rip tides known as *canales* can sweep you a long way out in a short time. If you get caught, don't fight it by trying to swim straight back to the beach; swim to right or left to escape the rip, then curve in to the beach.

Places to Stay

Turn left at the lighthouse, then take the first right and you come to the *Restaurant Playa Escondida*. Bare little rooms, just about clean and with mosquito nets, cost 22 pesos (shower and toilet separate) or 30 pesos (with private toilet). This and similar places will also rent you a hammock to sleep in or let you sling your own for 8 pesos.

Two blocks in the opposite direction from the lighthouse, then left towards the sea, the seafront *La Puesta del Sol* has big, clean rooms with two double beds, fan and private bath for 100 pesos at the front, 80 pesos behind. Other places on the same 'street' have dirtier rooms at around 30 pesos a single, 55 pesos a double. Off-season you can bargain them down a bit. Also up this end of town is *La Casa Diana*, with a choice of bed, hammock or tent accommodation, which claims to be clean with good food, plenty of fresh water, and rock'n'roll music.

The top place is the *Hotel Arista Bugambilias* (☎ Tonalá 3-07-67), towards the north end of Boulevard Zapotal, where clean, air-con rooms with TV cost 135 pesos each. They're nothing fancy but a step up from everywhere else. The hotel has a pool and a garden reaching to the beach.

Places to Eat

Every second beachfront palapa will serve fried fish, eggs or soup any time of year but for slightly more choice and similar prices try *La Puesta del Sol* on the seafront two blocks north of the lighthouse. A good mojarra grande (a big perch-type fish) with salad and tortillas here is 16 pesos.

Getting There & Away

Colectivo taxis go to Puerto Arista from the corner of Matamoros and 5 de Mayo in Tonalá for 5 pesos per person. They leave when full (six passengers). From Tonalá zócalo, walk two blocks south along the main street, Hidalgo, then turn right down 5 de Mayo for one block to Matamoros.

Transportes Rodulfo Figueroa buses also go from Tonalá to Puerto Arista, about half-hourly from 7 am to 5 pm, for 1.75 pesos.

Continue along 5 de Mayo for one block past the colectivo stop, then turn left on to Juárez. The stop is almost immediately on the right.

Boca del Cielo

About three km from Puerto Arista on the Tonalá road, a turning to the right (southeast) leads to this little fishing settlement at the mouth of an *estero* (estuary) 17 km away. There are some very relaxed palapa seafood restaurants and you can take a launch along the mangrove-fringed estuary or to a beach.

Getting There & Away Rodulfo Figueroa runs a few buses from Tonalá to Boca del Cielo (3.25 pesos, 1¼ hours) each day. From Puerto Arista to Boca del Cielo you could wait for one of these buses at the junction three km inland, or take a taxi for about 28 pesos.

TAPACHULA
* *pop: 220,000*

Most travellers come to Mexico's southernmost city only because it's a gateway to Guatemala, though for ruins buffs Izapa, 11 km east, is worth a visit.

Tapachula is the 'capital' of the Soconusco, and a busy commercial centre. You may notice some blonde Mexicans and Chinese names in Tapachula; these are mostly the descendants of German immigrants from the Nazi era and Kuomintang supporters who fled China in the 1940s. All this, plus the informal dress dictated by the sticky heat, gives the place a livelier atmosphere than most Chiapas towns.

Tapachula is overlooked by the 4092-metre Tacaná volcano to its north-east, the first of a chain of volcanoes stretching down into Guatemala. The village of Unión Juárez, 40 km from Tapachula, supposedly provides good views of the volcano, and the surrounding country has hiking possibilities.

Orientation

The axes of Tapachula's street grid are Avenida Central, running nearly north-south, and Calle Central (east-west), but the large zócalo, Parque Hidalgo, is between Avenidas 6 and 8 Norte, three blocks west of Avenida Central, with Calle 5 Pte on its north side. Accommodation is mostly near the zócalo. Bus stations are scattered north, east and west. Avenidas are even-numbered west of Avenida Central, odd-numbered east of it, and suffixed Norte or Sur depending on whether you're north or south of Calle Central. Calles are even-numbered south of Calle Central, odd-numbered north of it, with the suffix Ote or Pte (East or West).

Information

Tourist Office The tourist office (☎ (962) 6-54-70, fax 6-55-22) is at Avenida 4 Nte 35, a few doors north of Hospedaje Colonial, on the 3rd floor, and has few customers.

Money Several banks around the city centre will change dollars and quetzals, but for a little extra commission. The Casa de Cambio Tapachula on the corner of Calle 3 Pte and Avenida 4 Nte is quicker and open longer – from 7.30 am to 7.30 pm Monday to Saturday and 7 am to 2 pm Sunday.

Post & Telecommunications The post office is several blocks from the centre on the corner of Calle 1 Ote and Avenida 9 Nte and is open 8 am to 6 pm Monday to Friday, 8 am to noon Saturday. Tapachula's postal code is 30700.

There are Lada casetas on Calle 17 Ote, 1½ blocks west of the Cristóbal Colón bus station, and in the Farmacia Monaco across from Hotel Don Miguel on Calle 1 Pte.

Foreign Consulate The Guatemalan Consulate (☎ (962) 6-12-52) is at Calle 2 Ote 33, between Avenidas 7 and 9 Sur. It's open 8 am to 4 pm Monday to Friday. Visas are issued quickly.

Soconusco Regional Museum

The Museo Regional del Soconusco on the west side of the zócalo has archaeological and folklore exhibits, including some finds from Izapa. Entry is 10 pesos.

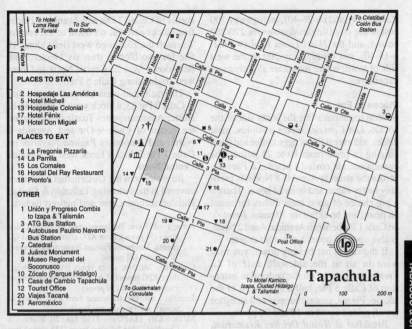

PLACES TO STAY
2 Hospedaje Las Américas
5 Hotel Michell
13 Hospedaje Colonial
17 Hotel Fénix
19 Hotel Don Miguel

PLACES TO EAT
6 La Fregonia Pizzaría
14 La Parrilla
15 Los Comales
16 Hostal Del Ray Restaurant
18 Pronto's

OTHER
1 Unión y Progreso Combis to Izapa & Talismán
3 ATG Bus Station
4 Autobuses Paulino Navarro Bus Station
7 Catedral
8 Juárez Monument
9 Museo Regional del Soconusco
10 Zócalo (Parque Hidalgo)
11 Casa de Cambio Tapachula
12 Tourist Office
20 Viajes Tacaná
21 Aeroméxico

Tapachula

0   100   200 m

Places to Stay – bottom end

The friendly *Hospedaje Las Américas* (☎ (962) 6-27-57), at Avenida 10 Nte 47 north of the zócalo, has rooms with fan and private bath for 23/30 pesos a single/double.

Hospedaje Colonial (☎ (962) 6-20-52), at Avenida 4 Norte 31, half a block north of Calle 3 Pte, has clean, bright rooms with private baths along a balcony for 22 pesos per person. Ring the bell to enter.

Around the corner (one block west) from the Cristóbal Colón bus station is the *Hospedaje Chelito* (☎ (962) 6-24-28), at Avenida 1 Nte 107 between Calle 15 Pte and 17 Pte. Rooms are clean, pink and pretty. For a black and white TV, fan and private bath you pay 55 pesos; for 75 pesos you get a colour TV and air-con. Attached is a small café.

Places to Stay – middle

The *Hotel Santa Julia* (☎ (962) 6-31-40), Calle 17 Ote 5, next door to the Cristóbal Colón 1st-class bus station, has clean singles/doubles with TV, telephone and private bath for 105/125 pesos.

Hotel Fénix (☎ (962) 5-07-55), Avenida 4 Norte 19 near the corner of Calle 1 Pte, a block west of the zócalo, has an encouraging lobby and room service but a mixed bag of medium-sized rooms within. Some fan-cooled ones at 90 pesos are less dilapidated than some air-con ones at 110 pesos. The nearby modern *Hotel Don Miguel* (☎ (962) 6-11-43), at Calle 1 Pte 18, is probably the best city centre hotel. Rooms are clean and bright with air-con and TV for 175/210 pesos. There's a good restaurant here too.

A half-block east of the zócalo, on Calle 5 Pte 23, the *Hotel Michell* (☎ (962) 6-88-74) has comely 2nd and 3rd-storey rooms with air-con, TV, big closets and desks for 130/165 pesos for a single/double.

Places to Stay – top end

The town's two top hotels, both with air-con rooms and swimming pools, are the *Motel*

Kamico (☎ (962) 6-26-40), on highway 200 east of the city (singles/doubles for 220/260 pesos), and the *Hotel Loma Real* (☎ (962) 6-14-40), just off highway 200 on the west side of town, where rooms are slightly more expensive.

Places to Eat

Several restaurants line the south side of the zócalo. *Los Comales* serves antojitos, meat dishes, and a breakfast of eggs, coffee and juice, ranging in price from 10 to 25 pesos. The comida corrida costs 18 pesos. *La Parrilla,* across the street at Avenida 8 Norte, is probably better value, and open 24 hours. There's a big choice of good meat dishes for about 18 pesos, and breakfast for 10 pesos. *Pronto's,* on Calle 1 Pte between Avenidas 4 and 2 Norte, is also open 24 hours but is a bit dearer.

If the sun is not beating down, you may want to sit at the sidewalk café of *La Fregonia Pizzaría,* on the pedestrian extension of Calle 5 Pte, half a block west of the zócalo. Pizzas, pastas, burgers and antojitos are all priced between 10 and 20 pesos.

Breakfast at *Hostal Del Rey Restaurant,* Avenida 4 Norte 17 near Calle 3 Pte, with its quiet music, waiters in pink bow ties and cummerbunds, and pretty decor, is a nice way to begin the day. An early meal of hotcakes, fruit, eggs and coffee costs 18 pesos. Later in the day you may want soup and salad or antojitos for 13 pesos, or aves or carne for 20 to 35 pesos.

Getting There & Away

Air Aeroméxico (☎ 6-20-50) has daily nonstop flights to/from Mexico City: a 1½-hour flight for 380 pesos. Its office is at Avenida 2 Norte No 6. Aviacsa (☎ 6-31-47) flies daily to/from Tuxtla Gutiérrez (40 minutes, 285 pesos) and Mexico City (2½ hours, 380 pesos). Viajes Tulum on Calle 1 Pte between Avenidas 2 and 4 Norte, and Diverti Viajes on the corner of Calle 1 Pte and Avenida Central Norte, sell Aviacsa, Aeroméxico and Mexicana tickets.

Bus Cristóbal Colón is the only 1st-class bus line serving Tapachula. Its terminus is on the corner of Calle 17 Ote and Avenida 3 Norte, five blocks east and six north of the zócalo. To reach the zócalo go west (left) along 17 Ote for two blocks, then six blocks south (left) down Avenida Central Norte and three west (right) along Calle 5 Pte.

The main 2nd-class bus stations are Sur, at Calle 9 Pte 63, a block west of Avenida 12 Norte; Autotransportes Tuxtla Gutiérrez, on the corner of Calle 9 Ote and Avenida 3 Norte; and Autobuses Paulino Navarro, on Calle 7 Pte 5, half a block west of Avenida Central Norte.

Buses to/from the Guatemalan border are covered in the following Talismán & Ciudad Hidalgo section. Other destinations include:

Arriaga – 245 km, 3½ hours; eight Cristóbal Colón buses (34 pesos); three ATG afternoon buses (22 pesos); Autobuses Paulino Navarro buses every 30 minutes (22 pesos)
Comitán – 260 km, seven hours (via Motozintla); three ATG buses (45 pesos); several courtesy of Paulino Navarro (50 pesos)
Juchitán – 380 km, six hours; three ATG buses (44 pesos); several daily Sur buses
Mexico City (TAPO) – 1150 km, 20 hours; six Cristóbal Colón 1st-class buses (155 pesos); two Plus afternoon buses (175 pesos)
Oaxaca – 650 km, 11 hours; two Cristóbal Colón buses (64 pesos); one evening Plus (78 pesos); and one Sur 2nd-class evening bus
Salina Cruz – 420 km, seven hours; two ATG daily buses (55 pesos)
San Cristóbal de Las Casas – 350 km, eight hours; 15 Cristóbal Colón buses (via Tuxtla) (50 pesos); three ATG buses (38 pesos)
Tonalá – 220 km, three hours; eight Cristóbal Colón 1st-class buses daily (26 pesos); three ATG buses (20 pesos); several courtesy of Sur
Tuxtla Gutiérrez – 400 km, seven hours; 15 Cristóbal Colón buses (45 pesos); six ATG buses (36 pesos); two courtesy of Sur

Train The station lies just south of the intersection of Avenida Central Sur and Calle 14. Only masochists, the dull-witted and the hopelessly adventurous take the train.

Getting Around

To/From the Airport Tapachula airport is 18 km south of the city off the Puerto Madero road. Transporte Terrestre (☎ (962) 6-12-87) at Avenida 2 Sur 40-A charges 12 pesos to the airport and will pick you up from any hotel in Tapachula. A taxi costs 28 pesos.

IZAPA

If this site was in a more visited part of Mexico it would have a constant stream of visitors, for it's not only important to archaeologists as a link between the Olmec and the Maya but it's also interesting to walk around. It flourished from approximately 200 BC to 200 AD. The Izapa carving style – typically seen on stelae with altars placed in front – is derived from the Olmec style and most of the gods shown are descendants of Olmec deities, with their upper lips grotesquely lengthened. Early Mayan monuments from lowland north Guatemala are similar.

Northern Area

Most of this part of the site has been cleared and some restoration has been done. There are a number of platforms, a ball court, and several carved stelae and altars. The platforms and ball court were probably built some time after Izapa was at its peak.

Southern Area

This is less visited than the northern area. Go back about 0.75 km along the road towards Tapachula and take a dirt road to the left. Where the vehicle track ends, a path leads to the right. The three areas of interest are separated by less-than-obvious foot trails and you may have to ask the caretaker to find and explain them. One is a plaza with several

A *na*, or Mayan thatched-roof hut

stelae under thatched roofs. The second is a smaller plaza with more stelae and three big pillars topped with curious stone balls. The third is a single carving of jaguar jaws holding a seemingly human figure.

Getting There & Away

Izapa is 11 km east of Tapachula on the road to Talismán. You can reach it by the combis of Unión y Progreso which depart from Calle 5 Pte, half a block west of Avenida 12 Norte in Tapachula. The main (northern) part of the site is marked on the left of the road.

TALISMÁN & CIUDAD HIDALGO

The road from Tapachula to Guatemala heads 20 km east past Izapa to the border at Talismán bridge, opposite El Carmen, Guatemala. A branch south off this road leads to another border crossing at Ciudad Hidalgo (38 km from Tapachula), opposite Ciudad Tecún Umán. Both crossings are open 24 hours.

At the time of writing it was possible to obtain Guatemalan visas as well as tourist cards at the border, but check this in advance; availability may depend upon your nationality. There's a Guatemalan Consulate at Central Ote 10 in Ciudad Hidalgo, as well as the one in Tapachula. The Guatemalan border posts may make various small charges as you go through, and insist on being paid in either dollars or quetzals – so get some before you leave Tapachula.

Getting There & Away

The combis of Unión y Progreso shuttle between Calle 5 Pte in Tapachula (half a block west of Avenida 12 Norte) and Talismán every few minutes for 2.75 pesos. A taxi from Tapachula to Talismán takes 20 minutes and costs 12 pesos.

Autobuses Paulino Navarro makes the 45-minute journey between Tapachula and Ciudad Hidalgo for 4 pesos, every 15 minutes.

There are two daily Cristóbal Colón 1st-class services between Talismán and Mexico City for 155 pesos.

Many of the longer-distance buses leaving the Guatemalan side of the border head for Guatemala City (about five hours away) by the coastal slope route through Retalhuleu and Escuintla. If you're heading for Lake Atitlán or Chichicastenango, you need to get to Quetzaltenango (Xela) first, for which you may have to change buses at Retalhuleu or at Malacatán on the Talismán-San Marcos-Quetzaltenango road. For details of travel in Guatemala, see Lonely Planet's *Guatemala, Belize & Yucatán: La Ruta Maya*.

Tabasco & Chiapas
Top: Na Bolom, San Cristóbal de Las Casas (TW); Temple of the Cross, Palenque (DT)
Bottom: Lagos de Montebello (JN); Templo del Carmen, San Cristóbal de Las Casas (TW)

Tabasco & Chiapas
Top: View of the Palace from the Temple of Inscriptions, Palenque (DT)
Bottom: Cañón del Sumidero (PW)

The Yucatán Peninsula

When you cross the Río Usumacinta into the Yucatán Peninsula, you are crossing into the realm of the Maya. The appearance of the countryside changes, as do the houses and the people in them. Heirs to a glorious and often violent history, the Maya live today where their ancestors lived a millennium ago. The Maya are proud to be Mexican, but even prouder to be Maya, and it is the Mayab (the lands of the Maya) that they consider their true country.

Though it's flat and hot, the Yucatán Peninsula has surprising diversity. There are archaeological sites galore, several handsome colonial cities, Mexico's most popular seaside resort and quiet coastlines populated mostly by exotic tropical birds.

The Yucatán Peninsula's rainy season is from mid-August to mid-October. During this time it's normal for an afternoon shower to come down most days. A good time to visit is in November and early December, when it's less crowded and less pricey.

HISTORY
The Maya

At the height of Mayan culture during the Late Classic Period (600 to 900 AD), the Mayan lands were ruled not as an empire but as a collection of independent but also interdependent city-states. Each city-state had its noble house, headed by a king who was the social, political and religious centre of the city's life.

By the end of the Late Classic Period, the focus of Mayan civilisation had shifted from Guatemala and Belize to the northern part of the Yucatán Peninsula, where a new civilisation developed at Chichén Itzá, Uxmal and Labná.

In the 9th and 10th centuries, during the Early Postclassic Period, classic Mayan civilisation collapsed. Weakened, the Maya were prey to a wave of invaders from central Mexico. It's thought that Toltecs from Tula (near present-day Mexico City) sailed eastwards to the Yucatán Peninsula. They

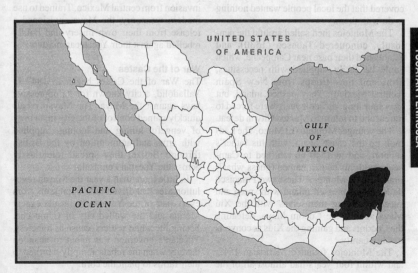

were led by a fair-haired, bearded king named Kukulcán or Quetzalcóatl, who established himself in Yucatán at Uucil-abnal (Chichén Itzá). He left behind in Mexico, and then in Yucatán, a legend that he would one day return from the direction of the rising sun. The culture at Uucil-abnal flourished after the late 10th century, when all of the great buildings were constructed, but by the 14th century the city was abandoned.

For more on Mayan history and culture, see the Maya and Toltecs sections under History in the Facts About the Country chapter at the beginning of the book.

The Spaniards

Cortés's expedition of 1519, departing from Cuba, first made landfall at Cozumel off the Yucatán Peninsula. After their conquest of central Mexico, the Spaniards turned their attention to the Yucatán Peninsula. The Spanish monarch commissioned Francisco de Montejo (El Adelantado, The Pioneer) with the task of conquest, and he set out from Spain in 1527 accompanied by his son, also named Francisco de Montejo. Landing first at Cozumel on the Caribbean coast, then at Xel-ha on the mainland, the Montejos discovered that the local people wanted nothing to do with them.

The Montejos then sailed around the peninsula, conquered Tabasco (1530), and established their base near Campeche, which could be easily supplied with necessities, arms and new troops from New Spain (central Mexico). They pushed inland, but after four long, difficult years were forced to retreat and to return to Mexico City in defeat.

The younger Montejo (El Mozo, The Lad) took up the cause again, with his father's support, and in 1540 he returned to Campeche with his cousin named (guess what?) Francisco de Montejo. These two Francisco de Montejos pressed inland with speed and success, allying themselves with the Xiú Maya against the Cocom Maya, defeating the Cocoms and gaining the Xiús as converts to Christianity.

The Montejos founded Mérida in 1542, and within four years had almost all of the Yucatán Peninsula subjugated to Spanish rule. The once proud and independent Maya became peons, working for Spanish masters without hope of deliverance except in heaven.

Independence Period

When Mexico finally won its independence from Spain in 1821, the new Mexican government urged the peoples of the Yucatán Peninsula, Chiapas and Central America to join it in the formation of one large new state. Central America went its own way but the Yucatán Peninsula and Chiapas, after some flirtation with Guatemala, joined Mexico.

Mayan claims to ancestral lands were largely ignored and the criollos (descendants of the Spanish colonists) created huge plantations for the cultivation of tobacco, sugar cane and henequén (agave). The Maya, though legally free, were enslaved by debt peonage to the great landowners.

Not long after independence, the Yucatecan ruling classes again dreamed of independence, this time from Mexico, and perhaps of union with the USA. With these goals in mind, the *hacendados* made the mistake of arming and training their Mayan peons as local militias in anticipation of an invasion from central Mexico. Trained to use modern weaponry, the Maya envisioned a release from their own misery and boldly rebelled against their Yucatecan masters.

War of the Castes

The War of the Castes began in 1847 in Valladolid, a city known for its oppressive laws against the Maya. The Mayan rebels quickly gained control of the city in an orgy of vengeful killing and looting. Supplied with arms and ammunition by the British through Belize, they spread relentlessly across the Yucatán Peninsula.

In little more than a year the Mayan revolutionaries had driven their oppressors from every part of the Yucatán Peninsula except Mérida and the walled city of Campeche. Seeing the white settlers' cause as hopeless, Yucatán's governor was about to abandon the city when the rebels abruptly returned to their farms to plant the corn.

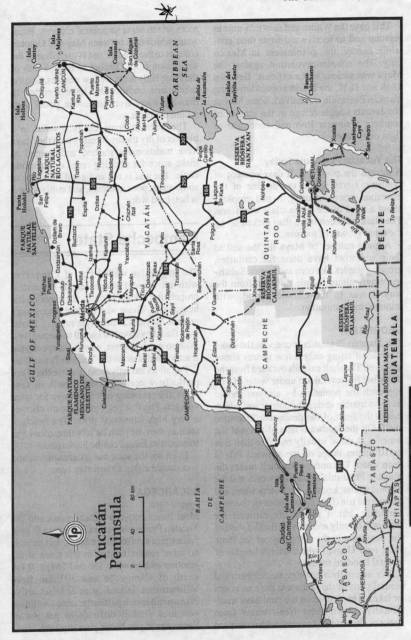

Yucatán Peninsula

CARIBBEAN SEA

Isla Contoy
Isla Mujeres
Isla Cozumel
San Miguel de Cozumel

Chiquilá
Puerto Juárez
CANCÚN
Kantunil Kin
Puerto Morelos
Playa del Carmen

Isla Holbox

Bahía de la Ascención

Bahía del Espíritu Santo

Banco Chinchorro

Akumal
Xel-Ha
Tulum
Tulum

RESERVA BIÓSFERA SIAN KA'AN

Río Lagartos
San Felipe
PARQUE NATURAL RÍO LAGARTOS

Cobá
Chemax
Popolnah
Nuevo Xcan
Valladolid

Felipe Carrillo Puerto

Acalak
Ambergris Caye
San Pedro
CHETUMAL
Consejo
Corozal
Orange Walk

Punta Hololoh

Tizimín
Espita
Dzitas

Chichén Itzá

Tinsuco

Laguna Kana

Bacalar
Cenote Azul
Xul-Ha
Caldeitas
Calderitas
Consejo

BELICE
BELIZE

To Belize

Río Hondo

PARQUE NATURAL SAN FELIPE

Dzilam de Bravo

Buctzotz
Kantunil
Izamal

Peto
Santa Rosa
Bencanchén

Polyuc

Nohbec

Kohunlich

QUINTANA ROO

Telchac Puerto
Progreso
Chicxulub
Dzibilchaltún

Motul
Acanceh
Telchaquillo
Yaxcaba

Santa Elena

Xpujil

RESERVA BIÓSFERA CALAKMÚL

GULF OF MEXICO

Sisal
Yucalpetén
Hunucmá
Kinchil

MÉRIDA
Umán
Hoctún

Izamal

Tixkokob
Mayapán
Tekax
Xlapak
Sayil
Kabah
Bolonchén de Relón
Hopelchén

Dzibalchén

Xmaben
V Guerrero

RESERVA BIÓSFERA CALAKMÚL

Río Bec

PARQUE NATURAL FLAMENCO MEXICANO DE CELESTÚN

Celestún

Maxcanú
Muna
Ticul
Uxmal
Oxkutzcab
Tzucacab

Becal
Calkiní
Tenabo

CAMPECHE

Edzná

Tenabo
Sihochac
Champotón

YUCATÁN

BAHÍA DE CAMPECHE

Isla Aguada
Isla del Carmen
Zacatal
Ciudad del Carmen
Laguna de Términos

Sabancuy
Escárcega
Candelaria

Río

Laguna Misteriosa

GUATEMALA

RESERVA BIÓSFERA MAYA

Sabancuy
Puerto Real

CAMPECHE

TABASCO
CHIAPAS

Frontera
VILLAHERMOSA
Jonuta
Macuspana
Catazajá

San Pedro

TABASCO

YUCATÁN PENINSULA

0   40   80 km

LP

This gave the Whites and mestizos time to regroup and to receive aid from their erstwhile enemy, the government in Mexico City. The counter-revolution against the Maya was vicious in the extreme. Between 1848 and 1855, the Indian population of the Yucatán Peninsula was halved. Some Mayan combatants sought refuge in the jungles of southern Quintana Roo and continued to fight until 1866.

The Yucatán Peninsula Today

Although the post-WW II development of synthetic fibres led to the decline of the henequén (rope) industry, it still employs about a third of the peninsula's workforce. The slack has been more than picked up by the rapid growth of tourism.

A good number of Maya till the soil as their ancestors have done for centuries, growing staples like corn and beans. Subsistence agriculture is little different from the way it was in the Classic period, with minimal mechanisation.

GEOGRAPHY

The Yucatán Peninsula is one vast flat limestone shelf rising only a few metres above sea level. The shelf extends outward from the shoreline for several km under water. If you approach the peninsula by air, you should have no trouble seeing the barrier reef which marks the limit of the peninsular limestone shelf. On the landward side of the reef the water is shallow, usually no more than five or 10 metres deep; on the seaward side is deep water. The underwater shelf makes the Yucatán Peninsula's coastline wonderful for aquatic sports, keeping the waters warm and the marine life (fish, crabs, lobsters, tourists) abundant, but it makes life difficult for traders. The only anomaly on the flat shelf of the peninsula is the low range of the Puuc Hills near Uxmal, which attains heights of several hundred metres.

Because of their geology, the northern and central parts of the peninsula have no rivers or lakes. The people on the land have traditionally drawn their fresh water from cenotes, limestone caverns with collapsed roofs which serve as natural cisterns. Rainwater which falls between May and October collects in the cenotes and is used during the dry season from October to May. South of the Puuc Hills there are few cenotes, and the inhabitants traditionally have resorted to drawing water from limestone pools deep within the earth.

The Yucatán Peninsula is covered in a blanket of dry thorny forest, which the Maya have traditionally slashed and burned to make space for planting crops or pasturing cattle. The soil is red and good for crops in some areas, poor in others, and cultivating it is hot, hard work.

Campeche State

The impressive walled city of Campeche, with its ancient fortresses or baluartes, propels the visitor back to the days of the buccaneers. Those who explore the region's ancient Mayan Chenes-style ruins of Edzná may find they have the site all to themselves. With so much interest, why is Campeche the least-visited state in the Yucatán Peninsula?

For all its attractiveness, Campeche is not particularly tourist-friendly. Hotels are few, often disappointing and expensive for what you get. The fine regional museum charges a very high admission price. The beaches, such as they are, can be less than clean and transport to Edzná can be haphazard.

Even so, the state has its attractions, and you should enjoy a short stay here.

ESCÁRCEGA

• *pop: 18,000*

Most buses between Villahermosa and the Yucatán Peninsula stop in Escárcega to give passengers a refreshment break, but there is no other reason to stop in this town at the junction of highways 186 and 261, 150 km south of Campeche and 301 km from Villahermosa. Indeed, as most buses arrive in town full and depart in the same condition, you may find it difficult to get out of Escárcega if you break your trip here.

The town is spread out along two km of highway 186 toward Chetumal. It's 1.7 km between the ADO and Autobuses del Sur bus stations. Most hotels are nearer to the Autobuses del Sur bus station than to the ADO; most of the better restaurants are near the ADO bus station.

XPUJIL & SURROUNDS

Highway 186 heads due east from Escárcega through the scrubby jungle to Chetumal in the state of Quintana Roo, a 2½-hour ride (32 pesos). Right on the border between Campeche and Quintana Roo near the village of Xpujil, 153 km east of Escárcega and 120 km west of Chetumal, are several important Mayan archaeological sites: Xpujil, Becan, Chicanna and Río Bec.

These pristine unrestored sites, largely free of tourists, will fascinate true ruins buffs, but be forewarned that those expecting park-like sites such as Uxmal and Chichén Itzá will be disappointed. Most of what you see here is jungle and rubble.

Orientation

The village of Xpujil is the landmark where the buses stop. The Xpujil ruins are visible from the highway; those of Becan are eight km west of Xpujil and 200 metres north of the highway. Chicanna, 2.5 km to the west of Becan, is only about 500 metres south of the highway. If you want to do all these ruins in a day, hop on an early bus from Escárcega, cajole the driver to drop you at Chicanna, go on to Becan, then Xpujil and wait here in the village for a bus to take you onward to Chetumal, or return to Escárcega. If the driver won't stop (as is usual), you'll have to start your explorations in the village of Xpujil.

Xpujil

The latticed towers of Xpujil's pyramid greet you as you explore the village. This temple is the only truly excavated building on the site. It is built in the Río Bec style (see below). There are two sculpted masks carved into the rear of the temple. New excavations are under way. The site flourished from 400 to 900 AD, though there was a settlement here much earlier.

Becan

Becan means 'Path of the Snake' in Maya. It is well named, as a two-km moat snakes its way around the entire city to protect it from attack. Seven bridges used to provide access to the city. Becan was inhabited from 550 BC until 1000 AD.

Still to be excavated from Becan's profuse jungle cover are subterranean rooms and passages linked to religious ritual. Archaeologists have dug up some artefacts from Teotihuacán here, but still must determine whether they got here through trade or conquest. There's little to thrill the eye, though a few of the monumental staircases stimulate the imagination.

Chicanna

Buildings at Chicanna are in a mixture of Chenes and Río Bec styles. The city flourished about 660 to 680 AD, when the eight-room 'palace' here was probably occupied by nobles. The palace's monster-mask façade symbolises Itzamná, the Mouth of the Serpent. Each inner room in the palace has a raised bench of stone; the other rooms show signs of having had curtains draped across their doorways for privacy.

Río Bec

This site actually includes about 10 groups of buildings placed here and there in a site of 50 sq km. The sites are difficult to reach; a 4WD and guide are recommended.

Río Bec gave its name to the prevalent architectural style of the region characterised by long, low buildings that look as though they're divided into sections, each with a huge serpent-mouth for a door. The façades are decorated with smaller masks, geometric designs and columns. At the corners of the buildings are tall, solid towers with extremely small, steep steps, topped by small temples. Many of these towers have roofcombs as well.

CAMPECHE

• *pop: 185,000*

Filled with historic buildings, the centre of Campeche is quite appealing. Local people make their living fishing for shrimp or digging for oil, and the prosperity brought by those two activities is apparent in the town.

Originally part of the state of Yucatán, Campeche became an autonomous state of Mexico in 1863.

History

Once a Mayan trading village called Ah Kim Pech (Lord Sun Sheep-Tick), Campeche was invaded by the conquistadors in 1517. The Maya resisted and for nearly a quarter of a century the Spaniards were unable to fully conquer the region. Campeche was founded in 1531, but later abandoned due to Mayan hostility. By 1540 the conquistadors had gained sufficient control, under the leadership of Francisco de Montejo the Younger, to found a settlement here which survived. They named it the Villa de San Francisco de Campeche. The settlement soon flourished as the major port of the Yucatán Peninsula, but suffered from pirate attacks from an early date. After a particularly appalling attack in

1663 which left the city in ruins, the Spanish crown ordered construction of Campeche's famous baluartes which put an end to the periodic carnage.

Orientation

Though the baluartes still stand, the city walls themselves have been razed and replaced by streets which ring the city centre just as the walls once did. This is the Avenida Circuito Baluartes, or Circular Avenue of the Bulwarks.

Besides the modern Plaza Moch-Cuouh, Campeche also has its Parque Principal, also called the Plaza de la Independencia, the standard Spanish colonial park with the cathedral on one side and former Palacio de Gobierno on another.

According to the compass, Campeche is oriented with its waterfront to the north-west, but tradition and convenience hold that the water is to the west, inland is east. The street grid is numbered so that streets running north-south have even numbers, while east-west streets have odd numbers; street numbers ascend towards the south and the west.

Information

Tourist Office The State Tourism Office

Pirates vs Campeche

As early as the mid-1500s, Campeche was flourishing as the Yucatán Peninsula's major port under the careful planning of Viceroy Hernández de Córdoba. Locally grown timber, chicle and dyewoods were major exports to Europe, as were gold and silver mined from other regions and shipped from Campeche.

Such wealth did not escape the notice of pirates, who arrived looking to share the wealth only six years after the town was founded.

For two centuries, the depredations of pirates terrorised Campeche. Not only were ships attacked, but the port itself was invaded, its citizens robbed, its women raped and its buildings burned. In the buccaneers' Hall of Fame were the infamous John Hawkins, Diego the Mulatto, Laurent de Gaff, Barbillas and the notorious 'Pegleg' himself, Pato de Palo. In their most gruesome of assaults, in early 1663, the various pirate hordes set aside their jealousies to converge upon the city as a single flotilla, massacring many of Campeche's citizens in the process.

It took this tragedy to make the Spanish monarchy take preventive action, but not until five years later. Starting in 1668, 3.5-metre-thick ramparts were built. After 18 years of construction, a 2.5-km hexagon incorporating eight strategically placed baluartes surrounded the city. A segment of the ramparts extended out to sea so that ships literally had to sail into a fortress, easily defended, to gain access to the city.

With Campeche nearly impregnable, the pirates turned their attention to ships at sea and other ports. In response, in 1717, the brilliant naval strategist Felipe de Aranda started attacking the buccaneers and in time made the Gulf safe from piracy. ∎

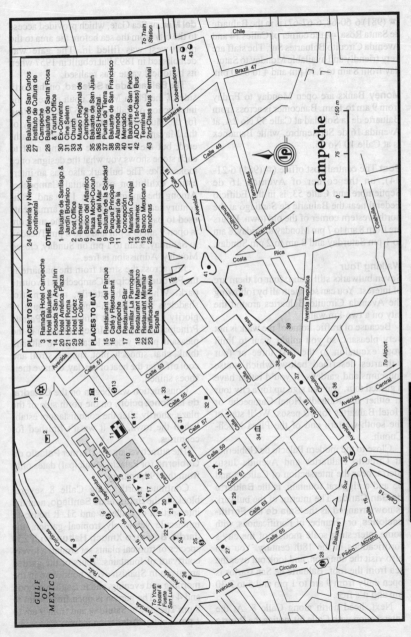

Campeche

PLACES TO STAY

3 Ramada Hotel Campeche
4 Hotel Baluartes
14 Posada San Angel Inn
20 Hotel América Plaza
21 Hotel Roma
29 Hotel López
32 Hotel Colonial

PLACES TO EAT

15 Restaurant del Parque
16 Café y Restaurant
   Campeche
17 Restaurant-Bar
   Familiar La Parroquia
18 Restaurant Marganzo
22 Restaurant Miramar
23 Panificadora Nueva
   España

24 Cafetería y Nevería
   Continental

OTHER

1 Baluarte de Santiago &
  Jardín Botánico
2 Post Office
5 Bancomer
6 Banco del Atlántico
7 Plaza Moch-Cuouh
8 Puerta del Mar
9 Baluarte de la Soledad
10 Parque Principal
11 Catedral de la
   Concepción
12 Mansión Carvajal
13 Banamex
19 Banco Mexicano
25 Banobras

26 Baluarte de San Carlos
27 Instituto de Cultura de
   Campeche
28 Baluarte de Santa Rosa
   & Tourist Office
30 Ex-Convento
31 Cine Selem
33 Church
34 Museo Regional de
   Campeche
35 Baluarte de San Juan
36 IMSS Hospital
37 Puerta de Tierra
38 Baluarte de San Francisco
39 Mercado
40 Baluarte de San Pedro
41 ADO (1st-Class) Bus
   Terminal
42 Banamex
43 2nd-Class Bus Terminal

YUCATÁN PENINSULA

(☎ (981) 6-60-68, 6-67-67) is in the Baluarte de Santa Rosa, on the corner of Calles 14 and Avenida Circuito Baluartes Sur. The staff are very friendly and available Monday to Saturday from 8 am to 2.30 pm and 4 to 8.30 pm.

Money Banks are open Monday to Friday from 9 am to 1 pm. Bancomer is across from Baluarte de la Soledad at Calle 59 No 2A, at Avenida 16 de Septiembre, while Banamex is at Calle 10 No 15.

Post The central post office (☎ (981) 6-21-34), on the corner of Avenida 16 de Septiembre and Calle 53, is in the Edificio Federal near the Baluarte de Santiago at the north-western corner of the old town. Hours are from 8 am to 7 pm Monday to Friday, 8 am to 1 pm Saturday and 8 am to 2 pm Sunday.

Walking Tour

Seven bulwarks still stand; four of them are of interest. You can see them all by following the Avenida Circuito Baluartes around the city on a two-km walk.

Because of traffic, some of the walk is not very pleasant, so you might want to limit your excursion to the first three or four baluartes described below, which house museums and gardens. If you'd rather have a guided tour, you can sign up for a city tour at either the Ramada Hotel Campeche or Hotel Baluartes for 70 pesos. We'll start at the south-western end of the Plaza Moch-Cuouh.

Close to the modern Palacio de Gobierno, at Circuito Baluartes and Avenida Justo Sierra, near the intersection of Calles 8 and 65 and a ziggurat fountain, is the **Baluarte de San Carlos**. The interior of the bulwark is now arranged as the **Sala de las Fortificaciones**, or Chamber of Fortifications, with some interesting scale models of the city's fortifications in the 18th century. You can also visit the dungeon, and look out over the sea from the roof. Baluarte de San Carlos is open daily from 9 am to 1 pm and 5 to 7.30 pm and it's free.

Next, head north along Calle 8. At the intersection with Calle 59, notice the **Puerta**

del Mar, or Sea Gate, which provided access to the city from the sea before the area to the north-west was filled in. The gate was demolished in 1893 but rebuilt in 1957 when its historical value was realised.

The **Baluarte de la Soledad**, on the north side of the Plaza Moch-Cuouh close to the intersection of Calles 8 and 57, is the setting for the **Museo de Estelas Maya**. Many of the Mayan artefacts here are badly weathered, but the precise line drawing next to each stone shows you what the designs once looked like. The bulwark also has an interesting exhibition of colonial Campeche. Among the antiquities are 17th and 18th-century seafaring equipment and armaments used to battle pirate invaders. The museum is open 9 am to 2 pm and 3 to 8 pm Tuesday to Saturday, 9 am to 1 pm on Sunday, closed Monday. Admission is free.

Just across the street from the baluarte is the **Parque Principal**, Campeche's favourite park. Whereas the sterile, modernistic, shadeless Plaza Moch-Cuouh was built to glorify its government builders, the Parque Principal (Plaza de la Independencia) is the pleasant place where locals go to sit and think, chat, smooch, plot, snooze, stroll and cool off after the heat of the day, or have their shoes shined.

Construction was begun on the **Catedral de la Concepción**, on the north side of the plaza, shortly after the conquistadors established the town, but it wasn't finished for centuries.

The attractive, arcaded former **Palacio de Gobierno** (or Palacio Municipal) dates only from the 19th century.

Continue north along Calle 8 several blocks to the **Baluarte de Santiago**, near the intersection of Calles 8 and 51. It houses a minuscule yet lovely tropical garden, the **Jardín Botánico Xmuch Haltun**, with 250 species of tropical plants set around a lovely courtyard of fountains. Tours of the garden are given in Spanish every hour or so in the morning and evening, and in English at noon and 4 pm. The garden is open from 9 am to 8 pm Tuesday to Saturday and from 9 am to 1 pm Sunday. Admission is free.

From the Baluarte de Santiago, walk east (inland) along Calle 51 to Calle 18, where you'll come to the **Baluarte de San Pedro**, in the middle of a complex traffic intersection which marks the beginning of the Avenida Gobernadores. Within the bulwark is the **Exposición Permanente de Artesanías**, a regional exhibition of crafts, open Monday to Friday from 9 am to 1 pm and 5 to 8 pm. Admission is free.

To make the entire circuit, head south from the Baluarte de San Pedro along the Avenida Circuito Baluartes to the **Baluarte de San Francisco** at Calle 57 and, a block farther along at Calle 59, the **Puerta de Tierra**, or Land Gate. The **Baluarte de San Juan**, at Calles 18 and 65, marks the southwesternmost point of the old city walls. From here you bear right (south-west) along Calle 67 (Avenida Circuito Baluartes) to the intersection of Calles 14 and 67 and the **Baluarte de Santa Rosa**.

Museo Regional de Campeche

The Regional Museum (☎ 6-91-11) is set up in the former mansion of the Teniente del Rey, or King's Lieutenant, at Calle 59 No 36, between Calles 14 and 16. Architecture, hydrology, commerce, art, religion and Mayan science are all dealt with in interesting and revealing displays.

Hours are from 8 am to 2 pm and 2.30 to 8 pm Tuesday to Saturday, and from 9 am to 1 pm Sunday. Admission is an unreasonable 20 pesos.

Mansión Carvajal

Campeche's commercial success as a port town is evident in its stately houses and mansions. Perhaps the most striking of these is the Mansión Carvajal, on Calle 10 between Calles 51 and 53, mid-block on the left (west) side of the street as you come from the Plaza de la Independencia.

It started its eventful history as the city residence of Don Fernando Carvajal Estrada and his wife Sra María Iavalle de Carvajal. Don Fernando was among Campeche's richest hacendados, or hacienda-owners. The monogram you see throughout the

building, 'RCY', is that of Rafael Carvajal Ytorralde, Don Fernando's father and founder of the fortune.

Mansión Carvajal

Other Sights

Walk through Campeche's streets – most especially Calles 55, 57 and 59 – looking for more beautiful houses. The walk is best done in the evening when the sun is not blasting down and when the lights from inside illuminate courtyards, salons and alleys.

Forts

Four km south of the Plaza Moch-Cuouh along the coast road stands the Fuerte de San Luis, an 18th-century fortress of which only a few battlements remain. Near the fort, a road off to the left (south-east) climbs the hill one km to the Fuerte de San Miguel, a restored fortress now closed to the public. The view of the city and the sea is beautiful, but the walk uphill is a killer.

To reach the Fuerte de San Luis, take a 'Lerma' or 'Playa Bonita' bus south-west along the coastal highway (toward Villahermosa); the hostel is out this way as well (see Places to Stay).

Beaches

Campeche's beaches are not particularly inviting. The **Balneario Popular**, four km south of the Plaza Moch-Cuouh along the coastal road just past the Fuerte de San Luis, should be avoided. A few km farther along is **Playa Bonita**, which has some facilities (including restaurant, lockers, toilets) but water of questionable cleanliness and, at the weekends, wall-to-wall local flesh.

If you're really keen for a swim, head south-west to the town of **Seybaplaya**, 33 km from Plaza Moch-Cuouh. The highway skirts narrow, pure-white beaches dotted with fishing shacks, the water is much cleaner, but there are no facilities. The best beach here is called **Payucan**.

Edzná Ruins Tours

Should you want to visit the ruins at Edzná from Campeche, you can go on a tour organised by one of the larger hotels (about 80 pesos). See the upcoming section on Edzná for more information.

Places to Stay – bottom end

Campeche's *Hostel* (☎ (981) 6-18-02), on Avenida Agustín Melgar, is 3.5 km south-west of the Plaza Moch-Cuouh off the shore road; the shore road is Avenida Ruiz Cortines in town, but changes its name to Avenida Resurgimiento as it heads out of town toward Villahermosa. Buses marked 'Lerma' or 'Playa Bonita' will take you there. Ask the driver to let you off at the Albergue de la Juventud and you'll cross some train tracks and pass a Coca-Cola/Cristal bottling plant before coming to the intersection with Avenida Agustín Melgar, near which the bus will drop you. Melgar is unmarked, of course. Look for the street going left (inland) between a Pemex fuel station and a VW dealership – that's Melgar. The hostel is 150 metres up on the right-hand side.

It is actually a university youth-and-sports facilities complex. To find the hostel section, walk into the compound entrance and out to the large courtyard with swimming pool, turn left and walk 25 metres to the dormitory building. The rate is less than 14 pesos per person per night. There is a cafeteria which serves inexpensive meals.

Places to Stay – middle

The cheapest hotels – *Reforma, Castelmar, Roma* – are dumps. *Hotel Colonial* (☎ (981) 6-22-22), Calle 14 No 122, between Calles 55 and 57, offers much more comfort for just a bit more money. The hotel was once the mansion of Doña Gertrudis Eulalia Torostieta y Zagasti, former Spanish governor of Tabasco and Yucatán. The well-furnished rooms have fans and good showers with hot water. The price is 72/90/108 pesos a single/double/triple.

Hotel América Plaza (☎ (981) 6-45-88, fax 1-16-18), Calle 10 No 252, is a fine colonial house with large rooms overlooking the interior court costing a somewhat expensive 120/130 pesos a single/double with fan.

Posada San Angel Inn (☎ (981) 6-77-18), Calle 10 No 307, between Calles 55 and 53, has rooms which remind one of a cell block, but they're modern and clean, with fan for 110 pesos a double, 130 with air-con.

Hotel López (☎ 6-33-44), Calle 12 No 189, between Calles 61 and 63, is not as well kept as it should be to charge 140 pesos a double.

Places to Stay – top end

The best hotel in town is the 119-room *Ramada Hotel Campeche* (☎ (981) 6-22-33), Avenida Ruiz Cortines No 51. Prices are 360/400/450 pesos a single/double/triple.

Just south of the Ramada is its competition, the older but still comfortable *Hotel Baluartes* (☎ (981) 6-39-11). The Baluartes' well-used rooms are air-con and comfortable, with sea views, and cheaper at 225/245 pesos a single/double.

Places to Eat

Inexpensive Among the best eateries is the *Restaurant Marganzo* (☎ 6-23-28), Calle 8 No 265, between Calles 57 and 59, facing the sea and the Baluarte de la Soledad. Breakfast costs 7 to 14 pesos, sandwiches 12 to 16 pesos; seafood is more than twice that much.

Cafetería y Nevería Continental (☎ 6-22-66), Calle 61 No 2, on the corner of Calle 8, serves ice cream, cakes, desserts and drinks, but they have a few items from which to make a good, cheap lunch: filete de pescado, for example, or the hearty soup named caldo xochitl.

If you'd just like to pick up some sweet rolls, biscuits, bread or cakes, head for the *Panificadora Nueva España*, Calle 10 on the corner of Calle 61, which has a large assortment of fresh baked goods at very low prices.

The *Café y Restaurant Campeche* (☎ 6-21-28), Calle 57 No 2, opposite Parque Principal, is in the building which saw the birth of Justo Sierra, founder of Mexico's national university, but the restaurant is very simple, bright with fluorescent light bulbs and loud with a blaring TV. The *platillo del día* usually costs less than 14 pesos.

In the same block facing the plaza is the *Restaurant del Parque* (☎ 6-02-40), Calle 57 No 8, a cheerful little place serving fish, meat and shrimp. It opens early for breakfast.

Mid-Range *Restaurant Miramar* (☎ 6-28-83), corner of Calles 8 and 61, specialises in Campeche's seafood. Full meals cost between 45 and 70 pesos. It's open from 8 am to midnight Monday to Friday, till 1 am Saturday, and from 11 am to 7 pm Sunday.

Perhaps the best known restaurant in town is the *Restaurant-Bar Familiar La Parroquía* (☎ 6-80-86), Calle 59 No 8. The complete family restaurant-café-hangout, La Parroquía serves breakfasts priced at 8 to 13 pesos from 7 to 10 am Monday to Friday and substantial lunch and dinner fare like chuleta de cerdo (pork chop), filete a la tampiqueña, shrimp cocktail or shrimp salad and even fresh pampano, for 16 to 40 pesos.

Entertainment
On Friday evenings at 8 pm (weather permitting) from September to May, the state tourism authorities sponsor Estampas Turísticas – performances of folk music and dancing – in the Plaza Moch-Cuouh. Other performances, sponsored by the city government, take place in the Parque Principal on Thursday, Friday and Saturday evenings at about 7 pm. Be sure to confirm these times and places with the tourist office.

Getting There & Away
Air The airport is west of the train station at the end of Avenida López Portillo (Avenida Central), across the tracks about 800 metres away, or 3.5 km from Plaza Moch-Cuouh. You must take a taxi (18 pesos) to the city centre.

Bus Campeche's 1st-class ADO bus terminal is on Avenida Gobernadores, 1.7 km from Plaza Moch-Cuouh, or about 1.5 km from most hotels. The 2nd-class terminal is directly behind it. For village buses to Cayal, Pich and Hool (for Edzná), go to the market at the eastern end of Calle 53 across Avenida Circuito Baluartes Este.

Here's information on daily buses from Campeche:

Cancún – 512 km, nine hours; many buses; change at Mérida

Chetumal – 422 km, seven hours; three 1st-class buses (60 pesos) by ADO

Edzná – 66 km, 1½ hours; irregular village bus service from the market; it is possible to take a faster 1st or 2nd-class bus to San Antonio Cayal (45 km), but you'd have to hitch south the remaining 20 km

Mérida – 195 km (short route via Becal), three hours; 250 km (long route via Uxmal), four hours; 33 1st-class buses (30 pesos) by ADO around the clock; 13 2nd-class buses (24 pesos) by Autobuses del Sur

Mexico City (TAPO) – 1360 km, 21 hours; two 1st-class buses (190 pesos) by ADO

Palenque – 362 km, 5½ hours; one 1st-class (50 pesos) direct bus by ADO at 6.30 pm; many other buses drop you at Catazajá (Palenque turnoff), 27 km north of Palenque village

San Cristóbal de Las Casas – 820 km, 14 hours; change at Palenque or Villahermosa

Villahermosa – 450 km, seven hours; 15 1st-class buses (55 pesos) stopping at Catazajá (Palenque junction) on the way

Train The train station is three km north-east of the city centre, south of Avenida Gobernadores on Avenida Héroes de Nacozari in the district called Colonia Cuatro Caminos. Buses departing from a stop to the right (west) as you leave the station will take you to the centre.

CAMPECHE TO MÉRIDA – SHORT ROUTE (HIGHWAY 180)

This is the fastest way to go and if you simply buy a bus ticket from Campeche to Mérida your bus will follow this route. If you'd prefer to go the long way via Edzná, Kabah and Uxmal, you must ask for a seat on one of the less frequent long-route buses. If you'd like to stop at one of the towns along the short route, catch a 2nd-class bus.

Hecelchakan, Calkini & Becal

At Hecelchakan, 77 km north-east of Campeche, is the **Museo Arqueológico del Camino Real**, where you will find some burial artefacts from the island of Jaina, as well as ceramics and jewellery from other sites. The museum is open from Monday to Saturday from 9 am to 6 pm, closed Sunday. The **Church of San Francisco** is the centre of festivities on the saint's day, 4 October. From 9 to 18 August a popular festival called the Novenario is held, with bullfights, dancing and refreshments.

After Hecelchakan, it's 24 km to Calkini, site of the 17th-century **Church of San Luis de Tolosa**, with a plateresque portal and lots of baroque decoration. Each year the Festival of San Luis is celebrated on 19 August.

Becal is eight km from Calkini just before you enter the state of Yucatán. It is a centre of the Yucatán Peninsula's Panama hat trade. The soft, pliable hats, called *jipijapa* by the locals, have been woven by townsfolk from the fibres of the huano palm tree in humid limestone caves since the mid-19th century. The caves provide just the right atmosphere for shaping the fibres, keeping them pliable and minimising breakage.

From Becal it's 85 km to Mérida.

CAMPECHE TO MÉRIDA – LONG ROUTE (HIGHWAY 261)

Most travellers take the long route (highway 261) from Campeche to Mérida, in order to visit the various ruin sites.

Edzná

The closest ruins to Campeche are at Edzná, south of highway 261.

Edzná, meaning House of Grimaces or House of Echoes, may well have been host to both, as there has been a settlement here since about 800 BC. Most of the carvings are of a much later date: 550 to 810 AD. Though a long way from such Puuc Hill sites as Uxmal and Kabah, some of the architecture here is similar to Puuc style.

The site is open daily from 8 am to 5 pm, for 14 pesos admission.

Although the archaeological zone covers two sq km, the best part is the main plaza, 160 metres long and 100 metres wide, surrounded by temples. Every Mayan site has huge masses of stone, but at Edzná there are cascades of it, terrace upon terrace of bleached limestone.

The major temple here, the 30-metre-high Temple of Five Levels, is to the left as you enter the plaza from the ticket kiosk. Built on a vast platform, it rises five levels from base to roofcomb, with rooms and some weathered decoration of masks, serpents and jaguars' heads on each level. A great central staircase of 65 steps goes right to the top. On the opposite (right) side of the plaza as you enter is a monumental staircase 100 metres wide, which once led up to the Temple of the Moon. At the far end of the plaza is a ruined temple that may have been the priests' quarters.

Getting There & Away The ruins of Edzná are 20 km south of the village of San Antonio Cayal, which is 44 km east of Campeche on highway 261.

From Campeche's market, at the eastern end of Calle 53 across Avenida Circuito Baluartes Este, catch a 2nd-class village bus early in the morning headed for Edzná. This will probably mean taking a bus going to the village of Pich, some 15 km south-east of Edzná, or to Hool, about 25 km south-west. Either bus will drop you at the access road to the site. A sign just north of the junction says 'Edzná 2 km', but don't let it fool you. The ruins are just 500 metres beyond the sign, only about 400 metres off the highway. Coming from the north and east, get off at

San Antonio Cayal and hitch or catch a bus 20 km south to Edzná.

When you leave you'll have to depend on hitching or buses to get you to San Antonio Cayal, from where you can hitch or catch a bus west back to Campeche, or to the north-east towards Uxmal.

If you're coming from the south (Palenque) in your own car and you don't plan to visit Campeche, you can bypass that city and head directly for Edzná via the village of Hool. This road bypasses Campeche completely, turning east and north from the coast near Champotón.

Alternatively, guided tours (80 pesos per person) are set up by the larger hotels in Campeche if they have enough people.

Bolonchén de Rejón & Xtacumbilxunaan

Heading 40 km east from San Antonio Cayal, brings you to Hopelchén, where highway 261 turns north. The next town to appear out of the flat, dry jungle is Bolonchén de Rejón, after 34 km. The local festival of the Santa Cruz is held each year on May 3rd.

Bolonchén is near the Grutas de Xtacumbilxunaan, located about three km south of town.

You can visit the cavern by taking a 30 to 45-minute tour with the guide/caretaker for the price of a tip. The cave is 'open' whenever the caretaker is around, which is most of the time during daylight hours.

Highway 261 continues into Yucatán state to Uxmal, with a side road leading to the ruin sites of the Puuc Route. See these sections, in the Yucatán State section after Mérida, for more information.

Yucatán

The state of Yucatán is a pie-shaped slice at the northern end of the Yucatán peninsula. Until the development of Cancún and the peninsula's Caribbean coast, the state of Yucatán was the most important area of the peninsula. Historically and culturally, it still is. This is where you'll find Yucatán's most impressive Mayan ruins (Chichén Itzá, Uzmal) and finest colonial cities (Mérida and Valladolid), as well as several small, interesting coastal communities.

MÉRIDA

• *pop: 600,000*

The capital of the state of Yucatán is a proud, charming city of narrow streets, colonial buildings and shady parks. It has been the centre of Mayan culture in Yucatán since before the conquistadors arrived; today it is the peninsula's centre of commerce as well. There are lots of hotels and restaurants of every class and price range and good transportation services to any part of the peninsula and the country.

Mérida seems busiest with tourists in high summer (July and August) and winter (December through March).

History

Francisco de Montejo the Younger founded a Spanish colony at Campeche in 1540. From this base he was able to take advantage of political dissension among the Maya, conquering Tihó (now Mérida) in 1542. By the end of the decade, Yucatán was mostly under Spanish colonial rule.

When Montejo's conquistadors entered defeated Tihó, they found a major Mayan settlement of lime-mortared stone which reminded them of Roman architectural legacies in Mérida, Spain. They promptly renamed the city after its Spanish likeness and proceeded to build it into the colonial capital. Mérida took its colonial orders directly from Spain, not from Mexico City, and Yucatán has had a distinct cultural and political identity ever since.

During the War of the Castes (1847-55), only Mérida and Campeche were able to hold out against the rebel forces; the rest of the Yucatán Peninsula came under Indian control. On the brink of surrender, the ruling class in Mérida was saved by reinforcements sent from central Mexico in exchange for Mérida agreeing to take orders from Mexico City. Though Yucatán is certainly part of

Mexico, there is still a strong feeling of local pride in Mérida, a feeling that the Mayab are a special realm set apart from the rest of the country.

Orientation

Odd-numbered streets run east to west, with higher numbered streets to the south; even-numbered streets run north to south, with higher numbered streets to the west. Most hotels and restaurants are within five blocks of the main plaza, or Plaza Mayor. House numbers may progress very slowly; Calle 57 No 481 and Calle 57 No 544 may be one block or ten blocks apart. Perhaps for this reason, addresses are usually given in this form: Calle 57 No 481 X 56 y 58 (between Calles 56 and 58).

Though the centre of Mérida is around the Plaza Mayor, many important buildings and services are along the grand Paseo de Montejo, a wide boulevard which begins nine blocks north of the plaza and extends northwards to the outskirts of the city.

Information

Tourist Office There are information booths of minimal usefulness at the airport and the 1st-class bus station. Preferable is the Tourist Information Centre (☎ (99) 24-92-90, 24-93-89), on the corner of Calles 60 and 57, in the south-west corner of the huge Teatro Peón Contreras, less than two blocks north of Plaza Mayor. Also worth noting is the recent establishment of a toll-free telephone hotline service for tourists who have experienced unfair or threatening treatment at the hands of police or government officials. The number is (☎ 91-800-00148, and the operators speak English.

Money Casas de cambio, though they may charge a fee for changing money, offer faster, better service than banks. Try Finex (☎ (99) 24-18-42), Calle 59 No 498K, near the Hotel Caribe on Plaza Hidalgo. In addition, there are lots of banks along Calle 65 between Calles 60 and 62, the street one block behind Banamex/Palacio Montejo (that is, one block south of the Plaza Mayor). Banking

hours are generally from 9.30 am to 1.30 pm Monday to Friday.

Post & Telecommunications The main post office (☎ (99) 21-25-61) is in the market area on Calle 65 between Calles 56 and 56A, open Monday to Friday from 8 am to 7 pm and Saturday from 9 am to 1 pm. There are postal service booths at the airport and the 1st-class bus station, open on weekdays. There is an American Express office which holds mail for clients at the Hotel Los Aluxes, Calle 60 No 444, on the corner of Calle 49.

To make long-distance telephone calls, go to the casetas at the airport, on the corner of Calles 59 and 62 or Calles 64 and 57, or on Calle 60 between Calles 53 and 55. There are Ladatel phones in front of the TelMex office and on the main plaza.

Foreign Consulates A number of countries have consulates in Mérida. If yours is not listed here, call your embassy in Mexico City.

Belgium
  Calle 25 No 159, between Calles 28 & 30 (☎ (99) 25-29-39)
Belize
  You can get information about travel in Belize at the British Vice-Consulate (see below), weekday mornings from 9.30 am to noon
Denmark
  Calle 32 No 198 at Calle 17, Colonia Garcia Ginerés (☎ (99) 25-44-88)
France
  Avenida Itzaes 242 (☎ (99) 25-46-06)
Spain
  Km 6, Carretera Mérida-Uman (☎ (99) 29-15-20)
UK
  Calle 53 No 489, at Calle 58 (☎ (99) 21-67-99, 28-39-62), open Monday to Friday from 8.30 am to 5 pm
USA
  Paseo de Montejo 453, at Avenida Colón (☎ (99) 25-50-11, 25-86-77), open Monday to Friday from 8 am to 4 pm

Laundry The Alicia on Calle 64 near the corner of Calle 55, and the laundry on Calle 61 between Calles 62 and 64 both charge around 2 pesos per kilo to wash your clothes.

Bookshops Librería Dante Peón (☎ 24-95-22), in the Teatro Peón Contreras on the corner of Calles 60 and 57, has some English, French and German books as well as Spanish ones. It's open seven days a week. At the south-west corner of Parque Hidalgo is Hollywood (☎ 21-36-19), Calle 60 No 496, which has a selection of international newspapers, magazines and some novels and travel guides.

Plaza Mayor

The most logical place to start a tour of Mérida is in Plaza Mayor. This was the religious and social centre of ancient Tihó; under the Spanish it was the Plaza de Armas, or parade ground, laid out by Francisco de Montejo the Younger. Surrounded by harmonious colonial buildings, its carefully pruned laurel trees provide welcome shade. On Sunday, the main plaza's adjoining roadways are off-limits to traffic. Plaza Mayor is bound on all sides by some of the city's most impressive buildings.

Catedral On the east side of the plaza, on the site of a Mayan temple, is Mérida's huge, hulking, severe cathedral, begun in 1561 and completed in 1598. Some of the stone from the Mayan temple was used in the cathedral's construction.

Walk through one of the three doors in the baroque façade and into the sanctuary. The great crucifix at the east end of the nave is Cristo de la Unidad, Christ of Unity, a symbol of reconciliation between those of Spanish and Mayan stock. To your right over the south door is a painting of Tutul Xiú, cacique of the town of Maní, paying his respects to his ally Francisco de Montejo at Tihó (Montejo and Xiú jointly defeated the Cocoms; Xiú converted to Christianity and his descendants still live in Mérida).

Look in the small chapel to the left (north) of the principal altar for Mérida's most famous religious artefact, a statue of Jesus called Cristo de las Ampollas, or the Christ of the Blisters. Local legend has it that this statue was carved from a tree in the town of Ichmul. The tree, hit by lightning, suppos-edly burned for an entire night yet showed no sign of fire. The statue carved from the tree was placed in the local church where it alone is said to have survived the fiery destruction of the church, though it was blackened and blistered from the heat. It was moved to the Mérida cathedral in 1645.

The rest of the church's interior is plain, its rich decoration having been stripped by angry peasants at the height of anticlerical feeling during the Mexican Revolution.

Palacio de Gobierno On the north side of the plaza, the Palacio de Gobierno houses the state of Yucatán's executive government offices. It was built in 1892 on the site of the palace of the colonial governors. The palace is open every day from 8 am to 8 pm.

See also the historical murals painted by local artist Fernando Castro Pacheco. After 25 years of work, the murals were completed in 1978.

In vivid colours, the murals portray a symbolic history of the Maya and their interaction with the Spaniards. Over the stairwell is a painting of Mayan sacred corn, the 'ray of sun from the gods'. On Sunday at 11 am, there's usually a concert (jazz, classical, pop, traditional Yucatecan) in the Salón de la Historia of the Palacio de Gobierno.

Palacio Municipal Facing the cathedral across the square, the Palacio Municipal is topped by a clock tower. Originally built in 1542, it has twice been refurbished, in the 1730s and the 1850s.

Today the building also serves as the venue for performances of Yucatecan dances (especially the *jarana*) and music at the weekly Vaquería Regional, a regional festival held to celebrate the branding of the cattle on haciendas. Performances are on Monday evenings at 9 pm.

Every Sunday at 1 pm, the city sponsors a re-enactment of a colourful mestizo wedding at the Palacio Municipal.

Casa de Montejo From its construction in 1549 until the 1970s, the mansion on the south side of the plaza was occupied by the

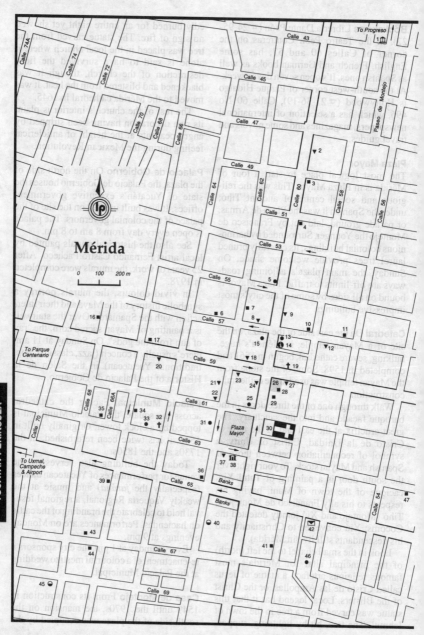

To Progreso

Calle 43

Calle 45

Calle 47

Calle 49

Calle 51

Calle 53

Calle 55

Calle 57

Calle 59

Calle 61

Calle 63

Calle 65

Calle 67

Calle 69

Paseo de Montejo

Calle 74A

Calle 74

Calle 72

Calle 70

Calle 68

Calle 66

Calle 64

Calle 62

Calle 60

Calle 58

Calle 56

Calle 54

Calle 68

Calle 66A

Calle 70

Mérida

0   100   200 m

To Parque
Centenario

To Uxmal,
Campeche
& Airport

Plaza
Mayor

Banks

Banks

Plaza
Mayor

2

3

4

5

6   7

8   9

10

11

12

13

14

15

16

17

18

19

20

21

22

23

24

25

26   27

28

29

30

31

32

33

34

35

36

37   38

39

40

41

42

43

44

45

46

47

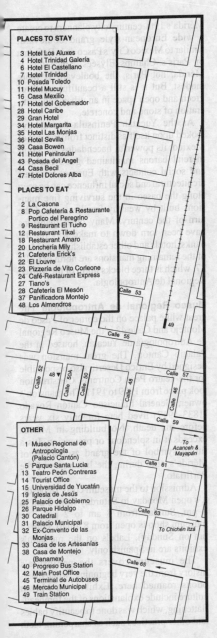

PLACES TO STAY

3 Hotel Los Aluxes
4 Hotel Trinidad Galería
6 Hotel El Castellano
7 Hotel Trinidad
10 Posada Toledo
11 Hotel Mucuy
16 Casa Mexilio
17 Hotel del Gobernador
28 Hotel Caribe
29 Gran Hotel
34 Hotel Margarita
35 Hotel Las Monjas
36 Hotel Sevilla
39 Casa Bowen
41 Hotel Peninsular
43 Posada del Angel
44 Casa Becil
47 Hotel Dolores Alba

PLACES TO EAT

2 La Casona
8 Pop Cafetería & Restaurante
  Portico del Peregrino
9 Restaurant El Tucho
12 Restaurant Tikal
18 Restaurant Amaro
20 Lonchería Mily
21 Cafetería Erick's
22 El Louvre
23 Pizzería de Vito Corleone
24 Café-Restaurant Express
27 Tiano's
28 Cafetería El Mesón
39 Panificadora Montejo
48 Los Almendros

OTHER

1 Museo Regional de
  Antropología
  (Palacio Cantón)
5 Parque Santa Lucia
13 Teatro Peón Contreras
14 Tourist Office
15 Universidad de Yucatán
19 Iglesia de Jesús
25 Palacio de Gobierno
26 Parque Hidalgo
30 Catedral
31 Palacio Municipal
32 Ex-Convento de las
  Monjas
33 Casa de los Artesanías
38 Casa de Montejo
  (Banamex)
40 Progreso Bus Station
42 Main Post Office
45 Terminal de Autobuses
46 Mercado Municipal
49 Train Station

Montejo family. Sometimes called the Palacio de Montejo, it was built at the command of the conqueror of Mérida, Francisco de Montejo the Younger. These days the great house shelters a branch of Banamex and you can look around inside whenever the bank is open (usually from 9 am to 1.30 pm Monday to Friday).

If the bank is closed, content yourself with a close look at the Plateresque façade, where triumphant conquistadors with halberds hold their feet on the necks of generic barbarians (who are not Maya, but the association is inescapable). Also gazing across the plaza from the façade are busts of Montejo the Elder, his wife and his daughter. The armorial shields are those of the Montejo family.

Walking Tour

A block north of the Plaza Mayor is the shady refuge of **Parque Hidalgo**. The park's benches always hold a variety of conversationalists, lovers, taxi drivers, hammock pedlars and tourists.

At the far end of the park, several restaurants, including Café El Mesón and Tiano's, offer alfresco dining. Tiano's often has a marimba band in the evening. The city sponsors free marimba concerts here on Sunday mornings at 11.30 am as well.

Just to the north of the parque rises the 17th-century **Iglesia de Jesús**, also called the Iglesia El Tercer Orden. Built by the Jesuits in 1618, it is the surviving edifice in a complex of Jesuit buildings which once filled the entire city block. Always interested in education, the Jesuits founded schools which later gave birth to the Universidad de Yucatán nearby. The 19th-century General Cepeda Peraza collected a library of 15,000 volumes, which is housed in a building behind the church.

Directly in front of the church is the little **Parque de la Madre**, sometimes called Parque Morelos. The modern madonna-and-child statue, which is a common fixture of town squares in this nation of high birth rates, is a copy of a statue by Lenoir which stands in the Jardin du Luxembourg in Paris.

Just north of Parque de la Madre you

confront the enormous bulk of the great **Teatro Peón Contreras**, built from 1900 to 1908 during Mérida's henequén heyday. Designed by Italian architect Enrico Deserti, it boasts a main staircase of Carrara marble, a dome with frescos by Italian artists imported for the purpose and, in its southwest corner, the Tourist Information Centre.

The main entrance to the theatre is on the corner of Calles 60 and 57. A gallery inside the entrance often holds exhibits by local painters and photographers; hours are usually from 9 am to 2 pm and 5 to 9 pm Monday to Friday, and from 9 am to 2 pm Saturday and Sunday. To see the grand theatre itself, you'll have to attend a performance.

Across Calle 60 from the theatre is the entrance to the main building of the **Universidad de Yucatán**. Though the Jesuits provided education to Yucatán's youth for centuries, the modern university was only established in the 19th century by Governor Felipe Carrillo Puerto and General Manuel Cepeda Peraza. The story of the university's founding is rendered graphically in a mural done in 1961 by Manuel Lizama. Ask for directions to the mural.

The central courtyard of the university building is the scene of concerts and folk performances every Tuesday or Friday evening at 9 pm (check with the Tourist Information Centre for performance dates and times).

A block north of the university, at the intersection of Calles 60 and 55, is the pretty little **Parque Santa Lucia**, with arcades on the north and west sides. When Mérida was a lot smaller, this was where travellers would get into or out of the stagecoaches which bumped over the rough roads of the peninsula, linking towns and villages with the provincial capital.

Today the park is the venue for orchestral performances of Yucatecan music on Thursday at 9 pm and Sunday at 11 am. Also here on Sunday at 11 am is the Bazar de Artesanías, the local handicrafts market.

Paseo de Montejo

The Paseo de Montejo was an attempt by Mérida's 19th-century city planners to create a wide European-style grand boulevard, similar to Mexico City's Paseo de la Reforma or Paris's Champs Elysées. Since this is Mérida, not Paris, the boulevard is more modest. But it is still a beautiful swath of green and open space in an urban conglomeration of stone and concrete.

As the Yucatán Peninsula has always looked upon itself as distinct from the rest of Mexico, its powerful hacendados and commercial barons maintained good business and social contacts with Europe. Europe's architectural and social influence can be seen along the paseo in the surviving fine mansions built by wealthy families around the turn of the century. Many other mansions have been torn down to make way for the banks, hotels and other establishments. Most of the remaining mansions are north of Calle 37, which is three blocks north of the Museo Regional de Antropología.

Museo Regional de Antropología

The great white palace on the corner of Paseo de Montejo and Calle 43 is the Museo Regional de Antropología de Yucatán, housed in the Palacio Cantón. The great mansion was designed by Enrico Deserti, also responsible for the Teatro Peón Contreras. Construction took place from 1909 to 1911. The mansion's owner, General Francisco Cantón Rosado (1833-1917) lived here for only six years before his death. No building in Mérida exceeds it in splendour or pretension. It's a fitting symbol of the grand aspirations of Mérida's elite during the last years of the Porfiriato.

Admission to the museum costs 18 pesos; it's open Monday to Saturday from 8 am to 8 pm, Sunday from 8 am to 2 pm. The museum shop is open from 8 am to 3 pm (2 pm on Sunday). Labels on the museum's exhibits are in Spanish only.

The museum covers the peninsula's history from the very beginning, when mastodons roamed here. Exhibits on Mayan culture include explanations of the forehead-flattening, which was done to beautify babies and other practices such as sharpening teeth and implanting them with tiny jewels. If you plan to visit archaeological sites near Mérida, you can study the many exhibits here – lavishly illustrated with plans and photographs – which cover the great Mayan cities of Mayapán, Uxmal and Chichén Itzá, as well as lesser sites.

Monumento a la Patria At the intersection with Avenida Colón is the Parque de las Américas, which boasts trees and shrubs collected from many countries of the western hemisphere. Walking north two blocks from Avenida Colón brings you to the Monument to the Fatherland, an elaborate sculpture in neo-Mayan style executed in 1956 by Rómulo Rozo. The fatherland, here, takes on a distinctly Mayan appearance.

Parque Centenario
On the west edge of the city, 12 blocks from the Plaza Mayor, lies the large, verdant Parque Centenario, bordered by Avenida de los Itzaes, the highway to the airport and Campeche. There's a zoo in the park which specialises in the fauna of Yucatán. To get there, take a bus westwards along Calle 61 or 65.

Festivals
Prior to Lent in February or March, Carnaval features colourful costumes and nonstop festivities. It is celebrated with greater vigour in Mérida than anywhere else in Yucatán. During the first two weeks in October, the Cristo de las Ampollas (Christ of the Blisters) statue in the cathedral is venerated with processions.

Places to Stay – bottom end
Prices for basic but acceptable double rooms in Mérida range from about 50 to 100 pesos. This price can get you a small but clean room with fan and private shower, only a short walk from the plaza. All hotels should provide purified drinking water at no extra charge (ask for *agua purificada*).

Hotel Las Monjas (☎ (99) 28-66-32), Calle 66A No 509 at Calle 63, is one of the best deals in town. All 28 rooms in this little

place have ceiling fans and running water (sinks or private baths with hot and cold water). Rooms are tiny and most are dark, but they are clean. Room No 12 is the best, quiet because it's at the back, light and cool because its windows provide good cross-ventilation. The price is 50 to 58 pesos a double with fan, 68 with air-con.

Hotel Margarita (☎ (99) 23-72-32), Calle 66 No 506, between Calles 61 and 63, is a favourite with foreigners because of its low price and convenient location. The rooms, which are small, dingy and not always spotless, cost 43/61/72/90 pesos a single/double/triple/quad with fan and running water. Air-con costs a few dollars more.

Hotel Mucuy (☎ (99) 28-51-93, fax 23-78-01), Calle 57 No 481, between Calles 56 and 58, has been serving thrifty travellers for more than a decade. It's a family-run place with 26 tidy rooms on two floors facing a long, narrow garden courtyard. Sra Ofelia Comin and her daughter Ofelia speak English. Rooms with ceiling fan and private shower cost 55/65/80 pesos a single/double/triple.

Casa Bowen (☎ (99) 28-61-09), Calle 66 No 521B, near Calle 65, is a large old Mérida house converted to a hotel. The narrow courtyard has a welcome swath of green grass. Rooms are simple, even bare, and some are dark and soiled, but all have fans and showers for 62 pesos a double with fan, 75 pesos with air-con. Get receipts for any payment.

Casa Becil (☎ (99) 24-67-64), Calle 67 No 550C, between Calles 66 and 68 near the bus station, is a house with a high-ceilinged sitting room/lobby and small guest rooms at the back. With private shower and fan, the price is 65 to 80 pesos a double. The family management tries hard to please.

Hotel Sevilla (☎ (99) 23-83-60), Calle 62 No 511, on the corner of Calle 65, offers a whisper of faded elegance, but most rooms are musty and dark. The price is not too bad: 55/65/80 pesos for a single/double/triple.

Hotel Trinidad (☎ (99) 23-20-33), Calle 62 No 464 between Calles 55 and 57, is decorated with modern Mexican paintings and the tiny courtyard is filled with plants. The hotel could use some paint. The guest rooms are all different, and range in price from 70 for a small double with sink to 155 pesos a double for a large room with private bath and air-con. Washing clothes in the sink nets you a 50-peso fine, though.

The Trinidad's sister hotel, *Hotel Trinidad Galería* (☎ (99) 23-24-63, fax 24-23-19), Calle 60 No 456, on the corner of Calle 51, was once an appliance showroom. There's a small swimming pool, a bar, art gallery and antique shop, as well as presentable rooms with fans and private showers renting for similar rates.

Hotel Peninsular (☎ (99) 23-69-96), Calle 58 No 519 between Calles 65 and 67, is in the midst of the market district. You enter down a long corridor to find a neat restaurant and a maze of rooms, most with windows opening onto the interior spaces. It costs 58/68/86 pesos a single/double/triple with private bath and fan; add a few dollars for air-con.

Places to Stay – middle
Mérida's mid-range places provide surprising levels of comfort for what you pay. Most charge 125 to 250 pesos for a double room with air-con, ceiling fan and private shower; and most have restaurants, bars and little swimming pools.

Hotel Dolores Alba (☎ (99) 21-37-45), Calle 63 No 464, between Calles 52 and 54, 3½ blocks east of the plaza, is one of the top choices in Mérida because of its pleasant courtyard, beautiful swimming pool and clean, comfortable rooms for 100 a double (slightly more for air-con).

Posada del Angel (☎ (99) 23-27-54), Calle 67 No 535 between Calles 66 and 68, is two blocks north-east of the bus station and is quieter than most other hotels in this neighbourhood. It's modern and convenient, and has a restaurant, but is a bit expensive at 100 pesos a double, 120 with air-con.

Hotel Caribe (☎ (99) 24-90-22, fax 24-87-33), Calle 59 No 500, on the corner of Calle 60 on the Parque Hidalgo, is a favourite with visiting foreigners because of its central

location, its rooftop pool, and its two restaurants. Most rooms have air-con and range in price from 120 pesos for a small single with fan to 275 pesos for a large double with air-con.

Gran Hotel (☎ (99) 24-77-30, fax 24-76-22), Calle 60 No 496, between Calles 59 and 61, is on the southern side of the Parque Hidalgo. Corinthian columns support terraces on three levels around the verdant central courtyard, and fancy wrought-iron and carved-wood decoration evoke a past age. All 28 rooms have air-con and cost 165 to 325 pesos a double.

Casa Mexilio (☎ fax (99) 28-25-05), Calle 68 No 495, between Calles 59 and 57, is Mérida's most charming pension, a beautifully restored and decorated house with comfortable rooms for 225 pesos a double, breakfast included.

Posada Toledo (☎ (99) 23-16-90, fax 23-22-56), Calle 58 No 487 at Calle 57, three blocks north-east of the main plaza, has a courtyard with vines, a dining room straight out of the 19th century and small, modernised rooms with fan or air-con overpriced at 130/165 pesos a single/double.

Hotel del Gobernador (☎ (99) 23-71-33), Calle 59 No 535, at Calle 66, is an attractive, modern hotel favoured by Mexican business executives. The price is good for what you get: 220 to 250 pesos a double.

Places to Stay – top end
Top-end hotels charge between 250 and 600 pesos for a double room with air-con. Each hotel has a restaurant, bar, swimming pool and probably other services like a newsstand, hairdresser, travel agency and nightclub.

Holiday Inn Mérida (☎ (99) 25-68-77; in the USA 800-465-4329), Avenida Colón 498 at Calle 60, half a block off the Paseo de Montejo behind the US Consulate General, is one of Mérida's most luxurious establishments. Its 213 air-con rooms cost 490 pesos.

For all-round quality, convenience and price, try the *Hotel Los Aluxes* (☎ (99) 24-21-99, fax 23-38-58; toll-free in USA 800-782-8395), Calle 60 No 444, at Calle 49. This relatively new 109-room hotel has all the services, plus modern architecture and an intriguing name: *aluxes* ('ah-LOO-shess') are the Mayan equivalent of leprechauns. Rates are 300 pesos a single or double, 400 pesos a triple.

Hotel El Castellano (☎ (99) 23-01-00), Calle 57 No 513, between Calles 62 and 64, is a favourite with business travellers and tourists. Its 170 rooms cost 295 pesos for a single or double, 375 pesos for a triple/suite.

Hotel El Conquistador (☎ (99) 26-21-55, fax 26-88-29), Paseo de Montejo No 458, at Calle 35, has 90 rooms in a modern nine-storey structure. Rates are 300 pesos for a single or double, 350 a triple.

The 90-room *Hotel Montejo Palace* (☎ (99) 24-76-44, fax 28-03-88), Paseo de Montejo 483-C, and the older *Hotel Paseo de Montejo* (☎ (99) 23-90-33), Paseo de Montejo 482, face one another across the Paseo at Calle 41. Both hotels are under the same management and charge 240 to 300 pesos a double.

Mérida's newest and most luxurious hotel is the 17-storey, 300-room *Hyatt Regency Mérida* (☎ (99) 25-67-22, fax 25-70-02), Avenida Colón and Calle 60, 100 metres west of Paseo de Montejo and about two km north of the Plaza Mayor. Rooms with all the comforts cost 520 to 580 pesos.

Places to Eat

Inexpensive Walk two blocks south from the main plaza to Calle 67, turn left (east) and walk another two or three blocks to the market. Continue straight up the flight of steps at the end of Calle 67. As you ascend, you'll pass the touristy Mercado de Artesanías on your left. At the top of the ramp, turn left and you'll see a row of market eateries with names like *El Chimecito, La Temaxeña, Saby, Mimi, Saby y El Palon, La Socorrito, Reina Beatriz* and so forth. Comidas corridas here are priced from 10 to 14 pesos, and big main-course platters of beef, fish or chicken with vegetables and rice or potatoes go for 9 to 14 pesos. The market eateries are open from early morning until late afternoon every day.

El Louvre (☎ 21-32-71), Calle 62 No 499, corner of Calle 61 at the north-west corner of the Plaza Mayor, opens early in the morning, and has a loyal local clientele. The comida corrida costs 22 pesos, though it's not what you'd call a gourmet treat. If they put something on your table that you didn't order, send it back or you'll pay for it. *Cafetería Erick's*, just up the street, is even cheaper than El Louvre.

The *Lonchería Mily*, Calle 59 No 520 between 64 and 66, opens at 7 am and serves cheap breakfasts (7 pesos), a two-course comida corrida (11 pesos) and cheap sandwiches. It closes at 5 pm, and is closed Sunday.

For takeaway food, try the *Pizzería de Vito Corleone* (☎ 23-68-46), Calle 59 No 508, at 62. This tiny eatery suffers from loud street noise, so many customers take their pizzas to the Parque Hidalgo instead. Pizzas are priced from 14 to 40 pesos, depending upon ingredients. Vegetarian varieties are available.

The best cheap breakfasts can be had by picking up a selection of pan dulce (sweet rolls and breads) from one of Mérida's several *panificadoras* (bakeries). A convenient one is the *Panificadora Montejo* on the corner of Calles 62 and 63, at the south-west corner of the main plaza. Pick up a metal tray and tongs, select the pastries you want and hand the tray to a clerk who will bag them and quote a price, usually 7 pesos or so for a full bag.

Mid-Range Those willing to spend a bit more money can enjoy the pleasant restaurants of the Parque Hidalgo on the corner of Calles 59 and 60.

The least expensive, yet one of the most pleasant restaurants here, is the *Cafetería El Mesón* (☎ 21-92-32) in the Hotel Caribe. Meat, fish and chicken dishes are priced from 16 to 35 pesos, but sandwiches and burgers are less. El Mesón is open from 7 am to 10.30 pm.

Right next to El Mesón is *Tiano's* (☎ 23-71-18), Calle 59 No 498, a fancier version of El Mesón. In the evening the restaurant often hires a marimba group to entertain its patrons, as well as the dozens of hangers-on in the square. Have sopa de lima, puntas de

---

Yucatecan Cuisine

Called by its Maya inhabitants 'the Land of the Pheasant and the Deer', Yucatán has always had a distinctive cuisine. Here are some of the Yucatecan dishes you might want to try:

Frijol con Puerco – Yucatecan-style pork and beans, topped with a sauce made with grilled tomatoes, and decorated with bits of radish, slices of onion, and leaves of fresh *cilantro* (coriander); served with rice

Huevos Motuleños – 'Eggs in the style of Motul'; fried eggs atop a tortilla, garnished with beans, peas, chopped ham, sausage, grated cheese and a certain amount of spicy chile – high in cholesterol, fat and flavour

Papadzules – Tortillas stuffed with chopped hard-boiled eggs and topped with a sauce of marrow (squash) or cucumber seeds

Pavo Relleno – Stuffed turkey. The Yucatecan *faisán* (pheasant) is actually the *pavo* (ocellated turkey). Slabs of turkey meat are layered with chopped, spiced beef and pork and served in a rich, dark sauce

Pibil – Meat wrapped in banana leaves, flavoured with achiote, garlic, sour orange, salt and pepper, and baked in a barbecue pit called a *pib*. The two main varieties are *cochinita pibil* (suckling pig) and *pollo pibil* (chicken)

Poc-chuc – Tender pork strips marinated in sour orange juice, grilled and served topped with a spicy onion relish

Puchero – A stew of pork, chicken, carrots, marrow (squash), potatoes, plantains and *chayote* (vegetable pear), spiced with radish, fresh coriander and sour orange

Salbutes – Yucatán's favourite snack: a hand-made tortilla, fried, then topped with shredded turkey, onion and slices of avocado

Sopa de Lima – 'Lime soup'; chicken broth with bits of shredded chicken, tortilla strips, lime juice and chopped lime

Venado – Venison, a popular traditional dish, might be served as a *pipián*, flavoured with a sauce of ground marrow (squash) seeds, wrapped in banana leaves and steamed ■

---

filete, dessert and a drink and your bill might be 60 pesos. You can eat for less, though. Tiano's is supposedly open 24 hours a day, though you'll see it locked up tight from about midnight to 7 am.

Across Calle 60, facing the Parque Hidalgo, is an old Mérida standard, the *Café-Restaurant Express* (☎ 21-37-38), Calle 60 No 502, south of Calle 59. Busy with a loyal crowd of regulars and foreigners, Express is a bustling and noisy meeting place, but the food is okay, service is fast and prices are fair. The comida corrida costs 20 pesos. Hours are daily 7 am (more or less) to midnight.

For vegetarian meals, try *Restaurant Amaro* (☎ 28-24-51), Calle 59 No 507, between Calles 60 and 62, open daily from 9 am to 10 pm. Yucatecan meals are served, as is Yucatecan beer, along with a few vegetarian dishes.

Pop Cafetería (☎ 21-68-44), Calle 57 between 60 and 62, is plain, modern, bright,

air-con, and named for the first month of the 18-month Mayan calendar. The menu is limited but adequate, with hamburgers, spaghetti and main-course platters such as chicken in mole sauce for 13 to 35 pesos. Breakfasts cost from 10 to 15 pesos.

Restaurant Tikal, Calle 57 No 485, next to the Hotel Flamingo, is small, nicely decorated, and moderate in price. Try the filling sopa de lima.

Expensive Among the city's most dependable dining places is the *Restaurante Portico del Peregrino* (☎ 21-68-44), Calle 57 No 501, between Calles 60 and 62, right next to Pop. This 'Pilgrim's Refuge' consists of several pleasant, almost elegant traditional dining rooms (some are air-con) around a small courtyard replete with colonial artefacts. Yucatecan dishes are the forte, but you'll find many Continental dishes as well. Lunch (noon to 3 pm) and dinner (6 to 11 pm) are served every day and your bill for a full meal might be 65 to 90 pesos per person.

La Casona (☎ 23-83-48), Calle 60 No 434 between Calles 47 and 49, is a fine old city house now serving as a restaurant. Dining tables are set out on a portico next to a small but lush garden; dim lighting lends an air of romance. Italian dishes crowd the menu, with a few Yucatecan plates to top it off. Plan to spend anywhere from 45 to 75 pesos per person. La Casona is open every evening for dinner; on weekends, you might want to make reservations.

Los Almendros (☎ 21-28-51), Calle 50A No 493 between Calles 57 and 59, facing the Plaza de Mejorada, specialises in authentic Yucatecan country cuisine, although some readers have complained that quality has suffered recently. You can try pavo relleno negro (grilled turkey with hot peppered pork stuffing), papadzul, sopa de lima, or Los Almendros' most famous dish, the zingy tomato-onion-and-pork poc-chuc. Full meals cost 35 to 60 pesos. Some people are disappointed at Los Almendros because they go expecting delicacies; this is hearty food.

How about entertainment as you dine Yucatán style? The *Restaurant El Tucho* (☎ 24-23-23), Calle 60 No 482 between 57 and 55, features Yucatecan specialities in a dining room fashioned to look like an enormous *na* (Mayan thatched hut), with thatched roof and bamboo walls. It's a place where the locals come for eating, drinking and singing, from 6 pm to midnight, seven days a week. Most main courses cost 30 pesos and a full meal can be yours for 60 or 75 pesos. Beware of the high prices for drinks.

Entertainment
Concerts & Folklore Proud of its cultural legacy and attuned to the benefits of tourism, the city of Mérida offers nightly folkloric events by local performers of considerable skill. Admission is free to city-sponsored events. Check with the tourist office for the schedule.

Cinemas Many English films, some of fairly recent release, are screened in Mérida with Spanish subtitles. Buy your tickets (usually about 7 pesos) before showtime and well in advance on weekends. The popular Cine Cantarell, Calle 60 No 488, next door to the Restaurant Express, and Cine Fantasio, facing Parque Hidalgo between the Gran Hotel and Hotel Caribe, are convenient. There's also the Cine Premier, on the corner of Calles 57 and 62, and the Cinema 59, Calle 59 between Calles 68 and 70.

Things to Buy
From standard shirts and blouses to Mayan exotica, Mérida is *the* place on the peninsula to shop. Purchases you might want to consider include traditional Mayan clothing such as the colourful women's embroidered blouse called a huipil, a Panama hat woven from palm fibres, local craft items and of course the wonderfully comfortable Yucatecan hammock, which holds you gently in a comfortable cotton web.

Guard your valuables extra carefully in the market area. Watch for pickpockets, purse-snatchers and slash-and-grab thieves.

Mérida's main market, the Mercado Municipal Lucas do Gálvez, is bound by Calles 56 and 56A at Calle 67, four blocks south-east of the Plaza Mayor. The market building is more or less next door to the city's main post office and telegraph office, on the corner of Calles 65 and 56. The surrounding streets are all part of the large market district, lined with shops selling everything one might need.

The Bazar de Artesanías, Calle 67 on the corner of Calle 56A, is set up to attract tourists. You should have a look at the stuff here, then compare the goods and prices with independent shops outside the Bazar.

Handicrafts The place to go for high-quality craft and art items is the Casa de los Artesanías, Estado de Yucatán on Calle 63 between 64 and 66; look for the doorway marked 'Dirección de Desarrollo Artesanal DIF Yucatán'. It's open Monday to Friday from 8 am to 8 pm, Saturday from 8 am to 6 pm. This is a government-supported marketing effort for local artisans. The selection of crafts is very good, quality is usually high and prices reasonable.

You can also check out locally made crafts at the Museo Regional de Artesanías on Calle 59 between Calles 50 and 48. The work on display is superlative, but the items for sale are not as good. Admission is free and it's open from 8 am to 8 pm Tuesday to Saturday and from 9 am to 2 pm Sunday.

Panama Hats Panama hats are woven from jipijapa palm leaves in caves and workshops in which the temperature and humidity are carefully controlled, as humid conditions keep the fibres pliable when the hat is being made. Once blocked and exposed to the relatively drier air outside, the panama hat is surprisingly resilient and resistant to crushing. The Campeche town of Becal is the centre of the hat-weaving trade, but you can buy good examples of the hatmaker's art in Mérida.

The best quality hats have a very fine, close weave of slender fibres. The coarser the weave, the lower the price should be. Prices range from a few dollars for a hat of basic quality to 90 pesos or more for top quality.

A store famous for its Panama hats is appropriately named Becal and is located at Calle 56 No 522. Another is El Becaleño, Calle 65 No 483, on the corner of Calle 56A. A third is La Casa de los Jipis, Calle 56 No 526 near Calle 65.

Getting There & Away

Air Mérida's modern airport is several km south-west of the centre off highway 180 (Avenida de los Itzaes). There are car-rental desks there. A Tourism Information office can help with questions and hotel reservations.

Most international flights to Mérida are connections through Mexico City or Cancún; the only nonstop international services are Aeroméxico's two daily flights from Miami and Aviateca's flights to Guatemala City. Domestic flights are operated mostly by smaller regional airlines, with a few flights by Aeroméxico and Mexicana.

Hammocks

The fine strings of Yucatecan hammocks make them supremely comfortable. In the sticky heat of a Yucatán summer, most locals prefer sleeping in a hammock, where the air can circulate around them, rather than in a bed. Many inexpensive hotels used to have hammock hooks in the walls of all guest rooms, though the hooks are not so much in evidence today.

Yucatecan hammocks are normally woven from strong nylon or cotton string and dyed in various colours; there are also natural, undyed versions. In the old days, the finest, strongest, most expensive hammocks were woven from silk.

Hammocks come in several widths. From smallest to largest, the names generally used are: *sencillo* (about 50 pairs of end strings, 45 pesos), *doble* (100 pairs, 50 to 65 pesos), *matrimonial* (150 pairs, 65 to 90 pesos) and *matrimonial especial* or *quatro cajas* (175 pairs or more, 80 pesos and up). You must check to be sure that you're really getting the width you're paying for. Because hammocks fold up small and the larger hammocks are more comfortable (though more expensive), consider the bigger sizes.

During your first few hours in Mérida you will be approached on the street by hammock pedlars. They may quote very low prices, but a price is only as good as the quality is high and street-sold hammocks are mediocre at best. Check the hammock very carefully.

You can save yourself a lot of trouble by shopping at a hammock store with a good reputation. La Poblana (☎ 21-65-03), at Calle 65 No 492 between Calles 58 and 60, is fairly good. Some travellers report slightly cheaper prices for good quality at El Aguacate, Calle 58 No 604 at the corner of Calle 73. El Campesino, at Calle 58 No 548 between Calles 69 and 71, is cheaper but provides less guidance – so you should really know what you are looking for and check quality.

It's interesting to venture out to the nearby village of Tixcocob to watch the hammocks being woven. A bus runs regularly from the Progreso bus station south of the main plaza at Calle 62 No 524 between Calles 65 and 67. ■

Operators include the following:

Aerocaribe (☎ (99) 24-95-00, 23-00-02), Paseo de Montejo 476A, flies between Mérida and Cancún (morning and evening flights, US$75 one way, US$110 return-trip excursion), Chetumal, Mexico City, Oaxaca, Tuxtla Gutiérrez (for San Cristóbal de Las Casas), Veracruz and Villahermosa

Aerolíneas Bonanza (☎ (99) 28-04-96, 24-62-28), Calle 56A No 579, between Calles 67 and 69, flies return trips twice daily from Mérida to Chetumal and once daily to Ciudad del Carmen

Aeroméxico (☎ (99) 27-95-66, 27-92-77), Paseo de Montejo 460, has a few flights as well

Aviacsa (☎ (99) 26-32-53, 26-39-54, fax 26-90-87), at the airport, flies nonstop to Cancún and Villahermosa, and direct to Tuxtla Gutiérrez, the airline's home base. They also have routes linking Tuxtla with Chetumal, Mexico City, Oaxaca and Tapachula

Aviateca (☎ (99) 24-43-54) at the airport, flies to Tikal and Guatemala City several times a week

Litoral (☎ toll-free 91-800-2-90-20), based in Veracruz, flies to Ciudad del Carmen, Veracruz and Monterrey

Mexicana (☎ (99) 24-66-33), Calle 58 No 500 has nonstop flights to/from Havana, Cancún and Mexico City

Bus The main Terminal de Autobuses (☎ 24-37-43), operated by the Unión de Camioneros de Yucatán, is on Calle 69 between Calles 68 and 70, about six blocks south-west of the main plaza. Facilities here include a bank, a travel agency, a Yucatán state tourism booth, an instant B&W photo booth and a bank of Ladatel coin-operated long-distance phones, as well as a public fax machine.

ADO has a ticket window in the Terminal, but also has its own modern terminal on Calle 71 between 70 and 72. The UNO deluxe line has its own terminal less than a block west of the main terminal, on Calle 69 between 70 and 72.

A dozen different companies use the Terminal de Autobuses. Each company specialises in services to a certain part of the region or the country, but some companies' territories overlap. Shop around a bit before you buy your ticket, as fares, travel times and comfort can vary from one company to the next. Here's a quick rundown on the companies

(their abbreviated name appears after the company name):

Autobuses de Oriente (ADO) – long-haul 1st-class bus routes to Campeche, Palenque, Villahermosa, Veracruz and Mexico City

Autotransportes Peninsulares (A Peninsulares) – frequent 1st-class buses to Chetumal

Autotransportes de Oriente Mérida-Puerto Juárez (A de O M-PJ) – frequent 1st and 2nd-class buses between Mérida and Cancún stopping at Chichén Itzá, Valladolid and Puerto Juárez (for Isla Mujeres boats); they also run buses to Tizimín and to Playa del Carmen (for Cozumel boats)

Autotransportes del Sur (A del Sur) – frequent 1st and 2nd-class buses to Uxmal, Kabah and Campeche and one bus a day to Villahermosa

Autotransportes del Caribe (A del Caribe) – nine 1st-class buses daily to Ticul; also 1st and 2nd-class buses to Felipe Carrillo Puerto, Bacalar, Chetumal, Tulum and Akumal

Autotransportes del Sureste en Yucatán (A del Sureste) – one 2nd-class bus daily to Palenque and one to Tuxtla Gutiérrez

Expresso de Oriente – deluxe buses Mérida-Valladolid-Cancún-Playa del Carmen-Tulum

UNO – several deluxe buses daily on long-haul routes such as to Cancún, Villahermosa and Mexico City

Here's information on daily buses to/from Mérida. The times are by 1st-class bus (2nd class may be slower):

Akumal – 350 km, six to seven hours; three 2nd-class buses (36 pesos) by A de O M-PJ and three by A del Caribe

Bacalar – 420 km, 8½ hours; four 1st-class (50 pesos) and four 2nd-class (42 pesos) buses by A del Caribe

Campeche – 195 km (short route via Becal), 2½ hours; 250 km (long route via Uxmal), four hours; 26 1st-class buses (30 pesos) by ADO and 13 2nd-class buses (24 pesos) by A del Sur

Cancún – 320 km, 3½ to five hours; very frequent in all classes (24 to 40 pesos); deluxe nonstops vía cuota (by the toll road) are fastest

Chetumal – 456 km, 6½ hours; seven 1st-class buses (45 pesos) by A Peninsulares and six by A del Caribe; four 2nd-class buses (36 pesos) by A del Caribe

Chichén Itzá – 116 km, two to 2½ hours; many 1st-class (18 to 22 pesos) and 2nd-class (18 pesos) buses by A de O M-PJ heading for Valladolid and beyond; return-trip excursion bus by A de O M-PJ leaves Mérida at 8.45 am and returns from Chichén Itzá at 3 pm

Felipe Carrillo Puerto – 310 km, 5½ to six hours; two
1st-class buses (33 pesos) by A del Caribe (others
of this line may stop there as well) and one
2nd-class bus (25 pesos) by A de O M-PJ

Kabah – 101 km, two hours; six 1st-class buses (12
pesos) by A del Sur; ADO tour bus to Uxmal and
the Puuc sites (see below)

Mexico City (TAPO) – 1550 km, 28 hours; six 1st-
class buses (200 pesos) by ADO

Palenque – 556 km, 10 or 11 hours; three 1st-class
buses (75 to 90 pesos) by ADO; many more will
drop you at Catazajá, 27 km north of Palenque,
from which there are taxi and shuttle-bus services

Playa del Carmen – 385 km, seven hours; six 1st-class
(44 pesos) and six 2nd-class (39 pesos) buses by
A de O M-PJ

Progreso – see below

Ticul – 85 km, 1½ hours; nine 2nd-class buses (10
pesos) by A del Caribe

Tizimin – 210 km, four hours; three 1st-class buses
(28 pesos) by A de O M-PJ, or take a bus to
Valladolid and change there for Tizimin

Tulum – 320 km, six hours; three 2nd-class buses (38
pesos) via Cobá by A del Caribe and three (40
pesos) via Cancún by A de O M-PJ (eight hours)

Tuxtla Gutiérrez – 995 km, 16 hours; one deluxe by
Cristóbal Colón (120 pesos); one lunchtime 2nd-
class bus (80 pesos) by Autotransportes Tuxtla
Gutiérrez (ATG)

Uxmal – 80 km, 1½ hours; eight 2nd-class buses (11
pesos) by A del Sur, or take a bus bound for
Campeche or beyond by the inland (longer) route
and get off at Uxmal; ADO has a special tour bus
to Uxmal and the Puuc sites (see below)

Villahermosa – 700 km, 10 hours; 11 1st-class buses (66
pesos) by ADO; one evening UNO bus (costs more)

If you take an all-night bus, don't put anything valuable in the overhead racks, as there
have been several reports of gear being
stolen at night.

ADO has a special tour bus to Uxmal and
the Puuc sites departing daily at 8.30 am,
stopping at each of the Puuc Route sites for 30
minutes, then Uxmal for two hours, returning to Mérida by 4 or 4.30 pm, for 35 pesos.

For buses to Progreso and the ruins at
Dzibilchaltún, go to the Progreso bus station
1½ blocks south of the main plaza at Calle
62 No 524 between Calles 65 and 67. Buses
depart every 15 minutes on the run to the
Dzibilchaltún access road (15 km, 30
minutes, 4 pesos) and Progreso (33 km, 45
minutes, 4.50 pesos).

Travellers heading to the Celestún fla-

mingo region can choose from several departures a day from the Autotransportes del Sur
station at Calle 50 No 531 on the corner of
Calle 67.

To Río Lagartos or San Felipe, Autotransportes del Noroeste buses depart three
times daily from Calle 52 between Calles 63
and 65.

Train Buses are preferable to trains in that
they are faster and safer and also because rail
robberies in some areas (between Mérida,
Campeche and Palenque in particular) have
reached epidemic proportions. There are no
dormitorios to lock on trains travelling this
route – just vulnerable seating.

If you still want to get between Mérida and
other points by rail, the station is at Calle 55
between Calles 46 and 48, about nine blocks
north-east of the main plaza.

Car There are three ways to visit the old
Mayan capital of Mayapán and the Puuc
Route archaeological sites of Kabah, Sayil,
Labná, Xlapak and Loltún: you can take a
tour, take a bus to Kabah and walk many km
(with the occasional hitchhike) in the hot
sun, or you can rent a car.

Assume you will pay about 150 pesos per
day for the cheapest car offered, usually a
bottom-of-the-line VW or Nissan. If you can
find others to share the cost, car rental is the
best way to see the Puuc Route sites. If you
rent for more than a day or two, the price
should go down to 120 pesos or so per day.

You might start your price comparisons at
a small local firm such as Mexico Rent a Car
(☎ (99) 27-49-16, 23-36-37), Calle 62 No
483E between Calles 59 and 57, owned and
operated by Alvaro and Teresa Alonzo and
their daughter Teresa. They also have a desk
on Calle 60 at the car park entrance next to
the Hotel del Parque, just north of the Parque
Hidalgo. There are numerous other agencies,
small and large, nearby.

The big international car-rental companies all have agencies in Mérida, the most
active of which is Budget Rent-a-Car
(☎ (99) 27-87-55), Paseo de Montejo Prolongación 497.

Getting Around

To/From the Airport Bus 79 ('Aviación') travels infrequently between the airport and the city centre for 2 pesos. Most arriving travellers use the Transporte Terrestre minibuses (14 pesos) to go from the airport to the centre; to return to the airport you must take a taxi (28 pesos).

To/From the Bus Terminal A taxi from the bus terminal to the Plaza Mayor costs about 10 pesos. To walk from the Terminal de Autobuses on Calle 69, between Calles 68 and 70, to the Plaza Mayor, exit the terminal to the street in front (Calle 69), turn right and walk three blocks, passing the Church of San Juan de Dios and a park, to Calle 62. Turn left on Calle 62 and walk the remaining three blocks north to the plaza.

Bus Most parts of Mérida that you'll want to visit are within five or six blocks of the Plaza Mayor and are thus accessible on foot. Given the slow speed of city traffic, particularly in the market areas, travel on foot is also the fastest way to get around.

The city's bus system is confusing at best, with routes meandering through the city, finally terminating in a distant suburban neighbourhood. For exact route information, ask at the tourist office.

The bus system is supplemented by minibuses, which are easier to use as they run shorter and more comprehensible routes. The minibus (colectivo) you're liable to find most useful is the Ruta 10 (2 pesos), which departs the corner of Calles 58 and 59, half a block east of the Parque Hidalgo, and travels along the Paseo de Montejo to Itzamná.

DZIBILCHALTÚN

This was the longest continuously utilised Mayan administrative and ceremonial city, serving the Maya from 1500 BC or earlier until the European conquest in the 1540s. At the height of its greatness, Dzibilchaltún covered 80 sq km. Today there is not much left of the original site except a few ruined pyramids, a sacbe (ceremonial road) or two,

the interesting little **Temple of the Seven Dolls** and a cool, clear cenote swimming pool. A new **archeological museum** has also recently opened, situated between the Universidad del Mayab and the archaeological zone. While it opened too recently for us to take a look, it may be worth checking out.

Dzibilchaltún (Place of Inscribed Flat Stones) is a large site, open daily from 8 am to 5 pm; admission costs 10 pesos.

Getting There & Away

Buses depart every 15 minutes from Mérida to the Dzibilchaltún access road (15 km, 30 minutes, 4 pesos) on the right (east) side of the highway. It's five km from the highway to the entrance of the ruins along a sleepy country road and through a little village; the best time to hitch a ride is in the morning. From the site entrance, it's another 700 metres to the building housing the museum, ticket window and soft drinks stand.

PROGRESO

• pop: 30,000

This is a seafarers' town, the port for Mérida and north-western Yucatán. The Yucatecan limestone shelf declines so gradually into the sea that a muelle (pier) 6.5 km long had to be built to reach the deep water.

This same gradual slope of land into water is what makes Progreso's long beach so inviting. The waters are shallow, warm and safe from such dangers as riptide and undertow.

Progreso is normally a sleepy little town, but on weekends, especially in summer, it seems as if all of Mérida is here.

Orientation

Progreso is long and narrow, stretched out along the seashore. Though it has an apparently logical street grid, it is illogically subject to two numbering systems fifty numbers apart. One system has the city centre's streets numbered in the 60s, 70s and 80s, another has them in the 10s, 20s and 30s. Thus you might see a street sign on Calle 30 calling it Calle 80 or on a map Calle 10 might also be referred to as Calle 60. We've included both systems on our map.

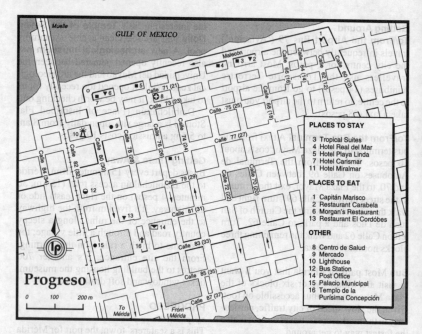

Muelle

GULF OF MEXICO

Malecón

Calle 71 (21)

Calle 73 (23)

Calle 75 (25)

Calle 77 (27)

Calle 79 (29)

Calle 81 (31)

Calle 83 (33)

Calle 85 (35)

Calle 87 (37)

Calle 82 (32)

Calle 84 (34)

Calle 80 (30)

Calle 78 (28)

Calle 76 (26)

Calle 74 (24)

Calle 72 (22)

Calle 70 (20)

Calle 68 (18)

Calle 66 (16)

Calle 64 (14)

Calle 62 (12)

Calle 60 (10)

Progreso

0   100   200 m

To Mérida

From Mérida

PLACES TO STAY
3 Tropical Suites
4 Hotel Real del Mar
5 Hotel Playa Linda
7 Hotel Carismar
11 Hotel Miralmar

PLACES TO EAT
1 Capitán Marisco
2 Restaurant Carabela
6 Morgan's Restaurant
13 Restaurant El Cordóbes

OTHER
8 Centro de Salud
9 Mercado
10 Lighthouse
12 Bus Station
14 Post Office
15 Palacio Municipal
16 Templo de la
    Purísima Concepción

The bus stations are near the main square. It's six short blocks from the main square to the Malecón and the muelle.

Places to Stay

Progreso is a resort, and thus a bit expensive. On Sunday in July and August, even the cheapest hotels fill up.

The best of Progreso's budget inns is the *Hotel Miralmar* (☎ (993) 5-05-52), Calle 77 No 124 on the corner of Calle 76, offering rooms with private shower, fan and one double bed for 65 pesos, with two beds for 78 pesos. Rooms on the upper floor are preferable – they're not as dungeon-like as the ground-floor rooms.

Several good lodging places are located right on the Malecón facing the sea. *Hotel Playa Linda* (☎ (993) 5-11-57), Malecón at Calle 76, is a simple little two-storey place with rooms renting for 72 pesos a double with two beds. You get a private shower, a fan and lounge chairs on the front terrace.

Three blocks east on the corner of Male-cón and Calle 70 are two more hotels. *Tropical Suites* (☎ (993) 5-12-63) is perhaps the nicest in this part of town, with tidy rooms with showers and fans going for 80 to 145 pesos a double. Some rooms have sea views.

Hotel Real del Mar (☎ (993) 5-05-23), between Calles 70 and 72 behind the Restaurant Pelicanos, is an older hostelry which looks its age sometimes, but is still a good deal as it's right on the Malecón. Rooms with shower and fan cost 70 pesos a single or double with one bed, 88 pesos a double/triple with two beds, or 100 pesos for a suite.

Hotel Carismar (☎ (993) 5-29-07), Calle 71 No 151 between 78 and 80, has cheap rooms for 68 pesos a double with bath.

Places to Eat

Seafood is the strong point on the menus of Progreso's restaurants, of course. Note that if you come on a day trip to Progreso, you can often change clothes at the *vestidores* (changing cubicles) attached to most beach-front restaurants.

An all-purpose inexpensive eatery on the north side of the main square is *Restaurant El Cordóbes*, on the corner of Calles 81 and 80, open from early morning until late at night. Standard fare – tacos, enchiladas, sandwiches, chicken etc – is served at good prices.

About the best prices you can find at an eatery on the Malecón are at *Morgan's*, between Calles 80 and 78, a Mexican beach restaurant where you can get a full fish dinner for about 45 pesos, everything included.

As you move eastward along the Malecón, restaurant prices rise. *Restaurant Carabela*, Malecón between Calles 68 and 70, is the spot for the young and hip beach crowd who come for the high-volume rock music (the bass notes shake the tables). Hamburgers are 18 pesos, fish plates twice as much.

At the east end of the Malecón between Calles 62 and 60, almost one km from the muelle, stands *Capitán Marisco* (☎ 5-06-39), perhaps Progreso's fanciest seafood restaurant and certainly one of its most pleasant.

Getting There & Away

Both Dzibilchaltún and Progreso are due north of Mérida along a fast four-lane highway that's basically a continuation of the Paseo de Montejo. If you're driving, head north on the Paseo and follow signs for Progreso. Those travelling by bus must go to the Progreso bus station, 1½ blocks south of the main plaza in Mérida at Calle 62 No 524 between Calles 65 and 67.

Progreso is 18 km (20 minutes) beyond the Dzibilchaltún turnoff. A bus from Mérida to Progreso costs 4.50 pesos one way.

CELESTÚN

Famed as a bird sanctuary, Celestún makes a good beach-and-bird day trip from Mérida. Although this region abounds in anhingas and egrets, most birdwatchers come here to see the flamingos.

The town is located on a spit of land between the Río Esperanza and the Gulf of Mexico. Brisk westerly sea breezes cool the town on most days. The white-sand beach is appealing, but on some days fierce afternoon winds swirl clouds of choking dust through the town. The dust makes the sea silty, and therefore unpleasant for swimming in the afternoon. Row upon row of fishing boats outfitted with twin long poles line the shore.

Given the winds, the best time to see birds is in the morning. Hire a lancha from the bridge on the highway one km east of the town. The rental should run to about 60 pesos for a 90-minute tour of the flamingo-inhabited areas.

Orientation

You come into town along Calle 11, past the marketplace and church (on your left/south) to Calle 12, the waterfront street.

Yucatán flamingos

Places to Stay

Hotels are few, and filled on weekends. A daytrip from Mérida is the best way to visit, but you can try for a room at the places listed below:

Turn left (south) along Calle 12 from Calle 11 to find the *Hotel Gutiérrez* (☎ (99) 28-04-19, 28-69-78), Calle 12 No 22, at Calle 13, the top budget choice, with well-kept rooms with fan and bath costing 75 pesos. *Hotel Maria del Carmen*, just south of it, is similar; enter from Calle 15.

Turn right (north) from Calle 11 along Calle 12 to find the *Hotel San Julio* (☎ 1-85-89), Calle 12 No 92, at Calle 9, where singles/doubles with fan and bath cost 44/54 pesos.

Places to Eat

The junction of Calles 11 and 12 has many small restaurants, including the *Celestún*, *Playita*, *Boya* and *Avila*, most with sea views and seafood. The cheaper eateries, as always, are inland.

Getting There & Away

Buses run from Mérida's Autotransportes del Sur station on Calle 50 No 531 at Calle 67. There are several per day on weekdays, increasing on the weekends to run hourly until 2 pm and every two hours thereafter until 10 pm. The 92-km trip takes about 1½ to two hours and costs 8.50 pesos.

UXMAL

Set in the Puuc Hills, which lent their name to the architectural patterns in this region, Uxmal was an important city during the Late Classic period (600-900 AD) in a region which encompassed the satellite towns of Sayil, Kabah, Xlapak and Labná. Although Uxmal means 'thrice built' in Maya, it was actually reconstructed five times.

That a sizeable population flourished at all in this area is a mystery, as there is precious little water in the region. The Mayan cisterns (chultunes) must have been adequate.

History

First occupied in about 600 AD, the town has been architecturally influenced by highland Mexico, and features well-proportioned Puuc style which is unique to this region.

Given the scarcity of water in the Puuc Hills, Chac the rain god was of great significance. His image is ubiquitous here in stucco monster-like masks protruding from façades and cornices.

There is much speculation as to why Uxmal was abandoned around 900 AD. Drought conditions may have reached such proportions that the inhabitants had to relocate. One widely held theory suggests that the rise to greatness of Chichén Itzá drew people away from the Puuc Hills.

Rediscovered by archaeologists in the 19th century, Uxmal was first excavated in 1929 by Frans Blom. Although much has been restored, there is still a good deal to discover.

Chac mask on a building at Uxmal

Orientation & Information

As you come into the site from the highway, you'll enter a car park (the cost is 4.50 pesos per car); the Hotel Villa Arqueológica is to the left at the end of a short entrance road. You enter the site through the modern Unidad Uxmal building, which contains the Restaurant Yax-Beh. Also in the Unidad Uxmal are toilets, a small museum, an auditorium, and shops selling souvenirs, crafts and books.

The archaeological site is open daily from 8 am to 5 pm, and admission costs 21.60 pesos. The Unidad Uxmal building stays open till 10 pm because of the 45-minute Luz y Sonido (Light & Sound) show, held each evening in English (12 pesos) at 9 pm and in Spanish (10 pesos) at 7 pm.

Pyramid of the Magician

This tall temple, 39 metres high, was built on an oval base. The smoothly sloping sides have been restored; they date from the temple's fifth incarnation. The four earlier temples were covered in the rebuilding, except for the high doorway on the west side, which has been retained from the fourth temple. Decorated in elaborate Chenes style, the doorway proper takes the form of the mouth of a gigantic Chac mask.

The ascent to the doorway and the top is best done from the west side. Heavy chains serve as handrails to help you up the very steep steps.

From the top of the pyramid, you can survey the rest of the archaeological site. Directly west of the pyramid is the Nunnery Quadrangle. On the south side of the quadrangle, down a short slope, is a ruined ball court. Further south stands the great artificial terrace holding the Governor's Palace; between the palace and the ball court is the small House of the Turtles. Beyond the Governor's Palace are the remains of the Great Pyramid, and next to it are the House of the Pigeons and the South Temple. There once were many other structures at Uxmal, but most have been recaptured by the jungle and are now just verdant mounds.

Nunnery Quadrangle

Archaeologists guess that this 74-room quadrangle might have been a military academy, royal school or palace complex. The long-nosed face of Chac appears everywhere on the façades of the four separate temples which form the quadrangle. The northern temple, grandest of the four, was built first, followed by the south, east and west temples.

Several decorative elements on the façades show signs of Mexican, perhaps Totonac, influence. The feathered serpent (Quetzalcóatl) motif along the top of the west temple's façade is one of these. Note also the stylised depictions of the *na*, or Mayan thatched hut, over some of the doorways in the northern and southern buildings.

Ball Court

Pass through the corbelled arch in the middle of the south building of the quadrangle and continue down the slope to the ball court, which is much less impressive than the great ball court at Chichén Itzá.

House of the Turtles

Climb the steep slope up to the artificial terrace on which stands the Governor's Palace. At the top on the right is the House of the Turtles, which takes its name from the turtles carved on the cornice. The frieze of short columns or 'rolled mats' which runs around the top of the temple is characteristic of the Puuc style. Turtles were associated by the Maya with the rain god Chac. According to Mayan myth, when the people suffered from drought so did the turtles and both prayed to Chac to send rain.

Governor's Palace

The magnificent façade of the palace, nearly 100 metres long, has been called 'the finest structure at Uxmal and the culmination of the Puuc style' by Mayanist Michael D Coe. Buildings in Puuc style have walls filled with rubble, faced with cement and then covered in a thin veneer of limestone squares; the lower part of the façade is plain, the upper part festooned with stylised Chac faces and

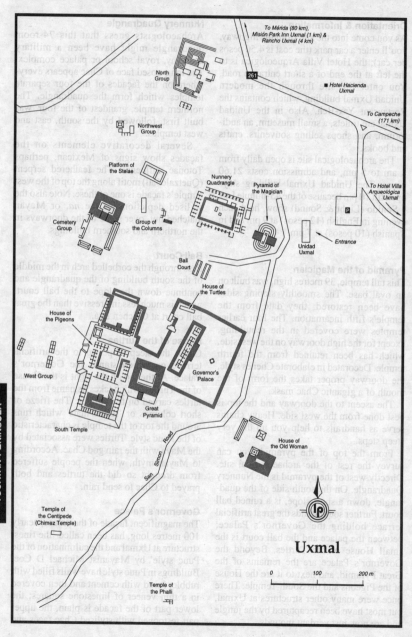

To Mérida (80 km),
Misión Park Inn Uxmal (1 km) &
Rancho Uxmal (4 km)

261

■ Hotel Hacienda
Uxmal

To Campeche
(171 km)

To Hotel Villa
Arqueológica Uxmal

North Group

Northwest
Group

Platform of
the Stelae

Nunnery
Quadrangle

Pyramid
of the Magician

Cemetery
Group

Group of
the Columns

P

Entrance

Unidad
Uxmal

Ball
Court

House of
the Turtles

House of
the Pigeons

West Group

Great Pyramid

Governor's
Palace

South Temple

San Simon Road

House of
the Old Woman

Temple of
the Centipede
(Chimez Temple)

Temple of
the Phalli

Uxmal

0   100   200 m

YUCATÁN PENINSULA

The Yucatán Peninsula
Top: Sound and light show, Uxmal (TW)
Bottom: Nunnery Quadrangle, Uxmal (RB)

The Yucatán Peninsula
Top: Xel-ha Lagoon (RB)
Bottom Left: Stairway, Chichén Itzá (DT)
Bottom Right: Musicians in the plaza, Mérida (DT); Yucatán folk dancers, Mérida (JL)

geometric designs, often lattice-like or fretted. Other elements of Puuc style are decorated cornices, rows of half-columns and round columns in doorways. The stones forming the corbelled vaults in Puuc style are shaped like boots.

Great Pyramid

Adjacent to the Governor's Palace, this 32-metre mound has been restored only on the northern side. There is a quadrangle at the top which archaeologists theorise was largely destroyed in order to construct another pyramid above it. This work, for reasons unknown, was never completed. At the top are some stucco carvings of Chac, birds and flowers.

House of the Pigeons

West of the great pyramid sits a structure whose roofcomb is latticed with a pigeon-hole pattern – hence the building's name. The nine honeycombed triangular belfries sit on top of a building which was once part of a quadrangle. The base is so eroded that it is difficult for archaeologists to guess its function.

House of the Old Woman & Temple of the Phalli

Both sites are located between the main highway and the San Simon road, south-west of the Governor's Palace. The House of the Old Woman, which is now largely rubble, was according to Mayan mythology the home of a dwarf magician's mother, a sorceress. Just to the south sits the Temple of the Phalli, which is festooned with phallic sculptures. Some of these served as spouts to drain water from the roof. Some archaeologists think the temple was constructed by later invaders, as the Maya are not believed to have had any phallic cult.

Cemetery Group

Lying on the path west of the ball court, these stone altars have skull-and-crossbone sculptures, but there is no real evidence that this was a cemetery.

Places to Stay & Eat – bottom end

As there is no town at Uxmal, only the archaeological site and several top-end hotels, you cannot depend upon finding cheap food or lodging.

Campers can pitch their tents five km north of the ruins on highway 261, the road to Mérida, at *Rancho Uxmal* (☎ in Ticul (997) 2-02-77) for 12 pesos per person. Several serviceable guest rooms with shower and fan go for 100 pesos a double (expensive for what you get, but then this is Uxmal), and there's a restaurant. It may take you 45 to 55 minutes to walk here – in the hot sun – from the ruins, but there's some possibility of hitching a ride.

The *Posada Uxmal Restaurant Nicté-Ha*, just across the highway from the road to the ruins, on the grounds of the Hotel Hacienda Uxmal, is a simple eatery open daily from 12.30 to 7 pm offering sandwiches, fruit salads and similar fare at prices slightly lower than those at the Yax-Beh. Often staff will allow you to use the hotel's swimming pool after you've bought a meal.

Places to Stay & Eat – top end

The *Hotel Hacienda Uxmal* (☎ (99) 24-71-42), 500 metres from the ruins across the highway, originally housed the archaeologists who explored and restored Uxmal. High ceilings with fans, good cross-ventilation and wide, tiled verandas set with rocking-chairs make this an exceptionally pleasant and comfortable place to stay, and the beautiful swimming pool is a dream come true on a sweltering hot day.

Simple rooms in the annexe cost 150 pesos a single or double; the nicer rooms in the main building range from 235 to 435 pesos a single, 260 to 470 pesos a double. Meals are mediocre and moderately priced. You can supposedly make reservations in Mérida at the Mérida Travel Service in the Hotel Casa del Balam (☎ (99) 24-88-44), on the corner of Calles 60 and 57, but they seem not to know the correct room prices and always say the hotel is fully booked, even if it isn't.

Hotel Villa Arqueológica Uxmal (in Mérida, ☎ (99) 24-70-53, Apdo Postal 449) is the closest lodging to the ruins. Run by Club Med, this attractive modern hotel offers a swimming pool, tennis courts, a good French-inspired restaurant and air-con guestrooms for 235/270/325 pesos a single/double/triple.

The *Hotel Misión Park Inn Uxmal* (in Mérida ☎ /fax (99) 24-73-08) is set on a hilltop two km north of the turnoff to the ruins. Many rooms have balcony views of Uxmal. Rooms with fan are priced at 320 pesos a single or double.

Getting There & Away

Air An airstrip is under construction near Uxmal. When it is finished routes from Cancún will be developed, making it possible for Cancúnites to visit Uxmal on a day excursion.

Bus Several readers have written to complain of poor-quality tours booked from Mérida hotels. It's better to make the trip on your own. From Mérida's Terminal de Autobuses it's 80 km (1½ hours) to Uxmal. ADO operates a special tour bus which departs Mérida at 8.30 am, visits each Puuc

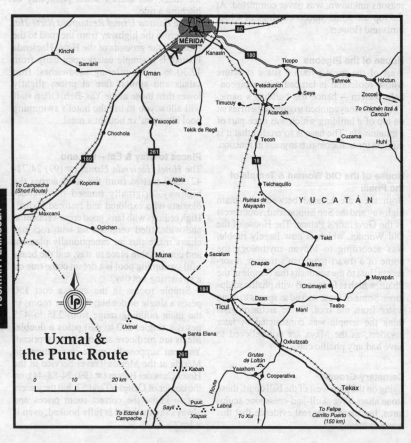

Uxmal & the Puuc Route

Route site for 30 minutes, stops at Uxmal for two hours, then returns to Mérida by 4 or 4.30 pm, for 35 pesos. This is perhaps the best way to tour if you have no wheels of your own.

Eight 2nd-class buses (8 pesos) of the Autobuses del Sur line make the trip daily and there are other buses as well. They'll drop you right at the turnoff to the ruins, only 400 metres away. For the return trip to Mérida, some buses depart from the car park at the archaeological site entrance; others must be flagged down on the main road. In late afternoon there may be standing room only.

If you're going to Ticul, hop on a bus heading north, get off at Muna and get another bus eastwards to Ticul.

For buses to Kabah, the Puuc Route turnoff and points on the road to Campeche, flag down a bus at the turnoff to the ruins.

THE PUUC ROUTE

Uxmal is undoubtedly the finest Mayan city in the Puuc Hills, but the ruins at Kabah, Sayil, Xlapak and Labná, and the Grutas de Loltún, offer a deeper acquaintance with the Puuc Maya civilisation. The Palace of Masks at Kabah and El Palacio at Sayil are especially worth seeing. The Grutas de Loltún (Loltún Caves) are also impressive. ADO operates a special tour bus which departs Mérida at 8.30 am, visits each Puuc Route site for 30 minutes, stops at Uxmal for two hours, then returns to Mérida by 4 or 4.30 pm, for 35 pesos.

Kabah

The Zona Arqueológica Puuc and the ruins of Kabah, just over 18 km south-east of Uxmal, are right astride highway 261. The site is open from 8 am to 5 pm; admission costs 10 pesos.

The guard shack and souvenir shop are on the east side of the highway as you approach. Cold drinks and junky snacks are sold.

Undoubtedly the most impressive building here is the **Palace of Masks**, or Codz Poop, set on its own high terrace on the right-hand (east) side of the highway. It's an amazing sight, with its façade covered in

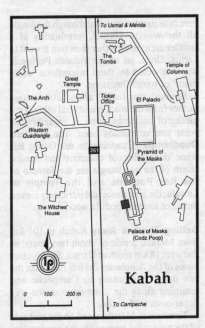

nearly 300 masks of Chac, the rain god or sky serpent.

To the north of the Palace of Masks is a small **pyramid**. Further north is **El Palacio**, with a broad façade having several doorways; in the centre of each doorway is a column, a characteristic of the Puuc architectural style. Walk around the north side of El Palacio and follow a path into the jungle for several hundred metres to the **Temple of Columns**, called the Tercera Casa, famous for the rows of semi-columns on the upper part of its façade.

Cross the highway to the west of El Palacio, walk up the slope and on your right you'll pass a high mound of stones that was once the Gran Teocalli, or **Great Temple**. Continue straight on to the sacbe, or cobbled and elevated ceremonial road, and look right to see a ruined monumental arch with the Mayan corbelled vault (two straight stone surfaces leaning against one another, meeting at the top). It is said that the sacbe

YUCATÁN PENINSULA

here runs past the arch and through the jungle all the way to Uxmal, terminating at a smaller arch; in the other direction it went to Labná. Once, all of the Yucatán Peninsula was connected by these marvellous 'white roads' of rough limestone.

Beyond the sacbe, about 600 metres farther from the road, are several other complexes of buildings, none as impressive as what you've already seen. The **Western Quadrangle** (Cuadrángulo del Oeste) has some decoration of columns and masks. North of the quadrangle are the **Temple of the Key Patterns** and the **Temple of Lintels**; the latter once had intricately carved lintels of tough sapodilla wood.

Getting There & Away Kabah is 101 km from Mérida, a ride of about two hours, or just over 18 km south of Uxmal. Six 1st-class buses of the Autobuses del Sur line make the run daily, continuing to Campeche and returning along the same route; a one-way ticket costs 6.25 pesos.

To return to Mérida, stand on the east side of the road at the entrance to the ruins and try to flag down a bus. Buses in both directions are often full, however, and won't stop, so it may be a good idea to try organise a lift back with some other travellers at the site itself. Many visitors come to Kabah by private car and may be willing to give you a lift, either back to Mérida, or southward on the Puuc Route. If you're trying to get a bus to the Puuc Route turnoff, five km south of Kabah, or to other sites along highway 261 farther south, stand on the west side of the highway.

Sayil

Five km south of Kabah a road turns east: this is the Puuc Route. Despite the interesting archaeological sites along this route, there is not much traffic and hitchhiking can be difficult. The ruins of Sayil are 4.5 km east of the junction with highway 261, on the south side of the road. Sayil is open daily from 8 am to 5 pm; admission costs 10 pesos.

El Palacio Sayil is best known for El Palacio, the huge three-tiered building with a façade

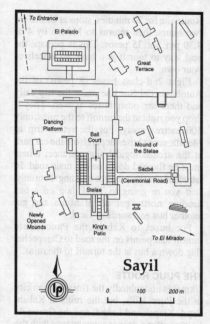

some 85 metres long that makes one think of the Minoan palaces on Crete. The distinctive columns of Puuc architecture are used here over and over, as supports for the lintels, as decoration between doorways and as a frieze above the doorways, alternating with huge stylised Chac masks and 'descending gods'.

Climb to the top level of the Palacio and look to the north to see several *chultunes*, or stone-lined cisterns, in which precious rainwater was collected and stored for use during the dry season. Some of these chultunes can hold more than 30,000 litres.

El Mirador If you take the path southwards from the palace for about 800 metres you come to the temple named El Mirador, with its interesting rooster-like roofcomb once painted bright red. About 100 metres beyond El Mirador by the path to the left is a stele beneath a protective palapa. It bears a relief of a phallic god that has become severely weathered over the centuries.

Xlapak

From the entrance gate at Sayil, it's six km east to the entrance gate at Xlapak ('shla-PAK'). The name means Old Walls in Maya and was a general term among local people for ancient ruins, about which they knew little. The site is open from 8 am to 5 pm; admission is 7 pesos.

The ornate palace at Xlapak is smaller than those at Kabah and Sayil, measuring only about 20 metres in length. It's decorated with the inevitable Chac masks, columns and colonnettes and fretted geometric latticework of the Puuc style. To the right is the rubble of what were once two smaller buildings.

Labná

From the entrance gate at Xlapak, it's 3.5 km east to the gate at Labná. The site here is open from 8 am to 5 pm; admission costs 4 pesos.

The Arch Labná is best known for its magnificent arch, once part of a building which separated two quadrangular courtyards. It now appears to be a gate joining two small plazas. The corbelled structure, three metres wide and six metres high, is well preserved

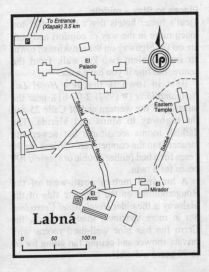

To Entrance
(Xlapak) 3.5 km

P

El
Palacio

Eastern
Temple

Sacbe (Ceremonial Road)

Sacbe

El
Mirador

El
Arco

Labná

0   50   100 m

and stands close to the entrance of Labná. The mosaic reliefs decorating the upper façade are exuberantly Puuc in style.

If you look at the ornate work on the north-eastern side of the arch, you will make out mosaics of Mayan huts. At the base of either side of the arch are rooms of the adjoining building, now ruined, including upper lattice patterns constructed atop a serpentine design.

El Mirador Standing on the opposite side of the arch and separated from it by the limestone-paved sacbe is a pyramid with a temple atop it called El Mirador. The pyramid itself is poorly preserved, being largely stone rubble. The temple, with its five-metre-high roofcomb, true to its name, looks like a watchtower.

Palace Archaeologists believe that at one point in the 9th century, some 3000 Maya lived at Labná. To support such numbers in these arid hills, water was collected in chultunes. At Labná's peak there were some 60 chultunes in and around the city; several are still visible.

The palace, the first edifice you come to at Labná, is connected by a sacbe to El Mirador and the arch. One of the longest buildings in the Puuc Hills, its design is not as impressive as its counterpart at Sayil. There's a ghoulish sculpture at the eastern corner of the upper level of a serpent gripping a human head between its jaws. Close to this carving is a well-preserved Chac mask.

Grutas de Loltún

From Labná it's 15 km eastward to the village of Yaaxhom, surrounded by lush orchards and palm groves which are surprising in this generally dry region. From Yaaxhom a road goes another four km north-east to Loltún.

Loltún Caves are the most interesting grutas in Yucatán. More than just a fine subterranean realm for spelunkers, Loltún has provided a treasure trove of data for archaeologists studying the Maya, as well as some impressive artefacts. The caves contain

YUCATÁN PENINSULA

spectacular stalactite and stalagmite formations, and carbon dating has provided evidence that they were first used by humans as long as 2500 years ago.

There is no sign on the road to tell you that you've arrived at the grutas, so you must look for a park-like enclosure with a gravel road entrance.

Loltún is open daily from 9 am to 5 pm, and the fee is 25 pesos. To explore the 1.5-km labyrinth, you must take one of the scheduled guided tours at 9.30 and 11 am, or at 12.30, 2 and 3 pm; these tours may depart early if enough people are waiting. The guides may be willing to take you through at other hours if you offer a substantial tip (a few dollars). Occasionally there is a guide on the premises who speaks English – check to see if the tour will be in a language you understand. The guides, who are not paid by the government, expect a tip at the end of the hour-long tour.

For refreshments there's the *Restaurant El Guerrero* near the exit of the caves, a walk of eight to 10 minutes (600 metres) along a marked path from the far side of the parking lot near the cave entrance. Once you get to the restaurant you'll find that their comida corrida costs about 32 pesos. Icy-cold drinks are served at high prices.

Getting There & Away Loltún is on a country road leading to Oxkutzcab (eight km) and there is usually some transport along the road. Try hitching, or catch a paying ride in one of the colectivos – often a *camioneta* (pickup truck) or *camión* (truck or lorry) – which ply this route, costing about 2.50 pesos for the ride. A taxi from Oxkutzcab may charge 25 pesos or so, one way, for the eight-km ride.

Buses run frequently every day between Mérida and Oxkutzcab via Ticul.

If you're driving from Loltún to the Puuc Route site of Labná, drive out of the Loltún car park, turn right and take the next road on the right, which passes the access road to the restaurant. Do not take the road marked for Xul. After four km you'll come to the village of Yaaxhom, where you turn right to join the Puuc Route westwards.

TICUL

Ticul, 30 km east of Uxmal, is the largest town south of Mérida in this ruin-rich region. It has several serviceable hotels and restaurants, and good transport. It's also a centre for fine huipil weaving – the embroidery on these dresses is extraordinary. For both quality and price, Ticul is a good place to buy this traditional Mayan garment. Ticul's main street is Calle 23, sometimes called the Calle Principal, going from the highway north-east past the market and the town's best restaurants to the main plaza.

Places to Stay – bottom end

Hotel Sierra Sosa (☎ (997) 2-00-08, fax 2-02-82), Calle 26 No 199A, half a block north-west of the plaza, has very basic rooms for 36 pesos a single or double. A few rooms at the back have windows, but most are dark and dungeon-like. Be sure the ceiling fan works.

Similarly basic but more expensive is the *Hotel San Miguel* (☎ (997) 2-03-82), Calle 28 No 195, near Calle 23 and the market. Singles at the San Miguel cost 40 pesos with fan and bath, doubles 44 to 50 pesos.

Places to Stay – middle

Ticul's better hotels don't really offer too much more in the way of comfort and both are on the highway on the outskirts of town, an inconvenient two-km walk from the centre, but fine if you have a car.

Best in town is the new *Hotel Las Bougambillias* (☎ (997) 2-07-61), near the junction of the western end of Calle 25 and the highway to Muna and Mérida. The darkish rooms are simple but newer and cleaner than the competition's. Prices are 70 pesos for a bed (either double or single), 100 pesos for a twin.

A hundred metres north-west of the Bougambillias on the opposite side of the highway is the older *Hotel-Motel Cerro Inn*. Set in more spacious, shady grounds, the Cerro Inn has nine well-used rooms with private shower and ceiling fan going for 60 to 70 pesos a double.

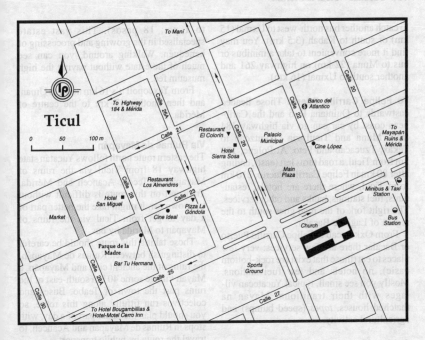

Places to Eat

Inexpensive Ticul's lively market provides all the ingredients for picnics and snacks. It also has lots of those wonderful market eateries where the food is good, the portions generous and the prices low. For variety, try out some of the loncherías along Calle 23 between Calles 26 and 30.

Should you want a sit-down meal, there's the cheap *Restaurant El Colorín* (☎ 2-03-14), Calle 26 No 199B, just close to the Hotel Sierra Sosa half a block north-west of the plaza. *Pizza La Góndola*, Calle 23 at Calle 26A, is tidy, with two-person pizzas cooked to order for 18 to 30 pesos.

Mid-Range *Restaurant Los Almendros* (☎ 2-00-21), Calle 23 No 207, between 26A and 28, is set up in a fortress-like town house with a large courtyard and portico. The air-con restaurant, open every day from 9 am to 8 pm, is fairly plain, but the food is authentically Yucatecan. The *combinado yucateco*,

or Yucatecan combination plate, with a soft drink or beer, will cost less than 40 pesos.

Getting There & Away

Ticul's bus station is behind the massive church off the main square. Numerous companies make the 85-km, 1½-hour run between Mérida and Ticul for 10 to 12 pesos. There are also three buses to Felipe Carrillo Puerto (25 pesos), frequent ones to Oxkutzcab (4 pesos), and five a day to Chetumal (12 hours, 55 pesos).

You can catch a minibus (combi) from the intersection of Calles 23 and 28 in Ticul to Oxkutzcab (that's 'osh-kootz-KAHB'), 16 km away, and from Oxkutzcab a minibus or pickup truck to Loltún (eight km); ask for the camión to Xul ('SHOOL'), but get off at Las Grutas de Loltún.

Minibuses to Santa Elena (15 km), the village between Uxmal and Kabah, also depart from the intersection of Calles 23 and 28, taking a back road and then leaving you to catch another bus north-west to Uxmal (15 km) or south to Kabah (3.5 km). You may find it more convenient to take a minibus or bus to Muna (22 km) on highway 261 and another south to Uxmal (16 km).

To Felipe Carrillo Puerto Those headed eastwards to Quintana Roo and the Caribbean coast by car can go via highway 184 from Muna and Ticul via Oxkutzcab to Tekax, Tzucacab and Peto. At Polguc, 130 km from Ticul, a road turns left (east), ending after 80 km in Felipe Carrillo Puerto, 210 km from Ticul, where there are hotels, restaurants, fuel stations, banks and other services. The right fork of the road goes south to the region of Lago de Bacalar.

From Oxkutzcab to Felipe Carrillo Puerto or Bacalar there are few services: very few places to eat (those that exist are rock-bottom basic), no hotels and few fuel stations. Mostly you see small, typical Yucatecan villages with their traditional Mayan na thatched houses, *topes* (speed bumps) and agricultural activity.

Getting Around
The local method of getting around is to hire a three-wheeled cycle, Ticul's answer to the rickshaw. You'll see them on Calle 23 just up from the market, and the fare is less than 4 pesos for a short trip.

TICUL TO MÉRIDA
Via Muna & Yaxcopoil
From Ticul to Mérida you have a choice of routes. The western route to Muna, then north on highway 261, is fastest, with the best bus services.

Muna$IMuna (Yuc), an old town 22 km north-west of Ticul, has several interesting colonial churches, including the former Convento de la Asunción and the churches of Santa María, San Mateo and San Andrés.

The hacienda of Yaxcopoil, 29 km north of Muna on the west side of highway 261, has numerous French Renaissance-style buildings which have been restored and turned into a museum of the 17th century (open from 8 am to 6 pm, Sunday from 9 am

to 1 pm; 18 pesos). This vast estate specialised in the growing and processing of henequén. Walking around, you can see much of the estate without paying the high museum fee.

From Yaxcopoil it's 16 km north to Uman, and then another 17 km to the centre of Mérida.

Via Ruinas de Mayapán
The eastern route north follows Yucatán state highway 18 from Ticul via the ruins of Mayapán to Tecoh, Acanceh and Mérida. Transport on this route is difficult without your own car. It might take the better part of a day to get from Ticul via the ruins of Mayapán to Mérida by bus.

Those taking this route should be careful to distinguish between Ruinas de Mayapán, the ruins of the ancient city, and Mayapán, a Mayan village some 40 km south-east of the ruins past the town of Teabo. Buses and colectivos run fitfully along this route, so you should plan the better part of a day, with stops in Ruinas de Mayapán and Acanceh, to travel the route by public transport.

If you're driving, follow the signs from Ticul north-east via Chapab to Mama (25 km), which has a peculiarly fortress-like church, then farther north-east to Tekit (seven km). At Tekit, turn left (north-west) on Yucatán state highway 18 toward Tecoh, Acanceh and Kanasin; the Ruinas de Mayapán are eight km north-west of Tekit on the left (west) side of the road.

RUINAS DE MAYAPÁN
The city of Mayapán, once a major Mayan capital, was huge, with a population estimated at around 12,000. Its ruins cover several sq km, all surrounded by a great defensive wall. Over 3500 buildings, 20 cenotes and traces of the city wall were mapped by archaeologists working in the 1950s and early '60s. The city's workmanship was inferior to the great age of Mayan art; though the Cocom rulers of Mayapán tried to revive the past glories of Mayan civilisation, they succeeded only in part.

History

Mayapán was supposedly founded by Kukulcán (Quetzalcóatl) in 1007, shortly after the former ruler of Tula arrived in Yucatán. His dynasty, the Cocom, organised a confederation of city-states which included Uxmal, Chichén Itzá and many other notable cities. Despite their alliance, animosity between the Cocoms and the Itzaes led to the storming of Chichén Itzá by the Cocoms during the late 1100s, which forced the Itzá rulers into exile. The Cocom dynasty under Hunac Ceel Canuch emerged supreme in all of the northern Yucatán Peninsula and obliged the other rulers to pay tribute.

Cocom supremacy lasted for almost 2½ centuries, until the ruler of Uxmal, Ah Xupán Xiú, led a rebellion of the oppressed city-states and overthrew Cocom hegemony. The great capital of Mayapán was utterly destroyed and was uninhabited ever after.

But there was no peace in Yucatán after the Xiú victory. The Cocom dynasty recovered and frequent struggles for power erupted until 1542, when Francisco de Montejo the Younger founded Mérida. The ruler of the Xiú people, Ah Kukum Xiú, submitted his forces to Montejo's control in exchange for a military alliance against the Cocoms. The Cocoms were defeated and – too late – the Xiú rulers realised that they had willingly signed the death warrant of Mayan independence.

Information

At the caretaker's hut 100 metres in from the road, pay the admission fee of 10 pesos and enter the site any day between 8 am and 5 pm. If you have camping equipment, the caretaker may grant you permission to camp near his hut. Facilities consist of a latrine and a well with a bucket.

Ruins

Jungle has returned to cover many of the buildings, though you can visit several cenotes (including Itzmal Chen, a main Mayan religious sanctuary) and make out the large piles of stones which were once the Temple of Kukulcán and the circular Caracol. Though the ruins today are far less impressive than those at other sites, Mayapán has a stillness and a loneliness (usually undisturbed by other tourists) that seems to fit its melancholy later history. The entry fee to the ruins is 7 pesos.

RUINAS DE MAYAPÁN TO MÉRIDA

About two km north of the Ruinas de Mayapán is **Telchaquillo**. Beneath the village plaza is a vast cenote filled with rainwater, which is still used as a water source during the dry months.

From Telchaquillo it's 11 km north to **Tecoh**, with its church and well-kept Palacio Municipal separated by a green football pitch. From Tecoh it's only 35 km to Mérida, but you should plan a short stop in Acanceh.

The road enters **Acanceh** and goes to the main plaza, which is flanked by a shady park and the church. To the left of the church is a partially restored pyramid (entry fee 7 pesos), and to the right are market loncherías if you're in need of a snack. In the park, note the statue of the smiling deer; the name Acanceh means Pond of the Deer. Another local sight of interest is the cantina Aqui Me Queda (I'm Staying Here), a ready-made answer for wives who come to the cantina to urge their husbands homeward.

Continuing north-west you pass through Petectunich, Tepich, San Antonio and Kanasin before coming to Mérida's periférico (ring road).

IZAMAL

• *pop: 40,000*

In ancient times, Izamal was a centre for the worship of the supreme Mayan god Itzamná and the sun god Kinich Kakmó. A dozen temple pyramids in the town were devoted to these or other gods. Perhaps this Mayan religiosity is why the Spanish colonists chose Izamal as the site for an enormous and very impressive Franciscan monastery.

Today Izamal is a small, quiet provincial town with the atmosphere of life in another century. Its two principal squares are surrounded by impressive arcades and dominated by the gargantuan bulk of the

Convento de San Antonio de Padua. There are a few small, cheap hotels and eateries.

Convento de San Antonio de Padua

When the Spaniards conquered Izamal, they destroyed the major Mayan temple, the Popul-Chac pyramid, and in 1533 began to build from its stones one of the first monasteries in the western hemisphere. The work was finished in 1561.

The monastery's principal church is the Santuario de la Virgen de Izamal, approached by a ramp from the main square. Walk up the ramp and through an arcaded gallery to the Atrium, a spacious arcaded courtyard in which the fiesta of the Virgin of Izamal takes place each 15 August.

Entry to the church is free. The best time to visit is in the morning, as it may be closed during the afternoon siesta. The monastery and church were restored and spruced up for the papal visit of John Paul II in August 1993.

If you wander around town, you may come across remnants of the other 11 Mayan pyramids. The largest is the temple of Kinich Kakmó; all are unrestored piles of rubble.

Getting There & Away

There are direct buses several times daily from Mérida (72 km, 1½ hours, 12 pesos). Five 2nd-class buses (2 hours, 15 pesos) serve Izamal from Valladolid; if you don't catch one of these, you must change buses at Hóctun. If you're driving eastward, turn north at Hóctun; if westward, at Kantunil.

CHICHÉN ITZÁ

The most famous and best restored of the Yucatán Peninsula's Mayan sites, Chichén Itzá will awe even the most jaded of visitors. Many mysteries of the Mayan astronomical calendar are made clear when one understands the design of the 'time temples' here. But one astronomical mystery remains: why do most people come here from Mérida and Cancún on day trips, arriving at 11 am, when the blazing sun is getting to its hottest point, and departing around 3 pm when the heat finally begins to abate? You'd do better to stay the night nearby and do your exploration

of the site either early in the morning or late in the afternoon.

Should you have the good fortune to visit Chichén Itzá on the vernal equinox (20 to 21 March) or autumnal equinox (21 to 22 September), you can witness the light-and-shadow illusion of the serpent ascending or descending the side of the staircase of El Castillo. The illusion is almost as good in the week preceding and the week following the equinox.

History

Most archaeologists agree that Chichén Itzá's first major settlement, during the Late Classic period between 550 and 900 AD, was pure Mayan. In about the 10th century, the city was largely abandoned for unknown reasons.

The city was resettled about 1000, and shortly thereafter, Chichén seems to have been invaded by Toltecs who had moved down from their central highlands capital of Tula, north of Mexico City. Toltec culture was fused with that of the Maya, incorporating the cult of Quetzalcóatl (Kukulcán in Maya). (See the Toltecs section of History in Facts about the Country for more on this.) You will see images of both Chac, the Mayan rain god, and Quetzalcóatl, the plumed serpent, throughout the city.

The substantial fusion of highland central Mexican and Puuc architectural styles make Chichén unique among the Yucatán Peninsula's ruins. The fabulous El Castillo, the Temple of Panels and the Platform of Venus are all outstanding architectural works built during the height of Toltec cultural input.

After a Mayan leader moved his political capital to Mayapán while keeping Chichén as his religious capital, Chichén Itzá fell into decline. Why it was subsequently abandoned in the 14th century is a mystery, but the once-great city remained the site of Mayan pilgrimages for many years.

Orientation

Most of Chichén's lodgings, restaurants and services are ranged along one km of highway in the village of Piste ('PEESS-teh'), to the

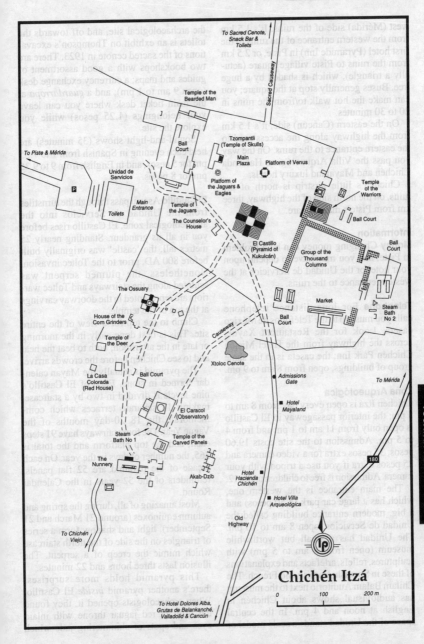

To Sacred Cenote,
Snack Bar &
Toilets

Sacred Causeway

Temple of the
Bearded Man

Ball Court

Tzompantli
(Temple of Skulls)

Main
Plaza

Platform of Venus

To Piste & Mérida

P

Unidad de
Servicios

Main
Entrance

Toilets

Platform of
the Jaguars &
Eagles

Temple of the Jaguars

The Counselor's
House

El Castillo
(Pyramid of
Kukulcán)

Temple of
the Warriors

Ball Court

Ball Court

Group of the
Thousand
Columns

The Ossuary

House of the
Corn Grinders

Temple of
the Deer

Market

Steam
Bath
No 2

La Casa
Colorada
(Red House)

Ball Court

Causeway

Xtoloc Cenote

To Mérida

Admissions
Gate

El Caracol
(Observatory)

Hotel
Mayaland

Steam
Bath No 1

Temple of the
Carved Panels

The Nunnery

Akab-Dzib

180

Hotel
Hacienda
Chichén

Hotel Villa
Arqueológica

To Chichén
Viejo

Old
Highway

Chichén Itzá

0   100   200 m

To Hotel Dolores Alba,
Grutas de Balankanché,
Valladolid & Cancún

YUCATÁN PENINSULA

west (Mérida) side of the ruins. It's 1.5 km from the western entrance of the ruins to the first hotel (Pyramide Inn) in Piste, or 2.5 km from the ruins to Piste village square (actually a triangle), which is shaded by a huge tree. Buses generally stop at the square; you can make the hot walk to/from the ruins in 20 to 30 minutes.

On the eastern (Cancún) side, it's 1.5 km from the highway along the access road to the eastern entrance to the ruins. On the way you pass the Villa Arqueológica, Hacienda Chichén and Mayaland luxury hotels.

Chichén's little airstrip is north of the ruins, on the north side of the highway, three km from Piste's main square.

Information

Money Changing money can be a problem in Piste, and you may have to depend upon your hotel or the Unidad de Servicios at the western entrance to the ruins.

Telephone For long-distance telephone calls you must go to the Teléfonos de México caseta. Look for the Restaurant Xaybe, across the highway from the Hotel Misión Chichén Park Inn; the caseta is in the same group of buildings, open from 8 am to 9 pm.

Zona Arqueológica

Chichén Itzá is open every day from 8 am to 5 pm; the interior passageway in El Castillo is open only from 11 am to 1 pm and from 4 to 5 pm. Admission to the site costs 19.60 pesos, 35 pesos extra for a video camera and 25 pesos extra if you use a tripod with your camera. Admission is free to children under 12.

The main entrance is the western one, which has a large car park (4.50 pesos) and a big, modern entrance building called the Unidad de Servicios, open 8 am to 10 pm. The Unidad has a small but worthwhile museum (open from 8 am to 5 pm) with sculptures, reliefs, artefacts and explanations of these in Spanish, English and French. The Chilam Balam Auditorio next to the museum has audiovisual shows about Chichén in English at noon and 4 pm. In the central space of the Unidad stands a scale model of

the archaeological site, and off towards the toilets is an exhibit on Thompson's excavations of the sacred cenote in 1923. There are two bookshops with a good assortment of guides and maps; a currency exchange desk (open 9 am to 1 pm); and a *guardarropa* at the main ticket desk where you can leave your belongings (1.25 pesos) while you explore the site.

Sound-and-light shows (35 minutes) are held each evening in Spanish from 7 to 7.35 pm for 5 pesos, and in English from 9 to 9.35 pm for 8 pesos.

El Castillo As you pass through the turnstiles from the Unidad de Servicios into the archaeological zone, El Castillo rises before you in all its grandeur. Standing nearly 25 metres tall, the 'castle' was originally built before 800 AD, prior to the Toltec invasion. Nonetheless, the plumed serpent was sculpted along the stairways and Toltec warriors are represented in the doorway carvings at the top of the temple.

Climb to the top for a view of the entire site. This is best done early in the morning or late in the afternoon, both to beat the heat and to see Chichén before the crowds arrive.

The pyramid is actually the Mayan calendar formed in stone. Each of El Castillo's nine levels is divided in two by a staircase, making 18 separate terraces which commemorate the 18 20-day months of the Vague Year. The four stairways have 91 steps each; add the top platform and the total is 365, the number of days in the year. On each façade of the pyramid are 52 flat panels, reminders of the 52 years in the Calendar Round.

Most amazing of all, during the spring and autumn equinoxes (around 21 March and 21 September), light and shadow form a series of triangles on the side of the north staircase which mimic the creep of a serpent. The illusion lasts three hours and 22 minutes.

This pyramid holds more surprises: there's another pyramid *inside* El Castillo. When archaeologists opened it, they found the brilliant red jaguar throne with inlaid eyes and spots of shimmering jade which still lies within. The inner sanctum also holds a Toltec chac-mool figure.

The inner pyramid is only open from 11 am to 1 pm and 4 to 5 pm. Entry is not a good idea for claustrophobes or those who hate close, fetid air.

Principal Ball Court The principal ball field, the largest and most impressive in Mexico, is only one of the city's eight courts, indicative of the importance the games held here. The field is flanked by temples at either end and bound by towering parallel walls with stone rings cemented up high.

There is evidence that the ball game may have changed over the years. Some carvings show players with padding on their elbows and knees and it is thought that they played a soccer-like game with a hard rubber ball, forbidding the use of hands. Other carvings show players wielding bats; it appears that if a player hit the ball through one of the stone hoops, his team was declared the winner. It may be that during the Toltec period the losing captain, and perhaps his team-mates as well, were sacrificed.

Along the walls of the ball court are some fine stone reliefs, including scenes of decapitations of players. Acoustically the court is amazing – a conversation at one end can be heard 135 metres away at the other end, and if you clap, you hear a resounding echo.

Temple of the Bearded Man & Temple of the Jaguars The structure at the northern end of the ball court, known as the Temple of the Bearded Man and named for a carving inside it, has some finely sculpted pillars and reliefs of flowers, birds and trees. See also the temple at the end of the court facing out on El Castillo. This Temple of the Jaguars (the south-eastern corner of the ball court) has some rattlesnake-carved columns and jaguar-etched tablets. Inside are faded mural fragments depicting a battle, possibly between the Toltecs and the Maya.

Tzompantli The Tzompantli, a Toltec term for Temple of Skulls, is between the Temple of the Jaguars and El Castillo. You can't

mistake it because the T-shaped platform is festooned with carved skulls and eagles tearing open the chests of men to eat their hearts. In ancient days this platform held the heads of sacrificial victims.

Platform of the Jaguars & Eagles Adjacent to the Temple of Skulls, this platform's carvings depict jaguars and eagles gruesomely grabbing human hearts in their claws. It is thought that this platform was part of a temple dedicated to the military legions responsible for capturing sacrificial victims.

Carving of a jaguar eating a human heart, Platform of the Jaguars & Eagles

Platform of Venus Rather than a beautiful woman, the Toltec symbol for the planet Venus is a feathered serpent bearing a human head between its jaws, of which you can see many examples on this structure.

Sacred Cenote A 300-metre rough stone road runs north (a five-minute walk) to the huge sunken well that gave this city its name. The Sacred Cenote is an awesome natural well, some 60 metres in diameter and 35 metres deep. The walls between the summit and the water's surface are ensnared in tangled vines and other vegetation. There are ruins of a small steam bath next to the cenote, as well as a modern drinks stand with toilets.

Although some of the guides enjoy telling

Dredging the Sacred Cenote

Around the turn of the century Edward Thompson, a Harvard professor and US Consul to Yucatán, bought the hacienda which included Chichén Itzá for US$75. No doubt intrigued by local stories of female virgins being sacrificed to the Mayan deities by being thrown into the cenote, Thompson resolved to have the cenote dredged. He imported dredging equipment (some of which is on display in the Unidad de Servicios), and set to work. Valuable gold and jade jewellery from all parts of Mexico and as far away as Colombia was recovered, along with many other artefacts and a variety of human bones. Many of the artefacts were shipped to Harvard's Peabody Museum, but many have since been returned to Mexico.

Subsequent diving expeditions in the 1920s and 1960s – some of them important ones sponsored by the US National Geographic Society – turned up hundreds more valuable artefacts. It appears that all sorts of people, including children and old people, the diseased and the injured, as well as the young and the vigorous, were forcibly obliged to take that eternal swim in Chichén's Sacred Cenote. ■

---

visitors that female virgins were sacrificed by being thrown into the cenote to drown, divers in 1923 brought up the remains of men, women and children.

Skeletons were not all that was found in the Sacred Cenote. Artefacts and valuable gold and jade jewellery from all parts of Mexico were recovered.

The artefacts' origins show the far-flung contacts the Maya had (there are some items from as far away as Colombia). It is believed that offerings of all kinds, human and otherwise, were thrown into the Sacred Cenote to please the gods.

Group of the Thousand Columns Comprising the Temple of the Warriors, Temple of Chac-Mool and Sweat House or Steam Bath, this group takes its name from the forest of pillars in front.

The platformed temple greets you with a statue of the reclining god, Chac, as well as stucco and stone-carved animal deities. The temple's roof, once supported by columns entwined with serpents, disappeared long ago.

Archaeological work in 1926 revealed a Temple of Chac-Mool beneath the Temple of the Warriors. You may enter via a stairway on the north side. The walls inside have badly deteriorated murals of what is thought to be the Toltecs' defeat of the Maya.

Just east of the Temple of the Warriors lies the rubble of a Mayan sweat house, with an underground oven and drains for the water.

The sweat houses were regularly used for ritual purification.

Ossuary The Ossuary, otherwise known as the Bonehouse or High Priest's Grave, is a ruined pyramid. As with most of the buildings in this southern section, the architecture is more Puuc than Toltec.

La Casa Colorada La Casa Colorada, or The Red House, was named by the Spaniards for the red paint of the mural on its doorway. This building has little Toltec influence and its design shows largely a pure Puuc-Maya style. Referring to the stone latticework at the roof façade, the Maya named this building Chichán-Chob, or House of Small Holes.

El Caracol Called El Caracol (The Giant Conch Snail) by the Spaniards for its interior spiral staircase, the observatory is one of the most fascinating and important of all of Chichén Itzá's buildings. Its circular design resembles some central highlands structures, although, surprisingly, not those of Toltec Tula. In a fusion of architectural styles and religious imagery, there are Mayan Chac rain god masks over four external doors facing the cardinal directions.

The windows in the observatory's dome are aligned with the appearance of certain stars at specific dates. From the dome the priests decreed the times for rituals, celebrations, corn-planting and harvests.

Nunnery & Annexe Thought by archaeologists to have been a palace for Mayan royalty, the Nunnery, with its myriad rooms, resembled a European convent to the conquistadors, hence their name for the building. The Nunnery's dimensions are imposing: its base is 60 metres long, 30 metres wide and 20 metres high. The construction is Mayan rather than Toltec, although a Toltec sacrificial stone stands in front. A small building added onto the west side is known as the Annexe. These buildings are in the Puuc-Chenes style, particularly evident in the lower jaw of the Chac mask at the opening of the Annexe.

Akab-Dzib On the path east of the Nunnery, the Akab-Dzib is thought by some archaeologists to be the most ancient structure excavated here. The central chambers date from the 2nd century. Akab-Dzib means Obscure Writing in Maya and refers to the south-side Annexe door whose lintel depicts a priest with a vase etched with hieroglyphics. The writing has never been translated, hence the name. Note the red fingerprints on the ceiling, thought to symbolise the deity Itzamna, the sun god from whom the Maya sought wisdom.

Chichén Viejo Chichén Viejo, or Old Chichén, comprises largely unrestored, basically Mayan ruins, though some have Toltec additions. Here you'll see a pristine part of Chichén without much archaeological restoration.

Grutas de Balankanché
In 1959 a guide to the Chichén ruins was exploring a cave on his day off. Pushing against a cavern wall, he broke through into a larger subterranean opening. Archaeological exploration revealed a path that runs some 300 metres past carved stalactites and stalagmites, terminating at an underground pool.

The Grutas de Balankanché are six km east of the ruins of Chichén Itzá, and two km east of the Hotel Dolores Alba on the highway to Cancún. Second-class buses

heading east from Piste toward Valladolid and Cancún will drop you at the Balankanché road. You'll find the entrance to the caves 350 metres north of the highway.

As you approach the caves, you enter a pretty botanical garden displaying many of Yucatán's native flora, including many species of cactus. In the entrance building is a little museum, a shop selling cold drinks and souvenirs and a ticket booth. Plan your visit for an hour when the compulsory tour and Light & Colour Show will be given in a language you can understand: the 40-minute show (minimum six persons, maximum 30) is given in the cave at 11 am, 1 and 3 pm in English, at 9 am, noon and 2 and 4 pm in Spanish and at 10 am in French. Tickets are available between 9 am and 4 pm (last show) daily. Admission costs 14.60 pesos.

Places to Stay
Most of the lodgings convenient to Chichén are in the middle and top-end price brackets. No matter what you plan to spend on a bed, be prepared to haggle in the off season (May, June, September and October) when prices should be lower at every hotel.

Places to Stay – bottom end
Camping There's camping at the *Pirámide Inn & Trailer Park* (☎ (985) 6-26-71 ext 115) on the eastern edge of Piste (closest to the ruins). For 18 pesos per person you can pitch a tent, enjoy the Pirámide Inn's pool and watch satellite TV in the lobby. There are hot showers and clean, shared toilet facilities. Those in vehicles pay 55 pesos for two for full hook-ups.

Hotels Unfortunately, there's not much. *Posada Chac-Mool*, just east of the Hotel Misión Chichén on the opposite (south) side of the highway in Piste, is now overpriced and dingy at 80 pesos for a double with shower and fan. *Posada El Paso*, a few dozen metres west of the Stardust Inn, is a much better choice, at the same price. *Posada Poxil* (☎ (985) 6-25-13 ext 116 or 123), at the western end of the town, charges the same for relatively clean, quiet rooms.

Places to Stay – middle

Hotel Dolores Alba (☎ in Mérida (99) 21-37-45), Carretera Km 122, is just over three km east of the eastern entrance to the ruins and two km west of the road to Balankanché, on the highway to Cancún. (Ask the bus driver to stop here.) There are more than a dozen rooms surrounding a small swimming pool. The dining room is good (breakfasts 12 to 15 pesos, dinner 35 pesos), which is important as there is no other eating facility nearby. They will transport you to the ruins, but you must take a taxi, bus or walk back. Single/double rooms with fan and shower cost 65/80 pesos; with air-con, 100/120 pesos.

Stardust Inn, next to the Pirámide Inn in Piste and less than two km from the ruins, is an attractive place with two tiers of rooms surrounding a palm-shaded swimming pool and restaurant. Air-con rooms with TV cost 160 pesos per single or double.

The *Pirámide Inn* next door has been here for years. Its grounds are very pretty, having had years to mature, and its swimming pool is a blessing on a hot day. There's a selection of different rooms, some older, some newer (look before you buy), all air-con and priced at 140/175/200/235 pesos a single/double/triple/quad. Here, you're as close as you can get to the archaeological zone's western entrance.

Places to Stay – top end

All of these hotels have beautiful swimming pools, restaurants, bars, well-kept tropical gardens, comfortable guest rooms and tour groups coming and going. Several are very close to the ruins. If you are going to splurge on just one expensive hotel in Mexico, this is a good place to do it.

Hotel Mayaland (☎ in Mérida (99) 25-21-22; reservations ☎ (99) 25-23-42, 25-22-46; toll-free in USA 800-235-4079; fax 25-70-22), a mere 200 metres from the eastern entrance to the archaeological zone, is the oldest (1923) and most gracious in Chichén. From the lobby you look through the main portal to see El Caracol framed as in a photograph. Rooms are priced at 400 pesos a double.

A sister hotel to the Mayaland is the *Hotel Hacienda Chichén*, just a few hundred metres farther from the ruins on the same eastern access road. This was the hacienda where the archaeologists lived when excavating Chichén. Their bungalows have been refurbished and new ones built. It's the choice of the discerning traveller who wants to avoid the crowds of the tour buses yet have some comforts. Rooms in the garden bungalows have ceiling fans and private baths, but no TVs or phones. These are available for 360 pesos a double. The dining room serves simple meals at moderate prices. The Hacienda Chichén usually closes from May to October. For reservations, call as for the Mayaland.

The *Hotel Villa Arqueológica* (☎ (985) 6-28-30), Apdo Postal 495, Mérida, is a few hundred metres east of the Mayaland and Hacienda Chichén on the eastern access road to the ruins. Run by Club Med, it's a modern layout with a good restaurant, tennis courts and swimming pool. Rooms are fairly small but comfortable and air-con and priced at 300/350/375 pesos a single/double/triple.

On the western side of Chichén, in the village of Piste, the *Hotel Misión Chichén* (☎ (985) 6-26-71 ext 104; toll-free in USA 800-648-7818) is two km from the ruins entrance on the north side of the highway. It's comfortable without being distinguished. Singles/doubles cost 285/325 pesos.

Places to Eat

The cafeteria in the *Unidad de Servicios* at the western entrance to the archaeological zone serves mediocre food at high prices in pleasant surroundings.

The highway through Piste is lined with little restaurants, most of them fairly well tarted up in a Mayan villager's conception of what foreign tourists expect to see. Prices are fairly high for what you get and most of these places serve only table d'hôte meals at lunch, which means you must pay one set price for a full-course meal; you can't pick and choose from a menu or just order something light as one might want to do in the heat.

Of the Piste restaurants, the *Restaurant*

Sayil, facing the Hotel Misión Chichén, is probably the cheapest; it's a plain little *restaurante económico* serving cochinita or pollo pibil for 12 pesos, rice with garnish for 4.50 pesos and egg dishes for 7.50 pesos. Another simple eatery with wooden benches and tables is the *Restaurant Parador*.

Prices are only slightly higher at the attractive, family-run *Restaurant Carrousel*, where you can order a platter of pollo pibil or cochinita pibil for under 30 pesos, eggs and a few antojito choices for even less. The big palapa-covered dining room is pleasant and open from 10.30 am to 6.30 pm.

If you are willing to spend the money, the *Restaurant Xaybe* opposite the Hotel Misión Chichén has good cuisine, usually served buffet style in a surprisingly formal, air-con dining room for the tour bus clientele. Figure on paying 45 pesos for lunch, and just slightly more for dinner, for all you can eat. Customers of the restaurant get to use its swimming pool for free, but even if you don't eat here, you can still swim for about 8 pesos.

Most tarted up of the restaurants in Piste is the fantastical *Restaurant Fiesta*, which is worth a look if not a meal. The luncheon table d'hôte goes for 45 pesos, but you can order from the menu in the evening, when substantial portions of meat cost 25 pesos, and tacos 12 to 23 pesos.

The luxury hotels all have restaurants, with the Club Med-run *Villa Arqueológica* serving particularly distinguished cuisine. If you try its French-inspired Mexican-Mayan restaurant, it'll cost you about 90 pesos per person for a table d'hôte lunch or dinner, and almost twice that much if you order à la carte – but the food is good.

Getting There & Away

Air Aerocaribe runs one-day return-trip excursions by air from Cancún to Chichén Itzá in little planes, charging 360 pesos for the flight.

Bus Most of the considerable bus traffic between Mérida, Valladolid and Cancún, both 1st and 2nd-class buses (at least two dozen daily), passes by Chichén Itzá. The fastest services are on the buses which use the cuota (toll road) for at least part of the journey. Here are some bus routes from Piste:

Cancún – 205 km, two to three hours, 18 to 30 pesos
Izamal – 95 km, 1½ to two hours, 13 pesos, you may have to change buses at Hóctun
Mérida – 116 km, two to 2½ hours, 18 to 22 pesos
Valladolid – 42 km, 30 to 45 minutes, 3 to 4.50 pesos; frequent buses

Getting Around

Be prepared for walking at Chichén Itzá: from your hotel to the ruins, around the ruins, and back to your hotel, all in the very hot sun and humidity. For the Grutas de Balankanché, you can set out to walk early in the morning when it's cooler (it's eight km from Piste, less if you're staying on the eastern side of the ruins) and then hope to hitch a ride or catch a bus for the return.

A few taxis are available in Piste and sometimes at the Unidad de Servicios car park at Chichén Itzá, but you cannot depend upon finding one unless you've made arrangements in advance.

VALLADOLID

• *pop: 80,000*

Valladolid is only 40 km (half an hour) east of Chichén Itzá and 160 km (about two hours) west of Cancún but as it has no sights of stop-the-car immediacy, few tourists do stop here; most prefer to hurtle on through to the next major site. It's just as well, for this preserves Valladolid for the rest of us who want to enjoy it.

History

The Mayan ceremonial centre of Zací was here long before the Spaniards arrived. The initial attempt at conquest in 1543 by Francisco de Montejo, nephew of Montejo the Elder, was thwarted by fierce Mayan resistance, but the Elder's son Montejo the Younger ultimately conquered the Maya and took the town. The Spanish laid out a new city on the classic colonial plan.

During much of the colonial era, Valladolid's distance from Mérida, its humidity and surrounding forests kept it isolated from royal rule and thus relatively autonomous. Banned from even entering this town of pure-blooded Spaniards, the Maya rebelled, and in the War of the Castes of 1847 they made Valladolid their first point of attack. Besieged for two months, Valladolid's defenders were finally overcome; many of the citizens fled to the safety of Mérida and the rest were slaughtered by the Mayan forces.

Orientation & Information

Odd-numbered streets run east-west, even-numbered streets run north-south. Recommended hotels are on or close to the main plaza, known as the Parque Francisco Cantón Rosado. The plaza is bound by Calles 39 and 41, and 40 and 42.

The old highway goes right through the centre of town, though all signs will direct you to the Cuota, north of town. To follow the old highway eastbound, follow Calle 41; westbound, Calle 39 or 35. The bus terminal is on Calle 37 between Calles 54 and 56, eight blocks from the plaza.

The post office is on the east side of the main plaza at Calle 40 No 195A. Hours are Monday to Friday from 8 am to 6 pm, Saturday from 9 am to 1 pm.

Church of San Bernardino de Siena & Convent of Sisal

Although Valladolid has a number of interesting colonial churches, the Church of San Bernardino de Siena and the Convent of Sisal, 1.5 km south-west of the plaza, are said to be the oldest Christian structures in Yucatán. Constructed in 1552, the complex was designed to serve a dual function as fortress and church.

If the convent is open, go inside. Apart from the miracle-working Virgin of Guadalupe on the altar, the church is relatively bare. During the uprisings of 1847 and 1910, angry Indians stripped the church of its decoration.

To get to the church, walk west on Calle 41 one km, then turn left and walk 500 metres to the convent. If you're riding a bicycle to the Cenote Dzitnup, you can stop at the convent on your way.

Other Churches

The Cathedral of San Gervasio, with its pretty garden, faces the Plaza San Roque, on the corner of Calles 41 and 42. It has an exhibition hall of Mayan artefact photographs. Other churches include Santa Ana on the corner of Calles 41 and 34, La Candelaria at Calles 44 and 35, San Juan Iglesia on the corner of Calles 49 and 40, and Santa Lucía on the corner of Calles 40 and 27.

Cenotes

Cenotes, those vast underground limestone sinkholes, were the Maya's most dependable source of water. The Spaniards used them also. The Cenote Zací, Calle 36 between Calles 39 and 37 is Valladolid's most famous.

Set in a pretty park which also holds the town's museum, an open-air amphitheatre and traditional stone-walled thatched houses, the cenote is vast, dark, impressive and covered with a layer of scum. It's open daily from 8 am to 8 pm; admission costs 7.50 pesos for adults, half-price for children.

More beautiful, but less easily accessible, is Cenote Dzitnup (Xkakah), seven km west of Valladolid's main plaza. Follow the main highway west towards Mérida for five km. Turn left (south) at the sign for Dzitnup and follow the road for just under two km to get to the site, on the left. A taxi from Valladolid's main plaza charges 36 pesos for the excursion there and back, with half an hour's wait.

Another way to reach the cenote is on a bicycle rented from the Refaccionaría de Bicicletas de Paulino Silva, on Calle 44 between Calles 39 and 41, facing Hotel María Guadalupe; look for the sign 'Alquiler y Venta de Bicicletas'. Rental costs 4 pesos per hour. The first five km are not particularly pleasant because of the traffic, but the last two km are on a quiet country road. It should take you only 20 minutes to pedal to the cenote.

Another way to get there is to hop aboard a westbound bus, ask the driver to let you off

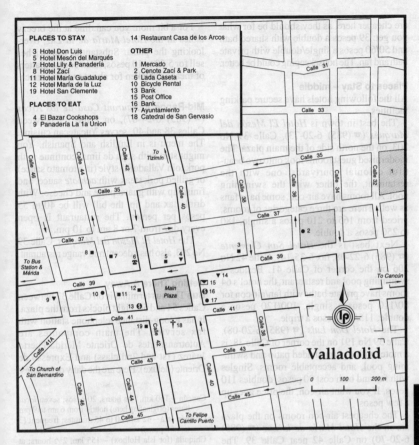

PLACES TO STAY

3 Hotel Don Luis
5 Hotel Mesón del Marqués
7 Hotel Lily & Panadería
8 Hotel Zací
11 Hotel María Guadalupe
12 Hotel María de la Luz
19 Hotel San Clemente

PLACES TO EAT

4 El Bazar Cookshops
9 Panadería La 1a Union

14 Restaurant Casa de los Arcos

OTHER

1 Mercado
2 Cenote Zací & Park
6 Lada Caseta
10 Bicycle Rental
13 Bank
15 Post Office
16 Bank
17 Ayuntamiento
18 Catedral de San Gervasio

Calle 31
Calle 33
Calle 35
Calle 37
Calle 39
Calle 41
Calle 41A
Calle 42
Calle 43
Calle 44
Calle 45

Calle 46
Calle 44
Calle 42
Calle 40
Calle 38
Calle 36
Calle 34
Calle 32

To Tizimín
To Bus Station & Mérida
To Cancún
To Church of San Bernardino
To Felipe Carrillo Puerto

Main Plaza

Valladolid

0   100   200 m

YUCATÁN PENINSULA

at the Dzitnup turning, then walk the final two km (20 minutes) to the site. Cenote Dzitnup is open daily from 7 am to 6 pm and entry 5 pesos.

As you approach, a horde of village children will surround you, each wanting to be your 'guide' to the cenote, 10 metres away. Even if you don't appoint one, they will accompany you down into the cave.

Places to Stay – bottom end

The best budget choice in town is the *Hotel María Guadalupe* (☎ (985) 6-20-68), Calle 44 No 188 between Calles 39 and 41. Kept

clean and in fresh paint, the simple rooms here go for 35/40/55 pesos a single/double/triple with private shower and fan. Arrive early in the day to get a room.

Hotel Zací (☎ (985) 6-21-67) is at Calle 44 No 191, between Calles 37 and 39. The Zací's rooms are built around a quiet, pleasant garden courtyard complete with swimming pool. Choose from rooms with fan for 60/90/125 pesos a single/double/triple or with air-con for about 6 to 10 pesos more.

Across the street and down a few doors is the *Hotel Lily* (☎ (985) 6-21-63), Calle 44 No 190, between Calles 37 and 39. Rooms are cheaper here, as they should be for what you get: 39 pesos a double with shared bath and 50/60 pesos a single/double with private bath and fan. The housekeeping could be better.

Places to Stay – middle

All the following hotels have secure parking facilities.

The best in town is *Hotel El Mesón del Marqués* (☎ (985) 6-20-73), Calle 39 No 203, on the north side of the main plaza. The modernised guest rooms look onto two beautiful colonial courtyards, one with the restaurant, the other with the swimming pool. All rooms have air-con, some have fans as well. There are three categories of rooms, priced from 165 to 210 pesos a single, 180 to 250 pesos a double.

Next best is the *Hotel San Clemente* (☎ (985) 6-22-08, fax 6-35-14), Calle 42 No 206 on the corner of Calle 41. Besides a swimming pool and restaurant, the hotel's 64 rooms have private baths with fan/air-con for 80/110 pesos a single, 100/120 pesos a double, 115/130 pesos a triple.

The *Hotel Don Luis* (☎ (985) 6-20-08), Calle 39 No 191 on the corner of Calle 38, is a motel with a palm-shaded patio and swimming pool, and acceptable rooms. Singles with fan and bath cost 90 pesos, doubles 110 pesos. If you want air-con, the price goes up a few pesos.

The cheapest air-con rooms on the plaza are in the *Hotel María de la Luz* (☎ (985) 6-20-70) on Calle 42 near Calle 39. The rooms surround a tiny court with trees and a much-used swimming pool. Rooms are 110 pesos a single or double with private bath and air-con, a bit cheaper with fan.

Places to Eat

Inexpensive *El Bazar* is a collection of little open-air, market-style cookshops on the corner of Calles 39 and 40, the north-east corner of the plaza. This is a great place for breakfast. At lunch and dinner time, a comida corrida of soup, main course and a drink costs around 15 pesos. There are a dozen eateries here open from 6.30 am to 2 pm and from 6 to about 9 or 10 pm.

For a bit more you can dine at the breezy tables in the *Hotel María de la Luz*, overlooking the plaza. Substantial sandwiches sell for 5.50 to 10 pesos, main course platters of meat or chicken for about twice as much.

Mid-Range *Restaurant Casa de los Arcos* (☎ (985) 6-24-67), on Calle 39 between Calles 38 and 40, serves Yucatecan cuisine. The menu is in English and Spanish. You might start with sopa de lima, continue with pork loin Valladolid-style (in a tomato sauce) or grilled pork steak with *achiote* sauce, and finish up with guava paste and cheese. With drink, tax and tip, the bill will be 40 to 55 pesos per person. The restaurant is open every day from 7 or 8 am to 10 pm.

The *Hotel El Mesón del Marqués*, Calle 39 No 203, also has a decent mid-range restaurant.

Getting There & Away

Bus The bus terminal is on Calle 37 between Calles 54 and 56, eight blocks from the plaza. It has a long-distance telephone station with fax service. The main companies are Autotransportes de Oriente Mérida-Puerto Juárez (1st and 2nd class) and Expresso de Oriente (deluxe). Here are the daily departures:

Cancún – 160 km, two hours, 20 pesos; seven *local* buses (originating here) hourly from 6 am to 9 pm

Chichén Itzá – 42 km, 30 to 45 minutes; frequent (3 to 4.50 pesos)

Chiquilá (for Isla Holbox) – 155 km, 2½ hours; at least one 2nd-class bus (18 pesos)

Cobá – 106 km, two hours; two 2nd-class buses (15 pesos)

Izamal – 115 km, two hours; five 2nd-class buses (15 pesos) by Autobuses del Centro del Estado de Yucatán

Mérida – 160 km, three hours; seven *local* buses (originating here) hourly from 6 am to 9 pm, 1st class (22 pesos)

Playa del Carmen – 230 km, 3½ hours; two 1st-class buses (32 pesos)

Río Lagartos – 103 km, two hours; one local 2nd-class bus (15 pesos) at 10 am; or change at Tizimin

Tizimin – 51 km, one hour; two 2nd-class buses (7.50 pesos) at 10 am and 1.30 pm by Autobuses del Noreste en Yucatán

Tulum – 360 km, six hours; two 1st-class buses (40 pesos)

Taxi A quicker, more comfortable, but more expensive way to Cancún is by taking one of the shared taxis parked outside the bus station, which leave as soon as all seats are filled. The trip costs approximately twice the bus fare.

TIZIMIN

Many travellers bound for Río Lagartos change buses in Tizimin (Place of Many Horses), the second-largest city in the state of Yucatán. There is little to warrant an overnight stay, but the main plaza is pleasant.

Two great colonial structures, the Convento de los Tres Reyes Magos (Monastery of the Three Wise Kings) and the Convento de San Francisco de Assisi (Monastery of Saint Francis of Assisi) are worth a look. Five lengthy blocks from the plaza, northwest on Calle 51, is a modest zoo, the Parque Zoológico de la Reina.

The Banco del Atlantico, next to the Hotel San Jorge on the south-west side of the plaza, changes money between 10 am and noon Monday to Friday. Banco Internacional is open from 9 am to 1.30 pm.

Places to Stay

Hotel San Jorge (☎ (986) 3-20-37), Calle 53 No 411, near Calle 52, on the south side of the plaza, is perhaps the town's best and boasts a swimming pool the size of a hot tub. Basic but serviceable rooms with private bath cost 85/110 pesos for a double with fan/air-con.

Hotel San Carlos (☎ (986) 3-20-94), Calle 54 No 407, 1½ long blocks from the plaza, is built like a motel, and charges identical prices.

Posada María Antonia (☎ (986) 3 23 84), Calle 50 No 408, on the east side of the Parque de la Madre, also has comfy rooms. Those with fan cost 85 pesos; doubles with air-con cost 100 pesos. The reception desk is also a Lada caseta.

Places to Eat

The market, a block north-west of the bus station, has the usual cheap eateries.

Perhaps the best dining in town is at *Restaurant Los Tres Reyes* (☎ 3-21-06), on the corner of Calles 52 and 53. It opens early for breakfast and is a favourite with town notables who take their second cup of coffee around 9 am. Lunch or dinner costs 11 to 18 pesos.

Tortas Económicas La Especial, on the main square, has cheap sandwiches and drinks, as does the *Cocina Económica Ameli*.

Otherwise, there's *Pizzería Cesar's*, on the corner of Calles 50 and 53, facing the Parque de la Madre. Pizza and pasta are the attractions here, in the evening (5.30 to 11 pm) only. You can eat in air-con comfort for 9 to 22 pesos.

Restaurant Los Portales is near the august portals of the Palacio Municipal on the north-east side of the plaza. It's a simple place, good for a quick sandwich or burger and a cold drink. *Restaurant La Parrilla*, on the north-west side of the plaza, is another unpretentious place open for lunch and dinner only.

For snacks, make-your-own breakfasts and bus food, drop by the *Panificadora La Especial* on Calle 55, down a little pedestrian lane from the plaza.

Getting There & Away

Autobuses del Noreste en Yucatán operates daily buses from Valladolid to Tizimin (51 km, one hour, 7.50 pesos) at 10 am and 1.30 pm. From Cancún and Puerto Juárez, there are several direct buses to Tizimin (215 km, four hours, 25 pesos). There are several daily 1st and 2nd-class buses between Tizimin and Mérida via Valladolid. For Río Lagartos there are three 1st-class bus departures and five daily 2nd-class buses which continue to San Felipe.

RÍO LAGARTOS

It is worth going out of your way to this little fishing village, 103 km north of Valladolid and 52 km north of Tizimin, to see the most spectacular flamingo colony in Mexico. The estuaries are also home to snowy egrets, red egrets, great white herons and snowy white ibis. Although Río Lagartos (Alligator River) was named after the once substantial

YUCATÁN PENINSULA

Great white heron

alligator population, don't expect to see any as hunting has virtually wiped them out.

The town of Río Lagartos itself, with its narrow streets and multihued houses, has little charm, though the panorama of the boats and the bay is pleasant. Were it not for the flamingos, you would have little reason to come here. Although the state government has been making noises about developing the area for tourism, this has not happened yet.

At the centre of town is a small triangular plaza, the Presidencia Municipal (Town Hall) and the Conasupo store.

Flamingos

If you walk some of the 14 km along the beach from the lagoon out to Punta Holohit on the sea, you will most likely see colourful bird life. Species common to the area include egrets, herons, flamingos, ibis, cormorants, stilts, pelicans and plovers.

A short boat trip (two to three hours) to see a few nearby local flamingos and to have a swim at the beach costs a high 130 to 150 pesos for a five-seat boat, and prices are enforced by a newly-created boat owner's union. (If you can find a fishing boat owner who is not a member of the union, the price drops almost in half.) The much longer voyage (four to six hours) to the flamingos' favourite

haunts costs 400 pesos or so for the boat, or about 80 pesos per person for a full load.

Places to Stay & Eat

The *Hotel María Nefertiti* (☎ 1-4-15), Calle 14 No 123, a hulk of a place, charges 75 pesos for rooms with bath and fan. An alternative is to rent one of the two cabañas in the yard of Tere and Miguel's house for 50 pesos a double. Tere will make coffee for you. Ask any local where to find them.

As for food, try the *Restaurant Isla Contoy*, Calle 19 No 134, which does a particularly good pescado a la Veracruzana for 20 pesos.

Getting There & Away

Autobuses del Noreste en Yucatán operates daily buses from Valladolid to Tizimín (51 km, one hour, US$2) at 10 am and 1.30 pm. The 10 am bus goes on to Río Lagartos (103 km, two hours, US$4); if you miss this one, you must change buses in Tizimín. There is also one direct bus daily between Tizimín and Mérida.

SAN FELIPE

• *pop: 400*

This tiny fishing village of painted wooden houses on narrow streets, 12 km west of Río Lagartos, makes a nice day trip from Río Lagartos. While the waters are not Caribbean turquoise and there's little shade, in spring and summer scores of visitors come here to camp. Other than lying on the beach, bird-watching is the main attraction, as just across the estuary at Punta Holohit there is abundant bird life.

There are no hotels in San Felipe, but the proprietor of La Herradura grocery store near the pier will tell you about inexpensive house rentals. Spartan rooms are sometimes available for rent above the Cinema Marrufo. Campers are ferried across the estuary to islands where they pitch tents or set up hammocks.

The town's sole eatery, *Restaurant El Payaso*, is cheap and quite good for seafood.

Some buses from Tizimín to Río Lagartos continue to San Felipe and return. The 12-km ride takes about 20 minutes.

Quintana Roo

In the past two decades, Mexico's once-sleepy Caribbean coastline has been subject to furious development. From being one of the country's most backward and sparsely populated areas, Quintana Roo is well on the way to becoming just the opposite.

Why? Long stretches of beautiful beach, warm water, luxuriant undersea coral reefs, interesting islands and a lust for bucks. The Quintana Roo coast is nature in the service of Mammon.

CANCÚN
• *pop: 250,000*

In the 1970s Mexico's ambitious tourism planners decided to build a brand new world-class resort on a deserted sand spit offshore from the little fishing village of Puerto Juárez. The island sandspit was shaped like a lucky '7'. The name of the place was Cancún.

The Yucatán Peninsula's major international airport is here, as are doctors, modern hospitals, consular representatives, rental car agencies and many other services.

Dozens of mammoth hotels march along the island's shore as it extends from the mainland nine km eastward, then 14 km southward, into the turquoise waters of the Caribbean. At the north the island is joined to the mainland by a bridge which leads to Ciudad Cancún; at the south a bridge joins a road leading inland to the international airport.

The Mexican government built Cancún as an investment in the tourism business. Cancún's reason-for-being is to shelter planeloads of tourists who fly in (usually on the weekend) to spend one or two weeks in a resort hotel before flying home again (usually on a weekend). They have a good time. This is the business of tourism.

Orientation
Ciudad Cancún is a planned community on the mainland. On the 23-km-long sandy island is the Zona Hoteles, or Zona Turística, with its towering hotels, theme restaurants, convention centre, shopping malls, golf course and so on.

Several landmarks will help you find your way around this vast resort. In Ciudad Cancún, the main north-south thoroughfare is called Avenida Tulum; it's a one-km-long tree-shaded boulevard lined with banks, shopping centres, noisy hotels, restaurants and touts selling time-share condominiums.

Two traffic circles on Avenida Tulum, with monuments at their centres, mark the northern and southern limits of downtown Cancún. Prominent here is the city hall, marked 'Ayuntamiento Benito Juárez' and set back from the roadway across a wide plaza. The bus station is half a block north-west of the northern traffic circle. The road out to the Zona Hoteles begins at the southern traffic circle.

Coming from Ciudad Cancún, the main road to Isla Canún is Boulevard Kukulcán (sometimes called Avenida or Paseo Kukulcán), a four-lane divided highway which goes east along the top of the '7'. The hostel and the few moderately priced hotels are located in the first few kms of Boulevard Kukulcán. After nine km, the road reaches the convention centre near Punta Cancún, and turns south for another 14 km to Punta Nizuc and then rejoins the mainland.

Cancún international airport is about eight km south of Avenida Tulum. Puerto Juárez, the port for passenger ferries to Isla Mujeres, is about three km north of Avenida Tulum. Punta Sam, the dock for the slower car ferries to Isla Mujeres, is about five km north of Avenida Tulum.

Information
Tourist Offices There are tourist kiosks at several points along Avenida Tulum. Sometimes they are even staffed.

The State Tourism Office for Quintana Roo (☎ (98) 84-80-73) is in a stone-faced building on the corner of Avenida Cobá and Avenida Carlos J Nader, a block off Avenida Tulum on the way to the Zona Hoteles, on the left-hand side of the road.

The 'Department in Defense of the Tourist', 26 Avenida Tulum, is next to the

Multibanco Comermex, to the left (north) of the municipality. It's the place to go with problems or complaints.

Money Banks on Avenida Tulum are open from 9 am to 1.30 pm, but many limit foreign exchange transactions to between 10 am and noon. Casas de cambio usually are open from 8 or 9 am to 1 pm and again from 4 or 5 pm till 7 or 8 pm; some casas are open seven days a week.

Post The main post office (Oficina de Correos, Cancún, Quintana Roo 77500) is at the western end of Avenida Sunyaxchén, which runs west from Avenida Yaxchilán; the post office is four or five short blocks from Avenida Yaxchilán. Hours for buying stamps and picking up Lista de Correos (poste restante) mail are from 8 am to 7 pm Monday to Friday, and from 9 am to 1 pm Saturday and holidays. For international money orders and registered mail, hours are 8 am to 6 pm Monday to Friday, 9 am to noon Saturday and holidays, closed Sunday.

Telecommunications You'll find Ladatel phones in both the arrival and departure terminals of Cancún's airport, in the bus station off Avenida Tulum and in front of the post office at the western end of Avenida Sunyaxchén. There are also special Ladatel phones which accept credit cards in the Plaza Caracol Shopping Centre on Isla Cancún, near the McDonald's restaurant and in the hall near the Gucci shop.

Foreign Consulates The US Consular Agent (☎ (98) 84-24-11) is located at the offices of Intercaribe Real Estate, 86 Avenida Cobá, one block east off Avenida Tulum as you go towards the Zona Hoteles. If the agent is not available, call the US Consulate General in Mérida (open weekdays from 7.30 am to 3.30 pm) at ☎ (99) 25-50-11; in an emergency after hours or on holidays, call ☎ (99) 25-54-09. There is always a duty officer available to help in an emergency.

Other countries have consular agents

reachable by telephone. If yours is not listed here, call your consulate in Mérida, or your embassy in Mexico City (see the Mexico City chapter).

Canada
   (☎ (98) 84-37-16)
Costa Rica
   (☎ (98) 84-48-69)
Germany
   In the Club Lagoon (☎ (98) 83-09-58, 83-28-58)
Italy
   (☎ (98) 83-21-84)
Spain
   (☎ (98) 84-58-39)
Sweden
   In the office of Rentautos Kankun in Ciudad Cancún (☎ (98) 84-72-71, 84-11-75)

Bookshops A store with periodicals and books in several languages is Fama Cancún, Avenida Tulum 105, near the corner with the southern end of Tulipanes.

Medical Services There are several hospitals and clinics, including the large IMSS (Social Security) and Cruz Roja (Red Cross). Contact the American Hospital at ☎ (98) 84-64-30, 84-60-68).

Laundry There are several shops offering this service. The Lavandería Maria de Lourdes, near the hotel of the same name, is on Calle Orquideas off Avenida Yaxchilán. You might also try the Lavandería y Tintorería Cox-Boh, Avenida Tankah 26, Supermanzana 24. Walk toward the post office along Avenida Sunyaxchén; in front of the post office, bear right onto Avenida Tankah and Cox-Boh is on the right-hand side of the street.

Laundry costs 13 pesos per kg for bulk service. Cox-Boh is open every day except Sunday.

Mayan Ruins

Zona Arqueológica El Rey, on Isla Cancún, is fairly unimpressive – a small temple and several ceremonial platforms. Heading south along Boulevard Kukulcán from Punta Cancún, watch for the marker for Km 17.8. Just past the marker there's an unpaved road

PLACES TO STAY
1 Hotel Posada Mariano
2 Hotel Uxmal
3 Hotel María Isabel
5 Hotel El Alux
6 Hotel Plaza Caribe
8 Hotel Cotty
9 Hotel Tankah
10 Hotel Canto
14 Hotel Parador
15 Hotel Novotel
16 Hotel Margarita
17 Hotel Suites
   Caribe Internacional
18 Hotel Hacienda Cancún
24 Hotel Plaza del Sol
31 Hotel Antillano

PLACES TO EAT
4 El Rincón Yucateco
19 Mandarin House
21 Mercado Municipal 28
22 Restaurant-Jazz Club
   100% Natural
23 Perico's

25 La Habichuela
26 Restaurant Pop
29 Restaurant El Pescador
32 Cafetería San Francisco
33 Rosa Mexicano
34 El Tacolote
36 Pizza Rolandi
42 Los Almendros

OTHER
7 Bus Station
11 Lada Caseta Central
12 Monument to the History of Mexico
13 Aerocaribe & Aero Cozumel
20 Main Post Office
27 Ayuntamiento Benito Juárez
28 Department in Defense of the Tourist
35 Fama Cancún Bookstore
35 Monument to the North-South Dialogue
37 Quintana Roo State Tourism Office
38 US Consular Agency
39 Aeroméxico
40 Mexicana
41 Aviacsa
43 Plaza de Toros

Ciudad Cancún

0   150   300 m

YUCATÁN PENINSULA

on the right which leads to the ruins, open from 8 am to 5 pm every day; admission costs 7 pesos.

For just a quick glimpse, continue on Boulevard Kukulcán 700 metres past the Km 17 marker and up the hill. At the top of the hill, just past the restaurant La Prosperidad de Cancún, you can survey the ruins without hiking in or paying the admission charge.

The tiny Mayan structure and chac-mool statue set in the beautifully kept grounds of the Sheraton Hotel are actually authentic ruins found on the spot.

Archaeological Museum

The Museo de Antropología y Historia, next to the Convention Centre in the Zona Hoteles, has a limited collection of Mayan artefacts. Although most of the items, including jewellery, masks and skull deformers, are from the Postclassic period (1200-1500), there is a Classic-period hieroglyphic staircase inscribed with dates from the 6th century as well as the stucco head which gave the local archaeological zone its name of El Rey (The King).

Beaches

The dazzling white sand of Cancún's beaches is light in weight and cool underfoot, even in the blazing sun. That's because it is composed not of silica but rather of microscopic plankton fossils called disco-aster (a tiny star-shaped creature). The coolness of the sand has not been lost on Cancún's ingenious promoters, who have dubbed it 'air-con'. Combined with the crystalline azure waters of the Caribbean, it makes for beaches that are pure delight.

All of these delightful beaches are open to you because all Mexican beaches are public property. Several of Cancún's beaches are set aside for easy public access, but you should know that you have the right to walk and swim on any beach at all. In practice it may be difficult to approach certain stretches of beach without going through a hotel's property, but few hotels will notice you walking through to the beach in any case.

Starting at Ciudad Cancún and heading out to Isla Cancún all the beaches are on the left-hand side of the road; the lagoon is on your right. The beaches are: Playa Las Perlas, Playa Linda, Playa Langosta, Playa Tortugas, Playa Caracol, and then Punta Cancún, the point of the '7'. South from Punta Cancún are the long stretches of Playa Chac-Mool and Playa del Rey, reaching all the way to Punta Nizuc at the base of the '7'. The beach at the Club Méditerranée, near Punta Nizuc, is noted for its nude bathing.

Beach Safety As any experienced swimmer knows, a beach fronting on open sea can be deadly dangerous and Cancún's eastern beaches are no exception. Though the surf is usually gentle, undertow is a possibility and sudden storms (called *nortes*) can blacken the sky and sweep in at any time without warning. The local authorities have devised a system of coloured pennants to warn beachgoers of potential dangers. Look for the coloured pennants on the beaches where you swim:

Blue: Normal, safe conditions
Yellow: Use caution, changeable conditions
Red: Unsafe conditions, use a swimming pool instead

Getting There & Away To reach the beaches, catch any bus marked 'Hoteles' or 'Zona Hoteles' going south along Avenida Tulum or east along Avenida Cobá. The cost of a taxi depends upon how far you travel. For details, see Getting Around at the end of the Cancún section.

Places to Stay

If you want to stay right on the beach, you must stay in the Zona Hoteles, out on the island. With the exception of the hostel, there are no budget hotels here. You can choose from among the few older, smaller, moderately priced hotels, or the many new, luxurious, pricey hotels.

Places to Stay – bottom end

Though there are more than 20,000 hotel rooms in Cancún, this resort offers the low-budget traveller the worst selection of cheap

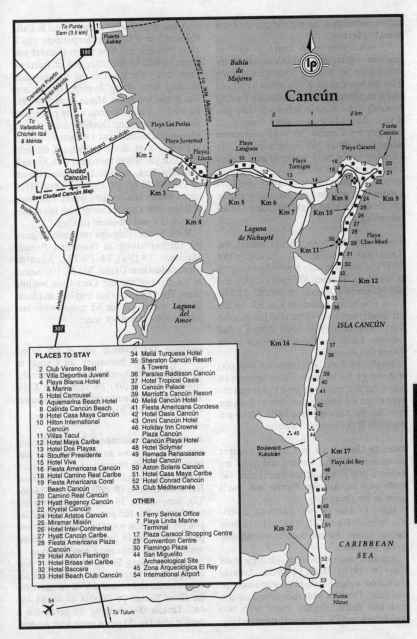

Bahía de Mujeres

Cancún

Punta Cancún

Playa Las Perlas

Playa Juventud

Playa Linda

Playa Langosta

Playa Tortugas

Playa Caracol

Ciudad Cancún

See Ciudad Cancún Map

Km 2

Km 3

Km 4

Km 5

Km 6

Km 7

Km 8

Km 9

Km 10

Km 11

Km 12

Km 14

Km 17

Km 20

Laguna de Nichupté

Laguna del Amor

Playa Chac-Mool

ISLA CANCÚN

Playa del Rey

CARIBBEAN SEA

Punta Nizuc

Boulevard Kukulcán

To Punta Sam (3.5 km)

Puerto Juárez

Carretera Puerto Juárez-Mérida

To Valladolid, Chichén Itzá & Mérida

Boulevard Kukulcán

Avenida Bonampak

Avenida Tulum

Avenida Cobá

180

307

54 To Tulum

PLACES TO STAY

2 Club Verano Beat
3 Villa Deportiva Juvenil
4 Playa Blanca Hotel & Marina
5 Hotel Carrousel
6 Aquamarina Beach Hotel
8 Calinda Cancún Beach
9 Hotel Casa Maya Cancún
10 Hilton International Cancún
11 Villas Tacul
12 Hotel Maya Caribe
13 Hotel Dos Playas
14 Stouffer Presidente
15 Hotel Viva
16 Fiesta Americana Cancún
18 Hotel Camino Real Caribe
19 Fiesta Americana Coral Beach Cancún
20 Camino Real Cancún
21 Hyatt Regency Cancún
22 Krystal Cancún
24 Hotel Aristos Cancún
25 Miramar Misión
26 Hotel Inter-Continental Cancún
27 Hyatt Cancún Caribe
28 Fiesta Americana Plaza Cancún
29 Hotel Aston Flamingo
31 Hotel Brisas del Caribe
32 Hotel Baccara
33 Hotel Beach Club Cancún

34 Meliá Turquesa Hotel
35 Sheraton Cancún Resort & Towers
36 Paraíso Radisson Cancún
37 Hotel Tropical Oasis
38 Cancún Palace
39 Marriott's Cancún Resort
40 Meliá Cancún Hotel
41 Fiesta Americana Condesa
42 Hotel Oasis Cancún
43 Omni Cancún Hotel
46 Holiday Inn Crowne Plaza Cancún
47 Cancún Playa Hotel
48 Hotel Solymar
49 Ramada Renaissance Hotel Cancún
50 Aston Solaris Cancún
51 Hotel Casa Maya Caribe
52 Hotel Conrad Cancún
53 Club Méditerranée

OTHER

1 Ferry Service Office
7 Playa Linda Marine Terminal
17 Plaza Caracol Shopping Centre
23 Convention Centre
30 Flamingo Plaza
44 San Miguelito Archaeological Site
45 Zona Arqueológica El Rey
54 International Airport

accommodation at the highest prices of any place in Mexico.

To make your room search as easy as possible, we've arranged our hotel recommendations on walking itineraries starting from the bus station. If you arrive by air and take a minibus into town (see under Getting Around), your minibus driver will drop you at your chosen hotel at no extra charge.

In general, Cancún City's cheapest rooms range from 90 to 165 pesos a double, tax included, in the busy winter season. Prices drop 15% to 20% in the less busy summer months. For this amount of money you'll get a room with private bath, fan and probably air-con and the hotel might even have a small swimming pool.

Hostel Four km from the bus station, the Hostelling International (formerly the IYHF) hostel is the only low-budget lodging in the Zona Hoteles. Officially called the *Villa Deportiva Juvenil* (☎ (98) 83-13-37), it's at Boulevard Kukulcán Km 3.2, on the left-hand (north) side of the road just past the Km 3 marker as you come from Ciudad Cancún. Look for the sign which reads 'Deportiva Juvenil'.

Single-sex dorm beds (there are over 600 of them) go for 36 pesos. Camping costs 18 pesos; for that price you get a locker and the right to use the hostel's facilities, as there are none for the camping area itself. Meals are available in the hostel's cafeteria.

Avenida Uxmal All of Cancún's cheaper hotels are in Ciudad Cancún and many are within a few blocks of the bus station. Go north-west on Avenida Uxmal and you'll come to the cheap lodgings:

Hotel El Alux (☎ (98) 84-06-62, 84-05-56), Avenida Uxmal 21, is only a block from the bus station. Air-con doubles with shower go for 140 pesos.

Across Uxmal on the south side is the *Hotel Cotty* (☎ (98) 84-13-19, 84-05-50), Avenida Uxmal 44, a motel-style place that's more or less quiet. Doubles with shower and air-con cost 140 pesos, slightly more with two double beds and TV. There's off-street parking.

A few steps farther along Uxmal is Calle Palmera, one of Cancún's loop streets: you'll cross Palmera and then the next street you come to will be the other end of Palmera. Look down the street at the first junction heading west along Avenida Uxmal and you'll see the *Hotel María Isabel* (☎ (98) 84-90-15), Calle Palmera, a tiny place with a quieter location. Doubles with private shower and air-con cost 130 pesos.

Farther west along Uxmal, on the left-hand side just before the corner with Avenida Chichén Itzá, stands the *Hotel Uxmal* (☎ (98) 84-22-66, 84-23-55), Uxmal 111, a clean, family-run hostelry where 125 pesos will buy you a double room with fan and/or air-con, TV and off-street parking.

Rock-bottom lodgings are available just a bit farther along at the *Hotel Posada Mariano* (☎ (98) 84-39-73), Avenida Chichén Itzá near Uxmal, SM 62, 100 metres to the right of the big Coca-Cola bottling plant. The lobby door has iron bars and basic double rooms go for 65 pesos with fan, private shower and hot water.

Avenida Yaxchilán If you've not found what you want, backtrack on Uxmal to Yaxchilán. Near Avenida Sunyaxchén is the *Hotel Canto* (☎ (98) 84-12-67), on Calle Tanchactalpen. Rooms with private shower and air-con cost 130 pesos.

Avenidas Sunyaxchén & Tankah Staying here puts you close to the post office and Mercado 28 with its good, cheap eateries.

Just off Yaxchilán stands the *Hotel Hacienda Cancún* (☎ (98) 84-12-08, 84-36-72), Sunyaxchén 39-40, on the right-hand (north) side. For 165 pesos (single or double) you get an air-con room with colour TV and private bath, use of the hotel's pretty swimming pool and patio and a good location.

Continue along Sunyaxchén to the post office and bear right onto Avenida Tankah. Watch on the right-hand side of the street for the *Hotel Tankah* (☎ (98) 84-44-46, 84-48-44), Tankah 69, charging 90 pesos for a double with fan, 25 pesos more with air-con.

Places to Stay – middle

Mid-range hotel rooms cost from 180 to 350 pesos in the busy winter season, somewhat less during the summer. During the very slow times (late May to early June, October to mid-December), prices may be only half those quoted here, particularly if you haggle a bit. These hotels offer air-con rooms with private bath and colour cable TV, a swimming pool, restaurant and perhaps some other amenities such as a bar, lifts (elevators) and shuttle vans from the hotel to the beach.

Near the Bus Station Directly across from the bus station is the *Hotel Plaza Caribe* (☎ (98) 84-13-77, toll-free 91-800-2-15-15; fax 84-63-52), offering very comfortable air-con rooms and all the amenities for 270 pesos a double in summer, 350 pesos in winter.

Avenida Tulum The *Hotel Parador* (☎ (98) 84-13-10, fax 84-97-12), Avenida Tulum 26, is a modern building with 66 rooms, all with two double beds, charging 215 pesos a single or double.

Directly across Avenida Tulum from the Parador is the *Hotel Novotel* (☎ (98) 84-29-99, fax 84-31-62), Tulum 75 (Apdo Postal 70). Despite its name, it is not a member of the French hotel chain. With fan, rooms go for 160 pesos a single or double; with air-con, 235 pesos. They have triples and quad rooms as well.

Our favourite hotel is the *Hotel Antillano* (☎ (98) 84-15-32, fax 84-18-78), Calle Claveles. The 48 guest rooms offer good value for money at 180/235/290 pesos a single/double/triple.

Avenida Yaxchilán *Hotel Plaza del Sol* (☎ (98) 84-13-09, fax 84-92-09), Avenida Yaxchilán 31, corner of Jazmines, has 87 nice rooms with two double beds priced at 270/325 pesos a single/double, as well as all the services.

A block farther along Yaxchilán stands the *Hotel Margarita* (☎ (98) 84-93-33, fax 84-92-09), with management, services and prices similar to the Plaza del Sol.

Across Yaxchilán from the Margarita is the *Hotel Suites Caribe Internacional* (☎ (98) 84-30-87, fax 84-19-93), Avenidas Yaxchilán con Sunyaxchén 36. The 80 rooms here include normal double rooms, but also junior suites with two beds, sofa, kitchenette with cooker and refrigerator, and a living room. Prices for doubles are similar to the Plaza del Sol, with the suites a bit higher.

Zona Hoteles A few of the older, smaller or simpler hotels on Isla Cancún charge rates around 360 pesos for a double room during the high winter season. In summer, many more bargains are to be had. Going along Boulevard Kukulcán from Ciudad Cancún, all are on the left-hand (north or east) side of the road, and you will come to them in the order given below. Note that the km markers given in the text and on the map of Isla Cancún are as accurate as we can make them but may not be precise – many of the hotels have very wide frontages.

The *Playa Blanca Hotel & Marina* (☎ (98) 83-03-44; in the USA 800-221-4726), Apdo Postal 107, is at Km 3.5; it's a 161-room hotel with lush gardens, comfortable air-con rooms, several bars and three restaurants.

The *Aquamarina Beach Hotel* (☎ (98) 83-14-25, in the USA toll-free 800-446-8976; fax 83-17-51), Boulevard Kulkulcán Km 3.5 (Apdo Postal 751), was built with tour groups of young sunlovers in mind. Some rooms have a kitchenette and refrigerator.

Hotel Maya Caribe (☎ (98) 83-20-00), Boulevard Kukulcán Km 6 (Apdo Postal 447), has 64 rooms, each with two double beds, mini-bar, balcony, hammock and a view of either the ocean or the lagoon. This one is a favourite of Mexican and Mexican-American vacationers.

Places to Stay – top end

Cancún's top places range from comfortable but boring to luxurious full-service hostelries of an international standard. Prices range from 550 to 900 pesos and more for a double room in winter. All the top places are located on the beach, many have vast grounds with rolling lawns of manicured grass, tropical gardens, swimming pools (virtually all with

YUCATÁN PENINSULA

swim-up bars – a Cancún necessity), and facilities for sports such as tennis, handball, water-skiing and sailboarding. Some are constructed in whimsical fantasy styles with turrets, bulbous domes, minarets, dramatic glass canopies and other architectural mega-lomania. Guest rooms are air-con, equipped with mini-bar and TV linked to satellite receivers for US programs.

Isla Cancún is now seriously overbuilt, and hoteliers are willing to offer good deals in order to fill their rooms. To get the most advantageous price at any of these luxury hotels, you should sign up for an inclusive tour package which includes lodging. If you have not come with a group, you can find the best value for money at the *Hotel Viva* (☎ (98) 83-01-08) at Boulevard Kukulcán, Km 8 or the *Hotel Aristos Cancún* (☎ (98) 83-00-11) at Km 9 (Apdo Postal 450).

Other places to look for good value are these:

Km 4 *Calinda Cancún Beach* (☎ (98) 83-16-00, in the USA 800-221-2222) facing the Playa Linda Marine Terminal. Decor here is of red tiles, white stucco and modern muted colours, all with a light, airy feel.

Km 8.5 *Fiesta Americana Cancún* (☎ (98) 83-14-00, in the USA 800-343-7821) is an oddity, resembling nothing so much as an old-city streetscape, an appealing jumble of windows, balconies, roofs and other features.

Camino Real Cancún (☎ (98) 83-01-00, in the USA toll-free 800-228-3000; fax 83-17-30), Apdo Postal 14, was one of Cancún's first luxury hotels and thus had the best pick of locations. Situated at the very tip of Punta Cancún, the Camino Real enjoys panoramic sea views, a lavish country club layout, lots of restaurants and bars and full luxury service.

Hyatt Regency Cancún (☎ (98) 83-09-66, in the USA toll-free 800-228-9000; fax 3-13-49), Apdo Postal 1201, shares Punta Cancún with the Camino Real. It's a gigantic cylinder with a lofty open court at its core and the 300 guest rooms arranged around it.

Km 14 *Cancún Palace* (☎ (98) 85 05 33, in the USA toll-free 800-346-8225; fax 5-15-93), Boulevard Kukulcán (Apdo Postal 1730), works extra hard to offer good value to guests. The 421 rooms and suites have all the amenities you'd expect, including balconies with water views and all the services.

Places to Eat

Nowhere in Mexico have we found more mediocre food at higher prices than in Cancún. Don't expect too much from Cancún's restaurants and when you get a memorable meal (and you will have at least a few) you'll be pleasantly surprised. Restaurants in the city centre range from ultra-Mexican taco joints to fairly smooth and expensive places where the Zona Hoteles people come to 'find someplace different for dinner'.

Inexpensive As usual, market eateries provide the biggest portions at the lowest prices. Ciudad Cancún's market, near the post office, is a building set back from the street and emblazoned with the name Mercado Municipal Artículo 115 Constitucional. Called simply Mercado 28 (that's 'mercado veinte y ocho') by the locals, it has shops selling fresh vegetables, fruits and prepared meals.

In the second courtyard in from the street are the eateries: *Restaurant Margely*, *Cocina Familiar Económica Chulum*, *Cocina La Chaya* etc. These are pleasant, simple eateries with tables beneath awnings and industrious señoras cooking away behind the counter. Most are open for breakfast, lunch and dinner, and all offer full meals (comidas corridas) for as little as 14 pesos, and sandwiches for less.

El Rincón Yucateco, Avenida Uxmal 24, across from the Hotel Cotty, serves good Yucatecan food. Service is from 7 am to 10 pm every day. Main courses cost 11 to 18 pesos.

El Tacolote, on Avenida Cobá across from the big red IMSS hospital, is brightly lit and attractive with dark wood benches. Tacos – a dozen types – are priced from 3.50 to 15 pesos. El Tacolote (the name is a pun on taco and *tecolote*, owl) is open from 7 to 11.30 am for breakfast, then till 10 pm for tacos.

Between the Hotel Parador and the Ayuntamiento is the *Restaurant Pop* (☎ 4-19-91), Avenida Tulum 26, a modern place with an air-con dining room and shaded patio tables out the front. The food is not exciting, but there's yoghurt, fresh fruit salads, hamburgers and sandwiches, soups, spaghetti, cakes and desserts. Expect to spend about 22 or 35 pesos for a filling meal, more if you're very hungry or drink several cervezas. Pop (the name is that of the first month of the 18-month Mayan calendar) is open from 8 am to 10.30 pm (closed Sunday).

The *Cafetería San Francisco*, in the big San Francisco de Assisi department store on the east side of Avenida Tulum, has welcome air-con. You can spend as much as 60 pesos for a full, heavy meal with dessert and drink, but most people keep their bill below 30. The cafetería is open daily from 7 am to 11 pm.

Mid-Range If you're willing to spend between 55 and 90 pesos for dinner you can eat fairly well in Cancún.

Most of the moderately priced restaurants are located in the city centre. The *Restaurant El Pescador* (☎ 84-26-73), Tulipanes 28, has been serving dependably good meals since the early days of Cancún. The menu lists lime soup and fish ceviche for starters, then charcoal-grilled fish, red snapper in garlic sauce and beef shish kebab. El Pescador is open for lunch and dinner (closed Monday).

Pizza Rolandi (☎ 84-40-47), Avenida Cobá 12, between Tulum and Nader just off the southern traffic circle, is an attractive Italian eatery open every day. It serves elaborate one-person pizzas (18 to 35 pesos), spaghetti plates and more substantial dishes of veal and chicken. Watch out for drink prices. Hours are 1 pm to midnight (Sunday, 4 pm to midnight).

Every visitor to Cancún makes the pilgrimage to *Los Almendros* (☎ 84-08-07), Avenida Bonampak at Calle Sayil across from the bullring, the local incarnation of the Yucatán Peninsula's most famous restaurant. Started in Ticul in 1962, Los Almendros set out to serve *platillos campesinos para los dzules* (country food for the bourgeoisie, or townsfolk). The chefs at Los Almendros (The Almond Trees) claim to have created poc-chuc, a dish of succulent pork cooked with onion and served in a tangy sauce of sour orange or lime. If you don't know what

to order, try the *combinado yucateco*, or Yucatecan combination plate. A full meal here costs about 75 pesos per person. Come any day for lunch or dinner.

Restaurant-Jazz Club 100% Natural (☎ 84-36-17), Avenida Sunyaxchén at Yaxchilán, is an airy café. Though the menu lists several natural food items such as fruit salads and juices, green salads and yoghurt, they also serve hamburgers, enchiladas, wine and beer.

Perico's (☎ 4-31-52), Avenida Yaxchilán 71 at Calle Marañón, is quintessential Cancún, a huge thatched structure stuffed with stereotypical Mexican icons: saddles, enormous sombreros, baskets, bullwhips etc. The army of señors and señoritas dressed in Hollywood-Mexican costumes doesn't serve you so much as 'dramatise your dining experience'. Oh, well, if you're in the mood for dinner à la Disney, Perico's will do. The menu is heavy with the macho fare most popular with group tourists: filet mignon, jumbo shrimp, lobster, barbecued spareribs. After the show, you'll be forking out between 75 to 110 pesos per person to pay your bill. Perico's is supposedly open from noon to 2 am, but may in fact serve only dinner.

You can get Chinese food at *Mandarin House* (☎ 84-71-83), Avenida Sunyaxchén at Avenida Tankah. The menu features a range of Cantonese classics, and is open daily except Tuesday for lunch and dinner from 1 to 10.30 pm. A full meal can cost less than 45 pesos.

Expensive Traditionally, Mexican restaurants have followed the European scheme of simple decor and elaborate food. Cancún, however, caters mostly to the sort of sunbaked North Americans who seem to prefer simple food served in elaborate surroundings. Half the menus in town are composed of such grill-me items as steak, jumbo shrimp, fish fillet and lobster tail. Thus Cancún's expensive restaurants are elaborate, with rhapsodic menu prose, lots of tropical gardens, mirrors, waterfalls, paraphernalia, even fish tanks and aviaries of exotic birds. The food can be good, forgettable or execrable. If the last, at least you'll have pleasant music and something to look at as you gnaw and gag.

The exceptional places are listed below.

Ciudad Cancún A long-standing favourite is *Rosa Mexicano* (☎ 84-63-13), Calle Claveles 4, the place to go for unusual Mexican dishes in a pleasant hacienda decor. There are some concessions to Cancún such as tortilla soup and filete tampiqueña, but also squid sautéed with three chiles, garlic and scallions and shrimp in a *pipían* sauce (ground pumpkin seeds and spices). Dinner, served daily from 5 to 11 pm, goes for 90 to 150 pesos.

Another dependable favourite (since 1977) is *La Habichuela* (☎ 84-31-58), Margaritas 25, just off Parque Las Palapas in a residential neighbourhood. The menu tends to dishes easily comprehended and easily perceived as elegant: shish kebab flambé, lobster in champagne sauce, jumbo shrimp and beef tampiqueña: 110 to 150 pesos per person for dinner. Hours are 1 pm to about 11 pm, every day of the year. La Habichuela ('LAH-b'CHWEH-lah') means 'The Stringbean'.

Isla Cancún Visiting gringos flock to *Carlos 'n' Charlie's* (☎ 83-13-04), Boulevard Kukulcán Km 5.5, opposite the Casa Maya, because they enjoy the who-cares atmosphere, jokey waiters, purple menu prose, decent food, and they don't mind paying 110 to 150 pesos for dinner. Trendy Mexican dishes (guacamole, fajitas, ceviche) join the requisite steaks, shrimp and lobster on the menu.

Entertainment
Most of the nightlife is loud and bibulous, as befits a supercharged beach resort. If the theme restaurants don't do it for you, take a dinner cruise on a mock pirate ship.

The local *Ballet Folklórico* performs some evenings at various halls for about 145 pesos per person, which includes dinner. The dancers come on at 8.30 pm. Don't expect the finesse and precision of the performances in Mexico City.

Bullfights (four bulls) are held each Wednesday afternoon at 3.30 pm in the Plaza de Toros at the southern end of Avenida Bonampak, across the street from the Restaurant Los Almendros, about one km from the centre of town. Tickets cost about 50 pesos and can be purchased from any travel agency.

Getting There & Away
Air Cancún's international airport is very busy. Be sure to ask your travel agent about charter and group flights, which can be quite cheap, especially in summer.

For information on transport to/from the airport see the following Getting Around section.

Aerocaribe is a regional airline owned by Mexicana Inter; it offers a special fare deal called the Mayapass, good for a series of flights at reduced prices. Aerocaribe has flights to points in the Yucatán Peninsula and beyond, in small and medium-sized planes. Here are the one-way (single) fares to various points; return fares are twice these:

Chetumal – 360 pesos
Cozumel – 150 pesos
Mérida – 175 pesos
Mexico City – 325 pesos
Oaxaca – 900 pesos
Tijuana – 670 pesos
Villahermosa – 650 pesos

Excursion fares offer better deals than these simple one-way fares.

Aerocaribe are also presently running flights on an experimental basis between Cancún and Belize City and Cancún and Flores (for Tikal) in Guatemala. A one-day tour from Cancún to Tikal and return costs US$150. Aerocaribe and the Guatemalan airlines Aviateca and Aeroquetzal also fly daily to/from Guatemala City; some routes are via Belize City.

Aviacsa is a regional carrier based in Tuxtla Gutiérrez, Chiapas, with flights from Cancún to Mérida, Mexico City, Oaxaca, Tapachula, Tuxtla Gutiérrez, Villahermosa and points in Guatemala. Airline contact addresses are:

Aerocancún – Oasis building, Boulevard Kukulcán (☎ (98) 83-21-44)

Aerocaribe – Avenida Tulum 29, at the traffic circle intersection with Avenida Uxmal (☎ (98) 84-20-00)

Aeroméxico – Avenida Cobá 80, between Tulum and Bonampak (☎ (98) 84-35-71, fax 86-00-79)

American Airlines – at Cancún airport (☎ (98) 86-00-55, toll-free 91-800-5-02-22)

Aviacsa – Avenida Cobá 55 (☎ (98) 87-42-14, toll-free 91-800-0-06-22; fax 84-65-99)

Aviateca – Plaza México, Avenida Tulum 200 (☎ (98) 84-39-38)

Continental – at Cancún airport (☎ (98) 86-00-40; toll-free 91-800-9-00-50)

LACSA – Edificio Atlantis, Avenida Bonampak at Avenida Cobá (☎ (98) 87-31-01)

Mexicana – Avenida Cobá 39 (☎ (98) 87-44-44)

Northwest – at Cancún airport (☎ (98) 86-00-46)

TAESA – Avenida Yaxchilán 31 (☎ (98) 87-43-14)

United – at Cancún airport (☎ (98) 86-01-58, fax 86-00-25)

Bus Several companies share the traffic to/from Cancún, including Autotransportes de Oriente Mérida-Puerto Juárez SA, Autotransportes del Caribe, and Espresso de Oriente. Services are 2nd, 1st or deluxe class.

The bus station on Avenida Uxmal just west of Avenida Tulum serves them all. The station has a cafeteria, snack shops and a newsstand. The guarda equipaje costs 5 pesos 'for one hour or 24 hours'.

Across from the bus station entrance is the ticket office of Interplaya, which runs shuttle buses down the Caribbean coast to Tulum every 20 minutes all day, stopping at major towns and points of interest along the way.

Here are some major routes:

Chetumal – 382 km, seven hours; 12 buses in all classes (40 to 48 pesos)

Chichén Itzá – 205 km, two to three hours; same frequency as Mérida, in all classes (18 to 30 pesos)

Mexico City (TAPO) – 1772 km, 27 hours; six deluxe or 1st-class buses (160 to 200 pesos)

Mérida – 320 km, 3½ to five hours; all classes (24 to 40 pesos), with departures at least every half-hour

Playa del Carmen – 65 km, one hour; Interplaya 2nd-class buses (6 pesos) every 20 minutes; 12 1st-class buses (10 pesos)

Puerto Morelos – 36 km, 40 minutes; Interplaya 2nd-class buses (4 pesos) every 20 minutes; 12 1st-class buses (7 pesos)

Tizimin – 212 km, three hours; four 2nd-class buses (20 pesos) via Valladolid

Tulum – 132 km, two hours; Interplaya 2nd-class buses (11 pesos) every 20 minutes; 1st-class buses (15 pesos) every two hours

Valladolid – 161 km, two hours; all classes (14 to 18 pesos), same frequency as Mérida

Villahermosa – 915 km, 14 hours; five 1st-class buses (90 pesos) by ADO

Getting Around

To/From the Airport Orange-and-beige airport vans (Transporte Terrestre, 22 pesos) monopolise the trade, and will often overcharge you for a private taxi-style ride when you should be paying for a shared ride.

The route into town is invariably via Punta Nizuc and north up Isla Cancún along Boulevard Kukulcán, passing all the luxury beach-front hotels before reaching the hostel and Ciudad Cancún. If your hotel is in Ciudad Cancún, the ride to your hotel may take as long as 45 minutes. At the end of the ride, many passengers tip the driver.

The alternative to the van is to take a taxi, or hire a van for a private trip, straight to your hotel. This should cost 40 pesos; settle on the price in advance.

If you walk out of the airport and follow the access road, you can often flag down a taxi which will take you for less because the driver is no longer subject to the expensive regulated airport fares. Walk the two km to the highway and you can flag a passing bus, which is very cheap.

To return to the airport you must take a taxi (40 pesos), or hop off a southbound bus at the airport junction and walk the two km to the terminal.

Bus Although it's possible walk everywhere in Ciudad Cancún, to get to the Zona Hoteles catch a 'Ruta 1, Zona Hoteles' local bus heading southward along Avenida Tulum. The fare depends upon distance travelled, but is usually 2.50 pesos.

To reach Puerto Juárez and the Isla

Mujeres ferries, take a Ruta 8 bus ('Pto Juárez' or 'Punta Sam', 5 pesos).

Taxi Cancún's taxis do not have meters so you must haggle over fares. Generally, the fare between Ciudad Cancún and Punta Cancún (Hyatt, Camino Real and Krystal hotels and the Convention Centre) is 15 or 18 pesos. A ride to the airport costs 40 pesos. To Puerto Juárez you'll pay about 15 pesos.

Ferry There are frequent passenger ferries to Isla Mujeres. Local buses (Ruta 8, 5 pesos) take about 20 minutes from stops on Avenida Tulum to the Puerto Juárez and Punta Sam ferry docks if you're going to Isla Mujeres. Taxis cost about 15 pesos. See the Isla Mujeres section for more details.

ISLA MUJERES

• *pop: 13,500*

Isla Mujeres (Island of Women) has a reputation as a 'backpackers' Cancún', a place where one can escape the high-energy, high-priced mega-resort for the laid-back life of a tropical isle – at bargain prices. Though this was true for many years, it is less true today. Cancún has been so successful that its version of the good life has spilled over onto its neighbouring island.

The chief attribute of Isla Mujeres is its relaxed social life in a tropical setting with surrounding waters that are turquoise blue and bathtub warm. If you have been doing some hard travelling through Mexico, you will find many travellers you met along the way taking it easy here. Others make it the site of a one to two-week holiday.

History

Although it is said by some that the Island of Women got its name because Spanish buccaneers kept their lovers here while they plundered galleons and pillaged ports, a less romantic but still intriguing explanation is probably more accurate. In 1519, a chronicler sailing with Hernández de Córdoba's expedition wrote that when the conquistadors' ships were forced by high winds into the island's harbour, the crew reconnoitred. What they found onshore was a Mayan ceremonial site filled with clay female figurines.

Today, some archaeologists believe that the island was a stopover for the Maya en route to worship their goddess of fertility, Ixchel, on the island of Cozumel. The clay idols are thought to represent the goddess.

Mayan glyph for Ixchel, goddess of fertility

Orientation

The island is about eight km long and from 300 to 800 metres wide. The good snorkelling areas and some of the better swimming beaches are to the south along the western shore; the eastern shore faces open sea and the surf can be dangerous. The ferry docks, the town and the most popular sand beach (Playa Cocoteros) are at the northern tip of the island. The small grid of narrow streets in the town is easily comprehensible even though there are few street signs.

The main plaza, which also serves as the basketball court, is just inland from the ferry docks.

Information

Tourist Office The Delegación Estatal de Turismo (State Tourism Department, ☎ (987) 7-03-16) faces the basketball court in the main plaza.

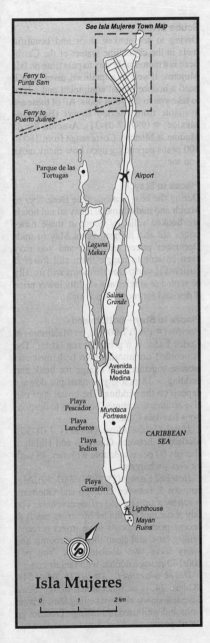

Isla Mujeres

0   1   2 km

See Isla Mujeres Town Map

Ferry to Punta Sam

Ferry to Puerto Juárez

Parque de las Tortugas

Airport

Laguna Makax

Salina Grande

Avenida Rueda Medina

Playa Pescador

Mundaca Fortress

Playa Lancheros

Playa Indios

CARIBBEAN SEA

Playa Garrafón

Lighthouse

Mayan Ruins

Money The island's Banco del Atlantico, at Juárez 5, and Banco Serfin, at Juárez 3, are so packed during the two hours a day (Monday to Friday from 10 am to noon) when foreign currency may be exchanged that many travellers change money at a lower rate at a grocery store, their hotel or at the tourist office.

Post The post office, next to the market, is open Monday to Friday from 8 am to 7 pm, Saturday and Sunday from 9 am to 1 pm.

Laundry Lavandería Automática Tim Phó, Avenida Juárez at Abasolo, is modern and busy.

Playa Cocoteros

Walk north-west along Calles Hidalgo or Guerrero to reach Playa Cocoteros, sometimes called Playa Los Cocos, the town's principal beach. The slope of the beach is very gradual and the transparent and calm waters are only chest-high far from the shore. However, the beach is relatively small for the number of sunseekers.

Playa Lancheros

Five km south of the town and 1.5 km north of Garrafón is Playa Lancheros, the southernmost point served by local buses. The beach is less attractive than Cocoteros, but there are free festivities on Sunday.

Parque Nacional Garrafón

Although the waters are translucent and the fish abundant, Garrafón is perhaps a bit over-rated. Hordes of day trippers from Cancún fill the water during the middle of the day, so you are more often ogling fellow snorkellers than aquatic life. Furthermore, the reef is virtually dead, which makes it less likely to inflict cuts but reduces its colour and the intricacy of its formations.

The water can be extremely choppy, sweeping you into jagged areas. When the water is running fast snorkelling is a hassle and can even be dangerous. Those without strong swimming skills should be advised

YUCATÁN PENINSULA

that the bottom falls off steeply quite close to shore; if you are having trouble, you might not be noticed amidst all those bobbing heads.

Garrafón is open daily from 8 am to 5 pm and the earlier you get here (see Getting Around at the end of this section), the more time you will have free of the milling mobs from Cancún. Admission to the park costs 12 pesos. There are lockers for your valuables at an extra charge. Snorkelling equipment can be rented for the day at 20 pesos. Garrafón also has a small aquarium and museum.

Mayan Ruins

Just past Parque Nacional Garrafón, at the southern tip of the island, are the badly ruined remains of a temple to Ixchel, Mayan goddess of the moon, fertility and other worthy causes. The temple has been crumbling for several centuries, and Hurricane Gilbert almost finished it off in 1988.

There's really little left to look at here other than a fine sea view and, in the distance, Cancún. The clay female figurines were pilfered long ago and a couple of the walls were washed into the Caribbean.

You can walk to the ruins, beyond the lighthouse at the south end of the island, from Garrafón.

Mundaca Fortress

The story behind the ruins of this house and fort are more intriguing than what remains of them. A slave-trading pirate, Fermin Antonio Mundaca de Marechaja, fell in love with a visiting Spanish beauty. To win her, the rogue built a two-storey mansion complete with gardens and graceful archways as well as a small fortress to defend it. While Mundaca built the house, the object of his affection's ardour cooled and she married another islander. Brokenhearted, Mundaca died and his house, fortress and garden fell into disrepair.

The Mundaca fortress is east of the main road near Playa Lancheros, about four km south of the town. Look for signs.

Scuba Diving

Diving to see sunken ships and beautiful reefs in the crystalline waters of the Caribbean is a memorable way to pass time on Isla Mujeres. If you're a qualified diver, you'll need a licence, rental equipment and a boat to take you to the good spots. All of these are available from Mexico Divers (Buzos de México, ☎ (987) 7-01-31), Avenida Rueda Medina at Madero. Costs range from 180 to 300 pesos depending upon how many tanks you use.

Places to Stay

During the busy seasons (late December to March and midsummer), many island hotels are booked solid by noon; at these times prices are also highest. From May to mid-December prices are lower and you may even be able to haggle them still lower if business is slack. Double rooms will usually be rented as singles at a slightly lower price if demand for rooms is not high.

Places to Stay – bottom end

Poc-Na (☎ (987) 7-00-90), on Matamoros at Carlos Lazo, is a privately run hostel. The fan-cooled dormitories take both men and women together. The charge for bunk and bedding is 18 pesos; you must put down a deposit on the bedding. The hostel staff can also arrange discounted boat trips to destinations like Isla Contoy.

Hotel Caribe Maya (☎ (987) 7-01-90), Madero 9, between Guerrero and Hidalgo, charges 60 pesos a double with fan, 85 with air-con – a bargain.

Hotel El Caracol (☎ (987) 7-01-50), Matamoros 5, between Hidalgo and Guerrero, is run by a smiling and efficient señora. The tidy restaurant off the lobby serves meals at decent prices. Rooms have insect screens, ceiling fans, and clean tiled bathrooms, and many have two double beds. You pay 100/140 pesos a double with fan/air-con.

Hotel Martínez (☎ (987) 7-01-54), Madero 14, is an older hotel. Some rooms have sea views, all have ceiling fans, private baths and well-used furnishings. Doubles go for 65 pesos.

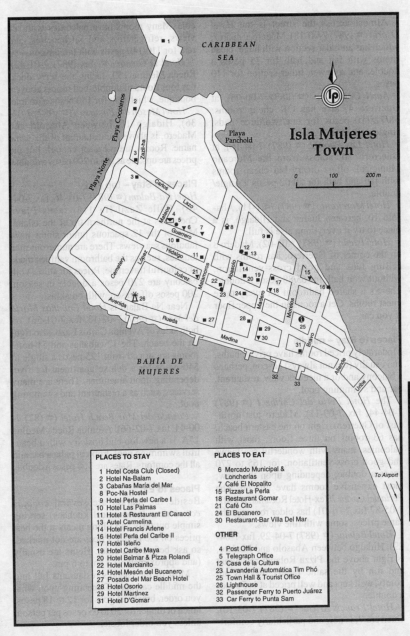

CARIBBEAN SEA

Playa Cocoteros

Playa Norte

Playa Panchold

Isla Mujeres Town

0   100   200 m

BAHÍA DE MUJERES

To Airport

PLACES TO STAY

1   Hotel Costa Club (Closed)
2   Hotel Na-Balam
3   Cabañas María del Mar
9   Poc-Na Hostel
9   Hotel Perla del Caribe I
10 Hotel Las Palmas
11 Hotel & Restaurant El Caracol
13 Autel Carmelina
14 Hotel Francis Arlene
16 Hotel Perla del Caribe II
17 Hotel Isleño
19 Hotel Caribe Maya
20 Hotel Belmar & Pizza Rolandi
22 Hotel Marcianito
24 Hotel Mesón del Bucanero
27 Posada del Mar Beach Hotel
28 Hotel Osorio
29 Hotel Martinez
31 Hotel D'Gomar

PLACES TO EAT

6   Mercado Municipal & Loncherías
7   Café El Nopalito
15 Pizzas La Perla
18 Restaurant Gomar
21 Café Cito
24 El Bucanero
30 Restaurant-Bar Villa Del Mar

OTHER

4   Post Office
5   Telegraph Office
12 Casa de la Cultura
23 Lavandería Automática Tim Phó
25 Town Hall & Tourist Office
26 Lighthouse
32 Passenger Ferry to Puerto Juárez
33 Car Ferry to Punta Sam

Almost across the street is the *Hotel Osorio* (☎ (987) 7-00-18), Madero at Juárez, which has an older section with huge, clean rooms with fan and bath for 75 pesos a double; and a newer, tidier section for 110 pesos.

Autel Carmelina (☎ (987) 7-00-06), at Guerrero 4, also has OK cheap rooms: 58/72/110 pesos for one/two/three beds, single or double.

Hotel Las Palmas (☎ (987) 7-04-16), at Guerrero 20, across from the Mercado Municipal, offers dreary but cheap rooms with fan and bath for 50/62 pesos a single/double.

Hotel Marcianito (☎ (987) 7-01-11), Abasolo 10, between Juárez and Hidalgo, is a place to try if everything else is full.

Hotel Isleño (☎ (987) 7-03-02), Madero 8 on the corner of Guerrero, has rooms with ceiling fans and good cross-ventilation, without/with bath for 65/88 pesos a double. There's a shared bathroom for every three guest rooms. Get a room on the upper floor if you can.

Places to Stay – middle

Moderately priced rooms have private baths, and usually (but not always) air-con, perhaps a balcony and/or a nice sea view, restaurant, bar and swimming pool.

The *Hotel Perla del Caribe I* (☎ (987) 7-04-44, fax 7-00-11), Madero just northeast of Guerrero, right on the eastern beach, has 63 rooms on three floors, most with balconies, many with wonderful sea views and good cross-ventilation, for 165 to 270 pesos a double, depending upon the view; most expensive rooms have air-con. The *Perla del Caribe II* (ex-Hotel Rocamar, ☎ (987) 7-05-87 fax 7-01-01) has older rooms at the same prices, some with fine views.

Hotel Belmar (☎ (987) 7-04-29, fax 7-04-29), Hidalgo between Abasolo and Madero, is right above the Pizza Rolandi restaurant and run by the same family. Rooms are comfy, well kept and well priced at 165 pesos a double.

Hotel Francis Arlene (☎ (987) 7-03-10), Guerrero 7, is new and particularly comfortable. Many rooms have balconies with sea views, refrigerators and kitchenettes, and rent for 110/140 pesos with fan/air-con.

Hotel D'Gomar (☎ fax (987) 7-01-42), Rueda Medina 150, facing the ferry dock, has four floors of double-bed rooms above a boutique, which rent for 140 pesos a double.

Hotel Mesón del Bucanero (☎ (987) 7-02-36), Hidalgo 11, between Abasolo and Madero, is above the restaurant of the same name. Rooms are pleasant enough but the prices are upscale at 165 to 200 pesos a double.

Places to Stay – top end

Hotel Na-Balam (☎ (987) 7-04-46, fax 7-04-46), Calle Zazil-Ha 118, faces Playa Cocoteros at the northern tip of the island. Most of the 12 spacious junior suites have fabulous sea views. There are numerous nice touches, such as the bathroom vanities made of colourful travertine. Prices for suites with balcony are 270 pesos a double in season, 200 pesos off season, with breakfast.

Near Na Balam is *Hotel Cabañas María del Mar* (☎ (987) 7-02-13, fax 7-01-56), on both sides of Avenida Carlos Lazo, also right on the beach. The 12 cabañas and 51 hotel rooms are priced from 125 pesos a single to 540 pesos for a deluxe apartment for five, depending upon amenities. There are many services, such as a restaurant and swimming pool.

Posada del Mar Beach Hotel (☎ (87) 7-00-44, fax 7-02-66), Avenida Rueda Medina 15A, is a new top-end hostelry with a beautiful swimming pool, tropical palapa bar and all the comforts. Rates are 360 pesos a double.

Places to Eat

Beside the market are several *cocinas económicas* (economical kitchens) serving simple but tasty and filling meals at the best prices on the island. Prices are not marked, so ask before you order. Hours are usually (and approximately) 7 am to 6 pm.

Most of the island's restaurants fall into the middle category. Depending upon what you order, breakfast goes for 12 to 18 pesos, lunch or dinner for 30 to 65 pesos per person, unless you order lobster.

Café Cito, a small place at Juárez and Matamoros, has a New Age menu: croissants, fruit, 10 varieties of crepes and the best coffee in town. The menu is in English and German. Come for breakfast (8 am to noon, about 18 pesos), or supper (6 to 10 pm, about 36 pesos).

Café El Nopalito, on Guerrero near Matamoros, serves delicious set breakfasts from 8 am to noon and daily special plates for 22 to 30 pesos, specialising in healthful but fancy food.

El Bucanero (☎ 7-02-36), Avenida Hidalgo 11 between Abasolo and Madero, has a long menu: breakfast omelettes of ham and cheese (12 pesos), fried chicken or fish (18 pesos) and Mexican traditional foods (enchiladas, tacos etc) for about the same. Besides the usual, they serve offbeat things like asparagus au gratin with wholemeal bread.

Pizza Rolandi (☎ 7-04-30), across the street, serves pizzas and calzones cooked in a wood-fired oven, and pastas with various sauces, for 18 to 32 pesos per person. The menu includes fresh salads, fish and some Italian specialities. Hours are daily from 1 pm to midnight, Sunday from 6 pm to midnight.

Pizzas La Perla, Guerrero 5, formerly the Restaurant La Peña, serves soup, pasta, steak, chicken and the like in a glass-walled dining room overlooking the sea. Meals cost about 36 pesos and are served from 8 am to midnight.

The *Restaurant El Sombrero de Gomar*, Hidalgo at Madero, has movie-Mexican decor on two levels, blasts rock music, and offers an all-you-can-eat luncheon buffet for 36 pesos, or à la carte choices for 15 to 50 pesos. The menu is eclectic and international.

Facing the ferry docks is the *Restaurant-Bar Villa Del Mar* (☎ 7-00-31), Avenida Rueda Medina 1 Sur, which is fancier in decor and ambience but not much higher in price.

Entertainment

The first place to go is the main plaza, where there's always something to watch (a football match, a basketball or volleyball game, an impromptu concert or serenade) and lots of somebodies watching it.

As for discos, there's *Buho's* (☎ 7-00-86), which is also a restaurant and bar, in the Hotel Cabañas María del Mar, Avenida Carlos Lazo 1, at Playa Cocoteros. It's been here a while and is usually satisfactory. Nearby is the *Bad Bones Café*, next to the north lighthouse, for a change of pace.

Tequila Video Bar (☎ 7-00-19), on the corner of Matamoros and Hidalgo, is a favourite with locals (who don't feel they must be near the beach), but draws a respectable number of foreigners as well. Hours are 9 pm to 3 am daily except Monday.

Getting There & Away

Most people travelling to Isla Mujeres from Cancún take a Ruta 8 bus heading north on Avenida Tulum (5 pesos) or a taxi (15 pesos) to Puerto Juárez, about three km north of Ciudad Cancún's Avenida Tulum; a Cancún airport minibus will take you to Puerto Juárez on a private trip for about 80 pesos, but it'd be cheaper to ride the minibus with others into Ciudad Cancún and then take a taxi from there.

To get to Punta Sam, take the Ruta 8 bus (5 pesos, 25 minutes) heading north from Avenida Tulum, or a taxi (20 pesos, 15 minutes).

There are three points of embarkation on the mainland for the ferry to Isla Mujeres, 11 km off the coast. Two are north of Ciudad Cancún, the other is on Isla Cancún.

To/From Puerto Juárez The official schedule says that passenger ferries depart every hour on the half-hour from 8.30 am to 8.30 pm, with extra boats at 6 and 10 am. In practice, the schedule depends upon demand and if few people show up for a particular voyage, it'll be cancelled. A one-way fare is 8 pesos (30 to 40 minutes), or 15 pesos if you take the fancier and more comfortable *Caribbean Express* or *Caribbean Miss* (15 to 20 minutes). Return schedules from Isla Mujeres are equally frequent; most hotels on the island have schedules posted.

To/From Punta Sam The dock at Punta Sam, about five km north of Avenida Tulum and 3.5 km north of Puerto Juárez, is the departure point for car ferries to Isla Mujeres. These offer greater stability (and less chance of seasickness) than the Puerto Juárez passenger ferries, but the car ferries are less frequent and slower, taking 45 minutes to an hour to reach the island.

Ferries leave Punta Sam at 7.15 and 9.45 am, at noon and at 2.30, 5.15, 7.45 and 10 pm. Departures from Isla Mujeres are at 6, 8.30 and 11 am and at 1.15, 4, 6.30 and 9 pm. Passengers pay 6 pesos; a car costs 30 pesos. If you're taking a car, be sure to get to the dock an hour or so before departure time. Put your car in line and buy your ticket early or you may have to wait for the next voyage.

To/From Playa Linda Marine Terminal
Four times daily, *The Shuttle* (☎ (98) 84-63-33, 84-66-56) departs from Playa Linda on Isla Cancún for Isla Mujeres. Voyages are at 9 and 11.15 am and 4 and 7 pm from Playa Linda; return voyages depart Isla Mujeres at 10 am, 12.30, 5 and 8 pm. The return fare is 50 pesos, but this includes free beer and soft drinks on board.

Show up at the Playa Linda Marine Terminal, Boulevard Kukulcán Km 4 on Isla Cancún, just west of the bridge between the Aquamarine Beach and Calinda Cancún hotels, at least 30 minutes before departure so you'll have time to buy your ticket and get a good seat on the boat.

Getting Around

Bus & Taxi By local bus from the market or dock, you can get within 1.5 km of Garrafón; the terminus is Playa Lancheros. The personnel at Poc-Na hostel can give you an idea of the bus's erratic schedule. Locals in league with taxi drivers may tell you the bus doesn't exist.

If you walk to Garrafón, bring some water – it's a hot, two-hour, six-km walk. By taxi, it costs about 8 pesos to Garrafón, just over 4 pesos to Playa Lancheros. Rates are set by the municipal government and are posted at

the ferry dock, though the sign is frequently defaced by the taxi drivers.

Bicycle & Moped Bicycles can be rented from a number of shops on the island, including Sport Bike, on the corner of Juárez and Morelos, a block from the ferry docks. Before you rent, compare prices and the condition of the bikes in a few shops, then arrive early in the day to get one of the better bikes. The costs are 12 to 18 pesos for four hours, only a bit more for a full day; you'll be asked to plunk down a deposit of 50 pesos or so.

When renting mopeds, shop around, compare prices and check these items: new or newer machines in good condition, full gas tanks and reasonable deposits. Cost per hour is usually 18 to 22 pesos with a two-hour minimum, 80 pesos all day, or even cheaper by the week. Shops away from the busiest streets tend to have better prices, but not necessarily better equipment.

When riding, remember that far more people are seriously injured on motorbikes and the like than in cars. Your enemies are inexperience, speed, sand, wet or oily roads and other people on motorbikes. Don't forget to slather yourself with sunblock before you take off. Be sure to do your hands, feet, face and neck thoroughly, as these will get the most sun.

AROUND ISLA MUJERES
Isla Contoy Bird Sanctuary

You can take an excursion by boat to tiny Isla Contoy, a national bird sanctuary, about 25 km north of Isla Mujeres. It's a treasure trove for bird watchers, with an abundance of brown pelicans, olive cormorants and red-pouched frigates, as well as frequent visits by flamingos and herons. There is good snorkelling both en route and just off Contoy.

Getting There & Away For a private trip, contact Ricardo Gaitan and he will take you to Contoy in his 10-metre sailboat, *Providencia*. Gaitan will supply food and snorkelling equipment for the two-day venture at roughly 110 pesos per person. You will need sunblock, insect repellent and a sleeping bag. To find him, just ask around – he's well-known in the area.

If you just want a one-day excursion, for about 75 pesos, ask at the Sociedad Co-operativa Transporte Turística 'Isla Mujeres' (☎ (98) 82-02-74), on Avenida Rueda Medina to the north of the ferry docks.

ISLA HOLBOX

If you're looking to be close to nature, Isla Holbox (pronounced 'HOHL-bosh') might appeal to you, but note that the most basic facilities are in short supply and the beaches are not Cancún-perfect strips of clean, air-con sand. To enjoy Isla Holbox, you must be willing to rough it.

The 25-km by three-km island has sands that run on and on, as well as tranquil waters where you can wade out quite a distance before the sea reaches shoulder level. Moreover, Isla Holbox is magic for shell collectors, with a galaxy of shapes and colours. The fishing families of the island are friendly – unjaded by encounters with exotic tourists or the frenetic pace of the urban mainland.

However, the seas are not the translucent turquoise of the Quintana Roo beach sites, because here the Caribbean waters mingle with those of the darker Gulf. Seaweed can create silty waters near shore at some parts of the beach. While there are big plans to develop Isla Holbox one day, at the time of writing there is only one modest hotel, the aptly named *Hotel Flamingo* (with doubles for 25 pesos) and a few snack shops. Most travellers camp or stay in spartan rooms rented from locals.

Getting There & Away

To reach Isla Holbox, take the ferry from the unappealing port village of Chiquilá on Quintana Roo's north coast. Buses make the 2½-hour trip three times a day from Valladolid to Chiquilá and in theory the ferry is supposed to wait for them. However, it may not wait for a delayed bus or may even leave early (!) should the captain feel so inclined. If you're coming from Cancún,

you'll probably need to change buses at the highway junction to Chiquilá.

It is therefore recommended that you reach Chiquilá as early as possible. The ferry is supposed to depart for the island at 8 am and 3 pm, and takes an hour. Ferries return to Chiquila at 2 and 5 pm. The cost is 6 pesos.

Try not to get stuck in Chiquilá, as it is a tiny, fairly dismal place with no hotels, no decent camping and very disappointing food.

PUERTO MORELOS

Puerto Morelos, 34 km south of Cancún, is a sleepy fishing village known principally for its car ferry to Cozumel. There is a good budget hotel here and travellers who have reason to spend the night here find it refreshingly free of tourists. A handful of scuba divers come to explore the splendid reef 600 metres offshore, reachable by boat.

Places to Stay & Eat

For good, basic, budget lodging, stay at the *Posada Amor* (no phone). Family-run, the Posada is a wood and white-stucco place with lots of plants and a happy atmosphere. Rooms with fan and a clean shared bathroom cost 130 pesos, per single or double. Good meals are served in the cosy dining room.

North of the centre, the *Cabañas Puerto Morelos* (☎ (987) 1-00-04; in the USA (612) 441-7630) has two comfy apartments rented out by Bill and Connie Butcher, formerly of Minnesota. Rates for two persons are 275 per week in summer, 450 in winter. Write for reservations: Apdo Postal 1524, 77501 Cancún, Q Roo. *Los Arrecifes* (☎ (987) 1-01-12) has beachfront rooms for 55 a double in summer, 65 in winter.

The *Caribbean Reef Club* (☎ (987) 4-29-32, in USA 800-322-6286; fax (98) 83-22-44) is a beautiful, very comfortable, quiet resort hotel right on the beach. Lots of water sports and helpful owners are the bonuses when you pay these rates, customarily quoted in US dollars: $110 to $140 per night from mid-December to late April, about 30% cheaper in summer.

For a fine, moderately priced meal, try the

Doña Zenaida Restaurant, on Avenida Javier Rojo Gómez, just south of the centre on the beach.

Getting There & Away

Interplaya buses drop you on the highway, two km west of the centre of Puerto Morelos. Additionally, regular 2nd-class and many 1st-class buses stop at the main square in Puerto Morelos coming from, or en route to, Cancún, 34 km (45 minutes) away. These buses generally come by every couple of hours during the day.

The car ferry (transbordador; in Cozumel ☎ (987) 2-08-27, 2-09-50) to Cozumel leaves Puerto Morelos daily. Departure times vary by the day of the week and from season to season.

Unless you plan to stay for awhile on Cozumel, it's hardly worth shipping your vehicle. You must get in line two or three hours before departure time and hope there's enough space on the ferry for you. Fare for the 2½ to four-hour voyage is 200 pesos per car, 30 pesos per person; you needn't have a car in order to steam over to Cozumel on this boat, of course. Note that rough seas often prevent the ferry from sailing. At times, it has remained in port for up to a week until the weather cleared.

Departure from Cozumel is from the dock in front of the Hotel Sol Caribe, south of town along the shore road. Be there several hours ahead of departure time in order to get in line.

PLAYA DEL CARMEN

For decades, Playa (or Playacar, as it's also called) was just a simple fishing village on the coast opposite Cozumel. With the construction of Cancún, however, the number of travellers roaming this part of the Yucatán Peninsula increased exponentially. Now Playa has taken over from Cozumel as the preferred resort town in the area. Playa's beaches are better and the nightlife is groovier than Cozumel's, and the reef diving is just as good. (One handy tip for those wanting to dive but who normally wear glasses – the Wet Dreams dive shop down on the beach a

couple of blocks from the Blue Parrot hires out lensed masks, so you won't miss any of the underwater action.) On the beaches, tops are optional everywhere; nudity is optional about a km north of Playa town centre.

What's to do in Playa? Hang out. Swim. Dive. Stroll the beach. Get some sun. Catch the Interplaya shuttle to other points along the coast. In the evening, Avenida Quinta, the pedestrian mall, is the place to sit and have a meal or a drink, or stroll and watch others having meals and drinks. Early evening happy hour (5 to 7 pm), with two drinks for the price of one, is an iron rule. It is impossible to order a single beer – the waiter automatically brings two!

Places to Stay

Playa del Carmen is developing and changing so fast that almost anything written about it is obsolete by the time it's printed. Expect many new hotels by the time you arrive, and many changes in the old ones. The room prices given below are for the busy winter season. Prices are substantially lower in the off season.

Places to Stay – bottom end

Camping La Reina, at the beach end of 2 Calle, has about 30 designated hammock-hanging spots which cost 16 pesos each, including a locker for your stuff. If you have no hammock, you can rent one for 5 pesos. There are camping sites as well.

The hostel, or *Villa Deportiva Juvenil*, 1.2 km from the ferry docks, is a modern establishment offering the cheapest clean lodging in town, but it's quite a walk to the beach and you sleep in single-sex dorm bunks. On the positive side, the hostel is cheap at 20 pesos per bunk.

Posada Lily, on Avenida Juárez (Avenida Principal) just a block inland from the main square, offers clean rooms with private shower and fan for 80 pesos a double. If it's full, try the *Hotel Dos Hermanos*, on Avenida 30 at Calle 4, for the same price. A half-block from the Dos Hermanos is the similar *Mom's Hotel* (☎ (987) 3-03-15).

Posada Sian Ka'an (☎ in Mérida (99)

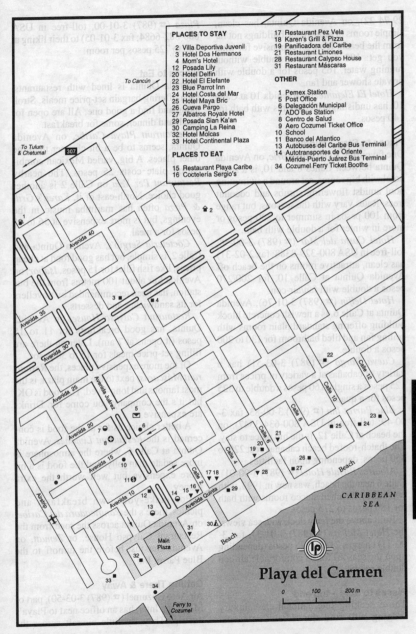

PLACES TO STAY

2   Villa Deportiva Juvenil
3   Hotel Dos Hermanos
4   Mom's Hotel
12 Posada Lily
20 Hotel Delfin
22 Hotel El Elefante
23 Blue Parrot Inn
24 Hotel Costa del Mar
25 Hotel Maya Bric
26 Cueva Pargo
27 Albatros Royale Hotel
29 Posada Sian Ka'an
30 Camping La Reina
32 Hotel Molcas
33 Hotel Continental Plaza

PLACES TO EAT

15 Restaurant Playa Caribe
16 Coctelería Sergio's

17 Restaurant Pez Vela
18 Karen's Grill & Pizza
19 Panificadora del Caribe
21 Restaurant Limones
28 Restaurant Calypso House
31 Restaurant Máscaras

OTHER

1   Pemex Station
5   Post Office
6   Delegación Municipal
7   ADO Bus Station
8   Centro de Salud
9   Aero Cozumel Ticket Office
10 School
11 Banco del Atlantico
13 Autobuses del Caribe Bus Terminal
14 Autotransportes de Oriente
    Mérida–Puerto Juárez Bus Terminal
34 Cozumel Ferry Ticket Booths

To Cancún

To Tulum
& Chetumal

307

Avenida 40

Avenida 35

Avenida 30

Avenida 25

Avenida Juárez

Avenida 20

Avenida 15

Avenida 10

Avenida Quinta

Alrededor

Calle 12

Calle 10

Calle 8

Calle 6

Calle 4

Calle 2

Main
Plaza

Beach

Beach

CARIBBEAN
SEA

Ferry to
Cozumel

Playa del Carmen

0   100   200 m

29-74-22), on Avenida Quinta, has clean, simple rooms in semi-rustic buildings not far from the beach. It's a bit expensive for what you get: 100 pesos for a double without running water, 165 pesos for a double with private shower and fan.

Hotel El Elefante, on Avenida 10 at Calle 10, has undistinguished rooms with bath for 140 pesos.

Places to Stay – middle

One favourite, *Hotel Maya Bric*, on Avenida Quinta between Calles 8 and 10, is a small hotel with big rooms, set around a swimming pool amidst flowering shrubs and coconut trees. Rates vary with the seasons, but range from 100 pesos in summer to 200 pesos or more in winter for a double with bath.

Hotel Costa del Mar (☎ (987) 3-00-58, toll-free in USA 800-329-8388; fax 2-02-31) has clean, attractive rooms on the beach off Avenida Quinta at Calle 10, for 200/270 pesos a double with fan/air-con.

Hotel Delfín (☎ (987) 3-01-76), Avenida Quinta at Calle 6, is a newish concrete block building offering standard plain rooms with ceiling fan and tiled bathroom for 130 to 200 pesos a double.

Cueva Pargo (☎ (987) 3-03-51) has a variety of cabañas at a variety of prices from 125 pesos a single, 160 pesos a double to 325 pesos for a quad.

Blue Parrot Inn (☎ (987) 3-00-83, fax 3-00-49; toll-free in USA 800-634-3547), on the beach at Calle 12, is the hip place to stay. The thatch-roofed beach cabañas cost 220 to 350 pesos, depending upon facilities.

Albatros Royale Hotel (☎ (987) 3-00-01), Calle 6 near the beach, was new in 1993, with two-storey thatched stucco rooms with bath for 180 pesos to 275 pesos.

Built above the ferry dock with sea views, the *Hotel Molcas* (☎ (987) 3-01-34, fax 3-00-71) charges 215 to 325 pesos (depending upon the season) for its comfortable air-con double rooms.

Places to Stay – top end

Those seeking international-class luxury lodging will find the *Hotel Continental Plaza* (☎ (987) 3-01-00, toll-free in USA 800-882-6684; fax 3-01-05) to their liking at 500 to 725 pesos per room.

Places to Eat

Avenida Quinta is lined with restaurants, each offering bargain set-price meals. Stroll along and find a good one. All are open for lunch and dinner, some for breakfast.

Restaurant Playa Caribe, on Avenida Quinta, seems to be a bit cheaper than the other places. A big, varied Mexican combination plate costs 25 pesos. The nearby *Restaurant Pez Vela* on Calle 2 is another good choice. North-east of it, *Karen's Grill & Pizza* often has marimba music in the evenings, but is more expensive at 36 to 45 pesos for a meal.

Coctelería Sergio's, Avenida Quinta and Calle 2, is simple, but has good food at cheap prices, like fish fillet for 15 pesos. *Isabor*, on Avenida Sur about 100 metres from the bus station, has been recommended by travellers for its sandwiches and desserts.

Restaurant Calypso House, on Avenida Quinta, has good breakfasts for 11 to 15 pesos (it opens at 7 am). Later on there are filling set-price meals for 15 to 30 pesos.

Of the more expensive places, the *Restaurant Máscaras*, next to the main plaza, is the most famous and long-lived. The food is OK, but it's the company you come for. Drinks are expensive.

A better choice as far as the food is concerned is the *Restaurant Limones*, Avenida Quinta at Calle 6, where the atmosphere is more sedate than jolly, and the food is a bit more expensive but well worth the extra money.

For make-your-own breakfasts and picnics, there's the *Panificadora del Caribe*, on Avenida Quinta across the road from the Restaurant Calypso House, or *Zematt*, on Avenida Sur just before the turnoff to the Blue Parrot Inn.

Getting There & Away

Air Aero Cozumel (☎ (987) 3-03-50), part of Mexicana Inter, has an office next to Playa's airstrip. They fly little aircraft across the water from Cozumel to Playa in seven minutes every two hours from 8 am to 6 pm during the winter season. In summer there are usually four flights per day in each direction, departing from Cozumel at 9 and 11 am, and 3 and 5 pm, returning from Playa del Carmen 20 minutes later. The flight costs 70 pesos one way.

Bus Numerous companies serve Playa del Carmen (see map for terminal locations). Besides the Interplaya buses running up and down the coast every 20 minutes, there are Autotransportes Playa Express buses every 30 minutes, charging 10 pesos from Playa to either Tulum or Cancún.

Cancún – 65 km, one hour; 6 to 10 pesos; Interplaya buses every 20 minutes; others 12 times daily

Chetumal – 315 km, 5½ hours; at least a dozen buses (30 to 40 pesos) daily

Cobá – 113 km, two hours; several Autotransportes de Oriente and Expresso de Oriente buses (1st-class 14 pesos, 2nd-class 11 pesos) on the Tulum-Cobá-Valladolid route

Mérida – 385 km, seven hours; six 1st-class (45 pesos) and six 2nd-class (35 pesos) buses by Autotransportes de Oriente M-PJ via Valladolid and Chichén Itzá; six 1st-class buses by Expresso de Oriente and several by A del Caribe via Oxkutzcab, Ticul and Muna

Tulum – 63 km, one hour; lots of buses, including the Interplaya and Playa Express shuttles for 10 pesos

Valladolid – 230 km, 3½ hours; fast *ruta corta* (short route) via Tulum and Cobá (see Cobá); slower Autotransportes de Oriente buses to Mérida stop at Valladolid (32 pesos 1st-class, 29 pesos 2nd-class)

Ferry A variety of watercraft ply the seas between Playa del Carmen and Cozumel, taking between 30 and 75 minutes to make the voyage and charging 18 to 35 pesos one way. Schedules, particularly in summer, may change, so buy a one-way ticket. That way, if your chosen boat doesn't materialise for a scheduled return trip, you can buy a ticket on another line.

The fastest boats are the waterjets *México* and *México III*, charging the top price and running about every two hours from dawn to dusk, but voyages may be cancelled at the last moment if the boat breaks down or if there aren't enough passengers. Note also that 'fast boat' emblazoned on ticket offices and billboards may not mean 'waterjet', and the 'fast boat' may actually be slower than the waterjet.

The next best boat is the *Playa del Carmen*, offering only slightly less in the way of comfort, speed and price.

The slowest, oldest, least comfortable but cheapest boats are the *Xel-Ha* and *Cozumeleño*, best avoided by those prone to seasickness.

COZUMEL
• *pop: 175,000*

Cozumel (Place of the Swallows) floats in the midst of the Caribbean's crystalline waters 71 km south of Cancún. Measuring 53 km long and 14 km wide, it is the largest of Mexico's islands. Cozumel's legendary Palancar Reef was made famous by Jacques Cousteau and is a lure for divers from all over the world.

Though it has that beautiful offshore reef, Cozumel does not have many good swimming beaches. The western shore is mostly sharp, weathered limestone and coral, and the eastern beaches are too often pounded by dangerous surf.

History

Mayan settlement here dates from 300 AD. During the Postclassic period, Cozumel flourished both as a commercial centre and as a major ceremonial site. The Maya sailed here on pilgrimages to shrines dedicated to Ixchel, the goddess of fertility and the moon.

Although the first Spanish contact with Cozumel in 1518 by Juan de Grijalva was peaceful, it was followed by the Cortés expedition in 1519. Cortés, en route to his conquest of the mainland, laid waste to Cozumel's Mayan shrines. The Maya offered staunch military resistance until they were conquered in 1545. The coming of the Spaniards brought smallpox to this otherwise surprisingly disease-free place. Within a generation after the conquest, the island's

YUCATÁN PENINSULA

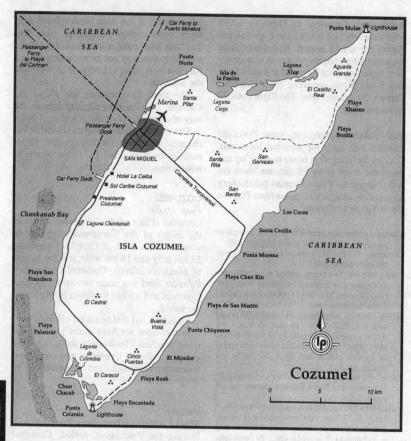

Cozumel

0   5   10 km

YUCATÁN PENINSULA

population had dwindled to only 300 souls, Maya and Spaniards.

While the island remained virtually deserted into the late 17th century, its coves provided sanctuary and headquarters for several notorious pirates, including Jean Lafitte and Henry Morgan. Pirate brutality led the remaining populace to move to the mainland and it wasn't until 1848 that Cozumel began to be resettled by Indians fleeing the War of the Castes.

At the turn of the century, the island's population, which was now largely mestizo, grew thanks to the craze for chewing gum.

Cozumel was a port of call on the chicle export route and locals harvested chicle on the island. Although chicle was later replaced by synthetic gum, Cozumel's economic base expanded with the building of a US air-force base here during WW II.

When the US military departed, the island fell into an economic slump and many of its people moved away. Those who stayed fished for a livelihood until 1961, when underwater scientist Jacques Cousteau arrived, explored the reef and told the world about Cozumel's beauties. A resort destination was born.

Orientation

It's easy to make your way on foot around the island's only town, San Miguel de Cozumel, where most of the budget lodgings are. Some of the mid-range places are here as well. For top-end hotels, take a taxi up or down the coast. The airport, two km north of town, is accessible only by taxi or on foot.

The waterfront boulevard is Avenida Rafael Melgar; on the west side of Melgar south of the ferry docks is a narrow but useable sand beach. Just opposite the ferry docks (officially called the Muelle Fiscal) on Melgar in the centre of town is the main plaza.

Information

Tourist Office The local tourist office (☎ (987) 2-09-72) is situated in a building facing the main square to the north of the Bancomer, on the 2nd floor. Opening hours are Monday to Friday from 9 am to 3 pm and 6 to 8 pm.

Money For currency exchange, the casas de cambio located around the town are your best bets for long hours and fast service, though they may charge as much as 3.5% commission.

Bancomer and Banco del Atlantico, off the main plaza, change money only from 10 am to 12.30 pm Monday to Friday, and the queues are long. Banpaís, facing the ferry docks, will change your travellers' cheques from 9 am to 1.30 pm Monday to Friday for a 1% commission.

Most of the major hotels, restaurants and stores will change money at a less advantageous rate when the banks are closed. ATMs, which issue cash dollars or pesos against your cash or credit card, are beginning to appear.

Post & Telecommunications The post and telegraph office (☎ (987) 2-01-06) is south of Calle 7 Sur on the waterfront just off Avenida Melgar. Hours are Monday to Friday from 9 am to 1 pm and 3 to 6 pm, and Saturday from 9 am to noon. Cozumel's postal code is 77600.

The TelMex telephone office is on Calle Salas between Avenidas 5 and 10 Sur. There are Ladatel phones in front, and they sell telephone cards in the office.

Laundry The clean and tidy Margarita Laundromat, Avenida 20 Sur 285 between Calle Salas and Calle 3 Sur, is open Monday to Saturday from 7 am to 9 pm, Sunday from 10 am to 6 pm. It charges 7 pesos to wash a load (1.50 pesos extra if you don't bring your own detergent), 3.50 pesos for 10 minutes in the dryer. Ironing and folding services are available at an extra charge. Look for the sign reading 'Lavandería de Autoservicio'.

Bookshop The Zodiac Bookstore, on the south-east side of the plaza, 40 metres from the clock tower next to Bancomer, is open seven days a week selling English, French, German and Spanish books, and English and Spanish magazines and newspapers.

Island Museum

The Museo de la Isla de Cozumel, Avenida Rafael Melgar between Calles 4 and 6 Norte, has nautical exhibits covering the history of the island. It's open from 10 am to 6 pm for 13 pesos; closed Saturday.

Activities

Scuba Diving For equipment rental, instruction and boat reservations, there are numerous dive shops on Avenida Melgar along San Miguel's waterfront. Generally, a two-tank, full-day scuba trip will cost 235 to 300 pesos and an introductory scuba course about 425 pesos.

The most prominent scuba destinations are: the five-km-long Palancar Reef, where stunning coral formations and a 'horseshoe' of coral heads in 70-metre visibility offer some of the world's finest diving; Maracaibo Reef, for experienced divers only, which offers a challenge due to its current and aquatic life; Paraíso Reef, famous for its coral formations, especially brain and star coral; and Yocab Reef, shallow yet vibrantly alive and great for beginners.

Snorkelling You can go out on a boat tour for 75 to 110 pesos or, far cheaper, rent gear for about 30 pesos and snorkel at the following places: Chankanab Bay, Playa San Francisco, La Playa Ceiba near the car ferry dock (where a plane was purposely sunk for the film *Survive*), Presidente Hotel and Palancar.

Boat Trips You can enjoy the coral formations and aquatic life by taking a tour by glass-bottomed boat. The boats are supposed to leave the car ferry dock area every day at 10 am, noon and 2 pm, but generally wait until they are filled. They cost 35 to 55 pesos, but outside the tourist high season, bargain for a lower price.

Places to Stay – bottom end

Camping To camp anywhere on the island you'll need a permit from the island's naval authorities. Permits are obtainable 24 hours a day, for free, from the naval headquarters south of the post office on Avenida Rafael Melgar. The best camping places are along the relatively unpopulated eastern shore of the island.

Hotels All rooms described below come with private bath and fan, unless otherwise noted.

Hotel Flamingo (☎ (987) 2-12-64), Calle 6 Norte No 81, off Melgar, is not the cheapest, but it's undoubtedly the best value for money. Run by an efficient señora, the 21 rooms go for 90 to 125 pesos a double, depending upon the season.

Hotel Marruang (☎ (987) 2-16-78, 2-02-08) at Calle Salas 440 is entered from a passageway across from the municipal market. A clean room with one double and one single bed costs 80 to 100 pesos.

Hotel Cozumel Inn (☎ (987) 2-03-14), Calle 4 Norte No 3, has rooms for only 75/95 pesos a double with fan/air-con in summer.

Hotel Posada Edém (☎ (987) 2-11-66, 2-15-82), Calle 2 Norte 12, between Avenidas 5 and 10 Norte, is uninspiring but cheap at 48/80 pesos a single/double.

Posada Letty (☎ (987) 2-02-57), on Avenida 15 Sur near Calle 1 Sur, is among the cheapest lodgings in town at 60 pesos in summer, 80 pesos in winter.

Hotel Saolima (☎ (987) 2-08-86), Calle

Salas 268 between Avenidas 10 and 15 Sur, has clean, pleasant rooms in a quiet locale for 58/65 pesos a single/double in summer.

Places to Stay – middle

Most mid-range hostelries offer air-con and swimming pools. All have private bathrooms.

Hotel Vista del Mar (☎ (987) 2-05-45, fax 2-04-45), Avenida Melgar 45, at Calle 5 Sur, has a small swimming pool, restaurant, liquor store and travel agency, and offers car rental. Some rooms have balconies with sea views. The price in summer is 145 pesos a double, rising to 180 pesos in winter.

Tried and true, clean, comfortable lodgings are yours at the *Hotel Mary-Carmen* (☎ (987) 2-05-81), Avenida 5 Sur 4, half a block south of the plaza. The 27 tidy air-con rooms cost 145 pesos a double in winter. Equally pleasant and similarly priced is the *Hotel Suites Elizabeth* (☎ (987) 2-03-30), Calle Salas 44. Air-con bedrooms have kitchenettes here.

Hotel Pepita (☎ (987) 2-00-98), Avenida 15 Sur 2, corner of Calle 1 Sur, has well-maintained rooms around a delightful garden for 90 pesos in summer, 125 pesos in winter. Most rooms have two double beds, insect screens, fans and little refrigerators as well as the air-con.

Bazar Colonial Hotel & Suites (☎ (987) 2-13-87, fax 2-02-09), Avenida 5 Sur No 9, has studios and one-bedroom suites (some of which can sleep up to four people) with kitchenette, air-con and pretensions to decor for 150 to 180 pesos a double in summer, 180 to 215 pesos in winter. The similar *Hotel Bahía* (☎ (987) 2-02-09), Avenida Melgar at Calle 3 Sur, is under the same management.

Hotel El Pirata (☎ (987) 2-00-51), Avenida 5 Sur 3-A, offers decent air-con rooms for 110 pesos a double in summer, 145 pesos in winter, while *Hotel Maya Cozumel* (☎ (987) 2-00-11, fax 2-07-18), Calle 5 Sur No 4, has good TV-equipped rooms and a pool for 125/145/165 pesos a single/double/triple in winter.

Hotel Kary (☎ (987) 2-20-11), Calle Salas at Avenida 25 Sur, is five blocks east of the plaza and a bit out of the way, but cheaper at

San Miguel de Cozumel

0   200   400 m

To Punta Norte
To Airport
Boulevard Aeropuerto

Costera Norte
Avenida 5 Norte
Avenida 10 Norte
Avenida 15 Norte
Avenida 20 Norte
Avenida 25 Norte
Avenida 30 Norte

Calle 12 Norte
Calle 10 Norte
Calle 8 Norte
Calle 6 Norte
Calle 4 Norte
Calle 2 Norte

Main Plaza

Melgar
Rafael
Avenida Benito Juárez

Calle 1 Sur
Calle 3 Sur
Calle 5 Sur
Calle Morelos
Calle Salas

Avenida 5 Sur
Avenida 10 Sur
Avenida 15 Sur
Avenida 20 Sur
Avenida 25 Sur
Avenida 30 Sur

Calle 7 Sur
Calle 9 Sur

Muelle Fiscal
Ferry to Playa del Carmen
Costera Sur
To Car Ferry Dock & Luxury Hotels

PLACES TO STAY
2   Hotel Flamingo
4   Hotel Cozumel Inn
6   Hotel Posada Edém
9   Hotel Posada Cozumel
9   Hotel Mesón San Miguel
12 Hotel Mary-Carmen
14 Hotel El Pirata
15 Bazar Colonial Hotel & Suites
19 Hotel Pepita
20 Posada Letty
23 Hotel Suites Elizabeth
24 Hotel Bahía
27 Hotel Saolima
28 Hotel Marruang
30 Hotel Kary
31 Hotel Maya Cozumel
33 Hotel Vista del Mar

PLACES TO EAT
1   Pizza Rolandi
5   The Sports Page
16 Pizza Prima
17 La Cocina Italiano
18 Cocina Económica Mi
22 Pepe's Grill
26 Restaurant La Choza
32 Lonchería Las Gemelas
36 Restaurant Costa Brava

OTHER
3   Museo de la Isla de Cozumel
8   Banpais
10 Tourist Office &
    Zócalo Bookstore
11 Bancomer
13 Banco del Atlantico
21 Mercado Municipal
25 Telmex
29 Margarita Laundromat
34 Post & Telegraph Office
35 Lighthouse
37 Naval Headquarters

80 to 115 pesos for a double with fan and 129 to 138 pesos with air-con. There's even a pool.

Hotel Plaza Cozumel (☎ (987) 2-27-11, fax 2-00-66), Calle 2 Norte 3, just off Avenida Melgar a block north of the plaza, is a new, modern, comfortable hotel with a rooftop swimming pool, colour TV with satellite hook-up, and prices of 200 pesos in summer, 320 pesos in winter.

Hotel Mesón San Miguel (☎ (987) 2-03-23, fax 2-18-20), Avenida Juárez 2-B, on the north side of the plaza, has a little pool, blissful air-con, a restaurant and 100 rooms with balconies. There's also a separate beach club with water sports facilities seven blocks from the hotel on the water. Rates are 165/245 pesos a double in summer/winter.

Places to Stay – top end

Several km south of town are the big luxury resort hotels of an international standard, which charge 540 to 1000 pesos for a room during the winter season. North of town along the western shore of the island are numerous smaller, more modest resort hotels, usually cheaper than the big places, but catering mostly to package-tour groups.

South of town, the *Presidente Cozumel* (☎ (987) 2-03-22, fax 2-13-60), Carretera a Chankanab Km 6.5, is hard to miss with its 259 rooms, many with sea views, set amidst tropical gardens. *Sol Caribe Cozumel* (☎ (987) 2-70-00, fax 2-13-01), Playa Paraíso Km 3.5 (Apdo Postal 259), Cozumel, Quintana Roo 77600, has 321 luxurious rooms and a lavish layout with tropical swimming pool complete with a large 'island'. For reservations at either hotel, call ☎ 800-343-7821 in the USA.

Meliá Maya Cozumel (☎ (987) 2-02-72, fax 2-15-99), Playa Santa Pilar, is a 200-room resort with a full list of water sport equipment. Another Meliá hotel, the *Sol Cabañas del Caribe* (☎ (987) 2-01-61, 2-00-17, fax 2-15-99) caters mostly to divers. For reservations, call ☎ 800-336-3542 in the USA.

Places to Eat

Inexpensive The cheapest of all eating places, with fairly tasty food, are the market loncherías located next to the Mercado Municipal on Calle Salas between Avenidas 20 and 25 Sur. All of these little señora-run eateries offer soup and a main-course plate for less than 15 pesos, with a large selection of dishes available. Hours are from 6.30 am to 6.30 pm daily.

Lonchería Las Gemelas, Avenida 5 and Calle 5, is a cheap little mom-and-pop eatery open for all three meals every day. Try also the *Comida Casera Toñita*, Calle Salas between Avenidas 10 and 15 Sur, open from 8 am to 6 pm.

Restaurant Costa Brava, on Avenida Rafael Melgar just south of the post office, is among the more interesting – read funky – places to dine on the island. Cheap breakfasts (7 to 13 pesos), and such filling dishes as chicken tacos, grilled steak and fried fish or chicken for 13 to 30 pesos, are served daily from 6.30 am to 11.30 pm.

Restaurant La Choza, Calle Salas 198, specialises in authentic Mexican traditional cuisine, which is not all tacos and enchiladas. Have the pozole, a filling, spicy meat-and-hominy stew. With a soft drink, you pay 30 pesos for a huge bowl.

The *Cocina Económica Mi Chabelita*, Avenida 10 Sur between Calle 1 Sur and Calle Salas, is a tiny, fairly cheap eatery run by a señora who serves up decent portions of decent food for 20 pesos or less. It opens for breakfast at 7 am and closes at 7 pm.

La Cocina Italiana, Avenida 10 Sur No 121, at Calle 1 Sur, has rustic wooden tables and rustic pizzas and pastas: 25 to 45 pesos for a full meal.

Mid-Range Our favourite is *Pizza Prima* (☎ 2-42-42), Calle Salas between Avenidas 5 and 10 Sur, open from 1 to 11 pm (closed Wednesday). The American owners produce home-made pasta and fresh pizza as well as excellent Italian specialities. Dine streetside, or upstairs on the patio, for about 30 to 50 pesos.

Pizza Rolandi, Avenida Rafael Melgar between Calles 6 and 8 Norte, serves good one-person (20-cm diameter) pizzas for 28 to 36 pesos. It's open from 11.30 am to 11.30 pm; closed Sunday.

Cozumel is so Americanised that it has its own sports buffs' watering hole, *The Sports Page* (☎ 2-11-99), a block north of the plaza on the corner of Calle 2 Norte and Avenida 5 Norte. A plate of fajitas costs 45 pesos.

Expensive Cozumel's traditional place to dine well and richly is *Pepe's Grill* (☎ 2-02-13), Avenida Melgar at Calle Salas. Flaming shrimps, grilled lobster, Caesar salad and other top-end items can take your bill to the lofty heights of 150 or 180 pesos per person.

Entertainment

Nightlife in Cozumel is pricey, but if you want to dance, the most popular disco is *Disco Neptuno*, five blocks south of the post office on Avenida Rafael Melgar. The cover charge is 18 pesos, with drinks (even Mexican beer) for 10 pesos and up. Another hot spot, similarly priced, is *Disco Scaramouche* at the intersection of Avenida Melgar and Calle Salas. For Latin *salsa* music, try *Los Quetzales*, Avenida 10 Sur at Calle 1 Sur, a block from the plaza. It's open every evening from 6 pm.

Things to Buy

Near the plaza and along Avenida Rafael Melgar are numerous boutiques selling the favourite local souvenir, jewellery made with black coral. Legitimate shops will probably not try to cheat you on quality, but beware the cut-price merchants who substitute black plastic for the real thing. True black coral is 'weathered', with gold-coloured streaks in it. It is very light – lighter than the plastic fakes – and true coral will not burn, as does plastic.

Getting There & Away

Air Cozumel has a surprisingly busy international airport, with numerous direct flights from other parts of Mexico and the USA. Flights from Europe are usually routed via the USA or Mexico City. There are nonstop flights on Continental (☎ (987) 2-02-51) and American (☎ (987) 2-08-99) from their hubs

at Dallas, Houston and Raleigh-Durham, with many direct flights from other US cities via these hubs. Mexicana (☎ (987) 2-02-63) has nonstop flights from Miami and direct flights from Mérida and Mexico City.

Aero Cozumel (☎ (987) 2-09-28, 2-05-03), with offices at Cozumel airport, operates flights between Cancún and Cozumel about every two hours throughout the day for 150 pesos one way. Reserve in advance.

Ferry For details on ferries from Playa del Carmen, see that section. Car ferries run from Puerto Morelos (see that section).

Getting Around

To/From the Airport The airport is about two km north of town. You can take a minibus from the airport into town for less than 8 pesos, slightly more to the hotels south of town, but you'll have to take a taxi (15 or 18 pesos) to return to the airport.

Bus & Taxi Cozumel's taxi drivers have a lock on the local transport market, defeating any proposal for a convenient bus service. A single bus leaves daily from the tourist booth on the plaza in town (near the ferry) at 11 am, heading south toward Chankanab bay, returning at 5 pm. The fare is 8 pesos. The walk from the Stouffer Presidente Hotel south to Chankanab is about one km.

For other points on the island you will have to take a taxi. Fares in and around town are 15 pesos per ride, or roughly 90 pesos per hour. From the town to Laguna Chankanab is 36 pesos.

Car & Moped Rates for rental cars are upwards of 200 to 250 pesos per day, all inclusive. You could probably haggle with a taxi driver to take you on a tour of the island, drop you at a beach, come back and pick you up, and still save money; keep this shocking fact in mind when you consider renting a car.

Rented mopeds are popular with those who want to tour the island on their own. It seems that every citizen and business in San Miguel – hotels, restaurants, gift shops, morticians – rents mopeds, generally for 110 to

140 pesos per day (24 hours), though some rent from 8 am to 5 pm for 80 pesos. Insurance and tax are included in these prices. It's amusing that a 24-hour rental of two mopeds (for two people) almost equals the cost of renting a car (for up to four people) for the same period of time.

You must have a valid driving licence, and you must use a credit card, or put down a hefty deposit (around 225 pesos).

The best time to rent is first thing in the morning, when all the machines are there. Pick a good one, with a working horn, brakes, lights, starter, rear-view mirrors, and a full tank of fuel; remember that the price asked will be the same whether you rent the newest, pristine machine or the oldest, most beat-up rattletrap. (If you want to trust yourself with a second-rate moped, at least haggle the price down significantly.) You should get a helmet and a lock and chain with the moped.

When riding, keep in mind that you will be as exposed to sunshine on a moped as if you were roasting on a beach. Use plenty of sunblock (especially the backs of your hands, and your feet, neck and face), or cover up, or suffer the consequences. Also, be aware of the dangers involved. Of all motor vehicle operators, the inexperienced moped rider on unfamiliar roads in a foreign country has the highest statistical chance of having an accident, especially when faced by lots of other inexperienced moped riders. Ride carefully.

AROUND COZUMEL

In order to see most of the island (except for Chankanab Bay) you will have to rent a bicycle, moped or car, or take a taxi (see the previous Getting Around section). The following route will take you south from the town of San Miguel, then anticlockwise around the island.

Chankanab Bay Beach

This bay of clear water and fabulously coloured fish is the most popular on the island. It is nine km south of San Miguel.

You used to be able to swim in the adjoin-ing lagoon, but so many tourists were fouling the water and damaging the coral that Chankanab lagoon was made a national park and decreed off-limits to swimmers. Don't despair – you can still snorkel in the sea here and the lagoon has been saved from destruction.

Snorkelling equipment can be rented for 30 pesos per day. Divers will be interested in a reef offshore; there is a dive shop at the beach, and scuba instruction is offered.

There is also a restaurant and snack shop. The beach has dressing rooms, lockers and showers, which are included in the 13-peso admission price to the national park, open 9 am to 5 pm daily. The park also has a botanical garden with 400 species of tropical plants.

Getting There & Away There's one daily local beach bus which leaves San Miguel at 11 am, returns at 5 pm and costs 8 pesos. The taxi fare from San Miguel to Chankanab Bay is about 35 pesos.

Playa San Francisco & Playa Palancar

Playa San Francisco, 14 km from San Miguel, and Playa Palancar, a few km to the south, are the nicest of the island's beaches. San Francisco's white sands run for more than three km, and rather expensive food is served at its restaurant. If you want to scuba dive or snorkel at Palancar Reef, you will have to sign on for a day cruise or charter a boat.

El Cedral

To see these small Mayan ruins, the oldest on the island, go 3.5 km down a paved road a short distance south of Playa San Francisco. Although El Cedral was thought to be an important ceremonial site, its minor remnants are not well preserved.

Punta Celarain

The southern tip of the island has a picturesque lighthouse, accessible via a dirt track, four km from the highway. To enjoy truly isolated beaches en route, climb over the sand dunes. There's a fine view of the island from the top of the lighthouse.

East-Coast Drive

The eastern shoreline is the wildest part of the island and highly recommended for beautiful seascapes of rocky coast. Unfortunately, except for Punta Chiquero, Chen Río and Punta Morena, swimming is dangerous on Cozumel's east coast due to potentially lethal riptides and undertows. Be careful! Swim only in coves protected from the open surf by headlands or breakwaters. There are small eateries at both Punta Morena and Punta Chiquero and a hotel at Punta Morena. Some travellers camp at Chen Río.

El Castillo Real & San Gervasio Ruins

Beyond where the east-coast highway meets the Carretera Transversal (cross-island road) that runs to San Miguel, intrepid travellers may take the sand track about 17 km from the junction to the Mayan ruins known as El Castillo Real. They are not very well preserved and you need luck or a 4WD vehicle to navigate the sandy road.

If you are a real ruins buff, there is an equally unimpressive ruin called San Gervasio on a bad road from the airport. 4WD vehicles can reach San Gervasio from a track originating on the east coast, but most rental car insurance policies do not cover unpaved roads such as this. The jungle en route is more interesting than the ruins.

Punta Molas Beaches

There are some fairly good beaches and minor Mayan ruins in the vicinity of the north-east point, accessible only by 4WD vehicle or foot.

BEACHES – CANCÚN TO TULUM

Some of the world's most beautiful beaches lie between Cancún and Tulum.

Xcaret (Km 290)

Look for the *Restaurant Xcaret* on the east side of the highway; this marks the access road to this beautiful spot. Once a turkey farm, Xcaret has now been Disneyfied into what one might call Mayapark (entry 60 pesos): several small Mayan ruins, a cenote for swimming, a beautiful inlet *(caleta)* filled with tropical marine life where you can swim with the dolphins (180 pesos), a restaurant and other amusements.

Swim with the dolphins at Xcaret

Pamul (Km 274)

Although Pamul's small rocky beach does not have long stretches of white sand like some of its Caribbean cousins, the palm-fringed surroundings are inviting. If you walk only about two km north of Pamul's little hotel, you will find an alabaster sand beach to call your own. If you're collecting coral, try the shores just south of Pamul. The least rocky section is the southern end, but watch out for spiked sea urchins in the shallows offshore.

Giant sea turtles come ashore here at night in July and August to lay their eggs. Why they return to the same beach every year is a mystery to zoologists. If you run across a turtle during your evening stroll along the beach, keep a good distance from it and don't use a light, as this will scare it. Do your part to contribute to the survival of the turtles, which are endangered: let them lay their eggs in peace.

Places to Stay & Eat The *Hotel Pamul* offers basic but acceptable rooms with fan and bath for 75/90 pesos a single/double. There is electricity in the evening until 10 pm. The friendly family that runs this somewhat scruffy hotel and campground also serves breakfasts and seafood at their little restaurant for reasonable prices.

The fee for camping is 25 pesos for two people per site. There are showers and toilets.

Puerto Aventuras (Km 269.5)

The Cancún lifestyle spreads inexorably southward, dotting this previously pristine coast with yet more sybaritic resort hideaways. One such place is the *Puerto Aventuras Resort* (☎ (987) 2-22-11), PO Box 186, Playa del Carmen, Quintana Roo, a modern luxury complex of hotel rooms, swimming pools, beach facilities and other costly comforts.

Laguna Yal-Ku (Km 256.5)

One of the secrets of snorkelling aficionados, Laguna Yal-Ku is not even signposted. Its dirt road turnoff is across from a stone-walled house with a windmill. The tiny lagoon is a good place to snorkel, filled with a delightful array of aquatic life. Best of all, you may have the place all to yourself.

Yal-Ku is basically for day trips, as there is little shade and not much in the way of decent places to pitch a tent. Bring your own refreshments and snorkelling gear.

Akumal (Km 255)

Famous for its beautiful beach, Akumal (Place of the Turtles) does indeed see giant turtles come ashore to lay their eggs during the summer.

Activities There are two dive shops here where you can rent snorkelling gear. The best snorkelling is at the north end of the bay; or try Laguna Yal-Ku, 1.5 km north of Akumal.

World-class divers come here to explore the Spanish galleon *Mantancero* which sank in 1741. You can see artefacts from the galleon at the museum at nearby Xel-ha. The dive shops will arrange all your scuba excursion needs. Beginners' scuba instruction can be provided for less than 435 pesos; if you want certification, the dive shops offer three-day courses. They will also arrange deep-sea fishing excursions.

Places to Stay The least expensive of this resort's three hotels is the *Hotel-Club Akumal Caribe Villas Maya*, where basic two-person air-con cabañas with bath, and the amenities of tennis and basketball courts, cost 325 to

450 pesos a double. Make reservations through Akutrame (☎ (915) 584-3552, or toll-free outside Texas 800-351-1622), PO Box 13326, El Paso, Texas 79913, USA.

The *Hotel Akumal Caribe* on the south end of the beach is an attractive two-storey modern lodge with swimming pool, boat rental and night tennis. Spacious air-con rooms equipped with refrigerators cost 400 pesos. These can sleep six people.

On the north side of the beach you will find the cabañas of *Las Casitas Akumal* (☎ (987) 2-25-54), consisting of a living room, kitchen, two bedrooms and two bathrooms. Bungalows cost 575 pesos in the busy winter season, 400 pesos in summer. For reservations write to Las Casitas (in the USA ☎ (201) 489-6614, fax (201) 489-5070), 270 River St, Box 522, Hackensack, NJ 07602, USA.

Places to Eat Even the shade-huts near the beach are expensive for light lunches and snacks, considering what you get. Just outside the walled entrance of Akumal is a grocery store patronised largely by the resort workers; if you are day-tripping here, this is your sole inexpensive source of food. The store also sells tacos.

Las Aventuras (Km 250)

Developers got the first chance at Las Aventuras, which now has a planned community of condominiums, villas and the beautiful *Aventuras Akumal Hotel*, which has double rooms for about 410 pesos.

Chemuyil (Km 248)

Here there's a beautiful sand beach shaded by coconut palms, and good snorkelling in the calm waters with exceptional visibility. Admission costs 8 pesos.

Chemuyil is being developed, with some condos already built. During winter's high season there are a fair number of campers here (14 pesos per person).

The cheap accommodation is spartan, screened shade-huts with hammock hooks. Enquire about availability at the bar; they cost 75 pesos, and showers and toilets are communal.

Local fare is prepared at the bar, including some seafood.

Xcacel (Km 247)

Xcacel ('shkah-CELL') has no lodging other than camping (25 pesos per person), no electricity and only a small restaurant stall. This is actually fortunate, because if Xcacel was more developed, this magnificent Caribbean beach would be overrun. As it stands, you can enjoy this patch of paradise in relative privacy for a day-use charge of only 9 pesos.

For fine fishing and snorkelling, try the waters north of the campground. The rocky point leads to seas suitable for snorkelling, and the sandy outcropping is said to be a good place to fish from. Swimming, like snorkelling, is best from the rocky point to the north end of the beach.

Xcacel offers good pickings for shell collectors, including examples of that aquatic collector, the hermit crab. There are also some colourful and intricate coral pieces to be found. When beachcombing here, wear footgear.

Take the old dirt track which runs two km north to Chemuyil and three km south to Xel-ha, and you may spy parrots, finches or the well-named clockbird (mot-mot) with its long tail.

Xel-ha Lagoon (Km 245)

Once a pristine natural lagoon brimming with iridescent tropical fish, Xel-ha ('SHELL-hah') is now a Mexican national park with landscaped grounds, changing rooms, restaurant-bar and ripoff prices. The fish are regularly driven off by the dozens of busloads of sun-oiled daytrippers who come to enjoy the beautiful site and to swim in the pretty lagoon.

Should you visit Xel-Ha? Sure, so long as price is no object, you come off-season (in summer), or in winter first thing in the morning to avoid the tour buses. Bring your own lunch and drinks as the little restaurant here is overpriced. Entry to the lagoon area costs 25 pesos (children under 12 free); it's open from 8 am to 4.30 pm daily. You can rent snorkelling gear; the price is high and the equipment leaky.

Museum & Ruins The small maritime museum contains artefacts from the wreckage of the Spanish galleon *Mantancero*, which sank just north of Akumal in 1741. In 1958 Mexican divers salvaged guns, cannons, coins and other items. Admission costs 3.50 pesos.

There is a small archaeological site on the west side of the highway 500 metres south of the lagoon entry road, open from 8 am to 5 pm for 8 pesos. The ruins, which are not all that impressive, date from Classic and Postclassic periods, and include El Palacio and the Templo de los Pájaros.

TULUM

The ruins of Tulum (City of the Dawn, or City of Renewal), though well preserved, would hardly merit rave notices if it weren't for their setting. And what a setting: the grey-black buildings of the past sit on a palm-fringed beach, lapped by the turquoise waters of the Caribbean.

Don't come to Tulum expecting majestic pyramids or anything comparable to the architecture of Chichén Itzá or Uxmal. The buildings here, decidedly Toltec in influence, were the product of Mayan civilisation in decline.

Tulum's proximity to the tourist centres of Cancún and Isla Mujeres makes it a prime target of tour buses. To best enjoy the ruins, visit them either early in the morning or late in the day. The ruins are open from 8 am to 5 pm. There is a 18-peso admission charge (plus 36 pesos for a video camera!); admission is free on Sunday.

History

Most archaeologists believe that Tulum was settled in the Early Postclassic period (900-1200). When Juan de Grijalva's expedition sailed past Tulum in 1518, he was amazed by the sight of this walled city with its buildings painted a gleaming red, blue and white, and

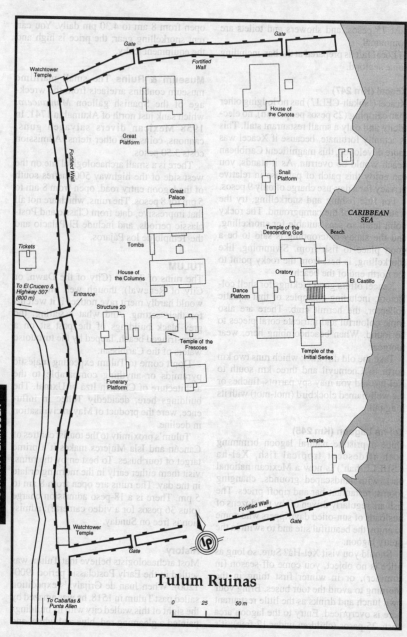

Tulum Ruinas

0   25   50 m

a ceremonial fire flaming atop its seaside watchtower.

The ramparts that surround three sides of Tulum (the fourth side being the sea) leave little question as to its strategic function as a fortress. Averaging nearly seven metres in thickness and standing three to five metres high, the walls protected the city during a period of considerable strife between Mayan city-states.

The city was abandoned about three-quarters of a century after the Spanish conquest. Mayan pilgrims continued to visit over the years and Indian refugees from the War of the Castes took shelter here from time to time.

In 1842, John L Stephens and Frederick Catherwood visited Tulum by boat. They made substantial drawings and notes which, published in 1848, aroused the curiosity of the outside world. Subsequent expeditions were mounted, the most important being the 1916-22 investigations by the Carnegie Institute.

Orientation

There are two Tulums, Tulum Ruinas and Tulum Pueblo. The ruins are 800 metres south-east off highway 307 along an access road. The village (pueblo) of Tulum straddles highway 307 about three km south of the Tulum Ruinas access road, or two km south of the Cobá road.

South of Tulum Ruinas, a road passes several collections of beachfront bungalows before entering the Reserva Biósfera Sian Ka'an. The road, unpaved, continues for some 50 km past Boca Paila to Punta Allen.

Tulum Pueblo has one lodging-place; no doubt more will open in the near future. The junction of highway 307 and the Tulum Ruinas access road, called El Crucero, has several little hotels and restaurants. The bungalows south of Tulum can provide shelter and food as well.

Structure 20 & the Funerary Platform

As you enter the Tulum city gate, look to the first building on your right, Structure 20. The roof caved in about 1929, making it a bit

difficult to envision what once was a royal palace. Fragments of paintings remain on the walls. Just to Structure 20's right is a Funerary Platform with a cross-shaped grave in its centre. Here archaeologists found skeletons and animal offerings, the latter to provide sustenance for the deceased on the journey to the next world.

Temple of the Frescoes

Thought initially to have been built about 1450, the temple has been added to on several occasions. Here you will see a carved figure very much in evidence at Tulum, the diving god. Equipped with wings and a bird's tail, this fascinating deity has been linked by some archaeologists with the Venus morning-star symbol of Quetzalcóatl. On the western façade are stucco masks thought to symbolise Quetzalcóatl in another form.

Inside the temple, the best preserved of the greenish-blue on black murals may be seen through protective bars. The mural is painted in three levels demarcating the three realms of the Mayan universe: the dark underworld of the deceased, the middle order of the living and the heavenly home of the creator and rain gods.

Mural in the Temple of the Frescoes

Great Palace

To the left of the Temple of the Frescoes, as you face the sea, is the Great Palace. Smaller than El Castillo, this largely deteriorated site contains a fine stucco carving of a diving god.

El Castillo

Tulum's tallest building is a watchtower fortress overlooking the Caribbean, appropriately named El Castillo by the Spaniards. Note the serpent columns of the temple's entrance.

Look down to the north from El Castillo and you will see a good small beach, great for sunning and a refreshing dip. There's a bit of an undertow here, so swim with caution.

Temple of the Descending God

The Temple of the Descending (or Diving) God has a good stucco relief of a diving god above the door. If you ascend the inner staircase, you will see paint fragments of a religious mural.

Temple of the Initial Series

This restored temple is named for a stele now in the British Museum, which was inscribed with the Mayan date corresponding to 564 AD. At first this confused archaeologists, who had evidence that Tulum was not settled until some time later. Today, scholars believe that the stele was moved here from a city founded much earlier.

Places to Stay

El Crucero Right at the junction of highway 307 and the Tulum access road are several hotels and restaurants, including the dismal *Motel El Crucero*, expensive at 55 to 75 pesos a double. The restaurant and shop selling ice, pastries, snacks and souvenirs are more useful.

Facing the Motel El Crucero across the access road are the *Hotel Acuario* and *Restaurant El Faisan y El Venado*, which is newer but also overpriced at 125 to 180 pesos a double.

Boca Paila/Punta Allen Rd South of the archaeological zone is a paradise of palm-shaded white beach dotted with collections of cabañas, little thatched huts of greater or lesser comfort, and simple wooden or concrete bungalows. Most of these places have little eateries at which you can take your meals, and some have generators which provide electric light for several hours each evening. There are no phones.

The cheapest way to sleep here is to have your own hammock, preferably with one of those tube-like mosquito nets to cover it; if you don't carry your own, several of the cheaper places will rent you what you need. If you have candles or a torch, they'll come in handy here. In the cheapest places you'll also have to supply your own towel and soap.

Unfortunately, these lodgings are located some distance south of the ruins and there is no public transport along the road. Though you may occasionally be able to hitch a ride, you can depend only upon your own two feet to get you from your bungalow to the ruins, which may be up to seven km away.

We'll start by describing the places closest to Tulum ruins, then head south to describe the places farther and farther away.

Closest to the ruins are *Cabañas El Mirador* and *Cabañas Santa Fe*, on the beach about 600 metres south of the Tulum ruins parking lot. Of the two, the Santa Fe is preferable, though a bit more expensive, charging 11 pesos per person for a campsite, 28 pesos to hang your hammocks in a cabin, single or double.

One km south of the parking lot is *Cabañas Don Armando*, perhaps the best of the bottom-end cabaña places. For 58 pesos (single or double) you get one of 17 cabins built on concrete slabs, with lockable doors, hammocks or beds (you pay a deposit for sheets and pillows), mosquito netting, good showers and a good, cheap restaurant. Lighting in the rooms is by candle, and the hotel employs two security guards for added peace of mind. This place is fun, right on the beach, and still only a 10-minute walk to the ruins.

The *Hotel El Paraíso* (☎ in Cozumel (987) 2-17-17), just 1.5 km south of the ruins, approaches a conventional hotel in its services. The newer rooms, with two double beds and private bath, cost 150 to 220 pesos. There's a nice little restaurant with a good sea view. There's electricity until 10 pm. *Gato's Cabañas*, 700 metres south, charge slightly less.

A road goes off to the right to join the main highway. South of this junction are *Cabañas Nohoch Tunich* and *Cabañas Mar y Sol*, five km south of the ruins. These are fairly rustic, charging 60 pesos a double. Just south the paved road gives way to a good sand track.

Osho Oasis Retreat (☎ (987) 4-27-72 ext 174, fax 3-02-30), Apdo Postal 99, Tulum, Q Roo 77780, is a resort for plain living and high thinking. There's a meditation hall and facilities for yoga, Zen, Kundalini and massage, as well as the beach. Readers of this guide report that sometimes the staff act holier-than-thou. Cabañas cost 110 to 250 pesos a double in high season; meals are 25/22/50 pesos for breakfast/lunch/dinner. *Cabañas de Anna y José*, two km farther south, has both older and newer cinder-block bungalows for 140 to 160 pesos a double.

Just south is *Cabañas Tulum*, over seven km south of the ruins, where older concrete bungalows look out through palms to the sea and the beach. The rate is 110 pesos per night, single or double. The electric generator runs (if it's working) from dusk to 10 pm each evening.

Places to Eat

Tulum Ruinas Small restaurants used to be clustered around the entrance to the site, but work is under way to move all such commerce to the other end of the access road at El Crucero. You should be able to find small mom-and-pop eateries serving sandwiches and grilled chicken meals for 10 to 20 pesos.

Motel El Crucero has a popular, very simple but somewhat expensive restaurant. Stick to the simpler items.

At the *Restaurant El Faisan y El Venado* across the street, the surroundings are a bit more attractive, the food similar, the prices even higher.

Getting There & Away

The access road between El Crucero and Tulum archaeological site is to be closed to most traffic, with visitors being shuttled back and forth on little rubber-tired trains. Let's hope that there is some sort of easy transport made available to the lodging-places south of the ruins as well. To head north or south from Tulum, wait at El Crucero for an Interplaya or regular intercity bus.

TULUM TO BOCA PAILA & PUNTA ALLEN

The scenery on the 50-km stretch from Tulum Ruinas past Boca Paila to Punta Allen is the typically monotonous flat Yucatecan terrain, but the land, rich with wildlife, is protected as the Reserva Biósfera Sian Ka'an. The surfy beaches aren't spectacular, but there's plenty of privacy.

It's important to have plenty of fuel before heading south from Tulum as there is no fuel available on the Tulum-Punta Allen road.

Reserva Biósfera Sian Ka'an

Over 5000 sq km of tropical jungle, marsh, mangrove and islands on Quintana Roo's coast have been set aside by the Mexican government as a large biosphere reserve. During 1987 the United Nations appointed it a World Heritage Site – an irreplaceable natural treasure.

A trip into Sian Ka'an (Where the Sky Begins) reveals thousands of butterflies as well as varied fauna: howler monkeys, foxes, ocelots, pumas, vultures, caimans (crocodiles), eagles, raccoons, giant land crabs and – if you're very lucky – a jaguar. Unrestored Mayan ruins are everywhere. Though small and mostly unimpressive, it's still a thrill to visit one of these quiet sites which has lain here unheeded for centuries.

Treks into the reserve are run from Cancún and Playa del Carmen. For details on the reserve, contact Amigos de Sian Ka'an (☎ (98) 84-95-83, 87-30-80), Plaza América, Avenida Cobá 5, 3rd Floor, Suites 48-50, Cancún, Q Roo 77500.

YUCATÁN PENINSULA

Boca Paila

Boca Paila is 25 km south of Tulum. One of the two hotels on the road to Punta Allen is *La Villa de Boca Paila*, where luxury cabañas complete with kitchens cost about 325 pesos per double, including two meals. The clientele is predominantly affluent American sport fishers. For reservations write to Apdo Postal 159, Mérida, Yucatán.

Ten km south of Boca Paila you cross a rickety wooden bridge. Beyond it is *El Retiro Cabañas* where you can hang hammocks or camp for a few dollars.

Fishing for lobsters in Punta Allen

Punta Allen

Once a pocket of wealthy lobster fishers in a vast wilderness, Punta Allen suffered considerable damage from the ferocious winds of Hurricane Gilbert in 1988. The hurricane and overfishing have depleted lobster stocks, but a laid-back ambience reminiscent of the Belizean cayes gives hope for a touristic future.

Punta Allen does have some rustic lodgings. The *Cruzan Inn* (fax (983) 4-03-83) has cabañas with hammocks for about 90 pesos a double. The couple who run it prepare breakfast and lunch at a cost of 24 pesos per person and charge 50 pesos for dinner. They can arrange snorkelling and fishing expeditions, or visits to the offshore island of Cayo Colibri, known for its bird life. To write for reservations, the address is Cruzan Inn, c/o Sonia Lillvik, Apdo Postal 703, Cancún, Quintana Roo 77500.

The *Bonefishing Club of Ascension Bay*, run by Jan Persson, specialises in guided fishing expeditions, but also has two rooms for rent in the house which is its headquarters. Family-style meals are served.

Let It Be Inn has three thatched cabañas with comforts such as private bath (with hot water), porches hung with hammocks and sea views. For reservations write to Rick Montgomery, Let It Be Inn, Apdo Postal 74, Tulum, Q Roo 77780.

If you wish to camp on Punta Allen's beach, simply ask the Maya in front of whose house you would be sleeping for permission.

COBÁ

Perhaps the largest of all Mayan cities, Cobá, 50 km north-west of Tulum, offers the chance to explore mostly unrestored antiquities set deep in tropical jungles.

History

Cobá was settled earlier than Chichén or Tulum, its heyday dating from 600 AD until the site was mysteriously abandoned about 900 AD. Archaeologists believe that this city once covered 50 sq km and held 40,000 Maya.

Cobá's architecture is a mystery; its towering pyramids and stelae resemble the architecture of Tikal, several hundred km away, rather than the much nearer sites of Chichén Itzá and the northern Yucatán Peninsula.

Some archaeologists theorise that an alliance with Tikal was made through marriage to facilitate trade between the Guatemalan and Yucatecan Maya. Stelae appear to depict female rulers from Tikal holding ceremonial bars and flaunting their power by standing on captives. These Tikal royal females, when married to Cobá's royalty, may have brought architects and artisans with them.

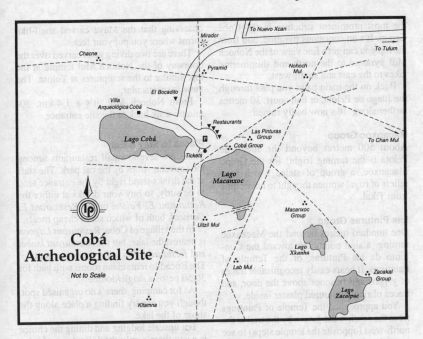

Cobá Archeological Site

Not to Scale

To Nuevo Xcan

Mirador

Chacne

To Tulum

Pyramid

Nohoch Mul

El Bocadito

Villa Arqueológica Cobá

Restaurants

Las Pinturas Group

Cobá Group

To Chan Mul

P

Tickets

Lago Cobá

Lago Macanxoc

Macanxoc Group

Uitzil Mul

Lago Xkanha

Lab Mul

Zacakal Group

Kitamna

Lago Zacalpuc

Archaeologists are also baffled by the network of extensive stone-paved avenues or sacbeob in this region, with Cobá as the hub. The longest runs nearly 100 km from the base of Cobá's great pyramid Nohoch Mul to the Mayan settlement of Yaxuna. In all, some 40 sacbeob passed through Cobá. The sacbeob were parts of the huge astronomical 'time machine' that was evident in every Mayan city.

The first excavation was by the Austrian archaeologist Teobert Maler. Hearing rumours of a fabled lost city, he came to Cobá alone in 1891. There was little subsequent investigation until 1926 when the Carnegie Institute financed the first of two expeditions led by J Eric S Thompson and Harry Pollock. After their 1930 expedition not much happened until 1973, when the Mexican government began to finance excavation. Archaeologists now estimate that Cobá contains some 6500 structures of which just a few have been excavated and restored.

Orientation

The small village of Cobá, 2.5 km west of the Tulum-Nuevo Xcan road, has several small, simple, cheap lodging and eating places. At the lake, turn left for the ruins, right for the upscale Villa Arqueológica Cobá hotel.

Cobá archaeological site is open from 8 am to 5 pm; admission costs 18 pesos, free on Sunday.

Be prepared to do considerable walking – at least five to seven km – on jungle paths. Dress for heat and humidity, and bring insect repellent. It's also a good idea to bring a canteen of water; it's hot and there are no drinks stands within the site, only at the entrance. Avoid the midday heat if possible. A visit to the site takes two to four hours.

Cobá Group

Walking just under 100 metres along the main path from the entrance brings you to the Temple of the Churches, on your right, the most prominent structure in the Cobá Group. It's an enormous pyramid, and from the top you can get a fine view of the Nohoch Mul pyramid to the north and shimmering lakes to the east and south-west.

Back on the main path, you pass through the Juego de Pelota, or ball court, 30 metres farther along. It's now badly ruined.

Macanxoc Group

About 500 metres beyond the Juego de Pelota is the turning (right) for the Grupo Macanxoc, a group of stelae which bore reliefs of royal women thought to have come from Tikal.

Las Pinturas Group

One hundred metres beyond the Macanxoc turning, a sign points left toward the Conjunto de las Pinturas, or the Temple of Paintings. It bears easily recognisable traces of glyphs and frescoes above the door, and traces of richly coloured plaster inside.

You approached the Temple of Paintings from the south-west. Leave by the trail at the north-west (opposite the temple steps) to see several stelae. The first of these is 20 metres along beneath a palapa. A regal figure stands over two others, one of them kneeling with his hands bound behind him. Sacrificial captives lie beneath the feet of a ruler at the base. Continue along the path past another badly weathered stele to the Nohoch Mul path, and turn right.

Nohoch Mul – The Great Pyramid

A further walk of 800 metres brings you to Nohoch Mul. Along the way, just before the track bends sharply to the left, a narrow path on the right leads to a group of badly weathered stelae. Farther along, the track bends between piles of stones – obviously a ruined temple – before passing Temple 10 and Stele 20. The exquisitely carved stele bears a picture of a ruler standing imperiously over two captives. Eighty metres beyond the stele stands the Great Pyramid.

At 42 metres high, the huge Great Pyramid is the tallest of all Mayan structures in the Yucatán Peninsula. Climb the 120 steps,

observing that the Maya carved shell-like forms where you put your feet.

There are two diving gods carved over the doorway of the Nohoch Mul temple at the top, similar to the sculptures at Tulum. The view is spectacular.

From Nohoch Mul, it's a 1.4-km, 30-minute walk back to the site entrance.

Places to Stay & Eat

There are several small restaurants among the souvenir shops by the car park. The staff at the drinks stand right by the entrance tend to be surly, so buy your drinks at either the *Restaurant El Faisan* or the *Restaurant El Caracol*, both of which serve cheap meals.

In the village of Cobá, *Restaurant Lagoon* is nearest the lake, but the *Restaurant Isabel* and *Restaurant Bocadito* are more popular. The Bocadito rents clean rooms with bath for 36/50 pesos a single/double.

As for camping, there's no organised spot, though you can try finding a place along the shore of the lake.

For upscale lodging and dining the choice is easy: there's only the *Villa Arqueológica Cobá* (☎ in Cancún (98) 84-25-74; in the USA 800-528-3100). The pleasant hotel has a swimming pool and good restaurant. Aircon rooms cost 250/290/325 pesos a single/double/triple. Lunch or dinner in the good restaurant might cost 70 to 100 pesos.

Getting There & Away

Numerous buses trace the route between Tulum and Valladolid. Be sure to mention to the driver that you want to get out at Cobá junction; the road does not pass through the village, which is 2.5 km west of the highway.

Leaving Cobá is problematic, as most buses are full when they pass here. If you're willing to stand for the 50-km ride to Tulum or the 50 km to Nuevo Xcan (120 km to Valladolid), you have a better chance.

A more comfortable, dependable but expensive way to reach Cobá is by taxi from the car park at El Crucero near Tulum Ruinas. Find some other travellers interested in the trip and split the cost, about 70 to 100 pesos return, including two hours (haggle for three) at the site.

By the way, many maps show a road from Cobá to Chemax, but this road is not passable.

FELIPE CARRILLO PUERTO

• *pop: 17,000*

Now named for a progressive governor of Yucatán, this town was once known as Chan Santa Cruz, the dreaded rebel headquarters during the War of the Castes.

History

In 1849 the War of the Castes went against the Maya of the northern Yucatán Peninsula, who made their way to this town seeking refuge. Regrouping their forces, they were ready to sally forth again in 1850, just when a 'miracle' occurred. A wooden cross erected at a cenote on the western edge of the town began to 'talk', telling the Maya they were the chosen people, exhorting them to continue the struggle against the Whites, and promising victory. The talking was actually done by a ventriloquist who used sound chambers, but the people nonetheless looked upon it as the authentic voice of their aspirations.

The oracular cross guided the Maya in

battle for more than eight years, until their great victory in conquering the fortress at Bacalar. For the latter part of the 19th century, the Maya in and around Chan Santa Cruz were virtually independent of governments in Mexico City and Mérida. In the 1920s a boom in the chicle market brought prosperity to the region and the Maya decided to come to terms with Mexico City, which they did in 1929. Some of the Maya, unwilling to give up the cult of the talking cross, left Chan Santa Cruz to take up residence at small villages deep in the jungle, where they still revere the talking cross to this day. You may see some of them visiting the site where the cross spoke, especially on 3 May, the day of the Holy Cross.

You can visit the **Sanctuario del Cruz Parlante** five blocks west of the Pemex fuel station on the main street (highway 307) in the commercial centre of town. Besides the cenote and a stone shelter, there's little to see in the park, though the place reverberates with history.

Places to Stay & Eat

El Faisán y El Venado (☎ (983) 4-00-43), across from the Pemex station 100 metres

---

Time Among the Maya

The history of the Talking Cross is not over. Every year on 3 May, the Feast of the Holy Cross, Mayas gather in Felipe Carrillo Puerto – known as Noh Cah Santa Cruz Balam Na to them – to celebrate the cross as the symbol of ancient Mayan traditions, and specifically the Talking Cross as the last great symbol of Mayan independence.

Just a short drive inland from Carrillo Puerto, Mayan villagers observe many aspects of traditional life, including even the use of the ancient Mayan calendar.

In the mid-1980s, English writer Ronald Wright came here in search of Mayas who still understood the Long Count and lived by the dictates of the tzolkin, or ancient Mayan almanac. Wright wrote about his experiences in a fascinating book, *Time Among the Maya*, published by Weidenfeld & Nicolson (New York) in 1989.

Wright found what he was seeking in X-Cacal Guardia and nearby villages, where descendants of the survivors of the 19th-century War of the Castes settled. Enveloped in the Yucatecan jungle, away from the wealth and centres of power which the government in Mexico City sought to control, they guard their ancient crosses and religious beliefs while accepting innovations like electric light, automobiles and Coca-Cola.

Within the 25-metre-long church at X-Cacal Guardia, guarded by men with rifles, is a holy-of-holies, to be entered only by the Nohoch Tata (Great Father of the Holy Cross) himself. It may be that Chan Santa Cruz's famous Talking Cross, spirited away from the doomed city by the Mayas retreating from the last battle of the War of the Castes, has come to rest here. ■

south of the traffic circle, has 13 cheap rooms with private showers and ceiling fans. Prices are 55/95 pesos a single/double. They have a restaurant with surprisingly good food and service, too. The ADO bus station is on the south side of the restaurant. Just a few dozen metres to the south is the *Restaurant 24 Horas*, which is a bit cheaper.

Just off the main plaza is the *Hotel Chan Santa Cruz* (☎ (983) 4-01-70), with drab rooms around a courtyard priced similarly to those at El Faisán y El Venado.

Getting There & Away

Buses running between Cancún (224 km, four hours, 30 pesos) and Chetumal (155 km, three hours, 22 pesos) stop here, as do buses travelling from Chetumal to Valladolid (160 km, three hours, 22 pesos). There are also a few buses between Felipe Carrillo Puerto and Ticul (200 km, 3½ hours, 30 pesos); change at Ticul or Muna for Uxmal. Bus fare between FCP and Tulum is 14 pesos.

Note that there are very few services such as hotels, restaurants or fuel stations between Felipe Carrillo Puerto and Ticul.

LAGUNA BACALAR

Nature has set a turquoise jewel in the midst of the scrubby Yucatecan jungle – Laguna Bacalar. A large, clear freshwater lake with a bottom of gleaming white sand, Bacalar comes as a surprise in this country of tortured limestone. Bacalar, for all its beauty, has hardly been developed at all. While this preserves its beauty, it also makes it difficult to put up here for the night.

The small, sleepy town of Bacalar, just east of the highway some 125 km south of Felipe Carrillo Puerto, is the only settlement of any size on the lake. It's noted mostly for its old fortress and its swimming facilities.

The fortress was built over the lagoon to protect citizens from raids by pirates and Indians. It served as an important outpost for the Whites in the War of the Castes. In 1859, it was seized by Mayan rebels who held the fort until Quintana Roo was finally conquered by Mexican troops in 1901. Today, with formidable cannons still on its ramparts,

the fortress remains an imposing sight. It houses a museum exhibiting colonial armaments and uniforms from the 17th and 18th centuries. The museum is open daily from 8 am to 1 pm and has a small admission charge of 4 pesos.

A divided avenue runs between the fortress and the lakeshore northward a few hundred metres to the balneario, or bathing facilities. Small restaurants line the avenue and surround the balneario, which is very busy on weekends.

Costera Bacalar

The road which winds southward along the lakeshore from Bacalar town to highway 307 at Cenote Azul is called the Costera Bacalar. It passes a few lodging and camping places along the way.

About 2.5 km south of the town is the *Mesón Nueva Salamanca*, Costera 51, with tidy little motel-type rooms for 90 pesos a double. There's no restaurant, but a little shop sells cold drinks and snacks.

Hotel Laguna (☎ (983) 2-35-17 in Chetumal, (99) 27-13-04 in Mérida), 3.5 km south of Bacalar town along the Costera, is only 150 metres east of highway 307, so you can ask a bus driver to stop here for you. The Laguna is a hidden paradise: clean, cool and hospitable, with a wonderful view of the lake, a nice swimming pool, breezy terrace and restaurant, and bar. Rooms cost 150 pesos a single or double with fan and private bath.

Only 700 metres past the Hotel Laguna along the Costera is a nameless little campground on the shore run by a family who live in a shack on the premises. You can camp in the dense shade of the palm trees for 22 pesos per couple. Bring your own food and drinking water, as the nearest supplier is the restaurant at the Hotel Laguna.

Cenote Azul is a 90-metre-deep natural pool on the south-western shore of Laguna Bacalar, 200 metres east of highway 307. A small sign purveys the traditional wisdom: 'Don't go in the cenote if you can't swim'. Being a cenote there's no beach, just a few steps leading down to the water from the vast palapa. The palapa also shelters a restaurant which serves main-course dishes of fish or meat for around 18 to 40 pesos; an average meal here might cost between 32 to 50 pesos.

Getting There & Away

Coming from the north, have the bus drop you in Bacalar town, at the Hotel Laguna, or at Cenote Azul, as you wish (check before you buy your ticket to see if the driver will stop).

From Chetumal, catch a minibus from Combi Corner. Departures are about every 20 minutes from 5 am to 7 pm for the 39-km (40 minutes, 11 pesos) run to the town of Bacalar; some northbound buses (7.50 pesos) departing from the bus station will also drop you near the town of Bacalar. Along the way they pass Laguna Milagros (14 km), Xul-ha (22 km) and the Cenote Azul (33 km), and all of these places afford chances to swim in fresh water. The lakes are gorgeous, framed by palm trees, with crystal clear water and soft white limestone-sand bottoms.

Heading west out of Chetumal, you turn north onto highway 307; 15.5 km north of this highway junction is a turn on the right marked for the Cenote Azul and Costera Bacalar.

CHETUMAL

• *pop: 130,000*

Before the Spanish Conquest, Chetumal was a Mayan port for shipping gold, feathers, cacao and copper from this region and Gua-temala to the northern Yucatán Peninsula. After the conquest, the town was not actually settled until 1898 when it was founded to put a stop to the illegal trade in arms and lumber carried on by the descendants of the War of the Castes rebels. Dubbed Payo Obispo, the town's name was changed to Chetumal in 1936. In 1955, Hurricane Janet virtually obliterated Chetumal.

During the rebuilding, the city planners laid out the new town on a grand plan with a grid of wide boulevards. In times BC (Before Cancún), the sparsely populated territory of Quintana Roo could not support such a grand city, even though Quintana Roo was upgraded from a territory to a state in 1974. But the boom at Cancún brought prosperity to all, and Chetumal is finally fulfilling its destiny as an important capital city.

Chetumal is also the gateway to Belize, and you may encounter groups of Belizeans coming to the 'big city' to shop.

Orientation

Despite its sprawling layout, the centre is easily manageable on foot. Once you find the all-important intersection of Avenida de los Héroes and Avenida Alvaro Obregón, you're within 50 metres of several cheap hotels and restaurants. The best hotels are only four or five blocks from this intersection.

The city's new bus station is three km north of the centre of town at the intersection of Avenida de los Insurgentes and Avenida Belice.

Tiny riverside village typical of the Yucatán region

Information

Tourist Information A tourist information kiosk (☎ (983) 2-36-63) on Héroes at the eastern end of Aguilar, across from the market, can answer most questions. Hours are 8 am to 1 pm and 5 to 8 pm. The state tourism authorities may be reached on ☎ 2-02-66.

Money For currency exchange, most banks are located along Héroes in the centre of town. For instance, there's a Bancomer (☎ (983) 2-02-05) at Héroes 6 and a Banamex (☎ (983) 2-27-10) at the intersection of Obregón and Juárez. Banking hours are from 9.30 am to 1 pm Monday to Friday.

Post The post office (☎ (983) 2-00-57) is at Plutarco Elias Calles 2A. The postal code for Chetumal is 77000.

Foreign Consulates The Guatemalan Consulate (☎ (983) 2-85-85) is at Avenida Chapultepec 354. It's open from 9 am to 2 pm Monday to Friday and offers quick visa service. The Belizean Consulate (☎ (983) 2-28-71) is at Obregón 226A.

Things to See

No one comes to Chetumal for sightseeing. Most of what's worthwhile in the area is outside Chetumal (see Around Chetumal). The exception is the new, huge **Museo Cultura Maya** up from the tourist information kiosk, which should be open by the time you arrive.

Places to Stay – bottom end

The hostel, *Villa Juvenil Chetumal* (☎ (983) 2-05-25), on Calzada Veracruz near the corner with Obregón, is the cheapest place in town. It has a few drawbacks: single-sex dorms, 11 pm curfew, and a location five blocks east of the intersection of Héroes and Obregón. The cost is 18 pesos for a bunk in a room with four or six beds and shared bath. Breakfast costs 14 pesos and lunch or dinner 16.50 pesos in the cafeteria.

Hotel María Dolores (☎ (983) 2-05-08), Obregón 206 west of Héroes, above the Restaurant Sosilmar, is the best for the price, with tiny, stuffy rooms for 40 pesos a single and 50 to 60 pesos a double with fans and private bath.

Hotel Ucum (☎ (983) 2-07-11), Avenida Mahatma Gandhi 167, is a large, rambling old place with lots of rooms around a bare central courtyard and a good cheap little restaurant. Plain, cheap rooms equipped with fan and private bath cost 33/50/62 a single/double/triple.

Hotel Cristal (☎ (983) 2-38-78), Cristóbal Colón 207, between Juárez and Belice, is run by an energetic señora who offers clean rooms for 40/58 pesos a single/double with fan, 80 pesos a double with air-con.

Hotel Jacaranda (☎ (983) 2-03-20), on Obregón just west of Héroes, is plain and bright with fluorescent lights. Rates are 45/58 pesos a single/double, about 11 or 13 pesos higher with air-con. Note that this hotel has many noisy rooms; choose carefully.

Want a very clean, quiet room with good cross-ventilation, fan, TV and private bath for only 55/75 pesos a single/double with air-con? Then find your way to the *Posada Pantoja* (☎ (983) 2-17-81), Lucio Blanco 95, one km north-east of the tourist information kiosk in a peaceful residential area. Ask at the Restaurant Pantoja for directions.

Places to Stay – middle

The new *Hotel Caribe Princess* (☎ (983) 2-09-00), Obregón 168, has lots of marble and good air-con rooms for 150 pesos a double.

Hotel El Dorado (☎ 2-03-15), Avenida 5 de Mayo No 42, has large, tidy rooms for 65/75/95 pesos a single/double/triple with fan, 110/125/140 pesos with air-con.

Places to Stay – top end

Hotel Los Cocos (☎ (983) 2-05-44, fax 2-09-20), Avenida Héroes at Chapultepec, is the best in town, with a nice swimming pool set in grassy lawns, guarded car park and decent restaurant. Air-con rooms with TV, rich in nubbly white stucco, cost 300 pesos a single or double.

Chetumal

0   100   200 m

To Bus Station,
Hotel Principe
& Calderitas

To Venus Bus
Station (Belize)

BAHÍA DE CHETUMAL

To Airport, Escárcega,
Belize & Cancún

PLACES TO STAY
1   Posada Pantoja
2   Hotel Cristal
5   Hotel & Restaurant Ucum
8   Hotel Continental Caribe
13 Hotel Los Cocos
17 Hotel & Restaurant Jacaranda
19 Villa Juvenil Chetumal
22 Hotel María Dolores &
    Restaurant Sosilmar
25 Hotel El Dorado
26 Hotel Caribe Princess

PLACES TO EAT
6   Restaurant Pantoja
15 Restaurant El Taquito
21 Restaurant Pollo Brujo
23 Panadería La Muralla &
    Restaurant Campeche
24 Sergio's Pizzas & Maria's
    Restaurant

OTHER
3   Museo Cultura Maya
4   Combi Corner
7   Mercado
9   Tourist Information Kiosk
10 Hospital Morelos
11 Centro de Salud
12 Telmex
14 Post Office
16 Banca Serfin
18 TAESA Office
20 Banamex
27 Banco Internacional
28 Banamex
29 Palacio de Gobierno

YUCATÁN PENINSULA

Two blocks north of Los Cocos along Héroes, on the right-hand side near the tourist information kiosk, is the *Hotel Continental Caribe* (☎ (983) 2-10-50, fax 2-16-76), Héroes 171. Its comfortable rooms overlook several swimming pools, a restaurant and bar, and cost 175/210 pesos a single/double; junior suites are 250/300 a single/double.

Places to Eat

Near the intersection of Héroes and Obregón is the quaint old *Restaurant Campeche*, in a Caribbean-style wooden building which may give way to the bulldozers and rampant modernisation at any moment. Until it does, you can enjoy cheap food in an old Chetumal atmosphere.

Next door is the *Panadería La Muralla*, providing fresh baked goods for bus trips, picnics, and make-your-own breakfasts.

Restaurant Sosilmar, next along Obregón west of Héroes below the Hotel María, is perhaps the cleanest and brightest Chetumal eatery. Prices are listed prominently; filling platters of fish or meat go for 15 to 22 pesos.

To the west of the Sosilmar is *Pollo Brujo*, a roast chicken place where you can roll your own burritos.

The family-owned and operated *Restaurant Pantoja*, on the corner of Avenida Mahatma Gandhi 164 and 16 de Septiembre 181, is a neighbourhood favourite which opens for breakfast early, and later provides a comida corrida for 16.50 pesos, enchiladas for 11, and meat plates such as bistec or liver and onions (higado encebollado) for 18 pesos. The nearby *Restaurant Ucum*, in the Hotel Ucum, also provides good cheap meals.

To sample the typical traditional food of Quintana Roo, head for the *Restaurant El Taquito*, Avenida Plutarco Elias Calles 220 at Juárez. You enter past the cooks, hard at work, to an airy, simple dining room where good, cheap food is served. There's a daily comida corrida for 14 pesos.

Sergio's Pizzas (☎ 2-23-55), Obregón 182, a block east of Héroes, is actually a full-service restaurant. Look for the stained-glass windows, enter the delightfully air-con dining room, order a cold beer in a frosted mug or one of the many wines offered, and select a pizza priced from 18 pesos (small and plain) to 75 pesos (large and fancy). The pleasant wood-panelled dining room has paintings and soft classical music. Sergio's is open from 1 pm to midnight every day. *María's Restaurant*, right next door on the corner, is similar, with a menu of pizzas, steaks and Continental dishes.

Getting There & Away

Air Chetumal's small airport is less than two km north-west of the city centre along Obregón and Revolución.

Aerocaribe (☎ (983) 2-66-75 at the airport) operates flights between Chetumal and Mérida, Cozumel and Cancún.

Aviacsa (☎ (983) 2-76-89/76; at the airport 2-77-87) flies nonstop to Mexico City, and also to Tuxtla Gutiérrez. From Tuxtla you can fly to Mérida, Oaxaca, Tapachula or Villahermosa.

Aerovías, a small Guatemalan airline, flies to Guatemala City three times weekly, with stops at Belize City on two days. Otherwise, for flights to Belize City (and on to Tikal) or to Belize's cayes, cross the border into Belize and fly from Corozal.

Bus Chetumal's large new bus station is three km north of the city centre. There's a left-luggage room charging 1 peso per hour. The dominant company is Autotransportes del Caribe, but ADO buses stop here as well. For Belize, Batty's Bus Service runs from the Chetumal bus station; Venus Bus Lines runs from the intersection of Regundo and Calzada Veracruz, two km north of the centre.

Destinations include:

Bacalar – 39 km, 45 minutes; nine 2nd-class buses (6 pesos)

Belize City – 160 km, four hours (express 3¼ hours); Venus (36 pesos) on the hour from 6 am to 6 pm; Batty's (36 pesos) every two hours from 4 am to 6 pm

Campeche – 422 km, seven hours; 1st-class buses (44 pesos) at 12.30 and 7 pm

Cancún – 382 km, seven hours; six 1st-class (48 pesos) and six 2nd-class (40 pesos) buses

Corozal (Belize) – 30 km, one hour with border formalities; see also Minibus, below

Felipe Carrillo Puerto – 155 km, three hours; five 1st-class (22 pesos) and nine 2nd-class (19 pesos) buses

Kohunlich – 67 km, 1¼ hours; Xpujil and Escárcega buses drop you just before Francisco Villa, a nine-km (1¾-hour) walk to the site

Mérida – 456 km, 6½ hours; seven 1st-class buses (45 pesos) by A Peninsulares; eight 1st-class and nine 2nd-class buses (36 pesos) by A del Caribe

Muna (for Uxmal) – 375 km, seven hours; nine 2nd-class buses (32 pesos)

Playa del Carmen – 315 km, 5½ hours; at least six 1st-class (40 pesos) and six 2nd-class (30 pesos) buses

San Cristóbal de Las Casas – 700 km, 13 hours; one 1st-class (100 pesos) evening bus by ADO

Ticul – 352 km, 6½ hours; nine 2nd-class buses (40 pesos)

Tulum – 251 km, four hours; six 1st-class (32 pesos) and six 2nd-class (26 pesos) buses

Valladolid – 305 km, five hours; two 2nd-class buses (40 pesos)

Villahermosa – 575 km, nine hours; one deluxe (80 pesos) by Cristóbal Colón at 10.45 pm; eight 1st-class buses (70 pesos) by ADO

Xpujil – 120 km, two hours; three 2nd-class buses (22 pesos)

Minibus Not far from the tourist information kiosk are several minibus departure and arrival points. Volkswagen combi minibuses run from here to points in the vicinity of Chetumal such as Laguna Bacalar and the Belizean border at Subteniente López. Combi Corner, as it is known, is the intersection of Avenidas Primo de Verdad and Hidalgo, two blocks east of Héroes (four blocks north-east of the market).

AROUND CHETUMAL
Calderitas
If you want to go out to a beach, catch a Calderitas bus on Avenida Belice between Colón and Gandhi, just by the market, for a 15 to 20-minute, six-km ride to Calderitas Bay and its rocky beach. Palapas here shelter you from the sun; refreshment stands provide snacks and drinks. If you wish to pitch a tent, there's a campground. Note that on Sunday the beach is packed with locals and their families enjoying their day off.

KOHUNLICH RUINS
West of Chetumal along highway 186 is the archaeological site of Kohunlich. It is only partly excavated, with many of its nearly 200 mounds still covered with vegetation. The surrounding rainforest is thick, but the archaeological site itself has been cleared selectively and is now a delightful forest park. Kohunlich's caretaker, Señor Ignacio Ek, may offer you a tour, after which a tip is in order. Otherwise, the site is open from 8 am to 5 pm daily and admission costs 15 pesos. Drinks are sold at the site, but nothing else.

These ruins, dating from the late Preclassic (100-200 AD) and Early Classic (250-600 AD) periods, are famous for the impressive **Pyramid of the Masks**: a central stairway is flanked by huge, three-metre-high stucco masks of the sun god. The thick lips and prominent features are reminiscent of Olmec sculpture. Though there were once

eight masks, only two remain after the ravages of archaeology looters. The masks themselves are impressive, but the large thatch coverings which have been erected to protect them from further weathering also obscure the view; you can see the masks only from close up. Try to imagine what the pyramid and its masks must have looked like in the old days as the Maya approached it across the sunken courtyard at the front.

The hydraulic engineering used at the site was a great achievement; nine of the site's 21 hectares were cut to channel rainwater into Kohunlich's once enormous reservoir.

Getting There & Away

There is no public transport running directly to Kohunlich. To visit the ruins without your own vehicle, start early in the morning, and take a bus heading west from Chetumal to Xpujil or Escárcega, then watch for the village of Nachi-Cocom some 50 km from Chetumal. About 9.5 km past Nachi-Cocom, just before the village of Francisco Villa, is a road on the left (south) which covers the nine km to the archaeological site. Have the bus driver stop and let you off here, plan to

walk and hope to hitch a ride from tourists in a car. To return to Chetumal or head westward to Xpujil or Escárcega you must hope to flag down a bus on the highway.

SOUTH TO BELIZE & GUATEMALA

Corozal, 18 km south of the Mexican/Belizean border, is a pleasant, sleepy, laid-back farming and fishing town, and an appropriate introduction to Belize. There are several decent hotels catering to a full range of budgets, and restaurants to match. For complete details on travel through, within and beyond Belize, get hold of Lonely Planet's *Guatemala, Belize & Yucatán: La Ruta Maya* and/or *Central America*.

Buses run directly from Chetumal's bus station to Belize City via Corozal and Orange Walk. From Belize City you can catch westward buses to Belmopan, San Ignacio, and the Guatemalan border at Benque Viejo, then onward to Flores, Tikal and other points in Guatemala.

A special 1st-class bus service goes directly between Chetumal's bus terminal and Flores (near Tikal in Guatemala) once daily (350 km, nine hours, US$40).

Glossary

Note: For food and drink terms, see Food and Drinks in Facts for the Visitor; for bus and train terms, see the Getting Around chapter.

AC – *antes de Cristo* (before Christ); equivalent to BC

adobe – sun-dried mud brick used for building

aduana – customs

agave – family of plants including the *maguey*

aguardiente – literally 'burning water'; strong liquor usually made from sugar cane

Alameda – name of formal parks in several Mexican cities

albergue de juventud – youth hostel; often dormitories in a *villa juvenil*

alfarería – potter's workshop

alfíz – rectangular frame around a curved arch; an Arabic influence on Spanish and Mexican buildings

Altiplano Central – dry plateau stretching across north central Mexico between the two Sierra Madre ranges

amate – paper made from tree bark

Ángeles Verdes – Green Angels: government-funded mechanics who patrol Mexico's major highways in green vehicles; they help motorists with fuel, spare parts and service

antojito – traditional Mexican snack or light meal

Apdo – abbreviation for *Apartado* (Box) in addresses; hence *Apdo Postal* means Post Office Box

arroyo – brook, stream

artesanías – handicrafts, folk arts

atlas (s), **atlantes** (pl) – sculpted male figure(s) used instead of a pillar to support a roof or frieze; a *telamon*

atrium – churchyard, usually a big one

autopista – expressway, dual carriageway

azulejo – painted ceramic tile

bahía – bay

balneario – bathing-place, often a natural hot spring

baluarte – bulwark, defensive wall

barrio – neighbourhood of a town or city, often a poor neighbourhood

billete – bank note

boleto – ticket

brujo, -a – witch-doctor, shaman

burro – donkey

caballeros – literally 'horsemen', but corresponds to 'gentlemen' in English; look for it on toilet doors

cabaña – cabin, simple shelter

cabina – Baja Californian term for a *caseta de larga distancia*

cacique – Aztec chief; in more recent times used to describe a provincial warlord or strongman

calle – street

callejón – alley; small, narrow or very short street

calzada – grand boulevard or avenue

camarín – chapel beside the main altar in a church; contains ceremonial clothing for images of saints or the Virgin; also, a type of sleeping compartment on a train

campesino, -a – country person, peasant

capilla abierta – open chapel; used in early Mexican monasteries for preaching to large crowds of Indians

casa de cambio – exchange house; place where currency is exchanged, faster to use than a bank

caseta de larga distancia – long-distance telephone station, often in a shop; see *Lada, Ladatel*

cazuela – clay cooking-pot; usually sold in a nested set

cenote – a limestone sinkhole filled with rainwater, used in Yucatán as a reservoir and sometimes for ceremonial purposes

central camionera – bus terminal

cerro – hill

Chac – Mayan rain god

chac-mool – pre-Hispanic stone sculpture

of a hunched, belly-up figure; the stomach may have been used as a sacrificial altar

charreada – Mexican rodeo

charro – Mexican cowboy

Chilango, -a – citizen of Mexico City

chinampas – floating gardens of the Aztecs; versions still exist at Xochimilco near Mexico City

chingar – literally 'to fuck'; it has a wide range of colloquial usages in Mexican Spanish equivalent to those in English

chultún – cement-lined brick cistern found in the *chenes* (wells) region of Yucatán in the Puuc hills south of Mérida

Churrigueresque – Spanish late-baroque architectural style; found on many Mexican churches

cigarro – cigarette

Coatlicue – mother of the Aztec gods

colectivo – minibus or car which picks up and drops off passengers along a predetermined route

Coleto, -a – citizen of San Cristóbal de Las Casas

colonia – neighbourhood of a city, often a wealthy residential area

comedor – literally 'dining room', an eating stall or small, cheap restaurant

comida corrida – fixed-price menu with several courses, offered in restaurants; cheaper than eating à la carte

completo – no vacancy, literally 'full up'; a sign you may see at hotel desks

conasupo – government-owned store that sells many everyday basics at subsidised prices

conde – count (nobleman)

conquistador – early Spanish explorer-conqueror

cordillera – mountain range

Correos – post office

coyote – person who smuggles illegal Mexican immigrants into the USA

criollo – Mexican-born person of Spanish parentage; in colonial times considered inferior by peninsular Spaniards (see *gachupines, peninsulares*)

Cristeros – Roman Catholic rebels of the late 1920s

cuota – toll; a *vía cuota* is a toll road

damas – ladies; the sign on toilet doors

Danzantes – literally 'dancers'; stone carvings at Monte Albán

DC – *después de Cristo* (after Christ); equivalent to AD

de lujo – deluxe; often used with some licence

delegación – a large urban governmental subdivision in Mexico City comprising numerous colonias; equivalent to a *municipio*

descompuesto – broken, out of order

DF – Distrito Federal (Federal District); where Mexico City is located

ejido – communal landholding

embarcadero – jetty, quay

encomienda – a grant made to a *conquistador* of labour by or tribute from a group of Indians; the conquistador was supposed to protect and convert the Indians, but usually treated them as little more than slaves

enramada – thatch-covered, open-air restaurant

enredo – wrap-around skirt

entremeses – theatrical sketches; performed during the Cervantino festival in Guanajuato

escuela – school

esq – abbreviation of *esquina* (corner) in addresses

estación ferrocarril – train station

estípite – long, narrow, pyramid-shaped, upside-down pilaster; the hallmark of Churrigueresque architecture

ex-convento – former convent or monastery

excusado – toilet

faja – waist sash used in traditional Indian costume

feria – fair

ferrocarril – railway

ficha – locker token available at bus terminals

fonda – eating stall in market; small restaurant

fraccionamiento – subdivision, housing development; similar to a *colonia*, often modern

frontera – border between political entities

gachupines – derogatory term for the colonial *peninsulares*

gringo, -a – North American (and sometimes European, Australasian etc) visitor to Latin America; not a very respectful term

Grito – literally 'shout'; the 'cry' for independence by parish priest Miguel Hidalgo y Costilla in 1810 which sparked the struggle for independence from Spain

gruta – cave, grotto

guarache – also *huarache*, woven leather sandal, often with car-tyre tread as the sole

guardería de (or **guarda**) **equipaje** – room for storing luggage, eg in a bus station

guayabera or **guayabarra** – man's shirt with pockets and appliquéd designs up the front, over the shoulders and down the back; worn in place of a jacket and tie in hot regions

güero, -a – fair-haired, fair-complexioned person; a more polite alternative to *gringo*

hacha – flat carved-stone object from the Classic Veracruz civilisation; connected with the ritual ball game

hacienda – estate; Hacienda (capitalised) is the Treasury Department

hay – there is, there are; you're equally likely to hear *no hay* (there isn't, there aren't)

henequén – agave fibre used to make sisal rope; grown particularly around Mérida in Yucatán

hombres – men; sign on toilet doors

huarache – see *guarache*

huevos – eggs; also slang for testicles

huipil, -es – Indian woman's sleeveless tunic(s), usually highly decorated; can be thigh-length or reach the ankles

iglesia – church

INAH – Instituto Nacional de Antropología e Historia; the body in charge of most ancient sites and some museums

indígena – indigenous, pertaining to the original inhabitants of Latin America; can also refer to the people themselves

INI – Instituto Nacional Indigenista; set up in 1948 to improve the lot of Indians and to integrate them into society; sometimes

accused of paternalism and trying to stifle protest

isla – island

IVA – *impuesto al valor agregado*, or 'eebah'; a 10% sales tax added to the price of many items

ixtle – maguey fibre

jaguar – panther native to Central America; principal symbol of the Olmec civilisation

jai alai – the Basque game *pelota*, brought to Mexico by the Spanish; a bit like squash, played on a long court with curved baskets attached to the arm

Jarocho, -a – citizen of Veracruz

jefe – boss or leader, especially a political one

jorongo – small poncho worn by men

Kukulcán – Mayan name for the plumed serpent god Quetzalcóatl

Lada – short for *larga distancia*

Ladatel – automatic coin or card-operated long-distance telephone

ladino – more or less the same as *mestizo*

lancha – fast, open, outboard boat

larga distancia – long-distance; usually refers to telephones

latifundio – large landholding; these sprang up after Mexico's independence from Spain

latifundista – powerful landowner who usurped communally owned land to form a *latifundio*

libramiento – a free road running parallel to a toll highway

licenciado – university graduate, abbreviated as Lic and used as an honorific before a person's name; a status claimed by many who don't actually possess a degree

licuado – drink made from fruit juice, water or milk, and sugar

lista de correos – literally 'mail list', a list displayed at a post office of people for whom letters are waiting; similar to General Delivery or Poste Restante

lleno – full, as with a car's fuel tank

machismo – Mexican masculine bravura

madre – literally 'mother', but the term can

be used colloquially with an astonishing array of meanings

maguey – a type of agave, with thick pointed leaves growing straight out of the ground; *tequila* and *mezcal* are made from its sap

malecón – waterfront street, boulevard or promenade

mañana – literally 'tomorrow' or 'morning'; in some contexts it may mean 'sometime in the future'

maquiladora – assembly-plant operation in a Mexican border town or city; usually owned, at least in part, by foreigners and allowed to import raw materials duty-free on the condition that the products are exported

mariachi – small ensemble of street musicians playing guitars and trumpets; from the French *mariage* (wedding), at which such groups played during the French intervention in Mexico (1864-67)

marimba – wooden xylophone-type instrument, popular in Veracruz

mercado – market; often a building near the centre of a town, with shops and open-air stalls in the surrounding streets

Mesoamerica – the ancient Mexican and Mayan cultures

mestizaje – 'mixedness', Mexico's mixed-blood heritage; officially an object of pride

mestizo – person of mixed (usually Indian and Spanish) ancestry, ie most Mexicans

metate – shallow stone bowl with legs, for grinding maize and other foods

mezcal – strong alcoholic drink produced from maguey cactus

milpa – peasant's small cornfield, often cultivated by the slash-and-burn method

mirador, -es – lookout point(s)

Moctezuma's revenge – Mexican version of Delhi-belly or travellers' diarrhoea

mordida – literally 'little bite', a small bribe to keep the wheels of bureaucracy turning; giving a mordida to a traffic policeman may ensure that you won't have to pay a bigger fine later

mota – marijuana

Mudéjar – Moorish architectural style, imported to Mexico by the Spanish

mujeres – women; seen on toilet doors

municipio – small local-government area; Mexico is divided into 2394 of them

na – Mayan thatched hut

NAFTA – North American Free Trade Agreement (see *TLC*)

Nahuatl – language of the Nahua people, ancestors of the Aztecs

naos – Spanish trading galleons

Noche Triste – the 'Sad Night', when the Spanish conquistadors suffered big losses retreating from Tenochtitlán

norteamericanos – North Americans, people from north of the US-Mexican border

Nte – abbreviation for *norte* (north), used in street names

Ote – abbreviation for *oriente* (east), used in street names

palacio de gobierno – state capitol, state government headquarters

palacio municipal – town or city hall, headquarters of the municipal corporation

palapa – thatched-roof shelter, usually on a beach

palma – long, paddle-like, carved-stone object from the Classic Veracruz civilisation; connected with the ritual ball game

pan integral – wholegrain bread

panadería – bakery, pastry shop

parada – bus stop, usually for city buses

parado – standing up, as you often are on 2nd-class buses

parroquia – parish church

paseo – boulevard, walkway or pedestrian street; also the tradition of strolling in a circle around the plaza in the evening, men and women moving in opposite directions

Pemex – government-owned petroleum mining, refining and retailing monopoly

peña – evening of Latin-American folk songs, often with a political protest theme

peninsulares – those born in Spain and sent by the Spanish government to rule the colony in Mexico (see *criollo, gachupines*)

periférico – ring road

pesero – Mexico City's word for *colectivo*

petate – mat, usually made of palm or reed

peyote – hallucinogenic cactus

pinacoteca – art gallery

piñata – clay pot or papier-mâché mould decorated to resemble an animal, pineapple, star etc; filled with sweets and gifts and smashed open at festivals, particularly children's birthdays and Christmas

playa – beach

plaza de toros – bullring

plazuela – small plaza

Poblano, -a – person from Puebla, or something in the style of Puebla

pollero – same as a *coyote*

Porfiriato – Porfirio Díaz's reign as president-dictator of Mexico for 30 years until the 1910 revolution

portales – arcades

presidio – fort or fort's garrison

PRI – Partido Revolucionario Institucional (Institutional Revolutionary Party); the political party which has ruled Mexico since the 1930s

propina – tip; different from a *mordida*, which is closer to a bribe

Pte – abbreviation for *poniente* (west), used in street names

puerto – port

pulque – thick, milky drink of fermented maguey cactus juice; a traditional intoxicating drink which is also nutritious

quechquémitl – Indian woman's shoulder cape with an opening for the head; usually colourfully embroidered, often diamond-shaped

quetzal – crested bird with brilliant green, red and white plumage, native to Central and northern South America; quetzal feathers were highly prized in pre-Hispanic Mexico

Quetzalcóatl – plumed serpent god of pre-Hispanic Mexico

rebozo – long woollen or linen shawl covering the head or shoulders

Regiomontano, -a – person from Monterrey

rejas – wrought-iron window guards

reserva biósfera – biosphere reserve; area dedicated to conservation and research, with visits usually allowed only by permit

retablo – altarpiece; or small painting on wood, tin, cardboard, glass etc, placed in a church to give thanks for miracles, answered prayers etc

río – river

s/n – *sin número* (without number); used in street addresses

sacbe (s), **sacbeob** (pl) – ceremonial avenue(s) between great Mayan cities

sanatorio – hospital, particularly a small private one

sanitario(s) – toilet(s), literally 'sanitary place'

sarape – blanket with opening for the head, worn as a cloak

Semana Santa – holy week, the week before Easter; Mexico's major holiday period, when accommodation and transport get very busy

sierra – mountain range

sitio – taxi stand

stele, -ae – standing stone monument(s), usually carved

supermercado – supermarket; anything from a small corner store to a large, North American-style supermarket

Sur – south; often seen in street names

taller – shop or workshop; a *taller mecánico* is a mechanic's shop, usually for cars; a *taller de llantas* is a tyre-repair shop

talud-tablero – stepped building style typical of Teotihuacán, with alternating vertical *(tablero)* and sloping *(talud)* sections

Tapatío, -a – citizen of Guadalajara

taquería – place where you buy tacos

taquilla – ticket window

telamon – statue of a male figure, used instead of a pillar to hold up the roof of a temple; see also *atlas*

telar de cintura – backstrap loom; the warp threads are stretched between two horizontal bars, one of which is attached to a post or tree and the other to a strap around the weaver's lower back, and the weft threads are then woven in

teleférico – cable car

templo – church; anything from a wayside chapel to a cathedral

teocalli – Aztec sacred precinct

tequila – vodka-like liquor; like *pulque* and *mezcal*, it is produced from maguey cactus

Tex-Mex – Americanised version of Mexican food

Tezcatlipoca – Aztec god; as a smoking

mirror he could see into hearts, as the sun god he needed the blood of sacrificed warriors to ensure he would rise again, and as Quetzal-cóatl he was the lord of life and enemy of death

tezontle – light-red, porous volcanic rock used for buildings by the Aztecs and conquistadors

tianguis – Indian market

típico, -a – typical or characteristic of a region; particularly used to describe food

TLC – Tratado de Libre Comercio, the North American Free Trade Agreement (NAFTA)

topes – anti-speed bumps; found on the outskirts of many towns and villages, they are sometimes marked by signs

tzompantli – rack for the skulls of Aztec sacrificial victims

UNAM – Universidad Nacional Autónoma de México (National Autonomous University of Mexico)

universidad – university

viajero, -a – traveller

villa juvenil – youth sports centre, often the location of an *albergue de juventud*

voladores – literally 'flyers', the Totonac Indian ritual in which men, suspended by their ankles, whirl around a tall pole

War of the Castes – bloody Mayan uprising in the Yucatán peninsula (1847-66)

were-jaguar – half-human, half-jaguar being, portrayed in Olmec art

yácata – ceremonial stone structure of the Tarascan civilisation

yugo – U-shaped carved-stone object from the Classic Veracruz civilisation; connected with the ritual ball game

zaguán – vestibule or foyer, sometimes a porch

zócalo – main plaza or square; a term used in some (but by no means all) Mexican towns

Zona Rosa – literally 'Pink Zone'; an area of expensive shops, hotels and restaurants in Mexico City frequented by the wealthy and tourists; by extension, a similar area in another city

Index

ABBREVIATIONS

Agu	Aguascalientes	Gua	Guanajuato	Que	Querétaro
BCN	Baja California (Norte)	Gue	Guerrero	QR	Quintana Roo
BCS	Baja California Sur	Hid	Hidalgo	Sin	Sinaloa
Cam	Campeche	Jal	Jalisco	SLP	San Luis Potosí
Chi	Chiapas	Méx	México	Son	Sonora
Chih	Chihuahua	Mic	Michoacán	Tab	Tabasco
Coa	Coahuila	Mor	Morelos	Tam	Tamaulipas
Col	Colima	Nay	Nayarit	Tla	Tlaxcala
DF	Distrito Federal	NL	Nuevo León	Ver	Veracruz
	(Mexico City)	Oax	Oaxaca	Yuc	Yucatán
Dur	Durango	Pue	Puebla	Zac	Zacatecas

MAPS

Acapulco 510
  Old Acapulco 515
Aguascalientes 605
Alamos 365

Bahías de Huatulco 767
Baja California 301
Barra de Navidad 485
Barranca del Cobre 374
Bonampak Ruins 833

Cabo San Lucas 344-5
Campeche 855
Cancún 907
  Ciudad Cancún 905
Cañón del Sumidero 800
Catemaco 710
Central Gulf Coast 662
Central North Mexico 382
Central Pacific Coast 444
Chetumal 947
Chiapas 776
  Chiapas Highlands 790
Chichén Itzá 891
Chihuahua, Central 392
Cholula 261
Ciudad Juárez, Central 385
  East Ciudad Juárez 386
Ciudad Victoria 419
Cobá Ruins 941
Colima 583
  Around Colima 587
Comitán 837
Copper Canyon, see Barranca
  del Cobre
Copper Canyon Railway 372

Córdoba 700
Cozumel 926
  San Miguel de Cozumel 929
Cuautla 270
Cuernavaca 276

Dolores Hidalgo 636
Durango 400

El Tajín 678
Ensenada 310-11

Guadalajara 529
  Around Guadalajara 546
  Guadalajara City Centre 532
Guanajuato 625
Guaymas 359

Hermosillo 354

Isla Mujeres 915
  Isla Mujeres Town 917
Ixtapa, Around 498
Iztaccíhuatl 241

Jalapa, see Xalapa

Kabah 884
Kohunlich 949

La Crucecita 768
La Paz 332-3
Labná 885
Lago Pátzcuaro 569
Lagos de Montebello 839
Loreto 327
Los Mochis 369

Los Tuxtlas 705

Manzanillo 487
  Around Manzanillo 489
Matamoros 415
Matehuala 619
Mazatlán 446
  Old Mazatlán 451
Mérida 864-5
Mexicali 316-17
  Central Mexicali 318
Mexico
  colour map, between 16 & 17
  Mexican States 42
Mexico City 152-3
  Around Mexico City 226-7
  Central Mexico City 158-9
  Chapultepec & Polanco 176
  Coyoacán 187
  Mexico City Metro 222
  San Ángel 183
  Zona Rosa 172
Mitla 745
Mixteca 748
Monte Albán 739
Monterrey 423
  Central Monterrey 425
  Monterrey Bus Station
    Area 431
Morelia 551

Navojoa Bus Stations 361
Nogales Border Area 350
North-East Mexico 404
North-West Mexico 348
Northern Central Highlands 590
Nuevo Laredo 407

957

Oaxaca (city) 720
   Central Oaxaca 726
Oaxaca Central Valleys 737
Oaxaca State 716
Orizaba 703

Palenque (town) 830-1
Palenque Ruins 824
Pátzcuaro 564
Pie de la Cuesta 520
Playa del Carmen 923
Popocatépetl & Iztaccíhuatl 241
Progreso 876
Puebla & Cholula 259
   Central Puebla 251
Puerto Ángel 761
Puerto Escondido 753
Puerto Vallarta 468
   Around Puerto Vallarta 471
Puuc Route 882

Querétaro 654

Reynosa 411

Saltillo 439
San Blas 459
San Cristóbal de Las Casas 804
San José del Cabo 339
San Luis Potosí 611
San Miguel de Allende 641
San Miguel de Cozumel 929
San Patricio-Melaque 482
Sayil 884

Tabasco & Chiapas 776
Tampico 665
Tapachula 845
Taxco 285
Teotihuacán 233
Tepic 462
Tepoztlán 267
Ticul 887
Tijuana, Central 304-5
Tlaxcala 245
Toluca 295
Tula Zona Arqueológica 229
Tulum Ruinas 936
Tuxpan 672
Tuxtla Gutiérrez 793

Uruapan 574
Uxmal 880
Uxmal & the Puuc Route 882

Valladolid 899
Veracruz 692
   Central Veracruz 695
Villahermosa 778
   Central Villahermosa 782
   Parque-Museo La Venta 779

Western Central Highlands 524

Xalapa 684
   Central Xalapa 686

Yagul 743
Yaxchilán Ruins 835
Yucatán Peninsula 851

Zacatecas 594
Zempoala 681
Zihuatanejo 503
   Around Zihuatanejo & Ixtapa
   498

TEXT

Maps are in **bold** type

Acanceh (Yuc) 889
Acapulco (Gue) 508-20, **510**
   Old Acapulco **515**
Acatepec (Pue) 263
Acatlán de Osorio (Pue) 265
Acaxochitlán (Hid) 674
Acayucan (Ver) 712
accommodation 88-9
Acolman (Méx) 231
Actopan (Hid) 238
Agua Azul (Chi) 820-1
Agua Prieta (Son) 351
Aguascalientes (city) 602-8, **605**
Aguascalientes (state) 602
air travel 129-33
   to/from Australasia 132
   to/from Europe 130-2
   to/from Guatemala
      & Belize 132
   to/from Latin America &
      the Caribbean 133
   to/from the USA &
      Canada 129
   within Mexico 139
Ajijic (Jal) 547-8
Akumal (QR) 934
Alamos (Son) 361, 366-7, **365**

Aldama (Tam) 417
Allende (NL) 435
Alvarado (Ver) 704
Amatenango del Valle (Chi) 817
Amecameca (Méx) 242, 243
Amozoc (Pue) 264
Angahuan (Mic) 578
Angangueo (Mic) 559-60
Aquismón (Ver) 669
archaeological sites
   around Madera 390
   around Nuevo Casas
      Grandes 390
   Balcón de Montezuma 420
   Becan 853
   Bonampak 833-6
   Cacaxtla 247
   Calixtlahuaca 297
   Chicanna 853
   Chichén Itzá 890-5
   Cholula 260-3
   Cobá 940-3
   Comalcalco 786-7
   Copilco 183
   Cuernavaca 275
   Cuicuilco 185
   Dainzú 741
   Dzibilchaltún 875
   Edzná 858, 860-1

El Castillo Real 933
El Cedral 932
El Rey 904
El Tajín 676-80
Grutas de Loltún 885-6
Ihuatzio 568
Isla Mujeres 916
Izamal 889-90
Izapa 847-8
Kabah 883-4
Kohunlich 949-50
La Quemada 601-2
Labná 885
Lambityeco 742
Loltún 885
Malinalco 298
Mitla 744-5
Monte Albán 737-41
Palenque 821-7, 833
Paquimé ruins 389
Puuc Hills 883
Pyramid of Tepozteco 266
Río Bec 853
Ruinas de Mayapán 888-9
San Gervasio 933
Sayil 884
Tamuín 669
Templo Mayor 164-5
Tenayuca 180

Teotenango 298
Teotihuacán 232-6
Tingambato 571
Tizatlán 246
Tlatelolco 178
Toniná 819
Tres Zapotes 706-7
Tula 228-31
Tulum 937-9
Tzintzuntzan 568
Uxmal 878-83
Xel-ha Lagoon 935
Xlapak 885
Xochicalco 282-3
Xpujil 853
Yagul 742
Yaxchilán 833-6
Yohualichán 264
Zempoala 681-2
architecture 49-51
    baroque 50
    Churrigueresque 50
    Mayan 15
    plateresque 49
    pre-Hispanic 49
Arriaga (Chi) 842
Arroyo de Cuchujaqui (Son) 367
Arroyo los Monos (Chih) 390
art 46-9
    Mayan 15
artesanías 97-128
    books on Mexican
        handicrafts 128
    buying handicrafts 100-1
    festival crafts 127-8
    see also under individual crafts
Atl, Dr 48, 167, 174
Atlixco (Pue) 265
Atotonilco (Gua) 650
Atotonilco El Grande (Hid) 239
Ayutla (Oax) 745
Aztecs 18-19, 47, 147, 164, 298,
    523, 560, 568, 651, 663, 715,
    770
    religion 18
azulejo tiles 50, 249

Bacalar (QR) 944
Bahía Cacaluta (Oax) 767
Bahía Chahué (Oax) 767
Bahía de Matanchén (Nay) 458
Bahía de Santa Cruz (Oax) 766
Bahía Kino (Son) 356-7
Bahía Maguey y Organo (Oax)
    767
Bahía San Agustín (Oax) 767
Bahía Tangolunda (Oax) 767

Bahías de Huatulco (Oax)
    765-70, 767
Baja California 300-46, 301
Bajío 589
Balcón de Montezuma (Tam)
    420
ball courts
    Chichén Itza 893
    Dainzú 741
    El Tajín 679, 680
    Guiengola 771
    Monte Albán 738
    Tenango del Valle 298
    Tingambato 571
    Tula 229, 230
    Uxmal 879
    Yagul 743
ball game 17, 662, 676, 679,
    741, 893
bark paintings 121
Barra de Navidad (Jal) 483-6,
    485
Barra El Tordo (Tam) 418
Barranca del Cobre 371, 374
    see also Copper Canyon
        Railway
baseball 53
baskets 125
Batopilas (Chih) 378, 380
beaches 751
    Akumal 934
    Bacocho 752
    Bahía Cacaluta 767
    Bahía Principal 751
    Bahía San Agustín 767
    Bahías de Huatulco 766
    Boca del Río 691
    Calderitas 949
    Campeche 858
    Cancún 906
    Carrizalillo 752
    Chachalacas 682
    Chemuyil 934
    Ciudad Madero 664
    Costa de Oro 691
    Estacahuite 761
    Isla Mujeres 914
    Jicacal 711
    Mandinga 691
    Mazunte 765
    Mocambo 691
    Pamul 933
    Payucan 858
    Península Pichilingue 336
    Playa Bonita 858
    Playa Cocoteros 915
    Playa Conejos 767
    Playa del Carmen 922
    Playa del Panteón 761

Playa La Entrega 766
Playa La India 767
Playa Lancheros 915
Playa Maguey 767
Playa Miramar 666
Playa Norte 671
Playa Organo 767
Playa Palancar 932
Playa Punta Arena 767
Playa San Francisco 932
Playa Santa Cruz 766
Puerto Ángel 761
Puerto Angelito 752
Puerto Arista 843
Puerto Escondido 751
Revolcadero 522
San Agustinillo 764
San Felipe 902
Seybaplaya 858
Tecolutla 680
Tulum 935
Zicatela 751
Zipolite 763, 764
Becal (Cam) 860
bird-watching 40, 877
    Cañon del Sumidero 800
    Isla Contoy 920
    Laguna de Tamiahua 670
    Laguna San Ignacio 324
    Manialtepec 758
    Río Lagartos 901
    San Felipe 902
    Xcacel 935
blankets 107
    Oaxaca city 733
boat travel
    Boca del Cielo 844
    Bonampak 834
    Cabo San Lucas 342
    Cancún 919
    Canón del Sumidero 800
    Chiquilá 921
    Cozumel 925, 928
    Guaymas to Santa Rosalía 360
    Isla Cancún 920
    Isla Contoy 920
    Isla Holbox 921
    Isla Mujeres 914, 919
    La Paz to/from Mazatlán &
        Topolobampo 335
    Lago Pátzcuaro 568
    Manialtepec 758
    Mazunte 765
    Palenque to/from Flores
        (Guatemala) 137
    Playa del Carmen 925
    Puerto Juárez (QR) 919
    Punta Sam (QR) 920
    Río Lagartos 902

boat travel *cont*
Santa Rosalía to/from
Guaymas 325
Topolobampo to La Paz 370
Yaxchilán 834
Boca del Cielo (Chi) 844
Boca Paila (QR) 940
Bochil (Chi) 798
Bolonchén de Rejón (Cam) 861
Bolsón de Mapimí 398
Bonampak (Chi) 833-4, **833**
books 74-77
culture, art & architecture 75
fiction 76-77
history & society 74-75
travel & description 76
travel guides 75
border crossings
to/from Belize 836, 950
to/from Guatemala
136, 833, 836, 842, 848
to/from the USA 133, 308, 320,
350, 351, 381, 388, 409, 412,
416, 436
Brownsville (USA) 416
bullfights 52
Aguascalientes 604
Cancún 912
Chihuahua 395
Guadalajara 542
Mexico City 209
Tijuana 306
Zacatecas 596
bus travel
classes 140
terminals & schedules 140
to/from Guatemala &
Belize 137, 950
to/from Mexico City 214-6
to/from the USA 133
within Mexico 139, 140-1, 145
business hours 69

Cabo San Lucas (BCS) 341-6,
344-5
Cacaxtla (Tla) 247
Calderitas (QR) 949
Calderitas Bay (QR) 949
Calixtlahuaca (Méx) 297
Calkiní (Cam) 860
Campeche (city) 854-9, **855**
Campeche (state) 852-61
Cananea (Son) 351
Cancún (QR) 903-14, **905, 907**
beaches 906
getting around 913-4
getting there & away 912-3
places to eat 910-2

places to stay 906-10
things to see 904-6
Cañón de la Huasteca (NL)
434-5
Cañón del Sumidero (Chi) 800,
800
Cañón San Bernardo (BCS) 336
Cañón San Dionisio (BCS) 336
Cañón San Pablo (BCS) 324
Cañón San Pedro (BCS) 336
car & motorbike travel 134-6
accidents 144
breakdown assistance 143
buying a car in the USA 134
driver's licence 135
in Mexico City 218
fuel 142
insurance 135
parking 143
rental 144
road conditions 143
service 142
to/from the USA 134-7
vehicle permits 135-6, 406
within Mexico 142-4
Cardel (Ver) 682
Cárdenas, Lázaro 494-5, 525
Carlota, Empress 26, 174, 273
Carnaval 70, 692, 867
Casas Grandes (Chih) 389-90
Cascada Cusárare (Chih) 378
Cascada de Basaseachi (Chih)
378, 396
Cascada de Tamul (Ver) 669
Cascada de Tzaráracua (Mic)
576
Cascadas Cola de Caballo (NL)
435
Castillo de Teayo (Ver) 673
Catemaco (Ver) 709-11, **710**
caves
Cueva del Ratón 324
Cueva Grande 390
Grutas de Bustamente 435
Grutas de García 434
Las Grutas de Cacahuamilpa
292
Ceballos (Dur) 398
Celestún (Yuc) 877-8
Cempoala, *see* Zempoala
Cenote Azul (QR) 944-5
ceramics, *see* pottery
Cerocahui (Chih) 372
Cerro de Cubilete (Gua) 632
Cerro Potosí (NL) 435
Chacahua (Oax) 758
Chachalacas (Ver) 682
Chalma (Méx) 299
Chamela (Jal) 480

Chankanab Bay (QR) 932
Chapala (Jal) 546-7
charreadas (rodeos) 53
Chihuahua 395
Guadalajara 542
Zacatecas 596
Chemuyil (QR) 934-5
Chetumal (QR) 945-9, **947**
Chiapa de Corzo (Chi) 798-800
Chiapas (state) 34, 775, **776**,
787-91, **790**
Chichén Itzá (Yuc) 17, 890-7,
891
Chichimec people 560, 589,
591, 603, 638
Chihuahua (city) 391-6, **392**
Chihuahua al Pacífico Railway,
see Copper Canyon Railway
children, travel with 63
Chilpancingo (Gue) 522
Chinkultic (Chi) 840
Chipinque (NL) 426-8
Chiquilá (QR) 921
Chol people 791
Cholula (Pue) **259**, 260-3, **261**
Chupaderos (Dur) 402
Ciudad Acuña (Coa) 436
Ciudad Constitución (BCS) 329
Ciudad Cuauhtémoc (Chi) 841-2
Ciudad Hidalgo (Chi) 848
Ciudad Jiménez (Chih) 397
Ciudad Juárez (Chih) 381-8,
385, 386
Ciudad Lerdo (Dur) 397-8
Ciudad Madero (Tam) 664-8
Ciudad Mante (Tam) 420
Ciudad Obregón (Son) 361
Ciudad Valles (SLP) 668-9
Ciudad Victoria (Tam) 418-9,
419
Classic Veracruz civilisation
17, 662
climate 36
Coahuila (state) 436
Coatepec (Ver) 688
Coatzacoalcos (Ver) 713
Cobá (QR) 940-3, **941**
Cofre de Perote (Ver) 688
Coixtlahuaca (Oax) 748
colectivos 145
Colima (city) 580-6, **583, 587**
Colima (state) 579
Colonia del Valle (NL) 426-8
Colonia Juárez (Chih) 390
Columbus (New Mexico) 388
Comala (Col) 586
Comalcalco ruins (Tab) 786-7
Comitán (Chi) 836-9, **837**
Complejo Anasazi (Chih) 390

Complejo Ecoturístico Arareko (Chih) 377
Copper Canyon, *see* Barranca del Cobre
Copper Canyon Railway 347, 367, 371-80, **372**, 391, 395-6
copper crafts
Santa Clara del Cobre 570
Cordillera Neovolcánica 548
Córdoba (Ver) 699-701, **700**
Corozal (Belize) 950
Cortés, Hernán 20-22, 240, 260, 272, 273, 663, 688, 776, 925
Costa Esmeralda (Ver) 680
Costera Bacalar (QR) 9445
costs, *see* money
Cozumel (QR) 925-33, **926**
San Miguel de Cozumel 927-32, **929**
crafts, *see* artesanías
Creel (Chih) 376-80
Cristero rebellion 522
Cuauhtémoc (Chih) 396
Cuauhtémoc, Emperor 20, 293
Cuautla (Mor) 269-71, **270**
Cuernavaca (Mor) 271-82, **276**
courses 278
getting there & away 281-2
places to eat 280-1
places to stay 278-80
things to see 273-7
Cuetzalán (Pue) 263-4
Cueva Grande (Chih) 390
Cuilapan (Oax) 745
Culiacán (Sin) 371
Cusárare (Chih) 378
customs 64-65
Cuyutlán (Col) 492-4
cycling 87, 144, 808

Dainzú (Oax) 741
dance 51-52
Day of the Dead, *see* Día de los Muertos
Desemboque (Son) 356
deserts 39, 320, 398
Desierto Central (BCN) 320
Día de los Muertos (Day of the Dead) 70, 127
Díaz, Porfirio 27, 148, 546, 609, 663, 689, 691, 715
Dinamita (Dur) 398
Distrito Federal (state) 146
diving 87
Akumal 934
Cabo San Lucas 342
Cozumel 925
Isla Mujeres 916
La Paz 331

Laguna de Tamiahua 670
Mulegé 325
near Veracruz 692
Hidalgo del Palancar Reef 932
Playa del Carmen 922
Puerto Escondido 752
Puerto Morelos 921
Divisadero (Chih) 372, 373, 378
Dolores Hidalgo (Gua) 634-7, **636**
drinks 94-96
Durango (Dur) 399-402, **400**
Dzibilchaltún (Yuc) 875

economy 41-44
NAFTA 34, 43
Edzná (Cam) 860-1
ruins 858
Ejido de Alta Cumbre (Tam) 420
Ejutla (Oax) 747
El Carmen (Guatemala) 848
El Carrizal (Ver) 688
El Castillo Real (QR) 933
El Cedral (QR) 932
El Chalotón (Son) 367
El Cielo Reserva de la Biósfera (Tam) 420
El Espinazo del Diablo (Dur) 402
El Fuerte (Sin) 370-1
El Mezquital (Tam) 417
El Paso (Texas) 381-8
El Salto (Dur) 402
El Sásabe (Son) 351
El Tajín (Ver) 662, 676-80, **678**
El Tule (Oax) 741
electricity 74
embassies 61-63
Empalme (Son) 360
Ensenada (BCN) 308-13, **310-11**
Erongarícuaro (Mic) 570
Escárcega (Cam) 852

fauna 39-41
birds 40, 41, 438, 940
butterflies 558
crickets 602
dolphins 465, 765
elephant seals 323
flamingos 877, 901, 902
sea turtles 40, 322, 764, 933, 934
whales 40, 41, 465
fax services 73
Felipe Carrillo Puerto (QR) 943-4
ferry travel, *see* boat travel
festivals 54, 69-71
Aguascalientes 606
Carnaval 70, 692, 867

Colima 582
Día de los Muertos (Day of the Dead) 70
Dolores Hidalgo 636
El Día del Jumil (Taxco) 287
Feria Nacional (Durango) 399
Festival Internacional Cervantino (Guanajuato) 629
Festival of San Francisco (Real de Catorce) 620
Fiesta de Enero (Chiapa de Corzo) 799
Fiestas de Octubre (Guadalajara) 536
Guadalajara 536
Guelaguetza (Oaxaca City) 723-4
Mexico City 191-2
Morelia 554
Pátzcuaro 563
San Miguel de Allende 644
Semana Santa 70, 808
Uruapan 572
Veracruz 692
fiestas, *see* festivals
fishing 87
Boca Paila 940
Cabo San Lucas 342
Corozal 950
La Paz 331
La Pesca 417
Laguna de Tamiahua 670
near Madera 390
permits 64
Presa El Mocuzari 367
Presa Vicente Guerrero 418
Punta Allen 940
San José del Cabo 338
Tuxpan 671
Xcacel 935
flora 39
food 89-94
Oaxaqueña cooking 729
Yucatecan cuisine 870
football (soccer) 52-53, 209, 542
Fortín de las Flores (Ver) 701-2
Francisco Villa (QR) 950
Fresnillo (Zac) 600-1

Galeana (NL) 435
gay travellers
Acapulco 517-18
Mexico City 208
Puerto Vallarta 474, 477
gems 123
around Torreón 398
San Juan del Río 658
geography 35
Gogorrón (SLP) 617-8

Gomez Farías (Chih) 390
Gómez Farias (Tam) 420
Gómez Palacio (Dur) 397-8
Sandoval, Gonzalo de 579
government 41
Grutas de Balankanché (Yuc) 895
Grutas de Bustamente (NL) 435
Grutas de Cacahuamilpa (Gue) 292-3
Grutas de García (NL) 434
Grutas de Loltún (Yuc) 885-6
Grutas de Xtacumbilxunaan (Cam) 861
Guadalajara (Jal) 525-45, **529, 532**
  festivals 536
  getting around 545
  getting there & away 543-5
  places to eat 538-40
  places to stay 536-8
  things to see 528-36
Guadalupe (BCN) 313
Guadalupe (Zac) 599-600
Guanajuato (city) 622-32, **625**
  getting around 632
  getting there & away 632
  places to eat 630-1
  places to stay 629-30
  things to see 624-8
Guanajuato (state) 622-50
Guaymas (Son) 357-60, **359**
Guelatao (Oax) 749
Guerrero (state) 265, 522
Guerrero Negro (BCS) 320-1
Guerrero, Vicente 25, 293, 746, 766
guitars 120
  Paracho 577
Guzmán, Nuño de 524, 526, 560, 569

Hacienda de San Diego (Chih) 390
hammocks 126, 872
handicrafts, see artesanías
hats 126
  panama hats 860, 872
headdresses 117
health 78-84
  altitude sickness 82, 241
  hospitals & clinics 84
  medical problems & treatment 80-4
  predeparture preparations 78
  protection against mosquitoes 79
  women's health 84
Hecelchakan (Cam) 860

Hermosillo (Son) 351, 356, **354**
Hidalgo (state) 237, 238
Hidalgo del Parral (Chih) 396-7
Hidalgo y Costilla, Miguel 25, 148, 391, 394, 526, 622, 623, 626, 634, 635, 636, 638
history 12-35
  Aztecs 18-22
  Classic Veracruz civilisation 17
  colonial era 22
  Maya 13, 14, 17, 19
  Mexican Revolution 27-28
  Mexican-American War 26, 405, 437
  Olmecs 12-13
  Spanish conquest 20
  Teotihuacán 14
  Toltecs 17
  War of Independence 25, 391
hitchhiking 145
horse racing 53, 759
horse riding
  Alamos 362
  Parque Nacional Sierra San Pedro Mártir 314
  Pie de la Cuesta 521
  Playa Troncones 507
  Puerto Vallarta 471
  Revolcadero 522
  San Cristóbal de Las Casas 807
  Valle de Bravo 297
hot springs
  Aguascalientes 602, 604
  Atlixco 265
  Balneario de Gogorrón 617
  Cuautla 269, 270
  El Carrizal 688
  Escondido Place 650
  Ixtapan de la Sal 299
  near Madera 390
  near San Miguel 649-50
  Oaxtepec 269
  Ojo Caliente 604
  Parador del Cortijo 650
  Recohuata Hot Springs 378
  Santa Veronica 650
  Taboada 649
Huajuapan de León (Oax) 749
Hualahuises (NL) 435
Huamantla (Tla) 248
Huapalcalco (Hid) 239
Huasca (Hid) 239
Huastec people 20, 45, 662, 664
Huauchinango (Pue) 674
Huautla de Jiménez (Oax) 749
Huehuetla (Hid) 239
Huehuetzingo (Pue) 263

Huejutla (Hid) 670
Huichol people 45, 54, 620
Huixtán (Chi) 817
hunting 64, 417, 418

Iguala (Gue) 293
Ihuatzio (Mic) 563, 568
independence movement 148, 634
Indian clothing 102-6
  Oaxaca city 733
Indians 23, 44-45, 46
  ceremonial brotherhoods 816
  languages 55
  religion 54
Isla Cedros (BCS) 321
Isla Contoy (QR) 920-1
Isla Cozumel, see Cozumel
Isla de los Monos (Ver) 709
Isla Holbox (QR) 921
Isla Janitzio (Mic) 563, 568
Isla Mujeres (QR) 914-20, **915, 917**
Isla Tiburón (Son) 356
Islas San Benito (BCS) 323
Isthmus of Tehuantepec 770
Iturbide (NL) 435
Iturbide, Agustín de 25, 168, 293, 699, 788
Ixcateopan (Gue) 293
Ixmiquilpan (Hid) 238
Ixtapa (Gue) 497-507, **498**
Ixtapan de la Sal (Méx) 299
Ixtlán (Oax) 749
Izamal (Yuc) 889-90
Izapa (Chi) 847-8
Iztaccíhuatl (Méx) 240-4, **241**
Izúcar de Matamoros (Pue) 265

jai alai 53, 209, 303
Jalapa, see Xalapa
Jalisco (state) 525
Jamiltepec (Oax) 759
Jarácuaro (Mic) 563
Jerez (Zac) 601
jewellery 122-3
  Oaxaca city 733
  San Juan del Río 658
Jicacal (Ver) 711
Jocotepec (Jal) 548
Juárez, Benito 26-27, 163, 391, 394, 398, 715, 722, 749
Juchitán (Oax) 773-4
jumping beans 366

Kabah (Yuc) 883-4, **884**
Kahlo, Frida 49, 174, 186, 188

Kino Nuevo (Son) 356-7
Kino Viejo (Son) 356-7
Kohunlich (QR) 949-50, **949**

La Aduana (Son) 367
La Antigua (Ver) 688
La Bocana (Oax) 767
La Bufa (Chih) 378
La Carbonera (Tam) 417
La Crucecita (Oax) 766, **768**
La Junta (Chih) 396
La Malinche (mountain) (Tla)
    248
La Malinche (woman) 20, 186
La María (Col) 586
La Mesilla (Guatemala) 842
La Paila (Coa) 442
La Paz (BCS) 330-6, **332-3**
La Pesca (Tam) 417
La Quemada (Zac) 601-2
Labná (Yuc) 885, **885**
Lacandón people 791
lacquerware 118
Lago Arareco (Chih) 378
Lago de Chapala (Jal) 546-8
Lago Pátzcuaro (Mic) 568, **569**
Lagos de Montebello (Chi)
    839-41, **839**
Laguna Bacalar (QR) 944-5
Laguna Catemaco (Ver) 709
Laguna de Montebello (Chi)
    840, **839**
Laguna de Sánchez (NL) 435
Laguna de Tamiahua (Ver) 670
Laguna de Tequisquitengo
    (Mor) 283
Laguna del Chairel (Ver) 664
Laguna La Canada (Chi) 840
Laguna La María (Col) 586
Laguna Madre (Tam) 417
Laguna Ojo de Liebre (BCS)
    320-1
Laguna San Ignacio (BCS) 324
Laguna Tziscao (Chi) 840
Laguna Verde (Ver) 680
Laguna Yal-Ku (QR) 934
Lagunas de Colores (Chi) 840
Lambityeco (Oax) 742
language 54-59
    Huastec 664
    Indian 55
    Mayan 791
    Mayance 664
    Nahua 249
    Spanish 54
language courses 88, 191, 278
    Ensenada 309
    Guadalajara 535
    Guanajuato 628

Morelia 553
Oaxaca city 723
San Cristóbal de Las
    Casas 808
San Miguel de Allende 643-4
Taxco 287
Laredo (Texas) 409
Las Aventuras (QR) 934
Las Casas, Bartolomé de 23, 788
Las Cruces (Mex) 243
Las Grutas de Cacahuamilpa
    (Gue) 292
leather 122
    Jerez 601
    León 633
    Quiroga 570
    San Miguel de Allende 648
    Zacatecas 598
León (Gua) 633-4
Linares (NL) 435
Loltún (Yuc) 885
Loreto (BCS) 326-8, **327**
Los Alamos (Dur) 402
Los Barriles (BCS) 336
Los Mochis (Sin) 367-70, **369**
Los Tuxtlas (Ver) 704, **705**
lucha libre (wrestling) 53

machismo 45
Madera (Chih) 390
Madero, Francisco 27
Malinalco (Méx) 298
Mama (Yuc) 888
Mame people 791
Manialtepec (Oax) 758
Manzanillo (Col) 486-92, **487**
Mapimí (Dur) 398
maps 77, 143
maquiladoras 383
Maracaibo Reef (QR) 927
mariachi bands 51
    Guadalajara 531
    Mexico City 207
masks 116
Mata Ortiz (Chih) 390
Matamoros (Tam) 412-7, **415**
Matehuala (SLP) 618-9, **619**
Maximilian of Hapsburg 26,
    174, 273, 275, 391, 651, 655,
    776
Maya people 13, 19, 45, 46
    civilisation 776, 787, 819, 833,
        840, 849-52, 925
    history 13-14
    language 791
    religion 16
    time 943
Mayapán (Yuc) 888-9
Mazahua people 45

Mazatec people 45, 717
Mazatlán (Sin) 443-54, **446, 451**
Mazunte (Oax) 765
McAllen (Texas) 412
media 77-78
Mennonites 378, 389, 391, 396
Mérida (Yuc) 861-75, **864-5**
    getting around 875
    getting there & away 872-4
    places to eat 869-71
    places to stay 867
    things to see 863-7
Mesoamerican civilisation 775
metalwork 122-4
Metepec (Méx) 297
Metztitlán (Hid) 670
Mexicali (BCN) 314-20, **316-17,
    318**
Mexican Revolution 27-28, 715
Mexico
    around Mexico City 224-99,
        226-7
    central Gulf coast 661-713,
        662
    central north Mexico 381-402,
        382
    central Pacific coast 443-522,
        444
    north-east Mexico 403-42, **404**
    north-west Mexico 347-80,
        348
    northern central highlands
        589-660, **590**
    western central highlands
        523-88, **524**
Mexico City 146-223, **152-3**
    airline offices 212-3
    Alameda 166-7
    Anahuacalli 189-90
    Basílica de Guadalupe 179-80
    Bazar Sábado 181
    bookshops 156
    Bosque de Chapultepec 172,
        175-7, **176**
    bus terminals 213-4
    Catedral Metropolitana 163
    central Mexico City **158-9**
    Copilco 183
    Coyoacán 186-90, **187**
    Cuicuilco 185
    embassies & consulates 155-6
    emergencies 157
    entertainment 206-9
    festivals 191-2
    getting around 219-23
    getting there & away 211-18
    Insurgentes Sur 180-1
    laundry 156
    Lomas de Chapultepec 178

Mexico City *cont*
　Lotería Nacional 170
　maps 157
　markets 210-1
　medical services 157
　Metro 221-3, **222**
　money 151-4
　Monumento a la Independencia
　　(El Ángel) 172
　murals 148, 165-6, 167, 169,
　　174, 180, 184
　Museo de Arte Carrillo
　　Gil 182
　Museo Nacional de
　　Antropología 174-5
　Museo Nacional de Arte 168
　Palacio de Bellas Artes 167-8
　Palacio Nacional 162-3
　Parque Nacional Desierto
　　de los Leones 191
　Paseo de la Reforma 171-2
　places to eat 198-206
　places to stay 192-8
　Plaza de la República 170-1
　Polanco **176**, 177-8
　pollution 161
　post 154
　safety 161
　San Ángel 181, **183**
　shopping 210-1
　telecommunications 154
　Templo Mayor 164-5
　Tenayuca 180
　Tlatelolco 178-9
　tourist offices 150-1
　Universidad Nacional
　　Autónoma de México
　　(UNAM) 184-5
　Xochimilco 190-1
　Zócalo 162
　Zona Rosa 172, **172**
Michoacán (city) 548-9
Michoacán (state) 525
Minas Nuevas (Son) 367
Minatitlán (Col) 588
Minatitlán (Ver) 713
Mineral del Chico (Hid) 239
Mineral del Monte (Hid) 239
mineral springs, *see* hot springs
Miramar (Son) 360
Misión San Francisco Javier
　(BCS) 328
Misol-Ha (Chi) 821
Mitla (Oax) 744-5, **745**
Mitontic (Chi) 817
Mixe people 717, 745
Mixtec people 20, 45, 47, 249,
　715, 717, 738, 745, 746, 747,
　759

Mixteca (Oax) 747, **748**
Moctezuma 18, 20, 272
Molango (Hid) 670
Monclova (Coa) 436
money 65-68
　bargaining 67
　consumer taxes 67
　costs 67
　credit cards 66
　tipping 67
Monte Albán (Oax) 13, 46,
　737-41, **739**
Montemorelos (NL) 435
Montepío (Ver) 711
Monterrey (NL) 420-34, **423, 425**
　bus station area **431**
　getting there & away 432-3
　places to eat 430
　places to stay 428-30
　things to see 422-8
Morelia (city) 549-58, **551**
　getting around 558
　getting there & away 557-8
　places to eat 556-7
　places to stay 554-6
　things to see 550-3
Morelos (state) 265
Morelos y Pavón, José María
　269, 550
motorbike travel, *see* car &
　motorbike travel
Motozintla (Chi) 841
mountain climbing 87
　Iztaccíhuatl 240-4
　Picacho del Diablo 313
　Pico de Orizaba 704
　Popocatépetl 240-4
　Volcán de Fuego
　　de Colima 587
　Volcán Nevado
　　de Colima 587
　Volcán Paricutín 577
movie locations 402
Mulegé (BCS) 325-6
murals 29, 46, 47
　Bonampak 834
　Cacaxtla 247
　Cuernavaca 273
　Mexico City 148, 165-6, 167,
　　169, 174, 180, 184, 194
　Oaxaca 719
　Tulum 937
　Zacatecas 592
Museo Amparo (Puebla) 250
Museo de Antropología (Xalapa)
　683
Museo Nacional de
　Antropología (Mexico City)
　47, 174-5

music 51
　folk 758
　guitars 120, 577
　mariachi bands 207, 531
　musical instruments 120

Nachi-Cocom (QR) 950
Naco (Son) 351
Nahua people 45, 249, 263, 391,
　670, 674
national parks & reserves 40-1
　El Cielo Reserva de
　　la Biósfera 420
　Grutas de Cacahuamilpa 292
　Parque Nacional Cofre
　　de Perote 688
　Parque Nacional Constitución
　　de 1857 313
　Parque Nacional
　　de Montebello 840
　Parque Nacional Desierto
　　de los Leones 191
　Parque Nacional Eduardo
　　Ruiz 572
　Parque Nacional El Chico 239
　Parque Nacional Garrafón
　　915-16
　Parque Nacional Lagunas
　　de Chacahua 758
　Parque Nacional Lagunas
　　de Zempoala 282
　Parque Nacional Sierra San
　　Pedro Mártir 313
　Parque Natural del Gran
　　Desierto del Pinacate 351
　Reserva Biósfera Bolsón de
　　Mapimí 398-9
　Reserva Biósfera El
　　Vizcaíno 321
　Reserva Biósfera Sian
　　Ka'an 939
　Santo Desierto del Carmen 298
　Santuario de Mariposas El
　　Rosario 558-60
　Xel-ha Lagoon 935
Nativitas (Tla) 247
Nautla (Ver) 680
Navojoa (Son) 361, **361**
Nayarit (state) 461
Nevado de Toluca (Méx) 297
Nochixtlán (Oax) 749
Nogales (Son) 347-50, **350**
Nopoló (BCS) 326
Nuevo Casas Grandes (Chih)
　389-90
Nuevo Laredo (Tam) 405-9,
　407
Nuevo León (state) 420

Oaxaca (city) 717-36, **720**, **726**
  festivals 723-4
  getting around 736
  getting there & away 734-5
  places to eat 729-32
  places to stay 724-9
  shopping 733-4
  things to see 719-23
Oaxaca (state) 714-17, **716**
  Central Valleys 736-7, **737**
Oaxaca Indian people 717
Oaxtepec (Mor) 268-9
Obregón, Alvaro 28-29, 182
Ocampo (Mic) 560
Ocampo, Melchor 552
Ocosingo (Chi) 818-9
Ocotlán (Oax) 747
Ocotlán (Tla) 244-5
Ojinaga (Chih) 388
Ojo de Talamantes (Chih) 397
Ojuela Mine (Dur) 398
Olmec people 12-13, 46, 775
  civilisation 787
  culture 661
  Olmec heads
    San Lorenzo 712
    Santiago Tuxtla 706
    Villahermosa 779, 780
    Xalapa 683
Olympic Games 30, 148, 178
Orizaba (Ver) 264, 702-4, **703**
Orozco, José Clemente 28, 48,
  165-6, 167, 174, 182
Otomí people 45, 238, 651
Oxchuc (Chi) 817

Pachuca (Hid) 236-8
Pahuatlán (Pue) 674
Palancar Reef (QR) 927
Palenque (town) (Chi) 827-33,
  830-1
Palenque ruins (Chi) 821-33,
  824
Palomas (Chih) 388
Pamul (QR) 933
Papantla (Ver) 674-6
Paquimé ruins (Chih) 389
Paracho (Mic) 577
Paraíso (Col) 492-4
Paraíso Reef (QR) 927
Parras (Coa) 442
Paso de Cortés (Méx) 242-4
Paso de Doña Juana (Ver) 682
Pátzcuaro (Mic) 560-8, **564**
peseros 145, 223
peyote 45, 54, 373
photography 78
Picacho del Diablo (BCN) 313
Pichilingue (BCS) 335

Pico de Orizaba 264, 704
Pie de la Cuesta (Gue) 520-2,
  520
Piedras Negras (Coa) 436
piñatas 71
Pinotepa de Don Luis (Oax)
  759
Pinotepa Nacional (Oax) 759
pirates 854
Piste (Yuc) 890
Plateros (Zac) 600
Playa Azul (Mic) 495-7
Playa Bagdad (Tam) 414
Playa Balandra (BCS) 336
Playa Caimancito (BCS) 336
Playa Conejos (Oax) 767
Playa Coromuel (BCS) 336
Playa Coyote (BCS) 336
Playa del Carmen (QR) 922-5,
  923
Playa Escondida (Ver) 711
Playa La India (Oax) 767
Playa Palancar (QR) 932
Playa Palmira (BCS) 336
Playa Pichilingue (BCS) 336
Playa Punta Arena (Oax) 767
Playa San Francisco (QR) 932
Playa Santiago (Col) 490
Playa Tecolote (BCS) 336
Playa Tesoro (BCS) 336
Pochutla (Oax) 759-60
Popocatépetl (Méx) 240-4, **241**
population 44-46
Posada Barrancas (Chih) 372,
  373
postal services 71-72
pottery 110-15
  Colima 579
  Dolores Hidalgo 637
  Mata Ortiz 390
  Metepec 297
  Oaxaca city 733
  Paquimé 389
  Pátzcuaro 567
  Puebla 249
  San Bartolo Coyotepec 746
Poza Rica (Ver) 673-4
Pozos (Gua) 650
Presa de la Amistad (Coa) 436
Presa El Mocuzari (Son) 367
Presa Falcón (Tam) 412
Presa Vicente Guerrero (Tam)
  418
Presidio (Texas) 388
Progreso (Yuc) 875-7, **876**
Promontorios (Son) 367
public holidays 69, 71
Puebla (Pue) 248-60, **251**, **259**
  getting there & away 257-8

Museo Amparo 250
  places to eat 255-7
  places to stay 254-5
  shopping 257
  things to see 250-4
Puebla (state) 239, 263
Pueblo La Playa (BCS) 338
Puente Cogante (Chih) 390
Puente de Dios (NL) 435
Puertecitos (BCN) 320
Puerto Ángel (Oax) 760-3, **761**
Puerto Arista (Chi) 843-4
Puerto Aventuras (QR) 934
Puerto Escondido (Oax) 750-8,
  753
Puerto López Mateos (BCS) 329
Puerto Marqués (Gue) 522
Puerto Morelos (QR) 921-2
Puerto Peñasco (Son) 351
Puerto San Carlos (BCS) 329
Puerto Vallarta (Jal) 465-79, **468**
  entertainment 476-8
  getting around 478-9
  getting there & away 478
  places to eat 474-6
  places to stay 472-4
  things to see & do 467-72
Punta Allen (QR) 940
Punta Celarain (QR) 932
Punta Holohit (Yuc) 902
Punta Mirador (BCS) 341
Punta Molas (QR) 933
Purépecha (Tarasco) people 523,
  548, 560
Putla (Oax) 748
Puuc Hills (Yuc) 852, 878-83
Puuc Route (Yuc) **882**, 883-6
Pyramid of Teopanzolco (Mor)
  275
pyramids
  Acanceh 889
  Castillo de Teayo 673
  Cerro del Gallo 708
  Chichén Itzá 892
  Cholula 260, 261
  Cobá 942
  Comalcalco 786
  Cuernavaca 275
  El Tajín 679
  Izamal 890
  Kabah 883
  Kohunlich 949
  Palenque 823
  Teotihuacán 234-5
  Tepoztlán 266
  Toniná 820
  Uxmal 879, 881
  Xochicalco 282
  Zempoala 682

Querétaro (city) 651-7, **654**
Querétaro (state) 651
Quetzalcóatl 14, 17, 18, 20, 162, 230, 664, 889
Quintana Roo (state) 903
Quiroga (Mic) 570
Quiroga, Vasco de 560, 569

Real de Catorce (SLP) 619-22
rebozos 103
  Santa María del Río 617
Recohuata hot springs (Chih) 378
Reform War 526
religion
  Christian 53-4
  Indian 373
  Jewish 54
  Mayan 16
retablos 125
Revolcadero (Gue) 522
Reynosa (Tam) 409-12, **411**
Río Balsas 525
Río Cupatitzio 576
Rio Grande 383, 403
Río Grijalva 777, 791, 800
Río Huápoca 390
Río Lagartos 90-2
Río Lerma 525
Río Oteros 378
Río Pánuco 664
Río Papaloapan 705
Río Urique 372, 378
Río Usumacinta 787
Rivera, Diego 28, 48, 162, 165-6, 167, 169, 174, 181, 182, 188, 189, 273, 625
rodeos, see charreadas
Rodrigo Gómez Dam (NL) 435
Rosarito (BCN) 308
rugs 107
  Oaxaca city 733
Ruinas de Mayapán (Yuc) 888-9
ruins, see archaeological sites & individual entries

Sabinas Hidalgo (NL) 435
safety 85-6, 265, 750, 751, 763, 815, 820, 906
Salina Cruz (Oax) 772-3
Saltillo (Coa) 436-41, **439**
San Agustinillo (Oax) 764
San Andrés Larraínzar (Chi) 817
San Andrés Tuxtla (Ver) 707-9
San Antonio (Col) 586
San Bartolo Coyotepec (Oax) 746
San Blas (Nay) 457-61, **459**
San Carlos (Son) 360-1
San Cristóbal de Las Casas (Chi) 800-14, **804**

getting around 814
getting there & away 813-14
places to eat 811-3
places to stay 808-11
shopping 813
things to see 803-7
San Felipe (BCN) 320
San Felipe (Yuc) 902
San Fernando (Tam) 417
San Francisco de la Sierra (BCS) 324
San Gervasio (QR) 933
San Ignacio (BCS) 323, 324
San José del Cabo (BCS) 338-41, **339**
San Juan Chamula (Chi) 816
San Juan Cosalá (Jal) 548
San Juan del Río (Que) 658-9
San Juan Teotihuacán (Méx) 236
San Lorenzo (Ver) 712-3
San Luis Potosí (city) 609-17, **611**
San Luis Potosí (state) 608-9
San Luis Río Colorado (Son) 351
San Miguel de Cozumel, see Cozumel
San Miguel de Allende (Gua) 637-49, **641**
  getting around 649
  getting there & away 648-9
  places to eat 646-7
  places to stay 644-6
  things to see 640-3
San Miguel del Milagro (Tla) 247
San Nicolás (Chih) 396
San Pablito (Pue) 674
San Patricio-Melaque (Jal) 480-3, **482**
San Pedro Amuzgos (Oax) 748
San Pedro Chenalhó (Chi) 817
Santa Ana Chiautempan (Tla) 245
Santa Ana del Valle (Oax) 742
Santa Anna, Antonio López de 25
Santa Catarina (NL) 435
Santa Clara del Cobre (Mic) 570
Santa Cruz Huatulco (Oax) 766
Santa María del Río (SLP) 617
Santa Rosalía (BCS) 324-5
Santiago Tuxtla (Ver) 705-6
Santo Tomás Jalieza (Oax) 747
Santuario de Mariposas El Rosario (Mic) 558-60
Santuario de Plateros (Zac) 600
sarapes 103
  Quiroga 570
Sayil (Yuc) 884, **884**
Scammon's Lagoon, see Laguna Ojo de Liebre

scuba diving, see diving
Semana Santa 70
Seri people 356
shopping
  artesanías 100-1
  ceramics 257
  silver 287, 290
Sierra de La Laguna (BCS) 336
Sierra Madre de Chiapas 790
Sierra Madre de Oaxaca 258, 715
Sierra Madre del Sur 715
Sierra Madre Oriental 435
Sierra Norte de Puebla 263-4
silver 122
  Alamos 362
  Oaxaca city 733
  San Miguel de Allende 648
  Taxco 284, 287, 290-1
Sinaloa (state) 367
Siqueiros, David Alfaro 28, 48, 165, 166, 167, 174, 178, 180, 182, 275
snorkelling 87
  Akumal 934
  Bahías de Huatulco 766
  Chankanab Bay 932
  Cozumel 927
  Isla Mujeres 914
  Laguna Yal-Ku 934
  Palancar Reef 932
  Puerto Ángel 761
  Puerto Escondido 751
  Punta Allen 940
  Zcacel 935
soccer, see football
Soconusco (Chi) 790, 842
Sonoita (city) 351
Sonora (state) 347, 352
Sontecomapan (Ver) 711
Soto La Marina (Tam) 417
Spanish conquest 20-22, 524, 526, 580
Spanish language 54
straw goods
  Tzintzuntzan 569
student cards 63
Suchitlán (Col) 586
surfing 87
  La Pesca 417
  Puerto Escondido 750
  Punta Mirador 341
  San José del Cabo 338
  Zipolite 763
sweaters, see wool sweaters

Tabasco (Tab) 775-7, **776**
Talavera pottery 110-15
  Dolores Hidalgo 637
Talismán (Chi) 848

Tamaulipas (state) 403, 405
Tamazunchale (Ver) 670
Tamiahua (Ver) 673
Tampico 663-8, **665**
Tampumacchay (Col) 588
Tamuín (SLP) 669
Tancanhuitz (Ver) 669
Tapachula (Chi) 844-7, **845**
Tarahumara people 372, 373, 376, 377, 391
Tarascan league 560, 568
Tarascan people 20, 253, 560
Tarasco people, see Purépecha people
Taxco (Gue) 283-92, **285**
taxi 145
Tecali (Pue) 264
Tecate (BCN) 308
Tecoh (Yuc) 888, 889
Tecolutla (Ver) 680
Tehuacán (Pue) 264-5
Tehuantepec (Oax) 770-2
Tehuilotepec (Gue) 293
Tekit (Yuc) 888
Telchaquillo (Yuc) 889
telephone services 72-73
Tenancingo (Méx) 298
Tenango de Doria (Hid) 239
Tenango del Valle (Méx) 298
Tenejapa (Chi) 817
Tenochtitlán 18-19, 21-22, 147
Teotenango (Méx) 298
Teotihuacán (Méx) 14, 46, 232-6, **233**
Teotitlán del Valle (Oax) 741
Tepeaca (Pue) 264
Tepehua people 239
Tepic (Nay) 461-4, **462**
Teposcolula (Oax) 748
Tepotzotlán (Méx) 225-8
Tepoztlán (Mor) 265-8, **267**
Tequila (Jal) 548
Tequisquiapan (Que) 659-60
textiles 102-9, 813
  Mitla 745
  San Miguel de Allende 648
  Santa Ana del Valle 742
Tezcatlipoca 17, 228
Ticul (Yuc) 886-8, **887**
Tijuana (BCN) 302-8, **304-5**
time 74
Tingambato (Mic) 571
tinplate crafts 124
  Oaxaca city 733
Tizatlán (Tla) 246
Tizimin (Yuc) 901
Tlachichuca (Pue) 264
Tlacolula (Oax) 742
Tlacotalpan (Ver) 705

Tláloc 14, 18, 46
Tlamacas (Pue) 240, 242, 243
Tlaquepaque (Jal) 534-5
Tlaxcala (city) 244-6, **245**
Tlaxcala (state) 239
Tlaxiaco (Oax) 748
Todos Santos (BCS) 337-8
Tolsá, Manuel 163, 168, 169
Toltec civilisation 849
Toltec people 17, 47, 228, 389, 662, 890
Toluca (Méx) 294-7, **295**
Tonalá (Chi) 843
Tonalá (Jal) 535
Tonantzintla (Pue) 263
Toniná (Chi) 819-20
Topolobampo (Sin) 370
Torreón (Coa) 397-8
Totonac people 20, 45, 662, 675, 677
tourist cards 60-61
  extensions & lost cards 61
tourist offices 69
tours 137
  Bahías de Huatulco 767
  Bonampak 834
  Edzná ruins 858
  Guadalajara 536
  Guanajuato 628
  Morelia 554
  near Creel 377-8
  Oaxaca city 723
  Palenque 827
  Pico de Orizaba 704
  Puerto Escondido 752
  San Cristóbal de Las Casas 808
  Tequisquiapan 659
  Yaxchilán 834
train travel
  classes 141
  Copper Canyon Railway 371-80
  El Constitucionalista 632, 657, 659
  El División del Norte 599, 608, 633, 657
  El Jarocho 698
  El Oaxaqueño 258, 735
  El Purépecha 558, 567, 576
  El Regiomontano 617
  El Tapatío 543
  Estrella del Pacífico 543
  schedules 142
  tickets 142
  to/from Mexico City 216-8
  to/from the USA 134
  within Mexico 141-2
trekking 87, 243
  Cañón San Dionisio 336

Iztaccíhuatl 243
Parque Nacional Sierra San Pedro Mártir 313
Popocatépetl 243
Tres Zapotes (Ver) 706-7
Triqui people 717, 748
Trotsky, Leon 48, 188-9
Tula 17, 228-31, **229**
Tulancingo (Hid) 239
Tulum (QR) 935-9, **936**
Tututepec (Oax) 758
Tuxpan (Ver) 671-3, **672**
Tuxtepec (Oax) 749
Tuxtla Gutiérrez (Chi) 791-8, **793**
Tzeltal people 45, 791, 815, 817
Tzintzuntzan (Mic) 523, 563, 568
Tziscao people 840
Tzotzil people 45, 791, 798, 815, 816
Tzurumútaro (Mic) 563

Unión Juárez (Chi) 844
Uruapan (Mic) 571-6, **574**
Uxmal (Yuc) 878-83, **880**

Valladolid (Yuc) 897-901, **899**
Valle de Allende (Chih) 397
Valle de Etla (Oax) 736
Valle de los Monjes (Chih) 378
Valle de Tlacolula (Oax) 736
Valle de Zimatlán (Oax) 736
Velasco, José María 47, 168
Veracruz (city) 688-99, **692, 695**
  getting around 699
  getting there & away 697-8
  places to eat 696-7
  places to stay 692-4
  things to see 690-2
Veracruz (state) 661
Villa del Oeste (Dur) 402
Villa Rica (Ver) 680
Villa, Pancho 27, 383, 388, 391-2, 393, 397, 591, 595
Villahermosa (Tab) 777-86, **778, 782,** 798
  Parque-Museo La Venta 779-80, **779**
Virgin of Guadalupe 53, 179
visas 60-3
voladores 51, 174, 671, 677
Volcán de Fuego de Colima (Col) 579, 580, 586-8
Volcán Nevado de Colima (Col) 579, 586-8
Volcán Paricutín (Mic) 577-8
Volcán San Martín (Ver) 707
Volcán Tacaná (Chi) 844

Walker, William 330
War of Independence 623, 626
waterfalls
  around El Salto 402
  Cascada Cusárare 378
  Cascada de Basaseachi
    378, 396
  Cascada de Tamul 669
  Cascada de Tzaráracua 576
  Cascadas Cola de Caballo 435
weaving 105, 107, 886
  Teotitlán del Valle 741
weights & measures 74
whale-watching 40
  Bahía de las Banderas 465
  Ensenada 309
  Laguna Ojo de Liebre 320
  Laguna San Ignacio 324
  near Ciudad Constitución 329
  Puerto Adolfo López Mateos
    329
  Puerto San Carlos 329
  Reserva Biósfera El Vizcaíno
    321
windsurfing 336
women travellers 85
woodwork 119
  carved furniture (Comala) 586

inlaid woodwork
  (Santa María del Río) 617
  Quiroga 570
wool sweaters
  Quiroga 570
work 86
wrestling, see lucha libre

Xalapa (Ver) 682-8, **684, 686**
  Museo de Antropología 683
Xcacel (QR) 935
Xcaret (QR) 933
Xel-ha Lagoon (QR) 935
Xico (Ver) 688
Xicoténcatl 244
Xicotepec (Pue) 674
Xilitla (Ver) 670
Xlapak (Yuc) 885
Xochicalco (Mor) 282-3
Xpujil (Cam) 853

Yaaxhom (Yuc) 885
Yagul (Oax) 742, **743**
Yanhuitlán (Oax) 747
Yaxchilán ruins (Chi) 833-6
Yaxcopoil (Yuc) 888
Yepachi (Chih) 396
Yocab Reef (QR) 927

Yohualichán (Pue) 264
Yucatán Peninsula 849-950, **851**
Yucatán (state) 861

Zaachila (Oax) 746
Zacatecas (city) 591-9, **594**
Zacatecas (state) 590-1
Zacateco people 591
Zacatepec (Oax) 745
Zacualtipán (Hid) 670
Zamora (Mic) 579
Zapata, Emiliano 28, 265, 269
Zapatista National Liberation
  Army 789, 801, 818
Zapatista rebellion 788
Zapotec people 13, 19, 45, 714,
  717, 737, 744, 746, 770
Zaragoza (Chih) 390
Zempoala (Ver) 681-2, **681**
Zempoaltépetl (Oax) 717, 745
Zihuatanejo (Gue) 497-507, **503**
Zinacantán (Chi) 816-7
Zipolite (Oax) 763-4
Zirahuén (Mic) 570
Zona del Silencio (Dur) 398
Zongolica (Ver) 704
Zoofari (Mor) 283
Zoque people 791

THANKS

Thanks to all the many travellers who wrote in with comments about our last edition, and with tips and comments about Mexico (apologies if we've misspelt your name):

Louis Adams (USA), Beatrice Aebi (E), Raimon Alamany (E), Lualdi Alberto (I), Judy Almeranti (USA), Gail Anderman (USA), Lisa Audouin (UK), Jon Aves (UK), Anni Baker (AUS), Bryan Bakker (USA), Erika Cortes Barba, Sophie Barker (UK), Greg Barnacle (UK), Stephen Barr (USA), Giles Barrow (UK), Cristiana Barzaghi (I), Heather Beach (USA), Raymond Beer (USA), Robert Begotka (USA), Steve Bell (UK), Mr & Mrs F Bennett (UK), Amos Benvered (IL), Mario Bevione (I), Hiro Bhojwani (CDN), Margaret Billington (UK), J M Bithell (UK), Julie Bostrom (USA), Pam Bowers (UK), Mike Boyce (USA), Bernard Brahm (USA), Demara Brake (USA), B Breed (USA), Ian Brodie, Valerie Broom (UK), A Brouwer (NL), Luciana Brugnoli (UK), Marleen Brulles (NL), Jill Buckingham (NZ), Graziano Bullegas (I), Antoinette Burnham (USA), Dr P Burstin (AUS), Daniel Bush (USA), Giuseppe Cacciato, Nan Caldwell (USA), Virginia Campbell, William Cannady (USA), Timothy Cannon (USA), Yuen Ka Yi Carrie (HK), Ismael Carrillo Jr (USA), Stuart Carter (USA), Dennis Cavagnaro (USA), Wim Ceuppens (B), Rustin Chrisco (USA), James L Citron (USA), Margaret Clarke (D), Craig Coben (USA), Paul Coleman (UK), Mikail J Collins (CDN), Don Conrad (USA), Peter Converse (AUS), Maire Conway, Dennis Conway (USA), Kathleen Cooke (USA), Flore Coumau (F), Mark Crawford (UK), Scott Cunningham (USA), Monika Curlin (USA), Erich Dahlmanns (D), Lorraine Daoust (CDN), Russell Davidson (CDN), Stefan De Keersmaecker (B), Carlos Lozano de la Torre, Carmen Dekell (USA), Barry J DeMillion (USA), R E den Braasem (NL), Mark E Denney (USA), Steve Derne, Ken Dickson (AUS), Franz X Diemer (A), A M Diffley (USA), Tamar Dothan (USA), Desmond Dubbin (UK), Neil Dunkin (UK), Katharine Edey (UK), Caroline Edwards (USA), Ronny & Diane Eijckman-Gielen (B), Simon Elms, Ralf Emig (D), William Engel, Emmanuel Ermidis (USA), Ursula Etter (CH), Fernanda Fabre, C Feierabend (USA), Clint & Ina Ferguson (NL), Thomas Fetzer (UK), Arnold Fieldman (USA), Hugh Finsten (CDN), Vivienne Flanagan (IRE), Francisca Flores, Donna Franklin (USA), Gavin Fredric (NZ), Jurg Furrer (CH), Judy Gabriel (USA), Donald Gaby (USA), Jason Gay (AUS), Alison Gayland (USA), Faye Gishen (UK), Roy Goff (USA), Sharlya Gold, Ruth Goldberg (USA), Bruce Graham (NZ), John Grant (CDN), Helen Grant (UK), Rachel & Laurie Greenberg (USA), Bridget Grounds (AUS), Dr Matteo Gulmanelli (I), Cindy Halvorson (USA), Steven Hankey (AUS), Kathy Hanneson (CDN), Stefan Hansson (S), Anne-Maroe Harbers (NL), Ole-Johan Harm (N), Kelly & David Harnett, Fred A Haskett (USA), Tina Hawker (USA), Dr Barbara Hayes-Roth (USA), Steven Heller (CDN), Martin Hendriks (NL), Kai Hermann (D), Pat Hickey (USA), Kevin Hill (UK), Tina M Hocker (USA), Peter Hollings (USA), Jan Phillip Holscher (S), Ed Holub (USA), Prudence Huff-Butt (USA), Caron M Hughes (UK), D Hulse (USA), Iain Jackson (UK), Ruth James (UK), Olga Jansen (NL), Steen B Jensen (DK), Helle Johnsen (DK), Nij & Nadia Johnson (UK), Judith Jones (USA), Peter Jordan (UK), Henny Kanen (NL), Kami Kanetsuka (CDN), Stanley Kaplan (USA), Angus Kennedy (UK), Roy Kesey (USA), Michael Klein (USA), Bill Kornrich (USA), Robert Kozak (CDN), Petra Kranse (NL), Marlene Kratzer (CH), Kenneth Kristensen (DK), Jorgen Kristensen (DK), Ulf Kristofferson (S), Earl Krygler (USA), Gerald Kuhl (D), Maureen Kurtz (USA), Jenny Landen (USA), Stefan Landmann (D), Brian Latimer (CDN), D Lawrence (USA), William Lawrence (USA), Cale Layton (USA), F Lebour (NL), Stephen & Barb Lee (CDN), Elaine Lee (USA), Justine Lees (AUS), Roland Lehmann, Damian Lilly (UK), Ineke Lint (NL), D H Livingstone (CDN), Rob Lober (UK), Helga Loebell, Ciaran Logan, Patti Lohr (USA), Kathy & Ruth Lotscher, J Louveaux (UK), Markus Low (USA), Iain Mackay (UK), Clyde Magill (USA), P A Martin (UK), Steve Mathias (USA), M McClure, Peter McCormack (CDN), Bruce McDonough (USA), Jim McGowan (USA), Steven McKay (D), Lawrence McNamara (AUS), N R McWhinnie (AUS), Perry McWilliams (USA), Nathan Meyer (USA), Jeremy Michael (UK), Keith Miller (USA), Mauro Molteni (I), Michael Moody (USA), Chris Morey (UK), Paula Suarez Moya (USA), Marilyn Moyer (USA), Kerry Mullen (UK), Daniel Muller (USA), Henk Muller, Brian Murphy (USA), Dan Muruve (CDN), Louis Nef (B), Graeme Neilson (UK), Paul & Marion Nelissen (NL), Chris & Kay Nellins (UK), David Nelsin (USA), L Nevaer (USA), Andrea Nguyen (USA), Thomas Nielson (DK), Karen Nienaber (AUS), Kip & Ron Nigh, Anna Nilsson, Jane & Simon Nixon (UK), Jim O'Daniel, Wayne O'Sullivan (AUS), Arthur Olof (NL), Erik Olsen (USA), Anton Opperman (NL), Nancy Orr (USA), Catherine Orton (UK), Chris Parry (AUS), David Paton, Jo Pearce, Antoine Pecard (F), Margery Perlmutter (USA), Paul & Valerie Pieraccini (USA), Sanya Polescuk (UK), Markus Pomper (USA), B Pottier (USA), Peter & Anna Proudlock, Judith Rabbit (USA), Steven Rainey (USA), Penelope Ralph (UK), Angel Rangel, Caral Ann Raphael (USA), Joel Rapp (IL), Keith Reay (UK), David Reiss, Bruce Richardson (CDN), Prentiss Riddle (USA), Mike Roach (USA), Ralph L Robinson (CDN), Mrs Barbara Rogers (UK), Jens Rohark (D), Janette Rosbroy (USA), Patricia & Marv Rosen (USA), Lori Rubens (USA), Federico G Russek,

Maarten & Barbara Ruygrok (NL), Elena Sacchi (I), Angela K Salmon (NZ), Pascal Sartoretti (CH), Nancy Schave (USA), Lawrence Schneck (UK), Martin Schneider (D), Stephan Schneider (D), Richard R Schrader (USA), Ellen Schulze, Axel Schwingenheuer (D), E B Seeman (UK), Miss A Shanley (UK), Kathleen Shields (IRE), Alan Sirulnikoff (CDN), Kristina Small (USA), Michael Smith (UK), Pernille & Ole Sonne (DK), Steen M Sorensen (D), Robin Soroka (USA), Les & Cynthia Southgate (UK), Madeleine Speed (CDN), Anne Spencer (UK), D Spoetter (D), Robert Starek (USA), Terry Stein (USA), Lynn Stewart (USA), Dorothy Strickland (USA), N Sylvester, Steve & Gaby Telander, Detlef Thedieck (D), Ron Toews (CDN), Tony Tresigne (UK), Amanda Triggs (UK), Craig Uhler, Jens Ulmer (D), Sabrina Vadala (I), James Valentine (UK), Arthur van den Elzen (NL), Onno van der Salm (NL), Miriam J De Villagomez, R Walker (CH), Emma-Jane Waller, A L Watson (UK), Mary Jo Weir (USA), David Weisberg (USA), Dirk Weisheit, Ronit Weiss (IL), Don & Alicia Welker (USA), Darren Welsh (USA), Oda Weyers (NL), Maxine White (USA), Linda White (USA), Juliet Whitlock (AUS), Ed Wilde (USA), Ian Wilkie (UK), K & P Willemen (B), Jim Williams (AUS), Sheila Wilmot (CDN), Mr B & Mrs M Wilson (UK), Rosemary Wiss (AUS), Martin & Nikola Woodhams (USA), Anthony Woodruff (AUS), Sr Manuel Zepeda (MEX), Alice Zinkevich (USA), Luc Hachez (B).

A – Austria, AUS – Australia, B – Belgium, CDN – Canada, CH – Switzerland, D – Germany, DK – Denmark, E – Spain, F – France, HK – Hong Kong, I – Italy, IL – Israel, IRE – Ireland, MEX – Mexico, N – Norway, NL – Netherlands, NZ – New Zealand, S – Sweden, UK – United Kingdom, USA – United States of America

LONELY PLANET JOURNEYS

JOURNEYS is a unique collection of travellers' tales – published by the company that understands travel better than anyone else. It is a series for anyone who has ever experienced – or dreamed of – the magical moment when they encountered a strange culture or saw a place for the first time. They are tales to read while you're planning a trip, while you're on the road or while you're in an armchair, in front of a fire.

JOURNEYS books will catch the spirit of a place, illuminate a culture, recount a crazy adventure, or introduce a fascinating way of life. They will always entertain, and always enrich the experience of travel.

FULL CIRCLE
A South American Journey
Luis Sepúlveda
Translated by Chris Andrews

Full Circle invites us to accompany Chilean writer Luis Sepúlveda on 'a journey without a fixed itinerary'. Extravagant characters and extraordinary situations are memorably evoked: gauchos organising a tournament of lies, a scheming heiress on the lookout for a husband, a pilot with a corpse on board his plane . . . Part autobiography, part travel memoir, *Full Circle* brings us the distinctive voice of one of South America's most compelling writers.

THE GATES OF DAMASCUS
Lieve Joris
Translated by Sam Garrett

This best-selling book is a beautifully drawn portrait of day-to-day life in modern Syria. Through her intimate contact with local people, Lieve Joris draws us into the fascinating world that lies behind the gates of Damascus.

ISLANDS IN THE CLOUDS
Travels in the Highlands of New Guinea
Isabella Tree

This is the fascinating account of a journey to the remote and beautiful Highlands of Papua New Guinea and Irian Jaya. The author travels with a PNG Highlander who introduces her to his intriguing and complex world. *Islands in the Clouds* is a thoughtful, moving book, full of insights into a region that is rarely noticed by the rest of the world.

LOST JAPAN
Alex Kerr

Lost Japan draws on the author's personal experiences of Japan over a period of 30 years. Alex Kerr takes his readers on a backstage tour: friendships with Kabuki actors, buying and selling art, studying calligraphy, exploring rarely visited temples and shrines . . . The Japanese edition of this book was awarded the 1994 Shincho Gakugei Literature Prize for the best work of non-fiction.

SEAN & DAVID'S LONG DRIVE
Sean Condon

Sean and David are young townies who have rarely strayed beyond city limits. One day, for no good reason, they set out to discover their homeland, and what follows is a wildly entertaining adventure that covers half of Australia. Sean Condon has written a hilarious, offbeat road book that mixes sharp insights with deadpan humour and outright lies.

SHOPPING FOR BUDDHAS
Jeff Greenwald

Shopping for Buddhas is Jeff Greenwald's story of his obsessive search for the perfect Buddha statue. In the backstreets of Kathmandu, he discovers more than he bargained for . . . and his souvenir-hunting turns into an ironic metaphor for the clash between spiritual riches and material greed. Politics, religion and serious shopping collide in this witty account of an enlightening visit to Nepal.

LONELY PLANET TRAVEL ATLASES

Lonely Planet has long been famous for the number and quality of its guidebook maps. Now we've gone one step further and in conjunction with Steinhart Katzir Publishers produced a handy companion series: Lonely Planet travel atlases – maps of a country produced in book form.

Unlike other maps, which look good but lead travellers astray, our travel atlases have been researched on the road by Lonely Planet's experienced team of writers. All details are carefully checked to ensure the atlas corresponds with the equivalent Lonely Planet guidebook.

The handy atlas format means no holes, wrinkles, torn sections or constant folding and unfolding. These atlases can survive long periods on the road, unlike cumbersome fold-out maps. The comprehensive index ensures easy reference.

- full-colour throughout
- maps researched and checked by Lonely Planet authors
- place names correspond with Lonely Planet guidebooks
  – no confusing spelling differences
- legend and travelling information in English, French, German, Japanese and Spanish
- size: 230 x 160 mm

Available now:
Thailand; India & Bangladesh; Vietnam; Zimbabwe, Botswana & Namibia

Coming soon:
Chile; Egypt; Israel; Laos; Turkey

LONELY PLANET TV SERIES & VIDEOS

Lonely Planet travel guides have been brought to life on television screens around the world. Like our guides, the programmes are based on the joy of independent travel, and look honestly at some of the most exciting, picturesque and frustrating places in the world. Each show is presented by one of three travellers from Australia, England or the USA and combines an innovative mixture of video, Super-8 film, atmospheric soundscapes and original music.

Videos of each episode – containing additional footage not shown on television – are available from good book and video shops, but the availability of individual videos varies with regional screening schedules.

Video destinations include: Alaska; Australia (Southeast); Brazil; Ecuador & the Galápagos Islands; Indonesia; Israel & the Sinai Desert; Japan; La Ruta Maya (Yucatán, Guatemala & Belize); Morocco; North India (Varanasi to the Himalaya); Pacific Islands; Vietnam; Zimbabwe, Botswana & Namibia.

Coming soon: The Arctic (Norway & Finland); Baja California; Chile & Easter Island; China (Southeast); Costa Rica; East Africa (Tanzania & Zanzibar); Great Barrier Reef (Australia); Jamaica; Papua New Guinea; the Rockies (USA); Syria & Jordan; Turkey.

The Lonely Planet TV series is produced by:
Pilot Productions
Duke of Sussex Studios
44 Uxbridge St
London W8 7TG UK

Lonely Planet videos are distributed by:
IVN Communications Inc
2246 Camino Ramon
California 94583, USA

107 Power Road, Chiswick
London W4 5PL UK

Music from the TV series is available on CD & cassette.
For ordering information contact your nearest Lonely Planet office.

PLANET TALK

Lonely Planet's FREE quarterly newsletter

We love hearing from you and think you'd like to hear from us.

When...is the right time to see reindeer in Finland?
Where...can you hear the best palm-wine music in Ghana?
How...do you get from Asunción to Areguá by steam train?
What...is the best way to see India?

For the answer to these and many other questions read PLANET TALK.

Every issue is packed with up-to-date travel news and advice including:

* a letter from Lonely Planet co-founders Tony and Maureen Wheeler
* go behind the scenes on the road with a Lonely Planet author
* feature article on an important and topical travel issue
* a selection of recent letters from travellers
* details on forthcoming Lonely Planet promotions
* complete list of Lonely Planet products

To join our mailing list contact any Lonely Planet office.

Also available: Lonely Planet T-shirts. 100% heavyweight cotton..

LONELY PLANET ONLINE

Get the latest travel information before you leave or while you're on the road

Whether you've just begun planning your next trip, or you're chasing down specific info on currency regulations or visa requirements, check out the Lonely Planet World Wide Web site for up-to-the-minute travel information.

As well as travel profiles of your favourite destinations (including interactive maps and full-colour photos), you'll find current reports from our army of researchers and other travellers, updates on health and visas, travel advisories, and the ecological and political issues you need to be aware of as you travel.

There's an online travellers' forum (the Thorn Tree) where you can share your experiences of life on the road, meet travel companions and ask other travellers for their recommendations and advice. We also have plenty of links to other Web sites useful to independent travellers.

With tens of thousands of visitors a month, the Lonely Planet Web site is one of the most popular on the Internet and has won a number of awards including GNN's Best of the Net award.

http://www.lonelyplanet.com

LONELY PLANET PRODUCTS

Lonely Planet is known worldwide for publishing practical, reliable and no-nonsense travel information in our guides and on our web site. The Lonely Planet list covers just about every accessible part of the world. Currently there are eight series: *travel guides, shoestring guides, walking guides, city guides, phrasebooks, audio packs, travel atlases* and *Journeys* – a unique collection of travellers' tales.

EUROPE

Austria • Baltic States & Kaliningrad • Baltic States phrasebook • Britain • Central Europe on a shoestring • Central Europe phrasebook • Czech & Slovak Republics • Denmark • Dublin city guide • Eastern Europe on a shoestring • Eastern Europe phrasebook • Finland • France • Greece • Greek phrasebook • Hungary • Iceland, Greenland & the Faroe Islands • Ireland • Italy • Mediterranean Europe on a shoestring • Mediterranean Europe phrasebook • Paris city guide • Poland • Prague city guide • Russia, Ukraine & Belarus • Russian phrasebook • Scandinavian & Baltic Europe on a shoestring • Scandinavian Europe phrasebook • Slovenia • St Petersburg city guide • Switzerland • Trekking in Greece • Trekking in Spain • Ukrainian phrasebook • Vienna city guide • Walking in Switzerland • Western Europe on a shoestring • Western Europe phrasebook

NORTH AMERICA

Alaska • Backpacking in Alaska • Baja California• California & Nevada • Canada • Hawaii • Honolulu city guide • Los Angeles city guide • Mexico • Miami city guide • New England • Pacific Northwest USA • Rocky Mountain States • San Francisco city guide • Southwest USA • USA phrasebook

CENTRAL AMERICA & THE CARIBBEAN

Central America on a shoestring • Costa Rica • Eastern Caribbean • Guatemala, Belize & Yucatán: La Ruta Maya • Jamaica

SOUTH AMERICA

Argentina, Uruguay & Paraguay • Bolivia • Brazil • Brazilian phrasebook • Buenos Aires city guide • Chile • Easter Island • Chile travel atlas• Colombia • Ecuador & the Galápagos Islands • Latin American Spanish phrasebook • Peru • Quechua phrasebook • Rio de Janeiro city guide • South America on a shoestring • Trekking in the Patagonian Andes • Venezuela

Travel Literature: Full Circle: A South American Journey

ANTARCTICA

Antarctica

ISLANDS OF THE INDIAN OCEAN

Madagascar & Comoros • Maldives & Islands of the East Indian Ocean • Mauritius, Réunion & Seychelles

AFRICA

Arabic (Moroccan) phrasebook • Africa on a shoestring • Cape Town city guide • Central Africa • East Africa • Egypt • Egypt travel atlas• Ethiopian (Amharic) phrasebook • Kenya • Morocco • North Africa • South Africa, Lesotho & Swaziland • Swahili phrasebook • Trekking in East Africa • West Africa • Zimbabwe, Botswana & Namibia • Zimbabwe, Botswana & Namibia travel atlas

MAIL ORDER

Lonely Planet products are distributed worldwide. They are also available by mail order from Lonely Planet, so if you have difficulty finding a title please write to us. North American and South American residents should write to Embarcadero West, 155 Filbert St, Suite 251, Oakland CA 94607, USA; European and African residents should write to 10 Barley Mow Passage, Chiswick, London W4 4PH; and residents of other countries to PO Box 617, Hawthorn, Victoria 3122, Australia.

NORTH-EAST ASIA

Beijing city guide • Cantonese phrasebook • China • Hong Kong, Macau & Canton • Hong Kong city guide • Japan • Japanese phrasebook • Japanese audio pack • Korea • Korean phrasebook • Mandarin phrasebook • Mongolia • Mongolian phrasebook • North-East Asia on a shoestring • Seoul city guide • Taiwan • Tibet • Tibet phrasebook • Tokyo city guide

Travel Literature: Lost Japan

INDIAN SUBCONTINENT

Bangladesh• Bengali phrasebook• Delhi city guide • Hindi/Urdu phrasebook • India • India & Bangladesh travel atlas • Indian Himalaya • Karakoram Highway • Nepal • Nepali phrasebook • Pakistan • Sri Lanka • Sri Lanka phrasebook • Trekking in the Indian Himalaya • Trekking in the Karakoram & Hindukush • Trekking in the Nepal Himalaya

Travel Literature: Shopping for Buddhas

SOUTH-EAST ASIA

Bali & Lombok • Bangkok city guide • Burmese phrasebook • Cambodia • Ho Chi Minh city guide • Indonesia • Indonesian phrasebook • Indonesian audio pack • Jakarta city guide • Java • Laos • Lao phrasebook • Laos travel atlas • Malay phrasebook • Malaysia, Singapore & Brunei • Myanmar (Burma) • Philippines • Pilipino phrasebook • Singapore city guide • South-East Asia on a shoestring • Thailand • Thailand travel atlas • Thai phrasebook • Thai audio pack • Thai Hill Tribes phrasebook • Vietnam • Vietnamese phrasebook • Vietnam travel atlas

MIDDLE EAST & CENTRAL ASIA

Arab Gulf States • Arabic (Egyptian) phrasebook • Central Asia • Iran• Israel & the Palestinian Territories• Israel & the Palestinian Territories travel atlas • Jordan & Syria • Jordan, Syria & Lebanon travel atlas • Middle East • Turkey • Turkish phrasebook • Trekking in Turkey • Yemen

Travel Literature: The Gates of Damascus

ALSO AVAILABLE:

Travel with Children • Traveller's Tales

AUSTRALIA & THE PACIFIC

Australia • Australian phrasebook • Bushwalking in Australia• Bushwalking in Papua New Guinea • Fiji • Fijian phrasebook • Islands of Australia's Great Barrier Reef • Melbourne city guide • Micronesia • New Caledonia • New South Wales & the ACT • New Zealand • Northern Territory • Outback Australia • Papua New Guinea • Papua New Guinea phrasebook • Queensland • Rarotonga & the Cook Islands • Samoa • Solomon Islands • South Australia • Sydney city guide • Tahiti & French Polynesia • Tasmania • Tonga • Tramping in New Zealand • Vanuatu • Victoria • Western Australia

Travel Literature: Islands in the Clouds • Sean & David's Long Drive

THE LONELY PLANET STORY

Lonely Planet published its first book in 1973 in response to the numerous 'How did you do it?' questions Maureen and Tony Wheeler were asked after driving, bussing, hitching, sailing and railing their way from England to Australia.

Written at a kitchen table and hand collated, trimmed and stapled, *Across Asia on the Cheap* became an instant local bestseller, inspiring thoughts of another book.

Eighteen months in South-East Asia resulted in their second guide, *South-East Asia on a shoestring*, which they put together in a backstreet Chinese hotel in Singapore in 1975. The 'yellow bible', as it quickly became known to backpackers around the world, soon became *the* guide to the region. It has sold well over half a million copies and is now in its 8th edition, still retaining its familiar yellow cover.

Today there are over 180 titles, including travel guides, walking guides, language kits & phrasebooks, travel atlases and travel literature. The company is one of the largest travel publishers in the world. Although Lonely Planet initially specialised in guides to Asia, we now cover most regions of the world, including the Pacific, North America, South America, Africa, the Middle East and Europe.

The emphasis continues to be on travel for independent travellers. Tony and Maureen still travel for several months of each year and play an active part in the writing, updating and quality control of Lonely Planet's guides.

They have been joined by over 70 authors and 170 staff at our offices in Melbourne (Australia), Oakland (USA), London (UK) and Paris (France). Travellers themselves also make a valuable contribution to the guides through the feedback we receive in thousands of letters each year.

The people at Lonely Planet strongly believe that travellers can make a positive contribution to the countries they visit, both through their appreciation of the countries' culture, wildlife and natural features, and through the money they spend. In addition, the company makes a direct contribution to the countries and regions it covers. Since 1986 a percentage of the income from each book has been donated to ventures such as famine relief in Africa; aid projects in India; agricultural projects in Central America; Greenpeace's efforts to halt French nuclear testing in the Pacific; and Amnesty International.

Lonely Planet's basic travel philosophy is summed up in Tony Wheeler's comment, 'Don't worry about whether your trip will work out. Just go!'

LONELY PLANET PUBLICATIONS

Australia
PO Box 617, Hawthorn 3122, Victoria
tel: (03) 9819 1877 fax: (03) 9819 6459
e-mail: talk2us@lonelyplanet.com.au

USA
Embarcadero West, 155 Filbert St, Suite 251,
Oakland, CA 94607
tel: (510) 893 8555 TOLL FREE: 800 275-8555
fax: (510) 893 8563
e-mail: info@lonelyplanet.com

UK
10 Barley Mow Passage, Chiswick,
London W4 4PH
tel: (0181) 742 3161 fax: (0181) 742 2772
e-mail: 100413.3551@compuserve.com

France:
71 bis rue du Cardinal Lemoine, 75005 Paris
tel: 1 44 32 06 20 fax: 1 46 34 72 55
e-mail: 100560.415@compuserve.com

World Wide Web: http://www.lonelyplanet.com